THE CAMBRIDGE HISTORY OF IRAN

IN SEVEN VOLUMES

Volume 6

THE CAMBRIDGE HISTORY OF IRAN

Volume 6

THE TIMURID AND SAFAVID PERIODS

edited by

PETER JACKSON

Lecturer in History,
University of Keele

AND

the late LAURENCE LOCKHART

CAMBRIDGE
UNIVERSITY PRESS

Published by the Syndics of the Cambridge University Press
The Pitt Building, Trumpington Street, Cambridge CB2 1RP
40 West 20th Street, New York, NY 10011–4211, USA
10 Stamford Road, Oakleigh, Victoria 3166, Australia

First published 1986
Reprinted 1993

Printed and bound in Great Britain by
Woolnough Bookbinding Ltd, Irthlingborough, Northamptonshire

Library of Congress Catalogue Card Number: 67–12845

British Library Cataloguing in Publication Data

The Cambridge history of Iran.
Vol. 6: The Timurid and Safavid periods.
1. Iran—History
I. Jackson, Peter II. Lockhart, Laurence
955 DS272

ISBN 0 521 20094 6

UP

BOARD OF EDITORS

CONTENTS

PLATES

Between pages 744 and 745

1–2 An astrolabe made in 1127/1715 by 'Abd al-A'imma, the younger (Victoria and Albert Museum, London item no. 458–1888. Reproduced by courtesy of the Director).

3 Khusrau and Shīrīn, ascribed to Bihzād, dated 1490 (From the *Khamsa* of Niẓāmī, British Library, Add. 25,900, fol. 3. Reproduced by courtesy of the Trustees).

4 Woollen knotted carpet, Persia, first half of the 16th century (The Metropolitan Museum of Art, New York, purchase 1910, Hewitt Fund).

5 Multiple woollen prayer rug, Persia, first half of the 16th century, (Staatliche Museen Preussischer Kulturbesitz, Museum für Islamische Kunst, Berlin).

6 Woollen knotted carpet, the so-called Ardabīl carpet, Persia, dated 1539–40 (Victoria and Albert Museum, London).

7 Woollen knotted carpet, Persia, dated 1522–3 (Museo Poldi Pezzoli, Milan).

8 Woollen knotted carpet, "north-west Persian medallion carpet", first half of the 16th century (Victoria and Albert Museum, London, McMullan Collection).

9 Woollen knotted carpet, "Herat carpet", 16th century (Österreichisches Museum für angewandte Kunst, Vienna).

10 Woollen knotted carpet, "Vase carpet", Persia, first half of the 17th century (Victoria and Albert Museum, London).

11 Woollen knotted carpet, "Portuguese carpet", Persia, first half of the 17th century (Österreichisches Museum für angewandte Kunst, Vienna).

12 Woollen knotted carpet, "Sanguszko group", Persia, second half of the 16th century (Musée des arts décoratifs, Paris).

13 Silk knotted carpet, "Hunting carpet", Persia, 16th century (Österreichisches Museum für angewandte Kunst, Vienna).

14 Silk tapestry-woven carpet, Kāshān, latter half of the 16th century (Österreichisches Museum für angewandte Kunst, Vienna).

15 (*a*) Silk knotted carpet, Persia, 16th century (The Metropolitan Museum of Art, New York, bequest of Benjamin Altman).

(*b*) Silk knotted carpet with gold and silver brocade, the so-called "Polonaise carpet", Iṣfahān, first quarter of the 17th century (Staatliche Museen Preussischer Kulturbesitz, Museum für Islamische Kunst, Berlin).

16 Cope, knotted in silk with brocade, Iṣfahān, beginning of the 17th century (Victoria and Albert Museum, London. Reproduced by courtesy of the Director).

17 Velvet, enriched with metal thread, Persia, 16th century (The Keir Collection, London).

18 Satin, Persia, beginning of the 17th century (Musées Royaux d'art et d'histoire, Brussels).

19 (*a*) Yazd. Masjid-i Jāmi', portal (Photograph, Laurence Lockhart).

(*b*) Yazd. Masjid-i Jāmi', view of court and sanctuary *aivān* (Photograph, Laurence Lockhart).

20 Turbat-i Shaikh Jām. Masjid-i Kirmānī, east wall, transverse vaults (Photograph, Lisa Golombek).

21 (*a*) Iṣfahān. Masjid-i Jāmi', *miḥrāb* of the adjoining *madrasa* (Photograph, Lisa Golombek).

(*b*) Samarqand. Shāh-i Zinda. Detail of portal of the tomb of Terken Āqā (From *Historical Monuments of Islam in the U.S.S.R.* no. 25).

22 (*a*) Samarqand. Shāh-i Zinda. Detail of façade of the mausoleum of Tūmān Āqā (From *op. cit.* no. 29).

(*b*) Samarqand. Gūr-i Mīr, general view (From *op. cit.* no. 51).

23 Turkistān. Mausoleum of Aḥmad Yasavī, south elevation of the "complex" containing mosque, mausoleum, *khānqāh* and library (From Hill and Grabar, *Islamic Architecture and its Decoration*, pl. 106).

24 (*a*) Mashhad. Gauhar Shād mosque, sanctuary *aivān* (Photograph, Laurence Lockhart).

(*b*) Mashhad. Gauhar Shād mosque, detail of foundation inscription (Photograph, Bernard O'Kane).

25 (*a*) Mashhad. Gauhar Shād mosque, southeast *aivān* (From *SPA*, pl. 433).

(*b*) Herat. Gauhar Shād Muṣallā. Dome of the mausoleum of Gauhar Shād (Photograph, Derek Hill).

26 Herat. Gauhar Shād Muṣallā. Interior of the mausoleum of Gauhar Shād (Photograph, Josephine Powell).

27 Herat. Gauhar Shād Muṣallā. Inside of the dome of the mausoleum of Gauhar Shād (Photograph, Josephine Powell).

28 Khargird. Madrasa of Ghiyāṣ al-Dīn, interior of eastern domed room (Photograph, Lisa Golombek).

29 Herat, Gāzur Gāh. Detail of faience in sanctuary *aivān* (Photograph, Lisa Golombek).

30 (*a*) Iṣfahān. Darb-i Imām, façade (Photograph, R. Pinder-Wilson).

(*b*) Iṣfahān. Darb-i Imām, detail of faience (Photograph, R. Pinder-Wilson).

31 (*a*) Tabrīz. Blue mosque, main sanctuary, northwest side (Photograph, Basil Gray).

(*b*) Tabrīz. Blue mosque, main sanctuary, northeast side (From *SPA*, pl. 456).

32 (*a*) Tabrīz. Blue mosque, detail of main portal (Photograph, Basil Gray).

(*b*) Tabrīz. Blue mosque, interior (Photograph, Josephine Powell).

Between pages 808 *and* 809

33 Woollen knotted carpet, "Garden carpet" (Burrell Collection, Glasgow Art Gallery and Museum).

34 Velvet, metal thread ground, Persia (Museo Civico Correr, Venice).

35 Velvet, metal thread ground, Persia (Badisches Landesmuseum, Karlsruhe).

36 Khusrau at the palace of Shīrīn. Tabrīz, dated 1505. Miniature added to a manuscript of the *Khamsa* of Niẓāmī (The Keir Collection, London).

48 *Khamsa* of Niẓāmī, arrival of Khusrau at the palace of Shīrīn. Baghdad, 1386–8 (British Library, MS Or. 13,297, folio 80a).

49 (*a*) *Iskandar-nāma* of Niẓāmī, Iskandar sleeping. Shīrāz, *c.* 1440 (British Library, MS Or. 13,529, folio 19).

(*b*) *Anthology* of Iskandar Sulṭān, Iskandar visits a hermit. Shīrāz, 1410–11 (British Library, MS Add. 27,261, folio 230a).

50 *Anthology* of Iskandar Sulṭān, illuminated frontispiece. Shīrāz, 1410 (Calouste Gulbenkian Foundation, Lisbon, LA 161, folio 3b).

51 *Shāh-nāma* of Firdausī, Isfandiyār slaying Arjāsp in the Brazen Hold. Herat, 1430 (Gulistān Library, Tehran).

52 *Shāh-nāma* of Firdausī, Isfandiyār slaying Arjāsp in the Brazen Hold. Herat, *c.* 1440. (Royal Asiatic Society, London, *per* British Library: folio 278b).

53 *Ta'rīkh al-rusul wa'l-mulūk* of Ṭabarī, Bahrām Gūr attacking a lion. Tabrīz, 1470 (Chester Beatty Library, Dublin, MS 144, folio 157b).

54 *Kalīla va Dimna*, The Fable of the Four Friends. Tabrīz, 1450–60 (Gulistān Library, Tehran, folio 48a).

55 *Khamsa* of Niẓāmī, the battle of the tribes of Lailā and Majnūn. Herat, *c.* 1490 (British Library, MS Add. 25,900, folio 121b).

56 *Manṭiq al-ṭair* of 'Aṭṭār, funeral procession at the gate of a *ḥaẓīra*. Herat, *c.* 1487 (The Metropolitan Museum of Art, New York, folio 35).

57 *Shāh u Darvīsh* of Hātifī, Darvīsh conducting a school. Bukhārā, dated 1542 (Pierpont Morgan Library, New York, MS 531, folio 13).

58 (*a*) Brass wine jar decorated with gold and silver, showing the dedication to Ḥusain Bāīqarā under the foot, with the date A.H. 903 (A.D. 1497) and signature of Muḥammad b. Ismā'īl Ghūrī. Herat, 1497 (British Museum, reproduced by courtesy of the Trustees).

(*b*) Silver gilt tankard, chased and engraved with the name of Qāsim b. 'Alī. Date, *c.* 1400 (Hermitage Museum, Leningrad).

59 *Jamāl u Jalāl* of Āṣafī, Jalāl before the turquoise dome. Tabrīz, 1504–5 (Uppsala University Library, folio 57b).

60 *Dīvān* of Ḥāfiẓ, the feast of 'Id. By Sulṭān Muḥammad, dedicated to Sām Mīrzā, Tabrīz, *c.* 1530 (Private collection, Geneva).

61 *Khamsa* of Niẓāmī, King Nūshīrvān and his vizier at a ruined village. By Mīr Muṣavvir, Tabrīz, 1539–43 (British Library, MS Or. 2265, folio 15b).

62 *Tuḥfat al-aḥrār* of Jāmī, East African with a mirror. Mashhad, 1556 (Courtesy of the Smithsonian Institution, Freer Gallery of Art, Washington, D.C., folio 221b).

63 (*a*) Portrait of a chamberlain, by Mīr Muṣavvir, Tabrīz, *c.* 1535–40 (British Museum, Department of Oriental Antiquities, 1930-11-12-02).

(*b*) Album of the Amīr of Bukhārā, a young falconer at the court. Attributed to Ṣādiqī Beg, Qazvīn, *c.* 1590 (Pierpont Morgan Library, New York, MS 386).

64 *Shāh-nāma* of Firdausī, Bīzhan drawn up from the well by Rustam. Iṣfahān, 1614 (New York Public Library, Spencer Collection, folio 432).

65 (*a*) A girl holding a fan, by Āqā Riżā, Qazvīn, *c.* 1595 (Freer Gallery of Art, Washington, D.C.).

(*b*) A girl holding a wine cup and flask, by Muḥammad Yūsuf, Iṣfahān, *c.* 1645 (Formerly Y. Dawud Collection, London).

66 *Khamsa* of Niẓāmī, Shīrīn discovers the murder of her husband Khusrau, by Muḥammad Zamān, Iṣfahān, dated 1675 (Pierpont Morgan Library, New York, MS 469, folio 128).

67 Lacquer-painted book-cover, Tabrīz, *c.* 1540 (Reproduced by courtesy of the Trustees of the British Museum. 1948-12-11-027/28).

68 Tooled and gilt leather binding, Tabrīz, *c.* 1550–60 (Ledermuseum, Offenbach-am-Main, Frankfurt, no. 78).

69 Panel of polychrome tiles in cuerda seca technique, from a pavilion in the Chahār Bāgh, Iṣfahān, *c.* 1640 (Victoria and Albert Museum, London).

70 Steel helmet, with carved and gilt decoration: dedication to Shah 'Abbās I with the date 1625–6 (British Museum, Henderson Collection, 1878).

71 *Shāh-nāma* of Firdausī, Rustam recovers Rakhsh. Herat style. From the *Shāh-nāma* of Shah Ṭahmāsp, folio 295a. Tabrīz, *c.* 1520–1530 (Private collection).

72 *Shāh-nāma* of Firdausī, Bahrām Gūr pins the coupling onagers. From the *Shāh-nāma* of Shah Ṭahmāsp, folio 568a. Tabrīz, *c.* 1520–1530 (The Metropolitan Museum of Art. Gift of Arthur A. Houghton, Jr, 1970).

TEXT FIGURES

MAPS

TABLES

PREFACE

The period of Iranian history from the death of the last important Īl-Khān, Abū Sa'īd, in 1335 down to the mid 18th century has scarcely received adequate notice from western historians. Since this volume was first conceived, the void has been filled partially by two works in English, *The Aqquyunlu* by J. E. Woods (1976) and R. M. Savory's *Iran under the Safavids* (1980). But there is as yet no authoritative monograph on Tīmūr or the Timurids (with the qualified exception of Barthold's work on Ulugh Beg and on the court of Ḥusain Bāīqarā); and the standard work on the Qarā Quyūnlū is in Turkish. It is not the least merit of Professor Roemer's first four chapters, therefore, to make the pre-Safavid era as a whole accessible and intelligible to the Western reader.

The relative neglect from which late medieval and early modern Iran has suffered is all the more remarkable when it is borne in mind that this period witnessed the first emergence of Iran as a "national" state enjoying a recognisable continuity with the present day. To a large extent this was of course fortuitous rather than a matter of conscious policy on the part of the Safavid rulers. The defeat at Chāldirān ensured that the Safavids would not extend their power into Anatolia, just as the simultaneous rise of the Uzbeks and of the Mughal empire curtailed attempts to enter into the Timurid political legacy in the east. Yet the fact remains that under the Safavid dynasty, which contrived to last longer than any of its predecessors since the Islamic conquest, Iran came to constitute a single political entity roughly within its present-day boundaries. The part played in this process by the adoption of Shī'a Islam as the state religion; the reshaping of the Persian monarchic ideal; the need to resolve the conflicts inherent in Iranian society, as for instance between tribal and non-tribal elements – all these are problems which merit detailed investigation.

The period has other fascinations for Western Europe. If diplomatic contact between Iran and the West had begun under the Īl-Khāns, it had nevertheless been shortlived. Not until the late 15th century, in the time of the Āq Quyūnlū, did such exchanges become a regular phenomenon, fortified under both Uzun Ḥasan and his Safavid heirs by the common hostility of the parties concerned towards the Ottoman empire. These contacts, and the growing attractiveness of Iran also to Western merchants in search of manufactures and raw materials, endow the Safavid period especially with a wealth of European travellers' reports which are among our principal sources for the country's political, economic and social history.

This volume was first planned in 1961, when Laurence Lockhart was appointed editor, and invitations to most of the contributors had been sent out by the end of 1963. Several chapters were as yet unfinished or awaited translation into English at the time of Lockhart's death in 1976. Professor J. A. Boyle, who had produced the fifth volume in this series, then took over the editorship of volume 6, but had been able to do very little when he in turn died two years later. It has fallen to me, as editor since the autumn of 1979, to receive the chapters still outstanding, to edit and prepare the entire manuscript for the press. Some of the contributors – Professor Savory, Dr Hillenbrand and Mr Gray – have revised their chapters within the last few years; and we are indebted to Professor Schimmel and Professor Yarshater for adding, at somewhat short notice, two valuable chapters to the literature section of the volume. The remaining chapters were drafted earlier, and consequently the most recent research has not been taken into account. For this, of course, the authors themselves are not to blame. It should also be mentioned that the maps and genealogical tables were drafted by me and not by the authors of the chapters within which they are located.

Every effort has been made to achieve a high degree of standardisation throughout the volume. I have adhered, on the whole, to the system of transliteration followed in volume 4 and to the practice adopted there of using italics only for the first appearance of technical terms, and roman characters thereafter, within each chapter. A major difficulty has arisen from the fact that, even in the period covered by this volume, Arabic names and terms are by no means totally eclipsed by Persian ones, and that it is necessary to employ different transcriptions (Arabic *th*, *dh*, *ḍ*, and *w* for Persian *s̱*, *ẕ*, *ẓ̇* and *v*). The results may occasionally seem startling, as when the convention is applied to the titles of books written by the same author but in different languages; or in the case of the Islamic months and of religious and philosophical terminology, which have been given in their Arabic form (thus *qāḍī* rather than *qāẓ̇ī*, except where part of a proper name, as in Qāżī Burhān al-Dīn). The ligature used in previous volumes, indicating that the roman letters concerned represent a single consonant in the Arabo-Persian alphabet, has been discarded. Diacritical marks are also omitted, for example, in the names of dynasties where these are anglicised (thus Ṣafaviyya, but Safavids) and in such titles as shah unless an integral part of a proper name (thus Jahān Shāh, Shāh Jahān; but Shah 'Abbās). For Turkish and Mongol words and names I have slightly modified the system of transcription found in volume 5; and in any case those dynasties which held extensive sway over Iranian territory, as did the later Qarā Quyūnlū and Āq Quyūnlū rulers, have been treated as if they were Persian. It is hoped that the adoption of these admittedly complex principles will have proved more vexatious to the editor than to the reader.

It remains to thank those who contributed to the completion of this volume. Hubert Darke, the Editorial Secretary for the Cambridge History of Iran, has been of considerable assistance with the bibliography, plates and figures. I have benefited also from the help of Iain White, who sub-edited the manuscript. My colleagues and friends at Keele have had to live with me while I wrestled with editorial tasks; I should like finally to thank them for their patience and good humour.

The Publishers and the Editorial Board of *The Cambridge History of Iran* are grateful for a generous donation from The Yarshater Fund, Columbia University.

PETER JACKSON

Keele, April 1985

CHAPTER I

THE JALAYIRIDS, MUZAFFARIDS AND SARBADĀRS

THE LAST CHINGIZIDS

The end of the Il-Khanid empire resulted in Persia, if not in the creation of a vacuum, at any rate in a dilution of power, which worked in favour of various forces contending for authority in the state. The rivals involved in the struggles which now began fall into three categories. The most obvious of these were princes from several lines of the dynasty of Chingiz Khān, who looked to a restoration of centralised Mongol rule. They set about their task partly on their own initiative and partly as mere figureheads put up by legitimist groupings in the background. A second group was the representatives of local dynasties or highly placed families, who had served the Īl-Khāns as generals or senior servants of the state, and also the leaders of powerful tribal associations. And there were, finally, other groups for whom what mattered was not dynastic or aristocratic considerations but religious adherence to Shīʿī or extremist movements.

The power struggles that went on within or between these groups lasted for half a century. Though one or other of the rivals might for a time contrive to establish a certain measure of political and economic stability in his area of effective control, none had any lasting success, and there was no question of their unifying the country alone and unaided. Whatever the hardships Persia suffered as a result of divisions and chaotic conditions, even greater sacrifices were demanded of the people when, at the beginning of the eighties of the 8th/14th century, reunification was finally achieved: imposed, in fact, from outside by the conqueror Tīmūr. Pressing forward from Central Asia, he soon swept aside the contending parties or merely allowed them to fade into insignificance.

It is typical of Persia that in spite of the troubles of the decades between the end of the Il-Khanid empire and the appearance on the scene of Tīmūr, Persian culture was not submerged, as one might have expected, but achieved, in its intellectual life, for example in the sphere of poetry, a distinction hardly equalled in any other period. The flowering of poetry which reached its highest point in the unique figure of

Ḥāfiẓ of Shīrāz is a striking phenomenon in the cultural history of 8th/14th century Persia. In marked contrast, public life and political affairs were throughout most of this period in a sorry state. Political confusion, the tyranny of petty princes, bloody conflicts between local powers, and devastating invasions were a constant menace, not only to the general well-being but to people's very existence, even when they managed to save their skins in the apocalyptic horrors which now descended on their homeland, depopulating many towns and laying waste entire areas. The collapse of the Mongol empire of Iran, struggles for the Mongol inheritance and the horrors of another conquest and occupation of the country at the hands of Tīmūr made up the fate of the luckless inhabitants of Iran in this century; a fate which was all the more keenly felt as the memory of the halcyon days under the last of the Īl-Khāns was no doubt still widely treasured.

Strangely enough, the very time at which – with the death of the Īl-Khān Abū Sa'īd and the passing of Hülegü's dynasty – the end of their empire became imminent, was the year in which Tīmūr was born, the man who a few decades later incorporated Persia into an empire destined eventually to extend from the Jaxartes to Asia Minor. Though he himself was actually of Turkish origin, throughout his life, and even when he had become the most powerful man on earth, he set the greatest store by his Mongol family connections – a plain indication of the high regard in which Chingiz Khān and his descendants were held even long after the fall of the Il-Khanid empire.

Of course, the extinction of the line of Hülegü need not necessarily have implied the end of the Persian Mongol empire, and there is no doubt that many people in Persia at this time were convinced that Mongol rule would survive, for there was plainly no lack of influential Mongol leaders and politicians, nor of princes belonging to the most diverse lines of descent from Chingiz Khān who could theoretically have provided for the continuation of the empire. Abū Sa'īd's successor Arpa Ke'ün, for instance, belonged to the family of Tolui. He was a competent prince, who might have been able to secure Mongol control of Persia had he not met his end a few months after his accession as a result of a conflict with a general who was seeking to put another Chingizid in power. But he was the last of the princes who emerged, or were thrust forward in these struggles for power, to show any competence, at least in terms of their success in re-establishing a united Iranian empire. Not one of them was able to assert control, nor could any of their military or nomadic backers. The disappearance of centralised authority not only opened the way for Mongol princes and influential military leaders or tribal chieftains to engage in political adventures; it was also the signal to local rulers who had hitherto been submissive to Mongol power to make a bid for independence.

The Chingizids' control of Iran was at an end by half way through the 8th/14th century. This is true whether one chooses to take as critical the year 740/1340, in which Ḥasan-i Buzurg, the founder of the house of the Jalayirids, took power personally in Baghdad in place of his figurehead Jahān Temür, a descendant of the Īl-Khān Gaikhatu (690–4/1291–5), or whether one prefers the year 754/1353, in which an equally insignificant Chobanid caused the last coins to be minted bearing the name of the puppet khan Anūshīrvān and, in addition, the last Chingizid, Togha Temür, was murdered by a Sarbadār. From then on until Tīmūr's invasion of the country, Iran was under the rule of various rival petty princes of whom henceforth only the Jalayirids could claim Mongol, though not Chingizid, descent. They ruled from Baghdad and were later significantly involved in the history of the country with the conquest of Āzarbāījān. In the east, especially in the Khurasanian city of Sabzavār, the Sarbadārs increased in power, while in Fārs and Iṣfahān members of the house of Īnjū sought to assert themselves over the Muzaffarids. In the south-east, princes of the Kart (or Kurt) dynasty at Herat were active on the political scene, just as they had been under the Īl-Khāns. Later, Türkmen confederations appeared, thrusting forward from eastern Anatolia towards the Iranian highlands. These were the Qarā Quyūnlū and the Āq Quyūnlū, of whom the former were already beginning to influence the fortunes of Persia in the 8th/14th century.

It is necessary to discuss the political scene at this time, grim and unedifying though it is, because it forms the background to a significant epoch in Iranian intellectual life; and also because it shows up in clear colours the negative reasons for Tīmūr's successes on Iranian soil. Before tracing the main lines of this development, which extended over some fifty years, it will be as well to try to clarify the situation of the time by means of a table setting out the most important political forces which began to operate after the fall of the Il-Khanid empire. Although the plan which follows is not exhaustive, it does demonstrate the fragmentation of the country. It is evident from the dates given, which in many cases can only be tentative, that various of these régimes survived the conquest by Tīmūr or in some cases even the entire Timurid era:

The Chobanids in 'Irāq-i 'Ajam, Āzarbāījān and Armenia, until 744/1343;

The Jalayirids in 'Irāq-i 'Arab and later also in the territory of the Chobanids, until 835/1432;

The Qarā Quyūnlū in Āzarbāījān, and later with further extensions of influence to Fārs and Khurāsān, till 873/1468–9;

The "Īl-Khān" Togha Temür in western Khurāsān and Gurgān, until 754/1353;

The Sarbadārs in western Khurāsān, until 783/1381;

The Sayyids of Māzandarān, until 794/1392, and Gīlān down to 1370;

The Kārkiyā in Lāhījān, until 1060/1650;

The Kartids (Kurtids) of Herat in eastern Khurāsān and Afghanistan, with influence extending into Sīstān and Kirmān, until 791/1389;

The Injuids in Fārs and Iṣfahān, until 758/1357;

The Muzaffarids in Kirmān and Yazd, and later also in the former territory of the Injuids, until 795/1393;

The *maliks* of Shabānkāra in the area lying between Fārs and Kirmān on the Persian Gulf, until 756/1355;

The governors (*ḥukkām*) of Lār, until 983/1575;

The maliks of Hurmuz, until 1031/1622;

The atabegs of Greater Luristān (Lur-i Buzurg), until 828/1425;

The atabegs of Lesser Luristān (Lur-i Kūchak), until 1006/1597.

A number of these princely houses and their representatives such as Togha Temür, the Chobanids, and particularly the conflict of the "two Ḥasans", i.e. the Chobanid Shaikh Ḥasan-i Kūchak and Shaikh Ḥasan-i Buzurg of the Jalāyir tribe, have been treated elsewhere,[1] and the Qarā Quyūnlū will be dealt with later; others are of such minor significance in the history of Iran, in this period at least, that no more than a brief reference can be made to them here. We shall therefore summarise the most important events in three brief sections on the Jalayirids, on the Īnjū family and the Muzaffarids, and on the Sarbadārs and their rivals.

[1] On the Chobanids, see Boyle, in *CHI* v, 373–416; for Togha Temür, *ibid.*, 413–16, and Minorsky, "Tugha Tīmūr", *EI*[1]; for the racial affinities of the Jā'ūn-i Qurbān who supported him, Aubin, "L'ethnogénèse", p. 67.

THE JALAYIRIDS

The name Jalāyir is derived from that of a large and important Mongol tribe.[1] The dynasty of the same name, whose rule began in 740/1340 with Shaikh Ḥasan-i Buzurg's seizure of power in Baghdad and ended with the death of Ḥusain II at the siege of al-Ḥilla, is also quite often referred to as the Īlkā dynasty or the Ilkanids. The name originates with Shaikh Ḥasan's great-grandfather Ilge (<Īlkā) Noyan, who as one of Hülegü's generals took a significant part in the Mongol conquest of Central Asia and the Near East. His sons likewise attained to high rank in the military aristocracy of the Il-Khanid empire, and several of them were able to take princesses of the house of Hülegü in marriage. Thus Ilge's grandson Ḥusain (d.722/1322) married a daughter of the Īl-Khān Arghūn named Öljetei, who became the mother of Shaikh Ḥasan, the founder of the dynasty.

Shaikh Ḥasan-i Buzurg, who under Abū Sa'īd and again under Arpa Ke'ün had attained to the highest offices as *ulus beg* and deputy, proved to be the strongest personality in the massive struggles for power which took place at the end of Mongol rule in Iran, though he was frequently hard pressed in the conflicts with the Chobanids, and especially with Shaikh Ḥasan-i Kūchak and, after the latter's murder in 744/1343, with his brother Malik Ashraf. If we are to credit a recent interpretation, he was more interested in seeing restoration of the Il-Khanid empire than its overthrow, which of course he did in fact bring about.[2] He is said never to have assumed any title other than *ulus beg* ("amīr of the state", from Tu. *beg*, "amīr", and Mo. *ulus*, "state, people") and to have recognised the legitimate Chingizids – Togha Temür (739/1338–9, 741–4/1340–4), Jahān Temür (740/1339–40) and Sulaimān (747/1346) – and subsequently, in the period 747–57/ 1346–56, to have left the throne unoccupied. The remarkable thing is that this prince was able to maintain his position in these troubled times right up to his death in 757/1356. "No one in his position has lived to such an age nowadays", commented

[1] In "Īlāt", *EI*², Professor Lambton discusses a manuscript said to be taken from the state papers of the Safavid Sulṭān Ḥusain, in which the distribution of tribes at the beginning of the 12th/18th century is surveyed and a distinction drawn between Persian and non-Persian tribes: here the Jalāyir in Khurāsān are listed in the former category.

[2] The view of Smith, "Djalāyir, Djalāyirids", *EI*². According to Spuler, *Die Mongolen in Iran*, p. 133, and Boyle, *CHI* v, 415, however, Shaikh Ḥasan began his autonomous rule in Baghdad with the deposition of Jahān Temür. On this question Shaikh Ḥasan's coinage appears relevant: cf. Spuler, p. 303, n.7.

in amazement Ibn Bazzāz; and he finds a supernatural explanation for the fact – namely the good relationship which (in contrast to the Chobanids) Ḥasan-i Buzurg had established with the saintly Shaikh Ṣafī al-Dīn of Ardabīl, who had died twenty-two years previously.[1]

He was succeeded by Shaikh Uvais, a son of Ḥasan and the Chobanid princess Dil-Shād Khātūn. In the same year – as had happened once before, at the death of Abū Sa'īd – an attack was launched by the Golden Horde against Persia, namely in Khurāsān and Āzarbāījān. However, the khan Jānī Beg (Jambek) Jalāl al-Dīn Maḥmūd, who had defeated and executed Malik Ashraf, the ruler in Āzarbāījān, was forced to withdraw as a result of developments in the northern part of his realm. When he died in the following year, his son Berdī Beg, whom he had left as governor in Persia, also returned to Sarāī. This amounted to the abandonment of the Persian conquests, even if we regard Akhīchūq, one of Ashraf's amīrs, who placed himself at the disposal of the conquerors after the defeat, and following their withdrawal twice took possession of Tabrīz, as belonging to the Golden Horde; for he, too, was unable to maintain his position for any length of time. In 761/1360 Uvais, who had at first recognised the overlordship of the Golden Horde, conquered Āzarbāījān, which his father had lost to Shaikh Ḥasan-i Kūchak twenty years earlier. Thus another attempt to restore Mongol rule in Iran, this time from the direction of the Golden Horde, had also failed. Shaikh Uvais' success had not been achieved at the first attempt, however. It was preceded by an abortive attack on his part and a campaign led by Mubāriz al-Dīn Muḥammad b. al-Muẓaffar of Yazd, which had thoroughly weakened Akhīchūq's fighting power. In the years that followed, Shaikh Uvais intervened in the power struggles of the Muzaffarids. To Shāh Maḥmūd, who acknowledged his sovereignty and married one of his daughters, he handed over Iṣfahān and recognised his conquest of Shīrāz.

These great successes were offset by many difficulties and setbacks with which Shaikh Uvais had to contend. Thus in the winter of 766/1364, during a campaign against the Shīrvān-Shāh Kai-Kā'us b. Kai-Qubād, news reached him of the revolt of his governor in Baghdad, Khwāja Mirjān, and he was obliged to return and restore order in his own capital city. Among his worst enemies were the Qarā Quyūnlū

[1] Cf. Glassen, *Die frühen Safawiden*, p. 43. Good relations with the Ardabīl order continued into later times, as may be seen from an edict of the Jalayirid Aḥmad of 1372: see Massé, "Ordonnance".

in Diyārbakr, the same Türkmen federation which later, at the beginning of the 9th/15th century, was to put an end to his dynasty. In the spring of 767/1366 he marched against them and defeated Bairām Khwāja, their leader, at the battle of Mūsh. Eventually he also brought to heel the Shīrvān-Shāh, who had twice exploited his absence from Āzarbāījān to launch attacks on Tabrīz. In Ray he defeated Amīr Valī, who ruled in Astarābād after the death of Togha Temür, but was forced to break off the campaign when news was brought of the death of his brother Amīr Zāhid in Ūjān, which made necessary his return to Āzarbāījān. He placed the governorship of Ray in the hands of Qutlugh Shāh, one of his amīrs, who was followed in the post two years later by 'Ādil Āqā.

Although Shaikh Uvais retained Baghdad as his capital, his military enterprises and political considerations repeatedly took him to Persia, and he died finally in Tabrīz (776/1374). It is not only his military and political achievements that mark him out as unquestionably the most eminent prince of his line; it is particularly his human qualities and the impetus he gave to cultural life. The latter embraced both efforts to revive commercial enterprise in the devastated regions of Iran and his own personal contribution to civilised living, his patronage of and interest in art and literature – to which no doubt we are also indirectly indebted for many of the detailed facts concerning his life and activities found in a chronicle whose author was apparently his official court chronicler, the *Tārīkh-i Shaikh Uvais* of Abū Bakr al-Quṭbī al-Ahrī. But in addition he wrote verses himself and won renown as a calligrapher and painter.

Shaikh Uvais's efforts towards an extension of Jalayirid power to central and eastern Persia, which was clearly to have been initiated by the campaign against Ray, met with no success. Nor were the rulers who followed him any more successful in this direction. Indeed, the decline of Jalayirid power set in immediately and relentlessly after his death. His eldest son, Ḥasan, failed on account of his general unpopularity and was executed by the top-ranking amīrs. The succession passed to his brother Ḥusain (776–83/1374–82).[1] He experienced immediate difficulties with the Muzaffarids, first with his brother-in-law Shāh Maḥmūd, who marched from Iṣfahān to occupy Tabrīz, though he was obliged to

[1] According to Rabino, "Coins of the Jalā'ir", p. 106, Ḥusain's *laqab*, which is usually given as Ghiyāṣ al-Dīn, appears on his coins as Mughīṣ al-Dīn. Perhaps it should also be read thus in the document published by Herrmann, "Ein Erlass des Ǧalāyeriden Solṭān Ḥoseyn".

withdraw from the town as a result of illness and died shortly afterwards. His successor Shāh-i Shujā' also made all haste to occupy Tabrīz if he could, but again the attempt failed. Disturbances in the city, the inclemencies of a hard winter, and an uprising in Qazvīn forced him to return to Iṣfahān. Not until the summer of 778/1376 was Ḥusain again able to take up residence in Tabrīz, only to be compelled in the following spring to march again, against Bairām Khwāja and his Türkmens, who were thrusting eastwards once more, this time from the direction of Erzerum.

These operations were successful, but Ḥusain soon found himself caught up in problems of an internal nature, in which his brothers Shaikh 'Alī, Aḥmad and Bāyazīd were involved. The situation was further aggravated by his support of 'Ādil Āqā, whose exceptional rise to power provoked the hostility of other influential amīrs. Incessant troubles at home, uprisings by local potentates and battles with the Muzaffarids consumed Ḥusain's resources. To all this was added the breach with 'Ādil, who had meanwhile risen to a position of unchallengeable power. So he found himself by Ṣafar 784/the end of April 1382 defenceless against an attack by his brother Sulṭān Aḥmad when he advanced with an armed force from his territory around Ardabīl and occupied Tabrīz. Aḥmad, who took over the succession, had his brother executed.

Amīr 'Ādil countered by proclaiming Prince Bāyazīd, who had managed by the skin of his teeth to escape from Tabrīz, as sultan in Sulṭāniyya. Aḥmad, now subjected to attack from several directions, could find no other expedient in the circumstances than to seek help from the arch-enemies of his family, the Qarā Quyūnlū under Qarā Muḥammad. His brother, Shaikh 'Alī, who had advanced from Baghdad to attack Tabrīz, was killed in the fighting against them. A treaty providing for the cession of Āzarbāījān to Sulṭān Aḥmad, 'Irāq-i 'Ajam to his brother Bāyazīd, and 'Irāq-i 'Arab jointly to Aḥmad and 'Ādil, proved to be shortlived, so that it was in a state of utter disunity and discord that the Jalayirids were hurled into the great conflicts of Tīmūr, on the one hand with the Golden Horde under Tokhtamïsh and on the other with the Ottomans under Bāyezīd I Yïldïrïm. This will be dealt with in the next chapter.

The contributions to cultural life made by various princes of the Jalayirid dynasty provide a welcome contrast to the disastrous rôle played in Iranian politics by this princely house (especially its later members), with their endless disputes and feuds. Miniature painting is the most significant area. Their artistic activities were centred on Tabrīz and especially Baghdad, where impressive examples of their architecture have been preserved. In the period we are dealing with the Jalayirids were largely Turkicised, or at least Turkish-speaking; and they have been credited with establishing the Turkish element in Arabic Iraq on a firmer foundation so that Turkish became the language most commonly spoken after Arabic.[1] But this did not prevent them from acquiring a reputation as patrons of Persian poets: as a prime witness to this fact we may quote no less a name than Salmān Sāvajī.

In the religious sphere the Jalayirids display unmistakably Shī'ī features, as in their preference for such names as 'Alī, Ḥasan and Ḥusain. A still clearer indication is to be seen in the dying wish of the founder of the dynasty, Shaikh Ḥasan-i Buzurg, to be buried in Najaf, where according to tradition 'Alī b. Abī Ṭālib had found his last resting place. Nevertheless, as Mazzaoui points out,[2] the conversion of ruling princes to Shi'ism at this time did not necessarily assume a spectacular form or result in the conversion of their subjects. Whether this circumstance helps to explain the virtual absence of references to the Shī'a on Jalayirid coins must remain an open question. Rabino has found no evidence demonstrating even Shī'ī sympathies among the coins – over 150 of them – minted by the Jalayirids which he has examined. In a group of 35 other coins preserved in the Mūza-yi Āzarbāījān, Tabrīz, only one bears the names of the Twelve Imāms rather than those of the Orthodox caliphs, namely a coin of Ḥasan-i Buzurg minted at Āmul in 742/1341–2.[3] A recent find at 'Aqarqūf, 20 km west of Baghdad, contained 227 Jalayirid silver coins, of which 50 belong to Shaikh Uvais and the remainder to Sulṭān Aḥmad. Shī'ī characteristics were totally lacking, and the coins of Uvais bore the names of the Orthodox caliphs.[4]

[1] Yınanç, "Celâyir", p. 65. [2] *Origins of the Ṣafawids*, p. 64.

[3] Sayyid Jamāl Turābī-Ṭabāṭabā'ī, *Sikkahā-yi shāhān-i islāmī-yi Īrān* II (Tabrīz, 1350/1971), 110; cf. *idem*, *Rasm al-khaṭṭ-i uighurī va sā'irī dar sikka-shināsī* (Tabrīz, 1351/1972), p. 58, for two other strikings of Ḥasan-i Buzurg, in Baghdad 745/1344–5 and 744/1343–4, which both bear the names of the Orthodox caliphs.

[4] Mahāb Darwīsh al-Bakrī, "Iktishāf nuqūd jalā'iriyya fī 'Aqarqūf", *al-Maskūkāt* III (1972), 77–80 (reference kindly supplied by Dr Dorothea Duda): the details are unfortunately very scanty.

JALAYIRIDS, MUZAFFARIDS AND SARBADĀRS

I. *The Jalayirids*

- Ḥusain
  - Shaikh Ḥasan-i Buzurg
    - Shaikh Uvais
      - Ḥasan
      - Ḥusain
      - Sulṭān Aḥmad
      - Shaikh ʿAlī
      - Bāyazīd
    - Amīr Zāhid

II. *The Muẓaffarids*

- Sharaf al-Dīn Muẓaffar
  - Mubāriz al-Dīn Muḥammad
    - Jalāl al-Dīn Abu'l-Favāris Shāh-i Shujāʿ
      - Sulṭān Uvais
        - Sulṭān Abū Isḥāq
      - Zain al-ʿĀbidīn ʿAlī
      - Sulṭān Shiblī
    - Shāh Maḥmūd
    - Shāh Muẓaffar
      - Shāh Manṣūr
      - Shāh Yaḥyā
    - Sulṭān ʿImād al-Dīn Aḥmad

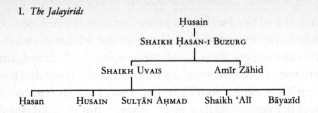

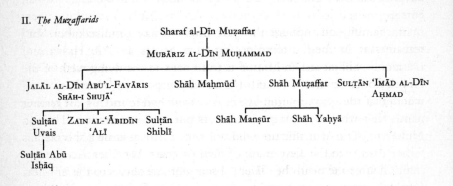

THE ĪNJŪ FAMILY AND THE MUZAFFARIDS

The Jalayirids had been unable to bring any lasting pressure to bear on 'Irāq-i 'Ajam and Fārs. On the contrary, the advances made by the Muzaffarids from these areas against their sphere of control, including even the repeated occupation of Tabrīz, can be regarded as a pointer to the debilitated condition to which they were so often reduced.

The Muzaffarids originated in an Arab family in Khurāsān which had been settled there since the Islamic conquest but which, on the advance of the Mongols, had withdrawn to Yazd where they had entered the service of the local atabeg, 'Alā' al-Daula. Various members of the family had then seen service under Hülegü, while others had remained in Maibud, a town not far from Yazd. Here the eponym of the family, Sharaf al-Dīn Muẓaffar, was finally appointed governor. He served under several Īl-Khāns, the last of whom was Öljeitü, as commander of the gendarmerie, with the task of exterminating the robber bands that were springing up in many parts of the country. His son Mubāriz al-Dīn Muḥammad, who was only thirteen years old when his father died, lived at first at the Īl-Khān's court but then returned to Maibud after the death of Öljeitü. From here he succeeded after a few years in bringing down the atabeg of Yazd and himself taking possession of the city. Soon after this he was obliged to engage in a whole series of battles with the Negüderis, a Mongol tribal group which was seeking at that time to intervene in the fortunes of Persia from the south-east.[1]

For the coup in Yazd, Mubāriz al-Dīn had a helper in Amīr Ghiyāṯ al-Dīn Kai-Khusrau of the house of Īnjū. This family, whose destiny is closely linked with that of the Muzaffarids, exercised control in Fārs and in various centres of 'Irāq-i 'Ajam from 703/1304, the beginning of the reign of the Īl-Khān Öljeitü, until their fall from power in 758/1357. They owed the name Īnjū to the circumstance that their ancestor Sharaf al-Dīn Maḥmud Shāh, the father of the Kai-Khusrau already mentioned, was responsible for administering the royal domains (Mongol: *injü*). Sharaf al-Dīn was reputedly descended from the well-known mystic of Herat, 'Abd-Allāh Anṣārī (d. 481/1089). The well-nigh absolute control he had managed to establish by 725/1325 in Fārs aroused the suspicion of Abū Sa'īd, who therefore summoned him

[1] For the origin and early development of the Negüderis as "le troisième groupe pré-Qaraunas", see Aubin, "L'ethnogénèse", pp. 73ff.

to his court and appointed another governor to replace him in Fārs. However, the latter was unable to take up his office because Amīr Ghiyās̱ al-Dīn, who ruled in his father's name in Shīrāz, refused to hand over the management of affairs to him, and some time later, on the news of the death of the Īl-Khān, took him prisoner and sent him to Āzarbāījān. Even during Abū Sa'īd's lifetime Sharaf al-Dīn had been imprisoned in Tabrīz after an abortive attempt on the life of his successor. When Arpa Ke'ün had him executed, his sons, who were present in the royal encampment (*ordo*), took flight, Amīr Jalāl al-Dīn Mas'ūd Shāh finding refuge with Shaikh Ḥasan-i Buzurg in Rūm, and Shaikh Abū Isḥāq with Amīr 'Alī Pādishāh in Diyārbakr.

Arpa Ke'ün later fell into the power of his rival Mūsā Khān and was handed over to Mas'ūd Shāh, who exacted a bloody revenge for his father's death. The same Mas'ūd Shāh forthwith advanced to the position of vizier to Muḥammad Khān, who succeeded Mūsā Khān as ruler in 736/1336, and after the murder of his master fled to Shīrāz, where Kai-Khusrau had meanwhile set himself up as his father's successor. In the struggle for power between the two brothers which promptly began, Mas'ūd Shāh emerged as the stronger but was unable to rid himself of the dispute with Kai-Khusrau until the latter went the way of all flesh a few years later (739/1338–9). But Mas'ūd Shāh was destined to have little joy of his reign. The very next year his brother Shams al-Dīn Muḥammad, whom he had been holding prisoner in the fortress of Qal'a-yi Safīd, escaped and threw in his lot with the Chobanid Pīr Ḥusain. The two men marched at the head of Mongol troops to Shīrāz and conquered the city; and Mas'ūd Shāh fled from there to Luristān. By his murder of Shams al-Dīn Muḥammad, Pīr Ḥusain forfeited all hope of support from the population, so that he again had to withdraw from Shīrāz. His attempt to gain possession of the city the following year also came to nothing. In his disputes with other Chobanids he finally sought refuge with Ḥasan-i Kūchak. The latter, however, had him executed; and shortly after this was himself murdered (27 Rajab 744/15 December 1343).

The two surviving sons of Sharaf al-Dīn Maḥmūd Shāh also tried to make their way with the aid of the Chobanids; and likewise it proved their undoing. Mas'ūd Shāh struck up an alliance in Luristān with Yaghï Bastï and marched with him to Shīrāz. He met the same fate as his brother and in the same year – murdered by his ally. Abū Isḥāq, the last of the Injuids, who had tried to appropriate Yazd to himself when the rule of the Īl-Khāns came to an end, had been entrusted by the above-mentioned Pīr Ḥusain with Iṣfahān; he had also successfully asserted his claim on Shīrāz at the collapse of the Chobanids, which followed immediately on the death of Ḥasan-i Kūchak. His efforts to extend his power into Kirmān, beginning in 748/1347, brought him into conflict with the Muzaffarid Mubāriz al-Dīn Muḥammad, a conflict which he only succeeded in intensifying by a campaign against Yazd (751/1350–1). Two years later his troops were defeated in open battle and the Muzaffarid besieged him in Shīrāz. He was compelled to capitulate, but managed to make good his escape and – with the aid of the Jalayirid Ḥasan-i Buzurg – to establish himself again in Iṣfahān, only to be besieged there in turn by Mubāriz al-Dīn. He had to capitulate once more, was taken prisoner and executed (758/1357).

With this triumph on the part of Mubāriz al-Dīn the fate of the Injuids was sealed, and it might well be thought that their passing would have gone quite unlamented. But it was not so. ʿUbaid-i Zākānī, one of the most famous poets of the time, deplored the death of Shaikh Abū Isḥāq in an elegy, and no less a figure than Ḥāfiẓ praised the happy days in Shīrāz under the reign of the last of the Injuids. The latter had been a generous patron of poetry – he was indeed not alone in this among the members of his house – and on this score secured his recognition in world literature in spite of the warmongering intrigues into which he had all too often recklessly blundered. With the victory of Mubāriz al-Dīn, which also found its way into the history of literature (if only in the negative sense that the victor is recalled as an implacable fanatic who made life hard for literary men), the happy days of Shīrāz and its buoyant poets seemed to have come to an end, and both social and public life were placed under the watchful eye of the supervisor of markets and public morals (*muḥtasib*). That this situation did not, however, erect insuperable obstacles for the poetic muse, but even added a certain stimulus to its life – by obliging poets to be discreet and operate with metaphors and ironic allusions – can be read between the lines in a number of passages in Ḥāfiẓ's *Dīvān*.[1]

The capture of Shīrāz and Iṣfahān gave Mubāriz al-Dīn, the first of the Muzaffarid princes, a dominant position in Iranian politics. The little country town of Maibud had served them as a springboard to Yazd; they had then pressed on to Kirmān, and now – with Fārs and

[1] See Lescot, "Chronologie".

'Irāq-i 'Ajam taken – they possessed two of the most important provinces of the country. Mubāriz al-Dīn Muḥammad made Shīrāz his capital. The fame of his military exploits caused the khan of the Golden Horde, Jānī Beg, who was in Tabrīz at the time, to invite him to enter his service. He was in a position to be able to decline the invitation, and when the khan, and shortly afterwards also his son and successor Berdī Beg, had withdrawn from Tabrīz, he promptly marched his forces to Āzarbāījān, defeated Akhīchūq, the khan's governor, at Miyāna, and occupied Tabrīz. But his triumph was shortlived, for when Jalayirid troops moved up from Baghdad he found himself unable to hold on to his conquests and retreated from Tabrīz. This meant the failure of an undertaking which could be regarded as an attempt to solve the major problem of Persia in the half-century between the fall of the Il-Khanid empire and the emergence of Tīmūr, namely the establishment of centralised control.

Mubāriz al-Dīn Muḥammad's bleak tyranny did not endure long after the removal of the house of Īnjū from the scene. His intolerance, combined with severity and treachery, inspired fear and hostility in his own sons. One of them, Abu'l-Favāris Shāh-i Shujā'[1], took him prisoner, had his eyes put out, and incarcerated him in Qal'a-yi Safīd. He contrived to improve his lot quite soon afterwards, but never again managed up to his death (765/1364) to secure a dominant influence in government, not even by means of a plot hatched by his supporters against his son. The period of his rule in Shīrāz stands out in stark contrast to the cultivated standards of the city with which we are familiar from contemporary literary evidence.

Under the new ruler, Shāh-i Shujā', the liberal spirit of freedom and tolerance that had been enjoyed before was once again in vogue, and was jubilantly greeted by Ḥāfiẓ. Though his long reign (759–86/1358–84) reintroduced an atmosphere of liberty and meant the end of narrow bigotry, yet it was anything but a period of undisturbed peace. The constant squabbles of the prince with his brothers and his attempts to extend his power produced even worse conditions than under the Jalayirids and the Injuids – namely, almost unremitting warlike entanglements with alternations of success and failure. As early as 765/1363 Shāh-i Shujā' marched against his brother Shāh Maḥmūd, who ruled in Iṣfahān. Although a reconciliation was initially effected, he met

[1] [For the form of the name, see Aubin, "La fin de l'état Sarbadâr", pp. 101–2 n. 32. (Ed.)].

with a reverse somewhat later when Maḥmūd, with the support of his father-in-law, the Jalayirid Shaikh Uvais, who ruled in Baghdad, invaded the province of Fārs, besieging and finally conquering Shīrāz. It was three years before he could again take possession of his capital city.

The idea of uniting the north-western areas of Persia with the Muzaffarid territories had not died with Mubāriz al-Dīn Muḥammad and his abandonment of Tabrīz; in fact, various further attempts were made to achieve it. The first impetus was given by the complex situation involved in the succession to the throne of Tabrīz (described above) after Shaikh Uvais had died there in 776/1374. At that time Shāh Maḥmūd had challenged his brother-in-law Ḥusain's claim to his father's inheritance, but was forced by a sudden severe illness to yield up Tabrīz, which he had by then occupied – just as his father had done before him. Not long after this he died (776/1375), and Iṣfahān passed into the hands of Shāh-i Shujā', who now himself sought to annex Āzarbāījān. In spite of a victorious advance on Tabrīz, he too was denied success, fundamentally because conditions in Fārs were not sufficiently stable for him to risk being absent for any length of time. This fact was quickly made plain when his nephew Shāh Yaḥyā, now installed in Iṣfahān, rose in revolt. He therefore acceded to a compromise arrangement with Ḥusain, hoping to secure his position by marrying his son Zain al-'Ābidīn to a sister of the Jalayirid ruler. This proved to be an illusory hope, for the Jalayirids, particularly Amīr 'Ādil, promptly prepared to strike back. They got no further than Sulṭāniyya, however, where Shāh-i Shujā' managed to halt them. He now contrived to draw over to his side the Jalayirid Bāyazīd, who had been proclaimed sultan there by Amīr 'Ādil, by making him his deputy; but even this move failed to save the town from falling into the hands of Sulṭān Aḥmad.

Shortly before his death in 786/1384 Shāh-i Shujā' appointed his son Zain al-'Ābidīn as his successor and his brother 'Imād al-Dīn Aḥmad as governor of Kirmān. This arrangement was far from satisfying Shāh Yaḥyā, who advanced against Shīrāz. However, a peaceful settlement of the conflict was reached. Shāh Yaḥyā was unable to hold onto Iṣfahān for long, but was driven out by the populace, which even at that period was prone to riots and disturbances,[1] and found refuge in Yazd; whereupon Iṣfahān was placed under the supervision of Muẓaffar-i Kāshī, an uncle of Zain al-'Ābidīn.

[1] See Roemer, "Das frühsafawidische Isfahan als historische Forschungsaufgabe", *ZDMG* CXXIV (1974), 320ff.

The final end of the Muzaffarids proved to be as bloody as the period of their rule. They fell at the hands of Tīmūr, who invaded Persia just when Shāh-i Shujā''s days were approaching their end. He was already on his deathbed when he wrote a letter to the conqueror – in the autumn of 786/1384 – in which he commended his sons to the benevolence of Tīmūr on the strength of their good relationship. The discovery of Tīmūr's real attitude towards the members of his house was an experience he was spared.

However bleak the record of political and social conditions under the Injuids and the Muzaffarids, the cultural achievements of the period were impressive. Many representatives of the two houses had a share in these, either as generous patrons or – like Shāh-i Shujā' with his poetry – as active participants. We have already indicated that this is one of the most brilliantly productive periods in Persian literature. But it is also important to mention the great contribution made by the two dynasties to the art of book illumination. Another area of significant achievement was that of architecture, which contributed not only to shaping the style of the metropolis, Shīrāz, but gave many towns their distinctive cast, as for instance Yazd, Kirmān and Iṣfahān.

As for the religious sphere, in contrast with the Jalayirids the Sunnī allegiance of the two princely houses cannot seriously be doubted. Nūr-Allāh Shushtarī does list the Injuids among the dynasties he regards as Shī'ī,[1] but the evidence he adduces is vague and unconvincing. If Shāh-i Shujā' is sometimes aligned with the Shī'a it is on account, it would seem, of his close relationship with Ḥāfiẓ, whom many writers describe as Shī'ī. However, it is no longer possible to sustain the view of that prince of poets as belonging within this religious category.[2] On the contrary, Shāh-i Shujā''s Sunnī religious persuasions are demonstrated conclusively by his recognition, in 770/1368, of the 'Abbasid shadow caliph of Cairo, al-Mutawakkil I.

THE SARBADĀRS AND THEIR RIVALS

As had so often been the case in the course of history, Khurāsān, whose contacts with central Persia are restricted by the mountains in

[1] *Majālis al-mu'minīn* I, 147.

[2] Rypka, *HIL*, p. 265, describes Krymsky and Muḥammad Qazvīnī as representing the extremities of the two views: the former roundly declares Ḥāfiẓ to have been a Shī'ī, whereas Qazvīnī regrets that he was not.

the north and the desert in the south to a narrow strip of settlements, played a special part in events at the end of the Persian Mongol empire. Here too, a pretender to the throne was to be found in the person of Togha Temür,[1] who could trace his ancestry back over six generations to Jochi Qasar, a brother of Chingiz Khān, and had contrived to attract support from the powerful figures in the province. The situation of Khurāsān, more or less isolated as it was from the rest of Persia, provided what was effectively a favourable precondition for his plan of restoring the Il-Khanid empire. Nevertheless, the several attempts he made to achieve his object were doomed to failure.[2] This was due partly to various developments in eastern Persia of greater interest to the historian than the campaigns undertaken by Togha Temür or even certain successes he achieved at home in temporarily stabilising conditions in limited areas.

Of these developments it is especially those concerned with the Sarbadār state that are of interest. Its beginnings and further growth are among the strangest in the Islamic world, the history of which is certainly not lacking in odd political structures. Whereas the founders of the principalities we have been discussing in other parts of Iran based their claims to authority on their relationship to individual Mongol rulers, or on an office conferred by them or by one of the shadow khans, the Sarbadārs of Sabzavār were usurpers, principally belonging to the Shīʿī creed, who certainly entertained no such legitimist notions. Certain social characteristics of the Sarbadār movement – if we accept this description as a meaningful one – have attracted the attention of socialist historians and have led them to indulge speculative views that are far from being adequately borne out on all points by the evidence available. The community they created differed from other systems in that it was not dynastic but a realm without kings. But it also displayed other unusual features, the most striking of which were its religious aspect and, associated with this, the part played by dervishes of an extreme form of Shiʿism.

Various interpretations have been offered for the name by which the Sarbadārs have gone down in history, none of which can be seen to be totally appropriate. It may be derived from an utterance of ʿAbd

[1] I have kept to the form of the name employed in *CHI* v. Smith, *Sarbadār Dynasty*, pp. 181ff., argues from the vocalisation of al-Ahrī and from the Uighur spelling of the name in favour of Taghai (Ṭaghāy) Temür.

[2] See Boyle, in *CHI* v, 414–16.

al-Razzāq, one of its best known representatives, intended to express the idea that the political success aimed at was worth the risk of hanging (*sar ba-dār*, "head on gallows").[1] And not only has it been the name that has produced varying interpretations; right up to the present day the same is true of evaluations of the Sarbadārs' historical importance. Whereas many commentators continue to dismiss them as a robber state, another interpretation would see them in terms of a socially orientated reform movement having the character of a class struggle, in which the unmistakable faith in a Mahdī, i.e. a kind of messianic belief, and a striving for a theocratic order, were no more than passing features of minor importance.[2] Both interpretations – robber state *and* the socio-critical view – have met with sharp opposition from John Masson Smith.

Togha Temür and the Sarbadārs, however, were not the only rivals for power in Khurāsān. Another contender was the Kart dynasty in Herat.[3] They were descended from an eminent dignitary of the Ghurids named Shams al-Dīn, who had succeeded in establishing his authority out of the wreckage of his masters' realm when the territory was recovering from the marauding expeditions of the Mongols around the middle of the 7th/13th century. He himself and his descendants ruled, as Mongol vassals, from Herat over Balkh and Sīstān and in the east as far as the Indus. Notwithstanding their Indian connections, they were from the outset also orientated towards the west, and not only kept a careful eye on the struggles for power going on in Khurāsān and other parts of Persia at the end of the period of Mongol rule, but also pursued their own interests by military and political means. For instance, they supported the opponents of the Muzaffarid Mubāriz al-Dīn in Kirmān, and were involved in the conflict between the Īl-Khān Abū Sa'īd and his generalissimo Amīr Choban. Their efforts did not always meet with success, in fact: in spite of their military intervention, Kirmān did pass into the hands of Mubāriz al-Dīn, and in 727/1327, on the insistence of Abū Sa'īd, Amīr Choban had to be executed in Herat, where he had taken refuge – an action which resulted in a severe loss of prestige for the Kart prince. When he and two of his successors died within a brief interval, many of their

[1] [Faryūmadī calls them *Sarbadālān*.]

[2] Petrushevsky, "Dvizhenie", trans. Kishāvarz, "Nahżat". The possible meanings of the term are listed in Büchner, "Serbedārs", in Smith, *Sarbadār Dynasty*, p. 108, and in "Dvizhenie", pp. 119, 121–22 (tr. Kishāvarz, pp. 161, 165).

[3] The name occurs both as "Kart" and as "Kürt": I have followed Ahmed Zeki Velidi (Togan), "Kert-mi Kürt-mü?", *TüMe* II (1928), 392-6.

subjects saw this as a punishment from God for the treachery committed against Amīr Choban as one seeking asylum. These shortlived rulers were followed in 732/1331–2 by Mu'izz al-Dīn Ḥusain, who was later to intervene actively in the power struggles in Khurāsān.

The situation in Khurāsān at the start of the succession conflicts following the death of Abū Sa'īd is thus none too easy to trace out. It appears still more confused if we bear in mind certain ethnic factors of political importance. These are ethnic strands which had arisen in eastern Khurāsān and on the frontiers with India since the Mongol invasion as a result of a racial mixing due partly to military dispositions and affecting various elements, particularly Mongol and Turkish ones; and partly to environmental associations, for example with the Indian population. Several of them were to be found under the name Qarā'ūnās in the area of their origin, and also in other regions of Central Asia and the Middle East, as well as in Egypt. Research on the complex relationships between these ethnic groups has recently progressed as a result of Aubin's work, though many questions remain unanswered at the present stage. We have already come across the Negüderis, who belong in this context. We have now to deal with the Jā'ūn-i Qurbān. By an unjustified analogy with the known family connections of their leaders, they are often referred to as Oirats, but in fact they arose from what was known as a "little thousand" (*hazāracha*) which, under the command of Amīr Arghūn Āqā (d. 673/1275), had been formed out of the Mongol army by the detachment of three (*je'ün*) soldiers in every hundred (*qurban*), that is to say, irrespective of tribal membership. In 736/1335 a grandson of this military leader, named Amīr Arghūn Shāh, was in command of this unit, which at the time was deployed over the area of Nīshāpūr, Mashhad and Abīvard, and also north-west of these cities as far as the upper course of the Atrak.

It is to the historian and geographer Ḥamd-Allāh Mustaufī (d. some time after 740/1339–40), who hailed not from Khurāsān but from Qazvīn, that we are indebted for certain details important to our understanding of the developments we must now consider.[1] According to his account, the large number of viziers and officials in the Mongol financial administration who came originally from Khurāsān had contrived so to arrange things that their home province, together with Quhistān, Qūmis, Māzandarān, and Ṭabaristān, had been

[1] For the relevant passage from *Nuzhat al-qulūb*, see Smith, *Sarbadār Dynasty*, pp. 95ff.

grouped together as a special tax area; and its governors were permitted to hold in reserve a considerable sum from the tax yield, under the pretext that it was required for the payment of troops. Some years before the death of Abū Sa'īd, it seems, his vizier Ghiyāṣ al-Dīn Muḥammad b. Rashīd al-Dīn had taken steps to abolish this abuse, calling upon the support of Shaikh Ḥasan-i Buzurg, the recently appointed amīr of the ulus, Shaikh 'Alī Qushjī, and 'Alā' al-Dīn Muḥammad Faryūmadī, who had been ordered to Khurāsān for this very purpose. It is evident that those who chiefly suffered from this measure were Togha Temür, Amīr Arghūn Shāh and 'Abd-Allāh b. Mulai, the master of Quhistān.

We may end this introduction to the major political figures by some reference to Shaikh 'Alī b. 'Alī Qushjī who has just been mentioned. He had been ruling as the Īl-Khān's governor in Khurāsān since 729/1328–9. After the death of his master he proposed as his successor the Chingizid Togha Temür, and having gained the support of the amīrs of Khurāsān, caused the prince's name to be adopted on the coinage (*sikka*) and in the official prayers (*khuṭba*). He thus secured an influential position with the new khan, who in any case was not a strong personality. Allowing also for the fact that about this time (737/1337) the pretenders Arpa Ke'ün and Mūsā Khān had already failed in their claims, there was no question of Togha Temür being recognised without friction in other parts of the realm, where of course control was generally in the hands of fairly strong princes. A campaign to the west, his first military undertaking, was aimed at restoring the Il-Khanid empire under his own sceptre. But even during the march rivalries broke out between the amīrs, in which Arghūn Shāh and 'Abd-Allāh b. Mulai, alarmed at the growing power of 'Alī Qushjī, deserted and set off back with their troops. Their defection was indeed counterbalanced by the addition of large numbers of Mongol troops whom Ḥasan-i Buzurg had defeated, including their leader Mūsā Khān, to whom reference has just been made. Nevertheless, the campaign ended in catastrophe; for the Jalayirid prince inflicted a crushing defeat on this army as well in a battle at Sulṭāniyya – an encounter whose outcome Togha Temür did not even wait to witness in person.

Now Amīr Arghūn Shāh's hour had come. He captured his rival, Shaikh 'Alī Qushjī, who was already in flight, in Bisṭām, had him executed, and sent his head to Ḥasan-i Buzurg, with whom, it will be recalled, the victim had cooperated in abolishing the privileges of the Khurāsānīs. Then he again joined up with Togha Temür and became his military commander (*amīr al-umarā'*). A governor whom Ḥasan-i Buzurg had appointed for Khurāsān, a man named Muḥammad-i Mulai, was defeated and executed. It looks very much as though the Jalayirid, in thus attempting to gain control of eastern Persia, had turned against Arghūn Shāh, but not against Togha Temür. This is supported by his loyal attitude to the Chingizids, referred to above, and by subsequent developments.

Even at this time he may have reckoned on the khan's readiness to make concessions, realising that the latter's only concern was the restoration of the Persian Mongol empire under his rule. And in fact this assessment proved well grounded in the case of an offer of alliance which he made to Togha Temür in the summer of 738/1338, after his defeat in battle against the Chobanid Ḥasan-i Kūchak. The khan accepted the offer and once more led his troops west; again ineffectually, however, for Ḥasan-i Kūchak had sown doubts about him in the mind of his ally by sending him a letter written in the khan's own hand. This contained the statement that he, the khan, was prepared to take up an offer of alliance made by Ḥasan-i Kūchak, to marry Amīr Choban's widow Sātī Beg, the sister of Abū Sa'īd, and thus to revive the Il-Khanid empire with Chobanid assistance. Shocked by such blatant disloyalty, Ḥasan-i Buzurg agreed to the alliance proposed by his old adversary, and in view of the opposition now ranged against him Togha Temür was left with no other choice but to withdraw to Khurāsān. The harmony between the Jalayirids and the Chobanids did not, in fact, endure for any length of time, and after various disagreements with his ally which worked out to his disadvantage, Ḥasan-i Buzurg again turned to the khan of Khurāsān. A new agreement he made with him managed to survive for three years, until 744/1343–4. Coins struck at Baghdad and other Mesopotamian mints which bear his name are evidence that the Jalayirid recognised Togha Temür's suzerainty at this time.

Although his accord with the Jalayirid prince had ensured the recognition Togha Temür so desired over large areas of Persia, indeed even in Iraq and eastern Anatolia, this lasted only for a short period in each case. And the price he paid for this episode in his career, the fleeting dream of an Il-Khanid restoration, was its devastating results. A mere few years of ill-advised policy had been enough to deplete the military strength of Khurāsān and its economic resources to a point from which no regeneration was possible. Worse still, the way was now open for political forces to come into play with which neither Togha Temür nor anyone else in Khurāsān could contend.

These forces burst out in the rising of the Sarbadārs, a revolt which in all probability was a reaction to fiscal burdens imposed on the amīrs and leading men of Khurāsān by 'Alā' al-Dīn Muḥammad, mentioned earlier, to cover the increased costs of maintaining the Khurāsānī, and no doubt also the Jalayirid, troops, and coming on top of the increases provided for in the financial reforms carried out only a few years before by the vizier Ghiyāṣ al-Dīn (see above). That Sabzavār itself was the centre of the disturbances may possibly be connected with the fact that the city, and Bāshtīn, which belonged to it, lay in the area administered by 'Alā' al-Dīn himself and would thus be hit by the full severity of the new measures. The rebellion cannot be precisely dated, but it seems most likely that it took place at a time when the Khurāsānī troops were otherwise engaged and not available for use in Sabzavār. Various interconnections would suggest the period shortly before the first Khurāsānī–Jalayirid alliance.

Of the various conflicting accounts we possess of the beginning of the rising, Ḥāfiẓ-i Abrū's seems the most inherently probable version. According to this, Amīr 'Abd al-Razzāq, the son of a very powerful figure and himself a highly placed person, killed a government official (*'āmil*), probably a tax-collector, in the township of Bāshtīn, which formed part of the district of Sabzavār, and then fomented a rising in order to avoid punishment. The motive for the killing is explained as an act of protest against oppressive methods used to collect increased taxes. By chance, the murdered official was a nephew of 'Alā' al-Dīn. Although 'Abd al-Razzāq found support, which enables us to conclude that the situation was tense, it is stretching the available evidence too far to talk, as does Petrushevsky,[1] of angry masses consisting of peasants, impoverished town-dwellers and artisans; nor is there sufficient warrant for the class struggle, racial friction or national antagonisms which he adduces as additional factors to support his hypothesis of a peasants' revolt. The solid fact of the matter which we should keep in mind is that 'Abd al-Razzāq belonged to the feudal ruling class of Khurāsān, which had plainly been made to bear the brunt of considerable increases resulting from 'Alā' al-Dīn's tax reforms. Had he belonged to the class of small landowners, there would have been no

[1] Petrushevsky, "Dvizhenie", pp. 94, 115 (tr. Kishāvarz, "Nahżat", pp. 130, 156) *et passim*.

plausible reason for his action: for the rise in taxation applied only to the wealthy and powerful in the land and not to the peasants and small landowners, whose own taxes, moreover, had been cancelled at the same time as these increases were imposed.

Immediately after the start of the rising, the ranks of the rebels, who – no doubt following well-tried precedents – had fallen back into the mountains, were so heavily swollen as a result of their successes against the militia and raids on caravans and herds of cattle that in the summer of 738/1337 they were able to take possession of the city of Sabzavār. ʿAbd al-Razzāq, who now assumed the title of amīr and had himself named on the coinage and in the official prayers, was stabbed to death by his brother Vajīh al-Dīn Masʿūd shortly afterwards in the course of a marauding expedition. The incident did take place in hot blood, during an argument between them, but may also have had deeper political motives. At all events, Masʿūd, who now took over the leadership of the Sarbadārs, for the moment abandoned the policy of confrontation in favour of one of compromise. He recognised Togha Temür and solemnly undertook to pay taxes to him. This change is authenticated by coins from Sabzavār. Both sides gained advantages from the new *modus vivendi*: the khan no longer needed to fear raids by the Sarbadārs, which had seriously jeopardised supplies for his troops, and the Sarbadārs were not exposed to government sanctions.

By taking the city of Sabzavār, the Sarbadārs had not only acquired a considerable political centre but had also established contact with an ideological movement which was to exercise a powerful influence on their future development: above all it provided them with new adherents and strong religious stimuli. In contrast to other places in Khurāsān, it contained a large number of Shīʿīs whose zeal for the faith had shortly before been roused to a pitch of intensity by the preaching of a mystic from Māzandarān named Shaikh Khalīfa. The Sunnīs must have regarded his activities as dangerous; at all events, they had him murdered. After his death one of his disciples, Ḥasan Jūrī, took over his rôle, scoring even greater successes in his propagandistic travels from one town of Khurāsān to another. His activities aroused the suspicion of the government authorities; in Shawwāl 736/May 1336 he had to take refuge in flight and went to ʿIrāq-i ʿAjam. When he later returned, by a circuitous route, Arghūn Shāh had him arrested (740/1339–40). It is quite possible that Masʿūd had a hand in his eventual release: later, Ḥasan's personal influence and wide popularity induced him not only to join the order as a novice (*murīd*) but also – following a practice seen among the earlier Sarbadārs – to give Ḥasan a joint share in government, for in the official prayers Ḥasan's name was mentioned first, before that of Mas'ūd. The shaikh proclaimed the imminent return of the Twelfth Imām. He had earlier founded a secret organisation to prepare for Shī'ī theocratic rule; this included an armed force which was apparently organised along the lines of the *futuwwa*[1] and was composed of artisans and merchants.

Though the oddly matched joint rulers began by cooperating well, tensions were present from the outset. In the first place, there was Ḥasan Jūrī's popularity among the Shī'ī population of Sabzavār, with which Mas'ūd could not compete. Then there were the totally different objectives of the two men. Ḥasan continued to hold to his Shī'ī and theocratic idea of the state, whereas Mas'ūd regarded Khurāsān as an integral part of an Il-Khanid empire that was in the very nature of things essentially Sunnī, at first under the rule of Togha Temür and then – as we shall see – under Chobanid lordship. Finally, Ḥasan's adherents, with their markedly religious orientation, were devotedly intent on furthering radical Shī'ī ideas, whereas those of Mas'ūd, in so far as they were Shī'ī at all, supported a moderate line. This led to the emergence of two groups of Sarbadārs, namely the original followers of 'Abd al-Razzāq and Mas'ūd, and those of Ḥasan Jūrī, who were called Shaikhiyān to distinguish them from the others. It was the latter in particular who were responsible for the reputation the Sarbadārs have had with many commentators – even earlier ones – as robbers and riff-raff.

Although Vajīh al-Dīn Mas'ūd's reign lasted only six years, i.e. until the summer of 745/1344,[2] it brought about a quite remarkable expan-

1 Cf. Cahen and Taeschner, "Futuwwa".

2 [A slightly different chronology for the early Sarbadār rulers is given by Faryūmadī, MS Yeni Cami 909, fol. 287^{r}:

Mas'ūd, killed 27 Dhu'l-Qa'da 743/23 April 1343;

Muḥammad Ai-temür, ruled 3 Jumādā II 743–Muḥarram 747/3 Nov. 1342–April or May 1346:

*Kallū Isfandiyār, killed 10 Rabī' II 748/20 July 1347;

Amīr Shams al-Dīn, ruled Rabī' II – Sha'bān 748/July – Nov. 1347;

Khwāja 'Alī-yi Shams al-Dīn, killed Dhu'l-Qa'da 752/Dec. 1351 or Jan. 1352;

Khwāja Yaḥyā Karābī, murdered 13 Jumādā II 757/14 May 1356;

Khwāja Ẓahīr Karābī, deposed Shawwāl 757/Oct. 1356 and killed at the end of Dhu'l-Qa'da/ Nov.;

Ḥaidar Qaṣṣāb, killed 25 Dhu'l-Qa'da 757/19 Nov. 1356.

Amīr Luṭf-Allāh b. Amīr Mas'ūd, deposed mid-Dhu'l-Qa'da 759/Nov. 1358 by Ḥasan Dāmghānī. (Ed.)]

sion of the Sarbadār state. What made this possible was the efficient army he created, said to consist of 12,000 well armed mounted peasants and 700 Turkish slave troops as his personal bodyguard, together with Ḥasan Jūrī's dervishes, the Shaikhiyān. The first blow was directed in 741/1340 against Arghūn Shāh's Jā'ūn-i Qurbān, who were obliged to give up Nīshāpūr and retreated to Ṭūs. As coins with Togha Temür's name were minted in Sabzavār in the very next year, the Sarbadārs must have assumed that the khan, who had been away on operations in the west at the time of their campaign, would overlook this liberty. He did not, however, but marched against them. His troops were routed, and while fleeing to Māzandarān such eminent figures as the vizier 'Alā' al-Dīn Muḥammad and 'Abd-Allāh b. Mulai were killed; indeed even the khan's brother 'Alī Ke'ün, lost his life. The victors occupied Jājarm, Dāmghān and Simnān, together with Togha Temür's capital, Gurgān.

By this victory a totally different situation had been created. When they took Nīshāpūr the Sarbadārs had come up against a population which was almost exclusively Sunnī, and by conquering Simnān they had become neighbours to the Chobanids, who were also Sunnī. Naturally, they considered the suzerainty of Togha Temür as having lapsed, and Mas'ūd recognised in his place the Chobanid Ḥasan-i Kūchak and the shadow khan Sulaimān whom he had appointed; though the decision can hardly have been taken in consultation with his co-regent, since these were Sunnī princes. Differences had in fact already arisen between them because Mas'ūd rejected the idea of forcibly converting the Sunnīs of the conquered territories to Shi'ism.

The dominions of the Sarbadārs now embraced a territory the size of Ireland. But with the recognition of Ḥasan-i Kūchak they were confronted with a real threat emanating from the Kartid of Herat, Mu'izz al-Dīn Ḥusain, whose father, it will be remembered, had killed Amīr Choban when he was in flight from Abū Sa'īd and sought refuge at his court. Furthermore, Ḥusain was an ally of Togha Temür. The Sarbadārs attempted to scotch this danger by means of a preventive strike. The armies met at Zāva (13 Ṣafar 743/18 July 1342), and the battle initially went in favour of the Sarbadārs. But when Shaikh Ḥasan Jūrī fell, the fortunes of war changed, since the dervishes broke off the engagement, assuming – probably not without justification – that their shaikh had not died at the hands of the enemy but had been struck down by an assassin hired by Mas'ūd. The battle thus resulted not only in defeat but also in an unleashing of hostilities and tensions that had been latent in the relations between the moderate supporters of Mas'ūd and the radical Shaikhiyān for a long time past. The total implications of this clash of views, however, did not become plain until later. At first Mas'ūd may well have thought that he could attain his objectives even without the dervishes. In his next expedition, two years later, he aimed to eliminate Togha Temür, who had withdrawn to the region of Āmul, secured the support of local princes, and was blocking the Sarbadārs' lines of communication with their Chobanid allies in the west. Although the campaign got off to a good start, it ended in catastrophe. On the march from Sārī to Āmul the Sarbadār army was trapped in a pincer movement by the enemy. Mas'ūd himself was taken prisoner and executed.

Their two defeats, one in the east, the other in the west of their dominions, had thrown the Sarbadārs back upon the starting-point of their operations, the region of Sabzavār and probably also Juvain and Nīshāpūr. Nevertheless, they had no need to fear for their survival. None of their rivals was in a position after all these years of heavy fighting to subject the whole of Khurāsān to his control, let alone to extend his power beyond its frontiers. For much the same reasons, there was little danger from the outside. The princes of Khurāsān came to a compromise agreement. Togha Temür was free to return to Astarābād and Gurgān, having settled for the recognition of his suzerainty on the part of the Sarbadārs; and even Arghūn Shāh in the east was once more able to exercise his authority as leader of the Jā'ūn-i Qurbān.

The Sarbadārs of Khurāsān survived by almost forty years the death of Mas'ūd, who had more than a dozen successors. Since one of them, 'Alī-yi Mu'ayyad, managed to stay in power for twenty years (763–83/1361–81), their very number is evidence of how troubled the period from 745/1344 to 763/1361 must have been. The chief feature of these years was in fact incessant fighting and quarrelling over the rulership. The way these disputes are recorded in the evidence we have is not free of contradictions; but the details are in any case only of limited importance for the history of the region and certainly for the history of Iran. In the context we are considering it is sufficient to trace the main lines of development.

How important the division into two parties (the moderate adherents of Mas'ūd and the party of the radical dervishes) was for the further progress of events, requires a more closely differentiated treatment. John Masson Smith[1] reckons among Mas'ūd's supporters not only the members of his family such as his son Luṭf-Allāh, (who, incidentally, later himself reigned for a short time), but also the gentry of Bāshtīn, as well as his army, to which – apart from professional soldiers – belonged also escaped slaves, former bandits and Turkish slave troops (*ghulāmān*). On the other side there was the group of the Sabzavārīs, of which Ḥasan Jūrī's dervish organisation has already been mentioned. It also included the Sabzavārī aristocracy (*khwājazādagān*) and the trade guilds, which may have been organised on the principles of the futuwwa. Not only were the two main parties at odds with each other, but each lacked internal unity as well. For example, there were considerable points of difference within the Sabzavārīs arising from the theocratic concepts of the extreme dervishes. These did not meet with the approval of all Shī'īs, for there were moderate groups even among them who leaned more towards cooperation with the Sunnīs than towards the acceptance of such radical ideas. All in all, this kind of analysis of Sarbadār society would appear to do more justice to the facts than Petrushevsky's division into "popular masses" of peasants, urban poor, and artisans in opposition to the feudal lords consisting of small Iranian landowners and a Mongol-Turkish nomad aristocracy, and his hypothesis of class struggle and racial hostilities in the period.

Vajīh al-Dīn Mas'ūd's first three successors came from the group of his adherents: these were two of his military commanders and his brother Shams al-Dīn b. Fażl-Allāh. All fell from power after the briefest time, and the periods of their rule total only three years. Meanwhile, the alliance with the Chobanids was abandoned; their power in any case came to an end with the fall of Ḥasan-i Kūchak about this time. In addition, the death in 743/1343 of Arghūn Shāh, the leader of the Jā'ūn-i Qurbān, proved convenient to the Sarbadārs, since his son and successor Muḥammad Beg, giving up his alliance with Togha Temür, established friendly relations with them; so that, with one exception, there were no further clashes with this neighbour.

Not until Shams al-Dīn 'Alī, a dervish of the Sabzavārī group, came to power was there again a personality of stature in charge of affairs. The achievements of his five years of government (748 to 752/1347 to

[1] *Sarbadār Dynasty*, pp. 122ff.

1351–2) are praised by the historian Daulatshāh. He records that the people lived under quite reasonable conditions. The officials were paid in cash. Notes (*barāt*) were no longer issued to cover salaries and soldiers' pay on tax payments due, an abuse which was evidently quite common. The new ruler carried out effective tax reforms, by means of which he reorganised the shaky finances of the state. Thus he was able to maintain efficient fighting units, with which he effectively protected his territory, now extending from Nīshāpūr in the east to Dāmghān in the west. He admittedly failed to take the city of Ṭūs, but did succeed in putting down a revolt in Dāmghān. By his simple manner of life, through the honesty and thrift on which he insisted in the conduct of state affairs, he won the affection of large sections of the population. His measures against prostitution, drugs, and alcohol are also worthy of mention.

The swift decline of Mas'ūd's adherents and the passing of power to a Sabzavārī may be seen as indications of the growth of this party. In fact the strength of Mas'ūd's adherents and his troops had been severely weakened by his unfortunate military enterprises, whereas the dervishes, who had taken no further part in his campaigns since the death of Shaikh Ḥasan Jūrī, had suffered no losses. Nevertheless, it must have been consideration for the forces of Mas'ūd, predominantly Sunnīs or moderate Shī'īs, that kept Shams al-Dīn 'Alī, who had belonged to Ḥasan's intimate circle and therefore must in all probability himself have been a Shī'ī, from officially introducing the Shī'ī confession. For ten years, from 748/1347 to 758/1357, the government of the Sarbadārs was Sunnī, as shown by the coins of which details have been published to date.

In spite of his efforts for the common weal – perhaps even because of them – Shams al-Dīn 'Alī soon made some bitter enemies, especially among those who distrusted him for his connections with extreme Shī'īs, i.e. the dervishes; among the libertines, who disliked his puritanical ways; and finally among the corrupt servants of the state, who lost out as a result of his reforms. One of the latter, Ḥaidar Qaṣṣāb, whose name suggests that he was a member of an artisan guild, was responsible for his murder. Although the immediate motive for the act was revenge for a punishment he had received for irregularities in the conduct of the tax collection for which he was responsible, it looks very much as if he also had backers in the circles of those of higher rank who were dissatisfied.

The elimination of Shams al-Dīn 'Alī is probably not to be traced, as might be supposed, to the adherents of Mas'ūd, but to the Sabzavārīs, that is to say, the group to which he himself belonged, as also did his successor, Yaḥyā Karāvī (752 to 756/1351–2 to 1355–6), a member of the Sabzavārī aristocracy. Under his rule the power and extent of the Sarbadār state reached a new peak. But first it was necessary to remove the major danger that had threatened this state from the beginning, the khan Togha Temür. In spite of the reverses he had had to endure in his struggle with the Sarbadārs, he regarded them as rebels who were to be destroyed at the earliest possible opportunity. They might be tolerated under the pressure of sheer circumstance, but they could not be recognised. Togha Temür's dominions had indeed been severely reduced in size, most recently by the defection of the Kartid of Herat, who had previously paid tribute to him, and of the Jā'ūn-i Qurbān and the Turkish tribes in the steppelands around Herat. Nevertheless, with his tribal units living in Gurgān and Astarābād, estimated at 50,000,[1] he was a potential danger to the Sarbadārs, who had only 22,000 men under arms at the time. Yaḥyā successfully attempted to lull the khan into a sense of false security by promising to recognise his suzerainty (a fact which is authenticated by many coins bearing his name struck in Sabzavār), and by undertaking to pay taxes as well as to make loyal visits once every year to demonstrate his obedience. When in Dhu'l-Qa'da 754/November–December 1353 he went to the Mongol winter camp of Sulṭān-Duvīn in the vicinity of Astarābād, accompanied by only a small military train, his appearance must have been associated with such a visit which was just about due. At all events, he was able to make his way unchallenged through the camp and into the tent of the khan. The men with him assassinated Togha Temür and cut down his courtiers. In order to eliminate any possibility of a successor, the Mongol troops were done to death and the khan's herds, without which the nomads were deprived of the very basics of life, were all slaughtered. Though Luqmān, a son of the murdered khan, constantly reappears up to the year 790/1388 in the struggle for mastery in Khurāsān, the fall of Togha Temür put paid once and for all to any idea of a restoration of the Il-Khanid empire.

The power of the Sarbadārs now once more reached those far-flung

[1] No doubt this is how we should understand the quotation from Ibn Baṭṭūṭa given in Petrushevsky, "Dvizhenie", p. 146 (tr. Kishāvarz, "Nahżat", p. 194).

frontiers which Mas'ūd had achieved by his conquests and then forfeited by his recklessness; indeed, it even spread beyond them – in the west into the area around Ray, in the east as far as Ṭūs, and in the north-west to Astarābād and Shāsmān in the region of Gurgān.

Even these great efforts in the cause of Sarbadār power could not spare Yaḥyā Karāvī the fate which had come to be almost customary for Sarbadār princes, namely murder by his opponents. From the evidence available it is not possible to say with certainty who was behind the assassination. It could have been adherents of Mas'ūd who would have preferred to see one of their number in power. The likely candidate would have been Mas'ūd's son Luṭf-Allāh, who in fact did later become ruler. It has even been argued[1] that he had, strictly speaking, already succeeded by the time of his father's death, but that in view of his youth others had exercised the regency on his behalf.

If the state had had to contend up to this point with external enemies, it was from now on affected by severe internal crises. These could well have threatened its very existence, and that they did not was only because there were no strong external enemies to be confronted at the time. Ḥaidar Qaṣṣāb, whom we have already mentioned, now promptly arrived from Astarābād to bring Yaḥyā's murderers to justice. He installed Yaḥyā's nephew Ẓahīr al-Dīn Karāvī as ruler, but soon afterwards seized power himself when the latter failed to fulfil his expectations. Lacking sufficient supporters, he had in fact overreached himself by this action. As will be recalled, he had originally been a member of Shams al-Dīn 'Alī's party, which is the reason why he found no friends among the adherents of Mas'ūd; later he had murdered his master and thereby had forfeited also the sympathies of the dervishes (the Shaikhiyān).

Meanwhile, in Isfarā'in, the most important city of the Sarbadārs after Sabzavār, Luṭf-Allāh's royal tutor and atabeg Naṣr-Allāh had fomented a rebellion with the aid of those of Yaḥyā's murderers who had escaped the vengeance of Ḥaidar Qaṣṣāb. Ḥaidar now turned upon the rebels. But before the issue could be decided in the field, he was struck down by the dagger of an assassin hired by Ḥasan Dāmghānī. Now Luṭf-Allāh's hour had come, and since there were still certain circles with sympathies for his father he could well have succeeded in founding a dynasty for the Sarbadārs. But this opportunity was lost when, in

[1] Petrushevsky, "Dvizhenie", pp. 141, 150 (tr. Kishāvarz, "Nahżat", pp. 184, 201).

the conflict with Ḥasan Dāmghānī which ensued with inevitable rapidity, he was defeated. As a result the party of his father's supporters was to all intents and purposes annihilated.[1]

These events in themselves show how feeble were the foundations of the state; but the civil war which now began demonstrated how utterly incapable it was of coping with the centrifugal forces that threatened it. Ḥaidar Qaṣṣāb's move out of Astarābād had left a vacuum which encouraged Amīr Valī, a son of the previous governor of the province, to return from the refuge he had been granted by a prince of the Jā'ūn-i Qurbān. He claimed to be representing the interests of Luqmān b. Togha Temür in his absence from Māzandarān, in order to gather the latter's sympathisers around him, but had not the remotest intention when he arrived there of actually handing over power to him. For in the meantime he had beaten in succession two expeditionary corps sent against him by Ḥasan, and finally he defeated Ḥasan himself, so that he was in a position to extend his power over other territories of the Sarbadārs as well.

In eastern Khurāsān a radical Shī'ī named Darvīsh 'Azīz[2] rose in revolt and established a theocracy in Mashhad in the name of the Twelfth Imām, Muḥammad al-Mahdī (d. 329/940). This sort of enterprise was in the air at the time: Ḥasan Jūrī and Shams al-Dīn 'Alī, after all, had themselves wanted to establish the theocratic state of the Mahdī, and we may assume that the Shaikhiyān of Sabzavār were represented among the supporters of Darvīsh 'Azīz. At any rate his successes in Mashhad, which were continued still further with the conquest of Ṭūs, must have electrified the Sabzavārī dervishes, who were of course also devoted to the idea of a theocratic state. Ḥasan Dāmghānī recognised the danger that this implied for him, marched east and put an end to the Mahdist state. Darvīsh 'Azīz went into exile in Iṣfahān.

While Ḥasan Dāmghānī was fully engaged in the north-western and eastern parts of his country, another danger was brewing for him in Dāmghān, to the west. Here 'Alī-yi Mu'ayyad rose in revolt and gathered around him the troops of Ḥasan's enemies who had been defeated and were in flight. He also sent for Darvīsh 'Azīz in Iṣfahān and joined

[1] Smith, *Sarbadār Dynasty*, p. 141, gives the year 759/1357–8 for Luṭf-Allāh's execution [see p. 24, n. 2 above (Ed.)], whereas Petrushevsky, "Dvizhenie", p. 150 (tr. Kishāvarz, "Nahżat", p. 201) supplies 30 Rajab 762/5 June 1361.

[2] Petrushevsky, *locc. cit.*, calls him 'Azīz Majdī.

his order; and together they prepared for the conflict with Ḥasan Dāmghānī. When the latter was laying siege to the castle of Shaqqān, near Jājarm, after taking Mashhād and Ṭūs, they captured Sabzavār in a surprise attack (763/1361–2). They succeeded in acquiring not only the possessions of Ḥasan's followers but also their families. 'Alī-yi Mu'ayyad's demand to Ḥasan's followers, that they should depose their master and send him his head as a sign of their loyalty, therefore produced the desired result.

Authority among the Sarbadārs was now vested in a duumvirate which shows striking similarities to that of Vajīh al-Dīn Mas'ūd and Ḥasan Jūrī. As in the former situation, the condominium worked quite well to begin with, in fact for ten months. Though 'Alī-yi Mu'ayyad, who was himself a Shī'ī, played his part in raising Shi'ism to the state religion, he resisted certain notions dear to the heart of Darvīsh 'Azīz as to what the Mahdist state should be; and this led, just as before, to severe tensions, culminating in the removal of the dervish leader. Again the decisive moment came during a campaign against Malik Ḥusain of Herat, except that 'Alī's men did not wait until they met up with the enemy, but picked a quarrel with the dervishes while still on the march. Darvīsh 'Azīz and many of his adherents were killed as they attempted to escape.

'Alī-yi Mu'ayyad did not leave it at this but seized his opportunity to rid himself of the threat from the dervishes once and for all. He smashed their organisation and hounded them out of Sabzavār; he even went so far as to have the graves of Shaikh Khalīfa and Ḥasan Jūrī destroyed. But although he had broken the power of his enemy for the time being, banishing the dervishes from his immediate entourage, they were still not done away with altogether. They found a welcome from Malik Ḥusain in Herat, from the Jā'ūn-i Qurbān and from the Muzaffarid Shāh-i Shujā' in Shīrāz. It goes without saying that from these places of refuge they now bided their time; nor, if things ran to the form familiar to contemporaries, would it be long in coming. In fact, in the final phase of the Sarbadār state which now began, the dervishes were a significant element and contributed their share to its downfall.

'Alī-yi Mu'ayyad managed to remain ruler for twenty years and even survived Tīmūr's invasion. Although it would be quite wrong to infer that this long reign was a period of peace and quiet, a certain degree of stabilisation does seem to have taken place, at least for a time. There is evidence of this in the steady quality of the coinage to begin with, although only up to the middle of his reign, when against a background of stormy political events a decline in quality set in which was never to be halted. ʿAlī-yi Mu'ayyad is described as a just and efficient prince, in so far as anyone could be in the conditions of the day, and he did in fact improve the lot of the peasants by a reform of the tax system.

The unsolved external problems of the Sarbadār empire which ʿAlī-yi Mu'ayyad had taken on when he assumed power in Sabzavār had a determining influence on his reign. Though the Jā'ūn-i Qurbān gained control of Ṭūs again, there do not seem to have been any further conflicts with them. There was a conflict, however, with Amīr Valī, who had in the past enjoyed their protection and was related by marriage to one of their leading men. Ḥasan Dāmghānī had had trouble with him in his time but had not been able to put him down. He had extended his control over Bisṭām and Simnān, whereas Astarābād, where between 767/1365–6 and 770/1368–9 Sarbadār coins were struck, was at least for a time subject to the government at Sabzavār before falling back again into the hands of Amīr Valī. ʿAlī-yi Mu'ayyad in fact avoided bringing the dispute to a head, because he saw this rival's area of control as a convenient buffer state against the Jalayirids. At the time they were beginning to evince rapacious designs on Khurāsān, with the result that Amīr Valī was obliged to mount campaigns against them in the region of Ray and Sāva.

ʿAlī-yi Mu'ayyad found himself drawn into a critical situation as a result of what was happening among the Kartids of Herat when in 771/1370 Malik Muʿizz al-Dīn Ḥusain died and the succession passed to his two sons Ghiyāṣ al-Dīn Pīr ʿAlī and Malik Muḥammad. Pīr ʿAlī, a grandson of Togha Temür through his mother Sulṭān Khātūn, saw ʿAlī-yi Mu'ayyad as sympathising with the murderers of his grandfather and stirred up against him the Sabzavārī dervishes now living as emigrants in his own territory. The Sarbadār leader retorted by conspiring with Pīr ʿAlī's stepbrother Malik Muḥammad, who ruled over the smaller portion of the Kartid empire from the city of Sarakhs. When Pīr ʿAlī marched against Malik Muḥammad, ʿAlī-yi Mu'ayyad rescued him in a flanking attack by overcoming one of Pīr ʿAlī's castles near the frontier whose captains were emigrant Sabzavārī dervishes. This was not only a blow struck at his own enemies; it also induced Pīr ʿAlī to come to a compromise with his brother. So commenced the years of fighting against Pīr 'Alī which tied down the Sarbadārs to Nīshāpūr, the most important place in the eastern part of the country, and inevitably prejudiced the defence of their capital. This situation proved to be a challenge to 'Alī-yi Mu'ayyad's opponents in the west, especially the dervishes who had fled to Shīrāz, who had found an enterprising leader in Rukn al-Dīn, a disciple of their unsuccessful master Darvīsh 'Azīz. Together with Iskandar, Pīr 'Alī's former governor of Nīshāpūr, he now mounted against Khurāsān a campaign which was supported with money and arms by Shāh-i Shujā'. They conquered Sabzavār (778/1376–7); and 'Alī-yi Mu'ayyad was forced into flight and found refuge with Amīr Valī.

The new condominium in Sabzavār, which promptly set about establishing a radical Shī'ī régime based on the teachings of Ḥasan Jūrī, was followed at once by a still more drastic reduction of the Sarbadār state, which had in any case severely contracted. Nīshāpūr was conquered by Pīr 'Alī, and it was not long before Amīr Valī appeared before the gates of Sabzavār. His entourage included Shāh Manṣūr, the rival of the Muzaffarid Shāh-i Shujā' of Shīrāz, and 'Alī-yi Mu'ayyad, whom Amīr Valī reinstated as ruler after the capture of the town. The alliance between Amīr Valī and the Sarbadār leader did not endure for long. By 783/1381 Amīr Valī was once again besieging the city. In his extremity 'Alī-yi Mu'ayyad turned to Tīmūr; and his appeal for help was destined not to go unheeded. It afforded the immediate pretext for Tīmūr's invasion of Persia. This did not yet mean the final end of the history of the Sarbadārs of Khurāsān, even though it was the end of their autonomy as a state. It will be necessary to refer to their later fortunes when discussing Tīmūr's appearance on the Persian scene.

At this point, however, some comment is required on various effects of, and parallels with, the rule of the Sarbadārs, extending to regions outside Khurāsān. We shall not consider the Sarbadārs of Samarqand,[1] since they do not directly form part of the history of Persia; but some mention should be made, if only in broad outline, of events in Māzandarān, Gīlān and Kirmān.

In the reign of Shams al-Dīn 'Alī an adherent of Ḥasan Jūrī, named 'Izz al-Dīn, together with a group of co-religionists who like him were not prepared to accept the conditions in Sabzavār, resolved to

[1] See Barthold, "Narodnoe dvizhenie"; also Yakubovsky, "Timur", pp. 56–8, who on the authority of 'Abd al-Razzāq's *Maṭla'* refers to the Samarqand rebels as "Sarbadārs", though whether they themselves employed the term is doubtful.

return to his homeland of Māzandarān. However, he died en route, and his son Sayyid Qivām al-Dīn, known as Mīr-i Buzurg, took his place. He managed to settle in Āmul and to found a state in conjunction with Kiyā Afrāsiyāb b. Ḥasan Chulābī, who in 750/1349 had brought down the local dynasty of the Bavandids, which had lasted for seven hundred years.[1] This state ran in many respects along the lines of that of Sabzavār. The dichotomy between a ruler who leant towards secular attitudes and a dervish aiming at a theocratic structure again led to a conflict, which ended with the victory of the religious fanatic. This state lasted until its destruction by Tīmūr in 794/1392, but after his death it emerged briefly once more.

With the aid of the Māzandarānī dervishes a group of Shī'ī shaikhs also gained control in Gīlān under the leadership of Shaikh Amīr Kiyā. The state he called into being endured for over two centuries – which was doubtless largely due to its geographical remoteness – until it was finally absorbed in 1000/1592 into the Safavid empire.

In 774/1373 a revolt took place in Kirmān against Shāh-i Shujā', the prince of Shīrāz, fomented by Pahlavān Asad b. Toghan Shāh. The rebellion received military support from 'Alī-yi Mu'ayyad, whose relations with Shāh-i Shujā' have already been discussed, but was put down in Rajab 776/December 1374 by troops sent from Shīrāz.

Seen as a historical phenomenon, the Sarbadārs of Khurāsān are a quite typical product of the situation in Persia after the collapse of the Il-Khanid empire, but they display certain noteworthy differences from what is found elsewhere. Khurāsān resembled other parts of the empire in that it lacked a single dominant power, and possessed in Togha Temür a descendant of the Mongol rulers who was too weak to assert effective control. But what distinguishes the Sarbadārs from practically all contemporary rulers in Persia is the absence of any legitimist claims on their part. It was not only that none of them could claim descent from a Mongol or other princely house or the warrant of having previously exercised high office; they plainly did not even consider it necessary to seek to establish any legitimate claim to rule. None of them had a Mongol shadow khan or marriage ties with a highly placed family, and there was no serious attempt to found a dynasty.

Another point of difference is the religious aspect, which played so great a part among the Sarbadārs. It was expressed particularly, though

[1] B. Nikitine, "Afrāsiyābids", *EI*². R.N. Frye, "Bāwand", *ibid.*

not exclusively, in the share the Sabzavārī dervishes had in Sarbadār rule, whether in the form of a condominium with a secular ruler, or as observers keeping at a discreet distance, or as rivals with a keen eye to their chances or even occasionally as sole rulers. It is undoubtedly significant that the population of their capital city had a strong Shīʿī component and that also, we may assume, many of their rulers, perhaps even the majority of them, belonged to the Shīʿa. But none of this was decisive, any more than the basic opposition between Shīʿa and Sunna in this particular situation. Moderate Shīʿīs in this period could, and in some cases actually did, reach a *modus vivendi* with Sunnīs more easily than with the dervishes. The stumbling-block for both parties was rather the dervishes' adherence to a rigid organisation with unambiguous ideas of what the state should be, ideas which they advanced with uncompromising firmness. The goal of the dervishes was a Mahdist state, a theocracy with an extremist Shīʿī state religion, and hence a utopia which admitted of no compromise with other conceptions of statehood.

It appears very much as if the princes who did not come from the ranks of the Shaikhiyān were at first not fully conscious of this aim. How else are we to explain the numerous attempts at establishing a condominium together with committed supporters of the dervishes? Not even so far-reaching a concession as joining the dervish order as a novice (murīd) saved those rulers who did so from the painful discovery that the theocracy the dervishes demanded was not to be reconciled with their own divergent conceptions of the state, nor even, in fact, with Shīʿī ideas on the subject. Practical illustrations of this are not far to seek, and at bottom it was this very incompatibility of other attitudes with an ideological conception of government which was the undoing of the Sarbadār state. In spite of numerous successes scored by each party over the other, the dichotomy of the Sarbadār state displays a balance of forces leading not to a *modus vivendi* but to decades of conflict, the net result of which was to weaken both parties. Masʿūd's adherents were unable to exclude the dervishes; nor again were the dervishes powerful enough to supplant their opponents. The result was a process of mutual exhaustion, a gradual attrition that had virtually extinguished the Sarbadārs' will to survive by the time Tīmūr advanced against Persia.

The Shaikhiyān must of course be reckoned among the many religious movements in the Islamic world that strove for power and in a fair number of instances actually gained control. Iran seems to have been good soil for such movements, as can be seen from a number of comparable phenomena from both earlier and later periods. It was the tragedy of the Sabzavārī dervishes that in their time and in their country there were also other political forces at work, especially among the provincial nobility, who were aiming at power simultaneously with them; and that it was impossible either to win these over or subject them – so that, in the end, there was nothing left for any of them but to sink together.

But apart from the conflict of interests at home, the Sarbadārs were also threatened by external enemies. They did manage to overcome Togha Temür after some time, but not his less impressive successor Amīr Valī. Though there were conflicts with the Jā'ūn-i Qurbān, for a long time peaceful relations prevailed; while the struggle against the Kartids of Herat remained indecisive. All these opponents kept up a state of feud with the Sarbadārs, irrespective of which of their two parties happened to have provided the ruling figure of the time. Although the Sarbadārs' rule started with a rising against the Mongols or their representatives, their further history cannot be thought of exclusively from this point of view. Once they had compelled Togha Temür to tolerate them in principle, their policies were no longer determined solely by an anti-Mongol attitude, so that eliminating Togha Temür was ultimately only a matter of choosing the right moment.

As for the question of their constituting a robber state, it is doubtful whether such a view is justified by any of the circumstances of their history – neither the frankly dubious name they chose to go by, nor their lack of or indifference to a legitimate claim, nor the absence of a dynastic line, nor the conflicts waged against established rulers of somewhat questionable legitimacy. The fact that the Sarbadārs in their campaigning were not given to considerate treatment of their enemies or the civilian population is hardly an argument to be used against them, since it is hard to imagine any belligerent party of the time which would have behaved differently. To this extent, therefore, the estimate we make of the Sarbadārs need be no different from that applied to their rivals or any other rulers in contemporary Persia. This view is also supported by the fact that they were not without their share of cultural activity or at least various efforts in this direction. We may mention just two examples: the efforts made by Shams al-Dīn 'Alī to develop Sabzavār architecturally, which led to the building of a Friday mosque (masjid-i jāmi') and a warehouse affording work for artisans. Another aspect was their interest in poetry, as evidenced by their panegyrist Muḥammad Ṭughrā'ī, known as Ibn-i Yamīn, who made a name for himself in literary history[1]. At the battle of Zāva he fell into the hands of the Kartids, spent some time as court poet in Herat, and eventually managed to escape and return to the Sarbadār dominions. Finally we may mention the relations of 'Alī-yi Mu'ayyad with the eminent Shī'ī theologian Ibn Makkī al-'Āmilī,[2] who was responsible for so important a Shī'ī book of law as *al-Lum'a al-Dimashqiyya*. This sort of evidence is also not easily fitted into the notion of a robber state.

If not a robber state, then, what of the interpretation of the Sarbadārs as the social revolutionary movement of which Petrushevsky speaks? This view is certainly correct to the extent that the phenomenon is traceable back to a revolt by suppressed and exploited sections of the population. But proof is lacking that it was a rebellion of the mass of the producing class against the exploiters. 'Abd al-Razzāq, with whom, in this view, the beginnings of the rising are very closely associated, was neither a peasant nor a representative of the lesser gentry who had espoused the peasants' cause because the latter were not in a position to press their own case. In fact, he belonged precisely to that aristocratic class of society at which the revolt of the exploited masses would have needed to be aimed. Moreover, the sources bearing on the social class of the various leading figures only rarely give any lead to speak of, so that any coherent interpretation on the pattern of socio-critical models is a dubious undertaking in the present state of knowledge.

Nevertheless, it is still legitimate to ask whether the dervishes of the Shaikhiyān may not properly be seen as a socially progressive group: in other words, whether the radical ideas they stood for in religious matters did not also have social implications or effects going beyond the principles of their order and their idea of a theocratic state. It is possible to infer an answer to this question from the particular manifestations within whose framework the Shaikhiyān are located. We are very well informed on one of these, which had experienced a spectacular upsurge at this very period, namely the Ṣafaviyya of Shaikh Ṣafī al-Dīn

[1] He is regarded as a convinced Shī'ī. Possibly this is to be seen as the reason for his flight from Herat: cf. Rypka, *HIL*, p. 261, and "Ibn-i Yamīn", *EI*[2].

[2] Most recently treated by Mazzaoui, *Origins of the Ṣafawids*, pp. 66ff.

Isḥāq (d. 735/1334). This was the religious-cum-political nucleus from which, at a later time, Shah Ismāʿīl I's state was to emerge. Even though at this time – in contrast to the Shaikhiyān – it was not yet Shīʿī, certain approaches of the two orders may very well have corresponded closely to each other. Reduced to a brief formula: both orders were groups based on religious principles with an unmistakable orientation towards political influence and claims to secular power, except that in the case of the Shaikhiyān the political component was already much more strongly developed than in the Ṣafaviyya.[1] This may have been due to differences in local conditions, but was probably due also to the markedly theocratic inclinations of the dervishes of Sabzavār, aimed as they were at the establishment of a Mahdist state. Social effects may occasionally have come about in the process. But these are rather to be understood as ingredients of the religious programmes of politically motivated groups, and most certainly not the other way round. Interpretations of the Shaikhiyān as a social revolutionary movement go beyond the limits imposed on the historian by the available evidence.

The cliché of a social-progressive movement or group does not apply to the Shaikhiyya of Sabzavār, any more than the label of a robber-state applies to the Sarbadār movement. The designation "Sarbadār dynasty" is hardly adequate, given the absence of a hereditary succession, which is the characteristic feature of a dynasty.[2] It would be possible, rather, to speak of an oligarchy and even, in a very limited sense, of a republic,[3] if one is unwilling to retain the definition of "a kingdom without kings",[4] which is most suited to the conditions of this period.

[1] Glassen, *Die frühen Safawiden*, p. 43, nevertheless reaches the conclusion: "The early Ṣafawīya were a mass movement ... Ṣafī ad-dīn had no wish to be the leader of an esoteric *ṭarīqa* in the midst of an élite association of disciples, but consciously devoted his whole energy to winning over the broad masses." Even Bina-Motlagh, *Scheich Safi von Ardabil*, pp. 53–68, gives detailed consideration to Shaikh Ṣafī's political connections, though he tends to see him rather as a saint (p. 126: "totally set apart from earthly things").

[2] The title of John Masson Smith's book is not to be understood, of course, in a genealogical sense.

[3] Aubin, "La fin de l'état Sarbadâr", p. 95: "... un État ... organisé en 'république', sans dévolution héréditaire de l'autorité, par les représentants de divers courants politiques". On p. 117, in the same context, he even speaks of the "phénomène d'auto-gouvernement iranien".

[4] Aubin, in *JESHO* XIV (1971), 382.

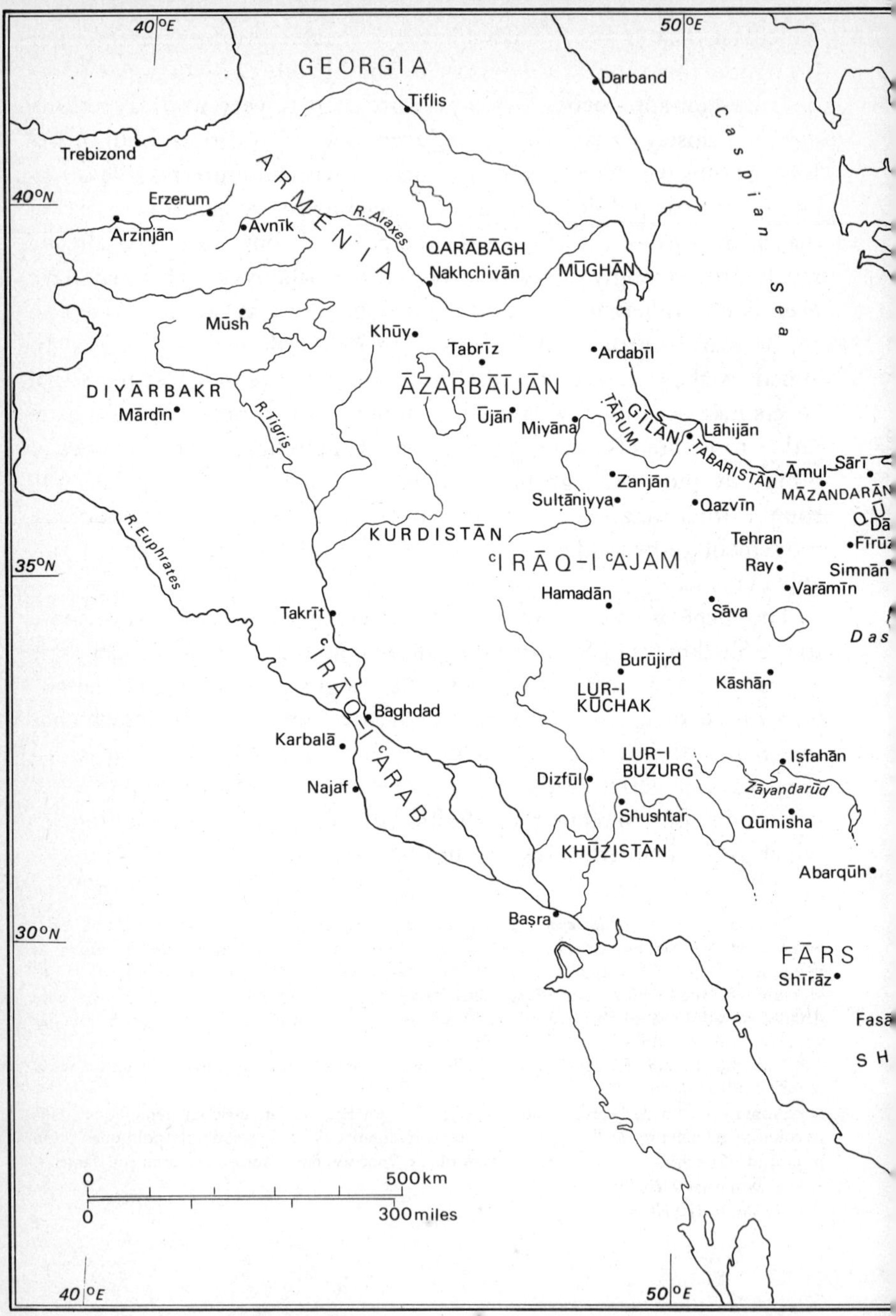

Map. Iran at the advent of Tīmūr

60°E
70°E
40°N
Samarqand
TRANSOXIANA
R. Oxus
R. Atrak
Abīvard
Marv
Balkh
gān
ābād
stām
Jājarm
JUVAIN
Isfarā'in
Rādkān
Kalāt
Ṭūs
Sarakhs
R. Murghāb
Sabzavār
Nīshāpūr
Mashhad
Zāva
Jām
35°N
Kābul
GHARCHISTĀN
KHURĀSĀN
Herat
QUHISTĀN
Isfizār
Dasht-i Lūt
Qandahār
ZAMĪN-DĀVAR
SĪSTĀN
Kirmān
30°N
KIRMĀN
Sīrjān
RA
Furg
R. Indus
HURMUZ
MAKRĀN
60°E
70°E

CHAPTER 2

TĪMŪR IN IRAN

Tīmūr's advances from Transoxiana into the Near East radically transformed conditions in Iran. The resulting changes were not confined to political affairs or to the structure of the state but also affected to a considerable degree the ethnic composition of Persia, the economic and social situation in the country and its cultural development.

In the decades following the demise of the Īl-Khān Abū Sa'īd the state of Iran was fragmented and there was widespread evidence of the collapse of national power. In itself, this might well have aroused the expansionist appetites of neighbouring states much earlier, but with the exception of the Golden Horde they simply lacked the military strength to take advantage of the situation. The Ottoman empire, as yet in its early stages, was just one of countless Anatolian principalities and constituted even less of a threat to Iran than any of the Türkmen tribal groups, such as the Qarā Quyūnlū, that were still struggling to obtain a political status. Nor is there any record of military advances by Egypt into Iran. The vast distances and the almost insurmountable geographical barriers involved make it unlikely that even the Mamlūk sultans contemplated such invasion plans,[1] and certainly any hopes the Muzaffarid Shāh-i Shujā' may have entertained when he granted recognition to the token caliph al-Mutawakkil 'alā'llāh Abū 'Abd-Allāh Muḥammad of Cairo were to remain unfulfilled. The situation was quite different, however, as far as the Golden Horde was concerned. At the court of Sarāī a keen interest was shown in events in Persia, and the ruling khans of the period were greatly attracted by the idea of gaining influence there. Indeed, as we have seen, attacks had already been made on Khurāsān and Āzarbāījān in 758/1357, as a result of which Tabrīz remained occupied for several years. The successes of the khans Jānī Beg and Berdī Beg proved ephemeral in view of the fifteen-year period of civil strife in the Golden Horde that followed their deaths, but Iran was to play a significant part in the duel between Tīmūr and Tokhtamïsh

[1] For details of Egypto-Persian relations during this period, see Sulaimān 'Aṭīya Sulaimān, *al-'alāqāt al-siyāsiyya baina Miṣr wa gharb Āsiyā (min wafāt Īlkhān Abī Sa'īd ilā daulat Āqquyūnlū)*, unpubl. Master's thesis, Univ. of Cairo (Kullīyat al-ādāb), 1952.

Khān and influence the actions and decisions of the two rivals over a long period, a subject that will be discussed in detail later.

TĪMŪR'S EARLY CAREER

First, some reference must be made, if only briefly, to Tīmūr's origins and the early stages of his life. At roughly the same time as central power was breaking down in Il-Khanid Persia, its eastern neighbour, the *ulus* of Chaghatai, named after its founder, Chingiz Khān's second son, was also undergoing severe political and religious disruption. In the process the Chaghatayid empire was split up into two khanates. One of these was Mughalistān, on the river Ili in eastern Turkestan, a land ruled by Mongols in which Mongol tradition was so staunchly upheld that even Islam failed to gain a footing there. The other was Transoxiana, an area peopled by strongly Turkicised Mongols who were being converted to Islam in ever increasing numbers. They were in time given the name Qarā'ūnās, a term originally applied only to the Mongols of mixed race living in the Indo-Iranian border area.[1] By the year 747/1346 Qarā'ūnās amīrs had replaced the Chaghatayid khans who had previously ruled the area. From now on the amīrs were the *de facto* rulers, although each of them raised to the throne a shadow khan and exercised power in his name. These khans no longer came exclusively from the line of Chaghatai, some of them being descendants of his brother Ögedei.

It was natural that the name Qarā'ūnās should be transferred to the Chaghatai Mongols, for this people in Transoxiana had become assimilated to its original population so as to form a distinct culture. By the middle of the 8th/14th century, the process of assimilation was complete throughout Transoxiana and beyond, even as far as Sīstān. Among those affected were the Barlās in the valley of the Qashqa-Daryā, the tribe of Tīmūr (Tu. *temür*, "iron"), whose name has been corrupted, via the Persian Tīmūr-i Lang ("the lame"), into the European form Tamerlane. This, in rough outline at least, was the milieu

[1] See Aubin, "L'ethnogénèse", and "Le khanat de Čaġatai", p. 18. Three possible meanings of the term Qarā'ūnās have to be taken into account: (1) the mixed Mongol population originating in the Indo-Iranian border area; (2) the Turco-Mongol population of Transoxiana; and (3) the Turco-Mongol dynasty of amīrs ruling in Transoxiana after the death of Qazan Khān in 1346. For the Timurid chroniclers the designation Qarā'ūnās ("half-castes") was taboo because the Mughals came to use it as their nickname for the Chaghatais. See Barthold, *Ulugh Beg*, p. 11, quoting Marco Polo and Mīrzā Ḥaidar Dughlāt. For their part the Chaghatais called the Mughals *jete* ("robbers").

into which he was born on 25 Sha'bān 736/8 April 1336, in Kish (Shahr-i Sabz), where he spent his childhood and probably also his youth. Although not a wealthy man, Tīmūr's father Amīr Taraghai was highly regarded within the Barlās tribe. A burial inscription ascribes to the family a common ancestry with Chingiz Khān, but during his lifetime Tīmūr never laid claim to such a relationship. Indeed, when he had come to power, he even installed puppet Chingizid khans in Samarqand: first Soyurghatmïsh Khān (proclaimed in 771/1370; d. 786/1384), a descendant of Ögedei, and then his son Sulṭān Maḥmūd Khān (d. 805/1402). This suggests that he felt his rule stood in need of legitimisation. He called himself Amīr, claiming the title *Amīr-i buzurg, Amīr al-kabīr* or the like, in addition to the attribute Kūrgān, which derives from the Mongol *küregen* ("son-in-law"): this last was a reference to his marriage connection with the Chingizids, of which we shall speak later. In accordance with the customs of tribal life Tīmūr learned in his youth every skill a warrior needed, especially horsemanship and archery. In addition to the Turkish language of his tribe he also acquired Persian, although he did not learn to read or write. The spread of Islam, which was making great strides in Transoxiana at that time, had also affected the Barlās tribe. Tīmūr, who can scarcely be described as a particularly religious man, was to value the conversation of dervishes and pious shaikhs throughout his life, a habit which may perhaps be ascribed to the influence of his father's spiritual adviser, whose name is given as Shams al-Dīn Kulāl.

Even in his early days Tīmūr found such recognition amongst his contemporaries in the Barlās tribe that some of them aligned themselves with him more closely as liegeman (*nöküt*, sing. *nökür*). His qualities as a leader and the success with which his various enterprises were crowned swelled the number of his followers. When considering the nature of these enterprises it must be borne in mind that in those times Transoxiana, just like Persia, was largely in a state of anarchy. They were in fact adventures typical of the circumstances of the time, warlike and predatory raids, mostly on a local scale – in other words nothing unusual in the nomadic milieu with which we are concerned. Reports of skirmishes in Sīstān, where civil wars were then a common occurrence, show that Tīmūr gradually extended his sphere of action. His involvement in this area may have had something to do with the Qarā'ūnās or Negüderis living there. Of course, whether one chooses to regard the leader of such exploits as an ambitious tribal warrior or as a bandit and robber chieftain depends on one's point of view. What the court chroniclers thought of them is fairly obvious, since they pass over this phase of Tīmūr's career in stubborn silence.

Several attempts were made from Mughalistān to re-establish the unity of the former *ulus* of Chaghatai under Mongol rule. The murder in 759/1358 of Amīr Qazaghan, who in 747/1346 had founded a line of Qarā'ūnās princes in Transoxiana, prompted Tughluq Temür Khān to launch a campaign against the region, as a result of which the governor of Qashqa-Daryā, Ḥājjī Barlās, took flight. Tīmūr, also convinced that it was pointless to put up any resistance, did not flee but acknowledged the authority of the khan, who then transferred to him the governorship of Qashqa-Daryā. This compact was short-lived, however, because Tīmūr then allied himself with Amīr Ḥusain, a grandson of Amīr Qazaghan who initially ruled the territory from Balkh to Kābul, but with Tīmūr's support managed after a long struggle to reconquer the lands of his grandfather. In one of these exchanges Tīmūr received the injuries to the right shoulder, the right hand and the right thigh which account for his nickname and traces of which were detected on his skeleton by the archaeological commission which opened up his sarcophagus in the Gūr-i Mīr in 1941. For the present Tīmūr cemented the alliance with Ḥusain by marrying one of his sisters, named Öljei Terken. Then, taking advantage of the increased social prestige this afforded him, he entered into further marriage alliances with the aristocracy of Central Asia.

Yet in the long run neither the alliance, nor the fact that they were related, nor even their shared experience of danger, imprisonment, defeats and eventual victories could prevent the two princes from becoming rivals. Tīmūr finally laid siege to Balkh and conquered it. Although he had granted Ḥusain safe conduct he allowed one of the local princes to murder him in revenge for the killing of his brother ten years earlier. Thus sovereignty over Transoxiana passed to Tīmūr. He now married Sarāī Mulk Khātūn, a member of Ḥusain's harem. She was a daughter of the Chaghatayid khan Qazan, who had ruled until 747/1346, and it was on this connection that Tīmūr based his claim to the epithet Kūrgān (son-in-law, that is, of a member of the dynasty of Chingiz Khān).[1]

The events just discussed took place against a background of great social upheaval and change for the population of Transoxiana. In part

[1] For the document of 804/1401 recording this, see Fekete, *Einführung*, pp. 71–5 and plates 3–6.

this was due to the fact that political power passed from the hands of the Mongol khans and their adherents to Qarā'ūnās amīrs who of course had their own followers. It is known that Amīr Ḥusain ousted from their positions and estates numerous amīrs and landlords, many of whom took refuge with Tīmūr. The social consequences are particularly clear in the case of Sarbadārs of Samarqand, to whom brief reference has already been made. They managed to save the city from attack by the Mongols but were subsequently destroyed by Amīr Ḥusain, apart from those who escaped to Tīmūr or were rescued by him. Another notable factor is the change from a nomadic to a more settled way of life. An example of this is Ḥusain's fortification of Balkh, a task he undertook despite Tīmūr's warnings. In the eyes of the nomads this was tantamount to a criminal offence, since they regarded it as a matter of principle never to settle permanently in any one place but constantly to renew their migrations. Yet the impulse to establish a permanent capital city, if not to adopt a wholly settled way of life, was so strong that even Tīmūr succumbed to it. Once he had eliminated his rivals, he too set about fortifying and architecturally developing his capital, Samarqand.

THE CONQUEST OF EASTERN IRAN

Tīmūr's advances to the south and west are in no way linked to a population explosion or to a mass migration of peoples. They lacked the spontaneity associated with the rise of Chingiz Khān. Tīmūr planned his campaigns against Afghanistan and the Iranian uplands with as much care as the early part of his career up to 1370 with which we have so far been concerned. Indeed, so thorough were his plans that more than a decade went by before he proceeded to put them into operation. Although he now had at his disposal the troops of his defeated rival, who had switched their allegiance to him, his forces were still not strong enough to outmanoeuvre the Qarā'ūnās amīrs, who had been watching his advancement with envy and suspicion. In order to ensure himself against surprise attacks in Transoxiana as he marched into the Near East he had either to eliminate them or to win them over to his side. To secure his position at the rear it was also necessary to subjugate Khwārazm.

At this time a variety of links existed between Transoxiana and Khurāsān. Following the murder of the Mongol ruler of Astarābād,

Togha Temür (754/1353), there remained in eastern Persia three significant political powers. These were the realm of the Kartids of Herat, the state of the Sarbadārs of Sabzavār, and the dominion of the Jā'ūn-i Qurbān around Ṭūs. Tīmūr had to deal with all three, and in each case the issue was settled differently.

With the Kartids, who lived closest to his home territories, Tīmūr established links at an early date. Malik Muʿizz al-Dīn Ḥusain (732 to 771/1331–2 to 1370), who after his victory over the Sarbadārs at Zāva (743/1342) had carried out various successful campaigns against the *ulus* of Chaghatai, took Tīmūr into his service. He had himself proclaimed Sultan (750/1349), which was tantamount to abrogating Mongol supremacy and was a measure typical of the increasingly strong tendencies in Herat at that time towards a revival of Islam. Although married to a Chingizid princess, the daughter of Togha Temür, the malik was not himself of Mongol descent and thus according to the law of Chingiz Khān, the Yasa, he did not qualify for sovereign rule. From his Mongol father-in-law he had nothing to fear ; it was Amīr Qazaghan, exercising power in the name of a Mongol puppet khan, who moved against him and forced him to give up his independence. The alliance with Tīmūr came to an end as a result of a predatory raid by the Kartid that impinged upon his immediate sphere of influence. After the death of his father, sovereignty over the Kartid empire passed to Ghiyās̱ al-Dīn Pīr ʿAlī, except for Sarakhs and part of Quhistān, which were the inheritance of his stepbrother Malik Muḥammad. In the struggle to gain absolute power that inevitably ensued, each of the two brothers attempted to secure his position by enlisting Tīmūr's support. The prince of Herat sent an embassy to him, and his brother even arrived in person, seeking asylum after being driven out of Sarakhs. This did not prevent Tīmūr from proposing to Ghiyās̱ al-Dīn Pīr ʿAlī that they should renew "the old ties of friendship" and indeed strengthen them by means of a marriage between one of his nieces and Ghiyās̱ al-Dīn's eldest son, who for this purpose came to Samarqand. Not until two years later was he allowed to return to Herat, and then only as a result of pressure from his father. Scarcely were the marriage celebrations in Herat at an end when Ghiyās̱ al-Dīn was summoned by Tīmūr to a great council (*quriltai*). This summons may well suggest that Tīmūr was beginning to doubt the loyalty of the prince of Herat, probably because of conspicuous defence works that the latter had undertaken. When Ghiyās̱ al-Dīn now made all sorts of excuses to try to postpone the date of his departure, Tīmūr armed himself for battle and arrived with his troops outside the city in Muḥarram 783/April 1381. This was the prelude to one of the greatest catastrophes in the history of Iran.

There is no lack of evidence to suggest that Tīmūr was well informed about the desperate political plight of Persia, the breakdown of power and the widespread internecine strife within the country. Moreover, some important figures in Iran actually wanted Tīmūr to intervene. Evidence of this can be seen from a letter sent by Mu'īn al-Dīn Jāmī, the aged vizier of Mu'izz al-Dīn Ḥusain, in which Tīmūr was openly invited to make his way to Khurāsān. When Tīmūr was nearing their city, the shaikhs of Jām, who were related to the vizier and had great political influence in the country, called upon all the dignitaries to go out and welcome the conqueror: almost without exception they did so. It is likely that Tīmūr was similarly encouraged by those Khurasanian emigrés and refugees who were in his camp, such as the Kartid prince of Sarakhs and Togha Temür's son Luqmān. No doubt they held hopes of being restored to power by Tīmūr, hopes which, incidentally, were often fulfilled.

Despite the city's strong fortifications Tīmūr had no difficulty in taking Herat. Ghiyāṣ al-Dīn Pīr 'Alī, who was by no means as skilful or capable as his father, had failed to arouse in the population the strength of will to defend the city. Tīmūr showed effective command of the tactics of psychological warfare by promising to spare the lives and possessions of those who took no part in the battle. He went even further when he made the magnanimous gesture of releasing some two thousand prisoners of war. After the city had been occupied the fortifications were dismantled, although not the citadel of Ikhtiyār al-Dīn. A fairly large group of respected citizens, including theologians and other scholars, was deported to Shahr-i Sabz in Tīmūr's more immediate homeland, and a high tribute was exacted from the population. Ghiyāṣ al-Dīn had no choice but to submit to the authority of his father's former liegeman and could count himself lucky to be reinstated as Tīmūr's vassal. In 785/1383, however, his career was terminated when he was suspected of complicity in a plot hatched by members of the house of Herat. Tīmūr's son Mīrān Shāh, the Chaghatayid governor, managed to nip the rebellion in the bud and annexed Herat. In 798/1396 he was to murder the other surviving Kartids at a banquet to which he had invited them. Thus ended, after 130 years, the sway of a local dynasty of no little significance in the history of Iranian civilisation.

In the very year he conquered Herat, Tīmūr turned his attention to the west, where 'Alī Beg Jā'ūn-i Qurbānī, who had succeeded his brother as ruler of Kalāt and Ṭūs, had ignored the summons to assist in the campaign against Herat. After a long siege Tīmūr took him prisoner, sent him to Transoxiana and shortly afterwards had him killed. A sizeable contingent of the Jā'ūn-i Qurbān was deported to Samarqand and the surrounding area, where they were later to attract the notice of chroniclers.[1]. Tīmūr installed one of their number, Ḥājjī Beg, as governor (*ḥākim*) of Ṭūs, thus entrusting to him a Chaghatayid protectorate which he was to administer until his rebellion in the year 791/1389.

It is sometimes maintained that the sovereign of the Sarbadār state of Sabzavār, Khwāja 'Alī-yi Mu'ayyad, suffered a fate similar to that of the ruler of the Jā'ūn-i Qurbān. The proponents of this view would have us believe that Tīmūr subjected him to his overlordship, only to dispose of him a few years later when he had outlived his usefulness. However, as Jean Aubin has recently shown, this version of events is not only inaccurate but also runs counter to the general policy pursued by Tīmūr in Persia. Already, towards the Sarbadārs of Samarqand, it will be recalled, Tīmūr had adopted a more or less friendly attitude. It is reasonable to suppose that he also established friendly contacts with the Sarbadār leader in Khurāsān before embarking on his westward advance from Herat. When he arrived in the region of Nīshāpūr, Khwāja 'Alī was there to pay him homage. What he had to offer the conqueror may have been no more than a modest remnant of the once glorious Sarbadār state, but the offer suited Tīmūr's plans well. His policy was not to dismantle established political structures but to make use of them whenever it was possible to do so without risk to himself.

Tīmūr was right to anticipate possible risks in western Khurāsān, as the conflicts with 'Alī Beg Jā'ūn-i Qurbānī had already shown. In addition there were the activities of Amīr Valī, self-appointed guardian of the interests of the Il-Khanid prince Luqmān. As we have already mentioned, Khwāja 'Alī-yi Mu'ayyad sought assistance from Tīmūr against him when he was already close to conquering Sabzavār. Tīmūr promptly relieved the pressure on the leader of the Sarbadārs by

[1] See Roemer, in *Šams al-Ḥusn*, pp. 99 ff., quoting Shāmī II (commentary), 46, 48, 49, 76.

actions against Gurgān and the possessions of Amīr Valī in Māzandarān, but above all by the brutal treatment he meted out to the latter's forces and the population of Isfarā'īn. In Rādkān, as he was returning from the campaign in Māzandarān, Tīmūr confirmed the appointment of Khwāja 'Alī-yi Mu'ayyad as governor of Sabzavār.

Khwāja 'Alī remained loyal to Tīmūr until the end, fulfilling his military obligations towards him until 788/1386, when he died as a result of a wound sustained in battle in Lesser Luristān. His loyalty was respected by Tīmūr, who did not occupy Sabzavār with a Chaghatai garrison. Khwāja 'Alī may have forfeited his independence, but he did retain control of the local administration and – although this did not always protect him from the encroachments of Chaghatai finance officers – even enjoyed in principle exemption from taxation. How can one reconcile this picture of events with the reported rebellion of 785/1383 in Sabzavār and the terrible retribution that followed it? The answer is quite simple. The scene of the uprising was not the capital of the Sarbadārs but a place in eastern Khurāsān that lay some 70 miles south of Herat and was furthermore called Isfizār.[1] Nor had the ringleader of the rebellion, Shaikh Dā'ūd-i Khiṭaṭāī, any connection with the Sarbadārs. He was a military man who, having left the service of the Kartids to join Tīmūr, had been made governor of the place. The rebellion was thus the work of the petty aristocracy of the Kartid empire.

The death of Khwāja 'Alī did not mean that his family ceased to play an active rôle in Tīmūr's empire. The territory of the Sarbadārs was divided up amongst several of his relatives, possibly in imitation of the Turkish or Mongol principle of inheritance. The army of Sabzavār and a number of Khwāja 'Alī's relations featured in several campaigns, usually playing a loyal part. Only Mulūk Sabzavārī allowed himself to become involved in the rebellion of Ḥājjī Beg of Ṭūs, to which we have already referred. After its failure he sought refuge with the Muzaffarid Shāh Manṣūr in Iṣfahān, but was eventually pardoned by Tīmūr and made governor of Baṣra at the beginning of 796/end of 1393.

When they had quelled the rebellion of Sabzavār/Isfizār, Tīmūr's forces marched on Sīstān. After heavy fighting they captured the capital Shahr-i Sīstān, and plundered and destroyed it. They then devas-

[1] Aubin, "La fin de l'état Sarbadâr", pp. 109ff., traces the origin of the confusion to Shāmī I, 91: Barthold had already correctly equated Sabzavār with Isfizār in 1903 in *Istoricheskiĭ-geograficheskiĭ obzor Irana* (see now his *Sochineniya* VII, 84)

tated the country, destroying especially irrigation works vital to its agriculture, a factor often cited as contributing to the continuing backwardness of the region even to this day. Qandahār was to suffer a similar fate in the course of the army's return march.

One other advance can be seen as part of this first phase of Tīmūr's operations against Iran. Begun in 786/1384, it took him back initially to Māzandarān. The Il-Khanid prince Luqmān, a son of Togha Temür who himself had found refuge in Samarqand in his day, was appointed governor of Astarābād. This was not, however, the sole aim of the offensive. Tīmūr advanced further, against the Jalayirid Sulṭān Aḥmad in Āzarbāījān, but failed to capture him either in this campaign or later. As a result of the latter's flight, however, Tīmūr had little difficulty in conquering the ancient Il-Khanid capital Sulṭāniyya, where he halted his advance. After going into winter quarters in Ray, he returned to Samarqand. Persia was to be further subjugated in the course of Tīmūr's three famous campaigns, the three-year campaign of 788–90/1386–8, the five-year campaign of 794–8/1392–6 and the so-called seven-year campaign[1] which he began on 4 Sha'bān 801/11 April 1399. These will be dealt with later.

MOTIVATION AND METHODS

An account has now been given of the most important stages of the military operations by means of which Tīmūr in the space of less than five years imposed his sovereignty on the east and south-east of Iran, i.e. Māzandarān, eastern and western Khurāsān, and Sīstān. Already a few typical features have emerged, a number of which were to recur in later operations against Iran. Particularly striking is the thorough preparation of each individual operation. It is obvious that all the military possibilities were carefully considered, as well as the means needed to put them into operation. Without prior reconnaissance this would certainly have been impossible. Members of Islamic orders, dervishes and itinerant monks (*qalandarān*) all played a part in the gathering of secret military information. For a Sunnī Tīmūr was relatively indifferent in his personal attitude to religion but he treated the champions of

[1] When Tīmūr died on 18 Feb. 1405, six years had elapsed since the start of the campaign and the seventh had begun only thirteen days previously, i.e. on 4 Sha'bān 807/5 February. The traditional designation "Seven Year Campaign" is therefore somewhat problematical, unless perhaps it derives from some plan of Tīmūr's.

the Islamic faith with obvious benevolence. Descendants of the family of the prophet Muḥammad (*sayyid*, pl. *sādāt*), shaikhs, Ṣūfīs, dervishes and judges of the religious law (*quḍāt,* sing. *qāḍī*) all enjoyed his special protection. Their lives or property were never in jeopardy when he was taking terrible reprisals against a captured city. Even when tributes were being raised, when the rest of the population had to surrender money and other belongings under threat of death or were forced by torture to reveal the whereabouts of hidden valuables, they were able to move about freely in the streets and squares. On occasion, indeed, they were able with some hope of success to intercede for one or another of the victims of Tīmūr's myrmidons. Naturally, they proved grateful for such great privileges, and Tīmūr could count on many of them whenever he was in need of their help. The mobility of this class of people and the widespread organisation of their orders made them ideal agents of reconnaissance.

The objects of Tīmūr's military ventures and campaigns were various: they might be designed to eliminate a permanent military threat, as in the case of the Golden Horde; to secure political influence, as in India or Anatolia; or to impose his own power in the face of dangerous rivals in the Chaghatayid heartlands, as was the case with the struggle against the Qarā'ūnās amīrs in Transoxiana and the subjection of Khwārazm. The invasion of Iran, however, had none of these aims. When he began his advance into Khurāsān, Tīmūr never contemplated annexing the territory or incorporating it into his homelands, as is quite clear from his endeavours to maintain existing political structures in being rather than destroy them. His objective was to neutralise other rulers, that is, to extend his own sphere of influence by setting up protectorates. The rulers were, of course, obliged to give up their independence and required to pay considerable sums in tribute. Although only one of the three protectorates, that of the Sarbadārs of Sabzavār, lasted for any length of time, whereas the other two – the empire of the Kartids and the realm of the Jā'ūn-i Qurbān – were liquidated soon after they had been established, this was due solely to the rebellions that occurred there after Tīmūr had withdrawn.

Increased political power was, however, by no means the only motive for Tīmūr's invasion of Iran. Economic considerations must have played an equally important part. In this connection it is worth bearing in mind the economic situation in Chaghatayid Transoxiana. It was far inferior to that of Iran even after almost three decades of confusion and civil war had, it would appear, reduced to ruins the Il-Khanid empire, which had attained a particularly high level of development thanks to the reforms of Ghazan Khān. Culturally, too, the Chaghatais were backward in comparison with the people of Iran. It would therefore be reasonable to assume that Tīmūr with his pragmatic cast of mind was concerned to redress the situation in favour of his Central Asian homeland. His idea was, as far as it was possible, to transfer material goods to Transoxiana in order to lay the foundations of economic prosperity and to give his authority as ruler a fitting air of splendour. His advances into Iran may have been predatory raids, but they were carefully considered and executed in accordance with previously established plans, unlike those of nomadic peoples attracted by the material wealth of sedentary populations. From Iran and other countries, therefore, the means were to be acquired to develop Transoxiana's economy and to transform Tīmūr's capital Samarqand into a splendid metropolis appropriate to so great a monarch. In fact, Tīmūr was not content to strip the cities he conquered or occupied of their treasures and objects of value, but also seized movable property of all kinds, including riding-horses and pack animals, domestic animals, herds of cattle, weapons, provisions and supplies of consumable commodities. No less important was the acquisition of human labour-forces, prisoners who could be used as slaves, especially qualified men such as craftsmen and artisans who could be put to work to improve and develop the homelands; although theologians and scholars were also included.

The description just given of the economic aspects of Tīmūr's conquests conforms to the type normally found in books. It is not wrong, but it is somewhat summary and lacking in concrete information. More recent investigations have served to clarify the picture, and though they may differ as regards points of detail, what emerges most strikingly from them is Tīmūr's essentially systematic and consistent approach. They provide an insight into the methods used when exacting tribute, ransom money and capital levies or confiscating property; and the extent to which such measures succeeded in individual cases can also be seen. In addition, they tell us what sort of means the army leaders used either to hold in check their soldiers' rapacity when it threatened to have an adverse effect on the superior claims of official revenue or, conversely, how they gave them free rein when the situation demanded it, i.e. when reprisals no longer worked or concessions had to be made to sustain the fighting spirit of the troops.

It was the normal military custom for troops on the march to live off the land, but the occasional mention of a requisition order suggests that they did not always go about it in an irregular manner. As far as they could be obtained, lists of businesses and tax registers were used as a basis for levying tribute. Responsibility for implementing the levies was entrusted to the tax-collectors (*muḥaṣṣilān*) of the Supreme Dīvān, to whom military assistance was also made available. The first step was to seal off all but one of a city's gates, sometimes even to wall them up. At any rate they were closely guarded, with two different aims in mind: to prevent the inhabitants from escaping or removing possessions that they were required to surrender, and to stop the troops who were eager for plunder from entering the city before the appointed time. Accompanied by torturers, the tax-collectors then moved through those areas of the city that had been assigned to them, confiscating money and possessions, carrying out house searches and extracting forced confessions from inhabitants whom they suspected of concealing valuables or possessing information about the circumstances of others who were liable to pay tribute. All takings were to be delivered to specified collection centres where they were registered, loaded and dispatched under the supervision of responsible amīrs. As the means of transport available for removing the confiscated possessions was often inadequate, particularly intensive searches were made for pack-animals. The ransom money (*māl-i amānī*) with which a city could buy immunity from plunder was usually distributed amongst the amīrs. Tīmūr's efforts to persuade every city he arrived at with his forces to capitulate by negotiating a ransom sum show that economic considerations weighed heavily with him. Naturally the desire to spare his own troops was also a significant factor, but above all he was concerned to secure the expected booty or tribute which would be considerably reduced, if not totally lost, as a result of the plundering that inevitably followed any seizure by force. As a rule the soldiers were only given permission to plunder, and then on a specific signal, when the officials of the dīvān had completed their requisitions; although such a regulation was no longer applicable when a city had been taken by storm. Tīmūr only resorted to military force when negotiations of surrender had failed, but when this happened he took extremely aggressive action, showing the city's inhabitants little or no mercy.

The economic and administrative aspect of Tīmūr's conquests – a feature common to all of them, not only those in Iran – has not received such clear recognition until now. This is probably because one's attention is all too easily distracted from such details by the descriptions of acts of cruelty and brutality found in reports. On the other hand, an economic approach to events must not be allowed to disguise the fact that bestial atrocities were commonplace. Indeed, to quote one historian, "The Great Amīr regarded terror as *the* means of government"[1] and all the more of waging war. The most horrifying atrocities were committed in the course of reprisals ordered by Tīmūr when his negotiators or officials sent into a city after its capitulation were attacked or killed, when a city prevented negotiations by attacking the forces besieging it, or when a conquered city subsequently rose up once more against the victors. In such cases punishment took the form of a bloodbath (*qatl-i 'āmm*), the slaughter of the entire population. While the menfolk were murdered, women, boys and girls were violated, but this did not necessarily mean that they escaped death. Only old people and very young children under the age of five had any chance of survival, providing they did not die of starvation later. Otherwise the inhabitants of conquered cities were considered as part of the booty, sold as slaves and deported to Transoxiana. Many of them – often one in two – died of exhaustion, starvation or disease on the way.

The pyramids (*minārahā*) of skulls that Tīmūr had erected outside the gates of cities punished in this manner may be regarded as direct symbols of his unbridled cruelty. The worst instance of this was in Iṣfahān, where in 790/1388 the population had attacked the tax-collectors. The historian Ḥāfiẓ-i Abrū, renowned for the reliability of his historical accounts, records how, in the aftermath of the reprisals, he walked with a friend half way round the periphery of the city and counted twenty-eight such towers, each consisting of roughly 1,500 heads. He also mentions similar towers on the other side of Iṣfahān, though not so many. Figures mentioned in the sources of 70,000 heads taken by Tīmūr's troops from the bodies of slain inhabitants of Iṣfahān may not, therefore, exceed the bounds of possibility. Tīmūr may have taken as his model the massacres carried out by the Mongols during their conquest of the Middle and Near East, but nothing they did equalled this degree of inhumanity. Nor could they rival in ingenuity the act of bestiality perpetrated in Sabzavār/Isfizār after the suppression of the above-mentioned uprising.

[1] Aubin, "Comment Tamerlan prenait les villes", p. 122.

Two thousand prisoners were heaped up in a living mound, which was then walled in with clay and fragments of brick.[1]

The conquest of a particular area could also be followed by resettlement operations on a fairly large scale.[2] Their significance is not always easy to determine, but as a rule they were probably carried out for reasons of security. This was the case with the group of the Jā'ūn-i Qurbān whose deportation has already been mentioned, and perhaps also with the Qarā Tatar who were moved from Amāsya and Qaiṣariyya to Central Asia in 806/1403.[3]

The principles by which Tīmūr proceeded in his conquest of Iran were scarcely ever so rigid as not to admit of exceptions. From time to time even a city in revolt, like Yazd in 798/1396, was able to benefit from his flexibility. Tīmūr gave orders that it was neither to be plundered nor held to ransom, and it was even spared the biennial tax normally imposed in such cases. On the other hand, thousands of the city's inhabitants had already starved to death during the siege that led to its eventual capitulation. Yazd was a centre of textile manufacture, and it may be that Tīmūr dealt with the city relatively leniently because he was concerned about a possible demise of the local industry. A bloodbath of the kind suffered by quite a number of cities could reduce them to a state of almost total depopulation and economic collapse. Nevertheless, the majority were able to recover after some time. That this was so is probably due to the fact that even when the collective murder of a population was involved Tīmūr imposed certain limits on the use of arbitrary violence and ensured that these limits were observed. As we have already noted, sayyids, shaikhs, qāḍīs and other members of the religious classes could be granted protection against murder and pillage. We have also encountered one example of a city where the dignitaries were given exceptional treatment, namely Herat in 783/1381. In fact, the leading members of a city's aristocracy or "the rich", as they were sometimes called, were generally spared, together with their relatives and servants: it was not unknown for Tīmūr to

[1] Shāmī I, 91.

[2] Cf. the case of the Ṣūfiyān-i Rūmlū, who were the descendants of liberated prisoners of war from Anatolia. Returning from his campaign against Bāyezīd in the spring of 806/1404, Tīmūr is said to have handed them over to the Safavid leader Khwāja 'Alī in Ardabīl at the latter's request (Hinz, *Irans Aufstieg*, pp. 15ff.): on the authenticity of this meeting, see Horst, "Tīmūr und Ḫōğä 'Alī," pp. 25, 38; also below, pp. 80, 205–6.

[3] For details, see Barthold, "Tatar", *EI*[1]. The later history of this tribal group is considered in Roemer, *Šams al-Ḥusn*, p. 97.

protect this section of society from the fate suffered by the remainder of the population by ordering a military cordon to be thrown around the closed districts in which they lived.

No direct comparison can be made between the planning of Tīmūr's advances into Iran and that of his other military enterprises, such as his campaigns against the Golden Horde, India and Anatolia. This is apparent even from the earliest of his operations which we have so far discussed. The subjugation of the Kartids of Herat, the removal of the Jā'ūn-i Qurbān and the partnership with the Sarbadārs of Sabzavār were not simply conceived as predatory raids, whatever gains they brought in terms of booty. Nor was there any intention, at least from the outset, to annex these territories. Tīmūr aimed rather at eliminating or, more precisely, at neutralising these hitherto more or less independent political entities by turning them into Chaghatai protectorates. His first raids on Sīstān, Gurgān and Māzandarān may be regarded as flanking manoeuvres to secure the principal territories of Khurāsān. The conquest of eastern Persia owed its success, as we have shown, to several carefully planned operations. There were good reasons for proceeding in so calculated a manner. Tīmūr had to tread cautiously because the internal situation in Transoxiana was only gradually returning to stability and because he saw danger threatening from his neighbours, the White Horde and the Golden Horde to the north, and the Mughals from the region of the river Ili in the north-east.

THE GOLDEN HORDE

The offensive of 786/1384 against Sulṭāniyya in itself makes it clear that Tīmūr's conquests in eastern Persia were not designed merely to establish a glacis for his Chaghatayid empire, but were the beginning of a campaign to subjugate Persia as a whole. In this connection a brief consideration of the political situation in Central Asia is necessary, and in particular of Tīmūr's relations with Tokhtamïsh. The latter, after clashing with Qïpchaq princes, had sought refuge with Tīmūr, who gladly welcomed him, not so much out of respect for his Chingizid descent, if he had such respect at all, but because he recognised the opportunity this offered to weaken the position of his northern neighbours, the White Horde and possibly also the Golden Horde. The campaigns Tokhtamïsh fought in Tīmūr's service all ended in defeat, but eventually he gained dominion over the White Horde and even over the Golden Horde. From then on his actions were quite the opposite of what Tīmūr had expected from him. He strove to make his territory a major power, first by invading Russia and plundering and destroying Moscow, then by pursuing ambitions in Transoxiana and Iran which led to attacks across the Jaxartes in the east and over the Caucasus in the west. Although there are coins of Tokhtamïsh that were minted in Khwārazm in 785/1383, it is not clear whether it was his incursion into this area that prompted Tīmūr to return to Samarqand from his first campaign to Āzarbāījān, instead of pursuing the Jalayirid Sulṭān Aḥmad, who had retreated from Sulṭāniyya to Tabrīz. On the other hand, all the evidence indicates that Tokhtamïsh kept a careful eye on Tīmūr's movements in Persia and began making preparations for an attack on Tabrīz on receiving news of his return to Central Asia. After advancing via Darband, his troops captured and plundered the city in the winter of 787/1385–6.

At the outset of the three-year campaign the Chaghatai forces aimed initially for the Jaxartes, a line of attack which might lead one to conclude that Tīmūr had in mind a show of force against Tokhtamïsh. There is, however, greater reason to believe that it was a diversion designed to cover up Tīmūr's real objectives, which were central and western Persia together with the invasion routes leading there from Qïpchaq. In fact his forces first went into action against the Lurs, on the pretext that they had been ambushing caravans of pilgrims bound for Mecca. But it is more likely that the slaughter Tīmūr inflicted upon them was designed to make secure the route to Mesopotamia because of its possible strategic importance in the struggle against Sulṭān Aḥmad Jalāyir. To suppress him was, after all, clearly one of the principal objectives of Tīmūr's campaign. Soon after the withdrawal of the Qïpchaq forces, Sulṭān Aḥmad had recovered control of the city of Tabrīz, and Tīmūr lost no time in marching there once the operation in Luristān had been completed. He had no difficulty in capturing the city in the summer of 788/1386, but the Jalayirid, whose army and resources had been seriously weakened by Tokhtamïsh's attack, had again managed to evade him by taking flight. The inhabitants of Tabrīz, still quite prosperous through their trading connections, were forced to pay a heavy tribute, and scholars, artists and craftsmen were deported to Samarqand. The Chaghatai court remained in residence in Tabrīz throughout the summer, and the rulers of the surrounding territories came to pay homage. Amīr Valī, who as Sulṭān Aḥmad's city commandant in Tabrīz had been swept away by Tokhtamïsh's forces, led a rebellion in Māzandarān, but it was put down, and the ringleaders were captured and executed. A nephew of Tīmūr, Muḥammad Sulṭān, was eventually made governor, and the Chaghatai troops moved on.

They now began a campaign against Georgia, the first of six invasions whose object was not only to subjugate and exploit the local population but also to cut off the approach routes normally used by the armies of the Golden Horde for their attacks on the Iranian uplands. As a result of these operations, the territory of Georgia was devastated and depopulated. The Georgians, a Christian people, were usually more than capable warriors, but they proved no match for the ferocious Chaghatais. The city of Tiflis, which was difficult to capture and tenaciously defended, was taken by storm in the very first campaign. King Bagrat V was imprisoned together with his wife Anna Comnena, a princess of Trebizond. Only by accepting Islam was he able to save his life, but subsequently he apostatised and as a result his country suffered further calamities.

In the winter the Qïpchaq forces again advanced through Darband to attack Persia. They were defeated by Mīrān Shāh, who then went with his prisoners to Qarābāgh, an Armenian territory where Tīmūr had set up his winter quarters. Against all expectations and contrary to his usual practice, Tīmūr treated the prisoners leniently. He set them free with no more than a warning, thus clearly making one last effort to convince Tokhtamïsh that he still enjoyed the goodwill of his former protector and at the same time discouraging him from further hostilities.

THE END OF THE MUZAFFARIDS

Reference was made in the previous chapter to the official dispatch that Shāh-i Shujā' issued shortly before his death, in which he sought to commend to Tīmūr's favour the members of his dynasty[1]. Tīmūr's mistrust of foreign rulers and the intrigues by individual relatives of the recently deceased Muzaffarid prince made him unwilling to take this document at face value. After the struggles in Armenia and Georgia he might have been expected to continue the pursuit of Sulṭān Aḥmad Jalāyir into Mesopotamia, but he chose first to establish order and stability in those territories of central Persia as yet not touched upon in his campaigns. A letter was dispatched to Zain al-'Ābidīn 'Alī,

[1] See above, p. 16.

the son and successor of Shāh-i Shujāʿ, reminding him of the latter's declaration of loyalty. As this had no effect, Tīmūr marched on Iṣfahān, whose governor, Muẓaffar-i Kāshī, surrendered the keys to him. The citizens would probably have suffered no more than the tribute imposed upon them, harsh though it was, had not a rebellion against the Chaghatai tax gatherers aroused Tīmūr's wrath and resulted in the slaughter of the population as was described above. On Tīmūr's approach, Zain al-ʿĀbidīn fled from his capital Shīrāz, intending to go to Baghdad. Near Shushtar he encountered his cousin Shāh Manṣūr, who treated him kindly at first but subsequently had him taken prisoner and thrown into gaol. In the circumstances Shīrāz easily fell prey to the Chaghatai troops. Along with ʿImād al-Dīn Aḥmad and other Muzaffarid princes and local rulers, Shāh Manṣūr then came to Tīmūr's court in the city to pay homage to the conqueror. As before, Tīmūr resorted in this instance to his old practice of reinstating the members of previously ruling families as governors in his service or allowing them to continue in office. Such a course of action was particularly advisable in this case, as reports of incursions by Tokhtamïsh called for his immediate return to Transoxiana. He entrusted the administration of Shīrāz to Nuṣrat al-Dīn Shāh Yaḥyā, a nephew of Shāh-i Shujāʿ.

It was obvious that Tīmūr's successes in Transoxiana and Persia, the bloodbath of Iṣfahān and the plundering of Shīrāz had all failed to teach the Muzaffarids a lesson, for they resumed their old feuds as soon as he had departed. Shāh Manṣūr, a particularly enterprising prince, set about re-establishing the old sphere of influence of the Muzaffarids. He first gained control of Shīrāz, forcing Shāh Yaḥyā to flee to Yazd. Then he captured Abarqūh, but his attempts to conquer Iṣfahān met with less success and he returned to Shīrāz. Meanwhile Zain al-ʿĀbidīn had escaped from prison and proceeded to Iṣfahān, where the inhabitants gave him a warm welcome. His cousin Shāh Yaḥyā tried to form an alliance with him and Sulṭān Aḥmad, the ruler of Kirmān, against Shāh Manṣūr. Negotiations took place in Ṣafar 793 (began on 8 January 1391) in Sīrjān,[1] at the home of the local ruler, a Muzaffarid by the name of Abū Isḥāq. The common front agreed upon against Shāh Manṣūr, however, was soon to crumble. When they were met by the latter's troops near Furg on the border of Kirmān, Shāh Yaḥyā's

[1] On the location of Sīrjān, which A.A.K. Vazīrī Kirmānī, *Tārīkh-i Kirmān* (*Sālāriyya*) (Tehran, 1340/1961), equates with Qalʿa-yi Sang, see Aubin, "Deux sayyids", p. 13, n. 1, and "La question de Sīrǧān au XIIIe siècle", *StIr* VI (1977), 285–90.

forces were not on the spot, and Sulṭān Ahmad retreated in the direction of Nairīz, accompanied by his son Ghiyāṣ. He eventually joined battle at Fasā, but lost the day and fled to Kirmān. Zain al-'Ābidīn for his part repaired to Iṣfahān, pursued by Shāh Manṣūr. When he attempted to slip away into Khurāsān he was captured in Ray by the local ruler Mūsā Jaukār and handed over to Shāh Manṣūr, who had him blinded and imprisoned in Qal'a-yi Safīd. The following year Shāh Manṣūr devastated the city of Yazd and its hinterland. He then appeared before the gates of Kirmān and tried to persuade Sulṭān Aḥmad and Shāh Yaḥyā, who had sought refuge there, to join him in an alliance against Tīmūr. When his efforts failed, he clearly recognised that he was in no position to capture the city, for he returned to Shīrāz, probably with the intention of strengthening his forces. At all events, he renewed his attacks on Yazd and Kirmān soon afterwards, though again without success except in terms of pillage and destruction. He failed to take Kirmān, so it is said, because a number of his officers defected to Sulṭān Aḥmad.

Such was the state of affairs in Fārs, in 'Irāq-i 'Ajam and in Kirmān when Tīmūr left Transoxiana on 14 Dhu'l-Qa'da 794/3 October 1392 to begin his new five-year campaign against Iran. In the interim he had been involved in conflicts with the powers that had invaded Iran during his absence, and with those who had aided and abetted them, i.e. the khans of the Golden Horde, the khans of Mughalistān and the ruler of Khwārazm. Since these campaigns are only indirectly connected with the history of Iran, a few brief references to them will suffice for our purposes. By now respect for Tīmūr's military genius had grown to such an extent that the mere news of his approach was sufficient to scatter the troops of his enemies, who were wreaking havoc in Transoxiana. But he was not content to let matters rest there. He launched a campaign against Khwārazm, plundering and destroying Ürgench, the country's flourishing capital, and emptying it of its inhabitants, who were abducted as slaves. This raid meant the end of the local Ṣūfī dynasty, whose last representative, Sulaimān Ṣūfī, sought refuge with the Golden Horde. After two campaigns against Mughalistān, where sovereignty had passed to Khiżr Khān, Tīmūr then prepared to strike against Tokhtamïsh. At the head of powerful forces he marched to Qïpchaq and inflicted a heavy defeat on his former protégé by the river Qundurcha, to the north of the city of Samara (15 Rajab 793/18 June 1391). Even though Tokhtamïsh had suffered heavy losses and was forced to flee, the foundations of his power had by no means been destroyed, as events were soon to show. A new khan was installed by the grace of Tīmūr, but this measure was of no lasting consequence because the Chaghatai troops soon withdrew once more.

Nevertheless Tīmūr was able to march to the west again in the following year without having to worry about the situation in Samarqand and Transoxiana, his departure having been delayed only by a serious illness. If the account in Yazdī's *Ẓafar-nāma* can be relied upon, Tīmūr's route took him through Gurgān and Māzandarān. The "heretical Sayyids", of whom he killed many in this area, may have been adherents of the Ḥurūfī sect. Its founder Fażl-Allāh Abu'l-Fażl, whom Tīmūr's son Mīrān Shāh executed with his own hands in Dhu'l-Qa'da 796 (began 6 November 1393) at the fortress of Alīnjaq near Nakhchivān, was a native of Astarābād and had many followers in the region.[1] However, this was probably no more than a minor action. Tīmūr's advance was aimed principally against the Muzaffarids or, to be more precise, against the one particularly active representative of the family, Shāh Manṣūr. Even though it meant conflict with his own relatives, the latter was doing everything in his power to re-establish the political dominance of his dynasty, and this in open opposition to Tīmūr. When he received the news of Tīmūr's departure from Samarqand, of his activities in Māzandarān and of his further advance, begun in Ṣafar 795/at the end of December 1392, via Dāmghān, Ray, Kurdistān and Burūjird, Shāh Manṣūr resolved initially to make Iṣfahān his defensive base. However, he was persuaded to drop this plan by the Sarbadār Mulūk, who had switched his allegiance to him, and instead remained in Shīrāz. He dispatched Mulūk to Kāshān as commandant (*dārūgha*) of the city, with the task of protecting the northern frontier of the Muzaffarid territory and of keeping him informed of the movements of the Chaghatai forces. By Rabī' II 795/the beginning of March 1393 Tīmūr had advanced to Dizfūl and Shushtar, where he installed the Sarbadār Khwāja Mas'ūd as governor. On the way he freed prince Zain al-'Ābidīn from imprisonment in Qal'a-yi Safīd, treated him kindly and promised to exact vengeance from Shāh Manṣūr on his behalf. At the approach of the Chaghatais Shāh Manṣūr had first left Shīrāz, but thinking better of it he turned back to face Tīmūr and

[1] Ritter, "Die Anfänge der Ḥurūfīsekte"; cf. Aubin, "La fin de l'état Sarbadâr", p. 100.

fought with great personal courage at the head of a feeble contingent whose numbers were further decreased by desertions. Wounded several times, he finally attempted to fight his way through to Shīrāz but was captured by prince Shāh Rukh's forces and decapitated.

This conflict was also of vital concern to the other princes of the house of Muẓaffar, and its outcome served to convince them of the futility of all further resistance. Arriving to announce their submission to Tīmūr, they were given an honourable reception, but on 10 Rajab 795/22 May 1393 in Qūmisha, to the south of Iṣfahān, a supreme order was issued for their execution. So ended the rule of the Muzaffarids. Only Zain al-'Ābidīn and Sulṭān Shiblī, the eldest and the youngest sons of Shāh-i Shujā', were spared and sent to Samarqand.

For an insight into conditions in general in Iran during the eighty years (713–95/1313–93) in which the Muzaffarids were politically active we have already had recourse to the testimony of Ḥāfiẓ (d. 791/1389 or 792/1390), whom many literary experts consider the greatest poet in the Persian language. His dīvān provides outstanding evidence of the cultural and intellectual situation at the time. It is significant both as a poetic masterpiece and as a rich source for the history of ideas, not least because of the style in which it is written, a subtle interplay of normal sense usage and mystical hidden meaning. Although the dīvān contains verses that are cheerful in mood, it does not of course follow that the circumstances of its author and his contemporaries were happy ones. On the contrary, the vein of melancholy which again and again predominates in the work carries rather more conviction. It is a reflection of the sceptical and often pessimistic attitude to life that was widespread amongst the people of Iran as a result of numerous national catastrophes, foreign domination, despotism and tyranny, typified especially by the beginning and end of the Mongol empire.

Strangely enough, these conditions of existence, however wretched and miserable they may have been, did not inhibit the development of strong cultural energies in the country, as has been indicated in the previous chapter. We have mentioned Shāh-i Shujā''s patronage of Ḥāfiẓ, but this was not an isolated example. Even a prince like Shāh Manṣūr took an interest in literature and promoted the Khwāja. Mubāriz al-Dīn Muḥammad, too, though his interest was more narrowly religious, encouraged certain intellectual disciplines, as can be seen from his generous patronage of 'Aḍud al-Dīn al-Ījī (d. 756/

1355), the distinguished Shāfi'ī jurist and Ash'arī theologian.[1] When the latter was in Iṣfahān, Shāh-i Shujā' took the opportunity of studying under his guidance the commentary of Ibn Ḥājib (d.626/1229) on *al-Mufaṣṣal fi'l-Naḥw*, a study of Arabic grammar by al-Zamakhsharī (d.538/1144).[2] Finally, one could point to the example of Shaikh Majd al-Dīn Ismā'īl, whose reputation for scholarship prompted the famous traveller Ibn Baṭṭūṭa (d.780/1378) to visit Shīrāz.[3] The Muzaffarids may have failed to rescue Persia from the chaos of civil wars and disruption that followed the collapse of the Il-Khanid empire: indeed their fratricidal warring brought untold disaster to countless inhabitants of the country and facilitated its almost effortless conquest by Tīmūr. Yet they managed reasonably well to maintain a minimum of public order and security, thus making possible cultural achievements such as we have just mentioned, achievements that are of greater significance in the history of Iran than the Muzaffarid rulers themselves.

THE CONQUEST OF THE JALAYIRIDS

Tīmūr's only adversary in Persia after the defeat of the Muzaffarids was Sulṭān Aḥmad Jalāyir, whose sphere of influence stretched from Āzarbāījān into Mesopotamia as far as Baghdad. Normally his summer residence, Baghdad had served him as a refuge from the Chaghatais ever since he had taken flight during Tīmūr's first advance on Sulṭāniyya. Hoping to surprise him by attacking in the hottest part of summer, Tīmūr took only eight days to march at the head of his advance guard from Fārs to Mesopotamia and arrived at the gates of Baghdad on 30 Shawwāl 795/29 August 1393. He caught his opponent unawares but failed to defeat him, for although Sulṭān Aḥmad had no time to prepare for the defence of Baghdad he did manage to withdraw to the west bank of the Tigris, taking with him what ships he could and scuppering the rest, as well as destroying all the bridges. To no avail, for Tīmūr wasted no time on the fortifications of the city, which at this period stood only on the east bank; nor did he halt at the Tigris. Showing great foresight, he had equipped his troops with planks and

[1] Van Ess, "al-Īdjī", *EI*², and *Die Erkenntnislehre des 'Aḍudaddīn al-Īǵī*, (Wiesbaden, 1966).

[2] Cf. Brockelmann, *GAL* I, 303 (*GAL*² I, 367) and *Supplement* I, 531–9, where no such commentary, however, is listed.

[3] Ibn Baṭṭūṭa, trans. Gibb, II, 300–5. We are here dealing with the *qāḍī* Ismā'īl b. Yaḥyā b. Ismā'īl, whose father and grandfather before him had also held the office of qāḍī of Shīrāz.

beams by means of which they were able to cross the river both above and below the city. Nevertheless, they arrived too late. Sulṭān Aḥmad narrowly escaped them, just as he did later when his pursuers came within a hair's breadth of capturing him near Karbalā. He fled to Syria, where his request for asylum was granted by the ruler of the Mamlūk empire, Sultan Barqūq (784–801/1382–1399).

Tīmūr occupied Baghdad without a fight. Several writers, including two eye-witnesses,[1] have left detailed accounts of the Chaghatai troops' behaviour in Mesopotamia, and we also have data on specific outrages and atrocities they committed. Yet it would appear that the population of Baghdad itself, in so far as they remained within the city walls, were treated relatively leniently, albeit at the price of a high ransom that was extorted from them. Plunder and confiscation were succeeded by dearth and famine when Tīmūr marched away again some two months later. On this occasion too, scholars and artists were deported, including the masters of the renowned Baghdad school of book illumination, who had enjoyed the protection of Sulṭān Aḥmad. Tīmūr also had captives, both male and female, taken away to be sold as slaves.

The governorship of Baghdad was conferred upon Khwāja Mas'ūd Sabzavārī, a nephew of Khwāja 'Alī-yi Mu'ayyad, the last Sarbadār prince of Sabzavār. His force of Sarbadārs, however, though 3,000 strong, was not sufficient to defend the city when Sulṭān Aḥmad marched back again a year later. Instead of giving battle, Khwāja Mas'ūd withdrew his troops from Baghdad to Shushtar. Sulṭān Aḥmad was thus able to re-establish his control over Baghdad. As if nothing had happened, he proceeded to live in the same unrestrained fashion as before, thus giving many a leading figure in his entourage cause to criticise him. In 800/1397–8 this discontent found expression in a conspiracy, and although he triumphed over the conspirators Sulṭān Aḥmad no longer felt secure. Secretly leaving the city, he sought assistance from the Qarā Quyūnlū chief Qarā Yūsuf, but when the latter's Türkmen cavalry arrived in the outskirts he had a hard task preventing them from occupying and – almost inevitably – plundering the city. Eventually, however, he persuaded them to turn back. Despite the air of nonchalance he usually displayed, Sulṭān Aḥmad was well aware of the danger of his position. Even though an attempt by Mīrān

[1] Shāmī I, 139. 'Azīz b. Ardashīr Astarābādī, *Bazm u razm*, ed. Kilisli (Istanbul, 1928), p. 19.

Shāh to advance against him from Tabrīz in the summer of 800/1398 had to be abandoned, it provided, along with other signs, clear evidence of a recurring Chaghatai interest in Mesopotamia. Two years later, when news reached him of Tīmūr's presence in Anatolia, he left Baghdad. Subsequently, when Tīmūr was occupied in Syria, he returned for a short while and handed over command of the city to Amīr Faraj, one of his army leaders, before taking refuge himself with the Ottomans.

Sulṭān Aḥmad's fear that a new Chaghatai advance against Baghdad was in the offing proved well grounded. After his numerous military successes, to which we shall return later, Tīmūr must have been especially irritated by the thought that the Jalayirid prince remained undefeated. In addition, of course, Baghdad was still an important centre of trade and communications. It was also strategically significant as a possible base for campaigns directed against the rear or the flank of those of his units active in Anatolia or Syria, and thus constituted a threat to the very operations that occupied his mind at this time. The disaster Sulṭān Aḥmad had anticipated soon occurred. It befell Baghdad in May 1401, when a Chaghatai division Tīmūr had sent out from Mosul to exact tribute met with vigorous resistance outside the city from Türkmen units and bands of bedouins called to the scene by Amīr Faraj. Even when Tīmūr's troops received reinforcements the resistance did not slacken, for the commandant of the city clearly had no idea that he was dealing with Tīmūr himself. As it was, the latter had arrived in person at the head of comparatively small forces, leaving behind the main body of his troops in the Kurdish mountains in view of the summer heat. There they had the benefit not only of a better climate but also of rich grazing grounds.

Although all Baghdad's supplies were exhausted in a siege that lasted forty days, Tīmūr's hopes of a bloodless surrender were disappointed. As a result, when the city was taken by storm on 27 Dhu'l-Qa'da 803/9 July 1401, he ordered a ruthless massacre of the population from which not even women and children were exempted. The only people whose lives were spared were theologians, shaikhs and dervishes. The city's fortifications were then demolished and its public buildings, including some from the 'Abbasid period, destroyed; the only exceptions were mosques, universities and hostels. By all accounts the depopulation and destruction of the city were carried to such lengths that Tīmūr had no need to instal a governor. Despite all this Sulṭān Aḥmad returned to Baghdad soon afterwards and set about rebuilding the city. In the middle of winter he had another narrow escape when a Chaghatai raiding party advancing from Kurdistān caught him unawares. Nevertheless he arrived back in his city again a few months later, this time accompanied by Qarā Yūsuf. The friendship between the two princes was not to last long. When they quarrelled, Sulṭān Aḥmad was expelled by the Türkmen leader.

Any hopes he entertained of being kindly received and granted asylum by the Mamlūks a second time proved illusory. Sultan Faraj (801–815/1399–1412), who in the meantime had succeeded his father Barqūq on the Egyptian throne, imprisoned the Jalayirid in a stronghold because he feared Tīmūr's vengeance. Here Sulṭān Aḥmad was to meet up again a short time later with Qarā Yūsuf, who in the autumn of 806/1403 was driven out of Baghdad by Abā Bakr, a grandson of Tīmūr, and similarly sought refuge with the Mamlūks. In prison the two of them formed a new alliance, but despite all guarantees it proved shortlived when they regained their liberty some time later. Qarā Yūsuf moved to Tabrīz, whilst Sulṭān Aḥmad returned to Baghdad and again assumed power. He retained it for five difficult years before Qarā Yūsuf defeated him in battle, took him prisoner and executed him. The victor handed over Baghdad to his son Shāh Muḥammad Qarā Quyūnlū, who conquered the city on 5 Muḥarram 814/29 April 1411. Thus began the Türkmen phase of the city's history. Elsewhere, notably in Khūzistān, Jalayirid rulers managed to retain power until as late as 835/1432.[1]

Apart from the Sarbadārs, who won Tīmūr's favour by promptly establishing good relations with him and continuing to serve him loyally, the Jalayirids were the only political force of any importance on Persian soil that survived the conqueror, though not by many years. The price Sulṭān Aḥmad had to pay for his survival was not only unsettled and precarious, but also depended on an uncertain alliance with his rivals, the Qarā Quyūnlū. This alliance was bound to end in a trial of strength, and when it finally came he proved no match for them

[1] Duda, "Buchmalerei", p. 32, lists (following Shīrīn Bayānī) the remaining Jalayirids: Sulṭān Valad (813–14/1410–11); Sulṭān Uvais II (814–24/1411–21); Sulṭān Maḥmūd (824–8/1421–4); and Sulṭān Ḥusain II (828–36/1424–32). Of these the first three were sons of Sulṭān Ahmad, and Ḥusain his grandson. In Yınanç, "Celâyir", the successor of Uvais is named as Muḥammad, and it is alleged that Valad's widow Tandū Khātūn bint Jalāl al-Dīn Ḥusain (previously married to the Egyptian Sultan Barqūq) paid homage to the Timurid Shāh Rukh and ruled over Wāsiṭ, Baṣra and Shushtar until her death in 819/1416.

either in Tabrīz or in Baghdad. Sulṭān Aḥmad's survival also entailed the sacrifice of a considerable cultural inheritance. His family had made Tabrīz and more particularly Baghdad into important cultural centres, and in both cities a miniaturist school of the highest rank was crippled, if not entirely destroyed, when Tīmūr carried off the best painters to Central Asia. Scholars and other representatives of intellectual, religious and artistic life were also deported. In the nine years that remained to him after 803/1401, Sulṭān Aḥmad was quite incapable of repairing the damage caused by this drain on his cultural resources, even though he did everything in his power to try to restore Baghdad.

In terms of his character and rôle, about which we have considerable detailed evidence, the Jalayirid prince was probably a typical figure not only of his dynasty but of his times in general, for he was a man of startling contrasts. He was both a patron of the arts and a practising artist in his own right : none other than the famous 'Abd al-Ḥaiy taught him drawing. He was a miniaturist, a skilled calligrapher, well versed in music, and a poet whose Arabic and Persian verses were collected in a dīvān. On the other hand he is described as cruelly despotic, fratricidal, disloyal and avaricious. Others depict him as a courageous warrior, in spite of his tactical retreats in conflicts with Tīmūr and his generals, and also as a protector of scholars and poets. We have already mentioned the court poet Jamāl al-Dīn Salmān Sāvajī (b. *c.*700/1300, d. 778/1376), who was highly esteemed by Sulṭān Aḥmad's father, Shaikh Uvais. Primarily a panegyrist, he was also a master of the romantic epic and of lyric poetry. A measure of the respect he enjoyed is the quatrain, ascribed to Ḥāfiẓ, in which he is praised as "chief among the cultured men of the age" (*sar-āmad-i fuẓalā-yi ẓamāna*). One unusual feature of his poetry is that he takes real events as his subject matter – a rare phenomenon in the classical literature of Iran. This is true of his *Firāq-nāma* ("Book of Separation"), in which he describes Shaikh Uvais's pain at the loss of one of his favourites, first when he disappears from the court, then when he is away on a military campaign, and finally when he dies unexpectedly.[1] Salmān is mentioned here as just one example of the many poets,

[1] For a detailed consideration of Salmān, see *LHP* III, *passim*, and *HIL*, pp. 261–2; Bozorg Alavi in *Kindlers Literatur-Lexicon* (Munich, 1974) IX, 3433f. (*Firāq-nāma*), 3767 (*Jamshīd va Khūrshīd*), and XIX, 8432ff. (*Sāqī-nāma*); Abdul Muqtadir, *Catalogue of the Arabic and Persian MSS in the Oriental Public Library at Bankipore*[2] I (Bihar 1962): "Ġazaliyyāt-i Salmān". Rypka considers the Ḥāfiẓ quatrain to be wrongly attributed.

famous and less well known, who lived under the Jalayirids and were patronised by them.

With their liking for ostentation at court, it was also natural that several of the Jalayirids should distinguish themselves as builders, but many of the architectural achievements for which they were renowned have been destroyed. One of the buildings of Khwāja Mirjān, who was the Jalayirid governor of Baghdad on more than one occasion, has survived, however. It is the Islamic university (*madrasa*) in Baghdad, which was later named Jāmi'-i Mirjān.[1] The Spanish ambassador Clavijo, usually a reliable observer, records having seen a palace of gigantic proportions in 804/1401 in Tabrīz which was called Daulat-khāna and had been erected by Uvais. His observations could well be based on fact. Lastly, Sulṭān Aḥmad's repeated efforts to improve or restore the architecture of Baghdad are emphasised in many sources.

The most impressive legacy of the Jalayirids is their painting. Examples of miniatures from Tabrīz and Baghdad that have been preserved derive for the most part from the Sultans Uvais, Ḥusain and Aḥmad. The Jalayirid schools suffered greatly as a result of the deportations ordered by Tīmūr, but the Baghdad school at least survived the first conquest of 795/1393 and did not finally come to an end until the second in 803/1401. This is demonstrated by works of art produced during the intervening period.

The cultural and intellectual achievements of the Jalayirids, particularly the complex and controversial subject of iconography, its genesis and styles, will be considered in more detail in later chapters. Here we have been content to give a general sketch of the world that Tīmūr destroyed in his efforts to eliminate the political and military power of the dynasty. Although Sulṭān Aḥmad personally succeeded in eluding Tīmūr's grasp, the blows he suffered sapped the vitality of his empire. Each military defeat drained away more of its cultural and intellectual energies until by the time of the conflicts with the Türkmens it had exhausted all its strength, and neither Sulṭān Aḥmad nor his successors could bring about its regeneration.

THE INDIAN CAMPAIGN

For the history of Iran the most important outcome of the five-year campaign was that the country became an integral part of Tīmūr's

[1] For Khwāja Mirjān and his architectural activities, see al-'Azzāwī, *Ta'rīkh al-'Irāq* II, 84–129.

sphere of influence. Opponents such as Sulṭān Aḥmad Jalāyir, the Türkmen Qarā Yūsuf Qarā Quyūnlū, or individual Georgian princes who managed to elude the grasp of the Chaghatais, constituted at most a latent threat. In practice they were reduced to living as best they could either as exiles abroad or in border areas of Iran to which access was difficult. Yet Tīmūr by no means underestimated the possibility of trouble from them. Contemplating as he did further conquests, he had to guard against all eventualities in his rear.

His plans did not stop at the destruction of the military power of the Qïpchaqs. For Mongol supremacy to be restored, as he envisaged, he would need to subjugate India and China too, not to mention areas of the Near East outside Persia. His grandson, Pīr Muḥammad b. Jahāngīr, who since 794/1392 had occupied the "throne of Maḥmūd of Ghazna" and had the closest knowledge of Indian affairs, was ordered to march against the Punjab in the autumn of 800/1397. This was the prelude to Tīmūr's Indian campaign of the next two years, culminating in the sack of Delhi in 801/1398. No political reasons for the expedition are mentioned in the sources. Since it was directed not solely against non-Muslim princes but also, indeed primarily, against Muslim rulers, the view that the campaign was motivated by a desire to spread Islam cannot be accepted without qualification. The weakness of the Indian princes and the fact that they were in conflict with one another may well have prompted Tīmūr's decision to attack, for booty and the payment of tribute seem to have been his principal aim. As a consequence the Indian territories affected suffered devastation and slaughter on an unimaginable scale, together with disease and famine, as one can see from Ghiyāṣ al-Dīn 'Alī's record of the expedition.

THE FINAL CONFLICT WITH TOKHTAMÏSH

Our summary of the fortunes of the later Jalayirids has taken us well beyond the period of Tīmūr's five-year campaign (794–798/1392–1396). The time has now come to pick up the thread of events following Tīmūr's departure from Baghdad in the late autumn of 795/1393, events which took place not in Iran itself but in border areas and neighbouring countries. In what follows they will be considered in more or less detail depending on the extent to which they affected Persian history.

When Tīmūr moved on up the Tigris after conquering Baghdad, it was not clear what his next military objective would be. Syria, Egypt, western or eastern Anatolia and the Caucasus were all possible targets, and the news of Tīmūr's military successes as well as his brutal methods of waging war not only perturbed the rulers of these territories but also struck fear into the hearts of their populations. Nor was the situation eased when the conqueror sent envoys to numerous princes and rulers, inviting them to establish friendly relations or demanding that they should submit to his sovereignty, as was the case with Sultan Barqūq of Cairo, who had granted asylum to Sulṭān Aḥmad Jalāyir, and with Aḥmad's Türkmen ally, Qarā Yūsuf of the Qarā Quyūnlū confederation. One other act of Tīmūr was probably designed to strike terror in the hearts of his rivals. This was the spectacular feat of capturing the fortress of Takrīt on the Tigris, which had been considered impregnable. Its commandant and garrison were slaughtered, and pyramids of skulls were erected for all to see. After the capture Tīmūr held a military parade on the west bank of the Tigris to demonstrate to the world the strength of the Chaghatai forces.

Such demonstrations had their effect, though not in the way Tīmūr had desired. They resulted in intensive diplomatic exchanges on the part of his adversaries. The ruler of Sīvās informed Barqūq of his fears and asked him for support. The Ottoman Sultan Bāyezīd made contact with the Egyptian ruler and sent him subsidies. Tokhtamïsh and Barqūq also entered into an alliance, which was of particular significance since it showed that Tīmūr's campaign against Qïpchaq in 793/1391 had failed to neutralise or at any rate intimidate the khan of the Golden Horde.

Nevertheless, Tīmūr now delayed, in fact for a whole year, before deciding on his next major blow. In the meantime he turned his attention to operations on a geographically limited scale. As well as the Artuqids in Mārdīn, he again attacked the Georgians. This was the prelude to later offensives against their territory, that of 1395 under the command of Mīrān Shāh and those of 1399 and 1403 which Tīmūr was again to lead himself. Qarā Yūsuf and his Qarā Quyūnlū, at this time Tīmūr's most dangerous enemy south of the Caucasus, were also engaged in battle. They lost the fortress of Avnik on the Araxes, and its commandant, a brother of Qarā Yūsuf called Miṣr Khwāja, was taken captive and sent to Samarqand together with his family. Events of importance on the personal level at this time were the birth of Ulugh Beg, a son of Shāh Rukh who was to become Tīmūr's favourite grandson, and the death of the conqueror's oldest surviving son, 'Umar Shaikh, which must have come as a severe blow. Summoned to the court from Fārs, where he was governor, he was fatally wounded by an enemy arrow while besieging a Kurdish stronghold en route.

A letter of 8 Jumādā I 797/1 March 1395[1] shows that Tīmūr made one last effort to effect a reconciliation with Tokhtamïsh. Even though it failed, it provides further evidence of his concern to remain loyal to the descendants of Chingiz Khān. Another communication, addressed to the Ottoman sovereign,[2] indicates that at this time – and perhaps even earlier – Tīmūr was contemplating something quite different. This was an expansionist policy on a grand scale, stretching as far as eastern Europe. As his starting point, Tīmūr took the old division of the *ulus* of Jochi into two parts, i.e. the area east of the river Dnieper as the left flank (*sol qol*), the empire of the Golden Horde, and the territories west of the Dnieper as the right flank (*oŋ qol*), together with the Ukraine, the lands of the Lithuanians and Poles, who were the allies of Tokhtamïsh. In his letter Tīmūr praised Bāyezīd's achievements in the holy war (*jihād*) against the Christian princes in the Balkans and suggested that they should establish mutual spheres of interest. The right flank, that is the area extending west of the Dnieper to the Balkans, was to be allotted to Bāyezīd, the left flank or all territory to the east of the Dnieper to Tīmūr. The letter also reveals that two of the basic principles behind Tīmūr's global political strategy were the spread of Islam throughout the world and the restoration of the worldwide supremacy of the Mongols. If, as Togan assumes,[3] Tīmūr's new campaign against Tokhtamïsh was designed not merely to punish a disloyal ally, but "to put into effect a comprehensive plan for eastern Europe", it failed because the sultan was not prepared to cooperate with him. At that time Bāyezīd regarded a siege of Constantinople and operations in northern Greece as more important than any far-reaching projects Tīmūr was contemplating.

Be that as it may, the spring campaign of 797/1395 turned out to be more urgent than any other actions Tīmūr may have been considering, such as operations against the Mamlūks in Syria and Egypt or indeed against Bāyezīd himself. For this there were two reasons. First, the attempts to negotiate an alliance between the Golden Horde and Cairo,

1 Sharaf al-Dīn Yazdī I, 523ff.
2 For the text, with detailed commentary, see Togan, "Timurs Osteuropapolitik".
3 *Ibid.*, p. 290.

which cannot have escaped the attention of the Chaghatai high command, meant that the ruler of Iran faced the risk of being hemmed in between these two powers, as was the situation of the Il-Khanid Empire and other Iranian empires before it. Secondly – and here the danger was no less acute – incursions into Tīmūr's domain in the Caucasus provided clear evidence of hostile intentions on Tokhtamïsh's part. When, in addition, Tokhtamïsh replied in unsatisfactory terms to Tīmūr's conciliatory message, the Chaghatai troops received the order to march against him that same spring. The decisive battle, in which both rivals personally took part, was fought in the valley of the river Terek in the northern Caucasus. It ended in a crushing defeat for the Qïpchaq army. The way was now clear for Tīmūr to advance into the Volga area and to strike against the capital of the Golden Horde, Sarāī. It was looted and plundered together with other cities of the lower Volga, the Crimea and the northern Caucasus. An immeasurable amount of booty was carried off, and many of the native people, not just soldiers but women and children too, were abducted into slavery. Stories of Tīmūr advancing as far as Moscow have no basis in fact, although he did make raids on cities in southern Russia that were close to the frontiers of the Golden Horde.

The country was so devastated and depopulated, its economic potential so effectively destroyed, that the Qïpchaq empire never again recovered. Moreover, with the severance of the trade routes and the destruction of key transfer-points, long-distance trade between the Far East and Europe, in so far as it passed via the Golden Horde, was virtually paralysed. Tīmūr had probably intended to ruin the country's economy in this way, for it is unlikely that he thought of usurping power there even though he helped Temür Qutlugh, a pretender of his choice, to assume control. Tokhtamïsh, who lost his throne as a result of the defeat, still had a rôle to play in later eastern European conflicts, but any ambition he or the Golden Horde had in Transoxiana or Iran were thwarted once and for all. Although its effects were to be felt for some time, Tīmūr's brutal punishment of the Qïpchaqs came to an end in the spring of 798/1396 when he marched to Persia via Darband. Isolated operations in Georgia, Āzarbāījān, Fārs and other areas of Iran, including the suppression of a rebellion in Yazd, brought the five-year campaign to a close. In the summer the Chaghatai troops set out on the return journey to Samarqand, where Tīmūr was to make his most protracted sojourn prior to embarking on the Indian campaign we have already noticed.

THE CAMPAIGNS IN SYRIA AND ANATOLIA

Tīmūr had scarcely recovered from a severe illness suffered on the return march from India to Transoxiana when not long after his arrival back in Samarqand, in May 1399, he began preparations for a new campaign. This was the so-called seven-year campaign against the West. A mass of information reaching him from that quarter led Tīmūr to decide on this course of action. All was not well in the realm of his son Mīrān Shāh, who reigned "on the throne of Hülegü" in Sulṭāniyya and Tabrīz. The situation was eased somewhat by the death in 801/1399 of Barqūq, the Mamlūk Sultan of Cairo, and the succession of his son Faraj, a boy of ten. On the other hand, it was aggravated by the constant and apparently irresistible rise to power of the Ottoman Sultan Bāyezīd I. On 25 September 1396 he had won a spectacular victory over an army of crusaders at Nicopolis on the lower Danube. Later, during Tīmūr's Indian campaign, he had enjoyed success in Anatolia in operations against the princes of Qaramān. Other news to reach Samarqand at this time was that of the death in 1398 of the emperor T'ai-tsu, who thirty years earlier had brought the Yüan dynasty to an end and expelled the Mongols from China. No doubt this greatly interested Tīmūr, but not enough to make him waver in his resolve to take action first against the threats looming in the west.

When the Chaghatai troops set off for Persia, a detachment under the command of Sulaimān Shāh, one of Tīmūr's nephews, was sent on ahead to investigate the charges that had been made against Prince Mīrān Shāh. Doubts had arisen about his loyalty because he had alluded in letters to his father's advanced age and incapability. The charges also concerned his failure to deal with instances of unrest and refusal to pay taxes in the area he ruled, as well as the loss of the stronghold of Alïnjaq, a pocket of resistance of great importance to the Jalayirids[1] where Georgian troops had come to the relief of Prince Ṭāhir, a son of Sulṭān Aḥmad Jalāyir. Far from making difficulties, Mīrān Shāh actually came forth with Sulaimān Shāh to meet his father. Tīmūr deposed him, and without further punishment assigned him to his retinue, where he was to remain for the next four years. His friends

[1] See more fully Minorsky, "Transcaucasica", pp. 91–112. Alïnjaq had already been attacked by Tīmūr in 789/1387. It was to offer the most stubborn resistance of all the fortresses he conquered, for it did not fall until 803/1401, after the Georgian campaign with which we shall shortly deal.

and advisers, some of them well known figures in cultural life, were not treated so lightly. They were severely punished, and some of them even executed, for allegedly corrupting the prince and leading him astray; this despite the fact that he was by now thirty-three years of age.

Tīmūr personally directed operations to restore order in north-western Persia. Then he moved into winter quarters in Qarābāgh, a stretch of country in the bend of the river Araxes that offered good winter shelter, especially for cavalry. From here he launched a punitive raid against the Georgians that was interrupted only by adverse weather conditions. The very next spring saw the start of a new campaign against the Georgians, the fifth in all, in the course of which Tiflis was again stormed. Tīmūr had demanded that the Jalayirid Ṭāhir, who had sought refuge with the Georgians, be handed over, but King Giorgi VII allowed him to escape just in time, and he made his way to the Ottoman Sultan Bāyezīd. In view of the destruction caused by the Chaghatais and the heavy losses sustained by his troops and people, the Georgian king was forced to open negotiations with Tīmūr, in the course of which he agreed to pay a considerable tribute and to furnish a contingent of troops for the conqueror's army.

Even though Sultan Barqūq had now died, Tīmūr still had a score to settle with the Mamlūks because of the support they had given to Sulṭān Aḥmad Jalāyir, their attempts to form an alliance with the Golden Horde, and above all the murder of his ambassador to Cairo. Although some years had elapsed since the murder took place, Tīmūr could scarcely allow it to go unexpiated, if only for reasons of prestige. Another factor he had to consider was the position of Mesopotamia. The presence of a strong opponent in Egypt would pose a real threat to its security and might leave one flank dangerously exposed, should he ever contemplate an expedition to Anatolia. Nor can one entirely rule out the possiblity that Tīmūr, with his respect for Mongol tradition, felt an obligation to avenge the historic defeat that the Mamlūks had inflicted upon the Mongols in 658/1260 at 'Ain Jālūt in Palestine. Lastly, it can scarcely have escaped his attention that since the death of Barqūq and young Faraj's elevation to the throne rivalries among the military commanders had made the internal situation in the Mamlūk kingdom highly unstable, a state of affairs that positively invited intervention on his part.

Such were the considerations that led to the advance of the Chaghatais against Syria in the autumn of 803/1400. Setting off from Malaṭya, the armies marched via 'Ainṭāb and captured the city of Aleppo. There they laid siege to the citadel, forcing it to surrender within four weeks. Not long afterwards Ḥamā, Ḥimṣ and Ba'labakk also fell. Early in Jumādā I/at the end of December Tīmūr arrived outside Damascus. Sultan Faraj, who had arrived with his forces from Cairo a few days earlier, was encamped in the Ghūṭa, not far from the city. He did not join battle, however, but marched off again, ostensibly because of rumours of an impending coup in Cairo. The sultan's withdrawal was a shattering blow to the morale and resistance of the Damascenes. The surrender of the city was followed by that of the fortress. The tribute Damascus had to pay was so high that all its resources were exhausted. Even so, the city was thrown open to the Chaghatai troops for three days of general pillage in the middle of March 1401. They committed untold crimes and atrocities despite Tīmūr's orders to spare the population.

For Tīmūr the Syrian campaign reaped a rich reward in terms of goods and valuables confiscated and slaves captured. For the country itself it meant economic ruin, the devastation of its cities, the decimation of its population and the destruction of countless businesses and trades. This state of collapse, which was to last for many years, suited Tīmūr's plans perfectly. Together with the unstable political situation inside Egypt, it offered, for the time being at least, the best possible guarantee against dangerous activities on the part of the Mamlūks, let alone any revival of the idea of an alliance between them and the Ottomans. Conscious of the success he had thus achieved and perhaps influenced by the warnings of a Western observer, Bertrando di Mignanelli, of a possible attack from the rear by the Ottoman Sultan, Tīmūr resolved to refrain from advancing further southwards against Egypt and to turn his attention once more to activities in Anatolia. Before doing so, however, he still had to avert the danger threatening from Baghdad. Thus, in the summer he proceeded to carry out the terrible revenge on that city to which we have already referred.

Just as Sulṭān Aḥmad Jalāyir and the Qarā Quyūnlū prince Qarā Yūsuf had sought refuge with the Ottoman sovereign, so Anatolian chiefs came to ask Tīmūr for asylum, having lost their dominions to the Sultan of Edirne. They were able to ensure that the Chaghatais were kept well informed about developments in the Ottoman sphere of influence. Although no military confrontation had yet taken place,

Tīmūr and Bāyezīd Yïldïrïm ("the Thunderbolt") had already been in opposition to one another for some time. When Tīmūr had invaded eastern Anatolia in the preceding year, the Sultan had been besieging Constantinople and was unable to react, first because of the great distance involved and secondly because of the impossibility of confronting the enemy with his troops before the onset of winter. He was thus unable to relieve the city of Sīvās, which he had captured only a few years previously from the renowned Qāżī Burhān al-Dīn Aḥmad. In revenge for the devastation of the city, he conquered Arzinjān in 1401, deposing for the time being its commandant, a protégé of Tīmūr named Ṭaharten.[1]

Bāyezīd was only too well aware, however, that much more was at stake than this or that stronghold in eastern Anatolia, than one more city or less pillaged by the Chaghatais. Tīmūr's plans for global conquest, long since a topic of daily conversation in every kingdom, were now jeopardising the very existence of the Ottomans. Up to now Bāyezīd had succeeded not only in centralising power in his own empire but had also subjugated the Balkan states within a few years and won a brilliant victory over the Hungarian King Sigismund at Nicopolis. If he wished for further success in this direction he simply had to eliminate the Chaghatai threat. He was now confronted by a new situation, for in his desire to expand he had so far looked principally to the west and north-west. Raising the siege of Constantinople, he marched eastwards with his army. In doing so he planned to force Tīmūr, who had again spent the winter in Qarābāgh, into fighting a battle at a spot on the upper reaches of the Euphrates where conditions would be much less favourable to Tīmūr than to his opponent. By strategically skilful manoeuvres Tīmūr managed to avoid the confrontation. Indeed, he even lured Bāyezīd into what, for him, proved a fatal race to reach Chubuq-ovasï, a plain north-west of Engüriye, on the site of present-day Ankara, where he, Tīmūr, contemplated fighting the decisive engagement. Arriving a few days earlier on the field of battle, the Chaghatais from the outset enjoyed an advantage over the Ottomans, who were late on the scene and, what is more, exhausted after days of forced marches in the summer heat. Tīmūr made good use of

[1] The forms Tahirten and Mutaharten, which are probably corruptions of Muṭahhar al-Dīn, also occur: cf. Uzunçarşılı, *Anadolu beylikleri*, p. 165.

his start by fortifying his camp and cutting off the enemy's access to water.

Sources differ as to the precise date of the battle. The most likely date is 27 Dhu'l-Ḥijja 804/28 July 1402.[1] There are also considerable discrepancies in the figures quoted for the strength of the two armies, the highest estimates being those of the Bavarian, Johann Schiltberger, who himself participated in the battle and was captured by the Chaghatais – namely, 1,600,000 Chaghatai and 1,400,000 Ottoman troops. A modern historian, after taking into account every known or accessible circumstance, particularly the distances marched and the movement of supplies, puts the figure for each side at a maximum of 20,000 men.[2] Apart from a few dozen Indian elephants on Tīmūr's side, the most important difference between the two armies was the strong representation in the Ottoman ranks of Janissaries, who were crack troops. In contrast to the bulk of the Chaghatais, however, these were not mounted forces.

In the first phase of the battle it was by no means clear which army would be victorious, which was hardly surprising since some of the most successful and efficient fighting troops of that time had come face to face. A turning point was reached only when whole contingents of the Sultan's army left the field en bloc or went over to Tīmūr's side. This was the result of earlier propaganda by the Chaghatais, helped by the Anatolian princes who had taken refuge with Tīmūr after being deposed by Bāyezīd. Although the Sultan lost all his cavalry in this way, he fought stubbornly on together with his Janissaries. They struggled with a courage born of despair, but had no chance against the might of the Chaghatai cavalry: in the end they were massacred, and Bāyezīd, who fell from his horse in a last minute attempt to escape, was taken captive.

If the battle of Ankara did not seal the fate of the Ottoman empire, it was because Tīmūr failed to exploit his victory to the full. Some of his generals did pursue fleeing enemy contingents, but quite a number of them escaped across the Sea of Marmora to Europe. Tīmūr also advanced further to the west, but at an unusually slow pace attributed by Roloff in part to the depleted strength of the Chaghatai forces after the battle and to the delay in reinforcements from the east. In spite of

[1] The date decided upon by Alexandrescu-Dersca, pp. 116–19.
[2] Roloff, "Die Schlacht bei Angora", pp. 253–6.

the many places he conquered (and they included the former Ottoman capital Bursa); in spite of his advance to the Aegean, where at the end of 1402 he stormed the stronghold of the Knights of St John at Smyrna (İzmir) and afterwards received the homage of the lords of several Aegean islands, there can be no question of Tīmūr's having truly eliminated the Ottomans. Nor did he set up a Chaghatayid administration in Anatolia. Instead he was content for the most part to re-establish under his suzerainty the regional principalities that the Sultan had abolished. As far as Constantinople was concerned, he was happy to accept the offer of submission brought to him by the hastily dispatched envoys of Emperor Manuel II, and he did not concern himself with the Balkans. The Sultan himself was taken along as a prisoner in Tīmūr's retinue until his death in Aqshehir on 13 Sha'bān 805/8 March 1403. Even though suicide was relatively rare in the Islamic world, the possibility cannot be ruled out that he took poison because it had been divulged to him that he would have to accompany Tīmūr to Samarqand. Tīmūr's problems in Anatolia were more or less at an end when Prince Süleymān, one of Bāyezīd's sons, subsequently declared his submission. Since the conqueror used the same methods to subjugate Anatolia as he had in other countries – raising excessive tributes, plundering and destroying cities, depopulating and devastating the countryside – the result was that the country's economic strength was destroyed when the campaign ended and his troops marched off eastwards. Politically, too, the area had been effectively neutralised, because for the time being Tīmūr could rest assured that the Ottoman princes and the regional dynasts, both in Anatolia and in Europe, would be occupied with their own rivalries.

The Chaghatai victory at Ankara gave rise to numerous diplomatic exchanges, not only between Tīmūr's headquarters and oriental courts, but also with Western powers. These will be discussed in detail later, but it is worth mentioning at this point that even Sultan Faraj of Cairo made efforts to win Tīmūr's favour. Hitherto he had detained the latter's envoys, but he now gave them permission to leave and sent an embassy of his own to declare his submission, which Tīmūr accepted. The reaction of the Georgian King Giorgi VII was different. He had failed to congratulate Tīmūr on his victory over Bāyezīd. In late summer, when Tīmūr was approaching, he tried to make good the omission, but the conqueror rejected the gifts he sent, demanding that he should appear before him in person. He then resorted to various excuses, but could not prevent the Chaghatais from invading his country and again subjecting it to the most terrible devastation. Giorgi at first retreated without any show of resistance, but eventually he managed to appease Tīmūr by offering him valuable gifts, including droves of horses and gold coins struck in the conqueror's name. Tīmūr again spent the winter of 806/1403–4 in Qarābāgh, setting off on the return march to Transoxiana the following spring. If we were to accept the evidence of Safavid historians, it would have been in the course of this journey that he visited Ardabīl and agreed to a request from Khwāja 'Alī, the master of the Ṣafaviyya, for the release of his Ottoman prisoners of war.[1] He arrived back in Samarqand at the beginning of 807/the end of July or early in August 1404, after an absence of five years.

THE PLAN TO INVADE CHINA AND TĪMŪR'S DEATH

In the middle of the 8th/14th century the famous Arab traveller Ibn Baṭṭūṭa had written that Transoxiana, the kingdom of Sultan 'Alā' al-Dīn Tarmashirin, was surrounded by four of the world's great kings: the king of China, the king of India, the king of Persia and the king of the Golden Horde (Özbeg), all of whom sent gifts to the sultan, and honoured and respected him.[2] This statement gives some insight into the view of the world with which Tīmūr grew up. It is not difficult to imagine what it now meant to the ageing prince to have conquered all the renowned rulers who had played a rôle in his boyhood and youth – all, that is, except for the emperor of China. To appreciate the full significance of this, it has to be realised that Tīmūr considered it his mission to restore the former Mongol world empire, of which China had of course been a part. In fact, Mongol domination in China had actually outlasted the world empire, continuing as it did until the collapse of the Yüan dynasty in 1368. Chaghatayid court circles were of course familiar with the political situation in contemporary China. It was known, for instance, that just recently, in 1402, the Emperor Hui-ti, grandson and successor of the Ming Emperor T'ai-tsu who had died four years previously, had been deposed by his uncle Yung-lo. Information about Yung-lo's policy towards the Mongols was also available. The new sovereign was known to be a

[1] See n. 2 p. 56; also pp. 205–6.

[2] Ibn Baṭṭūṭa, trans. Gibb, III, 556.

particularly efficient warrior and thus probably represented a special challenge to Tīmūr.

As had been his custom prior to making a major decision, Tīmūr again summoned a quriltai. Concerning this assembly, which took place in September 1404 on the plain of Kān-i Gil close to Samarqand, we possess a report by the Castilian ambassador Clavijo, who had then just arrived to take up his post and attended the gathering together with his advisers. It amounted to a demonstration of power, designed not only to impress external enemies against whom military operations were planned, but also to bolster the confidence of Tīmūr's own forces. In addition to military consultations, Tīmūr held a gigantic review of his troops in which the various Chaghatai hordes appeared. In conjunction with the assembly magnificent banquets were given, including the marriage celebrations for several royal princes, notably Prince Ulugh Beg, Tīmūr's favourite grandson.[1] During the festivities and consultations in Kān-i Gil preparations for the expedition to China, which Tīmūr had already commenced from Anatolia, were in full swing. Thus his forces, which included numerous auxiliaries in addition to the hard core of Chaghatais, were able to begin their march soon afterwards. Tīmūr himself left Samarqand on 23 Jumādā I/27 November. The orders he issued regarding the government and administration of the capital and the country as a whole, as well as the measures he took to protect his advance and his supply lines, all pointed to a particularly long absence. Despite severe weather conditions Tīmūr pressed on with all speed. He left Āqsūlād, where it had been planned to spend the winter, even before December was over. The bitter cold and the snow made life very difficult for the troops with their numerous baggage trains, but on the other hand a thick covering of ice on the Jaxartes made the river easier to cross. Nevertheless, there were instances of both men and animals succumbing to the frost. In the middle of Rajab 807/January 1405 Tīmūr reached Utrār, some 250 miles from Samarqand. This city, the point of departure for caravans going to China by the route through Mughalistān north of the Tien Shan range, was to serve as the rendezvous for the planned operation.

Tīmūr lodged in the governor's palace. Although he had made use of a litter as on previous occasions when he had been unwell, e.g. on

[1] Roemer, *Šams al-Ḥusn*, pp. 21–3.

the return journey from India, the long trip had left its mark on the conqueror, who was now nearing the end of his sixty-ninth year. In Utrār he continued to suffer from the extreme cold, and when members of his entourage suggested holding a feast to relieve the general atmosphere of depression, he readily agreed. The celebration lasted three days, during which Tīmūr, in his efforts to keep warm, constantly drank wine and other alcoholic beverages, but touched no food. Although he became feverish and suffered from stomach and bowel trouble, rather as in cases of gastritis, he continued drinking until he eventually lost the power of speech. For all their efforts his court physicians were unable to bring him relief. When he finally recovered consciousness and was able to speak again, he himself announced that his end was near. His doctors, asked to tell him the unvarnished truth about his condition, could not in all seriousness contradict him. To the princes and dignitaries assembled around his sick-bed he declared his last will and testament, in which he appointed as his successor on "the throne of Samarqand" his grandson Pīr Muḥammad b. Jahāngīr. All the nobles present, whose spokesmen were Amīr Shāh Malik and Amīr Shaikh Nūr al-Dīn, had to swear a solemn oath that they would respect this stipulation. Tīmūr died in the night of 17 Sha'bān 807/18 February 1405.

The princes and generals resolved to abandon the projected expedition to China and to proceed only with the smaller scale action against Mughalistān, which had formed the first stage of the original plan and which Tīmūr had ordered to begin on 10 Sha'bān/11 February, even before he fell ill. They would in any case only have been carrying out an order given long ago, since prince Ulugh Beg had been appointed governor of Mughalistān on the occasion of his marriage in Kān-i Gil, and his retinue had already been assembled. In order to accomplish this much at least, it was decided to keep secret the monarch's death for the time being. Khwāja Yūsuf, who was charged with transporting Tīmūr's mortal remains to Samarqand, was to leave under cover of darkness so as to escape notice. In addition he was to spread the rumour that he was conveying the remains of a dead princess. Despite all attempts to cover things up, however, it quickly became common knowledge that the conqueror had passed away. As a result the planned campaign against Mughalistān was also abandoned.

Khwāja Yūsuf, who is said to have arrived in Samarqand by 23

February,[1] buried Tīmūr in total secrecy alongside his grandson Muḥammad Sulṭān b. Jahāngīr (who had originally been designated as Tīmūr's successor but had died on the return march from the Aegean in March 1403), in the vault that bore the latter's name, the Khāngāh-i Muḥammad Sulṭān. Later, probably in 1409 after Shāh Rukh's occupation of Samarqand, the body was removed – once more with that of Muḥammad Sulṭān – to its present resting place in the Gūr-i Mīr.

AN ASSESSMENT OF TĪMŪR

Before assessing Tīmūr's significance in the framework of Iranian history, a brief sketch of his personality will be given, especially those features not yet touched upon. For this we are indebted to several excellent studies of Tīmūr that have appeared in the course of the last sixty years. Concerning Tīmūr and his times there is an abundance of source materials. They provide details not only of his campaigns, actions, and policies but also of his person, character and outlook on life. We can even say with certainty what he looked like. He was tall in stature and broad-shouldered. His right thigh bone had coalesced with the kneecap, which made him drag his right leg, and similar deformities in the right shoulder and lower arm deprived him of the normal use of his right hand. This coincides with what Ibn 'Arabshāh, who was a fourteen-year old boy when he saw Tīmūr, later wrote about his appearance from memory. It is also borne out by the account of the Castilian ambassador Clavijo, who met the conqueror a few weeks before his death and thus also speaks of his great age, his weakening eyesight and his already clouded judgment. There exists, in addition, a modern reconstruction by the Soviet anthropologist and sculptor M. M. Gerasimov, of Tīmūr's head which gives a reasonably accurate likeness of his facial features inasmuch as it has been modelled on his preserved skull.[2] It is not, however, adequate to help determine whether any of the illustrations that have been preserved in miniature paintings has the character of a portrait.

The information available about Tīmūr's character and personality is of course far less reliable than the data just mentioned, which are based

[1] Barthold questioned the accuracy of this date in view of the great distance from Utrār to Samarqand (400 km) which would have had to be covered at an average rate of 80 km a day: see "O pogrebenii Timura", trans. Rogers, p. 81.

[2] Reproduced in Hookham, *Tamburlaine*, facing p. 32.

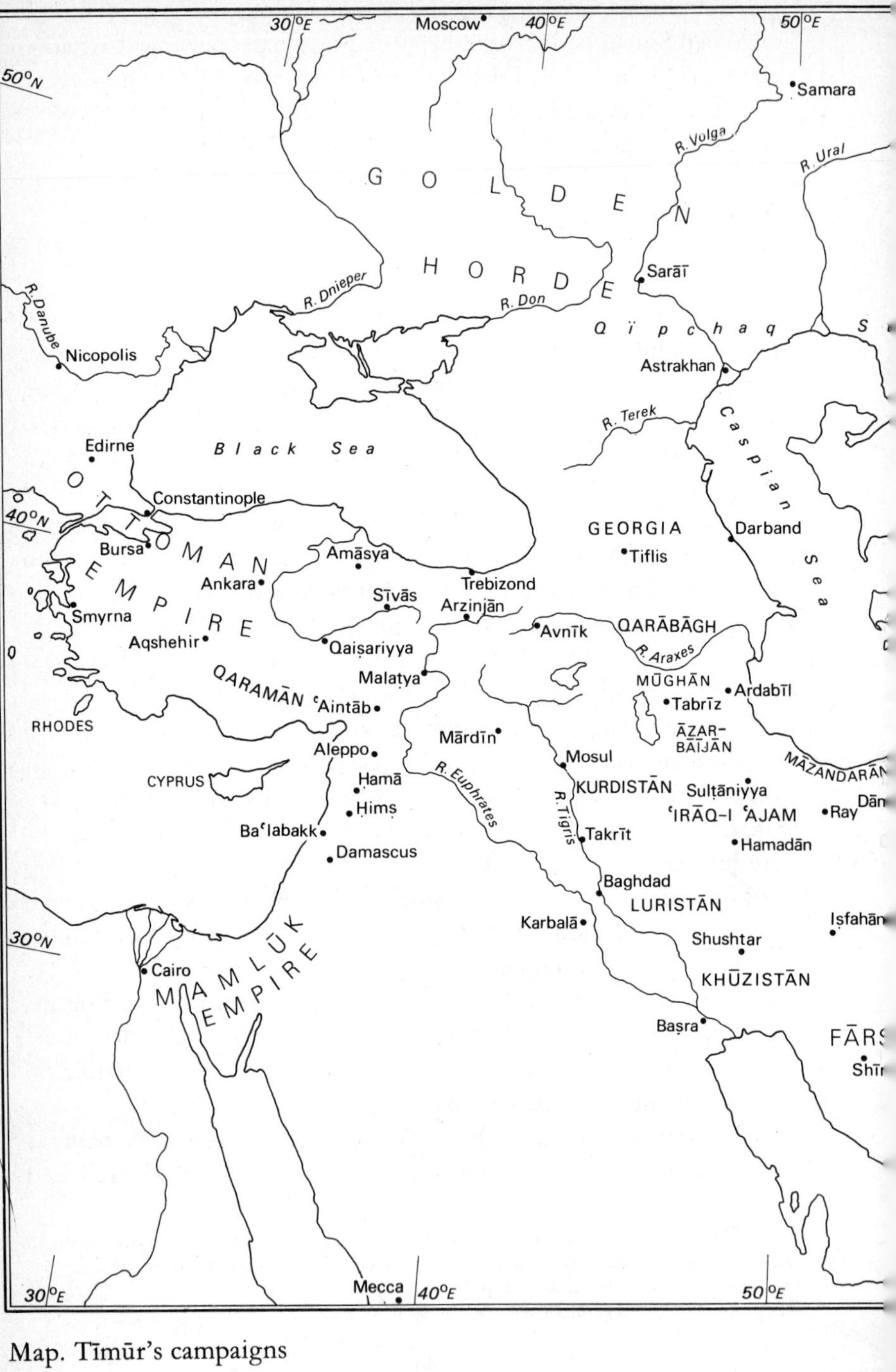

Map. Tīmūr's campaigns

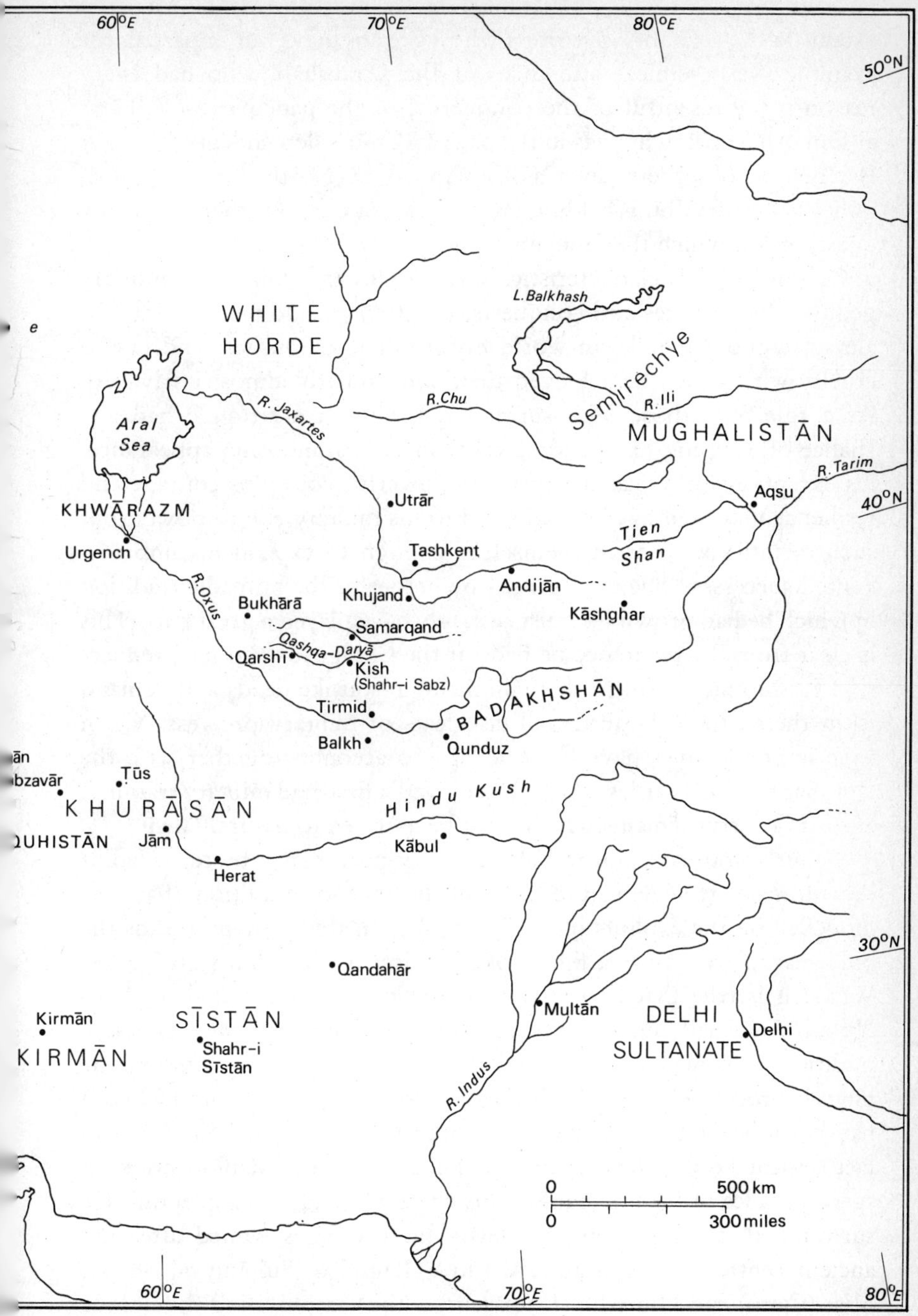
60°E
70°E
80°E
50°N
40°N
30°N
WHITE HORDE
Aral Sea
L. Balkhash
Semirechye
R. Ili
R. Chu
R. Jaxartes
MUGHALISTĀN
R. Tarim
Aqsu
KHWĀRAZM
Urgench
Utrār
Tashkent
Tien Shan
Andijān
Kāshghar
Khujand
R. Oxus
Bukhārā
Samarqand
Qashqa-Daryā
Qarshī
Kish
(Shahr-i Sabz)
BADAKHSHĀN
Tirmid
Balkh
Qunduz
Tūs
KHURĀSĀN
Jām
Hindu Kush
Kābul
Herat
Qandahār
Kirmān
SĪSTĀN
Shahr-i Sīstān
KIRMĀN
Multān
DELHI SULTANATE
Delhi
R. Indus
0 500 km
0 300 miles

on examinations of his skeleton. Here we are dependent to a large extent on the accounts of writers who were anything but impartial, for example the polemical utterances of Ibn ʿArabshāh, who had every reason to be resentful of the conqueror, or the panegyrics of Sharaf al-Dīn ʿAlī Yazdī, who was in the pay of Tīmūr's descendants. More or less neutral observers, such as Clavijo or the North African philosopher of history Ibn Khaldūn, are rare exceptions, but there are many questions on which they remain silent.

One of Tīmūr's characteristics was truly extraordinary: his military genius. His victories and conquests, his strategic and tactical feats are almost without parallel in world history. The callousness and bestial cruelty with which he achieved them are similarly almost unrivalled. As a rule only those who surrendered without a struggle had any chance of escaping his dreadful vengeance. His imposing appearance, his exceptional physical strength, his powerful voice, his courage and resilience may well have contributed to his military rise to power, but such qualities are not in themselves enough to explain his unprecedented successes. The example set by heroes of the nomadic tradition in which he had grown up must certainly have played a great part. This is clear from the reverence he had for the Chingizids and his predilection for Mongol customs that culminate in warlike deeds and demand from their adherents above all else feats of military prowess. When such imponderables have been taken into account, together with the fact that from his earliest youth he enjoyed a first-rate military training, a great deal still remains which must be ascribed to natural talent.

Tīmūr's immense political and military power may be regarded as the ultimate achievement of a nomadic warrior tradition that was modelled on the exploits of the Mongols, but this is by no means the only reason why he is a figure of historical interest and significance. Whilst it is true that he criticised his fellow warrior and rival Amīr Ḥusain for fortifying the city of Balkh and thus violating nomadic tradition, to which any idea of fixed settlements was utterly foreign, he himself proceeded to establish a fixed capital of his own after Ḥusain had been defeated. At first it was intended to be Shahr-i Sabz, but in fact it turned out to be Samarqand. Tīmūr, the descendant of nomads, spent decades of his life making this city more and more splendid. He surrounded it with a ring of newly built villages named after the ancient centres of the Islamic world – Baghdād, Sulṭāniyya, Shīrāz, Miṣr (Cairo) and Dimashq (Damascus) – thus emphasising the unique distinction and superiority of the new metropolis. His military campaigns provided the resources, materials and manpower needed to carry out the architectural projects he had in mind. The vast wealth of booty brought to Samarqand from the countries he had conquered, and the architects, craftsmen and artists selected from the populations of captured cities and deported to Transoxiana, all made it possible to develop the capital and other places as well. Many of the buildings Tīmūr had erected have been preserved to this day. Some have survived intact or have been restored, some are merely representative remains; but all testify to the artistic taste of the period and also, it is reasonable to assume, to the taste of their architect, Tīmūr himself.

The question now arises as to whether all this architectural activity stemmed from genuine cultural impulses or whether it was merely the product of Tīmūr's desire to provide as splendid a framework as possible for the power he had gained. We may perhaps be in a better position to answer this question if we first examine Tīmūr's attitudes to other areas of cultural life to see whether he had any feeling for such activities at all, and if so to what extent. Even though he could neither read nor write, Tīmūr had a command of Persian in addition to his Eastern Turkish mother tongue. Persian was the language not only of his court chroniclers, who had to read out their works for his critical comments, but also that of his chancellery.[1] His interest in history was not confined to contemporary chronicles but included also the past of the Turks, the Persians and the Arabs. Two other disciplines in which he is said to have shown an interest were medicine and astrology, although it is claimed that he did not avail himself of the latter for his personal use, preferring instead to seek guidance from oracles (*tafā'ul*) in the Qur'ān. Regarding his attitude to philosophy and logic the sources contain conflicting statements.

Tīmūr always had a number of scholars in close attendance, and he had a particular liking for the conversation of members of religious orders, theologians and representatives of spiritual life in general. Of these the most famous – if one ignores the meeting with Ḥāfiẓ which cannot be entirely ruled out but is not reliably documented – was Ibn Khaldūn (b. 732/1332, d. 808/1406). The Moroccan scholar has left us

[1] Evidence of this is provided by three documents: (1) Tīmūr's decree of 804/1401, referred to in n. 1 p. 45; (2) his letter to Charles VI of France, in Qazvīnī, "Nāma'ī"; and (3) his letter of 1395 to Bāyezīd, referred to in n. 2 p.72. It goes without saying that the use of Persian was not confined exclusively to Tīmūr's chancellery.

detailed accounts of the conversations he had with Tīmūr in January and February 1401, when they met on numerous occasions in the military camp outside Damascus. The very fact that the conqueror knew of Ibn Khaldūn's reputation as a historian and philosopher, immediately enquired after him in Damascus, and received him time and again for lengthy conversations is in this context highly significant. The various discussions are said to have been conducted in a friendly – indeed positively cordial – atmosphere. This was probably because the historian with his engaging appearance, elegant bearing, shrewdness and eloquence was soon able to gain Tīmūr's sympathy. The fact that he mentioned several prophecies from his younger days that might be interpreted as relating to Tīmūr may also have played its part. In view of the large number of audiences he was granted and the favours readily bestowed upon him for his personal security and that of his friends and colleagues, as well as unconditional leave to return to Cairo, one can scarcely describe Ibn Khaldūn's account of his friendly reception by Tīmūr as exaggerated. The historian's Moroccan homeland figured largely in the discussions. The conqueror, who knew little about it, not only made him talk at some length about the country but also caused him to write a fairly detailed exposé of the subject during those weeks in Damascus. It is likely that they devoted even more time to historical questions, discussing the heroes of classical antiquity, the ancient East and Iranian mythology, as well as more recent matters such as the continuation of the ʿAbbasid caliphate after the fall of Baghdad in the persons of the puppet caliphs at Cairo and the problem of their legitimacy. Tīmūr did not hesitate to recognise them, influenced as he probably was by the legitimist attitude which he himself observed towards his own Chingizid shadow khan, Maḥmūd, whose name had been duly inserted in the khuṭba of the Umayyad mosque following the capture of Damascus. The account of the conversations in Damascus conveys the impression that Tīmūr, even at an advanced age (he was then just completing his sixty-fifth year), was blessed with an active mind, intellectual curiosity, unclouded judgment and a remarkable degree of culture. Ibn Khaldūn expressly credits him with high intelligence, discernment and delight in the discussion of topics both familiar and unfamiliar.

As far as his religious attitudes were concerned, Tīmūr remained strongly attached to Mongol traditions; indeed, after his death his followers felt constrained to design his burial-place according to Mongol custom and in defiance of Muslim beliefs.[1] Yet he frequently stressed his faith in Islam, claiming that he would make it the dominant religion in the world. As an example of this attitude one need only point to his conflict with the Mughals, whom he quite justifiably regarded as unbelievers. In general the evidence for his religious beliefs is conflicting: some factors suggest a commitment to Islam, others cast doubt upon it. His relations with representatives of the Muslim faith – theologians, members of religious orders and dervishes – have already been mentioned, as has his predilection for religious debate. One could also point to the sums he spent on religious causes, on sacred buildings and visits to Muslim holy places. On the other hand, it is impossible to ignore the fact that his troops desecrated mosques, transgressed the laws of sanctuary, murdered prayer-leaders in the Umayyad mosque of Damascus and killed Muslim men, women and children or took them captive by the thousand in order to sell them as slaves. Ibn al-Shiḥna records hearing Tīmūr vent his anger upon troops who were found to have decapitated people alive instead of collecting human heads severed from corpses, as they had been ordered, but such evidence scarcely mitigates the overall picture of disregard for Muslim lives.

Another contradictory aspect of Tīmūr's behaviour was his simultaneous observance of both the customary law of the Mongols (*törü, tura*) and the Muslim religious law (*Sharī'a*). No less peculiar was his ambivalent attitude to the split within Islam between Sunna and Shī'a. In Māzandarān he punished Shī'ī dervishes for disparaging the Companions of the Prophet, whereas in Syria he appeared as the protector of the Shī'a and the descendants of 'Alī. Here one must assume that either his contemporaries and associates in general or he himself lacked all awareness of the acute polarisation between the two views of Islam, or that he acted in a purely opportunist fashion, adopting religious causes for reasons of political expediency. Despite conflicting evidence in the sources Tīmūr cannot be regarded as an adherent of the Shī'a. Yet even though he was not a religious man, his personal development was influenced to a great extent by three theologians. They were Shams al-Dīn Kulāl, his father's spiritual adviser, who was greatly attached to him in his childhood; Zain al-Dīn Abū Bakr Tāyabādī Khwāfī, who is said to have protected him from the start of his military career; and Sayyid Baraka, his own spiritual adviser.

[1] Barthold, "O pogrebenii Timura", trans. Rogers, pp. 81–3: on the grave (*qabr*) itself lay his clothes (*aqmisha*), on the walls hung his weapons (*asliḥa*) and his personal effects (*amti'a*).

Tīmūr's attitude to religion becomes somewhat clearer if it is seen against the background of his homeland Transoxiana. At that time the country was the meeting point of the Muslim sphere of influence (*Dār al-Islām*) and the as yet non-Islamic world (*Dār al-ḥarb*). The sedentary population, predominantly Persian, had adopted the Muslim faith. So too had the nomadic population, Chaghatai Turks and Mongols, although their Islamic beliefs were less orthodox and still left room for elements of Shamanism and other heathen notions. Alongside these were tribes which were totally unaffected by Islam and attracted the attention of itinerant Muslim mystics, who attempted to convert them. The majority of these were Ṣūfī dervishes whose views as a rule did not accord with strict Sunnī doctrine. One such itinerant monk was Ni'mat-Allāh Valī Kirmānī, the famous founder of a religious order, who when they met personally made so strong an impression on Tīmūr that the conqueror feared he might exert a suspect political influence and banished him from Transoxiana.[1]

The assertion that Tīmūr was a proponent of uncompromising orthodoxy does not bear investigation, any more than do attempts to compare him with Charlemagne, Charles V or Napoleon and other great historical figures. Not even the apparently convincing comparison with Chingiz Khān is well founded. The Mongol conqueror was a nomad, and remained a nomad all his life. The Chaghatai was himself no longer a nomad, even though he won his victories with predominantly nomadic troops and actually came from a nomadic environment. He had, after all, given up the vital principle of not becoming attached to any one place, at the latest when he made Samarqand his capital and set about developing it into a splendid metropolis with the help of the treasures, artists and craftsmen of the countries he had conquered. Of course he was familiar with the nomadic way of life and even liked to take part in it frequently, but from his earliest childhood he had connections with the settled rural population and also with city life, as can be seen from his knowledge of Persian alone.

Tīmūr, if one wants to characterise him aptly, was a Turkish aristocrat of Central Asian origin, in essence a military man but not lacking either in cultural interests or intellectual refinement. If anything, his respect for Mongol traditions strengthens rather than detracts from

[1] See Aubin's introduction to *Matériaux*, which contains three biographies of the saint; for a further biography recently discovered in Princeton by Muḥammad Taqī Dānishpazhūh, see *RK* XVI (1352), 285–7.

this view, as does his ideal of restoring Mongol world domination. His cruel methods of warfare were not unique to him, but corresponded to the almost inconceivably harsh practices of the period, as we have seen from those symbols of terror, the pyramids of skulls. What set him apart from all other contemporary princes was his mastery as a general and the unprecedented good fortune in battle that accompanied his career right up to the end. It is this that has guaranteed him a place not only in the annals of history but also in the popular legends and literatures of the East and the West even down to the present day.

Tīmūr's effective destruction of the military and economic might of the Golden Horde did a great deal to liberate Old Russia from the Tartar yoke under which it had suffered for so long. The catastrophic fall of the Ottoman empire after the defeat at Ankara and the capture of Sultan Bāyezīd, granted Constantinople, which was then close to falling, another fifty years' respite. In this way Tīmūr, who considered himself the standard-bearer of Islam, rendered the Christian powers valuable service. Needless to say, this was not his intention; indeed, it is doubtful whether he ever became aware of such causal connections. There can be even less question of agreements with the prince of Moscow and the Byzantine Emperor. It does, however, show that Tīmūr, who after all had undertaken to re-establish the Mongol world empire, was not always guided by global political considerations.

Just as it is difficult to discern any clear global policy behind his campaigns, so it is hard to see what were the objectives in his various campaigns in the case of victory. Nor is there much evidence of economic planning and consideration, apart from the primary need to supply Samarqand and a certain amount of assistance given to other cities of Transoxiana, notably Shahr-i Sabz. Tīmūr seems to have lacked any really clear sense of the need to make long term arrangements or to plan for the future. The conquered territories were held together as if in a vice by their fear of Tīmūr's policy of inexorable terror, as experienced by all those who disobeyed him or rebelled against him. In this sense the gruesome examples of Herat, Tabrīz, Iṣfahān and Baghdad had the desired effect, but in the long run they could not make up for Tīmūr's lack of statesmanly vision and his failure as a consequence to make appropriate structural changes.

Originally Tīmūr seems to have pursued a policy of setting up protectorates in the conquered territories under the control of members of the previously ruling dynasties who were loyal to him. However, this solution only proved practical in exceptional cases because the danger of such governors defecting was too great. As his sons and grandsons, along with other princes of his dynasty, gradually grew older, Tīmūr therefore reverted to the old Turkish principle of appointing princely governors from among his own family. In such cases an experienced amīr would be assigned to the younger princes as *atabeg* or tutor, whose job it was to ensure that they exercised power correctly. This, at any rate, was the policy Tīmūr applied in Iran soon after his very first advance against Khurāsān, though he did not necessarily adhere to it in other countries as well. Thus Amīr Shāh Malik was appointed governor of Damascus, and Prince Abā Bakr received Baghdad. But Tokhtamïsh, on the other hand, was replaced by one of his Mongol relatives, while in India power was similarly entrusted to a native regent, and it was an Ottoman prince who after the battle of Ankara was set up as ruler in the Ottoman dominions.

Basic to this principle was of course the idea that power belonged not only to the ruler but to his whole family, or more precisely to all its male members. As far as the continuity of the dynasty was concerned the concept was not without its attendant risks, for an almost inevitable consequence of the death of the ruler was the creation of minor principalities, a problem that duly arose in Tīmūr's realm. In such cases it was necessary, if the empire was not to become fragmented, to neutralise all those princes who were surplus to succession requirements. The Ottomans solved the problem by murdering them. Later, the Safavids were to confine them strictly to the harem and to exclude them from all the affairs of state. In the case of the Timurids the problem never became quite so acute, because their dominions collapsed before such a stage was reached.

In a recent study of administration and authority in Tīmūr's empire, Beatrice Forbes Manz points out that the information on the subject available in the sources is inadequate. The very fact that such data are scarce has led Gafurov to conclude that Tīmūr had no interest in setting up a new system of administration in his dominions.[1] The large number of different – indeed in themselves conflicting – settlements he is reported to have made do in fact suggest that he was more concerned to limit the powers of the governors, and leave himself as much oppor-

[1] *Istoriya tadzhikskogo naroda* II/1, 337.

tunity as possible for intervention, than to introduce unified and clearly defined forms of organisation. Certain features of Tīmūr's military organisation bear this out. Whereas the main body of the fighting forces remained under the control of the central authority, the governors had only relatively small contingents at their disposal. In this way units could be called away from a particular territory without any need to consult the local governor responsible. Even though we are only concerned with Iran, it is necessary at this point to consider some features at least of the Chaghatai military system, to which Tīmūr owed his victories and conquests. The nucleus of his armed forces was the Chaghatai units. Shortly after the invasion of Persia they were joined by Iranian troops such as, for example, the Khurasanian contingents under Sarbadār command, which were renowned for their efficiency and for which Tīmūr had a particularly high regard. In the tightness of their organisation and the strictness of their discipline Tīmūr's forces were more akin to the armies of Chingiz Khān than to any Islamic contingents of the period. No doubt this was Tīmūr's intention, but it would be wrong to assume that he modelled his forces on those of the Mongols in every respect. In fact, he also pursued quite new tactics of warfare to outwit his opponents, such as abruptly changing the direction of his marches, using novel methods of deployment and reorganising his troops into hitherto unknown combat units.

The military and administrative organisation of Iran under Tīmūr differed in essential points from that of Transoxiana. The seven *tümens* of Transoxiana had no equivalent in Persia. Instead the country was divided into provinces or areas controlled by governors of the kind that, with the exception of Farghāna, did not exist in Transoxiana. Here especially there was a lack of uniformity. The Persian gubernatorial districts differed in size, and their legal arrangements were neither uniform from case to case nor over the course of time. Two of them are particularly notable – both because of their size and because of their titles, which were derived from older traditions. They are Tabrīz (or Sulṭāniyya) and Qandahār. Prince Mīrān Shāh was expressly appointed to "the throne of Hülegü" when he received the governorship of Āzarbāījān, a post he occupied from 1396 until his dismissal in 1399. So too was his successor Muḥammad Sulṭān b. 'Umar Shaikh on his appointment in 1401. Three years later he was in turn followed by prince 'Umar, Mīrān Shāh's second son, who was to have jurisdiction over all the princes in western Persia, including Fārs and 'Irāq-i 'Ajam as well as Mesopotamia. This immense power was in turn curtailed when the highly influential amīr Jahān Shāh was appointed as his guardian. As governor of Qandahār, Pīr Muḥammad b. Jahāngīr received, along with the territories stretching west of the Hindu Kush to the Indus, "the throne of Maḥmūd of Ghazna". Since such high ranking princes were appointed to these two governorships – no less than three of them were designated successors to the throne – Tīmūr must have considered them very important territories, perhaps even the most important of all after Transoxiana. In the case of Āzarbāījān and the areas belonging to it this clearly makes sense, but it is not immediately obvious why Qandahār, which was economically no match for Tabrīz, should have carried such weight. Evidently, however, it had a certain military and political significance, above all by virtue of its glorious past under the Ghaznavids, but also on account of its sheer size. Even in 1383, long before the Indian campaign, when it was first conferred upon a Timurid prince (Mīrān Shāh), it comprised Herat, Balkh, Qunduz, Baghlān, Badakhshān, Khuṭṭalān and Ḥiṣār.

There were of course other large provinces in Iran, especially Fārs with its capital Shīrāz, which was conferred upon 'Umar Shaikh and later upon his son Pīr Muḥammad (not to be confused with his namesake, Jahāngīr's son, who was prince of Qandahār). In addition there were any number of medium-sized and small governorships, such as Iṣfahān under Rustam, Hamadān under Iskandar, Kirmān under the amīr Idikū, Ray under Sulaimān Shāh and Fīrūzkūh under Iskandar Shaikhī. Although the majority of the governors were descendants or relatives of Tīmūr, such posts were also open to other deserving military commanders.

Appointments of this kind, as the example of Fārs suggests, could take the form of fiefs, called *suyūrghāl*, which were either hereditary (*suyūrghāl-i abadī*) or granted for a fixed duration.[1] The suyūrghāl was an extension of the older *iqṭā'* that covered administration and jurisdiction in addition to taxes and duties.[2] It probably dates from the turn of

[1] According to Shāmī I, 135: *'Umar Shaikh Bahādur-rā ān mamlakat* [*sc.* Fārs] *ba-suyūrghāl farmūda ḥākim-i muṭlaq gardānīd.* This evidence is important because it is the sole instance mentioned by Shāmī of a large Persian territory being granted as suyūrghāl. The other examples he lists where a suyūrghāl was granted are: I, 77 (*īl va vilāyat*); I, 95 (Kāvkārsh in the Nisā area as *suyūrghāl-i abadī*); I, 122 (*vilāyatī mu'tabar*); I, 145 (*ān qal'at-rā*); and I, 153 (*vilāyat-i Akhlāṭ*). He employs the word *suyūrghāl(āt)* on numerous other occasions, but not with reference to enfeoffments. Cf. the etymology in *TMEN* I, 351–3.

[2] A view expressed time and again by Petrushevsky, e.g. in *Zemledelie*, p. 273.

the 7th–8th/13th–14th centuries, and thus cannot have been introduced by Tīmūr, as has been suggested,[1] but must have been in existence before his time. It was given specific form first by the Jalayirids,[2] then by the Türkmen confederations, and finally by the Safavids. Although further research into the matter is needed, the suyūrghāl appears to have had various functions in Tīmūr's time, such as the granting of territories, cities or strongholds, first to relatives of Tīmūr, secondly to deserving military commanders, and lastly to former holders of such possessions who had surrendered to the conqueror. Whether exemption from taxation was also granted in every case remains to be seen, although it was probably a regular feature of the last mentioned type of arrangement. What is certain is that the suyūrghāl was not yet of great importance during Tīmūr's reign, so that no comparison with the Safavid period is possible. Tīmūr's governors in Persia, even if they were his own close relatives and enjoyed wide ranging powers, were not given unlimited jurisdiction *vis-à-vis* the armed forces or the organs of civilian administration.[3] There is ample evidence to show that they were subject to direct supervision from above and that they could be deposed where necessary, as the fate of prince Mīrān Shāh demonstrates. When they were appointed, they were given the task of getting trade and business going again, putting the administration on a regular footing and bringing to heel or eliminating rebellious elements. In each case they were granted an initial period of a few years to accomplish such tasks, after which they were again required to report for military service.

Under this administration, however much it may have varied from one area to another, Iran as a whole gradually recovered from the heavy damage it had sustained during the period of turmoil resulting both from the collapse of the Il-Khanid empire and the conquest and subjugation of the country by the Chaghatais. No lesser an authority

[1] Belenitsky, "K istorii feodal'nogo zemlevladeniya", p. 46, and Yakubovsky, "Timur", pp. 66ff.

[2] The word suyūrghāl occurs fifteen times in Nakhchivānī's *Dastūr al-kātib*, dedicated to the Jalayirid Shaikh Uvais; but it is used not in the sense of "fief" or "transfer of territory" but rather of "favour", otherwise forming part of a compound verb meaning "to grant" or "to donate".

[3] In this respect it would be wrong to make too much of the fact that the formula *sözümiz* is used in documents of Mīrān Shāh dating from 796/1394 and 798/1396 and in a document of Muḥammad Sulṭān of 804/1401. It is particularly interesting to note that in addition to the preamble *Sulṭān Maḥmūd yarlīghīndīn*, which is common to all three documents, the last also contains the formula *Amīr Tīmūr küregen sözümindin*. Cf. Fekete, *Einführung*, no. 1 (reviewed by Herrmann in *Der Islam* LV [1978], 147–9), and Herrmann, "Zur Intitulatio".

than Barthold claimed that Tīmūr's constructive achievements were just as astonishing as the destruction he wrought, and he has been praised in particular for the security that prevailed in his dominions. For instance, the example of a merchant's widow travelling on business, accompanied only by two young Indian slaves, has been cited to show that the route from Qandahār to Diyārbakr was absolutely safe. In dangerous areas robbery and theft were effectively curbed by the introduction of severe sanctions and also by military or police operations against notoriously disruptive elements amongst the nomadic populations of Türkmens, Kurds and Lurs. Not only Iran but Tīmūr's entire empire also enjoyed the benefit of an efficient postal system.

Apart from these by no means negligible achievements of Tīmūr and his governors, what other benefits did the conqueror bring to Iran? We know of irrigation works in the steppes of Mūghān and in Khurāsān that he either had installed or had restored to working order.[1] He is said to have shown great enthusiasm for the reconstruction or restoration of cities and villages destroyed during his conquests; indeed it is claimed that he could not bear to see a patch of arable land lying fallow.

As far as cultural life is concerned, one can point to the fact that Persian poetry continued to flourish, although there is relatively little evidence of its being directly encouraged by Tīmūr. Persian historical scholarship owes a greater debt to him, for he commissioned several works of distinction.[2] One can also name Persian scholars who enjoyed his patronage, and who wrote their works exclusively or predominantly in Arabic, e.g. the theologian and grammarian Sa'd al-Dīn Mas'ūd al-Taftazānī (d. 791/1389 or six years later), the famous mystic and logician 'Alī b. Muḥammad al-Sayyid al-Sharīf al-Jurjānī (d. 816/1413) and the renowned lexicographer Abū Ṭāhir b. Ya'qūb al-Shīrāzī al-Fīrūzābādī (d. 817/1414).

The lack of any well organised, uniform system of administration, in conjunction with the basically destructive attitude to ruling authority which ceased to be latent among the Tīmūrids when their eponymous leader died, did not detract from the gradual process of recovery in Persia, at least during the last phase of the conqueror's life. Once the news of his death had spread, however, these factors proved fatal both

[1] Barthold, *K istorii orosheniya Turkestana*, p. 65.

[2] See *PL*, trans. Bregel' II, 787–828; Hinz, "Quellenstudien"; Yakubovsky, "Timur", pp. 42–6; and Roemer, *Šams al-Ḥusn*, pp. 1–14.

to the continued existence of the empire and to the unity of Persia. But as far as the cultural foundations of the empire were concerned, the situation was quite different. Within the broad framework of his sphere of authority Tīmūr once more, and for the last time, re-established the total cultural entity of Iran – from Transoxiana to eastern Anatolia, from the Aral Sea to Mesopotamia and from the Caucasus to the Indus. It is idle to speculate whether or not he was himself conscious of this fact. Certainly he personified the transition from a nomadic to a sedentary way of life, and in this his contact with Iranian culture played a decisive rôle. For him, indeed, Iran may well have been the very epitome of culture. This can be seen from his tireless efforts over a period of decades to develop his homeland, and in particular the metropolis of Samarqand, by means of buildings, works of art and other cultural achievements, the vast majority of which bore the imprint of Persian taste, Persian artistic sensibility and Persian craftsmanship. The fact that scholars, poets, artists and craftsmen were selected from the population of conquered cities and deported to Samarqand is also clear proof of this, for Iranian elements predominated in these cultural circles both outside Persia and within. Of course, as a result of this influx and in other ways, that section of the capital's population which was responsible for its cultural development also contained a sprinkling of Turkish and, to a lesser extent, Mongol elements: in certain particulars they too left their mark on the resulting culture, but they had no effect on its essential features.

With the development of Samarqand the centre of gravity of Persian culture was switched to the periphery, a process not without precedent in the history of Iran. After Tīmūr's death, however, this was offset by the enforced exodus of numerous people and by the development of new centres of Iranian culture under the Timurids. Not only did the culture of Iran survive the trials inflicted upon its representatives by Tīmūr and his Chaghatais, but it also conserved sufficient energy to experience a further development in the constituent states that were formed after 807/1405. This was true even of Samarqand under Ulugh Beg, who had a marked preference for Mongol traditions. Tīmūr thus laid the foundations for the culture of the Timurids, which was one of the most important epochs in Persian cultural history.

CHAPTER 3

THE SUCCESSORS OF TĪMŪR

The empire Tīmūr left behind at his death was of vast extent. But as there existed neither an effective disposition for the succession nor a firm political organisation for the realm, its unity immediately crumbled. In spite of this, large portions of the territory remained for a long period in the hands of Tīmūr's successors, some of them ruling over independent states, some in the manner of joint rulers and local princes as governors of the individual provinces in the daughter empires which now emerged. The distinction of this period was no longer military in character, nor political; it is to be sought rather in an astonishing upsurge of cultural and intellectual life, the shaping of which involved both Persian and Turkish elements under Timurid control and largely also Timurid patronage. After some years of violent conflict for the possession of the throne, the countries of Central Asia and the Near East again enjoyed periods of relative quiet in comparison with the reign of Tīmūr. During such periods many of the old wounds inflicted by Tīmūr in his campaigns and acts of devastation were healed. Conditions in individual regions, however, varied considerably, and hardly anywhere was there any sure guarantee of tranquil life, since local risings, disputes concerning the succession and incursions on the part of warlike neighbours were a constant possibility.

The period of Timurid government in Iran extends from 807/1405 to 913/1507. Successors of Tīmūr did in fact rule long after this period, in the Mughal empire in India founded by Ẓahīr al-Dīn Bābur. However, that state had no immediate influence upon the development of Persia – at least, none of any major consequence. The importance of the Timurid age for Iran lies in the intellectual, religious, and cultural developments which were beginning to take shape at that time. These led at the end of the 9th/15th and the beginning of the 10th/16th century to radical changes in many parts of the Islamic world and particularly in the Iranian area.

EARLY SUCCESSION DISPUTES

Of the conqueror's sons, Jahāngīr had died in 777/1375 and 'Umar Shaikh in 796/1394. The third, Mīrān Shāh, suffered from mental trouble as the result of an accident, while the fourth, Shāh Rukh, who had been born in 779/1377 and had a reputation for excessive modesty, peaceableness and personal piety, appeared to lack the necessary qualities to rule. Hence Tīmūr had appointed as his successor his grandson, Pīr Muḥammad b. Jahāngīr, who was thirty-one years of age and occupied at the time the governorship of Qandahār, the "throne of Maḥmūd of Ghazna". In the absence of support from his relatives he was unable to succeed to the throne and was murdered by his own vizier in 809/1407.

It was clearly the case that the great empire which had been built upon the conquests of three decades was all too dependent on the personal authority of its founder. His sons and grandsons, whom he had appointed as governors of individual countries and provinces, where they reigned in effect as joint rulers, had been obliged to defer to his authority. With his death, however, that authority was at an end, and now they ignored his dispositions for the succession. Any one of them who was in a position to do so had his name incorporated in the official prayers and inscribed on the coinage in his own domain, so claiming for himself the status of an independent ruler. The governmental pattern Tīmūr had given to his empire thus revealed its weakness. It based itself on the conception commonly accepted among Turkish peoples that the state belonged not to the ruler alone, but to the whole ruling family, and hence that the territory entrusted to the administration of any one member of the family was his property.[1] Under a monarch as strong as Tīmūr such notions might not endanger the unity of the empire; but it was a very different matter in the situation obtaining after his death, when no personality comparable in terms of personal authority was at hand to take over the succession. The empire disintegrated into a number of separate principalities; and although a large number of them were later for some decades reintegrated into one state, the territorial extent of Tīmūr's empire was never again attained. In the disputes over the succession and the confusions which now followed, various of his successors made war on one another, and certain amīrs who had deserved well of the state and had been entrusted by him with offices at court or in the provinces were inevitably drawn into the conflicts. Others involved were local princes

[1] For this and similar interpretations, see F. Köprülü, *Türk edebiyatında ilk mutasavvıflar* (Ankara, 1966), p. 161n., with reference to the Köktürks and the Saljūqs; O. Turan, *Selçuklular tarihi ve Türk-İslâm medeniyeti* (Ankara, 1965), p. 218, with reference to the Great Saljūqs; and Yınanç, "Akkoyunlular".

who derived their claims from the period before the reign of Tīmūr and who now came forward to urge their own particular demands by force of arms. These struggles lasted for some years.

At the death of Tīmūr the troops of the main army formed part of his immediate train. Their amīrs really wanted to prosecute the war against China, if only with the limited aim of striking a blow against the Mughals in eastern Turkestan. They abandoned the project, however, when on the news of Tīmūr's death the succession did not work out according to plan. Samarqand, Tīmūr's capital, fell into the hands of Prince Khalīl Sulṭān b. Mīrān Shāh (b. 786/1384), who had distinguished himself in the campaign in India, had in 1402 received the governorship of Farghāna, and had enjoyed his grandfather's particular favour. While still in Tashkent he had forthwith had his amīrs pay homage to him; and regarding himself as Tīmūr's successor, he took possession of his treasure, which he squandered, and transferred the title and authority of khan, which had hitherto always been vested in a direct descendant of Chingiz Khān, to a Timurid prince. Sulṭān Ḥusain, the son of one of Tīmūr's daughters, who at first had also been a pretender to the throne, relinquished his claim and joined forces with Khalīl Sulṭān; though after various adventures he was to finish up in captivity and was put out of the way by Shāh Rukh while under detention in Herat.

Shāh Rukh marched his army from his city of Herat to the Oxus, but made no further offensive move against Khalīl, no doubt because the latter's father Mīrān Shāh represented a serious threat, advancing at the head of his troops from Āzarbāījān – which had been given into his charge by Tīmūr – with Abā Bakr, another of his sons, to the support of Khalīl. He later withdrew, however, without having carried out his intentions. Although there were a series of more or less unproductive negotiations between Shāh Rukh and Khalīl Sulṭān, the latter was finally reduced after many clashes even though he had frequently been victorious. His attitude had provoked general disapproval in Samarqand. His amīrs could not condone the powerful influence permitted to his wife Shād Mulk, as a result of which individuals of low rank were elevated to high positions to the disadvantage of Tīmūr's old companions-in-arms, while the widows and concubines of Tīmūr, not without some pressure, it seemed, were married off to men of humble origin. A famine which affected the land contributed its share to the general mood of discontent. And finally Khalīl Sulṭān fell into the hands of Khudāīdād Ḥusain, a powerful tribal amīr, leader of the Dughlāt, a man who had once been his mentor. The latter accompanied him to Farghāna, had him proclaimed as ruler in Andijān, and himself went to join the Mughals in order to win their military support for further operations.

Meanwhile, on 27 Dhu'l-Ḥijja 811/13 May 1409, Shāh Rukh occupied his own home city of Samarqand without striking a blow. He declared his eldest son Ulugh Beg (b. 796/1394) governor of Transoxiana, with his seat of government in Samarqand, initially under the guardianship of Amīr Shāh Malik, one of Tīmūr's long-serving military commanders. Khalīl Sulṭān, whose wife had fallen into the hands of Shāh Rukh, now betook himself to his uncle in Samarqand, received his wife back from him and became governor of Ray. Shortly afterwards, however, on 16 Rajab 814/4 November 1411, he died there; whereupon Shād Mulk took her own life. Khalīl Sultān, whose generosity, liberality and credulity, and unquestioning love of Shād Mulk, contributed largely to his own failure, has gone down in history – not least for his literary and artistic leanings – as a romantic figure, difficult to place in the general picture of the age.

THE REIGN OF SHĀH RUKH

Now that, at a point in time marked at the latest by the death of Khalīl Sulṭān and following the execution of Sulṭān Ḥusain and the murder of Pīr Muḥammad, all immediate rivals had left the scene, Shāh Rukh became Tīmūr's successor. In spite of the fact that his father had not considered him for the succession, he had made him governor of Khurāsān, the most centrally situated province of his empire, which he administered from Herat. He plainly felt so attached to that city that he declined to move to Samarqand and conducted the government of the Timurid empire from Herat until his death in 850/1447. Some years before the acquisition of Transoxiana Shāh Rukh had extended his domains to include Gurgān and Māzandarān. Insubordination on the part of his nephew Bāīqarā b. 'Umar Shaikh led to his mounting an expedition to Fārs in 817/1414. Two years later he succeeded in subduing Kirmān, where Sulṭān Uvais b. Amīr Idikū Barlās had reigned since 811/1408 as an independent ruler. The area under his control was further extended as the pull of his steadily consolidated dominion made itself felt, either by voluntary subordination on the part of minor princes or by means of alliances. Thus it was not long after the fall of Khalīl

Sulṭān that in a single year emissaries presented themselves from the land of the Uzbeks, from the Qïpchaq steppes, from Shīrvān, Hazār-jarīb, Sārī, Fīrūzkūh, Garmsīr and Qandahār.

Up until 823/1420 Shāh Rukh was able to assert his power in the eastern areas of Tīmūr's empire, central and southern Persia, but not in Mesopotamia and Āzarbāījān. After the death of Tīmūr, the Jalayirid Sulṭān Aḥmad b. Uvais, who had been expelled by Tīmūr fifteen years previously, once again seized power, only to be driven out of Tabrīz by Abā Bakr b. Mīrān Shāh. Shortly afterwards, however, an opponent made his appearance on the scene for whom Abā Bakr was no match. This was Qarā Yūsuf Qarā Quyūnlū, who defeated him, first in 809/1406 at Nakhchivān and then again in 810/1408 at the battle of Sardrūd near Tabrīz, in which Mīrān Shāh met his death. In 813/1410 this Türkmen prince defeated and destroyed also Aḥmad Jalāyir when the latter attempted to reconquer Tabrīz. As a result of his conquest of Diyārbakr and Baghdad and successful operations against Georgia and Shīrvān, and above all by the conquest of Sulṭāniyya, Ṭārum, Qazvīn and Sāva in 822/1419, he established himself as a dangerous neighbour to the Timurids.

The threat which arose in this advance of the Türkmens remained for decades the great unresolved problem of the Timurid empire. Shāh Rukh attempted to solve it by political and – in three campaigns against Āzarbāījān – military means, but never achieved more than partial success. Qarā Yūsuf, the real founder of the princely power of the Qarā Quyūnlū, an energetic and battle-hardened man, ended his days in Dhu'l-Qa'da 823/November 1420 as Shāh Rukh entered Āzarbāījān in the course of the first of these campaigns, so that the Timurid troops were at first able to occupy not only Tabrīz but also Āzarbāījān and Armenia without difficulty; but even so Shāh Rukh was obliged to assert his sovereignty in the summer of the following year in a battle of several days' duration against the Türkmen prince's sons. However, as Iskandar b. Qarā Yūsuf contrived to re-establish the power of the Qarā Quyūnlū in the years that followed, another Āzarbāījān campaign proved to be necessary in 832/1429. Once again, Shāh Rukh won the day against the Türkmens. But his attempt to solve the problem by installing a Qarā Quyūnlū prince named Abū Sa'īd under Timurid suzerainty met with only short-lived success; for in 835/1431 Qarā Iskandar reoccupied Tabrīz and had Abū Sa'īd executed. Faced with the extension of Qarā Iskandar's control over an ever wider area, Shāh

Rukh early in 838/near the end of 1434 resolved upon his third and last campaign against north-west Persia. This campaign, although it did not achieve a final settlement of the Türkmen question, at least brought about one which was adequate for the remainder of his reign, namely the installation of Qarā Iskandar's brother Jahān Shāh as the Timurid governor of Tabrīz.

It is noticeable that Shāh Rukh, at least in the early part of his reign, frequently made transfers among the princes who held court as governors in the provinces of his empire. Among those transferred were not only Khalīl Sulṭān (from Samarqand to Ray) but also 'Umar Mīrzā (from Āzarbāījān to Astarābād), Iskandar Mīrzā (from Farghāna and Kāshghar to Hamadān and later to Shīrāz), and Bāīqarā Mīrza (from Shīrāz to Qandahār and Garmsīr), to mention only a few examples. It is reasonable to assume that the motive behind such measures, which were quite often directly connected with acts of insubordination on the part of those affected, was the desire to ward off possible hankerings after independence. Certainly Shāh Rukh, for all his precautions, was not spared dangerous rebellions on the part of the Timurid princes. And though he was not hard put to it to suppress them in the eastern parts of his empire, it was a different matter in his western dominions. Over and over again he had to intervene with armed might against recalcitrant relatives, as for instance in 816/1413 against his nephew Iskandar b. 'Umar Shaikh, who once before, in 812/1409, had encouraged his brother Pīr Muḥammad to attack Kirmān and, moreover, after the latter's murder had himself assaulted Iṣfahān and Kirmān, systematically devastating the country in the process. Mention has already been made of Shāh Rukh's campaign against Bāīqarā b. 'Umar Shaikh, who not long afterwards rose in rebellion in Shīrāz. Even shortly before his death, Shāh Rukh, already weakened by age and ill-health, again had to march to the west, where one of his grandsons, Sulṭān Muḥammad b. Bāīsunqur, had risen in revolt. In Ramaḍān 850/December 1446 he managed to bring the latter's supporters to justice in Sāva, but the prince himself had eluded his grasp and escaped to Luristān. Three months later, on 25 Dhu'l-Ḥijja 850/13 March 1447, Shāh Rukh died in winter quarters at Ray.

At first sight his long reign seems to yield a fairly favourable overall picture.[1] Although Tīmūr's enormous empire was not preserved in its

[1] For a particularly favourable view, see Togan, "Büyük türk hükümdarı Şahruh".

entirety under his rule, it remained a coherent dominion of considerable extent in Central Asia and the Near East. In spite of protracted and sanguinary conflicts at home, which inevitably brought misery and suffering to the populations affected, the state was preserved for four decades from the anarchy which threatened to engulf it upon Tīmūr's death; and in some parts of the empire there was an improvement not only in economic standards but also in cultural achievements. It must be admitted that the credit for the turn of the tide and these more hopeful developments was not all – perhaps not even primarily – Shāh Rukh's. Although certain aspects of his character are in marked and refreshing contrast to the hardness and ruthlessness of his father, there is no conclusive evidence to suggest that he should be credited with outstanding skill as a statesman, and even his character is not a matter of agreement amongst modern historians. It is rather the case that at the court of Herat other personalities exercised a more powerful influence on government than the ruler himself, especially his first wife, Gauhar Shād, who together with her sons and a few state officials made it her business to provide for orderly continuity in the state's affairs, which contributed to the welfare of wide sections of the population. The highest offices of state had indeed been entrusted to men of unusual ability, some of whom, moreover, remained in office for a very long period, with the result that they had full scope to develop their talents. Examples are Jalāl al-Dīn Fīrūz Shāh, who was for thirty-five years supreme commander of the armed forces; Ghiyāṣ al-Dīn Pīr 'Alī Khwāfī, who was supreme secretary for thirty-one years; and Amīr 'Alīka Kökültāsh, vizier in charge of the finances of the state for forty-three years.

Shāh Rukh's piety, indeed bigotry in religious matters, is well known. He regarded himself as an Islamic ruler for whose actions the prescriptions of the Sharī'a were authoritative, not the Mongol traditions which had of course meant so much to Tīmūr that he called himself Küregen (i.e. bound by marriage ties to the dynasty of Chingiz Khān) and was constantly accompanied by a Chingizid shadow khan even when he had reached the peak of his power. Shāh Rukh's son Ulugh Beg adhered to this tradition in Samarqand by taking the title Küregen and immediately after the deposition of Khalīl Sulṭān, whose Timurid shadow khan disappeared from Transoxiana simultaneously with him, appointed a Chingizid to be khan in Samarqand. In contrast, Shāh Rukh called himself neither Khān nor Küregen (though he did bear the title Bahādur accorded him by Tīmūr) and appointed no shadow khan in Herat.

Shāh Rukh's relations with China,[1] in which Ulugh Beg was also involved, are renowned. They were not restricted to the exchange of ambassadors but included also trading contacts. Other commercial links, too, especially with Egypt and India, were fostered. Source material contains in addition details of the encouragement of agriculture. River control and irrigation schemes in the Herat and Marv regions are also mentioned.

The reign of Shāh Rukh saw significant advances in cultural life, especially in the sphere of the arts and intellectual inquiry. These included painting, especially miniatures and calligraphy, architecture, music, historiography,[2] and the law and theology of Islam. The encouragement of artistic and intellectual achievement, however, was due not only to the ruler but also to his sons and other members of the family, and to certain highly placed members of his court. The interest of Prince Bāīsunqur (d. 837/1433) in promoting calligraphy is well known; so, too, is the patronage at Shīrāz of Prince Iskandar b. ʿUmar Shaikh, one of whose protégés was the mathematician and astronomer Ghiyāṡ al-Dīn Jamshīd b. Masʿūd Kāshī, who later lived in Samarqand. Poetry, too, in this period is marked by such distinguished names as those of the Ṣūfī poets Qāsim al-Anvār and Shāh Niʿmat-Allāh Valī. In addition to Persian literature the beginnings of an eastern Turkish literature are also to be discerned. Even though the cultural achievements of the Timurid age were only just moving towards their climax, however, the death of Shāh Rukh saw the onset of the decline of the Timurid empire as the leading political power in Central Asia and the Near East.

ULUGH BEG AND HIS RIVALS

Shāh Rukh had made no disposition for the succession, but it was understood that he would prefer to see Muḥammad Jūkī, a man of some forty years of age then ruling as governor in Balkh, as the next occupant of the throne. The latter, however, died three years before his father, so that of Shāh Rukh's five sons only Muḥammad Taraghai,

[1] Quatremère, "Mémoire" and "Notice"; also *A Persian Embassy to China ... from Zubdatu't Tawarikh of Hafiz Abru*, trans. K.M. Maitra, new ed. (New York, 1970); D.M. Dunlop, "Hāfiz-i Abrū's version of the Timurid Embassy to China in A.D. 1420", *Glasgow Univ. Oriental Soc. Transactions* XI (1942-4), 15–19; and H. Serruys, *The Tribute System and Diplomatic Missions, 1400–1600* (Brussels, 1967), p. 624.

[2] As instanced in the dedication of the *Muntakhab al-tavārīkh* to Shāh Rukh, on which see Hinz, "Quellenstudien", p. 362.

known as Ulugh Beg, survived him. Yet at the time of his father's death he was neither in the royal entourage nor in Herat. In fact he had only ever made an occasional appearance at court as a guest and had never been invited to share in the imperial government; since 812/1409 he had been merely a more or less independent local prince in Samarqand. He had up to this time had coins struck bearing the name of his father, though his edicts were issued in the name of the Chingizid shadow khan he himself appointed; and he had provided military contingents for his father's campaigns, but had never personally served in command. He appears not to have been required to make contributions to the central treasury in Herat, or at any rate he never in fact did make any. The question of the succession under the existing circumstances could have been a comparatively straightforward matter. Nevertheless, as early as 848/1444, when Shāh Rukh had fallen ill and his impending death had to be reckoned with, there had been a kind of prelude to the confusions which now ensued in real earnest. At that time, Muḥammad Jūkī had gone to Herat, hoping to succeed to his father's throne, while the troops, at the direction of Gauhar Shād, were quickly sworn in allegiance to 'Alā' al-Daula b. Bāīsunqur (b. 820/1417), in confident but, as things turned out, misplaced expectation of a change of ruler. The latter, together with Ulugh Beg's third son 'Abd al-Laṭīf, had previously been a supporter of the princess in her conduct of government affairs.

It looked almost as if the demise of Shāh Rukh was going to produce a repetition of what had happened at the death of Tīmūr. Again there was no one outstanding figure strong enough to assert himself against the aspirations to power of the numerous princes. But there the parallel ends, for on this occasion there was nobody on the scene, like Shāh Rukh in his day, to profit from the general turn of events or to enlist competent aides in order to build up a centralised administration and thereby to preserve the unity of the empire. It soon became evident, moreover, that what had been experienced at the time of Shāh Rukh's illness in 848/1444, far from easing the question of the succession, had if anything exacerbated it. Gauhar Shād, who had accompanied Shāh Rukh on his last campaign, induced 'Abd al-Laṭīf, who was also present in the royal camp, to take over supreme command of the army. Abu'l-Qāsim Bābur b. Bāīsunqur (b. 825/1422), together with Khalīl Sulṭān b. Muḥammad Jahāngīr, Shāh Rukh's daughter's son, plundered the main baggage-train of the army and marched to

Khurāsān. 'Alā' al-Daula, who had remained in Herat, at first played a waiting game, but then had himself proclaimed ruler when he realised how the situation was shaping. He distributed his grandfather's treasure among his troops and had Mashhad occupied. Ulugh Beg, who regarded himself as his father's only rightful successor, called his troops together and advanced as far as the Oxus. However, he found himself prevented from further immediate action because Mīrzā Abū Bakr, governor of Khuttalān, Arhang and Sālī Sarāī, had crossed the river ahead of him and occupied the region of Balkh, Shabūrghān and Qunduz as far as Badakhshān and expelled his brother Muḥammad Qāsim, to whom Balkh had been entrusted after the death of their father Muḥammad Jūkī.

Such was the situation at the beginning of the struggles for power which developed after the death of Shāh Rukh among his descendants, lasting the whole two years of Ulugh Beg's reign, and which has been described in detail by Barthold in his classic study of Ulugh Beg. In the struggle of each party against every other which now began, the fortunes of war ebbed to and fro, but no decisive victory was won, nor were clear alignments established. The various parties agreed to certain alliances, frontier settlements and other arrangements, which led in some instances to a temporary lull in hostilities. But these agreements were hardly ever kept for any length of time and their infringement in each case became the cause of renewed conflict. Various princes were captured, regained their freedom, or were killed.

Ulugh Beg did achieve a certain measure of success. He contrived, for example, to foil the plans of Prince Abū Bakr b. Muḥammad Jūkī, and in the spring of 852/1448 he won a victory over his nephew 'Alā' al-Daula at the battle of Tarnāb and occupied Mashhad, while his son 'Abd al-Laṭīf conquered the fortress of Herat. Yet his political and military skill was nowhere near sufficient to master the complexities of the situation. The occupation of Herat, important though it was in strategic terms and still more – as the former capital – in a psychological sense, was only a step in the right direction, since he did not wish to remain there but intended to make Samarqand the capital of the Timurid empire. The military enterprises he carried out from Herat did not bring about the consolidation of his power, but rather led to the most detrimental of results for the population of Khurāsān and their economic life through the devastation of the countryside which was involved. In Transoxiana at this period it was the same disastrous story. The continuing confusions had remained no secret to the Timurids' neighbours, especially the Türkmens in the west and the Uzbeks in the east. The first move was made by the Uzbek khan Abu'l-Khair, who invaded Transoxiana and marched through the region around Samarqand, looting and burning as he went.

When Ulugh Beg left Herat for Samarqand late in 852/at the end of 1448, taking his father's body with him, the problems of Khurāsān were no nearer solution than they had ever been, not to mention those of other parts of the empire: indeed he was not even able to march unimpeded to Transoxiana. First a detachment dispatched by Abu'l-Qāsim Bābur inflicted heavy losses on him; and then, to make matters worse, his troops were ambushed by the Uzbeks while crossing the Oxus before reaching their intended winter quarters at Bukhārā.

To summarise the first phase of the conflicts arising from the succession to Shāh Rukh, it remains only to be said that two years after his death no centralised form of government had been achieved, and what was emerging was rather a tripartite division of his empire. Ulugh Beg, who may be regarded as his father's rightful successor, evidently imagining that he could make Samarqand the capital once again as in the days of his grandfather Tīmūr, had – by yielding up Khurāsān as the real base from which to extend his rule over the whole of Shāh Rukh's territory – *de facto* limited the area of his control to Transoxiana. To begin with, Abu'l-Qāsim Bābur asserted himself in Khurāsān, conquering both Mashhad and Herat, while 'Alā' al-Daula, after the defeat at Tarnāb, was soon forced to abandon his plan of marching on Samarqand and had to be content with a small territory in south-western Afghanistan. From here he was able in the next few years to intervene in the struggle for Khurāsān, but without any enduring success. Central Persia ('Irāq-i 'Ajam) and Fārs passed into the control of Sulṭān Muḥammad b. Bāīsunqur, who after the death of his grandfather at once emerged from his hiding-place in Luristān and played a significant part in the ensuing struggles for the succession. Finally, the supremacy of the Timurids over the Türkmen principality of the Qarā Quyūnlū under Jahān Shāh in north-west Persia and eastern Anatolia, which Shāh Rukh had secured in three campaigns, had become virtually meaningless in the present circumstances. It was not to be long before Jahān Shāh's expansionist potential would be made evident, to the detriment of the Timurids.

Ulugh Beg had no further opportunity to put into effect his

intention of again subjugating Khurāsān in the spring of 853/1449, since his strained relations with 'Abd al-Laṭīf, who ruled in Balkh, led to the latter breaking into open rebellion around this juncture. During his time in Herat Ulugh Beg had on various occasions humiliated his son, in connection, it would seem, with the planned transference of the capital city. When his pent-up anger was still further increased after his father's departure, the result was a military confrontation in the autumn of 853/1449, the consequences of which were decisive. Ulugh Beg was defeated near Samarqand at the township of Dimashq. Previously a series of uprisings had broken out in the capital against Ulugh Beg's appointed governor, his youngest and favourite son 'Abd al-'Azīz, in which it would appear that representatives of the religious classes had played some part, just as they had in the downfall of Ulugh Beg's predecessor Khalīl Sulṭān in 811/1409. The ruler had been able to restore order, but dissatisfaction and resentment had continued. After his defeat, and plainly in association with these events, his stock had sunk so low that wherever he sought shelter he could find no refuge, not even in his own capital. He was only able to escape the imminent threat of being captured and handed over to his victorious son by voluntarily giving himself up. He received permission to undertake a pilgrimage to Mecca, as often happened in such cases, but was killed on the journey in accordance with the verdict which 'Abd al-Laṭīf had caused to be passed on him in his absence and without his knowledge at a false trial. This was in Ramaḍān 853/October–November 1449. Some days later the same fate overtook 'Abd al-'Azīz; but in his case no legal means had been invoked.

This sorry end after a rule of only two years, consisting of a series of political and military failures and errors, is by no means what has gone down in history as the dominant image of the man Ulugh Beg. What are remembered as significant are rather the cultural achievements brought about in the course of his reign of almost four decades as prince of Transoxiana, achievements either associated with his name or attributed to him personally. We may mention his initiation of building projects in Samarqand and Bukhārā or his interest in problems of Persian poetry, which he discussed in a correspondence with his artistically inclined brother Bāīsunqur. Mention may also be made of the fact that certain Chaghatai poets eulogised him in Turkish verse, though it is not known what attitude he adopted towards the eastern Turkish literature which was just emerging during his lifetime. A historical work, the *Tārīkh-i arba' ulūs*, a history of the four states which came into being at the disintegration of the Mongol empire, is reputed to have been written at his behest.

Though such interests and activities may have encouraged the view of him as "the scholar on the throne", they did not succeed in really validating it. What did, however, was his involvement in the *'ulūm-i riyāẓī va ḥukmī* – the exact sciences as one would say nowadays. In this he was in line with an attitude of mind that had prevailed in the Near East, and especially in Persia, since the rule of the Mongols and amounted to a view of scientific findings as being of lasting benefit to mankind in contrast to theology and literature, whose significance in terms of time and also – on account of language differences – in terms of space could only ever be limited. Among the scholars available to provide Ulugh Beg with instruction or collaborate with him in scientific research a number of astronomers and mathematicians are noteworthy, especially Ṣalāḥ al-Dīn Mūsā b. Qāżīzāda Rūmī, Ghiyāṣ al-Dīn Jamshīd b. Mas'ūd Kāshī, 'Alā' al-Dīn b. Muḥammad Qūshchī and Mu'īn al-Dīn Kāshānī.[1] Ulugh Beg's observatory in Samarqand, dating from 823/1420, is famous (its remains were excavated in 1908); yet the period during which it was in use did not outlast the death of its founder. His writings on astronomy won him an enduring reputation. His astronomical tables, usually known as *Zīj-i Ulugh Beg* or *Zīj-i jadīd-i sulṭānī*, represent a climax of achievement in that science, which declined in the Islamic world after his death.

Ulugh Beg's splendid style in Samarqand did not lag behind that of the court of Herat, even in his father's lifetime. However, he found his model not in Shāh Rukh but in his grandfather Tīmūr. The very choice of royal title, already mentioned, reveals that his pattern was not the figure of the Muslim prince but that of the Mongol ruler, for whom the prescriptions of the Yasa rather than those of the Sharī'a were authoritative. Thus he was given to such secular delights as cannot be reconciled with the religious law of Islam. In Samarqand there were carousals with music and singing. Wealthy inhabitants of other cities even had musicians and singers of both sexes come from Samarqand. As a result of his predilection for such pleasures Ulugh Beg came into conflict with certain religious circles, not the representatives of the official theology, on whose support he could broadly count, but the

[1] See below, chapters 10 and 11.

adherents of Folk Islam, as embodied in the manner of life of ṣūfīs and dervishes, usually adherents of the Naqshbandiyya order. The situation was therefore the precise opposite of that in Islamic lands situated further west, in which the theologians figured as the guardians of the religious law, whereas ṣūfīs and dervishes gave their allegiance to more liberal notions in which the requirements of the religious law could easily be relegated to an unimportant place.

Ulugh Beg was a cultured prince of keen intellectual interests; but he was not a man of action and he lacked political and military talent. Thus after a defeat which he had sustained in the spring of 830/1427 in a battle against a small force of Uzbeks he took no further part in any campaign for twenty years, and even in the dispute over the succession following the death of Shāh Rukh he did not distinguish himself through bold action or strategic acumen. In contrast to his pious, not to say bigoted, father he was a man of *savoir vivre* and cheerful demeanour. Towards his subjects he was, it seems, an easy-going if not a popular prince. At all events, he contented himself with a modest land rate, though he insisted implacably on the tax imposed on commerce and trades, the *tamghā* – a tax, moreover, which conflicted with the Sharīʿa.

ABŪ SAʿĪD AND THE LOSS OF WESTERN PERSIA

ʿAbd al-Laṭīf, who succeeded his father, was, like him, interested in secular scholarship. He introduced a stricter discipline among the population and the military than had been the case hitherto. However, by a pious personal life and respectful treatment of the dervishes he managed to secure the goodwill of those religious circles which had been offended by Ulugh Beg's habits. Since many amīrs could not forget the murder of his father and brother, a conspiracy was eventually mounted against him, to which he fell victim after a reign of only six months, in Rabīʿ I 854/May 1450.

ʿAbd-Allāh b. Ibrāhīm (b. 836/1433), another grandson of Shāh Rukh, who replaced him on the throne, also enjoyed only a short reign. Earlier, Fārs had been entrusted to him by his grandfather, but he had been obliged to withdraw from there in 851/1447 under attack from Sulṭān Muḥammad's troops. As an adherent of Ulugh Beg he had been imprisoned at the latter's fall. His release and installation as sultan, for which he had to show his recognition by handsome gifts of money to the troops, did not meet with universal approval. ʿAlāʾ al-Daula b.

Bāīsunqur, whose ambitions have already been mentioned in connection with the death of Shāh Rukh, rose against him, though with only passing success. Far more dangerous, however, was the reaction in Bukhārā, the traditional centre of dervishism in Transoxiana. There, Abū Sa'īd b. Muḥammad (b. 1424), a great-grandson of Tīmūr of the lineage of Mīrān Shāh, who had also been incarcerated at the death of Ulugh Beg, was released from captivity and proclaimed ruler. After some initial setbacks he eventually marched from Tashkent to Samarqand with the military support of the Uzbek Abu'l-Khair Khān, defeated his rival in Jumādā I 855/June 1451, took him prisoner and had him executed, causing himself to be enthroned instead. Abū Sa'īd was able to maintain his authority for some considerable time, in fact until the winter of 873/1468–9, and he even succeeded in bringing about a stabilisation of the internal situation in his dominions. However, these only embraced western Turkestan, Khurāsān, Māzandarān and parts of present-day Afghanistan (Kābulistān and Zābulistān), so that it is not possible to speak of a restoration of the Timurid empire, even to the extent of Shāh Rukh's territorial possessions. But even such limited successes were not achieved without warfare.

Since the fall of Ulugh Beg, changes had also come about beyond Transoxiana. Sulṭān Muḥammad b. Bāīsunqur, not content with Fārs and 'Irāq-i 'Ajam, had advanced on Khurāsān and compelled Abu'l-Qāsim Bābur in an initially victorious campaign culminating, in March 1450, in a battle at Mashhad, to cede to him certain parts of his domain. Somewhat later, however, the fortunes of war turned against him. Abu'l-Qāsim took him prisoner and had him executed, re-established his authority over the whole of Khurāsān, and then marched to Shīrāz to incorporate his vanquished opponent's lands into his own empire.

He had proceeded to appoint governors for Qum and Sāva when Jahān Shāh of the Qarā Quyūnlū, who had hitherto remained loyal to the vassal relationship instituted by Shāh Rukh, advanced westwards from Tabrīz and threatened the two cities. His action had in a sense even been provoked by Bābur, and not merely by the unstable political conditions prevailing in eastern Persia and Transoxiana; for Bābur, in spite of having placed his name on the coinage and in the public prayers, the privileges of the Muslim sovereign, had merely communicated the news of his victory over Sulṭān Muḥammad to him in a letter bearing the royal seal rather than in the form of an edict (*nishān*), with the demand which might be expected from a successor of Shāh Rukh, to the effect that henceforth Jahān Shāh must pay him tribute money (*bāj*), as formerly laid down by Shāh Rukh, and the taxes (*kharāj*) for the province of Āzarbāījān.

Bābur, who had already set off to relieve Qum and Sāva, was obliged to return to Herat, ostensibly because of the news of intrigues on the part of ʿAlāʾ al-Daula, in league with the Türkmens, but more likely as a result of the massive onslaught of the troops led by Pīr Būdāq, Jahān Shāh's son. The way was now wide open for the further expansion of the Qarā Quyūnlū. An additional factor was that they could count on a friendly attitude on the part of certain groups among the population in many places. Hardly one of the Timurid princes and other governors was able to hold at bay the Türkmen assault for any length of time. Thus in Rajab 856/August 1452 the control over almost the whole of Persia and Mesopotamia established by Tīmūr seventy years before came to an end, with the exception of Abarqūh, which was not taken until a year later, and Kirmān, which was temporarily reconquered and was intended to have served as a base position for more ambitious operations by the Timurid forces. These losses were final, and a few thrusts against Ray at a later date could do nothing to alter the situation.

An invasion of Transoxiana carried out by Bābur as a reply to the conquest of Balkh by Abū Saʿīd in the spring of 858/1454 from Herat led to the siege of Samarqand. Apparently it was only under pressure from the Naqshbandī shaikh ʿUbaid-Allāh Aḥrār that Abū Saʿīd resolved to defend the city. But hostilities were finally brought to an end by the mutual recognition of the Oxus as frontier. This was agreed in a treaty of peace which remained effective until the death of Bābur in 861/1457. Bābur's successor, his eleven-year-old son Maḥmūd, was forced out of Herat by Ibrāhīm b. ʿAlāʾ al-Daula after only a few weeks. The latter himself, however, had to flee in Shaʿbān 861/July 1457 from Abū Saʿīd, who had never abandoned the idea of annexing Khurāsān. Nevertheless, Abū Saʿīd did not succeed in capturing the citadel of Herat, but took up winter quarters in Balkh.

The conflicts going on among the Timurids induced Jahān Shāh, after his amazing successes in central Persia, Fārs and Mesopotamia, to attempt further advances eastwards. Having occupied Gurgān, he defeated Ibrāhīm in a battle near Astarābād. The vanquished Timurid withdrew to Herat, where he was joined shortly afterwards by his father ʿAlāʾ al-Daula and his forces. Yet there was no question of the pair offering resistance to Jahān Shāh, so that there was nothing left to them but flight, whilst the Türkmen prince made his entry into Herat on 15 Sha'bān 862/28 June 1458. Four months later Pīr Būdāq also arrived in the city with his troops, clearly in order to strengthen the Türkmen forces. Jahān Shāh, now installed in the capital city of his former overlord Shāh Rukh, promptly had his name incorporated into the official prayers and inscribed on the coinage.

It was soon evident, however, that he had outreached himself by his advance into such remote regions. He had to contend with the same handicap as the Timurids, namely the unceasing struggle for power on the part of the princes of his own house; ambitions which were all the more dangerous for him as his capital Tabrīz was so far distant. Faced with a revolt led by his son Ḥasan 'Alī, who had managed to escape from the fortress of Mākū where he had been held prisoner, he saw no other course open to him but to return to Āzarbāījān. Abū Sa'īd, who had not remained in ignorance of his opponent's tight situation, demanded in the ensuing negotiations that all Timurid possessions which Jahān Shāh had conquered should be handed back. In the event, all he secured was the return of Khurāsān.

Qarā Quyūnlū rule over Herat remained no more than an episode in the history of the Timurids without other direct results of any consequence. No more Türkmen operations were undertaken, nor were the Türkmen governors able to hold Khurāsān for any length of time after this. Quite soon, more or less friendly relations were established between Abū Sa'īd and Jahān Shāh, since each of them had enough to do to keep his own house in order. Thus we know of Türkmen missions in 1461, 1463, 1465 and 1466 which were amicably received in Herat. On balance, the whole train of events had tended to consolidate the power of Abū Sa'īd. In the very next spring he defeated 'Alā' al-Daula, Ibrāhīm and Sulṭān Sanjar b. Aḥmad b. 'Umar Shaikh in the vicinity of Sarakhs. He had Sanjar, who had fallen into his hands, executed, but the two other princes managed to escape. However, they both died soon afterwards, Ibrāhīm within only a few months and his father the following year. And as, in addition, Bābur's son Maḥmūd met his death about this time, Abū Sa'īd was able to consolidate his power still further, being rid of so many rivals, and even to extend it to Māzandarān and Sīstān.

Meanwhile, Prince Ḥusain Bāīqarā (b. 842/1438), a grandson of 'Umar Shaikh who had formerly lived in Khwārazm, had appeared upon the scene in Khurāsān. After Jahān Shāh's withdrawal from Herat he succeeded in defeating the latter's governor of Gurgān, Ḥusain Beg Sa'dlī, the chief of one of the most important Qarā Quyūnlū tribes, and taking over his territory. Although, to begin with, he recognised Abū Sa'īd's sovereignty, as soon as the latter was involved in putting down a rising in Transoxiana in 1460, he lost no time in occupying Māzandarān, and in Dhu'l-Qa'da 865/September 1461 he laid siege to Herat. Though his successes were not permanent and he was later compelled to seek refuge again in Khwārazm, he was nevertheless able in 868/1464 to undertake a pillaging expedition to Khurāsān with impunity.

Abū Sa'īd had gained power with Uzbek aid. In spite of this, Uzbek incursions across the Jaxartes into Transoxiana did not cease during his reign. The same Abu'l-Khair Khān who a few years previously had supported Abū Sa'īd in his struggle against 'Abd-Allāh and had then received a daughter of Ulugh Beg in marriage, was by 859/1454–5 granting Uvais b. Muḥammad b. Bāīqarā his assistance in a rising in the course of which Abū Sa'īd suffered a serious defeat. Another Timurid, Muḥammad Jūkī b. 'Abd al-Laṭīf, rose in revolt in 865/1461, marched through Transoxiana pillaging as he went, and finally took up a position in Shāhrukhiyya, where Abū Sa'īd besieged him from November 1462 to September 1463. The danger from the Mughals also became acute once again but receded after Abū Sa'īd had repulsed two attacks by the Chaghatayid khan Esen Buqa and from 860/1456 onwards lent his support to the latter's elder brother Yūnus, whom he had recognised as joint ruler in Mughalistān.

It would be wrong to conclude from the friendly relations which Abū Sa'īd maintained with Jahān Shāh after 863/1458 that he had given up the idea of re-establishing Timurid rule over the territory conquered by the Türkmens. This was plain when early in 872/at the end of 1467 Jahān Shāh, coming up against the rivalry of the Āq Quyūnlū Türkmens, met his death in a clash with their ruler Uzun Ḥasan. Abū Sa'īd was quite aware that the reconquest of the Iranian territories previously lost to the Qarā Quyūnlū and now passing into the hands of the Āq Quyūnlū might become a forlorn hope – indeed an absolute impossibility – if he did not succeed in checking the menacing rise of Uzun Ḥasan. In face of this danger the traditional alliance linking the Timurids with the Āq Quyūnlū no longer carried much weight.

Abū Sa'īd therefore embarked on a campaign to the west under the pretext of relieving Jahān Shāh's son Ḥasan 'Alī, who had asked for his assistance after an unsuccessful battle against the Āq Quyūnlū. Even the start of this operation, at the beginning of Sha'bān 872/end of February 1468, was clearly undertaken so impetuously and with so little planning that he did not wait for all the troops at his disposal to arrive, let alone ensure that he had adequate reserves. He did in fact manage to dislodge the Türkmen governors of 'Irāq-i 'Ajam and Fārs; and elsewhere, as in Gīlān, his sovereignty was once again recognised. But he continued his advance without paying due regard to establishing order in the hinterland, and failed to capture all the strongholds – Ray, for example, was one which was simply bypassed. Nor did he pay any attention to asseverations of friendship and peaceful intentions on the part of Uzun Ḥasan, which reached him en route.

The situation for Abū Sa'īd was in fact far from unfavourable. After the disastrous end of Jahān Shāh there were a fair number of amīrs and members of the Qarā Quyūnlū federation who were only awaiting the opportunity to throw in their fortunes with a new leader, especially in a campaign against Uzun Ḥasan. Thus when the Timurid army arrived in Miyāna, Jahān Shāh's son Yūsuf, a large number of amīrs of the Qarā Quyūnlū, and troops totalling allegedly some fifty thousand men joined him; so did Prince Ḥasan 'Alī b. Jahān Shāh with his son Amīrzāda 'Alī; and when he was about to take up winter quarters on the banks of the Araxes he was joined also by the Shīrvān-Shāh Farrukh-Yasār, who was in alliance with him.

In spite of this accession of strength, the Timurid army found itself in a critical situation at this time, caused not only by the inclemencies of the Āzarbāījān winter but also by serious supply problems. Not only were its supply routes to Khurāsān – extending some 1,250 miles – vulnerable in themselves, but to make matters worse Uzun Ḥasan succeeded within a short space of time in severing all routes by which reinforcements could be brought up. He cut off the access of supply ships from Shīrvān, intercepted a supply column (*jībakkhāna*) from Khurāsān and mounted attacks from Ray against his enemies' communications. The lack of food and winter clothing, the loss of riding and transport animals, and the constant surprise attacks by fast raiding groups of Türkmens undermined the morale of the Timurid troops. When Uzun Ḥasan succeeded, in addition, in persuading the Shīrvān-Shāh to defect from Abū Sa'īd and withdraw, the demoralisation of the army reached a nadir which manifested itself in numerous desertions. The depleted army marched via Ardabīl, low in spirit and with little heart for fighting, into the Mūghān steppes and was there met by the waiting Türkmen troops. After suffering heavy losses, Abū Saʻīd was taken prisoner. On 22 Rajab 873/5 February 1469 he was handed over to Yādgār Muḥammad, a great-grandson of Shāh Rukh who had sought refuge with Uzun Ḥasan. Yādgār Muḥammad took a belated bloody revenge on him for Gauhar Shād, the energetic wife of Shāh Rukh, who had been murdered in Herat twelve years previously on Abū Saʻīd's orders. With his overthrow the loss to the Timurid empire of all Persian territories west of Khurāsān was finally sealed.

The verdict on Abū Saʻīd as a man and a ruler is sometimes more favourable than his achievements warrant, not least because he succeeded in holding his own in the succession struggles of his day throughout eighteen years. This does not of course offset his failure to re-establish the previous extent of the empire and bring about peaceful conditions. He is best seen as a typical representative of the Türkmen military aristocracy. The main prop of his power was clearly the Turkish tribe of the Arghūn, who had elected him as their chieftain and on whom he could rely in his political and military ventures. The means he used to consolidate his power was the granting of fiefs (*suyūrghāl*), in which he indulged most liberally, and not only to leading members of the tribe, but also to his sons and to secular and religious dignitaries, to Turks and non-Turks alike. We should not fail to observe the religious element in the sultan's character. Ṣūfī shaikhs had a considerable influence on him, especially Khwāja ʻUbaid-Allāh Aḥrār. He described himself as a *murīd* of this particular dervish, who exercised absolute power in Samarqand under his government, persuaded him to reinstitute the religious law (the Sharīʻa) in Samarqand and Bukhārā, and even to give up the tax on commerce and trades (tamghā), which could not be reconciled with Islam. It was he, too, who fortified him in his fatal decision to undertake the campaign to the west from which he was never to return.

In the domestic sphere he can be seen to have shared the kind of interest in agriculture and the welfare of the peasants which we have observed earlier in the empire of the Timurids. His measures included tax provisions favouring agriculture and improvements in the irrigation system. In this connection his vizier Quṭb al-Dīn Simnānī was particularly active in organising the laying of the Jūī-yi Sulṭānī to the north of Herat. Source materials also speak of peasants' revolts, however, and it therefore needs to be clarified how far these measures in the area of agricultural policy may have been inspired only as a response to uprisings and the threat of violent action on the part of desperate peasants. As there is no lack of evidence of Abū Sa'īd's cruelty we should not simply attribute his tax reductions to motives of generosity and sympathy.

THE LINE OF ABŪ SA'ĪD IN TRANSOXIANA

With the passing of Abū Sa'īd the Timurid empire entered a new phase of disintegration. In the territory which Shāh Rukh had at least nominally ruled as one whole, three independent empires now emerged: in Persia, Transcaucasia and eastern Anatolia a Türkmen empire with its capital at Tabrīz, in which, however, it was no longer princes of the Qarā Quyūnlū who ruled, but the Āq Quyūnlū Uzun Ḥasan, until 882/1478, and later his son Ya'qūb (883–96/1478–90) and his successors; in western Turkestan, Timurid Transoxiana with its capital at Samarqand, in which Khwāja Aḥrār (d. 895/1490) was the dominant figure until his death, but where sovereignty passed to the sons of Abū Sa'īd, beginning with Sulṭān Aḥmad (b. 855/1451, ruled 873-899/1469–94); and finally Cisoxiana, i.e. the territory to the west and south-west of the Oxus together with Khurāsān and the greater part of present-day Afghanistan, where the great-grandson of 'Umar Shaikh, Sulṭān Ḥusain Bāīqarā (873–911/ 1469–1506), came to power. The latter ruled in Herat, with whose attractions Samarqand had not been able to compete since the days of Shāh Rukh, so that even Abū Sa'īd had transferred his seat of government there after finally managing to conquer the city in 863/1459.

While Uzun Ḥasan was engaged in raising his empire to a position where it commended itself even to Western powers as an ally against the Ottomans, things were going steadily from bad to worse with the two Timurid principalities. They were plagued with the age-old Turkish rivalry between princes, who operated in the cities and provinces entrusted to them as governors with an independence that grew in proportion to the weakness of the central power – fundamentally the inevitable result of that Turkish concept of the state referred to earlier, whereby the country did not belong to the ruler, let alone the people, but jointly to all the members of the ruling family.

The disintegration of power in Transoxiana was particularly drastic. Here, as previously, danger threatened from two eastern neighbours, the Uzbeks, who in 1447, under Abu'l-Khair Khān, a descendant of Shaiban (or Shībān), a son of Jochi and grandson of Chingiz Khān, had advanced their area of control at the expense of the Timurids as far as the Jaxartes; and the Mughals, who lived in the Semirechye, that is to say on the Issyk Kul and the rivers Talas, Ili, Yulduz and Manas. In spite of originally friendly relations between them, Abū Sa'īd had of course been obliged to defend himself repeatedly against Uzbek intrigues. Moreover, he had succeeded in weakening the offensive power of the Mughals by promoting the division of Mughalistān between two rival Chaghatayid princes. However, it proved to be his own protégé Yūnus Khān (866–892/1462–87) who later reunified the country under his rule, thus becoming so powerful that he was able to intervene in the disputes of the Timurids of western Turkestan. In this connection it should be remembered that these princes, regardless of their respective genealogies, even if they boasted descent from Chingiz Khān himself, were, like their peoples, Turks or Turkicised. It is doubtful, even in the case of the inhabitants of Mughalistān, who called themselves Mongols and were thus designated by other ethnic groups, whether by this time they spoke the Mongol language. Yūnus Khān, whom we have mentioned, had spent long years in Persia in his youth and had there acquired a degree of cultivation thanks to which he is described as the "most educated Mongol of all time". Sulṭān Aḥmad's brother 'Umar Shaikh, who ruled as prince of Farghāna from Andijān (not to be confused with Tīmūr's son of the same name, who had similarly governed Farghāna in his day), maintained friendly relations with him. 'Umar's wife, Qutluq Nigār Khānum, the khan's sister, was the mother of his son Ẓahīr al-Dīn Muḥammad Bābur (b. 888/1483), who was thus descended on his father's side from Tīmūr and on his mother's from Chingiz Khān: he later became the founder of the dynasty and empire of the Great Mughals in India.

The fall of Abū Sa'īd had been preceded in 872–3/1468 by the death of the Shaibanid Abu'l-Khair Khān. After years of heavy fighting with the Oirats pressing forward from western Mongolia he had finally been defeated and done away with by members of his own family who had earlier defected from him and taken up their abode in Mughalistān. In the same year his son Shaikh Ḥaidar had met his death in a conflict with Yūnus Khān. Thus the Uzbek menace to the Timurids had been brought under control, but only temporarily. A grandson of Abu'l-Khair named Muḥammad Shaibānī (b. 855/1451) had managed to survive after the death of his grandfather and uncle, until he found the opportunity of re-establishing himself in a position of power in the service of Maḥmud b. Yūnus Khān. When he finally marched across the Jaxartes into western Turkestan, there arose once more an Uzbek dominion: it was to spread rapidly at the expense of the Timurids, who were prevented from taking effective counter-measures by incessant family strife, and was to provide the basis for a powerful empire that endured for a century and played a significant rôle in the history not only of Central Asia but also of Iran.

Muḥammad Shaibānī's objective was of course Samarqand. At the same time, he had a Timurid competitor in Prince Bābur, of whom mention has just been made and who had succeeded his father in Andijān in 899/1494, when the latter was killed in an accident. His uncle Sulṭān Aḥmad promptly marched against him to take possession of Farghāna, since 'Umar Shaikh had withdrawn from his obedience under the protection of his Mughal allies and had even made attacks on territories belonging to Samarqand; but Bābur was saved by Sulṭān Aḥmad's sudden death in the course of his advance. Since his brother Maḥmūd, who succeeded him, died in the following year and none of the sons of Sulṭān Aḥmad was able to hold his own, Bābur occupied Samarqand in 903/1497, but then had to yield it up on account of a conspiracy in Andijān. The partition of Farghāna which he arranged with his brother Jahāngīr (who enjoyed the support of the Mughals) provided him with a free hand for a new move against Samarqand in competition with Muḥammad Shaibānī, in which he was, however, defeated. In 905/1500 the Uzbeks conquered Samarqand, and in the course of the fighting the ruling Timurid Sulṭān 'Alī lost his life. But shortly afterwards Bābur succeeded in taking the city by means of a *coup de main*. In Ramaḍān 906/April–May 1501, however, he was defeated at the battle of Sar-i Pul by the Uzbeks, following which he had to abandon Samarqand to them again. They were now able to establish a firm hold on Transoxiana, while he himself, losing even his homeland of Farghāna, which Jahāngīr now claimed for himself alone, set off on his celebrated wanderings and was not able to gain a foothold until 910/1504, in Kābul. Here, two years later, a plea for help reached him from Ḥusain Bāīqarā of Herat, who was now also being hard pressed by the Uzbeks.

ḤUSAIN BĀĪQARĀ

We must now trace out the beginnings of the Timurid empire of Herat, which had arisen shortly after the death of Abū Sa'īd. That state also had to struggle against heavy odds but, in contrast to the Timurid empire in Transoxiana, it was distinguished by great achievements in the sphere of intellectual and material progress, a continuation for more than three decades of the great age which had begun under Shāh Rukh and which had given the state of Herat that characteristic stamp that now reached its ultimate development under the rule of the Timurid Ḥusain Bāīqarā.

Sulṭān Ḥusain b. Manṣūr b. Bāīqarā, to give him his full name, had lost his father when he was only seven or eight years of age, and in 856/1452 had entered the service of Abu'l-Qāsim Bābur, interrupted for a brief time only after the latter's unsuccessful campaign against Samarqand. After the death of his master he led the irregular life of a wandering mercenary captain, the kind of man frequently found over the years among the auxiliary troops of various Timurids engaged in their struggles for power, until he eventually began to wage war on his own account, for a long time indeed without lasting success. To begin with, his interests lay in Māzandarān, then particularly in Khwārazm, whence he repeatedly set out on invasions or pillaging expeditions into Khurāsān. These won him the enmity of Abū Sa'īd, against whom he sought assistance from the Uzbek khan Abu'l-Khair. However, his overtures were brought to nothing by the latter's death, to which we have referred.

With the news of Abū Sa'īd's fall, a situation had therefore arisen in which Ḥusain Bāīqarā was no longer dependent on Uzbek aid. Seeing his opportunity, he forthwith exploited it. On 25 Sha'bān 873/10 March 1469 the news reached Herat of the events in the Mūghān steppes; on 2 Ramaḍān/16 March Sulṭān Maḥmūd, a son of the executed prince, arrived in the city with the remnants of his father's army, but had to quit it again shortly afterwards; and only a week later the official prayers were proclaimed in the name of Ḥusain Bāīqarā, who had meanwhile made his entry into the city. Although Sulṭān Aḥmad was already approaching Herat with a powerful force from Samarqand, he broke off his campaign to Khurāsān after meeting up with his brother Maḥmūd en route.

Nevertheless, Ḥusain Bāīqarā's succession did not remain undisputed. Uzun Ḥasan did not fail to exploit his victory over Abū

Sa'īd. He transferred his capital from Diyārbakr to Tabrīz, and not only occupied 'Irāq-i 'Ajam, Fārs and Kirmān but also declared Yādgār Muḥammad, the prince who had put Abū Sa'īd to death, as the only legitimate heir to the throne, sending him off with the Timurid soldiery who were in his company at the time to Khurāsān. A victory which Ḥusain Bāīqarā scored over him at Chinārān on 8 Rabī' I 874/15 September 1469 proved indecisive, because Uzun Ḥasan promptly sent reinforcements to the aid of his protégé. It was plainly his intention to extend his influence, if not his sovereignty, over Khurāsān. Thus he demanded from Ḥusain Bāīqarā, in vain as it turned out, the handing over of various Qarā Quyūnlū amīrs who had fled to Herat while he was occupying Kirmān. When Uzun Ḥasan's sons Zainal and Khalīl were brought in to support Yādgār Muḥammad, Ḥusain Bāīqarā found himself in a critical situation. So many of his troops deserted to the enemy that he even had to abandon Herat, where his rival made his entry on 9 Muḥarram 875/8 July 1470. The latter, in fact, could not rely on his troops either, especially the contingents of the Āq Quyūnlū, so that Ḥusain Bāīqarā, having assembled fresh forces and having met the three sons of Abū Sa'īd in a victorious engagement, reoccupied his capital six weeks later. Yādgār Muḥammad, who fell into his hands, was executed, and with him the last descendant of Shāh Rukh left the political stage. Since the line of Jahāngīr had ceased to play a political rôle only a few years after the death of Tīmūr, the activity of Tīmūr's heirs was now restricted to descendants of his two sons Mīrān Shāh and 'Umar Shaikh – that is to say, respectively the scions of Abū Sa'īd in Transoxiana, of whom only Bābur had a significant future, and Ḥusain Bāīqarā and his family in Khurāsān.

With the death of Yādgār Muḥammad the designs of Uzun Ḥasan on Khurāsān likewise came to an end. There were no further attempts to extend his territorial power over eastern Persia. And Ḥusain Bāīqarā, too, refrained from any move against his western neighbour. His frontier with the empire of the Āq Quyūnlū followed from the coast of the Caspian Sea a line west of Astarābād running in a southerly direction, then ran along the edge of the Dasht-i Lūt, finally reaching Lake Hāmūn. Both parties were intent on good-neighbourly relations, which were not affected by occasional frontier incidents.

Though he had achieved signal distinction through his courage and enterprise before his accession to the throne, Ḥusain Bāīqarā seems henceforth to have yielded to no further desire for military enterprises of any scope. Thus he substantially respected the Oxus frontier, though the incessant conflicts of his cousins beyond the river and their military weakness in fact represented a constant invitation to intervene. This is all the more remarkable since from his own experience and acquaintance with the personalities of the situation he knew only too well what dangers were lurking in the background; that is to say, how strongly the peoples who lived on the Jaxartes, particularly the Uzbeks, were pressing towards the west and developing into an immediate threat to him personally with every success they scored in western Turkestan. Before he found himself in direct confrontation with the Uzbeks at the end of his life, only incidents of a more or less limited significance took place on the Oxus frontier, with one exception: the campaigns carried out by Khurāsān forces against the Timurid Sulṭān Maḥmūd ruling in Ḥiṣār.

These in fact fruitless operations were connected with the conflicts which Ḥusain Bāīqarā had to fight out against his sons, especially in the second half of his reign. Fundamentally, the cause yet again was always the question of the authority enjoyed by the Timurid princes who ruled in the most important cities; a perpetual temptation to challenge the central power as soon as differences of opinion with the ruler arose. As early as 1490 Darvīsh ʻAlī, a brother of ʻAlī Shīr (see below), had – as guardian of Prince Ibrāhīm Ḥusain, a son of Ḥusain Bāīqarā who had his residence in Balkh – intrigued with Ḥiṣār, which apparently led to a campaign against the city. Years later, in the course of a further campaign, Ḥusain Bāīqarā's eldest son Badīʻ al-Zamān was transferred from his governorship in Astarābād to Balkh and rose in rebellion when his son Muḥammad Mu'min, whom he had left behind in Astarābād, was passed over for appointment as governor there. Badīʻ al-Zamān was defeated in battle, and chance decreed that his son, who had also risen in rebellion and had consequently been imprisoned in Herat, was executed at about the same time, though this had no connection with his father's defeat. A reconciliation was brought about, but this revolt was not the last, and in 1499 the prince even besieged Herat. Other sons, too, rose against the ageing ruler. As a result, there were frequent occasions for military operations but no upheavals, apparently, serious enough to endanger the state.

We have detailed knowledge of the Turkish and Persian figures of eminence in the empire on whom Ḥusain Bāīqarā depended in the business of government, even down to the details of court intrigues. Among these figures, one personality stands out, a man of distinction in both political and intellectual history. This is ʻAlī Shīr Navā'ī

(b. 844/1441), who had been closely connected with Ḥusain Bāīqarā even in his youth. He was a Turk born in Herat who had been present at Sulṭān Aḥmad's headquarters in 873/1469 and arrived in the capital only a few weeks after Ḥusain's accession to the throne. He was appointed keeper of the great seal, and in 876/1472 member (*dīvān begī*) of the great state council (*dīvān-i buzurg-i amārat*). The influence he exerted was so powerful that he is referred to as second only to the prince. In the course of time relations between ruler and adviser did indeed become strained, and this state of affairs took some years to pass, with 'Alī Shīr Navā'ī in 892/1487 going to Astarābād as governor for fifteen months. The high esteem in which he was held, which incidentally is not to be dissociated from his achievements in the cultural sphere, was strikingly evident in the ceremonies of mourning ordered by the prince on the occasion of his death in 906/1501.

The year 1501 ushered in a new era for both Central Asia and the Middle East involving the fall of the Timurids and the rise of new powers. It saw the consolidation of Uzbek power, as has been mentioned above, resulting from Muḥammad Shaibānī's final conquest of Samarqand, and the accession of Shah Ismā'īl I, with which the Safavid empire began. Ḥusain Bāīqarā, who had moved further and further away from the military prowess of his youth in the three decades of his rule in Herat, was prevented by advanced age and protracted illness from taking energetic decisions. As may be seen from his correspondence, he was at pains to avoid conflict with Shah Ismā'īl. For a long time – far too long, in fact – he closed his eyes to the immediate threat of a massive attack on the part of the Uzbeks, whose successes in Transoxiana could of course have been no secret to him, and trusted in his fortresses which barred the way to Khurāsān. Even Bābur's attempt to spur him to action against the common enemy was unable to prevail against this view. So it came about that the Uzbeks were able to cross the Oxus, conquering Khwārazm and carrying out pillaging expeditions against Khurāsān.

Ḥusain Bāīqarā did not live to see the collapse of his empire. He died on 11 Dhu'l-Ḥijja 911/4 May 1506, having finally marched against the Uzbeks. It was just at this very time that Bābur was making preparations to answer the appeal for help that he had received from Herat by advancing from Kābul with his troops. Though he received the news of Ḥusain Bāīqarā's death en route, he continued his march until, after four months, he reached his objective. In his memoirs he records of Badī' al-Zamān and Muẓaffar Ḥusain, two sons of the dead prince who were at odds over the succession, that they were no doubt experienced in matters of court ceremonial but not in the rules of warfare. Judging the military situation to be hopeless, he retreated without waiting to clash with Muḥammad Shaibānī. In the very next year he received news of the Uzbeks' entry into Herat and the flight of Ḥusain Bāīqarā's sons. Muẓaffar Ḥusain did not long survive the disaster; his brother found refuge first at the court of Shah Ismā'īl and afterwards in Istanbul, where he died in 923/1517.

It stands to the credit of Ḥusain Bāīqarā that in the thirty-seven years of his rule in Herat he gave the Timurid empire, in spite of everything, fairly peaceful conditions, albeit within a severely reduced area. Bābur speaks of his reign as a wonderful period, in which many significant men lived in Khurāsān. The able warrior he is described as being in the first half of his life was not only a famous sabre-fighter who plunged fearlessly into hand-to-hand fighting in battle, but also a cultivated man, actively interested in the intellectual and artistic life of his time, and a renowned patron of the arts. He himself wrote Turkish and Persian poetry under the pseudonym of Ḥusainī. It should, however, be said that his Turkish dīvān, which has come down to us, contains only poems of average merit. He also left behind a brief treatise in which his opinions and ideals are set out. He does not appear to have been strongly committed in a religious sense. He was entitled to plead the rheumatism he suffered from for years as an excuse for neglecting the prescribed prayers; but this and similar excuses cannot account for offences against the laws of fasting or for other derelictions from the religious law which appealed to him, such as daily indulgence in wine, pigeon-flying, ram-fighting and cock-fighting. His lack of political acumen and his all but apathetic absence of resolution in dealing with the Uzbeks – among the main contributory factors in the fall of the Timurid empire – may have been signs of senility, for he was generally credited with an alert mind which found expression not only in rapid utterance but also, at the beginning of his career, in swift decision.

THE EARLY CAREER OF BĀBUR

The Uzbek conquest of Khurāsān need not in itself have signified the end of the Timurids in Central and Western Asia, for Ẓahīr al-Dīn Bābur was still ruling in Kābul. Indeed, the idea of a Timurid restoration in these territories remained alive in him, and he was to be presented with the necessary opportunity a few years later, on the fall of Muḥammad Shaibānī. Although an incursion into India in 910/1505 shows a new direction of his ambitions, the march on Herat which he carried out at Ḥusain Bāīqarā's request reveals his sense of involvement in the Timurid heartlands and his hatred for the Uzbeks who had expelled him from them. In the fresh circumstances he was once again threatened in Kābul by the same enemy, and from two directions: in the north from Qunduz and the province of Badakhshān, and in the south-west from Qandahār. To begin with, he had to witness his younger brother Nāṣir Mīrzā falling back before the Uzbeks in Badakhshān. And when Muḥammad Shaibānī also laid siege to Qandahār, Bābur does seem temporarily to have given his cause up for lost. At all events he took care to evacuate his men from Kābul in order to march on India. Only because he was prevented from making a rapid advance by ambushes mounted by Afghan tribes did he learn en route that due to difficulties in the hinterland the Uzbeks had raised the siege of Qandahār after offering easy conditions to the besieged troops. At once he returned to Kābul.

Here he received news, some time later, of Shah Ismā'īl's victorious campaign against Khurāsān, the battle of Marv, in which Muḥammad Shaibānī had been killed on 1 Ramaḍān 916/2 December 1510, and the entry of Ismā'īl into Herat. In spite of the winter conditions he at once set off for Transoxiana. In Qunduz, where he was held up by Uzbek resistance, he was joined by his sister Khānzāda Begum, whom he had agreed to marry off to Muḥammad Shaibānī when he had been forced to give up Samarqand. She had fallen into the hands of the Persians at Marv and had now been sent to him by the shah. To this gesture of amity he responded by sending Prince Mīrzā Khān on a mission with presents and felicitations. The shah confirmed the ambassador in the governorship of Badakhshān and gave an assurance that Bābur should retain all the territories in Transoxiana he could take from the Uzbeks – on condition, however, that he converted to the Shī'a. Bābur accepted, although of course this implied recognising the sovereignty of the Safavids. On his advance through Transoxiana he took Ḥiṣār and Bukhārā. In Rajab 917/October 1511 he occupied Samarqand – for the third time – but was compelled to evacuate the city again in the following Ṣafar/May after a reverse in battle with the Uzbeks. Meanwhile, the initial jubilation at his return had subsided, and indeed had turned to disaffection and hatred, because the Sunnī population could not come to terms with the Shī'a. Though nothing more than mere verbal assent was involved for Bābur, the official prayers did include the name of Shah Ismā'īl, whose brutal treatment of eminent Sunnīs in Herat was common talk; and also the Shī'ī confession of faith. The same objections no doubt applied to the inscriptions on the coinage. Shortly afterwards, with the arrival of Persian auxiliaries under Ismā'īl's viceroy (*vakīl*) Yār Aḥmad Khūzānī, known as Najm-i s̲ānī,[1] Bābur realised that his position had become untenable. It was not merely that he was to be subjected to the military authority of the Persian general; the latter inspired terror and revulsion in the people as a whole for having, against Bābur's advice, slaughtered the entire population of the city of Qarshī which he had conquered. Thus at the battle of Ghujduvān on 3 Ramaḍān 918/12 November 1512, Bābur held back. The Uzbeks were victorious and the Safavid general was killed; while Bābur withdrew in all haste.

He remained in fact in Badakhshān for some considerable time after this before admitting to himself that there was no future for him in Transoxiana and Khurāsān. After 920/1514, the year of his return to Kābul, he turned his whole attention to India and undertook several campaigns in that direction, until on 8 Rajab 932/20 April 1526 he won a decisive victory against Ibrāhīm Lōdī, the sultan of Delhi, at the battle of Pānīpat. This was the moment at which the Mughal empire was born, a Timurid state founded on Indian soil, which endured until the 13th/19th century. And though parts of Afghanistan, and Kābul, which was not lost until it was conquered by Nādir Shāh in 1738, belonged to this empire, the fact is that its centre of gravity lay in India. This state of affairs was not altered by occasional later thrusts towards Khurāsān and Transoxiana, which led at best to ephemeral successes. In Central and Western Asia the Timurids had ceased to play a vital part on the political scene in 913/1507, with the Uzbek victory over the sons of Ḥusain Bāīqarā, and at the latest with the return of Bābur to Kābul in 920/1514.

THE POLITICAL TRADITIONS OF THE TIMURID EMPIRE

What, then, are the characteristic features of this Timurid period? The state which Tīmūr had left to his successors was made up, according to Barthold,[2] from components derived from the Turco-Mongolian military system, and ample trimmings of Islamic culture,

[1] On whom see Braun, *Aḥvāl-e Šāh Ismā'īl*, pp. 81ff., and Aubin, "Études Safavides I", pp. 68ff.
[2] *Ulugh Beg*, pp. 8ff.

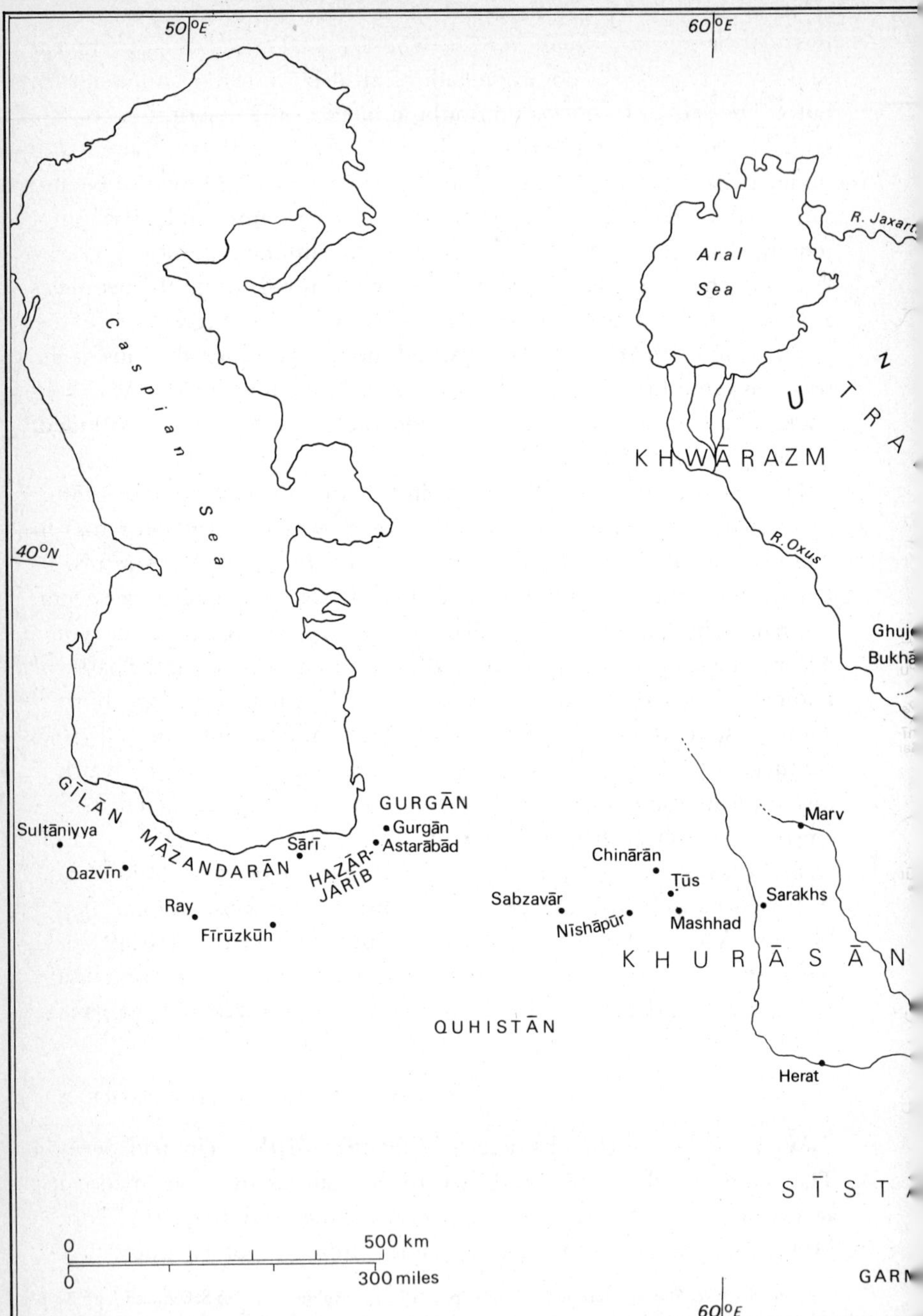

Map. Eastern Iran and Central Asia in the later Timurid era

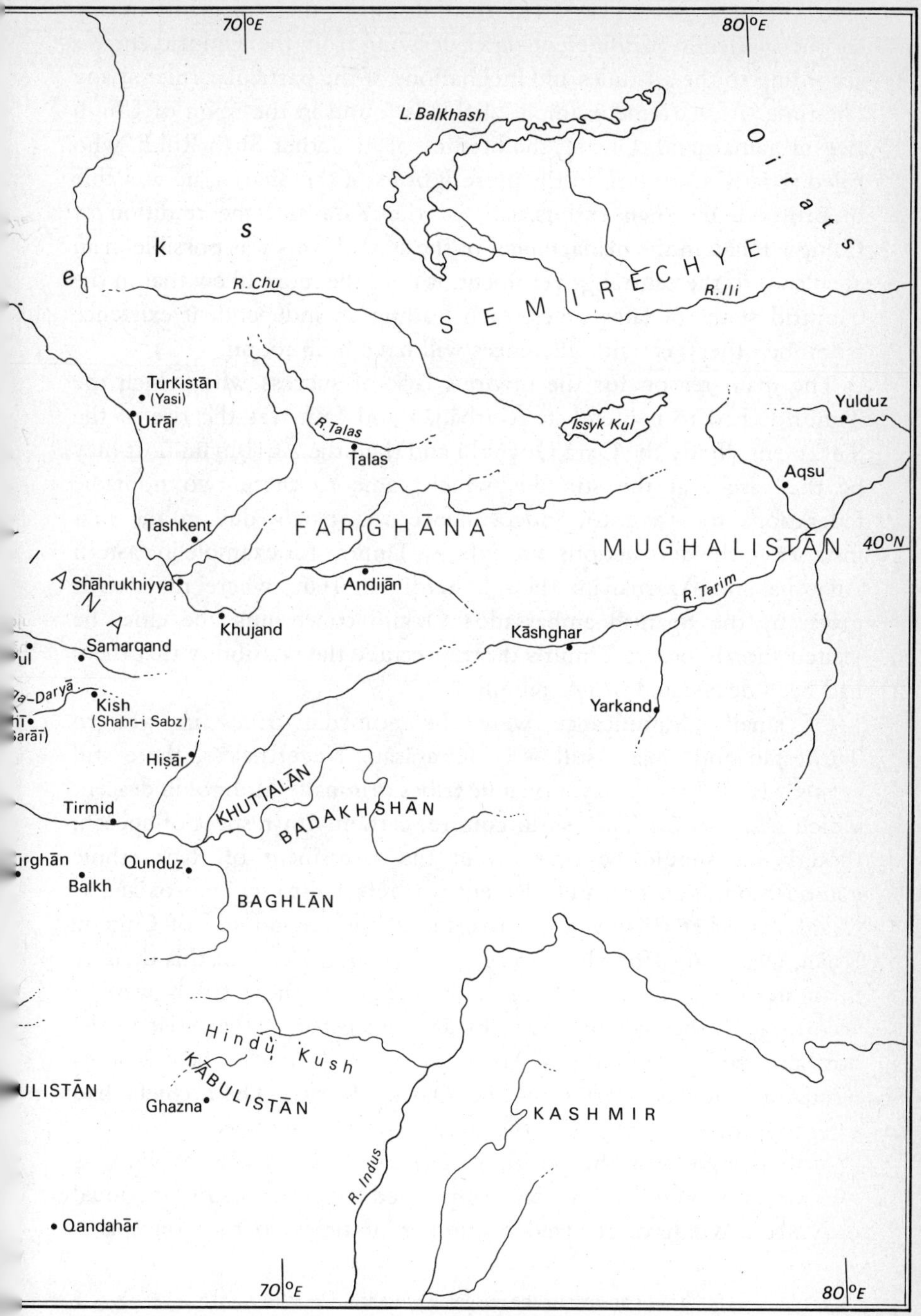
70°E
80°E
L. Balkhash
Oirats
SEMIRECHYE
R. Chu
R. Ili
Issyk Kul
Turkistān
(Yasi)
Utrār
R. Talas
Talas
Yulduz
Aqsu
Tashkent
FARGHĀNA
MUGHALISTĀN
40°N
Shāhrukhiyya
Andijān
R. Tarim
Khujand
Kāshghar
Samarqand
Kish
(Shahr-i Sabz)
Yarkand
Ḥiṣār
Tirmid
KHUTTALĀN
BADAKHSHĀN
Qunduz
Balkh
BAGHLĀN
Hindu Kush
KĀBULISTĀN
Ghazna
KASHMIR
R. Indus
Qandahār
70°E
80°E

generally of a Persian cast. The relationship of these elements to one another varied in the different states deriving from the Timurid empire according to the attitudes and inclinations of the particular ruler at any one time. An extreme example of this is found in the reign of Ulugh Beg in Samarqand. During the lifetime of his father Shāh Rukh, who ruled strictly according to the prescriptions of the Sharī'a, he was able to promote his own enthusiasm for the Yasa and the tradition of Chingiz Khān in the management of the state. If this was possible in an area loyal to the central government, it is all the more likely that in the Timurid states of later times, each leading an independent existence from the others, certain differences will have been found.

The main reason for the obvious lack of success with which the Timurids had to contend in Āzarbāījān and Iran was the rise of the Türkmens, firstly the Qarā Quyūnlū and then the Āq Quyūnlū. It may be the case that the stimulus which came to these two nomadic federations to strive for independence was partly due in the first instance to the destructions wrought by Tīmūr,[1] for example in eastern Anatolia and Āzarbāījān; though hardly in Iran, where the details given by the Spanish ambassador Clavijo concerning the cities he visited shortly before Tīmūr's death preclude the possibility that these had been devastated or not rebuilt.

Of smaller significance were the nomadic tribes in western Turkestan and – less still – in Khurāsān. Nevertheless, there still existed, as in Tīmūr's day, nomadic tribes originally Mongol in descent which had become Turkish in culture, certainly in respect of speech, though we should be cautious in the assessment of their ethnic composition. This nomadic element was referred to in Transoxiana as Chaghatai, after Chaghatai (d. 639/1242), the second son of Chingiz Khān, even long after there were any surviving khans of this dynasty in western Turkestan. The most important of these tribes were – according to the account given by Ibn 'Arabshāh – the Arlāt in the northern part of present-day Afghanistan, the Jalāyir in the region of Khujand, and the Barlās on the Qashqa-Daryā. Their chiefs had extensive sovereign rights in the areas in which they lived.

Still stronger was the position of those Timurid princes who, as joint or autonomous rulers, were appointed as governors in individual provinces. We have referred a number of times to the conception

[1] This is at any rate the reasoning of Cahen, *Der Islam* I, 331.

underlying their legal position, namely that the empire was not the sole possession of the ruler but belonged to all male members of the ruling family, and have drawn attention to the fateful results which followed from this assumption. Taken together with the absence of an effective disposition for the succession, this conception led to unending disputes over the rightful inheritance and to the fragmentation and diminution of the territory as a whole. At the same time, military strength crumbled, and when powerful opponents took the offensive, disaster followed.

One of the basic features of the Timurid state was feudalism, the material foundation of the military. The prime beneficiaries were the princes and those holding high military command, including tribal chieftains. From the beginning of Shāh Rukh's reign we come across the institution known as the *suyūrghāl*, a further development of the earlier *iqṭā'*. Etymologically, as we have seen,[1] this suggests a *beneficium*, an "act of largesse" or "reward" on the ruler's part towards persons employed in his service. *De facto* it was the granting of a territory as a fief, especially a military fief, which carried the obligation to serve in the army of one's lord and at the same time to make available a fixed number of armed warriors. In return, the fiefholder was guaranteed freedom from rates and taxes in his own territory but allowed the right to raise such contributions for his own benefit from the population, who of course did not share the privilege of this freedom. Unlike the iqṭā', this immunity not only applied to the fiscal sovereignty of the central authorities but extended also to their administrative and judicial sovereignty. A typical feature of the Timurid administration was the existence of extremely large fiefs of this kind embracing whole provinces. In time, the suyūrghāl acquired a hereditary character and was not restricted to military beneficiaries, being accorded also to civilians such as the holders of religious offices and dignities.

The organisation of the Timurid governmental machinery has been only inadequately researched as yet. Although it cannot be assumed that it remained even in broad outline uniform throughout the whole period from 807/1405 to 913/1507 or even among the various states existing alongside each other, we may nevertheless reasonably infer that certain basic characteristics were common, for instance the influences exerted by the different elements in the population on the organisation of the communities, or at any rate the Turkish/Persian dichot-

[1] See above, pp. 94 and n. 1, 95 n. 2.

omy. A brief consideration of the most important authorities among the supreme imperial institutions under Ḥusain Bāīqarā gives the easiest general picture.[1] The supreme body in the Herat administration was the Great State Council (*dīvān-i buzurg-i amārat*) already mentioned. As the designation *dīvān-i amārat-i tuvājiyān* is also found, it is to be assumed that it was identical with the *tuvājī dīvānï* frequently referred to.[2] Among yet other titles for the same institution, *türk dīvānï* is especially interesting as a reflection of the responsibility for army matters: the army was of course composed mainly of Turks and Turkicised Mongols. It was a sort of general staff with additional functions corresponding to the increased importance of the forces in maintaining a state constantly threatened by external and internal enemies. Its members were amīrs (= begs) with the title *amīr-i tuvājī* or *dīvān begī*. They took precedence in rank over all other amīrs. As inspectors of troops they had a wide area of responsibility. At court or in the military headquarters this included preparing and carrying out the receptions and parades given by the ruler. The secretaries of this dīvān were called *bakhshiyān* or *navīsandagān-i turk*, never *vazīr*. Of course, there were also viziers; but they were responsible for the financial affairs that fell within the competence of another dīvān, the *dīvān-i māl*, which appears to have been identical with the *dīvān-i 'ālī* and was also called *sart dīvānï* in order to distinguish it from the *türk dīvānī*. In contrast to the "Turkish secretaries" just referred to, in the case of this dīvān only the term "Persian secretaries" was used (*navīsandagān-i tājīk*). At its head stood the *amīr-i dīvān-i māl*. The superior status of the tuvājī dīvānï is suggested by the fact that it was also called the supreme dīvān (*dīvān-i a'lā*). This interpretation of the source material, incidentally, is not upset if we adopt the explanation of the function of the Great Amīr (*ulugh beg*), who is sometimes referred to, as that of supreme head of both the dīvāns we have considered. It must be admitted, though, that the schema suggested here need not offer the only possible explanation for what is a highly complex set of facts.

ECONOMIC AND COMMERCIAL LIFE

The economic life of the Timurid age was not so darkened by the destructions carried out by Tīmūr as might be imagined. In this connection the particularism of the Timurid princes and governors even

[1] Roemer, *Staatsschreiben*, pp. 169–72; Togan, "'Ali Şîr".
[2] See J. Deny, "Osmanli ancien tovïja (dovïja)", *JA* ccxxi (1932), 160–1; *TMEN* i, 260–4.

had favourable results; for they had a strong vested interest in rebuilding the cities which were their seats of government and – in the economic sphere – of putting the political, and more especially the cultural, aspirations which most of them cherished on a sound footing.

In most comparisons made of the cruelty and destructive fury of Tīmūr with that of the Mongols, Tīmūr comes off badly. Yet it is a fact that the desolation he wrought did not have such a lasting effect as those for which they had been responsible. Whereas whole cultivated areas were destroyed and reduced to pastureland as a result of Mongol campaigns, under Tīmūr public order was at any rate to some extent soon restored after the cessation of hostilities. Where the irrigation systems vital to agriculture had deteriorated as a result of devastation or lack of attention, they were put in order without delay. It is known of a number of rulers, for instance Shāh Rukh, Ulugh Beg and Abū Sa'īd, that they paid particular attention to the irrigation system and were renowned for their construction of famous installations. The holders of fiefs and benefices also had an interest in the development of the territories whose taxes and rates were under their control. There is evidence of specific measures to encourage agriculture in many places, not only in Transoxiana and Khurāsān, but for example also in the vicinity of Iṣfahān. In some places the pre-Mongol standard was reached or even surpassed. However, there were areas in which the destructions of the Mongols could not be made good. Care for agriculture is seen as one of the characteristic features of Timurid rule. Nevertheless, arbitrary increases in the rates imposed and abuses in the taxation system on occasion caused distress and poverty among the peasantry, sometimes proving so oppressive that revolts broke out.[1]

Under the Timurids there was a commercial life which was as active as it was important, and which did not stop at the frontiers. Tabrīz, due to its peripheral situation, was indeed not able to continue to play the same part in east-west trade as it had under the Mongols. Even the trade relations with Byzantium, the Ottomans and the Mamlūks in Egypt were now necessarily based on other routes. The trade routes to the east and the north, to China and the Golden Horde, ran via Samarqand and in part also via Herat, which was in addition an important stage on the trade route via Kābul to and from India. The *ortaq* system provided a remarkable trading institution. By means of this, merchant entrepre-

[1] Arunova, "K istorii narodnykh vystupleniĭ".

neurs invested loan capital for orders and for the benefit of their financial backers, of whom quite often the ruler himself was one.

In the taxation system Mongol traditions were quite unmistakably preserved: payments in kind made by the agricultural section of the population, and trade and craft taxes (tamghā) in the towns, levied to some extent as local and transit tolls. We do in fact often hear of such levies being waived or reduced, either because of the results of natural catastrophes, epidemics or crop failures, or for religious reasons on the occasions when a pious mystic or a theologian succeeded in steering his ruler back onto the path of the religious law (Sharī'a), whose prescriptions condemned such sources of revenue. But this sort of concession was rarely permanent; with the best will in the world, the rulers could usually not manage to forgo the tamghā, the most productive of all the taxes. Even the pious Shāh Rukh went no further than giving a semblance of legality when he attempted to declare trading taxes to be alms levies (*zakāt*) – by a simple change of terminology – just in order to rescue them from the odium of illegality that attached to the tamghā.

What has been said here of the restoration of public order, the recouping of losses due to destruction at the hands of Tīmūr, and the rebuilding of cities does not by any means imply that in Central and Western Asia under the Timurids peaceful and prosperous conditions everywhere prevailed. The long reigns of Shāh Rukh, Abū Sa'īd, and Ḥusain Bāīqarā did in each case bring about a certain stabilisation of affairs in comparison with earlier times and the intervening periods. Nevertheless, in view of the incessant risings, the incursions by the Türkmens in the west and the Uzbeks and Mughals in the east, the endless succession disputes and the concomitant military measures, troop movements, requisitionings and reprisals, it is not reasonable to speak of general peace and prosperity, even though the conjunction of all these things was generally confined to a few limited areas. The sufferings of the people in the districts and cities affected were protracted and had long-lasting effects. In the first half of the 9th/15th century reports from the province of Kirmān speak of the constant insecurity to which daily life was subject.[1] Here even a town such as Bam, described by Arabian geographers as a flourishing city with an important textile industry, fell back into village conditions with a mere four or five thousand inhabitants. In Khurāsān, too, a decline in

[1] Aubin, "Deux sayyids", and "Fragments historiques concernant Bam"; for conditions in Herat, cf. Boldyrev, "Ocherki iz zhizni", which was unfortunately inaccessible to me.

population density in contrast with the Mongol period can be observed which is recognisable in the changes that took place in the territorial pattern.[1] The constituent units of Timurid territory were larger than those of the Mongols; and the reason for older administrative units having been abandoned is clearly to be sought in a considerable reduction in the size of populations. Quhistān, for instance, formerly the largest district (*vilāyat*) belonging to Herat, was now no longer a unit administratively speaking, but only geographically.

RELIGIOUS AND CULTURAL ACTIVITY

This somewhat grim background of general conditions is eminently important for an understanding of the religious situation of the Timurid period. It is undoubtedly true to say that the larger part of the population should be thought of as belonging to a Sunnī form of Islam, yet this is an inadequate description of the pattern. Even the limitation that individual areas such as Gīlān, Māzandarān, Khūzistān and eastern Quhistān, and a few cities such as Ray, Varāmīn, Qum, Kāshān, and Sabzavār in Khurāsān, were traditional centres of the Shī'a – and especially of the Twelver Shī'a – amounts to no more than a rough amplification of what is only a crude sketch. In reality, it was a far more complicated matter. The facts show that much of the Islamic world was vigorously involved in religious change. This begins at the latest with the disappearance from the scene of the 'Abbasid caliphate, the rule of the Mongols and the resulting curtailment of the influence of the theologians in the Islamic east. The most important aspects of these changes were numerous manifestations of popular piety, an increase in Islamic monasticism (*ṭāriqa, taṣavvuf*), veneration of the saints, pilgrimages, belief in miracles, veneration of 'Alī and the *ahl al-bait* generally. Such phenomena often bore a Shī'ī stamp, but this is far from justifying the conclusion that they are evidence for religious assent and adherence to the Shī'a. For some time past the term Folk Islam has been applied to this kind of phenomenon,[2] usually in reference to conditions in Asia Minor; but there is no lack of convincing evidence for an analogous development further to the east, in the dominions of the Timurids.

[1] Aubin, "Un Santon quhistānī".

[2] The concept of Folk Islam, at least in the broad sense, is probably older and is to be found as early as Babinger's Berlin inaugural lecture of 1921, published as "Der Islam in Kleinasien"; see further Mazzaoui, *Origins of the Ṣafawids*, pp. 22ff, and *passim*.

The oscillation between Sunna and Shīʿa typical of Folk Islam also exercised a powerful influence on the political potentates of the age. The traditional formula which speaks of the Shīʿī Qarā Quyūnlū and the Sunnī Āq Quyūnlū can now no longer be sustained in its former exclusive sense.[1] It is undoubtedly truer to say that the princes of the two federations were hardly concerned about a religious issue but far more about political ones when they sought to achieve assent and more effective support among the population by favouring one side or the other. Similar motives of expediency – in addition to personal preferences, no doubt – may explain something of Abū Saʿīd's adherence to the Naqshbandiyya, the order of Khwāja Aḥrār, who was omnipotent in Samarqand and indubitably persecuted Sunnī attempts at a restoration of the Sharīʿa; or again, it would seem, when Ḥusain Bāīqarā, who after his succession to the throne in Herat had taken the first steps to introduce the Shīʿa, then abandoned the project at the instigation of ʿAlī Shīr; not to mention Ẓahīr al-Dīn Bābur's conversion to the Shīʿa on his third conquest of Samarqand, when his only concern was to secure the support of Shah Ismāʿīl for his plans.

All in all there developed in the atmosphere of Folk Islam favourable preconditions for heterodox tendencies and hence also for the Shīʿa, either because it formed a bridge to the popular variant of Shīʿa and thus advanced the Imāmiyya, or because it prepared the ground for extremist sects, which in the course of the 9th/15th century attracted many new adherents and had far-reaching effects.[2] The underground political-cum-religious activities of the time are vividly projected for a moment on 22 Rabīʿ II 830/21 February 1427 by an attempt on the life of Shāh Rukh, when an adherent of the Ḥurūfiyya attempted to stab him as he was leaving the Friday prayers.[3] This was by no means the first outbreak of heretical violence. It had been preceded by religiously inspired risings, immediately after the death of Tīmūr, in Sabzavār, where Shāh Rukh had only been able to exert his authority with difficulty, and a year later in Māzandarān, where an attempt was made to re-establish the amirate of the Shīʿī Marʿashī Sayyid. One rising

[1] "Le problème n'était pas pour les Qara Qoyunlu ou les Aq Qoyunlu de se montrer hostiles ou favorables au chiisme, mais d'adopter une politique qui leur garantît un large support parmi leurs sujets": Aubin, "Notes sur quelques documents Aq Qoyunlu", p. 132.

[2] Molé, "Les Kubrawiya"; Miklukho-Maklaĭ, "Shiizm".

[3] Most recently treated by Savory, "A 15th Century Ṣafavid Propagandist"; on the Ḥurūfiyya, see Bausani, "Ḥurūfiyya"; Ritter, "Die Anfänge der Ḥurūfīsekte"; Gölpınarlı, "Fadlallâh-i Hurûfi'nin oğluna".

which was successful, at least against the Timurid governor of Fārs and Khūzistān, was that of Sayyid Muḥammad b. Falāḥ (845/1441–2), who claimed to be the Mahdī and who made the city of Ḥavīza the official seat of an extremist provincial dynasty, the Musha'sha', which even outlasted the Timurids.[1] It must also be assumed that the revolt of Muḥammad b. Bāīsunqur in 849/1446 had a religious background. This would also explain the severity of Shāh Rukh, unusual for him in his dealings with Islamic aristocrats and scholars (*sādāt* and *'ulamā'*), when in Ramaḍān 850/December 1446 in Sāva his verdicts on the adherents of the rebellious prince – to the horror of many contemporaries – did not spare this category of persons the penalty of execution. In fact he thus dealt a severe blow to the Shī'a, which was spreading rapidly in Fārs, as elsewhere, from which it could not easily recover. This action of his is intimately connected with his religious attitudes and the rôle as restorer of orthodoxy and protector of the Sunnī theologians which he had assumed.

Even though it is difficult, and in many cases impossible, to classify individuals or indeed even particular orders as to their religious attitude – Sunna or Shī'a – this does not mean that all the distinctions were simply blurred. Orthodox theology existed under the Timurids as it had before. It had indeed passed its ultimate climax with 'Ażud al-Dīn al-Ījī (d. 756/1355), who had gathered its doctrines together in a new form in his *Mawāqif* – and in a challenging fashion.[2] His ideas were, moreover, still widespread among the theologians of the 9th/15th century. But they had long since ceased to be productive and had petrified into merely scholastic forms. With a few exceptions – one of them the *Sulūk al-mulūk* of Fażl-Allāh b. Rūzbihān al-Khunjī, written in the *Fürstenspiegel* tradition – the theological writings of the period have nothing to offer but commentaries and super-commentaries in devastating quantity, and glosses and manuals which in their use of abbreviations are barely comprehensible to the modern reader.

To be brief, the representatives of the Sunna were in no position to have their own way in the conflict with the rising tide of Shī'ī or heretical movements. The decisive blow was struck, as far as large areas of the Timurid territory were concerned, when one of these movements, that of the Safavids, succeeded in Persia in forcing through its religious ideas against the Sunna by the use of the military

[1] Minorsky, "Musha'sha'"; Caskel, "Ein Mahdī des 15. Jahrhunderts", and "Die Wālī's von Ḥuvēzeh".

[2] See above, pp. 63–4 and n. 1.

might which it had acquired through the support of fanatical adherents. However, it was unsuccessful against the mortal enemies of the Timurids, the Uzbeks, who now became the protective power of orthodoxy in the eastern Islamic world. The results of these events were, however, only clearly perceptible after the fall of the Timurid states of Central and Western Asia.

The intellectual life of the Timurid age may be traced through the ample evidence which has come down to us, the most noteworthy source being Daulatshāh of Samarqand. If their best historians do not quite approach the leading figures of Mongol historiography, they did leave behind works of a highly respectable quality. Their most important writers include such names as Ḥāfiẓ-i Abrū (d. 833/1430), ʿAbd al-Razzāq Samarqandī (d. 887/1482) and Mīr Khwānd (d. 903/1498). The lastnamed chronicler not only soon aroused the interest of historically minded groups in the Ottoman empire, but later intensively occupied Western historians, as can be seen by the numerous translations of his work, especially in the last century. Ḥāfiẓ-i Abrū offers in his works interesting evidence of the historical method and the historical interests of the age. His *Majmūʿa* embraces twelve works, of which a majority are based on earlier authors and the rest are his own work. His *Majmaʿ al-tavārīkh* with its four parts is a universal history, the fourth section of which, separately entitled *Zubdat al-tavārīkh-i Bāīsunqurī*, contains the history of Shāh Rukh up to 830/1427. ʿAbd al-Razzāq's work, entitled *Maṭlaʿ al-saʿdain*, is also in the nature of a universal history. Its treatment of the Timurid period is based primarily on Ḥāfiẓ-i Abrū and is a valuable source in itself for the events which its author experienced in person. Since the Timurid historical writings were mainly, if not exclusively, commissioned by princes intent on transmitting their own renown or that of their dynasties to posterity, we have of course to be prepared for much rose-coloured presentation of the facts. Furthermore, the lives and sufferings of the common people usually disappear in the aura of court history. In the area of religious and social history certain works of popular literature, especially hagiographical writings – which for some time now have been evaluated with remarkable results – are therefore of very considerable importance. Aspects of constitutional history and the history of finance are being illuminated by documents which to date indeed are only seldom available in their original form but frequently are to be found in the copies which figured in a literary genre highly appreciated at that time, the works called *Inshāʾ*. Analysis of these, too, has now been taken in hand.

While historical writing in the Timurid period, and also, it seems, the astronomical and mathematical work mentioned in connection with Ulugh Beg, was written in Persian, in the sphere of literature there figures also Chaghatai, an eastern Turkish language of which no literary monuments are preserved from the time before Tīmūr's reign. Its first known representative is Sakkākī, a poet from Transoxiana who died in the first half of the 9th/15th century. He may have been writing as early as the lifetime of Tīmūr, but at all events he is mentioned as court poet to Khalīl Sulṭān and Ulugh Beg. Outstanding among his successors is Luṭfī, the author of a dīvān and a verse narrative (*maṣnavī*) entitled *Gul u Naubahār*. His home was Herat, where he died in 1462 or 1463 at the age of ninety-nine. Turkish poetry was written by Timurid princes such as Khalīl Sulṭān, Abā Bakr Mīrzā and Abu'l-Qāsim Bābur. Chaghatai literature reached its peak under Ḥusain Bāīqarā, who personally contributed a dīvān and a *risāla*.[1] While his works lack the touch of real distinction, this is found in the numerous compositions of his famous minister and friend Mīr 'Alī Shīr Navā'ī, who not only finally raised Chaghatai to the level of a literary language but, in one of his works entitled *Muḥākamat al-lughatain* ("Arbitration on the Two Languages", i.e. Persian and Turkish), accorded Chaghatai the primacy for its greater expressiveness. The first history of Chaghatai literature, the *Majālis al-nafā'is*, came from his pen.[2] Among the other prose writings Ẓahīr al-Dīn Bābur's memoirs of the period 899–936/1494–1529, entitled *Vaqā'i'-i Bāburī* or more usually *Bābur-nāma*, occupy an eminent place from a biographical, a historical and a geographical point of view. There is no reason to conclude from Navā'ī's "Arbitration" that there existed any antagonism between the use of Turkish or Persian, if only because the authors of Turkish works usually had in addition Persian writings to their credit. Chaghatai poetry also has many if not most forms in common with Persian – and the same ones, moreover, as had been favoured by Persian poets as early as the 8th/14th century. Even the subject matter corresponds, except that Turkish poets show a somewhat stronger preference for subjects derived from popular literature. Evidence for the good relationship between Chaghatai and Persian literature is provided by Navā'ī himself with his Turkish translations of Jāmī's *Nafaḥāt al-uns* and 'Aṭṭār's *Mantiq al-ṭair*.

[1] Gandjeï, "Ḥusayn Mīrzā", and "Uno scritto apologetico".

[2] But although he held Persian to be of lesser value, this did not prevent him from using that language also: cf. Gandjeï, "Il canzoniere persiano".

The brilliant period of Persian literature before Tīmūr's invasion is not repeated after his death. One does come across Timurids who wrote in Persian, esteemed Persian poetry, and as patrons also reinvigorated court poetry. Favourable external circumstances of this kind increased the number of poets but not the intellectual and aesthetic worth of their production. The originality and richness of thought of the previous century declined, and adherence to poetic convention and heavy stress on formal elements took their place. As Indian style extended its influence, classicising rigidity was further encouraged. Such negative elements are a burdensome legacy even for considerable talents.

The increased tendency to turn for guidance to the religious orders, due to the troubles of the time, is matched by an increase in mystical poetry. Typical exponents are such saints as Shāh Ni'mat-Allāh Valī (d. 834/1431), the author of numerous works, some in Arabic and some in Persian, which display pantheistic emphases, and the poetically far more gifted Qāsim al-Anvār (d. 837/1433–4). The latter was born in Āzarbāījān, lived for a time in Herat, and was suspected of being involved in a heretical conspiracy in connection with the attempt on Shāh Rukh's life, but finally found asylum with Ulugh Beg in Samarqand. But in addition to this religiously orientated poetry, there are represented also love lyrics and romantic and heroic epics. The lyric poetry quite often shows the same weave of mystical and pseudo-mystical elements as is frequently found in the work of Ḥāfiẓ. This is particularly true of the writings of Kamāl al-Dīn Binā'ī (executed in 918/1512). In the romantic epic Kātibī of Nīshāpūr (d. between 1434 and 1436) earned a high reputation, while 'Abd-Allāh Hātifī (d. 927/1520), a nephew of Jāmī, is worthy of mention for his *Tīmūr-nāma*, a heroic epic in praise of Tīmūr.

These few examples would adequately characterise Persian poetry were it not for the fact that the century produced one other remarkable figure, Maulānā Nūr al-Dīn 'Abd al-Raḥmān Jāmī (b. 817/1414, d. 898/1492), who was outstanding not only as a poet and mystic but also as a scholar in various disciplines and as a powerful personality. True to his training under Sa'd al-Dīn Muḥammad Kāshgharī, the pupil and follower of the founder of the order, Bahā' al-Dīn Naqshband, he remained loyal throughout his life to the Sufism observed by the Sunna, in spite of the pantheistic ideas found in his works. He was a friend of 'Alī Shīr Navā'ī and Khwāja Aḥrār and had good connections with the court of Herat. He dedicated various of his works to Ḥusain Bāīqarā and Sulṭān Ya'qūb Āq Quyūnlū, the prince of Tabrīz. Yet he was never tempted into the conventional flattering panegyrics of his day. Nor did he take up an invitation to move to the Ottoman court, though he did not disdain travel, as is shown by his pilgrimages to Mashhad and Mecca and quite lengthy stays en route in Baghdad, Damascus and Tabrīz. As a scholar, Jāmī dealt with questions of theology, prosody, and Arabic grammar. In his poetry, an œuvre of unusual scope, almost all the traditional genres are represented. He left three dīvāns, and in seven long poems (mas̱navīs) under the general title *Haft aurang* he took up again the main themes of Persian poetry. As the mature expression of Persian thought, his works have commanded high regard and found numerous translators in Europe.

There is an apparent contradiction to be seen between the fair consolidation of outward conditions in the Timurid dominions, on the one hand, especially under the long reigns of Shāh Rukh, Abū Sa'īd and Ḥusain Bāīqarā, and the insecurity, distress and oppression, on the other, which obtained at particular stages and in many areas for the population of the plains and the provincial towns. This contradiction, however, is exceeded by the remarkable imbalance between the general social and economic conditions and the brilliance of some of the larger cities, especially the royal cities such as Samarqand, Shīrāz and Herat. The great pattern and standard the Timurids imitated was Tīmūr, who had applied his best efforts to making Samarqand the radiant metropolis of the Islamic world. We know that he deported master builders and artisans, artists and scholars for this purpose to Samarqand from the cities he conquered, in order to use their skills to enhance the beauty and renown of his capital. We find the same habit in his successors, if not to the same extent. We know, at any rate, the names of certain artists, poets and scholars who at the whim of the particular conqueror had to shift their sphere of operations away from various cities when these were occupied, to where the prince resided. Of course it should not be assumed that coercion was always used, since clearly the patronage of many princes had a powerful attraction for those involved in cultural life.

The most obvious expression of all this was to be found in the buildings of the Timurid empire, of which many are preserved and others are at least known from the descriptions of contemporary writers, of whom some were travellers from Europe. They bear testimony to a great flourishing of Islamic architecture at this time, which largely accounts for the phrase "Timurid renaissance" coming into vogue in Europe. One of the characteristic features was an adherence to existing architectural traditions, expecially – but not exclusively – Iranian traditions; another is a striking eclecticism. Both are seen by scholars as symptomatic of that coming together of professional artists, especially from central and southern Persia, which we mentioned above. And it was precisely this that preserved architecture from slipping away into provincialism. We cannot reject the suggestion that the personal taste of the clients also gave a new impulse to artistic creativity. This is a question which would merit detailed investigation. Finally, there is some *prima facie* evidence suggesting foreign influences, for instance from the Far East.

The beginnings of essentially Timurid architecture go back to the time of Tīmūr, and had already achieved their peak of perfection in the palace of the conqueror at Kish (Shahr-i Sabz), known from the description of the Spanish ambassador Clavijo, who saw it in 1404 before its completion, and in the Aḥmad Yasavī mosque at Turkistān, built 797/1394–5, and the Bībī Khānum mosque at Samarqand, completed five years later. A new era, the first Khurāsān period, occurs during Shāh Rukh's reign, in which his wife Gauhar Shād and their son Bāīsunqur (d. 837/1433) are remembered for the work they commissioned, and Qivām al-Din Shīrāzī as their builder. In contrast to the preceding era in Transoxiana it shows considerable progress in both design and decoration, as can clearly be seen by a simple comparison of the Gauhar Shād mosque at Mashhad (begun 808/1405–6 and completed 821–2/1418–9) with the Bībī Khānum mosque at Samarqand. This structure initiated the predominantly classical Timurid style of the next few decades. The basic architectural plan – as in the 8th/14th century – was the inner court with its four cloisters with pointed arches (*aivān*), connected by two-storey arcades, but now also extended by a portal. In the next architectural period, which lasted from the end of Shāh Rukh's reign to the fall of the Timurid empire of Herat, this type of structure only occurs once, namely in the Herat madrasa. Otherwise we find the covered mosque, which demanded less expenditure, or a kind of combined form, a mixture of covered and courtyard mosque, represented by Abu'l-Qāsim Bābur's mosque in Anau dating from 848/1444–5. As an example of the more common covered mosque we may cite the Masjid-i Shāh (1451) at Mashhad. As the period went on the statesman and writer Mīr ʿAlī Shīr Navāʾī won renown as the builder of a large number of edifices.

Among the striking innovations of Timurid architecture are not only the increase in expenditure involved and – especially in the first Khurāsān period – the tendency to magnificence seen in the greater height of the buildings, precious surface decorations, numerous cupolas and minarets and a greater number of rooms in contrast with former designs, but also new structural features such as the portal with stalactites in droplet form and – very typically – the tall pear-shaped cupola which now appears, in addition to the flat cupola which is still used. The first instance of this is found in the Gūr-i Mīr at Samarqand. It rests on a supporting cupola not visible from the outside, which, in addition to its function as a support, also serves to restore the normal height dimension to the space beneath. Still more important, though, indeed perhaps the most important feature, is the hitherto unprecedented wealth of colour. It is often found in the faience mosaics of the surface decoration, which is frequently embedded in stucco and covers the representational sides of whole buildings in a lavish display of plant and script motifs. Whereas the Timurid faiences of the early period have only a modest, somewhat austere range of colours, what develops in the course of time is a rich palette as great in its variety as in its aesthetic elegance which gives the whole architectural concept its characteristic fascination.

With the choice achievements of its architecture, in terms both of technical and decorative developments, Timurid civilisation undoubtedly reached its peak. It is part of the great artistic heritage which passed to the Safavids in the 10th/16th century and became the starting-point of a new development which so impressed itself on the outward appearance of Persia that it remains to this day one of the characteristic features of the country.

The initiative of the Timurid princes, no matter what may have been the motives and personal interest of the art-loving patrons among them, was responsible for the emergence of painting of high quality. No examples of mural or textile painting have been preserved, but specimens of miniature art are numerous. Illuminated manuscripts of the Timurid period constitute some of the most priceless treasures in the libraries and collections of east and west.[1] Even before Tīmūr's

[1] To give two examples: I. Stchoukine, "Un Gulistan de Saʿdī illustré par des artistes tîmûrides", *RAA* x (1936), 92–6; R. Ettinghausen, "An illustrated manuscript of Ḥāfiẓ-i Abrū in Istanbul", *KO* II (1955), 30–44.

time several generations of artists, influenced by the work of the Far East, and under Mongol and probably also Turkish influences, had awakened the art of old Iran to new life out of the petrifaction of obsolete forms. In the 9th/15th century, under Timurid – that is to say, essentially Turkish – patronage, the art of painting looks back to its Iranian past, and the influence of this past forces back the hitherto dominating influences.

Research to date places the origins of Timurid painting in the workshops of the Jalayirids in Baghdad and Tabrīz, perhaps also in those of the Muzaffarids in Shīrāz, attributing them to artists deported by Tīmūr to Samarqand after his conquest of these cities.[1] Since none of their work survives, it cannot be proved, though it may reasonably be assumed, that it was here that the roots of a syncretism of various different styles are to be found, and moreover those of totally different schools of painters, a syncretism which is characteristic of Timurid painting throughout the whole period of its existence. The political upheavals which followed the death of Tīmūr induced many artists to leave Samarqand and to seek their livelihood at the newly developing Timurid princely courts. This would account for the fact that the style of the period, in spite of the great distances that separated the individual centres, shows a remarkable unity in which the only differences are matters of nuance.

This style can only in fact be traced as an unbroken sequence at two places, Shīrāz and Herat. Under Iskandar b. ʿUmar Shaikh, who ruled from 812/1409 to 817/1414, painting in Shīrāz enjoyed a period of distinction strikingly marked by the refinement of its draughtsmanship and the delicacy of its colours. And in the following twenty years under Ibrāhīm (d. 838/1435), whom his father Shāh Rukh appointed governor of Fārs after the victory over Iskandar, the distinction of this school continued, even though its production was no longer quite of the same high standard. At the same time there grew up a powerful rival to it under the patronage of Shāh Rukh and his son Bāīsunqur in the form of the Herat school, which eventually reached and later even surpassed its achievements by its success in evolving new means of expression and a unique wealth of colour. Signs of age were already appearing in Timurid art when it once again had the good fortune to

[1] Stchoukine, *Manuscrits Tîmûrides*, p. 156, regards both Jalayirids and Muzaffarids as the precursors of the Timurid schools of painting, whereas Aubin, "Le mécénat timouride", p. 73, mentions only the Jalayirids.

acquire generous patrons in Ḥusain Bāīqarā and Mīr ʿAlī Shīr Navā'ī. Under their protection emerged the greatest painter of Muslim Iran, Kamāl al-Dīn Bihzād (d. *c.* 1535). Combining direct observation of nature with traditional elements, he was responsible for the renaissance of book illumination. He outlived the fall of the Timurids, went to Tabrīz, and achieved high renown at the court of the Safavids. As a result of his work and the wide circle of his pupils he introduced into Safavid miniature art what was to be a continuation of Timurid painting, distinguished by the brilliance of its achievements.

III. *The Timurids*

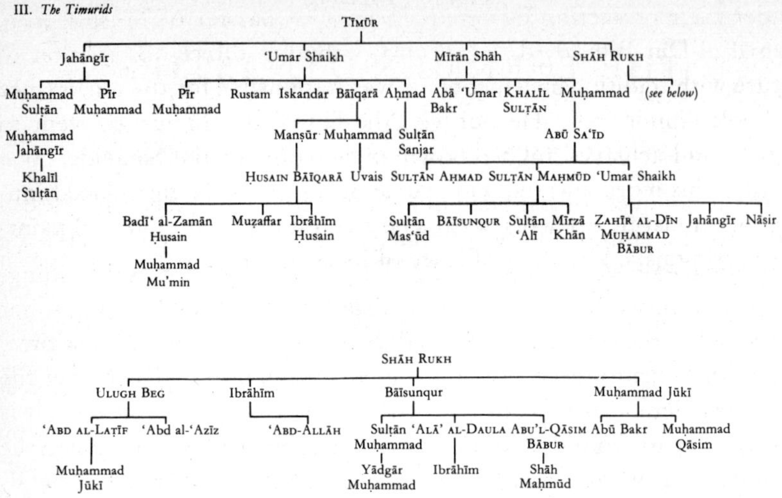

CHAPTER 4

THE TÜRKMEN DYNASTIES

INTRODUCTION: THE TURKISH BACKGROUND

With the conquest of Baghdad in 656/1258, the Mongols dealt a death-blow to the empire of the caliphate. This event, together with the dramatic circumstances that attended it, is often regarded as a dividing-line between two historical epochs. This view is justified only in so far as the fall of the caliphate destroyed the last tie which, up till that time, had with difficulty been holding together the world of Islam. Yet the historical significance of this event should not be over-estimated. It is true that, apart from the liquidation of the ʿAbbasids, it represented the prelude to new historical developments, such as the rise of the Il-Khanid dynasty, which was to be of great importance in the history of Persia. But its total effect on the history of the Islamic world was of a more or less superficial nature. For the political organisation of the caliphate which the Mongols had destroyed was little more than an outer shell, which had long been crumbling away, around heterogeneous structures which as a whole had very little to do with the Islamic empire of the early ʿAbbasids, and which indeed actually negated the *raison d'être* of a common polity.

In spite of the catastrophic effect of the Mongol assault upon the people of that time, and in spite also of the changes which it caused and the traces which, here and there, it left behind it, eighty years later it already belonged to the past. Of distinctly greater historical significance were other developments which had begun long before. One of the most important of these, though not the earliest chronologically, was the influx of the Turks into the Islamic world which, by the 5th/11th century, had reached considerable proportions, but had in fact begun in a small way as early as the 3rd/9th. The advance of Turkish peoples has been likened to the Teutonic migrations because by invading a unified ancient culture – the Teutons that of the West, the Turks that of Islam – both movements created the necessary preconditions for the rise of national states. It should be remembered that the Turkicisation of Anatolia did not begin in the 7th/13th century, as was once supposed, but had already started in the 5th/11th century, or even earlier: there is mention in the 3rd/9th century of the *Tourkopouloi* as auxiliary troops of the Byzantine emperor, presumably Oghuz Türkmens, who are known to have existed in Bukhārā towards the end of the 4th/10th century.[1]

Indeed, the political success of single Turkish groups and individuals within the world of Islam which had thus begun more than two centuries before the Mongol onslaught, was one of the most important prerequisites for later developments. The Turkish invasion did not merely bring about the fall of the Byzantine empire. In addition, the arrival in the Holy Land of victorious Turkish hordes furnished the pretext for the crusading movement in the West; it was Turkish forces which marched against the Crusaders as they drew near their goal; Turkish troops, this time under the Mamlūks, who halted the hitherto irresistible advance of the Mongols in the Syrian approaches to Egypt; and Turkish initiative, again, that prevailed during the jockeying for political power in the Near East after the end of Mongol hegemony. In fact, if the 20th century be disregarded, nearly all the later states of the Islamic world were of Turkish foundation. But of particular historical import in this connection were the events that took place during the 8th/14th and 9th/15th centuries, since they were the prelude to a development whose effects were to last until well into the 20th century.

Great though the Turkish share in this process may have been, it would not be correct to describe it as being exclusively Turkish. To speak of an age as being entirely Turkish is possible only with reserve and within very restricted limits for the reason that there was another and very significant factor at work. Even before the Turkish migration had reached the highlands of Iran other, Iranian, forces had begun the work of undermining and subverting the 'Abbasid caliphate, whose effective strength was by then already in decline. So the Turks in fact did nothing more than take over and continue the work that Persians had already begun: that work concerned the formation and development of indigenous forces in Iran, which in their turn succeeded in establishing political dominions without the central government in Baghdad being able to put a stop to their activities, but also without these forces having in view the removal of the caliphate. This political development was accompanied by a cultural one, for at about the same

[1] W. Björkman, "Die altosmanische Literatur", in *Philologiae Turcicae Fundamenta* II (Wiesbaden, 1964), 403.

time the New Persian literary language was reaching its zenith, and this manifested itself in literary achievements of the first order; it is but one example, though an especially striking one, of the cultural impulse then at work in Iran, which, together with its many other manifestations, is sometimes called Iranism.

It is true that none of the Iranian sub-principalities survived for long. But the cultural movements which were inspired or encouraged under their aegis are all the more remarkable. They set their stamp upon wide areas of the Islamic world, though in varying forms. The Turks who later made their appearance from Central Asia showed themselves particularly receptive to this Islamic culture. These migrating bands need not be seen as completely uncivilised barbarian hordes; the Turkish immigrants in Anatolia consisted predominantly of nomads, but there were also some sedentary elements.[1] Nevertheless it may be conjectured that even after the adoption of Islam they brought with them to the west the lightest of cultural burdens and were therefore quite remarkably open to new influences. At all events, the fact remains that Persian culture of that time exercised upon them a peculiar attraction to which they readily responded. Of course they did not take over everything that was proffered lock, stock and barrel, nor did they leave unchanged what they absorbed. In the place of the more or less unified Islamic culture which had been brought about by the ʿAbbasid empire, there arose something quite new, a Turco-Persian culture which is always to be found wherever Turks settled on Persian soil or wherever, after contact with Iranian lands and their cultural emanations, they appeared elsewhere. A new, and not uncontested, interpretation sees in this the initial phase of national political developments, a question which will be discussed in greater detail in connection with the Safavids.

Among the Turkish immigrants into the Near East the Oghuz, Türkmen peoples under leaders of the house of Saljūq, had been particularly successful as a result of founding several kingdoms, of which that in Anatolia with its capital Qonya, the former Iconium, is of special interest in our particular context. From the start, these Saljūqs were not the only Turkish princes in Asia Minor with political ambitions, since under their dominion, or alongside them, there were other families of high standing who were awaiting their opportunity.

[1] See Sümer, "Anadolu'ya yalnız göçebe Türkler mi geldi?".

That had arrived with the downfall of the Saljūq kingdom in Asia Minor in 708/1308, which was followed soon after, through the decline and final extinction of Mongol power, by a political vacuum, a challenge to men of enterprise. Among the principalities which were then formed or grew in strength was that of the Ottomans, later to take its place in world history, a destiny which at the time seemed by no means assured and indeed cannot yet have been envisaged. Seen in retrospect, the rise and fall of most of these ruling houses, some twenty in all, belong to the sphere rather of Ottoman than of Persian history, although all of them, not excluding the Ottomans themselves, came under that influence of Iranian culture already mentioned.

Yet some of them are of primary significance in the history of Iran, not only because of cultural ties but also for political, dynastic and religious reasons. Two of them, the principalities of the Āq Quyūnlū and Qarā Quyūnlū, which also fall within the immediate Ottoman context, are closely connected with Persia; at times individual rulers of these dynasties were able to bring large sections, even the whole, of Persian territory under their sway, and thus a rôle very nearly devolved upon them which in the event was to be reserved for others. At any rate, in the eyes of contemporary European observers in the 9th/15th century it seemed certain that here were the eastern counterparts to the dangerously expanding Ottomans. The impressive reports of these informants led the European powers to enter into negotiations with the Türkmens with a view to an alliance. Under their rule there were also Shīʿī movements which were to have far-reaching historical consequences. It is a measure of their importance that those who followed them, the Safavids, are seen as the successors of these same Türkmen princes, as a collateral, that is, of the ruling house of Āq Quyūnlū, with a different territorial area.[1]

ORIGINS AND EARLY HISTORY OF THE TWO TÜRKMEN GROUPS

While in recent times much new light has been shed on these Türkmens, their actual origin is still obscure.[2] The uncertainty begins with their very names. There is, indeed, nothing especially remarkable about

[1] The view of Aubin, "Études Safavides I".

[2] On the meaning of the word *Türkmen*, see Minorsky, "The Middle East", p. 439; I. Kafesoğlu, "Türkmen adı, manası ve mahiyeti", *Jean Deny Armağanı*, ed. J. Eckmann *et al.* (Ankara, 1958), pp. 121–33.

designations like Āq Quyūnlū, "those (tribes) with white sheep (*qoyun*)" and Qarā Quyūnlū, "those (tribes) with black sheep", among nomads whose flocks were among their most valuable possessions. But still the question remains as to how they should be interpreted. There is a tendency today to see them as referring to totem animals, to which, however, it must be objected that in ancient times – at least according to Rashīd al-Dīn Fażl-Allāh – Turks had been prohibited from eating the flesh of their totem animals. Had this proscription still been in force in this instance, such an interpretation would have to be rejected on grounds of practicality alone, in which case greater probability would accrue to a more mundane interpretation, namely that the designations in question are expressions of nothing more than the colour of the sheep exclusive to, or predominating in, their respective flocks. The designations must also have had an antithetical character in that they reveal the desire of the two groups to be clearly distinct one from the other. The dynastic emblems of the Āq Quyūnlū and Qarā Quyūnlū found on coins, documents and tombstones have no recognisable connection with their names.[1]

In considering the genesis of such groups it should be remembered that these are nomad confederations of which, in the course of time, the composition changes frequently under the influence of political, geographic or economic factors. A strong tribe may, by the successes it achieves, attract other tribes, absorb them into its alliance and eventually through such accretions become a major constellation. But the opposite process is also possible when an important tribe loses its renown, its power, its magnetism; until, perhaps, it finally disintegrates altogether, while its various components achieve independence or seek to join other tribes that are on the upward climb. This explains how one and the same name may attach now to a kinship, now to a tribe or even to a confederation of several tribes. It is obvious that some part is played in this by rivalry, feuds and military struggles. It is not always possible to trace the underlying events, because history scarcely records them – if indeed they are recorded at all – unless they are preserved in oral tradition or in legendary accounts. Not until a tribe

[1] For the Āq Quyūnlū, see Hinz, *Irans Aufstieg*, pp. 105ff.; for the Qarā Quyūnlū, Burn, "Coins of Jahān-Shāh"; Rabino, "Coins of the Jalā'ir", p. 102; Minorsky, "The Clan of the Qara-qoyunlu rulers". On the interpretation of these *tamghas* generally, see Uzunçarsılı, *Anadolu beylikleri*, pl. 49; H. Jänichen, *Bildzeichen königlichen Hoheit bei den iranischen Völkern* (Bonn, 1956), pl. 28, no. 24; L.A. Mayer, *Saracenic Heraldry* (Oxford, 1933), pls. 50, 51.

or confederation achieves prominence does its destiny attract the attention of historians, whereupon the question of its origin and provenance arises, but often without any satisfactory answer being found. What is discovered, then, in the sources is all too often confused, incomplete and contradictory.

Thus it is with the beginnings of the Āq Quyūnlū and Qarā Quyūnlū. It is not impossible that they once belonged to the same confederation, or perhaps even formed one tribe, later to separate and seek their fortunes, in both cases successfully, as independent tribes. By the time when they are clearly discernible historically, in the 8th/14th century, their names are no longer those of mere tribes, but of two confederations with numerous sub-tribes. Some of the names of these latter are known from earlier times, from the catalogue of the original twenty-four Oghuz tribes found in Rashīd al-Dīn and from other legendary accounts.[1] We are thus concerned with two confederations formed from various Türkmen tribes – those, in fact, which in all probability came with the Oghuz to Western Asia in the 5th/11th century, some of them no doubt getting as far as Anatolia. The sources give no direct information concerning these associations, but they must have been formed in the 8th/14th century after the fall of the Anatolian Saljūq dynasty and to some extent out of the latter's bankruptcy. At that precise moment, too, the disintegration of the Mongol hegemony by which they and their member tribes had been contained enabled them to pursue their aspirations in the area of the resulting power vacuum, namely eastern Anatolia, northern Mesopotamia and north-west Persia.

There is, indeed, no record of the names of the Āq Quyūnlū and the Qarā Quyūnlū in the pre-Mongol period, though there does exist a record of the principal kin-groups which were later to become the ruling families among their subjects: the Bayïndïr (Bayundūr) with the Āq Quyūnlū, and the Bahārlū, sometimes called Bārānī, with the Qarā Quyūnlū.

Bayïndïr is found in Rashīd al-Dīn's index of tribes mentioned above as the designation of one of the twenty-four Oghuz tribes, whereas in the *Kitāb-i Dede Qorqud*, a Turkish epic that was recorded about 1400, it is the name of an Oghuz ruler. It is supposed that the Āq Quyūnlū were a clan of the Bayïndïr tribe, but in the sources Bayïndïr or

[1] Cf. E. Rossi, *Il 'Kitab-i Dede Qorqut'* (Rome, 1952), pp. 16ff.

Bayïndïriyya is also found as a synonym for Āq Quyūnlū; at any rate the tribal name Bayïndïr is met with in the 8th/14th century in Asia Minor. Certain central Anatolian place-names which must go back to the Oghuz conquest give rise to the supposition that the Bayïndïr took part in the Saljūq conquest of Asia Minor. After the fall of the Āq Quyūnlū dynasty, the Bayïndïr settled in Tripoli and Aleppo, and also to the south of Sīvās.

The name Bahārlū borne by the ruling family of the Qarā Quyūnlū is sometimes connected with Bahādur,[1] but is almost certainly linked with the locality of Bahār north of Hamadān, the seat of a powerful Türkmen family also represented at Irbīl, Marāgha and Akhlāṭ: from the basin of Lake Urmiya, that is, to that of Lake Vān, as well as considerably to the north and south of these. The pressure of the Mongol invasion may have driven them completely into the area north of Lake Vān, where later the confederation of the Qarā Quyūnlū was to form. This connection can be deduced from the name Īvā'ī which is recorded as early as 629/1230 at Akhlāṭ and again with one of the last 'Abbasid caliph's most famous ministers, who came from the village of Bahār and was executed in 656/1258 in Baghdad by the Mongols. Īvā'ī is merely a derivative of Ïva or Yïva, which is the name of another of the original Oghuz tribes. The connection between the Qarā Quyūnlū and the Yïva is proved by the dynastic emblem common to both, and which the Qarā Quyūnlū dynasty must have taken over from the Yïva.[2] The designation Bārānī, as used in respect of the Qarā Quyūnlū, has not yet been satisfactorily explained. It has been supposed that it is the name of the tribe's ruling family, or that it is connected with a place-name,[3] two interpretations which need not be mutually exclusive.

The early history of the two Türkmen groups with which we are here concerned is closely bound up with the "social sickness", as a Turkish scholar has called the period of decline,[4] which set in with the end of Mongol hegemony throughout a large part of the Near East. Freelance mercenaries and adventurers, basing themselves upon nomadic tribes and robber bands, disrupted economic life in town and

[1] Sümer, "Kara-Koyunlular", p. 292, mentions a Bahādurlu tribe. There is no mention of the transition from *bahādur* to *bahār* amongst the many references collected by Doerfer, *TMEN* II, *s.v. bahādur*, apart from the *ba har* occurring in Caucasian languages (p. 373).

[2] Minorsky, "The Clan of the Qara-qoyunlu rulers"; idem, "Bahārlū", *EI*². On the Yïva tribe, see Sümer, "Yıva Oğuz boyuna dâir".

[3] See respectively Sümer, "Kara-Koyunlular", p. 292, and Minorsky, "The Clan of the Qara-qoyunlu rulers", p. 392.

[4] Yınanç, "Akkoyunlular", p. 258.

country, often bringing it to a complete standstill. They offered their services, or allied themselves, to any prince who seemed likely to succeed, but they never hesitated to abandon master or ally as soon as fortune beckoned elsewhere. Lust for booty, a thirst for power and a striving for territorial dominion, such were their motives. Only the successful could count on the following that perhaps might enable them to achieve political authority.

It was in these circumstances that the two confederations evolved, and under these conditions that they prospered, so that during the second half of the 8th/14th century they were both able to found dynasties, that of the Āq Quyūnlū in Diyārbakr, with its centre at Āmid, that is in the lands of the Tigris and Euphrates with Urfa and Mārdīn in the south and Baiburt in the north; that of the Qarā Quyūnlū immediately to the east, with a centre at Arjīsh on the north-east shore of Lake Vān, and spreading north to Erzerum and south to Mosul. The territories of both confederations were then occupied, as they had long been already, by a predominantly sedentary population, consisting of Armenians, Kurds, Aramaeans and Arabs, but at first including no Persian elements. While no doubt exploited and much oppressed by the Türkmens, these peoples were never driven out or exterminated. Individuals, families, and sometimes even much larger groups, might fall victim to circumstances, abandon their homes, or marry into one of the oppressor's tribes, but the ethnic pattern remained much the same, with groups surviving Türkmen overlordship and persisting in their own locality, in some cases actually until the present day. Their rôle in the political developments we have to consider was, with rare exceptions, non-existent; they were the suffering witnesses of events upon which, generally speaking, they could have no influence whatsoever.

The rise of the two confederations was accompanied, not only by endless conflicts with their neighbours, but also by mutual jealousies and rivalries: the destruction of Erzerum in 733–5/1332–4 resulted from the feud between them.[1] These quarrels and conflicts determined their policies of alliance and their choice of enemies, in other words, their entire destiny, until eventually the Āq Quyūnlū triumphed, destroyed the dominion of the Qarā Quyūnlū, assimilated not only their lands, but also many of their sub-tribes, and entered the ranks of the major powers of the Near East. In spite of certain peculiarities

[1] Ibn Baṭṭūṭa, trans. Gibb, II, 437.

distinguishing the two groups from one another, they have so much in common ethnically, politically, historically, culturally and economically, that their history is best considered in conjunction.

We are better informed regarding the political inception of the Āq Quyūnlū than about the first stages of the Qarā Quyūnlū. No doubt this is due to the nature of one of their first objectives, the Comnenian empire of Trebizond, which they set out with great determination to attain, their raids and conquests for the rest not being confined to eastern Anatolia, but extending into Mesopotamia and Syria. Their often repeated attacks on Trebizond after 741/1340 gave the Byzantine chroniclers every cause to write about them. Thus they mention Ṭur ʿAlī Beg, lord of the "Turks of Āmid", who had already attained the rank of amīr under the Īl-Khān Ghazan (694–703/1295–1304). When in 749/1348, under his leadership, the Türkmens reappeared before Trebizond, they again failed to take the town, but the youthful John Comnenus, soon to ascend the throne as Alexios III but never to achieve military fame, had evidently been so terrified that he, and no doubt also his advisers, deemed it politic to betrothe his sister, Maria Despina, to Fakhr al-Dīn Qutlugh Beg, son of the Türkmen leader, thus finally warding off the danger.[1] The calculation proved correct: Trebizond was spared for the time being, and later generations witnessed several other such unions between Comnenian princesses and Āq Quyūnlū chiefs. It may well be to these that the empire of Trebizond owed the respite which enabled it to survive until 865/1461, eight years after the fall of Constantinople. However this may be, we know that Uzun Ḥasan intervened with Meḥmed the Conqueror on Trebizond's behalf.[2]

From the Türkmen–Trebizond marriage of 753/1352, the first to be attested, was born the founder of the Āq Quyūnlū dynasty, Qarā Yoluq[3] ʿUs̱mān Beg who, in 791/1389, followed his brother Aḥmad Beg as head of the Āq Quyūnlū. The chief chronicle of the dynasty, Ṭihrānī's *Kitāb-i Diyārbakriyya*, not only mentions his grandfather, Ṭur ʿAlī Beg, the besieger of Trebizond, and his father, Qutlugh Beg, who presumably succeeded the latter in 764/1363, but traces his lineage

[1] Fallmerayer, pp. 208ff.; Miller, *Trebizond*, pp. 57–60.

[2] Minorsky, "La Perse au XVe siècle", p. 322; Babinger, *Mehmed the Conqueror*, p. 190.

[3] The form Ḳara Yoluḳ adopted by Minorsky, "Aḳ Ḳoyunlu", is corroborated by the contemporary European transcriptions "Caro Jolucho" and "Korolock" or "Karolackes": see P. H. Dopp, *L'Égypte au commencement du quinzième siècle d'après le Traité d'Emmanuel Piloti de Crète* (Cairo, 1950), p. 103, and Stromer von Reichenbach, "Diplomatische Kontakte".

through 51 generations back to Oghuz Khān, the legendary eponym of the Oghuz.[1] Such genealogical trees are, of course, notoriously unreliable, yet this is a significant point, revealing as it does the view which the Āq Quyūnlū held of themselves, since around 875/1470, the time of the chronicle, when they were in their heyday, they may well have regarded this genealogy not only as mere flattery but also as political legitimation. We do not know – indeed it is doubtful – whether this claim was made at the time of the dynasty's foundation, or in fact whether it could be made at all. At that time, a family alliance with the Comneni may in itself have represented political capital. In any case, Qarā 'Us̱mān followed the example of his father by marrying a Trebizond princess.

Seldom were the many conflicts in which the Āq Quyūnlū engaged so romantically resolved. Generally these were feudal struggles with neighbouring and usually local rulers, in which territorial expansion and spheres of influence were involved. In the course of his long life, Qarā 'Us̱mān carried out many more of these than his far from peaceable father, always impelled by the belief that he would succeed in establishing his tribal lands of Diyārbakr as a stable dominion. It is not necessary, nor possible, to describe in detail these never-ending quarrels, if only because accounts in the sources differ from each other in many respects and most have not yet been critically assessed. Yet they cannot be completely ignored, for in them can sometimes be discovered the lines of later development. This is usually so when one of the major powers is involved, as could of course happen even in a mere quarrel with any princeling whatsoever. This was the case with the rulers of Sīvās, to whose assistance the Ottoman Turks willingly hastened because the rise of the Āq Quyūnlū had filled them with foreboding and mistrust, especially when, as here, it was a question of lands in which they themselves were interested. The struggle ended in the year 800/1397 with the defeat and death of Qāżī Burhān al-Dīn, a man renowned as a poet, who had risen from being a lawyer to the rank of sultan of Sīvās.

There was also friction with the rulers of Egypt, the Mamlūks, whose possessions in northern Syria and southern Armenia were threatened by Qarā 'Us̱mān. This did not lead to more serious consequences at the time, perhaps because Barqūq (784–801/1382–1399), the

[1] For the genealogy, see also Ghaffārī, as cited in Hinz, *Irans Aufstieg*, p. 128.

sultan of Cairo, was compelled by a serious rising in Syria to devote all his energies to the preservation of that country, and even to the protection of his own throne and person.

But there was one adversary who, above all others, was dangerous to the Āq Quyūnlū and the political aims they pursued, namely their tribal kinsmen of the Türkmen Qarā Quyūnlū confederation. Their leader, Qarā Muḥammad, it is true, did not long survive 'Us̱mān Beg's father, against whom he had often fought. His successor, Qarā Yūsuf, however, showed himself uncommonly active and was, of course, determined to keep up the traditional feud. At first the issue remained undecided. Only when Tīmūr appeared in the Near East did a change seem imminent. The Qarā Quyūnlū, the first to encounter his troops, ignored his demands for surrender, opposed him and suffered defeat every time that battle was joined. This gave rise to a feud that persisted with Tīmūr's successors. There appear to have been many different accounts current at the time concerning the conqueror's character and his military methods. Whereas in Cairo he was still being referred to in 788/1386 as "a Mongol rebel by the name of Tīmūr", who was on his way to Tabrīz, in Persia and Mesopotamia his advance aroused so intense a state of terror as sometimes to induce a kind of paralysis. Qarā Yūsuf did not wait for a final military decision, but chose rather to seek refuge with the Ottoman Turks. Returning later, he again had to flee, this time to Syria where he was interned in a castle near Damascus by the governor because of his earlier activities against the Mamlūks.

His conduct, and the attitude of hostility towards Tīmūr adopted by the other Qarā Quyūnlū chiefs, may have been the incentive that determined the Āq Quyūnlū leader to join the conqueror and to offer him his services. This took place in 801/1399, in the Transcaucasian camp at Qarābāgh, where Qarā 'Us̱mān paid homage to Tīmūr. During the first campaign in Anatolia he was made commander of the vanguard, and his name is also mentioned in connection with the subsequent Syrian campaign. Next, in 804/1402, he took part in the battle of Ankara. The defeat and imprisonment of Bāyezīd I brought about a serious crisis in the Ottoman empire. Tīmūr awarded the title of amīr to the leader of the Āq Quyūnlū as a reward for his services, and conferred on him all the lands of Diyārbakr in fief.

Thus it seemed that the Āq Quyūnlū's dream of a principality had come true, for at that time there was no greater feudal lord in the Near East than Tīmūr. But their joy was shortlived; for when Tīmūr died in February 1405 during a campaign in the east, it was immediately apparent that the vast empire he had accumulated by his conquests lacked internal stability. The anarchy following his death saw the rise of a number of rulers. One of the main causes for the rapid decline of so great an empire was undoubtedly the fact that the princes of Tīmūr's house, scattered throughout the dominions as governors and ruling their provinces with virtually unlimited power, although they had submitted to the supreme authority of the conqueror, did not feel bound to any successor. This phenomenon has its parallel in the origins of many Turkish states and is also found, as we shall see, among the Türkmens. Notwithstanding these upheavals, a considerable empire survived, mainly in eastern Persia and in Afghanistan, under the rule of Tīmūr's son, Shāh Rukh, as it continued to survive under his successors for the next hundred years. But exert themselves as they might, these rulers were unable to overpower the Türkmens. The immediate effect of Tīmūr's campaigns is apparent in the fact that neither the Timurids nor the Ottomans nor yet the Egyptian Mamlūks succeeded in containing the political ambitions of the two Türkmen confederations, a circumstance that was to play a significant rôle in their subsequent development.

In the sorely afflicted countries of the Near East, the struggle continued after Tīmūr's death. Qarā 'Us̱mān, whose successes at Tīmūr's side had earned him considerable prestige in the eyes of his confederation and had won over a number of tribes of doubtful allegiance, waged war, usually with success, against many of the neighbouring princelings. His relations with Egypt were initially peaceful, but later he again attacked her possessions. In nearly all his undertakings against the Qarā Quyūnlū, still his main adversaries, he was unsuccessful, probably because in Qarā Yūsuf he had encountered an equal, if not a superior, antagonist. He remained loyal to Tīmūr's house, however, though the patronage of Shāh Rukh (807–50/1405–47) was very far from being as significant as that of his father, so that the alliance was therefore of small advantage to Qarā 'Us̱mān and was partly responsible for bringing about his death. During Shāh Rukh's three Āzarbāījān campaigns (823/1420, 832/1429, 838–9/1434–5), all conducted against the Qarā Quyūnlū, Qarā 'Us̱mān is found each time fighting on the Timurid side. Although Qarā Yūsuf had died at the very start of the first expedition, his troops had been dispersed, and Iskandar Beg, his second son and eventual successor, had been beaten, the Qarā

Quyūnlū were quick to recover. During the third campaign, when this same Iskandar fled before Shāh Rukh to take refuge with the Turks, Qarā 'Usmān, now almost eighty years old, tried to cut off his retreat. During a fight near Erzerum he was severely wounded, and died as a result in Ṣafar 839/at the end of August 1435. Returning from exile, Iskandar Beg passed through the town, had the Āq Quyūnlū leader's grave opened and the corpse decapitated, characteristically sending the skull to the sultan of Egypt, who caused it to be publicly displayed in Cairo.

'Usmān Beg's fearlessness and military fame were immensely admired by his contemporaries, yet when the results of his turbulent career are considered, it is found that he did little more than make a first attempt at founding a state. It is true that he had achieved royal status, had extended his dominions by the conquest of numerous lands including important places such as Rūḥā (formerly Edessa, now Urfa), Sīvās and Ṭoqat, and had consolidated his sovereignty shortly before his death by victories over al-Malik al-'Ādil Jikam, the governor of Aleppo and Damascus, as well as over al-Malik al-Ẓāhir 'Īsā, the commander of Mārdīn, but these achievements were to a large extent nullified by the violent disputes that broke out between his sons after his death. For a time their dynasty was eclipsed by that of the Qarā Quyūnlū, though it was later to make a brilliant recovery. Thus the initiative had now passed to the Qarā Quyūnlū, who entered on the period of their greatest expansion. Before considering their subsequent history, something should be said of the early years of this confederation, which have not been dealt with before because less significant than the founding of the Āq Quyūnlū state.

In the decades following the death of the Īl-Khān Abū Sa'īd (716–736/1316–1335), which brought Hülegü's dynasty to a close, various Mongol princes and other potentates attempted to subdue the Il-Khanid empire, or portions of it. The ensuing struggle for power quickly brought about the disintegration of the Mongol empire, part of which re-emerged as the dominion of the Jalayirids, extending across Mesopotamia, Āzarbāījān and, later, Shīrvān. During the reign of Shaikh Uvais (757–776/1356–1374), an energetic and successful representative of this dynasty, the Qarā Quyūnlū emerged for the first time as an undoubted political force. In the sources, their name is mentioned in connection with Bairām Khwāja and two of his brothers, who belonged to the Bahārlū tribe, of which we have already spoken as the sometimes unruly followers of Shaikh Uvais[1]. Although after the latter's death Bairām Khwāja did not shake off Jalayirid authority, he succeeded in acquiring Arjīsh, Mosul and Sinjār, as well as some places in Transcaucasia, so that on his death in 782/1380, Qarā Muḥammad, presumably his son but according to some sources his nephew, succeeded to dominions extending from Erzerum to Mosul.

Qarā Muḥammad, whom we have already encountered as the antagonist of Qutlugh Beg Āq Quyūnlū, the son-in-law of the Comneni, is generally regarded as the founder of the Qarā Quyūnlū ruling house, and rightly so if we consider the strength of his influence in the above-mentioned lands. His successes against the Artuqids, a dynasty of Türkmen origin that had existed for something like two centuries in and around Mārdīn, against the Āq Quyūnlū and against the Syrian nomadic Türkmen tribe of the Dögher under their leader Sālim[2], were threatened by Tīmūr's conquest of western Iran in 788/1386 and his campaign against the Qarā Quyūnlū in the very next year.

At the very beginning of his reign, Qarā Muḥammad had secured for the Jalayirid Aḥmad the succession against other pretenders; thus, though the dependent position of his dynasty *vis-à-vis* the Jalayirids was not actually reversed, it was at least converted into one of alliance, and hence of independence. In any event, there was now nothing to prevent him from trying to establish friendly relations with the Egyptian Mamlūks, and the report of Egyptian chroniclers that on the occupation of Tabrīz in 790/1388 he paid allegiance to Sultan Barqūq, declaring that the latter's name was to be mentioned in the Friday prayers and on the coinage, seems highly probable, since this ruler would appear to have been a perfect ally, both against the Āq Quyūnlū and against Tīmūr. However, his policy towards Egypt had to be temporarily abandoned for several reasons, not least because as early as the spring of 791/1389 Qarā Muḥammad was killed in a struggle with rival Türkmens.

We have already mentioned the flight of his son, Qarā Yūsuf, to the Ottomans, and it should be added that his stay in Turkish territory was Tīmūr's main incentive for his second Anatolian campaign, although by that time Qarā Yūsuf was already on his way back. Aḥmad Jalāyir had also taken refuge with the Ottomans, and the paths of the two princes crossed for the second time when, after their return from

[1] See above, pp. 7–8.
[2] See Sümer, "Döğerlere dâir".

Anatolia, they again fled before Tīmūr's troops, this time to Syria, in the domain of the Mamlūks. Here they received a welcome less kindly than that of the Ottomans; indeed they were interned in a castle near Damascus for having some time previously attacked and defeated Egyptian governors of northern Syria, and an order for their execution actually arrived from Cairo, having its origin either directly or indirectly in Tīmūr; but it was not carried out. Their imprisonment together led to a renewal of their former friendly relations, differences that had sprung up in the meantime were ironed out and an agreement was reached regarding spheres of influence that was intended to eliminate all dispute. According to this, Mesopotamia with Baghdad was to be an area of Jalayirid influence, and Āzarbāījān with Tabrīz an area of Qarā Quyūnlū influence.

When the two princes regained their freedom in the spring of 806/1404, this agreement turned out to be little more than a programme, for both dominions had meanwhile been incorporated into Tīmūr's empire and made over to one of his grandsons, Mīrzā Abā Bakr b. Mīrān Shāh, a prince who had already on a previous occasion defeated Qarā Yūsuf in battle. But circumstances soon changed. The Qarā Quyūnlū leader's personal renown and the successes that he soon achieved again won him a considerable following which increased on the death of Tīmūr: for this we have the evidence of the Spanish ambassador Clavijo, who encountered his troops in the summer of 1406 in the region of Khūy.[1] In the struggle against Abā Bakr he was victorious first in 809/1406, again in 810/1408, and on several subsequent occasions. The news that his former fellow prisoner, Aḥmad Jalāyir, had occupied Tabrīz was a severe blow, however, for not only was it a violation of the treaty we have mentioned, but it also put in jeopardy his eastward expansion which, in view of Ottoman resurgence and the tenacious resistance of the Āq Quyūnlū in the west, might well prove to be a question of life and death. Thus the occupation of the town of Tabrīz cut across Qarā Yūsuf's most vital plans and represented a pretext for war. He therefore marched against Aḥmad Jalāyir, who was defeated, taken prisoner and executed in 813/1410.

During the time of his Syrian imprisonment, a son, Pīr Būdāq, had been born to Qarā Yūsuf. This boy had been adopted at the time of his

[1] Clavijo, *Embajada*, pp. 239ff., trans. Le Strange, pp. 329ff. (especially p. 363, n.2).

birth in 1403 by Aḥmad Jalāyir, probably to demonstrate the sincerity of his friendship. It was probably owing to legitimist considerations that Qarā Yūsuf nominated this particular son, while still of tender years, lord of Tabrīz, even getting his adoptive father to appoint him by royal decree as his successor, while he himself retained only the regency. The Türkmen leader, not in other respects a scrupulous man, obviously had sufficient reason for thus reasserting his claims to independence when he made Tabrīz his capital city. He had repeatedly occupied it since 793/1391, but never held it firmly in his grasp.

With the elimination of the Jalayirids, the power of the Qarā Quyūnlū moved rapidly towards its zenith. The very next year, in 815/1412, Shāh Muḥammad, another of the prince's sons, conquered Mesopotamia and Baghdad which he retained, in spite of some disputes with his father, under the latter's overlordship, until driven out in 836/1433 by his younger brother, Aspand. Qarā Yūsuf himself fought successfully against the Āq Quyūnlū in eastern Anatolia, conquering parts of Georgia and Shīrvān, whose rulers had owed allegiance to the Jalayirids. While an advance into Persia, namely to Sulṭāniyya, the former capital of the Īl-Khāns, and to Qazvīn, Iṣfahān and Fārs, increased his military fame, it was a move that had serious consequences, for it made Shāh Rukh aware of the full extent of the danger that was threatening from the Türkmens. We have already seen that he did not remain idle in the face of that threat but led an expedition against Āzarbāījān. Qarā Yūsuf, though mortally ill, went out to meet him, but death overtook him before battle had even been joined.

In spite of the crisis brought about by Shāh Rukh's attack and the death of their leader, the Qarā Quyūnlū dynasty had foundations stable enough to withstand these perils. That this was so was due in large measure to the achievements of Qarā Yūsuf, who had not only created an efficient army and repeatedly held his own on the field of battle, but had so successfully conducted his internal affairs with justice and liberality, at the same time keeping a close watch over the conduct of his wayward governors and showing concern for his dominions' agriculture, that he is extolled as the most able statesman of his house.

His successor, Qarā Iskandar, while victorious in his battles against the Kurdish amīrs and the Shīrvān-Shāh, did not succeed in adding appreciably to the power of his confederation, though he was relatively successful in keeping their dominions intact. He was not, however, a match for the intrigues of the Timurids, whose intention it was to play off his ambitious brothers against him. It is true that he was able to assert himself in 835/1431 against Abū Sa'īd, who had been made governor of Tabrīz while he himself had been in exile. But when, after another defeat in 840/1436, he had to meet in battle his brother Jahān Shāh, the new governor of Āzarbāījān – another appointee of Shāh Rukh's – his soldier's luck deserted him once and for all. He was defeated near Tabrīz, in the locality of Ṣūfiyān, and retreated to Alīnjaq, a castle in the neighbourhood of Nakhchivān. There he was murdered soon after by his son Shāh Qubād in 841/1437.

JAHĀN SHĀH QARĀ QUYŪNLŪ

Under Jahān Shāh, the power of the Qarā Quyūnlū confederation reached its height, but his death was followed by an abrupt decline. Though he owed his rise to the political strategy of Shāh Rukh, by whose favour he had in fact become governor, he did not carry gratitude and loyalty beyond what was necessary to secure his sway over the principal lands of the Qarā Quyūnlū. As early as 850/1447 circumstances changed through the death of his overlord and, like his predecessors, he followed the basic tendency of his house, the Türkmen drive towards the east. His brilliant victories in the ensuing campaigns against the Timurids did not always lead to lasting gains, but they clearly demonstrate the growth of Türkmen influence in the history of Persia at that time; not through the occupation of Persian provinces alone, but also from an ethnological standpoint, for at the time of Jahān Shāh's seizure of power the second of three waves of Türkmen peoples flooding back into Persia from Anatolia was in full swing: they were to play a considerable part in the development of that country.

The fall of Qarā Iskandar had brought into Jahān Shāh's hands the Qarā Quyūnlū principality, with the exception, however, of central and southern Mesopotamia; here his brother Aspand, who had extended his dominion as far as Ḥavīza and Baṣra, refused him recognition. During two campaigns in Georgia similar to those which that country's Muslim neighbours had been waging for many years, he was able to try out his troops and allow free rein to their thirst for plunder. On the death of Aspand, when inheritance disputes afforded an opportunity for intervention, he conquered Baghdad and Mesopotamia.

The inevitable conflicts following the death of Shāh Rukh were a signal for Jahān Shāh to shake off the overlordship of the Timurids and to extend his power eastwards at their expense. He assumed the title of Sultan and Khaqan, immediately reoccupied Sulṭāniyya and Qazvīn, and seized Iṣfahān in 856/1452 and Fārs and Kirmān in the following year. After an advance upon Herat, the capital of Khurāsān, undertaken in 862/1458, he had clearly over-reached himself, but was wise enough to relinquish his conquest when a reserve army from Turkestan under the Timurid Abū Sa'īd marched against him, and impending danger in the Türkmen west necessitated his return. Soon after his arrival there he effectively subdued his son Ḥasan 'Alī's insurrection in Āzarbāījān. He faced a more difficult conflict with another of his sons, Pīr Būdāq (not to be confused with his namesake, Qarā Yūsuf's son, who had died as early as 816/1413), who had already proved unruly when governor of Fārs and who had now rebelled as governor of Baghdad. Not until the summer of 870/1466, after the city had been under siege for a year and a half, was he overthrown and killed, perhaps by his brother Muḥammadī, who took over the succession. Contemporary observers saw in Pīr Būdāq's execution, which directly contravened the promise of safe conduct, not only a breach of faith but a Pyrrhic victory because Jahān Shāh, already an old man, thus deprived himself of an exceptionally capable comrade-at-arms.

Indeed, Jahān Shāh's tactics were eventually to fail in confrontation with the Āq Quyūnlū confederation. This heralded a development which was to bring about the fall of the Qarā Qoyūnlū. Before going into this further, it would seem pertinent to consider briefly Jahān Shāh's character and the political system which he succeeded in setting up in opposition to the sovereign claims of the Timurids.

With Jahān Shāh's reign of almost thirty years, the principality of the Qarā Quyūnlū achieved not only independence from the Timurids but, as a result of territorial expansion from Lake Vān to the deserts which separated Persia from its eastern province of Khurāsān, and from the Caspian to the Persian Gulf, attained almost imperial dimensions. In asking ourselves what this kingdom was like, we must again recall the importance attached by the Qarā Quyūnlū to their appearance as legitimate successors of the Jalayirids. There was a further consideration underlying this, namely that the successors of the Jalayirids were also entitled to the inheritance of the Īl-Khāns. Whether or not Jahān Shāh really called himself "Īl-Khān", it is certain that the Qarā Quyūnlū adopted the political forms of the Persian Mongol empire, as is evident from the Mongol titles of "Khaqan", "Noyan" and

"Bahādur" adopted by them. Again, comparison of the available documents issued by their court chancelleries with those of the Jalayirids supports the assumption.[1]

While in this respect Jahān Shāh was merely following in the footsteps of his predecessors, his personality achieves greater definition when considered in the context of the Türkmens' cultural achievements. The rulers who preceded him seldom afford any opportunity for insight into the intellectual and artistic life of the times. Even allowing for the gaps in our knowledge and for the fact that the information we possess regarding the Qarā Quyūnlū derives for the most part from writers who were not well-disposed towards them and hence were sparing of expressions of praise and appreciation, yet the picture we have of their cultural activity is somewhat colourless, if their excessive religious enthusiasm and the literature it produced, discussed later on in this volume, are disregarded. Amongst the Türkmen leaders we have encountered up till now – mercenary characters for the most part, avid for power and spoils – Jahān Shāh stands out both for his military and political prowess and for his cultural merits. Traces of his building works remain in a number of Persian cities, an especially remarkable monument being the Blue Mosque in Tabrīz. His literary activity discloses rather more about him. Under the pseudonym Ḥaqīqī or Ḥaqīqat, we possess an anthology of his work consisting partly of Persian and partly of Turkish poems astonishing for their unusual and difficult verse-forms which are handled with considerable skill. Even if we are justified in suspecting that these are not the work of the ruler himself but of a ghost-writer, they nevertheless allow us to deduce a good deal respecting his cultural level and his literary tastes. Indeed Jahān Shāh is said to have patronised large numbers of poets and scholars, as well as himself being actively involved in intellectual matters.

These constructive traits, however, are not at all in keeping with the portrait on which the sources are virtually unanimous. They describe him, rather, as a grasping tyrant, a powerful and successful man perhaps, but of an unpredictable, malicious and merciless temperament

[1] For Qarā Quyūnlū documents, see Busse, *Untersuchungen*, p. 250; for Jalayirid documents, A. D. Papazian, "Dva novootkrytykh Il'khanskikh yarlyka", *Banber Matenadarani* VI (Erivan, 1962), 379–401. Further references in Roemer, "Arabische Herrscherurkunden aus Ägypten", *OLZ* LXI (1966), especially 329f., n.5.

who, on the slightest pretext, would fling his officers in gaol, invariably for life. His cruelty towards vanquished towns, such as Tiflis (843/1439–40) and Iṣfahān (856/1452), must be taken as proven. He was reputed to have a partiality for opium and wine, debauchery and licentiousness, and for that reason was known contemptuously at the Ottoman court as "the bat". He is reproached with lack of assiduity in prayer, with ignoring religious precepts and with heretical inclinations. Against all this calumny only one voice is raised in approval; and because it comes from so unexpected a quarter, it is a voice that commands a hearing. ʿAbd al-Razzāq Samarqandī, the court chronicler of the Timurid Shāh Rukh and his successors, praises Jahān Shāh's righteousness, his careful government and the good treatment meted out to his subjects;[1] his capital of Tabrīz, with its large and prosperous population, compares favourably with Cairo; even Jahān Shāh's model régime during the occupation of Herat comes in for praise.

Such contradictory judgments are difficult to reduce to a common denominator. One can only seek for an explanation as to how and why they arose. The suggestion that ʿAbd al-Razzāq was under an obligation to Jahān Shāh, perhaps because of certain gifts or favours bestowed upon him on the occasion of a not altogether implausible encounter in Herat, can have little foundation in view of the chronicler's name for impartiality in reporting his times.[2] It might, indeed, profit us more to assess the crimes and misdeeds of which Jahān Shāh has been accused in the context of the debased morality of those days, which might have led a well-disposed or even merely unprejudiced reporter of the 9th/15th century to see them in a milder light. Yet the idea is not to be arbitrarily dismissed that Sunnī – and perhaps also Safavid – writers depicted the prince's adverse characteristics in more lurid colours because of his heretical leanings or his hostile attitude towards the Safavids.

This brings us to the question of Jahān Shāh's religious attitude. If no clear picture is attainable of his qualities as a man, in this particular respect he proves still more elusive. Here we are concerned not only with the evaluation of his personality, but also with circumstances of political import. For he has sometimes been designated as a progenitor

[1] ʿAbd al-Razzāq, *Maṭlaʿ al-saʿdain*, pp. 1271–4.

[2] Barthold and Shafīʿ, "ʿAbd al-Razzāḳ al-Samarḳandī", *EI*².

of Shī'ī heresy[1] and his dynasty, on account of its heterodox views, as the virtual predecessors of the Safavids, who were just then beginning to make the Shī'a the basis of a political system that was to determine Persia's destiny for more than two hundred years and, so far as religious matters were concerned, even right up till the present.

How the Shī'a achieved such significance has not yet been adequately accounted for, although recently avenues have been opened up that promise new discoveries. What is known without doubt is that during the 8th/14th and 9th/15th centuries heretical movements of various kinds proliferated throughout the whole area of what had been the Il-Khanid empire.[2] It is incontestable that there were also Shī'ī tendencies among the Qarā Quyūnlū. Yet the thesis of their Shī'ī bigotry, culminating in the person of Jahān Shāh, is no longer altogether tenable. We know, indeed, that his brother Aspand, when governor of Baghdad (836–848/1433–1445), introduced the Twelver (Ithnā'ashariyya) Shī'a into Mesopotamia as the official religion, and this most certainly was not without Jahān Shāh's knowledge and consent. It is also a fact that Sulṭān Qulī, descendant of one of Jahān Shāh's nephews, who fled from Hamadān to India in 883/1478, embraced the Shī'a and became the founder of the Quṭbshāhī dynasty of Golkonda, who were well known for their Shī'ī views. No less incontestable is the occasional use of Shī'ī coin-inscriptions by Jahān Shāh. It is bewildering, but perhaps also characteristic, that his coins should as a rule have on their obverse side what was, from a Shī'ī point of view, a highly unacceptable enumeration of the Orthodox Caliphs. The suppression of a Ḥurūfī rising in Tabrīz is hardly compatible with the picture of an anti-Sunnī fanatic,[3] nor for that matter is the fact that he twice banished from Ardabīl, in about 852/1448 and again in 863/1459, the Safavid Shaikh Junaid, a man whom many people charge with Shī'ī views. These arguments justify us in concluding that Jahān Shāh cannot indeed have been the Shī'ī zealot depicted by many writers. This is

[1] Minorsky, "Ahl-i Ḥaḳḳ", *EI*[2] (French edition, I, 270: "Il est à relever que Djahānshāh ..., qui pour les Sunnites est un horrible hérétique, portait parmi ses adhérents le titre de *sulṭān al-'ārifīn*." This sentence is missing in the English edition).

[2] Babinger, "Der Islam in Kleinasien", pp. 58ff.; H. Laoust, *Les Schismes dans l'Islam* (Paris, 1965–9), pp. 258ff.; and recently K. E. Müller, *Kulturhistorische Studien zur Genese pseudo-islamischer Sektengebilde im Vorderasien* (Wiesbaden, 1967), *passim*. For an interesting example, see Ritter, "Die Anfänge der Ḥurūfīsekte".

[3] It is not absolutely certain, however, that this rising and its suppression took place in Jahān Shāh's reign: cf. Minorsky, quoted by Ritter, "Die Anfänge der Ḥurūfīsekte".

also substantiated by the dīvān mentioned earlier, which cannot really be cited as evidence of a Shīʿī mentality, especially when it is compared with that of Shah Ismāʿīl, where extreme heretical convictions are professed. Thus the thesis of heresy is based upon little more than certain Shīʿī inclinations not entirely incompatible with a Sunnī environment, as other examples go to show. A further contributory factor was the down-to-earth opportunism which, for better or worse, dictated a policy of compromise with the dangerous religio-political movements of the day.

Whatever Jahān Shāh's moral qualities and his religious convictions may have been, it is undeniable that his military and diplomatic skill acquired for the Qarā Quyūnlū a sizeable empire extending far into Persian territory, and testifying in many ways to a notable cultural achievement. Had this kingdom been granted time for peaceable development and the construction of an ordered polity, it would undoubtedly have exerted considerable influence on the subsequent course of Persian history. But that was not to be, for the very moment of time that marked the zenith of its power, also marked the beginning of its decline.

THE RISE OF UZUN ḤASAN ĀQ QUYŪNLŪ

We must now return to the history of the confederation of the Āq Quyūnlū, which we last noticed in 839/1435 when, in a battle against Iskandar Beg, Qarā ʿUs̱mān was mortally wounded before the gates of Erzerum. None of his many sons was of the same fibre as their warrior father, and for a whole decade it seemed as though the ruling house of the Āq Quyūnlū would be engulfed in the turbulence of endless strife and intrigue. It would be otiose to recount the details of this anarchy. We need only mention here that two of Qarā ʿUs̱mān's sons, first ʿAlī Beg (d. 842/1438), then Ḥamza Beg (d. 848/1444), strove to preserve their father's heritage, sometimes in conflict with the Egyptian sultans, sometimes with their support and that of the Ottomans, but either way without any marked success, failing in particular to repel Jahān Shāh's inroads into their dominions, which were eventually reduced to the region between Diyārbakr and Arzinjān. Nor was the decline of Āq Quyūnlū power affected by the recognition ʿAlī Beg had succeeded in eliciting from Shāh Rukh and the sultan of Cairo. Incidentally, after ʿAlī's death this was also to earn for Ḥamza the rank of an Egyptian amīr.

Circumstances began to change only with the accession of 'Alī Beg's son Jahāngīr. Under his rule some at least of the land seized by the Qarā Quyūnlū was recovered. But his endeavours to restore the previous territorial position and to consolidate his confederation were hindered by family disputes which constantly impelled him into conflict with his uncles and cousins. Particularly troublesome in this respect were his father's two brothers, Qāsim Beg and Shaikh Ḥasan. The one looked for support to the Egyptian Mamlūks, the other received it from the Qarā Quyūnlū, thus threatening Jahāngīr's very existence. He therefore sent his brother, Uzun Ḥasan, against his uncle. The battle ended with Shaikh Ḥasan's defeat and death. The good understanding between the two brothers – based, it would seem, on yet other services rendered by Uzun Ḥasan – subsequently proved illusory. At any rate there can have been no question of brotherly affection in the summer of 857/1453, if not actually earlier, when Uzun Ḥasan, during Jahāngīr's absence, seized the town of Diyārbakr (Āmid) by a ruse and at once became master of the Āq Quyūnlū. The resulting situation must have reflected the actual balance of power, for Jahāngīr, in spite of many and dogged attempts during the years that followed, was unable to regain his position and finally had to be content with retaining only Mārdīn, where he ended his days in 874/1469.

Uzun Ḥasan's rule not only led to the resurgence of the Āq Quyūnlū, but represents the most successful of all the Türkmen undertakings discussed so far. This cannot be attributed to unusually favourable circumstances, of which, except for the decline of Timurid power, there is no question. Not even the fortunes of war by which Uzun Ḥasan was so often, though by no means always, favoured suffice to explain his success. More important than any other circumstance were the outstanding qualities by which he was distinguished, not merely as a military leader, but also as a statesman.

It is questionable whether the conquest of Constantinople by Sultan Meḥmed II in 857/1453 was, in the eyes of oriental princes, so epoch-making an event as it was to the minds of Western observers, both then and later. There are many indications to show that the sultan failed to impress Uzun Ḥasan as a result. To the latter the Comnenian empire at Trebizond, even after 1453, was not a doomed structure, but a power factor with which, at least to a certain extent, its neighbours must continue to reckon. At any rate he carried on the tradition of his house, to which we have already alluded, marrying in 863/1458 Kyra

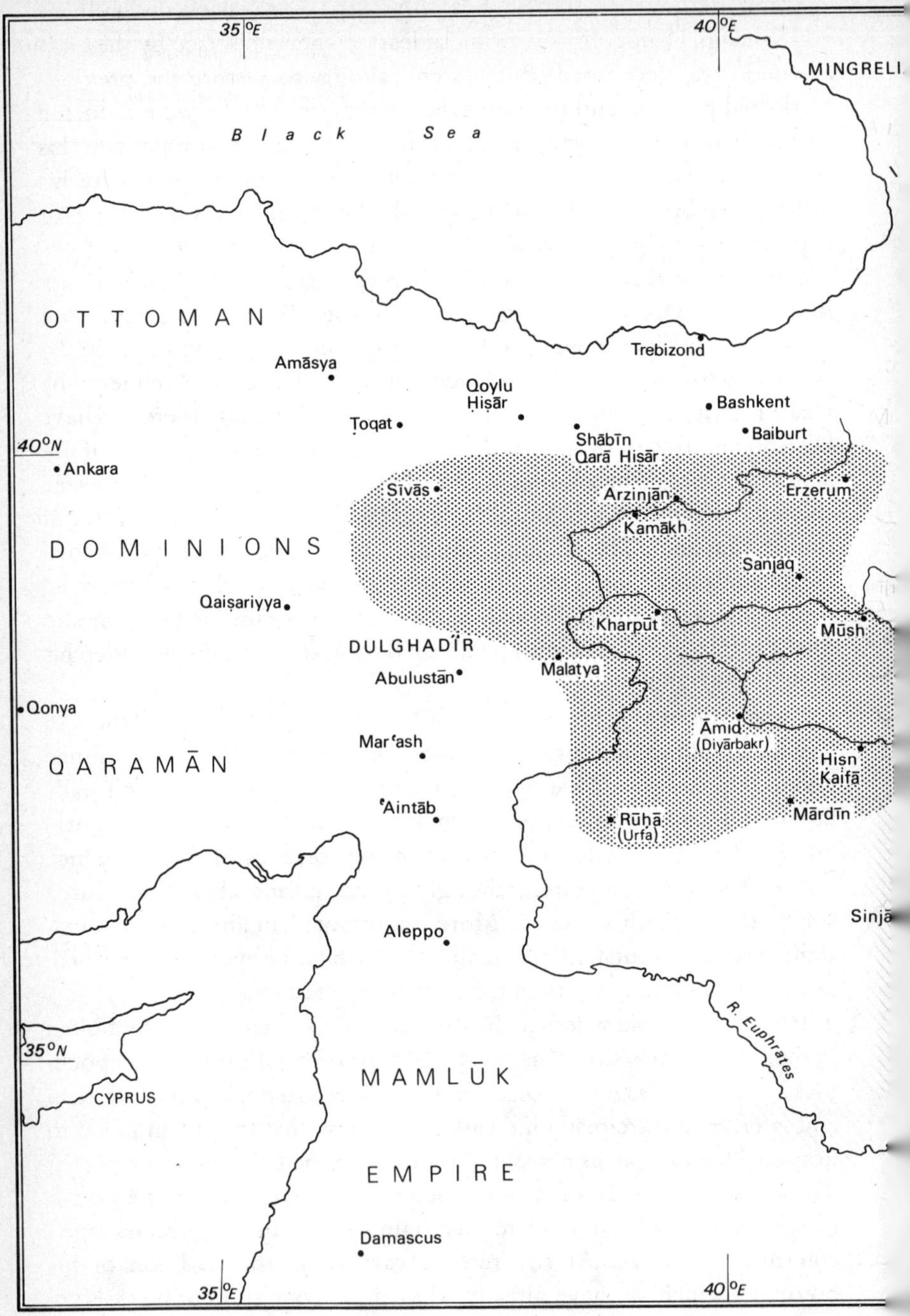

Map. Eastern Anatolia, the Caucasus and Āzarbāījān in the Türkmen period

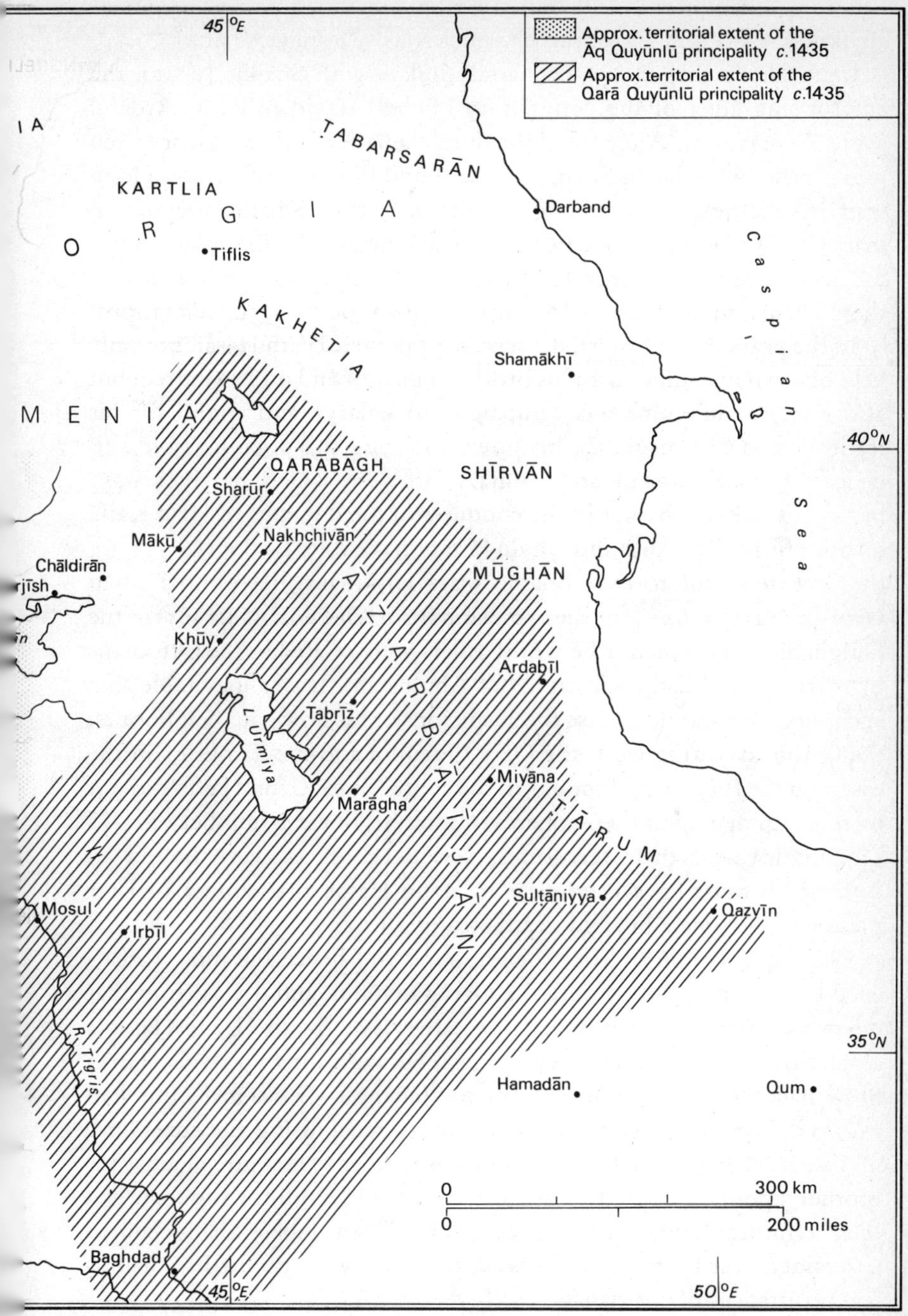
Approx. territorial extent of the Āq Quyūnlū principality c.1435
Approx. territorial extent of the Qarā Quyūnlū principality c.1435
45°E
TABARSARĀN
KARTLIA
O R G I A
Tiflis
KAKHETIA
Darband
Caspian Sea
Shamākhī
M E N I A
QARĀBĀGH
SHĪRVĀN
40°N
Sharūr
Mākū
Nakhchivān
Chāldirān
rjīsh
MŪGHĀN
ĀZARBĀYJĀN
Khūy
Ardabīl
Tabrīz
L. Urmiya
Miyāna
Marāgha
TĀRUM
Sulṭāniyya
Qazvīn
Mosul
Irbīl
R. Tigris
35°N
Hamadān
Qum
0
300 km
0
200 miles
Baghdad
45°E
50°E

Katerina, a daughter of the emperor Kalo Johannes, a princess generally known, even in European chronicles, as "Despina Khātūn".

Uzun Ḥasan forged another family link – with Shaikh Junaid, the enterprising chief of the community of the Safavid order at Ardabīl (851–64/1447–60). After the difficulties the latter had experienced ten years earlier with Jahān Shāh, he now found himself invited for a long visit by the new ruler who gave him his sister Khadīja Begum in marriage. While this course may have been dictated by the sympathy he felt for dervishes in general, and for the young shaikh in particular, there must certainly have been some dominant political considerations.

In the years that followed his seizure of power, Uzun Ḥasan not only held his own in conflict with his brother Jahāngīr and other kindred, but also engaged in numerous campaigns to enlarge and round off his territory and to consolidate his power. During that time he gave evidence of political skill and military prowess which nearly always brought success, whether in the conquest of the domains of Ḥiṣn Kaifā on the Tigris (866/1462) and Qoylu Ḥiṣār on the river Kelkit (863/1459), the capture of the fortress Shābīn Qarā Ḥiṣār, his first campaigns in Georgia (1459, 1462–3) or the expulsion from Kharpūt (869/1465) of the Dulghadïr (a Türkmen tribe whose rulers were related to the Ottomans by marriage and had their capital at Abulustān). It was inevitable that such successes should arouse the suspicions of his powerful neighbours, the Ottomans in the west, the Qarā Quyūnlū and the Timurids in the east, and the Egyptian Mamlūks in the south. Since Uzun Ḥasan did not merely impinge upon their spheres of interest, but in a number of cases actually invaded their territories, serious conflicts were bound to develop. It must have been clear to Uzun Ḥasan that sooner or later there would come a life and death struggle.

The Āq Quyūnlū's closest neighbours, and hence the most threatened by their expansion, were the Qarā Quyūnlū, and it was from that quarter that the first strong reaction came. Even before Uzun Ḥasan's seizure of power there had been a clash between the two rivals. Jahān Shāh had then been unable to break Jahāngīr's resistance, but had extorted from him a declaration of loyalty recognising the suzerainty of Tabrīz. A few years later Jahāngīr, as a defence measure against his brother's political coup, had asked the Qarā Quyūnlū for support. But their reinforcements were beaten back. When Jahān Shāh claimed suzerainty over Uzun Ḥasan as well, the latter went no further than to give assurances of allegiance.

In the long run this failed to satisfy Jahān Shāh, and in the spring of 871/1467 – that is, in the year following the conquest of Baghdad – he decided on a campaign against the Āq Quyūnlū in upper Mesopotamia. It may have been partly the pacific nature of Uzun Ḥasan's letters that led him to believe that there was no immediate danger and hence to spend the summer in the region of Khūy. When, at the end of Rabīʿ I 872/October 1467, he eventually entered the eastern Anatolian plain of Mūsh, he was overtaken by the premature onset of wintry conditions, interrupted his campaign against Uzun Ḥasan, sent the majority of his troops into winter quarters and with a small following made his way northwards. Uzun Ḥasan, who had been keeping a wary eye on his opponent's movements, was in no way put out by the change in weather, seeing it rather as an opportunity. While Jahān Shāh was encamped near Ṣanjaq in the Chapakchur region, Uzun Ḥasan took advantage of the negligence of the Qarā Quyūnlū to attack in the half-light of dawn on 14 Rabīʿ II 872/11 November 1467. Jahān Shāh was surprised in his sleep, after a night of of drunkenness, according to the sources. Though he succeeded at the last moment in making his escape, he was killed as he fled by one of Uzun Ḥasan's soldiers. The defeat was total, for his sons Muḥammadī, the crown prince, and Abū Yūsuf also fell into enemy hands, the latter being blinded, the former killed later on.

Jahān Shāh's death also brought about the dissolution of his kingdom. It is true that Ḥasan ʿAlī, one of his surviving sons, was able to take up the succession, but in spite of the considerable following that he collected at first, he was not long able to maintain his position. With the Āq Quyūnlū hot on his heels, he fled to the region of Hamadān where, in Shawwāl 873/April 1469, he committed suicide. His brother Abū Yūsuf, who had regained his freedom, also paid with his life for his attempt to restore the power of the Qarā Quyūnlū in Fārs. Thus the political rôle of the Qarā Quyūnlū in the Near East came to an end.[1] The fact that a few decades later one branch of the dynasty succeeded in founding a kingdom on Indian soil at Golkonda is outside the scope of this work. With the elimination of the ruling family both the state of the Qarā Quyūnlū and the confederation of that name disappeared. Their territories soon fell to Uzun Ḥasan. Individual tribes which had

[1] It has still to be determined how far the name of the Qarā Quyūnlū region in what was later the khanate of Mākū is connected with the confederation of that name: cf. Gordlevsky, "Kara Koyunlu".

belonged to their alliance looked for new affiliations; many found them with the victor, whose confederation thus gained in size and striking power.

HEYDAY OF THE ĀQ QUYŪNLŪ

With the unexpected victory over Jahān Shāh, Uzun Ḥasan took the centre of the stage of Persian history. Whereas previously he had been no more than an ambitious Türkmen prince with territorial interests outside Iran, the heritage of the Qarā Quyūnlū which he now took over brought him at one stroke dominion over nearly the whole of Persia. He also became the immediate neighbour of the Timurids, however, and while he and his forebears had remained their loyal allies since the days of Tīmūr, it seemed improbable that his sudden rise to power could fail to disturb them.

It will be remembered that Jahān Shāh's expansion eastwards after 850/1447, the year of Shāh Rukh's death, had occurred at the Timurids' expense. Herat, which he had later also occupied but had then relinquished, had been the price he had had to pay for a good understanding with Tīmūr's great-grandson Abū Sa'īd when in Ṣafar 863/December 1458 domestic problems had compelled his return to his home territory. It was to Abū Sa'īd also that Ḥasan 'Alī had successfully turned for support against Uzun Ḥasan after his father's death. Clearly in the hope that here was an opportunity to regain at little cost the territories lost to the Türkmens, the Timurid moved precipitately westwards. A contributory factor was, of course, the thought of the danger to the Timurids which so active a ruler as Uzun Ḥasan would represent if given free scope in a new Türkmen state extending from eastern Anatolia to the borders of eastern Persia. All endeavour to restrain Abū Sa'īd's impetuous advance by negotiation proved vain; vain, too, the reminder of the alliance maintained through some generations. It cannot have been with a light heart that Uzun Ḥasan marched to encounter so determined an enemy. But the fortunes of war continued to smile upon him. Abū Sa'īd, who with his cavalry had rushed ahead, careless of his lines of communication, was at the mercy of the Āzarbāījān winter, and finally suffered annihilating defeat on 14 Rajab 873/28 January 1469, after being surrounded on the Mūghān steppe beside the lower reaches of the Araxes river. He himself was taken prisoner and ten days later was executed.

After the fall of Abū Sa'īd, the Timurids, whose dominion in eastern Persia, Afghanistan and Turkestan continued to survive for several decades, presented no danger worthy of the name to the Āq Quyūnlū. It was only now that the latter could feel secure in the possession of the land they had seized after their victory over the Qarā Quyūnlū. They had risen to be virtually the only uncontested power in Persia. That Uzun Ḥasan was conscious of the rôle thus devolving upon him is apparent from his prompt transfer of his capital from Āmid in Diyārbakr, one of Anatolia's local centres of power, to Tabrīz. By so doing he chose a residence with an ancient tradition where not only the Qarā Quyūnlū had previously had their capital, but also the Mongol Īl-Khāns and their heirs, the Jalayirids. This procedure symbolised the assumption of power in Persia; it also led to a new phase, the second great wave of Türkmen population elements which flooded back from Anatolia into the Iranian highlands and for a century afterwards was to play a considerable rôle in the development of that country, as will presently be shown.

News of Uzun Ḥasan's astonishing rise spread not only among his eastern neighbours, but also among the Western powers. While their interest in the Near East during the first half of the 9th/15th century had been determined largely by the old idea of the crusade, that is to say the liberation of the Holy Sepulchre and the conquest of Egypt along with Syria and the Arabian peninsula, since the fall of Constantinople to the Ottomans in 857/1453 the new and most important motive had been the reconquest of that city, and even the word "crusade" had finally come to mean the struggle against the Ottomans. The fall of Constantinople, too, had made plain to the West the growing danger that Ottoman expansion represented. Pope Nicholas V had promulgated a bull on 30 October 1453 in which he called for a crusade against the Turk. At the same time he had sent to the east an ambassador, probably the Franciscan Ludovico da Bologna, to win allies behind the back of the powerful monarch. Even though the idea of a pact with non-Christian powers was not exactly popular in the West, it was far from being a new one, for Western powers had previously negotiated with the Mongols to effect an alliance behind the back of the Egyptian Mamlūks. Venice, too, who saw her interests in the eastern Mediterranean threatened, had already despatched a mission to "Persia" in 1454. Although at that early date Uzun Ḥasan had not shown himself prepared to discuss proposals for an alliance against the

Ottomans, he would seem to have been alive to its inherent possibilities and to have desired to show himself uncommitted; for a group of ambassadors of Anatolian princes arriving in Rome in 1460, whence they were to proceed to other European courts, included a Türkmen ambassador whose presence among envoys predominantly Christian aroused considerable attention.

Before long Uzun Ḥasan adopted a positive policy and, indeed, after 872/1467, became the moving force behind the busy interchange of diplomatic missions, a subject that will be treated in greater detail in a later chapter. This can be seen as a presage of the imminent struggle with the Ottomans, the more so since Uzun Ḥasan had been forced to witness the Ottoman conquest of Trebizond in 865/1461. The idea of an East–West anti-Turkish league had numerous and sometimes changing advocates both on the European side and on that of Asia Minor. The Curia, Venice, Naples, and other powers were the partnership that corresponded to the Trebizond, Georgian and Türkmen princes. But just as Venice was to become the principal spokesman in the West, so Uzun Ḥasan eventually assumed that position in the East. Preliminary agreements in 1458 were followed by an alliance in 1464, and this was further strengthened when relations culminated in the mission of Caterino Zeno. The latter left for Tabrīz in 1471, probably at the beginning of October, and did not return to Venice for another four years. Being personally acquainted with the East, and even related to Uzun Ḥasan through his wife, a niece of Despina Khātūn, he was particularly well-equipped for his mission. On account of the Turco-Venetian war (867–84/1463–79) the Türkmen alliance had certainly acquired a new significance for the Signoria, especially since the Ottomans had conquered the Morea, Lesbos, and also Euboea (875/1470), which had been in Venetian hands for 264 years. The object of all these negotiations was common and coordinated military action to destroy the Ottoman empire, as well as agreement on the distribution of eventual spoils. Over and above this, Uzun Ḥasan had expressed the urgent request that Venice should supply him with artillery and other firearms so that in this respect at least he could be a match for the Ottomans, who were already thus equipped. These weapons were despatched by decision of the Senate on 4 February 1473.

The Porte, naturally, was not unaware of what was going on. Through Uzun Ḥasan's rise to power, Sultan Meḥmed II, the conqueror of Constantinople, found himself increasingly in the same kind of situation as had existed on the eve of the catastrophe of 804/1402, except that this time his enemies both to the East and to the West were in agreement. There were precedents not only for the East–West confrontation but also for the involvement of Asia Minor. By his marriage with the Despina, Uzun Ḥasan had become part of an alliance directed against the Ottomans, thus joining forces with the rulers of Trebizond, Georgia and Qaramān, and in the following year, 1459, he had sent a mission to the Sublime Porte requesting that the latter should waive the contributions paid yearly by the emperor of Trebizond, while at the same time he reminded him of the annual presents formerly made by the sultan to the rulers of Diyārbakr. For more than fifty years this had not been paid. The negative outcome of the move can hardly have come as a surprise. None the less it provided a pretext for Uzun Ḥasan to attack the small principality of Qoylu Ḥiṣār on the river Kelkit which commanded the approaches from central to eastern Anatolia and to Trebizond. While this failed to bring him lasting success, he had at least shown that he regarded himself as the protector of the Comnenian dynasty. When in 865/1461 Meḥmed II advanced to attack Trebizond, Uzun Ḥasan sent his troops to meet him between Arzinjān and Kamākh, though after several unsuccessful skirmishes he was forced to acknowledge that he could not obstruct the sultan's intentions. He was clever enough to avoid a premature trial of strength, but sought rather to come to an understanding by despatching his mother, Sarāī Khātūn, into the Ottoman camp, not, it would seem, without success.

In spite of this reverse and his quite manifest desire for the moment to avoid a definite break with the sultan, he still did not relinquish his Anatolian ambitions; and indeed his western commitments hardly allowed him to do so. For if that alliance were to be fully effective, he must needs maintain direct contact with his European allies. How else, for instance, could arms reach him from Venice? Since at this time Cyprus was governed by King Jacques II de Lusignan, husband of the Venetian Catarina Cornaro, and so was open to Venetian ships, it was clear that Uzun Ḥasan must seek access to that part of the Anatolian coast facing the island. The way that led there passed through Qaramān country, where Uzun Ḥasan's interests clashed with those of the Ottomans and the Egyptians. A favourable opportunity arose when, in 868/1464, after the death of the Qaramanid Ibrāhīm, his eldest son Isḥāq was driven out by his brother Pīr Aḥmad, and sought help from his father's old friend, Uzun Ḥasan. This was forthcoming, and with Türkmen support he regained his throne. So important was Qaramān to Meḥmed, however, that by the spring he had restored the former status quo in Qonya, the Qaramān capital. Whether the ruler of the Āq Quyūnlū was deterred by the death of his protégé a short while after, or by fear of provoking the Porte, or by developments to the east of his territory, he did not seek to intervene when the sultan reinstated Pīr Aḥmad, nor yet when he drove him out again not long afterwards, to incorporate Qaramān within his own dominions.

If to modern eyes Uzun Ḥasan's actions seem predominantly aggressive, the impression of him that prevailed in Istanbul in his own time was one of moderation and readiness for compromise. Jahān Shāh's message to the sultan, which was accompanied by a request for support, that he was about to march against the Āq Quyūnlū, met with refusal on the grounds that the Porte had no cause for war with Uzun Ḥasan. It can only be assumed that a campaign in the east did not fit in with the sultan's plans. Doubtless, too, he also nourished the conviction that, if it came to a crisis, the ruler of Āmid would present a problem no greater than had any of the other potentates of the Anatolian hinterland, and could be dealt with as had recently those of Trebizond and Qaramān, a fatal miscalculation, as it turned out, when by his victories over Jahān Shāh and Abū Sa'īd Uzun Ḥasan had grown to be almost the leading power in the Near East. For not even Istanbul could dismiss as a mere Anatolian princeling a ruler having at his disposal the combined resources of eastern Anatolia, Mesopotamia, Āzarbāījān and Persia. Moreover, his Western alliance, of which the effects were gradually becoming perceptible, now appeared in a quite different light. With such an enemy in his rear, the sultan's hands were tied in regard to his far-reaching ambitions in the west and north-west, for were he to leave his eastern frontier exposed he would have to reckon with the threat of surprise attack.

Uzun Ḥasan did not hesitate to take advantage of the changed situation. Significantly, he began with Qaramān, returning for the first time to the plans which the sultan had thwarted in 1469. It would seem that he had already undertaken an expedition against Qaramān in 875/1471, but without success. The following year a strong force set out, ostensibly against the Dulghadïr in Abulustān, but in reality once more against Qaramān. To mislead the sultan and his informers in

Anatolia, Uzun Ḥasan simultaneously sent a mission to Istanbul, soliciting a pardon for the Qaramanids exiled from Qonya, while all the time these were marching on their country with the Türkmen levies. In August Türkmen troops laid waste Ṭoqat and pressed on through Sīvās to Qaiṣariyya and Qaramān. Certainly Uzun Ḥasan's immediate objective was to contact his western allies on the Mediterranean coast and to take delivery of the firearms which had arrived there meanwhile from Venice. Nevertheless, ultimately all his military activity was directed against the Ottoman sultan: it was a question of supremacy in Anatolia. If further proof was required in Istanbul of the gravity of the situation, it was forthcoming in the news that Admiral Pietro Mocenigo, well-known to the Turks from many a battle as a daring enemy, had entered Qaramanian waters with a fleet of ninety-nine Venetian, Neapolitan, Papal and Cypriot galleys and was conquering towns and fortified places on the coast.

Uzun Ḥasan's advance on Qaramān was intentionally planned for late summer because this meant that the sultan must first muster his troops, then bring them over a large distance, and hence would not be able to counter-attack before the winter, so that nothing was to be feared from that quarter earlier than the following spring. Under these circumstances it might have been expected that Uzun Ḥasan would shortly make his way south-west to join his allies in person. But this was not to be. When news of the destruction of Ṭoqat reached Meḥmed II, he knew that the time had come for action. Undeterred either by the lateness of the season or by the warnings of his cautious advisers, he demonstrated his intentions by transferring the royal camp to the Asiatic shore of the Bosphorus and made everything ready so that he could march on eastern Anatolia in the spring without any further delay, a plan which in fact he put in operation. At the first encounter between the two forces, which took place between Arzinjān and Tarjān, Uzun Ḥasan's troops were victorious. But in the decisive battle at which both rulers were present, on 16 Rabīʿ I 878/11 August 1473, near the village of Bashkent on the Otluqbeli, the Ottomans triumphed; and every detail of the battle is described in a victory document by Meḥmed II.[1] The Ottomans were already using gunpowder and fire-arms at the beginning of the 9th/15th century, and the

[1] R.R. Arat, "Fatih Sultan Mehmed'in yarlığı" *TüMe* VI (1936-9), 285–322. Salim, *Otlukbeli.*

effect of their artillery on the Türkmen cavalry in this battle was devastating.[1]

The result of this struggle was a peace treaty whereby the Euphrates became the western frontier of the Türkmen empire, a demarcation which Uzun Ḥasan and his successors were in fact to observe. While their defeat at Bashkent can be seen as an indication that the Türkmens had reached the limits of their expansion and had passed the zenith of their political development, the defeat was of little immediate consequence to the Türkmen empire, if only because Meḥmed II did not exploit his victory but refrained from the pursuit of his conquered foe. Perhaps this circumstance also explains why the Western powers so obviously underrated the extent and significance of the Türkmen defeat. How otherwise is it comprehensible that Venice should actually have intensified her efforts to involve Uzun Ḥasan in common action against the Ottomans after the disaster of 878/1473, although in retrospect it is obvious to historians that this had shattered the Western–Türkmen alliance? The defeat at Bashkent, which set the final seal upon Uzun Ḥasan's failure in Qaramān, did in fact preserve him from a clash with Egypt, the fourth of his powerful rivals, which would have been inevitable had he continued to press onwards towards the Mediterranean. As it turned out, however, his relations with the Mamlūks, which up till then had been clouded only by an occasional episode, were to remain more or less friendly until the end of his reign.

We have recounted in detail only those of Uzun Ḥasan's military operations which are of significance in the expansion of his kingdom or in the general field of politics, while lesser operations such as his campaigns in Georgia or his battles with the Kurds have been mentioned, if at all, only cursorily. Of the further struggles after 1473, only the rebellions of his sons, Ughurlū Muḥammad in Shīrāz and Maqṣūd in Baghdad (879/1474), and that of his brother Uvais in Rūḥā (880/1475) are worthy of note. In these, needless to say, his military skill did not again fail him.

More important than a detailed account of these occurrences, which we can now leave behind, is a survey of the forces which Uzun Ḥasan employed in the conquest of his kingdom and for the maintenance of order within it. Some reasonably reliable figures are available in a study

[1] V. J. Parry, "Bārūd: The Ottoman Empire", *EI*².

of an account of a review held by Prince Khalīl, governor of the province of Fārs, in 881/1476.[1] We are told that the standing army consisted of 25,000 horsemen and 10,000 infantry, with corresponding staff and commissariat. Besides these there were the contingents of the provincial governorships, among which Fārs led with an almost equal strength, while the rest of the provinces put up levies commensurate with their smaller capacity. All in all, Uzun Ḥasan probably had at his disposal an army of more than 100,000 men. The strength of that army lay in its exceptionally effective cavalry, according to the eye-witness account of the Venetian ambassador, Caterino Zeno; its weakness, as we have seen, was its lack of firearms, and particularly of artillery.

Besides military qualities, Uzun Ḥasan also possessed striking political ability. This was particularly apparent during the final phase of his reign, from about 875/1471 to 882/1478. To this time probably belongs the *Qānūn-nāma-yi Ḥasan Pādishāh*, a kind of legal code, of whose contents the greater part at least is known to us.[2] It concerns the codification of fiscal regulations as handed down, probably from ancient times, in many different parts of the Türkmen empire, and was compiled with the intention of protecting the people against arbitrary increases in existing taxation and the introduction of new taxes and levies. To gauge the significance of the introduction of binding and effective fiscal laws, one need only call to mind the ruthless exploitation of the people, the oppression and the horrors of war which, for more than a hundred and fifty years, had been the predominant characteristics of that region. Not only were these laws a determining factor in the population's welfare, but they were also the prerequisite for a healthy economic life. And, indeed, the "Codex Uzun Ḥasan", as this compilation might be called, was still in use many decades later in regions of the Türkmen empire by then in Ottoman hands and in Persia. Eastern writers of that time mention it with approval. Its originator thus exercised a lasting influence on government and finance and secured for himself an honourable place alongside another Near Eastern reformer, the great Mongol statesman Ghazan Khān.

When Uzun Ḥasan breathed his last on 1 Shawwāl 882/5 January 1478 at the age of barely 53, he left behind him a Türkmen empire even larger than that lost to him eleven years earlier by Jahān Shāh Qarā

[1] Minorsky, "A Civil and Military Review".
[2] Hinz, "Das Steuerwesen Ostanatoliens"; Barkan, "Osmanlı devrinde".

Quyūnlū. It extended from the upper reaches of the Euphrates to the Great Salt Desert and the Kirmān province in south Persia, and from Transcaucasia to Mesopotamia and the Persian Gulf. Uzun Ḥasan had made no provision for the succession; nevertheless, it seemed at first as though this kingdom, unlike so many other states of Turkish foundation, possessed enough internal stability to survive its founder. Even though his son Khalīl Sulṭān, who succeeded him on the throne, was able to hold it for only a few months, his younger brother Ya'qūb who overthrew him succeeded in preserving the kingdom through twelve comparatively peaceful years. In this he was favoured by the fact that Meḥmed the Conqueror's successor in Istanbul, Bāyezīd II (886–918/1481–1512), was an inferior warrior, and also by having less threatening neighbours in Ḥusain Bāīqarā (873–911/1469–1506), the ruler of the Timurid kingdom in Herat, and in the Egyptian sultan Qā'itbāī (872–901/1468–96).

The predominantly peaceful conditions at this time can be ascribed to the skill shown by the young ruler in obtaining the allegiance of the country's magnates. Thus secured against many an internal difficulty, he was able to devote his whole energy to domestic policy, to cultural interests and to such military matters as even he found unavoidable. Amongst these was a victory over an Egyptian force which had been despatched in 885/1480 to conquer Diyārbakr, and also a number of campaigns, such as those in Kirmān, Georgia, Gīlān and Māzandarān which were judged to be necessary during his reign.

From beginning to end, none of these operations presented any real threat. Such cannot have been Ya'qūb's estimation of the events of 893/1488, that is to say, the machinations of his cousin and brother-in-law, the young leader of the community of the Safavid order at Ardabīl. We have already seen his father, Shaikh Junaid, as the foe of the Qarā Quyūnlū and protégé of Uzun Ḥasan. Subsequently he had met his death in 864/1460 during a battle with the Shīrvān-Shāh Khalīl Sulṭān, whom he had provoked on the occasion of an attack upon the Circassians. His son and successor, Shaikh Ḥaidar, also waged a war against the Circassians the motives of which will be discussed in the chapter on the Safavids. In order to reach their country, which was not adjacent to Ardabīl but about 250 miles away, he had to march through Shīrvān, which was subject to the Āq Quyūnlū. Although he had not omitted to obtain Ya'qūb's permission, the increased power that accrued to him from the very active support of ṣūfī followers seems to have aroused suspicions in Tabrīz and as a result he was invited in 891–2/1487 to Ya'qūb's court, where he had to swear an oath of fealty. But only a year later, the Türkmen leader, happening to be at Qum, received a call for help from the Shīrvān-Shāh Farrukh-Yasār, his brother-in-law, whom the shaikh had attacked and beleaguered in his capital city, Shamākhī, while returning from a campaign against the Circassians. Circumstances cannot have left him long in doubt as to his course of action in regard to these two brothers-in-law, since he must have feared that the victorious Safavid shaikh, were he also to conquer Shīrvān, would become a serious menace to himself. He therefore despatched troops and set out himself for Shīrvān. On 29 Rajab 893/9 July 1488 the Safavid forces were vanquished by the Türkmens near the village of Dartanat at the foot of the Alburz mountains, Shaikh Ḥaidar being killed during the fighting.

It could not then have been predicted that, in spite of their annihilating defeat, the future belonged to the Safavids. The necessary preconditions did not arise until after Sultan Ya'qūb's sudden death in 896/1490, when the resulting continuous struggle for power among the Türkmen princes brought about a condition of chaos.

THE DECLINE AND END OF THE ĀQ QUYŪNLŪ

Under the last representatives of the Āq Quyūnlū dynasty, Bāīsunqur (d. 898/1493), Rustam (d. 902/1497), Aḥmad Gövde (d. 903/1497), Alvand (to 907/1502), Muḥammadī (d. 905/1500), and Murād (to 908/1503), the empire created by their grandfather Uzun Ḥasan fell into decay. Its future development had already been presaged when Sulṭān 'Alī, son of the Safavid Shaikh Ḥaidar, secured the succession for Rustam. Their friendship did not last long. Fleeing before the troops of his now mistrustful protégé, he was killed in 899/1494. It was reserved to his brother Ismā'īl, born in 892/1487, to secure the heritage of the Āq Quyūnlū for the Safavids – in Persia for good, but temporarily only in eastern Anatolia, until the Ottoman victory. In 907/1501 he ascended the throne in Tabrīz and defeated Alvand the following year. With the conquest of Mārdīn, held by the Āq Quyūnlū until some time prior to 913/1507,[1] and the almost simultaneous flight of Murād from Baghdad to Turkey, Türkmen rule came to an end.

[1] Minorsky, "Aḳ Ḳoyunlu", and "A Soyūrghāl of Qāsim b. Jahāngīr".

Historians of the West are not forward in praising Türkmen achievement, including that of the Āq Quyūnlū, and its subsequent influence in the field of culture.[1] This might, however, appear in a more favourable light if seen against the background of the appalling conditions brought about by the Mongol invasions and Tīmūr's campaigns. In the general devastation of the Near East, architectural activity such as that of the Āq Quyūnlū, especially of Uzun Ḥasan and Ya'qūb, however little of it may have survived, has a certain significance in that it formed a connecting link with later, happier times. The relations they established with Western powers were also to have certain repercussions. Finally, the intellectual life at the court of Tabrīz under Uzun Ḥasan and Ya'qūb was distinguished by the presence of a number of eminent men whose names have gone down in the history of Persian thought.

The Āq Quyūnlū are supposed to have belonged to the Sunna, and are therefore seen as directly contrasting with the Qarā Quyūnlū. This dichotomy may well be due to a failure in discrimination, itself perhaps the result of reliance on the classifications of eastern, and notably Shī'ī, writers. We have already seen that the Shī'ī zeal of the Qarā Quyūnlū has certain doubtful features, and probably much the same applies to Uzun Ḥasan's Sunnī orthodoxy, of which the pro-dervish policy, not only towards the Ardabīl shaikhs, is somewhat suspect. It should not be overlooked that the Sunnī label attaching to the Āq Quyūnlū, who repeatedly engaged in strife with the Safavids during the phase of their decline, is problematical, especially when based on later Shī'ī accounts. In future research rather more consideration should be given to the religious factor.

The political structure of the Āq Quyūnlū, like that of the Qarā Quyūnlū, was based in many respects upon Mongol foundations and the Jalayirids must be regarded in this instance as its mediators. Uzun Ḥasan's reforms have already been discussed. While his achievement appears to have been the stabilisation of existing principles of law so as to prevent arbitrary fiscal innovations, towards the end of Ya'qūb's reign there was an energetic attempt to eradicate utterly such principles of Mongol taxation as were out of step with the prescriptions of Islamic religious law, and to set up the latter in their stead. Although the attempt failed and Sultan Rustam (897–902/1492–7) returned to

[1] Spuler, *The Muslim World* II, 77.

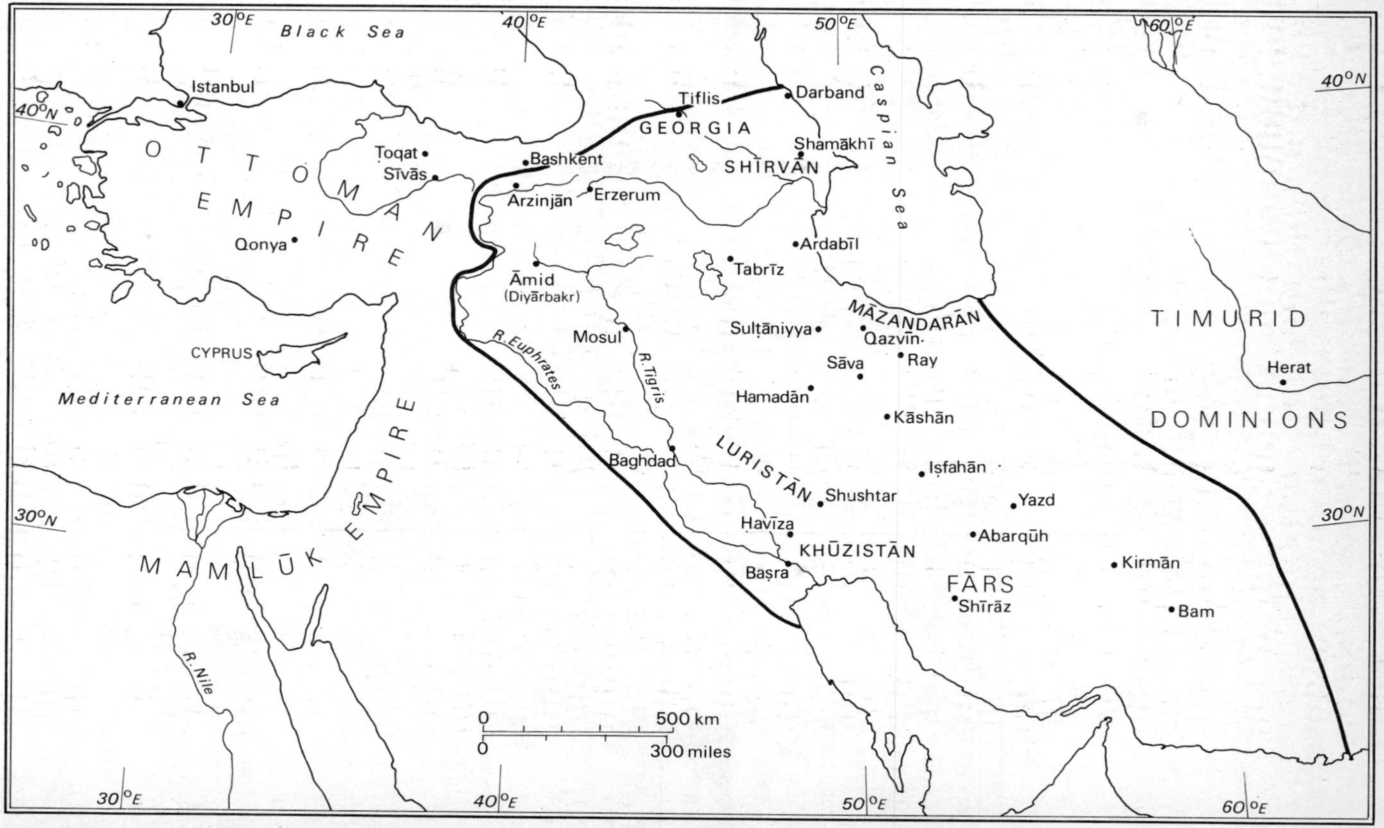

Map. The empire of Uzun Ḥasan

IV. *The Qarā Quyūnlū*

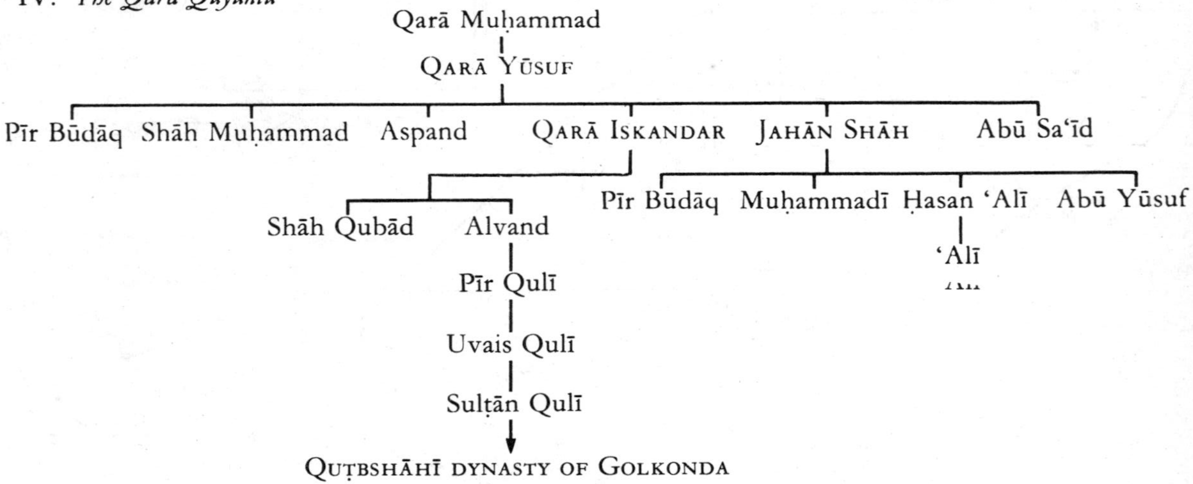

Qarā Muḥammad
Qarā Yūsuf
Pīr Būdāq
Shāh Muḥammad
Aspand
Qarā Iskandar
Jahān Shāh
Abū Sa‘īd
Shāh Qubād
Alvand
Pīr Qulī
Uvais Qulī
Sulṭān Qulī
Quṭbshāhī dynasty of Golkonda
Pīr Būdāq
Muḥammadī
Ḥasan ‘Alī
Abū Yūsuf
‘Alī

V. *The Āq Quyūnlū*

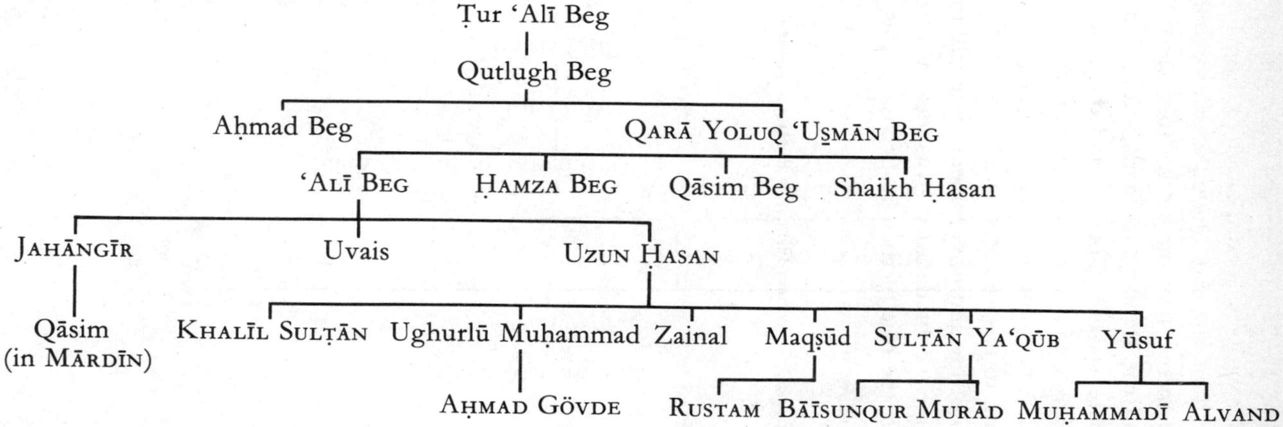
Ṭur ʻAlī Beg
Qutlugh Beg
Aḥmad Beg
Qarā Yoluq ʻUsmān Beg
ʻAlī Beg
Ḥamza Beg
Qāsim Beg
Shaikh Ḥasan
Jahāngīr
Uvais
Uzun Ḥasan
Qāsim (in Mārdīn)
Khalīl Sulṭān
Ughurlū Muḥammad
Zainal
Maqṣūd
Sulṭān Ya‘qūb
Yūsuf
Aḥmad Gövde
Rustam
Bāīsunqur
Murād
Muḥammadī
Alvand

the old customs,[1] it was repeated, once again without success, under Aḥmad Gövde ("the Dwarf"), who during the years of his exile had become familiar with the corresponding Ottoman regulations.

With the fall of the Āq Quyūnlū, the second wave of Turkish population elements flowing back from Anatolia to the east, to Āzarbāījān and the Iranian highlands, came to an end. When it had been in full spate, states had been founded that seemed full of promise, but their success was never of long duration. They were too closely bound up with exceptional individuals, and there was no sound political organisation to ensure their continuance. In the final analysis, the nomadic form of life and government were still too strong. Although neither Türkmen confederation was destined to have noteworthy reverberations, the rôle of their respective ethnic groups was not yet played out.

[1] Roemer, "Le dernier Firman de Rustam Bahādur Aq Qoyunlu?".

CHAPTER 5

THE SAFAVID PERIOD

In the summer of 906–7/1501,[1] after his victory over the Āq Quyūnlū, Ismā'īl entered the Türkmen capital Tabrīz, ascended the throne and took the title of Shah. He thereby founded the rule of the Safavid dynasty in Iran which was to last until 1148/1736. Thus after becoming Grand Master of the Ardabīl order on the death of his brother Sulṭān 'Alī, he finally attained the political power in pursuit of which his father and grandfather had already lost their lives.

Whether we think of this event as marking the beginning of modern Persian history or not, it certainly heralds a new era. The historical achievement of the Safavids was to establish a strong, enduring state in Iran after centuries of foreign rule and a lengthy period of political fragmentation. Although the preceding Türkmen dynasties, the Qarā Quyūnlū and the Āq Quyūnlū, created certain preconditions of this achievement and on the surface pursued similar aims for a short time – came near, indeed, to realising them – their success was only temporary. Despite all their military and political attainments in the late 8th/14th and 9th/15th centuries – for example, the way in which they maintained their independence *vis-à-vis* such powerful neighbours as the Ottomans, the Mamlūks and the Timurids, or founded new states culminating in the kingdoms of Jahān Shāh and Uzun Ḥasan – not one of their rulers succeeded in establishing a lasting political structure. Though their rule extended deep into Persian territory, it represents from the point of view of the history of Persia merely peripheral formations beyond or on the frontiers of Iran. Not until the Safavid era did Iran witness the rise of a state similar in importance to the Ottoman empire or the empire of the Egyptian Mamlūks. For more than two centuries the Safavid kingdom prolonged the older political and cultural tradition of Persia and endowed the country and its peoples with a unique character of historic significance, which has in part endured even up to the present day. Its typical features include the revival of the monarchist tradition, the acquisition of historically justified territory, the creation of a new military and political structure, the spread of a

[1] The date authoritatively established by Glassen, *Die frühen Safawiden*, p. 85.

Shīʿī creed as the state religion, the Iranicisation of Persian Islam, the continued progress of modern Persian towards becoming the language of politics and administration in modern Iranian history, and the development of a specific culture which reached its peak in architecture (still visible today), but which also produced remarkable results in the intellectual life of the Persian nation. The importance of this dynasty is not confined to the national history of Persia: it was the Safavids who led Iran back on to the stage of world history. Their conflicts with the Ottomans and their policy of alliance with the Western powers have a world-historical interest and a direct relevance to the history of Western Europe.

THE BACKGROUND OF THE SAFAVIDS

Who was this Ismāʿīl, who made such an impact on the Persia of his time and whose influence was still felt centuries later? His personality presents difficulties to the historian which cannot be resolved adequately by reference to either his biography or his career. Rather, they become clear and comprehensible only when one considers his origins and the strange intellectual climate which produced him. We have already met his father, Shaikh Ḥaidar, and his grandfather Junaid as notably enterprising characters in Türkmen history, politically ambitious representatives of the Ṣafaviyya, a widespread ṣūfī order centred on Ardabīl in the south-western coastal region of the Caspian Sea. The early history of this order differs little from that of other Islamic conventicles,[1] but the political development in which it culminates is quite unique. The order is named after Shaikh Ṣafī al-Dīn Isḥāq, whose lifespan (650–735/1252–1334) coincides almost exactly with the Persian Mongol empire of the Īl-Khāns, a circumstance which in several respects helped to determine his life and actions.

This era constitutes a special period in the history of Islam. With the destruction of the Caliphate by the Mongols and the decline of almost all the previous centres of power in the Islamic East, Islam was faced with a grave crisis, both political and religious; indeed, even its very existence seemed threatened. Moreover, after the numerous theological disputes and the endless wrangling between heretical sects in preceding

[1] See Kissling, "Aus der Geschichte des Chalvetijje-Ordens": the connection between the Ṣafaviyya and other orders is dealt with in Kissling's table I.

centuries, the chance of a reconciliation of the warring factions and a reversion to the essential elements of the faith might have been found in this very crisis. It cannot be said that the opportunity was exploited: even at this point Islam did not undergo a genuine renaissance or reformation. However, in the territories under Mongol rule at least, certain differences were pushed into the background, for example, the split between the four schools of law and the violent opposition between the Sunna and the Shīʿa, the origin of which – the question of the legitimate ruler of the Islamic world – had lost its immediate significance in the light of the Mongol victory. With the loss of the political background, the official theology, which had never been popular because of its rationalism, was deprived of much of its importance and influence. A popular religiosity became widespread, displaying several characteristics which had probably existed earlier but which had not prevailed owing to orthodox hostility. These included a marked willingness to believe in miracles, a cult of saints with the growth of much-frequented places of pilgrimage, and even the veneration of ʿAlī, the cousin and son-in-law of the prophet Muḥammad, an aspect fundamental to Shīʿī belief but which does not necessarily have the same importance in Folk Islam since even devout Sunnīs have venerated ʿAlī as *amīr al-muʾminīn*. They also included Islamic mysticism, which had flowered long before the Mongol invasion but now underwent a great revival. At the same time the ṣūfī orders which practised it expanded to unprecedented dimensions. Their shaikhs were known and loved by the masses and the great respect commanded by certain masters of the religious chapters filled the scholarly theologians with envy and resentment.

In this respect Shaikh Ṣafī was a typical religious leader, a representative of Folk Islam far removed from the official theology, whose spokesmen viewed his career with grave suspicion. But in no other regard: for even his origins as a member of a respected family which had lived in Ardabīl for generations, are by no means typical of the religious leaders of the time, who normally came from the lower classes. Although he was renowned for asceticism and piety, he displayed other qualities which for the most part accord ill with a propensity for the meditative existence of a recluse: self-confidence, enterprise, acquisitiveness and a militant activism. Shaikh Ṣafī is portrayed as a paradoxical personality in which the miracle worker and man of God combined with a sober, practical politician and a cunning merchant.

His teacher, Tāj al-Dīn Ibrāhīm Gīlānī, known as Shaikh Zāhid (b. 615/1218, d. 700/1301),[1] a familiar figure in the history of Islamic religious orders, is said to have perceived his extraordinary gifts at their very first meeting and – according to the legend – to have realised even then that he was destined to become conqueror of the world. At all events, Shaikh Zāhid allowed him to marry one of his daughters and appointed him as his successor.

Round about 1300, perhaps while his spiritual leader was still alive, Shaikh Ṣafī founded his own order in Ardabīl, the Ṣafaviyya. He never in fact conquered the world, but Shaikh Zāhid's assessment of his other qualities proved accurate. As grand master of his order, as one of the holy men who in those days ruled alongside the political leaders, he achieved extraordinary success. Unless we are very much mistaken, his cell even became the focal point of a mass religious movement. He was friendly with the secular rulers and enjoyed remarkable esteem on their part; undoubtedly their attitude was determined by the size of his following and his influence over the people. He became the protector of the poor and the weak, while his convent at Ardabīl became a refuge for the persecuted and the oppressed. In the last analysis he owed his popularity not merely to his reputation for sanctity, miracles and prophecies, but also to his political authority and to the wealth which he acquired in due course through the generous gifts of his supporters and admirers. His network of disciples and emissaries, so we are told, extended throughout the land from the Oxus to the Persian Gulf, from the Caucasus to Egypt. An emissary (*khalīfa*) of his is even said to have risen to a position of influence in Ceylon.[2]

The intertwining of religion and politics in Islam, such as is seen in the history of the Prophet Muḥammad himself, is also a characteristic feature of the Safavids which, as we can see, marks even the career of their founder. Although he was not very concerned with secular power, he certainly did not lack political influence. The integrity of his religious position is beyond question. Not only his good works and his asceticism, but also his missionary efforts to convert the Mongols, many of whom were not of the Islamic faith, and his influence on certain Turkish or Türkmen groups stamp him as a particularly conscientious Muslim. The theory[3] that he dreamed of a renewal of Islam

[1] Minorsky, "A Mongol Decree of 720/1320". [2] Glassen, *Die frühen Safawiden*, pp. 43, 130.

[3] Details *ibid.*, p. 50, where a change in the meaning of the word "ṣūfī" to something like "committed, active Muslim" is mentioned.

which would transcend the dogmatism of the theologians and the squabbling of the heretics is not without foundation. He certainly could not achieve so paramount a success during his lifetime, nor did the effects of his activities, once this success materialised later, cover the whole Islamic *oecumene*. But the religious revival and unification of Persia which came about two centuries later are unthinkable without the brotherhood he founded – although there is no direct connection between them. Whether on the other hand Shaikh Ṣafī envisaged a Shīʿī Persia is quite a different question, with which we shall deal later.

Nevertheless, his rôle in the Ṣafaviyya was not confined to founding the order and giving it his name; he also established a firm basis for future development through the great number of supporters which he won for it and the prosperity with which he endowed it.[1] The ancestors of the Safavid rulers are often depicted as unassuming monks, but this image does not really correspond to the historical facts even in the earliest phase. It is scarcely appropriate for the later period either. Although we have only meagre evidence about the immediate successors of Shaikh Ṣafī as masters of the Ardabīl order, we can conclude simply from occasional references in the sources that they were highly esteemed – by the early Ottoman sultans, among others.[2] How otherwise could one explain the ambitious plans and the political aspirations of Junaid and Shaikh Ḥaidar under the Türkmen princes of the latter half of the 9th/15th century – aspirations which were after all by no means entirely unfulfilled?

After his entry into Tabrīz, Shah Ismāʿīl immediately proceeded to institute the Shīʿī creed as the state religion. Until it is proved otherwise, we can assume that he took this decision out of religious conviction, not out of political expediency.[3] The precise nature of Ismāʿīl's commitment to the Shīʿī faith – to what extent he was familiar with and himself observed the precepts of the Shīʿa – remains to be seen. At present it will suffice to affirm that he desired to abolish the Sunna with

[1] For endowments set up in Shaikh Ṣafī's favour, see M.H.M. Nakhjuvānī, "Farmānī az farāmīn-i daura-yi Mughūl", *Revue de la Faculté des Lettres de Tabriz* v/1 (1953), 40–8.

[2] Babinger, "Der Islam in Kleinasien", p. 61.

[3] Political motives for his Shīʿī creed are imputed to Ismāʿīl by Efendiev, *Obrazovanie*, pp. 49, 51; E. Werner, *Die Geburt einer Grossmacht – Die Osmanen (1300–1481)* (Berlin, 1966), p. 303; and Guseĭnov and Sumbatzade, *Istoriya Azerbaĭdzhana* I, 210.

its veneration of the Orthodox Caliphs and to replace it with the belief in ʿAlī and the Twelve Imāms.

We know that Ismāʿīl's advisers voiced grave reservations about his intention because the entirely Sunnī population of Tabrīz would be violently opposed to the Shīʿa. But Ismāʿīl would not be deterred, and in fact achieved success. The first phase of Safavid rule does not lack a certain grotesque trait, in as much as theologians who were fully conversant with the Shīʿa must have been few and far between at that time. Detailed information about Shīʿī precepts was hard to come by; indeed, there was a lack of books from which this might have been culled. In the search for appropriate texts there eventually came to light a solitary volume of the *Qawāʿid al-aḥkām fī maʿrifat al-halāl wa'l-ḥarām* of Ibn Muṭahhar al-Ḥillī (d. 726/1325), a famous Shīʿī theologian of the Mongol period. Admittedly the book was in Arabic and therefore unsuitable for general use until it had been translated into Persian, for a knowledge of Arabic could by that time no longer be presupposed among the populace.

Given the tremendous importance of the introduction of the Shīʿa for Ismāʿīl's future and for Persia, we must ask ourselves what made him take this decision. It is not easy to find an answer. We do not know for certain who was the first member of the future dynasty to profess the Shīʿī faith. Was Ismāʿīl himself the first? Or were his father and grandfather adherents of the sect? Or must we go back even further, perhaps to Shaikh Khwāja ʿAlī, or even Shaikh Ṣafī in person? Circumstantial evidence of all kinds is adduced in this connection, but none is conclusive.

There are various reasons for our being still so much in the dark. First, there is the lack of evidence in the sources, or at least in the reliable ones; in this context we must certainly disregard most documents written under Safavid rule and many sources which originated among their enemies. The complex relationships within Folk Islam similarly constitute an obstacle to a clear understanding of the situation. This Shīʿī–Sunnī syncretism, as it might be termed, occurs in Iran from the time of the Mongol invasion, and even in the 8th/14th and 9th/15th centuries, after the decline of the Īl-Khāns, it continued to mould the religious outlook of the ordinary people. Finally, it is by no means impossible that if one or other of Ismāʿīl's ancestors had been a Shīʿī, he might have practised *taqiyya*, that is, he might have concealed his convictions; this is in fact prescribed by the Shīʿa whenever an open profession of the faith might be dangerous.

All these considerations should not be allowed to obscure the fact that even the question of what Shīʿa and Sunna meant in the 9th/15th century cannot at present be answered at all precisely. This would require careful examination of the theological writings of the age, and such an analysis we do not yet possess. For the time being we must be content to surmise that at this period the well-known definitions of earlier times were no longer entirely valid. Until we possess more detailed knowledge, we cannot define more closely the religious ideas of Ismāʿīl's ancestors.

In order to characterise the situation, the following factors may be emphasised. That Shaikh Ṣafī was a Sunnī is beyond all shadow of a doubt. Yet the orthodoxy of his beliefs should not be judged too rigidly since the mere ideas of the religious world in which he lived cannot be entirely reconciled with orthodox tenets. Significantly he belonged to the Shāfiʿī *madhhab*, that is, to precisely that school of religious law which is closest to the Shīʿa and therefore normally adopted by Shīʿīs who are masquerading as Sunnīs. For the first hundred years after his death we have so little information that we can do no more than surmise that his successors adopted a similar position. Shaikh Khwāja ʿAlī (d. 832/1429) could be linked with the Shīʿa on account of his name and especially because he is said to have seen ʿAlī, the fourth Caliph and son-in-law of the Prophet, in a dream, and sang his praises in verses which are still extant. Sunnī writers are particularly distrustful of Junaid, the grandfather of Ismāʿīl, because he is alleged to have compromised himself round about 1450 in Qonya in the presence of the famous theologian Shaikh ʿAbd al-Laṭīf through a pro-Shīʿī remark transmitted to us by a friend of the shaikh, the Ottoman historian ʿĀshïqpashazāde. We are told also that when Junaid died some of his followers began to call him God and his son Ḥaidar the Son of God. Admittedly this statement stems from an embittered enemy of the Safavids, Fażl-Allāh b. Rūzbihān Khunjī, the chronicler of Sulṭān Yaʿqūb Āq Quyūnlū, who later fled from Ismāʿīl to Transoxiana. Ḥaidar too is reported to have seen ʿAlī in a dream. This is supposed to be the origin of the "Ḥaidar cap", the red hat of the Qizilbāsh, whose twelve gores are explained by reference to the Twelve Imāms.

We could certainly draw conclusions from these reports if we had any certain knowledge of the dividing lines between Sunna and Shīʿa in the 9th/15th century. Since it is possible that these were no longer what they had been, we must be cautious. Yet it should be noted that not one of the relevant writers describes any ancestor of Ismāʿīl unambiguously as a Shīʿī – not even those authors who attack their religious attitude. It is also significant, on the other hand, that an unbroken, direct Shīʿī tradition extending from Junaid via Ḥaidar to Ismāʿīl is out of the question. Ḥaidar was not born until 864/1460, several weeks after his father's death, and was brought up at the court of his uncle Uzun Ḥasan in Āmid, in an environment which has so far not been suspected of sympathy towards the Shīʿī doctrine. Not until he was nine years old did he arrive in Ardabīl where again it is unlikely that any marked Shīʿī atmosphere predominated under Shaikh Jaʿfar. If Ḥaidar was actually converted to the Shīʿa later, he had no opportunity to introduce Ismāʿīl to the creed, for Ismāʿīl was born on 25 Rajab 892/17 July 1487, only a year before his father's death. Ḥaidar could not have achieved this indirectly through Sulṭān ʿAlī, his eldest son, either, as the latter was still a child. In the next seven years which the sons of Shaikh Ḥaidar spent in the custody of the Āq Quyūnlū, we cannot exclude completely the possibility that they were exposed to Shīʿī influence, for example on the part of their guardians, but neither can we impute this to them without further ado. Although we cannot speak of a direct transmission of ideas between those three generations, we must posit a certain virulence of Shīʿī thought in order to begin to grasp the course of events.

Perhaps the solution of the problem lies precisely in the fact that Shaikh Ṣafī and his descendants, possibly including Ismāʿīl until shortly before his seizure of power, must be seen in the framework of Folk Islam without ever having consciously or overtly gone over to the Shīʿa. In the case of adherents of a ṣūfī order such as they, this is a perfectly reasonable conjecture in the light of all that we know. We can pass over the question of whether the equation of *taṣavvuf* (Sufism) with the Shīʿa is justified or whether it oversteps the mark: what is certain is that the step from Sufism to heresy was a fairly small one. The Sunnī theologians had only too good a reason for their antipathy towards the dervishes and their religious brotherhoods. If it is permissible to link the Ardabīl order from the outset with Folk Islam, certain Shīʿī features become clear. Though in Folk Islam these Shīʿī elements were stronger or weaker depending upon the area and the period, they were surely always present. Therefore certain Shīʿī affinities in the case of Shaikh Ṣafī and his successors (who at all events bear the stigma of

Sufism in the eyes of the distrustful orthodox theologians) do not necessarily mean that they had abjured the Sunna and turned Shī'ī. Neither the name of Shaikh Khwāja 'Alī, the second successor and grandson of Shaikh Ṣafī, nor the manifestation of 'Alī in dreams which he and later Shaikh Ḥaidar are said to have had, nor his verses in praise of 'Alī therefore constitute clear signs of a Shī'ī faith, and they are perhaps no more than features of Folk Islam.

If one examines Ismā'īl's notions against the Folk Islam background, it is quite possible that the worship of 'Alī widespread in his environment grew more firmly rooted in him so that a tendency towards the Shī'a became predominant. This accords well with his youthful capacity for enthusiasm (he was only fourteen years old when Tabrīz fell). We see his enthusiasm in his collection of Turkish poems, particularly where religious ideas are concerned, but also with regard to the heroes of Iranian legend. What is so disconcerting about the introduction of the Shī'a is the violent hostility exhibited towards the Sunnīs, whereby the execration of the Caliphs Abū Bakr, 'Umar and 'Uthmān is far more strongly emphasised than the Shī'ī additions to the *shahāda*, which is what really matters. Even if propaganda purposes played a part in this, there remains an impression of youthful protest, perhaps because Ismā'īl had grown tired either of the compromises of Folk Islam or of the secretiveness of taqiyya.

We must not underestimate the importance for Ismā'īl's religious beliefs of his stay in Lāhījān which followed his escape from the soldiers of Sulṭān Rustam Āq Quyūnlū. From 899/1494 onwards he spent five years there under the protection of Kārkiyā Mīrzā 'Alī, the then ruler of Gīlān, who claimed to be a descendant of the Caliph 'Alī and was a Shī'ī. He appointed one of the theologians in his kingdom, one Shams al-Dīn Lāhījī, to be Ismā'īl's teacher. This man must have influenced his pupil to a certain extent, since he occurs again, immediately after Ismā'īl ascended the throne, as *ṣadr*, occupying the highest religious office in the realm; later we see him as tutor to the princes at court. There is scarcely any doubt but that he was a Shī'ī. And this would be certain if he should be identical with a disciple of the same name of Sayyid Muḥammad Nūrbakhsh, who along with Muḥammad b. Falāḥ, the famous Mahdī, had been trained by the well-known Shī'ī theologian Aḥmad b. Fahd al-Hillī. Whatever the truth about the religion of his forebears, where Ismā'īl himself is concerned we already have a valid explanation of the origin of his Shī'ī faith in the few years he spent with his tutor in Lāhījān. This factor lends credence to the suggestion that his religious attitude was determined by inner conviction.

His collection of Turkish poems mentioned above provides an insight into his religious ideas. The Shīʿī character of these verses is unmistakable. But clearly what we have here is not something that can be related to the High Shīʿa as delineated in Shīʿī theology, but rather rabid fanaticism. The worship of ʿAlī expressed here betrays an extremism which cannot be reconciled with the normal Shīʿī doctrine. ʿAlī is named before the Prophet Muḥammad and placed on a level with God. In these lines we see perhaps an unrestrained exaggeration of certain Shīʿī ideas which also occur incipiently in Folk Islam. It is also significant that the particularly extreme passages are only to be found in the oldest extant versions of the collection: later manuscripts do not contain them, presumably because they derive from a version expurgated under the influence of Shīʿī theologians. Anyway the creed which Ismāʿīl avowed on coming to power could not have been the Shīʿa of the theologians, no matter of what school. Even if he himself, lacking clear religious ideas, envisaged no more than changing from the Sunna to the Shīʿa, his poems proclaim very different notions. Nor can they be interpreted as a gradual transition from Folk Islam to the High Shīʿa. If one pursues Ismāʿīl's thought to its conclusion and relates it to his political intentions, one realises that he is proclaiming a Shīʿī theocracy with himself at its head as a god-king.

However Ismāʿīl's attitude may be judged from the point of view of the official theology, his claim to be venerated as a god (*sijda*) did not prevent him from favouring the Ithnāʿashariyya, the Twelver Shīʿa, among the manifold divisions of the Shīʿa existing at the time. This creed acknowledges not the Caliphs but only the Twelve Imāms as the legitimate successors of the Prophet Muḥammad; a succession commencing with ʿAlī and ending with the Mahdī Muḥammad Ḥujjat-Allāh who, his followers believe, did not die but was merely carried off on 24 July 874, to return once more at the end of the world.

It was on this theory of succession that the Safavids based their claim to be direct descendants of ʿAlī and thereby of the Prophet Muḥammad. It rests on a genealogy which links Shaikh Ṣafī via a line of twenty ancestors with Mūsā al-Kāẓim (d. 183/799), the Seventh Imām.

Clearly such a lineage lent great weight to Ismāʿīl's bid for power in the legitimist atmosphere of the Shīʿīs, perhaps also in the rather monarchist concepts of certain Iranian circles. However, this lineage has not gone unchallenged. It was attacked even during the Safavid period and likewise deemed a forgery in recent times by Persian and non-Persian scholars alike.[1] It is indeed possible that the family tree of the Safavids cannot bear any closer analysis than many another table of this kind. The question still remains whether Ismāʿīl invoked it, knowing it to be false, or even undertook or commissioned the forgery himself as alleged by the Ottoman historian ʿĀlī;[2] or whether he acted in good faith, convinced of the authenticity of this genealogy. The answer to this question determines whether he began his extraordinary career in the honest, though biased, belief that he had a legitimate claim to the throne, or whether right from the outset he was prepared to stoop to anything, even outright forgery, to achieve his aim. Given his numerous embittered enemies, it is not surprising that he has indeed been accused of deliberate deception – unjustly, as far as one can tell. For even the Shīrvān-Shāh Khalīl-Allāh addresses Junaid, Ismāʿīl's grandfather, in a letter the text of which has been preserved, as a descendant of the Sayyids; and the Turkish Sultan Bāyezīd II applies to Shaikh Ḥaidar epithets such as are only used for a scion of ʿAlī's family.[3] If therefore alien rulers who were opposed to the Safavids accepted this notion, why should not Ismāʿīl himself have believed in all honesty that he was descended from ʿAlī? This belief is also attested by the spontaneity and originality which characterise his dīvān, precisely at the points where he emphasises his ʿAlid blood. Finally, Ismāʿīl may also have been aware that Shaikh Ṣafī himself had allegedly claimed to be related to the Prophet's family.[4] At least in childhood

[1] Kasravī, *Shaikh Ṣafī*, followed by Togan, "Sur l'origine", who pointed to the different versions of the *Ṣafvat al-ṣafā*.

[2] Walsh, "Historiography", p. 207; cf. also Togan, *loc. cit.* For a detailed study of anti-Safavid propaganda, see E. Eberhard, *Osmanische Polemik gegen die Safawiden* (Freiburg i. Br., 1970).

[3] Ṣābitī (Thābitī), *Asnād*, pp. 375 f. Ferīdūn Bey, *Münshe'āt es-selāṭīn*[2] (Istanbul, 1274–5/1858–9) I, 303.

[4] Shaikh Ṣafī's remark, *dar nasab-i mā siyādat hast*, which is included even in the earliest MSS and could not therefore have been added in the Safavid period, is passed over by Togan as being too vague. But Togan thereby ignores the fact that this expression corresponds exactly to the attitude of a Sunnī who, though a descendant of ʿAlī, does not wish to draw too much attention to himself. Togan nevertheless concedes the possibility that Shaikh Ṣafī's son, Ṣadr al-Dīn Mūsā, as is claimed, could have ordered the *sharīf*, on the occasion of a *ḥajj*, to authenticate a genealogy going back to ʿAlī; given this, it is unfair to dismiss outright Ismāʿīl's good faith as he does.

and certainly at the time of his accession to the throne in Tabrīz, Ismā'īl was convinced that his family tree reached back to Caliph 'Alī. Whether he maintained this belief in later life, when perhaps he had access to more reliable sources of information, is another question.

Thus whether or not Ismā'īl was the first of Shaikh Ṣafī's descendants to embrace the Shī'a, he was certainly the first whose Shī'ī faith can be proved without a shadow of a doubt, and was viewed in this light by certain 10th/16th century writers.[1] The political ambitions which he combined with his faith were after all not without precedent in his family. We saw that Shaikh Ṣafī enjoyed respect and influence among political leaders of his time, even though he did not himself pursue any political goals. That his successors were not entirely remote from the affairs of this world may be judged from Tīmūr's legendary visit to Khwāja 'Alī, and we meet his son Ibrāhīm, described by a Christian eye-witness as the "cruel governor of Ardabīl", in the retinue of Jahān Shāh on a campaign in Georgia.[2] We have fairly detailed knowledge of the military and political exploits of Junaid, Shah Ismā'īl's grandfather. Since up to his father's death the leadership of the order had always passed from father to son, he could have inherited the office in 851/1447, and there is in fact a well-attested tradition which speaks of his accession in that year. Nevertheless, he might thereafter have lost the leadership again: this would not necessarily be recorded in the official history of the Safavids, which naturally sets out to portray Ismā'īl's grandfather in the appropriate light.

The point is that at this time not he, but one of his father's brothers, Shaikh Ja'far, was head of the order, while he himself was mostly away from Ardabīl, not always of his own accord. It is of secondary importance whether Ja'far functioned as his nephew's guardian or representative, or whether he personally was invested with the office of grand master. What interests us is that Ja'far too did not stay remote from and uninvolved in the political events of his age, for he mobilised against Junaid the powerful Jahān Shāh Qarā Quyūnlū,[3] who was the father-in-law of Ja'far's son Qāsim. Ja'far also had contacts with the Timurid Abū Sa'īd and went out to greet him when the latter reached Sulṭāniyya on his fatal campaign of 873/1469 to the Mūghān steppe.

[1] E.g.. al-Nahrawālī and al-Qaramānī: see Mazzaoui, *Shī'ism*, p. 215, n.203.
[2] Minorsky, "Thomas of Metsop'", p. 25. [3] See above, p. 167.

We also know about Ja'far's correspondence with the Shīrvān-Shāh Khalīl-Allāh, again to the detriment of his nephew.[1]

There is no doubt that, soon after Shaikh Ibrāhīm's death, around 852/1448 a serious estrangement occurred between Shaikh Ja'far and Junaid which was still not resolved at the time of Junaid's death. But we have no such certainty concerning its cause. The motive is sought in diverging religious beliefs. According to this explanation Ja'far, who remained faithful to the Sunna, quarrelled with his nephew because of the latter's Shī'ī proclivities. This is indeed possible, but finds no adequate support in contemporary sources; one cannot draw conclusions about Junaid's early years from records which refer to his behaviour in later life. In Fażl-Allāh Khunjī's royal chronicle of the Āq Quyūnlū, which is relevant here, we read that he diverged from the life of his forebears. This might of course allude to divergent religious beliefs, if the writer did not expressly state that he had something else in mind: he says that Junaid strove for secular power, was driven into alien lands by his lust for conquest, instigated revolts against individual provincial governors in Anatolia, and constantly suffered fresh onsets of folly. All this need not necessarily be connected with Shī'ī heresy. There were probably sufficient grounds for the conflict in Junaid's militaristic tendencies alone, for we read that his multitudinous supporters occasionally gave Ardabīl the appearance of an armed camp.

Junaid's career doubtless gave many of his contemporaries cause for admiration or criticism, especially those who clung to the pattern of a devout life as led by his famous ancestors. He was anything but the ideal religious leader whose life was composed of pious striving and progression along the path of mystic perfection. When first exiled from Ardabīl, he wandered for seven years through Āzarbāījān, Anatolia and northern Syria, probably in the manner of a travelling monk but without observing the limitations of this rôle. His ambition was political success and a military following that would help him attain it. His charismatic personality must have had a great impact especially on the adventurous elements among the Türkmen tribes which he visited. On the other hand, he rightly saw that his opportunity lay in the rivalry between the Qarā Quyūnlū and the Āq Quyūnlū. The hostility of Jahān Shāh Qarā Quyūnlū drove him to cultivate the latter's opponent

[1] Ḥasan-i Rūmlū, quoted in Hinz, *Irans Aufstieg*, pp. 47f.

in Āmid and eventually in 861/1456 he succeeded in being received there. Uzun Ḥasan welcomed him and showed him such favour that Junaid enjoyed his hospitality for three whole years and, after some time, was even allowed to marry his sister. Although at that time Uzun Ḥasan was not the famous potentate he was later to become, this connection represented for the young Safavid a gain in prestige which gave many an observer food for thought in that twilight world between religion and politics.

Such events are by no means typical of the career of a member of a religious order at that period. They cannot be explained by Junaid's eminent lineage nor by the sympathy which Uzun Ḥasan is supposed to have shown towards dervishes. It is more fruitful to suppose that the Türkmen potentate took this unusual step out of certain political expectations, for example, the hope of winning over along with Junaid the latter's militant followers for his own cause. But such an assumption would only be reasonable if Junaid had been at this time a man of some importance or at least potentially a great military leader. And that indeed appears to have been the case. We have to postulate a change in the conception of a religious order, which seems to have occurred with Shaikh Ṣafī's descendants. There is some evidence that with Junaid this development reached its climax. In order to understand it, we must remember that even the founder of the order had been reproached for allowing his disciples to grow too numerous for him to be able to instruct them in the precepts of the mystic initiation. In fact, he must have modified the mystic practice (such as he himself had followed under his teacher Shaikh Zāhid) which he handed down to his disciples; thus the word ṣūfī, originally denoting an Islamic mystic, seems to have declined even during his lifetime to the meaning "active Muslim", in accordance with the religious mass movement which in those days appears to have been centred on Ardabīl. The esteem which the order continued to command under Ṣafī's successors indicates that a similar situation also prevailed under their rule.

We can assume that during his stay in Anatolia and northern Syria Junaid exploited the contacts which the Ardabīl order enjoyed there and which in many cases it had maintained for a long time. We may even suppose that he did his best to strengthen those relations and to influence them according to his lights. Here lies the explanation of statements to the effect that at this time he had a lively following which increased during his years at the court of Āmid, and that from there he intensified recruitment by appointing new emissaries (*khulafā'*).[1] His success with Uzun Ḥasan must have endowed his ideas with a peculiar attraction in precisely those circles which mattered to him. At all events it is clear that his exploits must be seen in relation to the Ardabīl order; this is also indicated by the fact that he did not abandon the idea of returning to the home of the order, and in 863/1459 actually attempted to gain a footing in Ardabīl again – but without success.

Although several aspects of Junaid's personality remain at present obscure, there is no doubt that he gave military training to the adherents of the order who lived in his retinue and used them in military operations. Here lies the origin of the equating of the words *ṣūfī* and *ghāzī* ("soldier of the faith") which is taken for granted in the Safavid chronicles thereafter. The change in meaning of the word ṣūfī, which occurs even in the early Ṣafaviyya, reaches a new and far more advanced stage round about this time. The change is not confined to the semantic history of one word, but has a prominent political significance. Members of a ṣūfī order, whose mystical rule was probably preserved only as a more or less faded memory, were converted to the ideals of a Holy War which are inherent in Islam, trained as fanatical warriors and, as we shall see, actually led into battle.

The ghāzī idea has another historical bearing which should be mentioned here. Defenders of the faith known by this name played an important part as early as the first third of the 8th/14th century in western Anatolia, on the Byzantine frontier of the Ottoman heartlands. From the collapse of the Saljūq empire onwards, when the pressure of Mongol power on western Asia Minor lessened, they contributed substantially to the protection and extension of the frontiers with Byzantium, while the Ottoman empire was being established. Recent research shows, however, that the ghāzī concept was not limited to western Asia Minor but also existed in eastern Anatolia, where they are credited with the attacks of the Āq Quyūnlū on the Comnenian empire of Trebizond,[2] which was discussed earlier. That had been about the middle of the 8th/14th century. But the ghāzī concept appears to have survived even after that and to have finally been taken over by Shah Ismā'īl's two predecessors. This theory is supported by the fact that the Safavid chronicles prefer to use the word ghāzī to denote the military

[1] *Ibid.*, pp. 22–32, 37ff.

[2] Baykal, "Die Rivalität", pp. 443f.

followers of the master of the order – not exclusively, of course, but almost more frequently than ṣūfī or Qizilbāsh.

It remains to be seen whether in practice the Safavids were familiar with the Jihād, the Holy War, in this sense. In fact such seems to have been the case. A fairly conclusive instance of this is Junaid's attempt to conquer Trebizond in 860–1/1456, that is, prior to his appearance at the court of Uzun Ḥasan, from where he could not very well have launched such a venture since after all it would have been directed against his host's relatives. He was, moreover, on the point of conquering the city, but at the last moment had to relinquish his impending victory because the Turkish Sultan, seeing his interests in Trebizond threatened, despatched an armed force to the scene which would have proved too much for Junaid.

Other military adventures undertaken by Junaid can also be included under the ghāzī heading; although it is clear that in Junaid's case, just as elsewhere, other motives in addition to the ghāzī concept were instrumental in the attacks on non-Muslim peoples – the problems of feeding and paying a large military retinue, and the thirst of Junaid's adherents for adventure and plunder. We shall not examine these exploits in detail.[1] The last was a campaign against the Circassians of Ṭabarsarān, which he decided to undertake in 863/1459 after again being banished from Ardabīl on the orders of Jahān Shāh. This exploit met with success, but he was then attacked by the Shīrvān-Shāh Khalīl-Allāh, through whose territory he had marched and to whom the defeated Circassians may have been tributary, and on 11 Jumādā I 864/4 March 1460 was killed in battle.

If we sum up Junaid's life, we see an unruly spirit with political ambitions and military propensities, but not a religious reformer. Even if it is true that, as Khunjī claimed,[2] he was worshipped as a god after his death, this betokens the unbridled fanaticism of his followers or those of his successor, rather than the nature of his own religious beliefs. Although as a member of the order he may have been susceptible to the 'Alī-venerating or even Shī'ī tendencies in Folk Islam, he need not necessarily for that reason have been the wild Shī'ī fanatic which his enemies – especially Khunjī and 'Āshïqpashazāde – make him out to be. Even the quarrel with Shaikh Ja'far, as we saw, need not

1 Summarised in Sohrweide, "Der Sieg der Ṣafaviden", pp. 118–22.
2 Minorsky, *Persia in A.D. 1478–1490*, p. 66.

have been due to religious differences. It can easily be explained by the fact that after Ibrāhīm's death two strong personalities whose political ambitions were irreconcilable clashed in Ardabīl: Junaid's ambition may be gauged, after all, from the fact that he aspired to the headship of the order even though not his father's eldest son but only his sixth. Finally, it must remain an open question whether during his wanderings in Anatolia Junaid came across such strong Shī'ī tendencies among supporters of the Ardabīl order or among sections of the population which he hoped to win over, that he was compelled to profess the Shī'a, either out of expediency or out of conviction.[1]

However much recent scholars have concerned themselves with the rise of the Safavids, several features of this unusual phenomenon have yet to be satisfactorily explained. We know that Türkmen adherents of the Ardabīl order played an essential part, but how this participation came about cannot yet be elucidated in every detail. The question is vital not only because of the share of the Türkmen in founding the Safavid state, but also because during the first century of its existence the majority of its ruling class and, up to the time of 'Abbās I, virtually all the officers and men in the army were in fact Türkmens. That the Safavids themselves cannot be called Türkmens, in spite of their close ties and the blood relationship with the Āq Quyūnlū, simply makes the problem more complicated. How then did Türkmen tribes come to play such a crucial rôle?

Even their contemporaries in Persia probably racked their brains over this question. They searched for an explanation and found it – in a visit to Ardabīl by Tīmūr, a visit which he was supposed to have paid to the then head of the order, Khwāja 'Alī. It is said that the latter's miracles impressed him deeply, whereupon he made Khwāja 'Alī a present, at his request, of 30,000 prisoners of war whom he had brought with him from Anatolia. These were the forefathers of the Türkmens who a century later played a prominent rôle in the foundation of the Safavid empire. Tīmūr's visit to Ardabīl is likely to have occurred in the spring of 806/1404. That it was in honour of the Safavid leader, or that he even glimpsed the latter on this occasion, is not, it is true, out of the question, but neither is it anywhere attested. Moreover, the presentation of these Anatolian prisoners is pure myth,

[1] As Minorsky, "Shaikh Bālī Efendi", p. 439, maintains.

since the captive nomads deported from Anatolia by Tīmūr were Qarā Tatars and were subsequently settled not in Persia but in Transoxiana;[1] and the story is apparently a home-grown attempt to account for the Türkmen part in the founding of the Safavid empire.

A plausible explanation for their rôle can be found in something I have already mentioned, the spread and popularity of Islamic religious communities in the 8th–9th/14th–15th centuries. As will be recalled, in addition to the focal point of the order at the seat of the master (*murshid* [*-i kāmil*] or *pīr*), they had a following scattered over a wide area which kept in touch with the centre through so-called representatives or emissaries (khulafā'). We know that this following included numerous Türkmens, if not whole tribes or tribal groups. This is true in general of all such orders but especially of the Safavid order, which even in the founder's time had had Turkish or Türkmen supporters[2] and which seems later to have enjoyed an increasing popularity among the Türkmens. This Türkmen following probably extended in the main through Āzarbāījān, Anatolia and northern Syria. It was thus not fortuitous that Junaid visited precisely these areas on his raids. Here he could be certain of support and assistance. On the other hand the presence of an enterprising, even fascinating, descendant of the great Ardabīl Shaikh Ṣafī could not have failed to win recruits for the local ṣūfī groups.

Although our knowledge of the early history of the Türkmen tribes, whose names occur very frequently in the sources, is in several respects incomplete, certain tribal names which can be construed with certainty confirm that they originated in the areas mentioned: the Shāmlū must have had their home in Syria (Shām), the Rūmlū in Anatolia or, to be more precise, in the province later known as Sīvās but which earlier had been called Rūm. The name Takkalū points to the province of Tekke in southern Anatolia, and Dulghadïr, corrupted to the Arabic form Dhu'l-Qadr, had been since 1337 the name of a local Türkmen dynasty in Abulustān, the region between Jaiḥān and the Euphrates.

The intellectual atmosphere to which Junaid owed his success among the Türkmens - possibly too the impression which his personality left on these simple people, who were always inclined to believe in the miraculous and the extraordinary – must have lasted a long time after his death, long enough anyway for his son Ḥaidar to slip effortlessly, or so it seems, into his father's rôle. We do not know the exact

[1] See above, pp. 56, 80.

[2] Glassen, *Die frühen Safawiden*, p. 385.

point when this happened, or when he assumed the leadership of the Safavid order. He came to Ardabīl in 1470 when he was barely ten years old, from Āmid, where his childhood had been spent at the court of Uzun Ḥasan. Perhaps his uncle sent him to the home of the order in order to neutralise Shaikh Ja'far, whose once powerful protectors, the Qarā Quyūnlū Jahān Shāh and the Timurid Abū Sa'īd, were no longer alive.

It seems indeed that Ja'far was loth to accept and tolerate his great-nephew in Ardabīl. The man of religion, himself highly educated, appears to have consistently neglected to complete or at least improve Ḥaidar's religious training which had been totally overlooked in Āmid. Perhaps the love of arms which Uzun Ḥasan had inspired in the boy, together with a corresponding natural bent, had already grown too strong. Perhaps too the advanced politicisation of the order stood in the way of any change of heart. Unless we are very much mistaken, Ḥaidar's self-image already suggested the son of a secular prince rather than the future head of a mystical order. "Instead of the school bench, he sat on a horse, instead of mystic treatises he read mythical tales": in such words he is censured by Fażl-Allāh b. Rūzbihān Khunjī,[1] who at the same time testifies to his great courage and mastery of the arts of war. It is not surprising that under his leadership the secularisation of the order proceeded apace and its militarisation neared a climax. An external sign of this development was Shaikh Ḥaidar's introduction of a uniform for members of his order. Its characteristic feature was a red turban with twelve gores, called *tāj-i ḥaidarī*, the "Ḥaidar cap". Their enemies gave the wearers of this headgear the nickname *qïzïlbāshlar* ("Redheads"), a designation, however, which they soon proudly adopted as a title of honour.

The name Qizilbāsh for the followers of the Ardabīl shaikhs undoubtedly goes back, together with the introduction of the red turban, to the time of Ḥaidar. The word is not found in Ṭihrānī's *Kitāb-i Diyārbakriyya*, completed in 1470, but it is used by Khunjī fifteen years later in a derogatory sense. But whether even at that period as later this was bound up with a religious motif, the accusation of Shī'ī heresy on the part of opponents or the public profession of the Shī'a on the part of those concerned, or whether we have here the projection of subsequent conditions back to an earlier age, cannot be ascertained with

[1] Minorsky, *Persia in A.D. 1478–1490*, p. 66.

certainty, whether or not one accepts the explanation that Ḥaidar acted in accordance with a command given him by the Imām 'Alī in a vision. Were one to relate the twelve gores, as is usually done, to the Twelve Imāms, this does not necessarily indicate Shī'ī convictions, since the Twelve Imāms also had a place in the Folk Islam of those times. Even a Sunnī sectarian like Faẓl-Allāh Khunjī wrote a poem in praise of the Twelve Imāms which has been preserved.[1]

Thereby we come to the problem of Shaikh Ḥaidar's religious beliefs. Was he a Shī'ī or not? As we have seen, in the first ten years of his life in Āmid he scarcely had any religious education at all, and certainly not a Shī'ī one. In Ardabīl he came into contact with Shaikh Ja'far, whose orthodoxy (not, of course, to be measured by the standards of Sunnī theology but rather against the more moderate conditions of Folk Islam) has never been disputed. Again, it is Khunjī alone who questions Ḥaidar's orthodoxy, and even he does not accuse him of subscribing to the Shī'a, maintaining rather that his foolish followers worshipped Junaid as God and Ḥaidar as the Son of God. It is difficult to accept this at its face value, especially in the case of someone with such an underdeveloped religious sensibility as Ḥaidar. Normally, the influence exerted over him by his father's followers when he lived in Ardabīl is the reason put forward for his supposed conversion to the Shī'ī faith.

It is of course true that Türkmen supporters of the Safavids flocked to Ardabīl when it was learnt that the young shaikh was recruiting fighting men like his father before him, possibly in the aftermath of the collapse in 872/1467 of the Qarā Quyūnlū confederation, whose elements may now have striven for a new relationship with the Ardabīl shaikhs. One can therefore quite reasonably reckon on a strong Türkmen influence on Ḥaidar whereby religious zeal may have been a factor – but not necessarily the Shī'ī creed. Folk Islamic ideas, with a greater or lesser Shī'ī tinge, combined with the ghāzī concept, suffice to explain the process. And we may almost with certainty impute the ghāzī idea to a military mind like that of Shaikh Ḥaidar.

He too carried the Holy War into the land of the Circassians. Twice, in 888/1483 and 892/1487, his campaigns went according to plan. The third time, in 893/1488, there was again no need for complications, because Ḥaidar had obtained permission to march through Shīrvān.

[1] M.A. Khunjī, "Faẓl-Allāh b. Rūzbihān Khunjī", *FIZ* IV (1335), 178f.

But when he attacked the town of Shamākhī in order, we are told, to avenge his father, he came into conflict with Farrukh-Yasār, who had succeeded the Shīrvān-Shāh Khalīl-Allāh in 867/1462. With the support of troops of the Āq Quyūnlū sent to his aid by Sulṭān Ya'qūb, the Shīrvān-Shāh was victorious. Shaikh Ḥaidar fell in battle on 29 Rajab 893/9 July 1488 in Ṭabarsarān, not far from the spot where his father had been killed in 864/1460.[1]

As early as the Mongol period several Türkmen tribes had learnt to absent themselves from the arena of great events whenever danger threatened. In later times too this ability appears to have been shared by many Türkmen adherents of the Safavids, as when they vanished from the stage for many years after Junaid's death. Following Ḥaidar's death, they again withdrew into obscurity for more than a decade and bided their time, leading the unobtrusive life of nomads.

ISMĀ'ĪL I

Just as at the beginning of the 9th/15th century the leaders of the Āq Quyūnlū and the Qarā Quyūnlū expended all their energies in attaining military power and acquiring territorial sovereignty, so Junaid and Ḥaidar too were dedicated to the pursuit of political goals. Then as now the notion of warring for the faith appears to have figured as a welcome motive, if not as a pretext. Whether the two Safavids were driven by a more profound religious zeal, for instance by a desire to launch a Shī'ī mission, cannot at present be established and in fact seems doubtful, although in their case too the ideas of Folk Islam certainly included a series of Shī'ī features.

In Ismā'īl's case we are faced with different assumptions, inasmuch as he spent a lengthy period of his childhood in a Shī'ī enviroment and was apparently given instruction in the Shī'ī faith. Moreover, he must have had a well-defined religious sensibility, as can be seen from his dīvān. Here he calls 'Alī a manifestation of God and proudly asserts that he himself is a descendant of 'Alī and Fāṭima who came into the world at 'Alī's behest. Of course such notions cannot be reconciled with the Shī'a or the Shī'ī theology; but they originate in the world of the Shī'a rather than in that of Folk Islam.

[1] Savory, "Ḥaydar", *EI*², concludes that in view of the help rendered by the Āq Quyūnlū Ḥaidar must have had stronger forces than his father, whom the Shīrvān-Shāh had defeated without outside assistance.

Although Ismā'īl's statements are somewhat vague, they at least convey a marked sense of mission. This makes more comprehensible his decision in the summer of 905/1499, that is, at the age of twelve, to leave his refuge in Lāhījān, despite the warnings of his protector Kār-kiyā Mīrzā 'Alī, in order to try to emulate the deeds of his father and grandfather. However strange this venture may seem, it was very well timed from a political point of view. The power of the Āq Quyūnlū, in whose territory Ismā'īl lived, had been more or less paralysed by the dispute over the succession triggered off by the death of Sulṭān Ya'qūb in 896/1490. The rôle of the Timurids in Persia had been curtailed by the fall of Abū Sa'īd. Both the Ottomans in the west and the Uzbeks in the east were at this time unable – as yet, at least - to intervene in the affairs of Persia. And in Cairo, where the rule of the powerful Sultan Qā'itbāī had ended in 901/1496, a grave crisis was simmering, characterised by a rapid succession of new rulers. Apart from a few local dynasties of little influence, there was a political vacuum in Persia.

Since the death of his brother Sulṭān 'Alī in 899/1494, Ismā'īl had been grand master of the Ardabīl order. It is not known whether he himself underwent the mystical initiation and conveyed it afterwards to novices; in fact this seems unlikely.[1] His sufism seems rather to be confined to the extreme Shī'ī ideas which occur in his poetry. Nevertheless, after leaving Lāhījān he made straight for Ardabīl, the centre of the Safavid order. Emotional reasons may have influenced this choice, and probably too the hope that there he was most likely to attract the militant adherents of the order whom he now needed. This expectation was not in fact fulfilled, clearly because through the respect he commanded the local governor, who owed his appointment to the Āq Quyūnlū, deterred members of the order from openly supporting Ismā'īl. And because of this same governor Ismā'īl could not remain in Ardabīl. Uncertain what to do next, he decided – significantly – to lead a holy war (*ghazā-yi kāfirān*) against Georgia.

The messianic spirit which inspired Ismā'īl had its pendant in the religious mood of the people. Many seem to have had an apocalyptic awareness at this time. Insecurity caused by war, anarchy, bandits, catastrophes, plagues and famine had given rise to religious expectations typified by the hope – shared by others besides the Shī'a – of the

[1] That the Ardabīl shaikhs down to Junaid had practised mysticism emerges from their influence on other dervish orders: see Kissling, "Aus der Geschichte des Chalvetijje–Ordens" and "Bajrâmijje".

return of the Mahdī, which would mark the end of the world. There was evidence of a connection between the young Ismāʿīl and the Mahdī; there were even those who saw in him the returning Imām or at least his harbinger. Typical of this was the scene when Ismāʿīl arrived at the summer camp of the Türkmen tribe of the Ustājlū. When news of his approach reached them, the whole tribe, led by the elders (*rīshsafīdān*), went to greet him, singing and dancing, and escorted him just as centuries earlier the old Companions (*anṣār*) had welcomed the Prophet Muḥammad in Medina when he arrived there on the Hijra from Mecca. In the stories of these Türkmens he was seen as the messenger of the Lord of Time (*ṣāḥib al-zamān*).

Ismāʿīl's physical appearance must also have had some effect when he entered public life. The testimony of an eye-witness depicts him as being of truly regal bearing, gentlemanly and with engaging features, a fair complexion and reddish hair. If one thinks of the enthusiasm with which even today the mostly dark-skinned Persians greet a fair-headed youth, it is easy to imagine the impact made by the young head of the order, about whom various anticipatory legends were circulating, in that period of intense religious awareness. Ismāʿīl's descent from the shaikhs of Ardabīl, his personal appearance, his religious ideas and his sense of mission corresponded almost perfectly with the expectations which an oppressed people might nourish in their religious daydreams. His youthfulness, which arouses scepticism in the rational mind of the modern observer, must in the circumstances have fostered his plans. The great influence of the Ardabīl order, the propagandist and military endeavours undertaken by his father Ḥaidar and particularly by his grandfather Junaid among the Türkmens, now bore abundant fruit. He had already brought with him a group of Türkmen companions from Lāhījān, and other members of these tribes joined him during his first winter camp in Arjuvān on the Caspian Sea. The intention of finding further reinforcements was certainly one of the motives behind a campaign against Arzinjān in eastern Anatolia, upon which he embarked in the middle of Shaʿbān 905/March 1500. Finally his army grew to 7,000 men and he launched the intended holy war.

The ghāzī troops again marched on Shīrvān. This time, in Jumādā I 906/December 1500, at the village of Jabānī near the Shīrvān capital of Shamākhī, they clashed at the outset with the Shīrvān-Shāh, the same Farrukh-Yasār who had defeated Ismāʿīl's father twelve years previously. At that time he had been helped by the Āq Quyūnlū; on this occasion he was unaided. In spite of his superiority of numbers he was vanquished and killed. Thereby Ismā'īl not only avenged his father and grandfather, but also conquered a land which had enjoyed for long periods a certain independence under the family of the Shīrvān-Shāhs, although under different suzerains. Admittedly, he could not yet claim to have a firm grip on it, since several sons of Farrukh-Yasār had escaped and there were to be Shīrvān-Shāhs under Safavid suzerainty until 945/1538.

In the spring of 906/1501 Ismā'īl initiated from his winter camp at Maḥmūdābād measures to complete the subjugation of Shīrvān. Meanwhile news reached him that Alvand, the sultan of the Āq Quyūnlū, like himself a grandson of Uzun Ḥasan, had been disquieted by Ismā'īl's victory over the Shīrvān-Shāh and was mobilising against him; but that because of the disorderly circumstances in which Alvand lived, the time was ripe for a preventive blow. Ismā'īl therefore interrupted his enterprise in Shīrvān and for the time being also abandoned his plans for Georgia. Battle was joined at Sharūr in the Araxes valley and as a result Alvand took flight. This victory at the beginning of 907/in July or August 1501, opened up for Ismā'īl the way to Tabrīz, the Türkmen capital. His reign over Iran is usually dated from the occupation of that city, although the dynasty of the Āq Quyūnlū was not finally eliminated for some years, after the expulsion of Alvand, the victory over Murād at Hamadān on 24 Dhu'l-Ḥijja 908/20 June 1503 and the fall of Mārdīn still later.

In the existing political and religious situation the appearance and early successes of Ismā'īl must have had extraordinary results. I have already pointed to the way in which the activity of his father and grandfather stood him in good stead when he went among the Türkmen tribes. The departure of the first tribal groups doubtless hastened the decision of many others to follow suit, for as a result of the decline and final collapse of the power of the Āq Quyūnlū they were faced with the necessity of finding new connections – upon which nomadic peoples at the time depended if only for the sake of self-preservation – to replace their previous affiliation to the federation of the Āq Quyūnlū. Indeed many of them were only too willing to join Ismā'īl after he had given impressive proof of his enterprise and military skill in the battles at Jabānī and Sharūr. His unequivocal support for the Shī'a, which may have aroused hostility in some instances, for example among the urban population, would not have been a serious obstacle for these people, who subscribed to Folk Islam and were not interested in theological arguments.

A description of Ismā'īl's political career reveals how significant a part the Türkmens played in the founding of the Safavid state. In this his kinship with the Āq Quyūnlū is naturally a pertinent factor; but at least as important is the fact that his military strength was based on his rapidly growing retinue of Türkmen tribesmen. It was on their leaders that he drew when he had to fill military posts at court, posts in the civil administration and, as his conquest grew, in the provinces. A certain Shams al-Dīn Zakariyā Kujujī, who had been vizier to the Āq Quyūnlū, had earler presented himself at the winter camp at Maḥmūd-ābād and encouraged Ismā'īl to undertake the successful campaign against Alvand by describing the confused situation at the court of his erstwhile masters. He then became Ismā'īl's first vizier. Thereby a firm link was forged with the Türkmen tradition of government and administration, whose institutions were undoubtedly taken over following the capture of the previous centre of government at Tabrīz.

What is true of the military posts in the earliest Safavid administration – namely, that they were filled by Türkmen notables – is by no means true of the civil posts, for example in the treasury, or of the extensive sphere of religious law ranging from the judiciary and the administration of the pious endowments to the charitable institutions. These posts were not occupied by Türkmens, any more than under the Āq Quyūnlū or the Qarā Quyūnlū. As members of the military aristocracy they did not lay claim to them – nor would they have been suitable candidates for the vacancies. For some time past this type of administrative post had been staffed by the native Iranian bureaucracy, irrespective of which dynasty happened to be reigning. The Zakariyā Kujujī mentioned above belonged to this civil servant class.[1] To that extent Iranian personnel provided continuity between the Türkmen and the Safavid administrations.

The adoption of Türkmen institutions or the dependence on existing traditions does not, on the other hand, exclude the introduction of major changes. It was an innovation that the two groups of Türkmen soldiers and Iranian civil servants – the "lords of the sword" (*arbāb-i saif*) and the "lords of the pen" (*arbāb-i qalam*) – should be united even ethnically in the person of the Safavid ruler. In the Türkmen states discussed

[1] On his family, see Aubin, "Études Safavides I", pp. 60–3.

earlier, the sultans had always been Türkmen: the Safavid Shah combined in himself the blood of both Türkmen and Iranian ancestors. It is irrelevant, therefore, whether the founder of the dynasty, Shaikh Ṣafī, was descended from Iranian *dihqāns*, from 'Alī, or from Kurds, since Ismā'īl himself was connected equally with the military and the administrative aristocracy. The consequences of this remarkable dualism will be seen later.

But the divergence from the pattern of Türkmen government did not stop there. Ismā'īl, who ascribed to himself divine qualities as the representative of the Twelve Imāms, was also the head of a theocracy, which had not been the case with either the Āq Quyūnlū or the Qarā Quyūnlū. He was therefore infallible and could command divine veneration. Moreover, the state which he founded perpetuated the Ardabīl religious order. Ismā'īl was grand master (*pīr, murshid, murshid-i kāmil*) of the Ṣafaviyya. His adherents were therefore called *murīd* and *ṣūfī* or *ghāzī*. Their external appearance was again characterised by the tāj-i ḥaidarī, the turban with twelve red gores which had been introduced by Ḥaidar but which had grown less popular after his death. Thereby the name Qizilbāsh became common usage.

As far as can be ascertained, the overwhelming majority of Ismā'īl's militant supporters belonged to Türkmen tribes. What was demanded of them was *ṣūfīgarī*, "conduct becoming to a ṣūfī", though this can scarcely have meant the same duties as those normally incumbent upon members of an Islamic mystical order. We must leave unanswered the question of how far under Ismā'īl's rule the Safavid ṣūfīs had to discharge the religious duties of prayer and worship belonging to the mystic path (*ṭarīqa*), asceticism and a retiring life, vigils and fasts, litanies and the invoking of God. On the other hand, there is no doubt that, just as with the members of a dervish community, absolute obedience to the murshid was demanded of them.

We know that the Qizilbāsh soldiers fulfilled this obligation; they even accepted the king's claim to be venerated as a divine being. Their battle cry is significant:

Qurban oldïghïm pirüm mürshidim!
("My spiritual leader and master, for whom I sacrifice myself!")

Reports of their fanatical conduct in battle indicate that this cry truly conveyed their inner conviction, that they cared nothing for their own safety in war, either because they believed themselves to be invulnerable or because they positively longed for death as a direct access to paradise. The belief in Ismāʿīl's invincibility, repeatedly confirmed over the years, also contributed to the process of turning his hordes into an efficient fighting force. At that time, when the morale of almost every army was extremely low, a strong moral impulse and several intangible factors must have been necessary to organise a military force adequate to the task of conquering a country as large as Persia.

In order to understand further developments in the story, it is important to remember that the Türkmen tribesmen were grouped together in units or bands according to their tribe. Their tribal grouping also played a part in certain specialised units which were set up in due course.[1] It was of particular importance when it came to allocating provinces to the amīrs. Each one would take all or some of his fellow tribesmen with him to his new place of residence, and employ them to help carry out his decrees: he was thus able to exercise an almost regal authority. The survival of tribal loyalties subsequently had serious repercussions for the Safavid state.

Of the tribes which played a part in founding the empire, we have already mentioned the Ustājlū, the Shāmlū, the Rūmlū, the Takkalū and the Dulghadïr. Also important are the Turkmān, the Afshār and the Qājār. Besides these there were smaller tribes which had little or no influence on events; and there were other tribal groups which formed subdivisions of or clans within the main tribes.[2]

Apart from regarding himself as god-king, Ismāʿīl seems to have seen himself as the legitimate heir of his grandfather Uzun Ḥasan Āq Quyūnlū. His desecration of the graves of the Āq Quyūnlū rulers following his coronation does not necessarily contradict this. More pertinent are not only the fact that he preferred Tabrīz as his capital to other cities such as Ardabīl, but also his acceptance of the Türkmen administration described above, and the important contribution made by Türkmen tribes to his success. The same can be seen in his decision not to press further eastwards after the final expulsion of Alvand and the victory over Murād Āq Quyūnlū which established his control over Hamadān with central and southern Iran; instead he turned his attention to the old heartlands of Uzun Ḥasan, Diyārbakr and the

[1] Cf. Röhrborn, *Provinzen und Zentralgewalt*, p. 49.

[2] For further details, see Sohrweide, "Der Sieg der Ṣafaviden", pp. 131–7, and Minorsky, *Tadhkirat al-Mulūk*, pp. 189–95.

earlier capital, Āmid. Here in eastern Anatolia he even advanced as far as Mar'ash and Abulustān, the home of the Dulghadïr tribe, only a section of which had hitherto been numbered among his adherents.

Thereby he had reached the eastern frontier of the Ottoman empire. But he was clever enough not to provoke his powerful neighbour further. Although certain tensions had existed between them, peaceful relations still appeared possible at this point, particularly since Sultan Bāyezīd II was known to be a friend and protector of dervishes and ṣūfīs. Shortly before, he had granted an annual pension to a Qizilbāsh leader in southern Anatolia named Ḥasan Khalīfa,[1] and he had hitherto set great store by the cultivation of the traditional friendly relations between his dynasty and the Ardabīl order.

After the conquest of Āzarbāījān and eastern Anatolia Ismā'īl turned his attention to Mesopotamia; its conquest began before 1507 with the capture of Mārdīn, the last bastion of the Āq Quyūnlū, and was completed the following year with the capture of Baghdad. We do not propose to describe these campaigns in detail, but must discuss a little more closely a remarkable exploit which followed the conquest of Baghdad. This was a campaign to the southern Persian province of Khūzistān, directed against ultra-Shī'ī sectarians who had lived there since 840/1436 under the name of Musha'sha'[2]. According to the testimony of a Safavid chronicler[3] they had at that time a leader named Sayyid Fayyāż and professed the heretical belief that 'Alī, the fourth Caliph, was God and that finally their leader Sayyid Fayyāż was also an incarnation of God. We are also told that at their prayer meetings they recited verses about *'Alī Ilāhī* and so on, thereby achieving invulnerability: if they then tried to thrust a sword into their bodies, it left no wound – on the contrary, the blade would bend like a bow.

Certain aspects of the teaching of these sects, of which we have more detailed knowledge, bring to mind notions which we know to have occupied Ismā'īl, above all the exaggerated adulation of 'Alī. There seems to be further proof here that such ideas were in the air at the time. Naturally, it is easy to see that such extreme viewpoints could scarcely coexist harmoniously, the less so when they were linked with rival political claims. It is not surprising that Ismā'īl refused to tolerate in others religious demands similar to those which he voiced himself. The Khūzistān campaign ended the independence of the kingdom of

[1] Sohrweide, "Der Sieg der Ṣafaviden", p. 139.
[2] See above, pp. 136–7.
[3] Iskandar Munshī, trans. Savory, p. 57.

Ḥavīza. Sayyid Fayyāż was killed in battle. Soon, however, his brother Sayyid Falāḥ took his place. With him began a line of princes who were vassals of the Safavids except when they were prevented from fulfilling their allegiance by the Ottomans. Under their rule the border country of ʿArabistān around Ḥavīza formed a kind of buffer state between the Ottomans and the Safavids and rendered the Safavids in particular valuable services. We must not forget either the way in which the rulers of Ḥavīza mediated between the Persian and Arabic cultures.

Before the Ottoman–Safavid conflict – which we have touched upon several times already – could be resolved, there was a clash with another enemy of the Safavids, the Uzbeks of eastern Iran, who had begun to rise to power in Transoxiana around 1495. Their ruler, Muḥammad Shaibānī Khān, was waiting for a chance to annex the territory of the Timurids together with their capital Herat. There, since the fall of Abū Saʿīd in 873/1469, power had been in the hands of Ḥusain Bāīqarā, who had turned his capital into a splendid centre of Islamic culture. When he died in 911/1506, two of his sons quarrelled over the succession, so that the following year Herat fell an easy prey to the Uzbek khan. Thereby the western part of Khurāsān was also threatened. The information which Ismāʿīl received about these events, and certainly too the personal appeal of Badīʿ al-Zamān, Ḥusain Bāīqarā's son and heir, who had sought asylum at Ismāʿīl's court, led him to launch a campaign in the east. He defeated and slew the Uzbek ruler in battle at Marv at the beginning of the winter of 916/1510. Ismāʿīl captured Herat, appointed one of his amīrs governor, and withdrew again.

The fall of Muḥammad Shaibānī Khān did not remove the Uzbek threat to the Safavids; on the contrary, it remained acute until the end of the 10th/16th century. Two years after the battle of Marv there was another Uzbek attack which overwhelmed the Safavid troops in Khurāsān. Reinforcements sent by Ismāʿīl under the leadership of the famous general Najm-i s̱ānī proved no match for ʿUbaid-Allāh Sulṭān, the new khan, even though they were supported by the Timurid Bābur, who later founded the Mughal empire in India. After the catastrophic defeat of his forces at Ghujduvān on 3 Ramadān 918/12 November 1512[1], Ismāʿīl had to go to Khurāsān in person the following spring, in order to save the situation. His arrival brought about the withdrawal of the Uzbeks without any battle being fought.

[1] See above, pp. 126–7.

In a relatively short period Ismā'īl had won control over both the territory of the Āq Quyūnlū and the rest of Persia, with the exception of a few small areas. Apart from the Uzbek khan Muḥammad Shaibānī, he had not come across any truly dangerous opponent. Admittedly he had not been greeted everywhere by a jubilant populace. There were cities like Kāshān and Qum with an old-established Shī'ī population which clearly welcomed a Shī'ī ruler. In several places, too, the propaganda which preceded his arrival and the reputation of his fascinating personality doubtless prepared the ground; similarly, the far-reaching intellectual climate of Folk Islam had favourable consequences for him. These circumstances doubtless facilitated for many their conversion to the new faith. Nevertheless, it would be wrong to think that in the course of the expansion of the Safavid state the population of Persia was converted overnight from the Sunna to the Shī'a. The propagation of the Shī'a was not accomplished uniformly or with unqualified success or without conflict. There are even grounds for supposing that decades after the commencement of Safavid rule, for instance, in Khurāsān (where there was to be no lack of Sunnīs at the time of the Uzbek conquest in 997/1589[1]), and probably in other parts of the realm too, adherents of the Sunna continued to practise their creed in secret. But in the course of these conquests there were also fervent Sunnīs who refused to relinquish their religious principles and were not prepared even to make a pretence of being converted. In such cases – for example, in Baghdad or Herat – Ismā'īl reacted with brutal severity, ruthlessly executing theologians, scholars and even poets who refused to accept the Shī'ī faith.[2]

I have already alluded to the extensive spread of the Safavid order in Asia Minor. We also know that Ismā'īl prepared for his seizure of power by despatching envoys to mobilise his supporters in Anatolia. It has been suggested that the purpose of his march to Arzinjān may have been to shorten the march of the Qizilbāsh hastening to meet him from the west and thus to have them at his disposal at the earliest possible moment. It is true that many Anatolian Türkmens flocked to Ismā'īl's standard when he embarked on his first exploits. In the first ten years of his rule this influx grew year by year. The reason lay above all in his military successes, but also in his reputation for generosity in the

[1] Iskandar Munshī, trans. Savory, pp. 559, 584, 1073.
[2] Duri, "Baghdād", *EI*[2]. *LHP* IV, 63.

distribution of booty, news of which spread rapidly throughout the Near East. Adventurousness and religious zeal played their part. Although the desire to join Ismāʿīl's army at an opportune moment before the final triumph of the Safavid movement may have been a contributory factor, it was not merely that kind of motive which drove so many Türkmen tribesmen into the Safavid camp. An additional reason was the persistent economic crisis among the population of Asia Minor at this time, following natural disasters, plagues and famines.

When one realises that many of these Türkmens – in fact, all those who came from the province of Rūm – were Ottoman subjects, one readily appreciates that this occurrence, a movement of population which the Ottoman authorities could not fail to notice, was viewed in Istanbul with suspicion and growing disquiet. It was seen as a confirmation of certain separatist tendencies which had been evinced in the province of Rūm for some time. Even a ruler sympathetic towards the dervishes like Sultan Bāyezīd II could not look on indifferently: at least since the attempt on his life in 897/1492 by an Islamic wandering mystic, he knew what to expect of political fanatics who had donned the cowl. Although the would-be assassin had been a qalandar dervish, not a Qizilbāsh, the political aspirations of the Qizilbāsh had been clear enough to the Sublime Porte since the time of Junaid. Thus when Ismāʿīl appeared in Arzinjān, the Ottoman government feared an attack on the province of Rūm, which in the circumstances might only too easily result in the loss of this territory. It therefore made extensive military preparations, which were not abandoned until Ismāʿīl had turned his attention to the regions further to the east. Although the expected attack had not materialised, there remained grave concern about the continuing flow of Anatolian mercenaries into Ismāʿīl's armies.

In order to stem this massive emigration of able-bodied subjects and put an end to the reinforcement of a potential enemy, the sultan ordered in 907–8/1502 the first persecution of Qizilbāsh in Anatolia. Every inhabitant who was known to have Safavid sympathies was branded on the face and deported to the west, usually to Modoni and Koroni in southern Greece. The amīrs on the eastern frontier were ordered to prevent Qizilbāsh from crossing the border. However, these measures could have had little permanent effect in the conditions of the time, particularly in the case of a partly nomadic population whose religious and political loyalties were difficult to check. But the campaign was not a total failure either, as can be seen from Ottoman chroniclers who record that Ismāʿīl sent the sultan a written (and unsuccessful) appeal asking him not to forbid his adherents to cross the frontier.

Relations between the Ottomans and the Safavids worsened after Ismāʿīl's campaign of 913/1507 against the principality of the Dulghadïr, which lay within the Ottoman sphere of influence; though whether he also advanced into Ottoman territory proper is not known, since the sources contradict each other.[1] In any case the Ottoman military were provoked into taking new defensive measures which in the event again proved unnecessary. The extent of the threat to the province of Rūm, if not to the whole Ottoman empire, of Ismāʿīl's rise to power and of the movement he led, was not seen until several years later – and then not as the result of a military attack but through a grave internal crisis.

When the sons of Sultan Bāyezīd II began to quarrel over the succession even while their father was still alive, Prince Sulṭān Qorqud secretly left his city of Antalya at the beginning of 1511 and headed for Manisa, a town closer to the capital, from where he could more easily observe the developments at court. His departure, which did not in fact pass unnoticed, gave rise to rumours of the death of the sultan, who had been in poor health for years. This totally unfounded news brought to a head the resentment which had been simmering among the Qizilbāsh, especially in the province of Teke-Ili, of which Antalya was the capital, ever since the persecutions mentioned above; the tension had been increased by their fear of deportation and their anger at not being allowed to cross into Persia. Led by a certain Qizilbāsh called Shāh Qulī, who hailed from that area but whose origins are otherwise not completely clear, hordes of rebellious Türkmens, composed almost entirely of Qizilbāsh, roamed the region, murdering and looting. The rebels belonged to the landless rural classes who had nothing to lose but who believed themselves to be assured of paradise if they were killed. The economic distress in Anatolia should not be ignored as a motivating factor in the uprising. This social aspect combined with Shīʿī extremism is clearly discernible.

Wherever the rebels appeared they spread fear and panic. Villages whose inhabitants refused to join them were razed to the ground, the people – even women and children – were massacred, and all the animals

[1] Sohrweide, "Der Sieg der Ṣafaviden", p. 142.

slaughtered. Even mosques and Islamic monasteries were not spared their lust for destruction. Regular forces which intercepted them were defeated, whether under the command of the governor of Anatolia or of Prince Sulṭān Qorqud, who did battle with them on the plain of Alashehir. In the end Sultan Bāyezīd had to despatch his Grand Vizier Khādim 'Alī Pasha with a large army. The latter pursued Shāh Qulī and his bands, who had fled from him at Antalya, across wide stretches of Anatolia until finally on 2 July 1511 he caught up with them in the neighbourhood of Sīvās. The battle ended in catastrophe for both sides: the Grand Vizier was mortally wounded, and Shāh Qulī was killed either during or soon after the engagement. Despite heavy losses his adherents managed to escape across the Persian frontier. At Ray they joined Ismā'īl, who was probably filled with suspicion by their misdeeds. At all events the leaders were executed on his orders for committing robbery on Persian soil, and the others distributed among the fighting units, obviously because he feared the consequences of accepting such troops into his ranks as a separate and unified force. Although Shāh Qulī had begun as a supporter of the Safavids, in the later stages of the revolt he had been worshipped as God, Prophet and Mahdī and had thus relinquished his support for Ismā'īl. For this reason alone it is somewhat unlikely that the rebellion was instigated or assisted by the Safavids. Moreover, this is never suggested in the sources.

A very different situation prevailed subsequently. The revolt was not quelled by the battle of Sīvās and the death of Shāh Qulī. On the contrary, only after this did it break out properly in the province of Rūm. Here there are clear links between the rebels and the Safavids. The proximity of the Persian frontier allowed them in an emergency to evade their pursuers by withdrawing on to Safavid territory, there to plan fresh exploits. The rebellious Qizilbāsh even obtained support from members of the Ottoman royal house. Prince Shehīn Shāh, one of Bāyezīd's sons and governor of Qaramān, tried to reach an agreement with them but died suddenly before achieving anything. When his brother Aḥmed, whom the sultan had in fact chosen as his successor, saw his hopes of ascending the throne fade and rebelled as a result, his son Murād, who had been deputising for him in his capital Amāsya, negotiated with the Qizilbāsh and allowed them to occupy Amāsya in the middle of April 1512. The history of the revolt in Rūm is characterised by atrocities just as terrible as those committed in western Anatolia by Shāh Qulī and his followers. Whether the conduct of the rebels met with Murād's approval, we do not know. At all events he soon lost the initiative and had no alternative but to flee to Shah Ismāʿīl.

The revolt of the Anatolian Qizilbāsh contributed substantially to a turn of events which was highly unpropitious for the rebels: under pressure from his generals Sultan Bāyezīd abdicated in favour of his son Selīm, who ascended the throne on 7 Ṣafar 918/24 April 1512. The new sultan was not only energetic and determined, but was also a bitter enemy of Shah Ismāʿīl. He understood the true magnitude of the threat to his empire from the Qizilbāsh, for as governor of Trebizond he had watched from relatively close range the rise of the young Ismāʿīl, the orphaned son of a religious fanatic and political adventurer, to become the invincible God-King of Persia. He had seen too the fanatical valour of Ismāʿīl's warriors. He did not doubt that Ottoman rule, at least in the provinces of Asia Minor, was in jeopardy as long as the revolt of the Qizilbāsh in Anatolia was allowed to continue.

The developments in Persia and their repercussions in the eastern territories of the Ottoman empire - for this is how the revolt must have appeared to Selīm - had already given him enough grounds for concern: now, about the time of his accession, further disquieting information reached him. The Persian intervention which Istanbul, erroneously, had expected earlier at the time of Ismāʿīl's campaigns against Arzinjān in 905/1500 and Abulustān in 913/1507, had finally occurred. Not the shah in person, but his governor in Arzinjān, Nūr ʿAlī Khalīfa Rūmlū, had now invaded Ottoman territory on the orders of his master to assist the rebels in Rūm. He sacked several Ottoman towns and finally, together with Prince Murād, whom he had intercepted on his march towards Persia, the city of Ṭoqat. He inflicted a devastating defeat on an Ottoman general, Yular Qïsdï Sinān Pasha, who attacked him on his return march close to the frontier.

As soon as Selīm I had prevailed over his brothers, he ordered a pitiless repression of the Anatolian Qizilbāsh. Anyone who was known or suspected to be a member of the movement was called to account. All ascertainable Qizilbāsh were registered; some were executed, others imprisoned. On this occasion too the victims were nomadic Türkmen tribesmen or peasant villagers; townspeople as a rule showed little tendency to support extremist movements. The reason for the persecution was the repeated revolts of the Qizilbāsh and their connection with the Safavids – not their Shīʿī faith, even though this conflicted with the dominant Sunnī creed of the Ottoman empire. There were other Shīʿī groups who remained unscathed as long as they refrained from treasonable activities. It is possible that Selīm saw in the rebellion of the Anatolian Qizilbāsh the culmination of certain separatist tendencies which had troubled the province of Rūm for decades. At all events he did not draw the line at internal measures, but on 20 March 1514 set out for a campaign against Persia. Both his military advisers and his troops were loth to undertake this campaign, a factor which subsequently proved of some consequence.

If we have hitherto examined the relations between the Safavids and their Türkmen adherents in Anatolia primarily from a religious point of view, it is because this is the prevailing interpretation. However, a recently elaborated thesis,[1] according to which social and political factors outweighed religious motives, also deserves attention. According to this argument the Türkmen tribes of Asia Minor turned to Persia because they neither would nor could be integrated into Ottoman society. For one thing their own strong racial consciousness stood in the way of any integration (though in the event the Safavids too failed to bring about such an integration). For another, their leaders would have had no chance of promotion in the Ottoman army of this period because a Turkish military aristocracy had already been formed – whereas in Persia Türkmen amīrs had been offered a wide sphere of action not only in the conquest of territory but also in the political organisation and provincial administration of the empire.

This argument is not implausible, although its validity remains to be tested on some points, especially the idea that tribal interests overshadowed all other ties, even the religious ones, and that these Türkmens were in fact quite indifferent to the religious issue, being still close to the shamanistic faith of their forebears. Such assertions are not adequately supported by the sources discovered to date, and for the time being we must assume that the rise of Ismāʿīl was inspired by strong religious motives which must have impinged on his Anatolian adherents. There, even if one attaches no great significance to the religious motives of his father and grandfather, the matter must rest, until the opposite is proved to be the case.

Whatever the details of events in Anatolia, Selīm had of course good reason to view the development of the new Safavid state as a threat to

[1] Walsh, "Historiography", pp. 202f.

the Ottoman empire. With the far-reaching plans which he had doubtless already conceived and which shortly afterwards he put into effect with the conquest of Syria and Egypt in 922/1517, he could not accept the risk of being attacked on the flank or from the rear. But as he marched towards Persia in the spring and summer of 920/1514, he was dogged by the worry that he might not be able to engage the shah in battle. He could not be sure that Ismā'īl would fight, in spite of the provocation contained in the letters exchanged by the two rulers, the texts of which have come down to us. Should Ismā'īl seek to avoid doing battle, the march eastwards could not be continued indefinitely with troops who were already less than eager (there is a report of a mutiny among the janissaries). Spending the winter in eastern Anatolia was also out of the question, if only for climatic reasons. The whole difficulty of the operation was brought home when the Safavid governor of Diyārbakr retreated from his province as the enemy approached and implemented a scorched-earth policy against his pursuers.

In the end this anxiety proved to be unfounded: Ismā'īl did not avoid doing battle, although he must have known that the sultan commanded greatly superior forces. If certain sources can be relied upon, he deliberately relinquished certain advantages which would have accrued to him in his base in the mountains of Khūy in north-west Āzarbāījān, and instead marched down into the plain of Chāldirān. Moreover, we are told that he refused to attack the enemy before their troops had time to recover from the exertions of their long march and could be deployed in battle order, the advice of two of his generals, Muḥammad Khān Ustājlū and Nūr 'Alī Khalīfa, based upon their experience of fighting Ottoman troops. Although such information smacks slightly of the hindsight of participants, it is not impossible in view of the good fortune which had hitherto smiled on Ismā'īl's military ventures that he really did act in this way out of a feeling of invincibility.

In the battle of Chāldirān on 2 Rajab 920/23 August 1514 the shah suffered a shattering defeat. He himself managed to escape to his capital Tabrīz with a small band of followers, but his army was beaten and many of his generals were killed. The magnitude of the disaster may be judged from the fact that the royal harem with two of Ismā'īl's wives fell into the hands of the enemy. The reasons adduced for the Persian defeat include not only those already mentioned, especially the numerical superiority of the Turkish army, but also its possession of artillery and firearms which the Persians lacked almost completely[1] and which had a devastating effect on their cavalry, particularly on the plain. The brilliant solution of the logistical problem, the difficulties of which should not be underestimated, on such a long march mostly through loyal territory certainly contributed to the Turkish victory, although perhaps it did not play a decisive rôle.

However thorough Ismāʿīl's defeat had been, the Turkish Sultan was in no position to exploit his victory properly. He pursued the shah and captured Tabrīz, but a week later, on 13 September, he had to withdraw again westwards after failing, despite their impressive victory, to persuade his officers to winter in Tabrīz, let alone advance on the Iranian highlands as would have been necessary if the pursuit of the shah was to be continued. Here we see a situation from which the Safavids were often to profit in their subsequent conflicts with the Ottomans; the extended lines of communication, the difficulties of transportation and the harsh climate of eastern Anatolia and Āzarbāījān. Cleverly exploiting these circumstances, they avoided a decisive battle with the Ottomans after Chāldirān and caused their offensives to dissipate themselves, in the certain expectation that the approach of winter would force them to turn back.

Shortly after Selīm's withdrawal Ismāʿīl returned unopposed to Tabrīz. Yet he was unable to prevent the Turkish occupation and eventual annexation of the provinces of Arzinjān and Diyārbakr, losses which after 1517 were in fact never recovered.

For Shah Ismāʿīl Chāldirān did not mean merely the loss of a battle and of extensive tracts of land. In the eyes of his followers he had also lost the nimbus of invincibility, even if the defeat had done nothing to impair his reputation for sanctity. After all, the later Safavid monarchs were still considered sacred persons. However, his confidence must have been dealt a considerable blow. How else is one to explain the fact that thereafter in the ten years up to his death he never once summoned up the strength to take part in a military campaign, against either external or internal enemies? After Chāldirān there seems to have been little left of his old dynamism or of the boldness which he had still shown even on the battlefield of Chāldirān, although there was no lack of opportunity for military action, whether because of the revolt of

[1] Falsafī, "Jang-i Chāldirān", p. 53. Savory, "The Sherley Myth", pp. 73ff.

individual governors or because of attacks from outside, for example a new Uzbek invasion in 927/1521 under 'Ubaid-Allāh Khān. Tasks such as these he left to his officers. He himself appears to have lapsed into a persistent passivity, at least as far as the military defence of his throne and empire was concerned. Although he continued the customary transfer of the royal court and headquarters from one province to another, the alternation of summer and winter camps, he spent most of his time in hunting, competitive games and carousing. In the spring of 930/1524, on a hunting trip to Georgia, the shah fell ill, but recovered in Ardabīl on the way back and continued his journey. However, he developed a violent fever en route and succumbed to it in Tabrīz in the month of Rajab/May.

Before we proceed to discuss the later history of the Safavid empire, this is an appropriate point to assess Ismā'īl's personality and historical significance. Contemporary Italian reports convey a vivid picture of the appearance of the first Safavid shah. This is supplemented by a portrait which nowadays hangs in the Uffizi palace in Florence.[1] The Italian informants, who saw Ismā'īl with their own eyes, describe him as of prepossessing appearance, not too tall but of adequate stature, heavily built and broad-shouldered, with a fair complexion, clean-shaven except for a reddish moustache, and with apparently thinning hair.[2]

Ismā'īl is reputed to have been shrewd, to have had a lively mind and a quick intelligence. His personality as deduced from the sources does not lack positive features. The chronicles depict him as a just ruler who had the interests of his subjects at heart. His poems bespeak an unusual religious enthusiasm. Therein lies probably the key to his early political and military success: his ability to inspire others with his zeal – though the age was such that we may presuppose a certain susceptibility on their part. Courage and boldness together with physical strength and a masterly skill in the arts of war – he was said to be a superb archer – distinguished him in battle. But elsewhere too he did not lack courage, as is shown for instance by his decision to introduce officially the Shī'ī faith in Tabrīz, a city which had been hitherto two thirds Sunnī. These qualities characterise his conduct even at a very early age. We hear that while out hunting as a boy he fearlessly faced

[1] For a mediocre reproduction, see Falsafī, *Chand maqāla*, facing p. 40.

[2] Thus Ramusio, quoted in Hinz, *Irans Aufstieg*, pp. 74f.; also "The Travels of a Merchant in Persia", in *A Narrative of Italian Travels*, p. 202.

bears, leopards and lions. He was famed for his boundless generosity, especially when it came to distributing booty: of course his behaviour may not have been influenced by altruism alone but also by the realisation that this was the quickest way to win recruits.

However unstinting the shah may have been towards his adherents, he also showed merciless severity, for example towards arbitrary acts on the part of his governors. Opponents who refused to submit were pursued with unrelenting vengefulness and horrifying cruelty. We recall the faithful Sunnī executed on his orders or the refined tortures which, according to the chronicles, he inflicted upon some delinquents. His hatred could outlast the death of his opponents; for instance, he had the skull of the Uzbek Muḥammad Shaibānī Khān fashioned into a drinking vessel for his own use, and ordered the desecration of graves and corpses. One's revulsion at such horrors is scarcely mitigated by any allusion to the general barbarity of the age. A curious light is thrown on Ismā'īl's character by his passivity and his hedonism during the last ten years of his life. The transformation from a remarkable military and political ambitiousness to a life limited to the confines of the court and devoted to drinking bouts, hunting and contests, appears to have puzzled even his contemporaries. At all events their naive attempt to present the shah as the victim of the wiles of worthless courtiers such as the Grand Vizier Mīrzā Kamāl al-Dīn Ḥusain (murdered in 1523) or other Iṣfahān notables, suggests that this was the case.

CHARACTER OF THE EARLY SAFAVID EMPIRE

Two sections of the population of the Safavid empire stand out in particular, the Turks and the Iranians. They are distinct not only in language and customs, but also in origin and culture. Whereas the Turkish element is composed of Türkmen tribesmen, for the most part nomadic herdsmen and warriors, the Iranian consists of the old-established peasantry and the urban mercantile and artisan classes. In the figure of Ismā'īl the Turkish and the Iranian groups fused. It was not immediately apparent whether Ismā'īl would cast in his lot with one or the other of these two sections of the population, and if so which one he would choose.

Although the sultan had not been able to exploit his victory to the full, the battle of Chāldirān had immense repercussions not only on

Shah Ismāʿīl's personal conduct but also on the history of Persia. With the resulting loss of the Safavid territory in eastern Anatolia the capital Tabrīz found itself deprived of its more or less central location and placed on the frontiers of the empire; the geographical centre of gravity of the Safavid realm was thereby well-nigh compulsorily transferred to the Iranian highlands. Despite all Ismāʿīl's Iranian conquests as far as Khurāsān, it was by no means clear in the first phase of his rule whether his realm, whose western frontier with the Ottoman empire was marked by the upper stretches of the Euphrates, would develop into an Iranian state with a Turkish glacis to the west, or into a Turkish state with an Iranian perimeter to the east. Both were possible, although certain circumstances such as the inclusion of some Türkmen traditions in the administration and the army appeared to indicate a preference for the Turkish option. The defeat at Chāldirān did not indeed supply a final answer to this question, for Ismāʿīl still clung to Tabrīz as his capital and the seat of government was not moved to Qazvīn for another generation; but without doubt it caused Safavid policy to be directed towards the east, especially since Ismāʿīl accepted the new situation without endeavouring to reverse it.

It would be wrong to see in the distinction between Turks and Persians at this time something approaching a national bias, if only because nationalism in the modern sense came only much later from Europe to the Near East. On the other hand, the individual peoples were fully aware of the differences between themselves and others. In the Safavid empire discord and even violent antagonism deriving from the rivalry between Turks and Persians were not only common, they even exerted a strong influence on the internal development, at least in the 10th/16th century and, moreover, as early as Shah Ismāʿīl's own reign. From the outset there were on the one hand Turkish soldiers who could claim credit for having laid the political foundations of the new state, and on the other hand members of the Iranian aristocracy who were proud of the part they had played in organising and administering the realm.

For generations certain Iranian families had furnished civil servants for the chancellery and the highest positions in the administration. These families belonged to the native Iranian aristocracy. Irrespective of whether their rulers were Qarā Quyūnlū, Timurids or Āq Quyūnlū, the senior civil servants were always drawn from this Iranian aristocracy. Sometimes it can be ascertained that members of one and the same family, and occasionally even the very same men, served several dynasties. Ismā'īl too when he came to power had no alternative but to make use of the same class of experienced bureaucrats, just as earlier rulers had done, for there were no other qualified candidates to fill these posts, certainly none of Turkish or Türkmen origin.

We may ask ourselves whether, as is maintained,[1] Ismā'īl was really the symbolic representative of the Iranian population through whom they made their last and most successful attempt to win political power. What is certain is that in his case the recourse to the native aristocracy had quite different consequences than under earlier rulers such as the Türkmens. Hitherto the influence of Iranian officials had always been strictly limited by the interests of members of the royal house and of the Türkmen military aristocracy, as instanced in the fate of the reformer Qāżī Ṣafī al-Dīn 'Īsā Sāvajī in 897/1492.[2] With Ismā'īl, however, we see the effect of his own link with the Iranian feudal class – to which, without prejudice to his Türkmen ancestry, he after all belonged – in that he was no less sympathetic towards the Iranian element than towards the Türkmens. To this must be added the overwhelming influence of the Türkmen tribes who had helped him to victory. The part played by their leaders especially in his early years must have positively compelled him to be on the look-out for a counterbalance; and almost inevitably this could only be found in the Iranian aristocracy.

According to the traditional interpretation, there existed a sharp distinction in the Safavid empire before Shah 'Abbās I (995–1038/1587–1629) between military posts which were reserved for the Turkish tribal leaders, and civil and religious posts which were filled by members of the native aristocracy, that is by Persians, often called *Tājīk*. More recent studies have revealed that such a summary account does not adequately describe the position at the time.[3] Even under Shah Ismā'īl numerous significant departures from this schema can be ascertained. The bestowing of senior posts in the chancellery and of the highest authority over the pious endowments (the office of *ṣadr-i a'ẓam*) on Iranian notables is quite in line with the dichotomy described above. But it is no longer consistent with this principle that a man like

[1] Walsh, "Historiography", pp. 202f.

[2] Minorsky, "The Aq-qoyunlu and Land Reforms", *BSOAS* XVII (1955), 449–62 (repr. in *The Turks, Iran and the Caucasus*).

[3] Braun, *Aḥvāl-e Šāh Ismā'īl*, *passim*. Aubin, "Études Safavides I".

Qāżī Muḥammad Kāshī should have become simultaneously ṣadr and amīr. The abandonment of the principle becomes even clearer with the appointment of a deputy (*vakīl*) for the shah who had to combine in his own person the functions of commander-in-chief (*amīr al-umarā'*) and grand vizier (*vazīr-i a'zam*). Even the first occupant of this office, Shaikh Najm al-Dīn Mas'ūd Rashtī, was an Iranian, and the recruitment policy which he pursued in this high post was unequivocally directed towards the favouring of Iranian notables and the reduction of Turkish influence. On his death in 1509 another Persian, Yār Aḥmad Khūzānī, better known as Najm-i s̱ānī, was appointed as his successor, again with the double function, both military and civil. That he took the military section of his duties seriously is beyond all doubt, since in 918/1512 he led the royal armies against the Uzbeks and was killed in the battle of Ghujduvān. From 1509 to 1514 the appointment of commander-in-chief, or the more comprehensive office of vakīl, was in Iranian, not Turkish, hands. The position is illustrated by the examples cited, and one could quote many more. They show clearly that even under Ismā'īl I the highest military appointments and the military commands in the field were open to Iranian notables.

It can be shown that under Ismā'īl Iranian dignitaries used their influence to restrict the once well-nigh unlimited power of the Turkish amīrs, something which would scarcely have been possible without the agreement or acquiescence of the ruler. We know too that Shah Ismā'īl heaped tokens of his favour on the Iranian notables already mentioned and on their fellows, so that several of them acquired immense wealth. It does not require much imagination to picture the indignation and resentment of the Türkmen aristocracy when they witnessed such favouritism and particularly the serious encroachments on their privileges, real or imagined. Here lies the origin of the strained relations between Turkish and Iranian dignitaries which lasted throughout the 10th/16th century and are even characteristic of this period of Safavid rule. They will recur frequently in the subsequent history of the dynasty.

Ismā'īl was undoubtedly aware of these effects of his Iranophile policies, at least to a certain extent. It is therefore plausible to suggest that he had some definite purpose in mind, if only the combatting of the influence of the Turkish military, to whom can be imputed the desire to make him an instrument of their own ambitions. Be that as it may, the geographically determined Iranicisation of the Safavid empire, referred to above, was now compounded with the strengthening of the Iranian element or, to be more precise, the ruling class of the native population. For all the similarity with the previous empire of the Āq Quyūnlū, which had also fostered a certain Iranicisation through transferring the capital from Āmid to Tabrīz, through Uzun Ḥasan's defeat by the Ottomans in the battle of Bashkent in 878/1473 and through the appointment of Persian notables to posts in the government and the civil service, one observes under Ismā'īl's régime signs of more or less deliberate measures. It cannot be proved that he consciously attempted to bring about an Iranicisation of the country; but one can certainly postulate that he was familiar with the problem, if only in vague terms. This conclusion is justified by a letter written to him by Sultan Bāyezīd II. For this letter urges Ismā'īl to regard himself as an Iranian ruler and to confine his activities to the affairs of the inhabitants of Iran.[1] Admittedly the recipient of this advice bequeathed to posterity a collection of poems written in Turkish; but according to the testimony of his son Sām Mīrzā he also wrote Persian poems. We may credit him with an insight into the differences in culture and civilisation between the Persians and the Turks, differences which were probably not insignificant. However strong Ismā'īl's Turkish connections may have been, however important the contribution of the Qizilbāsh to his political success, the state which he founded could scarcely have been intended to be a Turkish empire.

The Iranian aristocracy favoured by Shah Ismā'īl's recruitment policy were essentially large landowners.[2] As everywhere else in the Near East, where latifundia and feudal-type institutions governed economic life, the territory annexed by Ismā'īl contained broad sections of population who lived in reduced circumstances, many in abject penury. This suggests that the religious movement which carried Ismā'īl to victory may have been inspired by social motives and aspirations, especially by a concern to remedy existing abuses. Before Ismā'īl's appearance on the scene there had in fact been movements of this kind often enough in the Islamic world, for instance the communistic uprisings under Shaikh Badr al-Dīn b. Qāżī Samāvnā and Bābā Bürklüje

[1] Cited in Falsafī, *Chand maqāla*, p. 7.

[2] An exception that proves the rule is the Grand Vizier Mīrzā Kamāl al-Dīn Shāh Ḥusain, an architect by profession: he was appointed to the office for having found Ismā'īl's favourite wife wandering about helplessly after Chāldirān and restored her to the shah. But he too acquired extensive areas of land through his position and the shah's favour: Aubin, "Études Safavides I", pp. 71f.

Muṣṭafā in western Anatolia at the beginning of the 9th/15th century.[1] If Ismā'īl originally showed some understanding of the social problem,[2] he did not introduce any social reforms when he became shah. The favouritism shown towards Iranian notables indicates rather that he did not wish to tamper with existing social conditions. Of course, no reforms could be expected from the Iranian aristocrats themselves, and the less so the more powerful they grew. But such ideas were also foreign to the Türkmen leaders with whom they were at loggerheads: the Türkmens thought of nothing but the defence of their own privileges which could best be achieved by the preservation of the old feudal order, and certainly not by its curtailment or abolition. Although new men were appointed to posts of responsibility, nothing changed in the sphere of economic and social conditions. The burdens which Ismā'īl's subjects had to bear at this time are all too clearly revealed by the long lists of taxes and dues found in documents relating to tax exemptions and immunities.[3]

The foundation of an empire whose frontiers corresponded approximately to those of present-day Persia, the political organisation of these lands, a certain internal consolidation, and protection from foreign enemies – such is Ismā'īl's incontestable achievement. The propagation of the Shī'a as the state religion, however dubious the methods employed, can be seen in retrospect to have made a limited contribution towards the unification of the empire and its peoples. On the other hand it had little immediate effect upon the antagonism between the predominantly nomadic Türkmens and the Iranian town-dwellers. The new state did not display any particular national character. This notion occurs in the older literature, but it must be dismissed, if for no other reason than that nationalist ideas (in the modern sense) did not exist at that time. Shah Ismā'īl I did not carry out any social or political reforms. The form of government which he adopted in his empire represents no advance upon that of preceding dynasties: it was an absolute monarchy, distinguished from other oriental political systems by its theocratic trappings.

[1] Cf. Kissling, "Badr al-dīn ibn Ḳāḍī Samāvnā", *EI*[2], and for the impulse he and his order derived from the Ṣafaviyya, "Bajrâmijje".

[2] See the view of Babinger, "Schejch Bedr ed-dīn", pp. 87f.

[3] For a list of such documents, cf. Busse, *Untersuchungen*, pp. 250–7.

ṬAHMĀSP I

Shah Ṭahmāsp I (930–84/1524–76),[1] Ismā'īl's eldest son, was only ten years old when he ascended the throne. At that age, clearly, he could not exercise any great influence on the government and to begin with other elements gained the upper hand with the result that it rapidly became evident on what weak foundations the Safavid empire still rested. The internal situation was marked by immense difficulties, among them the lust for power and the unbridled tribalism of the Qizilbāsh, which was henceforth to remain the main problem of Safavid domestic politics for decades. Immediately after Ṭahmāsp's accession, and again on successive occasions thereafter, disputes and intrigues among the Türkmen tribes crippled the military strength of the Safavids in the face of such powerful foes as the Ottomans in the west and the Uzbeks in the east. Historians usually pronounce a somewhat unfavourable verdict on the reign of the new shah, which lasted fifty-two years. However, if one considers the problems and perils which he had to face during this period – and which on the whole he overcame successfully – one cannot pass a purely negative judgment on his rule.

The first decade of his reign, the period from 930/1524 to 940/1533, has the appearance of an interregnum during which power was wielded not by the shah himself but by Qizilbāsh amīrs. In addition, it was in a sense a reaction against the last phase of Ismā'īl's rule. As will be recalled, the latter had lost much of his earlier self-confidence after his defeat at Chāldirān which deprived him of his aura of invincibility. Evidently in connection with this, there occurred a certain retreat from the theocratic system of government of the early years – and above all the attempt to circumscribe the power of the Türkmens by appointing Iranian dignitaries to the highest administrative and military posts. It is obvious that on Ismā'īl's death this policy terminated for the time being, that the Türkmen leaders immediately undid what had been achieved and saw to it as long as they were able that similar tendencies did not prevail under the new shah. Ṭahmāsp's tutor (*atabeg*), Dīv Sulṭān of the Rūmlū tribe, took over the direction of public affairs with the office of Great Amīr (*amīr al-umarā*). His position did not go unchallenged, however, since the other Türkmen tribes and particu-

[1] Dickson, "Fall of the Ṣafavī Dynasty", prefers the form Ṭahmāsb.

larly the strongest among them, the Ustājlū, who dwelt in Khurāsān and also in Tabrīz, were loth to accept this arrangement. Nevertheless, Dīv Sulṭān managed to assert his authority to the point of being able to enter the capital. But he had to make concessions: together with Köpek Sulṭān, an influential amīr of the Ustājlū tribe, and a leader of the Takkalū by the name of Chūha Sulṭān, he formed a triumvirate to rule the empire. In trying to oust his two co-regents, whom he regarded from the outset as his rivals, he came to grief or, rather, brought about conflicts in the course of which, from the spring of 932/1526 onwards, regular battles broke out between individual tribes. At first these were confined to north-west Persia, but later other parts of the country, above all Khurāsān, were also dragged into the strife. The result was civil war and chaos throughout the land, and fresh activity on the part of the Uzbeks in the east.

The Ustājlū suffered heavy losses in these battles and Köpek Sulṭān was killed. Thereupon Chūha Sulṭān Takkalū succeeded in winning the support of the shah and in poisoning his mind against Dīv Sulṭān Rūmlū, so that in the summer of 933/1527, before the assembled court, the shah shot an arrow at his atabeg, thereby giving the signal for his removal. The dominance of the Rūmlū tribe was now followed by that of the Takkalū, but only for three years. As early as 937/1530–1 there was a clash between the Takkalū and the Shāmlū, whose leader Ḥusain Khān, governor of Herat, went so far as to brawl with his opponents in the royal tent. Thereby Chūha Sulṭān met his death and Ḥusain Khān took his place. Just like the Ustājlū and the Rūmlū before them, the Takkalū were now ousted in favour of the Shāmlū. But Ḥusain Khān's days were also numbered: three years later he was overthrown and executed, although he was related to the shah through his mother, a sister of Shah Ismā'īl.

This brief outline of the Qizilbāsh interregnum must suffice. It is enough to illustrate the steady development of the Türkmen tribes into a kind of Safavid praetorian guard, an evolution characteristic of the 10th/16th century. It can readily be imagined how each of these coups brought with it an intrigue involving various individuals and the tribes to which they belonged or whose allies they were. The fall of a powerful amīr signified each time a severe blow for the government and the whole realm, because the situation at court had its repercussions in the provinces: each victorious amīr attempted to appoint fellow tribesmen or members of allied tribal groups to the most important positions both at court and in the provinces, naturally at the expense of the defeated faction. This process produced innumerable enmities.

The ousting of Ḥusain Khān denoted a turning point in this development. The young shah knew now what to expect from the Türkmen amīrs and did not hesitate to draw the appropriate conclusions. He rode roughshod over the allocation of offices already decided by the amīrs, by entrusting the command of the Shāmlū contingent not to one of the amīrs of that tribe but to his brother Bahrām Mīrzā and by once again nominating a Persian as the shah's viceroy (vakīl). This was Qāżī Jahān Qazvīnī, who had already held this post earlier. For the time being the enormous perils confronting both throne and empire as a result of the ambitions and cabals of the Qizilbāsh amīrs had been checked, but they were by no means eliminated. From time to time they continued to loom up with varying degrees of ominousness. The latent threat remained the same as under Ismā'īl. However, Ṭahmāsp succeeded in asserting his authority for forty years from 940/1533 onwards, until a new rebellion, similar in extent to that which troubled the beginning of his reign, again rocked the empire.

Scarcely less devastating were the effects of the strife among the Qizilbāsh on the external political situation of the Safavid empire. The Uzbek danger which we encountered in the reign of Shah Ismā'īl for a long time plagued his son in turn. It crystallised into five separate assaults, the first of which took place in the year of Ṭahmāsp's accession. It is unlikely that this initial attack was aimed at the conquest of Khurāsān, though mounted as it was by a strong force it was more than a mere raid in search of booty and indeed culminated in a prolonged but unsuccessful siege of Herat. On the other hand, this intention, which we have already observed in the case of the Uzbeks, is so clearly discernible behind the subsequent invasions that a modern writer has appropriately described the Persian–Uzbek conflicts between 930/1524 and 947/1540 as "the duel for Khurāsān".[1] It is not certain whether the decision to launch the first of the five Uzbek attacks was taken in the light of the events enacted at the Persian court after Ṭahmāsp's accession, since the evidence of the sources is contradictory, some placing the outbreak of hostilities prior to Ismā'īl's

[1] The title of Dickson's thesis: *Sháh Tahmásb and the Úzbeks (The Duel for Khurásán with 'Ubayd Khán ...)*.

death; but it is undoubtedly the case that these events influenced the course of the conflict.

The governorship of Khurāsān province together with that of the capital Herat was at that time in the hands of Ṭahmāsp's younger brother Sām Mīrzā. In view of his youth, power was exercised on his behalf by his tutor, Durmish Khān Shāmlū. Letters exchanged by the Uzbek prince 'Ubaid-Allāh Khān, Muḥammad Shaibānī's nephew, and the commandant of the fortress of Herat which he was investing, apparently during the winter of 932/1525–6, are still extant and convey a good impression of the situation. For in his summons to surrender, the Uzbek indicates that no assistance could be expected from the shah in view of the quarrelling among the Qizilbāsh amīrs. And indeed Dīv Sulṭān Rūmlū did not dare to weaken his army by despatching a force to relieve Herat. As it happened, there were no serious repercussions at this particular point because 'Ubaid-Allāh Khān was not prepared to prolong the siege until the enemy had been ground down. Some time later he withdrew empty-handed.

Shortly after that, however, he must have resolved to conquer Khurāsān, indubitably influenced by the unending squabbles among the amīrs of the shah, and perhaps too by news of the death of Durmish Khān. As early as 934/1528 he mounted a fresh attack, occupied Mashhad and Astarābād and appeared once again before the walls of Herat to begin a seven-month siege. This time a Persian relief force was organised and the shah accompanied it to Khurāsān. He intervened personally in the battle of Jām (10 Muḥarram 935/24 September 1528) and won a victory principally by methods which his amīrs had learnt from the Ottomans: for example, by the use of artillery, which was new to the Uzbeks. Unfortunately, the Safavid troops failed to exploit their victory, allowing the enemy to escape, and the following spring they marched westwards again in order to put down a revolt in Baghdad which had been instigated by Ẕu'l-Faqār Beg Mauṣillū.

Because of its connections with the Ottomans this uprising had a more than local significance for the shah. He considered it to be more dangerous than the Uzbeks, who would predictably return in the event of his own withdrawal. Indeed, he did not have to wait long for news of 'Ubaid-Allāh's third attack. After conquering Mashhad, 'Ubaid-Allāh this time achieved the surrender of the fortress of Herat by Ḥusain Khān Shāmlū, the tutor of Sām Mīrzā, in return for a guarantee of safe conduct out of the city. The reasons for this were firstly that

Herat had not yet recovered from the previous siege; and secondly that the court made no effort to go to the aid of Khurāsān, clearly because Chūha Sulṭān Takkalū had nothing to gain from assisting his enemy Ḥusain Khān. On the face of it relief was perfectly possible, for the shah had been able to resolve the problem in Baghdad with unexpected rapidity. Ẕu'l-Faqār had been murdered and with the collapse of this revolt Baghdad had fallen to Ṭahmāsp on 3 Shawwāl 935/10 June 1529. But instead of then returning to Khurāsān, the shah set up a summer camp at Abhar, and on top of that spent the winter in Qazvīn. Not until the following summer did he march towards Khurāsān at the head of a strong army. At the news of his advance, 'Ubaid-Allāh Khān's governors took flight. 'Ubaid-Allāh himself likewise retreated from Herat, tried to raise reinforcements in Marv and, when that failed, marched on to Bukhārā. The shah assigned Khurāsān to Prince Bahrām Mīrzā and appointed Ghāzī Khān Takkalū as his tutor. In spite of the lateness of the season he left Khurāsān again in mid-Rabī' I 937/at the beginning of November 1530, perhaps because the size of his army would have caused grave supply problems had he decided to winter there.

About this time the Persian court witnessed the fall of Chūha Sulṭān and the ousting of the Takkalū. The events connected with this were of such a spectacular nature that the Uzbeks must have learnt about them forthwith and conceived the idea of a fresh campaign against Khurāsān. An attack by the Ottomans on north-west Persia, with which we will deal later, was another contributory factor. As in 935/1528 the shah again reacted nervously to the Ottoman initiative and marched to Āzarbāījān, which not even a fresh Uzbek invasion in the spring of 938/1532 could induce him to leave. The reason for his different estimation of the foes on Persia's western and eastern flanks lay probably not only in the greater military potential of the Ottomans and the obvious success of their expansionist policies, but also in the geopolitical situation. The remote province of Khurāsān is connected with the Safavid central provinces only by a small colonised strip between the southern face of the Alburz mountains and the northern edge of the desert; an enemy like the Uzbeks, who were essentially interested only in Khurāsān, would scarcely venture beyond that strip in any large-scale actions (though they occasionally raided further, as in 939/1533, when they reached Ray). In Āzarbāījān, on the other hand, with its tracts of agricultural land, vital interests were at stake, including several access routes to the country's central provinces.

The fourth Uzbek assault on Khurāsān thus coincided with the shah's stay in Tabrīz. It led to the almost complete occupation of the province. Herat alone resisted the attack and a siege lasting a year and a half, which might still have achieved its aim had not ʿUbaid-Allāh suddenly retreated in mid-Rabīʿ I 940/at the beginning of October 1533. His action may have been determined by internal events in his homeland of Transoxiana, but scarcely by news of Shah Ṭahmāsp's advance, since the latter did not reach Khurāsān for another two months. The fact that the Herat garrison was equal to the hardships of a protracted siege is astonishing, the more so since the local Qizilbāsh had hitherto been dominated by the Takkalū, who had long since been ousted from the shah's immediate circle. Nevertheless, the new constellation now had its impact on Herat. Sām Mīrzā was again appointed governor, as before with a tutor from the Shāmlū tribe, called Aghzīvār Sulṭān. This time the shah wintered in Herat. In preparation for a campaign against the Uzbeks he sent troops to Marv and the territory of Gharchistān on the sources of the Murghāb. In Dhu'l-Ḥijja 940/June 1534 he himself departed for Balkh with the main force. There news reached him of an Ottoman raid on north-west Persia. He thereupon changed his plans and marched towards the west.

Before we discuss the events of the ensuing war in the context of Ottoman–Persian friction, we would do well to consider the course and temporary termination of the struggle against the Uzbeks. But we can record at this point that the Ottoman attack created the most dangerous crisis of Shah Ṭahmāsp's reign, because it was connected not only chronologically but also inherently with the machinations of the Qizilbāsh touched on earlier. That ʿUbaid-Allāh Khān made the most of the opportunity afforded him by the shah's involvement in the west and by the crisis at the Persian court is scarcely surprising. But we must dismiss the notion that the Turkish sultan conceived of an alliance with the Uzbeks in order to trap the Safavids in a pincer movement, or that similar ideas existed in Bukhārā. The latter supposition is refuted by the mere fact that ʿUbaid-Allāh did not mount his attack until the Ottomans had already begun to retreat.

It is quite another question whether ʿUbaid-Allāh had some connection with the rebellion of the Qizilbāsh, in the course of which, as we saw, Ḥusain Khān Shāmlū was executed. The consequences of this uprising for Khurāsān began with an official edict (*ḥukm*) from the Herat authorities, permitting the Türkmens to plunder the civilian population. The revolt of Sām Mīrzā, his tutor and his amīrs was revealed when without the shah's authorisation they undertook a campaign against Qandahār, which was part of the Mughal empire in India. The enmity existing between ʿUbaid-Allāh Khān and the Mughals, together with the fact that ʿUbaid-Allāh initially did not launch any offensive, but only minor thrusts against Herat, although the city had been left in a state of turmoil akin to civil war and entirely without any military protection – all this points to a secret understanding. It was undoubtedly known in Bukhārā that the Turkish sultan had already officially recognised Sām Mīrzā as shah in place of his brother Ṭahmāsp.

When in 942/at the end of 1535 ʿUbaid-Allāh Khān mounted his fifth offensive against Khurāsān, a revolt of the population against the Qizilbāsh was under way in and around Herat in consequence of the ruthless plundering to which it had been subjected. The rebels were so strong and numerous that they were able to place Herat under a regular state of siege. They put themselves at the disposal of ʿUbaid-Allāh, who was camped before Mashhad, and summoned him to Herat. Finally, treason on the part of Persian citizens delivered the town into the hands of the rebels and their Uzbek allies. With the conquest of Herat, ʿUbaid-Allāh, who meanwhile had been elected supreme khan of the Uzbeks, might have seen himself at the summit of his ambition to enter upon the heritage of the Timurids in their famous capital, had not the collapse of discipline in his army become all too evident. When news reached him that the shah was approaching after a victory over the Ottoman sultan, his amīrs refused to risk a battle with the Qizilbāsh and insisted instead on returning to Bukhārā and abandoning their conquests in Khurāsān.

Thus it came about that Herat was evacuated in mid-Shaʿbān 943/at the end of January 1537 and was occupied without a struggle by the new governor whom the shah had sent on in advance. He was Ṭahmāsp's eldest son, the future Shah Muḥammad Khudābanda, accompanied by a tutor from the Takkalū tribe, Muḥammad Khān Sharaf al-Dīn-ughlī, who as governor of Baghdad during the rebellion of his tribe had remained faithful to the shah. Ṭahmāsp remained in Khurāsān for six months, waged a campaign against the Mughals, thereby conquering Qandahār (if only for a brief interval), and sent his troops into action against various Uzbek dominions. When in Rabīʿ II 944/September 1537 he began his return march towards Tabrīz, the

Uzbek threat had been dispelled for a long time to come. Ṭahmāsp's prestige, founded on his triumphs over the Ottomans, Uzbeks and Mughals, but above all over his own Qizilbāsh amīrs, did not fail to have its effect.

The shah was now twenty-three years old, and had acquired experience from the events of his childhood and adolescence which, in conjunction with his political and military aptitude, had turned him into a ruler of considerable stature. He had survived with flying colours the long probation period of internal and external crises since his accession. The very circumspection of his reaction to the Uzbek attacks leads one to postulate a sound judgment in complicated situations. He may have known that 'Ubaid-Allāh Khān's aspirations in Khurāsān, however serious, were limited by the lack of internal stability in Transoxiana. In fact 'Ubaid-Allāh's ideas could not by any means have been identical with the plans of his generals. Whereas he envisaged an extension of Uzbek territory – namely the revival of the former Timurid glory – his followers had perfectly concrete, more modest ends in mind, that is, forays and expeditions to Khurāsān and what seemed to them to be the untold wealth of its settlements.

Ṭahmāsp was right: his most dangerous enemies were the Ottomans, not the Uzbeks. Naturally, he was not to know that his opponent Süleymān the Magnificent (926–74/1520–66) would go down in history as the most important sultan of the Ottoman empire. Whether the shah had adequate information right from the beginning of the conflict about the sultan's military strength and his dealings with the western powers, we do not know. The mere memory of his father's grave defeat at Chāldirān may have been sufficient to determine his estimate of the Ottoman threat. Although that battle had taken place as early as 920/1514, the year of Ṭahmāsp's birth, eye-witness accounts which he heard as a child doubtless had their effect in later years.

As an indication of the fact that the shah was none too well informed of the Ottomans' plans or at least exaggerated the potential danger, we might look at his reaction to the revolt of Ẕu'l-Faqār Sulṭān Mauṣillū Turkmān. It will be recalled that it was this uprising which, after the victory at Jām in the autumn of 935/1528, caused Ṭahmāsp to leave Khurāsān again with the greatest speed. Since news of the rebellion had reached him even before the Khurāsān campaign, the reason for his haste was probably that Ẕu'l-Faqār had recognised the authority of the Ottomans. Now the sultan had just returned from the conquest of Hungary and was preoccupied with a campaign against Austria, the attack which led to the siege of Vienna (27 September – 15 October 1529); he was thus scarcely in a position to pay much heed to the events in Baghdad, but this was clearly not so obvious from the point of view of the Persian court encamped in Jām.

Only with the Austrian ceasefire of 14 January 1533 and the peace treaty which quickly followed did a really serious situation arise for Persia, resulting in the first of three Turco-Persian wars waged during Ṭahmāsp's reign. Sultan Süleymān could scarcely have been under any illusion concerning the danger which a strong Safavid empire might represent for him and his ambitious plans in the west and north-west of his realm. Moreover the revolts of the Anatolian Qizilbāsh – especially that of Shāh Qulī but also others that had followed[1] - were still fresh in his mind. When the peace with Austria restored his freedom of action, he therefore proceeded to tackle this problem.

As will be recalled, the Takkalū had been ousted from their position of dominance in Persia in 937/1531. The ensuing persecution and harassment of the members of this tribe provoked one of their leaders, Ūlāmā Sulṭān, a governor of the shah in Āzarbāījān who had earlier fled to Persia from Anatolia, to seek refuge at the Ottoman court. Describing the precarious position of the shah, exposed as he was to tribal strife at court and in the provinces and to Uzbek attacks on Khurāsān, he drew attention to the favourable conditions for an Ottoman initiative. The sultan readily took up this suggestion, hoping in such circumstances to abolish a potential danger in his rear which might have grown acute at a time when he was engaged in campaigns in Europe. He sent Ūlāmā Sulṭān, who had meanwhile been given the rank of pasha, to Ḥiṣn Kaifā as governor with the task of conquering Bitlīs and supporting the Turkish offensive against Persia. In Muḥarram 941/July 1534 the Turkish Grand Vizier Ibrāhīm Pasha occupied Tabrīz and two months later Süleymān himself arrived in the city. He marched via Hamadān on Baghdad, which surrendered to the Turks at the end of November without a struggle. The shah, who had broken off his campaign against the Uzbeks upon learning of the Ottoman invasion, and had hastened a distance of some 1,200 miles to meet it, found himself in desperate straits. In Khurāsān there had been an

[1] Gökbilgin, "Süleyman I", pp. 109f. Sohrweide, "Der Sieg der Ṣafaviden", pp. 164–86.

attempt to poison him. The Shāmlū were in revolt, and more and more Qizilbāsh amīrs were leaving him in the lurch. This was the last of the great tribal feuds before the shah succeeded in asserting his authority and in taking over the government of the realm himself. Süleymān exploited this situation by making contact with the rebellious prince Sām in Khurāsān, whom he believed he could set on the Persian throne at the price of Āzarbāījān. The Shāmlū, and perhaps also the Takkalū, seem to have been behind this project. Contact between the Khurāsān rebels and the sultan may have been established by Ghāzī Khān Takkalū, who had been tutor to Bahrām Mīrzā during his governorship of Herat and now paid a brief visit to the Ottoman winter headquarters at Baghdad.

Nevertheless, Ṭahmāsp was able to reverse all of Süleymān's gains as soon as the latter retreated into Mesopotamia. This led the sultan to launch a fresh campaign against Persia in the following spring. The shah again refused to fight a pitched battle – indeed he was probably not in a position to do so. He confined his activity to attacking the Turkish rearguards and involving them in skirmishes. When the sultan began the return march to Istanbul at the end of 1535, his conquests were again completely lost, with the sole exception of Baghdad, which remained permanently Turkish, apart from a Persian interlude in the 11th/17th century. Sultan Süleymān had failed to achieve his goal of freeing himself from the Persian threat to his rear. His failure was all the greater in that Ṭahmāsp emerged strengthened from the grave crisis into which the Ottoman attack had plunged him. There is little doubt that the Turkish failure must once again be attributed to the rigours of the climate and to the extended lines of communication which presented the Ottoman armies with practically insoluble logistical problems. The Persian problem had been shelved, but not solved.

In the next fifteen years Safavid troops established several strong points along the Turkish frontier, yet without noticeably straining relations with the Ottomans. Not until Ṭahmāsp's brother Alqāṣ[1] Mīrzā, who had once played a prominent part in the struggle against the Uzbeks and had been made governor of Shīrvān, rebelled against the shah and was granted asylum at the Porte did relations once more grow perilously tense. On this occasion too a recent peace treaty with

[1] Alternative forms are Alqāṣṣ, Alqās, Alqāsb and Ilqās (for the last, see Röhrborn, *Provinzen und Zentralgewalt*, index).

Austria gave the sultan a free hand in any conflict with Persia. The encouragement of the Persian prince to this effect found a ready ear, especially since another refugee, a son of the last Shīrvān-Shāh, was working along the same lines. In the spring of 955/1548 the sultan attacked Persia. Again a two-year campaign ensued, and again the Ottomans failed to win any decisive gains. Tabrīz was captured, but only for a few days. With the sultan's permission, Alqāṣ Mīrzā launched a thrust towards Iṣfahān and other Persian towns, using not Turkish but irregular troops. Eventually, however, he fell into his brother's hands and was imprisoned in a fortress, where he soon met his death. While Süleymān withdrew to a winter camp at Aleppo, Ṭahmāsp laid waste large areas of eastern Anatolia. Thereby he achieved his aim: although the Turks sent a force into Georgia, they would not risk an engagement with the shah and in the late autumn of 956/1549 they began their retreat.

The repeated capture of his capital by the Turks must have demonstrated to the shah its exposed location. He therefore decided in 955/1548 to transfer his seat to Qazvīn.[1] It was to remain there for half a century until finally Iṣfahān became the capital. One may also see in this change a token of the increasing Iranicisation of the Safavid empire, for which the Türkmen tradition linked with Tabrīz had now lost its erstwhile importance.

That the second Persian campaign of Süleymān the Magnificent had likewise failed to fulfil its objective soon became apparent when shortly afterwards Ṭahmāsp's second son Ismā'īl Mīrzā invaded eastern Anatolia, invested various towns in the neighbourhood of Vān, captured Akhlāṭ and later Arjīsh, and defeated Iskandar Pasha, governor of Erzerum, before the gates of his own city. When similar exploits were repeated, the sultan decided on another campaign which initially he intended to entrust to one of his generals, but which in the event he led himself. In Jumādā II 961/May 1554 he left his winter camp in Aleppo for Āmid and advanced as far as the Armenian territory of Qarābāgh in the southern bend of the Araxes. But by the time he returned to Erzerum in Ramaḍān/August all that had been achieved was extensive pillaging and more or less insignificant skirmishes. Then a Persian envoy appeared and an armistice was negotiated. Clearly it

[1] The date given in Lockhart, *Persian Cities* (London, 1960), p. 69. The difficulty of tracing a record of the transfer in the sources may probably be ascribed to the fact that public affairs were dealt with mostly in the royal camp, i.e. in frequently changing locations.

was in the interest of both sides to terminate hostilities. For after Ṭahmāsp, whose pacific nature is often emphasised, had despatched another plenipotentiary the following spring, a peace treaty was concluded in the sultan's camp at Amāsya on 8 Rajab 962/29 May 1555, the first official peace between the Safavids and the Ottomans. It was observed until after the deaths of both rulers – in fact, until 986/1578.

Admittedly the Turkish attacks had deprived Ṭahmāsp of Baghdad and Mesopotamia, together with the fortress of Vān. But he had been able to prevent any further loss of territory, above all the loss of Āzarbāījān. Confronted by a foe who was at the height of his power, whose exploits had been crowned with success far into Europe, the shah had acquitted himself not at all badly. Thereby one is of course overlooking the repercussions of three decades of war in the east and in the west, combined with the simultaneous internal strife amongst the Qizilbāsh tribes, for the Persian economy and the material circumstances of the population.

Alongside the conflict with the Uzbeks and the Ottomans, Ṭahmāsp's relations with the empire of the Indian Mughals, which had been founded shortly before the beginning of his reign by Ẓahīr al-Dīn Muḥammad Bābur, the famous descendant of Tīmūr, were of secondary importance. Though in 943/1537 the shah had occupied the Mughal city of Qandahār, he omitted to take any retaliatory measures when it was shortly afterwards recaptured from the governor he had appointed. Some years later, when Bābur's successor Humāyūn sought refuge at his court, the shah placed at his disposal Persian troops, with whose help he retook the town. In fact, Qandahār did not revert into the shah's possession until the accession of the Emperor Akbar (963–1014/1556–1605).[1]

The Safavid empire possessed numerous frontier areas like Qandahār. Some of them were ruled as vassal states by native governors, who occasionally bore the title of *vālī*. The territories were often remote and differed from the rest of Persia in the language, culture and religion of their populations. Sometimes they formed a kind of buffer state between Persia and her powerful neighbours. In the course of time they

[1] For further details of Ṭahmāsp's relations with India, cf. the *Tārīkh-i Quṭbī* of Khūrshāh b. Qubād al-Ḥusainī: review of M.H. Zaidī's partial edition of this work in *Der Islam* XLV (1969), 169ff.

were integrated with the Persian state as provinces, thereby of course losing their special status. This tendency can be seen even in the reign of Ṭahmāsp I: in fact, from 943/1536–7, with the appointment of a governor in Lāhījān, where following the death of Ismā'īl's benefactor Kārkiyā Mīrzā 'Alī relations between the Safavid court and the ruler of east Gīlān had rapidly deteriorated; the appointment was short-lived, though another was made for a few years towards the end of the shah's reign.[1] Shīrvān lost its autonomy once and for all in 1538, Bākū followed some years later and Shakkī in 1551. Ṭahmāsp also appointed a governor over part of Māzandarān, but the latter could only maintain his position from 1569 to 1576. The rulers of 'Arabistān, the Musha'-sha', had remained loyal to the Safavids since their subjugation by Ismā'īl I. To be sure, Badrān b. Falāḥ found himself in a cleft stick when the Ottomans began their operations against Mesopotamia, and had no choice but to go to greet Süleymān the Magnificent on his advance from Hamadān towards Baghdad in 941/1534. Yet his son and heir Sajjād once again acknowledged the shah as his lord when Ṭahmāsp proceeded to Dizfūl in 948/1541. On this occasion Sajjād was confirmed as governor (*ḥākim*) of Ḥavīza.

Naturally there were also territories conquered by Ismā'īl I which were lost to his son; for example, Bitlīs on the Turkish frontier, which has already been mentioned, and Sīstān in the far south-east of Persia. Georgia – including the areas of Shīrvān and Shakkī – held a particular attraction for the Safavids, as indeed it did for the Ottomans and had also done for previous Muslim dynasties such as the Türkmens. Ṭahmāsp was following an established precedent, therefore, when he undertook no fewer than four Georgian campaigns, three of them in the period 947–61/1540–54. Great as was the attraction of this land for the Safavids, the difficulties confronting them there were no less daunting, both on account of its geography and because of the military prowess of the Georgians. Ṭahmāsp was not able to hold the capital Tiflis, although it had been captured several times by the Qizilbāsh, until he succeeded in establishing there as his governor the Bagratid David, a brother of King Simon I, who came to the Persian court, was converted to Islam and entered Ṭahmāsp's service. This, however, did not by any means solve the Georgian problem. Nevertheless, the oper-

[1] From 975/1567–8, according to Röhrborn, *Provinzen und Zentralgewalt*, p. 83. Minorsky, *Tadhkirat al-Mulūk*, p. 170, gives 1567.

ations of the Safavids in Georgia had a domestic significance which will be discussed below.

In order to elucidate the domestic repercussions of Safavid–Georgian relations, we must again recall the frequent revolts and mutinies of the Qizilbāsh amīrs, the civil wars unleashed by them at the beginning of Shah Ṭahmāsp's reign, their unbridled tribalism, individual cases of desertion to the Ottomans, and their attempt to depose Shah Ṭahmāsp in favour of his brother Sām Mīrzā – all alike basically the consequence of the failure of Ṭahmāsp, and still more of Ismā'īl I, to assimilate the old Safavid order, the Qizilbāsh, within the state. As has already been mentioned, such incidents had led occasionally under Ismā'īl, and all the more under Ṭahmāsp, to successive attempts either to oust the Qizilbāsh amīrs or to reduce their predominance. This was possible only if they could be dislodged from the most important military and administrative posts in the empire. We have seen what courses of action the two rulers adopted in order to attain this goal. They probably realised that although they could obtain partial success by playing off rival tribes or individuals one against the other, no definitive success could be achieved in this way. Shah Ismā'īl's practice of appointing Iranian dignitaries to the highest military posts indicates his awareness that a fundamental change could only be brought about by recruiting non-Türkmen elements.

In these efforts not only Persians play a rôle, but even more so Georgians[1] and Circassians (in the then accepted sense of anyone living north of Darband[2]), who as a rule were recruited into the army as bodyguards (*qūrchīs*). The commander of the royal guard (*qūrchī-bāshī*) was already gaining more and more importance during the second half of Shah Ṭahmāsp's reign, while the power and influence of the Great Amīr (amīr al-umarā') diminished. This process, which extended over several decades and eventually resulted in the undermining or even neutralisation of the Türkmen military aristocracy, the Qizilbāsh, did not, of course, escape the attention of the victims, even though to begin with it was not perhaps as apparent as the preference given to representatives of the Persian aristocracy under Shah Ismā'īl I. They were of course reluctant to accept this turn of events, and so repeated disturbances and

[1] In 1553–4 alone Ṭahmāsp brought back no fewer than 30,000 Georgian captives: Savory, "The Principal Offices ....during the reign of Ṭahmāsp I", p. 84.

[2] Minorsky, *Tadhkirat al-Mulūk*, p. 163.

rebellions ensued until Shah 'Abbās I succeeded in finally quelling the Qizilbāsh.

Yet before this point was reached, the Safavid empire had to survive another grave internal crisis, so grave indeed that its very existence was in danger. The trouble began at the end of Shah Ṭahmāsp I's long reign, when in October 1575 the aged ruler fell ill. Among the members of the royal family and the court, especially the chief amīrs of the Qizilbāsh, the question of the succession was inevitably debated. This matter was not governed by any set rules, any more than was the leadership of the Ardabīl order, in which, although it had been customary for the leadership to be handed down from father to son, the eldest son had not always been chosen and the rule does not seem in any case to have been followed invariably.[1] Nor had the shah made any explicit disposition by nominating a crown prince. Although he had for some time past shown favour to Prince Sulṭān Ḥaidar Mīrzā by inviting him to participate in affairs of state, he had nevertheless refrained from endowing him with any specific office.

Admittedly there were influential tribal leaders, among them amīrs of the Ustājlū and powerful Georgians, who looked upon Ḥaidar as the future shah. His elder brother Muḥammad Khudābanda was not considered a serious contender because he suffered from a major eye complaint. Yet Prince Ḥaidar was opposed by amīrs of the Rūmlū and Turkmān tribes, for instance, who like Ḥaidar's influential sister Parī Khān Khānum had a quite different candidate in mind, namely Prince Ismā'īl. The reasons for this choice are not very clear, for the prince in question had lived for eighteen years under close arrest in the fortress of Qahqaha, in the Savalān mountains west of Ardabīl. Presumably little more than tribal particularism lay behind it. Perhaps, too, one may adduce the fame that Ismā'īl had won through his victories over the Turks and which had never entirely faded, that very esteem combined with the common touch and a certain arrogance which may have induced Shah Ṭahmāsp to imprison Ismā'īl after all his unpleasant experiences with his brothers Sām Mīrzā and Alqāṣ Mīrzā. We cannot, however, dismiss the possibility that in spite of everything his father still considered Ismā'īl an eventual successor, since the shah sent a

[1] Hinz, *Irans Aufstieg*, p. 17. We can only assume that the traditions of the order were observed in the succession of the first Safavid shahs, since to date there has been no detailed study.

reliable bodyguard to protect him from any attempts on his life that might have been instigated by the fortress commandant.

Initially it seemed as if the discussions at the court of Qazvīn about the succession had been premature. Shah Ṭahmāsp recovered from his illness and devoted his attention as before to affairs of state. But the tensions among his entourage remained in spite of the king's attempts to dispel them by making changes in the personnel surrounding him. The tensions still prevailed when he finally died six months later, as a result of poison, on 15 Ṣafar 984/14 May 1576. Whether this was by accident or design has never been established.

Ṭahmāsp's death triggered off a series of dramatic events. Before proceeding to deal with these, however, we must dwell at least briefly on an assessment of his character and his fifty-two-year reign. In general the verdict of historians has tended to be adverse. They criticise his miserliness, his greed and his cowardice. They are also offended by the bigotry which he demonstrated at an early age, apparently following the failure of a poisoning attempt,[1] and which not only affected his personal conduct and his immediate retinue but was also responsible for a series of narrow-minded ordinances imposed on the population as a whole. The notion that he refused to conclude any treaties with the Christian powers of Western Europe on religious grounds can no longer be sustained.[2] But his bigotry is discernible in his stubborn attempts to convert the Great Mughal Humāyūn to the Shī'ī faith when the latter sought asylum at his court in 1541. A particularly repugnant act of treachery may be seen in his treatment of the Ottoman Prince Bāyezīd, who sought refuge in Persia in 1559 after rebelling against his father. The shah could have been in no doubt as to the impending fate of the prince and his four sons when he handed them over to an Ottoman delegation after negotiations lasting two years. Even if political considerations were involved – Süleymān had threatened military reprisals, in other words, the termination of the Peace of Amāsya – it is to Ṭahmāsp's discredit that he accepted payment for his collaboration in gold coin and territorial concessions.[3]

Such misdeeds, errors and weaknesses throw a murky light on

[1] Dickson, *Sháh Tahmásb and the Úzbeks*, pp. 261, 276ff., with the date 1534.

[2] Cf. now Palombini, *Bündniswerben*, especially p. 119.

[3] S. Turan, *Kanunî'nin oğlu*; more briefly Gökbilgin, "Süleyman I", pp. 140–3; Kramers, "Selīm II", *EI*[1].

Ṭahmāsp as a person and as a ruler. Yet a just appraisal of the shah cannot be reached on the basis of this evidence alone: we must also consider other factors together with his political achievements and behaviour. We should not forget that the first decade of Ṭahmāsp's life – the whole period prior to his accession – coincided with that phase in the career of his father Ismā'īl I during which the latter, clearly disillusioned and discouraged by his defeat at Chāldirān, could not bring himself to take any notable political or military initiative and therefore failed to inspire his son with any noble aspirations. On the other hand, we should not underestimate Ṭahmāsp's achievement in personally taking over the reins of power within a space of ten years, after the land had been at the mercy of plotting tribal chieftains. If in the first decade of his reign he was a puppet in the hands of Türkmen amīrs, he certainly cannot be accused of weakness during the next forty years.

What is remarkable is not only the skill with which he freed himself from the tutelage of the Qizilbāsh leaders but also the courage with which he faced the Uzbeks, particularly in the battle of Jām, and then in 941/1534, even before the Uzbek danger had been averted, took the correct decision to withdraw from the fighting in the east and march to meet the greater threat posed by the Ottoman invasion. He adhered steadfastly to this policy despite the Ottoman successes and despite the conspiracy of his brother Sām and the defection of most of his Türkmen generals. Only in this way did he succeed eventually in asserting his authority, quelling several revolts on the part of the Qizilbāsh (nowadays we would describe them as civil wars), retaining Khurāsān with Herat and Mashhad in defiance of five Uzbek attacks and even emerging relatively unscathed from three wars against the Ottomans.

Persia was able to absorb the loss of Baghdad, and the surrender of eastern Anatolia gave an impetus to the Iranicisation (at least in a geographical sense) of the Safavid empire, for which both its Türkmen forebear Uzun Ḥasan and the latter's son and heir Ya'qūb had, so to speak, established certain preconditions. Another instance of this development was manifest from 955/1548 onwards, when the Safavid capital was transferred from Tabrīz, now standing on the boundaries of the empire, to Qazvīn. Although Ṭahmāsp and his advisers probably had no conscious thought other than to avoid the ever-present threat to the capital from the Ottomans, the idea of a Türkmen state with its centre at Tabrīz and its fulcrum in eastern Anatolia, Mesopotamia and north-west Persia was thereby abandoned in favour of an empire centred on the Iranian highlands. At this time, therefore, arose roughly the same geopolitical situation that still prevails today. There is no reason to seek here the beginnings of a deliberate policy of Iranicisation. Yet the implications of the development are clear. At most one can speak of an involuntary Iranicisation that shows even fewer signs of being a conscious intention than the previously mentioned recruitment of non-Türkmen notables for the civil and military administration.

The shah's character also appears in a rather more favourable light when we learn that in spite of his cupidity piety led him to forgo highly lucrative taxes on the grounds that they offended against religious law; thereby rejecting an income of some 30,000 *tūmāns*.[1] The extant record of the speech he made on 19 July 1562 to the envoys of the Turkish sultan who had come to negotiate the extradition of Prince Bāyezīd betokens his political skill,[2] while his highly cultured mind, his scholarliness and his patronage of the arts ensure him a measure of sympathy. After all, under his aegis the art of book illumination attained between 1530 and 1545 a zenith of development that has never been surpassed.[3] Thus, if one carefully weighs up the positive and negative features that were combined in Ṭahmāsp's character, favourable qualities are by no means lacking. It must be counted a particular achievement that by the time of his death he had managed to preserve the essential fabric of his father's empire in the face of grave internal and external dangers.

ISMĀʿĪL II

That same day the explosive nature of the domestic political situation in the Safavid empire became evident. It was revealed less by the immediately erupting dispute over the succession than by the peculiar character of the antagonisms that now came to the fore. It was not only a matter of a conflict between rival interests which grouped themselves around the two contenders, but also (and to a far greater extent) of a struggle between Türkmen and non-Türkmen. Admittedly, the picture does not appear so clear-cut at first sight. On the one hand we find

1 Kütükoğlu, "Tahmasp I", p. 647: following Hinz, "The Value of the Toman in the Middle Ages", *Yād-nāma-yi Īrānī-yi Minorsky* (Tehran, 1348/1969), pp. 90–5, this is equivalent to 1,730 kg of pure gold.

2 On this report, see Hinz, "Zur Frage der Denkwürdigkeiten".

3 Stchoukine, *Manuscrits Ṣafavīs* pp. 189, 199ff.

Prince Ḥaidar supported partly by the Türkmen Ustājlū tribe but mainly by the Georgian leaders at court; on the other hand the party of Prince Ismāʿīl, who was still imprisoned at Qahqaha – a group led by Princess Parī Khān Khānum and supported partly by her Circassian uncle Shamkhāl Sulṭān but in the main by all the Türkmen tribes other than the Ustājlū.

Prince Ḥaidar considered himself not without good reason as the heir appointed by Ṭahmāsp, but did not even get a chance to take power: he fell into the hands of his opponents and was immediately murdered. Thereafter the way was open for his brother to ascend the throne as Ismāʿīl II. The eighteen months of his rule constituted a reign of terror unusual even by oriental standards. That the party which had suffered a defeat over the succession should have been exposed to the revenge of the victors is not surprising. What *is* remarkable is the merciless cruelty with which the new shah exterminated his brothers. Only one of them, the almost blind Muḥammad Khudābanda, eluded his assassin – and that only because Ismāʿīl died before the order could be carried out. This brutality is explained by the hypothesis that Ismāʿīl, whose health had been ravaged by the constant use of drugs during his long captivity, was on the verge of insanity when he succeeded to the throne and from then on acted purely out of paranoia. This theory may well be correct; but it is equally possible that he was deliberately imitating the example of the Ottoman court, where at this time, after several unfortunate experiences, the "superfluous" princes were systematically eliminated to ensure that the accession of the crown prince would not be threatened.[1] It can be assumed that Ismāʿīl, remembering his earlier battles with the Turks, continued to show an interest in developments in the Ottoman empire even during his captivity. We even know that he could draw on certain sources of information at Qahqaha. Why should he therefore not have come to the same conclusions as had been drawn in Istanbul? Perhaps the distrust and fear that he showed reflected his own attitude towards his father; they were certainly dictated by his father's bitter experience with his brothers Alqāṣ and Sām. There is no evidence that the murdered princes had given the new shah any concrete grounds for suspicion, with the exception of one of his cousins, Sulṭān Ḥusain Mīrzā, who set

[1] Cf. F. Giese, "Das Seniorat im osmanischen Herrscherhause", *MOG* II (1923–6), 248–56. That the Persian court was familiar with the Ottoman practice is clear from Sām Mīrzā's *Tuḥfa-yi Sāmī*, ed. Humāyūn Farrukh (Tehran, 1347/1969), p. 25.

up an independent principality in the remote region of Qandahār and who perished early in 1577 without Ismā'īl's contrivance.

If one looks for positive features to alleviate the sinister picture of Ismā'īl's personality during his brief reign, there is very little to fall back on. One could probably point to the success with which he re-established law and order in the land. In the last eight years of Ṭahmāsp's reign, we are told, conditions in Persia had grown very insecure. It is alleged that thousands of Persians were killed by bandits or as a result of the raids of Türkmen soldiery. Ismā'īl apparently succeeded in re-establishing law and order with relentless severity. One can also point to the glimmerings of Ismā'īl's military glory that may have preserved the country from attacks by foreign enemies, although news of events inside Persia, of the murder of the princes and especially of the strife between various Qizilbāsh tribes, which took a particularly violent turn in Khurāsān, might have been expected to arouse their interest and ever-present greed for plunder.

Even though Ismā'īl II had to proceed cautiously in his relations with the Ottomans, one of the most extraordinary measures that he attempted to carry out shortly after assuming power, namely the re-introduction of the Sunnī faith, can scarcely be explained in terms of his respect for their religious susceptibilities (although such a notion was current in the capital)[1] – not even in the light of the Ottoman demand in the Peace of Amāsya of 962/1555 that the execration of the Caliphs Abū Bakr, 'Umar and 'Uthmān that dated back to Shah Ismā'īl I should cease in Persia. What Ismā'īl's real motives for such a step may have been remains a mystery, at least in the present stage of knowledge. Naturally one can adduce his hatred for his merciless father and the corresponding endeavour always to do the very opposite of what Ṭahmāsp had deemed fit; in this case, therefore, to abandon the typical Safavid credo which Ṭahmāsp had maintained with such exaggerated piety. One could combine with this explanation the argument that a reaction against the previous Shī'ī fanaticism was inevitable. It is possible, however, that the step was dictated by a sober political consideration: Ismā'īl's concern about the excessively powerful position of Shī'ī dignitaries, which would have been undermined by a reintroduction of the Sunna.

Before the full repercussions of Ismā'īl's completely disastrous and aimless policies could be felt, he met his death on 13 Ramaḍān 985/24

[1] Hinz, "Schah Esma'il II", p. 80. See chapter 12 below.

November 1577 in an unexpected and mysterious fashion. Some accounts claim that he died of an overdose of drugs, others that he was poisoned by his ambitious sister Parī Khān Khānum, who had been instrumental in ensuring his succession but who had earned only ingratitude for her pains. Others again relate that he was murdered by Qizilbāsh amīrs who refused to tolerate his political measures, particularly the religious changes.

MUḤAMMAD KHUDĀBANDA

Some of Ismā'īl's relatives had escaped the systematic elimination of the royal princes. These included his eldest brother Muḥammad Khudābanda and four of his sons, the eldest, Sulṭān Ḥasan Mīrzā, having been murdered in Tehran shortly before on Ismā'īl's orders. In the council of the Qizilbāsh amīrs at court who met to discuss the succession various suggestions were made. Shāh Shujā', Ismā'īl's infant son, who was only a few weeks old; his eleven-year-old nephew, Sulṭān Ḥamza Mīrzā; and the latter's father, Crown Prince Muḥammad Khudābanda, who had been passed over at the time of Ṭahmāsp's death, were all mooted as successors. In each case Princess Parī Khān Khānum, who was at this time about thirty years old, hoped to be able to take over the regency – even when the choice finally fell on Muḥammad Khudābanda, for owing to an ophthalmic disease he was almost blind.

When he moved from Shīrāz, where he had escaped the fate of his brothers, to Qazvīn and ascended the throne on 3 Dhu'l-Ḥijja 985/11 February 1578, the land was delivered from a harrowing tyranny, but the ten years of his reign brought little joy to his people. What at first made him appear a mild ruler was the sheer contrast with Ismā'īl's cruelty. If one looks closer, his gentleness is seen to be really weakness, indifference and incompetence. Although his eye trouble was not conducive to an effective reign, it cannot explain completely his total lack of involvement in affairs of state. In these circumstances power soon passed into other hands. The shah lived so much in the background that some foreign observers evidently never became aware of his existence; this is the reason for Sulṭān Ḥamza Mīrzā being described more than once as a reigning monarch in the list of Safavid rulers – a position which in reality he never held.[1]

[1] Horst, "Der Ṣafawide Ḥamza Mīrzā"; Roemer, *Niedergang*, pp. 66ff.

The principal feature of the new shah's whole reign was the quarrelling and intrigues of the Qizilbāsh amīrs that had gone on for decades and were only quelled when a particular ruler was able to counter them either by force or by cunning. Since Muḥammad Khudābanda could do neither, their unruliness and jockeying for position reached a climax during his reign, until his son 'Abbās succeeded in suppressing them. When news of Ismā'īl's death was received, bloody conflicts immediately broke out among the Qizilbāsh, with the Shāmlū and Ustājlū on the one side and the Turkmān and Takkalū on the other. Although the Grand Vizier, Mīrzā Salmān Jābirī, a member of an aristocratic family from Iṣfahān which had served the Safavids from an early date,[1] managed to reconcile the warring parties for a time, these quarrels – sometimes amounting to serious rebellion and even civil war – were to remain the dominant factor in Persian politics for the next ten years. The mention of the grand vizier indicates that not only various factions among the Türkmen tribes, but also non-Türkmens such as members of the Iranian aristocracy took part in these clashes. This particular combination, which had already existed before even as early as the reign of Shah Ismā'īl I, foreshadowed future developments. Admittedly it would be wrong to speak of a confrontation between Türkmen and non-Türkmen, or even between Türkmen and Iranian. On the contrary, one finds elements of both groups on either side at any given moment.

On the death of Ismā'īl II the reins of power, as we have seen, were gathered together in the hands of Princess Parī Khān Khānum. She was supported by her Circassian uncle, Shamkhāl Sulṭān, the lord of the seal. As at the time of her father's death, the princess could muster considerable support among the Qizilbāsh and with their help was able to assert her claims. Thus it came about that the Grand Vizier Mīrzā Salmān, who had been appointed by the late shah in Rabī' I 985/June 1577 and did not find favour with the princess, soon left the capital ostensibly to pay his respects to the new shah but in fact prompted by a well founded fear for his own safety. Here we see an alliance of interests that is worth noting. In the retinue of the new shah it was evidently known what was to be expected of his reign. The way that he had exercised previous functions, most recently in Shīrāz, permitted the drawing of fairly reliable conclusions: neither his eye ailment nor

[1] Aubin, "Études Safavides I", pp. 76ff.

the indifference towards public affairs that he had shown previously was likely to change. The rôle of the royal spouse Khair al-Nisā Begum, known as Mahd-i 'Ulyā, would therefore be all the more important. She was an ambitious woman, born into the Māzandarānī nobility, and her enterprise and lust for power now found undreamed-of opportunities, after she had gone for months in constant fear of her life. When the grand vizier arrived in Shīrāz she must have welcomed him not only as a man fully conversant with the latest events in the capital, but also as a potential ally ideally suited to her purpose. He was familiar with the details of the administrative machinery and at the same time enjoyed no particular following among the Qizilbāsh, since he belonged to a famous Iranian family. Thus he was not likely to find any better opportunity than an alliance with the queen of such a weak ruler as the new shah. All the same, he could not have been unaware of certain dangers inherent in this community of interests.

To begin with, Mīrzā Salmān's calculations were apparently proved correct. He retained his high office even under the new ruler and saw his enemy Princess Parī Khān Khānum brought low when, along with her uncle Shamkhāl Sulṭān, she lost all influence shortly after the arrival of the court in Qazvīn and was murdered. Yet the grand vizier could scarcely have foreseen the extent to which the queen herself appropriated power, any more than had the Türkmen amīrs, who had presumably voted for Muḥammad Khudābanda not least because of his weakness and inadequacy. She was by no means content to exercise a more or less indirect influence on affairs of state: instead, she openly carried out all essential functions herself, including the appointment of the chief officers of the realm. In place of the usual royal audience, these high dignitaries had to assemble each morning at the entrance to the women's apartments in order to receive the Begum's orders. On these occasions the royal edicts were drawn up and sealed. Political affairs continued to be dealt with in such a manner for well over a year. By that time the amīrs were so infuriated by the regiment of women that they conspired against the queen, and openly demanded that the shah should remove her. They achieved their aim: the Begum was strangled in the harem on 1 Jumādā I 987/26 July 1579, on the pretext – whether justified or not, it is uncertain – of having entered into a love-affair with 'Ādil Girai, a brother of the khan of the Crimea.

The queen's murder was tantamount to the usurpation of power by the influential leaders of the Qizilbāsh. First there occurred a violent explosion of hatred against the Iranian aristocracy, particularly because of their entrenched positions of power in the central government and other branches of the administration. During the ensuing persecution of Iranians, especially the Māzandarānī supporters of the murdered consort, only those under the protection of powerful Türkmen amīrs survived unscathed and unmolested. One such man was the Grand Vizier Mīrzā Salmān Jābirī, who had joined the conspirators at an opportune moment even though he did not agree with them on every point. The difficulties that he had to face during the persecution of the Iranians may well have deceived the shah into overlooking his previous conduct. At all events the shah allowed him to remain in his high office.

The conspirators found it easy enough to persuade the shah to continue on the throne and to satisfy him with renewed protestations of their fealty. Naturally they emerged scot-free; for who could have called them to account? However, it is interesting that Muḥammad Khudābanda's address to the amīrs and the reproaches that he levelled at them contained clear allusions to the old relationship between the shah as ṣūfī master and the amīrs as his disciples (*ṣūfīgarī, 'aqīda-yi bāṭinī*). From this we may conclude that in theory the original basis of the Safavid empire was still adhered to, even though the religious bond with the shah had long since been dissolved, probably as early as the second half of the reign of Shah Ismā'īl I.

On this occasion Prince Ḥamza was proclaimed crown prince. Since he was only eleven years old the Qizilbāsh had nothing to fear from him for the moment. However, in time, as we have seen, he stepped into the limelight. He had a strong ally in the Grand Vizier Mīrzā Salmān Jābirī, who soon achieved a position of prominence once more. Naturally, the increasing influence of the prince and the vizier earned them the suspicion and ultimately the enmity of the Qizilbāsh amīrs. It is therefore not surprising that they both met a violent end.

In fact, they were not killed until 991/1583 and 994/1586 respectively. Before that the disputes and fighting among the Türkmen tribes grew so acute that the internal crisis of the Safavid empire, which had been simmering ever since Shah Ṭahmāsp's death, began to have wider repercussions: both in the east and in the west Persia's neighbours launched attacks on her. In the context of the present study a mere outline of the main events and their background will suffice.

An attack by Uzbek bands in the spring of 986/1578 was repulsed by Murtażā Qulī Sulṭān, the governor of Mashhad. This was perhaps a legacy of the Uzbek wars waged by Ṭahmāsp I, rather than a prelude to later Uzbek onslaughts of a greater magnitude. In the west the position was more serious. Whether one chooses to see the Turkish defeat at the hands of Don Juan of Austria at the battle of Lepanto in 1571 as a turning point in the history of Turkish power, or merely as one of many signs of incipient decline - perhaps even as an attempt to seek compensation in the east for reverses suffered in the west[1] – the Ottomans still remained by far the greatest threat to the Safavids. Relations between the Ottomans and their western and north-western neighbours were just as important a factor in determining the fluctuating extent of the danger as the strength or weakness of particular Safavid rulers. The confusion surrounding the accession of Shah Muḥammad Khudābanda created ideal conditions for Ṣultan Murād III (982–1003/1574–95) to mount military expeditions in the eastern part of his empire, because the Habsburg Rudolf II had shortly before paid him tribute and he could reasonably assume that he had nothing to fear from that quarter. The Grand Vizier Meḥmed Soqollū, who was inclined to accept the Persian offer to abide by the Peace of Amāsya, was unable to dissuade his monarch; the Sultan was bent on war. A series of uprisings in the Persian frontier areas among the Kurds and in Shīrvān, quarrels among the Georgian princes – some of whom inclined towards the Turks, others more to the Persians – favoured the Turkish plans. These tribesmen may well have had a presentiment of a new Ottoman–Safavid confrontation: indeed in some cases it was known that neighbouring Turkish governors were stirring up trouble on instructions from above.[2]

The Turko-Persian war (986–98/1578–90) was launched by the Porte with the dispatch of the third vizier Muṣṭafā Pasha, known as Lālā Pasha. He gained victories in Georgia, and also defeated Persian troops on Lake Chïldïr (some 30 miles north of Kārs) and invaded Shīrvān, but the decisive breakthrough into Persia eluded him. Although the khan of the Crimea also sent an expeditionary force into Shīrvān, there were no lasting gains to begin with, since the Safavids – despite great losses – harassed the initially victorious invaders, often

1 A contemporary view: Roemer, *Niedergang*, p. 90.

2 Minadoi, p. 25. Micheli, in *Relazioni degli Ambasciatori Veneti al Senato*, ed. E. Albèri, Serie IIIa, II (Florence, 1844), 261.

forcing them to withdraw. However, other Ottoman generals operated more successfully, with the result that ultimately Persia suffered considerable territorial losses not only in Transcaucasia but also in Kurdistān and Luristān and in 993/1585 she even lost Tabrīz.

Nothing could be wider of the mark than to suppose that such military disasters would have helped to terminate the fateful strife between the different factions among the Qizilbāsh tribes, or at least to keep it within tolerable bounds. As before, dissenting tribal interests remained the guiding principle of the amīrs' actions. They were blind to the interests of the empire as a whole, in the foundation of which their forefathers had played such a large part and whose very existence was now at stake. Their attitude naturally had repercussions on the military developments and aggravated the situation to a marked extent.

Particularly dangerous was a rebellion in Khurāsān that led in 989/1581 to this province temporarily seceding from the central government in Qazvīn. In order to understand this event we must recall that within the Safavid administrative framework certain Qizilbāsh amīrs, together with their tribes or individual groups of tribal followers, represented the central government in various provinces as viceroy (ḥākim, vālī) and wielded political authority on its behalf. Certain provinces were placed in the charge of royal princes who entrusted the duties of their office to the Türkmen amīrs attached to them as guardians or tutors. Thus we encountered Muḥammad Khudābanda, before his accession, as governor of Shīrāz. This post was bestowed on him eighteen months after the birth of his son 'Abbās on 1 Ramaḍān 978/27 January 1571, while Herat, which he had governed hitherto, was allotted to the new-born prince.

Khurāsān, which included parts of present-day Afghanistan, had two centres at this time, Mashhad and Herat. The importance of this land and the value placed upon it by the Safavids will be remembered from the earlier account of Shah Ṭahmāsp's Uzbek wars. It should be noted that Khurāsān produced centrifugal tendencies more than once in the course of Persian history owing to its remoteness from the central areas of Iran and to the narrow corridor that was its sole link with them between the Alburz mountains and the Kavīr desert. This separatism now manifested itself once again, as during the bloody strife between the Türkmen tribes the victory of any particular group was immediately countered by reprisals against the kinsfolk of the victors in another area. This escalation reached its peak when an alliance composed mainly of Turkmān and Takkalū triumphed over the more closely linked Shāmlū and Ustājlū at the royal court.

The man who had become tutor to Prince 'Abbās was one 'Alī Qulī Khān Shāmlū, who had originally been made governor of Herat by Shah Ismā'īl II and sent there with orders to eliminate the prince. However, he had not found the opportunity to carry out this commission when he learnt the news of the shah's death, and this enabled him to take up office without fulfilling his instructions. Thereafter, before the demands of Queen Mahd-i 'Ulyā that the prince be sent to the court could be met, she too perished. Thus in the dispute with the court, where his enemies were now all-powerful, and in the struggle with their representative in Mashhad, Murtażā Qulī Khān, the governor still possessed an important pawn. He defeated his rival and retained the upper hand even when the latter was reinforced by troops sent from the capital. Then fresh reprisals were taken at court against his fellow tribesmen and in consultation with confederate amīrs he resolved to have the prince proclaimed shah. The accession took place at Herat in Rabī' I 989/April 1581. However, Shah Muḥammad Khudābanda advanced into Khurāsān in such strength that the ambitious 'Alī Qulī Khān was worsted at Ghūriyān, then forced to retreat and was finally surrounded at Herat. He thereupon surrendered. Nevertheless, he remained governor of his province and guardian of Prince 'Abbās.

The motive force behind the counter-attack in Khurāsān had been the Grand Vizier Mīrzā Salmān Jābirī. He had gained more and more influence at court and even when the queen was murdered his career suffered no more than a temporary setback. In the perilous game in which he was involved he staked his fortunes on Prince Ḥamza, married off his daughter to him, made his eldest son Mīrzā 'Abd-Allāh the prince's vizier, and accompanied him on his campaign in Qarābāgh and Shīrvān. The grand vizier distinguished himself during this campaign, as also in the war against the Ottomans and in the battle against 'Ādil Girai Khān, the brother of the khan of the Crimea. The public token of this rise to power was the bestowal of the rank of governor or *iyālat*. Eventually Mīrzā Salmān enjoyed the same kind of authority as the shah's viceroy (vakīl) in the days of Shah Ismā'īl I,[1] though he was never given this particular title. His success aroused the suspicion and jealousy of the Türkmen amīrs and finally inspired them with a grow-

[1] See above, pp. 229–30.

ing hatred for him. They accused him of being hostile to the Qizilbāsh and of plotting against them, of harbouring a lust for power and interfering in military affairs which in their view could never be the concern of a vizier, an Iranian. The Herat campaign brought things to a head and they demanded that he be handed over (991/1583). Such was the bitterness of the amīrs that the shah and Prince Ḥamza had no choice but to abandon the grand vizier to his enemies.

His assassination demonstrates that in the eighty years since the beginning of Shah Ismā'īl's career the rift within the Safavid empire between Iranian and Turk had still not been healed. Shah Ismā'īl's plans to break the power of the Qizilbāsh by uniting the supreme administrative and military authority in the hands of a non-Turkish, Iranian vakīl had been frustrated despite five successive attempts to tackle the problem. Shah Ṭahmāsp I's endeavours had likewise met with little success. Although the office of viceroy existed during his reign, none of those appointed took a hand in military affairs after an initial attempt to do so had almost cost the vakīl his life. However, these experiences had left the Türkmen generals with an almost traumatic sensitivity towards possible military aspirations on the part of some leading Iranian even though no military rank had in this case been conferred. Since they felt it degrading to be under the command of an Iranian, they fought to defend their military privileges even when a political analysis would have revealed that their position could rather be strengthened by a unanimity to be displayed in the face of external enemies.

We have taken a somewhat closer look at the internal conflicts of the Safavid empire after the accession of Muḥammad Khudābanda in order to show the extent of the crisis caused by the advent of an incompetent ruler. The bloody quarrels among the amīrs, the murder of the queen and Mīrzā Salmān, and the attempted secession in Khurāsān were all merely symptomatic of this crisis. The tribal self-seeking of the Türkmen amīrs continued to make itself felt even after the assassination of the grand vizier. But it would be pointless to unravel the details of the ensuing intrigues. What is more important is the effect that the obvious weakness of the Persian government had on its external foes. Events among the Safavids offered them a temptation which soon proved irresistible. One result was a new Ottoman attack on north-west Persia in 992/1584. Prince Ḥamza was dispatched at the head of inferior forces to confront 'Osmān Pasha and Farhād Pasha, the commanders of the invading Turkish armies, but failed to recapture Tabrīz. Even in the face of the enemy he had to deal with quarrels among the Qizilbāsh. On 24 Dhu'l-Ḥijja 994/6 December 1586 he was assassinated in his camp in Āzarbāījān. It has been claimed, though never proven, that the murderer, a barber by the name of Khudāvardī, had been hired by a group of conspirators among his officers.[1] This new assassination triggered off a development of vital significance. It brought about the accession of Prince 'Abbās.

After the death of Prince Ḥamza amīrs of the Shāmlū and Ustājlū tribes at court managed to thwart the succession of the shah's next son, Prince 'Abbās, and instead had his younger brother Abū Ṭālib Mīrzā (b. 1574) proclaimed crown prince. This step led to immediate repercussions in Khurāsān, where by now the initiative no longer lay in the hands of 'Alī Qulī Khān Shāmlū, the governor of Herat, but in those of the new governor of Mashhad, Murshid Qulī Khān Ustājlū, who had succeeded in spiriting Prince 'Abbās off to Mashhad. He now proceeded to set in motion plans far more ambitious than those pursued by the governor of Herat in 989/1581 with his rebellion against the central government. He cleverly induced some Türkmen leaders in Khurāsān to lend him their support. In addition declarations of loyalty to Prince 'Abbās arrived from other parts of the country. Since the shah had left the capital with the crown prince and his military retinue, Murshid Qulī Khān ventured to ride with 'Abbās and a small escort – not more than a few hundred horsemen – to Qazvīn in order to make his ward shah in place of his father.

When he ascended the throne in Qazvīn on 16 October 1587, 'Abbās became the fifth shah of the Safavid dynasty. Muḥammad Khudābanda did not challenge the usurper even after returning to the capital. He continued to live in Qazvīn for a time, but was then banished from court, a measure probably connected with an attempt to restore him to the throne. According to the accepted version of events, he was taken with Prince Abū Ṭālib to Alamūt, where his son Ṭahmāsp Mīrzā was already being held: it is said that all three were blinded. Since, however, Iskandar Munshī records that Navvāb-i Sikandar-sha'n, as Khudābanda was known posthumously, died at Qazvīn in the ninth

[1] Bellan, *Chah 'Abbas I*, p. 14.

year of 'Abbās's reign[1] (that is, between 21 July 1595 and 10 July 1596), his imprisonment, if there is any truth in the above story, cannot have lasted very long.

'ABBĀS I

Murshid Qulī Khān Ustājlū, whom Shah 'Abbās appointed his viceroy (*vakīl-i dīvān-i 'ālī*), may well have counted on the sixteen-year-old ruler now giving him a free hand. This hope was rapidly dispelled. Before long the measures taken by the new government bore the hallmark of the young monarch himself.

The most urgent problems confronting him were the same as those which had constantly recurred in previous years. In the first place there was the internal problem of the Türkmen tribalism which had been fostered by the protracted weakness of the central government. From the beginning of the reign of the Safavids, all-powerful tribal princes had filled the military offices at court, while others held sway with their clans in the provinces as feudal lords, either as governors or as the guardians of princes who had not yet attained the age of majority. In some provinces it appears that certain tribes regarded it as their prescriptive right to hold the governorship and other administrative offices – for instance, the Dulghadïr in Fārs and the Shāmlū in Kirmān. At about this time another problem arose with the renewed rise to power of certain previously subjugated local dynasties, mostly in the frontier regions of the empire. However, the external difficulties of the realm were almost more acute than the domestic situation. The enemies of the Safavids, especially the Ottomans in the west and the Uzbeks in the east, had overrun large areas, totalling well-nigh half the territory bequeathed by Shah Ṭahmāsp to his successors; and now they were making preparations for fresh attacks on Persia. Under such conditions trade and industry suffered and the living standards of the people were correspondingly wretched.

Through determined and consistently applied policies Shah 'Abbās I overcame the crisis in which the country had found itself at the beginning of his reign. It took him many years and he repeatedly suffered grave setbacks. Yet his eventual success, like his personality, left a deep

[1] Iskandar Munshī, trans. Savory, p. 692.

impression on his people. The memory of this particular shah survived in Iran for generations and even to this day it has not completely disappeared. What interests us, however, is the question of how he found for these problems the solutions which had eluded his predecessors for so long. The most urgent problem at the time of the shah's accession was the feuding of the Türkmen amīrs, which had grown to the proportions of a civil war. As will be recalled, their power rested ultimately on the services rendered by their forefathers as soldiers of the Ardabīl order at the time of the foundation and expansion of the Safavid empire. Of course, there could no longer be any question of the old relationship between the shah as grand master of the order and the Qizilbāsh as his disciples, nor is there any doubt that the theocratic ideas of Ismā'īl I had lost their validity for Shah 'Abbās. If, however, the strength of the former religious ties had declined, this is not to say that they had been completely forgotten or had dwindled into insignificance. The erosion of these old ties has been amply demonstrated by the above-mentioned activities of the amīrs. But their decay is also demonstrated by 'Abbās's readiness to cast aside the old customs of the order whenever it was in his interest to do so. On the other hand he willingly obeyed or enforced them if it suited him. Naturally the conflict with the Qizilbāsh was in the first instance a political problem, but an element of the original religious relationship remained.[1]

Apart from this religious aspect the history of the Safavid empire up to 'Abbās I is synonymous with the history of the rivalry between the two leading ethnic groups within the state, the Türkmen and the Iranian elements. One can also view it as a conflict between town and country, between nomads and settlers. There were plenty of attempts to achieve a solution. It is an open question whether we should lay greater emphasis on the endeavour to break the dominant power of the Türkmen amīrs or on the effort to unite and reconcile Persian and Turk such as was represented in the person of individual members of the Safavid dynasty. Whichever view we take, the failure is obvious:

[1] Its foundations had already been undermined at Chāldirān, as pointed out by Savory, "The Principal Offices ....during the reign of Ismā'īl I", p. 91. But this leaves open the question how far the Safavid monarchs were still seen as masters of the order or laid claim to that rôle. At any rate, as late as 'Abbās's death in 1038/1629 attempts were made to obtain the consent of all available members of the order regarding the succession, in the traditional manner: Braun, *Das Erbe Schah 'Abbās' I*, p. 104; and below, p. 279 . See also Savory, "The Office of Khalīfat al-khulafā".

nobody succeeding in working out a compromise between these opposing elements.

The new shah tackled the Türkmen amīrs from the outset in a relentless and uncompromising fashion. He began by executing a group of tribal amīrs whom he held responsible for the murder of his brother Ḥamza. He continued by crushing savagely a conspiracy of tribal leaders who were plotting to depose him, and then eliminated his erstwhile guardian Murshid Qulī Khān Ustājlū, who had boycotted an expedition to relieve the siege of Herat by the Uzbeks because of his long-standing dispute with the city governor, 'Alī Qulī Khān Shāmlū. There were several other examples over the years, but we need not go into detail at this point. The experiences of the shah's youth, such as the assassination of his mother and his brother Ḥamza, undoubtedly helped to inspire his life-long suspicion of the Qizilbāsh. So ineradicable was this suspicion that he even removed an outstanding general for the sole reason that he considered him to have acquired too much power. In the end Shah 'Abbās succeeded in breaking the stranglehold of the Türkmen amīrs and in suppressing the constant squabbles among the tribes.

Shah 'Abbās's reign saw the beginning of the end for the Türkmens, the decline of their military and political influence and the eclipse of their social status. The contempt and distrust with which they were regarded by the ruler resulted in their being squeezed out of the most important military commands. We witness in effect the disbanding of the praetorian guard into which the Qizilbāsh had developed after the accession of Shah Ṭahmāsp I. This is not to say that they disappeared from the scene altogether: there were still Qizilbāsh units in Persia during the reign of Shah 'Abbās and even down to the collapse of his dynasty in the 12th/18th century. But henceforth they were no longer the sole military caste.

After they had been neutralised the structure of the Safavid empire was fundamentally transformed. Shah 'Abbās could only achieve a lasting success by creating a counterbalance to the Qizilbāsh on the one hand and by compensating for the loss of military striking power on the other. He employed various means to this end. One was a procedure associated with the term *shāhīsavanī* which aimed at polarising feeling among the Qizilbāsh. It took the form of a summons to "those loyal to the king", the royalists. It seems that in this way reliable elements among the Qizilbāsh were identified and then probably reorganised into fresh military units. However, we have no detailed knowledge of this.[1]

We know a good deal more about the establishment of a new corps in the Safavid army, the cavalry formation of royal squires (*qullar* or *ghulāmān-i khāṣṣa-yi sharīfa*) whose commander bore the title of *qullar-āqāsī*. These royal squires, mostly Muslim converts descended from Christians of diverse races, had either come to Persia as children or had been born of Georgian, Circassian, Caucasian and Armenian parents, often prisoners of war, who had already settled in Persia. This corps, which was raised by 'Abbās shortly after his accession, proved so valuable that the Qizilbāsh formations were soon reduced to a half or even less of their original establishment. As their first commander, a Georgian convert to Islam by the name of Allāhvardī Khān, won great esteem and was honoured with the title of Sulṭān. Qullar who proved their worth could rise to high office: they were employed as governors – Allāhvardī Khān himself succeeded in becoming governor of Fārs – or were even appointed commanders of Türkmen troops when the latter failed to produce suitable candidates for vacant positions from among their own ranks. In time they came to occupy about a fifth of all the key positions in the administration.

Among the royal squires there was a secondary troop, the corps of musketeers (*tufangchiyān*) which had already existed in a more modest way under Shah Ṭahmāsp I. It was composed of the most diverse ethnic elements, among them representatives of the Persian peasantry, Arabs and also Türkmens. In addition there was an artillery corps (*tūpchiyān*), a military arm of which the Persians were not particularly enamoured. Although the Safavids exploited it readily enough in siege situations, they did not make much use of artillery in the field. Sir Robert Sherley, an English adventurer, is usually credited with the introduction of artillery into Persia. He arrived at the Persian court in 1598 with his brother Sir Anthony and a group of other Europeans. It is a fact that Shah 'Abbās sought this man's advice on the question of military reforms and Allāhvardī Khān adopted his suggestions for the reorganisation of the army. He also supervised the production of artillery pieces. But he had nothing to do with the introduction of artillery

[1] *Shāhīsavanī kardan* is commonly used in documents dating back to Khudābanda's reign. From the synonymous phrase *ṣalā-yi shāhīsavanī kardan* it is clear that the meaning is not "to make Shah's friends", as in Tapper, "Shahsevan", p. 65, but rather "to proclaim: Let him who loves the Shah present himself at such and such a place". Cf. further Minorsky, "La Perse au XVe siècle", p. 326.

into Persia, because the Persians had long since been familiar with it.[1] By the end of the 10th/16th century the number of troops at the shah's disposal – in addition to the Qizilbāsh – amounted to 37,000 men. This total comprised the corps of royal squires (10,000), a bodyguard again formed by squires (3,000), and the corps of musketeers and artillery (12,000 each). The artillery was equipped with 500 cannons.[2] The essential characteristic of these new formations was that they were not tied to any one tribal organisation and hence were not commanded by members of the Türkmen military aristocracy. Moreover they were paid directly out of the royal chest, not out of the military appropriations like the Qizilbāsh.

These military and administrative reforms took many years to complete and it was some time before they bore fruit. They were of no help in the military crises which confronted Shah ʿAbbās I at the beginning of his career. What was needed there above all was astute political decisions – in the first place peace with the Ottomans, which could not have been easy for the shah to accept. But since he had no hope of defeating them as long as several provinces were in revolt and the Uzbeks were occupying Khurāsān, this was the only means open to him of securing a free hand to deal with his other, even more pressing problems.

Ottoman troops who had already invaded large areas of Persia in the reign of Muḥammad Khudābanda – parts of Āzarbāījān along with Tabrīz, parts of Georgia and Qarābāgh, the city of Erivan, Shīrvān and Khūzistān – extended their conquest of Persian territory still further after the accession of the new shah. Baghdad was lost to them in 995/1587 and shortly afterwards they took Ganja. Negotiations with the Porte led to the Peace of Istanbul on 21 March 1590. This put an end to twelve years of hostilities between the Ottomans and the Safavids. The conditions imposed on the shah were unusually harsh. They included the loss of Āzarbāījān and Qarābāgh together with Ganja, of Shīrvān and Dāghistān, of the Safavid possessions in Georgia, of parts of Kurdistān and Luristān, of Baghdad and Mesopotamia. Although Ardabīl, the seat of the Safavid order, remained in Persian hands, the old capital of Tabrīz, where Shah Ismāʿīl I had founded

[1] Savory, "The Sherley Myth".
[2] Figures from Savory, "Safavid Persia", p. 418. See also Lockhart, "The Persian army".

his empire, had to be relinquished. A clause which decreed that the Persians should desist from anathematising the Orthodox Caliphs – a practice instigated by the founder of the empire – added a particularly humiliating note to the peace treaty, for it involved the original hallmark, as it were, of the Safavid state. The peace which was bought at such a price gave the shah a free hand to solve urgent internal problems and to confront his foreign enemies in the east. (We shall discuss these measures later.) Yet the fundamentally unacceptable terms militated against a final peace settlement, and relations with the Ottomans were to occupy ʿAbbās for the rest of his life.

To begin with, however, he turned his attention to the Uzbeks, who had been occupying Khurāsān for the past ten years. Disputes concerning the succession in Transoxiana favoured his undertaking, and in 1007/1598-9 he reconquered Herat and Mashhad, also extending his control to include Balkh, Marv and Astarābād. But when, two years later, Bāqī Muḥammad Khān, the new ruler of Transoxiana, re-occupied Balkh, the Safavid troops found they were no match for him and were finally not only forced to withdraw, but lost the greater part of their new artillery in the process (1011/1602–3). That, for the moment, was the end of the Safavid–Uzbek conflict. In spite of their eventual losses, the Persians had gained from it by the reconquest of western Khurāsān, the area lying to the north of it and bordering the Türkmen desert and including Marv and Nasā, and eastern Khurāsān, including Herat, Sabzavār and Farāh. Later – in 1031/1622 – they also won back Qandahār, which the Mughal emperor Akbar had wrested from the Safavids in 1003/1594, when ʿAbbās had been in no position to put up an effective defence.

With the successes in the east the danger of a war on two fronts was checked, so that even by 1012/1603–4 the shah was able to risk a confrontation with the Ottomans. He now reconquered Āzarbāījān, Nakhchivān and Erivan. The Turkish supreme commander Chighālezāde Pasha, preparing to strike back, suffered a crushing defeat at Tabrīz. Although a new peace agreement was drawn up in 1612 at Istanbul which re-established the old Turkish – Persian frontier, the sultan tried once again a few years later, albeit in vain, to recover control of the ceded Transcaucasian and Persian conquests by means of another military expedition. A Safavid campaign against Mesopotamia in 1033/1623–4 re-established Persian control over the Kurdish territories of Daqūq, Kirkūk and Shahrazūr, Karbalā and

Najaf, and in addition over Baghdad, though in this case only for fifteen years; a further result was the occupation of Diyārbakr.

These had been preceded by further extensions of territory: in 1010/1601–2 the island of Baḥrain had been annexed, and in 1016/1607–8 Shīrvān had been reconquered. A series of campaigns brought extensive areas of Georgia into Persian hands. However, 'Abbās was not able to subdue Kakhetia, and was in fact obliged to recognise the government of King Theimuraz I. In 1031/1622 he succeeded – though only with the help of the English – in driving the Portuguese out of Hurmuz.

The chaotic state of affairs at home at the beginning of the reign of 'Abbās seemed to herald the dissolution of the Safavid empire or, more correctly, the rump state that was left after the depredations of neighbouring powers. This, it seemed, was what was likely to happen, with the development of various opposing small states under Türkmen princes, roughly comparable to the petty princedoms (*uc beylikleri*) of Anatolia in the 8th/14th century. It is not inappropriate to describe the situation by saying that Shah 'Abbās had to reconquer his own land "from the Türkmens and other military leaders who had to all intents and purposes become autonomous".[1] By throwing in his newly constituted forces, and by dint of an adroit policy at home, he managed to master this Sisyphean task. His perspicacity is particularly evident from the fact that in spite of the tough, even brutal measures he took, he did not allow himself to be swept into a rigid consistency of action which might have called forth a solid front on the part of the mutually disaffected tribal chieftains. Thus he not only preserved the old lifeguards (qūrchīs) but, as we have seen, retained in addition to the new military formations contingents of the old Qizilbāsh amīrs; and he did not touch the possessions of the Türkmen lords provided they remained loyal. Indeed, new fiefs (*tiyūl*)[2] were granted, and not only to Türkmen army officers but also to the non-Türkmen commanders of the new corps. His appeal to the old discipline of the order (ṣūfīgarī), to which reference has been made above, and the loyalty due to the shah as grand master of the order (shāhīsavanī) may well have reflected similar considerations.

[1] N. Keddie, "Iran und Afghanistan", in *Fischer Weltgeschichte* xv: *Der Islam* II. ed. G.E. von Grunebaum (Frankfurt am Main, 1971), p. 167.
[2] Minorsky, "Tiyūl", *EI*[1]; *TMEN* II, 667f.; see also below, chapter 9.

Nevertheless, during his reign of over forty years, the shah adhered consistently to the principle of centralisation for his state. Evidence for this is to be found not only in the reorganisation of the armed forces, with the creation of a standing army, the quashing of particularist tendencies on the part of the Qizilbāsh amīrs and the abolition of practically independent tribal rulerships such as those just mentioned, the Dulghadïr in Fārs or those of the Afshār in Kirmān, but also the annexation of the former vassal states of Māzandarān (1005–6/1596–8), Gīlān (1000/1592 Lāhījān, 1003/1595 Rasht) and Lār (1010/1601–2) and the resubjection or firmer attachment of independent areas such as the Georgian regions of Kakhetia (1029–30/1620–1) and Meskhetia (1032–3/1623–4) and the province of Makrān (1017/1608–9). The idea of centralisation is particularly in evidence in the way in which crown lands (*khāṣṣa* or *khāliṣa*) were systematically increased. There had in fact been royal demesnes in the Safavid empire prior to this. But it was 'Abbās I who began the process of incorporating whole provinces, indeed major provinces, into the crown lands, a practice to which his successors adhered. The implications of this can be assessed if we remember that between 996/1588 and 1014/1606 the provinces of Qazvīn, Kāshān, Iṣfahān, Kirmān (in part), Yazd, Qum, Māzandarān, Gīlān, Āstārā and Gaskar were finally, or at any rate for some considerable period, converted into royal demesne lands, so that their total revenue was reserved for the use of the shah, i.e. could neither be paid into the state treasury nor used for purposes of enfeoffment.

At the end of the 10th/16th and the beginning of the 11th/17th century, Shah 'Abbās had mastered the crisis which had shaken his country at the time of his accession, in respect both of external enemies and of disruptive forces at home. Iran now enjoyed the greatest territorial extent it ever reached under the Safavids. After security had been restored in the country, 'Abbās turned his attention to establishing an effective administration. In the development of transport routes, which he pursued with energy, particularly noteworthy is the network of caravansarais he created, many of which are still preserved today, either completely or in remarkable remains,[1] and take their place among the characteristic monuments of Persia. These and other measures invigorated trade and industry, so that the broad masses of the population also found that their standard of living was at first

[1] Siroux, "Les caravanserais routiers Safavids".

improved and ultimately reached a level never known up to that time. Whereas in other parts of the Islamic world around this period economic setbacks occurred, due to the recessions in Mediterranean trade and the extension of Atlantic trade, Persia – at any rate in this period – seems to have been spared these changes and the consequences of the decline of the Central Asian caravan routes, from which it was in any case largely cut off by its Uzbek neighbours.

Iṣfahān, which took the place of Qazvīn as the new capital of the country in 1006/1598 – Qazvīn having in its half a century as the metropolis undergone no significant development as a city – now became, as it were, the symbol of resurgence. ʿAbbās called on the services of architects, artists and craftsmen to develop it. Though basing their approaches on an older tradition in architecture, town planning and decorative style, they developed the specifically Safavid style to a point of such rare maturity that it still has power to captivate the observer of today. Some of its most beautiful monuments are grouped around the Royal Square (Maidān-i Shāh), which – according to the testimony of European travellers of the time – were without parallel anywhere, especially the Masjid-i Shāh, the ʿĀlī Qāpū gatehouse and the Shaikh Luṭf-Allāh Mosque. With these, a new array of jewels was added to the rich treasury of brilliant architectural achievements left by the earlier dynasties in Persia, and such as represented a culmination of the aesthetic standards of a whole epoch. The artistic creativity of the Islamic world once more attained to a peak of achievement, represented in the popular punning phrase *Isfahān nisf-i jahān*: "Iṣfahān, half the world".

The motives that led Shah ʿAbbās to move his capital from Qazvīn to Iṣfahān are not as clearly discernible as those of his grandfather Ṭahmāsp fifty years earlier, when he chose Qazvīn in place of Tabrīz.[1] The decisive element at that time had been fear of the Ottomans and, connected with this, a certain tendency towards Iranicising the Safavid empire, together with a mistrust of the Türkmen tribes and their influence (which was particularly strong in Āzarbāījān and Tabrīz). But it is possible that now, in changed circumstances, it was especially his desire for a centrally situated position within the reconstituted Persian empire that determined ʿAbbās to make the change, and the

1 For the background to the various Safavid changes of capital, see Roemer, "Das frühsafawidische Isfahan".

opportunities of developing the city according to his own ideas. And of course we must not underplay his personal preference for Iṣfahān, to which sources refer. It seems highly likely that another factor was the climatic advantages of the area, its ample supply of water and the fertility of the developed land in the vicinity, even though the population had from time immemorial not enjoyed the best of reputations for their tendency – attested by Khunjī, himself a native of the city – to indulge in rumour-mongering and intrigues of every kind.[1]

The shah succeeded in creating a position of parity for his new capital among the famous Islamic metropolises. As a result not only of its development architecturally, but also by virtue of its vigorous economic, social and political life, Iṣfahān was preserved from the odium of provincialism that Qazvīn had never been able to shake off. With the international repute that 'Abbās won for himself, the diplomatic contacts linking him to the potentates of his time also intensified. These included, in addition to the contiguous powers such as the Great Mughals of India, the khan of the Crimean Tartars and the Tsar of Muscovy, as also many Western powers, and there are many contemporary descriptions of the magnificence attending the comings and goings of emissaries from other countries. An associated factor was the presence of Western merchants, artists and monks, who were free to move around at will in the country provided they did not engage in proselytising activities among the Muslims. We know of Carmelites, Augustinians and Capuchins who paid visits to Iṣfahān and other places in the land, and to some of these we owe highly informative accounts of the shah's court and of life in the country and among the people, and accounts of events they witnessed at first hand.[2]

This period of distinction for Iṣfahān must be attributed in part no doubt to the shah's population policy, a matter we have already touched on in connection with his reform of the armed forces. This fed in elements, not only to the troops, but to the population at large, whose energy and skills in various crafts and whose trading enterprise benefited the economic life of the capital. It was particularly evident in the transfer of three thousand Armenian families from the Āzarbāījānī city of Julfā to Iṣfahān, where they were settled beyond the Zāyanda-rūd in a new part of the city which was then given the same name as their old home town, a name it still preserves. Many Georgians, too,

[1] Minorsky, *Persia in A.D. 1478–1490*, p. 38.

[2] See below, chapter 7.

were brought into the country as prisoners of war and around the middle of the 11th/17th century numbered 20,000 souls in Iṣfahān alone. Unlike the Armenians and also, incidentally, the members of the old Jewish community,[1] both of which groups adhered doggedly to their separate linguistic and religious traditions, they were assimilated fairly easily into the indigenous population.

The Iran of the end of the 10th/16th and the first quarter of the 11th/17th century: the rebirth of the Safavid state out of chaos; the emergence of a state enjoying high regard abroad among the powers of the Near East which had already begun to expand into Persian territory; widespread revival of economic life; the development of an indigenous cultural style, accompanied by an admirable flowering of the arts – all this was the work of Shah ʿAbbās I. And though his historical significance has long been known there has as yet been no adequate appraisal in the West of ʿAbbās as a ruler – for he was *the* ruler without whom Persia's transition to the modern age cannot be understood – in spite of the wealth of material available. In what follows we will attempt to trace out at least the most important features of his personality.

Robert Sherley, who of course knew the shah personally, speaks of him in the following terms: "His person is such as well-understanding nature would fit for the end proposed for his being – excellently well-shaped, of most well-proportioned stature, strong and active; his colour, somewhat inclined to a man-like blackness, is also more black by sun-burning; the furniture of his mind infinitely royal, wise, valiant, liberal, temperate, merciful; and an exceeding lover of justice, embracing royally other virtues as far from pride and vanity as from all unprincely sins or acts."[2] Of these qualities, it is his liberality of outlook which is expecially striking in contrast with his bigoted father, Ṭahmāsp I, not to mention other oriental potentates of the day. It was clearly evident in his tolerance towards Jews and Christians, for instance, not only in his permitting them to exercise their religion and to build churches, but in the fact that he himself even had a church built for the Armenians brought to New Julfā.

1 W. Fischel, "Isfahān – the Story of a Jewish Community in Persia", *Joshua Starr Memorial Volume* (New York, 1953), pp. 111–28.

2 Quoted in Welch, *Shah ʿAbbās and the Arts*, p. 17; for pictures of the shah, see, e.g., *ibid.*, p. 123; Browne, *LHP* IV, frontispiece.

There was no question of his indulging in libertarian attitudes in questions of religion. He is, rather, described as a good Muslim, and in this connection there is a reference to a pilgrimage to Mashhad which he made on foot;[1] we hear, too, of the repair work he had carried out to the mausoleum of the Eighth Imām, damaged by the Uzbeks, and his fondness for visiting the famous Shī'ī places of pilgrimage at Ardabīl, Mashhad, Karbalā and Najaf. It is significant that he insisted on keeping his rôle as master of the order of the Ṣafaviyya among the population, as can be seen on the occasion of his visits to Ardabīl. This is consistent with his having regarded himself as a sayyid, that is to say, his claiming descent from 'Alī, whose memory he held in honour along with that of the Twelve Imāms. In his personal life he kept in a high degree to the religious commandments except where he allowed himself to be driven into breaches of it by his fundamentally sensuous approach to life. Numerous pious foundations (*auqāf*) were the work of Shah 'Abbās, such as grants of land from his demesnes in Āzarbāījān, Qazvīn, Kāshān and Iṣfahān; and he maintained close relations with many religious scholars (*'ulamā*), especially those who eschewed worldly ambition.

In spite of his great tolerance towards non-Islamic confessions, there was a limit to his indulgence regarding the Sunnīs among his own subjects. Though he would go no further than to make unmistakeable allusions to his own Shī'ī faith in his dealings with the ambassadors of neighbouring Sunnī countries, his Sunnī subjects or Sunnī prisoners of war, especially theologians amongst them, could count on no consideration and clemency from him; far less the adherents of heretical movements, of which there were many at the time, e.g. the *ahl-i nuqṭa*, also known as the *Nuqṭaviyān*, followers of Maḥmūd Pāsīkhānī Gīlānī, who had proclaimed a doctrine with metempsychotic characteristics around the year 1400.[2] Enthusiasts for these and similar views, who were to be found in various Persian cities and in various social classes up to the highest strata of society, were persecuted on the orders of the shah, and where it was possible to arrest them or to trace them in his entourage, they were sentenced to death. Such movements were in fact not without a dangerous aspect, since they generally entailed political aims, as for instance in the case of Mullā Qāsim, a Nuqṭavī who challenged the

[1] Cf. also later authors such as Riżā Qulī Khān Hidāyat, *Rauẓat al-ṣafā* VIII (Tehran, 1339), 467.
[2] Kiyā, "Nuqṭaviyān".

shah's right to the throne. This being so, the shah's reaction was no different from those of his Sunnī opponents to the west and east of his empire in their attitude towards Shī'ī tendencies.

Though the shah was in advance of his time in many ways, he remained a child of his age in other respects, especially in the superstitious notions he entertained. It is possible to find a religious explanation for his putting on a shirt embroidered with verses from the Qur'ān when marching into battle, but not for the respect he showed to astrological predictions and the dreams he had, and to which he paid heed in reaching decisions. Such facets of his character are of course of no consequence in estimating his personality.

Of more interest is his relationship to art, especially representational art of various kinds; and this, of course, touches on religious issues in a number of respects. We are referring not to sacred architecture or its décor, mentioned above, but particularly to painting, which clearly implies some attitude to the Islamic prohibition of visual representation. Reference has been made to Ṭahmāsp's service to book miniatures: we should add that as he grew old, and under the influence of increasing bigotry, he turned more and more away from this interest. The case was quite different with Shah 'Abbās. He seems to have shared neither the personal engagement of his grandfather nor his religious scruples. It is natural that a man who had spent the greater part of his youth among the productions and abiding stimuli of Timurid art in Herat and Mashhad was not without sensitivity to the artistic expressions of his time. Indeed we can still see in the Shaikh Luṭf-Allāh mosque, with its textual scrolls and lacy roof ornamentation, a personal involvement of the shah in architecture and its development similar to that of his grandfather in the sphere of art; and with the transfer of the capital from Qazvīn to Iṣfahān the workshops attached to the royal court also had to move, and the artists employed there along with them. Thus it came about that the great painter Riżā-yi 'Abbāsī was able in Iṣfahān to develop an entirely new style, differing from that of Qazvīn, in whose traditions he had grown up and worked hitherto. It is plain that this sort of thing did not take place without the active interest and encouragement of the ruler. The latter's influence, however, hitherto a decisive factor in artistic developments, begins – precisely under Shah 'Abbās I – to decline, and to decline in favour of commercial influences. This is most evident in the sphere of ceramics, textiles, and carpet designing, all of them up to this time areas of largely individual creativity. With the introduction of workshops for export production – a departure for which the shah was responsible – their products lost their value as individual artistic achievements and sank to the level of industrial products. This change was also felt in book illustration. What was now produced in this sphere was no longer made for the ruler alone, or at any rate for governors of princely rank in the provincial capitals, but also for other customers, who included parties with a commercial interest.

Recent attempts to rescue the Safavids from the odium of indifference to creative writing,[1] if not indeed of its neglect or suppression, show that Shah 'Abbās took a positive attitude at all events to individual poets, for example to Sharaf al-Dīn Ḥasan Shifā'ī (d. 1037/1628), whom he appointed poet laureate, or to Shāmī, whom he had weighed in gold as a sign of his recognition, and to Kamālī Sabzavārī (d. 1020/1611–12), who celebrated his exploits in a verse epic entitled *Shāh-nāma* or *'Abbās-nāma*.[2] However, since relationships of this kind form the exception rather than the rule, they signify little. The criticism of Safavid poetry, whether justified or not, as lacking in originality, full of banalities and "endless verbal niceties" is not shaken by such evidence. Emigration of Persian poets, particularly to India, which had been going on at least since the time of Shah Ṭahmāsp, did not cease under 'Abbās. Indian courts, at which the old interest in courtly poetry continued, offered at any rate better opportunities than Iṣfahān with its Safavid traditions, and not only for poets but for other artists such as calligraphers and miniature painters, whose success was largely dependent on the ruler's attitudes to aesthetic matters.

The shah's interest in the intellectual and artistic culture of his time is unmistakeably evident, sometimes in the form of unique works of art, and certainly also in the large number of artistic achievements that appeared. But it is also unmistakeably the case that this influence was exercised, if not exclusively, at any rate largely, to resuscitate an older heritage, that of the Timurids; in other words, it was not always based on original conceptions. And in addition, these reversions to the past, however impressive they may be when seen from a distance or at a casual glance, reveal on closer inspection a more or less hasty manner

[1] E. Yar-Shater, "Safawid literature". Falsafī, *Zindagānī* II, 28ff. Cf. W. Heinz, *Der indische Stil in der persischen Literatur* (Wiesbaden, 1973).

[2] Mentioned by H. Ethé, "Neupersische Literatur", in *Grundriss der iranischen Philologie*, ed. W. Geiger and E. Kuhn (Strassburg, 1895–1904), II, 237.

of execution, a lesser degree of thoroughness than the originals, and the use of less costly materials.

Nevertheless, alongside the successes of the statesman, the general, and the far-sighted politician must be reckoned also the achievements of the builder of cities, the architect and the patron of the arts. Enterprise, energy, shrewdness and a degree of tolerance remarkable for his time went together in 'Abbās with intellectual curiosity, as is clear from his taste for conversations with Islamic and Christian theologians and with western diplomats and merchants, his aesthetic sensitivity and, albeit with certain limitations, his knowledgeability in artistic matters.

In spite of his many talents, the shah was unable to muster either the statesmanship or the personal qualities to contend with one momentous problem relating both to the political situation and to the personal sphere. This was the question of arranging the succession and the treatment of his sons; and here he may have been influenced by residual elements of the Turkish notion that authority did not reside exclusively in the reigning prince but was the property of the ruling family as a whole.[1] Among the eleven children of the shah known to us, five were sons: (1) Muḥammad Bāqir Mīrzā, usually called Ṣafī Mīrzā, (2) Ḥasan Mīrzā, (3) Sulṭān Muḥammad Mīrzā, also referred to as Rūzak Mīrzā or Muḥammad Khudābanda Mīrzā, after his grandfather, who died in the year of his birth (1006/1597–8), (4) Ismā'īl Mīrzā, and (5) Imām Qulī Mīrzā.[2] Of these princes, Ḥasan Mīrzā and Ismā'īl Mīrzā died while still in childhood.

'Abbās was not only conscious of problems with princes that had come the way of his immediate predecessors – some during his own lifetime - and, before that, of most of his forebears who had occupied the throne; he had himself come to the throne as the result of a *coup d'état*, had deposed his own father and banished him from the capital together with his two surviving brothers, whom he had caused to be blinded. To these memories was added the fear of possible acts of vengeance on the part of malcontents among the aristocracy of the empire, especially the relatives of tribal chieftains he had eliminated or

[1] See above, p. 99.

[2] The most reliable details are given in Falsafī, *Zindagānī* II, 170–207. In the genealogy provided by Röhrborn, *Provinzen und Zentralgewalt*, p. 158, "Sulṭān Ḥusain Mīrzā" should be deleted and Ismā'īl Mīrzā included in the penultimate position. A further son, Ṭahmāsp Mīrzā, mentioned in some of the sources, is apparently identical with Ḥasan Mīrzā.

stripped of power among the generals of the Qizilbāsh. With these things in the background, he developed attitudes of suspicion and mistrust that stayed with him all his life. In his efforts to rule out conspiracies and *coups d'état*, he kept his courtiers, especially the military men, away from his sons as far as it lay in his power to do so, and expressly forbade them to have dealings with his offspring, in several instances punishing infringements of his orders with cruel penalties. The princes were largely banished to the harem, where their social relationships were restricted to the princesses, the ladies of the harem, and the eunuchs. They received no training in either statecraft or soldiering and were likewise excluded from participating in their father's campaigns.

As a result of the sanguinary means by which the shah had seized and secured power, and of his rigid conduct of state affairs, he had indeed made many enemies. A number of these entertained sympathies for his eldest son, the crown prince Ṣafī Mīrzā, and would have liked to see him ruling in his father's place, particularly as he had the reputation of good character and warm personal qualities. The very fact of the increasing popularity of the prince was a thorn in the flesh to the shah. When, in addition, he encountered plans to depose him in Ṣafī Mīrzā's favour, he resolved to remove him from the scene. Upon warnings given by one of the court astrologers and the advice of his closest counsellors, he was persuaded to do away with the prince. He met his end at the age of twenty-seven while on a visit to Rasht, where, in 1024/1615, he was stabbed to death on his father's orders while returning from his bath. All the evidence suggests that the prince was innocent, as 'Abbās seems to have realised afterwards. At all events, he never recovered, to his dying day, from the horrific memory of his evil decision. Nevertheless, his concern for the security of the throne and his own life had such a grip on him that some time later he had the eyes put out of Prince Sulṭān Muḥammad Mīrzā, his grandson Sulaimān Mīrzā, the eldest son of Ṣafī Mīrzā, and even – at the very end of his life – the crown prince Imām Qulī Mīrzā, thus eliminating them from the succession, which in accordance with Islamic ideas is barred to pretenders who are blind.

The murder of Ṣafī Mīrzā aroused an enormous sensation of disquiet and horror not only in the shah's entourage but also among the people. In Rasht even riots ensued. But since the circle of those who knew the true facts was a small one, such expressions of anger or protest led to no further consequences. Persian historians, from whom the truth of these events was not hidden, have named Shah ʿAbbās "the Great", and so he is known in Iran to this day. In view of his splendid achievements and the services he rendered his country it is a title which can hardly be challenged. Possibly his actions can be judged in a somewhat more lenient light in view of the circumstances of the time in which he lived.

It is too easy for the observer of history, impressed by the record of Shah ʿAbbās's great achievements for his country, not only to be tempted to feel that the less spectacular ages which followed his reign were a period of decline, but to see his death as the beginning of the end of Safavid rule. This view is emphatically not justified. Apart from the outward and visible magnificence which continued under the later Safavids, there were in the remaining century of their rule in Iran still decades in which the empire maintained an impressive level of achievement and when large sections of the population were able to enjoy wealth or at least reasonable prosperity, even though the period of territorial expansion was over once and for all.

One fateful cause of the later decline of his dynasty and its power was indeed the work of Shah ʿAbbās himself, namely his neglect of the succession. The elimination of royal princes, whether by blinding them or immuring them in the harem, their exclusion from the affairs of state and from contact with the leading aristocracy of the empire and the generals, all the abuses of the princes' education, which were nothing new but which became the normal practice with ʿAbbās at the court of Iṣfahān, effectively put a stop to the training of competent successors, that is to say, efficient princes prepared to meet the demands of ruling as kings. The result was that from then on the princes who came to the throne had from their earliest youth been ruined by living in the women's quarters, by indulgence shown towards them by all around, by courtiers, eunuchs and concubines, and were not only quite useless in the performance of their duties but often totally uninterested.

ṢAFĪ I

When Shah ʿAbbās died at his summer palace at Ashraf in Māzandarān on 24 Jumādā I 1038/19 January 1629 none of his brothers and none of his sons was available to take on the succession. Those who were still alive had been blinded and were thus unsuitable to rule. He had appointed his grandson Sām Mīrzā, a son of the murdered Ṣafī Mīrzā as his successor, although in a not entirely unambiguous fashion. The decision to have the prince come to Ashraf to prepare him to take over the throne came too late, and the negotiations about what was to happen after his death, which the shah conducted with various leading figures from his deathbed, achieved no results. As it proved impossible to keep the shah's death a secret, and as the alternative possibility of unforeseeable developments such as the enthronement of another prince, local risings, or intervention by neighbouring powers, could not be ruled out, the leading figures in the empire who were present in Ashraf, especially the Grand Vizier (*vazīr-i aʿẓam*) Khalīfa Sulṭān and the commander of the guards (*qūrchī-bāshī*) ʿĪsā Khān, made every effort to arrange for the succession of Sām Mīrzā at the earliest possible moment. A document to this effect which was sent to Iṣfahān had the desired effect. Promptly on 28 January 1629, three weeks before the court entourage returned, he mounted the throne in accordance with the wishes of his grandfather, adopting the royal title Shah Ṣafī (I).

Reports on this change of rulers expressly stress the part played by members of the Safavid order and the fact that the observances of the order were fulfilled.[1] According to these reports, the leading aristocrats of the empire had assured themselves of the agreement of this group at the Ashraf meeting, and in Iṣfahān the rules of the ṣūfīs were observed at the enthronement. It may be legitimate to see in this regard a connection with the attitude of the dead shah, who repeatedly had attached the greatest importance to his position as pīr and murshid, i.e. master of the order and its spiritual leader. On the other hand, it is of some interest to note (especially in view of the observances of the order we have referred to, but of which we obtain no very precise details in the source materials), that Mīr Dāmād, equally famous as a philosopher and representative of "orthodox" Shīʿī theology, took part in the solemn ceremonies at Iṣfahān.

The details we have about the character of the new ruler, who began his reign at the age of eighteen, seem at first sight to be contradictory. On the one hand he is praised for his lavish generosity, and on the other he is reproached with unbounded cruelty. Foreign observers

[1] Iskandar Munshī, quoted in Braun, *Das Erbe Schah ʿAbbās' I*, pp. 104, 106.

who had personal contacts with him praise his charm and his uncomplicated character, which they contrast with the inscrutable and incalculable attitudes of his grandfather. Which of these estimates is correct? Was Shah Ṣafī a warm and generous ruler or a bloody despot? It is certainly the case that, for instance, at his enthronement he distributed lavish presents. But when we learn that so enormous a sum as 500,000 tūmāns was spent for this purpose, and Imām Qulī Khān, the grand beg of Fārs, was remitted a whole year's instalment (60,000 tūmāns) of the dues he owed, it is more appropriate to speak of wild extravagance than of generosity.

It can also not be denied that in the early years of his reign almost all the royal princes, including the sons of his predecessor's daughters and even the princes who in any case had been blinded, were systematically murdered and that, in addition, a large number of leading figures in the empire and servants of the court were done to death, for example – in 1630 – the commander-in-chief of the armed forces (*sipāhsālār-i kull-i sipāh*) Zainal Khān Shāmlū, in 1632 the generals of the guards (qūrchī-bāshī) 'Īsā Khān and Chirāgh Khān Zāhidī, in 1634 the Grand Vizier (vazīr-i a'ẓam) Mīrzā Ṭālib Urdūbādī and the lord marshal (*ishīk-āqāsī-bāshī*) Ughurlū Khān Shāmlū. These are merely a few names, quoted as examples which may stand for many more besides. Even if one is disposed, in view of the circumstances of this period, to see the liquidation of royal rivals as an understandable protective measure and even to attribute the execution of undesirable dignitaries in the state and army to the exigencies of *raison d'état*; indeed, if one assumes it to have been probable that the shah was heavily influenced by individuals in his immediate entourage, it is still not possible to acquit Ṣafī of the charge of exceptional cruelty.[1]

The study of the actions and attitudes of the new shah reveals no sign of a more human dimension to his personality which would explain the positive comments of European observers; rather, it is the features of a moody despot that stand out, one who kept those around him in a state of fear and trembling by assassination and arbitrary death sentences. Moreover, the degree of interest he evinced for the business of state was only peripheral in character, if not non-existent, and it seems likely that he took not the slightest part in the intellectual and cultural life of his people; for in spite of a number of efforts to begin, he had not even

[1] On Ṣafī's cruelty, see Falsafī, "Dasthā-yi khūn-ālūd", *Chand maqāla*, pp. 211–22.

managed to attain a reasonable standard in reading and writing. If we add to this the fact that he indulged with increasing frequency a taste for wine and that it had been prescribed, we are told, to counteract certain effects of opium, to which he had apparently become addicted at quite an early age, we are left with a somewhat grim picture of the ruler and the thirteen years he occupied the throne before death from excessive drinking carried him off.

Although he received instruction from several experienced leading figures of the empire in affairs of state, starting shortly after he ascended the throne, little appears to have been achieved through these efforts to influence the shah to take more than the slightest interest – a reaction which is clearly the result of his upbringing in the harem. The decisions that had to be taken therefore became the responsibility of other important personages, however much they may have contrived to suggest to their master that they emanated from him. With a simple-minded, uncomplicated personality, as his is described, this can hardly have been a very difficult matter, for he was quite incapable of keeping himself immune from the intrigues and insinuations of his courtiers. This was especially serious when such machinations were aimed at competent and unexceptionable people, whose fate was then almost invariably sealed.

If we enquire who were the real rulers in the state, we find that in the early years of the new reign four outstanding personalities emerge: the lord marshal (ishīk-āqāsī-bāshī) Ughurlū Khān Shāmlū; a Georgian named Rustam Beg, formerly imperial provost (*dīvān-begī*), and later in addition general commanding the musketeers (*tufangchī-āqāsī*) and commander-in-chief of the armed forces (sipāhsālār-i kull-i sipāh); Chirāgh Khān Zāhidī, who at first had no special office and later was appointed general of the guards (qūrchī-bāshī); and lastly another Georgian named Rustam Khān, who was town governor (*dārūgha*) of Iṣfahān and general of the royal squires (qullar-āqāsī) and had originally been known as Khusrau Mīrzā and also as Khusrau Khān. We may also assume that various ladies of the harem, for example the queen mother and, at least for a time, Zainab Begum, one of ʿAbbās I's daughters, exercised some influence. We have already come across the names of two of the people mentioned above, Ughurlū Khān Shāmlū and Chirāgh Khān Zāhidī, in connection with the victims of Shah Ṣafī's tyrannical rule. In 1630 Rustam Beg Dīvān-begī became grand beg (*beglerbegī*) of Āzarbāījān and his namesake

Rustam Khān moved from Kartlia to Tiflis to become governor (*vālī*).

Mention should be made at this point of the elimination of the most powerful and wealthy man in Iran after the ruler, and his sons. This was Imām Qulī Khān, the recipient of such munificence on the occasion of Ṣafī's accession. He was not only grand beg of Fārs and Kūhgīlūya, but also governor of Lār, Hurmuz (Jarūn), the Baḥrain islands, Gulpāīgān and Tūysirkān. In these offices he had followed in the footsteps of his father, Allāhvardī Khān, who had risen to high office under Shah ʿAbbās I. Shah ʿAbbās had even honoured him, a practice not unknown among the Safavids, by giving him one of his own wives in marriage. On the rather threadbare charge of conspiracy with insubordinate dignitaries in north-west Persia and Georgia, he and nearly all his numerous sons were put to death in 1632. The simultaneous conversion of the province of Fārs into crown lands was entirely in line with the policy of centralisation that Shah ʿAbbās had pursued on a grand scale by strengthening the shah's position as the central authority at the expense of the provinces controlled by state governors.

Ultimately, the dominant influence at the court of Iṣfahān came to be that of the Grand Vizier (*vazīr-i aʿzam-i dīvān-i aʿlā*) Mīrzā Muḥammad Taqī, usually known as Mīrza Taqī or Ṣārū Taqī ("Taqī of the fair hair"). Appointed in 1634, he had had a successful career in administration, where he had distinguished himself through services in the sphere of construction, including road building projects undertaken for ʿAbbās I in Māzandarān and the rebuilding of the sanctuary of Najaf on the orders of Ṣafī I, and through his activity as vizier of Māzandarān and of the whole of Gīlān after the rising stirred up there by Gharīb Shāh.[1] Ṣārū Taqī, who held office as grand vizier until the death of Ṣafī and for as long as three years afterwards, was not only an experienced specialist in administration but also a person of integrity, incorruptible and not at all intent on personal financial advantage. He so won the support and goodwill of the shah that he was able to get his way with all the authorities, in earlier years even including the military aristocracy. Efficient administrative measures, especially in finance, enabled him to raise revenues to a level never before known in Iran. He did indeed make use of a secret information service to this end, the

[1] Braun, *Das Erbe Schah ʿAbbās' I*, pp. 16f. Petrushevsky, "Narodnoe vosstanie".

activities of which, while it may have increased his popularity in some quarters, had quite the reverse effect elsewhere. In the course of time, moreover, he became so hardened and implacable, and so given to autocratic behaviour and contempt for others, that he not only played into the hands of his opponents but sometimes even offended against the interests of the state. Thus in 1638 his misplaced reluctance to compromise gave the impetus to the loss of Qandahār, when he insisted on withdrawing certain privileges in the payment of annual contributions to the Grand Dīvān from the local governor, 'Alī Mardān Khān, which had been granted by his predecessors. Instead of obeying the summons to appear at court, the governor proceeded to place himself and his province under the jurisdiction of the Mughal emperor Shāh Jahān.

This brings us to the question of Iran's foreign relations under Ṣafī I. Even under normal circumstances a change of ruler in the Safavid empire always touched off increased interest and, all too easily, covetous aspirations among neighbouring powers. Since Shah Ṣafī revealed himself only too soon as a weak, insecure and impressionable character, his neighbours lost no time in making appropriate moves. In the reign of Shah Ṣafī hostilities started up on the frontiers with the Ottoman empire, in Georgia, with the Uzbeks and with India, and these resulted in territorial losses or at all events in the necessity for counter-measures. The fact that Iran escaped fairly lightly is hardly attributable to its ruler, but was due rather to other circumstances.

The first disorders that occurred after the death of Shah 'Abbās were incursions on the part of Bedouin Arabs of the Banū Lām tribe into the area around Baghdad. These, however, had no significant effect upon the destinies of Iran; and even various conflicts among the Musha'sha' in the area of Ḥavīza (Ḥuvaiza), a tribe subject to the shah, which broke out after the murder of the governor of Shīrāz, Imām Qulī Khān, had no particularly momentous consequences. This was because 'Alī Pasha, the independent Turkish governor of Baṣra, who might have caused difficulties, was shrewd enough to avoid any involvement in these disputes.

Grave news, however, was arriving in Iṣfahān from the west, where under the young Sultan Murād IV (1032–49/1623–40) an enterprising and ruthless grand vizier had come to power in the person of Khüsrev Pasha. The object of his planning was clearly to exploit the easement achieved as a result of the renewal of the Peace of Szöny recently negotiated between the Porte and the Emperor Ferdinand II by mounting a blow against Persia. At the news of his approach in the summer of 1038–9/1629, the Persians did not find themselves unprepared. Zainal Khān Begdelī Shāmlū, the newly appointed commander-in-chief, moved at the head of the Persian forces to Hamadān, where the shah was also encamped with his court. Khüsrev Pasha, who had temporarily given up his original objective, Baghdad, and had advanced in the direction of Hamadān, scored a victory on 4 May 1630 at Māhīdasht. Though Hamadān then fell into his hands, he resisted the temptation to press on further into the interior of Persia and turned his attention to his real objective, Mesopotamia and Baghdad. As the Baghdad contingent under Ṣafī Qulī Khān held out against the Ottoman assault following heavy artillery bombardment, Khüsrev Pasha regarded the venture as a failure, and withdrew. It seems likely that his decision was prompted in part by the thought of the approaching winter – the attack took place between 8 and 12 November 1630 – and no doubt by the associated thought of how vulnerable his lines of communication to the rear would be, having regard to their length and particular geographical location. It proved not too difficult for the Persians to clear out the garrisons left behind by the Ottomans in the central part of the Euphrates region, and to bring to heel the Kurds, who had largely sided with the enemy. Although it at first looked as if peace could be brought about between the Ottomans and the Safavids, these hopes were destined to be dashed because the new Turkish Grand Vizier, Tabanyasï Meḥmed Pasha, observing the murder of the Persian princes and the Georgian resistance to the shah,[1] did not regard Persia as a dangerous enemy and had no interest in concluding a peace. Hence the next four years saw no end to frontier skirmishes in which the initiative and the outcome alternated from one side to the other constantly.

The Ottoman conquest of the fortress of Erivan in 1045/1635, at which the Sultan Murād IV was present in person, was a more serious matter. So was the subsequent advance on Tabrīz, which was plundered and laid in ruins, but not occupied. Shah Ṣafī himself took part in the Persian counter-offensive in the following spring, which ended

[1] See below, pp. 285–6.

with the reconquest of Erivan. Overtures of peace made by the Persians immediately afterwards were once more unavailing.

The reason for the Supreme Porte's reluctance to make peace was no doubt that Istanbul had not given up the idea of reconquering Baghdad. In fact, in 1048/1638 the sultan again undertook a campaign into Mesopotamia, by means of which he achieved the desired result, for Baghdad fell into his hands in mid-Sha'bān/the closing days of December without the Persians making any attempt to relieve their garrison in the city. From then until the First World War the city remained an Ottoman possession.

In spite of the atrocities that followed the conquest, the Persians entered into peace negotiations with the Ottomans. These resulted, on 14 Muḥarram 1049/17 May 1639 in the peace treaty of Ẕuhāb, as a consequence of which a settlement of frontiers was agreed that survived beyond the end of the Safavid empire and – apart from the northern sector, where a new situation was created by the advance of the Tsarist empire in the 12th/18th century – endured up to the present time. For Persia, it meant not only the loss of Baghdad, but also the final abandonment of the whole of Mesopotamia. Both parties abided by the terms of the treaty, and after this no more wars were fought between the Safavids and the Ottomans.

Nor were there any serious consequences from conflicts in the Transcaucasian petty states, especially the Georgian kingdoms and principalities, where Safavid and Ottoman interests overlapped. It will be remembered that Shah 'Abbās I had not only undertaken campaigns of conquest into Georgia, but had transplanted very large numbers of Georgians to Persia, where many of them, in connection with the reorganisation of the army, were taken into the Iranian forces and not infrequently rose to the higher and even to the highest military and governmental positions. Stubbornly though the Georgians clung to their own national ways in their homeland, even under Muslim rule, to their language, and to their Christian faith especially, in Persia they were quickly assimilated and, alongside Iranians and Turks, formed the third ethnic element of modern Persian society. In this they contrasted markedly with their Armenian neighbours, whose treatment under Persian tutelage was entirely comparable.

Shah Ṣafī's relations with Georgia have already been touched on in the context of the transfer of the governor of Iṣfahān, Rustam Khān. He held to the Islamic faith and had made his entire career in Persia up to this point; but in 1634 he succeeded in defeating Theimuraz and seizing power in Tiflis in the name of the shah. His success determined the lords of Imeretia, Mingrelia and Guria, who strictly owed allegiance to the Ottoman state and its ruler, to declare their willingness to accept the shah's authority. Even Theimuraz, who at first disappeared from the scene, but later managed to oust the Safavid governor of Kakhetia, finally placed himself under the Iṣfahān government, which confirmed his rule over Kakhetia – clearly in order thus to create a rival to Rustam and prevent his gaining excessive power. Conflicts between the two viceroys, Rustam and Theimuraz, were not slow to develop, but did not assume very serious proportions. Thus Rustam Khān, who remained in office until his death in 1658, was able to give his country a long period of peace and reconstruction, of which it was sorely in need after the serious devastations and losses of population resulting from the campaigns of Shah 'Abbās I. The exportation of Georgians to Persia, especially boys and girls, continued throughout the 11th/17th century, but it was no longer in the form of official, obligatory requisitions or forced deportations, as had formerly been the case, but was arranged by agents, who tackled the problem by means of bribes, persuasion, and cunning.[1]

There was more serious unrest on Iran's north-east frontier. A reconciliation was effected with the neighbouring Türkmens after they had invaded from Khīva (Khwārazm), when its Yadgarid ruler Isfandiyār Khān (1032–52/1623–42) apologised for the attack and in 1039/1630 handed over to the shah his brother Abu'l-Ghāzī, on whose shoulders he put the blame. Abu'l-Ghāzī, later Isfandiyār's successor and a celebrated historian, spent the next ten years at the shah's court. In contrast, the Uzbeks of Transoxiana, now under the rule of the Janid dynasty, kept the Persians fully occupied. The most important figures here were Imām Qulī Khān, the prince of Bukhārā (1020–51/1611–41), and his brother Nadr Muḥammad Khān, who was initially his governor in Balkh and was appointed by him as his successor in 1051/1641 when he himself had gone blind. Imām Qulī Khān set off on a pilgrimage to Mecca and only just managed to escape into Persian territory from pursuers sent after him on the orders of his brother, who at the last moment had resolved to prevent his leaving. He was received

[1] P. Oberling, "Georgians and Circassians in Iran", *Studia Caucasica* 1 (The Hague, 1963), 127–43.

there by the shah with the highest honours due to an eminent guest, and finally died in Arabian territory. Strangely enough, Nadr Muḥammad Khān in turn at a later date (1056/1646) had to seek refuge in Persia, and he too was received with great ceremony. Nevertheless, it would be quite wrong, on the evidence of the reception accorded by Safavid rulers to Uzbek princes in difficulties, to conclude that good neighbourly relations existed between the two powers. The opposite was, in fact, the case. As they had from the very beginning of Safavid rule, Uzbek incursions and plundering raids into Persia continued unabated during the 11th/17th century, and in the reign of Shah Ṣafī they reached a climax, with no fewer than eleven Uzbek campaigns against Persia. Even though most of these were no more than forays, we find that such large forces were involved – numbers amounting to 20,000 or 30,000 Uzbek warriors are mentioned – that the possibility that the Uzbeks intended a conquest of Khurāsān cannot simply be dismissed. Nevertheless, no significant results in this direction were achieved.

The tense relations between Shah Ṣafī and the Indian Mughals led, among other reasons, in 1636 to the severance of a strange Indo-Persian connection. ʿAbd-Allāh Quṭb Shāh, the lord of the principality of Golkonda in the Deccan (1020–1083/1626–72), and the descendant of a Shīʿī Qarā Quyūnlū refugee,[1] had attached himself for religious reasons to Shah ʿAbbās I and thereafter had caused the name of the Persian shah to be incorporated in the official prayers (khuṭba) and adopted on the coinage. He now abandoned his association with Persia and placed himself under the Great Mughal Shāh Jahān after the latter's victory over his neighbour to the west, the prince of Bījāpūr.

When Shah Ṣafī died unexpectedly on 12 Ṣafar 1052/12 May 1642[2] at the early age of thirty-one, he left behind him a country whose territory was quite considerably smaller than it had been at his succession, but which still embraced all the heartlands of Persia. From the point of view of the Iranicisation of the Safavid empire, the loss of the Mesopotamian territories – and these were by far the most extensive – was in any case of no very great importance. More significant was the fact that at the time of his death the country was not threatened by any serious external dangers, and especially that it was no longer at risk

[1] Minorsky. "The Qara-qoyunlu and the Quṭbshāhs", *BSOAS* XVII (1955), 55–73.

[2] Braun, *Das Erbe Schah ʿAbbās' I*, p. 117, says he died at Iṣfahān; Luft, *Iran unter Schah ʿAbbās II*, p. 207, n. 192, at Kāshān, though the date he supplies is in error.

from the Ottoman empire. This fairly positive state of affairs, however, could hardly be credited to Shah Ṣafī, but rather to various dignitaries in his empire distinguished by special competence, particularly the Grand Vizier Ṣārū Taqī. In Ṣafī's character we see clearly manifested some of the weak points in the structure of the Safavid empire which were to play a fateful rôle in its decline and final demise. These were especially the lack of preparation of the crown prince for the position of ruler and the unlimited power of a despotic monarch totally orientated on himself, and – since the time of Shah 'Abbās I – further strengthened by the exclusion of the Qizilbāsh amīrs and the increasing centralisation of the state. A figure possessing the personal qualities of a Shah 'Abbās could exploit such a position of omnipotence to the best advantage of Iran and its people. A man as weak as Ṣafī in mind and character – a man who was also physically weak – was not equal to the tasks involved in the office.

'ABBĀS II

Though Ṣafī cannot be compared with his grandfather 'Abbās in any respect, it is not proper to speak of the thirteen years of his reign as the beginning of the decline of Safavid power. It is true that the Safavid state at this time shows signs of ageing and also gives certain indications of decadence. But that it was still able to survive and guarantee its subjects good, if not outstandingly good, conditions in which to live, was evident under Ṣafī's son and successor, Prince Sulṭān Muḥammad Mīrzā, who ascended the throne on 16 Ṣafar 1052/15 May 1642 with the name 'Abbās II. Certainly there could be no question, to begin with, of his influencing the affairs of state, since the new shah was not quite ten years old at the time.[1] Since Ṣārū Taqī remained in office as grand vizier, it was inevitable that his should be the authoritative voice in government. Less self-evident was the part the queen mother played in state affairs. In the case in question, the practicalities of carrying out joint rule were in fact fairly simple, because the grand vizier was a eunuch, so that he was not subject to the usual prohibitions on access to the ladies of the court.

If there had been indications under the rule of Shah Ṣafī that the

[1] For a discussion of his date of birth, see Braun, *Das Erbe Schah 'Abbās' I*, pp. 132ff.

shift in power from the Türkmen tribal leaders to the shah and the tight centralisation that 'Abbās I had carried through would become a permanency, this now became clearer still. The grandees of the empire (*arkān-i daulat*), who were no longer dependent on or challenged by the Qizilbāsh aristocracy, now looked simply to the ruler. Indeed to such an extent was this so that the latter, if ever he should be unwilling to take action or if he should be as yet not of age to rule, could be represented for years by an efficient chancellor of the imperial court or grand vizier without such persons needing – as Mīrzā Salmān Jābirī had once needed – to fear the intrigues of the Türkmen military. This is far from saying that he was proof against the conspiratorial activities of other members of the court, especially the palace eunuchs and the ladies of the harem.

Even though the ruler still possessed supernatural powers in the estimation of his subjects, his rôle as master of the order now no longer had any practical significance. Perversions of what remained of this rôle, his alleged incapacity for doing any wrong (so that religious commandments and prohibitions did not apply to him), could have fateful results. The observances that derived from the rule of the order had been replaced by an ingeniously devised court ceremonial which is described in much detail by European observers living in Iṣfahān at the time. When the Türkmen military aristocracy was stripped of power, the rôle of the provinces as epicentres of central government was – as we have seen – reduced almost to nothing. There were among the leading figures of the empire, the incumbents of high office in the court, still some Türkmen tribal princes, but they had no significant power to fall back on in the provinces; they had to be content with fairly small governorships which might be associated with the court offices for which they were responsible. They no longer derived their influence from the fact that they belonged to particular tribes or from the economic power of their office in the provinces, but – like all other servants of the court, such as Georgians, Armenians or Circassians – from the favour of the ruler and, at times, of the grand vizier, largely depending on the degree of loyalty and competence they had shown. All in all, these are the typical characteristics of a court aristocracy. A significant aspect of the situation was that the court offices, which in the 10th/16th century had been largely only titular, now increasingly entailed specific functions, which on the one hand made their incumbents, i.e. the leading men in the empire, into pillars of the state (arkān-i daulat), and on the other invested them at particular times with considerable influence.

Although it is not intended here to examine the details of the Safavid governmental apparatus, it is worth casting a brief glance at the top échelons of the empire at the time of the new shah's accession. The ruler held solemn court at unspecified intervals for particular purposes. At these, affairs of state were discussed, ambassadors of foreign powers were received, and the conferment of offices announced. One noteworthy additional authority was the court and imperial council, one of whose functions was to supervise the work of governors and senior officials. Since it was responsible for enquiring into complaints from the population about abuses of authority, oppression and arbitrary government, there may well have been some connection with the *dīvān al-maẓālim* of earlier times. Any verdict it announced led to sentence being passed by the shah, who also had the right to exercise direct judicial power.

Among the members of the court and imperial council the grand vizier and the commander of the mounted guard (qūrchī-bāshī) occupied the first place. In addition, the commanders of the royal squires (qullar-āqāsī), of the musketeers (tufangchī-āqāsī) and of the artillery corps (tūpchī-bāshī) belonged to it, as did the dīvān-begī, the state privy clerk (*vāqiʿa-nivīs*), the lord marshal (ishīk-āqāsī-bāshī), and sometimes the imperial ṣadr (*ṣadr al-mamālik*). At the head of the financial administration, with partial responsibility for administering crown lands, was the imperial director of finances (*mustaufī al-mamālik*). Court administration was under the care of a supreme major-domo or intendant-general (*nāẓir-i buyūtāt*), who also had charge of the court workshops.

The Persian army, once the nucleus of Safavid power, had been weakened as a result of the tribal particularism and insubordination of the Qizilbāsh amīrs, but reformed both radically and effectively by Shah ʿAbbās I to represent a powerful striking force. Under Shah Ṣafī, in spite of the decimation of the generals, it had nevertheless so far contrived to preserve its strength that in 1058/1648 it proved itself a force to be reckoned with against the Indian invasion troops during the conflict over Qandahār. But quite soon afterwards the changed political situation began to take effect. The dangers which earlier on had threatened the existence of the state or its territorial integrity had either been averted or were no longer so menacing that they demanded trained troops in a constant high degree of readiness and in great numbers. As the government was no longer pursuing a policy of expansion, its military undertakings were confined to fairly small-scale punitive expeditions within the country or on the frontiers. The decline was first evident among the provincial contingents and not as yet among the main body of the royal army, which in 1654 was in fact increased by a small corps of bodyguard infantry, the *jazāʾirī*, consisting of 600 men to begin with, a number later increased to 2,000 men. The falling-off became plain among the artillery, which was the force least needed in long periods of peace and which had never been especially popular among the Persians with their marked preference for cavalry.[1] As time went on, the typical extravagance, luxurious living and idleness of the court did not fail to have a demoralising effect on the royal troops. Corruption in the intendant's office, inadequate provision for the lower ranks, casualness and neglect became the order of the day, and the shah's lack of interest added the finishing touches. Thus it was possible for it to happen that, in 1666, at a parade of troops, the same soldiers were marched past the shah several times over. The result of such abuses was that discipline disintegrated and the strength of units was allowed to fall, so that it was eventually said of the army that it was quite useful for military parades but no use at all for war.

Such, then, were the instruments of power available for the government of Iran when the new shah ascended the throne. If his personal share in the affairs of state was still confined for the time being to representative functions only, he nevertheless learned to make it more effective a few years later. To begin with, he had to catch up on the education he had been denied hitherto; and he made such good progress in reading and writing that it was soon possible to introduce him to religious texts. The foundations of his lifelong interest in theological questions may well have been laid at this time, and this interest may have provided the stimulus for a new Persian translation of al-Kulīnī's *Uṣūl al-kāfī fī ʿilm al-dīn*, the most important of the four books of the Shīʿī tradition. In addition to his intellectual training, which was not

[1] Against Chardin's assertion, however, that the artillery corps was disbanded after the death of its commander Ḥusain Qulī Beg in 1655, Luft (*Iran unter Schah ʿAbbās II*, p. 37) draws attention to the formation of a new artillery detachment in that very year.

confined merely to religious subjects, the shah also learned riding, archery, polo and other equestrian games.

Meanwhile, the real power lay in the hands of the trusted Grand Vizier Ṣārū Taqī, who did not shut himself off from the influence of the queen mother. He also willingly carried out ideas put forward by the Shīʿī jurists, who were deeply concerned to eradicate the excesses of Shah Ṣafī's reign that ran counter to the law. These included the tendency to wild extravagance at court and, in imitation of it, in the provincial capitals. The grand vizier insisted on the principle of economy and was able to curb the excessive drinking at court. However, the successes he achieved were not destined to last long, as in this respect ʿAbbās II later followed in his father's footsteps.

After the accession had been carried through smoothly there were more important concerns to worry about than the lax observance of the religious law at court. Experience taught that the fluid situation created by a change of ruler meant a challenge for discontented elements, power-hungry individuals, and centrifugal forces. Ṣārū Taqī met the new dangers with the classic ploys of generous tax concessions for the provinces and by confirming almost all of the highly-placed officials at the court and in the provinces. This policy had the desired effect. There were no disturbances or revolts when the change of ruler took place – with one exception. This was the trial of strength with the imperial field-marshal (sipāhsālār) Rustam Khān. He opposed the order to remain in Mashhad on account of the threat from Indian troops, having gone there to prepare a campaign, already planned but later abandoned, against Qandahār. He now set off for Iṣfahān, clearly with the intention of bringing pressure to bear on state policy with the change of ruler. The grand vizier reacted to this act of insubordination by promptly arranging for sentence of death to be passed on him. This was carried out in Mashhad on 9 Dhu'l-Ḥijja 1052/1 March 1643.

"Lord of the amīrs, servant of the poor", boasted Ṣārū Taqī in an inscription of 1053/1643 recording his foundation of a mosque he caused to be erected in Iṣfahān.[1] The death of Rustam Khān is not the only case in which he held to this principle. Integrity and incorruptibility were among the virtues for which he is remembered, and to which we have already referred. These alone made him many enemies. A compulsive urge to dominate, a contempt for people and the implac-

[1] Mihrābādī, p. 640. Cf. also Hunarfar, *Ganjīna*, p. 549.

able severity with which he proceeded against crooked dealings in the management of state affairs, and especially the system of spies employed in the collection of state taxes – each played its own part in increasing the number of people opposed to the grand vizier, who in any case does not seem to have been particularly popular even among the highest dignitaries in the land. Not surprisingly, a plot was hatched against him, led by Jānī Khān Shāmlū, the qūrchī-bāshī, who with five other conspirators attacked and murdered him in his home on 20 Sha'bān 1055/11 October 1645.

It was by no means certain whether what lay behind the murder was only the pent-up resentment of a fairly small group of officers or possibly – and perhaps more probably – a more ramified conspiracy of Türkmen tribal chieftains, such as those which may still have been remembered from the remote period of the Qizilbāsh conspiracies, aimed perhaps at dethroning the shah in favour of another prince. The crime was consequently followed by a period of some days in which bewilderment and confusion swept the court. Not until various senior officers and other dignitaries manifested their loyalty did the shah issue the order to proceed against the murderers and have them and their supporters put to death. It was again a Shāmlū amīr, Murtażā Qulī Khān Bījarlū, who was appointed to the position of qūrchī-bāshī. He occupied this office for four years and his place was then taken by Ḥusain Qulī Khān.

Ṣārū Taqī's successor was Khalīfa Sulṭān, who had been grand vizier once before, from 1623 to 1632, and now remained in office until his death (1064/1653–4). Shah Ṣafī had had four of his sons blinded at the time of the persecution of the princes. He was a pious man, concerned to see respect paid to the religious law, though his successes in this direction were at best only limited. It would seem that what he was able to achieve in the matter of prohibiting visual representation – in view of the many examples of portraiture and especially of miniature painting at the time – was just as modest as in the matter of drinking, which was a widespread habit, particularly at court, and could be suppressed only occasionally by imposing sharp penalties. It is well known that he made an effort to curb pederasty and to reduce prostitution by measures taken against the brothels that existed in many of the towns. In spite of his zeal in these directions, he seems on the whole – in welcome contrast to the severity, abruptness, and overbearing ways of his predecessor – to have been a conciliatory character, disposed to make allowances. Nevertheless, he was not without rivals at court. Since 1644 Allāhvardī Khān, the son of the Armenian Khusrau Khān, had been master of the hunt (*amīr-shikār-bāshī*). He was hardly less successful in securing the favour of the ruler than his namesake of earlier days with Shah 'Abbās I. He can be seen as almost the ideal embodiment of the courtier, and in his strategy as such he exploited especially the shah's passion for hunting. His brilliantly arranged *battues* secured him the shah's affection and indeed also bore testimony to the organisational skills which brought him the office of qullar-āqāsī when this position fell vacant; he held it until his death (*c.* 1663).

This high position, together with the unwavering goodwill of the shah, made it possible for him to manoeuvre one of his protégés into the position of grand vizier when Khalīfa Sulṭān died. This was Muḥammad Beg, a Tabrīz Armenian of modest origins, who up to that time had been intendant-general of the court (nāẓir-i buyūtāt) and had made a name as an efficient administrative and financial specialist. The problems he was required to solve, however, were beyond his capabilities. He did not succeed in reducing the immoderate outlay on the court and the high military expenditure as the situation demanded, not even by taking the necessary measures to reduce the quality of the coinage, attempting to foster mining, and further increasing the crown lands. His high-handed manner, his dismissal of several governors, and the disputes he was involved in with the Iṣfahān city administration created many enemies for him, among them some very influential people. When he finally became involved even in differences with the powerful Allāhvardī Khān, he was removed from office and compelled to take up permanent abode in Qum (18 Jumādā I 1071/19 January 1661).

The shah did not hurry to appoint his successor. The fact that ultimately Mīrzā Muḥammad Mahdī, scion of a highly respected family of theologians, who had been ṣadr-i mamālik for over ten years, was made grand vizier, may have been a concession to the Shī'ī jurists. Trouble had been fermenting in their ranks for a long time, not only on account of the libertarianism at court (the stricter discipline introduced after Ṣafī's death, with prohibition of wine and strict adherence to the other religious prescripts, had long since been allowed to go by the board), but also because of the magnanimity of the ruler towards Christians, and Christians only recently converted to Islam, who were able to attain to high office, indeed to the highest offices in the land.

In contrast to his predecessor, 'Abbās II took an active interest in the business of government, although he too had been raised in the seclusion of the harem and had received no preparation whatsoever for the throne. Exactly when he began to play an active rôle is impossible to determine, but it appears to have been at quite an early age, possibly in the period immediately following the assassination of Ṣārū Taqī, when he was scarcely more than fifteen years old. A distinctive feature of his reign was the consolidation of his power, which he achieved by pursuing policies of centralisation such as increasing the number of provinces belonging to the royal estates. In this respect he adhered firmly to the policy of Ṣārū Taqī who, under Shah Ṣafī, had already incorporated the province of Lār into the crown lands and who, only a year before his death, had also annexed the land of the Bakhtiyār, in consequence of a revolt against the local governor Khalīl Khān. Subsequently other territories such as Hamadān (1654), Ardabīl (1656–7) and Kirmān (1658) were also incorporated in the royal estates. The increased revenues and the greater power of the monarch resulting from these measures did not necessarily make for an improvement in the lot of the population. In certain instances they even proved detrimental, because the administrators of the crown lands, as the immediate subordinates of the shah, were frequently in a position to disregard constraints to which the former governors had been subject. On the other hand, it was not unknown for the shah to intervene against his provincial officials on receiving complaints from peasants or other of his subjects that they had been dealt with too harshly. This explains why European observers are able to contrast the well-being of the rural population in Persia with the very much worse plight of the peasantry in the West. The relatively favourable living conditions, also of course attributable to the fact that Persia was spared any serious involvement in major wars during this period, in turn help to explain why, for most of the time, the country remained peaceful internally and the roads were safe. When disorders and rebellions did develop they were confined, like the uprising of the Bakhtiyārs mentioned above, to border areas or vassal territories.

This was the case with various dominions in Georgia and Dāghistān which were either under Persian tutelage or loosely subject to the shah. Reference has already been made to Rustam Khān, who ruled as governor or viceroy (vālī) in Tiflis, and to conflicts between him and Theimuraz. These conflicts continued under 'Abbās II, in the first instance shortly after his accession, then again in 1648. Even though Theimuraz was eventually excluded from power and sent to Astarābād, fresh disturbances occurred, despite – or even because of – an attempt to restore peace by means of a special policy of colonisation and construction of fortresses, directed from Iṣfahān. Hostilities bordering on civil war were not brought to a conclusion until the beginning of the 1070s/1660s under a new viceroy called Shāhnavāz. Theimuraz himself, albeit in vain, had sought support from the government of the Tsar. His efforts were certainly not misplaced, for Cossacks had advanced as far as the river Terek around the year 1600. When, however, they proceeded to build fortifications commanding the approach routes to eastern Georgia, Persian troops were sent into action who destroyed their strongholds and put the garrisons to flight. To guard against renewed incursions by the Russians, or those of the Ottomans, any rebellions on the part of the princes of Dāghistān were quelled.

No account of the development of domestic politics under ʿAbbās II would be complete without a brief consideration of Western trading companies and their activities in Persia, although a later chapter will be devoted to a detailed discussion of this topic. By the beginning of the 11th/17th century, at the latest, these companies had become a significant factor not only in Persian history but also in the overseas history of various European powers, i.e. in the development of what nowadays would be termed Western imperialism and colonialism. We have already touched on the expulsion of the Portuguese with the aid of the English, who aimed at establishing secure trade relations with Persia.[1] Other European powers now endeavoured in much the same way to forge economic links with Iran and to set up suitable trade bases in the country.

Portugal had still been granted minor rights by the shah in a treaty of 1625, but when Muscat was conquered by the imām of ʿUmān in 1060/1650, she lost her foothold in the Persian Gulf and with it, simultaneously, her final opportunity for influence in Persia. It would, however, be quite wrong to conclude from their relations with the Portuguese that the rulers of Persia were in principle opposed to foreign trade delegations. They were in fact only too well aware of the benefits the country derived from the presence of Western trade representa-

[1] See above, p. 268, and below, chapters 7 and 8. For a brief recent survey, cf. Schuster-Walser, *Das ṣafawidische Persien*, pp. 67ff.

tives. These benefits were not confined solely to the economic sphere. Just how diverse they were can be gauged from two examples: the deployment of English ships in support of the Persian government, for instance, during the expulsion of the Portuguese, and the influence of Western art on that of Persia, which is of particular interest in view of the artistic inclinations of Shah 'Abbās II.

The English East India Company had been represented in Shīrāz and Iṣfahān since 1617. Later, in gratitude for the assistance it had given against the Portuguese, it was granted significant privileges by 'Abbās I and Ṣafī I, for example, a customs franchise in Bandar 'Abbās (Gombroon), which had replaced the Portuguese Hurmuz; representation by a permanent ambassador at the court; a guarantee of free trade throughout the country; independent legal authority; freedom of worship; the right to carry arms, and the pledge of greater supplies of silk. Despite all this it would be wrong to conceive of the activity of the company as being outstandingly successful. More often than not it encountered difficulties when seeking to exercise its privileges, and not infrequently it was obliged to relinquish them altogether. Moreover, the rôle of the company was dependent upon the prestige that the English homeland, about which they were quite well informed, enjoyed amongst the Persians; and this, particularly since the outbreak of the Civil War in 1642, was not exactly high.

Not many years after the English, the Dutch had also founded a settlement in Bandar 'Abbās. The Dutch East India Company was more successful in defending its interests than its English rival because, unlike the latter, it could count on the support of its government and also enjoyed greater freedom to act on its own authority. The privileges conceded to it by 'Abbās I were endorsed by the governments of both Ṣafī and 'Abbās II, though in the latter case not before drastic pressure had been brought to bear by sending a Dutch fleet from Batavia to the Persian Gulf.[1] The principal Dutch imports to Persia were spices, sugar and textiles. They purchased various silks, such as brocade, taffeta, velvet and satin, in addition to raw silk. A trade agreement remained in force until the end of the dynasty, but from time to time it proved damaging or problematical to one or other of the parties as the result of a stipulation obliging the Dutch to take agreed quantities of Persian silk at a fixed price, which proved ruinous for them.

[1] See Johann von der Behr, *Diarium*, as quoted in Schuster-Walser, p. 88.

French attempts to establish trade relations with the shah led to agreements, the contents of which were sanctioned by ʿAbbās II in a *farmān* issued shortly before his death, but for the time being nothing came of them in practice.

Apart from the exchange of goods they facilitated, the activities of the Western trading companies contributed to a certain opening up of Iran towards the West. The companies brought large numbers of Europeans to Persia, amongst them men of great acumen and intellectual curiosity who made it their ambition to really get to know the country and its inhabitants in depth, men who recorded their observations and experiences and subsequently published them. Reports of this nature not only provided the contemporary Western world with reliable information on Persia, but constitute to this day indispensable source-material for certain areas of study. Through the agency of the trading companies, for instance by using their ships, Persian merchants also visited European countries and were able to inform themselves of cultural conditions there. Western ideas reached Persia, where their influence is clearly discernible, if not so much on intellectual life, then certainly in the field of art and in the increasing refinement of Persian culture.

In discussing the European trading companies we have already moved to the subject of external relations, which were, as has already been indicated, predominantly peaceful in the reign of ʿAbbās II. The treaty of 1049/1639 proved a reliable basis for relations with the Ottomans. In other respects the judicious restraint of the shah paid dividends. He was not tempted by such favourable opportunities to expand his territory as arose, for instance, in Transcaucasia, where the risk of war was so acute that the governor of the Turkish border provinces had even evacuated the civilian population in expectation of a Persian attack, or in Baṣra, where the shah's aid had been sought to settle a struggle for the succession. Under these circumstances no danger threatened from the Ottomans, whether because the Porte was pursuing interests elsewhere – the conquest of Crete occurs in the period 1055–80/1645–69 – or because their desire for expansion was counterbalanced by considerable difficulties at home. A significant indication of the peaceful nature of relations between Persia and the Ottomans is the exchange of a number of legations.

Nor did any threat to peace emerge from the north-east, where in

Khīva a new ruler had ascended the throne in the same year as 'Abbās II. This was Abu'l-Ghāzī Khān, whom we have previously encountered as an exile in Iṣfahān. On the other hand, Persia was drawn into conflicts which arose amongst the Uzbeks of Bukhārā. Here we have in mind not those incursions by nomadic Uzbek tribes which did occasionally still occur, though no longer as frequently or on so large a scale as under Shah Ṣafī, but rather conflicts within the ruling dynasty. Just as Imām Qulī Khān had in his day arrived in Iṣfahān as a refugee from his brother Nadr Muḥammad Khān, so now this selfsame prince appeared seeking help at the Persian court after being banished from the throne by his son 'Abd al-'Azīz and having, if anything, further exacerbated the situation by asking the Great Mughal for military support. With Persian cooperation a settlement was arrived at between father and son, but it lasted only until the beginning of the fifties. The renewed strife, which had again led Nadr Muḥammad Khān to announce his arrival in Iṣfahān, was resolved by the latter's death.[1] From then on Persia seems to have had no further difficulties of any great significance with her Uzbek neighbours.

Nadr Muḥammad Khān's request for aid had reached Shāh Jahān as he was beginning preparations for an attack on Transoxiana with the initial aim of securing the approach route across the Hindu Kush, across Badakhshān and Balkh, a situation of which the khan of Bukhārā was completely unaware. Small wonder, then, that the Indian troops for whose support he was hoping had no other aim in mind than the annexation of his country. The Great Mughals, a Timurid dynasty, had consistently regarded the conquest and occupation of Central Asia as a hereditary commitment handed down from generation to generation, the legacy of their founder Ẓahīr al-Dīn Bābur, who, it will be recalled, had refused to give up the idea of a return to Samarqand even when it was a practical impossibility.

The Indian advance on Central Asia eventually ended in catastrophe. In Iṣfahān this led to a revival of the old plan to reconquer Qandahār which had had to be abandoned on the death of Shah Ṣafī. In the autumn of 1058/1648 the shah moved troops, supported by artillery, into Afghanistan and succeeded in conquering Qandahār and the fortresses of the surrounding district before the arrival on the scene of an

[1] Braun, *Das Erbe Schah 'Abbās' I*, p. 62, dates this crisis in 1653. According to Luft, *Iran unter Schah 'Abbās II*, p. 140, Nadr Muḥammad abdicated in 1650 and died later that year in Bisṭām while undertaking a pilgrimage to Mecca.

Indian relief force under the command of Prince Aurangzīb. A counter-attack by the Indians proved ineffectual and had to be abandoned. Even when, two years later, Shāh Jahān himself advanced at the head of an army with elephants and cannon, victory was denied him, despite a siege which lasted ten weeks. The Crown Prince Dārā Shukūh, who tried his luck in 1653, also failed. His attack was repulsed by Autār Khān, who, as a former member of a diplomatic mission to the country, was well versed in Indian affairs and now turned his experience to account as the shah's governor. Despite all efforts on the part of India, Qandahār remained in Persian hands even after the Safavid dynasty had come to an end, until the middle of the 12th/18th century, when it became a part of the emerging independent state of Afghanistan.

The illness of Shāh Jahān in Dhu'l-Qa'da 1067/September 1657 gave rise to a war of succession among his sons, of whom Prince Dārā Shukūh attempted to gain military support for his cause from the shah. It may well be the case that some form of intervention was contemplated in Iṣfahān, for a smallish contingent of troops was detailed for this purpose. However, no measures of great significance were taken and the prince eventually fell into the hands of his brother Aurangzīb, who had him executed in 1069/1659. It is possible that the prompt despatch of troops from Qandahār might have saved him.[1]

In the course of his struggle for power, in 1065/1655 and 1067/1657 respectively, Aurangzīb sent troops into the Deccan states of Golkonda and Bījāpūr, both of which had previously been under Persian suzerainty. He allowed them, however, to retain a certain measure of independence and it is possible that in view of this the authorities in Iṣfahān conceived the idea of playing off the Shī'ī princes of these states against the new Mughal emperor, himself a declared Sunnī. The sending of a Persian ambassador to the states would appear to support this conjecture. If it is correct, however, the shah must very quickly have convinced himself of the futility of such a scheme, for only a short time after the coronation of Aurangzīb, he resolved to recognise the Mughal's sovereign authority. Aurangzīb, whose position was still precarious, appears to have received this information with some sense of relief. If the shah's decision was motivated by concern for the security of Qandahār, he was to be disappointed, for when ambassadors were exchanged it transpired that the Indian monarch by no

[1] Riazul Islam, *Indo-Persian Relations*, p. 123.

means considered this particular question closed. Subsequently tensions between Persia and India increased to such an extent that the shah, even in his last days, when he was suffering from the illness which eventually killed him, was making preparations for a campaign against India. It was not, however, destined to be carried out.

A dominant feature of the reign of 'Abbās II is the indefatigable concern he personally showed for the affairs of state. This did not change even when, in 1073/ at the end of 1662, he displayed the first symptoms of what was to prove a long and painful illness, although his reactions to irregularities and maladministration on the part of individual dignitaries and officials became, from this point onwards, more severe and violent than in previous years. Executions for reasons of this nature were no longer a rarity. When a deterioration in the condition of the shah, who according to the descriptions of European reporters was probably suffering from syphilis,[1] forced him to recuperate in Māzandarān, he still retained sufficient energy to take charge of state business even from there.

At the age of thirty-three, in the autumn of 1077/1666, probably during the night of 26 Rabī' II/25–6 October,[2] 'Abbās passed away in Khusrauābād, a small mountain castle between Dāmghān and Gurgān. His body was brought to Qum, where he was buried next to his father Ṣafī. Not without reason is his name often mentioned in the same breath as those of Ismā'īl I and 'Abbās I as the three outstanding ruling figures of the Safavids. Because he might otherwise have been just the man to prevent the downfall of the Safavid kingdom, there is no lack of expressions of regret at his untimely end, either in the primary sources, of which the accounts of Western visitors to Persia have the first if not the sole claim to credibility, or in the writings of historians. The validity of such speculation can best be judged by a consideration of his personality.

Surviving portraits show the shah to have been a finely proportioned young man of medium height with a longish face, sharply defined features and a wide, sweeping moustache of the kind fashion-

[1] The testimony of Kaempfer, p. 36, as a physician, carries especial weight. Cf. also Chardin IX, 400.

[2] Braun, *Das Erbe Schah 'Abbās' I*, p. 142. Other sources give 25 Rabī' I (Luft, *Iran unter Schah 'Abbās II*, p. 103 and n.409) or 23 Rabī' I (the anonymous essay "Az ibtidā-yi Ṣafaviyya tā ākhir-i Qājāriyya pādshāhān-i Īrān har yak dar kujā madfūn and", *Yādgār* III/2 [1325], 9–22).

able at the time.[1] He was renowned for his skill in and enthusiasm for sporting activities such as riding and archery, as well as for his passionate interest in hunting.

'Abbās II adhered to the traditional conception of the divine kingship and sacred status of the Safavids and did not hesitate to dispute the views of those theologians who argued that until the return of the departed Imām, i.e. the Mahdī, temporal power belonged by right not to the Safavid shah but to the mujtahid of the time. On the other hand, he was concerned to foster good relations with the Shī'ī jurists, which explains in part why he chose his sisters' husbands from amongst their number. He did so also, of course, with the ulterior motive of precluding any issue eligible for succession to the throne, an eventuality he would have had to face had his brothers-in-law been members of the ruling dynasty or eminent military figures in the realm.

The desire to consolidate his own power, for decades the overriding concern of the Safavid monarchs, prompted 'Abbās II to have his nephews killed and his four brothers blinded. Nor was he content to follow the practice hitherto customary at the court, of rendering the cornea opaque, but ordered the actual removal of their eyeballs. This fear of potential rivals did not, however, extend to his own two sons, in spite of certain misgivings concerning them in court circles. A propensity to cruelty can also be discerned in certain directives issued when 'Abbās was in an inebriated condition. The prohibition imposed at the time of his accession by the Grand Vizier Ṣārū Taqī and representatives of the religious classes had been shortlived, and excessive consumption of alcohol, just as in the days of his father, had again become the order of the day at court. According to one chronicle,[2] probably the only activity the young shah preferred to a bout of heavy drinking was watching a game of polo. Another passion he indulged was his love of the fair sex, and it would seem that his early death was not unconnected with his lack of restraint in this regard.

Although such characteristics tarnish the image of the ruler somewhat, he was by no means lacking in conspicuously good qualities which earned the praise of native and foreign observers alike. Foremost amongst these was a pronounced love of justice. He would inter-

[1] See Braun, *Das Erbe Schah 'Abbās' I*, p. 136, and Luft, *Iran unter Schah 'Abbās II*, p. 260, n.587. Of the two portraits supplied in Welch, *Shah 'Abbās and the Arts*, pp. 85 and 98, the first is particularly impressive.

[2] Qazvīnī, *'Abbās-nāma*, p. 315; see also Braun, *Das Erbe Schah 'Abbās' I*, p. 137.

vene quite ruthlessly whenever corruption or despotism, irregularities or malpractices came to his notice, irrespective of whether it was a question of the normal administration of justice or the surveillance of political and administrative bodies, both civil and military. He even went to the length of personally devoting several days a week to the administration of justice, amongst other things initiating measures to promote public safety and above all to suppress banditry and highway robbery. The energy and drive displayed by 'Abbās in this and other areas of public life led not only to the eradication of particular abuses which had crept in since the death of his great-grandfather, but also to an overall reform of Safavid politics as such.

A clearer image of the ruler's personality emerges when one considers his attitude towards things spiritual, intellectual and artistic, something which has already been alluded to in passing. He valued the company of intellectuals and scholars as well as that of dervishes, on whom, incidentally, he lavished considerable sums. At court he would organise discussions and debates with them on topics chosen from their sphere of interest. On occasions, moreover, committed leaders of the faith such as his Grand Vizier Khalīfa Sulṭān succeeded in inciting him in his religious zeal to attempt to convert the non-Islamic minorities of the realm. Whereas the Christians emerged relatively unscathed because they were not pursued with any great rigour or stringency, the fate of the Jews, above all the sizeable Jewish community in Iṣfahān, was much worse. All kinds of coercive measures and underhand practices were employed to convert them to Islam.

Measures of this nature, however, seem only marginally to have affected the general climate of religious affairs under 'Abbās II, reliable accounts indicating as they do that, in contrast to other Islamic countries, religious discussions between Christians and Muslims were not merely permitted in Persia during this period, but actually took place frequently. Although the Islamic faith undoubtedly formed the undisputed basis of national and public life, there is ample evidence for the existence of liberal attitudes and, apart from the exceptions such as those just mentioned, the tolerance extolled by European observers of the time of 'Abbās I seems to have reigned during this period also. This can be seen, for example, from cases in which the shah intervened against Islamic judges who in legal disputes between Christians and Muslims had unfairly favoured the latter.

The ruler's attitude towards the fine arts shows him in a particularly sympathetic light. There was admittedly a long tradition of artistic inclination and aesthetic sensibility among the Safavids, but in 'Abbās II, who was himself a practising artist, these qualities found quite outstanding expression. The painting of the time owes its charm not least to the traces of European and Indian influence detectable in it. These are the result not only of the increasing number of pictures which found their way to Persia from Europe and India but also of personal contacts between Persian artists and European and Indian masters. 'Abbās II is himself the best example of this trend. After gaining experience of skilled craft-work in his early youth, he later received lessons in painting too, from European as well as Persian teachers.

The artistic interests of the ruler also extended to architecture and lengthy accounts of the buildings he erected in Iṣfahān are to be found in the sources. Apart from preservation and reconstruction work, however, no mention is made of the building of mosques, to which his great-grandfather owed his immortal renown as an architect. All the more significant and numerous, on the other hand, are his achievements in the field of secular architecture, such as caravansarais, bridges and palaces. Much that owed its inspiration to him has subsequently been destroyed, but to this day monuments have been preserved in the architecture of Iṣfahān which testify to his exquisite taste, such as, for instance, the most charming bridge Pul-i Khājū over the Zāyandarūd and above all the garden palace Chihil Sutūn, which in its combination of architecture and painting gives some impression of the radiance that adorned the royal household and the festivities of the shah.

ṢAFĪ II (SULAIMĀN)

With the death of 'Abbās II, who for all his faults was a just and magnanimous – if not a liberal – monarch, Persia came once and for all to the end of a long period of peace and prosperity. Problems began to arise even on the question of the succession, for which the late shah had made no provision. Was the eldest son, the approximately nineteen-year-old Ṣafī Mīrzā to succeed his father in accordance with the established custom of the Safavids, even though he had not been on particularly good terms with 'Abbās? Or would the throne fall to his favourite son Ḥamza Mīrzā, a mere seven-year-old? Despite initial support for Ḥamza Mīrzā's claim on the part of the Grand Vizier Mīrzā

Muḥammad Mahdī, the leading figures of the realm, assembled where 'Abbās had died, decided in favour of the older prince's succession, merely on the basis of representations made to them by his personal tutor and confidant, the eunuch Mīrzā Āqā Mubārak. Subsequently he ascended the throne on 1 November 1666 with the title Ṣafī II.[1]

The new shah, the son of a Circassian slave called Nakīḥat Khānum, had been raised, according to what by now had become the firmly established custom, in the wives' quarters, that is in the sole company of the ladies of the harem and eunuchs, without the slightest preparation for the throne. He lacked not only experience and observation of the practice of government but also those excellent human qualities his father had possessed, although he shared with the latter such vices as excessive drinking, cruelty, principally when under the influence of alcohol, and a tendency towards immoderate sexual indulgence. To a fondness for pomp and circumstance, evinced also by his father, came in addition an inordinate extravagance, at least in the early part of his reign. Later on, admittedly, he was to swing to the opposite extreme of avarice and covetousness, two qualities that remained with him until the end of his days. Engelbert Kaempfer, a German doctor, who lived in Iṣfahān in the years 1683–4, left behind an excellent account of the Safavid capital and of the administration of the court and country, including also a character sketch of the shah.[2] Alongside his more familiar faults and vices are listed irascibility, indolence and superstition, but a few good qualities also find mention: occasional acts of justice and clemency, piety, an unusual love of peace and winning social manners. Kaempfer testifies not only to the shah's kindheartedness but also to his popularity with his subjects.

The very beginnings of Ṣafī II's rule in Iran were anything but encouraging. The news from Māzandarān of his father's death and his own appointment to the succession had found him, just like his grandfather before him, in a state of total unpreparedness. Never before having set foot outside the harem, he was seized with panic and responded to the invitation to appear in the throne room for his coronation only after a considerable show of reluctance, because he assumed that he was being lured there simply to be murdered or blinded. Shortly after he came to the throne, prices soared in the capital and

[1] This and the second coronation are discussed in detail by Chardin, *Le couronnement de Soleimaan Troisième [sic], roy de Perse* (Paris, 1671), an account also included in his *Voyages* IX and X.

[2] Kaempfer, pp. 47–61.

there were outbreaks of famine and disease in the country. The province of Shīrvān suffered a violent earthquake and in the following year the Caspian provinces had to endure the predatory raids of Stenka Razin's Cossacks, whom the Persian forces were unable to subdue. Since all was not well with the ruler's health either, presumably because of the dissolute life he led, one of the physicians who were striving in vain to cure him hit on the idea that all these misfortunes – not only the shah's sickliness but all the untoward occurrences in the land – must stem from a miscalculation of the horoscope determining the date of his accession to the throne. It did not take long to find a court astrologer who confirmed this assumption, and the leading figures of the realm together with the shah duly concluded that the remedy to the situation lay in repeating the ceremony of accession.[1] A new horoscope indicated 20 March 1668, at nine o'clock in the morning, as the most propitious time. The second coronation, which was again observed in every ceremonial detail, was supposed to betoken a completely fresh start. Thus, on this occasion, the shah ascended the throne under a new name also, that of Shah Sulaimān, by which he is known in history.[2]

However, neither the renewed accession to the throne nor the adoption of a new name by the sovereign made for an improvement in the fortunes of the Safavid kingdom. The ruler was simply not a man of substance. The qualities he had lacked previously – energy, courage, decisiveness, discipline, initiative and an eye for the national interest – all these he subsequently proved incapable of acquiring. His fundamental indifference towards the tasks of government was reinforced, as before, by his fondness for alcohol and women. As the years went by, the respective grand viziers – initially Mīrzā Muḥammad Mahdī, who had served under 'Abbās II, then after the latter's death (*c.*1673) the Kurd Shaikh 'Alī Zangāna until 1690, and finally Mīrzā Muḥammad Ṭāhir Vaḥīd Qazvīnī – were granted less and less frequently the morning audience with the shah which previously had been the custom. More and more he made the harem the focal point of his existence, and whilst there he was inaccessible even to his grand vizier. Thus it

[1] On occasions one reads (cf. Stchoukine, *Manuscrits Ṣafavīs*, p. 32) that instead of Ṣafī II a self-appointed "usurper" ascended the throne at this time so that he could be the victim of the evil fate ordained in the stars. This is possibly connected with ancient eastern ideas: cf. K. Hecker, *Die Institution des Ersatzkönigs im alten Zweistromland*, probationary lecture in Freiburg, 9 Dec. 1970.

[2] Occasionally he is entitled Sulaimān I, to distinguish him from the ephemeral Sulaimān II, who ruled in Mashhad in 1163/1749–50: see Lockhart, *The Fall*, p. 510; below, p. 329.

happened that, even when important decisions had to be made, the grand vizier was often left entirely to his own devices or, alternatively, the shah would discuss affairs of state with his wives and eunuchs and communicate through a servant of the harem any decision arrived at in this manner. Indeed, the shah even set up a privy council in the harem, to which the most important eunuchs belonged, a kind of private administration which effectively deprived the real organs of government, i.e. the council of State (*dīvān*) and the court assembly (*majlis*) as well as the grand vizier, of their functions. In practice state dignitaries were reduced to the level of mere executive organs of this privy council. Even when the shah condescended to participate in consultations outside the harem it was hardly ever possible to discuss in detail problems that had arisen, because he had neither the inclination nor the patience necessary to familiarise himself with the facts of a complex situation; and the leading figures of the realm had learned from bitter experience not to be too energetic in their efforts to arouse his interest. Sovereignty resided in the harem, where eunuchs, princesses and concubines intrigued constantly.

The shah's indifference, bordering on apathy, with regard to questions of political administration inevitably gave rise to grave abuses. In the absence of any effective control or sanction against oppression and exploitation, corruption was rife. In the circumstances, the practice of bestowing favours, widespread in Persia, rapidly led to bribery in public life. Sinister developments in the armed forces, of which there had been indications even under 'Abbās II, now became widespread. Oblivious of their military duties, soldiers came to regard their pay as little more than a gratuity, in exchange for which no effort was required on their part. Some contingents, indeed, existed only on paper.[1]

Shah Sulaimān ruled for twenty-eight years, until 1105/1694. To judge from the observations of European travellers, the royal household was maintained with a pomp and splendour no less lavish than that which characterised earlier Safavid rulers. One reads, for example, of excursions organised by the shah with his estimated eight hundred ladies of the harem. At the beginning of his reign these took place once or twice a week, bringing the activities of whole areas of the city to a standstill,

[1] Minorsky, *Tadhkirat al-Mulūk*, p. 35.

because all males, even boys and old men, were banned under penalty of death (*qurūq*) from the streets through which the royal procession was due to pass.[1] The discrepancy between this outer veneer and the tawdry reality underneath becomes positively grotesque when one finds others, no doubt in all sincerity, reporting that the people revered this ruler and that life during his reign was not at all bad for them.[2] As a matter of fact, dissatisfaction with conditions in the country did not find expression in uprisings of any significance. How is one to explain this? Undoubtedly the Persian government's aggressive policy of centralisation since the reign of 'Abbās I had in the meantime borne fruit. Quasi-autonomous provincial administrations had been systematically eradicated. At the same time, those elements most likely to constitute a threat to the shah, especially the Qizilbāsh and their leaders, had been divested of power and ultimately suppressed. However, this is not of itself an adequate explanation. It is doubtless also significant that, according to Malcolm,[3] no events whatsoever of major importance occurred during the reign of Sulaimān. But what decisively influenced public verdict on the shah was probably the fact that he did not involve the country in war. His apathetic and nonchalant attitudes may well have been construed as a love of peace. In the judgement of the masses, reports of the dignified bearing and the external appearance of this blonde, blue-eyed man of great physical strength[4] are likely to have outweighed any evidence of lack of initiative.

It is true that in the sphere of foreign policy Sulaimān avoided doing anything that might lead him into difficulties. Although the Ottomans, owing to wars with Austria, Poland and Venice, would scarcely have been capable of action on any large scale in the eastern parts of their empire, he steadfastly refused to violate the peace treaty which his grandfather had made with the Porte in 1049/1639; this despite, for instance, repeated offers from Mesopotamia (1684, 1685) and from Baṣra (1690) to re-establish Persian suzerainty there. In addition, he allowed the Dutch East India Company to establish a base on the island

[1] Details in Kaempfer, pp. 179–85.

[2] Chardin, as cited in Minorsky, *Tadhkirat al-Mulūk*, p. 23.

[3] Quoted in Braun, *Das Erbe Schah 'Abbās' I*, p. 159.

[4] Braun, *ibid.*, p. 156, refers to a miniature depicting Sulaimān in the Chester Beatty collection, which is reproduced in *A Chronicle of the Carmelites* I, 405. The prohibition of illustrations of the shah referred to by Kaempfer, p. 48, cannot therefore have been as effective as Stchoukine, *Manuscrits de Shāh 'Abbās*, p. 37, assumes.

of Kishm in the Persian Gulf. Similarly he shunned conflict with Russia when the Cossacks, in the course of their increasingly frequent incursions on the southern coast of the Caspian Sea after 1662, requested on more than one occasion that they might be placed under Persian suzerainty.

The Uzbeks were able to make plundering raids on eastern Persia without fear of vigorous reprisals. Such raids, always undertaken when the Persians least expected them, were, however, relatively small-scale actions carried out by tribes of rapacious nomads not fully integrated into the sphere of influence of the khan. At all events they did not mar the good relations the shah enjoyed with successive rulers of Bukhārā, 'Abd al-'Azīz Khān and, after 1091/1680, the latter's brother, Subḥān Qulī Khān. In 1685 ambassadors were exchanged in an attempt to settle existing differences diplomatically.

Another neighbouring people from the north, the Kalmucks, a Western Mongolian race from the Ust-Urt region between the Caspian and Aral Seas, had already attracted the attention of the government in Iṣfahān in the time of 'Abbās II, at first because of an incursion into the province of Astarābād and later when a legation was sent to the Persian capital. The Kalmucks, clearly under the impression that Persia was militarily weak, made further attacks during Sulaimān's reign. From time to time they also sent ambassadors to the Persian court again. It is, however, unlikely that they were held in any great esteem there.[1]

In contrast to earlier periods there were no difficulties of note with the Georgian lands. In Kakhetia the previously mentioned governor Shāhnavāz had been succeeded in 1664 by his son Archīl Khān and in 1675, for a short period, by Herakleios I (Erekle), a grandson of the famous Theimuraz. All subsequent administrators were Persians. In Kartlia, on the other hand, a native dynasty, the Mukhranids, remained under Persian suzerainty.

Because of the pomp and circumstance associated with the reception of foreign legations, detailed accounts of the diplomatic activity of the period are given both by Persian sources and by foreign travellers. European missions figure prominently, such as those from Sweden, Russia and France. Their object was usually the development of trade relations, Persian silk in particular being in great demand.

On 29 July 1694 Shah Sulaimān died in Iṣfahān at the age of forty-

[1] Kaempfer, p. 206.

six. According to one version he suffered a stroke during a particularly heavy drinking bout.[1] According to another the cause of death was gout, which had already confined him to bed for two years. Other authorities see his death as the outcome of decades of debauchery.[2]

The brief sketch of his reign we have just drawn contains ample evidence of his failure as a ruler. The picture of Sulaimān the human being is no less shameful. Two instances of his insulting behaviour towards his Grand Vizier Shaikh 'Alī Zangāna will suffice to make the point. On one occasion, after forcing the grand vizier to imbibe intoxicating liquor, he spent hours revelling at the sight of his pathetic condition. On another occasion, after ordering the removal of the grand vizier's beard, he had the barber's hand chopped off because he had not done the job thoroughly enough. These and other still worse atrocities of which he was guilty are grotesquely incompatible with the "saint-like" and "unblemished" status to which he laid claim and which was attributed even to this shah by his subjects.[3]

Sulaimān's only redeeming feature might perhaps be his appreciation of art, specifically painting and the work of miniaturists. He must be regarded as an outstanding connoisseur if, as is likely, it is true that as a patron he influenced directly or indirectly some of the most impressive works of the three greatest painters of the late 11th/17th century, 'Alī Qulī Jabbadār, Muḥammad Zamān and Mu'īn Muṣavvir. His promotion on the one hand of the traditional style found in Mu'īn Muṣavvir and, on the other hand, of the new tendencies inspired by Western painting which mark the work of 'Alī Qulī Jabbadār and Muḥammad Zamān may well be evidence of an artistic taste that could, in more favourable circumstances, have led to the development of a new aesthetic sense.

SULṬĀN ḤUSAIN

Intrigues in the harem, which had played a decisive rôle in so many of his political affairs, seem also to have determined the choice of Sulaimān's successor. He himself had failed to nominate a crown prince. Instead, he is said to have advised the dignitaries gathered around his

[1] Gemelli-Carreri, *Voyage du tour du monde* II (Paris, 1719), 120, quoted in Schuster-Walser, *Das ṣafawidische Persien*, p. 21.

[2] For the last two versions, from Krusiński and the *Zubdat al-tavārīkh* respectively, see Braun, *Das Erbe Schah 'Abbās' I*, p. 157.

[3] Kaempfer, pp. 16f.

sick-bed during his last hours that if they were concerned to maintain peace and quiet they should make his elder son, the twenty-six-year old Sulṭān Ḥusain Mīrzā his successor; if, on the other hand, they wished to strengthen royal power and expand the empire they should rather appoint the latter's twenty-three-year old brother, 'Abbās Mīrzā. The ruler passed away at an unforeseen moment when no-one was present. His death was discovered by his aunt, Princess Maryam Begum, whose sympathies lay wholly with Prince Ḥusain. She informed the influential eunuchs and it is unlikely that she had any difficulty in winning their support for her favourite.

His coronation on 14 Dhu'l-Ḥijja 1105/6 August 1694 meant the continuation of his father's misrule, albeit in a somewhat different key. At the same time it was the prelude to the fall of the Safavid dynasty. Sulṭān Ḥusain had, it is true, a reign of twenty-eight years before him, but not one, however, destined to bring happiness to the empire. He and his country, which for more than two centuries had withstood serious crises within and powerful enemies without, were to suffer a catastrophe at the hands of an opponent as unforeseen as he was basically insignificant, but whom the shah and his army were powerless to repulse. Before considering this, however, we need to discuss his character, his outlook on life and his conduct of government.

Shah Sulaimān's statement concerning the choice of his successor, whether actually made or subsequently attributed to him, was well founded in the quite different personalities of his sons, the two eldest of a total of seven. Both had grown up in the seclusion of the harem and neither of them had received an education or preparation of any kind for the tasks which awaited a future monarch of Persia. Manliness, bellicosity, sobriety and adroitness were the main characteristics of Prince 'Abbās. Sulṭān Ḥusain was totally different: a placid, social personality, studious, abstemious and, even in his early years, pious to such a degree that he was given the nickname "Mullā Ḥusain" by those around him. His indifference towards the governmental duties assigned to him – in this respect he was just like his father – found expression in another nickname he was given, Yakhshidir ("very well!"), which was his stock response whenever matters of government were expounded to him.

In the good intentions with which he began his reign the new shah had the support of the Shaikh al-Islām Muḥammad Bāqir Majlisī

(b. 1037/1627, d. 1111/1699), a famous theologian on whom Shah Sulaimān had already conferred office. Initially, it looked as though this man, who had girded on Ḥusain's sword during the solemn investiture,[1] would prevent the young monarch from following in the evil ways of his predecessors. He was the driving force behind Ḥusain's first decrees, which forbade abuses of the religious code that had become widespread, such as unbridled consumption of alcohol. On his initiative too the ṣūfīs were banished from the capital, members of the very order of which the shah himself was master but with whom he no longer felt any affinity.

The influence exerted by Muḥammad Bāqir and his theologians inevitably roused the jealousy of the people of the harem, the eunuchs and the princesses. Anxious not to lose power, they did their utmost to counteract any attempts to weaken their position; and not without success, as shown by the fate of the ban on alcohol just mentioned. Cunningly exploiting the concept of moral infallibility associated with the office of shah, a Shī'ī version of the maxim "the king can do no wrong", they successfully tempted Ḥusain to indulge in wine drinking. Here again the Princess Maryam Begum, herself a hardened wine drinker, played a significant rôle.

Although at first sight these events appear to stem from a palace intrigue on the part of various pressure groups composed of court and state dignitaries, their real causes lie deeper. These will be dealt with in our concluding remarks, but at least some allusion to them is necessary at this point in the discussion. It will be recalled that Shah 'Abbās I had not only destroyed the military might of the Qizilbāsh but also neutralised the more strongly religious elements of the group, the ṣūfīs proper – by that time the arms-bearing ghāzīs could probably no longer be regarded as actually identical with the practising members of the ṣūfī order. 'Abbās I had put the latter firmly in their place in 998/1589–90 after a trial of strength to which they had challenged him. From then on he had suppressed their influence more and more, most effectively by a policy of ignoring them or treating them with contempt. After his death their standing suffered still further, especially when in the reign of Shah 'Abbās II a group of well-versed theologians appeared on the

[1] Lockhart, *The Fall*, p. 38, writes: "Sulṭān Ḥusain refused to let the Ṣūfīs gird him with the sword in the customary manner, and called upon the Shaikh al-Islām to do so instead." Ṣafī II (Sulaimān) had done the same at his coronation : Lambton, "Quis custodiet custodes?", *SI* VI (1956), 141f.; Braun, *Das Erbe Schah 'Abbās' I*, p. 50.

scene who were no longer prepared to recognise "the mystic vagaries of the earlier period".[1] This group, the 'ulamā', with the mujtahid at their head, advanced unassailable Shī'ī doctrines to refute the religious concepts of the ṣūfīs and resolutely strove, for their own part, to win power over the shah. In the case of Shah Sulaimān and, as will now be seen, Shah Sulṭān Ḥusain, they succeeded. Of the 'ulamā, the group which thus greatly increased in strength, a prominent representative was Muḥammad Bāqir Majlisī. As his theological writings prove, he was a man of great erudition, but this in no way diminished his interest in secular power. Nor, certainly, did it counteract a religious intolerance on his part from which not only Christians and Jews but also Sunnīs, the aforementioned ṣūfīs and even philosophers were made to suffer. The shah let him have his own way. Far from unifying the population of the country, this policy of intolerance, which was also pursued by Muḥammad Bāqir's grandson and successor Mīr Muḥammad Ḥusain, tended to sow dissension because it encouraged people to denounce one another. It was one of the factors that subsequently, in the hour of need, rendered religious commitment ineffective as a stimulus to popular resolve to defend the country.

A truly paradoxical situation characterises the final phase of Safavid rule. A monarch, pious to the point of bigotry, submits to the demands of orthodox Shī'ī theologians, the adversaries of his ancestors who had won over the nation to Shi'ism and preserved it in that belief. Of course these ancestors, especially Ismā'īl, the founder of the state, had held radically different views of Shi'ism from the theologians who now triumphed as power slipped from the hands of a weak and irresolute ruler. These did not use their power to the best advantage of the country, any more than did their rivals inside the harem, who with few exceptions were men of little ability. The decline in royal power, the indifference of the shah with regard to the affairs of state, his lack of initiative, energy and consistency ruled out all possibility of progress in the country, whether one considers trade and commerce, administration or agriculture, the national finances or the army. Nor were successes in foreign policy to be achieved in the prevailing circumstances. Nevertheless, the institutions of state continued to function, even if ominous signs of ossification and torpor became noticeable, for example, in the military sphere.

[1] See Minorsky, *Tadhkirat al-Mulūk*, p. 125.

Even cultural life continued on its way, in some fields with considerable achievements. Examples of craftwork, such as ceramics, metalwork and textiles, testify to the uninterrupted activity at the monarch's court workshops. Their products nowadays enjoy immense popularity amongst collectors and museums throughout the world. Architecture, too, remained productive. The shah was reponsible for the improvement and extension of his palace buildings and the Madrasa-yi Chahārbāgh, founded by his mother, is even one of the masterpieces of Safavid architecture. Contacts with Europe continued: we learn of legations from the courts of Louis XIV and Peter the Great in 1708, as well as a further legation from the Tsar in 1715. Persia herself sent diplomatic missions, for example to France. Although these exchanges were concerned primarily with specific problems of international trade, they were at the same time not without significance for the cultural and particularly the artistic development of the country. They brought aesthetic ideas from the West to Persia, European works of art such as paintings and even Western artists and craftsmen. Thus the already mentioned European influence on Persian art, especially painting, was enhanced. Clearly the shah himself did not stand in the way of this development, since he even agreed to pose for a Dutch portrait painter.[1] In this respect, at any rate, he had no religious scruples.

The religious policy just referred to, which was designed to impose Shī'ī Islam as the sole confession in Persia, naturally created a good deal of bad blood because of the forcible conversion of Zoroastrians, Jews, Christians and relatively small groups of Shī'ī sectarians, but it had positively devastating consequences for the more or less closed Sunnī sections of the population. If they lived near the borders, such communities reacted to the pressure of forcible conversion by developing separatist tendencies. This occurred in the Afghan areas of the Safavid empire, and it was there in the region of Zamīndāvar and Qandahār that the storm gathered which was eventually to cause the downfall of the shah.

The warlike tribe of the Ghalzai[2] had penetrated into these areas,

[1] Welch, *Shah 'Abbās and the Arts*, pp. 120-37. Stchoukine, *Manuscrits Ṣafavīs*, pp. 38–41. See also Lockhart, *The Fall*, frontispiece.

[2] Often linked with the Khalaj: cf. R.N. Frye, "Ghalzay (Ghaldjī, Ghilzay)", *EI²*; Köprülü, "Halaç", *İsl. Ans.*; on the language of the Khalaj resident in Persia, Doerfer, "Das Chaladsch – eine archaische Türksprache", *ZDMG* CXVIII (1968), 79–112, and "Das Chaladsch, eine neuentdeckte archaische Türksprache", *ZDMG Suppl.* I (1969), 719–25.

the population of which had been severely reduced during the reign of 'Abbās I with the resettlement of the Abdālīs in Herat. The Ghalzai policy of playing off the Persian governor of Qandahār against the Mughal governor in Kābul had so far helped them to overcome considerable difficulties. Inveterate Sunnīs as they were, the Ghalzai now attempted to counter Persian religious pressures by treating with India. Initially they had no intention of rebelling against the Persians, towards whom, if anything, they were more favourably inclined than to the Mughals. But a sudden switch in policy occurred when, as a result of an attack by the Balūchīs which the commandant of Qandahār proved powerless to resist, Gurgīn Khān (i.e. the former King Giorgi XI of Kartlia) was appointed governor-general in May 1704 and dispatched together with his forces from Kirmān to Qandahār. Brutal treatment at the hands of the Georgians now provoked a revolt amongst the Ghalzai. Gurgīn Khān suppressed them, took prisoner their leader, the wealthy and influential Mīr Vais, and sent him to Iṣfahān. Although Gurgīn Khān had warned that his prisoner was a dangerous man, Mīr Vais managed to gain the favour of the shah and even to arouse his suspicion against the governor-general. A few years later he returned to Qandahār a free man and Gurgīn Khān was unable to take any action against him. During his long stay in the capital he had gained a deep insight into the abuses of the government and central administration.

In April 1709, when a large proportion of the Georgian troops had left on an expedition in the provinces, Mīr Vais staged a carefully planned coup. Surprising the governor-general in a camp outside the fortress, he overpowered and defeated him together with his followers. Later, when the expeditionary force returned, it was unable to retrieve the situation. The man sent to quell the rebellion, Kai-Khusrau, prefect of Iṣfahān and a nephew of Gurgīn Khān, proved unequal to the task. It took him more than a year and a half even to arrive on the scene although the forces at his disposal – Georgians and Qizilbāsh, who were joined in Herat by a group of the Abdālī tribe, hereditary foes of the Ghalzai – were numerically strong. Despite initial successes, he was brought to a standstill outside the walls of Qandahār, and lack of reinforcements as well as the outbreak of an epidemic amongst his troops forced him to raise the siege at the end of October 1711. As he retreated the pursuing Ghalzai inflicted a crushing defeat which also cost him his life. The next commander to be entrusted with the reconquest of Qandahār, the qūrchī-bāshī Muḥammad Zamān Khān Shāman, fell ill and died en route in Herat long before his forces could make contact with the enemy.

Whether these failures helped to persuade the authorities in Iṣfahān that nothing could be achieved against the Ghalzai with forces of the quality hitherto dispatched, or whether the indifference of the shah had now spread to those members of the government who had so far retained an inclination for decisive action, Mīr Vais suffered no further attacks from the central government in the years up to his death in 1127/1715. He subjected the whole territory of Qandahār to his control and ruled it as an independent prince, if only under the modest title of vakīl ("administrator"). The plans sometimes attributed to him of marching on Iṣfahān, dethroning the shah and assuming sovereign command in Persia seem to have scarcely any foundation in fact and are probably embellishments of the truth in the light of subsequent developments.[1] The starting point of these developments may be discerned in the policies initiated by Mīr Vais, and he might even be regarded as a pioneer of Afghan independence, though not as its founder. Since his ambitions did not extend so far, that title is usually reserved for another tribal leader, Aḥmad Shāh Durrānī, who does not come to full historical prominence until thirty years later. One reason for this may be that the latter's tribe has greater claims to be called Afghan than the Ghalzai, namely the Abdālīs[2] of Herat, whom we have just encountered as the hereditary foes of the Ghalzai and allies of the luckless Kai-Khusrau. The Abdālīs, finding themselves in a plight similar to that of their adversaries in Qandahār, revolted against oppression and exploitation by representatives of the central government in Iṣfahān. The shah sent one force after another to suppress the uprising, but they all failed. Although the warlike spirit of the Afghans was a contributory factor, the lack of training and discipline on the part of the troops sent and the incompetence and inadequate fighting experience of their leaders was of greater account, as ample evidence from both Persian and Western sources shows.

In the face of such catastrophic information from the east of the

[1] Lockhart, *The Fall*, p. 92, and appendix VI, especially p. 543.

[2] Boldly speculative attempts are sometimes made to link the Abdālī tribe with the Hephthalites of the 5th and 6th centuries A.D.. Later the Abdālīs acquired the name Durrānī, by which they are still known today, after *Durr al-durrān*, an epithet attached to his name by the above mentioned Aḥmad Shāh. See Lockhart, "Abdālī"; M.E. Yapp, "Durrānī".

country – to which may be added the news of the occupation of Baḥrain and other islands of the Persian Gulf by Sulṭān b. Saif II, the imām of ʿUmān – Princess Maryam Begum, who still had a certain influence over the shah, tried to stimulate him to a more effective course of action. As a result he transferred his court in the winter of 1129–30/1717–18 to Qazvīn, hoping that he might be able to raise more efficient fighting troops in the north-west. During the three years he spent there, however, not a single successful expedition was made against the Abdālīs or the Ghalzai. Opportunities for effective intervention doubtless arose; it was merely a question of choosing the right moment. But in practice Sulṭān Ḥusain and his advisers allowed events in the east to take their course. During the turbulent period associated with the Abdālī uprising, which spread from Herat to Mashhad, events of vital interest to the shah were occurring, as it were, behind the scenes. For the brother and successor of the vakīl, ʿAbd al-ʿAzīz, intended in spite of all the opposition the idea aroused amongst his fellow tribesmen to announce his submission to Sulṭān Ḥusain. The intention proved fatal. In 1129/1717 it prompted Mīr Maḥmūd, a son of his late brother, to murder him and seize power. It seems that nobody at the Persian court was even aware of the opportunity that an arrangement with ʿAbd al-ʿAzīz might have offered. Similarly the Persians made little attempt to exploit the opportunities arising from the internal power struggles of the Abdālī leaders and failed to profit from the conflicts between the Abdālīs and the Ghalzai which soon developed. When Mīr Maḥmūd sent the shah the head of the Abdālī leader Asad-Allāh who had fallen in battle (1132/1719–20), the most obvious interpretation of the gesture – that it was a disarming ploy – never even occurred to him. Choosing instead to see it as a manifestation of loyalty, he appointed Mīr Maḥmūd governor-general with the title Ḥusain Qulī Khān and sent him a royal robe of honour.

The death-blow to the Safavid kingdom did eventually come from the east, but it was impossible to foresee that it would happen as it did. Nor, initially, did the government locate the principal danger in that direction. Given the incursions from Russia mentioned earlier, Peter the Great's interest in Persia should have given cause for alarm, and a Russian attack on the south-west coast of the Caspian Sea was in fact to occur in the summer of 1134/1722. By that time, however, Safavid might was in any case at the last gasp, and the Russians achieved little more than the capture of Darband.[1]

There was unrest amongst the Lezgians, a Sunnī people in the north-west of the country, even though one of their number was Grand Vizier. The Shīrvānīs, also Sunnī, were led by the intolerance of their Persian governors to appeal for aid to the Porte. This may have contributed to Durrī Efendī's being sent to Persia as ambassador, a move by which Istanbul probably hoped to gain a clearer picture of Persian affairs. In 1719 the Lezgians became involved in armed conflict, first with the Shīrvānīs, then with the Georgians under Vakhtang VI of Tiflis. The latter was just preparing to deal a final, crushing blow to the Lezgians when the government intervened to prevent him. Although the Lezgians were saved the future loyalty of the Georgian prince was forfeited. Rebellious Kurds occupied Hamadān and penetrated almost to the outskirts of Iṣfahān. In Khūzistān rivalry for the office of viceroy (vālī) led to unrest among the Musha'sha'. Balūchī tribes made plundering raids on Bam and Kirmān.

Since the government could not possibly contemplate dealing with all these potential threats simultaneously it chose to concentrate on what in its view was the most dangerous: the Arabs on the Persian Gulf and the imām of 'Umān, who in occupying the Gulf islands had of course already encroached on Persian territory. The Grand Vizier (i'timād al-daula) Fatḥ 'Alī Khān Dāghistānī entrusted the task to his nephew, Luṭf 'Alī Khān, the governor of Fārs, who assembled a force of 9,000 men which he intended to transport to 'Umān in Portuguese ships. But the project was not destined to reach fruition.

It seemed as if the government's attention was diverted from Qandahār as a result of this plan. There the young Maḥmūd – he was only eighteen years old when he seized power – was gaining the respect of his fellow tribesmen through his warlike bearing and his cunning. It suited his plans that the death of Aurangzīb in 1118/1707 had provoked a crisis in the Mughal empire, which meant that he was safe from surprise attacks on that flank. At the end of 1719 he gained an unqualified success when he advanced on Kirmān with 11,000 men. The startled governor took flight and the Ghalzai were able to occupy the city without difficulty. Soon, however, they were forced to march back to Qandahār because Maḥmūd's position there was threatened.

[1] Lockhart, *The Fall*, pp. 176–89.

The sudden attack on Kirmān must have caused Fatḥ 'Alī Khān to change his mind. At all events he endeavoured to divert the government's interest from the Persian Gulf and to concentrate it instead on Qandahār. He urged that all the armed forces should be marched there, the shah himself and the government taking part in the campaign in order to lend the desired weight to the operation for the benefit of external observers. The assembled court did in fact set off for the east at the end of 1132/beginning of October 1720, but it advanced no further than Tehran.

The grand vizier's standing at court was problematical, partly as he was a Lezgian and not a Persian proper, but above all because of his Sunnī beliefs which were considered unthinkable by those dignitaries still capable of reasoning in the old Safavid-Shī'ī categories. Moreover, he could not rely on the shah, apathetic, irresolute and inconsistent as he was. In these circumstances every member of the government and court strove to realise his own particular aims – or at least each pressure group did – and to thwart the opposing plans of others. In this way the proposed Qandahār campaign had met with violent opposition. The chief opponents of the grand vizier were the *mullā-bāshī*, Muḥammad Ḥusain, and the royal physician (*ḥakīm-bāshī*), Raḥīm Khān, in this case because of the increased power and prestige a successful campaign might bring him. With the help of a forged letter to a Kurdish tribal chief they made accusations of high treason against him to the shah. Fatḥ 'Alī Khān was alleged to be part of a Sunnī conspiracy to depose the monarch and assume power himself. Without investigating the charge, Sulṭān Ḥusain relieved him of his office and had him blinded and imprisoned. Luṭf 'Alī Khān was likewise accused of complicity in the plot, enticed from Shīrāz to Iṣfahān and there thrown into prison.

Any continuation of the march to Qandahār was now out of the question. The court turned back to Iṣfahān, where it arrived at the end of April 1721. Those of Luṭf 'Alī Khān's troops who had not already dispersed, now the only remaining operational force of the shah, were dispatched under a different command against the Afghans. As a result of various conflicts on the way, however, they were almost totally wiped out long before their destination was reached. Although by no means all authors agree in their judgment of Fatḥ 'Alī Khān Dāghistāni,[1] it is certain that in eliminating him and his nephew the shah had removed

[1] For the varying views, see *ibid.*, p. 106; Muḥammad Hāshim, *Rustam al-tavārīkh*, ed. M. Mushīrī (Tehran, 1348), p. 91 and n. 1.

the two strongest pillars of the now shaky edifice of his power. The accounts of the Turkish ambassador Durrī Efendī, who left Persia at this time, confirm precisely what his Russian counterpart Volynsky had reported to the Tsar two years earlier, namely that Safavid rule was on the point of collapse because of a lack of talented personalities in the government.

As a result of the fall of their tribesman Fatḥ ʿAlī Khān, unrest among the Lezgians increased. Together with fellow-Sunnīs from Shīrvān and other Transcaucasian areas they besieged and conquered the capital of Shīrvān, Shamākhī, taking terrible revenge for earlier Shīʿī oppression and placing themselves and the city under the sovereignty of the Sultan of Turkey. In the meantime the government had also lost its influence in the south and south-west of Iran, and chaos had supervened.

The Safavid empire was in flames, but it still enjoyed a respite which might have saved it from utter ruin – a respite, however, of which no advantage was taken. Immediately after his return from Tehran, Sulṭān Ḥusain repaired to his favourite castle of Faraḥābād on the other side of the Zāyandarūd and occupied himself with its further development, seemingly oblivious of the reasons for the campaign that he had intended to pursue only shortly before. Only when news arrived that Maḥmūd was again about to enter Kirmān did the government in Iṣfahān begin to appreciate the seriousness of the situation.

The Ghalzai had indeed arrived outside the city on 22 October 1721, but after suffering heavy casualties during an unsuccessful attack on the citadel Maḥmūd decided to forgo a renewed attempt, probably because of the risk of further losses, and marched on. A similar situation occurred in Yazd, where after an unsuccessful blockade Maḥmūd raised the siege in exchange for the payment of a high tribute and continued his march in the direction of Iṣfahān. Authorities there must by this time have realised that Maḥmūd was out to clinch matters, if reports are true that en route he was twice interrupted by messengers of the shah who were to offer financial inducements to halt his advance. Maḥmūd rejected such offers, rightly inferring that Sulṭān Ḥusain's preparations for defence could not be very strong.

In Sagzī, twenty-five miles east of Iṣfahān, he received intelligence of a Persian force advancing against him. He then continued his march only as far as the village of Muḥammadābād where he divided his troops, positioning them on three hills where they had an uninterrupted view over a plain stretching some 4,000 yards or more to the next village, Gulnābād. The Ghalzai forces were not all that strong: probably 10,000 men, to which must be added the support troops of the Hazāras and Balūchīs. Although details of the numerical strength of the two sides vary considerably in the sources, it is in all unlikely that Maḥmūd had more than 18,000 combatants at his disposal, and allowance must be made for the losses he had so far incurred: the abortive assault on the citadel of Kirmān alone had cost him 1,500 men.[1]

On 7 March 1722 the Persian forces arrived on the battlefield. Their army of 42,000 men was superior, numerically and in various other respects, to that of the Afghans. Although it contained a fairly large proportion of hastily assembled volunteers who were inadequately trained and armed, there were also experienced fighting troops such as the corps of royal squires (qullar), which included a four-hundred-strong guards unit under the command of the experienced Georgian general Rustam Khān; a 12,000 strong corps of Arab cavalry commanded by the vālī of ʿArabistān, who is said to have been called Sayyid ʿAbd-Allāh; two Lorian contingents of mounted tribal warriors, one under the command of ʿAlī Mardān Khān Failī, the other under ʿAlī Riżā Khān from Kūhgīlūya; and a detachment of artillery with twenty-four guns commanded by a Persian with the assistance of an experienced French master-gunner.

When battle commenced the following afternoon, the Persians gained initial successes that very nearly reduced Maḥmūd to a state of panic. It soon became apparent, however, that there was a total lack of coordination on the Persian side. There was no unified supreme command, responsibility being shared by two men who were, what is more, sworn enemies. They were the new Grand Vizier (iʿtimād al-daula) Muḥammad Qulī Khān Shāmlū and the vālī of ʿArabistān. The latter owed his position to the special favour of the shah whilst the Grand Vizier, as a former general of the guards (qūrchī-bāshī), was expected to possess military ability – a totally unwarranted assumption. The Persians' main asset, their heavy artillery, was scarcely of any account because the Afghans succeeded in eliminating it early in the battle. Whereas the absence of a clear hierarchy of command proved

[1] For a survey of the different figures for the strength of the two sides found in the sources, see Lockhart, *The Fall*, p. 136.

fatal to the Persians, the superior coordination of their own forces enabled the Afghans to make the best of a bad job even in awkward situations. By the end of the day the Persian forces had collapsed and were retreating in undisciplined fashion into Iṣfahān. Their losses are estimated at 5,000 men, whereas the Afghans are said to have lost only a tenth of that number. Only fear of an ambush prevented the Afghans from pursuing the defeated Persians into the city.

It seems that Maḥmūd did not immediately realise the full extent of the Persian defeat and the demoralisation it entailed. The fact that he had neglected to take the citadels of both Kirmān and Yazd during the course of his advance may well suggest that a military engagement with the shah was his major aim, but it does not necessarily imply that he had in mind the destruction of Safavid rule from the very outset of his campaign. At any rate, the victory does not appear to have deprived him of the capacity for making a realistic assessment of the possibilities open to him. It is difficult otherwise to explain why he let three days go by before resuming his march on Iṣfahān, now only nineteen miles away. On reaching the area south of the Zāyandarūd, he came upon Sulṭān Ḥusain's favourite castle of Faraḥābād. In spite of the existence of defence works, he was able to take it without a fight and set up his headquarters there. The Armenian suburb Julfā was then plundered and a tribute ruthlessly exacted from the inhabitants, to whom – rather than to Persian soldiers – it owed its defence. These actions suggest that the Afghan troops were still very much aware of the fact that they might suddenly have to retreat. Maḥmūd no doubt saw clearly that the victory of Gulnābād had been won to a large extent thanks to a combination of favourable circumstances; nor is he likely to have forgotten that at one moment during the battle he had been close to accepting defeat and retreating. Finally, he must have realised that in spite of the defeat the shah's military resources were as yet by no means exhausted.

One thing, for the moment at least, that the Ghalzai leader could not be expected to know was the absurd state of affairs that the shah, whenever a decision was required of him, was more or less guaranteed to choose the alternative least favourable or even fatal to his cause. Despite repeated disasters, he remained stubbornly faithful to those counsellors whose advice had constantly proved detrimental, especially the mullā-bāshī, Mīr Muḥammad Ḥusain, grandson and successor of the famous theologian Muḥammad Bāqir Majlisī, and the royal physician, Raḥīm Khān. Each of these men had, as we have seen, acted as evil genius to the ruler at an earlier stage. They were now joined by the vālī of 'Arabistān, for whom the shah had a particularly high regard despite his failure in the battle of Gulnābād. He persisted in his opinion when rumours too loud to ignore indicated that the governor was conspiring with the enemy and even when incontrovertible evidence of the fact came to light.

First in a whole series of fatal mistakes made by the shah was his decision to remain in Iṣfahān instead of mobilising fresh troops in other parts of the country to combat the Afghans. His peace proposal, which probably reached the Afghans as they were advancing on the capital, may more than anything else have given the game away and confirmed them in their intentions. On two occasions he then rejected Maḥmūd's offers of negotiation, one at the beginning of April, the other at the beginning of August 1722. He imposed a general ban on leaving the city and failed to evacuate the civilian population when it would still have been feasible. He successively dismissed the two royal princes Maḥmūd Mīrzā and Ṣafī Mīrzā from the position of crown prince and from their military functions, merely because of acts of intervention on their part of which his advisers disapproved.[1] In addition, he dispatched to Kāshān and Qazvīn the unreliable Prince Ṭahmāsp, who, instead of raising a relief force and returning with it to the sorely pressed capital as he had been commanded, engaged in dissolute pleasures. Finally, he even dismissed Aḥmad Āghā, the capable general of the royal squires (qullar-āqāsī), because in the heat of the moment his troops had taken revenge on some of the vālī's Arab cavalrymen who had left them in the lurch during a sortie.

At the beginning of April Maḥmūd succeeded in capturing a bridge in the 'Abbāsābād quarter and establishing a bridgehead. A little later he was able to link up with contingents based in the east and north, thus making it impossible to either leave or enter the city without risk. Given its size – Kaempfer set its circumference at 57 miles[2] – the Afghan troops were unable to encircle the city completely, but Maḥmūd did establish powerful strong points, between which units of cavalry constantly patrolled.

In the circumstances, living conditions in the city became increasingly difficult. Supplies of food ceased, and to prevent their being

[1] *Ibid.*, p. 147, for a more discriminating account than that given earlier by Lockhart in his *Nadir Shah*, p. 8.

[2] Quoted in Lockhart, *The Fall*, p. 477.

resumed in future Maḥmūd ordered all crops in the area to be destroyed. The shah made every effort to obtain relief. The most important fighting force, the Georgians, who could probably have dealt with the Afghans on their own, had to be ruled out when Vakhtang VI refused to come to the shah's aid because he had not yet forgotten the latter's intervention on behalf of the Lezgians. Other contingents such as the Bakhtiyār under Qāsim Khān, the Lurs of 'Alī Mardān Khān or the 10,000 strong force advancing under the command of Malik Maḥmūd Sīstānī, the governor of Tūn and Ṭabas, were either repulsed by the Afghans or ultimately had second thoughts, in part convinced by Maḥmūd of the pointlessness of their enterprise.

From mid-June onwards there was famine in Iṣfahān. All attempts to depose the shah or to persuade him to abdicate were of no avail. At the end of August, when the famine was at its height and more and more people were dying of starvation and disease, despair spread throughout the city. Cannibalism was rife, the dead could no longer be buried and thousands lost their lives in hopeless attempts to escape. In the end the coffers of both government and crown were empty and troops could only be paid out of funds loaned to the shah against the security of the crown jewels by the Dutch and, to a lesser extent, the British East India Companies.

By the beginning of October even the shah was convinced that further resistance was pointless, and he capitulated to Maḥmūd. The latter was not, however, prepared to receive him before 23 October 1722. The meeting took place in the morning of that day in the castle of Faraḥābād. The shah announced his abdication and the transfer of power to Maḥmūd, as a gesture of confirmation taking from his head the bejewelled tuft of heron's feathers (*jīqa*), the symbol of monarchy, and affixing it to Maḥmūd's turban with his own hands. Two days later Maḥmūd entered Iṣfahān in solemn triumph. Sulṭān Ḥusain rode at his left hand and, on arrival in the audience chamber of the royal palace, was obliged to acknowledge Maḥmūd as his successor once more, this time before the assembled military dignitaries, the viziers and the nobles of the realm.

THE LAST SAFAVIDS

Ghalzai supremacy was to represent only a brief interlude in the history of Persia, coming to an end as early as 1730 with the fall of Ashraf,

Maḥmūd's cousin and successor. Apart from the liquidation of the already tottering Safavid dynasty, it was scarcely of any significance. The Afghans were able neither to counteract Russian and Turkish incursions into Iranian territory nor to eradicate hotbeds of unrest in various parts of the country, whether these emerged before or after the fall of the Safavid empire. Least of all did they manage to restore the unity of Persia. They even proved incapable of reviving life in the sorely tried capital in which they now resided.[1]

The seventy-five years leading up to the end of the 12th/18th century have been not inaccurately described by Perry as a morass of anarchy[2] in which three periods, those of the Afshārs, the Zands and the early Qājārs, stand out like islands. During each a strong and relatively sensible government was headed by a figure of significance: Nādir Shāh, Karīm Khān Zand and Āghā Muḥammad respectively. The extent to which the traditions of the Safavids were taken over, preserved, adapted, diminished or enlarged by these rulers before they passed to the Qājārs and were finally handed down, via the 19th century, to the modern age, is a problem for the cultural historian. Within the narrower framework of Safavid history, our task is to investigate attempts to continue or resurrect the Safavid empire that were made either by members of the dynasty or with their assistance.

When the central government in Iṣfahān came to an end the Safavids were by no means totally eliminated. On the contrary, individual representatives of the dynasty were still to play a certain part in the political life of the country. Strictly speaking, there were Safavid puppet rulers and periods of partial Safavid rule until as late as 1187/1773, the year in which Ismā'īl III, last of the Safavid *rois fainéants*, died; and the efforts of genuine Safavid princes or impostors to gain power in various parts of Persia were of considerable significance.

No share in subsequent historical developments was granted to Sulṭān Ḥusain, nor is it likely that he sought any. During his lifetime, Maḥmūd ensured that he was well treated although, like all Safavid princes resident in Iṣfahān, he was imprisoned. He remained in prison

[1] The Persian forces are said to have lost 20,000 men in the course of the siege, and civilian losses are put at 80,000. If the population was really 650,000 at the end of the Safavid period, an enormous migration must have occurred as a result of the siege and the capture of the city by the Afghans. A census of 1882 lists only 73,654 inhabitants, and an estimate made by Schindler in 1893 gives 82,000. Even the rise in population in the last few decades has not yet caught up with the Safavid figure: see Lambton, "Iṣfahān", *EI*[2]; Lockhart, *The Fall*, pp. 169, 476ff.

[2] Perry, "The last Ṣafavids", p. 59.

until 1139/1726, when he was beheaded on the orders of Ashraf as a result of an insulting letter the latter had received from the Ottoman general Aḥmed Pasha, then operating in Persia. He called Ashraf a usurper and informed him that he considered it his duty to reinstate the legitimate ruler of Iran whom the Afghans had deposed. Only a year before, probably in a fit of persecution mania, Maḥmūd Shāh had killed the majority of the princes imprisoned with Sulṭān Ḥusain, some of them with his own hands.[1]

For wide sections of the population in Iran the collapse of the Safavid empire that occurred when Sulṭān Ḥusain relinquished the throne and power was assumed by Maḥmūd was a catastrophe greater than anything they could possibly have imagined. The result was an almost universal willingness to accept without question any sign of the continued existence of the dynasty or its possible revival – an ideal situation for pretenders! One source[2] lists eighteen of them in the Afghan period alone, and no less than twelve more are mentioned by chroniclers of the reigns of Nādir Shāh and his immediate successors. A number of these claimants found support in widely differing areas of the country and managed to occupy or conquer cities and strongholds. Not infrequently they were able to defeat strong regular troops, including even Ottoman invasion forces. Sooner or later, however, they failed because their supporters proved inadequate in numbers or lacked perseverance when really put to the test.

The claims of these pretenders to be Safavid princes – no fewer than three Ṣafī Mīrzās and three Ismā'īl Mīrzās emerged – were at best dubious and as a rule totally without foundation. Yet genuine princes of the fallen dynasty did exist, as well as others whose claims, whilst doubtful, could not simply be rejected out of hand. As we have already seen, Ṭahmāsp Mīrzā (b. 1704), appointed crown prince by Sulṭān Ḥusain, succeeded in breaking through the Afghan lines during the siege of Iṣfahān and managed to reach Qazvīn. There, as early as 30 Muḥarram 1135/10 November 1722, he had himself proclaimed shah, had the style of Shah Ṭahmāsp II included in official prayers and on the coinage, and issued decrees (*arqām*) in all parts of the country, announcing his accession to the throne. Although his was only a nominal

[1] Lockhart, *The Fall*, table following p. 472, names fifteen, although sometimes the numbers given are considerably higher.

[2] Muḥammad 'Alī Ḥazīn Jīlānī, cited in Perry, "The last Ṣafavids", p. 60.

rule, he reigned in fact for a good ten years.[1] In addition to Ṭahmāsp, another prince, Mīrzā Sayyid Aḥmad, son of Shah Sulaimān's eldest daughter,[2] had managed to escape. In 1139/1726 he rose to the level of ruler in Kirmān and proved to be a serious opponent in combats with the forces of both Ṭahmāsp II and the Afghans. He did indeed constitute a greater threat to the Afghans than Ṭahmāsp, and accordingly received more attention from them. Eventually he was defeated and brought as a prisoner to the Afghan chieftain, who had him executed in 1140/1728.

In foreign affairs, the greatest threat to Persia after the abdication of Sulṭān Ḥusain came from Russian and Ottoman designs on territory in the Caspian provinces and the north-west of the country respectively. Russian troops were already present in Darband and other places on the shores of the Caspian Sea. The Ottomans, for their part, were not slow to act. Sending a declaration of war in 1135/1723, they marched troops into Georgia and – via Kirmānshāh and Hamadān – into Persia itself. The policy of Ṭahmāsp II, who had been forced to withdraw from Qazvīn to Tabrīz by the Afghans, from there to Ardabīl by the Turks and ultimately via Ray to Māzandarān, again by the Turks, was dictated by the notion that his position at home would be consolidated if only the Russians and Ottomans could be induced to recognise him as the legitimate ruler of Persia. With this in mind he had sent negotiators to Istanbul and St Petersburg. As a result the Porte changed its view in his favour, but in a treaty for the division of western Persia, concluded by the Sultan and the Tsar for 2 Shawwāl 1136/24 June 1724, the two powers merely expressed a desire to help the shah to achieve "his legitimate rights". Moreover, he was to restrict himself to the territory in the west of the country, defined by the places Ardabīl, Sulṭāniyya and Qazvīn.

Ṭahmāsp II's first *vakīl al-daula* was Fatḥ 'Alī Khān Qājār. He was followed by Nadr Qulī Beg Afshār, a particularly capable military commander who successfully fought the Afghans and the Turks on his behalf and subjugated Āzarbāījān, Georgia and most of Armenia. In other respects, too, he did everything to gain the shah's favour. In 1138/1726 he had conferred upon him the title Ṭahmāsp Qulī ("servant of Ṭahmāsp") and by driving out the Afghan Ashraf he even made it

[1] For official documents he issued, see Fragner, "Ardabīl zwischen Sultan und Schah".

[2] Probably identical with the prince of the same name who is listed as a grandson of the princess in Lockhart's table referred to in p. 326, n. 1, above.

possible for the shah to return to Iṣfahān. It became increasingly clear, however, that the weak and unreliable shah was incapable of being anything more than a puppet in the general's hands, and when he suffered a heavy defeat in a battle with the Turks the latter's patience came to an end. He exposed the shah publicly as a drunkard and dethroned him.

He clearly still thought it advisable, however, to take account of popular sympathy for the Safavids, otherwise he would scarcely have nominated a new Safavid shah, the deposed monarch's eight-month-old son, who as 'Abbās III was puppet king from 1144/1732 to 1148/1736. The general then deposed him as well and mounted the throne himself under the name Nādir Shāh. Ṭahmāsp II and 'Abbās III were imprisoned and executed in 1740 at Sabzavār together with Ismā'īl, another son of Ṭahmāsp.

Although it is true that the Afshār tribe to which he belonged was one of the Qizilbāsh tribes which had contributed in large measure to the rise of the Safavids,[1] Nādir Shāh's general outlook by no means accorded with the Safavid conception of the state. Two things demonstrate this clearly: his religious policy, which involved a turning away from the Twelver Shī'a, and his decision to transfer the capital to Mashhad. Although this city lay in the middle of his Khurasanian homeland, the main reason for the transfer was more probably its central position within the extensive territory that Nādir Shāh thought of as his empire, as is shown by his campaigns in Central Asia, Afghanistan and India. His conception was, therefore, an imperial one that had nothing in common with the Safavids' idea of their realm, which was confined solely to Iranian lands. At any rate, Nādir's outlook could be compared to that of Tīmūr. It might be thought that the successes he enjoyed in realising this conception would have caused the glory of the Safavids to fade somewhat in the eyes of the Persian people. But the situation soon changed. When, after the murder of Nādir, the princes of his family were systematically eliminated, one of his grandsons, Shāh Rukh by name (b. 1734), was spared. Now his mother was a daughter of Sulṭān Ḥusain, and it was clearly the intention that a legitimate prince of Safavid descent should be available as puppet ruler in case renewed enthusiasm for the dynasty were to arise. At the time nobody could have foreseen that Shāh Rukh would rule over the

[1] F. Sümer, "Avşarlar'a dâir"; *idem, Safevî devletinin kuruluşu*, pp. 98–100, 145ff., 188–92.

inheritance of Nādir Shāh, or what still remained of it, from 1161/1748 to 1210/1796, albeit with some interruptions.

In the conflicts that followed upon the fall of Nādir Shāh, Mīr Sayyid Muḥammad, curator of sacred relics (*mutavallī*) in Mashhad, was also involved. Like the above mentioned Mīrzā Sayyid Aḥmad, he was a son of Shah Sulaimān's eldest daughter and was held in high regard. When, as the result of a mutiny, Shāh Rukh was deposed and blinded, he was the rebels' choice as a successor. In 1163/1750 (or shortly before)[1] he was elevated as shah in Mashhad with the style Sulaimān II. A move to Iṣfahān could not remotely be contemplated because quite different forces had in the meantime assumed effective control there. As it was, he fell victim to a conspiracy only a few weeks after his elevation to the throne, and Shāh Rukh, despite his blindness, returned to power in his place.

The concept of divine right, associated with the person of the shah in the thinking of the Safavids, cannot be ruled out as a significant factor in the stubborn survival of the dynasty. Developments in Iṣfahān and in central Persia generally at any rate suggest such an interpretation. Here, the downfall of Nādir Shāh left behind a vacuum into which streamed nomadic tribes from the Zagros mountains, e.g. Lurs, Bakhtiyārs, Kurds and also the Zands. Initially, the dominant figure in Iṣfahān was the Bakhtiyār leader ʿAlī Mardān Khān. He too seems to have regarded a Safavid figurehead as indispensable and found one in the person of the seventeen-year-old Prince Abū Turāb, the son of a marriage between Sayyid Murtażā and a daughter of Shah Sulṭān Ḥusain. He was crowned in 1163/1750, receiving the name Ismāʿīl III.[2] From then on ʿAlī Mardān himself bore the title of vakīl al-daula. It appears that the prince was not happy with the rôle assigned to him, but he had no other option.

In the battle of Chahār Maḥāll (spring 1165/1752), fought between the Bakhtiyār leader and Karīm Khān Zand, Ismāʿīl went over to the side of the Kurds with a section of the troops when he realised that his vakīl would be defeated. In subsequent conflicts between Karīm and

[1] According to Lockhart, *The Fall*, appendix I, he reigned from Dec. 1749 to Jan. 1750. Perry, "The last Ṣafavids", pp. 65ff., says that he was crowned in Jan. 1750 and deposed and blinded in the following month.

[2] Lockhart, *The Fall*, appendix I, says that Ismāʿīl III "ruled nominally in 1750 and again between 1752 and 1756". Perry also speaks of an "unsuccessful pretender Sulṭān Ḥusain II". See, in addition to the sources he mentions, Mīrzā Mahdī Khān Astarābādī, trans. T.H. Gadebusch, *Geschichte des Nadir Schah* (Greifswald, 1773), especially p. 423 (the only edition available to me).

Muḥammad Ḥasan Khān Qājār, he similarly chose to side with the stronger party, only to discover that the Qājār was eventually worsted. Handed over to Karīm Khān, he was greeted with the words *shāh-i namak ba-ḥarām* ("ungrateful Shah") and interned in the fortress of Ābāda, half way between Shīrāz and Iṣfahān. Nevertheless, Karīm was at first also content to be called vakīl al-daula. When in 1765 he opted for Shīrāz as capital city, he then changed his title to *vakīl al-ra'āyā* and occasionally *vakīl al-khalāyiq*, meaning roughly "Vice-regent of the people" and "Vice-regent of mankind" respectively. He would refuse to be addressed as "Shah", maintaining that the true shah was in Ābāda and that he was merely his deputy (*kadkhudā*). When Ismā'īl III passed away in 1187/1773, Karīm Khān, who outlived him by eight years, neither installed a new phantom ruler nor made himself shah.

The concept of the Safavid monarchy now ceased to exist. Although it had outlasted the fall of the Safavid empire by half a century, it had not been sufficiently strong to bring about a genuine restoration. The concept of monarchy as such was preserved in Iran. In the early 13th/late 18th century it was given a new lease of life by the Qājārs, who were successfully to unite the fragmented country within the territorial boundaries of the Safavid empire, albeit without Safavid participation.

One of the most important reasons for the fall of the Safavids was their failure to groom successive members of the dynasty for the task of ruling. Of all people, it was Shah 'Abbās I who abolished the original practice of assigning to the crown princes a large province in order to introduce them to the business of government, even if, until they attained their majority, they did nothing more than observe the governor at work and remained under the supervision of a tutor (*lālā*). 'Abbās I was also responsible for the fatal policy of confining the princes to the harem, thus not only preventing them from learning the practice of government, but also barring them from all contact with the outside world, making it impossible for them to associate with the aristocracy of the realm and giving them no opportunity to come to terms with the conditions of life in general.

Naturally there were other reasons for the fall of the dynasty. Amongst the most significant may be cited the increasing inefficiency of central authority within a system organised on centralist lines; the concomitant strengthening of local authorities such as respected tribal leaders; the ruin of the economy, which has been covered in detail elsewhere in this volume, and especially the disintegration of the armed forces which ultimately caused the shah to succumb even to an enemy as insignificant as the Afghans. The disintegration of the religious foundations on which the empire had been built also had fatal consequences. And finally, within the ruling classes there was a marked decrease in the supply of able personalities.

Depressing though conditions in the country may have been at the time of the fall of the Safavids, they cannot be allowed to overshadow the achievements of the dynasty, which were in many respects to prove essential factors in the development of Persia in modern times. These include the maintenance of Persian as the official language and of the present-day boundaries of the country, adherence to the Twelver Shīʿa, the monarchical system, the planning and architectural features of the urban centres, the centralised administration of the state, the alliance of the Shīʿī ʿulamā with the merchants of the bazaars, and the symbiosis of the Persian-speaking population with important non-Persian, especially Turkish-speaking, minorities.

A few of the most important factors – the peculiar antagonism between Persians and Turks, religious developments in so far as they were of political significance, and alterations in the monarchical system – will be considered in the following summary.

THE SAFAVID STATE

From the 8th/14th to the 10th/16th century, three waves of returning Turkish emigrants gravitated from eastern Anatolia and northern Syria towards the highlands of Iran. Each of them belonged to a particular tribal confederation and the leaders of each devoted all their energies to the establishment of political and territorial sovereignty. All three confederations succeeded in this, but only the third of them, the Safavids, had lasting success. The first of these Türkmen confederations, the Qarā Quyūnlū, began their endeavours in the 8th/14th century, establishing a principality the capital of which eventually became the Persian metropolis Tabrīz. In 872/1467, when at the height of their power, they were defeated in armed conflict by the rival Āq Quyūnlū, who after their victory also transferred their capital to Tabrīz. In 907/1501 the city then became the capital of the third confederation of Türkmens, the Safavids, after they had in turn overcome the Āq Quyūnlū. Like their two predecessors, the Safavids extended their domain to cover the whole of present-day Iran, an intervention in the fortunes of the country which proved of great significance for the whole development of Persia in the modern era.

How is one to explain these movements of population and the centuries-long interest of Turkish tribes in Iran, a country whose people were neither Turks nor Turkish speakers? True, the ancestors of the tribesmen in question had already been in Iran – during the course of the Oghuz migrations, mass movements of Turks into the Near East and Asia Minor – and come into contact with Iranian culture, some of them for the second time, since they had been exposed to the cultural influence of Iran in Central Asia even before their migration to the west. The state and court chancelleries of the confederations, as well as their chroniclers, used the Persian language, which in itself points to a certain degree of Iranicisation. This influence was, however, confined to a minute ruling class whose admiration for, and love of, Iran and its culture naturally cannot in themselves have triggered off migrations of whole tribes nor determined the particular direction of their movement. More important was the fact that, as a rule, the Türkmens in question had no access to the Ottoman army, any more than their leaders had to the Ottoman military aristocracy, which offered few real openings to them either before or after the battle of Ankara: The Qarā Quyūnlū leader Qarā Yūsuf was not even integrated into the Ottoman forces when he sought refuge with the Ottomans in flight from their mutual enemy Tīmūr. At this time Ottoman power did not extend as far as eastern Anatolia, let alone to Āzarbāījān or the Iranian highlands. In the power vacuum left behind after the death of Tīmūr and the fall of his empire these areas offered good opportunities for politically motivated tribal leaders interested in establishing independent domains. To the broad masses of the nomads the prospects of rich spoils of war from the civilised country of Iran and extensive grazing grounds for their herds were unfailing attractions. Together with the restlessness and spirit of enterprise typical of nomadic life, they probably constituted sufficient motive for the eastward thrusts of Türkmen tribes and their federations, at any rate for the first two waves, those of the Qarā Quyūnlū and the Āq Quyūnlū.

A quite different motive, however, underlay the third wave, that occurring under the Safavids. They were attracted by a ṣūfī order, the Ardabīl Ṣafaviyya and by a religious concept which, at the end of the 9th/15th century or perhaps somewhat earlier, had developed from vague beginnings in popular piety into a politico-religious ideology. This ideology aroused in its adherents enthusiasm, fanaticism and ultimately unconditional commitment – precisely those attitudes of mind associated with militant believers in Islam. The order's centre in Ardabīl had always attracted men of piety from near and far, including Türkmen tribesmen, long before the aspirations of its masters became unmistakeably political. But in the second half of the 9th/15th century the hitherto customary pilgrimages gave way to something quite different and the donations arriving in Ardabīl at that time, far from being mere oblations as before, had probably been given with other purposes in mind.

What had changed? With the travels of Shaikh Junaid in Anatolia and Syria an intensive phase of Safavid propaganda had begun, and his marriage with the Bayïndïr princess, a sister of Uzun Ḥasan, had both increased his prestige and made him, to a certain extent, an acceptable ally of the Türkmens. The importance of these two facts for subsequent developments can scarcely be overestimated. On the one hand the order was intensifying contacts with the outside world; on the other it was effacing the dividing line between the two key national groupings in the region. As the descendants of a line of Gīlānī landowners, the Ardabīl shaikhs were representatives of Persian agricultural life, and not Türkmens or nomads. Distinctions between nations of the kind familiar to us from later European nationalism were foreign to Islam and are scarcely applicable in this case. Yet the Persians and Turks incontestably sensed that they were essentially different, and this feeling frequently finds explicit expression in historical sources. Intermarriage between the two, in so far as it occurred at all, was not common. Junaid's marriage did not, however, remain the only example of a Tājīk-Türkmen union, and these initial indications of a symbiosis might perhaps help to explain just why Turkish nomads should have chosen as their leader the Persian-born master of a religious order.[1] Be that as it may, the activities of Junaid to which we have referred were significant factors in the formation of the third great Türkmen federation.

A brief look at the early history of the Safavid order should help to clarify these developments. The motives behind the formation of the

[1] A question last raised by S.H. Naṣr, in the Strasbourg colloquium *Le Shī'isme imâmite* (Paris, 1970), p. 243.

fraternity were certainly religious in nature, but it also played a considerable rôle in economic and political life, even in the time of Shaikh Ṣafī, who gave the family its name. Landed property, revenues from religious foundations, donations and other sources of income brought him economic influence, and in politics he was able to establish wide-ranging contacts, even with one so eminent as the Mongol Īl-Khān. His descendants, amongst whom the position of master of the order was usually handed down from father to son, likewise went on to achieve distinction in public life. Without going into further detail, it can now be seen that Junaid's intervention in politics did not represent a radically new departure. What was new was the way he, and afterwards his son and successor Shaikh Ḥaidar, set about militarising the order. The organisational measures and reforms they carried out must have been of lasting effect, for they remained in force until Ismā'īl came to public prominence decades later, in Muḥarram 905/August 1499, this despite the fact that their two initiators, and after them Sulṭān 'Alī, lost their lives on the battlefield – three masters of the order in the space of thirty-four years.

Recent research has thrown more light on these matters even if some questions still remain unanswered. We now have at least some notion of how the alliance between Ardabīl and its outposts worked, especially those in Anatolia and Syria that provided the main body of the forces which supported the Safavid seizure of power. Local cells existed under a headman, called a khalīfa. In individual cases, though not as a general rule, there was a supervisor, called a *pīra*, who was responsible for their coordination. At the head of the organisation was the khalīfat al-khulafā, who was also deputy of the master of the order (murshid-i kāmil). It has not yet been possible to ascertain exactly when this organisation was established, but it is known that there was a khalīfat al-khulafā as early as 1499, i.e. before Ismā'īl's accession to the throne. Once the decision to seize power had been taken, the organisation demonstrated its efficiency.

Assertions in some sources that the young Ismā'īl personally made this decision cannot be accepted at face value. Although he became master of the order five years earlier in place of his brother Sulṭān 'Alī, he was still merely twelve years old at the time of the march out of Gīlān. Even if one assumes that he was abnormally gifted, it is still inconceivable that a boy of that age could have carried out the complex political and military planning and preparation that must have preceded the uprising.

Who, if not Ismā'īl, could have taken the momentous decision and begun to put the operation into effect? Some time ago, Soviet historians referred, if only in vague terms, to the existence of Türkmen confidential agents as advisers of Ismā'īl.[1] More precise information has since come to light. They were in fact a group of leading Türkmen tribesmen, the *ahl-i ikhtiṣāṣ* ("those endowed with a specific responsibility" or "those legally empowered to act"), a sort of "central committee" as they were recently described in modern terminology.[2] These were the people who sustained Ismā'īl after the death of his brother, who made it possible for him to escape to Gīlān and kept him in hiding there, who took care of his education and ultimately persuaded him to march against the Āq Quyūnlū. In the light of this obviously convincing interpretation, the elaborate myth of Ismā'īl the child prodigy becomes superfluous. Even so, the events associated with his public appearances remain extraordinary enough and messianic elements, evident even at the outset of his career, are now no longer mere surmise but have actually been proved to exist.[3]

The hundred and fifty years of the Safavid order that culminated in the accession to the throne of Shah Ismā'īl not only have their place in the religious history of Islam but are from the outset of political significance. Although there had always been a certain influx of Türkmens into the order, it was not until the time of Shaikh Junaid that the strong links with Türkmen tribesmen were forged, that made for an increasingly tight-knit organisation. His years of propaganda in Anatolia, in Syria and, of course, also in Āzarbāījān ultimately unleashed the third wave of Turkish emigrants returning to the Iranian uplands and created the conditions necessary for the formation of the third Türkmen federation, which may be called the "Safavid" or perhaps, more accurately, the Qizilbāsh federation. This migration persisted, as has recently emerged,[4] right up to the death of Shah 'Abbās I, a time when the Qizilbash had decades previously forfeited their privileged rôle.

Closely linked to these occurrences is a religious phenomenon the origins and earliest development of which, despite new information, have still not been adequately investigated. This is the decisive trans-

[1] Guseĭnov and Sumbatzade, *Istoriya Azerbaĭdzhana* I, 224ff. I.P. Petrushevsky, *Islam v Irane* (Leningrad, 1966), pp. 370f.

[2] Savory, "Some Reflections".

[3] Glassen, "Schah Ismā'īl, ein Mahdī".

[4] Sümer, *Safevî devletinin kuruluşu*, p. 213.

formation due to the influence of the Shīʿa. The fact that present-day Persian adherence to the Shīʿa derives from the early Safavids, especially Shah Ismāʿīl I, might lead one in retrospect to conclude that a change of faith took place according to the principle *cuius regio eius religio*. But appearances are deceptive. In reality the transition was a lengthy and highly complex process, connected with the spread of certain Shīʿī ideas via Folk Islam or Islamic popular piety – a process which cannot be discussed in detail here.

On his accession to the throne, Ismāʿīl did in fact proclaim Shiʿism the official religion, or state religion, as it might be called. As he extended his sphere of influence, he then proceeded to implement it throughout Persia with the aim, so it is claimed, of distinguishing Persia from the Ottoman empire.[1] This may not, however, have been his sole intention or at all premeditated, but merely a more or less unconscious motive. What he proclaimed was ostensibly the Twelver Shīʿa, a creed which certainly cannot be reconciled with his own personal religious views. These we know from what is a quite unimpeachable source of personal testimony, his own poems. In them he claims to be the reincarnation of ʿAlī, an emanation of God and indeed God himself. Such notions have no place in the Shīʿa, indeed they are sheer heresy from an orthodox Shīʿī point of view, a fact which cannot be denied by arguing that they are perhaps merely the literary extravagances of a mystically impassioned youth, along the lines of such ṣūfī conceptions as *unio mystica*, union with God (*tauḥīd*). In fact they were by no means merely obsessive mystical speculations but articles of faith which were widely held by the supporters of the Safavids and had powerful practical consequences. Ismāʿīl's enthusiastic disciples (*murīdān*) took them so seriously that they were firmly convinced of his invincibility. Imbued with such ideas, they marched into battle, going from triumph to triumph until the whole of Persia had been subjected to the sway of the Safavids. Admittedly the defeat at Chāldirān destroyed Ismāʿīl's charisma, but even after this reverse he continued to be revered like a god by many of his subjects, and the same is also true, incidentally, of his son Ṭahmāsp.

The state founded by Ismāʿīl was a theocracy, comparable with the

[1] Lambton, "Quis custodiet custodes?", *SI* VI (1956), 126. As against this view, it would be worth investigating whether the Ottomans, who were then on the brink of turning to Shiʿism, did not rather have rapid second thoughts when the Shīʿa was raised to the level of state religion in Persia.

empire of the caliphs but based on Shīʿī rather than on Sunnī principles. The distinction is important because it meant that Shīʿī theories of the state and of succession, radically different from those of the Sunnīs, were to be authoritative. Instead of the elected caliph, the head of state was to be an imām descended from the Prophet Muḥammad, at any rate as long as such a person existed, i.e. until 260/873–4, the date of the disappearance of the Twelfth Imām. Subsequently the office passed to a vakīl whose entitlement did not depend on direct descent from the prophet, but rather on being nominated by a legitimate predecessor (*naṣṣ*). This regulation remained in force until 329/940–1, when the vakīl Abu'l-Ḥasan al-Samarrī passed away without having exercised his right to designate a successor. According to the doctrine of the Twelver Shīʿa, from that point onwards until the return of the Mahdī – i.e. for the duration of the great *ghaiba* which still continues today – a given mujtahid was to be considered as the latter's steward. The mujtahid is that singular dignitary who without being appointed, without either office or clearly defined responsibilities, has a commanding influence within the Shīʿa community in matters of religious law and practice purely by virtue of his personal authority, based on his learning and his exemplary conduct. It must be emphasised that neither the vakīl nor the mujtahid is required to be a descendant of the Prophet.

Bearing in mind these considerations, how legitimate was the Safavids' claim to sovereignty over Persia? Neither in Ismāʿīl's case nor in that of his father, grandfather or any other ancestor can there be any question of naṣṣ, and indeed none of them claimed to have been designated ruler by a legitimate predecessor. Nor was any one of them a mujtahid. In these circumstances, how could they have become sovereigns? Can it really be the case that so fundamental a qualification for the post of steward of the imām was disregarded, perhaps, as has been suggested, on account of Safavid propaganda, deliberately designed to divert attention from it?[1]

To consider the matter of Ismāʿīl's accession in such a theoretical light is in all probability inappropriate. Because it was markedly religious in character it is of course tempting to judge it from a theological point of view. But this is surely a mistake. Obviously Ismāʿīl was a personality with a pronounced sensitivity for things religious. For

[1] Savory, "The Emergence of the modern Persian State", especially p. 20.

some years he had received Shīʿī religious instruction, but he had certainly not acquired any theological knowledge. Nor can one assume that those around him possessed any. Moreover, the Shīʿa he caused to be proclaimed in Tabrīz by no means accorded with the theology of the Twelver Shīʿīs. True, this neglect of theological considerations was not to last, but for the situation to change Shīʿī theologians had to come from outside the country, a fact which in itself points to a certain paucity of theological knowledge at the outset of his reign. It would appear that the young Ismāʿīl and his advisers were not even aware of the meaning of the concept of naṣṣ.[1]

Although initially the sharp distinctions of theological concepts may have been foreign to the young Ismāʿīl's world of ideas, it by no means follows that he was totally ignorant of legitimist theories as such. He was probably just as familiar with general ideas of this kind as were his contemporaries. Whereas Sunnī theories of sovereignty allow for the recognition of a usurper, in Shīʿī teaching the principle of legitimacy finds particularly strong expression. It is encountered also in popular thinking, a concrete example of which is the quasi-legendary tale in which the hidden Imām performs the investiture of Ismāʿīl before the eyes of a dervish in a dream.[2] Here the underlying idea of the necessity for the ruler to be designated in accordance with divine wish or approval is unmistakeable, even though the concept of naṣṣ is not mentioned. To that extent the tale does not necessarily contradict our supposition that Ismāʿīl and his loyal supporters could scarcely have been familiar with so complex an idea.

Whether Ismāʿīl, in emerging from Gīlān, intended from the outset to win sovereignty over Iran remains debatable, however much subsequent reports suggest such an interpretation. Initially, of course, he had to establish himself as master of the Ardabīl order. This may explain the military campaigns and predatory raids he carried out which were similar to those of his father and grandfather before him with their bands of ghāzīs. Like them, he was probably inspired by the ghāzī concept and perhaps by the idea of vendetta as well. The turning-point was probably not reached until the emergence of Shams al-Dīn Zakariyā Kujujī, a native of Tabrīz who for many years had served the Āq Quyūnlū as vizier. For this man, whom Ismāʿīl made his own

[1] Glassen, "Schah Ismāʿīl I und die Theologen", p. 264.
[2] This story is analysed by Glassen, "Schah Ismāʿīl, ein Mahdī".

vizier, reported that his former masters were in a state of utter chaos.[1]

At all events, his reports demonstrated just how favourable an opportunity had arisen for seizing power. After all, Ismāʿīl was the grandson of Uzun Ḥasan. Why should he not ascend the throne of his grandfather instead of his cousins? A clear indication that Safavid rule was to represent a continuation of that of the Āq Quyūnlū is the fact that the Türkmen capital of Tabrīz was retained, whereas no mention is made of Ardabīl, which might equally well have been chosen as the royal residence. Further evidence of a desire to follow in the line of Türkmen rulers is Ismāʿīl's assumption of the title Pādishāh-i Īrān, previously held by Uzun Ḥasan. At the same time it provides documentary proof of the Persian monarchs' continued adherence to the concept of divine right – *khwarna*, "regal majesty", which under Islam was changed to *ẓill Allāh*, "the shadow of God [on earth]".[2]

Ismāʿīl's assumption of power in Tabrīz in no way affected his position as murshid-i kāmil, master of the order of the Ṣafaviyya. On the contrary, this office – which was relevant only to members of the order and not to his other subjects – had increased in significance as a result of his military and political successes, for in addition to his powers as sovereign it guaranteed him, by virtue of the pīr–murīd relationship, the particular loyalty of his armed forces, the Qizilbāsh. As we have seen, these were mostly Türkmen tribesmen from Anatolia, Syria and Āzarbāījān. Its importance was not to wane until the defeat of Chāldirān later destroyed the messianic radiance and charisma of the ruler, making him less sacrosanct in the eyes of his supporters. Not surprisingly, the khalīfat al-khulafā gained in influence, since he had to deputise for the shah to a large extent in his duties as master of the order. No outright confrontation between the two was to occur until half a century later, in the reign of Shah Ismāʿīl II, when members of the order made no secret of the fact that they felt a greater obligation to the khalīfa than to the monarch. This clear indication of the order's decline was followed by another confrontation, this time with ʿAbbās I in 998/1589–90, which practically speaking put an end to its respected status in the realm.

[1] Gruner, *Die Geschichte Schah Ismāʿīls I. aus der Chronik "Takmilat-al-aḫbār"*, pp. 88–90, 125, 133; the extract she uses is printed in facsimile in Efendiev, *Obrazovanie*.

[2] Most recently discussed by Savory, "The Ṣafavid State and Polity", p. 184; cf. Roemer's comments *ibid.*, p. 213, and Amin Banani in Savory, "The Emergence of the modern Persian State", p. 14.

More problematical than the two foundations of Safavid power we have discussed so far was its third basis, descent from the Prophet Muḥammad, i.e. the sayyid status of the dynasty. With a touch of dry irony Aubin remarks that the Safavids did not become Sayyids until late on, probably just before the middle of the 9th/15th century.[1] Since that other scion of the prophet, Sayyid Aḥmad Kasravī, made his violent attacks on the genealogy of the Safavids fifty years ago the arguments for and against their genuineness have constantly been the object of critical debate, but no clear-cut and definitive verdict has yet been reached.[2] Without pursuing the argument further here, we may confine ourselves to the observation that in the absence of proof to the contrary there is no reason to doubt the young Ismāʿīl's good faith with regard to his ancestry before he ascended the throne. That such a conviction cannot simply be dismissed as absurd is evident from the clearly unobjectionable testimony of a poet who, around the middle of the 8th/14th century, praises the then master of the Ardabīl order, Shaikh Ṣadr al-Dīn, as having emerged from the sea of the sayyids.[3]

Since, according to the doctrine of the Twelver Shīʿa, what determines the legitimacy of a ruler is designation by a rightful predecessor (naṣṣ) and not so much his genealogy, no particular significance should really be attached to descent from ʿAlī. Whether he is a sayyid or not, the man who seizes power without either naṣṣ or ijtihād is a usurper. This is a theory which still has its supporters today. Whether it is in fact applicable to the case of Ismāʿīl is, however, open to discussion. If it were, one would be obliged to deny the legitimacy even of his subjective claim to assume power. In that case the great significance the Safavids attached to their descent from ʿAlī would matter only in terms of the respect it brought them, the great proximity to divine truth resulting from it and the justification of their claim to sinlessness (*ʿiṣma*). This presupposes, however, that Ismāʿīl actually knew of the paramount importance of designation, which is probably the very opposite of the case. No evidence from the intellectual and spiritual

1 Aubin, "La politique religieuse des Safavides", especially p. 237.

2 For the present state of research, see Roemer, "Scheich Ṣafī von Ardabīl"; also M.R. Zamir-Dahncke, "The Problem of the Descent of the Ṣafavids", *Nashriyya-yi Dānishgāh-i Iṣfahān: Dānishkada-yi Adabiyyāt va ʿulūm-i insānī* VIII/9 (1352), 15–18.

3 M. Dirakhshān, "Pīrāmūn-i kalima-yi shaikh va sayyid", *Dānishgāh-i Ṭihrān: Majalla-yi Dānishkada-yi adabiyyāt va ʿulūm-i insānī* XXI/4 (1353), 153–62 (14–16), quoting from a qaṣīda by Nāṣir-i Bukhārāʾī written *c.* 1350, details of which are unfortunately not given.

sphere in which he lived, familiar to us both from the chronicles and from his own dīvān, supports the assumption that he had so sublime a knowledge of Shīʿī theory. In the long run, of course, with the increasingly dominant influence of theology, the Safavids must have discovered the existence of this doctrine. Exactly when they became acquainted with it remains to be investigated, but in this context it is not so important. Suffice it to say that no knowledge of it can be attributed to Ismāʿīl in the summer of 907/1501. The probability, rather, is that on the one hand he considered himself eligible to succeed by virtue of his descent from Uzun Ḥasan, and on the other hand he saw his ʿAlid lineage as giving him the advantage in legitimacy over his Āq Quyūnlū cousins and other claimants.

These are the decisive criteria for judging whether Safavid rule was from the outset established on the basis of a fraudulent manoeuvre, the only mitigating circumstances for which would be the tender age of the dynasty's founder and the unscrupulousness of his confidential advisers. Since Ismāʿīl's character was not without its sinister traits – it is sufficient to recall the inconceivable cruelty with which he imposed his authority and his religious views – one is inclined to believe him capable of any other misdeed. Yet his ruthless treatment of genuine and potential adversaries has to be seen against the moral background of his time and his immediate environment, in which humanity, magnanimity and clemency could prove fatal and were of as little account as in the West during the same period. Clearly allowance has to be made for a different scale of moral values, although it would be going too far to assume a total absence of ethical norms.

These reflections do not, however, do full justice to Ismāʿīl's seizure of power, because they leave out of account certain irrational factors that played a considerable rôle. A first-rate reliable source for these is, as has been mentioned, Khaṭāʾī's dīvān, Khaṭāʾī being the pseudonym he used as a poet. This collection of poetry shows him to be a man of great religious ardour and strong mystical impulse, surely evidence of a centuries-old tradition of sufism prevalent in his family. This is certainly borne out by his first emergence as a public figure. The ecstatic fervour he exudes is striking and transmits itself in an even more intense form to his adherents. Recognisably messianic features find a lively echo in contemporary expectations of the return of the Mahdī. It no more occurs to this religious revivalist to enquire into the theological minutiae of Shīʿī doctrine than to trouble himself with the details of what is essentially an established theory of succession, even assuming that he was familiar with it. For him, descent from ʿAlī, of which at this stage at any rate he may have been convinced, must have been the decisive factor in his entitlement to rule. If he knew anything at all about the concept of naṣṣ, one must suppose that he either equated or confused it with membership of the family of the Prophet (*dūdmān*), in other words with descent from the Seventh Imām, Mūsā al-Kāẓim, to which the Safavids laid claim. After all, when he ascended the throne, he had likewise not hesitated to make Shiʿism the official religion of the state, in spite of the heretical notions expressed in his dīvān.

The young master of a religious order, of Iranian rural stock but with forebears in Türkmen and Byzantine dynasties, seizes power, with the aid of fervently religious Türkmens, in Iran, a Persian-speaking country. He establishes a theocracy and proclaims a new faith, the Twelver Shīʿa, of which his knowledge is so superficial that he can equate it with his own quite personal belief which, precisely formulated, is a syncretism of metempsychotic Islam and Shamanism.[1] Such is the situation at the outset of the Safavid empire, under the auspices of which Persia crosses the threshold of the modern era. Inevitably this start was associated with a plethora of complex political and religious problems. The dynasty was to have two and a half centuries in which to solve them. In view of the continued influence and effect of their achievements down to the present day, one can scarcely say that the Safavids and their subjects failed in this task, even if the disintegration and catastrophe that marked the end of their empire makes it impossible to speak of total success. It is probably more accurate to see the Safavid era as a significant phase in the struggle for their identity which the Persians had to undergo as they entered the modern age.

Let us now return to the main problems which concern us, the antagonism between Persians and Turks, the religious developments and the changes in the monarchical system that occurred in Persia during this period. Without doubt the foundation of the Safavid state would have been impossible without the military effectiveness of the Qizilbāsh. There were also Qizilbāsh of non-Turkish descent, for

[1] Mélikoff, "Le problème ḳızılbaş", p. 52, speaks of a Qizilbāsh variant of Shiʿism in Anatolia which also existed, in a much more archaic form, in Iranian Āzarbāījān. Cf. also the phenomena discussed by Aubin, "La politique religieuse des Safavides", p. 237.

example Persians and Kurds,[1] but their numbers were small, probably even minute. The vast majority of the disciples who flocked to the Ardabīl order from the middle of the 9th/15th century onwards were members of nomadic Türkmen tribes or at times probably Türkmen peasants as well.[2] Whether, as has been discussed above, these were ethnic groups which had no connection with the foregoing confederations, the Qarā Quyūnlū and the Āq Quyūnlū, or whether on the contrary they comprised to a large extent their ethnic rump,[3] is a question that need not concern us here. What is important is the fact that Ismāʿīl's state so clearly bore the stamp of his Türkmen adherents that at first it scarcely differed from the principalities which preceded it and has justifiably been described as a direct continuation of them.

Given the powerful impetus which animated the Qizilbāsh, their rise to political power ought in itself to have brought about a Turkicisation of Persia, but things took a different course. Even though fewer and fewer historians still maintain the view that the Safavid empire was a Persian national state, it is undeniably true that the state founded by Ismāʿīl was from the outset exposed to strong Iranicising tendencies, which ultimately led to the integration of the Türkmens. At all events there can be no question of a Turkicisation of Iran at the hands of the Safavids. How is this to be explained?

To quote Minorsky, Türkmens and Persians, like oil and water, did not readily mix. According to him, the dualistic character of the population considerably affected both military and civil administration and can be seen, for example, in the dichotomy between Turkish "lords of the sword" and Persian "lords of the pen" which is mentioned in chronicles.[4] His diagnosis is accurate. The worst manifestation of antagonism between Persians and Turks had been eradicated within a century, but it would be utterly mistaken to ascribe this success to a gradual convergence of the two peoples. Rather was it the result of a lengthy and bloody confrontation which made the first half of the

[1] Cf. Efendiev, "Le rôle des tribus". An example is Ismāʿīl I's famous vakīl, Najm-i s̲ānī. The Tālish of north-west Persia referred to in Minorsky, *Tadhkirat al-Mulūk*, p. 14, as supporters of Ismāʿīl, were probably Qizilbāsh too.

[2] Sümer, *Safevî devletinin kuruluşu*, p. 213.

[3] Sümer's remark *ibid.* that Ismāʿīl's Türkmen helpers were "Anatolian Turks ... completely distinct from the Qarā Quyūnlū and Āq Quyūnlū confederations" cannot, of course, be taken to mean that elements belonging to these confederations were in no way involved in the foundation and rise of the Safavid empire. One has only to consider the Chepnī, to whom he himself refers and who had been part of the Āq Quyūnlū confederation. Cf. Sohrweide, "Der Sieg der Ṣafaviden", p. 121; Babinger, "Der Islam in Kleinasien", pp. 65ff.; Efendiev, "Le rôle des tribus".

[4] *Tadhkirat al-Mulūk*, p. 188.

Safavid era a time of ever recurring political crises both at home and abroad. These began immediately in the reign of Ismāʿīl I with constantly abortive attempts to combat the omnipotence of the Qizilbāsh generals by appointing an eminent Persian to the office of vakīl, the shah's deputy with regard to his political and military functions. They culminated in massive revolts on the part of the Qizilbāsh during the reigns of Shah Ṭahmāsp I and Shah Muḥammad Khudābanda and in the murders of Queen Mahd-i ʿUlyā (987/1579), mother of the subsequent Shah ʿAbbās, and the Grand Vizier Mīrzā Salmān Jābirī (991/1583).[1]

The final chapter of these dramatic events saw the destruction of Türkmen supremacy by Shah ʿAbbās I in the course of a thorough reform of the armed forces carried out at the beginning of his reign. The Türkmen tribal aristocracy was stripped of all power, new types of weaponry were introduced and a regular corps established which can be regarded as the model and source of later efforts to create a standing army. One of the most significant consequences of the reform was the fact that members of the Georgian, Armenian and Circassian ethnic groups were now recruited to the armed forces and the highest offices of state. The reorganisation of the armed forces, completed by the end of the 10th/16th century, also involved administrative and financial reforms. Payment of troops from the funds of the royal household replaced the feudal system on which the army had previously been based. Increasing numbers of provincial governorships, until now in the hands of Türkmen military commanders, were transformed into crown lands, with the result that their levies and taxes accrued to the shah and could be used for the maintenance of the new contingents.

The destruction of Türkmen autonomy was not the only consequence of these measures. They also led to large-scale social change and restratification which still await closer investigation. Qizilbāsh tribes continued to exist, and some of their leaders even retained their posts as governors, but all in all the reform of the army constituted an advance along the road towards the integration of the Türkmens with the Persian population. Even in the 12th/18th century, Türkmen tribes still supplied Persia with royal dynasties like the Qājārs whose rule

[1] See Savory, "The Significance of the Political Murder of Mīrzā Salmān"; Roemer, *Niedergang*, *passim*.

came to an end a mere fifty years ago. Alliances between Turkish and Persian elements – the example of Ismāʿīl's marriage was repeatedly followed by his successors – in the long run became a possibility for wider circles in the community. Even more important was the fact that just as Persian and other non-Turkish dignitaries could, from the end of the 10th/16th century onwards, occupy military commands and offices of state, so Türkmen tribesmen were able in time to play an active part in various spheres of Persian cultural life.[1] A few examples from the field of history alone will suffice: Ṣādiqī Beg Afshār and Ḥasan Rūmlū, both born shortly after 1530, and their younger contemporary, Iskandar Beg Turkmān, usually known as Iskandar Munshī, one of the greatest historians of Islamic Persia.

One final consequence of the reform of the army needs to be emphasised. The ensuing transformation into crown lands of provinces previously ruled by governors lasted for decades, indeed until the time of Shah ʿAbbās II (1052–77/1642–66), and went hand in hand with a strong policy of centralisation, affecting the administration and other spheres of life. This was of enormous importance for subsequent developments, even up to the present day. Ultimately it put an end to the polycentric system, inherited from the days of Tīmūr, which might have been of significance, especially in terms of artistic and intellectual development. A further contributory factor may have been ʿAbbās I's decision to discontinue the practice of appointing the royal princes to governorships in particularly important provincial cities.

At the start of Safavid rule, religious fanaticism, as we have seen, played a far more prominent part than theological knowledge, which would have been useful in confrontations with established Sunnī theology. At that time Persia was a largely Sunnī country, with numerous theologians of that persuasion. In the circumstances, the advisers of the new shah, and presumably Ismāʿīl himself, must quickly have recognised the disadvantages of their theological ignorance. Significant evidence of this is the search – albeit not exactly successful – for specialist literature on the subject, which is mentioned in a chronicle of the period.[2] Soon the situation changed as the call for Shīʿī theologians was answered. They came from areas in which there was a Shīʿī tradi-

1 Savory, "The qizilbāsh, education and the arts".
2 Ḥasan-i Rūmlū I, 61; cf. Mazzaoui, *Origins of the Safawids*, pp. 6, 28.

tion, from Baḥrain and from the Jabal 'Āmila in southern Lebanon, and brought Safavid religious views, which bore the imprint partly of popular piety and partly of the extremist currents of the early period of the empire, into line with the official tenets of the Twelver Shī'a. The extent to which they became respected in Persia can be judged, for example, from the fact that Shah 'Abbās the Great married the daughter of one of them, Shaikh Luṭf-Allāh Maisī from the Lebanese Mais al-Jabal, whose memory is kept alive to this day in what is one of the gems of Persian architecture, the little mosque on the Maidān-i Shāh in Iṣfahān which is named after him.

However, not all the consequences of this increase in the influence of Shī'ī theology proved welcome to the Safavids. The concept of divine right, so important to the shah's reputation, especially amongst large numbers of the common people, had no place in the doctrines of the Shī'ī theologians. They, of course, were familiar with the theory of naṣṣ, according to which any representative of the departed Imām needed to be designated by a legitimate predecessor. They were only too aware that the Safavids had not been designated in this way and could not make up for this deficiency by claiming descent from the Prophet. The dynasty had thus usurped the power which rightfully belonged to the mujtahid of the time. At first the theologians probably acquiesced in this without too much difficulty since both they and, of course, the mujtahid enjoyed a better position under the Safavids than under any Sunnī régime, however magnanimous. As their activities gradually influenced the beliefs and religious practices of the population, and the official doctrines of the Twelver Shī'a supplanted the heresy introduced by Ismā'īl, so the shah lost the preeminent position he had held previously in religious matters. Eventually, by the end of the 11th/17th century, he retained only executive power, and the people showed a greater devotion to the mujtahid. There is therefore a certain parallel here with previously discussed developments within the Safavid order, in which the khalīfat al-khulafā was able to assert his superiority over the shah in his capacity as murshid-i kāmil. More than a century later, the Qājārs, who after decades of indecision finally resolved to grant the Shī'ī theologians ('ulamā) their former privileged status, thus hoping to give their rule the semblance of legitimacy, were also disappointed. The theologians could not change their fundamental beliefs. Monarchs, no matter whether they were Safavids or Qājārs, were and remained in their eyes usurpers. Instead of supporting those to whom they owed a debt of gratitude, they contributed, in the case of both dynasties, to their downfall.

Shah ʿAbbās I may well have realised where things were leading. His ostentatious displays of religious devotion – from his visit to the shrine at Ardabīl to his pilgrimage to Mashhad – were primarily designed, although genuine religious motives cannot be ruled out, to establish a healthy relationship between monarchy and the Shīʿa. In vain: it fell to him not only to destroy the might of the Qizilbāsh; he was also the instigator of the most important measures of social discrimination against the ṣūfīs, which, according to the testimony of foreign travellers, had taken effect by the middle of the 11th/17th century. Within his own lifetime Shah ʿAbbās I was to witness the triumph in Persia of the representatives of Shīʿī orthodoxy, beginning with his famous contemporary Mīr Dāmād (d. 1630). The idea of the sanctity of the monarch had fallen into decay, the heretical beliefs of his great-grandfather had been banished and the Safavid order had declined.

One of the things modern-day Persia inherited from the Safavids had been the tradition of monarchy. Although initially it had taken the form of kingship by divine right, towards the end of the Safavid era the monarchy shed more and more of its supernatural aspects until ultimately it was completely devoid of them. Subsequent ruling dynasties held fast to the principle of monarchy but did not revive the idea of the shah as God incarnate. The Safavids, as we have seen, were obliged to pursue unconventional policies in order to achieve a reconciliation between the indigenous Iranians and the Türkmens their ancestors and they themselves had brought to the country, two ethnic groups with which they were, of course, linked by descent. Although they were unable to eradicate all antagonism between the two, they certainly managed to remove the most important obstacles to a reconciliation. Finally, it was as a result of their endeavours that Persia became a Shīʿī country, which it has remained to the present day. Two attempts to abolish the Shīʿa failed, the first under Shah Ismāʿīl II around 984/1576, the second a hundred and sixty years later under Nādir Shāh. The introduction of the Shīʿa to Iran is the most striking contribution of the Safavids to modern-day Persia because it is the factor that most clearly distinguishes the country from its neighbours.

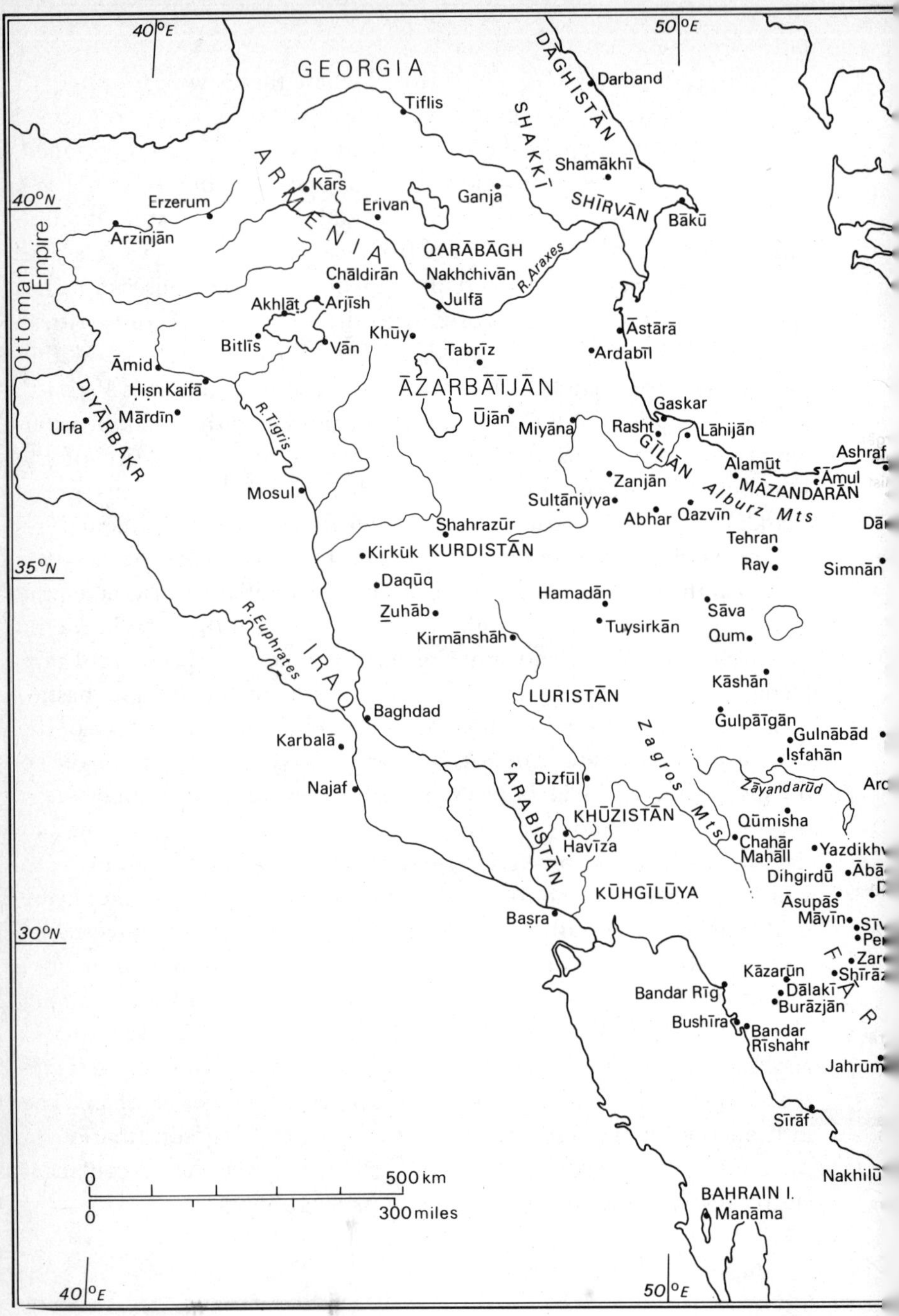

Map. Iran under the Safavids

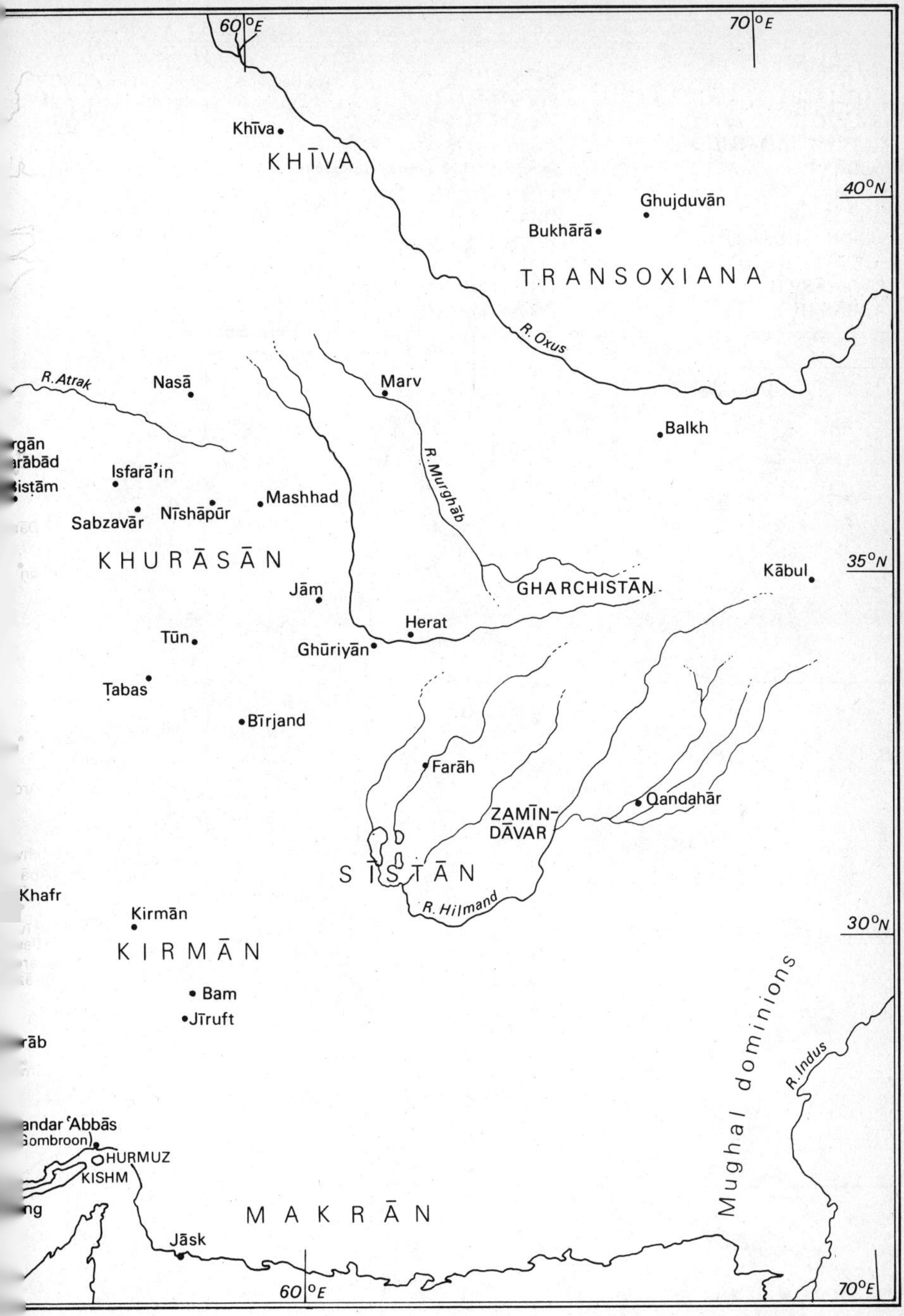
60°E
70°E
Khīva
KHĪVA
40°N
Ghujduvān
Bukhārā
TRANSOXIANA
R. Oxus
R. Atrak
Nasā
Marv
Balkh
rgān
rābād
istām
Isfarā'in
R. Murghāb
Mashhad
Nīshāpūr
Sabzavār
KHURĀSĀN
35°N
Kābul
GHARCHISTĀN
Jām
Herat
Tūn
Ghūriyān
Ṭabas
Bīrjand
Farāh
Qandahār
ZAMĪN-
DĀVAR
SĪSTĀN
R. Hilmand
Khafr
Kirmān
30°N
KIRMĀN
Mughal dominions
Bam
Jīruft
rāb
R. Indus
andar 'Abbās
Gombroon)
HURMUZ
KISHM
ng
MAKRĀN
Jāsk
60°E
70°E

Table VI. *The Safavids*

ISMĀ'ĪL I	907–930/1501–1524
ṬAHMĀSP I	930–984/1524–1576
ISMĀ'ĪL II	984–985/1576–1577
MUḤAMMAD KHUDĀBANDA	985–995/1578–1587
'ABBĀS I	(989)995–1038/(1581)1587–1629
ṢAFĪ I	1038–1052/1629–1642
'ABBĀS II	1052–1077/1642–1666
ṢAFĪ II (SULAIMĀN)	1077(1078)–1105/1666(1668)–1694
SULṬĀN ḤUSAIN	1105–1135/1694–1722
ṬAHMĀSP II	1135–1144/1722–1732
'ABBĀS III	1144–1148/1732–1736

CHAPTER 6

THE SAFAVID ADMINISTRATIVE SYSTEM

Before the principal phases in the development of the Safavid administrative system are discussed in detail, a brief outline of the Safavid administrative and social structure may be helpful. At the apex of this structure was the shah. Never was the Divine Right of Kings more fully developed than by the Safavid shahs. Shah Ismāʿīl I, who established the Safavid dynasty in 907/1501–2, considered himself to be the living emanation of the godhead, the Shadow of God upon earth, and the representative of the Hidden Imām by virtue of direct descent from the Seventh Imām of the Twelver (Ithnāʿashariyya) Shīʿa, Mūsā al-Kāẓim. It is axiomatic that such a ruler would command instant and unquestioning obedience from his subjects. Since the ruler was directly appointed by God, men were required to obey his commands whether just or unjust. Since the ruler, as the representative of the Hidden Imām, was closer to the source of absolute truth than were other men, opposition to him was a sin. This led inevitably to an assumption of kingly infallibility. In other words, the Safavid shahs usurped the function which the Ithnāʿasharī *mujtahids* had arrogated to themselves, namely, that of acting as the representative on earth of the Mahdī, the Ithnāʿasharī messiah. The net result of these various Safavid theories of kingship was absolutism.[1] In practice, however, there were well defined limits to this absolutism, even when the shah was a strong and capable ruler. Chardin declares emphatically that outside court circles there was no arbitrary exercise of power by the shah, and both Chardin and Malcolm assert that the awe in which the shah was held by the court and the nobility was the primary reason for the relative security and freedom from oppression enjoyed by the lower classes.

Minorsky has written: "It is a moot question how the idea of the State, if ever distinctly realised, was expressed in Safavid terminology". Though the term *daulat* was sometimes used as an abstract concept, he says, the nearest equivalent in a concrete sense was *mamālik-i maḥrūsa*, the "divinely-protected dominions".[2] This rather extreme statement

[1] Lambton, "Quis custodiet custodes?", *SI* VI (1956), 125ff.

[2] *Tadhkirat al-Mulūk*, p. 24.

must now be modified. There is abundant evidence that, long before the end of the Safavid period, the concept of the territories under Safavid jurisdiction as a state had crystallised into a more concrete form. During the reign of Shah Sulaimān (1077–1105/1666–94), the term *mamlikat-i Īrān* is found, but the historian Iskandar Beg Munshī, writing in 1025/1616–17, frequently uses terms of a similar nature with reference to the Safavid state at the time of Shah Ṭahmāsp I (930–84/1524–76): *mulk-i Īrān*; *mamālik-i Īrān*; *'arṣa-yi Īrān* (the last of these perhaps more geographical than political). Even if Iskandar Beg Munshī's use of these terms in regard to the reign of Shah Ṭahmāsp represents a case of prolepsis, it nevertheless indicates that, by the time of Shah 'Abbās I at least, Safavid rule had led to the emergence of a more definite concept of a state operating within fairly well-defined boundaries. The meaning of *daulat*, now the ordinary word for state, gradually evolved from the rather abstract concept of the "bliss" or "felicity" of the ruler, the aura of beneficence which surrounded him and sheltered his subjects, and came to be used in a more concrete sense. Roemer has pointed out that the existence of Iran as an administrative entity was acknowledged by the Ottomans from the time of the establishment of the Safavid state. A letter to Shah Ismā'īl I from the Ottoman sultan Bāyezīd II refers to him as *pādishāh-i Īrān*.[1]

The administrative organisation of the Safavid state was divided both horizontally, along ethnic lines, and vertically, by Barthold's classic "red thread", namely, "the division of all the organs of administration into two main categories, the *dargāh* (palace) and *dīvān* (chancery)".[2] On the ethnic plane, the Qizilbāsh, the Türkmen tribes which had been mainly responsible for bringing the Safavids to power, constituted the military aristocracy of the Safavid state, the "men of the sword" in traditional Islamic terms. The amīrs, or chiefs of these tribes, were the military governors of most of the provinces of the Safavid empire during its early period. They filled the most important offices of state, and held a dominant position in political as well as in military affairs. This state of affairs they considered to be no more than their due in view of their services to the Safavid cause. Differing from

[1] Savory, "The Ṣafavid State and Polity", p. 214 for Roemer's comments; *ibid.*, pp. 206–8, for further examples from Iskandar Munshī showing that Iran was viewed by that historian as a positive entity or state.

[2] Barthold, *Turkestan down to the Mongol invasion*, 3rd ed. (London, 1968, GMS n.s. v), p. 227.

the Qizilbāsh in race, language and culture were the Tājīks, or Persian elements of society, the descendants of those who had traditionally filled the ranks of the bureaucracy under a succession of alien Arab, Turkish, Mongol and Tartar rulers. From the Tājīk elements were drawn not only the viziers and the numerous classes of officials in the royal secretariat, but also the accountants, the clerks, the tax-collectors and other officials of the financial administration, and, in general, the "men of the pen" of classical Islamic society. In addition, the majority of the members of the religious classes (*'ulamā*): the *mujtahids*, the *qāḍīs*, the *sayyids*, the *khaṭībs*, and other functionaries of the religious institution, were Persians. The few who were originally of Arab blood had become thoroughly assimilated in the course of time, and thought of themselves as Tājīks. The head of the religious institution, the *ṣadr*, was always a Persian.

The administrative organisation of the Safavid state remained fluid during the whole of the period prior to the accession of Shah 'Abbās I (996/1588). Even when the actual administrative institutions assumed more rigid forms in the course of the administrative reorganisation carried out by 'Abbās I, some lateral mobility still existed, and officials were able to cross the boundary between the religious institution and the political institution with comparative ease. During the early Safavid period, the *dīvān*, or *mamālik*, branch was predominant. From the time of Shah 'Abbās I onwards, however, the power of that branch of the administration which was under the personal control of the ruler (in Safavid terminology: *khāṣṣa*) increased at the expense, and to the detriment, of the mamālik branch. Eventually (1077/1666–7), even the office of ṣadr was divided into a khāṣṣa and an *'āmma* (i.e., mamālik) branch.

The everyday business of the state was transacted by a council (*dīvān*; later: *jānqī*) of high-ranking amīrs (*arkān-i daulat*; *umarā-yi 'ālījāh*; etc.). The vizier (*vazīr*) was a member of this council. Later, other officials were nominated to it. They included an official known as the *majlis-nivīs*, or *vāqi'a-nivīs*, sometimes termed the *vazīr-i chap*, because he stood on the left of the shah, whereas the vizier proper stood on the shah's right. This official had three functions: he was the official court historiographer; he was the shah's private secretary; and, most important of all, he was a rapporteur to the shah.[1] In this last capacity he was

[1] Minorsky, *Tadhkirat al-Mulūk*, pp. 121–2.

in effect the head of a widespread intelligence system. The council of amīrs was presided over by the shah, or, in his absence, by the *vakīl-i nafs-i nafīs-i humāyūn* (later, by the *iʿtimād al-daula*). The amīrs who were members of the council resided at court. If any of them held another office in addition, such as a provincial governorship, he would delegate that function to his son, or to another amīr from his own tribe.

The head of the bureaucracy was the vizier. He had at his command a large staff of viziers of lesser rank, secretaries, and other officials, each of whom was in charge of a branch of the vizier's department, which was called the *daftarkhāna-yi humāyūn*, or royal secretariat. No letter of appointment to a post in the bureaucracy was valid without the vizier's seal. The various branches of his department dealt with such matters as the authorisation of assignments on the revenue, grants, pensions and immunities of many different kinds; the payment of troops, and the keeping of muster-rolls and other military records; and the keeping of the archives.[1]

Financial matters were ultimately the responsibility of the vizier, but the technical business of preparing and auditing the budget, assessing taxes (which were many and varied), and collecting the revenue – in short, the actual operation of the financial machine – was in the hands of a large staff of accountants, clerks, tax-collectors and financial agents under the control of the *mustaufī al-mamālik*, the comptroller of finance.[2] As the khāṣṣa side of the administration expanded, the office of *istīfā-yi mamālik*, like the *ṣadārat*, was divided, and the financial business of the khāṣṣa branch was conducted by an official termed *mustaufī-yi khāṣṣa*. In the final analysis, however, the latter seems to have been inferior in rank to the mustaufī al-mamālik.

The administration of the royal household was carried on by a separate department, headed by the *nāẓir-i buyūtāt*, or superintendent of the royal workshops (*buyūtāt-i khāṣṣa-yi sharīfa*), of which there were eventually about thirty-three.[3] "The artisans in the Royal Workshops were organised in royal guilds",[4] which continued to provide some of the court's needs. The royal workshops "made large profits for the Ṣafavid Shahs; they not only produced goods such as textiles and rugs for the court, but also sent expensive silks and textiles to Europe and

[1] *Ibid.*, pp. 44–6.
[2] *Ibid.*, pp. 54–5.
[3] *Ibid.*, pp. 48–50. See further Keyvani, pp. 166ff.
[4] Keyvani, p. 170.

India, and paid the profits made in this way to the Shah".[1] Each royal workshop was in the charge of a *ṣāḥib-jam'* and a *mushrif*, and the nāẓir-i buyūtāt had in addition many other subordinate officials who assisted him in the discharge of his multifarious duties. These included: the preparation of an estimate of the expenditure of the royal household (which was then submitted to the central vizier for approval); agreeing on the price of, and signing contracts for, foodstuffs and other goods supplied to the royal household; the supervision of the day-to-day expenditure of the various royal workshops; the payment of the workmen employed in the said workshops; the maintenance of all the buildings connected with the royal household; and the general supervision of the management of the royal stables and the arsenal. The administration of the harem (*ḥaram*) and the private quarters of the shah did not come within the purview of the nāẓir-i buyūtāt, but constituted an entirely separate branch, the internal palace administration, staffed mainly by eunuchs. The latter were initially all black eunuchs, but from the time of Shah 'Abbās I a number of white eunuchs, Georgian *ghulāms*, were employed in the palace. Not all the staff of the internal palace administration were eunuchs. The exceptions were: the royal physician; the royal astrologer; the comptroller of assay and other officials of the royal mint: and the keepers of various seals. All the officials of the internal palace administration were known under the general title of *muqarrab al-khāqān*. Officials whose duties lay at the entrance to, or outside, the harem and the private quarters of the shah, were classified as *muqarrab al-ḥaẓrat*. Included in this category were the officials of the department of the nāẓir-i buyūtāt, referred to above, and an extensive staff of doorkeepers, gentlemen-in-waiting, ushers, and the like.[2]

The administration of justice was a complicated affair. During the early Safavid period the ṣadr, as head of the religious institution, was ultimately responsible for the administration of canon law. The business of the courts, however, was in the hands of a number of other religious officials in addition to the ṣadr, including the *qāḍī al-quḍāt* and the *shaikh al-islām*. As a result, there was a considerable degree of conflict of jurisdiction. At some point, not yet determined, a new post was created in an attempt to draw all these strands together under one overriding authority. The holder of this new office was termed

[1] *Ibid.*, p. 166. [2] Minorsky, *Taḏhkirat al-Mulūk*, pp. 56ff.

the *dīvān-begī*. Although the ṣadr was supposed to possess superior authority in cases involving capital offences, the fact that such crimes were tried in the dīvān-begī's tribunal indicates that the supreme authority, in these as in other legal matters, in fact lay with the dīvān-begī. In addition, the dīvān-begī's court was the highest court of appeal. By the time of Phase Three (as defined below) of the development of Safavid administrative institutions, or possibly earlier, officials such as the mustaufī al-mamālik, the nāẓir-i buyūtāt, and the dīvān-begī, were classified as amīrs of the highest rank, and consequently were admitted to membership of the council of amīrs. By the end of the Safavid period, membership of this council stood at nineteen, but during the early period it was only about one-third of that size.

Safavid administrative institutions derived from two main sources: the administrative institutions of the Türkmens and the Timurids – rival dynasties which for a hundred years had disputed the succession to Tīmūr's empire in Persia – and the basic ṣūfī organisation of the Ṣafaviyya, the militant Shī'ī order which brought about the establishment of the Safavid state in 907/1501. Thus in part the Safavids were the inheritors of a bureaucratic system which resembled the traditional bureaucracy of a Persian Muslim state. The existence of the tightly-knit ṣūfī organisation of the Ṣafaviyya, however, constituted an essential point of difference between the Safavids and their predecessors. When Shah Ismā'īl became the first ruler of the Safavid dynasty in 907/1501, he was faced with the problem of incorporating this ṣūfī organisation in the administrative system of the Safavid state. In the event, the problem proved insuperable. As the Safavid administration system gradually evolved along more conventional lines, the remains of the original ṣūfī organisation continued to exist as a system within a system, but as an organism devoid of any real function within the state.

There are three main phases in the development of Safavid administrative institutions: first, the period between the accession of Shah Ismā'īl I and that of Shah 'Abbās I (907–96/1501–88); second, the reign of Shah 'Abbās I (996–1038/1588–1629); and third, the period from the accession of Shah Ṣafī to the overthrow of the Safavid dynasty (1038–1135/1629–1722). The first period was one of change and adjustment, during which the functions of the principal officers of state were not clearly defined. As a result, the powers of one official frequently clashed with those of another. During the second period, the administration of the Safavid state was reorganised on entirely new bases by Shah ʿAbbās I. The third period is one of gradual sclerosis and consequent decline.

PHASE ONE (907–96/1501–88)

At his accession, Shah Ismāʿīl, as mentioned above, was confronted by the problem of fusing very dissimilar elements into one harmonious administrative system. On the one hand were his Qizilbāsh followers, the ṣūfīs of the Safavid order who had brought him to power. These men accorded Shah Ismāʿīl adoration as a quasi-divine figure, since they regarded him as the Shadow of God upon earth and the representative of the Hidden Imām. He was also, as head of the Safavid order, their *murshid*, and they, as his *murīds*, gave him unquestioning obedience. From the ranks of the Qizilbāsh were drawn the *ahl-i ikhtiṣāṣ*, a small group of special staff officers, who maintained the Ṣafaviyya on an active service footing during the years that Ismāʿīl was in hiding in Gīlān (899–905/1494–9). These officers included a *lala* ("tutor", "guardian"), an *abdāl*, a *dada*, a *khādim* and a *khalīfat al-khulafā*. On the other hand were the Persian bureaucrats and ʿulamā, many of whom had held secular and religious posts respectively under the predecessors of the Safavids.

The task of combining a traditional mediaeval Muslim administrative system of the Persian type with what was in effect a theocratic organisation, would in any case have been a formidable one. It was rendered still more difficult by the fact that the élite of the Qizilbāsh fighting men were of Turkish stock, members of Türkmen tribes from eastern Anatolia and Syria, such as the Rūmlū, Dulghadïr, Takkalū, Ustājlū, and Shāmlū. The mutual suspicion and hostility between the Turkish and Persian elements in the state split the Safavid administration irrevocably along ethnic lines.

What steps did Ismāʿīl take in his attempt to effect a synthesis of these disparate elements? In the first place, he created the new office of *vakīl-i nafs-i nafīs-i humāyūn*. This official was to be the vicegerent of the shah and was to represent him both in his spiritual capacity (as *murshid-i kāmil* of the Ṣafaviyya) and his temporal capacity (as *pādishāh*). The powers of the vizier, traditionally the first minister and the head of the bureaucracy, were temporarily eclipsed by the overriding powers of this new official. The creation of this office clearly represented an attempt on the part of Ismāʿīl to bridge the gap between a theocratic form of government and a bureaucratic one. It was only natural that the first incumbent should be one of the ahl-i ikhtiṣāṣ, referred to above, the Türkmen officer Ḥusain Beg Lālā Shāmlū.

Secondly, Ismā'īl attempted through the office of ṣadr to forge a link between the political institution, which in the early Safavid period had a markedly military character and was dominated by the Türkmen aristocracy, and the religious institution, the Persian 'ulamā. The office of ṣadr had been inherited from the administrative system of the Timurids and the Türkmen dynasties, but the scope and purpose of the office under the Safavids was quite different. The chief function of the Safavid ṣadr, who was, of course, always a Persian, was the imposition of doctrinal uniformity throughout the Safavid state, and, as a corollary, the extirpation of heresy. This goal had largely been achieved by the end of Ismā'īl's reign in 930/1524. By establishing that the ṣadārat was subordinate to the political institution, Ismā'īl hoped to prevent that separation of secular and religious powers which in fact occurred under his successors. The predominantly military character of the early Safavid state is again shown by the fact that the ṣadrs often held military rank and not infrequently military command. At the critical battle of Chāldirān in 920/1514, for instance, the entire Safavid centre was under the command of ṣadrs and other members of the religious classes.

The other principal offices of state during the early Safavid period were those of the *amīr al-umarā*, the *qūrchī-bāshī*, and the vizier. The office of amīr al-umarā, or commander-in-chief of the Qizilbāsh tribal forces, was considered by the Qizilbāsh to be their prerogative. Apart from his military duties, this officer was one of the great amīrs of the supreme dīvān and played a considerable part in the affairs of state. Although, because of the predominantly military character of the Safavid state during this first phase, the terms "military" and "civil" cannot be used with precision in defining the functions of particular officials, it is clear that the amīr al-umarā was primarily a "military" officer who encroached on the prerogatives of the vizier and other top-ranking officials of the bureaucracy, to the extent permitted by the prevailing political situation. In the event that the shah was weak or a minor, the amīr al-umarā and the leading Qizilbāsh amīrs assumed full control of the machinery of government. Another high-ranking military officer was the qūrchī-bāshī, who later superseded the amīr al-umarā. During the early Safavid period, however, we hear little of the qūrchī-bāshī, and his function, which was distinct from that of the amīr al-umarā, remains obscure. Finally, we have the vizier, whose powers were drastically diminished during the early Safavid period by the creation of the office of vakīl-i nafs-i nafīs-i humāyūn, by the interference of the amīr al-umarā in political affairs, and even by the activities of the ṣadr, who, by virtue of his special rôle in the Safavid administrative system, wielded greater power than did his predecessors in the Türkmen and Timurid administrations.

Almost from the start, however, there were indications that the Turco-Persian condominium was not working smoothly. It seems clear that Ismā'īl made a mistake in allotting to one man, Ḥusain Beg Lālā Shāmlū, the two most important offices of state, that of vakīl-i nafs-i nafīs-i humāyūn and that of amīr al-umarā, so that too much power was concentrated in the hands of one individual. Ismā'īl's realisation of this fact can be seen in his dismissal of Ḥusain Beg from the *vikālat* only six years after the establishment of the Safavid state. From then on Ismā'īl, as a matter of deliberate policy, excluded the Qizilbāsh from the vikālat, and Ḥusain Beg was followed by a succession of five Persian vakīls between 913/1508 and 930/1524. But if Ismā'īl thought to balance the power of a Persian vakīl against that of a Türkmen amīr al-umarā, he was mistaken again. There was an immediate and violent reaction on the part of the Qizilbāsh against the appointment of Persians to the vikālat. Of the five Persian vakīls mentioned above, two were murdered by the Qizilbāsh, a third met his death as the direct result of the hostility between himself and the Qizilbāsh, and the remaining two held office for only two years each.

The decisive defeat suffered by the Safavids at the hands of the Ottomans at Chāldirān in 920/1514 had far-reaching effects, not only on the character and behaviour of Ismā'īl himself, but on his relations with the Qizilbāsh amīrs. This in turn affected the relative importance of the principal administrative offices, and the relations between the Persian and Turkish elements in the administration. Although the Qizilbāsh amīrs had suffered heavy losses at Chāldirān, Ismā'īl's virtual withdrawal from the conduct of both military and administrative affairs enabled the survivors to strengthen their position *vis-à-vis* the ruling institution, namely, the shah. An even more important effect of Chāldirān was the tacit assumption by the Qizilbāsh that their murshid's reputation for infallibility and invincibility was now in ruins. From the time of Chāldirān onwards, the Qizilbāsh by their actions demonstrated incontrovertibly that they considered that they need no longer in practice accord the shah the unquestioning obedience demanded of a murīd by his murshid. More and more their behaviour resembled that of turbulent barons, and, when Shah Ismā'īl I died in 930/1524 and was succeeded by Shah Ṭahmāsp, who was only ten and a half years old, they took advantage of the shah's youthfulness to assert their own power at the expense of the monarch. In the course of their internecine struggles to determine which tribe or coalition of tribes should rule the state, they showed so little respect for the shah's person or position that there were armed clashes between rival groups even in the presence of the shah, whose life was on one occasion endangered. The fiction of their loyalty to their spiritual director was maintained, however, and as late as 1629 Shah 'Abbās I was still recognised in theory as the murshid-i kāmil.

By the end of the reign of Ismā'īl, important changes had taken place in regard to three of the principal offices of state. First, after 920/1514, the term vakīl-i nafs-i nafīs-i humāyūn was abandoned, and the vikālat was referred to in terms more appropriate to the vizierate. There is no doubt that this marks the failure of the attempt to create in the person of the vakīl-i nafs-i nafīs-i humāyūn a superior authority who would be able, because he was the *alter ego* of the shah both in his spiritual and in his temporal capacity, to harmonise and co-ordinate the activities both of the political institution and of the religious institution. It marks, further, a decisive movement away from the concept of a theocratic state, and towards that separation of religious and temporal powers which became an accomplished fact under the later Safavids. Second, the task of imposing doctrinal uniformity, which had been the justification for the extraordinary powers wielded by the early Safavid ṣadrs, was virtually completed by the end of Ismā'īl's reign, and consequently there was from then on a progressive decline in the authority of the ṣadr, who had less and less influence in political matters. Third, Ismā'īl himself had taken steps to curb the power of the amīr al-umarā by appointing to that office in 915/1509–10 an officer of inferior rank. This proved effective, since the officer in question, although he held the office for fifteen years, does not figure prominently in the events of that period.

In 930/1524, the evolution of Safavid administrative institutions was rudely interrupted when the Qizilbāsh amīrs seized control of the state from the youthful Ṭahmāsp. For a period of ten years, different Qizilbāsh tribes, ruling either separately or in alliance with others, dominated the scene. The imposition of military government naturally had its effect on the Safavid administration. The Qizilbāsh had always considered the vikālat to be their prerogative, and the new rulers of the state dubbed themselves vakīl (but not, be it noted, vakīl nafs-i nafīs-i humāyūn) and/or amīr al-umarā. By vakīl they wished to indicate a rank superior to that of the vizier, who was a Persian and therefore, in their eyes, inferior and only fit to hold positions in the civil service. During this period, the fluidity of the administrative system was such that the sources often refer to two officials as vakīl simultaneously. This causes some confusion, but the military and political aspect of the vakīl's function is always uppermost in the one, and the administrative and bureaucratic aspect is predominant in the other. The former is always a Türkmen and may also hold the office of amīr al-umarā. The latter is always a Persian, and his office may also be referred to as the vizierate or *niẓārat-i dīvān-i 'ālī*.

About 940/1533, Shah Ṭahmāsp succeeded in imposing his authority on the Qizilbāsh amīrs. The immediate effect of the shah's assertion of himself as the ruling institution was the decline of the amīr al-umarā. In fact this officer disappears from the list of the officials of the central administration (although the title amīr al-umarā continued to be applied to the Qizilbāsh military governors of important provinces, particularly in times of crisis, up to the end of the reign of Shah 'Abbās I). His disappearance was accompanied by the rise of the qūrchī-bāshī, a formerly subordinate officer, to the position of commander-in-chief of the Qizilbāsh forces. Like the amīr al-umarā before him, the qūrchī-bāshī exercised his authority in political as well as in military affairs. During a period of some forty years (955–95/1548–87) prior to the accession of Shah 'Abbās I, the majority of the qūrchī-bāshīs were drawn from the Afshār Türkmen tribe. In addition, a marked hereditary tendency became apparent in appointments to this office. At first sight, this might suggest that the power of the qūrchī-bāshī was increasing. Although this may possibly be true in regard to individual qūrchī-bāshīs, I would suggest that both these tendencies reflect a weakening of the position of the Qizilbāsh as a whole within the state, and in their position relative to the shah. With the abandonment of the concept of the vakīl-i nafs-i nafīs-i humāyūn, and the disappearance of the amīr al-umarā, the qūrchī-bāshī had emerged as the most powerful military officer in the state. If the Qizilbāsh were prepared to allow this office to be monopolised by one tribe, several conclusions may be drawn. First, during this period the Qizilbāsh were not prepared to challenge the authority of the shah, a complete reversal of the position obtaining during the first decade of Ṭahmāsp's reign. Second, the Qizilbāsh tribes which had formerly been most prominent – the Shāmlū, the Ustājlū, the Takkalū and the Rūmlū – had either been weakened, or discredited, or both, by the decade of civil wars (930–40/1524–33). Thus the way had been opened for a hitherto less important tribe, the Afshār, to come to the fore. Third, the fact that the more powerful tribes acquiesced in the appointment of a succession of Afshārs to the office of qūrchī-bāshī again suggests that the shah's will now prevailed.

Another significant trend during the reign of Ṭahmāsp I (930–84/1524–76) was the continued decline in the power of the ṣadr. With the successful establishment of Ithnā'asharī Shi'ism as the "orthodox" form of Islam throughout the Safavid dominions, the special powers which had been conferred on the ṣadr at the inception of the Safavid state became less necessary. The ṣadrs ceased to play any significant part in political affairs and were largely preoccupied with routine religious matters, particularly the administration of the *auqāf* (bequests and endowments for pious purposes). Even their position as head of the religious institution was not secure, and there are certain portents during the latter part of Ṭahmāsp's reign of what became an established fact by the time of 'Abbās I, namely the eclipse of the ṣadr by the powerful theologians known as mujtahids, who emerged as the exponents of Shī'ī orthodoxy as it assumed more rigid doctrinal forms.

Finally, we may note the increased power and prestige of the vizier after the shah had brought the Qizilbāsh amīrs to heel about 940/1533. During the preceding decade, the viziers had been mere tools in the hands of the "military" vakīl/amīr al-umarā.

To sum up, we may recapitulate the following characteristics of the Safavid administrative system under Ṭahmāsp I: a continued movement away from the theocratic form of government associated with Safavid origins; a greater separation of temporal and spiritual powers; an increase, after an initial setback, in the authority of the ruling institution (the shah) and a corresponding curtailment of the influence of the Qizilbāsh in political affairs. In the second half of Ṭahmāsp's reign, the introduction into the Safavid state of elements of different ethnic origin, namely Georgians and Circassians, also militated against the Qizilbāsh supremacy. This will be considered in the next section.

PHASE TWO (996–1038/1588–1629)

PHASE TWO (996–1038/1588–1629)

It was stated above that Shah 'Abbās the Great reorganised the Safavid state on entirely new bases. Why was it necessary to do this? Briefly, Shah 'Abbās was forced to take drastic action to preserve the fabric of the state. In 982/1574 Shah Ṭahmāsp's physical powers began to fail, and this was the signal for the recrudescence of Qizilbāsh dissension. Ṭahmāsp's death in 984/1576 was followed by more than a decade of disastrous government by Ismā'īl II and Muḥammad Khudābanda, neither of whom was capable of effective rule. Various power groups took advantage of the situation to pursue their particular ends at the expense of the state, which was rent by their faction. The situation in 982/1574, however, differed from that obtaining in 932/1526 in one important respect. In 1526 the precarious balance between the Turkish and Persian elements in the administration had been upset when the Qizilbāsh seized control of the state, and the object of the civil wars which followed had been to decide which Qizilbāsh tribe, or tribal coalition, should dominate the rest. It was, so to speak, a domestic quarrel. In 1574 and subsequent years, however, the point at issue was whether the Qizilbāsh could maintain their privileged position in the state in the face of the threat posed by the new Georgian and Circassian elements which were beginning to oust them from administrative posts.

Where had these new elements come from? In the main, they were prisoners, or the offspring of prisoners, taken captive in four Caucasian campaigns fought by the Safavids between 947/1540–1 and 961/1553–4, and brought back to Persia. The rivalries of Georgian and Circassian women in the royal harem led to dynastic struggles based on ethnic considerations, of a type hitherto unknown in the Safavid state. Not all the Georgians were captives taken in battle. Some Georgian noblemen voluntarily entered Safavid service, and before the end of Ṭahmāsp's reign we hear of one such who held a provincial governorship.

In addition to anarchy at home, Shah 'Abbās was faced at his accession by a war on two fronts against the arch-enemies of the Safavid state, the Ottomans and the Uzbeks. The former had taken advantage of Persia's internal weakness to occupy more Safavid territory in the north-west than ever before; the latter had overrun Khurāsān in the north-east. 'Abbās had therefore to restore internal stability and then to expel the invaders from Persian soil.

In order to do this, 'Abbās desperately needed troops on whose loyalty he could rely. After enduring more than a decade of Qizilbāsh plots, intrigue and treachery, he decided he could place no further trust in them. He therefore formed, from the ranks of the Georgians and Circassians referred to above, several regiments of a new standing army, owing allegiance only to himself, and paid direct from the royal treasury. These men were known as ghulāms, *i.e.* "slaves" of the shah. This decision meant that a new source of income had to be found for the royal treasury. Hitherto the Qizilbāsh troops, which had constituted the greater part of the Safavid armies, had been paid by their Türkmen chiefs, who formed the military aristocracy of the early Safavid state and held all the important provincial governorships. The provincial governments were largely alienated from the control of the central government, and the provincial governors held the land under their jurisdiction in the form of assignments of various types, known by the general term *tiyūl.* They consumed on the spot the greater part of the revenue which they derived from these assignments, and remitted only a small portion, in the form of dues of various kinds, to the central government. Even then these funds were not under the direct control of the shah but were administered by a special "ministry of state lands". The shah's main source of income was crown lands, the revenues from which were collected by the royal agents. The solution adopted by Shah 'Abbās was to increase the revenue remitted to the royal treasury by converting some mamālik or "state" lands into khāṣṣa or crown lands. This policy was extended by his successors to such an extent that it became one of the principal causes of Safavid decline.[1]

Not all the ghulāms were trained for service in the newly-created regiments. Many were employed in the royal household and in the khāṣṣa administration in general. The latter necessarily expanded as it took over the administration of more and more state lands. Gradually the ghulāms made their presence felt at the higher levels of Safavid administration until they filled about one-fifth of the high administrative posts. Governorships of the khāṣṣa provinces went to ghulāms rather than to Qizilbāsh. Finally, in 1007/1598, a ghulām, Allāhvardī Khān, was appointed commander-in-chief of the armed forces. The old dichotomy between Turk and Persian had been further complicated by

[1] Lambton, *Landlord and Peasant*, pp. 107–9.

the emergence of the Caucasian elements as a powerful "third force". The numbers involved make it clear that Shah ʿAbbās had, in fact, effected a social revolution. For instance, in 1013/1604 20,000 Armenians were enrolled in the ghulāms. In 1025/1616 130,000 Georgian prisoners were brought back to Persia. In addition, in order to weaken tribal cohesion and to break down rigid social patterns, ʿAbbās moved large groups of Qizilbāsh tribesmen from one area to another and settled large groups of Caucasian immigrants in strategic areas.

As one would expect, this social revolution produced major changes in the administrative system. The abortive attempt by a Qizilbāsh amīr, at the beginning of the reign of Shah ʿAbbās, to constitute himself an old-style vakīl represented the last bid by the Qizilbāsh to regain their former position of dominance in the administration. When Shah ʿAbbās crushed this attempt, the title of vakīl lapsed, as to all intents and purposes did that of amīr al-umarā in so far as it denoted an officer of the central administration. Instead of these titles, associated specifically with the period of Qizilbāsh supremacy, we find the commanders of two of the new regiments ranked among the six principal officers of state, namely the *qullar-āqāsī* and the *tufangchī-āqāsī*. The former commanded the regiment of *qullar*, or ghulāms, and the latter commanded the regiment of musketeers. The commander of the Qizilbāsh forces still retained the title of qūrchi-bāshī, but since the Qizilbāsh constituted only one element of the Safavid army as reconstituted by Shah ʿAbbās, his influence in military and political affairs was necessarily curtailed. At best, he was now *primus inter pares*. The greater centralisation of the administration under ʿAbbās is reflected in the improved status of the vizier, the head of the bureaucracy and leader of the Persian elements in the administration. As a token of this new status, the vizier was commonly referred to as iʿtimād al-daula ("trusty support of the state") or *ṣadr-i aʿẓam* ("exalted seat of honour"). The ṣadr (with whom the ṣadr-i aʿẓam should not be confused) remained the head of the religious institution, but his position, as we saw above, was increasingly challenged by the mujtahids. The sixth and last of the principal officers of the realigned administration was the *ishīk-āqāsī-bāshī-yi dīvān*, who was naturally a Qizilbāsh amīr and whose duties as Grand Marshal were largely of a ceremonial nature.

The measure of the achievement of Shah ʿAbbās I – and for this reason alone he is deservedly called "the Great" – is that the administrative system of the Safavid state, as reorganised by him, continued to function for a century after his death, more or less under its own momentum because his successors, with the exception of ʿAbbās II, were weak and incompetent rulers. One must point out, however, that the germs of future decay were present in this system. The pernicious effect of the extension of the khāṣṣa system has already been mentioned. The reasons why it was pernicious are not hard to seek. Granted that the old-style Qizilbāsh military governors consumed the greater part of the provincial revenue *in situ*, and remitted little to the state coffers. But precisely because they enjoyed the use of this revenue it was in their own interests to maintain a flourishing economy in the area under their jurisdiction, and not so to tax the province that prosperity declined and the amount of revenue consequently decreased. In the khāṣṣa provinces, on the other hand, the taxes were farmed by the shah's agents or intendants, who had no material interest in the province in question, and whose sole concern was to increase the amount remitted to the royal treasury; by pleasing the shah in this way they ensured that they would retain their own jobs. The more rapacious the shah and his viziers, the harsher the burden of taxation imposed on the population of the khāṣṣa provinces. In contrast to the position obtaining in the mamālik provinces, little if any of the revenue collected from the khāṣṣa provinces was ever used to support the economy of those provinces.

The second major cause of subsequent decay was the growth of the ḥaram system. In the first phase of Safavid development it had been the practice for the shah to appoint his sons to provincial governorships. While they were still minors, the royal princes were placed under the guardianship of a Qizilbāsh amīr, termed lala (or, less commonly, *atabeg*, an echo of Saljūq practice). The lala was responsible for the moral and physical education of the prince committed to his charge, and the latter thus received a training which fitted him to take his place if need be, as ruler of the Safavid empire. In particular, he received first-hand training in the conduct of political and military affairs. The obvious danger inherent in this system was that an ambitious prince, or an overweening amīr, might seek to anticipate events by rebelling against the ruler. But when one observes the moral and physical degeneration of the dynasty which resulted from the practice, instituted by ʿAbbās I, of confining the royal princes to the harem, and entrusting their training to the court eunuchs, one is bound to feel that the possibility of treachery was the lesser of two evils.

PHASE THREE (1038–1135/1629–1722)

Almost a century elapsed between the death of Shah 'Abbās I and the usurpation of the Safavid throne by the Afghans. It was a period of gradual but continuous decline. This decline was checked, but not stopped, by Shah 'Abbās II (1052–77/1642–66). 'Abbās II was a strong ruler, who asserted his authority as the ruling institution. During his reign, however, the policy of bringing state (mamālik) lands under the direct administration of the crown was not only continued but extended. It has already been pointed out that this policy contributed largely to Safavid decline. Apart from the harmful effects resulting from the impersonal and oppressive administration of the khāṣṣa provinces by the shah's intendants, the loss of each successive mamālik province meant a proportionate reduction in the number of the Qizilbāsh, and a consequent decline in Safavid military strength. Although the Georgian and other ghulām regiments were loyal to the shah – indeed, by the end of the 11th/17th century they were almost the only troops on whose loyalty he could rely as fighting men – they were not comparable to the Qizilbāsh. In many cases, too, the reduction in the Qizilbāsh strength was not made good by a corresponding increase in the numbers of the ghulāms.

During the first phase of Safavid administrative development, the whole administrative system had a pronounced military character, as we have seen, and bureaucrats who had no military function had little influence. In Phase Two, Shah 'Abbās broke the power of the Qizilbāsh, and as a consequence of this, and of the increased centralisation of government, the power of the bureaucracy grew. In Phase Three, the transformation was completed. The military arm was weakened to the point where it was no longer possible to check the incursions of marauding tribesmen from Balūchistān and Afghanistan. At the same time, the bureaucracy expanded in size, and became more rigid in its organisation and operation, until it resembled the complex and ponderous machine described in the *Tazkirat al-mulūk*, a manual of Safavid administration, unique of its kind among Persian historical records, completed about 1726. The vizier became the most powerful officer of state and, in conjunction with the court and the harem, exercised undue influence over a succession of weak and debauched shahs.

We have already noted, in Phase Two, an increasing tendency

towards the separation of spiritual and temporal powers. In Phase Three, the separation between the political institution and the religious institution became complete. No longer subject to overriding political control, the religious classes tightened their grip on the nation, and their power reached its zenith during the reign of the two weakest Safavid shahs, Sulaimān and Sulṭān Ḥusain, who together ruled for fifty-six years (1077–1135/1666–1722). Particularly during the reign of the latter, the mujtahids, who had only reluctantly conceded the claim of the Safavid shahs to be the representatives of the Hidden Imām, took advantage of the weakness of the political institution to reassert their independence of it and to regain their prerogative as the representatives of the Mahdī. Some sources even suggest a period of "direct religious rule by means of a concourse of mujtahids above the monarch".[1] As E.G.Browne put it, the domination of the state by the "great ecclesiastics" "hardly made for either spiritual unity or national efficiency".[2] The founder of the Safavid state, Ismā'īl I, had recognised the potential dangers to the fabric of the state which would flow from unbridled intervention by the 'ulamā in political, economic and military affairs. It was for this reason that he had made the ṣadr a political appointee, charged with ensuring that the religious classes remained subject to political direction. This system worked only as long as the shah maintained a strong hand at the helm. According to Sir John Malcolm, however, under Shah Sulṭān Ḥusain the "meekness and bigotry" of the shah "proved more destructive to his country than the vices of Soliman [Shah Sulaimān: 1077–1105/1666–1694]. So great was his pious zeal, that none but Moollahs [*mullās*], or holy Syuds [sayyids], were appointed to high stations ...High nobles gave place, with feelings of resentment, to eunuchs and priests; but their discontent was only vented in complaints."[3]

Up to the time of Shah Sulaimān, the prosperous multicultural Safavid state, in which "strangers were encouraged and protected, and foreigners from every quarter of the globe, but particularly Europe, resorted to Persia"[4], continued to exist. Under Shah Sulṭān Ḥusain, however, the position of the Armenian merchants, whose commercial and financial expertise had contributed much to Safavid economic prosperity, declined greatly, since the shah was too weak to protect

[1] See Amin Banani, "The Social and Economic Structure of the Safavid Empire in its Heyday", paper presented to the Harvard Colloquium on Tradition and Change in the Middle East, December 1967, p. 6.

[2] *LHP* IV, 120.

[3] Malcolm, *History of Persia* I, 594–5.

[4] *Ibid.*, p. 592.

them from the "rapacious ministers and bigoted priests of his court"[1].

During the second half of the 17th century, the status of the ṣadr, an officer whose function was closely connected with the original concept of the Safavid state during Phase One, continued to decline. Shah 'Abbās II had deliberately restricted the power of the ṣadr, and in 1077/1666–7 the ṣadārat had been divided into a khāṣṣa and an 'āmma (mamālik) branch, a step which accurately reflected the current division of the Safavid administration and indicated that the ṣadr was no longer an official of the first importance. From the beginning of the reign of Sulṭān Ḥusain (1105/1694) at least, and possibly earlier, the supreme religious official was the *mullā-bāshī*.[2] The ṣadrs, however, continued to be primarily responsible for the administration of the auqāf and also assisted the qāḍīs in various juridical functions.

PROVINCIAL ADMINISTRATION

The provincial governments were, to a large extent, replicas in miniature of the central government. Some of the principal officers of the central government had their counterparts at the courts of provincial governors. Foremost among these were the vizier and the ṣadr. The provincial viziers and ṣadrs were, in general, appointed by the shah and not by the central vizier and central ṣadr respectively. If the provincial governor had more than one province under his jurisdiction, or if his province was of exceptional importance, the vizier who was in attendance at the seat of the provincial governor frequently controlled the activities of other viziers, subordinate to himself, who were resident at other large provincial centres. To denote the superior rank of the former, the term *vazīr-i kull* was used.

In appointing viziers and ṣadrs to the provincial administrations, the Safavids were once again following the practice of their predecessors, the Timurids, Qarā Quyūnlū and Āq Quyūnlū. Documentary evidence points to the continuity, at many levels, of the Persian bureaucratic tradition under a succession of Mongol and Türkmen rulers. In some instances the vazīr-i kull was hardly less influential than the vizier who was the organ of the central administration. In many cases the provincial vizierate was the stepping-stone to appointment to the central vizierate. Many families had a tradition of public service going back

[1] *Ibid.*, p. 627.	[2] Minorsky, *Tadhkirat al-Mulūk*, p. 110.

for several generations, but the facility and frequency with which provincial viziers were transferred from one part of the country to another militated against the growth of family dynasties or bureaucratic empires in the provinces.

The provincial ṣadr controlled the religious institution in his province, just as the central ṣadr was the head of the religious institution overall. He had authority over all members of the religious classes, and was responsible for the administration of the auqāf and the conduct of all transactions connected with them. During Phase One of the development of the Safavid administrative system, the provincial ṣadr, again like his central counterpart, not infrequently held the military rank of amīr. That this was no token appointment is shown by the fact that as late as 955/1548 we have evidence of a provincial ṣadr being in command of an actual military operation. Such was the predominantly military character of the Safavid administration during this first phase that not only ṣadrs, but also qāḍīs and other members of the religious classes, took part in military operations, in particular the defence of cities. In such cases, when qāḍīs moved to protect the lives and property of the citizenry, they were fulfilling the traditional rôle of the Persian 'ulamā as organisers of popular action. The lack of any clear boundary, during this first phase, between "political" and "religious", between "civil" and "military", is even more marked at the provincial level than in the central administration. Qāḍīs were frequently appointed to the vizierate and *vice versa*, and members of the religious classes often encroached on the preserves of temporal officials in regard to financial matters and the conduct of the business of the dīvān.

The remaining principal officers of state had no counterparts at the provincial government level. For instance, the *amīr al-umarā'ī*, or office of the supreme commander of the Qizilbāsh forces, had no provincial equivalent. The regional commanders of Qizilbāsh troops were, in the mamālik provinces, the military governors of the provinces concerned. These governors were termed indifferently *amīr*, *ḥākim*, and *beglerbeg* (*-ī*) (more rarely, *dārūgha* or *tiyūldār*). In times of crisis, however, the governors of the strategically important frontier provinces – in particular Āzarbāījān, Shīrvān and Khurāsān – were accorded the title of amīr al–umarā, in recognition of the fact that the military aspect of their office was all-important at such times.

From the time of 'Abbās I onwards, an increasing number of mamālik provinces were converted to khāṣṣa and brought under the direct administration of the shah. The administration of the khāṣṣa provinces was carried on in times of peace by viziers, drawn from the ranks of the ghulāms. If military officers were needed in the khāṣṣa provinces, they were furnished by one of the ghulām regiments. The number of provincial governors who were drawn from the ranks of the Qizilbāsh tribes was drastically reduced. As a result, the title of amīr al-umarā became increasingly uncommon, and in fact is rarely, if ever, used after the death of ʿAbbās I (1038/1629).

We saw previously that during the reign of Shah Ṭahmāsp the qūrchī-bāshī replaced the amīr al-umarā as the principal military officer of the central administration. As had formerly been the case with the amīr al-umarā, the qūrchī-bāshī did not have an equivalent in the provincial administrations, and for the same reason. When the term qūrchī-bāshī occurs in connection with provincial government, it denotes the commander of a local detachment of qūrchīs, or the commander of a small bodyguard of qūrchīs attached to the person of a royal prince, or has some other special connotation.

Finally, the vakīl-i nafs-i nafīs-i humāyūn (as he originally was), or the *vakīl-i salṭana* or plain vakīl (as he later became), naturally had no provincial counterpart. When the term vakīl occurs in the sources in relation to provincial government, it is used simply in the sense of "agent", "deputy", "representative". Not infrequently it is used to denote an official who seems to be subordinate to the provincial vizier.

CONCLUSION

The Safavids went down to defeat ultimately because they failed to reconcile the irreconcilable: Turk and Persian; tribal organisation and urbanism; the pastoral-nomadic tradition and the sedentary life of the agriculturalist; revolutionary sufism and dogmatic Shiʿism; theocracy and the complex bureaucracy required by an expanding empire; the "men of the sword" and the "men of the pen"; the claim of the mujtahids to constitute the only legitimate form of government in an Ithnāʿasharī Shīʿī state, and the imperatives of a multi-cultural state. The measure of their success is that they had a greater degree of success in dealing with these problems than had the Saljūqs, the Mongols and the Türkmens who had preceded them. The dynasties which followed them – the Afghans, Afshārs, Qājārs and Pahlavīs, all of whom were confronted by at least some of the same problems – were also to prove less successful in finding solutions to them. The Safavid administrative machine, with its complex system of checks and balances, worked with surprising efficiency, except when there was lack of effective direction from the centre. Life and property were secure; travel was safe; trade and commerce flourished; minorities were tolerated and protected; formidable foreign foes were kept at bay. Alone of all the countries of the Middle East, Iran resisted the most efficient military machine of its time, that of the Ottoman empire. The contrast with the position in the second half of the 18th century and the 19th century, after the breakdown of the Safavid administrative system, is startling: absence of effective central control; total lack of internal security; depopulation of the cities and economic decline; the unrestrained play of centrifugal forces; and the permanent annexation of Iranian territory by enemies in the north-west, north-east and east. In order to make a proper assessment of the merits and defects of the Safavid administrative system, one must take into account the ephemeral nature of the Türkmen dynasties which preceded it, and the chaos which followed its collapse. Despite the internal stresses and external pressures to which the system was subject, it gave Iran two and a quarter centuries of stable and prosperous government.

CHAPTER 7

EUROPEAN CONTACTS WITH PERSIA, 1350–1736

Although historians generally have regarded the Mongol irruption of the 7th/13th century into Persia and countries further to the west as an unmitigated disaster, this calamity may be taken as a starting point for this chapter because it in fact served one purpose that can be regarded as beneficial. The Mongol armies may have been motivated solely by lust for conquest and destruction, but even out of their evil sprang a positive development when they rent asunder the veil which had for so long shut off Persia and other Islamic countries from the West. For as a result of the Mongol invasions new contacts between the East and the West became established, though at first only slowly and with all the handicaps of much ignorance on both sides. As the pioneers in establishing this contact between East and West, such as William of Rubruck, the Polos, Marino Sanuto and Friar Odoric of Pordenone, all belonged to the period covered by the previous volume of this series, there is no need to say more here than to state that their achievements were of prime importance, since they showed the way for later travellers to follow. The East was no longer a closed book to the West, but as yet comparatively few pages had been turned. It must be borne in mind when studying the development of contact between Persia and the West that the "traffic" was not merely from West to East; there were also travellers in the opposite direction. On the whole, a good deal less has been heard of these visitors from Persia partly because they were fewer in number, and partly because their accounts did not, in the majority of cases, become widely known, if at all, in Europe.

One may begin this survey of contacts between Persia and the West by examining what were, on both sides, the main incentives for establishing and maintaining relations. These incentives were of a fourfold nature, but they were not, of course, always operative simultaneously; moreover, they were of varying intensity.

In the first category, but only in the West, there was the religious incentive. In consequence of the tolerant religious policy of the Mongol Īl-Khāns, towards the close of the 13th century a number of

Dominican and Franciscan friars visited northern Persia and some were allowed to establish themselves in Tabrīz. In 1318 Sulṭāniyya was made a metropolitan see, the first archbishop being Francus of Perugia, a Dominican. Between 1320 and 1329 bishoprics were established at Marāgha, Tabrīz and Tiflis, all the occupants being likewise Dominicans.[1] In 1350 Nakhchivān was made an episcopal see, and a century later, with the decline of Sulṭāniyya, became an archbishopric; it was destined to outlast all the other sees, surviving until 1745. A notable increase in the number of European missionaries occurred during the reign of Shah 'Abbās I, when his tolerant religious policy made possible the establishment in Persia of the Augustinians, Carmelites and other orders. Like the Dominicans, these missionaries had to learn Persian, Turkish and Armenian in order to be able to preach in those languages. Although the proselytising efforts of these missions among Muslims had meagre results, their members made important contacts, and many of their letters to Europe, particularly of the Carmelites and Jesuits, are most valuable sources of information.

Secondly, there was the desire for concerted military action by both East and West against the Ottoman Turks, whose growing power and aggressive nature constituted a serious threat not only to Persia but also to the Byzantine empire and other countries in the West. This desire led to the despatch of a number of diplomatic missions from various Western nations to Persia and also from the latter to the West. Though these attempted diplomatic exchanges were continued by both sides over a long period, they all failed. The reason for this failure was not lack of good will; it was the extreme difficulty of making and retaining close contact between East and West with a hostile Turkey in between. The consequence was that properly concerted and synchronised operations against the common foe proved to be impossible.

In the third place there was the commercial incentive. It was as advantageous to the Western nations as to the Persians to establish trade relations. The desire to forge commercial links resulted in the sending of a number of commercial missions by both Persia and the nations of the West.

In the fourth category of incentives to increased contact between Persia and the West were those travellers who passed through that country on their way to or from India or beyond. There were also

[1] Gams, pp. 454–5.

some persons who visited the country merely out of curiosity, as Persia was still a relatively unknown land.

Some of the earliest contacts between Persia and the West in the period covered by this chapter were made by the Dominicans and Franciscans, particularly the former. In March 1377 a Dominican named Johannes de Galonifontibus was appointed bishop of Nakhchivān. In August 1398 Pope Boniface IX made him archbishop of Sulṭāniyya.[1] Tīmūr, after his great victory over the Ottoman Turks near Ankara in July 1402, sent Archbishop Johannes on a mission to Venice, Genoa, London and Paris with tidings of his triumph.[2] To Henry IV of England and Charles VI of France Tīmūr sent letters in which he proposed to conclude treaties for the granting of reciprocal privileges for the merchants of his realm and for those of England and France. Both Henry IV and Charles VI replied in suitable terms and congratulated Tīmūr on his brilliant victory.[3] On his return to Persia, Johannes de Galonifontibus remained at Sulṭāniyya until his transfer to the Crimea about the year 1423.[4]

Tīmūr's victory over Bāyezīd transformed for a time the whole situation in the east and gave the already moribund Byzantine empire another half century of existence. In order to obtain up to date information on the results of this victory, Henry III of Castile and Leon decided to send a mission to Tīmūr under Ruy Gonzalez de Clavijo, Gomez de Salazar and Fr Alonso Paez de Santa Maria. He had already been in touch with Tīmūr, as two of his envoys, Pelayo de Sotomayor and Fernando de Palazuelos, were present at the battle of Ankara; moreover, when they returned to Spain Tīmūr sent with them an envoy of his own named Ḥājjī Muḥammad al-Qāżī.

The Clavijo mission left Spain in 1403. Not being able to reach Tīmūr while he was on his way back to Samarqand, Clavijo and his companions had to traverse the whole of northern Persia from west to east on the outward journey and in the reverse direction on the way back, the two routes differing slightly at certain points. Consequently, they were able to visit a number of important towns in northern Persia

[1] Eubel I, 457.

[2] For the confusion between Johannes de Galonifontibus and the English Franciscan John Greenlaw, bishop of Soldaia in the Crimea, who, so far as is known, was never in Persia, see Silvestre de Sacy, "Mémoire sur une correspondance inédite de Tamerlan avec Charles VI", *Mémoires de l'Académie des Inscriptions et Belles-Lettres* VI (1822), 509; also Loenertz, p. 172.

[3] For Henry IV's letter, see *Original Letters illustrative of English History*, ed. Sir H. Ellis, 3rd series (London, 1846) I, 54–8.

[4] Loenertz, p. 171.

and to meet many persons of note. Clavijo has given us a valuable account of these journeyings. Entering Persia on 1 June 1404, the mission travelled via Khūy to Tabrīz, a city which much impressed Clavijo. He described it as large and well laid out, with fine roadways and many great buildings. From Tabrīz the mission journeyed on to Sulṭāniyya, which was still enjoying its brief spell of importance. Clavijo noticed there the great concourse of merchants and traders who were attending the annual fair, held at Sulṭāniyya every summer and patronised by a number of Genoese and Venetians.[1] While at Sulṭāniyya, Clavijo and his colleagues were received by Mīrān Shāh, who, despite his mental instability, behaved very graciously on this occasion. From Sulṭāniyya the mission travelled via Tehran, Fīrūzkūh, Dāmghān and Nīshāpūr to Mashhad. In that town they were allowed to enter the tomb-chamber of the Imām 'Alī al-Riḍā, "whereby when travelling later through other parts of Persia it came to be noised abroad that we had been at Meshed and visited this holy place the people would come and kiss the hem of our robes, deeming that we were of those who had acquired merit for having made the pilgrimage to the shrine of the great Saint of Khurásán".[2] Of the remainder of the journey to Samarqand and of Tīmūr's reception of the mission in his capital no mention need be made because they are beyond the scope of this chapter. Nor does the return route, following the same itinerary as the outward one, except for digressions to Simnān and Qazvīn, need further comment. What is relevant is that when in March 1406 Clavijo and his companions reached Spain, they had done much to extend and strengthen European contacts with Persia.

Little can be said respecting the next contact between Persia and the West, for Nicolò de' Conti, the Venetian who made it, has left no records of much interest or value. Between 1420 and 1425 he sailed from Baṣra to Hurmuz, of which he gave some description. From Hurmuz he went along the Persian coast to a large town which he called Calabatia, where he claimed to have learned Persian; this place, like a number of others which he mentioned, cannot now be identified.

The Ottoman Turks, though so heavily defeated by Tīmūr in 1402, showed such powers of resilience that only twenty years later they were once again hammering at the gates of Constantinople. Although this

[1] Genoese merchants had been established at Sulṭāniyya since Il-Khanid times: Heyd II, 506.
[2] Clavijo, trans. Le Strange, pp. 185–6; p. 158 for Mīrān Shāh.

attack was beaten off, others followed, and in 1453, to the horror of the Christian world, the city fell and the Byzantine empire came to an end. Venice, with her far-flung commercial interests in the east, was gravely threatened by the ever-growing Turkish menace. For some time she and the other European powers which were exposed to this danger sought anxiously for some eastern ruler who, as Tīmūr had done, might attack the Turks from the rear, if possible in conjunction with a simultaneous onslaught from the west. At last it seemed that Uzun Ḥasan, the Āq Quyūnlū ruler of Persia, might be this ally. In 1458 Uzun Ḥasan made an alliance with the emperor David of Trebizond, whose niece Kyra Katerina, daughter of the penultimate emperor Kalo Johannes, he married. Though the Turks extinguished the empire of Trebizond in 1461, they were unable to overthrow Uzun Ḥasan. In 1463 the Venetian Signoria sent L. Quirini to Tabrīz to induce Uzun Ḥasan to join Venice in an attack on the Turks, but he failed to do so. Eight years later the Signoria despatched to Persia, with the same object, Caterino Zeno, a more suitable envoy than Quirini, as he was a nephew of Kyra Katerina (or Despina Khātūn, as she was pleonastically called after her marriage). In consequence, he was able to persuade Uzun Ḥasan to make war on the Turks. Although he was successful at first, the Türkmen ruler later met with a serious reverse. Unfortunately, no simultaneous attack was made from the west by the Venetians or other Western powers.

In 1473 the Signoria sent Giosafat Barbaro to Tabrīz to urge Uzun Hasan to renew his attack on the Turks, but he found the Türkmen ruler still smarting from his defeat and disinclined to cooperate. In other respects, however, Barbaro made an excellent contact with Uzun Ḥasan. He was able to visit many parts of Persia, of which he afterwards gave a valuable account. He was at Hurmuz not long after the visit of the horse-dealer Afanasiĭ Nikitin, the first Russian of whom we have any record in that part of the country.[1] Barbaro's efforts to make Uzun Ḥasan take up his sword again were soon reinforced by another Venetian envoy, Ambrogio Contarini, who brought with him an ambitious plan for a simultaneous attack on the Turks from both east and west. By this time, however, Uzun Ḥasan was in failing health and was preoccupied, moreover, with a revolt by one of his sons. In 1478 he

[1] For his description of Hurmuz, see Nikitin, *Khozhenie*, p. 21, and in Major, *India in the Fifteenth Century*, part 3, pp. 8–9.

died. Though Barbaro and Contarini failed in their main object, they brought back with them much information respecting Persia and its resources. Barbaro's account is the more valuable of the two, since he was very observant and had the advantage of knowing Turkish and also some Persian. On the other hand, Contarini's description of Uzun Hasan's appearance and character is more vivid than Barbaro's.[1]

Less than a decade after the failure of these Venetian efforts to combine with Persia against the Ottoman Turks, Bartholomeu Diaz rounded the Cape of Good Hope, but a threatened mutiny of his men prevented him from proceeding further. While Diaz was on his famous voyage, a Portuguese named Pero da Covilhã travelled across Egypt, sailed down the Red Sea and crossed the Indian Ocean. He was the first Portuguese to set foot on Indian soil. On leaving India, he landed on the island of Hurmuz, which he was likewise the first of his nation to visit. From Hurmuz da Covilhã returned to Egypt, where he wrote in great detail the report of his travels east of Suez. This report proved to be of great value to those responsible for planning Vasco da Gama's truly epoch-making voyage round the Cape of Good Hope to India. This was an achievement of capital importance: the Portuguese sea captains, trained in the tradition of Prince Henry the Navigator, had succeeded in outflanking Islam by sea. Moreover, as was apparent soon afterwards, they had also, commercially speaking, outflanked the Venetians and Genoese. Though it may be doubted whether Henry the Navigator had ever thought of Persia when he was formulating at Sagres his plans for ocean travel and discovery, it was undoubtedly his inspiration which led ultimately to the rounding of Africa and the inauguration of the long sea route from Europe to the Persian Gulf, India and beyond. This wonderful achievement had great effects on the relations between Persia and the West. Portugal, as the pioneer, was naturally the first to benefit and then make the contact permanent. With the additional route to Persia now open, there was soon to be a great increase in the number of travellers from the West to that country.

Shortly before the close of the century, a Genoese named Hieronimo di Santo Stefano, after a very hazardous journey to India and Ceylon, returned to Europe via Hurmuz, Shīrāz, Iṣfahān, Tabrīz, Aleppo and Tripoli. His account of Persia does not, however, add appreciatively to our knowledge of the country at that juncture.

[1] *Travels to Tana and Persia*, pp. 132–3.

Although there had been, as has been seen, quite a considerable interchange of travellers between Persia and the West in the course of the 15th century, it is improbable that more than a limited number of people in Europe had any precise knowledge of the country by its close. It must be borne in mind that the reading public of those days was small and that it was only in the latter part of the century that printed material became available. People were then on the whole more drawn to fabulous tales than to factual narrations. They liked to read of terrible monsters, of dog-headed men and of men with no heads at all. They were regaled with much material of this kind in the *Travels* of Sir John Mandeville, written about 1356, the real author of which was either Jean de Bourgogne or, less probably, Jean d'Outremeuse, both of them natives of Liège.[1] In the *Mirrour of the World*, which Caxton translated from Coussouin's *Image du Monde* and printed in 1480 or the following year, there occurs this passage:

Emonge alle other ther is a contree named Perse, and conteyneth xxxiii regyons: of which the first is the Royame of Perse, where is a science called Nygromancie was first founden, which science constrayneth the enemye, the fende, to be taken and holde prisonner. In this contree groweth a pese whiche is so hoot that it skaldeth the handes of them that holde it, and it groweth with encresynge of the mone, and with wayning it discreceth at eche tyme of his cours. It helpeth wel to them that ben nygromanciers.[2]

In the early years of the 16th century Ludovico di Varthema of Bologna, whose chief claim to fame is that he performed the pilgrimage to Mecca, landed at Hurmuz, which he described as a noble and extremely beautiful city. He went to Shīrāz, where he met a Persian merchant whom he had known at Mecca. This merchant took Varthema to his home at "Eri" (Herat), which he maintained was in "Corazani" (Khurāsān), but which was probably the village of Harāt-i Khurra, near Nairīz, in Fārs.[3] He and his merchant friend wished to go on to "Sambragante" (Samarqand), but could not do so because the "Soffi"[4] (Shah Ismā'īl) was ravaging the country and slaughtering the

[1] H.S. Bennett, *Chaucer and the Fifteenth Century* (Oxford, 1947), p. 199.

[2] Quoted from the Early English Text Society, no. 110, *The Mirrour of the World*, p. 81. The editor, O.H. Prior, points out that Caxton mistranslated as "pese" the word *poiz*, "pitch", which obviously makes much better sense.

[3] See Penrose, *Travel and Discovery*, p. 30. Varthema claimed to have travelled from the coast near Hurmuz to Herat in 12 days, which was manifestly an impossibility.

[4] A very early use of the term ("Sophy", a corruption of Ṣafī), unless it is a later interpolation.

Sunnīs. After spending some months at "Eri", Varthema returned to Hurmuz, whence he sailed to India.

Of far more importance than Varthema's visit to Persia was the arrival off Hurmuz in 1507 of a Portuguese fleet under the command of Affonso d'Albuquerque, who had come via the Cape of Good Hope. The twelve-year-old king of Hurmuz, Saif al-Dīn, was under the tutelage of his vizier, the audacious and cunning Khwāja 'Aṭṭār, who had received ample warning of the approach of the Portuguese fleet and had done his utmost to put Hurmuz in a state of defence. When Albuquerque demanded the surrender of the island, his demand was rejected. The Portuguese thereupon launched an attack which succeeded only after some hard fighting. The young king agreed to become a vassal of the king of Portugal and to pay an annual tribute.

Soon afterwards an official arrived from Shah Ismā'īl to collect the annual tribute due to him. In great perplexity the king and his advisers consulted Albuquerque as to their reply. Albuquerque, by way of answer, gave the official cannon balls, grenades and guns and bade him inform the shah that "this was the sort of money wherewith the King of Portugal had ordered his captains to pay the tribute of that kingdom that was under his command".[1] Albuquerque soon repented of this brusqueness, however, and sent the Persian official some valuable presents; while in 1513, still anxious to establish friendly contact with Shah Ismā'īl, he sent to him Miguel Ferreira as his envoy with suitable gifts and a message couched in appropriate terms.

The Portuguese fleet remained at Hurmuz until 1508, when some of Albuquerque's captains grew restive at the delay and began to intrigue with Khwāja 'Aṭṭār. Faced with open mutiny, Albuquerque was reluctantly compelled to abandon the island. He was so conscious of its great strategic and commercial importance, however, that he determined to recover it as soon as opportunity arose. When he had been able to collect a fresh fleet of sufficient strength in 1515, he again appeared off Hurmuz, seizing the island and this time holding it. Soon afterwards, Miguel Ferreira returned from the Persian court with an envoy from the shah. As Ismā'īl was still smarting from his defeat by the Ottoman Turks at Chāldirān in the previous year and as, in any case, he had no navy, he had no choice but to accept the Portuguese occupation of Hurmuz as a *fait accompli*. Albuquerque was thus able to

[1] Albuquerque I, 145.

conclude a treaty with Persia which confirmed that the king of Hurmuz was a vassal of the Portuguese crown. In return, the Portuguese were to help the Persians to recover the Baḥrain islands from the Arab dynasty of the Jabrids, to enter into an alliance against the Ottomans and to assist the Persian government to put down a revolt by a Balūchī tribe in Makrān.[1] One of the earliest Europeans to furnish particulars of Hurmuz after its seizure was Duarte Barbosa, who was probably an eye-witness of the event.[2]

Albuquerque, who had sent back with Shah Ismā'īl's envoy, following the conclusion of the treaty, his own ambassador Fernão Gomes de Lemos with presents double the value of those he had received from the shah,[3] then set out by sea for India, but died before he could reach Goa.

Thenceforward, for over a century, Portugal possessed not only a naval base controlling the approaches to the Persian Gulf but a commercial outpost of the first importance. Some years after their occupation of Hurmuz the Portuguese landed on the Baḥrain islands and expelled the Jabrid ruler; though instead of handing them over to Persia in accordance with the 1515 treaty they retained possession of them for eighty years. The fort which they built on the north coast of the main island a few miles to the west of Manāma is still to be seen but is now in ruins. In 1522 the Portuguese authorities on Hurmuz took over the customs there, but the conduct of their officials provoked a serious revolt, which spread from Hurmuz to the dependencies on the Arabian coast. They had meanwhile concluded a fresh treaty with the puppet king of Hurmuz which tightened their hold on the island even further.

In September 1523 Balthasar Pessoa headed an important Portuguese mission to the Persian court. Antonio Tenreiro, who was a member of this mission and afterwards wrote an account of it, describes Pessoa as "a man of much merit". Tenreiro himself was an acute observer who noted the differences between the Sunnīs and the Shī'a and correctly described the red caps of the Türkmen Qizilbāsh.[4] Shah Ismā'īl received the mission very graciously, but died shortly afterwards in May 1524.

During Shah Ismā'īl's reign endeavours had been made by him on

[1] For a summary of the terms of the treaty, see Sir A.T. Wilson, *The Persian Gulf* (Oxford, 1928), p. 121. [2] Barbosa I, 90–115. [3] Baião, *Itinerários*, pp. 33, 34.

[4] *Ibid.*, pp. 20–1. His account is more detailed and accurate than that of his Venetian contemporary, G.M. Angiolello: see *A Narrative of Italian Travels*, p. 115.

the one side and by the Emperor Charles V and King Ludwig II of Hungary on the other to conclude an alliance against the Turks. In 1516 Ludwig sent a Maronite friar named Petrus de Monte Libano to the shah with that object. Charles, while still king of Spain (he was not elected Emperor until 1519) also sent an envoy to the shah at this time for the same purpose. Shah Ismāʿīl's replies to these letters have not been preserved, but in the late summer of 1523 he sent a letter written in Latin to Charles V in which, after expressing astonishment that the Christian powers were fighting among themselves instead of combining to crush the Turks, he urged Charles to mobilise his forces and attack the common foe.[1] This same view was strongly expressed by Paolo Giovo somewhat later, in the second volume of his *Historia sui Temporis*, published in Paris in 1560. He maintained that the Christian powers, by their feuds and rivalries, had failed to crush the Turks while it was still in their power to do so, and that the Turks were now so strong that they were likely to conquer the whole world.

Ismāʿīl's letter did not reach Charles V until after the shah's death in 1524. It is noteworthy that the news of Shah Ismāʿīl's death and of Shah Ṭahmāsp's accession had not reached the emperor by February 1529, for he then addressed a further letter to Shah Ismāʿīl. This illustrates the parlous state of communications between Persia and the West at that time, which rendered impossible any concerted planning by the powers concerned.

In 1547 Sultan Süleymān the Magnificent took advantage of the revolt of Alqāṣ Mīrzā, Shah Ṭahmāsp's brother, to invade north-west Persia and occupy Tabrīz.[2] As it was then the policy of the French government to be on good terms with Turkey in order to be able to play off the sultan against the emperor, it was arranged for Gabriel de Luetz, Baron et Seigneur d'Aramon et de Vallabrègues, the French ambassador to the Porte, to accompany the sultan on this expedition. He was accompanied by two of his secretaries named Jacques Gassut and Jean Chesneau. As the Persians had, when they retreated, adopted a "scorched earth" policy, lack of provisions soon forced the sultan to withdraw his troops. He then laid siege to the citadel of Vān, which was held by the Persians. The Turkish artillery bombarded the citadel,

[1] For the Latin text, see *Correspondenz des Kaisers Karl V.*, ed. K. Lanz, 1 (Leipzig, 1844), 52–3, with the Hijra year incorrectly given as 924. Falsafī, *Tārīkh-i ravābiṭ*, pp. 163–4, has published a Persian translation of this letter, which he states was written in Shawwāl 929/13 Aug.–10 Sept. 1523.

[2] See above, pp. 242–3.

but their fire was ineffectual until, at the suggestion of d'Aramon, they moved one of their batteries to the other side of the fortress; the Persians were then forced to surrender.[1]

At the beginning of the second half of the 16th century steps were taken which soon led to the opening up of a trade route between England and Persia through Russia, thus turning the left flank of the Ottoman Turks just as the Portuguese and those who had followed them had outflanked them on the right. In 1553 a ship under the command of Richard Chancellor sailed round the north of Norway into the White Sea. Landing at Archangel, Chancellor travelled south to Moscow, where he was well received by the Grand Duke Ivan the Terrible. This visit laid the foundations for the overland trade with Persia via Russia, for which purpose the Muscovy or Russia Company was formed in 1555. Two years later Anthony Jenkinson and the brothers Richard and Robert Johnson set out from England, crossed Russia to Astrakhan and sailed from there down the Volga and across the Caspian Sea. This was truly a pioneering venture. In Jenkinson's words: "Note that during the time of our Navigation, wee set up the redde crosse of St. George in our flagges, for the honour of the Christians, which I suppose was never seene in the Caspian Sea before".[2] On this occasion, however, these pioneers went not to Persia but to Bukhārā, where they spent the winter. They were the first English merchants to set foot in Central Asia. Jenkinson and his companions returned to England by the route that they had followed on the outward journey.

Encouraged by this success, Jenkinson and his colleagues in 1561 set out for Persia, the company having in the meantime decided to include that country in its sphere of operations. Jenkinson took with him a letter from Queen Elizabeth to the grand duke and another to "the Great Sophie". On reaching Astrakhan, they sailed southwards and landed on the Persian coast near Shābrān, whence they journeyed to Shamākhī, the capital of Shīrvān. From Shamākhī they had to travel another twenty miles to the summer camp of 'Abd-Allāh Khān (Jenkinson's "Obdolowcan"), the governor-general of the province,

[1] Chesneau, pp. 84–8. See also Charrière, *Négociations* II, 66–9.

[2] Page, p. 114. It was probably this passage which led Marlowe to write, in *Tamburlaine the Great*:

And Christian merchants, that with Russian stems,
Plough up huge furrowes in the Caspian Sea.

who gave them a friendly reception. On 2 October Jenkinson set out via Ardabīl for Qazvīn, the then capital of Persia, where he was received by Shah Ṭahmāsp. At first all went well, but when the bigoted monarch discovered that Jenkinson was a Christian, he brusquely bade him depart. Nevertheless, the shah later relented, treated Jenkinson well, and gave him a handsome parting present when he left for England.

The success achieved on this occasion led to several other expeditions from England to Persia by the Russian route. During this period the Russia Company's traders visited a number of towns in Persia, penetrating as far south as Kāshān.[1] However, what with the ravages of plague in Persia, attacks by Tartar pirates on the Volga and a number of other troubles, accompanied by serious loss of life and goods, the undertaking was abandoned in 1581.

On 7 October 1571 the combined fleets of Spain, Venice and other Christian states gained a great naval victory over the Turks to the west of Lepanto. Pope Pius V thereupon wrote to Shah Ṭahmāsp urging him to attack the Turks and so share the fruits of victory instead of the toils of war. However, it was soon made clear from the account given by Vincentio d'Alessandri, who visited Persia in that year, that little or nothing could be expected of Ṭahmāsp. The shah had, he said, been immured in his palace for eleven years and cared only for women and money; he had no inclination for war; the country was in a bad state, there was much injustice and the roads were unsafe.[2]

Eight years later, another Venetian, Gasparo Balbi by name, travelled overland to Baṣra and sailed thence to Hurmuz. In his narrative Balbi gave rather more detail than was usual regarding his journey down the Persian Gulf, but his distortion of many of the names makes it difficult to identify the majority of them. Balbi's description of Hurmuz is of some value in affording particulars of the weights and measures in use there, together with other details of economic interest.[3]

Hard on Balbi's heels came that intrepid Elizabethan, John Newberie. The first Englishman to use the overland route via Aleppo and Baghdad, he reached Baṣra on 1 May 1581. Leaving Baṣra by ship, he arrived at Hurmuz on 22 June, after calling at Būshahr ("Abousher"), Nakhilū ("Necchel") and Kishm. Newberie spent six

[1] See Banister and Ducket, in Hakluyt, *Principal Navigations* II, 120–3.

[2] *A Narrative of Italian Travels*, pp. 215–25. [3] Balbi and Federici, pp. 123–8.

weeks in Hurmuz, where he met, among other people, a Venetian named Michiel Stropene, who aroused his suspicions by interrogating his servant very closely as to his affairs.[1] Crossing to the mainland, Newberie travelled by the caravan route via Lār to Shīrāz and thence to Iṣfahān, Kāshān, Qum and Tabrīz. From Tabrīz Newberie returned to England via Turkey. Not content with this journey, he soon set out on another, from which he was destined not to return. In company with Ralph Fitch, John Eldred, William Leeds, William Shales and James Story, he sailed to Tripoli in the *Tiger*. From Tripoli the party went to Aleppo and thence by the usual route to Baghdad and Baṣra. Leaving Eldred and Shales behind at Baṣra, the others sailed to Hurmuz, where they intended to establish trading connections. Shortly after their arrival, the Venetian merchants there, probably at the instigation of Stropene, denounced them to the Portuguese authorities as spies, with the result that they were placed under arrest and sent under guard to Goa for trial. Very fortunately, an English Jesuit named Thomas Stephens was able, with the help of Jan Huyghen van Linschoten and another Dutchman,[2] to procure their release on bail. It is beyond the scope of this chapter to record their further adventures and Newberie's tragic end. It seems that Shakespeare had read Fitch's *Journal*, published in 1598, for in Act I, scene 3, of *Macbeth* he made the first witch say, "Her husband's to Aleppo gone, Master o' th' Tiger". Incidentally, it is to be noted that Linschoten was apparently the first Dutchman to visit Persia, but as he confined himself to Hurmuz he saw nothing of the rest of the country.

In 1583 a new crisis arose in the relations between Turkey and certain of the Western powers. Pope Gregory XIII endeavoured to revive the crusading spirit in Europe and also the project of an alliance with Persia. In order to obtain up to date information on Persia and her military resources, the Pope sent Giovanni Battista Vecchietti, a native of Cosenza, to make a detailed report. As Vecchietti was an intelligent man and was something of an orientalist, he was well qualified for his task. He reached Persia towards the close of the reign of the weak Shah Muḥammad Khudābanda, when that monarch was merely a puppet in the hands of the Türkmen tribal leaders. Vecchietti found that the shah had only limited forces and no artillery whatever. He spent some time

[1] On Stropene, see Tucci, "Mercanti Veneziani", pp. 1092–3.
[2] Linschoten II, 186–8.

travelling around the country in order to acquire a more general knowledge of it. While he was in Persia war broke out between that country and Turkey, resulting in a number of defeats for Persia with loss of territory. Vecchietti returned to Europe in 1587, the year in which Shah ʿAbbās I was raised to the throne at the age of sixteen. It was clear from Vecchietti's reports that Persia was then in no position to give effective military aid to the West; on the other hand, no one could foresee the wonderful transformation in his country's fortunes which Shah ʿAbbās was going to effect in the years to come.

Pedro Teixeira, a Portuguese of Jewish descent, began his eastern travels in 1586, but did not reach Hurmuz until 1593. He spent several years on the island. He was probably the first European resident in Persia (if we can regard Hurmuz as being at that time part of the country) to study and, what is more, to attempt to write Persian history. He read Mīr Khwānd's *Rauẓat al-ṣafā fī sīrat al-anbiyā va'l-mulūk va'-khulafā*. With information taken from this source and from Tūrān Shāh's chronicle of the kings of Hurmuz (a work which is unfortunately no longer extant), he compiled his *Relaciones de P. Teixeira del origen, descendencia y succesión de los Reyes de Persia y de Hormuz y de un viaje hecho por el mismo autor desde la India oriental hasta Italia por tierra*, published at Antwerp in 1610. He included in this work an account of his journey from Hurmuz to Māzandarān and back. In spite of his use of Persian sources, his book has little merit as a historical work, while his record of his travels in Persia is distinctly jejune.

In November 1598 a mission headed by that adventurous but unscrupulous Englishman, Sir Anthony Sherley, arrived in Persia. This mission had been sent by the earl of Essex in order to endeavour to persuade Shah ʿAbbās to unite with the Christian powers against Turkey and also to take steps to improve trade between England and Persia. When Sherley was received by the shah, he was treated with much courtesy. The shah, besides promising to facilitate trade with the West, authorised Sir Anthony to go to Europe on his behalf to endeavour to enlist the support of the Western powers against the Turks. Leaving his younger brother Robert and five other members of his mission as hostages until he returned, Sherley set out for Europe via Russia. He was accompanied by the remainder of his suite and by a Persian named Ḥusain ʿAlī Beg Bayāt as joint ambassador, as well as some Persian secretaries and servants; one of the secretaries was the ambassador's nephew 'Alī Qulī Beg, while another was named Uruch[1] Beg Bayāt. After crossing Russia, the two ambassadors and their suites in October 1600 reached Prague, where the Emperor Rudolf treated them with great consideration.

The party arrived at Rome at the beginning of April 1601, but their audience with Pope Clement VIII was delayed because Sherley and Ḥusain 'Alī Beg could not agree as to which of them should have precedence. Eventually, the Pope received Sherley first, but when Ḥusain 'Alī's turn came, he claimed to be the real envoy and maintained that Sherley was merely his assistant.[2] The sojourn of the mission in Rome was far from being a placid one. The dissensions between the two ambassadors reached such a pitch that Sherley gave up his position as envoy in disgust. Ḥusain 'Alī Beg, though left as undisputed head of the mission, was greatly upset when several of his suite (one of them his cook) were converted to Christianity.[3] The ambassador, together with those of his suite who remained Muslims, went on to Valladolid, where Philip III received him in audience. The ambassador was deeply chagrined when his nephew 'Alī Qulī Beg and Uruch Beg both became Christians, with the king of Spain and his wife, Queen Margarita, acting as their godparents and giving them the names, respectively, of Felipe and Juan. So strongly were Ḥusain 'Alī Beg's feelings aroused over this conversion that he attempted to have Don Juan (Uruch Beg) murdered. With the aid of a Spanish licentiate named Alfonso Remón, Don Juan wrote in Spanish his *Relaciones*. In this book the account of the mission to Europe is prefaced by a history of the Caliphate, followed by that of Persia. In the last section, the early record of the Safavid dynasty is given in some detail and contains corrections of some errors made by Minadoi in his work referred to below. Don Juan's book was published in Valladolid in 1604. In the following year the unfortunate author, having got accidentally involved in a street brawl in Valladolid, was stabbed to death.

Before proceeding further with the record of the contacts between Persia and the West, it will not be out of place briefly to review the progress made during the 16th century. Much had been accomplished, though a vast amount yet remained to be done. So far, the Portuguese were the only people in the West to have direct and continuous contact

[1] Possibly a corruption of Ulugh, though Falsafī, *Zindagānī* I, 180, gives the name as Urūj.
[2] *The Fugger News-Letters, 1568–1605*, trans. P. de Chary (London, 1924), pp. 331–2.
[3] *Ibid.*, p. 243.

with Persia. The English had made their gallant but unsuccessful attempt to establish a trading relationship via Russia and the Caspian Sea. There had also been an interchange of envoys on a number of occasions. A notable feature of the second half of the century was the number of books which were written in Europe on the subject of Persia. There were, for example, the histories of the Turco-Persian wars by such writers as G.T. Minadoi, *Historia della Gverra fra Tvrchi et Persiani* (Rome, 1587), and P. Bizarus, *Rerum Persicarum Historia* (Antwerp, 1583). These works, though written at second- or third-hand, nevertheless often contained authentic material. In Italy the indefatigable Venetian Giovanni Battista Ramusio collected much valuable material concerning travel and discovery, which was first published in three volumes in Venice between 1550 and 1563 under the title *Delli Navigationi et Viaggi raccolte da M. Gio. Battista Ramusio.* In 1598 Richard Hakluyt, Ramusio's English counterpart, published *The Principal Navigations, Voiages, Traffiques and Discoveries*, in which he included material relating to Persia such as Ralph Fitch's record of his journeys.

In Elizabethan England there was a widespread idea of Persia as a land of great pomp and luxury. Spenser, in his *Faerie Queene* (Book I, canto iv, 7), referred to Persia as "the nourse of pompous pride". Furthermore, though there were no more "nygromanciers", fantasy and fable were not yet dead. In the closing years of the 16th century, Fr José Teixeira published a book supporting the claims of an impostor named Marco Tullio Catizone to be King Sebastian of Portugal, who, he maintained, had not been killed at the battle of al-Qaṣr al-Kabīr in Morocco in 1578 but had recovered from his wounds. He would not return to Portugal, which had been united to Spain in 1580, but wandered about the world under the title of the Chevalier de la Croix. Anthony Munday translated this book into English with the title of *The Strangest Adventure that ever happened ... containing a Discourse concerning the successe of the King of Portugall Dom Sebastian, from the Time of his Voyage into Affrique, when he was lost in the Battell against the infidels in the Yeare 1578, unto the sixt January, this present 1601.* On page 90 of this book Munday added that Sir Anthony Sherley had written from Persia to say that the Chevalier, with other gallant gentlemen, had taken service with the Persians and had fought valiantly against the Turks. There is, of course, not a word of truth in this assertion.

Shortly before Sir Anthony Sherley and the other members of his mission reached Rome, a Portuguese priest named Francisco da Costa had arrived there from India by way of Persia. He gave the Pope a most exaggerated idea of the state of the Christians in Persia, and he went so far as to allege that Shah 'Abbās was willing to undergo instruction in the Christian religion and that he would then, as a Christian, be all the more ready to make common cause with the rulers of Christendom against the infidel Turks.[1] He also said that the shah would welcome the advent of Christian missionaries, which was, however, nearer the truth, as will be seen below.

It was unfortunate that Pope Clement VIII decided to send this priest and a layman called Diego de Miranda as ambassadors to Iṣfahān in response to the Sherley mission. The two envoys quarrelled violently on the journey and continued their bickerings on reaching Persia. Furthermore, they behaved very badly in other respects. Fortunately for the good name of Christians in Persia, a mission consisting of three Portuguese Augustinians arrived in Iṣfahān in 1602 in order to establish a convent in the city. The missionaries, who had been encouraged to take this step by da Costa's assertions, were Antonio de Gouveia, Jeronimo da Cruz and Cristofero do Spirito Santo. They were all three of a very different type to da Costa and Miranda. Shah 'Abbās received them well and not only gave them leave to set up their convent in Iṣfahān and to build a church, but also paid for part of the cost of decorating the church. As time went on, the duties of the Augustinians in Iṣfahān grew more diplomatic than religious. The Prior of the Augustinians was also the representative at first of the king of Spain and, after the separation of Portugal from Spain in 1640, of the Portuguese king. This was the first permanent European diplomatic representation to be established in Persia.

In return for the embassy led by Sir Anthony Sherley and Ḥusain 'Alī Beg Bayāt, Rudolf II sent one to Persia under a Transylvanian nobleman named Stefan Kakasch de Zalonkemeny. Soon after this mission reached Gīlān, the unhealthy climate claimed a number of victims, among whom was the ambassador himself. George Tectander von der Jabel, Kakasch's assistant, thereupon took charge. As soon as news of the arrival of the mission on Persian soil reached Shah 'Abbās, he sent Robert Sherley to meet it. When Robert reached the members of the mission, he found that Kakasch was already dead. He thereupon took Tectander and the surviving members of his suite to Tabrīz,

[1] *A Chronicle of the Carmelites* I, 80–4.

where the court then was. When the shah received Tectander, he treated him graciously and then examined his letters of credence. While he was so occupied, a Turkish prisoner was brought in, and simultaneously a servant entered and gave two sheathed swords to the shah. Drawing one of these swords, the shah, with one swift stroke, cut off the unfortunate prisoner's head. Poor Tectander was terrified, thinking that his turn would come next. However, his fears were groundless, for the shah then turned to him and treated him kindly, and subsequently Tectander received as a gift the other sword which had been handed to the shah. Shortly afterwards, Tectander and the other members of the mission returned to Prague.[1]

Although Robert Sherley had been treated at first more or less as a hostage, he later entered the shah's service as a soldier and military adviser, becoming also, as has been stated, a diplomat. He fought valiantly in several battles against the Turks, and he was certainly of some assistance to the shah over the reorganisation of his army, though Samuel Purchas and some other writers have exaggerated his achievements in this respect. It was fortunate for Robert that he was able to justify himself to this extent, since his position at first was very difficult in view of his elder brother's failure to make good his promises.

At the beginning of February 1608 Robert married Teresa, the daughter of a Christian Circassian named Ismā'īl Khān, who was said to have been a relative of one of the shah's wives. Immediately after his marriage, Robert gave up his military duties for good, and went at the shah's orders as his envoy to Europe in order to endeavour to persuade the Christian rulers to combine against the Turks and also to take steps to improve the silk trade with Europe, in which the shah was personally interested, silk being a royal commodity in Persia. At Prague, Robert and his wife were well received by the emperor, who knighted Robert and made him a count palatine. From Prague he went to Rome, where he was again well received, being made a chamberlain and a count of the Lateran palace;[2] but as at Prague he made no real progress with the objects of his mission. He strongly urged Pope Paul V to do his utmost to induce the Christian powers to forget their rivalries and to join Persia in a league against the Turks. The letter from Shah 'Abbās to the Pope was couched in the same terms, though it contained nothing to support the statement in a Venetian source that

[1] Kakasch de Zalonkemeny, p. 50. [2] Purchas x, 377.

Robert had assured the Pope of Shah 'Abbās's willingness, after the overthrow of the Turks, to abjure Islam and become a Christian. It seems unlikely that Sherley would have made such an assertion, knowing the shah so well. On the other hand, many people had been misled by da Costa's mendacious statements, and in addition the shah's own behaviour lent some colour to the idea.[1]

From Rome Robert and his wife travelled to Spain. Although Robert made a better impression there than his brother had done, he failed in the end to achieve any concrete results. His position was rendered difficult when Antonio de Gouveia and Dengīz Beg Rūmlū arrived from Persia as rival envoys. Robert and his wife therefore went to England after he had received assurances that the fact that he had been in Spain as an envoy would not be detrimental to him. Although King James received him in kindly fashion at Hampton Court, Robert failed to persuade the hard-headed merchants of the Levant and East India Companies of the advantages of trading with Persia via Hurmuz. In consequence, he returned empty-handed to Persia in 1613. Details of his subsequent career will be given later.

Despite the fact that Robert Sherley was in Europe on his behalf, Shah 'Abbās in 1609 sent Antonio de Gouveia, and Dengīz Beg Rūmlū, a Persian, as envoys to Philip III of Spain and Pope Paul V. Iskandar Munshī, in his *Tārīkh-i 'ālam-ārā-yi 'Abbāsī*, described Dengīz Beg as "smooth-tongued".[2] They took with them a number of gifts for Philip III and the Pope and also fifty loads of silk for sale on the shah's personal behalf. They fared in Spain no better than Robert Sherley had done. While in Europe, Gouveia was made bishop of Cyrene and Apostolic Delegate. On their return to Persia in 1613 the shah had Dengīz Beg seized and executed in Gouveia's presence on charges of treasonable and corrupt actions while he was in Europe. Gouveia, fearing for his life, fled to the south. He was detained for a time at Shīrāz by Imām Qulī Khān, the governor-general of Fārs, but

[1] He would often discuss religious questions with the Augustinians in Iṣfahān and also with the Carmelites after their establishment in that city in 1608. When pressed by the friars as to whether he would become a Christian, he would pretend to agree, but when pressed further he would make an evasive reply. In Paris in 1606 an anonymous book entitled *Nouvelle Conversion du Roy de Perse avec la Defette de deux Cens Mil Turcs* was published, and ten years later, also in Paris, another with the title *Histoire véritable de toute qui s'est passé en Perse depuis la conversion du Grand Sophy*. Far more surprising, however, was the appearance in Paris in 1614 of an anonymous work supplying details of the conversion of the Ottoman Sultan!

[2] Iskandar Munshī, trans. Savory, p. 1074 (*mard-i charb-zabān*).

was later allowed to go on to Hurmuz. Imām Qulī Khān was very severely rebuked by the shah when he learnt of this action, as Gouveia was alleged to have given the silk to Philip III instead of having it sold for the shah's benefit. The shah therefore wished to recover the value of the silk from Gouveia. On reaching Hurmuz, Gouveia sailed to Baṣra, went overland to Syria and sailed from there for Portugal. His ship, however, was captured by Algerian corsairs and he himself was imprisoned and held for ransom. Truly, a diplomatic career in those days had its hazards and hardships.

As Shah 'Abbās had intimated to Philip III that he was tired of receiving friars as envoys and that he would prefer "some gentleman of note", Philip early in 1614 despatched Don Garcia de Silva y Figueroa as his ambassador to the shah. Philip had been much perturbed previously when the Persians had recovered the Baḥrain islands in 1602, and he was now worried by reports which he had received of the worsening situation in the Persian Gulf. Imām Qulī Khān had sought to regain the shah's favour by offering to recover from the Portuguese the strip of territory to the north of Hurmuz on which the small port of Gamrū was situated, but the shah refused permission. Soon afterwards, however, cruel and tactless action by the Portuguese commandant of Hurmuz led to the shah giving permission to Imām Qulī Khān to take this action, with the result that the Persians recovered this territory late in 1614.

Don Garcia reached Goa in October 1614, but the Portuguese authorities there, greatly angered at a Spaniard being sent on this mission instead of a Portuguese, detained him on various pretexts for over two years before he could set out for Hurmuz. There also the unfortunate envoy was detained for some time, with the result that he did not reach Iṣfahān until the summer of 1617. As the shah was at Qazvīn, Don Garcia had to travel there to present his credentials. It was not until the summer of 1619 that he could obtain a proper audience with Shah 'Abbās. Don Garcia then brusquely demanded the restitution of Kishm, the Baḥrain islands and the territory to the north of Hurmuz. He also demanded the exclusion of the English from the Persian markets. These demands so angered the shah that he broke off all relations with Don Garcia and gave him his *congé*. Don Garcia thereupon returned to Hurmuz, whence he sailed for Spain; he died, however, on the voyage. Under his supervision, one of Don Garcia's secretaries had compiled an interesting record of his mission.

In the meantime, Richard Steele, a factor of the East India Company, when travelling across Persia on his way to India, was struck with its potential value as an additional market. The company was then having difficulty in disposing of all its stocks of cloth in India. It therefore sent Steele and another factor called Crowther to negotiate with the shah. Shah 'Abbās received them well and gave them a *farmān* (royal rescript) enjoining his subjects to "kindly receive and entertaine the English Frankes or Nation" who might present themselves.[1] In consequence, the company, in December 1616, sent a mission to Persia under Edward Connock, who brought with him a cargo of cloth. Despite an attempt at interception by the Portuguese, Connock landed his cargo safely at Jāsk, and brought it to Iṣfahān early in 1617. In that year Connock opened factories at Shīrāz and Iṣfahān. Shah 'Abbās undertook to provide the company with between 1,000 and 3,000 bales of silk a year at a price of between 6s. and 6s. 6d per pound. It was also agreed that the staff of the company in Persia were to be allowed the free exercise of their religion, while the company's Agent or Resident at Iṣfahān was to be regarded as the ambassador of the king of England.

By this time Shah 'Abbās had determined to recover Hurmuz from the Portuguese, but he had no shipping. However, by threatening to withdraw its privileges, he forced the East India Company to make its ships cooperate with the Persian forces in an onslaught on the island. The consequence was that Hurmuz fell to the combined forces in May 1622. The loss of Hurmuz marked the beginning of the decline of Portuguese power in the Persian Gulf. On the other hand, this development had favourable results for the East India Company, which could never have competed successfully with the Portuguese had they been able to retain their long-established and highly successful entrepôt on the island. Shah 'Abbās made the company free of customs at Hurmuz and also promised that it should receive half the customs dues of the port. When soon afterwards Hurmuz was abandoned in favour of Gamrū (which the English called Gombroon and which was soon renamed Bandar 'Abbās), these privileges were, in theory, also to be enjoyed there. In practice, however, the company's share of the customs was almost always in arrears.

For nearly a century and a half the East India Company maintained

[1] Purchas IV, 279.

its trading connection with Persia; during this long period many of its employees served in that country. Some of these men who had served in India had learnt Persian there, as it was the language spoken at the Mughal court. By far the most outstanding scholar in its service in Persia was a Scotsman named George Strachan of the Mearns. He had an extremely good knowledge of Arabic and also knew Persian and Turkish well. Strachan, who may be regarded as ranking with his contemporaries Thomas Bedwell and T. van Erpe (Erpenius), was a keen collector of Arabic, Persian and Turkish manuscripts and books and became a close friend of the Italian traveller Pietro della Valle.

The East India Company, however, was not left long undisturbed in Persia. The Dutch, though they had cooperated with the English in fighting the Portuguese in the Persian Gulf, soon ceased to be allies and became rivals. With its greater wealth and its extremely vigorous methods, the Oost-Indische Compagnie soon gained and retained for a long while the ascendancy over its English rival. Like the English company, it established factories in many parts of Persia.

While Don Garcia de Silva y Figueroa was still in Persia, a traveller of a very different type arrived there. Pietro della Valle, an Italian of noble family and good education, had set out on his eastern travels in 1614 not for commercial gain or diplomatic duties, but primarily to cure himself of a broken heart. He spent much time in Istanbul learning Turkish, and then went on to the Holy Land, Syria and Mesopotamia. In Baghdad he cured his broken heart by marrying a local Christian lady called Maani Gioerida. With her he went on into Persia towards the close of 1616. Going first to Iṣfahān, he found that Shah 'Abbās was in Māzandarān, so he journeyed northwards to seek an audience. Given his knowledge of Turkish, which was the language spoken at the court,[1] he had no need of an interpreter when with Shah 'Abbās and his courtiers. He established very friendly relations with the shah, to whom he offered his services. He suggested that Persia might conclude an alliance with the Cossacks, who had for some time been raiding the northern coast of Asia Minor, against the Turks, though he did not explain how effective contact was to be made and maintained. He spent in all seven years in Persia, many parts of which he visited. To his friend Mario Schipano, of Naples, he sent voluminous letters describing his experiences and

[1] Du Mans, p. 134. See Thévenot II, 90, on the difference between the language as spoken in Turkey and the form employed in Persia.

doings. These letters, which have been published several times as his *Viaggi*, on the first occasion in 1650, constitute an invaluable record of Persia, its form of government and general conditions at that time. Gibbon, in his *Decline and Fall*, praised Pietro for his accurate descriptions, but accused him of being intolerably vain and prolix.[1]

More fortunate, or perhaps more circumspect, than Dengīz Beg Rūmlū was Ḥājjī Maḥmūd Shāhsavār, a native of the picturesque village of Navā, which is situated high in the Alburz mountains. On Shah ʿAbbās's behalf, Ḥājjī Shāhsavār travelled to Venice in 1613 and again eight years later. He also visited London, where he later became a permanent resident, dying there in August 1626.[2] Muḥammad, one of his sons, was with him in London and fell in love with the chambermaid of Lady Cokayne, whose husband Sir William was a high city dignitary (he was Lord Mayor in 1619–20). Muḥammad pressed his suit assiduously, offering the girl his whole estate and also promising to become a Christian. It seems that Muḥammad's wooing was unsuccessful, as there is no mention of him being accompanied by a wife when he left for Persia in the spring of 1627 in the same ship as the then youthful Thomas Herbert. The unfortunate Muḥammad never reached his native land, as he contracted "a burning fever" and died at sea. Herbert relates that "the captain of our ship honoured his funeral with the rending clamour of four culverins" as his coffin was committed to the deep.[3]

It is now time to return to Robert Sherley and to bring his story to its tragic conclusion. Robert and his wife reached India from England in 1613. From India they travelled overland to Persia via Qandahār. On their way they met that strange and whimsical character Thomas Coryate,[4] the author of the *Crudities*, who, having traversed Persia, was on his way to India on what was to prove his last journey. Soon after Robert's arrival in Iṣfahān, Shah ʿAbbās sent him to Europe again on another mission. He spent five years in Spain in further futile attempts to obtain agreement over the questions of the alliance against Turkey and the commercial treaty. Despairing of success in Spain, he went early in 1622 to England, where despite the hostility of the East

[1] Gibbon, *Decline and Fall* III, 223.

[2] For his curious epitaph, see W. Toldervy, *Select Epitaphs* (London, 1755), pp. 104–5.

[3] Herbert, *Travels in Persia*, p. 28.

[4] The "single-soled, single-souled and single-shirted Observer", quoted by D. Bush, *English Literature in the earlier Seventeenth Century* (Oxford, 1945), p. 173.

India and Levant Companies he had a promising audience with James I. Unfortunately, James died soon after, and Robert had to start all over again with Charles I. His position was greatly weakened by the arrival of a Persian named Naqd 'Alī Beg, who denounced Robert as an impostor and treated him with great rudeness. The English government thereupon decided to send an ambassador of their own to Persia, Sir Dodmore Cotton, who left England for Persia via Sūrat in March 1627. He was attended by a numerous suite, one of whom was a young man of good family named Thomas Herbert. Robert and Teresa Sherley left for Persia in the same convoy, as did Naqd 'Alī Beg, but he was sent in a separate ship. Before the mission reached Persia, Naqd 'Alī Beg, fearing condign punishment at the hands of the shah for his behaviour in England, committed suicide by taking an overdose of opium.[1] In due course, after travelling from Bandar 'Abbās via Shīrāz and Iṣfahān, Sir Dodmore, the Sherleys, Thomas Herbert and the other members of the mission were received by Shah 'Abbās at Ashraf, in Māzandarān, in May 1628. The shah was gracious to Sir Dodmore and promised Robert Sherley satisfaction for his treatment by Naqd 'Alī Beg. Thereafter, however, his attitude changed, owing, it is believed, to the hostility of Muḥammad 'Alī Beg, the shah's chief minister, who Herbert claims had been bribed to work against the English mission. When the shah left for Qazvīn, Sir Dodmore Cotton, his suite and Sherley and his wife accompanied him. On reaching Qazvīn, Sir Dodmore could make no progress with his negotiations, while Shah 'Abbās, despite all Robert's faithful services, treated him so harshly that he fell ill and died, apparently of a broken heart. A week later Sir Dodmore followed him to the grave, and the mission had perforce to return to England. Herbert wrote a most readable and entertaining account of the mission, with amusing descriptions of incidents at Shīrāz and elsewhere; and a more pedestrian record was compiled by Robert Stodart, another member of the mission.

Up to this time France had had but little contact with Persia. Père Joseph de Paris, the celebrated "Éminence Grise", having taken note of the success achieved by the English and Dutch East India Companies, determined that France must follow their example and have overseas interests as well as being a European power. For this purpose, he argued, Persia must be at least a stepping-stone for further penetra-

[1] Herbert, *Travels in Persia*, p. 31. On this mission, see Falsafī, *Tārīkh-i ravābiṭ*, pp. 140–4.

tion in the east. Père Joseph and Cardinal Richelieu, who shared his views, being aware that the Augustinians in Persia were exclusively Portuguese, while the Carmelite missions in the country contained a preponderance of Spaniards and Italians, in 1627 sent the Capuchin Père Pacifique de Provins as ambassador to Shah 'Abbās with a request to be allowed to open Capuchin missions in Iṣfahān and elsewhere. These missions were to be exclusively French in character. The shah readily agreed, with the result that the Capuchins established a mission at Iṣfahān and another at Baghdad, which was then in Persian hands. From that time on the Superiors of the Capuchins in Persia were regarded as representing the king of France.

Although Persia, after her wonderful efflorescence under Shah 'Abbās I, began to decline following his death in January 1629,[1] there was no appreciable change in her relations with the West. Missionaries of the Augustinians, Carmelites and, soon, the Capuchins continued to come and go, and so did the employees of the English and Dutch East India Companies. Furthermore, in 1636 a diplomatic mission from Duke Friedrich of Holstein arrived in Persia in order to arrange for the supply of raw silk for the industry, which he wished to establish in his newly founded town of Friedrichstadt. When Crusius and Brugman, the two envoys, reached Iṣfahān, Nicolaas Jacobus Overschie, the Agent of the Dutch East India Company, brusquely informed them that he had orders to do all in his power to frustrate their endeavours. The hostility of the Dutch and the bad behaviour of Brugman combined to make success impossible, and hence the mission returned empty-handed to Holstein in December 1637. Adam Olearius (Oelschläger), the secretary of the mission, subsequently wrote a record of it, which makes interesting reading.

Quite the most remarkable of the Capuchins to go to Persia was Père Raphaël du Mans, who in 1644 travelled from Baghdad to Iṣfahān in company with Jean-Baptiste Tavernier, the well-known French jeweller and traveller. Being a mathematician, Père Raphaël was warmly welcomed at the Persian court and was greatly esteemed by Shah 'Abbās II and by his successor Shah Sulaimān. Père Barnabas, a Carmelite, wrote of him that "he is constantly with the greatest persons of the country".[2] Besides conscientiously carrying out his religious

[1] Chardin III, 291: "Dès que ce grand et bon prince eut cessé de vivre, la Perse cessa de prospérer."

[2] *A Chronicle of the Carmelites* I, 398.

duties, he made a study of the Persian language and also spent much time and trouble in gathering together information respecting the country and its people. He compiled his *Estat de la Perse en 1660* for the guidance of Colbert when that able minister was collecting data on Persia prior to the formation of the Compagnie Française des Indes in 1664. During the rest of his long life (he remained in Persia until his death in 1696 at the age of 93) he continued to give what assistance he could to France and also to visitors from that country such as François Pétis de La Croix. Père Raphaël was also very helpful to Chardin, and Tavernier was much indebted to him for data respecting Persia, though this indebtedness was not always acknowledged.

Jean-Baptiste Tavernier was born in Paris in 1605. The son of a rich jeweller, he had, like Pietro della Valle, the means to gratify his desire to travel. Between 1636 and 1665 he paid six visits to the east. As already stated, in 1644 he travelled from Baghdad to Iṣfahān in company with Père Raphaël du Mans. In his book, the first edition of which was published in Paris in 1676, Tavernier had a great deal to say respecting the system of government in Persia, the religion of the people, their manners and customs, much of it provided by Père Raphaël. Tavernier had an agreeable style and had much of interest to relate, but his transcription of oriental personal and place names leaves a great deal to be desired. Voltaire took an unfavourable view of him saying that "il n'apprend guère qu'à connaître les grandes routes et les diamants".

The first Jesuit to visit Persia was Père François Rigordi. He was in Iṣfahān briefly in February 1646, when on an extensive journey to various Middle Eastern countries. In 1653 Père Rigordi, with another French Jesuit, Père Chezaud, came to Persia with letters of recommendation from Louis XIV in order to establish Jesuit missions there. Shah 'Abbās II received them well and allowed them to set up establishments in Julfā (Iṣfahān) and Shīrāz. Their advent brought the number of religious orders in Persia up to five, namely the Dominicans, Augustinians, Carmelites, Capuchins and Jesuits. Many of these missionaries were good linguists, as they had to preach in Persian, Turkish and Armenian.

Acting, apparently, on a suggestion made in a letter from a Persian Armenian named Khwāja Petros in 1650[1] to Queen Henrietta Maria,

[1] Bodleian Library, Carte MSS, vol. cxxx, fol. 145.

Charles II and his advisers, who were then in exile in Holland, sent Henry Ward, Viscount Bellomont, a former Fellow of King's College, Cambridge,[1] and an ardent Royalist, on a mission to Persia and India to raise funds. The intention was that Bellomont should endeavour to obtain from Shah 'Abbās II the sums due to the East India Company as its half share of the Gombroon customs receipts; sums which were, as was usually the case, very much in arrears. As England and Holland were then at war, Bellomont was given letters of introduction to the representatives of the Dutch East India Company in Persia, since he could hardly expect to receive any help from the English company, whose share of the Gombroon customs he was to endeavour to divert to Charles. In 1651 J.-B. Tavernier had written to the East India Company at Sūrat to warn them that Bellomont was on his way to Persia with this object in view. It is not therefore surprising that when Bellomont arrived he met with strong opposition from the representatives of the company in Persia, spending over a year in Iṣfahān in fruitless attempts to achieve his ends. As peace had by this time been signed between England and Holland, representatives of the Dutch East India Company were unable to give him active assistance. Finally, Bellomont had to make his peace with the English company by promising not to act against it in any way and was then given a passage in one of its ships to India. From Sūrat, which he reached in January 1656, he set out, after a brief stay, with his young Venetian companion Nicolò Manucci, for the Mughal court at Delhi, but on 20 June he died suddenly, apparently of heat apoplexy, soon after leaving Āgra.

Jean de Thévenot, like Pietro della Valle, was a man of independent means, and so was able to travel for the sake of gratifying his curiosity regarding foreign lands. Born in 1633, he travelled first extensively in Europe and later went to the Middle East. After traversing Mesopotamia, he entered Persia in August 1664 and travelled to Iṣfahān, where he stayed with Père Raphaël du Mans for five months. He had a sound knowledge of Turkish, which stood him in good stead, and also acquired some knowledge of Persian. From Iṣfahān he went to Bandar 'Abbās, intending to take ship to India. No ship, however, was available, and so he went to Shīrāz and thence to Persepolis. There he met Tavernier, Jean Chardin, and André Daulier-Deslandes, who had been sent to Persia to gather information for establishing commercial rela-

[1] A. Allen, *A Catalogue of all the Provosts...of the King's College* III, 1336–42.

tions between that country and France. With a view to returning to Europe via north-west Persia and Turkey, Thévenot set out for Tabrīz, but was seized with a fatal illness at Miyāna, where he died on 28 November 1667.

As already stated, the Compagnie des Indes Orientales was formed in 1664. The long delay in setting up this company was due to a number of causes, such as the Fronde rebellion and war with Spain. Immediately after the formation of the company, a mission consisting of Dupont, Béber and Mariage, representing it, and Nicolas Claude de Lalain and de la Boullaye le Gouz, who were accredited by Louis XIV to the shah, left France for Iṣfahān, which they reached in November 1665. Furious quarrels then broke out between the various members of the mission, and it was only with the greatest difficulty that Père Raphaël du Mans was able to patch up their differences sufficiently for them to open their negotiations with the Persian government. Notwithstanding the extremely unfavourable impression which these unseemly quarrels had produced, the shah agreed to grant the company exemption from tolls and customs dues for three years, together with the same trading rights as those which had already been granted to other foreigners. The Compagnie des Indes thereupon opened a factory at Bandar 'Abbās and began to trade with Persia, but neither Louis XIV nor the Compagnie sent any presents to the shah; nor was any attempt made to negotiate for a treaty to confirm its rights. The Compagnie later attempted to make amends by sending one of its senior officials from Sūrat, but he died on the way, and his place was taken by a young and inexperienced man named de Jonchères. In consequence, the Persian government did not take de Jonchères's attempts to negotiate seriously, a fact of which the English East India Company quickly took advantage. However, with the help of Père Raphaël du Mans and a Frenchman named Louis de l'Estoile, whose father had settled in Iṣfahān, he obtained permission for the Compagnie to trade freely, but without having any exceptional privileges. The Compagnie was, moreover, greatly handicapped by the active opposition of the English and Dutch East India Companies.

In 1665 Jean Chardin, a French Huguenot jeweller, first arrived in Persia. Between that time and 1677 he spent ten years in the country, mostly in Iṣfahān, during which he accumulated a vast amount of information regarding the country, its cities, its peoples and their modes of life. His *Voyages* is a veritable mine of information regarding

Persia in the latter part of the 17th century. Gibbon described Chardin as the master "of all our travellers of the last century",[1] praise which was fully deserved. Of particular interest is Chardin's account of Iṣfahān.[2] With his friend Herbert de Jager, of the Oost-Indische Compagnie, he used to wander through the streets and alleys of the city, noting down all that was of interest. De Jager took similar action, although his description of Iṣfahān cannot now be traced and only his account of Persepolis is extant.[3] So little has Iṣfahān changed in its essentials that it is still possible to use Chardin's *Voyages* as a guide to many parts of it. Of de Jager himself a few words must be said. By profession a physician, he had practised medicine in the East Indies and had then been sent by the Oost-Indische Compagnie to Persia. He was a remarkable linguist, being well versed in a number of oriental and other languages. Chardin described him as:

... Un très-savant homme... Il me suffira de dire, pour donner une idée de son mérite, que Golius, ce fameux professeur des langues orientales, le jugeoit le plus digne de tous ses disciples de remplir sa chaire et de lui succéder. Une passion commune de connoître la Perse et d'en faire de plus exactes et plus amples relations qu'on n'avoit encore faites, nous lia d'abord d'amitié, et nous convinmes, l'année suivante, de faire aussi, à frais et à soins communs, une description de la ville capitale, où rien ne fût omis de ce qui seroit digne d'être su.[4]

Pétis de la Croix was the son of Pétis, the secretary-interpreter of the king of France for Arabic and Turkish. Born in 1653, he was sent by Colbert to study Arabic, Turkish and Persian in the Levant, and also to collect manuscripts in those languages for the Bibliothèque du Roi. He spent two years in Persia, mainly in Iṣfahān, where Père Raphaël du Mans was of great help to him in his studies, besides nursing him through a serious illness. Under the guidance of the head of the Maulavī dervishes in Iṣfahān, he made a study of the *Maṣnavī* of Jalāl al-Dīn Rūmī. The Abbé Carré, who met Pétis in Baghdad in 1674, was greatly struck by his aptitude for oriental languages. Pétis returned to France in 1680 and fifteen years later succeeded his father as Professor of Arabic at the Collège du Roi in Paris. Before his death in 1713, he published translations of, *inter alia*, Sharaf al-Dīn Yazdī's biography of Tīmūr, entitled the *Ẓafar-nama*, and of the *Thousand and One Nights*, the latter translated from a Turkish text.

[1] Gibbon, *Decline and Fall* VI, 365.
[2] Chardin VII, 273–492, and VIII, 1–143.
[3] Included in F. Valentijn, *Oude en Nieuw Oost-Indiën* (Amsterdam, 1726).
[4] Chardin VII, 287–8.

In the latter part of the 17th century Sweden entered into diplomatic relations with Persia, her emissary being Ludwich (or Ludvig) Fabritius. He was born in Holland in 1649, but accompanied his step-father Beem to Russia in 1660 or the following year. Ludwich subsequently entered the Russian army and took part in the operations against Stenka (Stepan) Razin, the rebel Cossack leader. He was captured by the Cossacks in the Lower Volga region in 1670, but later escaped to Persia, where he remained until after the Razin revolt had been quelled. Instead of remaining in Russia after his return, he went to Sweden, where he later became naturalised. In virtue of his knowledge of Russian and Persian, the Swedish government sent him, in 1679, as envoy extraordinary to Russia and Persia. The object of this mission was, presumably, to induce Shah Sulaimān to attack the Turks, who were then threatening not only Poland but also the Swedish possessions to the south of the Baltic.[1] If this surmise is correct, nothing came of the request to make war on the Turks, because Shah Sulaimān was the least martial of monarchs and was, moreover, completely indifferent to affairs of state.

Fabritius returned to Sweden in 1682. In the following year Charles XI sent him again as envoy to Persia with the twofold object of inducing the shah to attack the Turks, who were then gravely threatening Vienna, and of concluding a commercial treaty. The secretary of this mission was a young German physician named Engelbert Kaempfer, of whom something more will be said later. Fabritius and his suite reached Iṣfahān in March 1684, and he was received in audience at the end of the month. Also in Iṣfahān at this time were an ambassador from Poland named Suski and an envoy from Siam. Fabritius could make no progress in his negotiations with the shah. More often than not, Sulaimān was drunk, and he, like Shah Ṭahmāsp, often shut himself up in his harem, sometimes for long periods.[2] Some while after Fabritius's return to Sweden, he was raised to the nobility, and in 1697 he went once again as ambassador to Persia. He died in Stockholm in 1729, aged eighty.

[1] Particulars of the mission and its objects are probably to be found in Johan Kempe, *Kongl. Swenska Envoijen Ludwich Fabritii Lefwerne*, which is apparently not available, however, outside Sweden. Some details are given in the *Svensk Uppslagsbok* (Malmö, 1954) IX, 66; see also Konovalov; David Butler, letter from Iṣfahān, 6 March 1671, in Struys, pp. 340–60.

[2] On one occasion for seven years, according to Muḥammad Muḥsin, *Zubdat al-tavārīkh*, Cambridge Univ. Library, Browne MS G. 15 (13), fol. 203r. See also *A Chronicle of the Carmelites* I, 408.

Kaempfer remained in Persia when Fabritius and his suite returned to Sweden in 1684. At the suggestion of Père Raphaël du Mans, he entered the service of the Dutch Oost-Indische Compagnie as a physician and served for some time in the Persian Gulf area and Bandar 'Abbās, leaving Persia for Japan in 1688. In his book *Ameonitatum Exoticarum* he gave an account of Shah Sulaimān, followed by a detailed description of the system of government and the duties of the court functionaries. His book was published in his native town of Lemgo in 1712, four years before his death.

Dr John Fryer, an M.A. of Cambridge University and in later life a Fellow of the Royal Society, arrived from India on a visit to Persia in March 1677, remaining in the latter country until the end of November 1678. During his visit he spent some time in Iṣfahān. Although ignorant of oriental languages, he afterwards wrote a very readable and interesting account of his experiences in the country, garnished with many classical quotations. Fryer gave the following unflattering description of Shah Sulaimān:

> Shaw Scholymon, the present Emperor; Who is a Man of a good Presence, and of no mean Capacity, unless by indulging his Body he thickens his Understanding as well as he has made his Body Gross; he is Tall and very Fleshy, so that when he stirs or laughs, all the Muscles of the Scapula, as well as Ribs, move together. In the beginning of his Reign, like another *Nero*, he gave good Specimens of his Inclinations, not unworthy the Heroes that were his Ancestors; but when he began to hearken to Flatterers, and give himself over to Idleness, he left off to Govern, and listed himself in the service of Cruelty, Drunkenness, Gluttony, Lasciviousness, and abominable Extortion, where he perpetrated things not only uncomely to be seen, but even offensive to the Ears; wherefore at his libidinous Feasts, to enquire what he transacts, or how he behaves himself, is fitter for an *Aretin* than a modest Author.[1]

Fryer made the following amusing comment on the great heat at Bandar 'Abbās: "... The Sailers had stigmatized this Place for its Excessive Heat, with this sarcastical Saying, *That there was but an Inch-Deal betwixt Gomberoon and Hell*".[2]

During the last two decades of the 17th century a number of ecclesiastics came to Persia, some of whom were French. Père Sanson, a French secular priest, reached the country in 1683 and remained until 1692. Soon after his arrival in Persia he accompanied Mgr François Picquet, the bishop of Babylon (Baghdad) and coadjutor-bishop of

[1] Fryer III, 51. [2] *Ibid.* II, 165.

Iṣfahān, to the court, where he spent some time. After the death of that prelate he was for long engaged in endeavouring to free from sequestration the bishop's effects at Hamadān. He thus had ample opportunity to observe the state of affairs at the court. In his book entitled *Voyage ou Relation de l'État présent du Royaume de Perse*, which was published in Paris in 1695, he described, *inter alia*, the stranglehold over the conduct of affairs which the court eunuchs had established owing to Shah Sulaimān's lack of interest in such matters. Apart from that, Père Sanson's book does not furnish anything of interest that is not to be found in Père Raphaël du Mans's more authoritative work. To judge from his book, Père Sanson's knowledge of the Persian language was not extensive.

Abler and better informed than Père Sanson was another French priest, Père (later Abbé) Martin Gaudereau, who went to Persia as a missionary some years before the end of the century. In 1698 he was appointed vicar-general to Mgr Pietro Paolo di San Francisco, the archbishop of Ancyra, when the latter reached Persia on his way to India as Apostolic Delegate. In so far as Persia was concerned, the objects of the mission were to obtain the renewal of privileges which had lapsed and to endeavour to win over to Catholicism the Gregorian Armenians of Julfā. The archbishop was successful in the case of these privileges, as Shah Sulṭān Ḥusain, who had succeeded his father Shah Sulaimān in 1694, was well-disposed towards Christians; he failed, however, in regard to the Armenians. Gaudereau left Persia for India with the archbishop and subsequently went back to France. Some years after his return to France Gaudereau was appointed secretary-general for oriental languages to the King. Besides writing the account of the archbishop's mission in Persia, Gaudereau was responsible for several other books on that country, which will be found in the bibliography at the end of this volume. More will be said of Père Gaudereau later, in connection with the mission of Muḥammad Riżā Beg to France in 1714–15.

Towards the close of the 17th century the Compagnie Française des Indes determined to expand its activities in Persia. In 1698 de Châteauneuf, the French ambassador at Istanbul, sent Jean Bilin de Cansevilles, an intelligent and enterprising merchant of Marseilles, to Iṣfahān to act ostensibly as secretary to the Capuchin mission there. The real object of this appointment was to enable de Cansevilles to obtain a thorough insight into trading conditions in Persia for the benefit of the

Compagnie Française des Indes. De Cansevilles remained in Persia until 1705, when he returned to France. In 1707 he was sent to Persia again, this time for a shorter visit. De Cansevilles obtained a great deal of data which he embodied in a series of memoranda, most of which have been preserved at the Ministry of Foreign Affairs in Paris, though some of them do not bear his name.

In the meantime, the French government had decided to send a mission to Persia in order to conclude a commercial treaty. The envoy selected was Jean-Baptiste Fabre, a native of Marseilles who had spent a good many years in the Levant. He was singularly ill-fitted for the task before him. Moreover, he was so much in need of money for his preparations that he had to borrow what he needed from his mistress Marie Petit. Fabre set out for Persia in March 1705. He was accompanied by his young son Joseph, his nephew Jacques Fabre, a surgeon called Louis Robin, a clock-maker named Jacques (or Jacob) Rousseau (a cousin of Jean-Jacques Rousseau) and a number of other persons; among these last was Marie Petit disguised as a "cavalier". Much difficulty was experienced in crossing Turkey, and it was not till January 1706 that the mission reached Erivan.

Fabre was well received by Muḥammad Khān, the governor of Erivan, and so was Marie Petit. Just before the mission was due to leave Erivan for the court, Fabre was taken ill with a violent fever from which he died shortly after. A scene of great confusion ensued. Some wished to make young Joseph the head of the mission, while others wanted to nominate Jacques. Marie Petit solved the problem by proclaiming herself the head, and at the beginning of December she and the youthful Joseph set out for the court via Tabrīz, accompanied by a Jesuit named Père Mosnier. Meanwhile, news of these startling developments had reached the Comte de Ferriol, the French ambassador to the Porte. He immediately sent one of his secretaries named Michel to supplant Marie Petit; so great was his haste that he did not pause to obtain proper credentials for Michel. Travelling post haste, Michel overtook the mission at Nakhchivān. However, while he had no credentials, Marie had been given an escort and provided with letters from the governor of Erivan, and so he was powerless to stop her. By different routes, they went on to Tabrīz, where Marie received every attention, but Michel met with a very cool reception and was refused permission to proceed. Marie thereupon went on to the court which was then encamped to the east of Tehran. In virtue of her letters from the governors of Erivan and

Tabrīz, Marie was well received by the I'timād al-Daula, who conducted her to the shah's harem, where she received "all possible honours".[1] Having achieved her great objective, Marie returned to Tabrīz. Meanwhile Michel had at last got leave to proceed to the court, but found that he could do nothing there. On returning to Tabrīz, in company with Mgr Pidou de Saint-Olon, the bishop of Babylon, he was arrested and thrown into prison with the bishop. They were, however, soon released and then found Marie in penitent mood. Michel bade her return to France and gave her a small sum in cash and a bond on Aleppo which proved to be worthless. On Marie's arrival in France, she was thrown into prison whence she emerged, years later, broken in health and penniless.

Michel's letters of credence having at last arrived, he was able to go again to the court at Iṣfahān, where, despite strong opposition by the English and Dutch East India Companies, he concluded a treaty on 16 September 1708 which, besides providing certain facilities for trade, gave protection to the Christian religious orders in Persia.[2] This was the first official treaty between France and Persia.

In return for Michel's mission, the Persian government decided to send an embassy to France. The envoy chosen was Muḥammad Riżā Beg, the *kalāntar* (mayor) of Erivan, who was to prove quite as unsuitable for the task before him as Fabre had been. He left Erivan for France in May 1714. After much difficulty in crossing Turkey, where he was imprisoned for a time, he eventually reached Marseilles in October 1714. For various reasons which are too lengthy to be mentioned here,[3] he did not arrive in Paris until the beginning of February 1715. His astounding whims and unpredictable outbursts of rage proved most trying to the unfortunate French officials, including Gaudereau, who had the misfortune to have to look after him. On 19 February 1715 the aged Louis XIV received Muḥammad Riżā Beg formally at Versailles. After handing over his letters of credence, the ambassador presented the casket containing the shah's gifts to Louis XIV. These gifts proved to be of poor quality; this fact, together with the strange behaviour of the envoy on a number of occasions, led many persons to believe that Muḥammad Riżā Beg was merely an impostor. They

[1] Evidence for the defence at Marie Petit's trial: Affaires Étrangères, Perse, vol. ii, fol. 259a.

[2] A French translation of this treaty by Pétis de la Croix is to be found in Affaires Étrangères, Perse, vol. ii, foll. 35–40.

[3] Herbette, *Une Ambassade Persane*, pp. 61–113.

included Montesquieu, who very probably derived the idea of writing his *Lettres Persanes* from this mission (see letter no. 92).

Negotiations thereupon ensued for the drafting of a new treaty to replace the one concluded by Michel. This new treaty, which was signed on 13 August 1715, was far more favourable to France than its predecessor.[1] Muḥammad Riżā Beg was given his final audience on the same day that this treaty was signed; it was the last public function to be attended by Louis XIV.

The departure of the ambassador for Persia was not unattended by surprise. As he embarked at Le Havre for Russia, a large case with a number of holes in it, said to contain his devotional books, was placed in his cabin. When the vessel was at sea, this case, on being opened, was found to contain a devotional object of a different kind, in the person of the young Marquise d'Epinay. She had fallen madly in love with Muḥammad Riżā Beg and had arranged to elope with him in this manner. The journey ended in tragedy, for Muḥammad Riżā Beg, realising that he had greatly exceeded his powers in signing such a treaty, committed suicide soon after reaching Persia. Madame d'Epinay is said to have embraced Islam and to have subsequently married Muḥammad Riżā Beg's brother.

One of the consequences of the conclusion of this treaty was the despatch of the Chevalier Ange de Gardane, the Seigneur de Sainte-Croix, to Persia to be French consul at Iṣfahān, accompanied by his younger brother François.[2] The Gardane brothers were destined to remain in Persia for sixteen years, during which they had to endure the privations and anxieties of the Afghans' siege of Iṣfahān in 1722 and the troubled years that ensued under the usurpers Maḥmūd and Ashraf. They were not able to return to France until after Nadr Qulī Beg, the future Nādir Shāh, had expelled the Afghans from Persia and restored the Safavid dynasty.

A number of other Europeans were in Persia during the Afghan period (1722–9). The one who has given the best and most detailed account of this troubled era was the Polish Jesuit Tadeusz Krusiński, who went to Persia in 1707. A man of energy and ability who became

[1] *Ibid.*, pp. 370–4, for the text.

[2] It is noteworthy that two other members of the Gardane family, likewise brothers, went on a mission to Persia just under a century later: Claude-Mathieu de Gardane, a distinguished general in Napoleon's service, and Ange-Paul-Louis, who, as secretary of the mission, wrote an account of it in his *Journal d'un Voyage dans la Turquie et la Perse, 1807–8* (Paris, 1809).

procurator-general of the Jesuit missions in that country in 1720, he had considerable linguistic gifts and often had to act as interpreter for the Persian court, thus playing a rôle like that of Père Raphaël du Mans in the previous century. After the siege of Iṣfahān, he was able to resume his activities at the court throughout the brief and terrible reign of Maḥmūd. He left Persia for Europe soon after the accession of Maḥmūd's cousin, Ashraf.

A valuable and so far unpublished record of the siege of Iṣfahān in 1722 is the *Dagregister* kept by Nicolaus Schorer, the Chief Merchant of the Oost-Indische Compagnie at Iṣfahān, and some of his assistants. It covers the period from the beginning of March up to the end of August 1722 and is by far the most detailed account of the siege that we possess. Owen Phillips and his Council of the English East India Company at Iṣfahān also contributed some valuable data regarding the siege and the succeeding period. Mention must also be made of William Cockell, who succeeded Owen Phillips as Resident of the East India Company at Iṣfahān. He was in Persia until February 1737, and was thus there throughout the brief reigns of Ṭahmāsp II and the infant 'Abbās III, as well as the beginning of Nādir's *de jure* reign as shah. Although not mentioned by James Fraser by name in his biography of Nādir Shāh, Cockell provided him with much of the material for the earlier part of that book.[1]

As the Safavid period came to an end with Nādir's usurpation of the throne in 1736, we may regard Cockell as the last of the contacts between the West and Persia during the period covered by this chapter. In looking back over the four centuries we have examined, we see that while progress in establishing contact between Persia and the West was slow at first, a great advance was made in the 16th century. Nevertheless, the progress then made pales into insignificance when compared with what was accomplished in the succeeding hundred years. Moreover, the contacts made in the 17th century with the establish-

[1] On p. iv of *The History of Nadir Shah formerly called Thamas Kuli Khan the present Emperor of Persia* (London, 1742), Fraser stated: "The Account of Nadir Shah's first Exploits I have been favoured with from a Gentleman now in England, who resided several years in Persia, speaks that Language, and has been frequently in Company with that Conqueror". After quoting Cockell's "Account" on pp.71–128, Fraser stated that Cockell (whom he referred to as "the Gentleman who favoured me with the above Memoirs") left Persia for India in February 1737. We learn from the Gombroon Diary (Vol. iv of *The Persia and Persian Gulf Records* of the East India Company of 9/20 February 1737) that Cockell was the only employee of the company to leave Persia for India in that month.

ment of the various religious orders and of the English, Dutch and French East India Companies were to prove of a more continuous and lasting nature. Furthermore, we have the narratives of a great number of travellers to, and residents in, Persia. Of these the most important were unquestionably Chardin and Pietro della Valle. For the first thirty-six years of the 18th century we have likewise a mass of material from a number of sources, such as Krusiński's works, which can be regarded as very reliable. To sum up, it may be said that by the end of the Safavid period in 1736, Persia had most certainly ceased to be a *terra incognita* in the West.

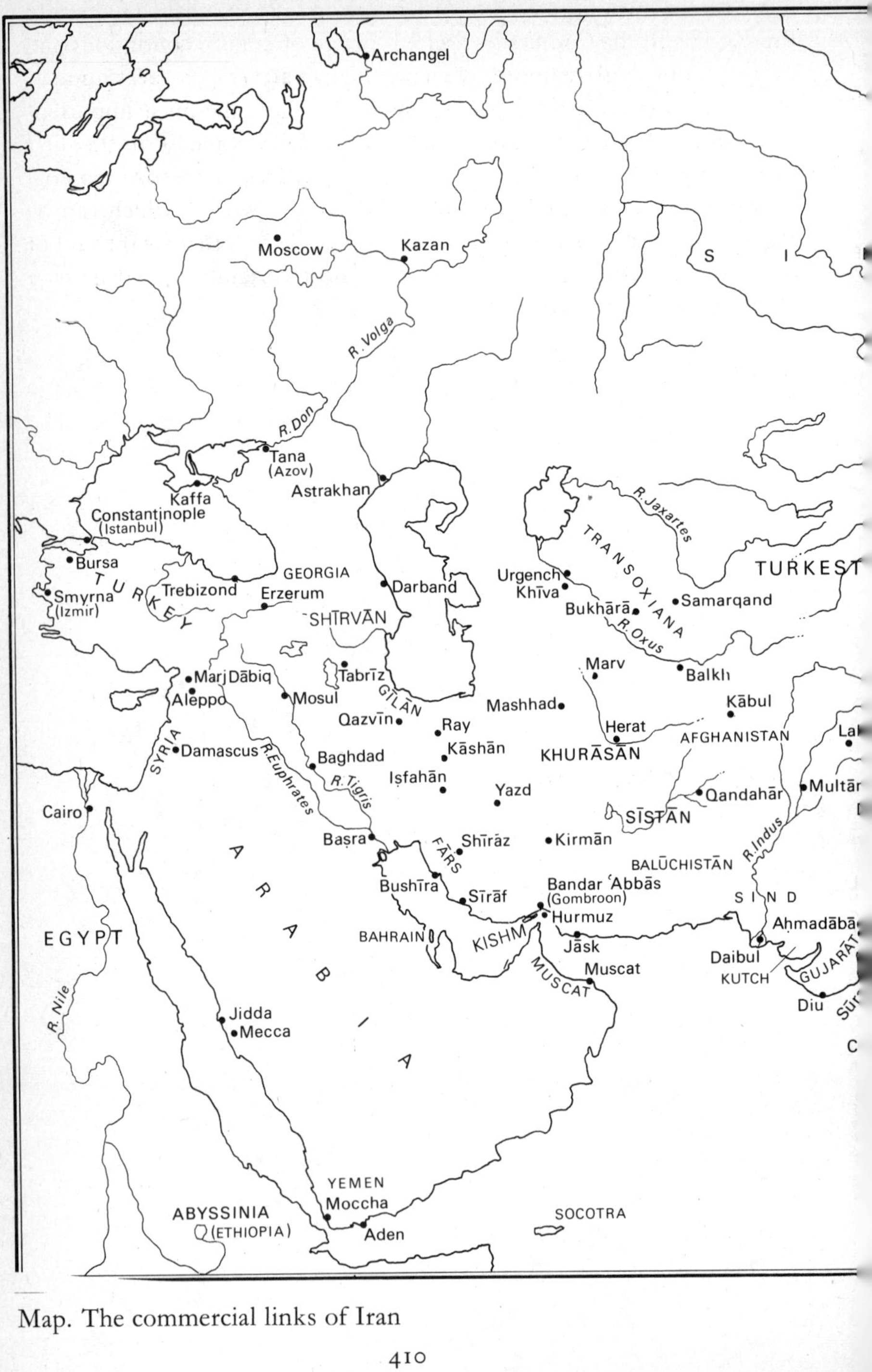

Map. The commercial links of Iran

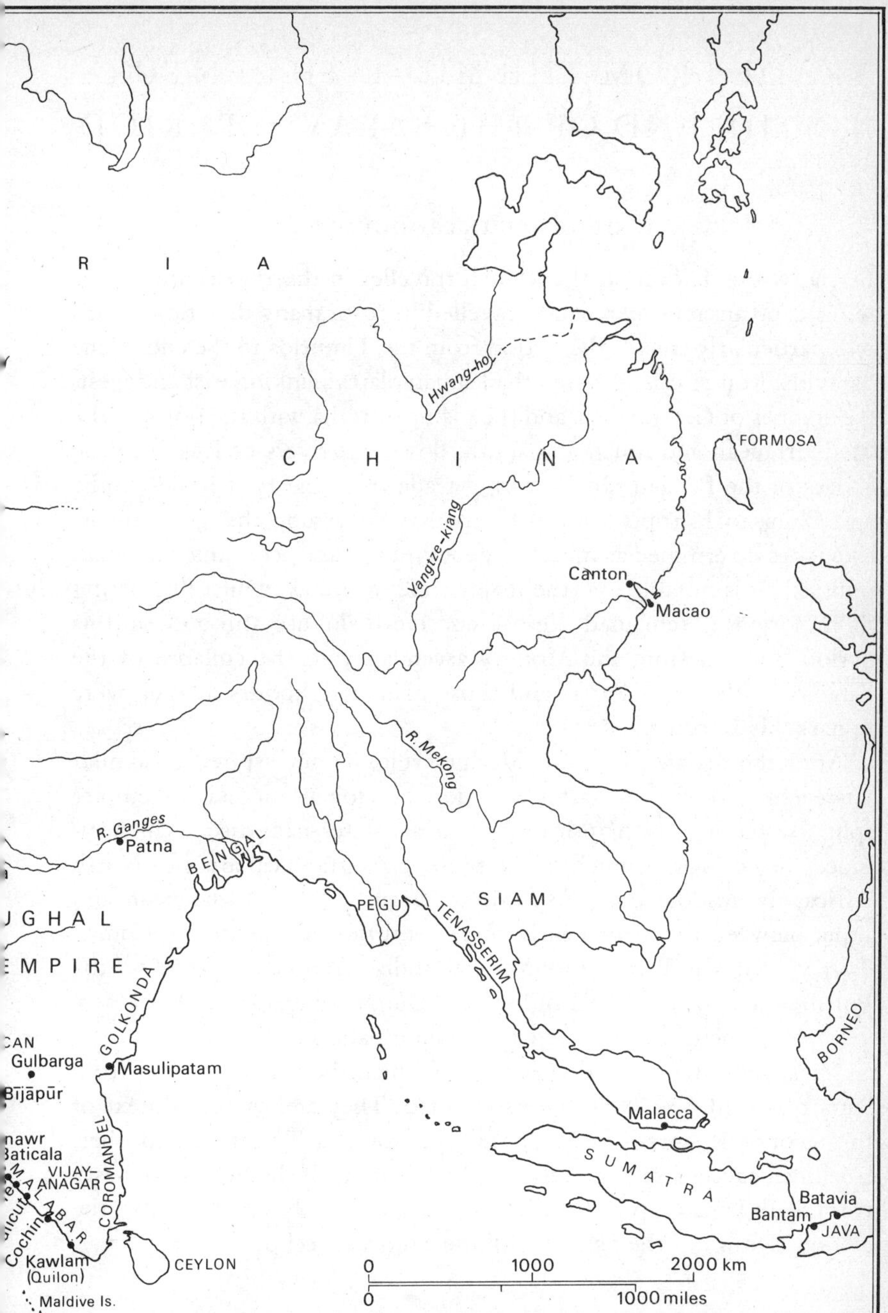
R I A
C H I N A
Hwang-ho
Yangtze-kiang
FORMOSA
Canton
Macao
R. Mekong
R. Ganges
Patna
BENGAL
PEGU
SIAM
TENASSERIM
UGHAL
EMPIRE
GOLKONDA
CAN
Gulbarga
Masulipatam
Bījāpūr
nawr
Baticala
VIJAY-
ANAGAR
MALABAR
COROMANDEL
Cochin
Kawlam
(Quilon)
CEYLON
Maldive Is.
BORNEO
Malacca
SUMATRA
Batavia
Bantam
JAVA
0
1000
2000 km
0
1000 miles

CHAPTER 8

TRADE FROM THE MID-14TH CENTURY TO THE END OF THE SAFAVID PERIOD

I. GENERAL INTRODUCTION

Persia, wrote Thévenot, the French traveller in the 17th century, was like a caravansarai: merchants travelled in from many directions. This was particularly true of the period from the Timurids to the end of the Safavids. Routes criss-crossed the Iranian plateau linking east and west, the steppes of Central Asia and the plains of India with the ports of the Mediterranean and north and south, down the rivers of Russia to the shores of the Persian Gulf carrying trade from the East Indies, India and China to Europe. Along the roads were strung the main towns, their sites determined as much by geographical and economic factors as political. It is notable that the major trading routes, whilst fluctuating in importance, remained almost constantly in use throughout this period, though from the Mongol ascendancy to the collapse of the Safavids the state of Persia and those of its neighbours in Asia were remarkably transformed.

After the disintegration of Mongol rule, Tīmūr aspired to similar far-reaching power but after a period of violent success his empire split. By the mid-10th/16th century three states had arisen which divided the control of much of the present geographical areas of North Africa, the Middle East, Asia Minor, Arabia, Iran, Afghanistan and India between them for nearly three centuries. These were Ottoman Turkey, Safavid Persia and Mughal India. Across the sea first the Portuguese and then the English and Dutch companies added a new maritime dimension to the ancient trading patterns.

There are three main divisions into which the general period from Tīmūr to Nādir Shāh can be subdivided. They are, in the context of this economic survey, firstly, the ages of the Timurids and their Türkmen successors, secondly, the first century of the Safavid dynasty from Shah Ismā'īl up to the accession of Shah 'Abbās and, thirdly, the second century of the Safavids till their ultimate eclipse.

2. THE TIMURIDS AND TÜRKMENS

(a) *The northern area*

The cruelty and destruction of Tīmūr's ruthless military campaigns are well known but amid the political confusion of much Persian history there is an astonishing recuperative capacity and fortitude in the midst of adversity. The reputed defiant encounter of Ḥāfiẓ with Tīmūr is an eloquent poetic expression of this spirit. In economic terms a recovery took place after the devastating effects of the post-Il-Khanid disorders and Tīmūr's relentless three decades of warfare in the last half of the 8th/14th century. At the beginning of the 9th/15th century Clavijo reported on the comparative prosperity of many parts through which he travelled on his embassy to Tīmūr. In Arzinjān he noticed "many opulent merchants" and "many caravans carrying much merchandise journey on their way, coming hither from Syria and bound for Turkey."[1] Tabrīz he thought "a very mighty city rich in goods and abounding in wealth, for commerce daily flourishes here." It was a wonderful sight, for "throughout the city there are fine roadways with open spaces well laid out: and round these are seen many great buildings and houses, each with its main doorway facing the square. Such are the caravanserais: and within are constructed separate apartments and shops with offices that are planned for various uses. Leaving these caravanserais you pass into the market streets where goods of all kinds are sold: such as silk stuffs and cotton clothes, crapes, taffetas, raw silk and jewelry: for in these shops wares of every kind may be found. There is indeed an immense concourse of merchants and merchandise here." He particularly remarked that "in certain of the caravanserais those who sell cosmetics and perfumes for women are established" and that it was the women who bought them, being "wont to use many perfumes and unguents."[2]

Clavijo was also impressed by Sulṭāniyya,[3] "a very populous city, but not so great as Tabriz: though it is a more important centre of exchange for merchants and their goods". In June, July and August of each year the city "is in a state of great commotion, and immense are the customs dues that accrue to the Treasury. Thus every year Sultáníyah is visited

[1] Clavijo, trans. Le Strange, pp. 129, 131. [2] *Ibid.*, pp. 152–3.
[3] *Ibid.*, pp. 158ff.

by numerous merchants from Lesser India who bring with them all kinds of spiceries. Hither too are imported the best sorts of the lesser spices that are not to be found on sale in the Syrian markets, such namely as cloves, nutmegs, cinnamon, manna, mace and the rest. These are prime spiceries that never reach the markets of Alexandretta and hence are not to be procured in the warehouses there." Apart from spices, silk was a commodity in great demand at Sulṭāniyya, whither was "imported all the silk that is produced in Gílán... where much of that commodity is produced and manufactured. This Gílán silk is exported from Sultáníyah to Damascus and other parts of Syria, also to Turkey and to Kaffa [in the Crimea] with the neighbouring lands. Further to Sultáníyah is brought all the silk made at Shamákhí [in Shirván] which is a place where much of this article is woven, and Persian merchants travel thither to buy it, also Genoese and Venetians." The importance of silk to the Persian economy was clear at that time.

It was not alone spices and silk that were marketed in Sulṭāniyya but "many kinds of cloth woven of silk or cotton and taffetas with crape-stuffs of various kinds" which "came from the country round and about Shíráz which lies towards the border of Lesser India." These textiles were joined by those from Yazd and the province of Khurāsān. From the port of Hurmuz came "a great quantity of pearls also many precious stones", in caravans which took sixty days to complete the journey. To Sulṭāniyya came "merchants from Christian lands, namely from Kaffa and Trebizond, with Moslem merchants from Turkey, Syria and Baghdad" meeting in the hostels which "were conveniently disposed for the accommodation of merchants who come to the city".

Samarqand, "rather larger than Seville", was another great city which Clavijo visited. Tīmūr had spared no effort to beautify and enrich it. It was a large emporium for produce and manufactured goods, for Tīmūr obliged artisans of all trades to settle in his capital. Many merchants, "Turks, Arabs and Moors of diverse sects, with Christians who were Greeks and Armenians, Catholics, Jacobites and Nestorians", besides Indians, traded there, for "the markets of Samarqand are amply stored with merchandise imported from distant and foreign countries", such as Russia, Tartary, China and India. The goods included leathers, linens, silk-stuffs, precious stones, unguents, herbs, spices, preserves with special emphasis on Chinese products which were regarded as the "richest and most precious of all those brought thither from foreign parts, for the craftsmen of Cathay are reputed to be the most skilful by far beyond those of any other nation".[1] Clavijo mentions an 800-camel caravan bringing merchandise from China which just preceded him to Samarqand. He writes that the journey from Peking took six months. One of the principal reasons for the trading prominence of Sulṭāniyya and Samarqand was their significance as the principal residences and military camps of the ruler of Western Persia, prince Mīrān Shāh, and Tīmūr himself. At a time when the administration and high command accompanied the ruler, such a base provided the central place of government and hence the focal point of buying and selling. This kind of organisational centre which existed in the Mongol, Timurid and Türkmen periods remained important too in Safavid times, when the purchasing power of the royal court and camp was a powerful economic factor.[2]

In Persia, where long distances had to be covered by caravans in a variety of exacting climatic and topographical conditions, the security and safety of the routes were vital. In periods of strong central authority there was a satisfactory system of post horses, caravansarais, road guards and market inspectors. It had been so in the heyday of the Achaemenian and Sasanian empires and existed for a time under the Īl-Khāns. It was also apparent in the Timurid period, for Clavijo commented on the post houses which had been built "at intervals of a day's journey apart, or sometimes of half a day's journey" with their horses for official use "kept stationed ready for use at post stages" and "cared for by men appointed to see to them". Amongst other places he was complimentary about the caravansarai at Miyāna "for the accommodation of travellers and for merchants on the road".[3] He reported that butchers and shoemakers who overcharged in the royal camp were penalised. In general from his descriptions of the main cities and others the picture which emerges is of much commercial and agricultural activity along the route that he travelled. Nīshāpūr was "very densely populated, and it is a most delightful place to live in"; Ṭūs, "a most pleasant township, and it has a greater population than any other place that we had come to since leaving Sultáníyah"; Bukhārā, where "the merchants here are very rich"; Simnān, "a very populous town";

[1] *Ibid.*, pp. 285, 288–9.

[2] Similarly in the Mughal empire, "those *bazar* dealers, so necessary for the support of an army in peace as well as in war": François Bernier, *Travels in the Mogul Empire*, ed. A. Constable (London, 1891), p. 43.

[3] Clavijo, trans. Le Strange, pp. 156–7.

Tehran, "a delightful abode being a city furnished with every convenience".[1]

Herat, unvisited by Clavijo, played then, and later, an important rôle in the Timurid trading pattern. "In the 14th Century it became the main centre of the north-east/south-west trade between the Golden Horde, Khwarazm and India and of the west-east trade between the empire of the Il-khans and the western provinces of China. It was soon acknowledged to be the pivot of the commercial and intellectual life of Central Asia."[2] Certainly not all cities were prospering: Erzerum, for example, which previously had been "the richest and greatest city of all those parts" [Anatolia], was not then well populated and similar misfortunes had befallen Qazvīn and Zanjān, where "most of the town is now uninhabited, but in former times they said this had been one of the greatest cities in all Persia". It was equally true that not all the roads at all times were safe from banditry and local extortions, as shown by Clavijo's efforts to avoid Qarā Yūsuf, the Qarā Quyūnlū chief, who was in revolt against Tīmūr, or his encounter with Cyril Cabasica, lord of "Zegan".[3] Yet generally whatever the political turmoil, trade had reasserted itself in the northern areas, from the Ottoman centre of Bursa to the Chinese capital of Peking through the roads and cities of Persia.

Yet later, as a result of the gradual fragmentation of the Timurid legacy, the increasing isolationism of the Chinese behind their Great Wall and the rising power of the Uzbeks, the full flow of trade through northern Persia and Central Asia from east to west began to lessen, though local trade persisted to south-west Asia and with India. Merchants were still passing along the routes from Tana on the sea of Azov to China in the time of Uzun Ḥasan, for the Venetians commented on Samarqand that it was "a verie great and well enhabited citie well replenished of artificers and merchaunts both". Furthermore, it was heard that "in these parties is verie great trafficque of merchaundize, specially jewells and clothes, as well of sylke as of other sortes, and from thense they go into the province of Catay".[4] Anthony Jenkinson, the English merchant-traveller, a century later in 1563 came across trade centering on Bukhārā. The overland trade with India too was of long standing and increased in importance with the rise of the Mughal empire. Ibn Baṭṭūṭa had mentioned the extensive overland trade in

[1] *Ibid.*, pp. 167, 181ff., 186, 302, 306.
[2] Allen, *Problems of Turkish Power*, p.8.
[3] Clavijo, trans. Le Strange, pp. 116ff., 139, 157.
[4] *Travels to Tana and Persia*, p.75.

horses, which were "exported to India (in droves), each one numbering six thousand or more or less. Each trader has one or two hundred horses or less or more,"[1] and they were taken to Sind through Multān, the capital. These were the horses valued for their "strength and length of pace". He noted that "there are manufactured at Naisābūr silk fabrics of *nakh*, *kamkhā'*, and other kinds, and these are exported from it to India".[2] They also exported by mounted post fruits from Khurāsān to India.

Ceramics and textiles were produced in Persia. In the Ottoman empire, Bursa had become a manufacturing city of much wealth and industry, as Clavijo had remarked on leaving Tabrīz when he "joined company with a caravan numbering some two hundred sumpter-horses carrying merchandise bound for the country of the Turks, the ultimate destination of the caravan being Brusa". Trade flowed between Persia and Turkey as Persian silk supplied most of the large requirements for the Ottoman looms. European merchandise reached Persia along the routes of Anatolia, the region of the upper Euphrates and by the Black Sea from Trebizond. It is towards the end of the 9th/15th century, after the Āq Quyūnlū under Uzun Ḥasan had asserted themselves over the Qarā Quyūnlū, that the complex relationship of mutual animosity and dependence developed between the Persians and Ottomans. Their empires and resources were too extensive for each to dominate the other completely; their economies were complementary.

The great Ottoman successes contemporary with the decline of the Timurids affected Venetian trade. The Venetians attempted to counter this by creating an alliance with Uzun Ḥasan against the Turks in 1472. This was no more successful than earlier attempts to enlist the services of Tīmūr against the Turks or, later, the Safavids against the common enemy of Persia and Europe. Venetian emissaries have left interesting descriptions of the state of trade in the late 9th/15th century. Since Clavijo's time, Sulṭāniyya had declined in importance, for "it is nowe but evill inhabited" with some 6–7,000 people in it. Tabrīz had taken its place as the capital and, according to Contarini, retaining its commercial prominence was a large city though not "very populous". "It abounds in all kinds of provisions but everything is dear. It contains many bazaars. A great quantity of silk passes through in caravans, bound for Aleppo, and there are many light articles of silk from the

[1] Ibn Baṭṭūṭa, trans. Gibb, II, 478. [2] *Ibid.*, III, 584.

manufactures of Jesdi [Yazd] and a great deal of fustians and merchandise of almost every kind."[1]

Yazd and Kāshān were recognised as important manufacturing centres by the Venetians. The former produced "clothe of golde, of sylke, and of damaskyne chamlette, lyned with sylke or furred with exceading faire armelynes and sables". It was a town of artificers, "as makers of sylkes, fustians, chamletts, and other like... of V myles in circuite, with very great suburbes, and yet in maner they all arr wevers and makers of divers kindes of sylkes which came from Straua [Āstārā], from Azzi, and from the parties towardes Zagatai". The articles produced were exported to other parts of Persia, India, China and Turkey and were so highly regarded that "lett him that woll bie good silkes of Soria, faire and well wrought, take of these". Apparently "they saie that towne requireth every daie twoo sompters of sylkes... As for chamletts, fustians, and such other, I saie nothing; for, by the sylke they make, it may easelie be gessed how much more they make of those." Kāshān too, well inhabited, was also renowned for its textiles, "wheare for the more parte they make sylkes and fustians in so greate quantitie that he wolde bestowe x^{ml} ducates in a daie may finde enough of that merchaundise to bestowe it on." Iṣfahān was well provided for the accommodation of merchants, whilst Shīrāz "conteigneth innumerable people, and is full of merchaunts.... Hither arr brought many jewelles, sylkes, both great and small, spices, rewbarbe, and semenzina". It was "a very sure dwelling without any disturbance". The Venetians marvelled at the diamonds, rubies and pearls they were shown. They were impressed with the carpets, the "most beautiful carpetts betweene which carpetts and those of Cairo and of Borsa [Bursa] (in my judgement), there is as much difference as betweene the clothes made of Englishe woolles and those of Saint Mathewes", which they saw in Tabrīz. The ingenuity of the carpenters was remarkable in spite of the shortage of suitable timber.[2]

Especially revealing were the comments on the organisation of the bazaars and the consideration paid to merchants. Writing of Yazd, the Venetian Barbaro wrote, "whan any merchaunt cometh to this towne for wares, he goeth into the Fondaco, rounde about the which arr certein litle shoppes, and in the middest a litle square place, likewise with shoppes, having twoo gates cheyned (bicause horses shulde not

[1] *Travels to Tana and Persia*, p. 127.

[2] *Ibid.*, pp. 60, 72–4.

passe through). This merchaunt with his companie, if they be acquainted with any place, resorte thither to sytt: if not, they may sytt wheare pleaseth them in any of those shoppes, beinge vj foote square a peece. And if they be divers merchaunts, lightly they take eche one a shoppe by himself. An howre aftre the sonne ryseng certein go about with sylkes and other wares on their armes, passeng rounde about without speaking. And the merchaunts, if they see ought that pleaseth them, call the seller; and looke on his wares: the price whereof is writen on a paper sowed unto it. If he lyketh them and the price, he throweth them into the litle shoppe, and so dispacheth them without moore wordes. For he that delivereth the stuff knoweth the owner of the shoppe, and therefore departeth without further question: which markett endureth till noone; and aftre dyner cometh the seller and receaueth his mooney; wheareas, if he fynde none that woll bye at his price one day, that he retorneth an other day: and so foorthe."[1] The caravansarais were locked at night for the protection of the merchandise.

As well as the main east–west route which went through Āzarbāījān, followed the foothills of the Alburz mountains and skirted the dangerous deserts of the interior, there was a more northerly route which crossed the Alburz dropping down to the Caspian Sea into the province of Shīrvān, Gīlān and Māzandarān, part of ancient Hyrcania. Some of the area had belonged to the old kingdom of Armenia, whose political influence had disappeared, but the industry and skill of individual Armenians survived the loss of the state. Armenians were to have a deep influence on the later course of trade in the 16th and, more particularly, the 17th centuries. The result of Tīmūr's campaigns and the resurgence of the Ottomans was to turn the northern provinces into political prizes for which the Persians and Turks contended at the expense of a succession of local rulers. The small pockets of Genoese traders whose principal bases were at Tana and Kaffa in the Crimea became isolated. Tīmūr had ruined the Tartar city of Astrakhan, the first of that name, which was the hub of trade up the Volga or westwards to the Crimea. This ended the Genoese and Venetian trade in the silks and spices there which, in the main, was re-routed through Syria.

This reduced the volume of trade in the former direction but did not stop it. Astrakhan was rebuilt and local trade over the Caspian resumed. The Russian merchant Nikitin, for example, travelled through

[1] *Ibid.*, pp. 73–4.

Astrakhan and over the Caspian with the ambassador of Shīrvān to Ivan III, Grand Duke of Russia (1462–1505). Conditions were not easy, for the behaviour of the Tartars was unpredictable and transportation insecure. Contarini wrote that the ships were kept on shore during the winter when they could not be used and were "called fishes, which they are made to resemble in shape, being sharp at the head and stern and wide amidships. They are built of timbers, caulked with rags, and are very dangerous craft. No compass is used, as they keep continually in sight of land. They use oars; although everything is done in a most barbarous manner, they look upon themselves as the only mariners worthy of the name." This Venetian voyaged to Astrakhan from Darband, with "thirty five persons, including the captain and six mariners; there were on board some merchants taking rice, silk and fustians to Citracan [Astrakhan] for the Russian market and some Tartars going to procure furs for sale in Derbent". Grounding on the shallows and shipwreck were not infrequent. It was said that an ambassador and a caravan left Astrakhan every year for Moscow "accompanied by a great many Tartar merchants who... take with them silk manufactured in Gesdi [Yazd] and fustian stuffs to exchange for furs, saddles, swords, bridles, and other things which they require".[1] On the Black Sea, some trade continued at Trebizond but did not represent a significant share of the total volume then entering or leaving Persia.

There was, therefore, in the Türkmen period as in that of the Timurids, a thriving textile industry, a considerable export of raw silk to Turkey, and a large import of spices. Whilst trade continued to follow the established pattern east and west across the north, though with diminishing importance as a long distance exchange, it was being augmented in the south by the remarkable rise of Hurmuz. This barren island, virtually devoid of natural resources, resembling a miniature polychromed waste land, became a poetic and real symbol of fabulous wealth. If the world was a ring, it was imagined, then Hurmuz was its jewel.

(b) *The southern area*

The other great axis of trade through Persia was longitudinal up from the Persian Gulf through the southern deserts, not easily passable in

[1] *Ibid.*, pp. 146–7, 151.

the hot summer, and along the eastern foothills of the Zagros to the northern junction towns of Āzarbāījān with principal spurs running east to west at Lār, Shīrāz, Ābāda, Iṣfahān, and Sāva. From very early times both the Red Sea and the Persian Gulf were frequented by traders. Recent discoveries of Achaemenian buildings near Bushīra have reinforced the literary evidence of Alexander's admiral, Nearchus, of an early Persian presence in the Gulf. The maritime interest of the Sasanians has been convincingly confirmed by the recent archaeological discoveries at Sīrāf. The importance of post-Islamic trade up the Persian Gulf is well attested by the Arab geographers and clearly proved by a number of scholars. In the time of the Mamlūks, Aden was especially notable for its spice trade and Ibn Baṭṭūṭa commented that "it is the port of the merchants of India, to which come great vessels from Kinbāyat [Cambay], Tānah, Kawlam [Quilon], Qāliqūt, Fandaraina, al-Shāliyāt, Manjarūr [Mangalore], Fākanūr [Bacanore], Hinawr [Honavar], Sindābūr [Goa], and other places. The merchants of India live there, and the merchants of Egypt also."[1] It retained a commercial importance to the mid 17th century. It was also a port of entry for pilgrims to Mecca.

Ibn Baṭṭūṭa visited Hurmuz some thirty years after the city was transferred from its mainland site to the adjacent island of Jarūn, shortly after 1300. Then, according to Ibn Baṭṭūṭa, it was "a fine large city, with magnificent bazaars, as it is the port of India and Sind, from which the wares of India are exported to the two 'Irāqs, Fārs and Khurāsān".[2] Lār too, with its "fine Bazaars" was becoming more important and the pearl fishing off Baḥrain was already renowned. Hurmuz retained its preeminent position at the head of the Persian Gulf for three centuries until it was ruined when the Persians took it in 1622 from the Portuguese, who had taken complete control of it under Albuquerque in 1515. Clavijo stressed the importance of Hurmuz in the trade of spices, precious stones and pearls, and stated that only the skilled men of Hurmuz could do the work of boring and stringing the pearls. The great Chinese admiral, Cheng Ho, brought fleets to Hurmuz, as well as Aden, in the early 15th century. There was no doubt about its wealth, for "foreign ships from every place and foreign merchants travelling by land all come to this country to attend the market and trade". Here were found a wonderful variety of fruits and

[1] Ibn Baṭṭūṭa, trans. Gibb, II, 372. [2] *Ibid.*, p. 400.

foods. The people of Hurmuz were "experts in every kind of art and craft", and they traded in all kinds of precious stones and textiles.[1]

Hurmuz was, in fact, the great emporium for the seaborne trade of the east which reached Persia and a vital link in the transhipment of trade between Europe and the Far East. There were a number of ports on which the long distance trade hinged and, as Albuquerque realised, they represented strategic keys for the domination of that trade. Besides Hurmuz, Aden, Goa, Calicut and Malacca were important staging ports, but trade was carried on elsewhere at a number of others along the coasts of India where Persian merchants were to be found. Evidence of this is widespread, notably in the accounts of 'Abd al-Razzāq, the ambassador of Shāh Rukh in 845/1441–2, and Afanasiĭ Nikitin, the Russian merchant, a generation later. According to 'Abd al-Razzāq, Hurmuz still continued to attract "the merchants of seven climates". They came from Egypt, Syria, Anatolia, all the provinces of Persia, Turkestan, southern Russia, China, Java, Bengal, Siam, Tenasserim, Socotra, Bījāpūr, the Maldives, Malabar, Abyssinia, Zanzibar, Vijayanagar, Gulbarga, Gujarāt, Cambay, Arabia, Aden, Jidda and the Yemen, bringing "those rare and precious articles which the sun, the moon and the rains have combined to bring to perfection, and which are capable of being transported by sea". The transactions were carried out either by money or by exchange.[2] There were indications of credit arrangements but it is probable that these were confined to merchants from the same towns as Ibn Baṭṭūṭa implied earlier or through family connections. 'Abd al-Razzāq said of the inhabitants of Hurmuz that they united the flattering character of the Persians with the profound cunning of the Indians. He was impressed with the security and justice of Calicut, to which merchants came from all quarters, and noted that people from Hurmuz resided at Vijayanagar as well as people from Khurāsān. Many Persians were employed in the Deccan. Nikitin also noticed this Persian presence, which he exaggerated by asserting that "the rulers and the nobles in the land of India are all Khorassanians". Nikitin remarked on the extensive trade in horses between Persia and India by sea, particularly at the port of Daibul in Sind. He, too, was impressed with Hurmuz, "a vast emporium of all the world; you find there people and goods of every description, and whatever thing is

[1] Ma Huan, *The Overall Survey of the Ocean's Shores*, trans. J.V.G. Mills (Cambridge, 1970), pp. 165, 167.

[2] Major, *India in the Fifteenth Century*, part 1, pp. 5–7.

produced on earth you find it in Hormuz. But the duties are high, one tenth of everything."[1]. He thought Chinese goods cheap, especially porcelain. Other travellers such as the Venetian Nicolò de' Conti support the evidence of widespread Persian involvement in the maritime trade with India. Conti refers to his friendship with some Persian merchants about 1440 and to Calicut being "a very noble emporium of the Persians". Just over fifty years later Hieronimo di Santo Stefano, a Genoese, after journeying from Cairo to India, returned home after innumerable adventures through Cambay and Hurmuz, where he was befriended by some Alexandrian and Damascene merchants. These helped him to reach Aleppo by way of Shīrāz, Iṣfahān, Sulṭāniyya and Tabrīz. He refers to Armenian merchants in Hurmuz. Another Venetian mentions that "the merchaunts that travaill either out of India into Persia or out of Persia into India, for the more parte do all arryve in this ilande".[2] All draw attention to the scorching heat and brackish water.

It is probable that Persian maritime trade with India in particular and the east in general reached a high level of activity in the last decade of the 15th century in both variety and volume. The Ottomans had not then won control over Egypt, Turkish–Persian relations were not affecting trade in the south to any great extent, Mughal dominion was not yet felt over India, and the Portuguese had not established themselves or disturbed the pattern of Asian trade. Not for another century and a half, in the time of Shah 'Abbās II, was maritime trade comparable, and then the Persians had to share it not only with Indian merchants, but also with the increasingly powerful Armenian merchant communities who were entrenching themselves in the main trading centres, and with the Dutch and English East India Companies.

The Portuguese noticed and admired the well-dressed, good-living inhabitants of Hurmuz, whose trading activities they were to control to their own advantage. Duarte Barbosa described the island in its greatest period at the beginning of the 16th century: "In this city are many merchants of substance, and many very great ships. It has a right good harbour where many sorts of goods are handled which come hither from many lands, and from here they barter them with many parts of India. They bring hither spices of all sorts, and divers kinds, to wit pepper, cloves, ginger, cardamoms, eagle-wood, sandal-wood,

[1] *Ibid.*, part 3, p. 19. [2] *Travels to Tana and Persia*, p. 79.

brasil-wood, myrobalans, tamarinds, saffron, indigo, wax, iron, sugar, rice (great store) and cocoa-nuts, as well as great abundance of precious stones, porcelain and benzoin, by all of which they gain much money. They have also great plenty of Cambaya, Chaul and Dabul cloths, and from Bengala they bring many *synbafos*, which are a sort of very thin cotton cloth greatly prized among them and highly valued for turbans and shirts, for which they use them. And from the city of Adem they bring to Ormus abundance of copper, quicksilver, vermillion, rose-water, many brocaded cloths, tafetas and ordinary camlets; also from the lands of the Xeque Ismael come a great quantity of silk, very fine musk and rhubarb of Babilonia. And from Barem and Julfar come seed pearls and large pearls, and from the cities of Arabia a great number of horses come, which they carry hence to India, whither every year they used to take one and at times two thousand horses, and each one of these is worth in India, taking good and bad together, three or four hundred cruzados, more or less according to the demand for them. And in the ships in which these horses are taken they carry also abundance of dates, raisins, salt and sulphur, also coarse seed pearls in which the Moors of Narsingua take great delight".[1]

The administration was competent and strict and, in spite of the necessity to import all the provisions of daily life, "all the open places are constantly full of all this food and wood (which also they bring from outside) in great abundance, and everything is sold by weight at fixed rates, with very strict regulations; and any person who gives short weight or departs from the fixed rate and orders given to him, is punished with great severity". The collection of customs was well organised, for "this king keeps his governors and collectors of revenue at those places in Persia and Arabia and the isles which pertain to his seignory". There would appear to have been an adequate supply of money without restrictions on its export and generally constant in its value. It is doubtful if gold was coined there, though it had a limited circulation, but it is probable that the special silver coinage, *lārīs*, which were like thin beans, were minted there, as Duarte Barbosa says. "All this money", Barbosa affirmed, "silver as well as gold, is in such plenty" that "as many ships as come to the city with goods, after they have sold their goods and bought the horses and *sinais* which they are to take away with them what balance soever remains over to them"

[1] Barbosa I, 93–5.

they take in this coin, "as it circulates much in India and has a good value there". This acceptance of the lārī facilitated trade. Barbosa specially mentioned connections with Daibul, to which horses were brought from Hurmuz; Goa, where "the harbour was exceeding good, had great trade, and many ships of the Moors, came thither from Mecca, the city of Aden, Ormus, Cambaya and Malabar", where horses were sold and where "the Ormus merchants take hence in their ships cargoes of rice (great store), sugar, iron, pepper, ginger and other spices of divers kinds, and drugs, which they carry thither".[1] Large quantities of rice were also obtained from the west coast of India at Baticala (Bhatkal), as well as sugar, for bartering for horses and pearls, and Bacanore, where it was bartered for copper, coconuts and molasses.

Other travellers at the same time corroborate the account of Duarte Barbosa, such as Tome Pires and Ludovico di Varthema. The latter comments on the extent of the trade of Bengal from which "fifty ships are laden every year in the place with cotton and silk stuffs... these same stuffs go through all Turkey, through Syria, through Persia, through Arabia Felix, through Ethiopia, and through all India".[2] Varthema also mentions, as does Tome Pires, Persian merchants at Pegu, a great centre for gumlac. This was probably exported in large olive-coloured jars with dragons and other Chinese motifs in relief and which were thereafter used for carrying holy water from the Ganges to Indian merchants residing in Persia. Tome Pires noted Persians and Armenians at Malacca. An interesting instance of the importance of local brokers in business transactions is described by Varthema as having taken place in Calicut and was probably paralleled elsewhere. Brokers and the money changers (*ṣarrāfs*) played extremely important parts in the organisation of trade.

There was no doubt at all of the extensive well-organised system of trading which operated along the sea routes. Doubtless greatly facilitated by a common religion and language in many parts among the traders as a result of the spread of Islam in previous centuries, it was nevertheless protected and encouraged by prince and producer for the wealth it brought and the revenues it sustained. The merchants were intrepid, for the voyages were dangerous, uncomfortable and dependent on the monsoons. The ships, apart from the great Chinese junks and the Portuguese galleons, were simple in construction, "the timbers

[1] *Ibid.*, pp. 165, 175–8. [2] Varthema, p. 212.

of which were sewn together with cords and the sails made of rush mats", or cotton. While the art of navigation was well understood, there was not a great deal of order on board ships, and there was the ever-present threat from pirates at sea and brigands on inhospitable coasts, the fear of shipwreck or at best loss of voyage or goods, or starvation in a voyage blown off course. A voyage from Hurmuz to Calicut would last three weeks or more and one from Aden to Calicut would take up to five weeks in normal conditions.

In assessing the particular trading rôle of Hurmuz from the 14th to the 16th centuries in Persian history, it is necessary to bear in mind the composite nature of the trade and the close connections of traders inhabiting the Persian Gulf on both its sides. Duarte Barbosa writes of Hurmuz that "the merchants of this isle and city are Persians and Arabs", and in considerable detail, if not always completely accurately, he enumerates all the places of the Gulf and the coastal districts of Arabia which were to a lesser or greater extent involved with the kingdom of Hurmuz. The trading was cosmopolitan but the kingdom itself was virtually autonomous, also administering part of the Persian mainland. There was no real effort to make it subject to the dynasties that rose and fell in southern Persia, which had neither the means to coerce it nor the power to supplant it whilst they benefited from the trade which was attracted to it. The Safavids sought early to change this state of affairs and make the kingdom of Hurmuz subject to them and sent officials to claim a yearly tribute. The vizier, Khwāja ʿAṭṭār, opposed the pretensions of the Safavids as much as the threats of the Portuguese. Shah Ismāʿīl sent an ambassador to Goa in 1510, before it had been taken by Albuquerque, to solicit assistance from the Goanese ruler in subjecting Hurmuz. Subsequently it was suggested to Albuquerque that the Portuguese and Persians should jointly effect this, but this and other requests were rejected. With the conquest of Hurmuz by Albuquerque in 1515, Persian claims to the island, even to its trading revenues, were unavailing for a century.

(*c*) *Conclusion*

There was, therefore, in Timurid and Türkmen times much commercial activity throughout Persia. The merchant had his standing in contemporary society and he had an assured place in the large towns where accommodation was provided and where retailing was carried out in the bazaars. Manufacturing centres at Yazd, Kāshān, Iṣfahān, Shīrāz, Kirmān, Tabrīz, to mention the major cities, produced a wide variety of textiles, ceramics, leather work and metal work for local consumption and export. The fine arts flourished; the main palace and mosque "so well built that I do not know how to describe it" at Tabrīz were regarded by a contemporary Venetian merchant as outstandingly beautiful. The transit trade was extensive from China to the Levant in which Persian merchants were prominent and Hurmuz was the entrepôt par excellence. Trade was only very loosely national in character, unlike that of the following centuries.

3. THE EARLY SAFAVID PERIOD

(*a*) *Introduction*

The rise to power of the Safavid dynasty in Persia did not generally, in the short term, have a profound effect on the Persian economy. During Shah Ismā'īl's early years of achievement, when he held off challenges to his own supremacy from the Turks and Uzbeks, Persia reacted to external events rather than took initiatives. There was, however, no mistaking the militant Shi'ism of Shah Ismā'īl, his religious fervour, irrespective of whether the motivation was political or spiritual. In his time he deliberately exploited Iran as the seat of a Shī'ī minority sect with all the devotion which such a feeling engenders. This initially may have proved a weakness, for not only did its self-conscious sense of self-righteousness make cooperation with Sunnīs difficult, but it led to extravagant claims and aggressive activities. Thus the Portuguese, in return for Persian assistance against the Turks, were requested, amongst other demands, to impose the Shī'ī creed in Goa, whilst early efforts to proselytise the Turks of Anatolia provoked wrathful reprisals from the Sultans. As in the previous century sea borne trade with India and beyond was maintained through Hurmuz, though the Persian revenues benefited little. Turkey remained the main market for silk exports, with increasing reliance on Venetians and Armenians as intermediaries.

It was on the periphery of Persia that the main events were taking place with such profound political and economic implications. Power was shifting from Central Asia to Anatolia. Many reasons have been advanced for this; many theories formulated. In part it is explained by the spectacular success of the Ottomans themselves. In part it is the triumph of the musket over the bow. In part it is the greater rise of industrial economies with manufacturing skills on a comparatively large scale which were being developed in Europe over peoples mostly exchanging raw materials: the facility of cash payments over bartering arrangements; the skills of navigation and shipbuilding construction over the mule and camel for transportation. Whatever the validity of these and other explanations, there is no doubt of the political and economic changes of the 10th/16th century. The Turks performed notable feats of administration, commerce and warfare. The Russians from Moscow broke free and stretched out from the Baltic to the Caspian along the Volga and east to Siberia. In Europe the fleets of Portugal, Spain, England and Holland were mastering the seas, adding a new dimension to the politics and trade of the period. The whole Mediterranean world teemed with activity. In Egypt the Mamlūk domination came to an end. The half century from 1510 to 1560 was particularly momentous. Shah 'Abbās and the later Safavids were to derive great advantages from a Persia placed in a decisive position between East and West.

(*b*) *The northern area*

As a result of the enmity between the Uzbeks and the Persians, which continued intermittently throughout the century, and the seizure of Herat by Shah Ismā'īl in 1510, which ended the golden age of that noble city, trade from Persia to Central Asia was reduced. Some trade continued to flow through Mashhad and Kābul to Bukhārā and Balkh as they remained centres distributing Indian and some European goods throughout Turkestan. In the second half of the century the Russians began actively promoting their trade there after they had defeated the Tartars and taken control of the Volga from Kazan down to the delta including Astrakhan. Anthony Jenkinson, who passed through the land of the Türkmens in 1561, reported that in Ürgench there was little trade out of Persia, "in most small quantitie not worth the writing", and that in Bukhārā, which gave some evidence of its former greatness as a yearly great resort of merchants, they were "so beggerly and poore that there is no hope of any good trade there to be had worthy the following". There was, however, some Persian trade there, for they "doe bring thither *Craska* [coarse linen] wollen cloth, linnen clothe, divers kindes of wrought pide silkes, Argomacks [Türkmen horses crossed with Arab stock] with such like, and doe carrie from thence redde hides with other Russe wares, and slaves", for which it was the largest market in Central Asia.[1] Besides the Russians, there were some merchants from India, "but golde, silver, precious stones, and spices they bring none". "I enquired", adds Jenkinson interestingly, "and perceuied that all such trade passeth to the Ocean Sea, and the vaines where all such things are gotten, are in the subiection of the Portingals." Jenkinson could not sell his cloth to the Persian merchants "for that they bring thither themselves, and is brought unto them as I have enquired from Aleppo in Syria, and the parts of Turkie". This was confirmed on his return journey, when he was again informed that "the chief trade of Persia is into Syria, and so transported into the Levant seas". The routes were dangerous, thieves abounded, and silver and copper coinage were in short supply and frequently debased. It was Russian interest which was to take in the widespread trade to Central Asia and eventually to culminate in their occupation of the area. On Jenkinson's return from his Central Asian journey he was accompanied by "two ambassadors, the one from the King of Boghar [Bukhārā], the other from the King of Balke [Balkh]..." and later "foure more Ambassadors sent from the King of Urgence, and other Soltans, his brethren, unto the Emperor of Russia...".

The acquisition of Siberia by Russia in the latter part of the 10th/16th century was also important in both a political and economic context. The area provided a vast store of furs, particularly sables and foxes, which became an important item of Russian trade to Persia, and some gold and silver. The southern Russian pivotal town for trade east to Central Asia and south to Persia was Astrakhan, 75 miles upstream on the lower Volga from the Caspian Sea. It had been important for centuries and during the 3rd/9th and 4th/10th centuries had been a link between the northern Viking communities and the Arab merchants. It acquired more importance in the Mongol period when Ibn Baṭṭūṭa described it as "one of the finest of cities, with great bazars", along with the "fine bazars and harbour" of Azov in the Crimea. As has been noted, in the 9th/15th century its trade declined, but with the southern and eastward expansion of Russia it gradually increased in importance after its capture in 1554 and its fortification in the 1580s. It did, how-

[1] Jenkinson, *Early Voyages* I, 72, 87–9.

ever, suffer greatly in the anarchical conditions of "the Troubles" over the Russian succession in the early 17th century.

Jenkinson on his first voyage described its trade as follows. "The chiefest commodities that the Russes bring thither are redde hides, redde sheepe skinnes, woodden vessels, bridles, and saddles, knives, and other trifles, with corne, bacon and other victualles. The Tartars bring thither divers kindes of wrought silkes; and they that come out of Persia, namely from *Shamackie*, do bring sowing silke, which is the coursest that they use in Russeland, Crasko, divers kindes of pide silkes for girdles, shirts of male, bowes, swoords, and such like things: and some yeeres corne, and wallnuts." At that time, however, less than a decade after its capture by the Russians, it was not an attractive place. There were "all such things in such small quantitie, the merchantes being so beggerly and poore that bring the same, that it is not worth the writing."[1]

The importance of Astrakhan in the third quarter of the 16th century in the context of Persian trade was twofold. Firstly, as a staging point in the route which stretched from the White Sea to the Caspian linking Europe and Asia, it was beyond the interference of the Spanish and Portuguese fleets. From the time of the first English voyage to Russia in 1553–5 a possible alternative route was available for spices, silkes and dyes, away from Turkish or Venetian control, and a potential market for exports of English cloth, which was then and for many years the staple English export item. As Jenkinson explained to 'Abd-Allāh, khan of Shīrvān, "if it would please the sayde Sophie and other princes of that countrey, to suffer our merchaunts to trade into those dominions, and to give us passeport and safe conduct for the same, as the sayde Turke hath graunted to the sayde Venetians, I doubted not but that it should growe to such a trade, to the profite of them, as never before had bene the like, and that they should bee both furnished with our commodities, and also have utterance of theirs, although there never came Turke into their land...".[2] Unfortunately Shah Ṭahmāsp, having just concluded a treaty with Ḥasan Āghā, the Turkish ambassador, in Qazvīn in November 1562, was unwilling to listen to Jenkinson's trade proposals at that time, lest he jeopardise his improved relations with the Turks. Laurence Chapman later reported Turkish hostility, their merchants pretending to be friendly "but

[1] *Ibid.*, pp. 58–9. [2] *Ibid.*, pp. 143–4.

secretlie they be our mortall enemies, searching by all meanes to hinder our sales". Arthur Edwards repeated this trade proposition later to Shah Ṭahmāsp when he promised to bring the merchandise as the Venetians did, "abundance of fine karsies, of broad clothes, of all sorts and coulers, as scarlets, violets, and other of the finest cloth of all the world... by the way of Moscovia, with more safetie and in much shorter time then the Venetians can bring them".[1] The shah was then agreeable and authorised the necessary privileges.

Secondly, as the most southerly Russian outpost Astrakhan threatened Ottoman interests in the Caucasian area. The six Persian voyages sponsored by the English Russia Company between 1560 and 1580 were a premature but interesting attempt to reorientate a portion of Persian trade from its east–west axis to a north–south one. It had attractions for a Persia that wished to be free from Turkish control over its existing major export routes. Shah Ṭahmāsp, in giving the Agent of the Russia Company, Arthur Edwards, the trading privileges and a list of the goods he wanted on 29 June 1566, made it clear that he "desireth to see of all sortes, which will be an occasion that the Venetians and Turkes shall be in lesse estimation than they are, for themselves doe feare and secretly say the same. And truely the Princes subiects intend to enter into trade with us for spices and other commodities that they were woont to sell unto the Venetians and Turkes." Thus at the outset of this trade one of the main objectives was to displace the Levant-routed merchandise, but neither then nor later throughout the rest of the Safavid period was this accomplished either in a northerly or southerly direction. Edwards realised that "to breake the trade betwixt the Venetians and the whole company of the Armenians" was not feasible on the resources he had available; it never was.[2]

As will already have been noted, trade to a greater or lesser extent had been carried on between Persia and the trading centres and ports of the Levant for centuries. The rise of the Ottomans, far from reducing its importance, increased it. Thus although the English merchants were in hopes of developing a profitable trade with Persia through Russia, neither the Venetians, the Armenians nor the Turks were disposed to surrender their markets lightly. What was at stake was mentioned by two Russia Company merchants, Thomas Banister and Geoffrey

[1] *Ibid.*, II, 413, 416.

[2] *Ibid.*, pp. 406, 410; see also p. 397. "I feare you shall be hindrd by the Venetians, if they may; for I knowe it will grieve them, that you doe trade into these partes."

Ducket, to Sir William Cecil in 1568: "This matter of Percia towchit the Etallians and straungers verye neare, for the Etallians have had the holle trayed of silks and also moche spyces brought by the Venetians, the Flamings; in lyke caise they have the stapill of all Spyces playsid at Andwarpe [Antwerp] by the Portingales, whereof a greate parte is utteride in England, so that if we might bringe the Spyces and silks this waye, they are all towchid, whiche they are not ignorant of."[1] Cloth, silk and spices – these were the main trading counters concerned in this new opening of trade which was definitely acquiring a national character.

What, then, did the English merchants discover in the Persia of Shah Ṭahmāsp in their "good hope for a beneffitiall trade of Spices, drugges and silkes out of Persia"? They were informed that "there is more silke brought into some one citie of Persia then is of cloth brought into the citie of London",[2] but, hyperbole aside, silk was the dominant Persian commodity. It was estimated that raw silk cost between 9/- and 10/- a lb., that is 60 *shāhīs*, at 6d each, a batman of six and a half lbs. at Qazvīn and a mule's lading was 60 batmans. It was thought possible to purchase 60,000–80,000 lbs. yearly at Qazvīn and at Ganja "(if it were not for the Turkes) for a two hundred thousandes pounds [over 400,000 lbs.] besides silke of all colours died in graine", for about 11s 6d per lb. There was no shortage of silk: "there is in those parts to be had three or foure thousand horses lading, every horse loade being 50 or 60 batmans, beside silke of Groine [Georgia]". The Turks, Venetians and Armenians had the edge over the English merchants not only in the regularity of their supplies, the security of their routes and their superior knowledge of local conditions, but also in their provision of ready money to facilitate sales. The Turks, according to Arthur Edwards, "bring great store of silver to be coyned, to wit, Dollars at ten *shaughes* the peece. The Hungarie Ducket is at 12 *shaughs*. And having monie in readiness at the time of the yeere, they buy silke the better cheap, when the country men bring it first to be sold."[3] For this reason it was requested "to send some bulion to be coined here; it will please the prince there, and be profitable to you".

The circulation of precious metals had become complex in the 10th/16th century, and with the introduction of large quantities of silver from South America it was to have increasingly different reper-

[1] *Ibid.*, p. 260. [2] *Ibid.*, p. 420. [3] *Ibid.*, p. 401.

cussions on national economies. In particular the Turkish economy suffered from a bad bout of inflation towards the end of the 16th century, exacerbating its relations with Persia. The movement of precious metals, particularly in the trade between west and east in the 11th/17th century, was a subject of acute controversy in the state treasuries. At this time in Persia, according to Vincentio d'Alessandri, "those who introduce silver from Turkey gain twenty per cent., gold fourteen and fifteen per cent., and copper sometimes eighteen and sometimes twenty per cent.; it is true that there are great expenses, as the exportation of metals is forbidden".[1] It was reported by the English merchants that "there is brought into Persia an incredible summe of Dutch dolers, which for the most part are there employed in rawe silke". In exchange for silk or spices English merchants could only provide cloth in quantity, and for this purpose Qazvīn, Tabrīz, Ardabīl and Kāshān were the places where resided the chief merchants; Tabrīz was "the principall place in this countrey for uttering of cloth or karsies". Kāshān was praised for "a towne that consisteth all together of merchandise, and the best trade of all the lande is there, beying greatly frequented by the merchauntes of India. Here our men bought great store of all maner of wrought silkes and some spices, and good store of Turkie stones." To the ordinary people who wore rough cloth, it was hoped to sell kerseys. The wealthier people wore broad cloth. "They talke such of London clothes" or those from Venice and preferred bright colours; "violets in graine and fine reds be most worne". However, though Shah Ṭahmāsp talked of taking 100,000 cloths, this did not materialise, nor was it likely. The shah might exercise a control over trade, especially of silk, but he was not a merchant. It was reported that "the Shaugh neuer tooke cloth unto his treasurie all the dayes of his life, and will not now beginne; his whole trade is in rawe silke, which he selleth alwayes for money to the Armenians and Turkes, and such other as use to buy it".[2] There was thus little chance of bartering cloth for silk directly with the shah. The English merchants were faced with strong competition from the Venetians and Armenians already entrenched in the complementary silk and cloth trade at Aleppo, for "the Armenians yeerely receaue at the Venetians hands kersies in barter for rawe silkes, giving sometimes 60 peeces of kersies for 70 batmans of silke of this countrey, and

[1] *A Narrative of Italian Travels*, pp. 225–6.

[2] Jenkinson, *Early Voyages* II, 411.

40 peeces for Grousine [Georgian] silke". It was reported that one Armenian village "yeerely carrieth 400 and 500 Mules lading of silke to Aleppo, and bringeth thence 800 or a thousand Mules laden with kersies and Venice clothes", a mule carrying 60 batmans of silk or 18 kersies.[1]

The same problem applied to spices, which were, however, in this period in short supply from Hurmuz owing to Portuguese–Indian hostilities, and the English merchants were advised to pay for them "one third part money, the rest, cloth and kersies fitted in coulers meet for this countrey".

Commodities thought exportable out of Persia for England through Russia included raw silk, pepper, ginger, nutmegs, mace, cinnamon, brimstone, alum, rice, galls, cloves and bow staves. Much good cotton was produced, some of which was exported to Aleppo. Manufacturing was carried on, and Khurāsān was mentioned by Alessandri where "they worked cloths of silk and especially velvets, which are equal in excellence to the Genoese; in other parts they work on smooth stuffs and damask, but not with the finish they have in Italy". Trade, however, by and large was not flourishing. There are frequent references to the interruption caused by the dearth of commerce at Hurmuz, or the effects of warfare around Aleppo, or the difficulties caused by disturbances within the country, or the Cossack brigands at the delta of the Volga. There was unrest with local notables, for example, in Shīrvān on the death of ʻAbd-Allāh Khān, and an almost perpetual state of Turkish – Persian hostilities. All this reached its climax in the anarchical state of Persia between the death of Shah Ṭahmāsp and the accession of Shah ʻAbbās I.

There does appear also to have been some deterioration in the accommodation and protection offered to travellers, for a number of the English merchants died or were slain on their journey in the last quarter of the century. The comments of the merchant Laurence Chapman, perhaps prejudiced, were far from flattering. "To travell in this countrey", he wrote, "is not onely miserable and uncomfortable, for lacke of townes and villages to harbour in when night commeth, and to refresh men with wholesome victualles in time of need, but also scarsitie of water, that sometime in three dayes journey together is not found any droppe fit for man or beast to drinke, besides the great danger we

[1] *Ibid.*, pp. 396–7.

stand in for robbing by these infidels, who do account it remission of sinnes to wash theyr hands in the bloud of one of us. Better it is, therefore, in mine opinion, to continue a begger in England during life then to remaine a rich merchant seven yeeres in this countrey, as some shall well finde at theyr comming hither."[1]

Yet, whatever the disturbances caused by local conditions, the Turks made strenuous efforts to procure the silk needed for the looms of Bursa and the revenues of the state. They used political pressure to supplement economic efforts in this as in other areas that touched their vital interests. Not only did the Turks control the routes across Anatolia which came through Erzerum, but they also controlled those to Aleppo along the Upper Euphrates valley after defeating the Persians at Chāldirān in 920/1514 and the Mamlūks at Marj Dābiq in 922/1516, and those across the desert as a result of their capture of Baghdad in 941/1534. Thus in the middle of the 10th/16th century the Turks controlled all the western outlets for Persian silk. It was not surprising that they reacted to the threat of a new northern outlet after the Russian capture of Astrakhan in 1554 and took counter measures.

In the first place there was a cessation of Turkish–Persian hostilities signalised by the Peace of Amāsya on 8 Rajab 962/29 May 1555. As a response to Russian probing advances to the Crimea, the Grand Vizier, Meḥmed Soqollū, conceived of the plan to isolate the Russians, link up with the Muslim khanates of Central Asia and deprive the Persians of their silk-growing territories. The Russians were not only a potential threat to the political and religious prestige of the Turks but a real threat to their trading interests. It was for these reasons that the Don–Volga canal project was opposed. "The Muslims were angry and afraid of Moscow gaining the great commercial roads and market places and thus bringing the trade of the Muslim countries into their own hands. The Ottoman Empire, struggling in the Indian Ocean with the Portuguese for the pilgrim and commercial routes, would certainly have wished to revive the central-Asian–Astrakhan-Crimean road. If a canal could be made at the point where the Don and the Volga are nearest to each other, supplies and ammunition could be brought directly by ships from the Black Sea to the Caspian... it would be possible to subjugate Shirvan, Karabagh and the whole of Georgia,

[1] *Ibid.*, p. 412.

and thus the Ottoman Empire could attack the innermost parts of Iran."[1] It was a geopolitical enterprise on a vast scale for the period, but it failed, for the idea outran the resources. Besides, Turkey and its Crimean allies were not only suspicious of each other but differed in their objectives. Astrakhan was sacked in 1569 and Moscow burnt by the Tartars a year later, but these were pyrrhic victories over a Russia that was then ill-prepared to sustain a long campaign, but which once more found its chief ally in the arduous winter climate.

The Turkish setback was serious but not irreparable. The Turks made peace with the Venetians and bided their time on their eastern front when they could strike a blow at Persia, which besides being an old enemy was the ally of two adversaries, Russia and Portugal. Indeed Persia "was a potential link between the two vast areas of the Portuguese 'oceanic' front and the Russian 'fluvial' front". Once again Persia was threatened because of its strategic position astride the land mass connecting Europe and Asia. The Turkish menace, however, then receded, but Persia's problems remained. The death of Shah Ṭahmāsp occasioned internal disorders in Persia of which the Turks took advantage and annexed most of Āzarbāījān, Georgia, Shīrvān, Luristān and parts of Gīlān. Turkey controlled the main ports on the Caspian and the silk-producing areas and eventually consolidated her hold by the treaty signed with the young monarch Shah 'Abbās in 998/1590. Thereafter, as long as Persian silk remained a commodity in request till the latter part of the 18th century, Turkish and Russian routes competed.

(c) *The southern area*

Hurmuz throughout the 16th century continued to play its important trading rôle, having a "greate traffique", according to Van Linschoten, for "it is the staple for all India, Persia, Arabia and Turkie, and of all the places and Countries about the same, and commonly it is full of Persians, Armenians, Turkes, and all nations, as also Venetians, which lie there to buy spices and precious stones, that in great abundance are brought thether [of all parts] of India, and from thence are sent overland to Venice, and also carried throughout all Turkie, Armenia,

[1] Allen, *Problems of Turkish Power*, p. 25. On earlier related aspects of the East Indies trade for the Turks and Persians, see H.J. Kissling, "Šâh Ismâ'îl Ier, la nouvelle route des Indes et les Ottomans", *Turcica* VI (1975), 89–102.

Arabia, Persia and every way. There are likewise brought thether, all manner of marchandises from the same Countries, that is from Persia – out of the Countrie called Coracone and Dias, and other places, great store of rich Tapestrie [and Coverlets] which are called Alcatiffas [carpets]: out of Turkie all manner of Chamlets: out of Arabia divers sortes of Drugges for Poticaries, as Sanguis Draconis, Manna, Mirre, Frankinsence and such like, divers goodly horses, that are excellent for breeding, all manner of most excellent Orientall Pearles..."[1] There appears to be no significant change in the goods and commodities passing through Hurmuz, in spite of the Portuguese pass system controlling the movements of local shipping or the exactions of Portuguese officials who claimed extra duties on trade there. Van Linschoten mentions the lārīs coined at Lār from fine silver and "brought thether in great quantities, whereby there is as great dealing with them, as with other merchandises, because of the greate gaine that is gotten by them and in India they goe very high". The treasure drain to India had commenced long before the arrival of European companies there in the 11th/17th Century. At Diu, Cambay and Chaul there continued to exist much traffic to Hurmuz, subject to Portuguese pass restrictions. An indication of the rising power of the Mughals was the growing importance of Āgra, which had become a "great resort of merchants from Persia and out of India, and very much merchandise of silk and cloth and of precious stones, both rubies, Diamonds and Pearls".

Van Linschoten stated that the reason for such a great traffic was that "every yeare twice there commeth a great companie of people over land which are called Caffiles or Carvanes, which come from Aleppo, out of the Countrie of Surie three dales iornie from Tripoli which lyeth uppon the west of the Mediterranean Sea,... in the months of April and September. There is a Captaine and certain hundreths of Iannisaries, which connvaye the said Caffila untill they come to the Towne of Bassora, from whence they travaile by water unto Ormus."[2] The merchants were informed of the movements of the caravans, which were protected against marauding Arabs. At Baṣra they regrouped on the way down to Hurmuz or up to Aleppo, "whereby all manner of merchandises, out of all places are brought thether in great abundance, by great numbers of traveling Marchants". It was, quite clearly, true

[1] Linschoten I, 47. [2] *Ibid.*, p. 48.

that "Baṣra continued to be, in the mid 16th century, an active centre of commerce with Asia".[1] Not only is the testimony of the customs registers conclusive, but contemporary literary evidence is corroborative. "There is a trade with Hurmuz, whence come all Indian wares: with Barhen, Catifa, Lasan, Persia, Baghdad, and all Arabia thereabouts".[2]

It was equally apparent that some Venetian merchants had established themselves well in Hurmuz, such as the Stropene family who resented the appearance of three English traders there in 1583. The Portuguese at Lisbon informed those on Hurmuz that "you shall take great heed that neither these people nor other similar ones be allowed in those parts, the which you shall order to be specially guarded against at the fortress of Ormuz, which is the gateway by which they are chiefly likely to enter".[3] This the Venetians did so successfully that the Portuguese authorities arrested the English merchants and sent them off to Goa, from which they subsequently escaped. In this case as over other Europeans, the Spanish and Portuguese, whose crowns were united in 1580, were very strict. It was not simply that there was rivalry in Europe but a sense of insecurity arising from the arrival of English and Dutch shipping, which was penetrating further and more frequently into oceans that had been considered exclusively for the use and benefit of the Spanish and Portuguese.

The Turks had reacted to the threat posed by the Portuguese astride their maritime routes to the east with seafaring expeditions mounted at great cost to challenge the Portuguese from 1520 to 1585. In spite of limited successes, they failed to dislodge the Portuguese; but they unsettled them. Because of this activity, the pertinacity of established traders, the increasing security of the routes across Arabia, the desire of Portuguese governors at Hurmuz to profit from trade and the ingenuity of local shippers, the Portuguese authorities were never able officially to operate an effective embargo on trade from the east through Hurmuz towards Baṣra and through Baghdad to Aleppo. The proportion of the total trade in Hurmuz may have fallen, but the volume remained significant and Hurmuz prospered. This state of affairs lasted till the end of the second decade of the 17th century. After Hurmuz

[1] R. Mantran, "Règlements Fiscaux Ottomans de la Province de Bassora (2e moitié du XVe siècle)", *JESHO* x (1967), 226.

[2] Teixeira, p. 29.

[3] Philip II of Spain to Viceroy of India, 25 Feb. 1585, quoted in Teixeira, p. xxviii. See also Tucci, "Mercanti Veneziani".

was captured by the Persians in 1031/1622 and practically destroyed, its place as a port was taken by Gombroon, renamed Bandar 'Abbās, on the mainland opposite, a mile or so away.

(*d*) *Conclusion*

Throughout the 10th/16th century, in spite of frequent Persian – Turkish hostilities, the external trade of Persia persisted. In terms of Persian exports the main commodity was silk, which was exported in quantity to Turkey where it was either consumed in the Turkish silk industry based at Bursa or purchased by Venetian merchants for European markets. The silk from the northern provinces of Persia also provided the raw material for the main weaving centres of Yazd, Kāshān, and Kirmān. Trade to and from Central Asia flagged and did not revive significantly till early in the 11th/17th century, when the Russian expansion to the Caspian was consolidated. The enterprise of English traders between 1560 and 1580 was an interesting development bringing a new trading force onto the Persian economic scene, but their efforts to re-route Persian trade from its Levant-orientated axis to a northerly one failed in the face of Turkish, Venetian and Armenian opposition. It did, however, demonstrate clearly the close connection between the cloth and silk trades, for they were a complementary exchange. Without cloth exports English traders would not have had the resources to pay for silk imports, lacking the greater Venetian supplies of silver currency. In the south, notwithstanding the arrival of the Portuguese in the Indian Ocean and their control over Hurmuz, goods from India and the East Indies continued to reach Hurmuz in quantities for onward shipment up the Gulf and across Arabia or through Persia to Mediterranean ports. Persia, though becoming a stronger power, did not reap the advantages from this transit trade owing to the Portuguese control over the revenues obtained at Hurmuz. Persia realised the importance of this trade but lacked the power to have its rights protected.

4. THE REIGN OF SHAH 'ABBĀS I

(*a*) *Introduction*

The economic, like the political, condition of Persia at the opening of the reign of Shah 'Abbās I was very unstable. The turmoil of the civil war prior to his accession had adversely affected trade. The arbitrary exactions of provincial governors, the lack of responsible central authority, tribal confusion and the atmosphere of uncertainty caused by two erratic monarchs and their courts were not conducive to trade. There were hostilities with the Turks, whose occupation of the main silk-producing provinces and whose incursions around the towns and along the routes severely affected the Persian silk trade and its connections with the eastern Mediterranean. The intermittent insurrections of parts of Georgia, Armenia and elsewhere were a constant drain on resources.

The southern trade which flowed into and up the Persian Gulf through Hurmuz and which was fairly strictly controlled by the Portuguese, both officially and unofficially, was gradually lessening. Although some Persian merchants and shipping continued to participate in the seaborne trade with north-west India, Arabia, the east coast of Africa and beyond, many of the caravans were bypassing Persia and going through Mesopotamia. The arrival of Dutch and English trading ships in the Indian Ocean to challenge Portuguese and Spanish dominance there upset the Portuguese navigational pass system whereby they had attempted to control the local shipping routes. As a result such shipping increasingly suffered. Although it was not completely damaged, it became more cautious in its sailings, so reducing the volume of its trade. In the north-east the disturbances among the Uzbeks and their incursions into Khurāsān hardly promoted trade. The overland routes through Kābul and Qandahār were suffering not only from Uzbek attentions but also from Akbar's activities to consolidate his empire. All these developments reacted adversely upon trade, disrupting but not entirely preventing it. Indeed one of the economic constants among the variables of economic history was concisely expressed by one of the first English traders to Persia in 1618: "Marchantes muste hazard that will trade."

Thus Shah ʿAbbās inherited an unpromising political and economic legacy. As long as the trading routes to the east were under the control of the Uzbeks, whilst the Portuguese dictated the course of trade in the south and the Turks possessed the silk-producing provinces in the north-west, Persia was almost economically strangled. Without revenue, Persia was without power. The manner in which Shah ʿAbbās defeated the Uzbeks, restored the silk-producing provinces to Persian sovereignty and acquired possession of Hurmuz is recounted in chapter 5. It was a prerequisite not only for the resumption of trading on the previous scale but for an expansion of Persian trade, upon which Shah ʿAbbās placed such a vital emphasis and to which he devoted so much effort.

(*b*) *Early policy*

There are two main aspects of Persian trade to be considered in this period. Firstly, there was the maximum advantage to be derived from exporting the produce and manufactures of Persia. Secondly, there was the revenue to be obtained from the transit trade, which was always a feature of Persian economic life by virtue of its position astride the great land routes connecting Europe and Asia. Shah ʿAbbās recognised that the key to Persian economic prosperity lay in silk, the export of which he fostered and controlled himself. This was the one commodity in which Persia was then pre-eminent. The provinces of Georgia, Shīrvān and Gīlān had the right climatic and soil conditions for the growth of mulberry trees, upon the leaves of which the silkworms fed before they became the chrysalises, having spun around their cocoon the light gossamer silk threads. The damp, close humid atmosphere was right for the rearing of silkworms and the region was famous for its silk industry. The total production of silk seems to have been increasing from the early part of the 10th/16th century not only in Persia, but in the Levant, the islands of the Aegean, and Italy. Silk became an important element in the Turkish economy and was contributing greatly to the revenue of the Ottoman treasury, apart from dues, services, hire, lodging and general expenses exacted from and disbursed by the caravans traversing the country.

For Persia the exports of silk were crucially important, for whilst Persia generally had an unfavourable balance of trade with the east, it was favourable with the west. With the proceeds from the sales of silk Persia principally imported cloth but, most important, coined money was acquired without which a circulating Persian coinage would have been almost impossible. Persia did not have any real gold or silver mines and as there were not enough exports to balance the imports of cotton goods, spices and drugs from the east, the balance was made up in money, part of the flow of precious metals eastwards. As the 10th/16th century progressed and the volume of silver arriving in Europe from South America increased, setting off with other factors a significant price rise, so did inflationary pressures mount and the Persian need for silver grow.

At the same time Turkey was also experiencing many of the same conflicting trading pressures on economic and social conditions. Some Turkish responses were to prohibit the export of precious metals to Persia, to insist on barter transactions in exchanging silk for cloth or to create more state industry to supplant Persian trade. These actions singly or together in various combinations were implemented at different times during the 10th/16th century. Their double object was to strengthen the Turkish economy and weaken that of Persia by denying it outlets for its major export, except under conditions strictly advantageous to the Turks, thus directly reducing Persian revenue and indirectly curbing its power by depriving it of the means to purchase strategic materials. Such measures were, however, never permanently effective or successful, for the two economies were too closely interdependent. Furthermore, the Turks never developed satisfactory alternative supplies of silk nor adequately enforced their restrictions.

Conversely, all the reasons pressing the Turks to extend their hold over the Persian silk trade applied to Persia; but, weaker both politically and militarily, Persia had been unable to exert much pressure on Turkey. Nevertheless it was not a state of affairs which could be long contemplated with equanimity by Shah ʿAbbās I. Whilst his enthusiasm for the possibilities of foreign trade may have been whetted by the opportune arrival of the English adventurer Sir Anthony Sherley in Qazvīn, when the shah had just returned in triumph from his victories over the Uzbeks in 1007/1598, there were earlier precedents for Persian attempts to bypass the Turks either through Russia or with Venetians. The range of possibilities, however, was extended as a result of the English and Dutch maritime presence in the Indian Ocean. The Cape route added a new dimension to the issue, for it would be invulnerable to Turkish countermeasures and as such had a strong appeal to Shah ʿAbbās. Yet more immediate was the need to restore the territorial integrity of Persia by reoccupying the silk-producing provinces and expelling the Turks. The shah envisaged that this could be accomplished in collaboration with certain European powers, to whom he despatched Sir Anthony Sherley. He was prepared to offer, in return for such assistance, a share in the monopoly of the Persian silk exports and privileged trading opportunities. He sought papal support by promising to tolerate the residence of Christian missionaries.

During the crucial two decades of his struggles with the Turks, Shah ʿAbbās waited vainly for any decisive intervention on the part of the European powers. The initial Sherleian mission failed because of its inability to persuade any of the countries visited to take any real action and because of mistrust amongst its members aggravated by the reciprocal antipathy of Sir Anthony Sherley and his Persian colleague, Ḥusain ʿAlī Beg. It was a pattern that was frequently repeated in the embassies of Shah ʿAbbās to Europe, which were more memorable for their internal dissensions than their actual successes. The Sherleian mission was followed by others to Venice, Rome and Spain. Venice was reluctant to jeopardise its relations with Turkey. The Pope was enthusiastic but ineffectual. Spain was interested, but Persia was insignificant compared to its more pressing problems of the Dutch and English penetrating oceans that were once considered exclusively within the Spanish and Portuguese sphere. These embassies produced no tangible evidence of a European commitment to an alliance with Persia against the Turks. Communications were long, distances great, trust ephemeral; and, besides, a certain trade with Turkey was not to be hazarded for a hypothetical one with Persia.

Another concerted attempt was made with the mission of Anthony Sherley's brother, Robert, who had been left behind by his brother in Persia as a hostage and had distinguished himself in Persian military service and as a minor provincial governor. He was sent in 1607 to persuade the Spaniards to establish a silk staple at Hurmuz and ship it to Europe in association with Persian and Armenian merchants. The Spanish were reluctant to become involved in such a trade, for they did not possess adequate facilities to handle it themselves and so would have had to rely upon others to dispose of the silk at no great profit to themselves. Also they were unwilling to waive customs and duties, thereby reducing the advantages to the Persians and Armenians in promoting such a trade. Furthermore, although the Spaniards and Portuguese had been united under one crown since 1580, they did not, as it were, speak with one voice. The Portuguese resentment of any Spanish interference in their affairs in the east resulted in the failure to formulate any agreed policy. It was a mass of contradictory decisions. Since Goa and Hurmuz would have been the main administrative and trading centres in such an enterprise, Portuguese cooperation was essential. Sir Robert Sherley's subsequent visits to Rome, Holland and England were also inconclusive. Although he was well received by the

English court he was rejected by the majority of English merchants.

Some time before Sir Robert Sherley returned to Persia in 1615, Shah 'Abbās had realised that an alliance was unlikely, for he had received little beyond missionary solicitude and expressions of support. After his victories over the Turks in 1608, with his recovery of much of the silk-producing area, a fragile peace ensued and he started to assert his authority in the south. His general, Imām Qulī Khān, reduced Lāristān and captured the mainland areas with the port and fort of Gombroon opposite the island of Hurmuz and took Baḥrain in 1614, which had been occupied by small Portuguese garrisons. These successes had an undoubted prestige value but were not militarily or economically significant whilst shipping was still controlled from Hurmuz itself. They marked, nevertheless, the determination of Shah 'Abbās to reassert Persian claims of sovereignty over lost territories, freedom for its trade, and an end to an intolerable political and religious situation aggravated by Portuguese behaviour. Carmelite missionaries had clearly remarked on the likelihood of such action some years before. Since the Persians were no match for Portuguese sea power and since the fort on Hurmuz was virtually impregnable to any assault unaccompanied by artillery, in which the Persians were deficient, there was no real danger to the Portuguese. The Persians for their part realised that they stood little chance of wresting Hurmuz from the Portuguese without naval and military assistance.

Before Shah 'Abbās could attempt to exploit his success in the south, three events occurred, each of which had its own significance and which taken together presaged important developments. Firstly, hostilities with the Turks, which had been smouldering, broke out again in 1024/1615, and the shah found himself hard pressed. So once again Persian silk exports were at risk without alternative markets. Secondly, Sir Robert Sherley arrived back from his disappointing European embassy and within a short time he was despatched again, primarily on a mission to Spain. His task was threefold: to renew the call for an alliance, to reassure the Spaniards over Hurmuz but maintain the Persian claims to the mainland, and to revive the proposals for trade. The third event was the arrival in Iṣfahān of two Englishmen, sent by the Council of the East India Company at Sūrat, to investigate the possibilities for trade with Persia. The English company, which had established itself in Sūrat in 1612 against Portuguese opposition, had failed to find adequate outlets for quantities of cloth, the main English export item, and was looking for other markets. The shah, impatient at his failure to induce the Spanish to take up the trade and still very anxious to lessen his dependence on Turkish-controlled export channels, affirmed the opportunities for trade and authorised the necessary permission and privileges to the English company. Perhaps his main consideration was that an English interest would more than counterbalance that of the Portuguese on Hurmuz and that he would be able to play one off against the other. He may also have been hoping for a supply of armaments, which he was being denied by the Portuguese but which he needed against the Turks.

At all events, the first English group of merchants arrived off Jāsk on 4 December 1616 to inaugurate trade with Persia, notwithstanding the lack of enthusiasm of the English ambassador to the Mughal court, Sir Thomas Roe. Roe was apprehensive over the attitudes of the Portuguese and the Turks, who would see their interests threatened if English trade became settled and who would take counter-measures to prevent its establishment. The ambassador was convinced that when Persia and Turkey made peace trade would return to its traditional channels and the shah would break his promises to divert it southwards. He doubted whether the volume of trade would support the expenditure or provide a sufficient exchange of commodities or enough money to make it profitable. His caution was reasonable. Although Shah 'Abbās had accomplished much, the state of the country was not really settled. The shah did not receive complete support and he was suspicious of the intentions of his family and court, as revealed by his later murder of his eldest son. Not all his court agreed that the warfare against the Turks should be sustained until the Persians had won decisively, and many proposed peace on terms that were unacceptable to the shah. Money was in extremely short supply, and only the shah himself was trading on any scale. The crisis was weathered and the shah emerged more powerful than ever. Peace was concluded with the Turks on satisfactory terms in 1027/1618 and the long "Hundred Years' War" with Turkey was almost over.

Shah 'Abbās, with his western and northern frontiers guaranteed and his trade routes to the Mediterranean again open, was free to turn his attention to the south and east. Conclusive evidence of his intentions is indicated by his attitude to the Spanish ambassador from Philip III, Don Garcia de Silva y Figueroa. He left him in no doubt in 1617 that he was not prepared to discuss Spanish claims to the mainland or return the island of Baḥrain. The English merchants, meanwhile, had not made an impressive appearance, for, lacking supplies, short of money, opposed by the merchants, abused by the officials and uncertain of their prospects, they were quite unprepared and unable to make any extensive purchases of silk, only obtaining 71 bales in their first two years. They persevered, expecting better prospects. The shah approved of their presence, even if he was disappointed with their purchases, for they might be persuaded to assist him one day against the Portuguese. Equally, he was not prepared to offend the Portuguese without cause, for he was still dependent upon their goodwill over the trade on Hurmuz. He had his reservations about the English, for he had seen little evidence of their power, but this opinion was changed as a result of the English company's successes at sea against the Portuguese off Hurmuz in 1621. The following year a pretext was found to hold the bales of silk bought by the English on the point of being shipped out. Restoration was made conditional upon the English company's fleet assisting the Persians to bombard the Portuguese forts on Kishm and Hurmuz and ferry Persian soldiers across the sea to assault the Portuguese garrison. Inadequately defending themselves, the Portuguese capitulated and the Persians under Imām Qulī Khān occupied Hurmuz.

(*c*) *Persian trade in the second decade of the 17th century*

Thus within four years Shah ʿAbbās had effectively freed Persia from the Turkish menace and the Portuguese blockade, and in the very same year he took Qandahār. All the frontiers were open and the routes free, two indispensable conditions for an expansion of Persian trade. What then was Persian trade at this time?[1] Firstly to be considered are Persian exports, and of those suitable for England silk was the most important. It is described as coming principally from four main areas: Georgia, which had three kinds, Ardass, Ardasett and Canaree and which produced about 60,000 *māns*, but in 1618 only produced 30,000 māns because "at present in regard of the last warrs in those partes the Countrye is much dyvasted and dispeopled" and it sold for 220 *shāhīs* a mān[2]; Gīlān, where silk came from several regions such as Lāhījān and

[1] The following account of Persian trade in the reign of ʿAbbās I is derived from the letters of two English merchants: see Ferrier, "An English View".

[2] Generally a mān was 12½ lbs, a shāhī 5d, and a tūmān worth £3.10s.

Rasht, producing about 81,000 māns selling for between 220 and 236 shāhīs a mān; Māzandarān, producing 57,000 māns selling for 200 shāhīs a mān; and Khurāsān, producing 34,000 māns of very fine silk which was unsuitable for carrying to Europe, but of which a considerable quantity was carried overland to India via Lahore or transported by ship from Hurmuz to Sind, worth between 350 and 360 shāhīs a mān. Some silk was also produced in Kirmān, Yazd and a few other places. Thus it was estimated that the total production of Persian silk then was 232,000 māns (2,900,000 lbs. or 125 tons), of which a third was retained for internal uses to be made into carpets or textiles.

Textiles included velvets made in Yazd and Kāshān of all colours, costing between 120 and 200 shāhīs a length of 6¾ yards, many satins, damasks and taffetas which were in good supply, usually 26 inches wide and 6¾ yards long, worth 48 shāhīs a piece. The taffetas were comparable to similar European kinds, but the other textiles were less esteemed. Cloths of gold and silver made in Iṣfahān, Kāshān or Khurāsān varied greatly in price according to the quality and work, from 200 to 2,000 shāhīs. There were bezoar stones from Kirmān, turquoises, a royal monopoly, from Khurāsān, civet, opium which was better than that grown in India, and all kinds of nuts and fruits such as walnuts, pistachios, almonds, prunes, raisins and dates.

Among the goods for India were *rūnās* (madder), used as a red dye, mostly grown around Ardabīl but procurable in Iṣfahān, costing 10 shāhīs a mān and carried overland in quantities into India via Qandahār; saltpetre, which although obtained at Lār was a royal monopoly and its export prohibited; pearls fished off Baḥrain, of which the best were supposed to be reserved for the shah and were better than any to be found elsewhere in the world; rosewater worth 6½ shāhīs for 1½ gallons and other essences, besides silk and textiles already mentioned.

First among the commodities from England vendible in Persia were cloths, either broad cloths in various bright colours, of which in lengths of 32 yards, costing £10–£12 pounds each, between 600 and 1,000 might be sold yearly for 34–36 shāhīs a yard, or kersies, a rougher cloth. Tin, of which 40–50 tons a year were used in Persia, came principally from Malacca and was worth 48–50 shāhīs a mān; brass was not required; quicksilver not much requested, being sold for 140–145 shāhīs a mān. Lead was almost as cheap as in England, for it was mined in the country, as was iron in Gīlān and Hamadān, worth 7 shāhīs a mān. Copper was greatly used for all kinds of utensils and, as it was an import prohibited by the Portuguese, was brought in overland from India at great charge: in plates it was worth 40–44 shāhīs a mān, in ingots 34–36 shāhīs a mān. Hides, of which 300–400 were sold annually, were used for saddles, coarse carpets and drinking vessels and worth, according to quality and size, 50–80 shāhīs each; furs were in demand, for "noe man in the cold season is without a coate lyned with one furre or other". A limited quantity of vermilion, worth 180–224 shāhīs a mān, and cochineal, worth 2,400 shāhīs a mān; some walrus teeth, 80–100 māns annually, worth 190–200 shāhīs a mān, and large coral beads, worth 24–30 shāhīs each depending on their size for use as prayer beads, would sell. Ornaments of all kinds were wanted.

Indian goods which could be disposed of in Persia included metals such as copper, iron and steel, the last of which was expensive in Persia owing to it being another commodity prohibited by the Portuguese and carried into Persia overland from India. White calicoes in particular and Indian cloth in general sold well in Persia in various qualities and kinds at differing prices to good profit. Sashes, of which there were innumerable varieties from different places such as Āgra and Patna, and coloured cloths from Aḥmadābād, Āgra and Lahore used for lining coats and quilt coverings had good sales. Powdered sugar was consumed from Bengal, Sūrat, Āgra and Lahore, and some 300 tons were sold yearly at 19–20 shāhīs a mān, as well as sugar candy. It was transported by ship or brought overland from India. Conserves, such as ginger and "mirabolins", had a limited sale of about 1,000 māns. Some cassia fistula, a medical product from the leaves of the Pudding Pipe tree, and aloes from Socotra had a limited sale. Of saffron from Daibul about 10,000 māns could be sold yearly, and of "cardemons" from Cannanore about 2,000 māns for 54–58 shāhīs a mān. Of gumlack from Siam, worth 64–70 shāhīs a mān, about 5,000 māns annually, and of indigo about 100 churls, worth 36–38 shāhīs a mān for the Biana kind and 22–24 for Serquess, were used for dyeing. A considerable amount of camphor, worth 230–240 shāhīs a mān, was imported for funeral purposes. Coffee brought in from Moccha costing 24–26 shāhīs a mān was drunk "heere as tobacco in England for idlenesse". About 2,000 māns of tamarind were sold for 6–8 shāhīs a mān. Packaging materials such as rough cloths, cord and cotton wool for bags and bales were expensive. Some 20,000 sheets of paper from Aḥmadābād were imported, costing about 3 shāhīs a sheet.

The main commodities received from the East Indian islands and

Ceylon were spices. It was thought that 100 tons of pepper were sold annually at 30–36 shāhīs a mān, 10 tons of cloves from 90–100 shāhīs a mān, and a small quantity of mace, nutmeg and cinnamon. Chinese goods imported included "all sorts of China ware [which] are heere both in greate esteeme and use which beinge sorted of all sizes, pryces and fashions will vend heere at least 100 tonns per annum", ginger, camphor and China roots. Logwood from Pegu in Siam or Cochin on the Indian coast was used in dyeing, some 5,000 māns being sold at 32 and 20 shāhīs a mān respectively.

Whilst this list seems reasonably complete, it must be remembered that it is primarily concerned with goods bought or sold in Persia, but not necessarily all consumed there. Furthermore, because it is concerned primarily with English interests there are some omissions. Wine, galls marketed in Hamadān, goat's and fine lamb's wool are not mentioned among the exports nor precious stones among the imports. Apart from textiles and carpets, it does not provide information on industry, such as saddlery and glass-making in Shīrāz, the copper and tinsmiths of Iṣfahān, Kirmān and Kāshān, the silversmiths of Tabrīz, the pottery of Kirmān or Mashhad. It is to be assumed that at this time most of those products were consumed within the country and did not form an appreciable percentage of exports.

(*d*) *The arrival of the English and Dutch trading companies*

Such then was the scope of Persian trade. What further measures or actions did Shah 'Abbās take to foster it? There was the deliberate attempt to encourage further foreign enterprise in Persia, not only to offset the dominant rôle of the overland Levant routes, but also to stimulate an expansion of trade in all directions. The Levant trade was, in any case, growing as the European trading companies became more established in Ottoman cities. Embassies were received. Relations with Bukhārā and Balkh and other Central Asian khanates were intensified, partly on political, partly on economic grounds. With the Portuguese weakening, the shah especially encouraged the English and Dutch trading companies. The English East India Company, with little option, had rendered singular service in helping the Persians to force the Portuguese from their base and emporium on Hurmuz. The Persians transferred the commercial organisation of Hurmuz to Gombroon, which was renamed Bandar 'Abbās. The buildings upon

Hurmuz were allowed to collapse and its fame and facilities withered away in neglect. The Persians hoped to force either the English or Dutch companies into attacking Muscat, then occupied by the Portuguese, with a view to extending Persian power to the western shore of the Persian Gulf and completely eliminating the Portuguese from the area. The English and Dutch, however, would not allow themselves to be used in this way and the Persians eventually reached an accommodation with the Portuguese in 1630 to grant them the use of the port of Kung with certain rights. This put an end to nearly twenty years of intermittent hostilities between them and opened the Persian Gulf to all shipping.

The opportunities offered to the English and Dutch companies were more important. The English company was granted special privileges including relief from customs for its imports, no liability for road taxes and the half of the customs revenue from Bandar ʿAbbās in return for its assistance in the capture of Hurmuz. Although possessed of them, it was not always accorded its rights, and only obtained about a tenth, at the most, of its share of the customs. The earliest agreement to trade had been obtained by Richard Steele and John Crowther in 1615 but was subsequently renegotiated and later confirmed on the accession of Shah Ṣafī in 1038/1629. It lasted with relatively little alteration till the reign of Shah Sulṭān Ḥusain and corresponded in broad terms to the treaties concluded with the Dutch in 1624 and the French in 1664.

In principle, the articles granted the residence of an English representative in Persia or a Persian one in England; and fair treatment at the ports of entry according to local conditions and charges so that traders would not be abused. In the event of shipwreck, no hindrance to salvage was to be offered or theft committed. There was freedom to travel anywhere within the country for the purpose of buying and selling goods without restrictions; religious toleration on all sides; and permission to keep and use arms in the defence of person or property. If a man was killed in the act of robbery, the English were not to be called to account for it, or if he was taken the robber was to be punished in the presence of the English; but if he was an Englishman, the English were to have the right to take what action they thought fit themselves. The possession of a residence was confirmed for the duration of their stay; the English Representative was responsible for the punishment of offending Englishmen without recourse to the local judiciary; respect was to be shown at all times to the nominated deputy of the chief representative. They were guaranteed protection against offences by local people wherever it might be; respect to be shown to all employees of the English and no man to be prohibited their service; the redemption of any slaves from Turkey proved to be English on due payment to the master; no interference in the estate of any Englishman dying in Persia and the right to a proper burial; the return of orphaned children born of Christian parents to the Representative. Ordinary English merchants were to pay no more customs than were exacted in the Ottoman empire at Aleppo or Istanbul, and if any losses occurred along the routes, the road guards were responsible for finding the goods or paying their value upon an affidavit sworn in the presence of a priest or representative. Any dispute between English merchants involving less than £66 was to be decided in the presence of an English representative according to Persian law, and if for a greater amount the same procedure was to be followed, but in the presence of the Representative. And lastly, any goods not disposed of were to be allowed to be returned without difficulty.[1]

The Dutch United East India Company first arrived in Persia on 20 June 1623, when Huybert Visnich, as chief merchant, landed from the *Heusden* at Bandar 'Abbās. He had been sent by Pieter Van den Broecke, who had been appointed the first Dutch director for Arabia, Persia and India in 1620. The Dutch soon made their presence felt and claimed and won the same customs privileges as the English. They soon became the leading importer of spices into Persia. An agreement was concluded in 1624. There was intense rivalry between the English and Dutch companies in the east, and the Dutch soon vaunted to the Persians their superior resources. The English, less well provided, resented this Dutch intrusion, for "they have builded uppon our foundations and reaped where wee had plowne". The Dutch mainly sold spices, purchased silk and obtained ready money through the favourable balance of trade which they were building up with Persia. The English, almost on the point of abandoning Persian trade in 1625, were reluctant to go, "lest our refusall should induce itts delyverie to the Dutch", and so remained after better assurances of support from the shah.

Meanwhile, in London from 1623 to 1626, Sir Robert Sherley on his

[1] The English treaties are to be found in the India Office [I.O.] Library: with 'Abbās I, E/3/5/661 (14 June 1618); with Ṣafī I, G/29/1 (1629); with Sulaimān, E/3/52/6416 (1697).

second mission was once again endeavouring to persuade English merchants to take a more active part in Persian trade. Now that the Portuguese had been removed from Hurmuz, the Persians, he argued, could defend their shores themselves if only they were provided with "prefabricated" galleys which could be assembled in the Persian Gulf. When English merchants claimed they could not cope with all the Persian silk exported, not having a sufficient range of suitable goods, nor adequate supplies of ready money, he suggested that Persian merchants "may passe ther goods in such Englishe shippinge as goes ordynarily thether, And which your Merchants are not able to lade themselves, paying such ffraytage as Merchants, with Merchants, may agree upon". It was a shrewd and interesting approach aimed at overcoming the inadequacies of Persian shipping and opening up new and unrestricted markets for Persian merchants by utilising the recently opened sea routes. At the same time it offered a means of overcoming the chronic shortage of ready money for foreign investments that afflicted English and most other European trading for most of the 17th century. James I was impressed with Sherley's advocacy and recommended the English merchants that "you take into your serious consideration and care both the furtherance and manner of settleing of it, as may bee best for the weale of our Kingdome". The king might propose it, but it was the merchants who decided. The East India Company was very reluctant to get entangled with Sherley, and the Levant Company objected to the idea.

At this stage Shah 'Abbās took the last of his diplomatic trade initiatives. He despatched embassies to England and Holland, the first under Naqd 'Alī Beg, which arrived early in February 1626 at Portsmouth in the *Star*, and the second under Mūsā Beg, which arrived on 9 February in the same year. Little is known of the exact circumstances in which these embassies were despatched, but certain explanations are likely. Shah 'Abbās probably recognised that the presence of both the English and Dutch companies in Persia was counterbalancing and favourable to Persia. He therefore probably decided to treat both countries impartially, and as he was hoping to conclude a treaty with the Dutch it was an opportune moment to confirm his interest in England. Be that as it may, it is likely that a renewal of hostilities between the Persians and Turks over Baghdad and unrest in Anatolia were adversely affecting trade again and raised once more the question of alternative markets. The Portuguese, dispossessed of Hurmuz, were still harrying the Persian coasts and interfering with shipping, so protection was necessary. The failure of a French embassy under Louis des Hayes, Baron de Courmenin, which was to have inaugurated French diplomatic and commercial relations with Persia, to materialise in 1626, together with the opposition expressed against certain Armenians at Marseilles, may have made the shah reluctant to count on French assistance. Neither of the embassies to England and Holland was particularly successful and both had their moments of *Comedia del arte* in Persian dress. The English responded with an embassy under Sir Dodmore Cotton, the account of which was written by Thomas Herbert but which achieved little except to offer lasting amity and goodwill. A Dutch–Persian treaty was eventually signed on 7 February 1630/1 in Holland, more formal than the agreement of 1624 in Persia.[1]

(*e*) *The encouragement of Armenians as traders in relation to the internal aspects of the trading policy of Shah ʿAbbās*

There are two major considerations: improvements in the local conditions for trade, and the rôle of the Armenians. The prosperity of transit trade depends on the amenities provided for merchants and the security of the roads. It is uncertain whether all the improvements in trading facilities ascribed to Shah ʿAbbās were in fact deliberate, but nevertheless it can be assumed that it was his concern which was responsible for the upsurge of public works throughout Persia. Doubtless in many cases the initiative taken and the costs incurred were the responsibility of the provincial governors. Sometimes buildings were due to competitive patronage, as was the case with Allāhvardī Khān's elegant architectural masterpiece, his bridge at Iṣfahān.

The result was an increase in the network of caravansarais at intervals along the main trading routes, a series of bridges spanning rivers at strategic sites, road improvements, such as the stone causeways constructed in the northern provinces of Gīlān and Māzandarān and in central Persia, the building of covered bazaars, of which the one surviving in Iṣfahān is a visible reminder of such attention to trade. Stringent regulations were enforced by the market inspectors on the quality and price of merchandise sold to the public. The status of the judiciary and local officials was enhanced. The stationing of road

[1] See Dunlop, *Bronnen*, pp. 677–82.

guards (*rāhdārs*) along the roads, for which a tax was exacted from merchants, increased the security of the routes. General attempts to improve administrative practice and the answerability of officials were not without their beneficial effects on trade. None of these measures was in itself an innovation, since many had already been applied earlier in Persia and elsewhere, particularly in Turkey; but they certainly had beneficial affects for the economy in general.

Perhaps, in the long term, the most vital contribution which Shah 'Abbās made to the Persian economy was his forced introduction into Persia of Armenians. There were many precedents for the transference of populations or groups of artisans. Tīmūr removed communities of craftsmen to embellish Samarqand, and Sultans Selīm and Süleymān had no scruples about uprooting people and settling them where they needed them. Shah 'Abbās made a virtue out of necessity in driving thousands of Armenians from their homelands around the north-western frontiers with Turkey in order to implement his "scorched-earth" policy against the invading Turks in 1604 and 1608. Many thousands he dispersed throughout Gīlān and Māzandarān to revive the silk-producing industry. Many died on the way or in the pestilential climate for which they were unprepared. Others were settled in areas around Iṣfahān to till the fertile plains there, or in areas of Āzarbāījān further from the Turkish frontiers, or in Kurdistān. Many fled north into Georgia or west to Turkey. A significant group already accustomed to trading were placed in a part of Iṣfahān, where they were eventually allowed to develop their own thriving and independent community in New Julfā, across the Zāyandarūd, and were free to follow their own national customs and their Christian practices and be governed by an Armenian of their own choice.

Shah 'Abbās had suffered from the malpractices of Persian merchants[1] and he was determined to manipulate the Armenian community to his own advantage. Apart from being thrifty, hard-working and shrewd, the Armenians had a facility for languages and an ability to travel light. They appealed to Europeans, in that they were Christian in faith, if not always in practice. Since the fall of their kingdom their successes as merchants in the time of their "diaspora" had been acquired in a hard school long before they were utilised by Shah

[1] An example being Dengīz Beg, who accompanied the Persian mission to Spain in 1609–13: see above, pp. 391–2.

'Abbās, for many Armenians had visited Europe on trading ventures. Some were playing an increasing part in Turkish life. Others were travelling eastwards to India and beyond. They had already opposed the English factors of the Russia Company in 1561 in Qazvīn. Armenians in the service of Shah 'Abbās first made their appearance in Venice. Gradually the Armenian community in Iṣfahān extended the range and scope of their trading activities under the patronage of the shah, assisted by his privileges and credit. The community began to prosper, and the wealthier members began building noble residences and stately churches. In 1618 they were opposing the efforts of the English factors to obtain silk when Shah 'Abbās set up an auction for it, the bidding going up to 50 tūmāns a load. The English complained that "the Armenians were made a stale to draw us on". Soon, however, the Armenians were freighting goods on the English company's shipping to and from Persia and India. In Europe their activities at Marseilles in 1621 aroused the wrath of French merchants who petitioned the French king "de vouloir interdire absolument à ces Arméniens et Persans toute descente de soie en votre Royaume à peine de confiscations".[1] Pietro della Valle in 1618 had advised Shah 'Abbās to break the Turkish hold on Persian trade by engaging the French, "since the intention of the King was that all the silk reach Europe without any whatsoever going through Turkey, to bring about which I say this (still with the intention of harming the Turks), that we needs must bring it about that the French come to Persia; and without them there is nothing to be done: for the French are those who bring to the Levant the most ready money."[2] There was some French and Armenian initiative afoot over Persian silk, for in 1625 the Secretary of the East India Company reported "the offer of the French Embassador of 2 millions yearely to ioyne with the English to bringe the Silke of Persia to Marsellis, but said hee had wholly discouraged him therein".[3]

[1] *Histoire du commerce de Marseille* IV, ed. L. Bergasse and G. Rambert (Paris, 1954), 66.

[2] Della Valle II/1, 299, letter no. 4, Qazvīn, 25 July 1618:
"...che l'intention del Rè era, che tutta la seta andasse in Europa senza che passasse punto per la Turchia. Per effettuar questo, io gli dissi (con intention sempre di far danno ai Turchi) che havrebbe bisognato procurare di far venire in Persia i Francesi; e che senza loro non si faceva niente: perche i Francesi eran quelli, che portavano in Levante la maggior parte del denaro in contanti".

[3] I.O., B/10, p. 58, 30 May 1625.

Yet, though the Armenians had only limited success in France, they fared better in Holland, where an influential group settled in Amsterdam and remained throughout the 17th and much of the 18th century. Indeed, it is in Holland that Robert Sherley's earlier suggestions of reciprocal trade which he had made to both the Portuguese and the English were most nearly accepted. In the Dutch–Persian treaty concluded in 1631 the Dutch "in return for privileges accorded to the Dutch in Persia conceded reciprocal benefits to Persian traders in the Netherlands". It was the Armenians who mostly benefited from this provision. Thus during the reign of Shah 'Abbās, whilst ostensibly remaining subordinate to the demands of the shah, who controlled the silk production and its disposal, the Armenians were already consolidating their position in the international trade of Persia and becoming an indispensable factor in its success.

(*f*) *Conclusion*

Shah 'Abbās I stimulated the overseas trade of Persia by concerted efforts to improve the local conditions, by encouraging new foreign traders to lessen dependence on older, more easily monopolised outlets, and by utilising the services of the enterprising Armenians to widen the search for new markets and products and expand the scope of the established routes. The sea routes opened to Europe then and later never supplanted the position of the traditional overland routes linking east and west through Anatolia or Mesopotamia across northern Persia, but they certainly supplemented them.

The impetus given to trade between India, Persia and the Levant which came as a result of the opening up of the Persian Gulf to all shipping was also significant. This reactivated local shipping, apart from increasing the volume and value of freight which was carried by the shipping of the Dutch and English companies. All this followed from the impressive Persian revival which was the political as well as the economic achievement of Shah 'Abbās; a legacy which, in spite of the enormous demands made upon it, outlasted the Safavids.

5. THE LATER SAFAVID PERIOD

(a) *Shah Ṣafī*

The pattern established by Shah 'Abbās remained substantially unaltered throughout the remainder of the Safavid period. Only in one respect was there a significant change. It concerned the royal silk monopoly which was discarded by Shah Ṣafī. The English merchants of the East India Company commented very clearly on the change evident in the early part of Shah Ṣafī's troubled reign, "these busie tymes where every upstart will have his voice". They reported that "the ould Emperor Shaw Abbas by his commands prohibited all men what nation soever to buy any silks unless from his hands, and to the ende all should be collected and brought into his Magazenes, hee sent his owne servants with ready Money to all places where silks grewe to buy from the Countrey people... att such rates as the owners could afforde itt, with this silke thus gained, hee complied yearlie with the English and Dutch nacons, could partt unto the Jullfaleyne Armenians att Ten Tomands the loade proffitt, which was transported by the way of Aleppo, some hee adventured with them on his proper account, and the rest hee hoarded upp in his Magazenes."[1] Shah Ṣafī, on the other hand, "gave lycence to buy Silks in all partts of his kingdome without restricon". When he failed to honour his contracts with the English merchants he justified himself to Charles I by claiming that "in my grandfather's tyme he made Crooke that no man could buy any but himselfe and of himselfe ... but since my tyme I have broken that Crooke, that Middlemen in my country might reape the benefitt thereof: and that those who are the owners of the silke might sell itt to whom they would".[2]

The merchants had no doubt about the reasons for the change and where the responsibility lay: "Jullfalleynes Armenians and other merchants of Guyland and Sherwan, who have their trade to Aleppo by their extreame bribes to his Ducks, Nobles and Ministers preventeth him".[3] The Armenians had consolidated their hold on Persian commerce, mostly over exports and imports of silk and cloth respectively, and had spread their interests into internal trade too, setting up

[1] I.O., E/3/12/1347, Gombroon to E. I. Co., 11 March 1630/1.
[2] Public Record Office, S.P. 102:40, part 1, fol. 190.
[3] I.O., E/3/13/1379, Iṣfahān to E. I. Co., 26 Sept. 1631.

shops in the bazaars with a network of contacts throughout the country. Against this monopoly the efforts of the English and Dutch merchants were ineffective. They never wrested the silk and cloth trades from the Armenians, however much they "earnestly solicited transport of silk to Bandar Abbas acquainting the Kinge how honourable and profitable an action it would be to him to restore and establish the Commerce of Ormous again which had in former tymes been the most famous mart in the World".[1] After the decision of Shah Ṣafī there was no hope of deflecting a major part of the silk and cloth trades to the seaborne routes in the face of opposition from the Armenians, with whom the European merchants had to come to terms.

After the reign of Shah 'Abbās there were few confrontations between Persia and the neighbouring countries, apart from some fighting with the Turks, during which Baghdad was lost in 1048/1638, and intermittent hostilities over Qandahār with the Mughals in 1636, 1642 and 1648. Persia was generally at peace. The relative prosperity and standard of living of Europe in the 17th century was growing; its trade with the rest of the world increased, and this involved Persia too. Reliable statistical information from the 17th century is difficult to find, quantify and interpret. This is particularly true in the case of Persia, where it is not easy to differentiate trade intended for local consumption and that in transit. It is possible that a comprehensive examination of sources not so far consulted in detail, such as Turkish and Russian customs archives, where they exist, would be revealing in this respect. If, however, the volume of silk purchases made by the English Levant Company, the greater part of which came from Persia, and the customs receipts obtained by the East India Company at Bandar 'Abbās are considered, there is no doubt at all that both on the Levant routes and the southern sea routes Persian trade expanded.

Moreover, Dutch and, to a lesser extent, French and Venetian purchases of Persian silk rose, not to mention direct Armenian transactions with buyers outside the main companies trading to the Levant. In the south through Bandar 'Abbās the English company's share of the customs, however imperfectly paid, rose over the century from 225 tūmāns in 1624 to 550 in 1631, 341 in 1634, 345 in 1637, 700 in 1640, 612 in 1643, 635 in 1648, 750 in 1651, 785 in 1652, and by 1672 it was generally assessed at 1,000. This represented only a part of the trade

[1] I.O., E/3/12/1317, Agent, Royal Camp, to E. I. Co., 6 Oct. 1630.

through the main ports of Bandar 'Abbās and Kung, for neither the Dutch nor the Portuguese paid customs. Furthermore many traders in little boats landed goods surreptitiously along the coast to avoid customs. Others made arrangements with the European companies to pass their goods off as belonging to the companies to escape customs, a procedure known as "colouring", greatly resented by the Persian officials but frequently used.

(*b*) *The seaborne trade to Persia*

(*i*) *The English and Dutch companies*

The direct involvement of the major European companies in the trade of Persia was almost entirely concerned with the southern routes, the seaborne traffic, although indirectly they bought Persian silk and sold cloth to Persia through Armenian middlemen, principally at Aleppo and less frequently at Smyrna and Istanbul. The English were first to land, at Jāsk in 1616, prematurely hopeful of obtaining 8,000 bales of silk on three years credit at 7/6d a lb. which was expected to sell for 16/- in England. Yet until the Agency of William Burt in 1627, business was uncertain, though probably some 1,700 bales of silk were shipped, purchased with ready money, English commodities and other goods, approximately a third of each. Then in a determined effort in the early 1630s, three separate "voyages" – trading ventures – were directed towards Persia, partly to test the market seriously and partly because conditions in India had deteriorated. Contracts were made with Shah Ṣafī, renewed, and then broken by him. Between 1630 and 1640 a little over 2,000 bales were obtained from the shah at prices ranging from 45 to 50 tūmāns a load. After these contracts finished the East India Company obtained little further supplies of silk from Persia, for the cost of obtaining it increased, its quality became unreliable and its profitability much reduced. The real reason was that the Armenian control of the market was almost complete. The East India Company realised that no progress could be made against Armenian competition and that only in association with them could they hope to increase their silk purchases and cloth sales. The mid 17th century in England, with its unsettled internal political conditions brought about by the Civil War and the three wars with the Dutch in the 1650s, 1660s and 1672, resulted in a diminished interest in Persian trade. Attention was concentrated on India, whose exports of calicoes, silk and silk goods satisfied demand.

However, after difficulties with the Mughal authorities in the 1680s, culminating in hostilities and the temporary loss of its position in Bengal, the East India Company turned seriously to Persia again and sought Armenian cooperation. Armenians who had settled in London pledged their collaboration. An agreement, therefore, was concluded in 1688 with them whereby in return for privileged treatment they would trade on behalf of the company particularly in India, where they were promised their own settlement, and elsewhere, with special reference to the silk and cloth trades. This was never very effective and in 1693 the East India Company attempted to enter into a more comprehensive agreement with five major Armenian merchants in Iṣfahān for a close trading partnership. A large consignment of goods amounting to £93,995.11s 7d, almost a third of all overseas investments for 1693–5, was sent to Persia to promote this association, concerning which the company wrote to the Armenians: "We shall God willing have much more to do with you of the same kind hereafter to such a degree, that your Nations shall not need to travel to Aleppo to sell their Silk or buy their Cloth, but may do both better and cheaper in their own Country and at their own doors."[1] There was no doubt about the purpose of this proposal, which was nothing less than "to turne the course of Trade between Persia and Aleppo, which hath continued many hundreds, it may be Thousands of Years, for the Persians etc. to buy vast quantities of Silk in the Province of Guiland, to carry it from thence to Aleppo etc., truck it there for Cloth and the Other Europe Goods, and bring that Cloth to Persia where it is finally consumed within the Limits of our Charter".[2]

This English proposition threatened the interests of the Armenians and they reacted strongly, for they were not prepared to enter into a contract on terms that were tantamount to a possible commercial hara-kiri. They replied that "As for bringing Silk to Ispahan, yt is but wind, for nobody will be so mad, when we carry it to Aleppo: we have more ways than one to dispose of it: for there are English, French, Venetians and Dutch; if we cannot sell them for ready money, part money, cloth, Cocheneal, amber, Coral, or false pearl; then we can carry it to Europe

[1] I.O., E/3/92, E. I. Co. to the Five Merchants, 3 Jan. 1693/4.
[2] I.O., E/3/92, E.I. Co. to Persia, 3 Jan. 1693/4.

our Selves; but if we bring it to Ispahan there is only you to buy it, and if you won't give us a price, then we must let you have it, as you will; and take cloth of what price you will, for you won't let us put it on board your Ships from England."[1] So the ambitious project of re-routing the silk and cloth trades again failed. The land routes had withstood the challenge from the sea. The experience of the East India Company underlined the importance of ready money to the European trader in the east, the tenacity of the traditional patterns, the crucial parts played by the local merchants and brokers and the close interdependence of the cloth and silk trades.

Though the English company failed to obtain a permanent foothold over the northern-orientated trade of Persia, it achieved more success in the south, though it is not easy to be sure how much of it was due to official policy and encouragement or how much was due to the personal initiative of the company's merchants both in India and Persia who traded on their own account. The first Agent, Edward Connock, tried to encourage local merchants to use the company's shipping, indicating the advantages, "their little charge in freight, their danger less and the brevity of time in their passage least of all". The policy was continued and freightage became an important element in trading to Persia, at least up to the First Anglo-Dutch War in 1652, when six English ships were destroyed off Hurmuz by the Dutch. Afterwards English shipping went into eclipse till the 1680s, when it revived again. This increased interest in Persia coincided with the Dutch company's differences with the Persians which led to their temporary occupation of Kishm in 1684 and caused a drop in their freightage. By the beginning of the 18th century Charles Lockyer, with some exaggeration, maintained that it was "a main Branch of the Company's Profit... So that I look upon English ships from Persia to Surat in the latter end of October and November, to be the richest Vessels on that side of the world", estimating them "sometimes to the Value of two or three hundred thousand Pounds".[2]

Such ships would also include goods purchased in India or elsewhere for delivery in Persia or Baṣra. This direct trade by sea had grown significantly since the 1630s as a result of improved security, at least until the piratical activities of the Muscat Arabs towards the end of the 17th century. The deflection of trade from the overland routes

[1] I.O., E/3/53/6417, Iṣfahān to E.I. Co., 15 July 1697.

[2] Lockyer, p. 251.

between India and Persia in the 1640s, as a result of hostilities around Qandahār, added to the growth of the sea routes, for much of this trade never returned to the old routes. Whilst English shipping brought sugar and cloth, the Dutch brought not only these goods, but spices and copper.

The Dutch company's share of Persian trade was proportionately larger than that of the English, commensurate with their greater resources and presence in the east throughout the 17th century. The Dutch too were interested in silk exports, obtaining their first deliveries in 1626, 352 bales. Thereafter, in the 1620s they were exporting about 1,200 bales a year and in the 1630s between 800 and 1,000 bales. In the 1640s they were curtailing their requirements as they had overcommitted their resources in Persia, and like the English merchants the Dutch were finding that the quality had declined and its cost increased, so they were only purchasing between 200 and 500 bales a year. In the early 1630s, it seemed as if another competitor for Persian silk might emerge. This was the duke of Holstein, whose mission left Hamburg for the first time in October 1633, travelled to Moscow, where it encountered many difficulties, and returned to Hamburg. Setting out again in October 1635, it reached Iṣfahān in August 1636 after travelling through Russia, voyaging down the Volga to Astrakhan and crossing the Caspian Sea, where the members of the mission were shipwrecked near Darband. The duke of Holstein hoped to import a considerable quantity of silk through Russia. He was quite unsuccessful, for the Russians proved obstructive, his mission incompetent, the Persians uncooperative and the English and Dutch companies hostile. The Dutch director, Nicolaas Overschie, with the connivance of the Armenians, made extensive purchases of silk to cause a shortage which put up the price. The mission departed empty-handed and rather ignominiously, after quarrelling with an Indian embassy then in Iṣfahān and behaving with an unfortunate disregard for Persian protocol.

As a result of straining resources for some years and the fraudulent practices of some directors, the Dutch authorities at Batavia of the United East India Company made a more vigorous attempt to keep a closer hold over their Persian Agency and to reassert themselves *vis-à-vis* the Persians. They tried to raise the price of Dutch imports, lower the price of silk, increase sales of Indian and other East Indian commodities and prevent abuses over the quality and deliveries of silk. The subsequent history of relations between the Dutch company and the

Persian authorities is basically one in which the Dutch are increasing their sales of imported commodities to Persia, reducing their purchases of silk and remitting the resulting trading imbalance in ready money. This policy became more important as the Japanese increasingly restricted the export of gold, silver and copper, upon which the Dutch had heavily relied for the availability of ready money. The Persians, concerned to balance their trade and reluctant to permit the flow of ready money out of the country, endeavoured to oblige the Dutch company to purchase at least 300 loads of silk yearly. These differing attitudes caused a tension in relations and resulted in mutual retaliatory activities. A Dutch embassy in Iṣfahān in 1644 considered itself abusively treated, and when there was a failure to reach an acceptable settlement the Dutch bombarded Bandar ʻAbbās and the island of Kishm in the following year. Temporarily they obtained better terms. Another mission in 1647 was inconclusive, and the Dutch were preparing for more hostile action but desisted as the English company was benefiting from these Dutch actions. In 1651 Johan Cunaeus arrived with an impressive embassy to settle the outstanding differences of claims and counter-claims and the question of silk contracts. A silk contract for 300 loads yearly at 48 tūmāns the load was agreed, but little else.

The real turning point in the Dutch company's fortunes in Persia resulted from the collapse of the English company's position there caused by losses to its shipping in the east from the First Anglo-Dutch War, which broke out in 1652. English energies were subsequently directed towards Europe and the West Indies against the Dutch. So during the Protectorate official interest in the east waned. The East India Company, for internal political considerations, was deprived of much of its authority and power which it did not begin to regain till after the Restoration in 1661. The Dutch, therefore, for three decades at least, had an almost free hand, for not only was there practically no English competition during this period but the Persians, deprived of the sufficiently counterbalancing power of the English, were forced to reach a less favourable arrangement with the Dutch company. Thus the Dutch exercised a dominating position in the southern trade, though not an exclusive one, for local shipping, in particular Indian and Armenian interests, was increasingly participating in that trade. The final eclipse of Portuguese power in the Persian Gulf with the loss of Muscat in 1649 stimulated trade on the Arabian side. When John

Fryer was at Bandar 'Abbās in 1675 he commented that "the English Company's Trade is but small here" and that "the greatest Traffick, next Indian Cloth, comes from the Spice Trade; which the Dutch engross, beside Sugar and Copper formerly; for which they carry off Fifty thousand *Thomands* worth of Velvets, Silk, Raw and Wrought, with Rich Carpets, besides many Tunn of Gold and Silver, Yearly".[1]

By the 1680s the price of Persian silk had fallen so low in Amsterdam that, in comparison with silk from India or brought to the Levant ports, it was unprofitable. The Dutch company was anxious to free itself from its Persian commitments and tried to accomplish this by intimidation, occupying Kishm in 1684, and by missions led by Reynier Casembroodt in 1683 and Johan Van Leenen in 1689–92, and negotiations. At that time, however, the English company was actively renewing its interest in Persia, so the Dutch did not hold all the advantage. There was, moreover, an increasing shortage of reliable ready money in Persia, caused by royal hoarding, non-productive luxury expenditure, the debasement of the currency and its eastward flow through Persia to India, in spite of efforts to prevent this taking place, and an increasing monetisation of the economy which exerted a growing pressure on supplies of reliable coinage. Thus the Persians were all the more reluctant to let the Dutch company continue to import on the same scale whilst reducing its silk purchases. Fortunately for Persia at this time, supplies of silk from India lessened and those from the Levant suffered from hostilities waged by England and Holland against France, which made the Mediterranean insecure for fleets. Therefore, in 1694 an agreement was reached for 300 loads at 44 tūmāns a load.

At this time, when the demand for Persian silk again outran supply, the Persians attempted to exert pressure on the English and Dutch companies to cooperate with them in an attack on Muscat, whose corsairs were attacking shipping and plundering along the Persian coast. Neither company was agreeable, though the Persians persisted in their efforts. When Jacobus Hoogkammer arrived in Persia in 1701 he was unable to renew the contract on the old terms, for the price demanded for silk was 48 tūmāns a load or 200 bales at 44 tūmāns with sufficient *douceurs*. This state of affairs lasted till the end of the Safavid period, the Dutch continuing to import spices and textiles on a large

[1] Fryer II, 163.

scale and refusing assistance over Muscat. Throughout this period there was a sizeable colony of Armenians in Amsterdam, who maintained a network of contacts throughout the Levant and who increasingly turned their attention to Russia.

(ii) The French and Portuguese

The French were not nearly so long represented in Persia as the English and Dutch companies, and exerted very little official influence in the 17th century, though many individuals successfully traded there, as the examples of Tavernier and Chardin show. French policy was strongly affected by the traditional friendship with Turkey and the commercial ties of Marseilles with the Levant. In spite of the early interest of Cardinal Richelieu and the establishment of a Capuchin mission under Père Pacifique de Provins in Iṣfahān in 1627, trading connections with Persia were insignificant, though some Armenians managed to trade under difficult conditions in Marseilles. It was not until the interest of Colbert had been aroused that some concerted action was taken to establish the real French presence in Persia. Colbert's objective was to "tirer de la main des Anglais et des Hollandais tout le commerce du Levant par une grande concurrence quelconque où les Français trouvassent un benefice".[1] This led to the establishment, on 26 May 1664, of La Compagnie des Indes.

On 11 July 1665 a mission from the company arrived in Iṣfahān composed of Messieurs de Lalin and de la Boulaye Le Gouz, nominated by the French king, and Messieurs Beber, Dupont and Mariage, appointed by the company. An agreement was reached for trading privileges, but the behaviour of certain members of the mission left an unfavourable impression and little resulted from its visit. In 1672 Louis XIV, who had become actively interested in and concerned about the persecution of Armenians who professed the Catholic faith, sent Sieur de la Jonchère with an impressive retinue and presents to confirm the privileges already granted and establish a trading base at Bandar 'Abbās. De la Jonchère unfortunately died on the way and the French director at Sūrat, Monsieur Gueston, took charge and an agreement was signed with Shah Sulaimān in December 1671. Although the French company appointed a director at Bandar 'Abbās there was, as John Fryer noted, little to occupy him, for "The French have as little

[1] *Histoire du commerce de Marseille* v, ed. R. Paris (Paris, 1957), 14.

to do at this Port as in other Places; and were it not for the Credit of their Interpreter, who gets good Profit by Wine, (he being priviledg'd with a Wine-press for that Nation at Siras, as well as the other Europe Nations), they could not subsist".[1] Colbert also encouraged Armenians to settle at Marseilles, admonishing the merchants there "de leur donner toute la protection que l'autorité de votre charge vous permettra de les garantir contre les chicanes des habitans... qui ne connaissent pas en quoi consister leurs avantages".[2] At Sūrat certain Armenians were suggesting loading silk on French vessels instead of transporting it overland through Turkey. Ultimately the policy of encouraging Armenians to bring their Persian trade to Marseilles foundered on the opposition of the French merchants. Ponchartrain, Colbert's successor, was obliged in respect of the Armenians to "leur imposer des conditions qui empêcheraient de faire tort au sujets de sa Majesté".[3]

In other respects, however, Ponchartrain persevered with his efforts "d'examiner les moyens d'introduire... les marchandises et manufactures du royaume et lever les obstacles qui pouvaient s'y opposer..., éntrer s'il était possible en concurrence avec le commerce qu'y font les Anglais et les Hollandais".[4] Jean-Baptiste Fabre was sent to Persia for this purpose. The Fabre mission was bedevilled with roguery, intrigues and misfortune, though it had its bizarre aspects when the disguised mistress of Fabre, Marie Petit, took charge of it on her lover's death in 1706. The mission was redeemed by Pierre Victor Michel, who succeeded in negotiating a treaty with the Persians on 14 September 1708, in spite of the hostility of the English, Dutch, Portuguese and Armenians. If the French were mainly concerned to assert their presence in Persia, increase trade and protect Catholic Armenians, the Persians were anxious to find a more effective ally against the Muscat Arabs. As a French envoy was pointedly informed by the Persians, "Le Roy de Perse t'ordonne de proposer au Roy de France que n'étant pas content des services qui luy rendent plus les Anglais contre les Mascatins ses ennemis bien qu'ils soient bien payés pour cela... nous envoyer équipes des vaisseaux et bombardes necessaires."[5] There is some similarity with the Persian predicament a century earlier, when they were forced to rely upon the English company to assist them in dislodging

[1] Fryer II, 164.
[2] *Histoire du commerce de Marseille* IV, 500.
[3] *Ibid.* V, 16.
[4] *Ibid.*, p. 422.
[5] Archives des Affaires Étrangères: Affaires Étrangères, Perse, vol. ii, fol. 313, mémoire, April 1711.

the Portuguese from Hurmuz. It was only in the reign of Nādir Shāh that tentative moves to form a Persian navy began, though in any case they proved abortive.

The Persians eventually followed up the Michel embassy with one of their own conducted by Muḥammad Rīżā Beg, who arrived in France on 23 October 1714. It fascinated the Parisian populace but exasperated the court officials, and in spite of a lavish reception, including the last public appearance of Louis XIV, it had little practical result. For whatever the interest of the royal entourage, trade with Persia had little appeal to French merchants, who advised, "n'écouter ladessus aucune proposition et de ne pas permettre de commerce de France aux merchands Persans... le commerce pourra faire tort au gens Marseillais".[1]

Taking a similar view to the English merchants trading to the Levant, the French merchants of Marseilles maintained their opposition for over a century. Their attitude was confirmed by the experience of the English and Dutch companies. The southern sea routes never supplanted the overland routes to Europe, for unless the trade was supplemented by Indian and other southern commodities it could not be balanced. The English company had its special privileges, the Dutch their spices, but the French merchants had no such inducements to enter a new trade which might jeopardise the old. For the majority of Armenians it held little interest in comparison with their trade through the Levant or later, from the end of the 17th century, through Russia.

The importance of the Portuguese in the trade of Persia after their loss of Hurmuz was negligible. Albuquerque believed, "This city of Ormuz is according to my idea the most important of them all." The English merchants reckoned that it was because of spices that the Portuguese "have made that barren island of Ormoze to yield them more profit than any (if not many) their Eastern trade besides". Kung, near Bandar 'Abbās, the port granted to them by Imām Qulī Khān provided them with a pale shadow of their former glory. It was used by Indian, Arab and Armenian merchants who wished to avoid Bandar 'Abbās, for little Portuguese trade passed through it. After the fall of Muscat in 1649 the Portuguese had even less hold over local shipping, for they were unable to enforce the pass system effectively and as they lost more ground to the Dutch in the east generally,

[1] *Ibid.*, vol. iv, fol. 165, 31 July 1715.

especially after the loss of Malacca, their trade further declined. Most of their effort was directed against the Arabs from Muscat, with whom they were engaged in almost incessant hostilities till the end of the 17th century.

(iii) Local shipping and trading

It early became obvious to the English merchants that one of the principal obstacles to a large trade with Persia was that sales of English commodities alone would not balance purchases of Persian goods and in consequence large supplies of ready money would be needed to make up the difference. This was, however, a problem which dominated eastern trade in the 17th and early 18th centuries. English merchants in general and the East India Company in particular did not then have sufficient ready money available. As the first Agent realised, "The want then of ready moneys to be extracted our land, being the life of all (the whole difficulty thereon consisting)". So efforts were made to participate in the local trade either from the East Indies with spices or from India with textiles, metals, drugs, foodstuffs etc. which were traditional Persian imports from these areas. The expectation was that "Your ships from the Southward may furnish with spices, from Suratt, if but only we bring the Moor and Banyan merchants (of whom we may receive great freights), all India commodities may also be supplied." Almost a century later the absolute necessity of such trading was echoed in comments from French merchants who maintained that trade to Persia alone from France would not pay without complementary commerce with India. The Dutch company certainly appreciated the point, for they not only took the position of the Portuguese as the chief suppliers of spices, but were very active in the Indian textile trade with Persia, particularly from Coromandel.

Nevertheless, the accusation that the English and Dutch were responsible for ruining trade in the Gulf or for eliminating local traders is unacceptable. In the two decades from 1612 to 1631 when the Portuguese were in conflict with the Persians, trade was already adversely affected and even from 1623 the joint Dutch and English convoys could only protect some of the merchants engaged in the trade for part of the time. With the granting of the port of Kung to the Portuguese in 1631 conditions became much more stable and the following decade saw a remarkable renewal of trade between India and Persia, much of it carried on in shipping constructed in India, particularly at

Sūrat. Gujarātī shipping reasserted itself not only in the Red Sea but also in the Persian Gulf. Armenian interests expanded in India both on their own and with Dutch and English assistance. Khwāja Nazar, who was head of the Julfā Armenian community, requested the East India Company's assistance in 1620 for Armenian merchants travelling by sea to India and their accommodation in Sūrat. By 1630 many Armenians were established at Bandar 'Abbās, with trading networks extending throughout India and into the East Indies. Khwāja Mīnas, originally from Iṣfahān, was operating from Sūrat on a large scale in the 1660s as principal buyer and creditor to the East India Company there and as the owner of much shipping. It was an Armenian who owned the *Queddah Merchant*, which was pillaged by pirates in 1690 and whose cargo was valued at £50,000. The Callendar family, with family connections in Iṣfahān, Sūrat and London, was associated with the East India Company in 1688 in its ambitious project to export Persian silk and import English cloth through Sūrat and Bandar 'Abbās. A similar scheme was proposed to the French in 1682 by Armenian interests, so there was no lack of initiative displayed by Armenian traders both with their own shipping and in freighting English and Dutch ships.

Indian participation in the trade to the Persian Gulf is also acknowledged. Much of the local trade was carried in the shallow-draught single-masted dhows of the time, which generally avoided the main ports of Bandar 'Abbās and Kung with their customs controls. This kind of clandestine trade continued in the Gulf up to the mid 20th century, so it is hardly surprising to find it existing in the 17th century. It is certainly true that there were a large number of Indian merchants, Banians, a rather loose term covering those coming principally from Gujarāt, who established themselves in the ports of Persia and the larger cities, such as Shīrāz, Kirmān, Kāshān, Iṣfahān, Tabrīz and Ardabīl. They had their own quarters in the bazaars. In Bandar 'Abbās they had frequent difficulties over their religious rites and beliefs. In addition to merchants, there were many Indian money-changers whose expertise in precious metals was widely acknowledged. Shah 'Abbās was very reluctant to agree to their presence, but under Shah Ṣafī and his successor their numbers increased and their knowledge became indispensable in the money markets. Many different coins entered Persia – piastres, chequins, rials, rijks dollars, ducats, pagodas, to mention a few – and the fluctuations in the exchange rates between themselves and in reference to the Persian silver coinage of 'abbāsīs and shāhīs and the unit of account, the tūmān, were carefully observed.

There was no doubt about the upsurge of trade between India and Persia in the third decade of the 17th century, after Sūrat had recovered from its famine and floods and peace was made with the Portuguese. The English Resident for India noted in 1637 that merchants "thrive and thronge yearely twixt Gombroone and Masulipatam". Earlier in 1633, according to the English Captain Weddell, merchants "finding the sweetnes of the trade, beginne, for want of shipping, to come hither in their own vessells". Hostilities between Persia and India over Qandahār in the middle of the century, which intermittently closed the overland routes, resulted in an increased volume of goods being carried by sea, much of which never reverted to the land. Thus in 1640 the English factors reported that the quantity of goods entering Bandar 'Abbās had quadrupled and that "never to any man's remembrance were soe many merchants and goods present at any one time in Surat" for Persia.

From the records it is clear that the range and variety of textiles being imported into Persia from India was growing and that throughout the century it remained a profitable investment for both European and local trader. The East India Company reckoned, probably conservatively, on goods from Āgra, that "From Disboursement of your mony, to the time it is returned, into your Cash, charge of Transport, way charges in Rhadaree, servants wages employed with Caphillaes, Customes of Surat and Broach, fraight to Gombroon and transport to Spahan, there cannot be lesse reconed then 40 or 45% one with another which being deducted, from the Spahan prizes there wilbe nonthelesse a Competent profitt, peradventure 35% one with another."[1] Indian merchants, purchasing more cheaply and with fewer overheads, would have traded even more profitably. Indeed, even in the spice trade, Indian merchants were not eclipsed by the Dutch, for they "carried on a traditional and considerable trade with Persia and Mocha". In the 1670s the names of 'Abd al-Ghaffur and Aḥmed Chelebī occur as shippers to Bandar 'Abbās amongst other places, and they were not alone. The increasingly aggressive activities of the Muscat Arabs towards the end of the century affected the security of shipping in the Gulf and more local trade began to be carried on European ships, either official

[1] I.O., E/3/14/1504, 24 March 1633; E/3/16/1658, 15 Jan. 1638/9; E/3/22/2216, 8 April 1651.

company ships or those in private ownership belonging often to English or Dutch merchants. This private trading is difficult to quantify, but the indications are that it was considerable and profitable.

The majority of local shipping came from Indian ports, much of it from Sūrat, where it was subject to control by the Mughal authorities. Thus during the hostilities over Qandahār in 1648 an embargo was placed upon shipping going to Persia. Occasionally Indian shipping expected special privileges to be arranged for it in Persia by the English merchants, such as those accorded to Mīr Jumla for his ships from Golkonda which entered customs-free. Frequently goods would be trans-shipped in ports from distant places and in this way goods from China were received, particularly china ware, which was much esteemed in Persia throughout the Safavid era. Sometimes shipping came from the East Indies, such as a vessel from Bantam in 1687, captained by an Englishman, Anderson, bringing spices. There was a brief exchange of trade with Siam in the 1660s. Furthermore, there was much local trade around the Arabian peninsula and along the Gulf to Baṣra. There were many small fishing and trading communities dotted about the coastline which contributed in some measure to the trade of the area.

(*c*) *Overland trade*

(*i*) *Turkey*

It has been said that "the silk trade between Persia and Turkey was a dominant element in the economies of both countries. The Ottoman silk industry was dependent upon Persian silk; moreover the trade brought an average of 70,000 alton a year into the treasury. In Persia, the currency in circulation was kept supplied by gold and silver earned on the Ottoman markets."[1] This was true of the 16th century, and it remained true of the 17th century, irrespective of the upheavals in the political and commercial relations between the two countries which virtually came to an end for almost a century with the Peace of Ẕuhāb in May 1639. The greatest part of Persian silk exports passed through Turkey, where it was either manufactured into textiles at Bursa or exported from Aleppo or Smyrna to London, Marseilles and, to a

[1] H. Inalcik, "Bursa and the Commerce of the Levant", *JESHO* III (1960), 131–47.

lesser extent, Venice and Leghorn. In Aleppo, Bursa, Smyrna and Istanbul the silk was traded principally for cloth or money, but other goods such as glass, arms, watches and objects of fashion were bought for import to Persia. It was well organised from the chain of trade silk-growing provinces to the Turkish market places. It suffered from the arbitrary behaviour of Turkish officials towards the Armenians at the beginning of the 18th century. The Armenians were the main intermediaries in this trade and were also well represented in other commercial and social affairs in Turkey.

(*ii*) *Russia*

There was a development of Persian trade to Russia towards the end of the Safavid era. Throughout the 17th century embassies had been exchanged between Persia and Russia. Shah 'Abbās received three, in 1618, 1623 and 1626. Some trade accompanied the embassies, for in 1648 a departing Persian ambassador for Russia "made Silke soe deare, hee carringe great quantities with him". The embassies, at least on the Russian side, were often elaborate, for in 1654 the Russian ambassador, Lobanov–Rostovsky, "went in greate pomp and state; he haveing Drums, Trumpetts and Flaggs carryed before him; accompanied with 250 or 300 Russians and had as many Camels for carryage of his present and Luggage".[1] A decade later a Russian ambassador "had a retinue of neerest 600 men of whom 400 sayd to be Merchants, att his entring the Citty rode 16 trumpets before him, 8 drums and 13 large Freezeland horses were led in state; its reported never the like beasts came into these parts before, being intended as presents for the King, with 2 Coaches extraordinary well made, with watches and clocks and abundance of other toyes, likewise bares and Doggs of all sorts".[2] There were also falcons and sables, which always made highly esteemed presents for the shahs. If there was not always real respect displayed on such visits, nevertheless the Persians recognised their value, for: "Le Moscovite est notre voisin, et notre ami et le commerce est establi entre nous d'ancienneté et sans interruption."[3]

If there was an element of exaggeration in this statement, there was more than a grain of truth, for by 1670 there were those suggesting to the Dutch traveller Jean Struys, "qu'il leur feroit bien plus facile de

[1] I.O., E/3/24/2288, 10 April 1654.
[2] I.O., G/36/104, 9 Sept. 1664.
[3] Chardin III, 171.

faire descendre leurs marchandises par la Wolga à Arcanguel, et de là en Hollande, que de les envoyer par terre à Smirne, où ils ne pouvaient les faire tenir sans les exposer à de grands perils, outre que les frais de cette voiture etoient immenses".[1] At this time from the middle of the century onwards, apart from the intermittently troubled period of the Cossack insurrections under Stenka Razin between 1664 and 1671, Armenian trade to Russia was increasing under Russian encouragement.

It was the Armenians who were the principal intermediaries in this trade. The importance of Astrakhan as an international entrepôt has been mentioned earlier, as have been the earlier efforts in the mid 16th century by Anthony Jenkinson to open up trade between Europe and Persia by the Volga. It was not surprising that Della Valle drew attention to the advantages of this land route over that by sea as advocated by a Russian embassy in 1622: "if the Muscovites have this in mind and are negotiating to facilitate it, having a sufficiency of money, at least to begin with, I believe it to be perfectly feasible for the English that they themselves can trade in Moscow by this route without such great risk of war."[2] The Armenians were singularly well placed to take an interest in the Persian–Russian trade, not only because of their local connections in the regions bordering the two countries, but because they had been involved to a greater or lesser extent in commercial affairs in Moscow since the end of the 15th century. Their activities increased as a result of the forward policy of Ivan IV, whose defeat of the Kazan khanate was a prelude to closer relations with the trading centres of Central Asia. Russian internal difficulties then checked this progress, but trade between Persia and Russia again developed depending on the security of the routes along the Caspian hinterland and the Volga. Contemporary accounts do not underestimate the dangers of travel in those regions.

Although Armenian merchants settled in the bazaars in Astrakhan during the reign of Shah 'Abbās I, it seems that the Russian encouragement of them becomes more evident in the second half of the century. After having conquered the Ukraine, contained the threat from Turkey

[1] Struys, p. 220.

[2] Della Valle II/2, 522, letter no. 18 from the ship *The Whale*, 18 Jan. 1623: "se i Moscoviti pensano a questo, e trattano di attendervi, havendo denaro a bastanza, almeno per cominciare; io l'hò per cosa assai riuscibile: ed a gl'Inglesi stessi, che pur' in Moscovia hanno traffico, per quella via, senza tanti pericoli di guerra."

and concluded an alliance with Poland, Russia felt able to turn her attention eastwards again. In 1660 Khwāja Zakar and nine companions from Iṣfahān were received by Tsar Alexis Mikhaĭlovich. In February 1666 another group of 40 Armenians arrived in Moscow, and after long negotiations a treaty of commerce was signed on 31 May 1667 with the Russian officials, Yury Dolgoruky and Ordin-Nastchokin. It gave the Armenians a concession to transport the goods of Asia to Europe by way of Astrakhan and Archangel on payment of customs of 5% ad valorem. The principal goods exchanged consisted of cloth, hides, furs, falcons and silk.

By the early 1690s the English factors in Persia were complaining about the competing supplies of cloth coming from Russia, but the strongest stimulus to Russian–Persian trade and relations in general followed the return of Peter the Great to Russia in 1698. He was determined to create a more powerful modernised Russia. Although for much of the time preoccupied by wars with Sweden, Poland and Turkey, Peter the Great successfully cultivated ethnic, religious and political links with Georgia and Armenia. In the troubled and weakened state of the northern Persian provinces, he particularly encouraged a closer trading association between the Russians and Armenians, which gradually grew as relations between the Armenians and Turks deteriorated. A Russian consul was established at Shamākhī and embassies sent in 1701 and 1708. In 1718 Artemiĭ Petrovich Volynsky negotiated a satisfactory treaty, including regulations and privileges regarding trade which permitted Russian merchants freedom of movement in Persia and unlimited purchases of silk. The impetus to trade given by Peter the Great survived his ill-fated campaign in 1722, for not only were Persian–Russian trading connections strengthened but the Dutch and English companies traded through Russia with Persia even after the demise of the Safavids till the mid 18th century. It had become obvious, as Jonah Hanway remarked, "that of all the nations who have endeavoured to establish a trade with the people of Persia, the Russians are most advantageously situated".

(*iii*) *Central Asia and India*

Mashhad was the main centre of Persian trade towards Central Asia in the later Safavid period, a gathering place for horses and the wool from the sheep and goats of the mountain pastures. Rhubarb and lapis lazuli were traded with Balkh and Bukhārā, which occasionally sent ambassadors to the shah's court. Here pottery, carpets and leather goods were made. Further east Herat and Farāh were strategic and commercial outposts but the nodal point of the overland trade between India and Persia was Qandahār, whose possession for half a century was disputed between the two countries. Two English merchants passing through Qandahār in 1615 noticed that "By reason of frequent passage of Caravans it is much enlarged lately, that the Suburbs are bigger then the Citie. For within this two yeare, that the way of Ormus is stopped up by the wars betwixt the Persians and Portugals, all Caravans which passe betwixt India and Persia, must of necessitie goe by this place. And here they doe hire Camels to go into India, and at their returne for Persia... Trade it yeelds not of it selfe, but accidentally by the meeting of Indian, Persian and Turkie Merchants, which are not willing to travel further at twentie per Cento profit."[1] These two merchants were accompanied into Persia by three Armenian and twelve Persian merchants. In 1628 Herbert noted the arrival in Qazvīn of a 40-camel caravan from India carrying tobacco.

There had always been a close connection between Khurāsān and India, particularly Golkonda and the Deccan. Shortly after Shah 'Abbās II had finally recaptured Qandahār an English traveller commented that "Qandahar brings vast Customes to the King of Pertia for theres noe way into the Northern parts of it from Multan and other India parts by land except it come by way of Sindy."[2] A few years later it was reported from Persia that, "By way of Candahar is arrived lately at Spahan near 1,000 camel loads of cloth and indico which hath caused said commodity to fall in price 15%." This was additional to the seaborne trade, of which it was written at about the same time that "Greater quantities of goods than usual arrived this year from India to Gombroon." So whatever the attractions of the sea route some caravans continued to travel throughout the 17th century between India and Persia and were only interrupted intermittently by the warfare around Qandahār. As a result of the raids of the Balūchīs and the disturbances with the Afghans at the beginning of the 12th/18th century, the roads then became less secure and the volume of goods carried decreased. An English merchant in Mashhad in 1697 remarked that it was difficult to sell cloth because the ways were blocked.

1 Purchas IV, 272–3.

2 "Richard Bell's Journal and Travels to the East Indies and the Mogul's Countrey in the year 1654", British Library, Sloane MS 811, fol. 6.

(*d*) *The routes*

In general the pattern of the routes did not change significantly in Safavid times. The means of transportation remained the camel, the horse and the mule, and the caravans depended upon local pasturage, food and, most crucial of all, water. Wheeled traffic was negligible. Political troubles might deflect the routes temporarily. Trade might, where practical, be moved by sea rather than land, but in the main, geographical conditions determined the choice of routes. In the same way the seasonal changes of the monsoons affected sailings. Ships came up from Indian ports to the Gulf generally from November to May at the latest, but from June to October there were only small local movements of shipping. A voyage from Sūrat to Bandar 'Abbās would take between three and six weeks, usually about a month, in a European vessel, such as a 300-ton carrack. The smaller Sūrat-built pinnaces of 100 tons would take about the same time, as well as the Arab-built dhows which crossed the Indian Ocean to East Africa or went round the Indian coast or across to the East Indies.

Once the merchandise had arrived at Bandar 'Abbās it was in one direction despatched either north-east through Jīruft, Bam, Kirmān, Yazd and Ardakān, where it joined up with the eastbound route which went to India across the Dasht-i Kavīr to Ṭabas, Bīrjand, Farāh and Qandahār or more easterly from Bam through Sīstān and the Hilmand valley to Qandahār, but this became more dangerous because of the Balūchīs. From Qandahār further routes went either north into Central Asia through Ghazna and Kābul or east into Multān and Lahore. The other way was north to Iṣfahān through Lār, Jahrūm, Khafr, Shīrāz, Zarqān, Māyīn, Ūjān, Āsupās, Dihgirdū, Yazdikhwāst and Qūmisha. Alternative routes were from Bandar 'Abbās to Shīrāz through Dārāb and Fasā and from Shīrāz to Iṣfahān through Sīvand, Dihbīd and Ābāda before rejoining the main route at Yazdikhwāst. Another route went north from Kung through Kuhkird, Bastak and Nimar, where it joined the main route at Lār. From the lesser ports at Bandar Rīg and Bandar Rīshahr routes converged near Burāzjān and the road to Shīrāz passed through Dālakī, Kāzarūn and the Dasht-i Arjan. These routes were subject to extraordinary variations in climatic conditions, scorching heat when only travelling at night was bearable and perishing cold when travel might be impossible. An English factor, Robert Loftus, noted in April 1628: "I stayed in Digerdoo [Dihgirdū] six daies until the Carravans had broken the waies, which otherwise I coulde not pass by reason of the extremitie of the snowe"; but his courier died on the way. There were many hazardous parts where the direction was confusing or the ground treacherous. John Fryer found the travelling hard in 1676 when "in the day, besides the Heat and Sands, the Winds brought with them another plague the Locusts... The Mountains gape, the Rocks cleft in Sunder, the Waters stagnate... Water...Thick, Troubled and Slimy", in all "a sensible Map of Purgatory".[1] Though accommodation in the main towns was satisfactory, Fryer experienced that it was not always so in the caravansarais along the way.

Throughout the 17th century the roads were reasonably secure and patrolled by rāhdārs who were responsible for guaranteeing the safety of the travellers and the protection of their merchandise. It was also a period of considerable building activity, with officials and merchants putting up caravansarais, bridges, water tanks, baths, and bazaars. In addition to the routes to India and Central Asia already mentioned through Farāh and Qandahār, another left Farāh through Herat to Mashhad. Coming into Mashhad were the routes from Balkh, Samarqand, Bukhārā and Khīva going through Marv. From Mashhad part of the old silk route was followed through Nīshāpūr, Sabzavār, Dāmghān, Simnān, Tehran, which was insignificant compared to the ancient town of Ray, and Sāva. There the routes divided. One went south through Qum and Kāshān, where it branched either in the direction of Iṣfahān and so south through Shīrāz to the coast or more south-easterly through Nā'īn, Ardakān and Yazd to Kirmān and Bam, where it either forked south to the coast or east towards India. Another turned west through Hamadān, where it divided, the northerly route going in the direction of Sanandaj, Mosul, Mārdīn and Urfa to Aleppo, the more westerly one going to Baghdad, where it divided once more, either north to Mosul along the Tigris or along the Euphrates through the desert to Aleppo. The third main route from Sāva passed north-westerly to Qazvīn, where it either went towards the Caspian to Rasht, Ardabīl and north to Shamākhī and Darband or went to Tabrīz through Sulṭāniyya and Miyāna. Tabrīz was an important industrial centre, a vital link with connections in all directions. One route went to Erivan, with a road going north to Tiflis and so to Georgia and Armenia, and then on to Turkey where

[1] Fryer II, 172–3, 185.

the first important town was Erzerum. From there routes went to the coast at Trebizond and through Anatolia to Istanbul or Bursa or to the Aegean at Smyrna. Another route from Tabrīz which went to Aleppo passed through Khūy, Bitlīs, Diyārbakr and Urfa, where it joined the route to Aleppo.

(*e*) *The trade*

(*i*) *Persian exports*

It was silk which was "the chiefest naturall commodity in and about this place" and which constituted Persia's principal export. As mentioned before, it was produced principally in the northern provinces of Georgia, Māzandarān and Gīlān and to a much lesser extent in Khurāsān and around Yazd. Production had declined in the last quarter of the 10th/16th century as a result of the Persian–Turkish wars, but Shah 'Abbās I made determined efforts to expand production. Statistics and terminology concerning the silk industry are unreliable, so that it is only possible to generalise on some of the main features. An estimate was given that in 1618 some 232,000 māns or 125 tons were being produced. Olearius, two decades later, suggested that production was 8,000 bales of 213 lbs. in Gīlān, 3,000 bales in Shīrvān, 3,000 bales in Khurāsān and 2,000 bales each in Māzandarān and Qarābāgh: about 192 tons, of which a twentieth perhaps was used in Persia. By Chardin's time production had increased, according to his computation, to some 270 tons, made up of 10,000 bales of 276 lbs. from Gīlān, from Māzandarān 2,000, from "Media and Bactria" 3,000 apiece, and 2,000 each from Qarābāgh and Georgia, totalling 22,000 bales. Struys, who is less reliable, put the total at 30,000 bales. By the end of the Safavid period in 1740 there was a 40% decline from peak production estimated at around 160 tons by Hanway. By this time Persian silk was meeting increased competition not only in the markets of Europe from Indian and Italian silk of middling and excellent quality, but in the Turkish market from Syrian and Greek silk.

In general the silk from Gīlān was most favoured, two main grades of which were imported to Europe: firstly, sharbassee, which was the best quality and according to Chardin "la meilleure soye pour les riches étoffes", and was also called legee, though the terms were not always synonymous; and secondly, ardasset, described by Chardin as "grosse, epaise et laide", which was coarser and cheaper and mostly came from Shīrvān. Other grades in lessening quality were called *Khadkudā pasand*, Carvarī and Canarī. Supply was influenced not only by political considerations but by climate and disease. Shah Ṣafī excused himself for the non-compliance of a contract in 1631 by referring to the disease ravaging the silkworms and the bad state of the mulberry trees. In 1721 the English Agent, Owen Philips, alluded to the increased cost of silk caused "by reason of great Loss of Silke and Wormes this year in an Earthquake". The European companies at first dealt almost entirely with the Court, and the tedious negotiations with the officials involved *douceurs* to those involved as well as presents on other occasions, such as the accession of the monarch, new appointments and at the festivities of Naurūz. Fluctuations in demand naturally influenced prices, and the Dutch complained that the arrival of the Holstein embassy increased the price of silk, though they contributed to this by extensive purchases to thwart them. Price increases were occasionally caused by the departure of an embassy carrying silk away. The English factors at first hoped to obtain a load of silk, 36 māns, for 40 tūmāns, about 6s. 3d a lb., but found their first consignment costing 50 tūmāns, about 7s. 6d a lb. It was generally marginally cheaper for ready money than in part exchange for other commodities and money. In general the price to the European companies fluctuated between 45 and 48 tūmāns a load, according to circumstances and quality. Exceptionally, in 1721 the English Agent reported Gīlān legee costing about 75 tūmāns a load.

The cost of transporting a load in 1617 from Iṣfahān to Bandar 'Abbās, some 550 miles, by camel in 45 days, ass in 40 days or mule in 30 days might cost 38 shāhīs in animal hire and $3\frac{1}{2}$ shāhīs for tolls. Packing, baling, wrapping and weighing in Iṣfahān, including materials, cost in 1639 25 shāhīs the load. Other costs included lighterage and porterage at port and freight charges, which to England were £20 a ton, about 75 shāhīs a load. Thus in 1640 silk costing 7s. 6d a lb inclusive was being sold in London for 17s. The prices and costs, however, fluctuated greatly, for in 1708 the East India Company was complaining to its Persian factors that the silk invoiced to them at 8s. 4d. was sold for 12s. 2d. on average, "so that considering freight, Custom, and Discount we have not our money again by a great deal besides all our Charges and Interest and Insurance lost".[1] The Dutch

[1] I.O., E/3/96, 9 Jan. 1708/9.

too became less enthusiastic over Persian silk, for it was often short in weight and dirty. At Aleppo costs were complicated by the interaction of cloth and silk prices and supplies, so that silk might be bought for 14 dollars a rotello in cash but 17½ dollars against a particular kind of cloth at a certain price depending on demand[1]. An appreciation of the interdependence of the silk and cloth trades in the Levant markets is of fundamental importance. In the early 18th century London prices for silk fluctuated between 20s. and 30s. a lb. in response to increased demand as a result of European hostilities which affected the security of shipping in the Mediterranean. Such silk was being bought for between 12s. and 14s. at Aleppo.

Other exports of Persia were of much less importance in comparison with silk. Kirmān wool, a fine quality from the goats found in that province, and a little from Mashhad, were exported by the European companies and also went through the Levant. Tavernier gives an amusing account of his experiences with an early consignment in 1654. The East India Company first requested it from its Persian factors in 1659 and within a decade they were requesting 10–12,000 māns yearly. During the 1670s about 150 bales were being exported yearly, "clean good, not to exceed 6d. or 8d. a lb. clear abroad, not black", for red was the preferred colour. The price obtained in London in the years 1669–77 ranged from 2s. 3d. to 6s. 3d. In 1693 392 bales were shipped, in 1697 254, and in 1698 338, with prices ranging between 5s. 7d. for the best and 3s. 5d. and 2s. 9d. for second grade. On the eve of the Afghan invasion the English factors had obtained 18,000 māns. The Dutch too exported considerable quantities of this wool, which was principally used in the making of hats and buttons. Of considerable interest is the fact that the production of this wool stimulated a local weaving industry which emerged in the 1670s, causing less supplies for the European companies. By the mid 1680s there was no doubt that the main reason for these restrictions was "the yearly increase of weavers who get their living by weaving that Commodity" in Kirmān.[2]

Textiles and carpets were important products of the industry of Persia, but whilst they now enjoy a remarkable reputation, this was not necessarily so in the 17th century, for artistic fashion changes. For example, in the 17th century travellers were unimpressed by Persian

[1] A dollar was 3s–5s, and a rotello 4 lbs 12 oz.

[2] I.O., G/36/92, 23 Feb. 1684/5.

painting, and manuscripts were obtained not for their aesthetic qualities but for their religious or historical interest.

The pearling industry off Baḥrain, which was nominally under Persian jurisdiction, was practically under the control of the strongest local sea power, which meant firstly the Portuguese and then the Muscat Arabs during the 17th century. The export of pearls, important though it was, brought little revenue directly to the Persian treasury. The best pearls were "to be round of good colour and clear, not yellow". An interesting development in the early 18th century was the idea of using a submarine to fish for the pearls. The East India Company was approached in the early 18th century in London "for making use of an Engine lately invented by which persons can continue underwater twenty fathoms deep for several hours. It is supposed great advantage might be made in the Pearl Fishery near Ormus." Bilin de Cansevilles, the French merchant and traveller, at the turn of the century had a similar idea, believing that a submersible machine used off Marseilles for recovering treasure from wrecks would be suitable for fishing "une grande quantité de perles orientales pendant toute la journée sans intermission".

Pearls were much used in the decoration of richly embroidered textiles as can be seen in contemporary Persian or European portraits. Red oxide and salt were exported steadily from Hurmuz. Rhubarb, which came from Central Asia to Qazvīn, was mostly exported to Aleppo, but occasional consignments were shipped from Bandar 'Abbās. Drugs, gums and medicaments such as lapis tuttia, oppoponax, salarmoniac, worm seeds, ammoniacum, galbanum, olibanum and assafoetida were exported in all directions and though the total volume was small the returns were considerable. An indication of this may be inferred from Lockyer's account of prices at Bandar 'Abbās in 1705, when lapis tuttia cost 7 shāhīs a Tabrīz mān of $6\frac{1}{4}$ lbs, galbanum 16 shāhīs and ammoniacum $6\frac{1}{2}$ shāhīs, whilst prices in London were reckoned in 1661 to be £5–£6, £10–£12 and in 1686 £3. 10s respectively. Dyestuffs included rūnās (madder), a red root from the Ardabīl area, which was especially in demand in India, and galls, a bitter excrescence forming on oak trees from the Hamadān and Kurdistān regions, which went mostly to the Levant.

Persian wine, especially that of Shīrāz, in spite of intermittent prohibitions, was highly esteemed in court circles and among the foreigners residing in the country. Tavernier in 1666 estimated the production of

Shīrāz wine at 154,688 imperial gallons, 4,125 barrels of 300 pints each (200,025 māns), of which a quarter was exported to India and another quarter consumed exclusively by the court. There were vineyards in many parts of the country where the climate was favourable, including Āzarbāījān around Lake Rizā'iyya, Qazvīn, Khurāsān, particularly about Nīshāpūr, districts in Georgia and Armenia, as well as Iṣfahān, Yazd and Shīrāz. Shīrāz, according to Tavernier, "is particularly famous for the most excellent wines of all Persia".[1] The grapes were fermented in large terra cotta containers before being bottled and transported wrapped with straw in cases. Jews, Armenians and Zoroastrians were those engaged in the trade. The wine of Shīrāz was highly esteemed by Europeans, who probably stimulated increased production from the beginning of the 17th century and who were granted special concessions to make their own, which was usually managed for them by Armenians. Tavernier reckoned that in 1666 50,000 māns were produced there for the Europeans and the rest by Jews, 100,000 māns of which much was exported to India. India also took rosewater, orange-flower essence and much fruit. In 1705 Lockyer stated that Shīrāz rosewater cost 120 shāhīs and Shīrāz wine cost 140 shāhīs a chest of 10 gallons, but in 1685 it was priced at 100 shāhīs with local brandy at 20 shāhīs a gallon.

(ii) Persian imports

The main imports were textiles either for internal consumption or for re-export to neighbouring countries. The principal kinds were firstly woollen cloths from Europe, particularly from England and to a lesser extent from Venice, France and Holland, which entered Persia mostly from the Levant, although the English East India Company especially made strenuous efforts at various times to expand its cloth sales through Bandar 'Abbās. Secondly, there was a wonderful variety of Indian cotton cloths which were brought in by local traders, the Dutch company and to a lesser extent the English Company. Most of the European cloth imported was English broadcloth, thick, well-woven and heavy, generally of the ordinary variety costing between 3s. 6d. and 5s. a yard dyed and called "Londra", which was the term given to it by Italian merchants towards the end of the 16th century when it was first appearing in the Levant. Though there were considerable varia-

[1] Tavernier I, 420; for quantity, see *ibid.*, 734.

tions in quality, weaving, dressing, pressing and dyeing, in general the cloths were some 40 yards long, slightly lengthening towards the end of the century, and between 4 ft. 6 ins. and 6 ft. in breadth and usually sold in bales of five cloths. The Persians preferred bright gay cølours and bought them at 30–36 shāhīs (10s.–12s.) a yard. Some sales were made of kersies, a coarse narrow cloth, some 27 ins. wide, woven from long wool. The newer style of cloths, lighter in texture, known as bays, and perpetuanos, the "new draperies", as they were termed in Europe, coming into fashion early in the 17th century, did not make much headway in the Persian markets. Middling and high quality cloths in rich colours such as scarlet, crimson or deep wine had limited sales and were often used for presents.

The Indian cotton cloths came mostly from Sind, Coromandel, Sūrat, which handled the production from Āgra, Broach, Aḥmadābād and other north-west Indian textile centres, Bengal and Kutch. The large number of Persians in India facilitated this trade and influenced its methods and patterns. The volume was great; perhaps a third of Indian textile production went to the Red Sea and Persia and onwards to Arabia, the Levant, Turkey, Russia and Central Aṣia. Fryer noticed the predominance of the textile and spice imports to Persia.

The Dutch involvement in the textile imports is well attested by Professor Raychaudhuri, who states that, "starting as a mere accessory to the spice trade in the Indies the Dutch trade with Coromandel developed before long into one of the chief pillars of the Company's Eastern commerce". and nowhere more so than to Persia.[1] The Dutch continued to the end of the Safavid period to import textiles and spices. Four Dutch ships arriving at Bandar 'Abbās in 1721 brought sugar, pepper, sappon wood, lack, cardamons, sugar candy, tin, cinnamon, cloves, nutmegs and a variety of textiles ranging in price from 8 to 138 shāhīs a piece, with the most numerous single kind being Cossas, of which there were 2,280 costing 56 shāhīs each.

In 1721 spices imported by the Dutch, who were not the exclusive but the largest traders in them, were valued in the Bandar 'Abbās customs house registers as follows: cardamons 70 shāhīs per Tabrīz mān, cinnamon 85 shāhīs 7 qazbaks, nutmegs 97 shāhīs, preserved nutmegs 200 shāhīs, pepper 11 shāhīs, cloves 142 shāhīs 8 qazbaks, preserved cloves 250 shāhīs, benjamin 18 shāhīs and more 40 shāhīs per

[1] T. Raychaudhuri, *Jan Company in Coromandel 1605–1690* (The Hague, 1962), p. 211.

100 misqāls. Turmeric and ginger were also imported, and rice. Wood was frequently imported in the south for building. Sugar was also an important import throughout this period.

Apart from these staple items, tin and iron were required and a wide variety of luxuries such as furs, jewels, watches, glassware, cutlery, amber for beads, coral, porcelain, ivory, falcons, exotic animals and fashionable bric-à-brac. Guns were always highly acceptable as presents in court circles and among officials, but there was no large-scale importation from European sources.

6. ORGANISATION OF TRADE

Shah ʿAbbās had trade organised as a state monopoly, almost on a personal basis. The reasons for this lay partly in his determination to centralise his administration, partly in the effects of the Turkish wars prior to his accession and partly as a consequence of the Portuguese hold over trade in the south, and not least because it was financially advantageous to him. Moreover, Persian merchants were short of capital to sustain trade on a large scale, as the English had noticed on their first arrival. As silk sales were a priority, Shah ʿAbbās encouraged the Armenian community he had settled in Iṣfahān. The shah, however, retained under his own control international trade, which was administered in accordance with his instructions by one of his ministers, Lālā Beg or Mullāʿīm Beg in the last fifteen years of his reign.

Under Shah Ṣafī the royal monopoly was greatly relaxed and under subsequent monarchs practically abandoned. The operations of the mints, which under Shah ʿAbbās were strictly supervised, became less effective and much of the foreign coinage entering the country was never taken to them. As a result of this and court hoarding, the amount of coinage in circulation failed to keep pace with financial requirements as the volume of business increased. Such a state of affairs had not yet become obvious by 1631, for remark was made of "Silver and Gould which is transported yearely from hence into India in great quantities by merchaunts of these parts",[1] but it had become a serious problem thirty years later. Raphaël du Mans noted that "la richesse de la Perse n'est donc que comme l'humidité de l'eau qui s'attache aux

[1] I.O., E/3/14/1503, 23 March 1633.

canaux cependant qu'elle passe pour aller se descharger dans son bassin... il reste quelque peu de chose sur le païs".[1]

Twenty years later still a critical situation had arisen with money in very short supply and the currency debased. "The unhappy Order of not suffering Gold nor Silver to be exported" was decreed and officers commissioned to enforce it, for "the Deputy who is now in towne [Bandar 'Abbās] hath given abunndance of trouble, threatning to open all chests and bales to seek for money, but the merchants at last made a general complaint and got leave for shipping their goods after he had searched all with running an Iron into both bales and chests".[2] This had some effect in the short term, but with the connivance of port officials and other more devious methods it was not long before the flow to India was continued, by which, according to Tavernier earlier, "those who understand the traffic well and carry hence gold or silver to the territories of the Great Mughal, always get 7% or 8%, provided they take care to shun the customs-house".[3]

As for the debasement in 1684, it was reported that "the money of Spahanne is soe very bad there is neither buying nor selling, and in fifty abassis there is not five Silver, soe that the Bazars are all shutt up, and noe trading at all, nor will be any until the King hath ordered this money to be cryed downe, and other good money made in the room of it, the which these people are now by the King's order every day at worke upon, but wee fear it will take some time (by reason of the Scarcity of good Silver) before they can gett quoined soe much as will serve soe great citty as Spahaune".[4] The problem continued to bedevil the Persian economy and was as much the result of the lack of administrative control in enforcing unpopular measures as economic. Practically all the silk was exported to the Levant, with little apart from European demand to balance the trade to the south and east, so that the imbalance was compensated by the export of precious metals. There was not such a shortage of these, for Venetian chequins came from the Levant, Hungarian ducats and rijks dollars from Russia. The Spanish real was still current. Much coinage, however, never reached the mints and so was not taxed, but exported directly.

The Armenians as a group seemed alone in possessing some kind of social as well as commercial cohesion, even a common school of busi-

[1] Du Mans, pp. 192–3.
[2] I.O., E/3/31/3504, 26 Oct. 1670.
[3] Tavernier II, 591–2.
[4] I.O., E/3/44, 5 Nov. 1684.

ness practice, but it must not be assumed that all Armenians everywhere had the same interests, for though some might mutually collaborate closely others were in violent opposition to each other. This became more obvious towards the end of the 17th century, when religious persecution, discrimination and competing commercial conditions began to disrupt their communal solidarity in Iṣfahān. There was similarly visible a clear reaction arising from the political, economic, social and religious factors throughout the Persia of Shah Sulṭān Ḥusain. This eventually resulted in its collapse and capitulation to the Afghans of Maḥmūd, described by a French observer as being "a body of eight thousand shepherds half unarmed". Banians and Jews too began to suffer more intervention in their affairs towards the latter end of the century, but in general Safavid Persia was more tolerant of its minorities than Mughal India and interfered with them less.

The bulk of direct European trade with Persia was conducted by the English and Dutch companies. This was regulated by treaties and decrees. Although a royal farmān authorising Christian merchants to trade in Persia with protection, privileges and exemption from tolls and customs was granted by Shah 'Abbās I to Sherley in 1599, the significant date is 1615, when Richard Steele and John Crowther obtained a farmān permitting the English East India Company to commence trade in Persia with the cooperation of the local officials. The first and second Agents, Edward Connock and Thomas Barker, proposed separate drafts, which if not formally accepted were used as the basis for normal relations until a formal agreement was accepted and issued by Shah Ṣafī in 1629. This lasted in force and in 1697 was confirmed and slightly expanded by Shah Sulṭān Ḥusain from eighteen to twenty articles. Similar arrangements were entered into by the Dutch with Persians in 1623 and a treaty signed on 29 December 1624. This was subsequently confirmed in 1631, 1642 and 1694.

These treaties established the framework in which the European companies operated in general, but secondly there were further *raqam*s required to cover more specific aspects which arose in the course of trading and which needed royal confirmation. These included freedom from *rāhdarī* (the road taxes), polite usage from local officials, permission to export an agreed number of horses annually, security of residence, freedom to make wine, provision of guards for caravans, supplies of water, permission to purchase Kirmān wool, restitution of goods or money unlawfully taken, and others. In 1697 nineteen such raqams were confirmed by Shah Sulṭān Ḥusain for the English company.

A third kind of official authorisation was that concerned with royal contracts such as those entered into between Shah 'Abbās I and Agent Burt or between Shah Ṣafī and Agents Burt, Heynes, Gibson and Merry for the English company between 1628 and 1640. These might concern the terms and conditions of the sale of Persian silk for English commodities such as cloth or tin or part exchange with money, or they might consist of instructions to certain officials or merchants to furnish a given amount of silk to the English company. The Dutch also required such raqams for their affairs, the granting of which often depended on the relationship between the personnel of the companies and the royal officials, the situation at court and the giving of presents.

In many ways the official most closely involved with the European companies was the *shāhbandar*, the port officer. There was a similar functionary for the Mughal emperor at Sūrat. He had the overall jurisdiction of the port, he collected the customs and controlled the customs-house, he regulated the movement of shipping, he authorised the landing and despatch of goods, he provided the lightering facilities which were essential at Bandar 'Abbās, and his goodwill was essential for the merchants. In the time of Shah 'Abbās I it appears that this appointment was in the gift of Imām Qulī Khān, the powerful governor of Fārs, but on his murder by Shah Ṣafī the appointment became a royal prerogative. The details are not certain: at first it seems to have been a salaried position, but in the latter part of the 11th/17th century it was a "farmed" post, at 24,000 tūmāns for Bandar 'Abbās.

By the middle of the reign of Shah 'Abbās I the facilities for merchants had improved. In the large cities the bazaars were functioning as the centre of trading. Each sector of the bazaar had its own particular kind of trade organised with its own guild administration for servicing the requirements of traders for wholesale and retail purposes, provision of porterage, transportation and stabling, the control of pricing and arbitration over commercial disputes. Food retailing was, however, organised differently and was distributed throughout the bazaar. The importance of the total bazaar complex and its relationship to the city is most clearly seen in Iṣfahān, where Shah 'Abbās included it among his religious, administrative and economic institutions centering on the great maidān. It is obvious too in a later example at

Shīrāz, where Karīm Khān Zand attached very much importance to his Bāzār Vakīl. Whilst the Armenians gradually dominated the silk and heavy cloth trades, Gujarātī merchants were prominent in the Indian trades of spices and light cloths and largely controlled the money exchanges. The European merchants were largely dependent on their local brokers, whose connections with the traders of the bazaar and the officials of the court were indispensable. The English and Dutch companies had their own quarters in Iṣfahān, but did little direct trading themselves after the reigns of Shah 'Abbās I and Shah Ṣafī. Along the trade routes a determined effort was made to supply sufficient caravansarais for the use of merchants on their journeys.

7. CUSTOMS AND REVENUE

The whole question of the Persian customs at the port of Bandar 'Abbās, which for most of the period handled by far the largest volume of seaborne trade to Persia, is confused in the absence of any reliable statistics, which is not surprising, given the nature and the methods of Safavid bureaucracy and the practices of merchants. Some tentative indications, based primarily on English sources, however, may be proposed with reservations. It was assumed in 1624 that the Portuguese obtained 180,000 rials (some £45,000 at 5s. per rial or some 14,616 tūmāns at £3. 6s. 8d a tūmān) yearly on customs set at 14% nominally at Hurmuz. The English company was entitled to half the customs taken at Bandar 'Abbās in recognition of the services it had provided for the Persians at the capture of Hurmuz. It was admitted that it received at the most only a tenth or even a fifteenth of what was due and in some years less than that or none at all, particularly towards the end of the 17th and beginning of the 18th centuries. The following amounts were received by the English East India Company for their share of customs in representative years: 1624 225 tūmāns, 1631 550, 1633 242, 1634 341, 1637 345, 1640 700, 1643 612, 1644 616½, 1648 635, 1649 200, 1650 612½, 1651 750, 1652 785, 1653 700, 1654 500, 1655 400, 1656 700, 1657 650, 1658 400, 1659 500, 1660 450, 1661 650, 1664 700, 1668 700, 1669 700, 1670 900, 1672 1,000. Subsequently it remained, though was not always delivered, at the agreed nominal figure of 1,000 tūmāns.

It is possible to hazard a possible cross-referencing of figures around 1670. If it is accepted that the English company only received a fifteenth of what was due to it, then this means that it should have had 15,000 tūmāns and the shāhbandar a like figure, or £50,000 each, giving a total of £100,000. Now it was calculated that the customs for 1669–70 trading period amounted to 29,000 tūmāns, some £96,666. In 1652 the Persian customs were reckoned to be £118,000. In 1682 in London it was believed that the English share of the customs was worth 12,000 tūmāns (£40,000) yearly in the period 1658–78. In 1661 Nicholas Buckeridge, the English Agent in Iṣfahān, overheard "the Vizeer of the Custome house acknowledge to his friends (supposing hee did not heare, or that hee did not understand him) that the King's Customes this year amounted to above 15 and 16 thousand Tomands ... [and] hath cheated the King and you, of more then would make it up 20 Thousand Tomands".[1] In 1674 customs were farmed out for 24,000 tūmāns. The duties were 10% of value. In 1656 and 1657 together some £444,500 worth of goods was cleared through the customs at Sūrat for Persia.

In attempting to extrapolate from these tentative figures the total value of trade, allowance has to be made for English and Dutch company trade, which was exempt from customs, though the private trade of the merchants was officially not so, but in fact was; the practice of offloading at secluded beaches; and the prevalence of "colouring", whereby local trade was brought in in the guise of company trade. An inspired guess for the total import trade of the southern ports might give a value of £700,000 in the middle of the 17th century, a little less from the Levant and somewhat less still from Russia, Central Asia and the overland trade from India: an overall total of £1¼m., of which a quarter might be re-exported. As for exports, the bulk of these were composed of silk exports. Chardin in the second half of the 17th century estimated the total production at about £5m. At between 45 and 50 tūmāns a load of 36 māns of 12½lbs per mān, the value of silk production was between £1½m. and £1,800,000. Perhaps a fifth of the total production was consumed in Persia, leaving a possible £1,750,000 for exports, though these figures varied greatly during the century according to the fluctuation of demand or supplies. Other exports in comparison were limited, and so in general it may be assumed that in the 17th century trade was balanced, but that after the collapse of the Safavids it deteriorated. In 1801 Sir John Malcolm reckoned that "the

[1] I.O., E/3/27/2894, Nicholas Buckeridge, Iṣfahān, to E.I. Co., 19 Aug. 1661.

annual amount of the imports and exports of Persia do not (if this statement is correct) much exceed two million and a half sterling... it is considered that at least one half of this only passes through the Kingdom on its way to others".[1] Thus the assumption that the value of the annual trade of Persia at the height of Safavid prosperity was £3m. is not unreasonable. In comparison, the imports and exports of the United Kingdom at this time were estimated at some £12m.

[1] Malcolm, *The Melville Papers*, ed. Sir A.T. Wilson, included in Charles Issawi, *The Economic History of Iran 1800–1914* (Chicago, 1971), p. 265.

CHAPTER 9

SOCIAL AND INTERNAL ECONOMIC AFFAIRS*

In discussing the economic situation of Iran from the 14th to the 18th century, it seems to us helpful to keep two essential sectors distinct from one another: on the one hand the economy of the open countryside (above all, agriculture, cattle-breeding, hunting, fishing and mining) and on the other hand the urban economy (commerce and industry). Let us turn initially to the sector of rural production, with agriculture and cattle-breeding as its predominant elements. This created to a great extent the basis for almost all the economic activities we shall encounter in the period we are to treat. Subsequently the development of the various forms and institutions of landholding will have to be examined. Thereafter we shall treat the urban sectors of the economy (home trade and industrial production), and we shall end with a description of the financial and taxation systems.

THE RURAL ECONOMY

In the framework of agrarian production we encounter above all two sharply demarcated social groups. While the settled peasants mostly devote themselves to agriculture, cattle-breeding is above all in the hands of nomads and semi-nomads. Let us first discuss some characteristic features of peasant production in our period.

The damage done to Iran's agriculture by the Mongol invasion showed its effects for centuries, and it is questionable whether the country, down to the end of the Safavid period, ever regained the degree of prosperity that distinguished Iranian agriculture from the 4th/10th to the 6th/12th century, though there were indeed regional exceptions. The reasons for this setback lay above all in the destruction of irrigation works, some of them centuries old, and in the deforestation and depopulation of the country: both of the latter were direct consequences of the Mongol invasion. Further devastation occurred in

* This chapter was completed in 1972. It has not been possible, therefore, to take into account work which has appeared since that date.

the course of Tīmūr's conquests. Nevertheless, there were phases of economic improvement around the middle of the 9th/15th century and above all in the 11th/17th century.

The village was the basis of rural production. Authority over the villages was exercised by landowners, fief-holders or tenants; when the ruler himself was the landowner, that is to say on crown lands, or when he had administrative control in some other way, he was represented in relation to the peasants by fiscal officials. We shall discuss this matter further below.

All peasants enjoyed equal rights as members of their village community; each of them, within his village, had a right to the use of a portion of land, to his own household, to the use of the communal pasture and the irrigation works of the village. The portion of land was usually calculated on the unit of a *juft* (*juft-i gāv*, "a yoke of oxen"); a juft was as much land as could be cultivated with a yoke of oxen, and it was an established principle that every peasant had the right to a juft. In this situation it was generally accepted that all the jufts of a village should be, as far as possible, of equal value with regard to the harvests they would yield. In some cases, in order to achieve this equal sharing among all the villagers, the jufts were reallocated after a period of several years.

Another possible method of establishing equal shares for the individual peasants was the allocation of a fixed quantity of water; in this case a village functionary, the *mīrāb*, saw to it that each peasant's portion of land was supplied with the necessary quantity of water from the irrigation system.

The peasant himself was regarded as a tenant of his landlord. In every case the cultivated ground, often also the implements, the draught animals, the water, and of course the irrigation works that cost so much to construct, belonged to the landlord. The human labour was of course supplied by peasants.

In conformity with the extent of these preconditions for agricultural production, the harvest of the village at any given time was divided up according to the terms of a "contract of lease" between landlord and tenant. If, for example, the landlord had provided the land, the draught animals, irrigation and seeds, and the peasants of the village concerned merely contributed their labour, then the latter had to be content with only one-fifth of the produce. This was the general rule for villages with straightforward field-tillage. With orchards, vineyards and vegetable plantations in the vicinity of towns, where irrigation was ensured by natural watercourses and not by expensive underground channels (*qanāt*), a different percentage was customary: here the peasant retained from one-third to one-half of the produce. In every case the peasants – the so-called *ra'āyā*, i.e. "the protected" (by the landlord and his representatives), "the flock" – formed a class on their own. They had, since the Jalayirid era, been increasingly bound to the soil and were not allowed to leave the region of their village without official sanction, as illustrated by a *farmān* of Shah Ṣafī issued in Rabī' I 1041/September – October 1631, in which there is mention of the return of Sīstānī peasants to their villages; they had fled to various parts of Khurāsān during an Uzbek raid.[1] Even though it may have held good for previous centuries that the landlord functioned as mediator between peasantry and bureaucracy and was thereby also the peasants' protector, this was hardly the case after the time of the Īl-Khāns: from the 8th/14th to the 12th/18th century we repeatedly encounter a tendency towards the development of a landowning class possessing far-reaching powers and authority. In general the peasants hardly ever came into contact with their landlords or their representatives; these lived almost entirely in towns, often far distant, so that the life of the villagers, especially of those living well away from the towns, was characterised by a high degree of isolation. The daily routine followed its course, year in, year out, entirely within the limits of the village community. Requisites for day-to-day use were made at home by the peasants themselves, or else the landlord provided such articles as implements of various kinds and eventually recovered their value by increasing his share of the produce. This fact is of fundamental importance, since it shows clearly that commerce was largely restricted to the urban sector of the economy and at best extended only to villages in the vicinity of towns. These villages supplied the towns with fresh fruit and vegetables. The relative prosperity of the peasants in such areas was by no means a characteristic of the inhabitants of the many remote villages. Their only contact with the outside world was when they met tax-collectors and the landlord's representatives, who had to bring in his share of the produce. It should also be said that these observations do not apply merely to the period under discussion here.

This also holds good when we consider the most important agricul-

[1] Ḥusain Dāvudī, "Asnād-i khānidān-i Kalāntarī-yi Sīstān", *BT* IV (1348), no. 5–6, pp. 9ff. (document no. 5). See generally Petrushevsky, *Kishāvarzī* II, 186–90.

tural products; as in earlier and later times, the main cereals were wheat and barley, the latter mainly as fodder. In the Caspian coastal areas rice-growing held first place; it was also to be found to a limited extent in the Iṣfahān area. Sugar-cane had already been cultivated in Khūzistān since the time of the Sasanians. Fruit-growing was not exclusively confined to plantations in the vicinity of towns; however, it always required favourable means of irrigation. Essentially the same kinds of fruit were cultivated as in our own day. Cotton-growing and the rearing of silkworms were widespread, the latter mainly around Yazd, in Khurāsān and in Gīlān on the Caspian coast. Wine-production was not unusual and mostly found in the vicinity of the vineyards themselves. It is, of course, not surprising that (Christian) Armenians and Georgians were especially active in this trade. Saffron, which was in great demand, came mostly from Khurāsān. In districts where there was hardly any frost in winter, figs and above all dates were harvested. There were extensive date-plantations everywhere in Khūzistān and also in the province of Kirmān and on the Caspian coast. Olives and citrus fruits were grown in the climatically favoured districts, limes especially in the fertile areas by the Persian Gulf, and Persian bitter oranges (*nāranj*) mainly on the shores of the Caspian and in Kirmān. The cultivation of sweet oranges (*purtaqāl*) also increased after the contacts with the Portuguese, i.e. in the 17th and 18th centuries, but it did not reach the same extent as today. Cultivation of poppies (for the extraction of opium) and hemp was widespread in all areas.

As has been indicated above, in Iran irrigation was a decisive factor for every kind of agriculture. The following irrigation techniques have been handed down from the 11th/17th century: surface irrigation with water from springs or rivers; "underground" irrigation from deep wells (*chāh*) fed by ground-water; and irrigation by means of qanāt (or *karīz*), underground channels, expensive to construct, which were driven through strata carrying ground-water. These methods are known well before the 8th/14th century and are still practised today.[1] Orchards and plantations, as we have already mentioned, required a greater supply of water than simple agriculture. We therefore find this type of cultivation mostly in places where surface irrigation with river-water was possible. In the crown provinces of the 11th/17th century the ruler had a monopoly of water and leased it to the holders of fiefs

[1] Chardin IV, 101. Ḥamd-Allāh Mustaufī, *Nuzhat al-qulūb*, text pp. 132, 133, 144, 145, 221, etc.

and to peasants. Thus the Band-i amīr dam in Fārs, for example, which went back to the Buyid epoch, is said to have brought in some thousand *tūmāns* annually for the royal treasury.[1] In a similar way, in other areas the landlord at any given time had special rights of ownership with regard to water and irrigation works. It hardly needs to be emphasised that the irrigation problem was of an entirely different character in the humid Caspian provinces.

Because of the limited range of the irrigation systems, agricultural operations were always restricted to a specific cultivation area; it therefore proved necessary to manure the exhausted and meagre soil regularly. For the most part the dung of asses, cattle, camels and sheep served the purpose, and the fertilising effect of human excreta was also highly esteemed. The cesspits of town houses were therefore emptied regularly by local peasants coming to market, in order that they could transfer this valuable material to their fields and gardens. Generally all the rubbish of the towns was – as it still is – carefully gathered up by peasants and used as fertiliser.[2] Ox and camel dung were also used as fuel. It was a very common practice to use the ground-up remnants of decayed mud walls, which had been made durable by an admixture of fermented straw and chaff and thus contained valuable chemicals. Pigeon droppings were held to be the most valuable fertiliser. Even today strangely shaped pigeon towers (*kabūtarkhāna*) are a characteristic feature of the environs of Iṣfahān; often up to ten thousand birds nest in them. These buildings, of which similar examples are found at al-Fayyūm in Egypt, date back to the 17th century. Every day considerable quantities of the precious salpetre-like substance were – and still are – obtained from them. In former times a fixed tax was levied by the state for the erection of these towers.[3]

Landlords and wealthy peasants used to store up large quantities of cereals for considerable periods. For this purpose they generally used large vessels, in which the goods to be kept were covered over with dry straw and sand. It was also customary to bury stores in large dry holes in the ground and cover them with sand. Apples, for example, could be kept for a whole year in this manner. Peasants often buried their harvest produce, to keep it out of the reach of tax-collectors, highwaymen or predatory nomads.

[1] Kaempfer, p. 94. [2] Du Mans, p. 233. Chardin IV, 103.
[3] Chardin III, 386–7.

We should add a word on mills and milling. There were mills in many districts; these, however, did not always belong to the peasant production sector, since their products (meal and flour, especially wheat-flour, and oils in the case of oil-mills) were in great measure intended for urban consumers. The meal needed for private use was generally ground by the peasants themselves. From the technological point of view there were mainly two types of mills: those driven by draught animals and – along watercourses – watermills. There was probably a trend towards an increasing number of watermills; these were in general use in the 17th century. There are also said to have been windmills in some parts of the country, e.g. in Khurāsān.[1]

The settled peasants practised cattle-breeding only to a limited degree, usually only for the reproduction of draught animals and possibly also to satisfy their own very modest demand for meat. Poultry – preferably chickens and pigeons, and in the Caspian regions also ducks – was bred mostly in the vicinity of the towns, obviously with a view to being sold in the markets. The major part in satisfying the demand for meat was played by the nomad cattle-breeders, whose extensive flocks and herds – mostly sheep and goats, camels, and in Khūzistān also buffaloes – were to be met with everywhere. There had been nomad tribes in Iran even before the arrival of the Turks and Mongols – Kurds, Bakhtiyārs, Lurs, Balūchīs (all of Iranian origin), and Bedouin Arabs (e.g. the Banū Ka'b) in Khūzistān ("'Arabistān"). In the period under discussion here, the tribes of Turkish origin were predominant. In addition, ethnically very heterogeneous tribes had developed in the Il-Khanid period under the leadership of Mongol soldiers; these probably succumbed to far-reaching Turkicisation during the 8th/14th and 9th/15th centuries. Each tribe had at its disposal a clearly defined and extensive pasture area, consisting of a summer pasture (*yailaq*) and a winter pasture (*qïshlaq*), which might often be at a great distance from one another. The summer pastures lay in the highlands, while the winter pastures were always to be found in extensive lowland tracts. The tribes were divided into sub-tribes and clans; the smallest organisational unit was a nomad household consisting of several tents (Turkish *ōba*). The total pasture territory of a tribe was called *yurt*.[2] The supreme authority over a yurt was exercised by the

[1] Petrushevsky, *Kishāvarzī* I, 263ff. Du Mans, p. 243.

[2] *TMEN* II, 132 ff. (no. 572). Petrushevsky, *Kishāvarzī* II, 77. For the yurt under Tīmūr, cf. Lambton, *Landlord and Peasant*, p. 100.

members of the tribal aristocracy, headed by the chief. Even though the flocks and herds were regarded as the communal property of the tribe concerned, they were in fact controlled by the leaders of the tribe, whose decisions were generally accepted because of their rank and prestige. The strict discipline prevailing within the tribes was also connected with the fact that every Turkish nomad tribe, down to the time of ʿAbbās I and to a lesser degree even later, was at the same time also a military unit and the tribal hierarchy was generally identical with the military hierarchy. We have already mentioned that the nomads met the demand for meat. Besides this, they also produced wool, supplied hides, did a small amount of tanning and made milk products of various kinds. They lived in tents; whereas the Mongolian felt tent (known as yurt) has been used in north-eastern Iran down to the present day, the type called the "black tent" came into general use in the central highlands and in western Iran from the Mongol period onwards. A "black tent" consisted of specially-cut pieces made of spun goat's wool. This was an excellent heat-insulating material, and the tents made of it were probably more mobile than the robust yurt. In Khūzistān the wandering herdsmen and shepherds also made themselves reed huts, which could be quickly erected. The economic aim of the nomad cattle-breeders was a constant enlargement of their stock; it must however be remembered that the annual increase was very much lessened by consumption for their own needs and by substantial surrendering of cattle to the state or the court and above all to the superiors of the tribe and to its leader. Cattle-dealing on a larger scale was carried on only by tribal leaders and their subordinates; these also made the greatest profits. More and more the leaders of tribes settled in the towns, above all in times of peace, and especially when they exercised administrative functions, as for example the Qizilbāsh governors. They thus became somewhat estranged from the way of life of their fellow-tribesmen, but never to such a degree as to risk losing their absolute authority. These were not the only circumstances in which there was a community of interests between the nomad leaders and the traditional landlords. As we shall see later, in the course of the 14th, 15th and 16th centuries, tribal chiefs were often the possessors of large "fiefs" or *beneficia* and thereby combined two social functions.

Hunting and fishing were probably always of limited economic importance. Hunting was practised as a sport by the genteel and rich; apart from this it was also one of the special characteristics of nomad life. Among the settled population, large-scale hunting and fishing were carried on only in the Caspian coastal areas, where game and fish were plentiful; there was also fishing in the waters of the Persian Gulf. For obvious reasons, the exploitation of fish was confined to the regions concerned. In general, the consumption of fish or game (chiefly gazelles, wild goats and game birds) was unusual among the town-dwellers of the interior of the Iranian plateau, except at court and in wealthy households, where such things were regarded as special delicacies. It gave ʿAbbās I particular pleasure to prepare with his own hands game that he had killed and to have it served to his guests and hunting companions.[1]

Finally, a few words about the exploitation of mineral resources. In the 17th century at least, the Crown held sovereign rights over mining, salt-production and pearl-fishing. The yield from these formed an essential source of revenue for the royal treasury. Among the most valuable mining products were the turquoises from the celebrated mines near Nīshāpūr. The exploitation of these mines was from time to time prohibited by the shah. Large quantities of copper were extracted in Khurāsān and above all in Kirmān, while the gold and silver mines of Iran were already so exhausted in the 11th/17th century that it was no longer possible to work them. Lead came mainly from Yazd and Kirmān; iron was extracted in Khurāsān. Lastly, sulphur, mercury and antimony were also mined.[2] The demand for salt was satisfied by the rich rock-salt deposits of Iran; there were also of course extensive salt-works in the Persian Gulf area, where sea-salt was obtained by evaporation. Travellers made particular mention of such salt-works, especially in Hurmuz.[3] We must also remember the mineral oil deposits in the Bākū and Khūzistān (Shushtar) area. Sometimes the exploitation of "oil-wells" (*chāh-i naft*) was incumbent upon local landlords; these wells were of course only gushers.[4]

We must also mention the dangers that threatened the existence of large parts of the population in every age – namely, natural disasters of various kinds. The most serious of these were crop failures and the ensuing famines: they were caused by lack of precipitation during the winter months, and they weighed most heavily on the rural population. The consequences of a period of drought affected not only the

[1] Falsafī, *Zindagānī* IV, 25.
[2] Kaempfer, p. 94.
[3] *Ibid. L'ouvrage de Seyfī Çelebī, historien ottoman du XVIe siècle*, ed. and trans. J. Matuz (Paris, 1968), pp. 142–3.
[4] Kaempfer, p. 94. Petrushevsky, "K istorii instituta 'soyurgala'", pp. 242ff.

settled peasants but also nomad herdsmen and cattle-breeders; it often took five years or more to re-establish a herd that had been decimated by drought and lack of pasture.

In the borderlands of the Great Desert the daily battle for water was coupled with fighting off the wind-borne sand that had for thousands of years been endeavouring to bury the settlements lying there. Walls had to be built to protect fields and gardens, and the advancing desert continually threatened to dry up the essential wells and destroy the irrigation systems.

Iran is one of the most restless tectonic zones on earth; in consequence of this, disastrous earthquakes occurred repeatedly. Those who suffered most from them were villagers living in frail mud huts, but hardly anyone escaped unhurt in an affected area.

Diseases and epidemics, often intensified by lack of water and absence of hygiene, also endangered many lives. The towns were especially prone to epidemics because of the crowded living conditions in high-concentration centres: the plague epidemic at Herat in the year 838/1435 as described by ʿAbd al-Razzāq Samarqandī is an instance of this. In such cases, the sparsely populated flat country proved to be a *cordon sanitaire* by which the epidemic could be prevented from spreading to other towns. In the rural areas, however, diseases like cholera, typhoid fever, dysentery and malaria were endemic, especially in Gīlān, Khūzistān and the coastal areas by the Persian Gulf; they were dreaded – not without cause – by European travellers, and in every age they were a danger to the rural population.

THE VARIOUS FORMS AND INSTITUTIONS OF LANDHOLDING

It is hardly possible to give a simple definition of all the forms of landholding which existed in the period under discussion. At one end of the scale there was private ownership; at the other there were beneficia, privileges and tax-farming ; while in between came grants somewhat reminiscent of the European "fief" and for which that term will be employed in this chapter, although it should be noted that they did not correspond to it at all points.

The institutions already existing in the Mongol period underwent various changes between the 14th and the 18th century. Furthermore in the course of time a number of new concepts and institutions arose, which in practice again changed rapidly and probably assumed different forms in different areas of Iran. Clarification of the problem of landholding is also complicated by the fact that the legal concepts of landlordship do not always give a true picture of the actual situation. In the following exposition we will try, as far as possible, to explain the various institutions on the basis of their legal definitions and to describe how they worked in practice, how they developed and changed in the course of time, and how new types of landlordship emerged.

In principle, the following categories of land were recognised from the ʿAbbasids onwards: (i) *dīvānī* land (state land), (ii) *mulk* land (private estates), (iii) *vaqf* land (charitable or religious endowment land), and (iv) *khāṣṣa* land (crown land).[1] However, this ideal scheme cannot be applied to our period without closer scrutiny. Within the category of "state land" in particular there was a bewildering mass of institutions by which the state's title to land was, to a greater or lesser degree, transferred to individuals. Let us first clarify the concept. All areas whose tax revenues were at the disposal of the state were regarded as dīvānī land. Part of this income was used to finance the civil service and the military; especially from the Mongol period onwards the authorities no longer restricted themselves to collecting the traditional *kharāj* (land tax), but levied a number of special taxes. These did not conform with the religious law, but were generally legitimised in the Il-Khanid period by the Yāsa, the code of Chingiz Khān. Their numbers, and the amounts required, varied at different times and in different places.[2] It was the normal practice for the tax officials (*ʿummāl*) of the time to collect the prescribed taxes on the spot. For centuries, however, this procedure had already been breached by the granting of fiscal privileges and beneficia. The most widespread forms of beneficium – already under the Buyids and particularly from the Saljūq period onwards – consisted of the various types of *iqṭāʿ*.[3] This institution was based on the procedure that high officials or military leaders were not paid in cash, but each received the tax revenue of a certain territory instead. In other words, the iqṭāʿ consisted above all in the state's yielding the right of tax collection to individual persons. In those cases where this procedure represented a substitute for salary,

[1] Cf. Petrushevsky, in *CHI* v, 515.

[2] Hinz, "Das Steuerwesen Ostanatoliens", especially p. 191. Minorsky, "The Aq-qoyunlu and Land Reforms". Minorsky and Minovi, "Naṣīr al-Dīn Ṭūsī on finance".

[3] Becker, "Steuerpacht", pp. 89 ff. Cahen, "L'évolution de l'iqtaʿ". Lambton, *Landlord and Peasant*, pp. 53ff. Petrushevsky, *Kishāvarzī* II, 45–65.

this right was attached to the performance of certain administrative or military duties within the framework of the state. It was therefore neither transferable nor hereditary on the part of the holder of the beneficium. This stipulation, however, remained legal theory, especially with regard to the military iqṭāʿ. The army of the Great Saljūq state was based on nomadic Turkish tribal formations, and every tribal unit was at the same time also a military unit. Just as the leader's rank was hereditary within the hierarchy of the tribe, so also his state function (as a military leader) passed to his heir, and thus the iqṭāʿ in question became *de facto* the basis of subsistence for several generations of tribal leaders. Niẓām al-Mulk had still required that the *iqṭāʿ-dār* (also *muqṭaʿ*, holder of an iqṭāʿ) should have no direct contact with the peasants of his iqṭāʿ and should confine himself exclusively to collecting the dues. However, towards the end of the 6th/12th century the iqṭāʿ-dārs regarded their beneficia as hereditary property. If one considers that the iqṭāʿ-dār's family had already held the beneficium for some generations and the iqṭāʿ-dār himself had military forces under his control, one can easily understand that he was interested in something more than the tax yield of the territory assigned to him. To an increasing extent he appropriated to himself sovereign rights over the territory, and at the beginning of the 8th/14th century the term iqṭāʿ signified not only the ceding of the beneficium but also the actual land concerned. The central power – insofar as one existed – and the legal institutions connected with it did not always recognise this state of affairs. They held fast to the principle that the iqṭāʿ was a beneficium attached to a person and his function. This proceeding was justified, insofar as the spreading and development of the military iqṭāʿ system in the time of the Great Saljūqs had undoubtedly played a large part in bringing about the collapse of their state. Moreover, there was probably little inclination to reconcile the legal recognition of the hereditary character of the iqṭāʿ, and the sovereign rights exercised by the iqṭāʿ-dār, with the principle of religious law that the Caliph or the ruler was the owner of all land.

Further development of the iqṭāʿ was stimulated in the Mongol period. Under the Īl-Khāns the military-nomadic element had gained the upper hand in every sphere of life. After the administrative and economic reforms under Ghazan Khān and his vizier Rashīd al-Dīn there existed a form of iqṭāʿ that no longer had anything much in common with the original fiscal beneficium: the iqṭāʿ-dār was the head of a military unit organised on a tribal basis, the commander of a force of anything from a thousand to ten thousand men. His iqṭāʿ was hereditary and his powers were so extensive that he was able to re-grant sections of his iqṭāʿ, as subinfeudations, so to speak, to subordinate commanders (tribal sub-leaders). The holders of the various subinfeudations were inspected annually, however, by state officials to make sure that they fulfilled all the duties arising from their grants, especially with regard to military service. Any such holder who was found unworthy was deprived of the right to his beneficium. This was a highly developed form of the authority of amīrs – military commanders, as can be deduced from the foregoing, and mainly of Turco-Mongolian origin – over what were often very extensive areas of cultivated land, including the settled population living on and dependent on this land for their livelihood. The break-up of the Il-Khanid state and the consequent weakening of all the elements of the central administration increased the independence of the amīrs in all parts of the country. From this form of a large-scale military iqṭāʿ in the Mongol period, as we have just described it, a new institution developed under the Jalayirids around the middle of the 8th/14th century which gave its beneficiaries the greatest power over cultivated land and its people that a landlord could achieve in the following centuries of Iranian history. This was the *suyūrghāl*, which we shall discuss later.

The development of the iqṭāʿ during the Saljūq and Mongol periods had of course not led to the disappearance of the iqṭāʿ in its original sense by the middle of the 8th/14th century or later. It had been customary, under the rule of all the dynasties with which we are concerned, to pay officials or clergy by granting them the tax revenue of certain places or districts, and by the Safavid period a whole series of modifications of this procedure had developed. These various forms differ from one another chiefly because of the fact that often only parts of the tax revenue were granted – shares of total amounts, or merely the yield of certain tax sources – or else because the areas on which the calculations were based might be of widely differing extent. Moreover, the grant might be subject to certain conditions.

The following methods of procedure are in part known from the Jalayirid period. Firstly, the *idrār*; an idrār grant gave the beneficiary the right to claim a fixed share of the kharāj revenues from a defined area. His title to this fixed sum was generally hereditary and was conferred, at least nominally, by the ruler. This procedure was basically the same as an earlier institution called *iqṭāʿ-i ijāra*.[1] It should be said incidentally that an idrār might consist not only of shares of agricultural taxes but also of shares of taxes on commerce and property (*tamghā*). A non-hereditary form of idrār was also known, namely the *idrār-i maʿīsha*, which was only valid for the beneficiary's lifetime. In both cases the idrār could be converted into a *muqāṣṣa* by decree of the ruler.

A muqāṣṣa differed from an idrār in that it granted not shares of taxes but regular shares of property; like the idrār, it was either for life only (*muqāṣṣa-yi maʿīsha*) or devisable. The hereditary nature of a grant was usually expressed by the term *abadī* ("eternal","perpetual") and sometimes by *sarmadī* ("eternal"), or else by a combination of the two words, *abadī va sarmadī*. For a hereditary muqāṣṣa there was also the formulation *muqāṣṣa-yi idrār*. In many respects the muqāṣṣa corresponded to the *iqṭāʿ-i tamlīk* of earlier periods.[2] With the establishment of a muqāṣṣa the land in question was removed from the authority of the dīvān, and in the case of an "eternal" muqāṣṣa there was little likelihood that the granted land would ever again be available for the profit of the dīvān. The holder of the muqāṣṣa also enjoyed some degree of administrative immunity; in a muqāṣṣa decree there appears the set formula which was still in use in the following centuries, *qalam va qadam kutāh va kashīda dārand* ("secured against the pen, protected against access", or *sine introitu iudicum*); this formula indicated the transfer of administrative rights from the official mentioned in the deed to the holder of the grant.[3] It is, however, possible that in this particular case the formula refers only to tax officials. The advantages of the muqāṣṣa over the simple idrār were above all that the holder of the muqāṣṣa not only had taxation rights but also received the landlord's shares of the crops due to him as part owner or exclusive owner. In any case, the rights accruing to the landlord from a muqāṣṣa-yi idrār were entirely similar to those attached to a large military iqṭāʿ. The decisive criterion was probably the size of the area in question. In terms of form, these two procedures had created the basis for the development of the suyūrghāl.[4] Idrār and muqāṣṣa – even when they were only *maʿīsha* ("for life") – carried too many advantages to the holder for them to be used exclusively for the purpose of paying salaries. It can

[1] Løkkegaard, p. 19.
[2] Cf. Lambton, *Landlord and Peasant*, pp. 28ff.
[3] Cf. Petrushevsky, *Kishāvarzī* II, 70, quoting Nakhchivānī, *Dastūr al-kātib*.
[4] *Ibid.*, pp. 66–72.

therefore be assumed that the recipients of idrār and muqāṣṣa could claim meritorious services as grounds for this distinction; they were probably deserving officials, the ruler's favourites, and religious dignitaries. These last were, in the 9th/15th century and also in the Safavid period, largely holders of smaller and medium-sized suyūrghāls, with which the muqāṣṣa had a good deal in common. On the other hand, the idrār was continued in later times in the form of payment of salaries by means of *barāt* (tax cheques; see below) and in the *mustamarrī*, which was, down to the Qājār period, understood as the payment of a pension to deserving persons. There are also connections between the idrār and the payment of a *vaẓīfa* in certain cases that are known from the later Safavid period. A vaẓīfa was understood as the payment of an annuity or the grant of certain rights of landholding to members of the religious class; normally *vaqf* land formed the basis of a vaẓīfa, and we shall return to this subject when discussing vaqf land. Vaẓīfa annuities could also be paid out of tax revenues from dīvānī land, and in this case we are strongly reminded of the idrār. The assignment of a vaẓīfa had, however, to be renewed every year.[1] The same condition existed in the case of a *yak-sāla* (in full, *barāt-i yak-sāla,* i.e. one-year tax cheque).[2] As this method of effecting payment out of tax revenues from certain areas – a method known from the Safavid period – was applied exclusively to salaries, we shall deal with it later on.

We see then that various forms of "feudal" rule were exercised not only by amīrs, local princes and provincial governors, who belonged to the *arbāb-i saif* ("men of the sword"), but also by civilian landlords, who belonged to the *arbāb-i qalam* ("men of the pen", officials) or to the *arbāb-i 'amā'im* ("men of the turbans", i.e. *'ulamā, shaikhs, sayyids,* teachers). But the most perfect forms of such "feudal" rule are encountered in the 9th/15th and as late as the 10th/16th century within the framework of the institution we have repeatedly mentioned here, the suyūrghāl. Before pursuing the history of this institution from the later 14th century to the early 18th century we will try to demonstrate some of its main characteristics.

The Mongol word *soyurghal* originally meant nothing more than "act of favour" (from the ruler), "grant", or "donation". The expres-

[1] Cf. Busse, *Untersuchungen*, pp. 112ff.; on a vaẓīfa from state funds, see *ibid.*, document no. 13.
[2] Chardin v, 420. Minorsky, *Tadhkirat al-Mulūk*, pp. 29, 153.

sion *suyūrghāmīshī* already had this general significance under the Īl-Khāns. The first known occurrence of the word as the designation of a certain kind of "fief" is in the Jalayirid period.[1] The holder of a suyūrghāl (*ṣāḥib-suyūrghāl*) enjoyed a number of rights over the estate in question. Above all – and this had already been characteristic of the iqṭā' – he was entitled to the tax yield of his area and in addition exercised rights of ownership over the tract of land in question (which was also called suyūrghāl). Furthermore, the suyūrghāl carried with it exemption from taxes; this point was always mentioned separately in the deeds conferring suyūrghāls. Thus a superficial inspection of the documents might give the impression that the privilege of tax-exemption (*mu'āfī, musallamī*) was a separate element from the suyūrghāl. This is not quite correct; every suyūrghāl grant shows at the same time the granting of immunity from taxes, and in many cases it is also stated that even in the event of an increase in the tax yield, e.g. of the kharāj by virtue of rising productivity, or of the poll-tax (*jizya*) when the population of non-Muslims living in the suyūrghāl area had grown, the surplus was to go to the holder of the suyūrghāl.[2] This usage can hardly be explained by saying that the dīvān authority had wanted to recognise the suyūrghāl only as a beneficium, in order to prevent too great a concentration of power in the hands of the landlord. The deed, as drawn up, rather served the landlord as a legal instrument that he could produce in order to defend himself successfully against the local and regional tax officials if they made tax claims on the suyūrghāl land. The same problem arises with the other privileges pertaining to a suyūrghāl "fief", namely those of administrative immunity and hereditary rights. Just as immunity from taxes was very often indicated by a detailed list of all the relevant dues, so also the previously mentioned formula for administrative immunity was in most cases preceded by a list of all the officials who were forbidden to set foot on the territory of the suyūrghāl or to make demands upon it. The formula we have already quoted, *qalam va qadam kutāh va kashīda dārand,* was usually employed for the administrative autonomy of the ṣāḥib-suyūrghāl. Besides this, the following expression might be used: *'ummāl ba-hīch vajh min al-vujūh dar ān madkhal nasāzand* ("the tax officials may not penetrate there under any circumstances"). This is

[1] Petrushevsky, "K istorii instituta 'soyurgala'", p. 228. For the etymology, see *TMEN* I, 351–4 (nos. 228, "soyūrġāl", 229, "soyūrġāmīšī").

[2] Busse, *Untersuchungen*, p. 98. Petrushevsky, "K istorii instituta 'soyurgala'", p. 238.

found in a deed of Rustam Āq Quyūnlū dated 27 Ramaḍān 902/29 May 1497. Otherwise the administrative and associated legal prerogatives were simply listed in full detail, as in suyūrghāl deeds of Jahān Shāh Qarā Quyūnlū dated 3 Rajab 859/19 June 1455 and of Shah Ismā'īl I dated 10 Rajab 915/24 October 1509.[1]

On the demise of the ṣāḥib-suyūrghāl the "fief" passed to his heirs; the Muslim law of inheritance was, however, not necessarily observed. The transfer was always confirmed by the drawing up of a deed, generally on the part of the ruler.[2] But this is not to be taken as implying that the heirs would always have needed the ruler's explicit assent. The rights to the existing suyūrghāl could be simply transferred to the heir or heirs. It was very much in the interests of the new holder of the suyūrghāl to have a deed recording the transfer; he could then use this against anyone who was trying to restrict his suyūrghāl territory or his prerogative. We can deduce from the text of many suyūrghāl deeds, especially from such confirmations, that particular clauses were inserted for specific reasons. The advantages the suyūrghāl brought to its holder were often accompanied by conditions, especially with regard to military service, or at least the obligation to provide a number of well-equipped warriors. But there were also suyūrghāls that were free from any obligations. This was especially the case with religious dignitaries to whom suyūrghāls were granted, a custom practised under the Timurids and also in the Türkmen and Safavid periods.[3] In such cases the suyūrghāl was in the nature of a distinction; moreover, this act on the part of the ruler was often interpreted as payment of the obligatory *zakāt* (alms tax),[4] since it was fundamentally a matter of pious conduct. With such an interpretation, attention could also be called to the fact that a large number of receivers of alms were supported out of the income of a religious suyūrghāl-holder, even though the beneficiaries might in many cases have been merely the working ra'āyā of the suyūrghāl. It was also possible for non-religious personages to receive such suyūrghāls of "distinction", as in the case of the poet Salmān Sāvajī. [5]

With smaller suyūrghāls it could happen that the material basis

[1] For these three documents, see respectively Roemer, "Le dernier firman", p. 286; Aubin, "Un soyurghal Qara-Qoyunlu", p. 161; Martin, "Seven Ṣafavid Documents", p. 180.

[2] 'Abd al-Razzāq, *Maṭla' al-sa'dain*, ed. M. Shafī' (Lahore, 1941–9), p. 682.

[3] E.g. Lambton, "Two Ṣafawid Soyūrghāls"; Khwānd Amīr IV, 431.

[4] Minorsky, "The Aq-qoyunlu and Land Reforms", p. 453. Busse, *Untersuchungen*, pp. 99–101.

[5] Daulatshāh, p. 260.

of the suyūrghāl was not the title to the entire tax yield from the suyūrghāl area, but only a claim to certain tax revenues. These were either defined as a specific sum of money or else limited to specific tax sources. In such cases the prerogative rights of the ṣāḥib-suyūrghāl were of course also reduced.

Suyūrghāl land could thus be of varying extent. There were suyūrghāls on villages, and indeed even on parts of villages; but small or large districts, and even entire provinces, could be granted as suyūrghāl. In the case of large suyūrghāls the prerogative rights and the material basis enjoyed by the holder were so extensive that he could acquire not only economic, but also political power. In any case, the institution of suyūrghāl formed a basis for all the forces in the state that were opposed to centralisation. It is therefore not surprising that we find the largest suyūrghāls, in terms of both territory and absoluteness of prerogative rights, in the 9th/15th century. In loose political confederations like those of the Qarā Quyūnlū and Āq Quyūnlū (and also the Timurids) large territories were granted as suyūrghāl. When new areas came under the sovereignty of the state the former territories of the local rulers were often returned to them as suyūrghāl. As one surveys the conditions and characteristics of the suyūrghāl and compares them with the administrative system of governorships in the 15th century, one comes to the inevitable conclusion that the governorships, in every case where the governor belonged to the military aristocracy or to the ruling house, to some extent represented gigantic suyūrghāls.[1] When, for instance, Uzun Ḥasan Āq Quyūnlū wanted to abolish the tamghā (the municipal trade taxes, which were forbidden by religious law), he had to give up his intention in face of the resistance of the amīrs, i.e. the Türkmen military leaders;[2] obviously most or all of them were entitled to a share of the tax yield not only of villages but also of towns. As the "fiefs" of the tribal military leaders (in fact, these very amīrs) in particular were not restricted to individual settlements but also included living-space for the members of their tribes, this practice is clear evidence for the territorial extension of their suyūrghāls – and it was certainly these that were involved, since the suyūrghāl had to a great extent superseded the other forms of military "fief" during the Türkmen period. It may be assumed that there were several towns in

[1] For such grants from the Timurid period, see Togan, "Büyük Türk hükümdarı Şahruh", p. 523; Yakubovsky, "Timur", sect. 4; Arunova, "K istorii narodnykh vystupleniĭ", p. 35.
[2] Schmidt-Dumont, *Turkmenische Herrscher*, p. 219.

each of their areas, and thus it was worth their while to defend their income from the yield of the tamghā. This example makes it plain that every attempt at building an empire, since it required centralisation of power and administration, had to work against the owners of the great suyūrghāls. A policy of weakening the suyūrghāls was in fact adopted under the Āq Quyūnlū rulers Ya'qūb and Aḥmad, and the Safavids too regarded the restriction of the suyūrghāl system as an important element in their internal policy.

Ya'qūb's vizier, Qāżī Ṣafī al-Dīn 'Īsā of Sāva, in his attempts to restrain the growth of the suyūrghāl system, directed his measures primarily against the holders of small and medium-sized suyūrghāls. It obviously seemed to him too dangerous to embroil himself with the great amīrs, and he therefore picked on those that had no condition of obligatory military service attached to them. Most of these, as we have shown above, belonged to religious dignitaries, and thus Qāżī 'Īsā got himself into a paradoxical situation. On the one hand he was basing his intentions on the argument that the abolition of the suyūrghāls served to assure the supremacy of the Sharī'a over the Yāsa, and on the other hand he was, on this pretext, actually taking drastic steps against the clergy! After this obviously abortive attempt the importance of the suyūrghāl increased steadily, and it is related of Rustam Āq Quyūnlū (898-902/1493-1497) that he granted more suyūrghāls than any prince of the Āq Quyūnlū or the Qarā Quyūnlū had ever done before.[1] His successor Aḥmad Beg Āq Quyūnlū, together with his high officials, renewed the struggle against the suyūrghāl holders, but this time with different methods from those used by Qāżī 'Īsā in his day. He declared the provisions of all the "perpetual" suyūrghāls granted under his predecessors to be invalid. Moreover, he deprived most of the religious holders of their various privileges, especially that of exemption from taxes. It is clear that this action angered the powerful military aristocracy against Aḥmad, and after only seven months as ruler he died in battle against insurgent amīrs (903/1497).

The Safavids did indeed grant suyūrghāls, but their policy in this field was clearly different from that of their predecessors. There were small and medium-sized suyūrghāls throughout the Safavid period, and the beneficiaries were generally arbāb-i 'amā'im, i.e. religious dignitaries. There were also cases where suyūrghāls were granted not to

[1] Petrushevsky, "K istorii instituta 'soyurgala'", p. 231, following the *Lubb al-tavārīkh*.

persons but to pious foundations. The *mutavallī* (administrator) of the foundation in question then had the benefit of such a suyūrghāl, and the whole business was probably a formal artifice to restrict the accumulation of prerogative rights in the hands of a single person.[1] In addition, various tax liabilities were imposed on the suyūrghāl holders; for example, in the late 17th and early 18th century the *ṣadr-i aʿẓam* received a percentage of the income from the suyūrghāls.[2] The progressive depreciation of the currency also played its part in weakening the suyūrghāls, especially those whose yield had from the start been defined as a specific sum of money.

When the Safavids assumed power the days of the great suyūrghāls were over. Recalcitrant great landlords were simply deprived of their latifundia by degree; other measures were also taken, such as the suspension of suyūrghāls in certain provinces (e.g. under ʿAbbās I in Āzarbāījān).[3] In the newly-arisen Safavid state governorships and large territories were granted to Qizilbāsh tribes or their leaders, but this was now done in the form not of suyūrghāl but of non-hereditary *tiyūl* (see below). Naturally – as the course of Safavid history shows – this procedure could not prevent the appearance of centrifugal tendencies; nevertheless the central power was considerably strengthened by avoiding the growth of large suyūrghāls, and its organs consciously directed their policy towards this end.

There is one peculiarity we should mention. In some Safavid deeds of grant vaqf estates are described as the suyūrghāl of their mutavallī. This is probably explained by the fact that in those days the functions exercised by a mutavallī were in practice identical with those of a ṣāḥib-suyūrghāl; they were entitled to tax revenues, enjoyed immunity from taxation, and exercised prerogative rights over their own territory. Moreover, their position was likewise hereditary, and their raʿāyā were bound to the soil. The suyūrghāl-holders belonged mainly to the religious class; according to Chardin none but religious families were beneficiaries of suyūrghāls.[4] The contamination of the two types of landlordship (*tauliyat*, i.e. administration of foundation property, and suyūrghāl) is no longer surprising, since the exercise of power was identical in both cases, even though their legal bases must be distinguished from one another.

[1] Busse, *Untersuchungen*, p. 99.
[2] Minorsky, *Tadhkirat al-Mulūk*, pp. 85ff.
[3] Martin, "Seven Ṣafavid Documents", pp. 203, 205 (document no. 7).
[4] Lambton, *Landlord and Peasant*, p. 115, quoting Chardin VI, 65.

Let us now recapitulate the most important characteristics and peculiarities of the suyūrghāl. It represented a hereditary grant of land with the title to the tax yield (or part of it), immunity from taxation, and prerogative rights which, in the case of large suyūrghāls, extended to administrative and judicial immunity. Further, it can be regarded as characteristic that the large suyūrghāls of the 15th century (Timurids, Qarā Quyūnlū, Āq Quyūnlū) were in the hands of powerful amīrs, mostly of Türkmen origin, and thus formed the basis of their political power. The lords of large suyūrghāls were more or less independent rulers over their own territories; they were, however, obliged to play an active part in the military operations of their sovereign. Restriction of the large suyūrghāls was a precondition for any attempt to centralise the state. The small suyūrghāls – of rather second-rate importance before 1500 even though they were widespread – represented the archetype of the suyūrghāl in the Safavid period. This type of suyūrghāl was less often connected with services to be rendered; it had rather the character of a distinction or honour for special merit. The holders of medium-sized and small suyūrghāls were from the start predominantly ʿulamā; in the late Safavid period there were probably hardly any suyūrghāls granted to persons who did not belong to the religious sphere.

We can see from this summary that the suyūrghāl involved the elaboration and fusion of a number of "feudal" institutions that had grown up by the middle of the 8th/14th century. In the small suyūrghāls, especially those of the Safavid type, we can easily recognise elements of the muqāṣṣa. Various types of the Saljūq iqṭāʿ survived in all the forms of suyūrghāl, and it is evident that the large suyūrghāl was a direct development from the Mongol military iqṭāʿ. The final form of the suyūrghāl was made possible mainly by the weakness of the central power in the successor states to the Il-Khanid empire. There is also the very significant fact that the ties between the legal system of that age and the Sharīʿa were relatively loose owing to the considerable influence of the Yāsa. This makes it much easier to codify the concept of suyūrghāl. The suyūrghāl had arisen in a period of weak central power, and in the 15th century the Timurids, Qarā Quyūnlū and Āq Quyūnlū found it a serious impediment to the development of lasting empires with a strong, centrally oriented monarchy. The large suyūrghāl was also one of the bases for the economic and administrative opposition between the (military-nomadic) Turkish elements in the population and the settled Persian elements.

We still have to ask the question whether the suyūrghāl was granted from state land and, if so, how far one could still speak of "state land" with reference to suyūrghāls. Again we have to distinguish between large and small suyūrghāls. The former undoubtedly represented a change in the character of dīvānī land, to which their territories had once belonged. With the smaller suyūrghāls this was not necessarily the case. They were not granted exclusively from state land, but rather from vaqf land and – above all in the 17th and 18th centuries – from crown land.[1] However, at that time it was possible for the ruler to encroach directly upon the interests of a governor and his officials by making a suyūrghāl grant from dīvānī land.

One of the most important constituents of the suyūrghāl was the privilege of fiscal immunity, which in medieval Europe was known as *exemptio*. This privilege had of course been practised long before the collapse of the Il-Khanid state, and in the period with which we are concerned it was by no means exclusively connected with a suyūrghāl grant. We know of many cases where tax exemptions were granted, and in practice any tax-paying subject could receive one. Here, in connection with the suyūrghāl, we intend to deal only with exemptions in the agricultural sector. The privilege of tax exemption was in principle designated by the terms *mu'āfī* or *musallamī* (pl. *musallamiyyāt*). Fiscal immunity reached back to pre-Mongol times; under the Īl-Khāns it was enriched with the qualities of a similar procedure introduced by Chingiz Khān. The Mongol privilege of immunity not only had the character of a mark of distinction or honour, but was also valid for the clergy of any recognised creed, for nobles, and for children. Some elements of this Mongol institution were still practised in the following centuries. It thus became the custom to grant exemptions to religious personages, and among these not only Muslim but also Christian (especially Armenian) clerics were included. Vaqf land was also subject to exemption. Fiscal immunity for aristocrats (probably mostly nomads) or nobles of the state might include a provision – also of Mongol origin and still in use under the Timurids – that the person in question was, in addition to the mu'āfī, also exempt from criminal prosecution for transgressions of the law, the number of offences that might go unpunished being precisely defined. Down to the 15th century the holder of a hereditary tax exemption for a particular tract of land was

[1] Busse, *Untersuchungen*, pp. 101-2. Lambton, *Landlord and Peasant*, *loc. cit.*

called *tarkhān*; the granting of this type of immunity and also the land concerned were called *tarkhānī*. Originally tarkhān was a term applied to Mongol nobles, but later it was extended to those who, without being themselves members or descendants of the Mongol nomad aristocracy, nevertheless enjoyed their privileges, particularly the hereditary tax exemption of their land. In these circumstances the tarkhānī represented a component that had entered into the institution of the suyūrghāl.[1]

The recipient of a mu'āfī could be a corporate body as well as an individual; as we have mentioned above, the 'ulamā and vaqf estates were exempted from taxes. Large mulk estates (see below) often enjoyed a mu'āfī, and tenant farmers (*musta'jir*), who were liable to pay taxes, could likewise be exempted. Tiyūls were also often combined with a mu'āfī. In the decrees we find, among others, the following formulae for exemption: *mu'āf va musallam dānand* ("to be recognised as exempted from liability to pay taxes"), *mu'āf va musallam va ḥurr va marfū' al-qalam dānand* ("to be recognised as freed from liability to pay taxes, disposing freely [of his territory] and secured from the pen"), *mu'āf va tarkhān va marfū' al-qalam* ("exempt from taxes, [made] tarkhān and secured from the pen") and *mafrūr va mustas̱nā shināsand* ("to be recognised as freed and excepted").

Exemptions could be granted en bloc; it was also possible to be exempted from individual dues, sometimes only up to a specified amount. In all cases more or less exact details were given in the decrees. Every decree dealing with a tax exemption was provided with a "tax list", which indeed often included not only the actual taxes of the time but also older ones that no longer existed; when this list was made up, dues from identical (or similar) sources of tax could be grouped together. This was often done in order to prevent the tax-collectors from using the pretext of formal objections, by which they might possibly have been able to collect the dues: this might be done merely by the insertion of previous deeds and by invoking certain chancery traditions. The issuing of decrees for fiscal immunity and the registration of them was the duty of the financial department of the *dīvān-i mamālik* (state land administration) or the *dīvān-i khāṣṣa* (crown land administration). In both cases the procedure generally resulted in the execution of a deed by the sovereign.

[1] Busse, *Untersuchungen*, pp. 102–3. For exempt Armenian clergy, cf. Papazian, *Persidskie dokumenty* I, nos. 1–6, 8–10, 14, 18.

The tiyūl[1] is an institution that is in many respects similar to the suyūrghāl. In post-Mongol times this term replaced the word iqṭā', and various procedures that had developed in the framework of the iqṭā' up to the early 14th century survived as a rule in the tiyūl. Thus tiyūl is really a later synonym of iqṭā', and the historians of the Safavid period used "iqṭā'" simply as an archaism for "tiyūl".[2] In the 15th century, when the members of the military aristocracy held their great suyūrghāls, the tiyūls were used to pay officials, and thus the tiyūls of officers of high rank may well have been in many respects similar to the medium-sized suyūrghāls of the higher religious dignitaries. For the sake of simplicity, let us set out the various manifestations of the tiyūl in the Safavid period.

The following characteristics apply to all tiyūls:

(i) The tiyūl was in principle subject to a time-limit and therefore not devisable; tiyūls were hardly ever recognised as hereditary.

(ii) The tiyūl was always involved with some service to be rendered, either the performance of an office or the obligation to raise an army or military units: it therefore represented the usual method of payment for this.

(iii) The fundamental constituent of the tiyūl was the grant of the tax yield from a particular area or of a part of that yield.

These are the formal basic elements that had been equally characteristic of the earlier iqṭā'. We must emphasise the word "formal" in this context: the economic, social and political effects of the various forms of tiyūl were in no way dependent on these three elements, but were rather related to the territorial and financial extent of the tiyūl in question and also to the additional rights granted to the tiyūl holder (*tiyūldār*) or claimed by him. The large tiyūls of the Safavid period were either "fiefs" of high officials or military "fiefs". As we have already said, under the Safavids the members of the military aristocracy were now granted their extensive territories as tiyūl and no longer as suyūrghāl. This was the case with governors (*ḥākim*, pl. *ḥukkām*), with Qizilbāsh nobles who occupied official posts, and with other military dignitaries, who were above all expected to raise troops. It is beyond doubt that the reason for avoiding suyūrghāl grants in such cases was

[1] *TMEN* II, 667 ff. (no. 1014).

[2] Lambton, *Landlord and Peasant*, pp. 102, 109ff. Minorsky, *Taḏhkirat al-Mulūk*, pp. 28ff. Kaempfer, p. 96.

the intention to restrict, at least formally, the autonomy of the high amīrs in the provinces. The fact that henceforward military functionaries (like the officials) were paid by tiyūl may also reflect the Safavids' endeavour to assimilate the predominantly Turkish military aristocracy to the higher bureaucracy, which was mostly of Persian origin. The exercise of rights of lordship by the great tiyūldārs was not noticeably different from the practice of the great ṣāḥib-suyūrghāls of the pre-Safavid era. This type of tiyūldār had absolute power over the land and its inhabitants, treated the peasants as he pleased and was assured of the non-intervention of the officials. In the time of Chardin, who travelled to Iran three times between 1655 and 1677, there were a number of tiyūls that had *de facto* become hereditary, so that the distinction between tiyūl and the earlier suyūrghāl was becoming blurred. Chardin also reported that the inhabitants of tiyūls that were in practice hereditary enjoyed better treatment than those of non-hereditary "fiefs".[1] This is easily understandable: the tiyūldār with a time limit was obviously very much interested in extracting the highest possible profits from his "fief". For the holders of intermediate and higher offices there were tiyūls attached to the office, so that on a new appointment to a post there was also a new grant of the tiyūl. This arrangement corresponded largely to the Ottoman *khāṣṣ*. Chardin's observation held good, and to an even higher degree, for the peasants of such "fiefs". However, it often happened that "special" salary contracts were concluded with new office-holders, which meant that they were granted additional tiyūls (probably only for life). In any case it held good for all these tiyūldārs that the competence of the organs of the state land administration extended to them only to a limited degree. The payment of ordinary officials and holders of minor military rank was likewise effected by procedures similar to tiyūls, but special forms had developed for this sector. An essential criterion for the significance of the small tiyūl with regard to landholding was whether the salary of the person concerned was assigned as global tiyūl for a village or at least part of a village, or whether this tiyūl was restricted to a specified (larger or smaller) sum of money – often with indication of the tax source. In the former case it could be assumed that the tiyūl holder had certain rights of exploitation over the ra'āyā. If, however, the tiyūl consisted only of relatively small individual sums, then the recipient of

[1] Chardin v, 418–20.

the salary was hardly in a position to influence production within the area of his "fief". In this context it is also an important question whether the tiyūldār had the tax yield (i.e. the income from his "fief") collected by persons subordinate to him, or whether this was effected by tax officials. (With governorships both definitions applied: the officials were subordinates of the ḥākim.) The answer to this question tells us a great deal about the degree of power that the tiyūldārs possessed in their territories. It is evident that those paid by way of partial tiyūls stood lowest in the hierarchy of the tiyūldārs. For them there were two main methods of payment: either a specified sum of money was awarded from a particular source and they could claim it every year, or the salary was reassigned annually on production of a certificate of employment. In both cases – and this also held good for somewhat more lucrative tiyūl grants – the central financial administration issued a tax-cheque (barāt) for the stipulated sum, to be collected from the relevant tax district; the recipient had to cash this cheque on the spot, and for this reason the category of barāt recipients was often contrasted with the possessors of (large) tiyūls. In the former case, this assignment of tax money (*ḥavāla*) was effected automatically, so long as there was no decree ordering a different procedure; a standing assignment of this kind was called *hama-sāla*. Most of the barāts were probably issued through the hama-sāla procedure. There was also a rather less common procedure called yak-sāla, which we mentioned earlier on in our discussion of the idrār: in this case the assignment was renewed every year.[1] Salaries assigned by barāt were called *mavājib* (i.e. dues, income). These mavājib were in practice usually a little less than the nominal value of the barāt. The salary of a subordinate recipient was often issued in the form of several small assignments of different types, with the further complication that the localities assigned for payment were often so far away from the recipient that he could not possibly make the journey because of the expense and waste of time. This led to the development of a special source of profit. Persons well provided with capital bought up the issued tax-cheques for less than their nominal

[1] From Minorsky, *Tadhkirat al-Mulūk*, p. 29, it is evident that payment of tiyūls was effected through the barāt system and that hama-sāla and yak-sāla were special cases of barāt. Consequently the concept of tiyūl applied to governors, officials of high or low rank and all subordinates in receipt of salaries, in so far as their salaries were in the form of assignments. It is therefore not altogether correct, in our view, to regard tiyūl, barāt and hama-sāla as procedures that differed basically from one another. Cf. Kaempfer, p. 96; Schuster-Walser, *Das ṣafawidische Persien*, p. 38.

value and then, either personally or through representatives, collected the full amounts on the spot. This procedure was employed especially with soldiers.[1] The Qizilbāsh warriors of the 10th/16th century still largely participated in the "fiefs" of their tribe (or in fact those of the tribal leader), in much the same way as with the military iqṭā' of the Mongols. Later they were more and more paid individually, naturally by way of assignments. The *ghulāmān* – the royal special troops since the time of 'Abbās I – were, however, paid in cash.[2]

We see that certain types of landholding survived in the Safavid tiyūl. Thus elements of the idrār and the muqāṣṣa can easily be recognised in the general salary system; the large tiyūls continued the tradition of the large suyūrghāls of the 9th/15th century, though they also showed some features of the Mongol tribal "fief". The replacement of suyūrghāl domination of the pre-Safavid type by tiyūl "fiefs" did not, in the long run, bring about any large-scale weakening of the great land-holders. The attempt to strengthen the powers of the central authority by the expansion of crown land was probably more successful; we shall say more about this later.

Different kinds of grants of tax revenue were subsumed, by formal criteria, into the concept of tiyūl. This led in the end to a confusion of concepts. Tiyūl, on the one hand, was used to convey the idea of grants in general, but also had the special sense of major "fiefs" which might have unmistakable suyūrghāl character. On the other hand, the term suyūrghāl had become rarer in the later Safavid period; it was used mainly for hereditary beneficia of distinguished and generally religious families. Clearly there was at no time any effort to define and codify, and eventually there was a certain confusion of the two ideas.

In conclusion we should mention that the holders of tiyūls in the later Safavid period had to pay dues for their "fiefs". The smallest amounts were paid for tiyūls connected with military service; with these the total dues came to about $3\frac{1}{2}\%$. More than 10% was collected for a hama-sāla, and more than 16% for a major tiyūl. Holders of suyūrghāls had to pay nearly a quarter of the revenue.[3]

The next category to be discussed is that of the mulk (pl. *amlāk*)

[1] Schuster-Walser, *Das ṣafawidische Persien*, p. 34, quoting Kaempfer, p. 75.
[2] Schuster-Walser, *ibid.*, pp. 30ff., following mainly Della Valle and Thévenot.
[3] Lambton, *Landlord and Peasant*, pp. 124–6, quoting *Taḏkirat al-Mulūk*, pp. 85–93.

estates. Mulk was understood as unconditional possession of land. The owner (*mālik*) could do what he liked with his land and was free to sell it or transfer it to other persons; it was devisable, mostly in accordance with the relevant Islamic rules, and there were no services of any kind attached to the possession of it. At the same time the concept of mulk included the ownership of irrigation works on the land in question and the water itself. There were precise legal regulations governing the conditions on which land could become mulk, but the practice of earlier centuries had already deviated from the rules. The essential characteristic of mulk land was that the features mentioned above (devisability, vendibility) were attached to the land itself, so long as no action had been taken to divest it of its mulk character. This also applied when there were various privileges connected with the mulk. An ordinary mulk was of course liable to tax: the normal dīvān taxes for mulk land were one-tenth of the revenue. On the other hand, an estate of the *mulk-i ḥurr* class gave its owner, to some extent automatically, the advantage of exemption from taxes. The tax officials carried mulk land of this type in their books as *isqāṭ* (approximately "dropped out", i.e. from tax liability). Land of the mulk-i ḥurr type could therefore be sold for a considerably higher price than normal mulk land of equivalent value. It might of course also happen that the owner himself, the mālik, was granted an exemption (mu'āfī) from taxes. However, in this case it was a matter of a strictly personal exemption which, understandably, could not be transferred by sale to other persons together with mulk land, even when the mu'āfī was hereditary.

We can distinguish two different types of mulk land. On large mulk estates the soil was cultivated by the local ra'āyā, and the relations between mālik and peasantry had a rather patriarchal character. Here the mālik was the beneficiary of his share in the yield. There was also, however, small-scale mulk land cultivated by the mālik himself, though this form of mulk was very much on the decline. Conquests and frequent changes of sovereign were a danger to the continued existence of mulk land, as it was always doubtful whether the mulk character of any piece of land would still be recognised under the new ruler. As we have already said, large amlāk were often converted into suyūrghāls. This made no difference to the actual circumstances within the land concerned; it did, however, mean the legal cancellation of its mulk status. Evidently the small mālik, in such situations, was particularly at the mercy of influential and powerful personages. It is therefore hardly possible to prove the existence of small amlāk in the Timurid period or later. In the Il-Khanid period very large amlāk came into being through sales and purchases. After the collapse of this dynasty the number of large amlāk increased rapidly, as many persons with the power to do so possessed themselves of Il-Khanid crown estates and ultimately incorporated them into their own property. At that time it was still possible to acquire large mulk property by purchase, as is shown by the increase in the amount of land owned by the early Safavids in the environs of Ardabīl (e.g. under Shaikh Ṣadr al-Dīn).[1] Subsequently the number of amlāk decreased. After the Safavids had taken over, many amlāk were confiscated in the course of efforts to ensure a concentration of power. A further decline of the amlāk was occasioned by the creation of crown land (khāṣṣa) under ʿAbbās I and probably even later; the shah forced the mulk owners to sell him their land at a low price, which almost amounted to confiscation.[2]

One special form of landholding was in many respects comparable with the mulk; this was the *khāliṣa*, an institution of Il-Khanid origin. It was understood in the 8th/14th century to be devastated and uncultivated (thus usually unirrigated) territory, forming part of either state land or crown land, which was given the advantages of a mulk (tithe, vendibility, etc.) for a limited period; in these circumstances the person who undertook the task of irrigating and cultivating the land was declared to be its landlord. Such a person was called *tānī* (pl. *tunnā'*, "resident").[3] This measure to repair the ravages inflicted on agriculture by the Mongol conquest was obviously a thoroughly practical one. There may still have been khāliṣa land in this sense under the Timurids. Later, however, this expression denoted a particular type of crown land (see below). We may perhaps see in this a hint of the future fate of land affected by this institution.

We hardly need to explain here the fundamental principles of the pious foundations (*vaqf*, pl. *auqāf*). We will merely remind the reader of a few important points. Anyone who possessed profitable movable

[1] Petrushevsky, *Kishāvarzī* II, 79, quoting *Manāqib-i Shaikh Ṣafī al-Dīn Ardabīlī*.

[2] Falsafī, *Zindagānī* III, 270ff. For the decline of the "arbābī" (i.e. mulk) estates, cf. Du Mans, p. 226; for confiscation, cf. also Kaempfer, p. 95.

[3] Petrushevsky, *Kishāvarzī* II, 25, and in *CHI* v, 526. Obviously the arrangements for khāliṣa estates differed from one part of the country to another.

or immovable property could, by fulfilling certain conditions, donate this for charitable or religious purposes. Suitable recipients for donations were mosques, the graves of holy men, *khānqāhs* (hospices for dervishes), institutions of general importance such as schools, caravansarais, bridges and wells, and also groups of persons, for example the donor's family or his descendants. In the latter case, the usual description was *vaqf-i ahlī*. Even fictitious persons could be made the recipients of a donation: 'Abbās I in 1015/1606–7 converted his private property into vaqf for the "Fourteen Immaculate Ones" (Muḥammad, Fāṭima and the Twelve Imāms). We shall return to this subject in a different context. In Persia there were also many auqāf for Christian (generally Armenian) institutions, especially under the later Safavids.[1] Here we shall deal mainly with donations of estates.

The donor appointed an administrator (mutavallī) for his vaqf. This office was normally hereditary and an annual stipend was assigned to its holder from the endowment. In general, foundations enjoyed a mu'āfī (exemption) from ordinary and special taxes. In the 8th/14th century the auqāf were controlled by the Islamic judges (*qāḍī*, pl. *quḍāt*) of the regions in question; for technical reasons special authorities were ultimately set up to deal with them. In the Safavid state – and even earlier – the control and administration of the auqāf, besides the safeguarding of the interests of Islamic law, were among the main duties of the *ṣadr*, who was head of the *dīvān al-ṣadāra* and to whom provincial ṣadrs were subordinated. The competent authority for the financial administration of the auqāf was the *mustaufī-yi mauqūfāt* (financial controller of foundations), who was head of an office for endowment affairs (*daftar-i mauqūfāt*). Chardin described this mustaufī as a "lieutenant des ṣadr".[2] Ṣadr authorities and mutavallīs ensured the fulfilment of the various purposes of the foundations; in addition they were themselves beneficiaries of the production from vaqf land and controlled the use of it. This does not mean that the mutavallī himself might have been a member of the ṣadr authorities: the situation was rather that the mutavallī exercised his hereditary office like a

[1] See, e.g., Papazian, *Persidskie Dokumenty* I, nos. 2, 4 (both pre-Safavid), 10, 11, 12, 15, 19; II, nos. 4, 14, 25, 26, 38. There are also Christian auqāf in the Lebanon.

[2] Minorsky, *Tadhkirat al-Mulūk*, p. 146. Chardin VI, 61. Lambton, *Landlord and Peasant*, p. 120. Petrushevsky, *Kishāvarzī* II, 29, states that the *ṣadr al-ṣudūr* was already the head of the *dīvān-i mauqūfāt* in the Il-Khanid period. According to Roemer, *Staatsschreiben*, pp. 143–5, however, there is no evidence for the office of ṣadr until the 15th century, and at the end of the Il-Khanid period endowment affairs were the responsibility of the *ḥākim-i auqāf-i mamālik-i maḥrūsa*.

landlord. Dismissal of a mutavallī was usually not within the powers of the representatives of the ṣadr authorities and the judges subordinated to them. The dīvān al-ṣadāra and especially the daftar-i mauqūfāt were merely the competent authorities for the affairs of the mutavallī and his vaqf property. The extent of the autonomy of the landlord in the later Safavid period is clearly illustrated by the fact (already mentioned in our discussion of the suyūrghāl) that in some deeds of grant the vaqf estates of a mutavallī are spoken of as his suyūrghāl. Obviously the mutavallī's exercise of power over the land entrusted to him differed only very little from that of a ṣāḥib-suyūrghāl. We must, however, bear in mind that at this time even the ṣāḥib-suyūrghāl was a religious dignitary.

Vaqf land could not be converted into another category of land and could, therefore, not be sold. In theory it could also not be confiscated, but in reality this was not always the case. Many auqāf had in fact been confiscated in the Mongol period, and even in later times, under the Safavids, it often happened that foundation land was removed from the competence of the dīvān al-ṣadāra. Nevertheless the landowner could largely keep himself out of the reach of the organs of the state and the ruler by converting his estates into auqāf and appointing himself (and his descendants) as mutavallī.

It was probably the theoretical impossibility of selling vaqf estates that caused the development of a special form of land tenancy; vaqf property was assigned to tenants (musta'jir) for a period of 99 years, in most cases probably in return for a lump sum. When this period had elapsed these tenants had to pay a sum equal to one year's tax yield of the area in question, whereupon the land was assigned to them for another 99 years. In some cases, however, a relatively small sum was collected annually as rent; the actual amount was determined by the size of the rented land.

The office of mutavallī appears, at any rate in some cases, to have been very profitable, especially with foundations for the great Shīʿī holy places in Iran. ʿAbbās II tried to counteract the concentration of administration of large vaqf estates in the hands of a few people by once again dividing up the estates among the mutavallīs.[1] It hardly made any difference to the raʿāyā whether they lived on a "fief" from dīvānī land or on vaqf land. In some places there may have been some

[1] Busse, *Untersuchungen*, p. 116, quoting Chardin vi, 63.

arrangements by which the mutavallī's or the musta'jir's share in the harvest was fixed as a lump sum. In consequence of the continual devaluation of the currency, however, it was in the landlord's interests to secure a definite percentage share of the harvest. Ultimately this way of determining the share was in general use, as we see in a farmān dated Rabīʿ II 1073/November–December 1662.[1]

One particular institution dates back to the time of Ṭahmāsp I, namely the foundations for the "Fourteen Immaculate Ones" (see above); the reigning sovereign of the time was appointed as their mutavallī. The best known of these foundations is the one which, as we have already mentioned, arose from the conversion of the private estates of 'Abbās I (1015/1606–7). Such foundation property from crown land, with the sovereign himself as mutavallī, was called *auqāf-i tafvīzī* (*tafvīz*, "mandate", "authorisation"). Simultaneously with this extensive increase in crown foundations the office of ṣadr was divided: a ṣadr-i khāṣṣa (ṣadr for crown foundations) was set up side by side with a *ṣadr-i 'āmma* (ṣadr for general foundations). However, the situation was not exactly that the competence of the ṣadr-i khāṣṣa was confined to regions in which there were foundations created by the sovereign from crown land; he was also competent for some other (defined) territories, and the ṣadr-i 'āmma was also often concerned with crown foundations. At certain times the two ṣadr offices were united in a single person.[2]

To sum up: it appears that in the sphere of the foundation system there was also a marked tendency to develop a fairly uniform type of landholding, of a kind that we have already seen in the tiyūl and the suyūrghāl. The growth of the crown foundations and the creation of the office of ṣadr-i khāṣṣa may be an indication that the Safavid central power was adjusting its policy, even with regard to the foundation system, so as to restrict the influence of these landlords.

Finally we have to consider the category of crown lands. The existence of estates of which the income was directly at the disposal of the court and especially the sovereign was not in itself anything new. As far back as the Il-Khanid period extensive areas, including whole towns, had been converted into crown property, and for these the

[1] Printed in Lambton, *Landlord and Peasant*, pp. 113–14, with commentary.

[2] *Tadhkirat al-Mulūk*, p. 42 (and Minorsky's comments at p. 111). The division of the office of ṣadr is mentioned by Kaempfer, p. 98.

Mongol term *injü* or the Arabo-Persian *(amlāk-i) khāṣṣa* was used.

After the collapse of the Il-Khanid empire there was a marked decrease in the extent of khāṣṣa land. The weakening of the central power in all regions of the former empire led to the conversion of large parts of earlier crown land into dīvānī or mulk land. It is clear, however, that even the post-Mongol dynasties had control of areas whose tax revenues were at the disposal of the sovereign and his nearest relatives and also the court.

We cannot take the formal distinction between crown land and state land to imply any opposition between the court and the state administration. In the 9th/15th and 10th/16th centuries crown estates were characterised by the fact that (at least in theory) sovereignty over them was not assigned to influential personages in the form of suyūrghāls or large tiyūls, as was the case with dīvānī land. They therefore not only served to finance the sovereign's personal expenditure but also formed a counterpoise against those tendencies towards feudal splintering of the land that we have seen with other categories of land. From this it is apparent that the strengthening of the monarchy and the central power under the Safavids was accompanied by growth in the size and importance of crown estates. Strictly speaking, even before 'Abbās I the crown estates were not free from "fiefs" of various kinds. However, the holders of these "fiefs" were very close relatives of the sovereign, and this was in complete accordance with the traditional character of the crown estates. These had become very substantial in the 10th/16th century; they included a number of more or less centrally situated provinces and formed a contrast to the governorships that had been bestowed as tiyūl, for example on the Qizilbāsh leaders. Such provinces which were entirely crown property were called khāṣṣa. Smaller crown estates, situated within other governorships, at that time generally bore the name of *khāliṣāt* (literally "free", i.e. from interference by the governor); these crown estates must not be confused with the 8th/14th century institutions that were also called khāliṣāt (see above).

The sweeping internal reforms of 'Abbās I (centralisation, repression of the Qizilbāsh, establishment of the *ghulāmān-i khāṣṣ*) and the increasing requirements of the court were among the causes of accelerating growth of crown estates under this ruler. This extension occurred in various ways. For example, a complaint from the inhabitants of a village near Naṭanz about the arbitrary attitude of the tax officials served the shah as a pretext for incorporating the whole district of Naṭanz into the crown lands.[1] Sometimes too the shah bought up private mulk estates: when this happened, the persons affected – as we have already mentioned – had to put up with a low price. Often the possessions or "fiefs" of dignitaries who had fallen into disgrace (for example Qizilbāsh leaders) were confiscated for the crown estates. In the end Iṣfahān, Kāshān, parts of Kirmān and Yazd, Qazvīn, Qum, Gīlān and Māzandarān all belonged to the sovereign's domains. The political aim of the extension of crown property was above all to break the power of the Qizilbāsh leaders, who ever since the beginnings of Safavid rule had been holding the governorships as tiyūl. As soon as a province was turned into khāṣṣa it also became free of Qizilbāsh troops as there was no longer any governor. This policy was continued under Shah Ṣafī and 'Abbās II. Ṣafī's vizier, Ṣārū Taqī, was one of its most important proponents, and it was he who instigated the incorporation of Fārs into the crown lands. The crown estates attained their greatest extent under 'Abbās II, but decreased again thereafter, as the threat of war once more necessitated the appointment of (Qizilbāsh) governors and these were naturally expected to raise troops.

A special administrative machinery for the crown estates had been built up and developed since the time of 'Abbās I. Viziers were put at the head of the khāṣṣa provinces. The various administrative affairs came gradually within the competence of the crown land administration (*sarkār-i khāṣṣa-yi sharīfa*).[2] As we have noticed above, there had been a ṣadr for the crown estates since the time of 'Abbās I, and now in addition a chancellery for the administration of crown property was established, with standing equivalent to that of the state chancellery. In the crown estates the Qizilbāsh were replaced by the troops of the ghulāmān-i khāṣṣ. The maintenance and payment of these forces made it necessary to depart from the previous practice of paying court and crown servants in cash. From 1026–7/1617–8 onwards the payment of all persons in the service of the domains administration was effected in the usual manner: officials and troops received tiyūls in the same way as others of their kind, or else barāt (hama-sāla and other mavājib assignments) from the tax revenues of crown estates.[3] In the

[1] Falsafī, *Zindagānī* III, 272.
[2] Minorsky, *Tadhkirat al-Mulūk*, pp. 25ff.
[3] Röhrborn, *Provinzen und Zentralgewalt*, p. 133, quoting Iskandar Munshī.

late Safavid period the "fiefs and appanages" part of the crown property grew to such an extent that it seemed advisable to bring together, as a new organisational group, the remaining crown estates from which neither tiyūls were assigned nor salaries allocated; the term khāliṣa found further employment as the name for this type of crown land.

It is indisputable that 'Abbās I and his successors, by their policy of extending the crown estates, achieved their object of a political and economic weakening of the Qizilbāsh tribes and their leaders. They were unable, nevertheless, to prevent the crown land from immediately developing forms of ownership similar to those that had existed previously in the other areas. In the end it made hardly any difference to the simple peasants whether their landlord was a tiyūldār on state or crown land. Moreover their situation was scarcely affected by the question whether their landlord exercised his absolute authority over them by reason of a tiyūl, a suyūrghāl, or an appointment as mutavallī. The peasants were perhaps more oppressed on the khāliṣa estates, where they were the victims of arbitrary treatment by the tax officials, than on tiyūl land or in areas that were used as beneficia for certain officials and dignitaries.

THE ECONOMIC LIFE OF THE CITIES: COMMERCE AND TRADE

In the Saljūq period Iranian foreign trade still extended far beyond the frontiers of the Islamic world. The Mongol conquest dealt a severe blow to this trade; nonetheless at the beginning of the 8th/14th century the big trading cities of Iran again appear as commercial links between east and west. This astonishingly rapid regeneration may well be connected with the fact that under the rule of the Chingizids Iran was brought politically closer to the countries of Central and Eastern Asia and, in consequence, served as a gateway to Europe for the traders of the entire Mongol empire – and *vice versa*. Moreover, as a result of the downfall of the 'Abbasid Caliphate, Iran's commercial activities had found a new focus: it is true that Baghdad continued to be an economically important city, but in the 8th/14th century Tabrīz, the seat of the Īl-Khāns, had taken precedence over all other cities in Iran. The ravages of the Mongol invasion, which had set other cities far back from their former stage of development, had long since been repaired in Tabrīz. In spite of the rapid reconstruction of the basic structures of Iranian economic life, however, the economic flowering which had been a characteristic of every large city in the land in the pre-Mongol period could not be achieved again.

At this point we should recall how enormously important for oriental foreign trade in all ages was the maintenance of the trade-routes. Commercial development depended in a high degree upon the quality and safety of the roads, the density of the communications network, the number of well appointed halting-places, watering-places, bridges, etc. The degree of development enjoyed by the cities was related ultimately to these factors also. For the city was above all a place of trade and exchange; its economic heart had always been the bazaars, the store-houses, the counting-houses; it was a vital necessity for the city to be attached to a supra-regional communications-network.

From this point of view the existence of well-organised, centralised states with the widest possible area of dominion was highly advantageous to the intensification of Iranian internal trade. The administrative organs of such a state-structure were much better able than an often shortlived, unstable local polity would have been to guarantee the quality, safety, and numerical sufficiency of the elements required by the economic infrastructure. For this very reason even trivial political changes frequently exercised an effect upon commercial life.

We have already referred to the importance of Tabrīz under the Mongols. From this city the main trade route led diagonally across northern Iran to the east, following the traditional silk-route, through Khurāsān to Samarqand and eventually to China. Commercial traffic from the interior of the Iranian highlands and from the south did not lead directly into Tabrīz, but through several entrepôts lying along this west – east route: Sulṭāniyya, Qazvīn, Ray and Nīshāpūr. As Sulṭāniyya had become the seat of the Īl-Khāns, it overshadowed the other centres. Since the supersession of the port of Sīrāf on the Persian Gulf by Hurmuz, through which the whole sea traffic between India and the Levant immediately began to flow, the trade-route between Sulṭāniyya and Hurmuz not only represented the north – south axis of internal Iranian trade, but made Iran the point of intersection of all existing trade links by land and sea between Europe and Asia in the 8th/14th century. The collapse of the Il-Khanid empire ushered in a gradual decline in the importance of Iran in the passage of trade between Europe and the Far East. The interest of the

Timurids was directed more at promoting the eastern Iranian trade centres such as Samarqand and Herat than at developing Iran's traditional position as the prime link in the chain of east–west trade. As a result of the opening up of the sea route to India round the southern cape of Africa, the importance of Iran for world trade rapidly declined, and constant military confrontations between the Timurids and the Türkmen states in the west, and the labile internal conditions of all these states created obstacles in the way of politico-economic concepts and considerations on a grand, supra-regional scale. When at last the country was consolidated under the Safavids, and the internal preconditions for the commercial recuperation of Iran were restored, it was already too late: world trade was now running along new tracks. As a result of the increasing importance of European commercial shipping in inter-continental trade, Iran found itself pushed onto the fringe of the world economic scene. It could no longer pride itself on playing an active part in world transit trade. To the European commercial powers Iran remained of interest chiefly on account of its products and raw materials. The economic flowering of Iṣfahān in the 11th/17th century is to be traced chiefly to this city's pre-eminence in internal trade. The capital of the Safavid period cannot, therefore, be compared with Tabrīz of the Mongol period, when it was a centre for international commerce.

A special mark of the merchant class, from the 8th/14th century onwards, was their close association with the great landowners. We have already mentioned the fact that the incumbents of suyūrghāls, the usufructuaries of vaqf land (mutavallīs, etc.) and the owners of mulk land preferred, unlike their antecedents in the early Islamic period, to live far away from their lands in the cities, where they were numbered amongst the most prominent citizens. Their large incomes enabled them to take part in a variety of commercial enterprises; they did this partly through capital investment, and partly by consigning large quantities of agricultural products to merchant-princes in exchange for a share in their profits. The preconditions for this were present, for ever since the Mongol domination the dues of the ra'āyā had increasingly come to be paid in kind. For their part the landowners invested a great deal of the wealth that they did not require for their own use in commercial enterprises. Even the rulers did not hesitate at times to invest considerable sums out of the privy purse in the businesses of commercial magnates. That this phenomenon is characteristic of the big business of that time can be seen from the name given to the merchant-prince, *urtāq* (Turkish *ortaq*, "partner", "shareholder").[1]

In the 11th/17th century foreign trade experienced a sharp increase in the volume of government commissions: the monopolisation by the crown of the silk trade, as well as of the production of precious stones and of other branches of industry, created the preconditions for this increase.[2] Under 'Abbās I there was a tremendous opening up of caravan routes and the provision everywhere of installations (inns, etc.) to serve the needs of commercial traffic. One of the most spectacular of these installations was the so-called *sang-farsh*, about 30 kilometres of paved roadway with several bridges across a swampy salt desert between Ardistān and Fīrūzkūh.[3] At a single stroke this road-system, built in a very short time, made Iṣfahān the centre of Iranian internal trade. As a result of these measures the whole commerce of the country naturally experienced an upsurge, but these efforts to extend and improve the communications network in Iran must also be assessed in terms of the commercial interests of the shah. At that time he was probably the biggest merchant-prince in the land; in the course of the 11th/17th century, under imperial protection, Armenians and European companies became the carriers of almost the entire export. Evidently the native merchants could only partially adapt to the mercantile requirements of the times and concentrated more on home markets, although even in the late 11th/17th century individual merchants were still keeping up commercial contacts with distant countries.[4]

In the centuries now under discussion, commerce in Iran was conducted solely in cash, with the clumsiness that this entailed. Money was packed in leather sacks in lots of 50 (silver) tūmāns and transported in the merchant caravans. The beginnings of non-cash transactions, which had evolved in the pre-Mongol period, seem to have been forgotten. In the second half of the 11th/17th century the Iranian commercial system made a rather poor impression on several European travellers. At that time the road network was becoming increasingly neglected, and the tradition-bound merchants of Iran were indeed

[1] Minorsky and Minovi, "Naṣīr al-Dīn Ṭūsī on finance", p. 84. Petrushevsky, in *CHI* v, 509. Hinz, "Ein orientalisches Handelsunternehmen", p. 334.

[2] Minorsky, *Tadhkirat al-Mulūk*, p. 20. Kaempfer, p. 94.

[3] A. Gabriel, *Die Erforschung Persiens* (Vienna, 1952), pp. 71, 85, quoting Della Valle and Thomas Herbert. Siroux, *Caravansérails*, p. 19. Tehrani, *Die Entwicklung*, pp. 53ff.

[4] Chardin IV, 167.

becoming less and less fit to stand up to the constantly increasing rivalry of European world trade.[1]

And yet the native merchants were well-off. Every year they made a profit of 30–40% on their business capital. In the warehouse of a merchant of Iṣfahān were found, during the Afghan siege of 1135/1722, silver coins worth 1,792 tūmāns (on the value of the tūmān see below.) This gives us some idea of the size of cash hoard a merchant-prince could command.[2]

Under the later Safavids export concentrated on the same products as those for which Iran had already become famous in the Mongol period: fabrics of all kinds, brocades, camel-hair, tobacco, precious stones, and, above all, silk; while during the Safavid era also the export of carpets steadily rose.[3] By contrast the supply of precious metals seems to have been more or less exhausted in this period. At no time, however, did the export of silver, mostly in coin and principally to India, ever cease. Those chiefly responsible for this export were the usurious Indian money-changers and money-lenders, who in the 11th/17th century plied their trade in every important centre of commerce. In Iṣfahān alone there are supposed to have been 10,000 of them. Their profit margin was allegedly much greater than that of the native merchants.[4] At all events they contributed to the universal shortage of money, which was aggravated also by the financial policy of the court, for in the later Safavid state cash payment was avoided and as much coin as possible hoarded in the treasury of the ruler.[5]

Inter-city trade was profitable only for commercial magnates with large capital, who were in a position to deal in costly luxury goods, and had the necessary trade connections and possibly also their own special organisations. The small merchant, who did not have these means, was basically restricted to trading in utility goods, chiefly in the produce from the countryside around his own city. High domestic tolls prevented him from undertaking lengthy overland transport: because of

[1] Minorsky, *Tadhkirat al-Mulūk*, pp. 20, 180. Chardin IV, 170. Rabino, "Banking in Persia", pp. 21ff. Ashraf, p. 321.

[2] Minorsky, *Tadhkirat al-Mulūk*, pp. 19ff., quoting the *Zubdat al-tavārīkh*.

[3] Chardin IV, 162ff. Petrushevsky, in *CHI* V, 508.

[4] Chardin IV, 64. Kaempfer, pp. 160, 178. Minorsky, *Tadhkirat al-Mulūk*, p. 19.

[5] Chardin V, 430. Kaempfer, p. 96. Du Mans, p. 193. Schuster-Walser, *Das ṣafawidische Persien*, p. 39. Minorsky, *Tadhkirat al-Mulūk*, pp. 182ff. Rabino, *Coins, Medals and Seals*, p. 6.

the variations in maximum prices from place to place, it was questionable whether he would make a profit.

Artisans, small merchants and other tradesmen – people who offered any kind of service – were organised in guilds (*ṣinf*, pl. *aṣnāf*). Everything Petrushevsky has said in the previous volume about these guilds in the 8th/14th century applies to the following period.[1] We do, however, have some additional information about these organisations as they existed under the Safavids. From the ranks of the "masters" (*ustād*) they elected representatives (*kadkhudā*, a term applied also to the head of a city-district), who in turn had to be accredited by an official called a *naqīb* (presumably the head of the sayyids of the city). Only then could the representative be officially installed by the *kalāntar*. The kalāntar was an official with functions similar to those of a western European mayor; but he was appointed by the central government and normally belonged to the aristocracy of his city. The office was often hereditary, and in the 8th/14th century the kalāntar still bore the title *ra'īs*. This great interest of the government in the guilds can best be explained by the part they played in the assessment of taxes on profits and of corvées (cf. below, the discussion of the tax-system). In other respects the competence of the heads of the guilds was rather limited. No one was permitted to open a new shop without their permission; and in addition it was their duty to present the monthly schedules for fixing the maximum prices to the *ṣāḥib-nasaq*, an official whose principal concern was with price control and related problems. This official was responsible to the *muḥtasib al-mamālik* ("overseer of market and morals for the whole realm"), who was represented in each city by the *nāyib* (literally "deputy"). Final decisions were made within the framework of this authority, so that the elders of the guilds exerted only an indirect influence on the price structure. Within the first three months of the tax-year the members of the guilds (most likely only the masters) assembled at the offices of the naqīb or before the kalāntar in order to discuss the apportionment of the prescribed dues.[2] There is no mention of any other "guild meetings". Chardin reports categorically that they never took place.[3] For the rest, the guilds were very loosely organised, but they did attend to the mutual support of their members, if these should become needy, and provided a not very binding instrument to

[1] Petrushevsky, in *CHI* v, 509, 511ff. On the rôle of the aṣnāf in Safavid Iran, see Ashraf, pp. 318ff. [2] Minorsky, *Tadhkirat al-Mulūk*, p. 81. [3] Chardin iv, 93.

represent the members' interests. All in all, their influence on society was slight. Only in a very restricted sense might we speak of communal self-government in the western European sense.

In the large cities every conceivable trade was to be found. Du Mans lists 35 different craft guilds in Iṣfahān in 1660.[1] To these must be added the service-trades – victual-dealers, bakers, cooks – and also such people as dancers, jugglers, beggars, dervishes and sayyids, all of whom belonged to guilds. This multiplicity of trades was not a special feature of the Safavid period: a government manual from the second half of the 8th/14th century lists a similar number of taxable trade associations in Tabrīz.[2] In medium-sized and small cities one often found a certain concentration of particular trades. In Yazd, for example, the manufacture of costly textiles predominated, while Kāshān was famous for its ceramics and, increasingly, for its carpets. Similar examples can be adduced for almost every city in the country.

Those engaged in commerce plied their trades chiefly in the great bazaars of the cities. The bazaar was often the property of the dīvān or of the crown, and in many cases bazaars were endowments.[3] The tradesmen then had to pay rents for their shops, which served also as workshops. This applied also to the city's cattle-markets, slave-markets, storehouses, caravansarais, bridges and baths, the rents from which provided an important source of income for the public treasury, the crown, or the vaqf administration. The central area of the bazaars in the large cities – the *qaiṣariyya* – was always crown property. The traders who exposed there for sale the choicest and costliest wares (e.g. expensive fabrics, jewels, luxury imports from distant lands) had to pay considerable sums of money for the privilege.[4]

At this point a particular form of bazaar must be mentioned. The royal headquarters sometimes moved from one place to another. This happened for a variety of reasons; e.g. war, or the search for climatically favourable summer- or winter-quarters. This habit was indulged especially by the Jalayirid, the Timurid, and the Türkmen rulers. On these occasions the whole court, led by the ruler, would forsake the capital city and take off for another, often far distant, part of the country where amid great pomp and ceremony a royal court encampment would be set up. The considerable needs of this encampment

[1] Du Mans, pp. 195–211.
[2] Hinz, *Resālā-ye Falakiyyā*, pp. 178ff.
[3] Petrushevsky, in *CHI* v, 506-8, and *Kishāvarzī* II, 28. Kaempfer, pp. 94ff.
[4] Kaempfer, p. 157.

were supplied by an army of scurrying tradesmen who on such occasions often came long distances to take advantage of this *urdū-bāzār* (i.e. "market of the court and army camp"). On the camp being struck, the provisional bazaar likewise was dissolved. This institution of the Īl-Khāns was still common under the Āq Quyūnlū, and provided the merchants with an enormous turn-over. Not until the time of the Safavids did the urdū-bāzār lose its importance. This market, too, was regarded as a crown institution, and the revenues from it were considerable.

Besides such institutions there were also industries, the income from which went to the public treasury, to the crown, or to the vaqf administration. The origin of these industries may be connected with the captive and enslaved workers who were set to work at various crafts in the palaces of the Īl-Khāns and, at a later date, of Tīmūr and even of his successors. At all events, from the 8th/14th century onwards such industries were to be found in many cities. The main industries of this sort were: tanning, pickling and preserving, soap-manufacture, paper-making, dyeing. The mints, too, must be listed among these "state" industries. The income from the mint, which came chiefly from mintage, that is the difference between the real and the nominal value of the coin, flowed constantly into the royal treasury.[1]

There was one special form of industry that mainly emerged in the Safavid empire: the *buyūtāt* (literally "houses") or "royal workshops". These court workshops and court industries of the Safavids were sited inside the royal palace grounds. Their function was chiefly the preparation of every imaginable product that the court might need. The buyūtāt comprised, firstly, departments connected in any way whatever with the supply of victuals for the court. Near the court kitchen were the food warehouse, the bakery, storerooms for drinking water and fruit juices, the wine-cellar, slaughterhouse, the coffee-kitchen, the pharmacy and the rest. Then there were storehouses and rooms of various kinds for firewood, torches and lamps, for tablecloths, plates and crockery, for carpets and robes of honour. The royal treasury, too, must be listed here. All the departments which employed manual labour for the provision of the needs of the court household were court workshops in the true sense. Thus the court controlled its own looms,

[1] Hinz, "Das Steuerwesen Ostanatoliens", p. 196. Rashīd al-Dīn Fażl-Allāh, *Mukātabāt*, ed. M. Shafī' (Lahore, 1945), p. 318. Yakubovsky, "Timur", pp. 72ff.

its own tailoring, shoemaking, and fur and leather industry. There was a goldsmith's workshop and a copper smithy, which supplied the court with all manner of tools and utensils; and there were many other departments as well. Finally, mention must be made of the harness-maker's workshop, the armoury, the ordnance-foundry, and the library in which manuscripts were not only collected but specially produced by a staff of artists. The stables and many other offices were also part of the buyūtāt.[1]

As a rule there was a director (*ṣāḥib-jam'*) and a controller (*mushrif*) over each department. This rule was broken, however, where, for operational reasons, several departments worked closely together and were therefore from time to time put under a single ṣāḥib-jam' or a single mushrif. In the late Safavid period the buyūtāt were entirely under the direction of the *nāẓir-i buyūtāt* ("overseer of the court workshops"). This had not always been so: at the beginning of the 11th/17th century the nāẓir-i buyūtāt had controlled only certain specific court industries and workshops. Later, however, he was *de facto* in charge of the whole royal household and was reckoned to be one of the most powerful and influential ministers of state.

Countless workmen and specialists with a variety of professional skills were employed in the court industries. In contrast to their colleagues in the bazaars they enjoyed a number of privileges. Each employee was given a deed of appointment which indicated precisely the manner of his work and his rate of pay. In the late Safavid period the annual wage of a workman ranged from two tūmāns to the considerable sum of 55 tūmāns. This was paid in the form of barāt – the assignment of certain tax returns. One of the employees was commissioned to cash these tax-cheques on the spot, so that in fact most employees got a cash payment, although forfeiting in the process 5–10% of the wage stated in their deed of appointment. Every third year an employee at a court workshop could count on receiving a wage-increase. In addition he had the right to specific allowances in kind (*jīra*). Emoluments in kind were calculated in terms of a unit known as the *qāb* ("dish"). Six or seven persons were supposed to be able to find subsistence from the food contained in one qāb. Highly paid workmen received a whole qāb, others only half or a quarter. On request one could have the jīra commuted into cash. As well as these

[1] Kaempfer, pp. 106ff. Chardin VII, 330ff. Minorsky, *Tadhkirat al-Mulūk*, p. 50.

regular wages the employees at the buyūtāt received premiums or "gifts" (*in'ām*), often amounting to as much as a year's wages. This occurred principally when a workman had distinguished himself by specially good work.[1]

An appointment in the buyūtāt was normally for life. In case of illness or unfitness for work the salary continued to be paid. Moreover, it also happened that many of the workmen worked not only by royal commission, but on their own account as well. All of these facts show that a post in court industry at a court workshop was in many respects a privileged post, and must have been much sought after.

In conclusion let us mention the activities of European workmen in the buyūtāt. Under 'Abbās I, Ṣafī I and 'Abbās II a series of painters worked at the court at Iṣfahān. There are several reports of watchmakers, but it is not clear whether these were always attached to the buyūtāt. Several European specialists were employed in the ordnance-foundry at court, and it is possible that their number increased under Shah Sulṭān Ḥusain (1105–35/1694–1722), for at this time the production of artillery was being stepped up.[2]

THE TAX SYSTEM IN THE POST-MONGOL PERIOD

During the centuries of the 'Abbasid Caliphate it had been customary to observe, formally at least, the tax regulations prescribed by the Sharī'a, even if the four canonical taxes – *kharāj* (tax on land and agricultural products), *'ushr* (tithe), *zakāt* (alms-tax) and *jizya* (capitation tax for non-Muslims) – covered the most heterogeneous institutions, and the rate of taxation differed greatly from place to place and from time to time, and special impositions had often assumed the character of regular taxes. In Iran this principle was overthrown during the first decades of Il-Khanid rule: the *qubchūr* tax took its place alongside the canonical kharāj and quickly proved to be the most oppressive taxation ever imposed upon the settled population.[3] In the Il-Khanid period the term qubchūr - originally a pasture-tax on the Mongol nomad herdsmen – denoted various types of tax. For the arable farming community the qubchūr was a levy assessed according to the quantity of the product, and had to be paid in cash. In many

[1] *Ibid.*, p. 21.

[2] *Ibid.* Schuster-Walser, *Das ṣafawidische Persien*, pp. 53ff. Busse, *Untersuchungen*, pp. 136ff.

[3] Petrushevsky, in *CHI* v, 530ff., and *Kishāvarzī* II, 228ff.

districts the qubchūr was a fairly uniform fixed tax on all subjects and thus a capitation levy on Muslims too.[1] Cattle-breeders also were liable for qubchūr dues, which again had to be paid in cash, not in cattle, as had originally been the custom with the Mongols. The zakāt was superseded by the tamghā, introduced by the Īl-Khāns. This was a set of taxes on trade and industry, the combined rate of which was several times greater than the 2½% of the canonical alms-tax. In addition, the Il-Khanid régime imposed a great number of oppressive special burdens upon the population of Iran, most of all upon the settled community. The exaction of taxes by the administrators of the Il-Khanid state had been brutal and capricious and had threatened the life of great sections of the Iranian peasantry. When reform came under Ghazan Khān (694–703/1295–1304), there was not by any means a return to the norms laid down in the Sharī'a. Such a course would have deprived the rulers of a substantial part of their income. What took place was, rather, the systematisation and codification of the practices that had been in operation since the middle of the 7th/13th century. On the basis of this reform the canonical taxes continued for the time being, but income for the public treasury was assured by the cataloguing of a wide range of additional dues. This seems nonetheless to have been to the advantage of the populace, because the fixing of the rate of taxation put a stop in some measure to the often immoderate demands of the tax-collectors.

The co-existence of canonical taxes and of levies that were not consistent with the Sharī'a, plus many special burdens – some of which admittedly had been customary even before the Mongol conquest of the Near East – is plainly characteristic of the post-Mongol period as well. As early as the 8th/14th century there appeared tendencies to obliterate the distinction between canonical and non-canonical taxes. Attempts to put a stop to this development were made repeatedly, as for example under the Timurid Shāh Rukh (811–50/1409–47), under the Āq Quyūnlū rulers Ya'qūb (883–96/1478–90) and Aḥmad (902–3/1497), and also under Shah Ṭahmāsp (930-984/1524-1576). Such intentions seem also to have played some part, albeit a limited one, in the tax reform of Uzun Ḥasan (857–82/1453–78).[2] The assimi-

[1] Minorsky and Minovi, "Naṣīr al-Dīn Ṭūsī on finance", pp. 79–80. Busse, *Untersuchungen*, p. 104. *TMEN* I, 387–91 (no. 266, "qubčur"). Barthold, "Die persische Inschrift", p. 261.

[2] Hinz, "Das Steuerwesen Ostanatoliens", p. 191; "Das Rechnungswesen", p. 121; and "Steuerinschriften", pp. 758ff. Minorsky, "The Aq-qoyunlu and Land Reforms", pp. 451ff., 458ff. Schmidt-Dumont, *Turkmenische Herrscher*, p. 219.

lation of non-canonical and canonical taxes was finally accomplished, it would seem, in the 11th/17th century, presumably under 'Abbās I. His fiscal measures came at the end of a continuous series of tax reforms. They were preceded by the codification and the regulation of the financial system during the second half of the 8th/14th century (the Jalayirid period) and by the creation of the *Qānūn-i* (or *Qānūn-nāma-yi*) *Ḥasan Pādishāh*, the tax book of Uzun Ḥasan Āq Quyūnlū. Common to all of these reforms is that, as we observed about the tax laws of Ghazan Khān, they have to do only in part with the introduction of totally new measures; for the rest they are concerned with the collating of detailed arrangements and of usages that had come into existence at an earlier stage. Thus, for example, the returns contained in the *Qānūn* of Uzun Ḥasan concerning eastern Anatolia – so important for our consideration – show tremendous variation from place to place, in respect both of the type of tax and of the rate of taxation. The reason for this can be traced to the fact that over a long period of time accepted local traditions had found their way into Ḥasan's code. And so, such returns as these give us some idea also of fiscal conditions before the codification of the *Qānūn*.[1] And there are some other sources which provide data concerning the tax system. As we explained in another context, records of tax exemptions always provide valuable evidence, for, in the form of tax lists, they indicate to which type of levy the exemption in question applied. On this subject the number of extant documents from the Safavid period is much greater than the number from the 9th/15th century or even earlier. Manuals of administration often supply valuable information on this score, and data of this kind in the records can be augmented from many reports by European travellers. We shall initially follow the development down the centuries of the most important regular taxes, and then discuss irregular special impositions.

The first thing to note is that soon after the collapse of the Il-Khanid state the terms kharāj and zakāt occur less frequently in the sources. This applies also to the Mongol expression qubchūr, presumably because in the popular mind this conjured up memories of the worst kind of fiscal exploitation. From the second half of the 8th/14th century onwards, in place of these terms we find *māl* and *jihāt*, and from the 9th/15th century onwards they are linked to form *māl-u-jihāt*. Both of

[1] Hinz, "Das Steuerwesen Ostanatoliens", p. 179.

these expressions possessed a comprehensive connotation: māl embraced the totality of the regular taxes that were payable in kind (that is, chiefly levies on agricultural products), whereas jihāt were indirect taxes to be paid in cash.[1] Amongst these were obviously the regular commercial taxes, but there were also the cattle levies, to be paid in cash (cf. below) and the taxation of land, in which certain elements of the traditional *misāḥa* regulations for the kharāj survived. In documents from the 9th/15th century onwards we find māl-u-jihāt along with *vujūhāt* (money-taxes of the most varied kinds, presumably mainly dues to officials) set in contrast to the *takālīf-i dīvānī* (special dues for the state household) and other extraordinary payments. In the manuals of administration, too, we meet this term māl-u-jihāt, but here, as we might expect, we find rather the specification of the separate classes of levy which made up the totality of the taxes. From this we are able to deduce that *māl-u-jihāt va vujūhāt* quite simply denoted all regularly collected taxes. It is clear that māl-u-jihāt in predominantly agricultural regions denoted chiefly taxes upon land and its produce, whereas in urban contexts it denoted chiefly taxes upon trade and industry.[2]

The rate of taxation of farm produce varied considerably from place to place and from time to time. Whereas under the Mongols after the reforms of Ghazan Khān the tithe had to be paid in kind, plus an additional high tax on produce in cash (one of the so-called qubchūr taxes), with the Jalayirids the tendency developed of shifting these cash qubchūr payments (tax on produce and the poll tax introduced by the Īl-Khāns) into the field of extraordinary taxation. This apparent easing of the burden of the tax on produce promptly made possible the collection of a larger proportion in kind as harvest tax. Under Uzun Ḥasan in most localities the tithe was replaced by the "fifth" (*khums, panj-yak*), and in many regions of Transcaucasia the harvest tax claimed as much as three-tenths of the whole harvest. In view of this severe oppression of the peasants it is scarcely conceivable that Uzun Ḥasan's regulations found a favourable reception. About a hundred years later in most districts the khums, or slightly less, was still in force. According to d'Alessandri, towards the end of the reign of Ṭahmāsp I (930–84/1524–76) only one-sixth of the harvest was claimed.[3] Chardin reports of the 11th/17th century, however, that on crown estates the

[1] Hinz, "Steuerinschriften", p. 765.
[2] Minorsky, "A Soyūrghāl of Qāsim b. Jahāngīr", p. 945. Hinz, *Resālä-ye Falakiyyä*, p. 129.
[3] Minorsky, *Tadhkirat al-Mulūk*, p. 178.

tax on produce accounted for one-third of the entire yield. In the region around Iṣfahān at the beginning of the 12th/18th century a quarter of the harvest (*chahār-yak*) was claimed.[1] These levies applied primarily to grain. Orchards and vegetable gardens were taxed on the basis of a tithe or a seventh part of the annual yield. In the 8th/14th, and in the first half of the 9th/15th, century vineyards were often subject to the khums, but under Uzun Ḥasan this levy was commuted into cash (in eastern Anatolia every hundred vines were assessed at the flat rate of about two Ottoman *aqchas*).[2] This may well indicate that at that time the greater part of the grape harvest was pressed, so that there was no point in claiming a levy on the fruit. The sale of the wine was subject to various commercial taxes, so that it paid the public treasury on the one hand to put a flat rate on the vineyards, and on the other to encourage wine production to the limit. This tax, known as *razkārī*, was in operation throughout the whole period under review, as one document from the year 1094/1683 demonstrates.[3]

Another māl tax in kind consisted in the supplying of hay, chaff, or firewood. According to the regulations of Uzun Ḥasan the tenant of a juft was liable to supply from one to four *kharvārs* (ass-load, cf. Hinz, *Masse u. Gewichte*, p. 14) of the materials indicated. All of these dues became payable at harvest, except the firewood, which had to be delivered in late autumn. The fixing of the precise quantities and sums to be given was the responsibility of the *mumayyiz* or *rayyā'*,[4] the assessor of the harvest, whose underlings performed this task a short time before the harvest. In order to protect himself from too high an assessment, the peasant had to pay the rayyā' and his staff both an assessment-due (introduced in the Āq Quyūnlū period) and also the so-called *taqabbulāt*. These dues became payable "when a tax-payer agrees to the assessment fixed by the revenue-officer."[5] Evidently this was a case of legalised bribery. Not without some amazement do we find the taqabbulāt, in an administrative manual of the early 18th century, among the regular state revenues.[6]

In this category must certainly be included the land tax collected in various regions – the *rasm-i juft*. Under Uzun Ḥasan the rasm-i juft passed in some districts as being consistent with the "old law".[7] Here

[1] Chardin v, 384, 392.
[2] Hinz, "Das Steuerwesen Ostanatoliens", p. 181.
[3] Busse, *Untersuchungen*, document no. 20.
[4] *Sic*! See Minorsky, *Tadhkirat al-Mulūk*, p. 150.
[5] Lambton, *Landlord and Peasant*, p. 441.
[6] Minorsky, *Tadhkirat al-Mulūk*, p. 76.
[7] Hinz, "Das Steuerwesen Ostanatoliens", p. 180.

we are dealing with a tax payable in cash and, under Uzun Ḥasan, varying in rate from district to district (and dhimmīs were further assessed at a higher rate than Muslims). D'Alessandri finds evidence for the existence of this tax in the late 10th/16th century, and Kaempfer puts the rate at five *'abbāsīs* per *jarīb* for the reign of Shah Sulaimān.[1] From Kaempfer and from Chardin we learn also that in the second half of the 17th century this category of payment included a contribution to the *bārkhāna-yi Shāh* ("royal goods-caravan"), claiming the choicest produce of the various regions. The yield from both taxes flowed into the coffers of the rulers. That these two interchangeable taxes represented a later form of the rasm-i juft can be seen from the fact that they were expressly catalogued among the regular taxes.

The same dichotomy in basic taxation can be observed in the realm of cattle-rearing, down to the second half of the 10th/16th century. By a decree of Ya'qūb Āq Quyūnlū dated 15 Ramaḍān 884/30 November 1479 the addressee of the document was exempted from paying the taxes of *mavāshī* (cattle-tax) and *marā'ī* (pasture-tax).[2] In the tax-regulations of Uzun Ḥasan both types of tax are mentioned. Let us first examine the cattle-tax. After the end of the Il-Khanid state it continued to be known for some time as *qubchūr-i rasmī* or *qubchūr-i aghnām*, expressions going back to the reforms of Ghazan Khān and current down to the Timurid period. In the *Qānūn-i Ḥasan Pādishāh* we find the above form mavāshī.[3] In eastern Iran in 1500 there existed a tax called *pāy-i gāvāna*, which clearly was identical with this cattle-tax.[4] Under Shah Ṭahmāsp, who was renowned for his piety, this undoubtedly non-canonical exaction was camouflaged in the colours of the Sharī'a, by being interpreted as one form of the alms-tax and named *zakāt-i gusfand va mavāshī*. Obviously, however, even this formal re-interpretation was not sufficient to calm the conscience of the sanctimonious Ṭahmāsp, for in 972/1565 he had it totally annulled as being unlawful.[5] From the time of 'Abbās I onwards the cattle-tax, now called *chūpān-bīgī*, once again took its place as a fixed element in the māl-u-jihāt and remained so until the 18th century.

Under Uzun Ḥasan in many districts the mavāshī tax consisted of

[1] Minorsky, *Tadhkirat al-Mulūk*, p. 179.

[2] Busse, *Untersuchungen*, document no. 3. On the term marā'ī, see Minorsky and Minovi, "Naṣīr al-Dīn Ṭūsī on finance", p. 78.

[3] Hinz, "Das Steuerwesen Ostanatoliens", p. 199, and "Steuerinschriften", p. 756. Busse, *Untersuchungen*, p. 107.

[4] Roemer, *Staatsschreiben*, p. 167.

[5] Hinz, "Steuerinschriften", pp. 759, 766.

two levies: one was a cash payment of from ⅔ to one aqcha for each wether-sheep or goat (in Anatolia), to which was added a herd-tax in kind – a stated number of livestock incurred, in varying amounts, fixed levies, for example one beast per year for every three hundred sheep. In addition female stall-cattle were taxed in cash: mares, cows, and asses incurred a tax of from 2 to 4½ aqchas per beast.[1] There are records from the reign of Ṭahmāsp of tax rates of 15 *bīstī* for every forty sheep (excluding tups) and 10 for each bullock.[2] Obviously these rates were in force before the above-mentioned cancellation of the cattle-tax in 1565. Under 'Abbās I, in the province of Khurāsān alone, the chūpān-bīgī yielded annually the sum of about 20,000 'Irāqī tūmāns, and this shows that here, too, we are dealing with a tax that had to be paid in cash.[3] Of the late 17th century Chardin reports, however, that the chūpān-bīgī for sheep had to be paid in kind: one-seventh of the lambs and the whole yield of fleeces. Foals were assessed at one-third of their fictive price (supposedly fairly assessed) in cash. In any case, in this period the ruler was the direct beneficiary of the income from the chūpān-bīgī.[4]

The pasture-tax, too, can be traced back to the period of Mongol rule in Iran, and is explicitly mentioned in the *Qānūn* of Uzun Ḥasan. Later on it frequently became merged with the categories of cattle-tax listed, but we have evidence that in the time of Ṭahmāsp I it was still separate.[5]

Regular taxation of urban commercial activity primarily affected trade and crafts – the latter at first only slightly. Of course the agricultural activity of individual city-dwellers is not in question here: in terms of the total tax yield from the cities revenues from this source were of no great importance.[6]

The most important of the levies imposed upon trade were the customs and sales taxes. From the time of Ghazan Khān these are to be reckoned as the most important regular revenues of the public treasury. Craft and industry were obviously liable to taxation on sales, but in addition at certain periods shops and workshops were taxable also. Most of these tariffs and taxes go back to the era of the Īl-Khāns, and in no way harmonised with the precepts of the religious law. First, let us

[1] Hinz, "Das Steuerwesen Ostanatoliens", p. 181.
[2] Minorsky, *Tadhkirat al-Mulūk*, p. 179, quoting d'Alessandri.
[3] Iskandar Munshī, trans. Savory, p. 774.
[4] Minorsky, *Tadhkirat al-Mulūk*, p. 180, following Chardin.
[5] Hinz, "Steuerinschriften", p. 764. Barkan, "Osmanlı devrinde", pp. 97, 104, 195, etc.
[6] Hinz, "Das Steuerwesen Ostanatoliens", p. 185.

take up a terminological problem. From the 8th/14th to the 10th/16th century all the taxes on trade and industry were described by the term "tamghā". There is documentary evidence that this originally Turkish word (primary meaning "herd-brand"; hence later "seal" or "stamp") had been applied to specific taxes in Iran since the late 7th/13th century. In every period the term was applied fundamentally to taxes that were raised on merchants and craftsmen and paid principally in cash. In the course of time the occasional payment in kind does, however, figure in the complex of tamghā taxes. We do not know exactly how the term tamghā came to be used in the fiscal realm. It is possible that the earliest tamghā dues were the customs dues paid by merchants on entry into a city, on all the goods they intended to sell in that city. This view is supported by an early 8th/14th century tradition, according to which, by order of the supreme authority, the tamghā dues of various cities had to be displayed in writing on the city gates, so that "the receivers of customs ...should not, under pretext of ...(an increase in the tamghā) ...collect more (than was prescribed) nor introduce any innovations".[1]

On the other hand Naṣīr al-Dīn Ṭūsī was already describing the tamghā as a kind of tax on sales.[2] In any case, towards the end of the Il-Khanid period, the term tamghā already possessed the character of a comprehensive concept covering all levies, often including extraordinary taxes, affecting trade and industry in the cities. The above-mentioned city customs dues, often designated by the word *bāj*, were part of this concept, as were also taxes on sales and profits. As none of these levies had anything to do with the tax prescriptions of Islamic religious law, the word tamghā, more often in its Arabicised plural *tamghāvāt*, was frequently used quite simply to denote all taxes that were contrary to the Sharī'a.[3] Hence the champions of the Islamic faith (arbāb-i 'amā'im) at all times fought for the abrogation of the tamghā, and this cause was taken up even by some of the rulers – either out of personal piety or from political considerations. But with all such "reforms" it was always a case of trying to resolve the contradiction that arose between religious ends and those forms of taxation which yielded the highest returns to the public purse and which the state economy simply

[1] *TMEN* II, 558, quoting Rashīd al-Dīn, *Jāmi' al-tavārīkh*.

[2] Minorsky and Minovi, "Naṣīr al-Dīn Ṭūsī on finance", p. 71.

[3] *Ibid.*, pp. 78f. See further Horst, "Zwei Erlasse", p. 302, for a document dating from late Ramaḍān 972/late April 1565.

could not do without. For this reason the success of every attempt to do away with the tamghā was very shortlived. The taxes and extraordinary dues embodied under this concept had to be forthwith reintroduced in another guise. From the reign of Shāh Rukh we learn about an even simpler solution. In order to satisfy the requirements of religion the term tamghā was simply replaced by the word zakāt.[1] In India Bābur and his successors frequently dispensed with the tamghā, a measure which must have produced almost no effect at all.[2] The most spectacular abrogation of the tamghā occurred in 972/1565 in connexion with a dream of the Safavid Ṭahmāsp. The story runs that this shah, notorious for his avarice, saw in a vision the Twelfth Imām, who commanded the sovereign to repeal the taxes, including the tamghā, that were contrary to the faith.[3] Naturally, these taxes disappeared from public life only for a short time. At all events there is evidence that from this time onwards the fiscal term tamghā was used less and less. In the 17th century the tamghā taxes did continue in various forms, but there seemed no longer to be any point in embracing them all together under the concept of tamghā.

The sales taxes which appeared under the Mongols were levied under the Jalayirids mostly at the rate of about 2½% – less than under the Īl-Khāns. Shāh Rukh's zakāt sales tax still ran at 2½% in 1440, but in Uzun Ḥasan's *Qānūn* it was fixed at 5%. Moreover, with the codification of the *Qānūn* efforts to abrogate the tamghā seem to have been effective, although the agents of this abrogation were unable to carry it out in face of the opposition encountered from the amīrs.[4] The rate went up under the Safavids (until Ṭahmāsp). For Christians it was as high as 10%. Particularly valuable goods such as pearls, jewels and musk were assessed at special low rates.

Sales taxes, as we have pointed out, were normally collected in cash. In several places, however, the tax on a few goods had to be paid in kind. Under Uzun Ḥasan wine was exempted from the sales tax but became liable to city customs dues and special tariffs, which did not, however, touch wine pressed inside the cities. Likewise possessing a special character was the sales tax on cattle, which in some places was

[1] Hinz, "Das Steuerwesen Ostanatoliens", p. 191. Ulugh Beg, on the other hand, obviously agreed with the concept of tamghā: Barthold, *Ulugh Beg*, p. 128.

[2] Beveridge, *The Bābur-nāma in English*, p. 555.

[3] Hinz, "Steuerinschriften", pp. 758–69. Horst, "Zwei Erlasse".

[4] Minorsky, "The Aq-qoyunlu and Land Reforms", p. 450. Hinz, "Das Steuerwesen Ostanatoliens", pp. 187, 190.

fixed at 4–5% of the selling price, in other places at a fixed sum (e.g. in Arzinjān at 10 aqchas for one ass). In order to distinguish the sales tax clearly from other tamghā taxes, under Uzun Ḥasan they were given the title *tamghā-yi siyāh* ("black tamghā").[1]

During the 17th century the sales tax declined somewhat in importance beside the great number of other taxes on trade and crafts. It is possible that they were exacted only in respect of specific goods. In this period certainly, they were calculated not as a percentage but on a flat rate. Olearius reported that in 1637 one paid one *'abbāsī* to sell a horse, one *muḥammadī* an ass, and one *qāzbakī* a sheep.[2] Silk, too, was liable to some such sales tax. This decline of the market tax under the later Safavids was certainly connected with the simultaneous restructuring of the financial administration, which we have still to discuss.

Because in Iran one could have the beasts one had bought (bullocks, sheep, lambs) slaughtered in the cattle yards (*khaṭīra*), the tamghā which fell due in such a case represented a combination of slaughtering-fees and sales tax. This slaughtering-tamghā could be paid partly or wholly by surrendering the skins to the city tannery, the heads and feet to the city pickling and salting works, or the offal to the gut-factory.[3] There is evidence of this custom as early as the second half of the 14th century; in the later 15th century the surrender of these parts of the animal may have become obligatory at least in certain districts. This special form of slaughtering fee is evidenced, however, not merely for eastern Anatolia and Āzarbāījān, but also for central Iran, for Qum, for example, where as well as the skins one had to give up half a sheep's liver and the fat – presumably the fat on the rump of the Persian sheep.[4]

After the sales taxes we come now to the customs dues. On this topic we must bear in mind that not all varieties of customs were regarded at all times explicitly as tamghā. At the moment, however, we do not wish to go any further into the question of formal classification. Up to the 16th century the most lucrative customs dues were the city customs (bāj, later also *durūb*), which presumably were always tamghā payments. They were not based upon some uniform tariff, but were made up of an ever-increasing number of levies, which often belonged neither to the category of māl nor to that of jihāt, but were officially

[1] *Ibid.*, pp. 190, 192.
[2] Schuster-Walser, *Das ṣafawidische Persien*, p. 36.
[3] Hinz, "Das Steuerwesen Ostanatoliens", pp. 194ff., and *Resālä-ye Falakiyyä*, pp. 176ff.
[4] Busse, *Untersuchungen*, document no. 4.

regarded as extraordinary impositions, although in practice certainly they very soon assumed the character of regular taxes.[1] Like the rest of the tamghā dues the system of city customs displays a continuous development from the Mongol period until the second half of the 16th century. Not until the time of ʿAbbās I do we find substantial changes. In the Il-Khanid period the goods carried by the caravans were still taxed at a flat rate, and one distinguished only between the rate for goods to be sold within the city and the rate for goods in transit. In the course of time, however, there evolved a refined system of deductions and "administrative fees" – for so we might describe those dues levied on the grounds that they reimbursed those engaged directly or indirectly in the work of collecting the customs dues. We will return to this topic in our discussion of extraordinary taxation.

Once again the data contained in the *Qānūn-i Ḥasan Pādishāh* are of assistance in providing a picture of the city customs. The basic levy was the due paid to the guard at the city gate, called the *rasm-i bavvābī*. This was a tax on the number of loads of goods that passed through the city gate, whether in or out, without distinction of quality, and irrespective of whether the goods were to be sold in the city or were merely in transit. If they were in transit, then they were taxed twice, once on entry, once on leaving.[2] Certain goods were exempt from the rasm-i bavvābī – for example, grain and milk products for the city's food supply. Peasants in the surrounding district could become exempt from the rasm-i bavvābī by paying additional dues in kind on their harvest. It might also happen, however, that in such cases the rasm-i bavvābī could be exacted in kind at the city gate. In Diyārbakr for fattened beasts, instead of this tax, one paid a levy of one aqcha for every six sheep that passed through the city gate, and this levy was called *tamghā-yi aghnām* ("sheep tamghā").

In addition to the dues paid to the guard at the gate there was a series of further customs charges, as, for example, the fee to the scribe (*rasm-i kitābat* or *rasm-i kuttābī*), and for caravans passing through there was a levy called *rasm-i qābiżāna*.[3] Duty on wine had to be paid in kind. There was a fee to the master of the court cellar, a fee to the commandant of the fort, and to the night watchman. In spite of these specific designations the quantities of wine collected as city customs

[1] Hinz, "Steuerinschriften", p. 766.

[2] Hinz, "Das Steuerwesen Ostanatoliens", p. 186.

[3] *Ibid.*, p. 187.

went into the royal cellars. A special group of different levies went to make up the silk tax, which had to be paid in cash. Certain textile goods were liable to an increased silk tax. The total revenue from city customs amounted in general to between 2% and 3% of the value of the goods. Hinz points out that in the 15th and 16th centuries the price of an article transported, say, from eastern Iran to Istanbul would double itself solely on account of the payment of local customs dues. Out-of-the-way cities sought to profit from this by enticing merchant caravans with the offer of lower customs rates.[1]

Not only at the city gates were tolls erected. Along the great caravan routes, at forts, guard posts and bridges, there were road tolls (*bāj-i shavāri'*) to be negotiated. For a long time these taxes, known as road-guard dues (*rasm-i rāhdārī*), had served to maintain the guards stationed everywhere along the highways; but these were not always regarded as a component of the tamghā.[2]

It is now time to look at the system of tolls and tariffs in the Safavid state of the 17th and early 18th century. Since the reign of 'Abbās I the dues on the highways and, even more important, at the ports had been allowed to supplant city tolls as the most important source of revenue for the public treasury. To this must be related the fact that trade with foreign, principally European, powers was constantly widening in scope during the 17th century. The rāhdārī dues had long since ceased to provide for the upkeep of the highway guards. Nevertheless their rate had been creeping up all the time, and this, along with the multiplication of the number of customs posts, had turned them into a public revenue source of the first order. A European traveller made the very pertinent observation, concerning the Iranian road system, that although one came upon scarcely any crossings or bridges one had nevertheless to pay up at every turn. The revenue from this abundant source had been flowing into the royal treasury very probably since the days of 'Abbās I.[3]

On the state frontiers the customs arrangements were not organised everywhere with the same thoroughness. The fiscal administration concentrated on taxing all goods imported into the country through the ports on the Persian Gulf, where the average rate ran at 10% of the estimated value of the goods. In the time of 'Abbās II (1052–

[1] *Ibid.*, p. 199. [2] Hinz, "Steuerinschriften", p. 768. Minorsky, *Tadhkirat al-Mulūk*, p. 76.
[3] *Ibid.*, p. 180. Kaempfer, pp. 132 ff. Schuster-Walser, *Das ṣafawidische Persien*, pp. 28ff.

77/1642–66), from Bandar 'Abbās alone the public treasury collected annually the sum of 24,000 tūmāns.[1] Later on, this source of revenue was somewhat neglected; under Sulaimān it brought in only 10,000 tūmāns, and the office of harbourmaster, to whom belonged the supervision of the machinery for collecting the tariffs, was finally leased out in 1674 for the relatively small sum of 2,700 tūmāns.[2] On the Persian Gulf there were three large ports: Bandar 'Abbās, Bandar Rīg, and Bandar Kangūn, each with its own independent customs house. On the inland frontiers and also on the Caspian Sea the customs were very irregularly organised. It is worth mentioning, however, that not all foreign merchants were taxed at the same rate. The British, the Portuguese, the Dutch and the French all paid at different rates, and all were entitled to specific tariff concessions.

Among the tamghā taxes abrogated by Ṭahmāsp in 1565 were the revenues from the mints. We must note that these revenues were of various kinds. Anyone who on his own initiative struck coin out of precious metal, or had foreign currency, also of precious metal, reminted – a practice that became mandatory in the 17th century – had to pay a fee to cover expenses. We know, however, from the later Safavid period that in addition the royal treasury claimed the difference between the real and the nominal value of every coin struck. W. Hinz and H. Horst argue convincingly that the mint tamghā was presumably this mintage deduction, averaging 2%, rather than the fees for minting.[3] At all events Ṭahmāsp's abrogation of the tamghā did not result in the revenues (*vājibī*) from this mintage being renounced for ever, for, as has been already pointed out, in the 17th century this tax appears as one of the most lucrative sources of revenue for the royal treasury, and in the first half of the 18th century the rate of mintage rose to over 15%.[4] When discussing the monetary system we will return to this question. Now we turn to the last significant group of tamghā taxes: taxes on crafts.

In the reign of the Jalayirids, and presumably under the Timurids as well, the taxation of crafts was operated within the framework of the existent sales taxes, on the principle that it was not the manufacture but the sale of a product that made it liable to taxation. Relevant, too, is the circumstance that in the tax codes the sales tax was not computed at a

[1] Minorsky, *Tadhkirat al-Mulūk*, p. 181. [2] *Ibid.* Kaempfer, p. 93.
[3] Hinz, "Steuerinschriften", p. 766, and "Das Steuerwesen Ostanatoliens", p. 188. Horst, "Zwei Erlasse", p. 306. [4] Minorsky, *Tadhkirat al-Mulūk*, pp. 130ff.

flat rate for a whole city, but specified for individual professions, artisan guilds (aṣnāf) and shops. From the models provided by an assessment book of the year 764/1363 for the city of Tabrīz we learn that a sales tax was presented for close on forty professional groups and guilds, which proves that this tax was clearly conceived as a means of taxing industrial production.[1] In the *Qānūn* of Uzun Ḥasan Āq Quyūnlū, about a hundred years later, we detect the beginnings of the attempt to tax industrial production itself, irrespective of the amount for which the product was sold. Obviously in the period before the compilation of the *Qānūn* of Uzun Ḥasan, the practice had become established of taxing weavers at a specified monthly or yearly rate for their looms. The *Qānūn* prescribed the tax on individual professions in various regions. This might be a tax on shops or workshops, as in the case of tradesmen, or it might be a straightforward tax on industry, as in the case of the bakers and cooks in the eastern Anatolian city of Kharpūt.[2] As a rule these taxes seem to have been payable in cash, but sometimes the rates referred to payment in kind. It is obvious that in the late 15th century and thereafter these taxes on industry were regarded as an extension of the previous system of taxing industry according to turn-over, for they were always conceived as tamghā levies.

The turning point in the development of some of the taxes, which we have placed at the beginning of the 17th century, can be perceived in the sphere of industry as early as the reign of Ṭahmāsp in the second half of the 16th century. The historical development of the tax on crafts had followed a different course from region to region. In contrast to this tax as operated by the Āq Quyūnlū and certainly as operated during the early decades of Safavid rule is the system which comprehensively taxed those engaged in industry. This system we find operating in the later period of Ṭahmāsp's reign. Because it embraced all urban manufacturers and subjected them to fixed levies, it was a much more efficient fiscal instrument than the codified usages of the *Qānūn-i Ḥasan Pādishāh*. In the often quoted administrative manual, *Taẕkirat al-mulūk*, this taxation system is vividly presented. In accordance with the guidelines set down by the dīvān, a high city official, the kalāntar (in several respects not unlike a European mayor, cf. above), assisted

[1] Hinz, *Resālä-ye Falakiyyä*, pp. 177–83.

[2] Barkan, "Osmanlı devrinde", p. 194. For the taxation of brothels (*bait al-lutf*) and gambling, see Hinz, "Das Steuerwesen Ostanatoliens", p. 188, and *Resālä-ye Falakiyyä*, p. 129; Minorsky, *Tadhkirat al-Mulūk*, pp. 139, 182.

by another dignitary, the naqīb (probably the most distinguished of the sayyids, i.e. descendants of the Prophet, in the city, cf. above), decided on the total extent of the taxes on industry due in their city. These taxes, known in Ṭahmāsp's time as *māl-i muḥtarifa*, were now called the *bunīcha*. Then the kalāntar summoned the heads of the districts (*kad-khudā*) and the elders of the guilds (*rīshsafīdān-i aṣnāf*) in order to apportion, in their presence, the bunīcha-quotas to the individual "guilds" and other institutions. The aldermen now became responsible for the collection of the amounts apportioned. The bunīcha payment was obligatory on all craftsmen, bazaar merchants, sellers at the rope market, cattle market, and other markets, on all bakeries, eating-houses, inns and baths (in so far as these were not crown properties and thus leased by the royal treasury, as, for example, in Iṣfahān), and at times on such notorious services as taverns and brothels.[1] In the crown provinces the revenues from the bunīcha, like all other levies, naturally flowed into the royal treasury, and in the other provinces they formed part of the *regalia*, so that in every case it was the sovereign who profited directly from the bunīcha.[2] Special value was attached to the tax on the production of silk and cotton. According to Chardin the ruler received a sum equivalent to one-third of the product, quite apart from the fact that the export of silk was one of the most important royal prerogatives. The flat rate assessment of the bunīcha was of advantage to the public treasury in yet another respect. If a particular producer was exempted from bunīcha levies, this in no way diminished the revenue from taxes, for the cost was shared out by the other members of the guild.[3]

Following Hinz's argument, we may regard the receipts from certain urban manufactures as a latent tax on industry. The fees levied, for example, by the city tanneries when someone brought a goatskin or sheepskin to have it tanned, or, as the case might be, took away the finished leather, were somewhat higher than the cost of running the industry. The surplus was claimed by the public treasury.[4] Certainly this did not apply in every case, nor to all manufactures. It also covered the processing of certain raw materials claimed as dues by fiscal

[1] Kaempfer, p. 94. On the bunīcha, see *Tadhkirat al-Mulūk*, pp. 81, 83; Hinz, "Steuerinschriften", p. 764.

[2] Kaempfer, *loc. cit.* Minorsky, *Tadhkirat al-Mulūk*, p. 180. Du Mans, p. 33.

[3] Minorsky, *Tadhkirat al-Mulūk*, p. 83.

[4] Hinz, "Das Steuerwesen Ostanatoliens", p. 196, following Barkan, "Osmanlı devrinde", pp. 185, 194.

fiscal officials. One recalls, for example, the dues payable on slaughtering an animal. Moreover, the products of these urban manufacturers were frequently the object of a fiscal device which, under the name of *ṭarḥ*, had been widespread since the Mongol period. The populace was compelled to sell certain raw materials to the fiscal office (explicitly, to the manufacturer) at an artificially low price, or, alternatively, to buy certain products from the fiscal office at an inflated price.[1] As with many other devices this one gave the tax officials ample scope for malpractice, as an inscription dated 981/1573 records concerning the compulsory sale of the products of the soap works at Nairīz.[2]

We now move on from the discussion of all those levies which were regarded up to the 16th century as tamghā, and which to some extent underwent special development during the 17th century. That does not mean that we have abandoned the sphere of regular taxation. To this sphere certainly belonged the jizya, the Quranic poll tax on non-Muslims. This tax affected Jews and Christians, both native and foreign (including Europeans). The principle underlying the jizya was fundamentally that every adult male dhimmī had to pay a specified annual sum. As with all the other taxes, the rate of the jizya varied from place to place and from time to time. In the middle of the 17th century, for example, Armenians and Jews liable to the jizya had to pay annually the equivalent of one *misqāl* of gold (i.e. 4.69 gm). Du Mans, to whom we are indebted for this information, tells us also that this tax was called either kharāj or jizya, an interesting indication of how little awareness there was in the 17th century of the original character of the canonical taxes.[3] We learn from a document of Sulaimān from the year 1094/1683 that the Quranic poll tax for Armenians in Julfā, south of Iṣfahān, was calculated at a flat rate and apportioned to the male members of the Armenian community by the kalāntar of the Armenians of Julfā in collaboration with the kadkhudās (heads of the districts, elders).[4] This procedure was very much in line with what we have already observed concerning the apportionment of the flat rate bunīcha tax. At that time the yield from the jizya for Julfā had reached the figure of 580 tūmāns. In 'Abbās I's time it had yielded only 180 tūmāns, which may indicate that the Armenians of Julfā in those days

[1] Petrushevsky, *Kishāvarzī* II, 289. Busse, *Untersuchungen*, document no. 5. Aubin, *Note préliminaire*, pp. 17ff. Lambton, *Landlord and Peasant*, p. 102. Hinz, "Steuerinschriften", p. 754.

[2] Aḥmad Iqtidārī, "Farmānī az Shāh Ṭahmāsp-i Ṣafavī", *FIZ* XII (1343), 319–22.

[3] Du Mans, p. 46.

[4] Busse, *Untersuchungen*, document no. 20.

had been taxed at a specially low rate, in order to encourage their settlement there. Under ʿAbbās I's successor Ṣafī (1038–52/1629–42) income from the jizya had already risen to 260 tūmāns. During the second half of the 17th century the income from the jizya raised in Julfā flowed into the purse of the queen mother.[1] From the document mentioned above we learn that at this time the jizya contribution of one of the richest Armenian merchants and his five sons added up to no less than 35 tūmāns.

Over and above the jizya, the dhimmīs were bound to pay other taxes as well. In the *Qānūn* of Uzun Ḥasan enhanced rates for certain taxes are indicated as applying to Christians, and we know that in the 16th century considerably higher tax rates were imposed upon Christian merchants and manufacturers than upon their Muslim colleagues, a fact already mentioned above. Since the time of ʿAbbās I a great Armenian colony had existed in Julfā. The above mentioned reduction in taxes which ʿAbbās granted the Armenians of this town did not continue to operate for long after his death. In the later 17th century the Christians of Julfā were particularly hard hit by tax impositions and other repressive measures. An additional burden upon the Armenian artisans of Julfā was that they were called upon much more frequently than were others to provide unpaid *corvée* labour. More will be said about this in the context of special impositions.

A special group of foreigners were the Indians, who had flocked to Iran in the 17th century. These, as we have observed, applied themselves to monetary business and usury. A specially assessed poll tax was imposed upon them, and was known as *sarāna-yi Hunūd*.[2]

Besides the jizya, there was yet another form of poll tax which must not be confused in any way with the canonical tax on non-Muslims: the universal poll tax on Muslims. Let us recall once again the concept qubchūr as it had been understood in the time of the Īl-Khāns. One of these qubchūr taxes had been a levy to which every subject was unconditionally liable. It was thus a poll tax on all Muslims, in strict contravention of the Sharīʿa. In spite of changes in the meaning of the term qubchūr, and its ultimate disappearance in the post-Mongol period, this tax continued in other forms, in such forms, indeed, that it could be listed officially amongst the extraordinary taxes, although exacted

[1] Chardin VIII, 114. Busse, *Untersuchungen*, p. 139. Hinz, "Das Steuerwesen Ostanatoliens", p. 182. Kaempfer, p. 68.

[2] Minorsky, *Taḏhkirat al-Mulūk*, p. 76.

with all the regularity of a regular tax. Under the Jalayirids this levy became known as *sarāna* or *sar-shumāra*, and in many districts the custom grew up of imposing a *khāna-shumāra* on a whole household instead of levying a poll tax in the true sense. In the *Qānūn* of Uzun Ḥasan we come across this "hearth-tax" (Hinz) in the context of extraordinary taxes.[1] It was still being exacted under the Safavids.

The same sort of thing happened in respect of the host of taxes in the form of "administrative dues". These too did not pass without reservation as regular taxes, and yet *de facto* were exacted on a regular basis and frequently formed an official component of regular levies, as was demonstrated above regarding the composition of the tamghā on wine. Such dues undoubtedly constituted an essential element in the comprehensive concept of vujūhāt to which we referred earlier. They were designated *ikhrājāt* (literally "expenses", signifying reimbursement of expenses incurred in the course of taxing and administering), *rusūm* or *ḥuqūq* (more or less "dues", to those in whose favour they were granted). A distinction was drawn between *muqarrarī* dues, which were regular exactions, and *khārijiyyāt*, which were *ad hoc* extraordinary dues.[2] It was undoubtedly true of many dues that their true application did not coincide with the purpose indicated by their title. This was especially obvious with those which were of long standing. For example, in Uzun Ḥasan's time and later, in certain districts of eastern Anatolia a *rasm-i tīmūrjak* was raised, a "Tīmūr due", when the conqueror had been dead and buried for fifty years. It is clear that in such a case an originally extraordinary imposition had become a regular tax.[3]

Obviously the contrary could also occur: the due reached the actual nominee. This probably happened all the time if the recipient were someone in a high position. Thus the *rasm-i nāyib* of Ḥasan's *Qānūn* most certainly found its way to the crown's deputy. Equally the *rasm al-vizāra*, known in the time of the Jalayirids, went to the vizier, whose upkeep at the end of the Safavid period was provided for almost entirely out of dues;[4] and the *rasm al-ṣadāra* was instituted for the benefit of the ṣadr. This latter tax had been in operation since the 15th century, and under the Safavids the suyūrghāls, too, were liable to it, as was mentioned in another context.[5] A characteristic of many dues was

[1] Petrushevsky, *Kishāvarzī* II, 278, quoting Nakhchivānī, *Dastūr al-kātib*. Hinz, "Das Steuerwesen Ostanatoliens", p. 182.

[2] Petrushevsky, in *CHI* v, 534.

[3] Barkan, "Osmanlı devrinde", p. 104.

[4] Minorsky, *Tadhkirat al-Mulūk*, p. 86 (§ 86).

[5] *Ibid.* (§ 87). Busse, *Untersuchungen*, documents nos. 3, 4. Hinz, *Resālä-ye Falakiyyä*, pp. 43, 48.

their persistence, often throughout several centuries: once such a perquisite was introduced, the recipient could hardly bring himself to renounce the income it brought. Thus the due for the governor of the city or the district (*shiḥna*, becoming *dārūgha* under the Timurids) was exacted under all the dynasties with which we are concerned as *rasm-i shiḥnagī, dārūghagāna* (under the Timurids) or *rasm-i dārūgha*.[1]

Another distinction may have lain in whether the due had been imposed for some higher official in the general administration (e.g. nāyib, ṣadr, vizier) or for an official who was actively engaged in the collection of one or more taxes. In the latter case the dues – at least at the time of their introduction – possessed the character of extraordinary taxes, as in the case of reimbursement fees for tax officials in general (*rusūm-i ʿummāl*, *ḥaqq al-taḥṣīl*) or dues destined for the assessor of taxes (though not to be confused with the aforementioned taqabbulāt). This had originally been the case with the rasm-i bavvābī and rasm-i kuttāb, which we mentioned along with the city gate customs, although by the time of Uzun Ḥasan they had already taken on the character of regular fiscal revenues. The same was true of the road customs dues (rāhdārī), which had originally maintained the highway guards but in the course of time became a component of regular state revenue or of the ruler's income.

Many dues had been conceived as supplementary levies, in the sense that their rate was computed as a percentage of other taxes. There were other dues, however, which had fixed rates.

A complete enumeration of all dues and a detailed exposition of their significance and development would go far beyond the framework of this present study. We must be content, therefore, with the foregoing reflections, and may sum up by stressing the fact that many of these impositions, although not by any means all of them, revealed a tendency to take on the character of regular state revenues, a tendency which expressed itself in the increasing alienation of the imposition from its original purpose as well as in the transition from "secondary rates", i.e. rates calculated as percentages of other taxes, to primary, fixed rates.

Another group of special impositions, fundamentally having something in common with the dues of which we have been speaking,

[1] Busse, *Untersuchungen*, pp. 108, 111 (*rasm-i dārūghagī*). Roemer, *Staatsschreiben*, p. 166. Barkan, "Osmanlı devrinde", p. 105 (*resmi şahnegî*). Hinz, "Steuerinschriften", p. 754.

comprised those levies imposed, originally at least, on particular occasions during the year. In this sphere, too, the tendency of extraordinary impositions to become regular taxes can be detected. We discover, for example, a feast-day levy and a wedding levy listed in the *Qānūn* of Uzun Ḥasan under the category of extraordinary impositions. It is quite clear, especially of the wedding levy, that these taxes, when first introduced, must have fallen due on the occasion of the particular event. The *Qānūn*, however, indicates that the term when both of these taxes fall due is the beginning of spring, which can only mean that these extraordinary impositions had become disguised as regular taxes on the population.[1]

The yield from genuine regular taxation – often described as *aṣl-i māl-u-jihāt* or, in respect of non-Muslims, as *aṣl-i jizya* – was augmented by surcharges in the form of specific percentages of the amounts yielded by the *aṣl*. These additions to regular taxes were known as *tafāvut* (literally "the difference"). In Mongol times the word used had been *far'*. The documents usually speak of *tafāvut-i māl-u-jihāt* and of *tafāvut-i jizya*. The original purpose of the tafāvut may have been to offset a putative increase in production without having to revise the fixed tax rates, an operation which would have involved considerable administrative expense. In fact, however, the tafāvut levies were little other than an easily contrived means of increasing the principal taxes. They had been exacted even in Mongol times and can be traced down to the late Safavid period.[2]

One special category of extraordinary taxes consisted of obligations which were not discharged directly through payment in cash or in kind. Here, too, the usage observed was essentially Il-Khanid in origin. First to be mentioned in this connexion are those services which peasants had to give to travelling officials, whom they had to accommodate along with their entire retinue. This service was called *qunalghā*. They were required also to provide for these people and their animals. In respect of persons, the obligation was called *'alafa* and, in respect of animals, *'ulūfa*. The word *ulāgh* denoted the duty of peasants to provide such officials and their retinues with mounts; while *ulām* denoted the obligatory service of providing local guides. The manner and form of exacting these services, even under the later Safavids, was very much in

[1] Hinz, "Das Steuerwesen Ostanatoliens", p. 182.

[2] Petrushevsky, *Kishāvarzī* II, 264, and "K istorii instituta 'soyurgala'", p. 239. See also Papazian, *Persidskie Dokumenty*, e.g. II, no. 28.

line with Il-Khanid usage.[1] The documents show that from the Mongol period until the end of the Safavid period other services were required which were known by the names *bīgār* and *shikār*. The latter term probably applied to unpaid service at the hunt, including possibly the supply of beaters. Bīgār denoted *corvée* services of all kinds, principally that of supplying agricultural labour. The number of days of such service prescribed for peasants could not at any time have been so very great. In Uzun Ḥasan's time, for example, only from one to three days a year were required, and exemption could be bought by payment of a moderate cash sum.[2]

The urban craftsmen, however, especially in the Safavid period, were subject to a much more exacting type of bīgār. They were called out to work chiefly on the large building projects of the shah. In this way it was possible for the ruler to execute large-scale plans without drawing too drastically on the treasury – one is put in mind of the architectural embellishment of the capital Iṣfahān by 'Abbās I and his successors. The organisation of such a comprehensive system of labour services was handled by precisely the same methods as the bunīcha, the tax on industry: the kalāntars decided on the quota of men required, and passed this on through the "guild" elders to the craftsmen in the guilds (aṣnāf). The Armenians of Julfā, called upon frequently on account of their manual skills to perform such unpaid work, presumably were not organised in guilds according to profession. The Armenian kalāntar of Julfā, in collaboration with the kadkhudās (heads of the separate residential districts), apportioned the work to the inhabitants of a city quarter who practised the particular craft.[3]

Finally, important revenues of the public treasury included every conceivable form of "gift", squeezed out of the people at every possible opportunity. There was scarcely a European traveller who was not moved to report in astonishing detail the unlimited appetite of Iranian rulers for an enormous range of valuable "gifts" from the provinces and from individuals, as well as their confiscation of property. In this, too, we see the persistence of Il-Khanid institutions and customs.[4]

[1] Busse, *Untersuchungen*, pp. 105 ff. Minorsky, "A Soyūrghāl of Qāsim b. Jahāngīr", p. 948. Petrushevsky, *Kishāvarzī* II, 294–300.

[2] Hinz, "Das Steuerwesen Ostanatoliens", p. 182. For bīgār, see Petrushevsky, *Kishāvarzī* II, 290–4.

[3] Chardin V, 404. Minorsky, *Tadhkirat al-Mulūk*, pp. 20, 181. Busse, *Untersuchungen*, document no. 20.

[4] Kaempfer, p. 93. Chardin III, 230, and V, 430. Minorsky, *Tadhkirat al-Mulūk*, p. 179. Petrushevsky, in *CHI* V, 535, quoting Rashīd al-Dīn.

The following observations are meant to provide a rough sketch of the administrative background to the tax system. During the period of our review, we can detect in general a far reaching continuity in state fiscal institutions. It must first be stated, however, that the division of the administration into two components under 'Abbās I and his successors brought about certain changes in this sphere also.

Together with the state chancellery the central finance administration formed the Grand Dīvān (*dīvān-i a'lā*), at the head of which stood the Grand Vizier. This linking of finance chamber and chancellery dates back, possibly, to Niẓām al-Mulk, the celebrated statesman of the time of the Great Saljūqs. One of its consequences was that the Grand Vizier was ultimately responsible for the financial affairs of the state. Nonetheless, the real head of the finance chamber was the *mustaufī al-mamālik*. Since the time of 'Abbās I his counterpart had been the *mustaufī-yi khāṣṣa*, who was responsible for the financial affairs of the crown estates.[1] At all events this sharing did not of necessity bring with it – at least not until the last decades of the 17th century – a twofold structure in all of the lower sections of the finance chamber.

Even in the time of the Īl-Khāns the mustaufī al-mamālik was assisted at the head of the finance chamber by two more high officials, although both were of lesser rank: the *mushrif al-mamālik* and the *nāẓir al-mamālik*. Obviously, in directing the financial administration the primary function of this trio was to exercise mutual control. The same trio was to be found in all provincial and regional finance chambers also. All regional mustaufīs were subject to the mustaufī al-mamālik, and, correspondingly, the mushrifs and nāẓirs were ultimately subject to the mushrif al-mamālik and nāẓir al-mamālik respectively. In the Safavid *nāẓir-i daftarkhāna-yi humāyūn-i a'lā* we can recognise the older nāẓir al-mamālik; and the mushrif al-mamālik was presumably the prototype of the Safavid *dārūgha-yi daftarkhāna*.[2]

The foundation of the tax system was the *qānūn*, the "book of levies". In this book were set down the rates of all taxes that had to be paid, based upon the data in what amounted to an archive and was comparable to a land register office. According to this book, the taxes should have been at the same level from year to year, but, as we have

[1] Hinz, "Das Rechnungswesen", p. 22. Minorsky, *Tadhkirat al-Mulūk*, pp. 25, 45. Röhrborn, *Provinzen und Zentralgewalt*, pp. 122ff.

[2] Hinz, "Das Rechnungswesen", p. 23. Minorsky, *Tadhkirat al-Mulūk*, p. 71. Busse, "Persische Diplomatik im Überblick," p. 240.

seen, this was not so in practice. For this reason, the qānūn had to be revised from time to time. In the later Safavid period the book of exactions, under the title *dastūr al-ʿamal*, was placed within the department of the *ṣāḥib-taujīh* (see below).[1]

In order to clarify the administrative procedures surrounding the actual collection of taxes we have to discuss two more concepts: tax farming and tax cheque (barāt). The raising of the various taxes in separate districts and regions was leased out, always under contract, to private persons or officials in the form of concessions which varied in range. On making application for such a concession, the applicant had to produce evidence of the state of his own property, for, if the application were granted, the lessee assigned his own property as surety for the sum to be raised. As the owners of tiyūls or suyūrghāls, as described above, always possessed the right to collect taxes, contracts had to be made with them also. But they did not have to provide any special evidence of their own financial standing, because in most cases they enjoyed an exemption from tax (muʿāfī), and so the public treasury had no claims upon them. Hence their contracts were different from those of the other tax-lessees, and were given the special name *taslīm-nāma*.[2] In all cases tax-cheques (barāt) were issued to the tax farmers (*musta'jir, mutaṣarrif*) by the central financial administration and made out on the basis of the terms and rates contained in the qānūn. The recipient had to cash these sums right away and at the end of the tax year balance his account, in accordance with the terms of his contract, whereupon he was discharged by the financial authorities. As we have seen, the barāt system also served to remunerate or reward officials. This was done by giving them tax cheques to the value of their salaries, drawn on a particular city or district where they could raise the fixed sums themselves or through an intermediary.

These procedures were put on record in two books of the finance chamber. Assigned tax cheques were entered in the *daftar-i taujīh* under the control of the ṣāḥib-taujīh.[3] In another book, the *daftar-i avārija*, appeared the current state of the tax fund for the whole territory, arranged by cities and provinces; and all financial transactions, including the making out of tax cheques, had to be noted in this book, which was kept by the *avārija-nivīs*. In the 17th century the book was sub-

[1] Hinz, "Das Rechnungswesen", p. 134. Minorsky, *Tadhkirat al-Mulūk*, pp. 143ff.

[2] Hinz, "Das Rechnungswesen", pp. 19ff. [3] *Ibid.*, p. 123. *Tadhkirat al-Mulūk*, p. 76 (§ 66).

divided according to the four traditional administrative regions – Āzarbāījān and Shīrvān, 'Irāq-i 'Ajam, Kirmān and Khurāsān – and each district was under its own avārija-nivīs.[1] Before making out a barāt on the tax income of any city or province, the subordinate officer of the ṣāḥib-taujīh had, therefore, always to consult the daftar-i avārija in order to make sure that he was not issuing an "uncovered" cheque in the event of the tax capacity of the region being exhausted. In the Safavid period all levies which, as *regalia*, flowed into the crown treasury, although not falling within the competence of the administration of the royal estates, were withdrawn from the "balance-sheet" of the avārija books and, from the first half of the 17th century, recorded in a special department headed by the *ẓābiṭa-nivīs*.[2]

In the Mongol period the custom had already become well established of taking the solar year as the fiscal unit of time. This year was based on the calculations of Naṣīr al-Dīn Ṭūsī. Since the time of the Timurids these solar years, reckoned from the beginning of spring, were given the year names from the Turco-Mongol twelve animal cycle. This manner of reckoning time – in comparison with reckoning in lunar years – simplified book-keeping and balancing, and eased the lot of the tax-payer, who otherwise – as still happened in the time of the 'Abbasid Caliphate – would have been taxed 33 times in the course of 32 harvests.[3]

OBSERVATIONS ON THE MONETARY SYSTEM

In Iran during the period under our review there existed throughout a two-tier, parallel currency, based upon gold and upon silver. Most coins were minted in silver, but there was always gold coinage too, even if seldom issued. Iranian coins in precious metal were always of a very high standard. Under Ghazan Khān the fineness of silver coins was 976/1000, and in later centuries the standard rose even higher.

From the 14th until the 18th century the coin chiefly to be found in currency was silver coin. This circumstance, like several other phenomena in economic life, is to be connected with the reforms of the Īl-Khān Ghazan. During his reign (694-703/1295-1304) a new unit of

[1] Hinz, "Das Rechnungswesen", pp. 120ff. Minorsky, *Taḏkirat al-Mulūk*, pp. 77ff., 174ff.

[2] *Ibid.*, pp. 76, 105ff.

[3] Hinz, "Das Rechnungswesen", p. 5. See further O. Turan, *Oniki hayvanlı Türk takvimi* (Dil ve Tarih Coğrafya Fakültesi Yayınlarından. Tarih serisi, 3. Istanbul, 1941).

currency was introduced: the silver dīnār, called the *dīnār-i rāyij*. One dīnār-i rāyij (silver) was equal to six *dirhams*. According to a statement of Rashid al-Dīn, in the time of Ghazan Khān the dīnār-i rāyij weighed 3 misqāl (at that time 4.3 gm). The dīnār thus weighed 12.9 gm. There were also dirham coins (2.15 gm) and coins valued at half a dirham – all in silver.[1] The unit of reckoning was the tūmān (from the Mongol *tümen*, i.e. 10,000), the equivalent of 10,000 dīnārs. Until the end of the 18th century the silver tūmān was never struck, so that in the period with which we are concerned there never were any silver tūmān coins. In his currency reform Ghazan Khān had taken as his model the "Chinese tūmān", which consisted of 10,000 *bālish* each of six dīnārs.[2]

At all events, this standardisation under Ghazan Khān broke with Islamic tradition, which set the dīnār as the unit of gold currency over against the dirham as the unit of silver currency. In Iran, from the Mongol period until its final disappearance, the dirham was regarded as a standardised subdivision of the (silver) dīnār, and this in turn remained the basis of reckoning for the whole monetary system of Iran throughout succeeding centuries, even though at a later stage it was no longer minted and other monetary denominations became common. In what follows the most important coins with their different names and their dīnār value will be presented, the gold value of the dīnār and the tūmān at different periods indicated, and some idea given, consequently, of the value of Iranian money in the course of the centuries with which we are dealing.

That it had been one of the intentions of Ghazan's reform to adopt the term dīnār primarily as a designation for the unit of silver currency can be seen from the fact that none of the gold coins of Ghazan Khān was named dīnār (or named as fractions of a dīnār or as a dirham, being a fixed fraction of a dīnār). This was so in spite of the fact that Ghazan's one misqāl gold coin corresponded by weight to one-third of a dīnār or two dirhams. For a gold coin weighing one dirham ($\frac{1}{2}$ misqāl, say 2.15gm) one used, obviously quite deliberately, the term *nīm-misqāl*.

Ghazan Khān's standard for the dīnār-i rāyij of three misqāl (12.9 gm) could obviously be maintained only for a few years. By the time

[1] Rabino, *Coins, Medals and Seals*, p. 4. Smith, "The Silver Currency", pp. 18ff. For a discussion whether *dīnār-i rāyij* or *dīnār-i rābiḥ* is preferable, see Herrmann and Doerfer, "Ein persisch-mongolischer Erlass", p. 17, n.60.

[2] Barthold, "Die persische Inschrift", pp. 251ff. Schroetter, pp. 697ff.

of the Īl-Khān Abū Sa'īd (717–36/1317–35) the silver dīnār weighed only 8.4 gm; but the original dīnār-i rāyij continued to be used as a unit of account.

In the period following the collapse of the Il-Khanid empire, namely in the second half of the 14th century, various monetary systems grew up in Iran. True to the Il-Khanid tradition, however, all of these were based upon the silver dīnār, subdivided into dirhams. Whereas a dīnār, divided into six dirhams following the tradition of Ghāzān's dīnār-i rāyij, was still minted in Tabrīz, we find in Baghdād, the capital of the Jalayirids, a dīnār divided into 12 dirhams, and another, called the *dīnār-i mursal*, divided into 10 dirhams.[1]

In Nishāpūr in the province of Khurāsān under Togha Temür (d. 754/1353) a silver dīnār weighing 4.21 gm and divided into 4 dirhams (at 1.05 gm) was minted. It was known also as a khurāsānī or a dīnār-i khurāsānī. However, in Khurāsān the dīnār-i rāyij at that time was still in use for account purposes.[2] Another currency based on a silver dīnār was to be found in Transoxiana: in the ulus of Chaghatai anonymous silver coins had been minted since the late 13th century. From the time of the reign of Kebek Khān (718–26/1318–26), however, these were struck with the name of a ruler, so that thereafter these coins were known as *kapakī* money. One silver kapakī dīnār weighed approximately 8 gm and was divided into 6 dirhams at from 1.3 to 1.4 gm.[3]

After 792/1390 Tīmūr had a new silver coin struck throughout the territories of Iran. At first it was introduced obviously only into Transoxiana and Khurāsān. This was the *tanga-yi nuqra* or silver *tanga*, a word which seems to be of Indian origin. Originally it denoted a unit of weight and was applied first to a coin probably under Maḥmūd of Ghazna. From the reign of Sultan Shams al-Dīn Iltutmish (607–33/1211–36) a silver tanga (tanga-yi nuqra) weighing 10.76 gm was being minted in Delhi. Tīmūr's tanga-yi nuqra followed this standard and weighed exactly half the tanga of Delhi, i.e. 5.38 gm. It was divided into four dirhams. Presumably Tīmūr's tanga soon ousted the above-mentioned lighter (dīnār-i) khurāsānī of four dirhams, for in the period around 844/1440 there is no further mention of the khurāsānī currency.

1 Rabino, "Coins of the Jalā'ir", pp. 103ff. Hinz, "Ein orientalisches Handelsunternehmen", p. 327, and *Resālä-ye Falakiyyä*, p. 14.

2 *Ibid.* Schroetter, p. 141. Smith, "The Silver Currency", p. 19. Herrmann and Doerfer, "Ein persisch-mongolischer Erlass", pp. 16–19.

3 Schroetter, pp. 141, 147. Hinz, "Steuerinschriften", p. 762, following the *Shams al-siyāq* of 'Alī Shīrāzī, MS Ayasofya 3986. On the kapakī dīnār, see further Barthold, *Ulugh Beg*, p. 8.

Under Shāh Rukh the weight of this silver tanga was reduced to 4.72 gm, which in his day was the weight of one mis̱qāl. In a very large part of the teritory under his rule, during the early decades of the 9th/15th century, the coin assumed the name *shāhrukhī*. Moreover, this Timurid tanga at one mis̱qāl was minted also in gold, although very rarely, and was called *tanga-yi ṭillā*. In later times it became the *ṭillā*, the current gold coinage of the Uzbek khans of Bukhārā, Khīva, and Khoqand.[1]

Even so, in the Timurid period various dīnār currencies persisted. There is evidence from 844/1440 of the existence of the following: in Transoxiana there was the kapakī dīnār at about 8 gm of silver. In western Iran there were as many as three different dīnār currencies, the relationship of which to the kapakī dīnār is known: the Baghdād or Shīrāz dīnār, the dīnār-i ʿIrāqī, and the Tabrīz dīnār. The dīnār-i ʿIrāqī seems traceable directly to the earlier Tabrīz dīnār-i rāyij, whereas the dīnār-i Tabrīzī of the 15th century must have appeared for the first time in Timurid times. At that time the relation between the four silver currencies was as follows: one kapakī dīnār was equivalent to three Baghdād (or Shīrāz) dīnārs, to six ʿIrāqī dīnārs and to nine Tabrīzī dīnārs. Thus we arrive at the following average weights for the various dīnārs: Baghdād or Shīrāz dīnār = *ca.* 2.7 gm; dīnār-i ʿIrāqī = *ca.* 1.35 gm; dīnār-i Tabrīzī = *ca.* 0.9 gm.[2]

There is one piece of information, likewise applicable to the period around 1440, that startles us: two kapakī dīnārs are supposed to have been equivalent to one tanga.[3] At first sight this would seem to contradict our affirmation that under Shāh Rukh a tanga of 4.72 gm had been minted. It is possible that meanwhile, at least in eastern Iran and Transoxiana, the name we have already mentioned, shāhrukhī, had become so popular for these smaller coins that the name tanga could be used for another species of coin. A similar process can be observed happening in the time of the Āq Quyūnlū in eastern Anatolia, where the terms tanga and shāhrukhī likewise denoted two different species of coin.[4] In the kingdom of Lār also there existed at a later date a monetary unit called a tanga, but this did not prevent a larger coin, the *lārī*, also being described as a tanga (cf. below).

In the second half of the 15th century the dīnār currency of Iran suffered an incredibly rapid decline. According to Hinz, in 1440 one

[1] Schroetter, pp. 680, 694. On the shāhrukhī, see *TMEN* II, 555.

[2] Hinz, in *Oriens* x (1957), 369.

[3] *Ibid.*, and "Steuerinschriften", p. 762.

[4] Barkan, "Osmanlı devrinde", pp. 100ff., 187.

tūmān-i 'Irāqī, i.e. 10,000 dīnārs, was still worth on the gold standard 3,250 German Gold Marks at pre-war standard (cf. below). Twelve years later the tūmān-i 'Irāqī had sunk to 1,200 Gold Marks. Under the Safavids the only currencies known were the 'Irāqī and Tabrīz dīnārs, and we may assume that the distinction between these soon became purely formal, both currencies becoming equal in value.[1] We may, therefore, equate the tūmān of 916/1510, that is of the reign of Ismā'īl I, with the tūmān-i 'Irāqī of 1440 and 1452: it was worth only 270 Gold Marks.

There is little information available on currency conditions under the Türkmen dynasties of the Qarā Quyūnlū and Āq Quyūnlū. In the time of Qarā Yūsuf, and presumably under all the other Qarā Quyūnlū rulers, the legal tender was the silver dīnār, at least in the form of the Tabrīz dīnār and the 'Irāqī dīnār. There are reports, however, which mention sums in tūmāns. Besides these there were silver tangas weighing 5 gm or 5.2 gm, and coins of Shāh Rukh and other Timurids were current also. What knowledge we have of the currency system in the Āq Quyūnlū state, at least in its territories in eastern Anatolia, comes from the records kept in these territories under the reign of the Ottoman Sultan Selīm I; and it is to these records, too, that we are indebted for our knowledge of Uzun Ḥasan's *Qānūn* (cf. above). There we find the following data: one *aqcha-yi 'Uṣmānī* (the Ottoman asper, the gold value of which at the time was calculated by Hinz to be 0.20 Gold Marks or 2.4d.) under the Āq Quyūnlū corresponded to three so-called *qaraja-aqchas*, also known as dirhams. One tanga is equated to two Ottoman aqchas, one *shāhrūqī* (clearly a corruption of shāhrukhī) to six Ottoman aqchas.[2] From this we may deduce:

1 tanga = 6 qaraja-aqcha
1 shāhrūqī = 3 tangas = 18 qaraja-aqchas

From this comparison we learn that one "shāhrūqī" had a gold value of 1.2 Gold Marks, which, at the end of the 15th century, was completely in line with the gold value of the shāhrukhī standardised at 4.72 gm under Shāh Rukh. In the second half of the 15th century the tanga of the Āq Quyūnlū period, of which we have just spoken, was worth only one-third of the shāhrukhī. This tanga was probably restricted to only a few provinces. Also in circulation was a silver coin with a

[1] Hinz, "Steuerinschriften", p. 762, quoting Chardin III, 156.

[2] Barkan, "Osmanlı devrinde", p. 187. Schroetter, p. 181. On the aqcha, see Schaendlinger, pp. 57ff.

standard weight of 4.6 gm (or 5.2 gm if we follow H.L. Rabino); and this coin, too, was called a tanga. In addition there were coins of half this weight, and even quarters and eighths of this unit. This tanga must have been the counterpart of the "shāhrūqī" we know existed in eastern Anatolia.[1] Under the Āq Quyūnlū, alongside a possibly multiple tanga currency, there was also in circulation the dīnār currency, principally the dīnār-i Tabrīzī.

A further brief note on the gold coins of the Türkmen dynasties: we know of a gold coin of Jahān Shāh Qarā Quyūnlū, weighing some 3.9 gm; the Āq Quyūnlū minted a gold coin weighing one *misqāl-i shar'ī*, i.e. a "canonical misqāl" of about 3.4 gm. Probably these two coins corresponded to the *ashrafī*; the second one almost certainly did. The ashrafī was an originally Egyptian gold coin which had been minted since 810/1407. It weighed 3.45 gm. There is proof that Mamlūk ashrafī coins were in circulation in the Āq Quyūnlū kingdom. There are, however, also records mentioning gold tangas of the Āq Quyūnlū rulers.[2]

We have already referred to the sharp debasement of the coinage in the course of the 15th century. This must be attributed to the fact that in the Safavid state the silver dīnār was no longer being minted. But the dīnār still remained what the tūmān had been from the beginning: a unit of account. In this period the 'Irāqī dīnār was already equated with the Tabriz dīnār as we mentioned above. This took place presumably as early as under Ismā'īl I. Other currencies based on the silver dīnār now existed only outside the frontiers of the Safavid state, with the exception of parts of Khurāsān.[3]

Under Ismā'īl I and Ṭahmāsp I, following the traditions of the 15th century silver tangas were still minted. But the early Safavid tanga no longer belonged to any special currency. Tanga was now the name for a coin of a specific weight, the value of which was expressed only in dīnārs or, which comes to the same thing, in fractions of the tūmān. In the early years of his reign, Ismā'īl's silver coins weighed four, two, and one misqāls (18.7 gm, 9.3 gm, and 4.7 gm). Later on their weight was reduced on several occasions. The silver coin weighing one misqāl was worth fifty dīnārs. The term tanga certainly applied to this coin, for its standard weight of one misqāl corresponded to the monetary

[1] Rabino, "Coins of the Jalā'ir", p. 127.

[2] *Ibid.* Schroetter, p. 42. Barkan, "Osmanlı devrinde", p. 101. Rabino, *Coins, Medals and Seals*, p. 14.

[3] *Ibid.*, p. 13.

standard of the silver tanga of the 15th century. Thus the double tanga was worth 100 dīnārs and the quadruple tanga 200 dīnārs.[1] Under Ṭahmāsp the new term *shāhī* supplanted the term tanga. One shāhī was equal to 50 dīnārs; the 100 dīnār coin was named the *dū-shāhī* ("double shāhī") and from 1540 weighed one misqāl (4.64 gm).[2] Under Muḥammad Khudābanda (985–95/1578–87) the name of the ruler established itself as the designation, *khudābanda* or *muḥammadī*, for the 100 dīnār coin. In the 17th century the name khudābanda was scarcely ever used. Under Muḥammad Khudābanda and at the beginning of the reign of 'Abbās I, the muḥammadī weighed one misqāl (about 4.7 gm).[3] For a short time it was the most minted coin, until under 'Abbās I (995–1038/1587–1629) a 200 dīnār piece appeared, the *'abbāsī*, which at first weighed two misqāls and hence corresponded to the Timurid tanga. In 1593 the weight of the 'abbāsī was reduced to 7.8 gm. Under 'Abbās I the following silver coins were minted: the *bīstī* worth 20 dīnārs, the shāhī worth 50 dīnārs, the muḥammadī worth 100 dīnārs, and finally the 200 dīnār piece, the 'abbāsī we have just mentioned. Besides these there were copper coins also called *qāz* or *qāzbakī*. One qāzbakī used to be worth five dīnārs. At the beginning of the 18th century there were "small"and "large" qāzbakīs, worth 5 and 10 dīnārs respectively. Copper coinage was minted in almost every city, but possessed its full value only in its region of origin; in the rest of the realm it possessed only half of its face value; it was re-minted annually.[4] From the second half of the 17th century more silver coins came into currency: the *hazār* (i.e. "thousand"), worth 1,000 dīnārs, and named also the *panj-'abbāsī*; and a *dah-shāhī* or *pānṣad-dīnār*, which, as the name indicates, was worth 500 dīnārs. In addition, under Sulaimān there were two different 'abbāsī coins: the "little 'abbāsī" worth 200 dīnārs and the so-called "large 'abbāsī" worth 250 dīnārs, also known as the *panj-shāhī*.[5] From the reign of 'Abbās I until the end of the 17th century the weight of the Safavid silver coins had scarcely altered.

[1] Here we accept Hinz's suggestion in "The Value of the Toman", p. 91, as against that of Rabino, *Coins, Medals and Seals*, p. 28, who argues that the 50 dīnār piece may have weighed 9.3 gm.

[2] Rabino, *Coins, Medals and Seals*, p. 15. This coin used to be called *ṣad-dīnār* or *ṣadī* also.

[3] *Ibid.* Hinz, "The Value of the Toman", p. 92. This coin was also known as a *maḥmūdī*: Schroetter, p. 1; Schuster-Walser, *Das ṣafawidische Persien*, p. 43.

[4] Schroetter, pp. 1ff. Rabino, "Coins of the Shahs", especially p. 350, and *Coins, Medals and Seals*, pp. 20ff., 32ff.

[5] Kaempfer, p. 54. Hinz, "The Value of the Toman", p. 94.

Only in the 18th century, under Sulṭān Ḥusain, did the ʿabbāsī, worth 200 dīnārs, drop to 5.4 gm.[1]

We have already mentioned that under Ismāʿīl I gold coins had been struck according to the monetary standard of the Mamlūk ashrafī at about 3.4–3.5 gm. Thus gold coins of 0.887 gm and 0.77 gm, struck in the name of Ismāʿīl, were $\frac{1}{4}$ ashrafīs.[2] Gold coins minted under Ṭahmāsp and Muḥammad Khudābanda exhibit by contrast the monetary standard of the Timurid (tanga-yi) ṭillā (the gold tanga), which lived on in the gold coinage of the Shaibanids and Janids in Transoxiana. One gold coin of ʿAbbās I weighed 2.3 gm; it represented a half-ṭillā, and thus followed the tanga standard, of Timurid origin.[3] Later the ashrafī completely ousted the gold tanga coinage. However, alongside the ashrafī currency gold coins were struck which followed the ʿabbāsī monetary standard current at the time. And so there were gold ʿabbāsīs, muḥammadīs, and so on. As has been explained already, these gold coins scarcely ever found their way into circulation. They were struck on special occasions and used chiefly by the shah as gifts. We must not fail to note, however, that foreign gold coinage, too, principally the Venetian ducat (*zecchino*, *ducato*) and the Florentine gulden (*fiorino*), were to be found all over the Middle East. In value they were always equivalent to the ashrafī.[4]

In conclusion we shall examine the Iranian currencies in circulation outside the Safavid state in the 16th and 17th centuries. One of the most popular coins around the Persian Gulf was the lārī, minted in Lār, the capital of Lāristān in southern Iran, a territory which in the 16th century did not yet belong to the Safavid empire. The lārī consisted of a double twist of silver purl, stamped on both sides, having a metal purity of 98% and weighing 4.8–5.1 gm.[5] This and the fact that in 1517 this curious coin was not only known as the lārī but sometimes was also designated as "tanga" causes us to surmise that the lārī, too, originally had been struck according to the standard of the Timurid tanga. In 1525 two lārī mintings were known: the "old lārī" equal to 3 tangas and 9 dīnārs, and the "new lārī" equal to 3 tangas and 10 dīnārs. In this

[1] Vasmer, p. 181.

[2] Rabino, *Coins, Medals and Seals*, p. 28.

[3] *Ibid.*, p. 34. Schroetter, pp. 681, 694.

[4] Du Mans, p. 33. Hinz, "Die spätmittelalterlichen Währungen", p. 303. Minorsky, *Tadhkirat al-Mulūk*, p. 59, arguing that *ashrafī-yi dū-butī* could have been the Venetian ducat. Vasmer, p. 138. J.L. Bacharach, "The Dinar versus the Ducat", *IJMES* IV (1973), 77–96.

[5] Hinz, "Die spätmittelalterlichen Währungen", p. 304. Cf. Rabino, *Coins, Medals and Seals*, p. 16.

context the tanga, as a fraction of the lārī, must not be confused with the name also commonly used of the whole lārī.[1] From these data we draw the following conclusion concerning the currency of Lāristān: its basis was the dīnār of Lāristān; 12 dīnārs made up one Lāristān tanga; an "old lārī", therefore, was valued at 45 dīnārs, a "new lārī" at 46 dīnārs. After the integration of Lāristān into the Safavid empire lārīs continued to be minted, although relatively seldom, but their value was determined from now on only by the Safavid currency, for obviously a native Lāristān currency no longer existed. And so: one (Safavid) lārī = 125 dīnārs = $1\frac{1}{4}$ muḥammadī = $\frac{1}{80}$ tūmān.[2]

In Hurmuz, which was under Portuguese rule in the 16th century, there were to be found in circulation at that time, besides lārīs, coins of a special dīnār currency. In the middle of the 16th century they seemed to have stood to the Safavid dīnār currency of the same period in the ratio of 4:1. At the beginning of the 16th century there was a 100 dīnār piece known as *ṣadī*, at that time the only silver coin in the dīnār currency of Hurmuz. The 1,000 dīnār piece called the hazār was of gold and was also called the "half ashrafī". One ashrafī, called by the Portuguese "xerafim", was thus equivalent to 2,000 Hurmuz dīnārs. In 1550 hazārs were also minted from silver. There was also a copper *fals* with a nominal value of 10 dīnārs. Until Hurmuz became absorbed into the Safavid empire in 1622, the Hurmuz currency steadily depreciated.

In Transoxiana, namely in the Uzbek khanates, the tanga currency continued after the days of the Timurids; but it was accompanied for some time by the kapakī dīnār currency. Rabino conjectures that the dīnār currency in circulation in Khurāsān in 1590 was identical with the kapakī dīnār currency and is to be traced back to the period of Uzbek rule in Khurāsān. Certainly at that time the value of the Khurāsān tūmān was less than that of the 'Irāqī (Tabrīz) tūmān of the Safavids by a quarter.[3]

In the following exposition we follow Hinz, whose research into the monetary system of Iran is of the highest importance.[4] We can arrive at a useful value-index of the various currencies by expressing them in terms of gold. A precondition for this is knowledge of the value ratio

[1] Hinz, "Die spätmittelalterlichen Währungen", pp. 304ff. (and cf. n.17).

[2] Rabino, *Coins, Medals and Seals*, p. 16. Hinz, "Die spätmittelalterlichen Währungen", p. 306, following Tavernier and Charles Lockyer, *An Account of the Trade in India* (London, 1711), p. 241.

[3] Rabino, *Coins, Medals and Seals*, p. 13, quoting Ḥasan-i Rūmlū.

[4] Hinz, "The Value of the Toman" and "Die spätmittelalterlichen Währungen".

of gold to silver – which was not the same at all times. This ratio was discovered by collating and assessing many data concerning money from various sources. In the 14th century the ratio was 1:12; in the middle of the 16th century it was 1:10; in 1622 it was again 1:12. About 1660 the ratio rose to 1:13¼ and by 1680 had reached the level of 1:15. In the early 18th century the ratio went back to 1:12. It is clear that when the gold value of silver fell, a silver coin of fixed weight lost in value, and *vice versa*.

Having taken these ratios into account, having assessed many parallel data concerning the nominal value of different coins and currencies, and having made use also of numismatic studies of monetary standards, we are at last in a position to make a statement concerning the gold value of the coinages underlying the currencies.

In the following tables, in accordance with Hinz, we will express the gold value of Iranian currencies and coins by means of German Gold Marks on the pre-war standard of 1913. The price of one gram of fine gold was then 2.81 Gold Marks. It should be noted that the equivalent of one German Gold Mark in English currency is one Gold Shilling; as far as French currency is concerned, 0.81 Gold Mark = 1 Gold Franc (all rates pre-war standard).

A. Iranian currencies based on silver dīnārs

year	*kind of dīnār*	*Approximate gold values of one tūmān (i.e. 10,000 dīnārs), expressed by equivalents in German Gold Mark on standard of 1913 (one gram of fine gold being 2.81 Gold Marks)*
	1. Pre-Safavid dīnārs	
c. 1300	dīnār-i rāyij (Ghazan)	29,400.- GM
c. 1320	dīnār (Abū Saʿīd)	24,500.- GM
c. 1380	kapakī dīnār	19,500.- GM
c. 1440	kapakī dīnār	19,500.- GM
c. 1440	dīnār-i Baghdād (d.-i Shīrāz)	6,500.- GM
c. 1440	dīnār-i ʿIrāqī	3,250.- GM
c. 1440	dīnār-i Tabrīzī	2,170.- GM
1452	dīnār-i ʿIrāqī	1,200.- GM
	2. Safavid dīnārs	
1510		270.- GM
1522		195.- GM
1530		165.- GM
1550		133.- GM
1577		162.- GM
1580		129.- GM
1593		100.- GM
1622		83.- GM
1660		77.- GM
1680		69.- GM
1711		63.5 GM
1718		66.5 GM
	3. dīnārs of Hurmuz	
c. 1520		50.- GM
c. 1550		33.6 GM
c. 1580		26.- GM
1618		22.7 GM

B. Currencies based on tangas

kind of tanga	*Approximate gold values of these tangas, expressed by equivalents in German Gold Mark on standard of 1913*
Tīmūr's tanga-yi nuqra with a weight of 5.38 grams (after 1390)	1.26 GM
Timurid tanga of the 15th century weighing 4.72 grams (the so-called shāhrukhī)	1.10 GM
"large tanga" equalling two kapakī dīnārs, *c.* 1440	3.90 GM
"small tanga", coined by the Āq Quyūnlū rulers in eastern Anatolia (late 15th century)	0.40 GM

C. Currency of Lāristān

year	*unit of currency*	*Approximate gold values expressed by equivalents in German Gold Mark on standard of 1913*
1525	"old" lārī	1.67 GM
1525	"new" lārī	1.70 GM
1525	so-called "small tanga" in Lāristān	0.44 GM
1554	lārī	1.43 GM
1615	lārī	1.25 GM
1627	lārī	1.05 GM

After the monetary integration of Lāristān into the Safavid empire one lārī equals 125 Safavid dīnārs

CHAPTER 10

THE EXACT SCIENCES IN TIMURID IRAN

Throughout the four centuries preceding the rise of Tīmūr, science had been actively cultivated in many parts of the Iranian plateau by practitioners who were in the forefronts of their respective disciplines. The dissipation of political power which attended the breakup of the 'Abbasid empire entailed also a dispersal of the scientists concentrated at Baghdad. But lines of inquiry opened by them were pursued by scholars supported at the various later dynastic centres. During this time trigonometry emerged as an independent branch of mathematics. The foundations of geometry were repeatedly re-examined, and steps were taken towards generalising the concept of number; solutions were given for extensive classes of algebraic equations. Advances were made in mathematical geography, and in astronomy, both in theory and in observation. In optics, a start was made in explaining the phenomenon of the rainbow. It is the object of this chapter to give an account of the extent to which these activities were continued during the century and a half between, say, 1350 and 1500. In point of fact, most of what follows describes the accomplishments of one man, Jamshīd Ghiyāṣ al-Dīn al-Kāshī (d. 832/1429), working at one place, Ulugh Beg's Samarqand observatory, and in one subject, numerical analysis. The names of a number of other scientists at Samarqand are known, and many more can be assembled from other localities, but only the writings of Jamshīd transcend competence and are contributions to knowledge.

This somewhat narrow picture may be changed at any time by the recovery of additional material. The ratio of scientific manuscripts studied to scientific manuscripts which exist is very low, though perhaps no lower for Timurid Iran than for Europe, or India, or the Far East. But meanwhile only what is known can be described. In what follows, modern mathematical symbols are used where convenient. There is no trace of this in the texts themselves; either the equivalent expressions are written out verbally or they must be inferred from the context.

DECIMAL FRACTIONS

If any system of representing numbers is to be used for major computations, it is necessary that it embody the notion of *place value*. This means that in the array of symbols which represents any particular number, the contribution of any individual symbol is determined not only by the symbol itself, but also by its place in the array; for instance, in the array 2027, the contribution of one of the 2's is two thousand, of the other, twenty. Only a finite number of different symbols is required, and this number is called the *base* of the system.

The first place value system to be invented was the sexagesimal representation (base sixty), in Mesopotamia, sometime in the second millennium B.C. Much later the now familiar decimal system appeared in India. Both were known and used by Islamic scientists from ʿAbbasid times on, but with inherited perversities which require explanation. Sexagesimals as written by the Babylonians incorporated no device analogous to the decimal point. It was as though with us 2027 could mean 2027000 ($=2027 \times 10^3$), or 20.27 ($=2027 \times 10^{-2}$), or .0002027 (2027×10^{-7}), or just 2027, or this times any other power of the base. Hence a set of cuneiform numeral symbols (digits) may represent one of many possible numbers, fractional or integer, and the reader must infer from the context which particular one the scribe had in mind. The Indian decimals, on the other hand, were used only for whole numbers (or common fractions), so that no decimal point was called for, and the representation was unique.

For the most part, the results of Islamic calculations were expressed neither in pure sexagesimals nor in pure decimals, but in a mongrel arrangement taken over from the Greeks. In it all symbols were alphabetical, the Arabic cognates of Greek letters. For the integer part of a number a non-place-value decimal system was used, the fractional part being in sexagesimals. But when it was necessary to multiply, divide, or extract roots of these numbers, they would first be transformed into a decimal expression in Indian numerals having a denomination of the smallest sexagesimal fraction present in the original expression. For example, the symbols (read from right to left) قك ه نج which may be transcribed as 120 5 53, stand for $120 + 5/60 + 53/60^2$. This number would be converted into the form: 432353 *seconds*, since $(120 \times 60^2) + (5 \times 60) + 53 = 432353$. Any desired operations having been performed on the decimal representations, the final result would be returned to the original alphabetical form, with sexagesimal fractions.[1]

Pure sexagesimals were by no means unknown in Islamic writings; they are to be found particularly in chronological tables, where the spans of days between pairs of epochs are often very large. Neither were decimal fractions completely unknown. Several occur in the 4th/10th century arithmetic of al-Uqlīdisī.[2] The medieval Chinese, in computing the appearance of new moons, measured time in days and in units consisting of one ten-thousandth of a day. This special variety of decimal fraction was well-known to Jamshīd from his work with the Chinese calendar.[3] It may have suggested to him the notion of the decimal fraction in full generality, which he proceeded to describe and to apply in his textbook of arithmetic, the *Miftāḥ al-ḥisāb*. So far as is known he was the first to do this, and in so doing anticipated the Fleming, Stevin, by almost two centuries.[4]

Jamshīd noticed that a sexagesimal representation can be thought of as two sequences of digits proceeding in opposite directions from the units digit. Thus in the representation

دلدكه طمح نو ثوالث,

which may be transcribed as

4 34 25 9 48 56 *thirds*

and which stands for

$$\mathbf{4}\times 60^2+\mathbf{34}\times 60^1+\mathbf{25}\times 60^\circ+\mathbf{9}\times 60^{-1}+\mathbf{48}\times 60^{-2}+\mathbf{56}\times 60^{-3},$$

the sequence 9, 48, 56 yields the fractional part of the number, and 25, 34, 4 the integer part. He observed further that the decimal system is completely analogous to the sexagesimal, and that to restrict the former to the writing of integers is to throw away, as it were, half the potential of the system. Therefore he adjoined a sequence of fractional digits to the integer sequence to give, say,

2953871 *decimal fourths*,

where we would write

295.3871.

It is worth remarking that his notation giving the power of the base by

[1] For an example, see Kennedy and Muruwwa, "Bīrūnī".

[2] See *Isis* LV (1964), 210.

[3] Kennedy, "The Chinese-Uighur Calendar", pp. 436–7.

[4] Juschkewitsch, pp. 236–48, 363–5.

which the rest of the representation is to be multiplied (instead of a mark to set off the fractional part) is precisely the "floating point" convention used nowadays in programming digital computers.

Having established the theoretical basis for decimal fractions, Jamshīd then went on to demonstrate their utility in the computation of areas, volumes, and other geometric problems. He gave rules and examples for converting common fractions into decimals, and conversely, and he worked out tables, still useful, for the conversion of sexagesimals into decimals, and vice versa.

The *Miftāḥ* was widely disseminated in manuscript copies. That its influence reached as far as Constantinople is demonstrated by an arithmetic written there, in Greek, sometime during the latter half of the 9th/15th century. This book contains one worked example of multiplication and one of division in which decimal fractions, converted from common fractions, are employed. The author ascribes the technique to "the Turks", and it is known that at least one of Jamshīd's colleagues at Samarqand, al-Qūshchī, eventually established himself in Constantinople. [1]

THE π-COMPUTATION

The important number now universally called π, definable as the ratio between the circumference and the diameter of any circle, has been an object of interest since the beginning of mathematics. In a treatise devoted entirely to it, *al-Risāla al-muḥītiyya*, Jamshīd criticises the approximations to π made by various individuals. He remarks, for instance, that the use of Archimedes' value, the familiar $3\frac{1}{7}$, to calculate the earth's circumference in terms of its radius would entail a possible inaccuracy of five *farsakhs*. He therefore proposes to compute π to such a degree of precision that if it is used to calculate the circumference of a circle with a diameter of 600,000 earth-diameters, the error involved will be less than the smallest linear unit known to him – the breadth of a horsehair. Presumably he chose this diameter as being that of the largest circle in the universe, a great circle on the sphere of the fixed stars. By use of the hierarchy of units between the horsehair and the earth-diameter, he shows that the imposed condition demands an order of accuracy of $1/60^9$ part of the result.

[1] Hunger and Vogel, pp. 32–5, 104.

His method of procedure, like that of all his predecessors, is to use the fact that if a regular polygon is inscribed in (or circumscribed about) a circle, the difference between the perimeter of the polygon and the circumference of the circle may be made arbitrarily small by sufficiently increasing the number of sides of the polygon.

From elementary geometric considerations, Jamshīd adduces relations expressible (in modern symbols) as follows:

Let a regular polygon be inscribed in a unit circle such that each side, a_n, subtends an arc $\alpha_n = 60°/2^{n-1}$, and let c_n be the chord of the supplement of this arc. Then, since $a_1 = \sqrt{3}$, the recursion relation

$$c_n = (2 + c_{n-1})^{1/2} \tag{1}$$

makes it possible to calculate any desired c_n by computing the second c in terms of the first, the third from the second, and so on. Moreover, the Pythagorean relation gives

$$a_n = (2^2 - c^2_n)^{1/2},$$

and the perimeter, an approximation to 2π, is the product of the length of a side, a_n, times the number of sides, $3 \cdot 2^n$.

Before beginning the actual computation, Jamshīd proceeds to determine how many iterations of (1) will be required to insure the degree of precision he has set himself, and to how many fractional sexagesimal places he must work. For this purpose, he makes a general estimate of the number of horsehairs which, laid side by side, will encircle the universe. And from this he concludes that the angle subtended at the centre by a single hair is greater than $1/60^8$ of a degree. Hence the required accuracy will be secured if the error is less than the latter. This condition is applied in the course of an involved sequence of inferences drawn from inequalities, and leading to the conclusion that, for a circle of radius sixty, an acceptable a_n must be less than $8/60^4$. Thereupon Jamshīd sets about successive halvings of $120°$ to produce the sequence of α's. It turns out that α_{28} is less than $6°/60^4$, and its chord, a_{28}, satisfies the condition given just above. The number of sides in the inscribed polygon finally used is therefore $3 \cdot 2^{28}$ $(= 805,306,368)$. In the sexagesimal representation this number has six digits. This consideration, combined with the requirement that the result must have eight significant fractional digits leads to the conclusion that, with numbers obtained in the course of the computation, digits beyond the eighteenth may safely be neglected, a requirement which is in fact unduly rigorous.

At this stage the calculation proper can commence. The main part of it consists of twenty-eight square root extractions, each one of which takes up an elegantly laid out page of the manuscript. In order to maintain a running check of the operation as it progresses, each successive square root is squared, and the result compared with the radicand.

The final result (in modern notation) is

$$2\pi = 6;16,59,28,1,34,51,46,14,50,$$

where the commas separate sexagesimal digits, and the semicolon is the "sexagesimal point".

For the benefit of people who are unaccustomed to this base, Jamshīd converts it into decimal fractions as

$$2\pi = 6.283\ 185\ 307\ 179\ 586\ 5,$$

correct to the last digit.

TRIGONOMETRIC TABLES

Trigonometry as an independent branch of mathematics was in large measure a creation of Muslim medieval astronomers. From the ninth century on, the standard trigonometric functions were made available in tables of continually increasing detail and precision. This trend reached its high point in Timurid Iran, and the function tables produced at the Samarqand observatory of Ulugh Beg are superior to all others of the time, a supremacy which was retained for a century.

The sine table alone in this set has a value for each minute of each degree up to ninety, hence 5,400 entries. But this number is doubled by the presence of a tabular difference (for each interpolation) for each entry. All of these are carried to five sexagesimal places, implying precision of the order of one to seven hundred million. These tables have been recalculated with electronic computers, and no error has been observed. The other trigonometric ratios were tabulated in analogous fashion at Samarqand, as well as many of the special functions encountered in spherical astronomy.

Implicit behind these masses of numerals is the knowledge of algorisms, computational schemes, which call for much more than patient and meticulous reckoning. An example is Jamshīd's method of determining the sine of one degree to any desired accuracy, the algorism which underlies Ulugh Beg's sine table.

The solution is related to the classical Greek problem of trisecting an angle. Jamshīd first derived a relation between the sine of any angle and the sine of its third, which we may write as

$$\sin 3\alpha = 3 \sin\alpha - 4 \sin^3\alpha. \tag{2}$$

The sine of three degrees, as it happens, is not difficult to calculate, by manipulating the functions of larger angles (like 30°) which are even easier to find. Let $x = \sin 1°$ and put $q = \sin 3°$, assumed to be known. Then (2) becomes

$$x = \frac{q + 4x^3}{3}, \tag{3}$$

which transforms the problem into that of finding a number x satisfying the cubic equation (3). The first sexagesimal digit of this root was already known, from earlier tables. Call this digit d_1; regard it as a first appproximation to the root, say $x_1 = d_1$, and try it out by substitution in (3). Symbolically, put $f(x) = (q + 4x^3)/3$, and calculate

$$x_1 - f(x_1) = r_2 \approx d_2,$$

where d_2 is formed from r_2 by dropping off all its sexagesimal digits save the first. Now regard d_2 as a correction to d_1 and add the two to obtain a better approximation to the root. I.e., put $x_2 = x_1 + d_2$, and repeat the above process to find a d_3. This means, form

$$x_2 - f(x_2) = r_3 \approx d_3.$$

The cycle of operations is then repeated. In general

$$x_n - f(x_n) = r_{n+1} \approx d_{n+1}$$

and

$$x_{n+1} = x_n + d_{n+1},$$

until the desired precision is attained.

This type of iterative algorism was used many centuries before the time of Jamshīd, and it is valid for categories of $f(x)$ much more general than this particular polynomial. But his is a particularly elegant example because the only operations involved are additions, subtractions, and multiplications. Furthermore, the process converges so fast that each iteration pinches off one more digit in the final result.[1]

[1] Computation described more fully in Juschkewitsch, pp. 319–24.

COMPUTING INSTRUMENTS – THE EQUATORIUM

Throughout the Middle Ages a great variety of scientific instruments were invented and produced in the countries of Islam, and in Iran in particular. These included astrolabes of many types, quadrants, celestial spheres, sundials, and mechanical or graphical devices designed to accept numerical data and to solve certain categories of problems in instances where tedious computation could be eliminated. Most of the known instruments of Timurid provenance are of types well known in previous periods. The one described briefly below, however, the equatorium invented by Jamshīd al-Kāshī, is in several ways unique.

For a given planet and a given time, the problem of determining its position in the celestial sphere has been of interest since early times. The operation is reducible to two parts: the determination of the planet's mean position, and the calculation of its "equation". Solution of the first part is simple indeed. The planet's motion is always in the vicinity of a fixed great circle called the ecliptic, and always generally forward on the ecliptic, but sometimes moving faster than its mean velocity, sometimes slower, and sometimes even backwards. It is customary to imagine a point, the "mean planet", which travels with the mean motion of the actual planet, sometimes on one side or the other of it but never exceeding a fixed distance on either side. The position of the mean planet at any time may be found by adding to its position at some known epoch the product of the time elapsed since epoch and the mean velocity.

The planet's equation at any time is the distance between the mean planet and the true planet at that instant; it is a measure of the irregularity of the true motion. The latter, in turn, is caused primarily by two effects, arising from the common character of the earth's and the planet's orbits about the sun. We view the planet from, as it were, a moving platform; hence its direction from us is affected not only by its own travels around the sun, but also by the changing point of view afforded by our own annual trip about the same object. Furthermore, neither orbit is quite a circle, and both earth and planet travel faster when they are nearer the sun.

The problem of determining the equation is therefore a complicated one. In medieval times the most precise method of solving it was to use a pair of tabulated functions, the "equation of the centre", and the "equation of the anomaly", and to modify the entry obtained from the one table by an involved interpolation procedure utilising the entry from the other table. Tables for determining the mean position, on the other hand, were very easy to use, since addition was the only operation required. A second method of solution would be to construct a scale model of the earth – sun – planet system, consisting essentially of the two orbits, the one being constrained to maintain its proper position relative to the other. Points properly fixed on the orbits represent the respective celestial bodies. For any particular time, a straightedge passing from the earth to the planet would indicate the planet's true position at that instant. A third way of solving the problem is to make a scale drawing of the configuration as of the time in question, whereupon the vector drawn from the image of the earth to that of the planet would yield the desired position.

Jamshīd's planetary equatorium can be characterised as an ingenious combination of the three types of approach sketched above: numerical, mechanical, and graphical. Mean positions were to be determined by numerical tables; hence they constituted the initial data fed into the machine. It consisted essentially of a large circular plate surrounded by an annular ring, graduated all around in degrees in order to serve as a 360° protractor. There were two moving parts, a graduated alidade, pivoted at the centre of the plate, and a graduated ruler, arranged so that it and the alidade together could be operated as parallel rulers. They served to transfer angular distances back and forth between the plate, which was used as a plotting board, and the protractor. Fig. 1 is a schematic representation of the instrument as set up to give a true position for the planet Mars. For purposes of simplicity, most of the graduations and rulings of the actual instrument have been left off the drawing. Of the two orbits required for each planet, one (called the deferent) was permanently engraved on the plate. The other (the epicycle) was never actually drawn, although it appears on our figure. The radius of the epicycle equals the segment *CD* on the alidade edge. By a rotation of the alidade, this length can be transferred to *CD'*, thence displaced to *EM*. Without going into details, it transpires that *C* can be regarded as the image of the earth and *M* that of Mars, whence the place where the alidade edge crosses the protractor ring gives the required true position. Thus the device yielded quick results, accurate, say, to within ten minutes of arc. Since the main motive for calculating planetary positions was for the casting of horoscopes, this degree of precision was ample.

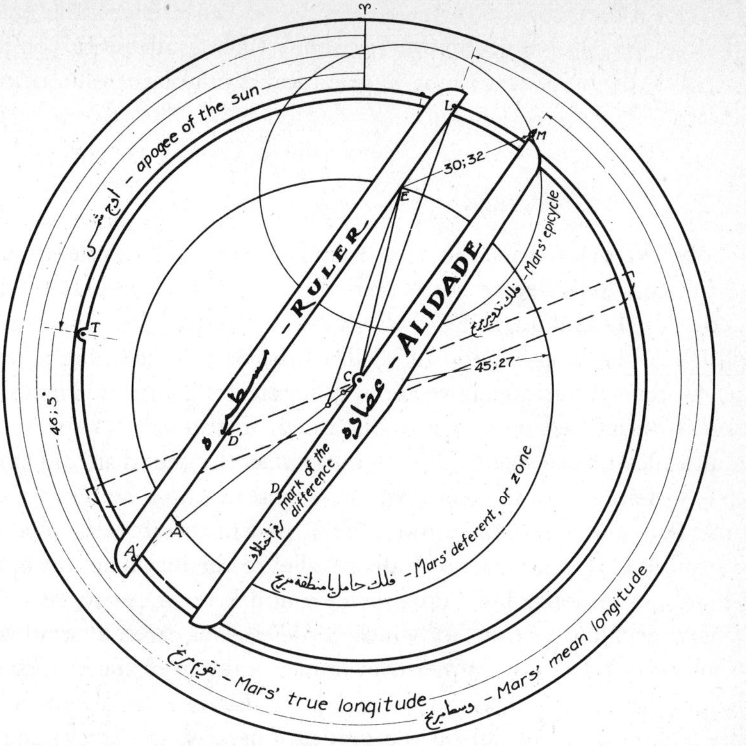

Fig. 1. A simplified representation of Jamshīd's equatorium as set up to give a true longitude for the planet Mars.

The basic idea of the equatorium reaches back into Hellenistic times, and several were constructed in medieval Europe, one by the poet Chaucer. So far, however, Jamshīd's version is the only example recovered from the lands of eastern Islam, and it is probably the most compact of all. In one respect it was far superior to others of its time in that it includes a method for determining planetary latitudes as well as longitudes.

The orbital planes of the planets lie almost in the ecliptic plane, and no great error is involved in assuming that the planetary motions take place in the ecliptic, as was done above. The problem is then two-dimensional and the motions are known as motions in longitude. In actual fact, however, the orbits diverge slightly from the ecliptic, and the amount of a planet's divergence at any time is called its latitude. The prediction of a latitude, since it adds a third dimension to the problem, is inevitably difficult. By applying what later came to be known as descriptive geometry, Jamshīd makes available to prospective users of his equatorium a graphical solution of the latitude problem.

OBSERVATIONAL ASTRONOMY

The observatory founded at Samarqand in 833/1430 by the astronomer-prince Ulugh Beg worthily carried on the tradition established by the Buyid, the Saljūq and the Il-Khanid dynasties. The observatory building, occupying the top of a hillock some 21 metres high, was a three-storey cylindrical edifice about 46 metres in diameter. The installation is dominated by an enormous mural instrument for measuring the altitudes of celestial bodies as they cross the meridian (fig. 2). It consists of an arc, in the meridian plane, and having a radius of about 40 metres. In order to make room for it, part of the arc was sunk into the ground between a pair of walls parallel to the meridian plane, and part was on masonry built up above ground level. The arc, or rather the narrow cylindrical surface which carries it, was carefully graduated in fractions of degrees. At meridian transit, a ray from the sun, or any other object being observed, would pass through an orifice at the centre of the arc and fall on the graduations, giving the altitude directly. Extensive remains of the building and instrument have been excavated, and are much visited by tourists in the Soviet Union. The instrument is an extreme example of an attempt to gain precision by great size.

Other instruments were in use there, but no complete listing can be given. There exists a letter by Jamshīd written from Samarqand back home to his father in Kāshān. In it he reports progress in the building of the observatory, saying that one armillary sphere had been completed, and that another was being made, as well as a diopter and an azimuth instrument with two quadrants. Both of the latter are types invented or elaborated upon at the Il-Khanid observatory at Marāgha. Jamshīd states further that before his arrival two massive brass rings had been cast, six cubits in diameter, to observe declinations after the manner of Ptolemy. He pointed out that the progress of the art had shown this technique to be faulty, and the sultan ordered the rings broken up and the metal used for other instruments.

Of other Timurid observatories we have no knowledge, nor can

Fig. 2. The meridian transit instrument at Ulugh Beg's Samarqand observatory.

much be said about actual observations. That the Samarqand observatory was used, follows from the fact that the stellar coordinates in the table of fixed stars in Ulugh Beg's *Zīj* are, for the most part, the result of independent observations. Jamshīd reports very completely three lunar eclipses he observed at Kāshān in 808/1406 and 809/1407.[1] There is no evidence to suggest that the elaborate observatories characteristic of late Islamic astronomy produced results which would have been unobtainable with less massive equipment.

RECAPITULATION AND ASSESSMENT

One general conclusion is clear – that the activity which had given Iran pre-eminence in science from late ʿAbbasid through Saljūq and Mongol times fell off markedly during the span of the Timurid dynasty. Steady and continuous progress had been made by Islamic mathematicians in the foundations of mathematics, in the solution of algebraic equations, and in geometrical optics. No Timurid additions can be exhibited in these fields, although competent practitioners continued to be plentiful. By way of contrast, vigorous work in trigonometry was now under way in Central Europe, and further west Oresme[2] was developing the concept of fractional exponents.

In one branch of mathematics, numerical analysis, brilliant work was done. Jamshīd's computational algorisms exhibited a feel for elegance, precision, and control which had never been seen before, and which was not to be surpassed for a long time to come.

The situation is much the same in astronomy. Writings of the Marāgha planetary theorists who later so strongly influenced Copernicus were known and debated in the group around Ulugh Beg.[3] But the available work done at Samarqand is purely Ptolemaic, unaffected by the newer planetary models. The equatorium of Jamshīd was matched by one turned out by a French contemporary of his, Fusoris. Whatever observations may have been made at Samarqand were less significant than the many hundreds recorded at Nuremberg alone by Walther[4] and his collaborators. All things considered, Iran's scientific output, though weakening, may have maintained her in a leading position through the 9th/15th century. Thereafter, the lead passed clearly to the West.

[1] *Zīj-i Khāqānī*, fol. 4r. [2] Juschkewitsch, pp. 401–9.
[3] Sayılı, "Ghiyāth al-Dīn al-Kāshī's Letter", pp. 99, 100.
[4] Pannekoek, p. 181.

CHAPTER 11

PERSIAN SCIENCE IN SAFAVID TIMES

One of the most distinguished European travellers drawn to Persia in Safavid times, Sir John Chardin, records a native saying in these terms: "Le doute est le commencement de la science; qui ne doute de rien n'examine rien, qui n'examine rien ne découvre rien, qui ne découvre rien est aveugle et demeure aveugle".[1] And he goes on to place both Persian and Chinese science next to that of Europe in achievement, qualifying his statement by adding that certain theorems which are regarded as new in the West are, in fact, to be found in the Persian and Arab books. But Chardin was impressed by the legacy of the past, for Islamic science, which had a strong Persian element, reached its zenith with Ibn Sīnā, al-Bīrūnī, 'Umar Khayyām, al-Khāzinī, and al-Ṭūsī, and, apart from a late burst of activity in Timurid times attributable to Ulugh Beg and his school, was then in decline. Medicine alone continued to make new advances.

There are, nevertheless, several influences which go to make this period in the history of science one of peculiar interest. Persia was a place of exchanges in ideas rather than a focus of original discovery. The protracted and bitter struggle between the Safavid monarchs and the Ottoman Turks, in the course of which the Persians became familiar with embassies from European courts, and Anthony Sherley is said to have suggested to Shah 'Abbās I an alliance with the Christian powers, not only generated an interest in technology, for the shah's armies were initially deficient in the heavier weapons of war; it also enabled Persia to know something of the scientific revolution which was gaining in momentum and influence in western Europe. Her traditional Islamic science, with a few Chinese accretions absorbed in the years of Mongol dominion, would soon be exposed to a discipline which might be called world science, for Persia was no longer in isolation from the effects of experimental method and the interpretation of its results in terms of mathematical analysis. Lest we be inclined, however, to exaggerate this impact upon the native science and culture, we are corrected at once by a predominant regard for the

[1] Chardin IV, 197.

established authors from Ulugh Beg and al-Ṭūsī right back to Galen, Ptolemy, Apollonius, and Euclid; by the perfection in Safavid times of the workmanship and art of the astrolabe, the favourite portable astronomical instrument of medieval Islam; by the persistence and further development of a medical tradition which owed much to India; and, not least, by the dead hand of orthodoxy. What the exhaustion and ravages of war failed to obliterate, the zealots of the Shī'ī faith strove to deny. In the struggle between the divine and the secular sciences the Legalities were in the ascendant, the Accomplishments in decline. To quote Mīrzā Muḥammad Qazvīnī on the Safavids: "... under this dynasty learning, culture, poetry and mysticism completely deserted Persia...".[1]

For two centuries there was a dearth of creative minds in literature, and many scholars perished in the siege of Iṣfahān in 1134–5/1722. The torch of learning which had burned brightest at the court of the ageing Sulṭān Ḥusain Bāīqarā in Herat in the early 10th/16th century now reappeared, rekindled at the Mughal court in Delhi, where thinkers and writers gathered from Persia under the liberal patronage of Humāyūn. Indeed it is from Persia's nearest neighbours, India and Turkey, that one may glean information which throws further light upon the condition of Persian science as well. This is not so surprising when it is realised that mathematics (*riyāẓiyyāt*), natural science (*ṭabī'iyyāt*) and metaphysics (*mā varā*, or *mā ba'd, al-ṭabī'at*) together comprised philosophy, and that in traditional Islamic science there was a strong *a priori* tendency inherited from the Greeks. Alchemy and astrology were still powers to be reckoned with, and times were harsh on those whose predictions failed to meet royal approval; but then it was not so different in Elizabethan England. It is impossible, as it was in medieval Latin Christendom, to sever science as a separate discipline from the whole corpus of learning, and at the courts of both Shah 'Abbās II in Iṣfahān and Akbar in Delhi there were poets who were physicians and physicians who were poets. Francis Bacon in England had still to ring the bell that gathered all the other wits together and so point the new way to scientific discovery. This period was one of transition in the West and, to a lesser extent, in Persia; thus it is necessary to evaluate the forces for change against a stable background of tradition.

[1] *LHP* IV, 26–8.

EMISSARIES, AMBASSADORS, AND CATHOLIC MISSIONS

Snippets of scientific information may be collected from the accounts of European travellers, many of whom settled and worked in the service of the shah. Thus, "Master Jeffrey Ducket, agent for the Muscovie companie" writes *c.*1574: "They have few bookes and lesse learning, and are for the most part very brutish in all kind of good sciences, saving in some kind of silke workes, and in such things as pertaine to the furniture of the horses, in which they are passing good".[1] Don Juan (Uruch Beg), who knew both Persia and the Catholic West, speaks[2] of "great numbers of water-wheels all along the banks of the rivers and lagoons, these being made after the fashion of the water-wheels and mills we see on the Tagus", and adds that armour of thin steel plate "cunningly forged" is made in large quantity and some "exported into Muscovy". On the subject of medicine he says: "In the matter of curing disease they do as with other nations of the barbarians, using herbs and ordering a strict diet. In acute illnesses, such as in cases of quinsy, pleurisy and the like, they bleed. The people are very superstitious, being given to regarding auguries, and imagine that by praying in the mosque they can favourably affect, or at least prognosticate, the issue of all their maladies." The writer knew of the splendours of Iṣfahān, its six hundred caravansarais at the entrance gates and its three hundred *ḥammāms*, and the stable system of communications in the reign of Shah 'Abbās the Great (995–1038/1587–1629).

William Parry, who accompanied Sir Anthony Sherley on his Persian travels in 1598–9, obviously makes a superficial observation when he says: "They are no learned nation, but ignorant in all kind of liberal or learned sciences..." and their writing is "as a wild kind of scribbling that hath therein neither form nor matter".[3] In fact, the Sherley brothers were bent upon diplomacy and military affairs, so that we learn only about the technology of ordnance. Abel Pinçon, also in the suite of Anthony Sherley, relates that the Persians had only a heavy armoured clothing and no artillery save that left behind by the Ottoman Sultan Selīm I in 920/1514. However, this statement has to be considered in relation to one made by Don Juan, to the effect that when the Turks of Sultan Murād III held the fortress of Tabrīz in

[1] Jenkinson, *Early Voyages* II, 436 (Hakluyt, *Principal Navigations* II, 129).

[2] Don Juan, trans. Le Strange, pp. 50–2.

[3] Ross, *Sir Anthony Sherley*, pp. 121–2.

993/1585 the Persians brought up two immense siege-guns whose bore at the open end "spanned a yard [*bara*] across, the length of the barrel being five yards".[1] Moreover, cannon seem to have been captured also from the Tartars, whilst at the height of his power Shah 'Abbās I appears to have drawn to his allegiance men who had deserted the Turks and were competent to manufacture new ones. Creasy[2] emphasises the undoubted superiority of the Turks in military engineering, but it may well be that after the encounter with the Sherleys the Persian artillery improved somewhat as a result of European contact: and this contact was maintained, for Philippe Colombe, a Frenchman, in charge of Persian ordnance under Shah Sulṭān Ḥusain, was killed in the battle of Gulnābād in 1134/1722. The immediate result of cooperation with Anthony Sherley, who is said to have brought a "gun-founder" in his company and to have shown the shah books containing "models of fortifications", is summed up in an exaggerated manner in the well-known quotation:

The mighty Ottoman, terror of the Christian World, quaketh of a Sherley-fever, and gives hopes of approaching fate. The prevailing Persian hath learned Sherleian arts of war, and he which before knew not the use of ordnance, hath now 500 pieces of brass, and 6,000 musketeers; so that they which at hand with the sword were before dreadful to the Turkes, now also in remoter blows and sulphurian arts are grown terrible.[3]

It is now clear that this statement cannot be taken at its face value, and that a more sober view should prevail: Savory gives first credit to the Portuguese and the Continental gunners in their service.

A still later English traveller, who was in Persia on the death of Shah 'Abbās I and who published his account some four years after returning to London, was Thomas Herbert. His comments on the state of Persian science are a useful general summary. Writing of the physicians, he says:

So well as I could apprehend, these are learned in the sciences, and few but are philosophers: nevertheless, their libraries are small; their books usually Arabic, but choice and useful, commonly such as advance their practice and profession; and in their proper art I perceived that they prefer plants and other vegetables before minerals... They are masters of much knowledge and not a little delighted with judicial astrology. Many Arabic writers, learned both in

[1] Don Juan, trans. Le Strange, p. 189.

[2] Sir Edward Creasy, *History of the Ottoman Turks* (London, 1878), p. 202.

[3] Purchas x, 376.

natural philosophy and the mathematics, have flourished in those parts, most of whose books they read, namely Hippocrates, Galen, Averroes, Alfarabius, Avicenna, Ben-Isaac, Abbu-Ally, Mahummed-Abdilla, Ben-Eladib, Abu-beer, Rhazis, Algazzallys, and Albu-mazar."[1]

Of the cities, Herbert says that Shīrāz "has a college wherein is read philosophy, astrology, physic, chemistry, and the mathematics; so as 'tis the more famoused through Persia",[2] whilst in Iṣfahān "Within the Maydan the shops"... show "greater variety of simples and ingredients of medicines than ever I saw together in any one city of Europe; and such as may give encouragement to physicians both to view and judge ..."[3] He also refers to the source of assafoetida as the region around Lahore and the River Indus, and remarks on the prevalence of mulberry forests for the rearing of the silkworm in the northern parts of the country (Persia). Like other travellers he notices in the people the veneration of tradition, such as adherence to the lunar calendar, and the general lack of enthusiasm for invention and innovation.

Without doubt our most valuable informant is Chardin. Knowledgeable in science, he gives the only systematic account of its condition in Safavid times. His travels took him to Persia in 1666, when he was in Iṣfahān on the death of Shah 'Abbās II, then to India, and back again to Persia in 1669. He returned to Paris in 1670 but was soon once more on his way to Persia, where he arrived in 1672 and stayed for four years. Finally he came to England, and was made Court Jeweller by Charles II, was knighted in 1681, and elected a Fellow of the Royal Society a year later. According to Chardin, the Persians "have a ready disposition to Sciences, and to the Liberal and Mechanick Arts ..." Astronomy and astrology are the most cultivated, especially since the latter affords an infallible key to the future. There are numerous astrologers in the capital Iṣfahān, and "the most celebrated originate from Corasson, where there is a little town called Genabad, and one illustrious family, noted for astronomy. The King draws his court astrologers only from Genabad, which has a school for training all the astronomers of Persia. In this region of ancient Bactria and Sogdiana, between the rivers Oxus and Jaxarte, where the air is pure, dry, and still, there have flourished for six hundred years the most competent astronomers."[4]

[1] Herbert, *Travels in Persia*, pp. 244–6: for explanatory notes on the proper names, see p. 329.
[2] *Ibid.*, p. 72. [3] *Ibid.*, p. 129. [4] Chardin IV, 211.

Chardin also has a chapter entitled "Of the Trees, Plants, and Druggs", for "Persia is a perfect Country for Physical Druggs";[1] and he goes on to relate an amusing story concerning the rivalry between astrologers and physicians at the Court:

Les astrologues sont toujours pleins de jalousie contre les médecins, comme également puissans, riches et recherchés; c'est à qui aura la faveur; les médecins veulent agir selon les phénomènes des maladies, et donner là-dessus les remèdes de l'art; les astrologues s'y opposent, et disent qu'il faut consulter les phénomènes célestes, pour savoir s'il est bon de prendre médecine, lorsqu'on en veut donner, et si l'opération en sera heureuse. Je me souviens d'avoir ouï dire à un astrologue à ce sujet: "Notre condition est bien différente de celle des médecins, dans l'exercice de notre profession. Car, si un astrologue fait une faute, le ciel la découvre; mais si un médecin en fait une, quelque peu de terre la couvre.[2]

Chardin records that the recognised authorities in science, who were highly regarded in Persia, were for astronomy and mathematics Ptolemy, for mathematics Archimedes, Euclid, Theodosius, Autolycus, Menelaus, and Apollonius, and for medicine Hippocrates and Galen; whilst in astronomy the leading native exponents were Abu'l-Ḥusain 'Abd al-Raḥmān b. 'Umar al-Ṣūfī (d. 376/986), Naṣīr al-Dīn Ṭūsī, Maḥmūd Shāh Khaljī,[3] and Mīrzā Ulugh Beg assisted by Jamshīd Ghiyās̱ al-Dīn al-Kāshī, Qāẓīzāda al-Rūmī, and 'Alī b. Muḥammad al-Qūshchī. Reliance upon tradition and established practice was widespread. Thus Chardin notes the retention of the original observations in al-Ṣūfī's star maps and, despite a knowledge of other instruments, the almost universal popularity of the astrolabe. He further adds to his list in astronomy and mathematics al-Ma'mūn, al-Kindī, al-Fārisī, and 'Umar Khayyām, and mentions Abu'l-Wafā' particularly for algebra, al-Fārābī for music and medicine, one "Ayran" (perhaps Ibn al-Haitham) for optics, and Abu'l-Fidā for geography. As in the quadrivium of medieval Latin Christendom there was in Islam a tradition of Euclidian geometry in which the straight line accounted for phenomena in optics, gnomonics, and perspective, whilst number ratios united mathematics with music. Of their libraries Chardin says that none exceeded four hundred volumes, and compared with those of Europe

[1] *Ibid.* III, 298 (translation from Lloyd II, 37). [2] Chardin IV, 355.

[3] Commentator (*c.* 852/1448–9) on the astronomical tables (*Zīj-i Īl-Khānī*) of al-Ṭūsī [He may, in fact, have been not the author but the dedicatee of the work: see *PL* II/1, 74, n.4. (Ed.)]: see Greaves, *Astronomica*.

"c'est une mouche auprès d'un éléphant",[1] whilst dependence upon the Ancients does not make many books nor many discoveries.

When in Iṣfahān Chardin lodged with the Superior of the Capuchin Order and obtained information on the astrolabe from the most famous maker, Muḥammad Amīn, who is remembered by two extant instruments dated 1086/1675–6 and 1097/1685–6. Chardin refers to him as the son of the astrologer Mullā Ḥasan 'Alī, but this son was Khalīl Muḥammad, known by nineteen extant astrolabes.[2] The distinguished Capuchin was Père Raphaël du Mans (Jacques Dutertre), who had accompanied Jean-Baptiste Tavernier to Iṣfahān and was helpful also to Thévenot and to Chardin.[3] He compared the Persian theory of the astrolabe with that of Jean Stoefflerin, whose *Elucidatio fabricae ususque astrolabii* had appeared in 1513, and Regiomontanus, and found them similar; according to Chardin's report the Persian version was the better and more accurate, being neater geometrically. A mathematician of note, Du Mans was held in high regard by Shah 'Abbās II and by Shah Sulaimān in turn. The first mission in Iṣfahān was Augustinian in 1602–3, and the last of the Catholic orders to establish itself there was the Jesuit in 1653. Contemporary Jesuit influence in China in the field of astronomy is significant, and there was a period when Chinese scholars knew of the telescope and of the heliocentric theory of Copernicus; in fact, the China Mission had already collaborated with native scientists to produce, between 1629 and 1635, a compendium on astronomy and the calendar entitled *Chhung-Chên Li Shu*. But we have as yet no record of such fruitful scientific cooperation between Jesuits and Persians at that time, though there is little doubt that both Iran and Turkey were gradually coming under the influence of Western science and technology, as we shall see from the next section.

ASTRONOMY AND RELATED SCIENCES

Islamic astronomy during the Safavid period lies at the end of a long tradition of geometrical representation, characterised mainly by the study of shadows cast upon surfaces by objects placed in the rays of the sun and by stereographic projections of heavenly bodies upon a circular plate (the astrolabe), and culminating in the observatories of Jai Singh II in India at a time when the telescope had found general

[1] Chardin IV, 220.   [2] Mayer, *Islamic astrolabists*, pp. 54–7.   [3] Chardin VIII, 109.

acceptance in Europe, thereby ushering in the optical period, and when Greenwich Observatory was beginning its regular observations.

Professor Kennedy has already enlarged upon the achievements of Timurid Iran in the previous chapter. The great Muslim institutions at Marāgha and Samarqand had had a short life and were now in ruins,[1] but they were perpetuated by their observational records, *Zīj-i Īl-Khānī* (*c.*670/1271) and *Zīj-i jadīd-i Sulṭānī*, which according to ʿAbd al-Munʿim al-ʿĀmilī (*c.*970/1562–3) were the tables of Ulugh Beg, completed in 841/1437. Versions of the latter tables, which were widely disseminated, appeared in Persian, Arabic and Turkish, and reached Oxford in the time of Charles I, whilst the fame of the gigantic meridian arc, which was the central instrument on the Samarqand site, being over 120 feet in radius, had spread to the astronomers in Istanbul and to a visiting Englishman, John Greaves. Efforts at emulation by the Safavid monarchs came to nothing. Shah Ismāʿīl I, founder of the dynasty, planned to restore the Marāgha observatory and charged Amīr Ghiyāṡ al-Dīn Manṣūr b. Amīr Ṣadr al-Dīn Muḥammad al-Shīrāzī (d.949/1542–3) with this task. Muslim astronomers had long considered, however, that to compile an adequate set of star tables would require extended observations over a period of thirty years corresponding with the revolution of Saturn, so Ismāʿīl abandoned the project. His successor Ṭahmāsp I (930–984/1524–1576) also had a scheme to build an observatory in a hall of the royal palace at Iṣfahān with the object of bringing the tables up to date, but this again failed to materialise. However, a valuable manuscript written in connection with the project as Iṣfāhan survives, and describes the design of instruments previously used at Alexandria, Marāgha and Samarqand.[2]

A word of explanation is required here concerning the brief life of Islamic observatories. There certainly were individual scientists who pursued their investigations for the sake of knowledge itself, as is clear from the prefaces to their writings, but the ruling powers had no such ideals, and the policies of the Safavid monarchs were dictated by expediency and the value attached to astrological speculation; thus the observatory was set up as a temporary institution for a restricted programme of work. Nevertheless, the Islamic observatory represents an

[1] The remains of the meridian transit instrument of Ulugh Beg's observatory are shown in fig. 2, p. 579.

[2] ʿAbd al-Munʿim al-ʿĀmilī, *Kitāb taʿlīm ālāt zīj*, British Library MS Add. 7702 (with diagrams): see Seemann.

important phase in the history of astronomy, and – in the absence of a Persian example – it is worth adding a few remarks about the contemporary Turkish building erected on a height overlooking the Tophane quarter of Istanbul from the south. Taqī al-Dīn Muḥammad al-Rashīd b. Ma'rūf, the director, who was also the author of a long account of the rectilinear propagation, reflection and refraction of light,[1] predicted that the comet of 985/1577 would bring good fortune to Sultan Murād III in his campaign against the Persians, so the observatory was completed in that year, and with the object of rectifying outdated astronomical tables. In its construction "Venetian Ducats were spent like sand", whilst the endeavours of the staff appear to have been crowned with success:

Sultan (to Taqī): Have you untangled knots from the firmament in a hair-splitting manner?
Taqī (to Sultan): In the Zīj of Ulugh Bey
There were many doubtful points, oh exalted King;
Now through observations the tables have been corrected.... [2]

There was an elaborate main building, with offices and a library, but with the large instruments mounted in the open. A smaller building nearby housed quadrants, an astrolabe, clepsydras, a terrestrial globe showing Africa, Asia, and Europe, and various geometrical instruments; such a small-scale observatory perhaps contained pilot instruments, but in any event it was not short of staff, four or five men being assigned to one instrument, two or three as observers, one as a recorder of readings, and the last for miscellaneous duties. We are indebted to the poet 'Alā' al-Dīn al-Manṣur for more detailed information about the work carried out. Thus he speaks of an armillary sphere for determining the latitudes and longitudes of stellar bodies; a mural quadrant for finding the declination of the sun and other "distances" from the equator; a large azimuthal quadrant for azimuths and elevations; a wooden or ruler-quadrant with two sights for investigating the motions of Mercury and Venus as well as determining angles of elevation and zenith "distances"; a parallactic ruler for all angles of elevation and the parallax of the moon; "an instrument with two holes" for studying apparent diameters of heavenly bodies and the phenomena of eclipses; "an instrument with cords" to determine the positions of the

[1] He wrote about these difficult investigations, "which are enough to make the hair turn white": see Winter, "Arabic Optical MSS".

[2] Sayılı, *The Observatory in Islam*, p. 293; "'Alâ al-Dîn al-Manṣûr's poems", text p. 455, trans. p. 482.

equinoxes, said to have been invented by Taqī al-Dīn to replace the equinoctial armilla; and finally *al-mushabbaha bi'l manāṭiq*. This was an invention of Taqī al-Dīn, based on Ptolemy's *Almagest*, whose purpose is not quite clear. al-Manṣūr writes of it:

> Moreover, with the help of the *mushabbaha*,
> And thanks to very carefully made observations,
> The radius of Venus' epicycle, in the third firmament,
> Became known with great precision...;

and of the sunaidī ruler, and a mechanical clock with a train of cogwheels,

> With the help of careful measurements and corrections made with the clock,
> The ascensions of stellar bodies were fixed,
> And with the firm and specially chosen ruler,
> That wonderful ruler to which the astronomers give the name "sanîdî"[1]
> All the symbols and signs of astronomical instruments
> Became extremely accurate.[2]

A comparison of the Istanbul instruments of Taqī al-Dīn with those of Tycho Brahe in Europe has been made by Miss Sevim Tekeli, and of those common to both astronomers the mural and azimuthal quadrants long used in Islam were then new to Europe, whilst the large fixed wooden or ruler-quadrant made by Tycho antedated by some years that of Taqī. Both used staircases to take readings. It is clear that there was a good deal of intellectual commerce between Turkey and the West, and also, despite crippling wars, with Persia, and that what we have described for the Istanbul observatory would have applied largely to any such establishment which might have arisen further east, even to Mughal India. Whilst the mechanical clock from Europe had entered the Ottoman observatory to rival the water-clock in the recording of duration, Islamic scientific information and ideas were percolating slowly westwards through Elia Misrachi (1456–1526), who travelled to Basle, and Regiomontanus when on a scientific mission to Hungary. The Islamic hypothesis of solid spherical shells was adopted by Peurbach. In fact, Sayılı remarks that "it seems probable that the

[1] Perhaps a geometrical instrument associated with the engraving of astrolabes etc.
[2] Sayılı, "'Alâ al-Dîn al-Manṣûr's poems", text p. 453, trans. pp. 478–9.

sudden rise in the level of astronomical work in Europe with Peurbach and Regiomontanus was the result of contacts with Eastern Islam".[1] Again, the Kassel Observatory of Landgrave Wilhelm IV of Hesse (1532–92), the first European institution comparable with the Islamic ones, was a royal observatory as its predecessors in Muslim lands had been. Of these latter Samarqand had greatest influence upon the West: Marāgha was rather too early, Istanbul perhaps rather too late. In this connection we must recall the name of John Greaves.

Greaves was one of those enterprising gentlemen associated with the rise of science in 17th-century England. Elected Professor of Geometry at Gresham College in 1630, he became interested in Islamic science, and encouraged by Archbishop Laud he left London seven years later in the company of the orientalist Edward Pococke with instruments to make astronomical observations and money to purchase books – in particular, the tables of Ulugh Beg. He collected in Istanbul in 1638, and went on to Alexandria and Cairo (where he says he found little), leaving Egypt in 1639 with his assembled manuscripts in Greek, Arabic and Persian. He had left Pococke in Istanbul with instructions to look for further scientific manuscripts. Back in England after a lapse of three years, he was to find himself deprived of his Gresham professorship through long absence and failure to deliver lectures. However, in 1643 we observe him occupying the Savilian chair of Astronomy at Oxford, where he settled down to the study of his oriental acquisitions. According to John Ward, Greaves collected five Persian manuscripts of the Samarqand Tables, translated them into Latin, and deposited the copy of his final revision with Archbishop Usher. "But Mr. Thomas Hyde of Queen's College in Oxford not knowing this, made a new version of them, which he published with the original, and a learned commentary, at Oxford 1665, quarto."[2] Ejected from his Oxford professorship, with his rooms ransacked, by the Parliamentary visitors in 1648, Greaves finally retired to London to work on his writings, and died there in 1652 in his fiftieth year.

Further attention has been directed to the problem of transmission, this time from West to East, by a letter written in 1624 to a Persian, one Zain al-Dīn al-Lārī, by the Italian traveller Pietro della Valle, who had spent several years in Persia. It relates to Tycho's system of the world and to the discoveries made with the Galilean telescope, and its

[1] Sayılı, *The Observatory in Islam*, p. 386.

[2] Ward, p. 149.

importance has recently been emphasised by a paper of Dr Aydin Sayılı entitled "An early seventeenth century Persian Manuscript on the Tychonic System".

As in the medieval quadrivium of Latin Christendom, the mathematical sciences in Safavid Persia were closely integrated by a common body of knowledge. Whilst accretions from further east were Sanskrit, transmissions to the West were Turkish. The *Ṭabaq al-manāṭiq*,[1] a planetary calculating device invented in Timurid times by Jamshīd Ghiyās̱ al-Dīn al-Kāshī (d. 832/1429?), inspired a similar instrument which is described in an early 10th/16th century *risāla* dedicated to Sultan Bāyezīd II. It will also be remembered that a colleague of al-Kāshī at the Samarqand observatory, 'Alī b. Muḥammad al-Qūshchī, established himself finally in Istanbul. Inevitably and deservedly, the fame of the Samarqand astronomers and mathematicians spread. Al-Kāshī's textbook of arithmetic, *Miftāḥ al-ḥisāb*, in which, according to Kennedy,[2] he anticipated Stevinus of Bruges by two centuries in the exploitation of decimal fractions, was widely disseminated through Turkey. From Mughal India came Persian versions of the *Līlāwatī* and *Vīja-gaṇita* of Bhāskara Āchārya, spreading the now common processes of decimal arithmetic and the solution of algebraic equations which had reached their final form with the Hindus in the 12th century. There were many writers of astronomical manuals in Persia: Mīrzā Qāżī b. Kāshif al-Dīn Muḥammad Yazdī (d. at Ardabīl in 1075/1664–5), Shaikh al-Islām, whose father had been a physician to Shah 'Abbās I, compiled a practical handbook of astronomy under the title *Tuḥfa-yi 'Abbāsiyya*. One of the best known of these writers was Bahā' al-Dīn Muḥammad b. Ḥusain al-'Āmilī (d. at Iṣfahān in 1031/1622), who was the author of *Tashrīḥ al-aflāk*, a work on astronomy in Arabic which was followed by Persian commentaries; *Tuḥfa-yi Ḥātimī*, a short treatise on the astrolabe, dedicated to Mīrzā Ḥātim Beg, vizier of Shah 'Abbās I; another very short composition in Arabic entitled *al-Ṣafīḥa*, brief enough to be inscribed on the plate of an astrolabe; and a successful Arabic compendium of arithmetic, *Khulāṣat al-ḥisāb*, which inspired commentaries in both Persia and India (e.g., Arcot, 1696) and was later printed with the *Tuḥfa-yi Ḥātimī* (Tehran 1316/1898–9). An emigrant to India, Muḥammad 'Alī "Ḥazīn" Jīlānī

[1] See Kennedy, "A Fifteenth-Century Planetary Computer".
[2] Kennedy, "The Chinese-Uighur Calendar", p. 437.

(b. in Iṣfahān in 1103/1692, d. in Benares in 1180/1766), composed a work on the elements of astronomy, *Risāla dar hai'at*, near the end of his life.

Indian mathematical influences are represented principally by Persian translations and commentaries on the first two sections of the *Siddhānta-śirōmani*, a Sanskrit astronomical treatise completed around 1150 by Bhāskara Āchārya of Bīdar in the Deccan. An edition of the opening section, *Līlāwatī*, dealing with arithmetic and geometry, was prepared in 995/1587 for Akbar by "Faiżī", a poet and scholar and brother of the emperor's chief minister Abu'l-Fażl; whilst the second section, *Vīja-gaṇita*, relating to algebra, was rendered in Persian under the title *Bīj ganit*, and dedicated to Shāh Jahān in 1044/1634–5, by 'Aṭā'-Allāh "Rushdī". "Rushdī" also wrote *Khulāṣa-yi rāz*, a metrical work on arithmetic, algebra, and mensuration which eulogised Shāh Jahān and Prince Dārā Shukūh (to whom it was dedicated). "Rushdī", "Muhandis" and Nūr-Allāh "Mi'mār" were the three sons of Nādir al-'aṣr ustād Aḥmad-i mi'mār-i Lāhaurī, the distinguished architect, who also had two grandsons and a great-grandson to perpetuate this tradition of science and learning. Luṭf-Allāh "Muhandis", "Rushdī's" younger brother, is known for his Arabic commentary on the *Khulāṣat al-ḥisāb* of Bahā' al-Dīn (mentioned above) and a Persian translation of al-Ṣūfī's famous book on the fixed stars, *al-Kitāb ṣuwar al-kawākib*. Incidentally, this last serves to emphasise the long-continued reverence for the masters of traditional Islamic astronomy.

This Muslim tradition in astronomy, reaching its peak in Samarqand, was perpetuated by the Mughal emperors, and came to its close with the observatories erected at Delhi, Jaipur, Mathurā (Muttra), Benares, and Ujjain, by Rāja Jai Singh Savā'ī, who had served Aurangzīb and his successors as a military commander. His tables *Zīj-i jadīd-i Muḥammad Shāhī*, completed in 1140/1728, were compiled with the object of correcting the earlier *Zīj-i Ulugh Beg, Zīj-i Khāqānī*, and *tashīlāt* composed for Akbar by Mullā Chānd and for Shāh Jahān by Mullā Farīd. Mullā Farīd al-Dīn Mas'ūd b. Ibrāhīm Dihlavī, Astronomer Royal to Shāh Jahān, had completed in 1039/1629 his *Zīj-i Shāh Jahānī*, based on Ulugh Beg and in the same format, and calculated for 1041/1631–2 in the new era Tārīkh-i Ilāhī-yi Shāh Jahānī.

Spherical trigonometry of the celestial sphere was equally valuable in terrestrial problems, such as the determination of the latitudes of cities and of the azimuth of the *qibla* (the direction of Mecca). The northern hemisphere had been divided into seven climates (*haft iqlīm*) according to a specific definition by latitude: thus, the first climate comprised regions having a maximum daylight of $12\frac{3}{4}$ to $13\frac{1}{4}$ hours, the second climate those having a maximum daylight of $13\frac{1}{4}$ to $13\frac{3}{4}$ hours, and so on. Most *zījāt* listed the geographical coordinates of cities, since apparent celestial positions are affected by the geographical position of the observer, and these appeared inscribed in the *umm* of astrolabes. But there is a dearth of information on cartography. After the maps of the Arab al-Idrīsī in mid-6th/12th century Norman Sicily, which superseded the medieval monastic maps and persisted in their influence for four hundred years, no maps appear from the Islamic world until the rise of Ottoman Turkey as a maritime power. The Turks were keen to amass geographical knowledge and obtained it either at first hand, as from the admiral Pīrī Re'is, who presented charts of the coasts and islands of the Mediterranean and Black Sea to Sultan Selīm in 927/1521 and had personal experience of the Indian Ocean and the China Sea, or from the scholars and cosmographers, such as Kātib Chelebī (Ḥājjī Khalīfa), the famous medical bibliographer, who translated in the mid-11th/17th century the *Atlas Minor* of Mercator and other European geographical works and drew upon Persian sources for his *Jihān-numā*. These latter included a Turkish version, made during the reign of Sultan Murād III (982–1003/1574–95), of a Persian *Qānūn-nāma*, written by a merchant and dedicated to Sultan Selīm I in 1516, a *Risāla* of Ghiyās̱ al-Dīn al-Naqqāsh, the painter, who was sent by the Timurid Shāh Rukh to the emperor of China in 822/1419, and another Persian work, entitled *Khiṭāī-nāma*, by Sayyid 'Alī Akbar-i Khiṭā'ī, who spent about three years (1505–8) in China. Persia was the intermediary through which knowledge of China passed westwards to the Turks and belatedly to Europe, as for example through the work of Banākitī (fl. 717/1317), of which the eighth section, on China, was translated in 1677; and this knowledge helps to supplement our meagre information concerning the period between Marco Polo and the Jesuits; whilst there is clear evidence of transmission in the opposite direction, e.g. Islamic influences upon Chinese porcelain of the early 10th/16th century. Following upon early Arab cartography, there is only one Persian map of the world extant, so far as I know, and this is in an English version derived from some unknown Persian author.[1] The impetus to the study of cartography which was provided in Turkey by her maritime exploits, and the enthusiastic translation of European geographies into Turkish, appear to have aroused no parallel activity in Persia.

THE ASTROLABE

Perhaps the most persistent feature of Safavid astronomy is the popularity of the astrolabe. The earliest dated instrument from Iṣfahān is one made by Aḥmad and Muḥammad b. Ibrāhīm in 374/984 (now in the Museum of the History of Science at Oxford), whilst in that same city seven hundred years later fine astrolabes were being produced by a number of distinguished astronomers and craftsmen. Astrolabes were fashioned in the royal workshops (*buyūtāt*), and to make and decorate one's own instrument became a work of art.

Chardin remarks on the fact that an astronomer was not regarded as a learned man who did not know how to make his own instruments, and "parmi le commun peuple même, chacun garde son astrolabe comme un bijou".[2] Derek J. Price has made an interesting study of the chronological distribution of astrolabes, which shows pronounced activity around the periods which gave birth to each new set of astronomical tables, whilst a great "peak" in the number of Western astrolabes around the year 1580 is seen to be followed by a lesser "peak" (rather more than half in number) of Eastern astrolabes a little later than 1700. This last phase coincides with the activity of Persian, Moorish and Mughal craftsmen which went on almost unabated from the mid-17th century to 1800, and embraces the outstanding achievements of ʻAbd al-A'imma the younger in Persia and of the Allāhdād family in Lahore. Price writes of the late activity in Islam during the period 1650–1750 as being in many ways a retransmission back from Europe of the popularity of the instrument. Such may well be one of the factors, but Persian craftsmen, with their long tradition, had no need of such a stimulus, whilst there were other influences: outside of the observatories, the portability and the reference data it supplied made the astrolabe popular, to the exclusion of almost all other instruments, with a people much taken with astrology. And again, this Persian renaissance of the astrolabe simply reflects in metalwork the artistic

[1] Bagrow, p. 209.
[2] Chardin IV, 332.

creativity of an age which produced worthy successors to Bihzād in miniature painting and reared those visionaries who conceived the gems of Mughal architecture in India.

Space forbids a full discussion of the theory of the astrolabe; an account by the present writer appeared in 1951 in the journal *Endeavour*, but for a complete treatment it is necessary to consult the article by Willy Hartner (in the *Survey of Persian Art*) or the treatise by Henri Michel. Chardin devotes a chapter to the theory and construction of the instrument as he understood them in Iṣfahān, and adds a geometrical illustration.[1] It will suffice to say here that of the two faces of the plate (umm or mater) of the plane astrolabe, one carried the alidade or sighter, used to determine stellar "altitudes", and secured to the centre of the plate by pin and horse; whilst the other face, together with a number of additional thin brass discs (*ṣafā'iḥ*) which could be placed singly over the central pin, enabled theoretical calculations to be made. Of these discs, the *'ankabūt* or rete, or spider (because of its open-work design), indicated the ecliptic, the signs of the zodiac, and by means of *shaẓāyā*, or pointed "branches", the positions of important fixed stars. In the case of a given latitude the face of the mater, acting as a disc or *ṣafīḥa*, represented the appropriate *stereographic* projection of the heavens upon the equator, whilst the 'ankabūt moving over it gave the path of the fixed stars around the north pole of the heavens. As an instance of the encyclopaedic value of the instrument we may refer to examples recently sold in London. A Safavid astrolabe[2] inscribed with the name Sayyid Radī al-Dīn Muḥammad b. Sayyid 'Alī al-Ḥusainī, but undated, carried on the 'ankabūt twenty-six named stars, and had five ṣafā'iḥ which showed hour lines, Babylonian hours as well as almucantars, azimuths, and unequal hour lines, for latitudes 22°, 25°, 30°, 32°, 34°, 35°, 37°, and 38°, and a tablet of horizons. In the umm itself was a gazetteer of longitudes and latitudes and *inḥirāf* (for defining the azimuth of the qibla of thirty-one towns, and the longitude and latitude for a further twenty-four towns. On the other face of the umm, over which rotated the alidade, was a sine graph, arcs of the signs of the zodiac with azimuths of the qibla, for Iṣfahān, Yazd, Herat, and two other places (illegible), a shadow square (containing also an astrological table), and a zodiac scale with the faces of the planets and other astrological data.

[1] *Ibid.*, pp. 331–51 and fig. XXVIII.
[2] Sotheby, *Catalogue*, 15 July 1963, item 186, p. 54 and plate.

It may be noted here that sometimes there is a cotangent scale as well as a sine graph, and an astrological table giving, in addition to the signs of the zodiac and the planets, the twenty-seven or twenty-eight mansions of the moon. This instrument, probably from the time of Shah Sulṭān Ḥusain, was 14.7 cm in diameter, about the usual popular size. An Indo-Persian astrolabe, in the same catalogue[1] and "inscribed in the blessed city of the port of Sūrat on the 13th of the holy month Muḥarram, year 1081 of the Hijra" (2 June 1670), carried on the front an ʻankabūt for fifty-five stars, six ṣafā'iḥ, some Italian hour lines being shown, and inside the umm a gazetteer of longitude and latitude for sixty-seven places; whilst on the back were engraved declination scales for the alidade, a zodiac and calendar scale giving Syrian solar months, a sine and cosine graph with arcs of sines and versed sines, arcs of the signs of the zodiac with a line of the sun's meridian altitude for latitude 21°30′ (suitable for Sūrat or Mecca), cotangent scales, and a shadow square within which was a table of the seven "climates" with their latitudes and the hours of the longest day.

The principal makers in Safavid Persia were ʻAbd al-A'imma the elder, who made a fine astrolabe for Shah ʻAbbās I in 986/1578–9; ʻAbd al-A'imma the younger, at least thirty-one of whose instruments made between 1688 and 1720 have survived, though they are perhaps not all by him (a fine example made by him in 1127/1715 is shown in Pls. 1, 2); ʻAbd al-ʻAlī b. Muḥammad Rafīʻ (al-Juz'ī?), who is remembered by seven examples made between 1707 and 1714, and especially by the superb astrolabe (now in the British Museum) constructed by him for Shah Sulṭān Ḥusain in 1124/1712 and decorated by Muḥammad Bāqir, the maker's brother;[2] Khālil Muḥammad b. Ḥasan ʻAlī, of whose instruments nineteen are known,[3] some of which are again decorated by Muḥammad Bāqir; Maḥmūd b. Jalāl b. Jaʻfar al-Asṭurlābī, who though flourishing near the beginning of our period represents a long line of tradition;[4] Muḥammad Amīn (who may be identical with Ibn Muḥammad Ṭāhir), Muḥammad Ṭāhir himself, and Muḥammad Amīn b. Amīrzā Khān al-Nakhaʻī al-Qumī; Muḥammad Mahdī al-khādim al-Yazdī, son of Muḥammad Amīn, maker and decorator of at least

[1] *Ibid.*, item 188, p. 56 and frontispiece.

[2] See W.H. Morley, *Description of a Planispheric Astrolabe constructed for Shāh Sultān Husain Safawī, King of Persia, and now preserved in the British Museum* (London, 1856). Gunther, p. 147.

[3] Josten, p. 12, and Maddison, *Supplement*, p. 25.

[4] Mayer, *Islamic astrolabists*, p. 58.

fifteen extant astrolabes;[1] Muḥammad Muqīm al-Yazdī, who had instruments decorated by the aforementioned Muḥammad Mahdī and in 1647 made, in the presence of Muḥammad Shafī', the astronomer of Janābād, an astrolabe for Shah 'Abbās II which was subsequently engraved by Fażl-Allāh al-Sabzavārī;[2] Muḥammad Zamān of Mashhad, whose name is perpetuated by four astrolabes and two celestial globes, and who constructed an astrolabe in 1677–8 for Subḥān Qulī Bahādur Khān of Bukhārā;[3] and finally Muṣṭafā Ayyūbī, who is known by two instruments of *c.* 1700.

The lastnamed is Ottoman, and it is of interest that few Turkish astrolabes of this period survive: if we are to judge from present evidence there was considerable activity in favour of sundials, which were in demand for mosques and madrasas. On the other hand, the Indo-Persian astrolabes form an interesting class of instruments of which a considerable number of fine examples exist. They are usually less ornate than the Safavid, and most were produced by the Allāhdād family in Lahore. A characteristic is the high triangular *kursī* which is decoratively pierced. A Mughal astrolabe recently sold[4] had an 'ankabūt for thirty-nine fixed stars, five ṣafā'iḥ for different latitudes (with azimuths drawn below the horizon line, and some lines for Babylonian hours), in the umm a gazetteer of latitudes and longitudes for forty-two places, and on the back (amongst other data) a sine/cosine diagram, scales of cotangents, and lines giving the meridian altitude of the sun throughout the year in latitudes 20°, 36°, and 38°. This instrument was made by Ḥāmid b. Muḥammad Muqīm b. 'Īsā b. Allāhdād and dated 6 Dhu'l-Qa'da 1086/22 January 1676. He was the maker of two other known examples, one of 1069/1658–9, the property of the Clockmakers' Company and in the Guildhall Museum, and the other of 1071/1660–1 in a private collection in Paris. An instrument signed by his father, Muḥammad Muqīm, and dated 1051/1641–2 has been described by Dr F. R. Maddison. Indeed the history of craftsmanship in this family can be traced back to its origina-

[1] Josten, pp. 11, 12; Mayer, *Islamic astrolabists*, pp. 70, 71.

[2] This instrument, formerly in the family of the amīr of Afghanistan, is now in the Evans Collection of the Museum of the History of Science, Oxford: Gunther, pp. 132–5; Mayer, *Islamic astrolabists*, pp. 74, 75.

[3] Now in the Museum of History, Uzbek Academy of Sciences, Tashkent: see M. Osipov, "Astrolabiya planisfera ili persidsko-arabskaya astrolabiya", *Protokoly zasedanii i soobshcheniya chlenov Turkestanskogo kruzhka lyubitelei arkheologii* (Tashkent, 1910), pp. 114–32.

[4] Christie's, London, *Catalogue*, 10 Nov 1964, p. 4 and plate.

tor, who signed an astrolabe made *c.* 1570 with the words: "Work of the Master, Allāh-Dād, the astrolabist of Lahore". [1]

MECHANICS AND TECHNOLOGY

We return to Chardin, who is a mine of information on Safavid technology. He pays particular attention to the technology of agriculture as it relates to the domestication of water:

They dig at the foot of Hills for Water, and when they have found a Spring, they guide it in subterraneous conduits to ten Leagues distance, and sometimes further, down Hill all the Way, that it may run the swifter. No People in the World know better how to Husband Water than the Persians. Those Conduits or Channels, are sometimes near fifteen Fathom deep; and I have seen some of them of that depth. They are easily measured for at every ten Fathom distance, there are Vent-holes, the Diameter whereof is as big as that of our Wells... Those subterraneous Ways are usually about nine Foot deep, and three Foot broad.[2]

And he adds that in Khurāsān there were at one time forty-two thousand of these underground kenses (*qanāts*).[3]

As to the distribution of the River and Spring water, it is made Weekly or Monthly, as occasion requires, in this manner. They lay on the Canal, which conveys the Water into the Field, a Brass Bowl, round and thin, with a little Hole in the Center of it, whereat the Water comes in by Degrees and when the Bowl sinks the Measure is full, and they begin again, till the quantity of Water agreed upon, be all run into the Field. The Cup is commonly near three Hours before it sinks. They make use likewise of that Contrivance in the East, to measure the Time by: 'Tis the only Clock and Sun-Dial they have in several Parts of the Indies, especially in Fortes, and in Noblemens Houses, where a Guard is set.[4]

A canal exceeding thirty miles in length, with a siphon arrangement, was built to the orders of Shah 'Abbās I, and later enlarged by Shah Sulṭān Ḥusain.[5]

In matters of cultivation and harvesting there was considerable enlightenment and ingenuity. Thus they "Plough with a Share drawn by lean Oxen (for the Persian Oxen do not grow fat as ours do) Yoked,

[1] See Maddison, *Supplement*, pp. 20, 22; also J. Frank and M. Meyerhof, *Ein Astrolab aus dem Indischen Mogulreiche* (Heidelberg, 1925).

[2] Chardin IV, 96–7 (translation from Lloyd II, 262–3).

[3] For a modern account of the *qanāt* system, see A. Smith, *Blind White Fish in Persia* (London, 1953), *passim*.

[4] Chardin IV, 98–9 (translation from Lloyd II, 264–5).

[5] Lockhart, *The Fall*, appendix III.

not by their Horns but with an Arch and a Breast-Leather". [1] As already pointed out by Needham, in respect of the breast-strap harness used by the Chinese, this is a superior arrangement.[2] Threshing is carried out, not with flails, but by drawing over the heaps of corn stalks small sledges with iron wheels. Each sledge (some 3 feet long by 2 feet wide) has three or four "round Sticks... which are instead of Axle-Trees; like our Pastry Cooks Rouling Pins, and go in some Iron Wheels, made something like the Wheels of our Jacks, but that they are dented sharp, most like the teeth of a Saw..." When drawn by an animal such as an ass, "Those Wheels break and cut the Straw, and squeze the Corn out of the Ears, without breaking it, because it slips between the Teeth..." As for the hulling of rice, this was done by a hinged-beam device, manually operated; the end of the beam (which was 4 feet long) fell on to the rice through an iron ring, half sharp, and 4 inches in diameter.[3]

Building and architecture afford scientific and artistic achievements of no mean order. A wooden crane, illustrated by Chardin (fig. 1), had a velocity ratio of approximately 5. It was used by the "Joyners; they are very skilful, and very ingenious in composing all sorts of Inlaid-work and Mosaick-work, and they make noble Ceilings of that Kind; they fit them all on the ground, and when they are done they raise them up over the top of the Building, on the Columns, that are to bear them up: I have seen a whole one of fourscore Foot Diameter, rear'd up, with the help of a Machine, like the Draught I present you with on the other side, not knowing whether our European Workmen have any such; the Persians use no other, and they raise every thing with a Pully... The Joyners sit on the Ground at their Work, their Plains are not like ours, for they thrust the Shavings out of the Sides, and not out of the Top, which seems to be a more expeditious way..."[4]

We have already commented on the state of Persian arms. Chardin in his chapter VII, Of Metals and Minerals, says: "The Persians don't make use of a Flint to their Guns, nor to strike Fire with. They have a Wood which serves them instead of a Steel and Flint, and has the same effect..."[5] Though they made their guns "alike strong and thick all

[1] Chardin IV, 101 (translation from Lloyd II, 266).

[2] J. Needham, *Science and Society in Ancient China* (Conway Memorial Lecture, London, 1947), pp. 16–17.

[3] Chardin IV, 106–7 (translation from Lloyd II, 270–1).

[4] Chardin IV, 127 (translation from Lloyd II, 289).

[5] Chardin III, 358–9 (translation from Lloyd II, 83).

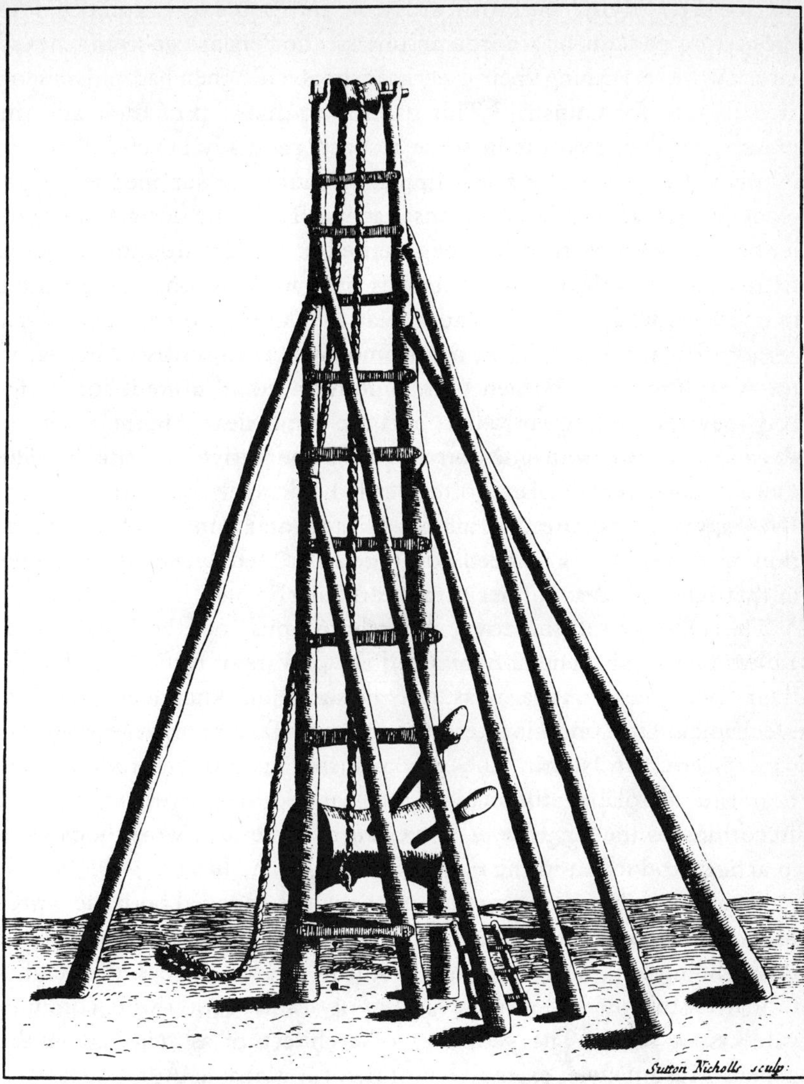

Fig. 1. Diagram of a wooden crane used by Persian builders in the 17th century.

along", the barrels were unnecessarily heavy and the open ends weak. In manufacture "they Soder the Breech of the Barrel with the heat of the Fire, and reject Screws, saying, that a Screw Breach going in without Stress, may be thrust out by the Violence of the Powder, and is not to be rely'd on".[1] Whilst Europeans and Turks were competent in the casting of ordnance in iron and brass, the Persians generally lacked interest in establishing their own industries and "they had rather send into Europe for Guns..."[2] This gradual opening up of trade and the influx of Europeans was in some respects mutually beneficial. In addition to gunnery experts, the French in particular supplied jewellers, clockmakers, and various artisans; Jacob (Jacques) Rousseau, a jeweller and clockmaker from Geneva, settled in Iṣfahān around 1707, and Chardin stresses the need: "Neither is there in Persia one single Native that knows well, how to mend a Watch".[3] On the other hand, "'Tis certain that the Dutch have much improved themselves in Persia, in the way of making Earthen Ware, and they would make it still better had they the same clear water, and the same clear Air they have in Persia." And Chardin goes on to praise the native craftsmen: "The Pieces which the Persian Potters called Cacoiper, or Earthen Ware Bakers, make best, are the Enamel Tiles painted and cut out in imitation of Moresk Work. Indeed nothing can be seen livelier and brighter in that Kind, or drawn finer or more regular".[4]

The function of the royal workshops must not be overlooked. Rulers have understandably retained the powers of technology within their own grasp. Akbar was not alone in his knowledge of "the Mechanick Arts" and his interest in the manufacture of weapons in his own palace. At Iṣfahān fine workmanship no doubt produced the exquisite astrolabes for which the Safavid monarchs are famed. According to the *Tazkirat al-mulūk*, thirty-three such workshops were in active production in the reign of Shah Sulṭān Ḥusain.

What might be called practical mathematics engaged both the writer of compendia and the engineer on the site; thus mensuration, the use of the right-angled triangle, the measurement of arcs, pulleys, the heights of inaccessible objects, and the laws of optical reflection were common subjects of study. The geometry of architecture as reflected in the superb Muslim style, exemplified in the Tāj Maḥal at Āgra (1638) and the tomb of Dilras Rābi'a Daurānī, wife of Aurangzīb, at Aurangābād (1666), displays a wonderful exploitation of symmetry in design and of calligraphy in decoration. Persia was already famous for faience in the

[1] Chardin IV, 138 (translation from Lloyd II, 299).
[2] Chardin IV, 91 (translation from Lloyd II, 257).
[3] Chardin IV, 89 (translation from Lloyd II, 256).
[4] Chardin IV, 129–30 (translation from Lloyd II, 291–2).

days of Tīmūr. We have previously mentioned the illustrious family of Lāhaurī. Nādir al-ʿaṣr ustād Aḥmad-i miʿmār-i Lāhaurī, who died in 1649, was the architect of the Tāj, whilst a nephew of his, Abu'l-Khair Khair-Allāh Khān "Muhandis", second son of Luṭf-Allāh "Muhandis" Lāhaurī, later became adviser to Jai Singh II of Jaipur in the building of his observatories and wrote a commentary on this distinguished Rāj-put's astronomical tables under the title *Shārḥ-i Zīj-i Muḥammad Shāhī.*

Finally, there are three small and unrelated items of technological information which deserve mention. The use of the mechanical clock in the observatory of Taqī al-Dīn recalls the present made by Queen Elizabeth to Sultan Meḥmed III in 1599. It was a mechanical organ, made by the famous Thomas Dallam, which incorporated a clock and other automatic devices.[1] In the fifth *tashkhīṣ* of the *Tuḥfat al-mu'minīn*, begun by Mīr Muḥammad Zamān Tunakābunī and completed by his son Muḥammad Mu'min-i Ḥusainī, there is a record of the weights used in medicine. An interest in natural history compelled Mīr Muḥammad Bāqir of Astarābād (pen-name Ishrāq), known as Mīr Dāmād (d. 1040/1630–1), to have constructed an observation hive of bees.

MEDICINE

We now enter a period of vernacular medical literature which, apart from the researches of Cyril Elgood, has been largely unexplored. Indian influences return, and valuable contributions were made by the Persians who had migrated to the Mughal Court. Medicine in Persia had suffered a great loss some two centuries earlier by the pillage of the Rubʿ-i Rashīdī, the quarter of Tabrīz upon which Rashīd al-Dīn Faẓl-Allāh, court physician to the Mongol Īl-Khāns, had lavished so much loving care by his establishment of hospitals, colleges, and libraries, where some fifty physicians from India, China and the Near East had each ten students in training, whilst surgeons, oculists, and bone-setters had each a quota of five. But now there were new clinical observations to supplement the traditional Arabic system exemplified in the *Qānūn* of Avicenna and the *Thesaurus* of al-Jurjānī,[2] and the pharmacology of the great botanist Ibn al-Baiṭār was augmented by a fresh exploitation of drugs. Thus Ghiyāṣ al-Dīn, a general practitioner

[1] H.G. Rosedale, *Queen Elizabeth and the Levant Company* (London, 1904), pp. 78–9. H. Bowen, *British Contributions to Turkish Studies* (London, 1954), p. 14.

[2] Browne, *Arabian Medicine*, pp. 109–11, 119–25.

in Iṣfahān who later went to Turkey, dedicated to Sultan Bāyezīd II in 896/1491 his *Mir'āt al-siḥḥa fi'l-ṭibb* ("Mirror of Health in Medicine"), in which a summary of the *Thesaurus* is amplified in the section dealing with drugs, and horizons are widened by a discourse on Turkish medical teaching. As for originality in observation and diagnosis we cannot do better than name Bahā' al-Daula, who, in the opinion of Elgood, was "the greatest physician who ever lived in Persia after the passing of the golden age of the caliphs of Baghdad".[1]

Muḥammad Ḥusainī Nūrbakhshī Bahā' al-Daula had studied under both Persian and Indian teachers at Ray and Herat, and was schooled in the works of Hippocrates, Galen, Avicenna, Rhazes, Sayyid Ismā'īl (al-Jurjānī), and Ibn al-Baiṭār, to which he soon added a wide and individual clinical experience in his only known work, written at Ray in 907/1501 under the title *Khulāṣat al-tajārib* ("The Quintessence of Experience"). In this book there is a description of an epidemic cough which was rife in Herat; this Elgood thinks may well have been the first account of whooping cough, on which the earliest publication in Europe was that by Willis in 1674. It also gives the earliest description of syphilis in the East. There is a chapter on eruptive fevers which accounts for three diseases, other than measles and smallpox, which could be chicken-pox, German measles, and the Fourth Disease. Further, in the chapter on diseases of the eye, there is described what is probably hay fever (not recognised in Europe until 1819), which Bahā' al-Daula found peculiarly resistant to treatment. In this last diagnosis it seems likely that he was helped by Rhazes, who had written an essay "On the Cause of the Coryza which occurs in the Spring when the Roses give forth their Scent". Nevertheless, Elgood points out: "Scattered through his works are observations which a physician of today can neither accept nor deny. They have never been considered" – for example, the appearance of pigmentary patches on the face or body of an epileptic denotes a cessation of the fits.

The second outstanding physician of Safavid times was 'Imād al-Dīn Maḥmūd b. Mas'ūd b. Maḥmūd of Shīrāz, who in later life attended patients at the shrine and hospital of Mashhad, where a regular medical service was provided for pilgrims and others. He wrote a monograph on *ātishak*, the Persian form of syphilis, in 1569.[2] China root, which

[1] Elgood, *A Medical History*, pp. 353–5.

[2] Trans. Elgood, in *Annals of Medical History* (New York, 1931), pp. 4ff.

was acclaimed efficacious in the treatment of this disease, was regarded as a universal panacea, and in an earlier treatise *Risāla-yi chūb-i Chīnī khwurdan* ("Essay on the Eating of China Root") he had already *c.* 1550 stressed its importance as an antidote in the arrest of a whole list of complaints. Another antidote (*bād-zuhr*) highly prized was the bezoar stone, a black or reddish stone found in the stomach and gall-bladder of the wild goat which roamed over the north-east extremity of Persia. Chardin in his account "Of the Trees, Plants and Druggs", which includes assafoetida, bezoar stone, musk, "Ambergrease", poppy, tobacco, and sugar, names it "a Counter Poison... a thing that has the upper-hand of Poison" and adds:

> The Bezoar is made use of with great Success in Sudorifics; they give it in Purple Fevers; they more especially prescribe it in Cordials, Confections, and Philtres. They say it warms and enlivens the Spirits, awakens Vigour, and confirms the Temperature of the Body... The Manner of using it in Persia, is to grate it with the Point of a Pen-knife, or to make it into Powder on a Marble, and the usual Dose is two or three Grains, in a Spoonful of Rose-water. [1]

In spite of its wide popularity in the 16th, 17th and 18th centuries, in both Persia and England, Chardin is honest enough to state that, though it was praised by the quacks, it was losing its esteem, and "will, in a short time, be entirely cry'd down, as I think it is already in Europe". The first monograph in Persia devoted to it was by 'Imād al-Dīn, and it remained in the English pharmacopaeias until around 1750.

Towards the end of our period the unsettled conditions forced Persian physicians to seek asylum at the Mughal court in Delhi. Among them was Mīrzā Muḥammad Hāshim 'Alavī Khān, who left Shīrāz in 1699, was presented to Aurangzīb and served his court, then that of Muḥammad Shāh, and finally the tyrant Nādir Shāh. Member of a medical family, he was the elder of two sons, both doctors, of Mīrzā Hādī Qalandarī. Other refugees from Shīrāz were Muḥammad Akbar Shāh Arzānī and Nūr al-Dīn Muḥammad 'Abd-Allāh b. Ḥakīm 'Ain al-Mulk. The latter wrote two important works, *Alfāz al-adviyāh* ("The Vocabulary of Drugs") for Shāh Jahān in 1038/1628–29, and the *Ṭibb-i Dārā Shukūhī* for Shāh Jahān's son and heir, murdered by Aurangzīb, which was the last great medical system written in Persian and con-

[1] Chardin III, 318–9 (translation from Lloyd II, 53).

tained a long section on syphilis. There had always been some contact, however slight, with Indian medicine, especially through Herat – thus Yūsuf b. Muḥammad b. Yūsuf, the son of a distinguished physician of that city, at an earlier date became secretary to Humāyūn (937–963/1530–1556) – and so subsequent adverse circumstances merely tended to foster the link.

The age which produced Bahā' al-Daula did not lack distinguished scholars. Poets and physicians thronged the court of Shah 'Abbās the Great as they did that of Akbar. Experimental science had not yet caused that expansion and fragmentation of knowledge which was the downfall of the medieval philosopher. The *a priori* approach of Muslim scientists, which can be explained by the classification of the natural sciences under a common heading of philosophy, inclined men to a respectful acknowledgement of traditional practice, especially in the conservative profession of medicine. It was Avicenna for his philosophy and system, Rhazes for diagnosis and treatment. As Rhazes had used apes in his pharmacological investigations, so other animals, such as dogs or fowls, might be used in certain experiments. Above all, it was the golden age of pharmacology, and many Persian compilers of *Qarabādīn* (*materia medica*), though they possessed additional specialised information of native or Indian origin, still revered Ibn Jazlā and Ibn al-Baiṭār as their model. The *Tuḥfat al-mu'minīn*, completed for Shah Sulaimān by Muḥammad Mu'min-i Ḥusainī in 1669, consisting chiefly of *materia medica*, persisted in numerous manuscript versions in both Arabic and Turkish (the court language of the Safavids). As for ophthalmology, a study of great importance in Islamic countries, little was achieved in Persia at this time and the main focus of effort was Cairo. The encyclopaedic mind, characteristic of the medieval world, prevailed. Bahā' al-Dīn 'Āmilī (Shaikh-i Bahā'ī), a theologian and philosopher whom we have mentioned earlier, studied mathematics under Mullā 'Alī Muẕahhib and Mullā Afżal of Qā'in; furthermore, he proceeded to learn medicine under 'Alā' al-Dīn Maḥmūd. Like Shifā'ī, he added prestige to the court of Shah 'Abbās the Great. Companion of the shah, court physician and "Plato of his time", Ḥakīm Sharaf al-Dīn Ḥasan Shifā'ī was praised by Riżā Qulī Khān in these words: "... his medicine eclipsed his scholarship, as his poetry eclipsed his medicine".[1] Physicians, druggists, and astrologers were members of families tradi-

[1] Browne, *Arabian Medicine*, p. 256. For his portrait, see British Library MS Or. 1372, fol. 7r.

tionally associated with learning, the tājiks. The principal court physician, *ḥakīm-bāshī*, advised on all matters relating to state medicine and the deployment of the country's doctors, and was assisted by the chief druggist, *'aṭṭār-bāshī*. Employees in the buyūtāt received free drugs and attention, whilst in Ṭahmāsp's reign a charitable dispensary was established. A good deal is known about the hospitals (*bīmāristān*; lit. "a place for the sick") in respect of location and buildings, but not much about their organisation and administration. Oddly enough, John Fryer omits to mention them. Unlike Herbert, who was not a medical man, he looked upon Persian medicine with less favour. Fryer says that "they stick to the *Arabian* Method as devoutly as to the Sacred Tripod... on which score Chymistry is hardly embraced; nor to the Pathological part do they think the Anatomical Knife can bring much Profit"; and since "Their Law forbids them to inspect a dead Carkass" so then in anatomy "their Practice is lame, and their Theory no more than the prating of a Parrot"; hence "they are imperfect in the Chyrurgeons Art...". They resort to phlebotomy. Unusual diets (e.g. camel's flesh) native to the country are recommended. Only certain specific remedies are tried, and these are of universal application "without respect had to difference of Temperament, or Constitution; nay, or even to the Distempers themselves..."[1] The bezoar-stone is highly regarded, especially in the treatment of Spotted Fever. Fryer, who reached Iṣfahān in August 1677 and was there at the same time as Père Raphaël du Mans, was particularly interested in the druggists, "all Jews", and the multiplicity of their wares. Sickness forced Fryer, who was a physician in the employ of the East India Company, to leave Persia, and after a period in Sūrat, he sailed for England, where in due course he was elected a Fellow of the Royal Society (1697). He was aware that chemistry, only recently a new science in England due largely to Boyle, had not yet emerged out of alchemy. Hülegü had had an alchemical laboratory attached to the observatory at Marāgha, and specific technical achievements in chemistry were not lacking, but it was the practice of an art rather than a science, and astrology and magic were close adherents. Even Baha' al-Daula, most eminent of clinical observers, believed that magic played some part in medical practice. The most significant reference to a technical process in chemistry seems to be that of Chardin when speaking of the production of rose-

[1] Fryer III, 94–7 *passim*; quoted *in extenso* by Elgood, *A Medical History*, pp. 401–7.

water by distillation; he refers to "its being Distill'd without Water, which is contrary to our Method... [1]

We return to the Catholic missions. It is appropriate to mention them here because of the close association of many of their members with medicine. Raphaël du Mans[2] describes an instrument for the extraction of soft cataracts by suction. This was not new, but was in the illustrious tradition of Arab eye-surgery, being the hollow needle, a forerunner of the injection syringe, invented by 'Ammār b. 'Alī al-Mauṣilī, who practised in Cairo in the late 4th/10th century. Though the Capuchin Fathers were given the title of physician, it is to the Carmelites, Père Matthéus and Père Ange de Saint Joseph, that we must turn for a definite record of achievement.[3] The former, first a physician in the important medical centre of Shīrāz, later travelled to India as a botanist and pharmacologist. Père Ange de Saint Joseph (Joseph Labrosse), the first serious student of Persian medicine, was responsible for the transmission of Persian medical terminology to Europe; on his return to Paris he published his *Pharmacopaeia Persica* in 1680, a work based upon the *Ṭibb-i Shifā'ī*, written by the pharmacist Muẓaffar b. Muḥammad al-Ḥusainī al-Shifā'ī before 963/1556. One might append here for the sake of completeness the name of Giovanni Tommaso Minadoi (1540–1615), who was also instrumental in the transmission of Persian and Turkish medical knowledge to Europe. After taking his medical degree Minadoi travelled for seven years in the Ottoman dominions, finally returning to Italy to become physician to the duke of Mantua and professor of medicine at the University of Padua.

We come to the end of our story, and it is left but to summarise. In this troubled period of Persian history conditions were not often conducive to scientific research. Physicians and astrologers who fell foul of their royal masters frequently found themselves on a swift journey to Paradise. Decisions were invariably dictated by expediency. Rather must we regard it as a period of culmination, in which the observatory in Islam, like the hospital before it, became an institution for the first time in human affairs. The long geometrical tradition in Muslim astronomy had reached its limits of accuracy in the erection of giant instruments and could progress no farther; so with the astrolabe we

[1] Chardin IV, 65 (translation from Lloyd II, 237).
[2] Du Mans, p. 178
[3] *A Chronicle of the Carmelites* I, 620.

have perfection at the end of an era of advancing craftsmanship. In the words of C.H.Josten, "In the middle of the seventeenth century the art of the Persian engravers reached its highest point. The precision and calligraphy of that period are without comparison. In spite of the most elaborate ornamentation the mathematical accuracy of the engraving is unimpaired".[1] It is perhaps only in medicine, especially in the acute clinical observations of Bahā' al-Daula, that we find the opening up of new vistas of enquiry, whilst Elgood still thinks that the study of the Persian pharmacology of the Safavid period is a profitable source of information. Science, circumscribed by native culture, was nurtured and confined in a few centres of learning: Iṣfahān, Shīrāz, and – on the Persian trade route to Bukhārā – Mashhad and Herat. Northern Khurāsān, through which the Indian merchants passed, also on their way to Bukhārā, was almost the only source of astronomers. Controlled experiment, in which concomitant variation could be examined, was lost after Ibn al-Haitham, and was only now being revived and appreciated in Europe; uncontrolled experiment had furnished, at Samarqand, the finest zīj of that time, though subsequently nothing like Kepler's Laws emerged from the data. But Persia stood upon the threshold. The door to the West was ajar, so that the light of a universal objectivity might one day come filtering through.

[1] Josten, p. 11.

CHAPTER 12

RELIGION IN THE TIMURID AND SAFAVID PERIODS

I. GENERAL CHARACTERISTICS OF THE TIMURID ERA

At the time of Tīmūr's death and under his immediate successors the religious situation in Iran was characterised by two complementary processes, which were the primary determinant of – or, minimally, ultimately resulted in – that particular form of religious reality known as Safavid Shi'ism.

The first factor is the great flexibility, bordering on prevarication, displayed by the religious world in fulfilling its cementing function between the political rulers and their subjects in the most disparate alliances between successive sovereigns and the local religious (and administrative) aristocracy, even when the diversity of *madhhab* professed by the two protagonists would lead one to expect an at least dual missionary activity rather than a day-to-day cooperation. It is true that there was a diversity of madhhab in a slightly broader and more equivocal sense, rather than in that usual connotation of the word which restricts it simply to the canonical schools. But it is indisputable that there was a rapprochement on the concrete plane which occurred at a time when, as all scholars admit, there was a "return" to the myth of the ideal sovereign, a "true Caliph", and consequently to a renewal of the hope in the advent of a leader in spiritual affairs and so too in religious affairs. This eagerly awaited leader was the Mahdī, a figure who was variously delineated and characterised in the different areas and *madhāhib* proclaiming and anticipating his coming.

The other decisive factor is a gradual trend towards Shi'ism among the "aberrant" currents of orthodoxy, including sufism, allied with the presence of strong "Twelver" elements in the movements consciously aiming at a centralist outlook, which transcended the traditional divisions of Muslim religious society. This analysis is acceptable only up to the advent of Shah Ismā'īl, after which any discussion of the religious situation in Iran must necessarily involve an examination of the religious policies followed by the various sovereigns in circumstances which, interesting though they may be, were less fluid and so easier to classify.

That these two processes were of a complementary nature is plain once one recognises the presence of ideological elements which provide us also with a key to the analysis of all the 9th/15th century religious movements. Muslim society explicitly embodied at that time, particularly in Iran, the backlash of reaction to the "paganism" of the Mongol hegemony during the preceding centuries.[1] The watchword was the restoration of Islam, conceived of as the restoration of the true *Sharī'a*, that is, the Sharī'a as expounded by the Prophet – and even more by his first Companions – which envisaged in a precise fashion a homogeneous society united under one leader. This led to an extension of the functions and prerogatives of the teachers of the Sharī'a, and in consequence to an exaltation of the ideological, and not merely the functional, values of the juridical madhhab to which the subjects had to conform. In religious terms, however, this is tantamount to admitting the possibility of the existence of an orthodox Sharī'a side by side with a faith open to innovations – a coexistence which was advocated and defended by many heresiarchs of those days.

The transition from the concept of an ideal sovereign acting as the leader of such a restoration, to that of a Mahdī representing the only hope of implementing the reform of Islam according to the dictates of the ancients, appears ever more natural. Typologically speaking, it is therefore more specific to recognise that religious trend of the Muslim world which, though representing the apotheosis of the waiting for the Mahdī in its most persistent form, is nevertheless always partial to an ever-delayed realisation of his coming as a sovereign: that is, the tradition of the Twelver Shī'a.

According to the ideal line of evolution, the lawful sovereign is considered at one time as an intermediary who wields the powers recognised as legitimately appertaining to that religious entity we call the Mahdī; then as his deputy and Caliph; and ultimately as the incarnation of the Mahdī. Tīmūr, the "refuge of the Caliphate",[2] the cosmic vindicator of all Islam, who punished the Shī'īs for their crimes against the Companions and the Damascenes for the wrongs they had inflicted upon the *Ahl al-bait*, represents the first and not altogether clear example of mediation between the Mongol heritage and the new complex of

[1] As opposed to the more immediate reactions to paganism implicit in irrationalism (Barthold), spirituality (Meier) or urban conscience (Köprülü) in Iranian Islam at the time of the Mongol domination, on which see A. Bausani, in *CHI* v, chapter 7.

[2] Cf. Ghiyāṣ al-Dīn 'Alī, in Barthold, "Khalif i sultan", p. 47 n. 144.

political and religious requirements of Islam. A significant case in point is his relationship, according to legend, with the Safavid Khwāja 'Alī, which thanks to the new sources published by Horst can now be even more legitimately considered as one of a number of attempts made by the throne to take advantage of the ṣūfī movements in order to acquire a wholly religious kind of legitimacy, which might be exhibited as one of the indispensable attributes of regality. For Tīmūr this may have been merely an *a posteriori* justification of an attempt to break with the preceding era that was to be emphatically endorsed by his successors and in particular by Shāh Rukh. The latter claimed to be the restorer *par excellence* of the Sharī'a and the Caliphate ("May God perpetuate his reign in the Caliphate of this world" are the words of the *khuṭba* which the Indian Khiżr Khān was required to utter in Ḥāfiẓ-i Abrū)[1] in the shadow of an increasing and deliberate philo-'Alidism which, although tempered by a prospective alliance with sufism, was destined to become gradually an Imamite form of 'Alidism. In this connection we must remember the aspirations of Ḥusain Bāīqarā ("ornament of the throne of the Caliphate"[2]), who, by trying to persuade Mīr Sayyid 'Alī Qā'inī to recite the khuṭba on behalf of the Twelve Imāms,[3] presented himself as the legitimate forerunner of a future authority which would automatically replace the principles of authority hitherto recognised.

This amalgam of the Shī'a, of sufism and of the awareness of the necessity for a Mahdī had an 8th/14th-century precedent in the Sarbadār movement, in which are discernible those elements that are typical of and common to all the religious protest movements of the century under consideration. Strictly speaking, the history of the Sarbadārs (Sabzavār 1337–1381) and its repercussions in the Caspian (Sayyids of Māzandarān, 1350–92; of Gīlān, 1370) and Kirmān (1373) areas do not concern us here, but a brief analysis of the nature of the movement will serve as an *ante litteram* case history of the subsequent relationship between the sovereign and the Musha'sha' or Qizilbāsh heretics. The Sarbadār opposition comprehended many kinds of heterogeneous elements: there were not only peasants and plebeians from the towns, but also members of the local landed gentry, who provided the first two military leaders of the movement – 'Abd al-Razzāq and Ma'sūd – and other elements also. These non-plebeian and essentially Iranian elements, faithful to the Firdausian traditions, did what they could to

[1] *Ibid.*, pp. 48–9. [2] Daulatshāh, p. 458.
[3] Petrov, "Dannye istochnikov", p. 77.

provide an opposition to the administrative aristocracy, many of whose members were also Shīʿī, and to the Sunnī *ʿulamā*, both of them groups which were enmeshed in the Il-Khanid policy. On the religious plane these aristocrats represent an idealisation of the true Sharīʿa, which lay beneath the expectation of the coming of the perfect prince, whereas the dispossessed, ready as they were to accept any leader provided one could be found, represent the longing for a brotherhood of all Muslims and thereby for one of the Mahdī's prerogatives, i.e. the establishment of social justice. Both components of the movement were at any rate Shīʿī. Thus, with the Sarbadārs, the Shīʿa became an effective form of protest. We are dealing here with a Twelver Shīʿa, despite the fact that some of its attitudes are reminiscent of the Zaidite revolts in the early years of the ʿAbbasid era which, though in a different way, were likewise obsessed with the idea of a legitimate sovereign. The Mahdī whose coming they awaited was to be a warrior and a conqueror, and the armed struggle they waged against constituted authority was directed towards hastening his coming by removing all possible obstacles. This explains the revival by the Sarbadārs of a custom witnessed by Yāqūt in 7th/13th century Kāshān: every morning the city authorities would lead a saddled horse outside the walls, in the always likely eventuality that the Mahdī should arrive.[1]

The ṣūfī movements, even under the Saljūqs and more especially during the years of Mongol domination, were characterised by a progressive socialisation, the first consequence of which was access to the "mystic path", open to those social classes who, because they were poor, were ready to accept any authority having the seal of religious legality, as opposed to the political reality which was proving more and more disappointing. The shaikhs to whom they had recourse appear to have represented a court of appeal for complaints, even when the only solution they could suggest was a disdainful liberation from worldly needs pending the arrival of better times.

This form of shaikh cult filled most of the gap between the Shīʿī outlook and sufism, thanks to the ever greater ideological affinity between imām and shaikh. The Sarbadārs were, in fact, Shīʿīs, but they were organised on military lines as a confraternity, and in this way a diarchy of power – religious and political – was created; this would seem to have posited the need for a kind of coexistence between an

[1] *Jacut's Geographisches Wörterbuch*, ed. F. Wüstenfeld, IV (Leipzig, 1869), 15.

amīr, responsible for maintaining order in temporal affairs, and a shaikh-Mahdī who would act as a guarantor of the truthfulness of the professed madhhab. As a result of this distribution of powers, the rôle of revolutionary elements and the task of introducing social reforms were entrusted to the shaikh-Mahdī, while the amīr acted as a moderator and hence as the mouthpiece of the claims of the minor aristocracy, whose chief aim was to supplant the Mongol rulers and their emissaries. In the 9th/15th century, when movements emerged of very different dimensions and religious significance, such as the Musha'sha' and the Qizilbāsh, the diarchy was combined in the hands of one man. The most typical examples are the first two Musha'sha' leaders – Muḥammad b. Falāḥ and 'Alī – and Shah Ismā'īl, whose careers display a certain similarity in evolving from a form of political and religious extremism. This led both Ismā'īl and 'Alī to consider themselves as partaking of a divine quality and thereby being in a position to grant favours of a mainly material nature – into a self-imposed limitation of their own prerogatives which they accepted in exchange for security of office (a development which was completed within Shah Ismā'īl's own lifetime, while in 'Alī Musha'sha'ī's case it extended to the rule of his successors).

Regardless of one's point of view, the religious history of Iran can be seen as being wholly reflected in the complex relationship of the Qarā Quyūnlū and Āq Quyūnlū with their subjects, in a complicated network of alliances and enmities which do not seem to have been dictated by any coherent religious policy; though it must be added that any such apparent policy would inevitably appear ambiguous owing to the individual sovereigns' wavering between orthodoxy and "heresy" in their own personal convictions.

It was in this climate of ambiguity and an uncertain political situation that heretical movements like those of the Ḥurūfīs and the Musha'sha' were born, and that the Qizilbāsh movement assumed the form of a military and religious organisation.

II. THE RELIGIOUS TOPOGRAPHY OF PRE-SAFAVID IRAN

Detailed information about the religious situation in the various provinces and cities of 15th-century Iran is lacking. Ḥamd-Allāh Mustaufī, however, has left us in his *Nuzhat al-qulūb* (*c.*740/1340) a fairly accurate religious topography of Persia during the preceding century, thus providing us with a starting-point for an analysis of the transformation of the Iranian mentality which, as we have seen, was characterised by an attempt to fuse sufism with the Shīʿa and by an increasing trend towards ʿAlidism. It needs to be said that this latter trend was extremely vague. The misfortunes of Jāmī, who in 877–8/1472 proclaimed himself a potential victim of both the Iraqi (Shīʿī) and the Khurāsān (Sunnī) *taʿaṣṣub*, are highly significant.[1] For the same reason, when the philosopher Jalāl al-Dīn Davānī, who was a Sunnī despite claims to the contrary,[2] devoted all his energies between 1467 and 1477 to a typical vulgarisation of a classical Shīʿī text such as the *Akhlāq-i Nāṣirī*, this did not seem to the 15th-century mind to be due to the eccentricity of a scholar, because in reality it formed part of a complex – and to some extent unconscious – official Sunnī attempt at annexing concepts or studies traditionally held to be part of the Shīʿī rationalistic heritage. In Davānī's case this was an abstract ethico-political theory, polyvalent by its very nature, which explains why both currents regarded him as their master. A more specific instance is provided by a fundamental work of Talibite genealogy, the *ʿUmdat al-ṭālib*, compiled at this time by Ibn ʿInaba (d. 828/1424) and dedicated to a patron who is generally believed to have been the reigning monarch, Tīmūr. While the historical validity of this dedication may be disputed, the work remains an indication of the popularity and the importance of the Ahl al-bait, which the religious mentality is inclined to regard as the common heritage of all Islam (at any rate such an attitude appears natural in this historical context, given the still more significant fact that *a posteriori* the work has been seen as written for Tīmūr). At Balkh the true (Iranian) *mazār* of ʿAlī was rediscovered and pilgrims flocked to Mashhad as a result of the growing importance of its shrine, whose influence was felt beyond the confines of the Imamite entourage and led the Timurids to embark on a whole range of imposing public works.

This was, in fact, the golden age of Mashhad, for after succeeding to the throne Shāh Rukh visited the city several times, paying homage to the tomb and making generous gifts to the local sayyids. The *Maṭlaʿ al-shams* records visits during the *Muḥarram* in 809/1406, 810/1407, 815/1412, 821/1418, 822/1419, and 840/1436. Shāh Rukh was also responsible for the embellishment of both the great Khurāsān shrines: the one we have just mentioned, at Mashhad, and the newly "discov-

[1] *LHP* III, 510–11.
[2] ʿAlī Davānī, *Sharḥ-i zindagānī-yi Jalāl al-Dīn Davānī* (Qum, n.d.).

ered" shrine at Mazār-i Sharīf, where his minister Ghiyās al-Dīn (d. 829/1425–6) was buried. The name of Mashhad, however, is connected above all with that of the sovereign's wife, Gauhar Shād, who was responsible for the erection of the mosque of the same name, built by a craftsman from Shīrāz between 808/1405 and 821/1418. Shāh Rukh's successors also venerated this shrine and the *Maṭla' al-shams* records visits by Ulugh Beg in 852/1448–9; by Abu'l-Qāsim Bābur in 856/1452–3 and on a second occasion before he died and was buried in the *madrasa* of Shāh Rukh in 861/1457; by his son Maḥmūd, who was crowned at Mashhad in the latter year; by Ḥusain Bāīqarā in 870/1465–6; and by Abū Sa'īd in 872/1467–8.[1] An "officially" Shī'ī dynasty could hardly have been more obsequious. In short, this was a period when the popular substratum played a leading rôle in official "sacred history" by introducing a kind of sentimentalism that might be described as group religiosity, and also had a share in formulating the language of sufism – for example in the "theology" of Vā'iẓ-i Kāshifī, who died in 910/1504–5 (the *Rauẓat al-shuhadā* is identical in terms of its contents with the classical Imamite texts, but its form is that of a narration, supplemented with a wealth of elements drawn from mythology and folklore), and in the mysticism of Shāh Ni'mat-Allāh Valī (d. 834/1431). As regards the other point, i.e. the intermingling of sufism and Shi'ism in the light of a reachieved Islamic unity, in accordance with the attempt to return to a kind of religious purism which, as we have seen, was a constant factor in Muslim society at that time, the man who was most effective and coherent in trying to bring about this synthesis was the Kubravī mystic, Sayyid Muḥammad Nūrbakhsh (d. 869/1464).

Nūrbakhsh derives his desire for unity from 'Alā al-Daula Simnānī, a Sunnī whose centralist outlook was typically Ash'arī but who, at the same time, was appointed by Öljeitü to preside over the Sunnī–Shī'ī council at Sulṭāniyya (1305) which ended with his "conversion" to the Shī'a. It should, however, be noted that this anti-rigorist attitude of both tendencies did not prevent Simnānī from replying to Shaikh Khalīfa, the theoretical founder of the Sarbadār movement, by throwing an inkpot at his head to punish him for his impertinence in declaring that he wanted something more than his master was able to give him.[2] Shaikh Khalīfa, in fact, had ventured to deny the validity of the

[1] Muḥammad Ḥasan Khān, *Maṭla' al-shams* II, 285–9.
[2] Petrushevsky, "Dvizhenie", p. 112.

juridical concept of the orthodox madhhab, to deny which was a very different thing from a sentimental attachment to 'Alidism. An equally centralist outlook, on the other hand, was shared by the most direct teacher of Nūrbakhsh, Aḥmad b. Fahd al-Hillī (d. 841/1437–8). This Twelver Shī'ī did not hesitate to pronounce a sentence of *takfīr* against his former pupil Muḥammad b. Falāḥ Musha'sha'ī when he too, although in circumstances different from those of the Nūrbakhsh case, claimed the prerogatives of a Mahdī.[1]

The position of Nūrbakhsh, which concerns us here more closely, is defined in a passage in his *'Aqīda*, which is, incidentally, coherently Shī'ī. In it he lays stress on a process which might be called one of "transfert", whereby the heir to the prophetic mission, i.e. he who is in the position of privilege of the Ahl al-bait, is the ṣūfī, whose own spiritual ancestor is 'Alī, while at the other extremity of the chain is the Mahdī. Within the history of the development of religious ideas in Iran this assertion is far more important than the reasons which later induced Nūrbakhsh to proclaim himself Mahdī, these reasons being based for the most part on astrological and cabalistic calculations as well as on a number of coincidences. Nevertheless, the religious topography of Iran that can be deduced from Mustaufī clearly reveals the possibility of the formation, in a promiscuous religious milieu, of a certain ambivalence and so that belonging to the Shī'ī rather than to the Sunnī confession would seem to be a matter of religious sensibility rather than one of ideological divergences or different juridical rites.

According to Mustaufī, in the big urban centres the majority of the inhabitants were Sunnīs, while the traditionally Shī'ī – or, to be more precise, Twelver – areas were, in addition to Gīlān and Māzandarān, the cities of Ray, Varāmīn, Qum and Kāshān, the province of Khūzistān and the Khurāsān region of Sabzavār. In those parts of Iran where it existed Shi'ism was widespread among the peasantry, but in the cities some of the aristocratic families were also Shī'ī and occupied leading posts in the administration during the Timurid era, and especially under the Sunnī Āq Quyūnlū.

Some significant examples, in this connection, are cited and developed by Aubin[2] to show the privileges granted to certain Shī'ī sayyids or whole families, in accordance with a policy of bestowing privileges upon them which began with Tīmūr and continued down to Uzun

[1] See below, pp. 626–8.

[2] Aubin, "Notes sur quelques documents aq-qoyunlu".

Ḥasan. On the other hand, as late as 1720–1 the Ottoman Durrī Efendī reported that a third of the population of Iran were Sunnīs.[1] Their numbers must have been more constant still outside the cities, a contributory factor being the ambivalent effects of *taqiyya*. It is pointless to ask what had happened during the period intervening between these two statements, unless one takes into account a fact of the greatest importance in the work of the earlier of the two writers. Mustaufī maintains that Shāfi'ī elements existed in almost every place he mentions, both in those where he speaks of the presence of Sunnīs and in the traditional centres of Shi'ism, and this provides evidence to support the supposition that the religious situation in Persia had a certain homogeneity, due not only to the factors mentioned above, but also to the influence of Shafi'ism, which from another point of view seems more capable than any other madhhab of absorbing methodologically different outlooks, thereby paving the way, in its turn, to a more complete amalgamation.[2]

As a partial confirmation of these suppositions let us consider an extreme case reported by Nūr-Allāh Shushtarī in the *Majālis al-mu'minīn*[3] when speaking of Kāshān, a city which, more than any other, provides frequent evidence of its adherence to the Shī'ī faith (the saddled white horse waiting for the Mahdī, the "death festival" of 'Umar,[4] etc.). Despite this, it was in Kāshān that, when Shah Ismā'īl ordered a public execration of the first three Caliphs, "the great and the worthy among the people of the Sunna in the land of Iraq took the path of exile", and it was in Kāshān that "there remained no traces of Sunnī *qāḍī* or *muftī*". For two years, whenever they wished "to ascertain the truth in their problems of Sharī'a", the people of Kāshān had to ask the *maulānā* Shams al-Dīn Muḥammad al-Khunfarī, "although he was not a specialist in the problems of *fiqh* and had no adequate text among his Shī'ī books". When formulating his *fatwā*, the maulānā used his common sense (a method used, in particular, by the Shāfi'ī school), pending the arrival in Kāshān of a Shī'ī jurist who, after examining the fatwās given by the maulānā, ratified them all because they were in accordance with

[1] *Relation de Dourry Efendy, ambassadeur de la Porte Ottomane auprès du Roi de Perse* (Paris, 1810), p. 54.

[2] On the Shī'ī side there is usually a tendency to stress the fact that the Shāfi'ī method was based on the Ja'farī system in order to explain certain undeniable analogies. This is of less interest to us, however, than the problem of finding a plausible explanation for the smooth transition from one system to the other in the everyday practice of the *istiṣḥāb*, which is a characteristic of both schools.

[3] Nūr-Allāh Shushtarī, *Majālis al-mu'minīn* (Tehran, 1268/1852), fol. 170r.

[4] *Ibid.*, fol. 18.

the principle of "rational beauty and ugliness", which was precisely the basic precept of the Imamite school. If we compare this valuable testimony with the fact that it was in Kāshān that a bitter enemy of the Safavids, the Sunnī (but Shāfi'ī) historian Fażl-Allāh b. Rūzbihān Khunjī (who was also the author of a poetical hymn in praise of the Twelve Imāms[1]), found a temporary refuge, we have more than a clue to the complexity of the situation. This will perhaps provide us with a basis for further inferences, for the existence of such a situation in one of the main centres of Persian Shi'ism, where it would seem that the jurists were Sunnī by nature and that one was a Shī'ī particularly in the writing of poetry, can serve to dispel much of the confusion surrounding the figure of Shaikh Ṣafī al-Dīn in connection with his proper place in the religious history of Ardabīl and his now undisputed original adherence to Sunnism.

According to Mustaufī, Ardabīl was a centre of Shafi'ism.[2] In particular, A. Kasravī has shown that Shaikh Ṣafī al-Dīn's Shafi'ism was an essential part of the religious mentality of the Shaikh and was certainly not due to any taqiyya, which would be unlikely at a time when Öljeitü was tending towards non-orthodox attitudes. Nevertheless, the example of Kāshān would seem to demonstrate that we cannot take the type of madhhab as an adequate basis for determining the nature of the faith professed by any Persian city. This does not cast any doubts on the position of Shaikh Ṣafī, but it does lead us to another question, the answer to which might help us to solve at least some of the outstanding problems concerning the religious evolution of the first Safavids. A certain simplification of terms, possible after the installation of Twelver Shi'ism in the whole of Iran, would seem to have been applied retrogressively to this period, which, as we have seen, was full of ambiguities. In particular, the claim made by Ṣafī al-Dīn's descendants to be Ḥusainī sayyids seemed for a long time to imply that they were Shī'ī, despite the fact that the authentic sources do not mention this title when referring to the shaikhs of Ardabīl. It would seem more likely that there was a gradual realisation of the importance of this claim – beginning with the vague remarks of Sadr al-Dīn, becoming explicit in the assertion of Ismā'īl, who described himself, though not always, as a Ḥusainī, and arriving finally at the generalisation of the

[1] Muḥammad Amīn Khunjī, "Fażl-Allāh b. Rūzbihān Khunjī", *FIZ* IV (1335), 178–9.
[2] Ḥamd-Allāh Mustaufī, *Nuzhat al-qulūb*, text p. 81.

title under Ṭahmāsp. In the traditional terminology, in fact, extremism and Shi'ism seemed to be more easily reconcilable than extremism and Shafi'ism, and it was impossible to give a typological definition of the Safavid *ghuluww* if the Shī'ī premisses were to be discarded.

The transition from Shafi'ism to the ghuluww, on the contrary, does not necessarily have to pass through a stage of claiming the *sayyāda*, this being no different from moderate Shi'ism, and there is another factor that might ultimately have proved disadvantageous to the sayyāda, i.e. to the Twelver Shi'ism, of the first Safavids, which may help to throw light on the situation. This was the Kurdish origin of the family, unequivocably demonstrated by Togan.

The inhabitants of Kurdistān were Shāfi'ī, and yet it was in Kurdistān that certain extremist heresies either had their origins or found fertile soil – for example, the *Ahl-i ḥaqq*. Such heresies were not offshoots of Twelver Shi'ism, but as a result of long contacts they were subjected to its influence to such an extent that after the accession of the Safavids they borrowed some of its forms. Moreover, the Ahl-i ḥaqq component seems obvious in the Qizilbāsh movement, in regard to which the Shaikhs of Ardabīl set themselves up as unquestioned and traditional leaders, and even today there are groups of Kurdish Qizilbāsh in Anatolia. Protected also by ṣūfī esotericism, the Shaikhs of Ardabīl seem to have submitted outwardly to a certain moderation, until they eventually found an outlet in a twofold kind of extremism: political when Shaikh Junaid indulged in extra-religious activities along lines apparently going back to the Zaidism of Gīlān, and religious when it reflected their relationship to their extremist followers.

This may enable us to hazard a definition of the components of the madhhab under the first Safavids: an extremist type of sufism – which did not prevent the profession of juridical Shafi'ism – influenced by the Kurdish (Ahl-i ḥaqq) and Turkish (Bektāshī) aspects of Qizilbāsh religious beliefs, but possibly also by Nuqṭavī elements known to have been present (see below) in Gīlān, the traditional refuge of the Shaikhs. Its approach was therefore of a heretical type which cannot be strictly characterised as Shī'ī or non-Shī'ī: such was Shāfi'ī sufism, which became the ideological banner of so composite a movement as that of the Qizilbāsh, engaged in difficult political manoeuvres with both the Shī'ī Qarā Quyūnlū and the orthodox Āq Quyūnlū, which were rendered even more complicated by innumerable ties of blood-relationship in no way determined by religious sympathies. Another instance of the coexistence of juridical Shafi'ism and heretical beliefs is provided by the case of the son of the Ḥurūfī Fażl-Allāh, who, when commenting on his flight from ruthless persecutors, claimed to have answered their question (to which madhhab he belonged) by professing a Shafi'ism which he did not subsequently renounce.[1]

This swinging of the balance of power from Āq Quyūnlū to Qarā Quyūnlū and *vice versa* was particularly noticeable in the first half of the 9th/15th century. Although, to a certain extent, it was a reflection of the sphere of political influence, there is no real parallel to this shifting of power in the far more subtle field of diplomatic and ideological relationships. Practically speaking, the latter were limited to the support given by princes to one another when they came into conflict with members of their own families. In such cases they exploited the idea of religious differences, which they seem to have regarded as being so many more strings to their own bows, and had the aim of encouraging the greatest possible confusion in their relationship to their subjects.

As examples one can cite the alliance between the Qarā Quyūnlū and the Sunnī Ottomans against the Āq Quyūnlū, who considered themselves the most direct heirs of Timurid power on account of the Il-Khanid princes' authoritative investiture; or conversely, the support given by an Āq Quyūnlū such as Uzun Ḥasan to the traditional enemy, embodied in this case by Ḥasan 'Alī, while the anti-Timurid Qarā Quyūnlū policy was being carried on by Iskandar. Such was the background in Iran to the fortunes of Mahdism, to the diffusion of the Ḥurūfī and Musha'sha' heresies and to the formation of Ahl-i ḥaqq (or rather their predecessors) and Qizilbāsh groups. All these things made it incumbent upon the sovereign to follow an elastic religious policy, ranging from broad-minded comprehension of equivocal or antithetical professions of faith on the part of his subjects to the inevitable exclusive adhesion to one group whenever the political situation became critical and the duties and ambitions of the sovereign were not limited to functioning merely as the guarantor of the *status quo*.

The two sovereigns who appear to have been the more or less involuntary mouthpieces of this complex religious world were Aspand and Jahān Shāh, both of whom were representatives *par excellence* of Qarā Quyūnlū heterodoxy, though the type of Shi'ism professed by each had different characteristics.

[1] Gölpınarlı, "Fadlallâh-i Hurûfî'nin oğluna", p. 45.

Aspand embraced Shi'ism after a grand council attended by both Sunnīs and Shī'īs, at a moment when the inhabitants of Iraq, who had always been Shī'īs, seemed at last to have found the leader for whom not only Khūzistān and Iraq, but the whole Islamic world, had been waiting – a man who, at all events at this stage, combined political audacity with an original religious syncretism, the Musha'sha' Muḥammad b. Falāḥ. Aspand's explicit acceptance of Shi'ism seems to have been a clever move on the part of a sovereign who was trying to reach a compromise with his non-orthodox subjects, to place himself on their religious level and to obtain – paradoxically enough, from his subjects – a more official investiture than that obtained by Shāh Muḥammad. For Aspand, becoming a Shī'ī meant minting coinage in the names of the Twelve Imāms, professing the Twelver cult and thus becoming – in effect – the champion of the pure madhhab of the Ahl al-bait.

By contrast, Jahān Shāh's Imamite profession of faith seems to have been dictated by more personal reasons, as he was a Shī'ī not merely by virtue of his minting coins with the names of the Twelve Imāms but also because he was troubled by more sincerely religious spiritual doubts, at least if we can judge from the dīvān which the ruler, designated Shams al-'ārifīn, either composed himself or at any rate claimed as his own.[1] In other words, while Aspand represents the high-level and probably demagogic realisation of the ruler-subject relationship which had been much more spontaneously anticipated by the vicissitudes of the Sarbadār movement, Jahān Shāh would appear to have been a forerunner of Shah Ismā'īl. The appropriateness of this analogy is evident in the negative attitude of both rulers towards the ghuluww, which they did not in any way try to appeal to in the name of a common background, either in a religious or in a political sense. Although Jahān Shāh was not the most outspoken denouncer of Hurufism, he could not accept it, not because his point of view coincided with that of such rulers as Tīmūr or Mīrān Shāh, who feared the danger – always latent in the Shī'a – of the discovery of the true sovereign, but because the chosen ruler had already been made manifest in his own person. Nor did his stubborn opposition to Hurufism create any real halo of ambiguity regarding the sincerity of his Shī'ī beliefs.[2] On the contrary, it would seem to have been due to the enthusiasm of one who felt that he had been entrusted with a super-

[1] Minorsky, "Jihān-shāh Qara-qoyunlu and his Poetry".

[2] But cf. chapter 4 above.

human task: as champion of the Twelfth Imām, he was the chosen leader and the repository (such was the esotericism of the Imamite agnostics) of a higher truth the need for which, directly or indirectly, had been repeatedly and insistently asserted in the course of the history of Twelver Shiʿism and had led to the *ʿārifs* being considered its trustee, sharing – to use an expression dear to Corbin – in the Body of which the Imām is the head.

III. THE ḤURŪFĪS

The Ḥurūfīs made their first appearance at the end of the 8th/14th century. Their founder Fażl-Allāh (possibly known earlier as ʿAbd al-Raḥmān) was born at Astarābād in 740/1340. The details of his life reflect all the ferments of his time: he was a sayyid, a mystic from childhood, an interpreter of dreams, an ardent pilgrim and a strict observer of the Sharī ʿa, as was only to be expected in the son of a qāḍī (hence his nickname, *ḥalāl-khur*). His actions were invariably determined by dreams; it was a dream that induced him to undertake the *ziyāra* to Mashhad immediately after the *ḥajj*; in another dream the names of the holiest mystics were revealed to him; and a dream of light foretold his mission by piercing his right eye (*ʿain*, which also means "essence" or "source") with the rays of the Star which rises in the East at intervals of centuries. His investiture immediately assumed the double form – indispensable in one who lays claim to being the repository of *sirr* in the Muslim world – of mediation in trans-human things (he acquired his first disciples by interpreting dreams and reading them in the mind) and of *ḥujja* in sub-human matters (the world of nature as represented by birds, whose language Fażl-Allāh, like all the Imāms, could understand). The community he gathered around him, however, had the same characteristics as the contemporary groups of dervishes: its members were of humble origin and were for the most part artisans; it practised frugality and rectitude. It was not until he had reached middle age, about 1396, that Fażl-Allāh was led to theopathy – from the authentic revelation of the meaning of the Prophecy to the dignity of Ṣāḥib al-zamān and the glory of the divine manifestation. He wrote the *Javīdān-nāma-yi kabīr*, and while his religious mission between Iṣfahān and Shīrvān naturally had a political significance, he went unarmed. He seems to have merely "besought" the potentates to join him, but Mīrān Shāh, whom he trusted, betrayed him, cast him into prison (during his imprisonment he wrote the *Vaṣiyyat-nāma*) and had him executed at Alïnjaq in 790/1394. Equally unfortunate was his first caliph, 'Alī al-'alā, when he tried to approach the new Qarā Quyūnlū leadership, embodied in this instance by Qarā Yūsuf. Yet though he was executed in 822/1419, he was nevertheless responsible for first spreading the Ḥurūfī doctrines within the Bektāshī-Anatolian environment. Subsequent external events and the various subdivisions and schisms are of only relative importance.

In substance, Hurufism is still an expression of Isma'ilism, in the sense that the theological terms defining it on the religious plane are not derived solely from Isma'ilism, i.e. the doctrine that the Creation is necessarily determined by the cosmic drama of which it is a pallid and imperfect reflection. Significantly, the definition of divinity was based on the absolute *ta'ṭīl* of the divine attributes and on a form of *tashbīh* which proceeded in an opposite direction to the orthodox, in the sense that the term of comparison was Man and it was to Man that the divine likeness was referred. But although this concentration of interest on the human figure as representing completely the ultramundane mystery is its closest link with Isma'ilism, Hurufism differs from the latter in its recognition of the real location of the *Ḥaqīqa* in the substance of the letters rather than in the person of the Imām. And hence a new type of Qur'anic *ta'wīl* related to what might be called the material rather than the symbolic form in which the word as revealed was incorporated in the sacred text. The Muslim mind has always been faced with the problem of a form of Qur'anic expressions capable of different and even conflicting interpretations, the various *tafsīrs* being merely approximate and incomplete catalogues of these that could be amplified. In this sense, for example, the letters *kn* symbolise the divine creative activity. The various heretical movements have always felt the need of clarifying the metaphysical content of such symbols by choosing – out of the various alternatives which were often suggested by orthodox as well as unorthodox thought – some that could represent Reality as a whole. By using among other things a cabalistic interpretation, Hurufism raises the letters' value to such a level that the dualism between Substance and Form is transformed into the equation: Reality of Substance = Determined Value of the Letter. This process of emphasis is, however, at the same time a process of simplification and, theologically speaking, instead of leading to an innovatory interpretation of the divine content, crystallises into a confessional creed of a static type, the revolutionary message of which is, paradoxically enough, entrusted to those practical measures which Muslim society regards as the inevitable consequences of any new religious choice. In any case, in the context of Hurufism, the thing that most plausibly transcends a strictly Shī'ī mentality is the claim to possession of the key to the Ḥaqīqa; this eliminates both the first intermediary (the Imām) and a leader like Jahān Shāh, claiming to be the second intermediary destined (as Twelver Caliph and Sovereign) to recognise the function of the Imām and to proclaim it to the world.

IV. THE MUSHA'SHA'

Aspand, too, had to deal with heresy, viz. the Musha'sha' movement which, on the social plane, had perhaps an even greater significance. His reaction, however, was quite different, and it has already been said that the ultimate aim of his persecution of the Musha'sha' was not so much their extermination as the hope of reducing their leaders to their rightful rank of vassals obedient to the wishes of their legitimate Shī'ī sovereign. The Musha'sha' movement originated in circles that, strictly speaking, were not Iranian and in areas where many of the inhabitants were Arabs, though it is true that Ibn Baṭṭūṭa located a Persian population in Ḥavīza, which was later to become their capital.[1] Typologically, however, this was an entirely Iranian heresy, so much so that the more modern Bābī offshoot of the Twelver Shī'a seems to have modelled itself upon it in its various stages of development and in its degrees of heretical intensity. Thus a description of the religious situation in Iran during the period in question would be incomplete without some reference to this movement.

The political situation, which is dealt with more fully in an earlier chapter, was characterised by an alteration of military successes and reverses on the part of the Musha'sha', who were initially helped by Aspand's policy of trying to win over to his side, in one way or another, the discontented and unreliable inhabitants of 'Arabistān, and by a sort of compromise whereby the legitimate authority of the Qarā Quyūnlū was acknowledged in exchange for a measure of frequently disputed autonomy in religious affairs which survived until Ismā'īl, like Jahān Shāh, compelled everyone to embrace orthodox Shi'ism. The

[1] Ibn Baṭṭūṭa, trans. Gibb, II, 321.

"conversion" of Aspand, in 840/1436–7, leaves open the question whether he took this step as a counter-offensive against the founder of the Musha'sha' heresy, who in that very year had launched his campaign among the local tribes, declaring that he was the Mahdī; or whether the public declaration by Muḥammad that he himself was the long-awaited Mahdī was possibly an unconscious reaction to the authority of Aspand, who since his conversion had become the legitimate religious – as well as political – leader. What is certain is that the grave economic situation in 'Arabistān, where problems existed that could not be solved by means of a new *siyāsa Shar'iyya*, gave the Musha'sha' movement plenty of scope for manoeuvre. It also gave them a kind of moral authority for their expansionist activities when they decided to set up an ideal structure, permeated by the wish to achieve consistency between the religious problems and the civil elements, in accordance with the principle of the perfect prince and a religious State that has remained an unrealised alternative throughout the history of Islam.

In any case, having recognised the complex nature of the relationship between the Shī'ī sovereign and the equally Shī'ī group facing him as his revolutionary opponent in the political as well as in the religious field, it is to the latter that we must turn our attention if we wish to provide analysis of some of the most typical stages of an evolution through which, it would appear, every heresy that can be called Iranian must necessarily pass.

The focal point of the Musha'sha' theory (known to us thanks to an unpublished *Kalām al-Mahdī* brought to light by A. Kasravī)[1] is the person of the Mahdī, which signifies the immanence of the Imām, conceived as a transcendent entity mediating between the Creator and his creatures in the metaphysically existential act which, through the process of creation, distinguishes the one from the other. Proceeding along these lines, the Musha'sha' (or, to be more precise, the two most interesting protagonists from the religious point of view, the founder Muḥammad b. Falāḥ and his son 'Alī) reached a halfway point in the ideal development of Mahdism, which began with the Ismā'īlī affirmation of the Imām's participation in the divine essence and ended with the Bābī movement, which claimed that the divinity had been manifested in the Imām. Muḥammad b. Falāḥ would seem, however, to

[1] Kasravī, *Tārīkh-i pānṣad-sāla*, pp. 1–46.

have progressed gradually in his religious evolution and in his career as leader of a community – unless of course this was merely tactical caution in the ever more explicit diffusion of his message. Two statements of his which were not necessarily intended as imposture can be quoted as cases in point: the declaration he made to the governor of Vāsiṭ, following the takfīr of his teacher Aḥmad b. Fahd, to the effect that he was a ṣūfī and a follower of the Sunna; and his words when, on being confronted with an *ʿālim* sent from Baghdad to refute his extremist position, he boasted that he had always applied the Sharīʿa. Now it is a fact that from the historical point of view the Mushaʿshaʿ (the etymology of the word is obscure, but it may be connected with the idea of "light" or "ray", from the root)[1] was one of those movements organised along the lines of a confraternity, the birth and development of which were realised in sufism – under whose authority they placed themselves – during the 7th/13th and 8th/14th centuries in particular.

The 9th/15th century organisations are different, principally by virtue of their platform of social and economic reform which frequently allowed them to set up a parallel military organisation among their disciples, as is clearly shown by the continually expressed desire of their leaders to observe scrupulously the law and the Sunna. Nevertheless, among the Mushaʿshaʿ the subsequent religious evolution was the result not of a group approach as in the case of the Qizilbāsh, but of their leaders' individual elaborations. Muḥammad b. Falāḥ began his career by proclaiming himself *walī* of the Mahdī (the Twelfth Imām), thus characterising himself as leader of the *jihād* in a typically Shīʿī sense, in order to bring about, in the name of the Mahdī, the indispensable moment of the Test, i.e. establishing who was for the Mahdī and who was against him.

This type of logic can be reconciled both with the most classical principles of Twelver ideology and with the most normal Shīʿī interpretation of Qurʾān x, 99–100, if one bears in mind that for the Shīʿīs each verse is always a *ẓāhir* expression of a more obscure substance. Muḥammad, however, denied that any such verification by the Mahdī himself was possible, since it was one of the Mahdī's prerogatives (and here we see the influence of contemporary social aspirations) that he was invincible and omnipotent, so that, *vis-à-vis* the Mahdī, both good and wicked men would be in an identical position, since they would be

[1] Caskel, "Ein Mahdī", pp. 91–2.

bound to recognise him. In this there was already a heresy, even though it was camouflaged by a sophism. Soon, however, caution was thrown to the winds, for the Test was to be followed by a period of *ẓuhūr* (manifestation) and Muḥammad b. Falāḥ declared that he was the *ḥijāb* (shield) of the Mahdī, while his son 'Alī went so far as to maintain that he himself was God, by a process based on one of those syllogisms so typical of extremist movements: the Mahdī is 'Alī; 'Alī is God; I, the Mahdī, am 'Alī; I am God. In any case, the fact remains that, although the respective positions of father and son may appear to have been different (in his correspondence with Pīr Būdāq, Muḥammad b. Falāḥ apologised for his son's conduct, comparing his position with that of 'Alī, who had allowed Abū Bakr to assume an office for which he was not destined, in the same way as God, in spite of his infinite foresight, had created Iblīs), the religious premiss is the same. This conception of the Mahdī was based on a clear distinction between the historical figure and his metaphysical nature, expressed in a terminology whose lucidity confirms the originality of the Musha'sha' way of thinking. Thus the Twelfth Imām, being alive as a category, might also be dead, and not merely "hidden" in the evanescent person of Muḥammad b. Ḥasan al-'Askarī. And following this line of thought there was no real difference between him and the Prophet, or between him and the other Imāms. All of them *were* the Twelfth Imām, and the actual death of any one of them was in its turn nothing but *ghaiba* on the conceptual plane from which their existence stems. It was therefore prophesied that each one of them would return, because the substance of the Imām was invariable, whereas the body in which he appeared was variable. In other words, in the actual prophetic cycle the divine function was expressed in the *silsila* leading up to the Eleventh Imām, whereas the function entrusted to the Twelfth (the Return *par excellence*) was now to be realised in his ḥijāb Muḥammad b. Falāḥ. The transition accomplished by 'Alī, in claiming to be the substance of the metaphysical principle of the Imām, seems to have been an esoteric stage of what his father had exoterically preached rather than an extremist extension of the concept from which it derived. And in the field of realisation it was 'Alī who plundered and defiled the tomb of 'Alī b. Abī Ṭālib, while it fell to the father to punish severely the *ghālī* even when they were his own followers, in a manner sometimes reminiscent of Kharijite ideas. (And yet this punctilious guardian of the Sharī'a was also the author of canonical formulae for the ziyāra to himself, on the lines of the classical Imamite formulae.)

It is also worth noting *how* the Qur'anic Christ, too, tends to be absorbed in this explanatory vision of the Imām. Strange tales were circulated concerning the dead Christ worshipped by Christians, almost as if he were a real, i.e. material, figure. The Qur'ān, on the contrary, tells not so much the "true story" of Christ as the story of Christ as an immortal, ever-present spirit. This duality, and the fact that the legends derived from Christological mythology differ from the Muslim versions, whether Shī'ī or orthodox, suggest Mandaean views were exerting their influence through a mechanism of borrowings whose starting-point cannot be established with any certainty. For example, the Christians' Jesus Christ is said to have had his head cut off and sent to a prostitute at Najaf, on the grounds that the cult practised there was idolatrous, since 'Alī was the living God, in Egypt (*sic*); in other words, Christ is John the Baptist, but the John of the Christians, whereas a quality attributed by the Mandaeans to the Baptist – that he could not be wounded with a sword – is also one of the miraculous attributes of the Musha'sha' Mahdī, just as the "death in the river" of 'Alī b. Muḥammad reminds us of the death of John according to the Mandaeans. Nor is this all, for the attribution to the "Magi", by Muḥammad b. Falāḥ, of the veneration of Bukht al-naṣṣar (Nebuchadnezzar), too hastily rejected as absurd by Kasravī, might also imply a Mandaean link with very ancient forms of Irano-Semitic syncretism.

On the other hand, much of our information on Musha'sha' beliefs (a striking example is the *dhikr* 'Alī Allāh) can be compared with what more recent writers have attributed to the Ahl-i ḥaqq. This and other analogies – the Safavid coin called Ḥuvaiza (Ḥavīza) used in initiations[1] – give us an idea of the continuity of the connective tissue in the religious life of the period in question, which leads on to broader and more composite issues, such as the complex problem of the Qizilbāsh.

V. THE QIZILBĀSH

The Qizilbāsh movement constitutes the meeting-point and the melting-pot of the various elements – or at any rate the most significant among them – of the religious life of the 9th/15th century. It is not, however, a zone of light amidst the obscurity characteristic of the period, for the presence of diverse motives in the movement produced

[1] *Ibid.*, p. 93.

composite, eclectic and contradictory results. The movement could be described as an ethnographical-religious complex localised, during the period we are discussing, in Asia Minor, principally in a geographical belt extending from the Lebanese – Syrian border to the Āzarbāījān frontier. Its members were drawn from Turkish tribes, but that the term Qizilbāsh (literally "men with red caps") was, ethnographically speaking, vague is demonstrated by the number of different connotations that it acquired at different times and in different places. Subsequent to its origination in Dzhungaria,[1] it was used in eastern Turkestan to denote the Shīʿīs;[2] in Asia Minor it was often used as an alternative for the term *ʿalavī*; for the Ottomans it meant a member of a secret society, a heterodox person, or, in the 16th century, the Safavid enemy; in Russia it became a synonym for Persian, and later, by extension, Asian; and among the Volga Tartars it was used to denote a cunning man (a merchant, often a Persian merchant).[3] The different ways in which this word was used independently of ethnical entities shows that it had an ideological content that became fused with the concept "Persian", i.e. schismatic, in the same way as the Persians themselves were defined in antithesis to the Ottomans. This, however, did not occur until a victorious Qizilbāsh movement under Shah Ismāʿīl had first made its contribution to Iranian religious life and then suffered what was essentially a repulse, being reduced, by a humiliating process of absorption, to the more commonplace, yet still heretical, connotation of official Safavid Shiʿism. The internal dialectic of all 15th-century extremist movements seems, in fact, to have led to a kind of self-camouflage, through which certain religious forms survive under different names or as original contributions to the great stream of Twelver Shiʿism. Despite this, the most striking innovatory feature, that particular religious attitude which could still be described as ghuluww and which acted as the catalyst of new social demands, was paradoxically eliminated at the very moment when a certain degree of political equilibrium might theoretically have enabled it to be utilised in a new type of society.

Whereas the Sarbadārs can be described as the first link in the ṣūfī chain leading to the Mushaʿshaʿ, its most outstanding element is undoubtedly represented by the Qizilbāsh. It now becomes self-evident that the particular kind of religious feeling permeating, with its longing for renewal, the conscience of the Iranian Islamic world at that

[1] E. Oberhummer and H. Zimmerer, *Durch Syrien und Kleinasien* (Berlin, 1899), p. 397.

[2] Le Coq, "Kyzylbasch", pp. 61–5.

[3] For all these, see Gordlevskiĭ, pp. 263, 264 n. 1.

time, had as its essential component a certain type of sufism. Or, to be more precise, we should speak, not of sufism, but of that particular evolution in the ṣūfī world, and in the relations existing between the members of the confraternities, which, as we have seen, was based on the communion – drawn from the Twelver Shīʿa – between the Shaikh as vicar of legitimate religious authority and his *murīds*; these latter in accordance with the classical Shīʿī procedure, were to be the "proofs" of his intentions, that is of his truthful madhhab. The gradual transition from the ascetic mission to identification with the task assigned by hagiography to the Mahdī, concludes with his declaring himself to be the Mahdī, and thereby the *maẓhar* of God in this world.

The Shaikhs of Ardabīl were precisely this in the eyes of those who turned to them, and the stages which they proposed are already comprehended in the evolution of the relationship between Shaikhs and their supporters. In other cases both the figure of the sayyid, though invested with an authority not solely due to his birth but recognised and demanded from below (the sayyids of Bam were examples of this during the first half of the 15th century), and that of the Shaikh, whose position was very similar to that of the Caliph, though in less universalistic terms (we need only think of Shāh Niʿmat-Allāh Valī), remain so to speak experiences crystallised in time, without any of that evolution which facts and circumstances seemed logically to require.

The union between Qizilbāsh and the Shaikhs of Ardabīl was a military relationship having, in its turn, no original features, which provided a practical solution for that reciprocity of duties and obligations which formed part of the relationship between the Shaikh and his followers. Seen in this light, the personal attitude of individual Shaikhs – that is to say, when they were "converted" to Shiʿism, the type of Shiʿism which they embraced and how much of the Qizilbāsh aberrations had entered into the religion of the man whom they recognised as their leader – becomes of secondary importance. The key element seems to be, above all, Junaid's awareness of the military potential latent in the order and the fact that in beginning preparations for his "reign" he developed it with the full consent of the Qizilbāsh, who then responded with fanatical enthusiasm to the appeals of the Shaikhs up to the time of Ismāʿīl's victory. Hence the particular reaction of the sovereigns then ruling Āzarbāījān who, whether they were Āq Quyūnlū or Qarā Quyūnlū, displayed a mistrust which sometimes erupted into open hostility. This is understandable when we remember the more or less conscious desire, on the part of authorities who were afraid of being bypassed, to surround themselves with a halo of religious legitimacy. It also explains the religious preparations for the reign of Ismā'īl, and the burden that he had to bear as a result of his presumed infallibility, which found expression in a theopathic enthusiasm, counterbalanced by his consent to the compromise offered by the Twelver Shī'a.

The religious folklore of the Qizilbāsh, in contrast to their spiritual ideas, which were typically Iranian, had been borrowed from Asia Minor, the religious outlook of which was by definition heretical, open to every kind of eclecticism and already endowed with a heritage of complex religious forms. On to the rites of an orgiastic nature with which the Qizilbāsh carry on extremely ancient Anatolian traditions, and on to the elements of a Christianity hostile to orthodoxy, Islam imposes a graft of plebeian social aspirations of a dissenting and vaguely communistic nature, such as those of the Qalandars and the Jalālīs, combined, in this specific case, with the expectation of the imminent coming of the Mahdī. From this point of view it is difficult to separate the religious forms of the Qizilbāsh from those of the Bektāshīs, who according to Gordlevskiĭ were the "codifiers" of the fluid Qizilbāsh religiosity maintained by the various wandering dervishes of the 16th century. The orthodox party accused them of forming secret societies, at the meetings of which ritual orgies were celebrated, including incest and pederasty, but these accusations do not differ greatly from the sins attributed by orthodox Islam to any heretical movement.

On the other hand, heresy did not prevent a movement which seems to represent the codification of that trend of Anatolian Qizilbāsh religiosity, which prevailed in the Kurdish area, i.e. the Ahl-i ḥaqq, from finding the necessary links with Twelver tradition. Indeed, were it not for the fact that the texts dealing with Ahl-i ḥaqq religious ideas are too modern to allow us to consider them here, it would seem more correct to regard the Bektāshī, Ahl-i ḥaqq and Qizilbāsh movements as slightly different expressions of the same religious form. For the Qizilbāsh as well as for the Bektāshī, authority was vested in a centralist leader who chose to rule the various communities his representatives – *dede* or *bābā* – who in their turn made use of an intermediary in dealing with the *ṭālib*. One of their distinctive signs was the ear-ring worn on the left ear, which in the case of a dede signified asceticism and chastity. Among the Bektāshīs, even today, the chiefs wear sleeveless robes like those of the Armenian peasants, but the most characteristic feature of their costume is the peaked twelve-banded red cap, the *tāj-i ḥaidarī*, variously explained as symbolising the Twelve Imāms or else resulting from Christian influence (the twelve Apostles), transmitted through the Armenians, from whom they have also borrowed certain practices relating to fasts. Another external sign is beard-kissing as a form of greeting – a beard being regarded as indispensable, for anybody dying without one is considered as doomed to unhappiness. A counterpart to these visible signs is an esoteric sign, understood only by initiates, viz. the star symbolising the light of the intellect and the soul, which shone in a Qizilbāsh and distinguished him from others. Incidentally, the Qizilbāsh are sometimes called *ot-dīnli*, or "worshippers of grass", owing to a belief (also current among the Bektāshīs), which might be characterised as of Dahrite origin, in the eternity of natural matter undergoing continual change. This belief led them to a pantheistic (or perhaps more precisely Ḥurūfī) attitude based on uninterrupted communication between God and his creatures; that is why, for instance, they swear by grass and by 'Alī while beating the ground with a stick. Another name for the Qizilbāsh is *chirāgh-söndüren* ("extinguishers of the light"), reminiscent of one of the Ahl-i ḥaqq sects which is similarly called Khamūshī in Persian, just as the name Dā'ūdī ("worshippers of David") applies both to some Ahl-i ḥaqq and to certain Qizilbāsh from Sīvās.

In addition to the normal veneration for 'Alī and the fraternal banquet – the Bektāshī "communion"– another custom, recorded, for example, among the Kach-Kiri Kurdish tribe, is the funeral banquet which may throw some light on the charge of cannibalism that has been brought against the Qizilbāsh,[1] believed to be in the habit of setting fire to their dead and eating them instead of burying them. As a matter of fact the funeral repast is consumed on the spot, on the tomb of the deceased, after the rite of lamentation, and consists of the scattering of yoghurt and morsels of a specially prepared sacred loaf, all of which is offered to the friends present at the ceremony. Another characteristic custom is the confession of their sins which the Qizilbāsh make to their dede. The latter ties a tape round the neck of the

[1] *Scheref Nameh ou Histoire des Kourdes*, tr. with notes by V. Velyaminov-Zernov, II (St Petersburg, 1862), 136.

penitent, who has then to bring the dede an offering, marking the door with a cross as he enters. After this the tape is removed and the sins are written down and burned. The person of the dede is considered sacred and everything he touches is thereby sanctified, and so too is the earth covering his tomb and the dust on which his horse has trodden, the latter being carefully collected because of its miraculous properties. On certain occasions the young women would come to kiss the dede, who singing mysterious songs would choose one of them to be his companion for the night; on the morning after the dede is washed and the water distributed among the various households. All these hybrid and non-Islamic elements exist side by side with a deep reverence for Shi'ism, as is shown not only by the link with 'Alī, who, with his attributes of holder of temporal authority and repository of the divine secret, is the central figure in this type of religious belief, but also by a social organisation reminiscent of certain Zaidite politico-social experiments, as well as by ṣūfī ideas, which, as we have seen, were impregnated with Twelver Shi'ism during the 15th century. The ṣūfī influence in its turn found its way into the Shī'a, at the popular level changing concepts into ritual practices and widening the devotional field, which previously had been limited to the Twelve Imāms.

VI. SHAH ISMĀ'ĪL

It was against a background of the kind that we have just described that there suddenly emerged the figure of Shah Ismā'īl, who personifies success in the historical and religious situation we are studying. In his own person he comprehended the qualities of a spiritual leader, a military commander, and a legislative reformer aware of the economic needs of his followers, as is clearly shown by, among others, Sanudo in his *Diarii*. These qualities were exemplified in his public career, for he realised the basic aspirations of the Qizilbāsh movement and those of the other heretical and dissenting bodies active at that time.

He was a ṣūfī, but in such a way as to transcend a shaikh's ordinary rôle, acting as an intermediary with God along lines which placed him closer to God than to the creatures to whom he gave witness. In this sense he was the long-awaited leader and his military successes were regarded as proofs of the superhuman nature of his task. His aspirations were identical with those of all the other "Messiahs" of the time, namely the creation of a State in which religious ideology would be identified with political necessity. Nevertheless, once he had risen to power, this did not prevent Ismā'īl from accepting political compromises and fusing them with his religious beliefs – and this not only on a personal level.

But in spite of his heretical acts – such as proclaiming himself 'Alī, or God, or disdaining to follow the dictates of the Sharī'a – Ismā'īl combined in his own person two conflicting aspirations of Islam, which, however, have not always led to antithetical consequences: a need for individualistic religious expression, which was the mainspring of sufism in the more generic significance of the term, and an urge to socialise every kind of experience by translating it into terms of the common weal. Ismā'īl was thus a typical Islamic *condottiere* – in other words, a "true Caliph", a new embodiment of what was symbolised by 'Alī throughout the history of Islam, whether orthodox or not.

Western sources describe Ismā'īl as a new prophet and provide us with evidence of the Mahdist and reforming aspect of his mission as well as of the fanaticism of his followers, whose relationship to their leader was of the peculiar military-religious type mentioned above. Ismā'īl is also depicted as a friend of the Christians, in contrast to the Ottomans who were considered the enemy *par excellence*. This is, in a way, a Venetian cliché, which, however, has some foundation as far as Ismā'īl's changing attitude to the jihād is concerned. Ever since Junaid's time the Shaikhs of Ardabīl, by extending their power to the temporal field, were conditioned in their tactics for its consolidation by the jihād, which presented the only religiously admissible method in a community as fundamentally Islamic as that of the Qizilbāsh. Their most natural enemies were obviously the Christians, firmly established to the north of the Ardabīl sphere of influence, but the wavering policy of the Qarā Quyūnlū produced what might be called a territorial landslide in the Shaikhs' interests when they became the heirs of this policy. The result was a new interpretation of the jihād, directed no longer against the Christians but against the Sunnī Ottomans, as soon as the buffer represented by the Āq Quyūnlū, who in their turn were also Sunnīs, was eliminated. The religious element in the Safavid conception of the jihād was gradually trivialised into the normal allegations of impiety in accordance with the classical formulae of disputes between Sunnīs and Shī'īs; but until the battle of Chāldirān the arguments used in this connection rank from the point of view of *kalām*, and even of Mu'tazilite kalām, among Ismā'īl's most outspoken affirmations of heterodoxy. At least, this is the case if we are to believe Sanudo's *Diarii*, of which the following is a typical passage:

> He took a Turk named Talisman and asked him where God was; and he replied that God was in Heaven, whereupon he caused the Turk to be cut in two. And then he took another man, a Christian priest from Armenia, and he asked him where God was; and he replied that God was in Heaven and upon earth and pointed to him who was listening. And he said: "Let him go, for this man knows where God is."[1]

In the Western sources Ismā'īl is called the *Sofi*, *Sophi*, *Sufi* or *Soffi*, a name which is also applied to his successors. That ṣūfī and Ṣafavī were confused, in the way exemplified by the passage where Pietro della Valle, speaking of the Ardabīl tombs, confuses the "Sofi" (Ismā'īl) with Ṣafī [al-dīn],[2] would explain why the "surname" of the Safavid dynasty is not given in any other form. For Europeans, in fact, the ṣūfīs are identical with the Safavid *ṭarīqa*.[3] This is the case even when a correct etymology and explanation of the word ṣūfī are given in the texts, e.g. in Rota[4] or in Don Juan of Persia,[5] who denies that it had any connection with the term "sophist", or again in the remark of an English traveller to the effect that the King of Persia would not be very pleased if he knew that in the West he was called the "Great Beggar".[6] In any case, since those Western texts which mention the word ṣūfī do not do so in order to stress its mystical connotation, the European interpretation of this term does not coincide fully with the local meaning, even if any hypothetical confusion is taken into account. In Persia mystics are not normally called ṣūfī, but the fact remains that contemporary Persian sources use the word to denote certain Safavid murīds, and in particular, to cite one example, to denote the seven dervishes who accompanied Ismā'īl when he left Gīlān and the reinforcements he subsequently received during the march from Lāhījān to Ṭārum;[7] later

[1] Sanudo, *Diarii* IV, cols. 191–2.

[2] Della Valle I/I, 407–8 (ed. Gaeta and Lockhart, p. 384).

[3] See, for example, T. Bulgarelli, *Gli avvisi a stampa in Roma nel Cinquecento* (Rome, 1967), p. 139 (copy of a letter from Andirnopoli written by Francesco Baiul to Rome, 1538): "...di questa sitta... fu un grande abbate detto Saich Caoder"; see also *Dell'origine, vita et facti d'arme del Gran Sofi al Doge di Venezia, per un maestro Giovanni Rota, nel 1505 di marzo*, MS Biblioteca Nazionale, Naples, Fondo MS XF 50, fol. 70r: the Ṣūfīs are called *qizilbāsh* because of the colour of their caps and "etnaseri" [*Ithnā'ashariyya*] because of the twelve bands on the same.

[4] *Dell'origine*, *loc. cit.*: "the religion of the Ṣūfīs lays down that, to show their humility, they should wear only woollen robes".

[5] Don Juan, trans. Le Strange, p. 50.

[6] Geofrey Ducket, in Hakluyt, *Principal Navigations* II, 126.

[7] Anonymous writer, in Ross, "The Early Years of Shah Ismail", p. 315; Ḥasan-i Rūmlū, *Aḥsan al-tavārīkh* I, 26.

on the term was also used to denote those members of the Safavid confraternity who were intimates of the shah, i.e. the *Shāhīsavanī*, especially those from the Shāmlū, Rūmlū and Qājār tribes.[1]

This is most probably the reason why the term reached the West as nothing but a synonym for Qizilbāsh or Safavid. The Qizilbāsh ṣūfīs provided the group from among which were chosen the various *khalīfas* and the *khalīfat al-khulafā*, i.e. the vicar-general of the *murshid-i kāmil*, the sovereign and only effective head of the brotherhood. The heaviest burden of the rules of honourable conduct towards the sovereign fell on the ṣūfī, and as late as the reign of Ismāʻīl II a ṣūfī who lied to his sovereign would be put to death;[2] ʻAbbās I used the term *nā-ṣūfī* to denote misbehaviour (1001/1592–3) and called a betrayal in the year 1023/1614–15 a *nā-ṣūfī-garī*.[3] Under ʻAbbās II and Sulaimān the ṣūfīs met in a hall called the *ṭāʼūs-khāna*, but gradually the importance of the category declined and some of the ṣūfīs were engaged in the humblest occupations, e.g. as sweepers, porters or executioners. At the time of its greatest splendour the Safavid confraternity granted to the ṣūfī the religious privileges that it conferred upon its leaders: a morsel of their food had the virtues of *shafāʻa* and the khalīfat al-khulafā granted remission of sins in public meetings, beating the penitents with a stick in accordance with the customs and rites of the Anatolian Qizilbāsh and Bektāshī communities which we have already mentioned. In this connection the report of an ambassador, Michele Membrè, who visited the court of Shah Ṭahmāsp on behalf of the Venetian Republic, contains a detailed account of the ceremony of public confession as practised in 1540 and lays particular stress on details of a ritual character (the fact that the sinners prostrated themselves when begging for remission and that they were publicly called upon to do so in a certain order) and on those of a cabalistic Ḥurūfī nature (the stick representing the letter *alif* etc.).[4]

In the religious career of Shah Ismāʻīl we can discern a veritable parabola. Between the time when he left Gīlān with the seven ṣūfīs and his coronation at Tabrīz he devoted himself with profound conviction to his mission as a new prophet-divinity; while the Qizilbāsh, against a background that was not only military and political but above all religious, represented the embryo of a new society that had still to be

1 Falsafī, *Zindagānī* I, 185–6.
2 Cf. the case of Bulghār Khalīfa: Iskandar Munshī, trans. Savory, pp. 318–9.
3 Falsafī, *Zindagānī* I, 187.
4 Membrè, *Relazione*, pp. 48f.

built up, and acted as a social element which, while accepting the new message, could provide the guarantees – necessary according to the Muslim way of thinking – that the declarations and appeals of the leader were genuine.

The official disavowal of this attempt came at Tabrīz when Ismā'īl recited the khuṭba in the names of the Twelve Imāms,[1] thus declaring his support for the Twelver Shī'a in the traditional way of a sovereign, which even found a reflection (admittedly merely formal) in the tenuous reform of the tāj-i ḥaidarī.[2] This fact, however, does not appear to have had a decisive influence on the religious personality of Ismā'īl, who continued to regard himself as the elected one and as a conqueror, that is to say as the Imām of his day according to Qizilbāsh ideas, which obviously went beyond any Twelver definition of the term Imām.

The peak of his religious crisis may be historically placed after the defeat at Chāldirān, which Ismā'īl seems to have accepted as a test designed to confute his divine mission. After that a change became apparent in his policy, which perceptibly turned Iran toward the east, as contrasted with the 15th-century tradition which regarded it as an alternative to Ottoman domination. It was at this stage that the great betrayal became irreversible, in respect not only of the Qizilbāsh ideal, but more specifically of the members of the brotherhood conceived of as the supporting structure of that now vanished ideal. A vivid echo of the religious vicissitudes of Ismā'īl and his followers can be found not so much in historical chronicles (e.g. the questionable events of 1512) as in the literary cycle revolving around certain Türkmen variants of the legend of Kïr-oghlu, apparently a hero of the *jalālī* type belonging to the Takkalū tribe, one of the most extreme among those making up the Qizilbāsh movement and also, partly for geographical reasons, one of the most susceptible to non-Islamic influences.[3]

To a fundamentally Shī'ī programme, based on the expectation of the Mahdī and the acknowledgement of the spiritual powers of the sovereign, were added various extremist elements of the Qarmato-Ismā'īliyya type, symbolised by communitarian ideas of the ideal State,

[1] See, however, Sanudo, *Diarii* IV, col. 192: "...and he has with him 40 governors, who are called *caliphani*, who also act and *celebrate the office* in his name, because he says that he is God...".

[2] Cf. the passage in the *Tārīkh-i jahān-ārā* quoted by Falsafī, *Zindagānī* I, 164.

[3] R. Mollov, "Contribution à l'étude du fond socio-historique du destan 'Koroglu'", *Études Balkaniques* VII (Sofia, 1967), 107-28.

reflecting perhaps an experience of the Sarbadār type. Despite the modifications of this legend to meet the circumstances (among the Uzbeks we find the extreme case of the hero being an enemy of the Qizilbāsh), everything seems to point here to a definitely Qizilbāsh conception of history – the key to which is provided by a Bulgarian variant in which it is definitely stated that Kïr-oghlu was a Qizilbāsh – more especially as regards the hero–sovereign relationship. We have on the one hand Bektāshī historical disengagement, which characterises the hero as a member of the ṭarīqa of ʻAlī, the Mahdī etc, and on the other a trend towards a more perceptive description of the hero as a victim of the shah, for whom, although no longer a Messiah, the hero continues to fight. The figure of the sovereign is deliberately left vague; he is not a symbol of oppression and betrayal, these tasks being normally left to an emissary, but an accomplice and supporter of the anti-ideal pursued to the disadvantage of Kïr-oghlu, who by definition is the shah's hero.

Another indication of Ismāʻīl's religious compromise stands out in typically legalitarian aspect against the background of the more and more "orthodox" character of his virtual conversion to what was obviously Twelver Shiʻism, even though its first manifestation is not chronologically defined by our sources: namely the claim to the *siyāda* which, explicit already in Ismāʻīl and even more precisely asserted by his successors, was retroactively attributed to his ancestors by the panegyrists and emendators of texts. On this point, too, the Western, and particularly the Venetian, sources are helpful. We need only remember the first items of information recorded by Sanudo.[1] Contemporary Eastern texts, when speaking of Ismāʻīl, still tend to call him *shaikh-oghlu* or even *Ardabīl-oghlu*[2] (cf. the term *shaikh-āvand* used to denote relatives of the sovereign), without normally referring to his title of *sayyid ḥusainī*. And yet this claim, which had its period of incubation and partial realisation in the years before the battle of Chāldirān, acquired in serving as a strongly anti-Qizilbāsh move the value of a well-planned political decision at a moment when the sovereign had given up his Imamite aspirations: his power was now supported by a new form of authority which, being more traditional, was endowed with sufficient legality to place a bond of obligation on

[1] It is true that in *Diarii* IV, cols. 253–7 and 312–13, the meaning is obscure, but the passage already quoted and cols. 500–2 are perfectly clear.

[2] Shukrī, *Salīm-nāma*, quoted in Barthold, "Khalif i sultan", p. 73, notes 307–8.

the Shīʿī Iranian aristocracy which had by now inherited the privileged position formerly held by the Qizilbāsh.[1]

VII. ṬAHMĀSP AND ISMĀʿĪL II

The history of this reciprocal granting of favours was repeated in a more decisive way under Ṭahmāsp, though with an irregular rhythm reflecting the religious involution of Ismāʿīl's successor, and it culminated in the violent and systematic repression of the Qizilbāsh carried out by ʿAbbās I. When the youthful Ṭahmāsp ascended the throne, he was steeped in the spirit of his preceptors and advisers; thus, like his father, he inaugurated his reign along the lines of Qizilbāsh teaching and then renewed, in a minor key, the experiment of transition to the traditional forms of Twelver Shiʿism. Obviously Ṭahmāsp was, so to speak, born a Twelver, and did not inherit from his father the pride in a mission to be accomplished by him as a prophet-Mahdī. But despite the conventional trappings with which he surrounded himself following his accession to the throne, his figure remained isolated amidst the orthodox Shīʿī establishment, which only later succeeded in obtaining his complete surrender. This was due to a particular conception of sovereignty, still strictly bound up with Qizilbāsh religious demands – which it would be wrong, because only very approximate, to describe as being autocratic – and determined by the ethico-political trend towards a unified conception of the State-religion hendiadys, which still demanded renewal, reforms, and the elimination of old structures. In this respect, Ṭahmāsp at first continued the anti-Ottoman policy, and it was precisely during the least Twelver phase of his reign – and perhaps not altogether by chance – that the religious aspect of Iran seems to have undergone an effortless change, with the result that Shiʿism acquired a greater degree of homogeneity. It seems legitimate to see in this grandiose phenomenon of conversion, not so much the abandonment of old systems or a break with juridical traditions, but

[1] The lack of unanimity in the documentary sources suggested to Kasravī that Ismāʿīl never proclaimed himself a *sayyid* (cf. Aubin, "Études Safavides I", pp . 44–5 and 44 n. 4), but to me it seems to denote uncertainty on Ismāʿīl's part, which is confirmed by the oft-quoted passage from Sanudo's *Diarii* IV, cols. 191–2: "...and his father said that he was a relative of Mahomet; and then his father died; ... and he says that my father was not my father, but he was my slave; and he says that he himself is God..." In other words, Ismāʿīl may have regarded the siyāda, at times, as a handicap in his mission. If this reasoning is correct, then Ismāʿīl was simply reaffirming, without conviction, a claim already made by his father Ḥaidar.

rather a transition towards a new conception of the State, which was accepted because it clarified – or at any rate set out to clarify – the relationship between the sovereign and his subjects, and consequently between political praxis and Islam. This did not imply a reaffirmation of those divine attributes which Ismā'īl had specifically renounced, since he had preferred a simple temporal investiture; but it did mean that there was a supreme idealisation of the temporal leader as a guarantor of the preparations for the blissful era of the Mahdī and also of the continuity of the Islamic past, as represented by the claim, from now on loudly proclaimed everywhere, that the sovereign belonged to the Ahl al-bait. And, at the same time, this could be considered the first actual manifestation of a nationalistic kind of claim, according to which regality was derived from the ancient rulers of Iran.[1]

An analysis of the situation in Tabrīz at three critical moments between 907/1501, the year of Ismā'īl's coronation, and 942/1535, the date of the reconquest of the city by Ṭahmāsp after it had been occupied by Süleymān, serves to validate our hypothesis of the conversion of Iran – or at least of the larger urban centres – to Twelver Shi'ism. In 907/1501 Tabrīz was in a position similar to that of Kāshān (see above), in the sense that there were neither Ja'farī texts nor, consequently, juridical experts – a circumstance which is normally attributed to the predominance of Sunnism in the first Safavid capital.[2] The sources do not record any drastic measures taken to remedy the situation, and this leads one to suppose that in Tabrīz, as in Kāshān, there was a slow evolution from a type of Shafi'ism towards a stricter form of Ja'farism. In 920/1514, when Selīm occupied Tabrīz after the battle of Chāldirān, he did not deem it necessary to take any repressive measures, probably because to him the city appeared to be still Sunnī (and this despite the fact that he had just ordered the massacre of 40,000 Anatolian Qizilbāsh). For the following twenty years, from this point of view, Tabrīz has, as it were, no history. When Süleyman arrived in 942/1535, however, it would seem that the city had completely changed; in other words it had become Shī'ī. Venetian sources tell us that many janissaries went over to the other side and that the populace rose against the Ottoman foe and greeted the Shī'ī Ṭahmāsp

[1] *Deposizione de persona fede degna del viaggio fatto al campo del Gran Signore verso Babilonia il 14 luglio 1535*, MS Biblioteca Marciana, Venice, classe VII, no. 882, fol. 7r.

[2] *LHP* IV, 53.

as a liberator.[1] The description of so oddly compliant – and yet complete – a conversion is confirmed by a passage in Membrè's report.[2] There Tabrīz is described as a typically Shī'ī and almost "modern" city, where by "modern" we refer to the "form" which characterises any Shī'ī Iranian city, distinguishing it from the towns of any other Islamic country, and which is not merely based on rituals such as the observance of Muḥarram or the public execration of the first Caliphs. It is also based on certain religious factors inspired both by sentiment and by folklore which, as we shall see, acquired a canonical form in the days of Majlisī and were based on a whole set of examples of "coexistence" with the Twelve Imāms, including prophecies, miracles, apparitions and dreams – all this in a setting which was halfway between the everyday life and the realm of myths. The modern originality of Persian Shi'ism has its roots here, and in this sense Ṭahmāsp can serve as a symbol: after a beginning marked by his Qizilbāsh background he soon fell under the influence of the Shī'ī 'ulamā, the first notable occasion being his contacts, during the 1530s, with the sayyids of Uskūya near Tabrīz.[3] Although the influx of new contingents of immigrants from Anatolia continued throughout his reign (at Qazvīn alone there were ten thousand new immigrants at the time of the sovereign's death, which would seem to indicate that Ismā'īl's betrayal had not taught them an effective lesson),[4] the administrative framework shows signs of the arrival of this new component on the political scene, although its influence was obviously by no means undisputed. Ṭahmāsp is thus the first modern Persian Shī'ī about whom we have information drawn not only from oriental sources (including the significant and searching autobiography of the sovereign himself) but also from reports by Western observers among which that of Membrè gives us a lucid account of the early period, while the better known work by d'Alessandri deals with the latter years of the monarch's reign. And as a conclusion to this theologico-sentimental edifice of which he was at once the champion and the victim, in his last years Ṭahmāsp was seized with a veritable mania for conservation: it replaced his already languishing anti-Ottoman ardour and led him to cut himself off from the world and to waste his time in commonplace activities that served as palliatives to his suspicions and fears, rendered more acute by con-

[1] *Deposizione*, fol. 3v; cf. the anonymous *Gran Rotta de lo exercito del Signor Turcho fatta de la gente del Sophi in Persia* (Venice, 1535), p. 6.
[2] Membrè, pp. 22–3, 46–8 etc.
[3] Iskandar Munshī, trans. Savory, pp. 229–30.
[4] Falsafī, *Zindagānī* I, 187.

tinual dreams which were his only guide whenever he had to make a public decision.

It seems that there could have been no logical reaction to Ṭahmāsp's clerical and bigoted Shiʿism other than an attempt to reintroduce into Iran "the impure and wicked commands of the damned Abū Bakr, ʿUthmān and others...", which is how Minadoi[1] describes Ismāʿīl II's efforts to restore Sunnism in his domains. In actual fact, Iran had been gradually tending towards definitely Shīʿī forms, especially in the larger cities, where the need to safeguard old-established interests by adopting an attitude as close as possible to that of the sovereign was most urgently felt. As invariably happens, the rural areas had revealed a more conservative spirit, though the character of the whole country was determined by the common denominator of an expected restoration of the old and pure Sharīʿa, as an antidote to economic difficulties that had never been solved. Ismāʿīl II's Sunnism was in its turn an invocation to the Sharīʿa, with the intention of providing himself with a weapon which would enable him to undermine the power of the Shīʿī ʿulamā by establishing a new balance of power between the Iranian aristocracy and the Qizilbāsh tribes still active in the political field, since, owing to their mutual rivalry, both these elements were not unwilling to give him a sure degree of support. At any rate, although it is possible to describe, with a certain approximation to truth, the political motivation of such a decision as anticlericalism, an appeal to the rural peasantry, an obligation of the Sharīʿa or diplomatic opportunism, yet the more specifically religious mechanism underlying it remains far from clear. Iran was rapidly becoming aware that it was the chosen land of the Imāms and that its inhabitants were the repositories of their ta'wīl, elements for which the presence of the sovereign, together with certain incipient national and religious ideas, had been a determining factor. To a certain extent the position of Ismāʿīl II would seem to posit a renunciation of these prerogatives and a greater sympathy for the more mundane needs of the country. Translated into religious terms, this meant a return to the situation that had brought Ismāʿīl I to the throne, by dint of combating the obscurantist tendencies of Ṭahmāsp's last years, almost in an attitude of anti-family reaction which was later carried to extremes, though within a framework which was again fully and conventionally Shīʿī, by Muḥammad Khudābanda.

[1] Minadoi, p. 11.

VIII. THE NUQṬAVĪS

For the reasons stated above it is once again a heresy that will help us to understand the spirit of the times more clearly than would a close examination of the official religious policy. The Nuqṭavī heresy (the word is derived from *nuqṭa*, "point", naturally in the cabalistic sense) began in Gīlān as an offshoot of Hurufism under the leadership of Maḥmūd Pāsīkhānī (hence the name Pāsīkhāniyān sometimes applied to its adherents) and towards the end of the 8th/14th century probably represented a form of opposition to the stagnant local Shi'ism with its Zaidite tendencies. It acquired, to a certain extent, greater significance during the rule of Ismā'īl II, while its end as an organised movement came in the reign of 'Abbās I. Its kinship with Hurufism, which explains the obvious Ismā'īlī influences present in Nuqṭavī ideology (though we should also bear in mind geographical proximity to Rūdbār), lies in the fact that it adopted a still more definite attitude, metaphysically speaking, towards the divine ta'ṭīl, and thereby towards a "Renaissance" appreciation of the value of human actions. Its relationship to the accepted Ḥurūfī theory that man is the starting-point for any form of superhuman knowledge is clear. For the Nuqṭavī deity, man does not represent an object of activity, and it is man himself who, through self-knowledge, can raise himself up to the divine sphere. Thus good and evil are measured against an extremely mundane yardstick and the realities of paradise and retribution occur on earth within a period of time which may exceed anybody's lifetime, through a process of metempsychosis corresponding to one's virtues and sins. This belief in metempsychosis, it should be noted, was stressed by a later writer, Riżā Qulī Khān Hidāyat,[1] whose remarks should be interpreted in the light of a possible subsequent Indian influence on the movement, since its followers, as a result of persecution, eventually fled to India. Instead of the resurrection of the body, however, Nuqṭavī metempsychosis appears to envisage a continual process of metamorphosis of matter, considered, in the Dahrite sense, as being eternal. To this we must probably add various residual elements that had been present for some time in the very promiscuous substratum of Gīlān, such as the belief in the visibility of the mid-day divinity (riding upon an ass like Dajjāl, who in Iran is not unconnected with Żaḥḥāk)

[1] Kiyā, "Nuqṭaviyān", pp. 43–4.

and, still more cogently, the classification of the appearance, bodily movements and qualities of human beings as ẓuhūr of the divine attributes.[1] The Nuqṭavīs, destined to be the alternative *par excellence* to official 16th-century Shiʿism, were persecuted by Ismāʿīl I after 1514 and, in a more reactionary manner, by the clerical Ṭahmāsp, who in 973/1565 had one of their leaders blinded and in 981/1573–4 carried out a large-scale repression of the sect at Kāshān. After the death of Ṭahmāsp, however, the movement clearly became the mouthpiece of two elements which in my opinion are of decisive importance in determining the religious attitude of Ismāʿīl II: on the one hand, an anti-Shīʿī trend, the theoretical basis of which consisted of the denial of any need for an official intermediary when dealing with the deity, irrespective of whether the intermediary were a walī-imām or the whole body of the Twelver *mujtahids* acting on behalf of and as substitutes for the Imām; and, on the other hand, the discontented plebeian element which was always ready to try the experiment of an organised protest. During the reign of Ṭahmāsp the most influential groups of Nuqṭavīs were to be found at Kāshān, Iṣfāhān, Shīrāz and especially at Qazvīn. The dervish Khusrau, a plebeian from Qazvīn, became their symbol and guide. His public activities show how closely involved with one another were the movements of this era and how primitive the demands which had led to their formation. The dervish Khusrau "clothed himself as a qalandar" and travelled all over the country before probing deeper into the Nuqṭavī doctrine. On his return to Qazvīn he began preaching in the mosque at meetings attended by other dervishes and the populace, and this annoyed the ʿulamā, who had him summoned to the court. In the presence of the shah – probably Ismāʿīl II – he questioned the dogmas of Islam and the "pure faith of the Imām", but "did not depart from the Sharīʿa", to improve his knowledge of which he had been attending fiqh lessons given by the ʿulamā themselves. He was pardoned in the name of Sharīʿa orthodoxy, which in the social spirit of Islam ranked higher than the ambiguities of pure kalām. Further information on the complex structure of the sect is provided by subsequent events (especially the increasing number of plebeians among his followers), culminating in the takfīr launched by ʿAbbās I, who had been present at a discussion between a famous

[1] Muḥammad b. Abī Ṭālib al-Dimishqī, *Cosmographie*, ed. A. F. M. Mehren (St Petersburg, 1866), p. 226.

Nuqṭavī known as Yūsuf the artisan and the qalandar Kūchik in the course of which the heretical nature of Khusrau's doctrine is said to have become clear, and the resulting "jest of the stars" (the title of a well-known *novella* by Akhundov), in which this same Yūsuf took the place of 'Abbās on the throne for three days before being killed (1002/1593–4).[1] The presence of an element that may be termed ṣūfī in the outward sense of its organic structure (compare, for instance, the *tekke* founded by the dervish Khusrau) has no bearing on the fact that the brotherhood spirit, strengthened in religious terms, now appeared to be paradoxically anti-mystical in so far as it was anti-individualistic. This would seem to have created around the movements influenced by it a margin within which it was possible to achieve a political compromise by means of an increasingly skilful use of the taqiyya, camouflaged under the officially recognised esotericism of the various ṭarīqas. On the other hand the Shī'ī religious class soon perceived the ambiguity of such an attitude, and the reaction to this new type of sufism took the form of a more precise limitation of the boundaries of Twelver Iran.

IX. THE HEYDAY OF THE SAFAVID ERA

The official religious history of the Safavid era, beginning with 'Abbās I, is in fact concerned with three fundamental problems: the condemnation of sufism; the juridical codification aimed at solving according to fiqh those contradictions and differences of opinion which would have been so much more dangerous if they had led to theological definitions (on the theological refinements reserved for privileged members and initiates of the so-called "school of Iṣfahān", see Chapter 13); and, lastly, the promulgation of the new Majlisian theology, a counterpoint to that feeling based on folklore and ritual which, as has been said, is typical of modern Shi'ism. In its official form anti-ṣūfī feeling in Safavid Iran after the reign of 'Abbās I was nothing but a return to the original standpoint of the Twelver Shī'a, traditionally averse to mystical experience. The importance of sufism in the evolution of religion during the 15th century lay in its functional and paradigmatic value. The typical religious forms tried out in the ṣūfī movements had been transplanted into the body of a dissenting and heretical

[1] Iskandar Munshī, trans. Savory, pp. 648–9.

Shīʿa, whence they were transmitted – emptied, however, of their revolutionary potential – to the official Safavid clergy. It was mainly a question of the link, equivalent to a precisely established hierarchical relationship, between Shaikh – Mahdī – sovereign and murīd – worshipper – subject; of the individualistic mechanism which, operating in connection with even the most heterodox demands, was in this case in symbiosis with a social and collectivist feeling that allowed a retrogressive check on the experiments carried out by the leader, who was the mouthpiece of aspirations which were indeed general but had been modified by refraction through the prism of his personal elaboration.

At a time when the Twelver religious class had been stabilised owing to a juridical organisation and a hierarchy stricter than in any other sector of Islam, to have permitted the survival of such elements outside the organisation would have implied the constant risk of decentralising for an authority already deeply engaged on both the religious and the political plane, which exhibited a high degree of parallelism and gave each other mutual support. Despite the continual agitation of the qalandars and the aftermath of the elimination of Qizilbāsh support within the state, the reign of ʿAbbās was therefore deeply marked by an anti-mystical spirit, so much so that the most advanced experiments in the religious sphere, viewed with suspicion by the authorities, were only externally tinged with sufism (e.g. the philosopher Mīr Dāmād), and the problems which arose melted away into a refined consciousness and love for theology, this being typical of the period.

In any case, the fact that the external appearance was ṣūfī in all matters that did not form part of the official Twelver religion brings us back to consideration of the question as to how far sufism was used as a taqiyya during the last century of Safavid rule, not only internally, i.e. to conceal extremist positions that had survived the process of standardisation, but also externally, in the sense that minority groups of Sunnīs embraced sufism in order to escape victimisation, for the most part fiscal but in some cases political. It is known that there were Sunnī groups at Qazvīn even in the immediate entourage of ʿAbbās, and also at Hamadān, where in 1017/1608 repressive measures were taken by ʿAbbās himself, who accused the Sunnī *raʾīs* of the city of ill-treating the Shīʿīs and stirring up his own co-religionists. Surkha, to the west of Simnān, was likewise the scene of persecution in 1599, but under Shah Ṣafī it would seem to have been still Sunnī, for in a farmān dated

1039/1630 he excluded this village from certain measures of tax-reduction.[1] The sole exception was Lāristān, whose tenacious Sunnism had been spared even by Shah Ismā'īl during the most political phase of his activity.

As confirmation of the fact that the definition of ṣūfī, a vague term inevitably arousing suspicion, covered more than one form of heresy (extremism, Sunnism) involving people whose common bond was dissatisfaction with the way political or religious power was exercised after its centralisation at the end of the Safavid era, we may mention the celebrated defence which Muḥammad Bāqir al-Majlisī, the mujtahid prince of the late Safavid period (d. 1111/1699–1700), attempted to make of his father's eclectic and ambivalent attitude to sufism.[2] A natural result of the ṣūfī question in the history of Twelver Shi'ism was the solemn takfīr proclaimed by the Uṣūlī Muḥammad 'Alī b. Muḥammad Bāqir Bihbihānī (d. 1216/1801–2),[3] which relegated it to that same sphere of obscurantism which according to official Islam – whether Shī'ī or Sunnī – was the domain of all broadly speaking illegal movements bearing the same burden of a general and typical accusation of immorality, contempt for the Sharī'a, the drinking of wine and so forth.

As regards the progressive simplification of ritual and theology, in the sense of an increasingly frequent appeal to an established authority and a fixed procedure for the various manifestations of religious life, the most striking example was the growth of a particular juridical spirit embracing every kind of religious problem and preparing the way for the theoretical – and not merely *de facto* – absorption of Twelver Shi'ism by the Islamic *umma*, as subsequently codified by Nādir Shāh. Progress towards the official recognition of the existence of another madhhab besides the four of the canon was marked by lively controversies with the Ottoman and Uzbek Sunnīs, and the instances given in the sources represent so many stages in an ideal evolution towards a steadily decreasing differentiation of the religious substance of things. By analysing three of these controversies – the correspondence between the Uzbek 'Ubaid-Allāh and Ṭahmāsp (936/1529–30),[4] an ex-

[1] Aubin, "Les Sunnites", p. 152.

[2] Mīrzā Muḥammad Tunakābunī, *Qiṣaṣ al-'ulamā*, p. 233.

[3] Āghā Muḥammad 'Alī b. Muḥammad Bāqir Iṣfahānī Bihbihānī, *Risāla-yi ḥairatiyya*, British Library MS described by Rieu, *Catalogue of the Persian MSS* I, 33–4.

[4] Ḥasan-i Rūmlū, *Aḥsan al-tavārīkh* I, 226–32.

change of letters between the 'ulamā of Mashhad and certain Uzbek 'ulamā dating from 997/1588–9,[1] and another dating from the first half of the 17th century between the Ottoman muftī Asad Efendī and his Persian colleagues[2] – we can establish a few of their fundamental theses. The views of the Shī'īs are still characterised by the condemnation of the first three Caliphs, which, however, in the letter from the 'ulamā of Mashhad is already considered as the affirmation, not of a religious, but of a political principle and definitely distinguished from the canonical execration, which is described as an "act worthy of ignorant Shī'īs". The dispute is restricted to the sphere of the public activity of the three Caliphs, to whom 'Ā'isha is naturally added, and the wrong done to 'Alī is not regarded as implying a religious fault in a general sense; it is treated merely as a juridical offence of such a kind that the guilty parties can still be held to be members of the umma. As regards the other side, in addition to the charge concerning the execration, which as we have seen drew a defensive reaction, only in the Ottoman letter is there a detailed list of charges, which are directed, however, against the Persian Qizilbāsh rather than against Shī'īs in general; controversy thus hinges on the wearing of moustaches and beards, the improper use of green clothing, the drinking of wine, sexual promiscuity and the like. Despite the possibility that such matters might be evidence of heretical tendencies, they are recalled in an argument more reminiscent of a legal dispute than a theological confutation and they are treated on the same plane as, or rather as supporting evidence for, the political and religious claims to priority, in relation to 'Alī, of Abū Bakr as the first convert, 'Umar as champion of the faith and 'Uthmān as editor of the Qur'ān. The more definite accusations belong to the category of political controversies directly involving the Safavid sovereigns. Conversely, on the Sunnī side stress was officially laid on the category of the "pure Imām" and, while in the letter to Ṭahmāsp there may still be some doubt concerning their identity, the subsequent Uzbek controversy shows that the path followed by the Sunnīs was that of the *Salafs* and the Twelve Imāms, both the former and the latter being guarantors of the true Sunna and of the *jamā'a*. The Twelve Imāms have always had a place in Sunnī devotional attitudes, especially during the pre- and proto-Safavid periods (the case of Khunjī may be cited as an example), but after the turbulent interven-

[1] Amoretti, "Una polemica". [2] Mordtmann, "Sunnitisch – Schiitische Polemik".

tion of the Qizilbāsh the Safavids must have seemed to the Sunnīs to be "asses of the Imāms", just as the Christians were called "asses of Christ", namely bearers overshadowed by a sacred burden.

At this stage, once political fanaticism had begun to subside, a contact between the two branches of Islam seemed to become feasible, subject to the proviso that there was full acknowledgment of the existence of single points of acceptable difference, whereas the more mature and original fruits of Persian-Shī'ī Safavid thought could be culled only within the narrow confines of the abstruse domain of abstract philosophical speculation, which on the one hand was ignored by official Sunnism and on the other was viewed with deep distrust by official Shi'ism. In the more strictly ecclesiastical Shī'ī camp, the lack of any definitely religious substance in these controversies was counterbalanced by the great flowering of religious-juridical codification which, though not insensible in its turn to strictly political demands, is of greater interest from the ideological point of view. In its general outlines the ideological complexity of Twelver Shi'ism at this stage, when it was adapting itself to its function as state religion, can be clearly discerned in the antithesis between the Uṣūlīs and the Akhbārīs, who during the Safavid era (after the compilation of the *Fawā'id al-madaniyya* by Mullā Amīn Astarābādī, who died in 1026/1617) assumed the character of well-defined currents within the body of the "Imamite school". The ethico-political foundation on which these two movements were based seems to have been formulated in terms offering a simplistic view of 15th-century problems. In Iran the Uṣūlīs represented the aristocratic element, which since the reign of Ismā'īl had reaffirmed its function as an indispensable link in the relationship between the sovereign and his subjects, as a result of the privileges granted on the basis of the well-known and uninterrupted tradition dating from the days of Tīmūr, and of its specific administrative functions. This was now enhanced by the corporate outlook of a youthful clergy whose spokesmen were drawn from the aristocracy, within which – as the sovereign's faithful ally – they became characterised as the instrument best suited to prevent any effective change in the balance of forces. When considering this dichotomy – which should not be viewed as a clear-cut religious contrast – it would definitely be going too far to attribute to the Akhbārīs the significance of symbolising a constant desire for reforms and progress; but within the Akhbārī movement, providing a proof of its greater vitality (in the purely religious sense) and of a certain availability which was at least consistent with the principles of a Shīʿī society, there later arose the shaikhī school, which in Iran was the only adequate testing-ground for new experiments that served to regenerate the normal Imamic conceptions when the Safavid era ended. The contrast is thus far more important than the struggle, *bāzārī* even if it was not pure folklore, between factions such as the Ḥaidariyya and the Niʿmatiyya. The disappointing and too fragmentary realisation of the promises implicit in the Akhbārī principles is certainly outside the scope of this study. Nor can we speak of a genuine Uṣūlī religious feeling, though it is permissible to talk of Uṣūlī and Akhbārī methods, which were divergent trends operating in the sphere of Majlisian Shīʿī society. Let us refrain from essaying a complete definition, but as one example of disagreement we can mention the interpretation of the ta'wīl, which was obviously the mainspring of any Shīʿī system. For the Uṣūlī the Sunna, through its interpretation entrusted to the reasoning (*ʿaql*) of the mujtahid, was the means of making effective (*ẓāhir*) the teachings of the Qur'ān. The ta'wīl was therefore entrusted to a special body which, necessarily provided with particular instruments, had the power to render practically equal to the text (*naql*) that which would otherwise have been only tafsīr, or, in legal terminology, *ijtihād* or *ẓann*. And it is precisely in its elaboration of the theory of ẓann that the originality and fascination of this school lie. The "cogency of conjecture" was a regrettable practical necessity, generating what was nothing better than a *credo quia incertum* and, in the administrative economy of the Safavid confessional State, an emphatic proclamation of a kind of *solve et repete* principle having a cosmic value, which required the acceptance in all cases of the decisions of the temporal authority, with the reservation that the real values – should they have been violated – would be re-established in the life to come.

In this way the Uṣūlīs cut themselves off from any prerogative of renewal, leaving the Imām with the sole function – which necessarily was never verifiable in space or time – of acting as the basis of their activity. They abandoned the pursuit of the ideals of perfect justice, realisable only through the Law which it was the Imām's task to convey to this world, and resigned themselves to the only realistic way of making the law consistent with changing circumstances, in an almost existential manner. From the religious point of view, reality was confined to direct and everyday experience of the Sharīʿa, while the Reality of Imamic dimensions was merely the logical instrument that made it possible to define this pure actuality. That Reality belonged to the plane of myths and not to that of metaphysics. A logical consequence of this was that no further revelation could be expected: the Imām was no longer considered as having the revolutionary potential of a Mahdī and his place was taken by a clergy well aware of the change that had been made to their own advantage. The Imām was no longer expected to arrive, because he was already there, living in the psyche and the dreams of the faithful. And these dreams were no longer a prerogative of saints and seers, but, by a kind of inflationary process, were from now on extended to all believers.

Ideologically the Akhbārīs were in a more classic situation, not because of any reversal of values *vis-à-vis* the Uṣūlīs, but merely because, unlike their opponents, they had retained certain options; recourse to the *akhbār* in an individualistic form, and ignoring the authority of the ijtihād, on the one hand prevented the constitution of any element that might become a substitute for the Imām, who remained active and indispensable; and on the other hand it also prevented the formation of a new naql as a ẓāhir of the Imamic Sunna, which was considered the only way of interpreting the prophetic message. The Sunna was thus the Qur'anic ta'wīl, and the tafsīr drawn from it did not exclude the possibility that the authentic interpretation of the Sunna in question should be the will of the Imām destined one day to change the Sharī'a as hitherto applied.

In a religious social conscience this still left room for the expectation of the Mahdī and his teaching and presupposed the possibility of a transformation of society starting from the top. Such a position (which was by no means unusual in the Shī'ī outlook, whose extreme manifestations extended in fact far beyond it in originality) now represented the only vital alternative to the rigorism introduced by the Safavids. All this is elucidated by the transformation which the theology of Majlisī brought about in Persian religious life, changing it into a cult and a spirit that were essentially nationalistic. Majlisī returned to the Sunna of the Imām and, without introducing any innovations in terms of its content, restored to the Safavid Shī'a the text of the various akhbār. The philological demand for new large "editions" of the material constituting the Sunna was one of the characteristics of this period, from which, in fact, date the new compilations of *ḥadīth*, the most important of these being Majlisī's *Biḥār al-anwār*. The new element that made its official appearance with Majlisī and was divulged in innumerable works of a popular type was the codification of what has been called the coexistence of the Imām and his followers. It is not the new miracles performed by the Imām that make it possible to perceive the transition (which was in fact reciprocal) between legend and theology, but the context within which these miracles, whether old or new, take place.

A striking example is the hagiography of the Imām 'Alī al-Riḍā,[1] virtually identical with that of Ibn Bābūya (4th/10th century). The miracles are foretold by luminous visions, by miraculous dreams and magic voices; generally they occur during a pilgrimage to the Imām, who speaks to his disciples "as if in a dream" and reveals unknown readings of the Qur'ān. Often the vows fulfilled by the Imām have detrimental consequences for the typical enemies of Persia at that time, the Uzbeks or the notables who thwarted the pietistic activities of good Persians and were probably Sunnīs. At the same time stress is laid on the sanctity of purely temporal requests from individuals and of demands for the granting of all kinds of privileges to the district of Mashhad, where the sanctuary of the Imām was situated and which was also a Shī'ī bulwark against the Uzbeks and Türkmens. The Imām, theoretically deprived of his function as a future effective head of the State, becomes the devout companion and the benevolent intercessor in everyday matters. This occurs as the result of a long series of visions, dreams and auspices which are not in any way mystical and represent the Iranian canonisation of everything that in Islam had remained outside orthodoxy (averse to anything that might detract from its pure monotheism), and confined within the barely tolerated sphere of religious sentimentalism manifesting itself in forms of ritual and a particular need of myths.

That is why the Shī'ī religion now takes on a nationalist hue based on figures such as the Eighth Imām, who represented the most perfect expression of Persian Shi'ism, with his typical characteristics, i.e. a conscious victim of his own sacrifice and a prophet of the greatness of Iran, destined to accept his *mashhad*. As a counterpoint to the fundamental theme of the *Insān al-kāmil*, which in the theology of Majlisī was recognised in the Iranicised version of the 'Alī al-Riḍā "type", pilgrimages to the tombs of the Imām and of the innumerable *Imām-zādas*, which had always been regarded as meritorious acts of devotion,

[1] Mullā Muḥammad Bāqir b. Muḥammad Taqī al-Majlisī, *Biḥār al-anwār* XII, 1–99.

acquired growing canonical status. Theoretically they were even placed on the same level as the ḥajj,[1] and to the popular mind they were perhaps more important than this, owing to a series of traditional and pietistic values which found expression in the accomplishment of the ziyāra, especially to Mashhad, which in the meantime had become one of the recognised centres of Twelver Shi'ism. The Shī'a still continued to revolve around the Iraqi axis of Najaf and Karbalā, but this infiltration of popular elements led to a veritable Iranicisation of the holy places, carried to such lengths that Imamism, at all events in its external manifestations, became a Persian religion, creating a homogeneous tradition destined to find its fulfilment in modern times. The compactness of the present Twelver world has sometimes led to misconceptions regarding the nature of the Shī'a in pre-Safavid times, because habits of thought and religious mechanisms have been attributed to it which as a matter of fact were present in the Shī'a only during the Safavid period of its development. The skill displayed by those who held the reins of power in creating national cohesion around the Shī'a, which the people of Persia embraced after a slow transition, prevented any anti-Shī'ī reaction at the time of the Afghan occupation. Such a reaction might well have offered Iran a Sunnī alternative founded on a system capable of solving the country's economic difficulties by doing away with the privileges of the ruling class; but the brutality of the Afghans, who were virtually isolated during their campaign and reduced to trying to solve problems with which they were incapable of dealing, merely served to strengthen the bonds between the Shī'a and Iran, thereby achieving the aim to which Ismā'īl had sacrificed his religious ambitions.

The Dasht-i Mūghān farmān of Nādir Shāh in 1736[2] was a recognition of this state of affairs. Like all the sovereigns of Iran he appealed to the local aristocracy to consider his act as one more step towards the recognition of the place of Iran within the framework of the Islamic world. The mujtahid at that time, 'Alī Akbar Mullā-bāshī, was officially the sovereign's adviser, and the execution of the edict was entrusted to an official who belonged to the great Safavid tradition, the vice-*ṣadr* Muḥammad 'Alī. The suggestion that there should be an ideal return to the period before the days of Ismā'īl, who had been responsible for the introduction of certain deplorable innovations (meaning thereby the

[1] Cf. the second "trustworthy" ḥadīth mentioned in Ḥājj Shaikh 'Abbās Qumī, *Kulliyāt-i mafātīḥ al-ẓinān*, p. 498.
[2] Petrov, "Ukaz", pp. 52–5.

execration of the first three Caliphs, subsequently abolished), was practically equivalent to the acceptance of Twelver Shiʿism with its juridical institutions, so that the mention of the mujtahid does not have the religious implications one would expect, just as to renounce the execration of the three Caliphs is not, for a Shīʿī, an indicator of theological aberration. The consequences of this edict are confined in practice to the final disappearance of the concept of jihād within the Muslim world, now divided no longer into *firāq* but into juridical schools, the fifth of which – the so-called Jaʿfarī school – is represented by the Twelver Shīʿa, in particular by Twelver Usulism. This led in Iran to an even greater isolation between actual religious life, entrusted to popular piety, and the task of the class destined to enforce the Sharīʿa, albeit according to the Jaʿfarī system. A positive result of this dualism – somewhat unusual from the Islamic point of view – was the adoption of a purely technical conception of whatever is the object of speculation in the sacred texts. The true Shīʿī ability to see problems through the prism of a highly developed juridical system without any interference of a religious-humanistic kind later contributed to a more ready acceptance – in comparison with other Muslim countries – of modernistic solutions to the various political and social problems.

CHAPTER 13

SPIRITUAL MOVEMENTS, PHILOSOPHY AND THEOLOGY IN THE SAFAVID PERIOD

THE BACKGROUND

The Safavid period is one of the outstanding epochs in the intellectual and spiritual history of Islamic Iran, although its artistic and political life is much better known to the outside world than what it created in the domains of sufism, philosophy and theology. Particularly in *Ḥikmat* – that combination of philosophy and gnosis which should be translated as theosophy rather than philosophy as currently understood in the Occident – the Safavid period is the apogee of a long development which reaches back to the 6th/12th century and the introduction of new intellectual perspectives into Islamic civilisation by Suhravardī and Ibn 'Arabī. Likewise, in sufism and the religious sciences the sudden flowering of activity in the 10th/16th century is based on the important but little studied transformation that was taking place in Persia since the Mongol invasion.

Persia did not become Shī'ī through a sudden process. Ever since the 7th/13th century Shi'ism was spreading in Persia through certain of the ṣūfī orders which were outwardly Sunnī – that is, in their *madhhab* they followed one of the Sunnī schools, usually the Shāfi'ī. But they were particularly devoted to 'Alī and some even accepted *wilāya* (or *valāyat*, in its Persian pronunciation), that is, the power of spiritual direction and initiation which Shī'īs believe was bestowed upon 'Alī by the Prophet of Islam. It was particularly this belief that made the transformation of Persia from a predominantly Sunnī land to a Shī'ī one possible. The Shī'īs consider Ṣafī al-Dīn Ardabīlī, the founder of the Safavid order, as a Shī'ī, whereas the research of modern historians has revealed him to be a Sunnī. The same holds true of Shāh Ni'mat-Allāh Valī, the founder of the Ni'matallāhī order, which is the most widespread ṣūfī order in contemporary Persia. In a sense both contentions are true depending on what we mean by Shi'ism. If we mean the Shāfi'ī school or madhhab, then these ṣūfī orders such as the

Ṣafavī and Ni'matallāhī were initially Sunnī and later became Shī'ī. If, however, by Shi'ism we mean the acceptance of the valāyat of 'Alī, then in this sense these orders were inwardly Shī'ī during this period and became also outwardly so during the Safavid era.

In any case the rôle of sufism in the spread of Shi'ism and the preparation of the ground for the establishment of a Shī'ī Persia with the Safavids remains basic both in the direct and active political rôle played by the Ṣafavī order and in the religious and spiritual rôle of other orders such as the Kubraviyya and especially the Nūrbakhshiyya, which more than any other order sought to bridge the gap between Sunnism and Shi'ism.[1] Shaikh Muḥammad Ibn 'Abd-Allāh, entitled Nūrbakhsh, who died in Ray in 869/1464–5, made indirect claims to being the Mahdī and sought to bring Shi'ism and Sunnism closer together through sufism. His successors Faiżbakhsh and Shāh Bahā' al-Dīn continued the movement in the same direction and finally became fully Shī'ī. A celebrated member of this order, Shaikh Shams al-Dīn Muḥammad Lāhījī, the author of the best-known commentary upon the *Gulshan-i rāz*, a work which is a bible of sufism in Persian, was thoroughly Shī'ī while being an outstanding ṣūfī. The story of his encounter with Shah Ismā'īl and the question posed to him by the shah as to why he always wore black, to which he replied that he was always mourning the tragic events of Karbalā, is well known.[2] And it indicates the complete transformation that had taken place within the Nūrbakhshī order so that it became totally Shī'ī in form. We observe the same process within the Ni'matallāhī and Ṣafavī orders. Both Shāh Ni'mat-Allāh, who came to Persia from Aleppo, and Shaikh Ṣafī al-Dīn from Ardabīl were at first ṣufīs of Sunnī background such as the Shāẕiliyya and Qādiriyya brotherhoods. But the inner belief in the valāyat of 'Alī gradually transformed the outer form of the orders as well into thoroughly Shī'ī organisations, although the inward structure of these orders, being ṣūfī, remained above the Shī'ī – Sunnī distinctions. The Ni'matallāhī order became Shī'ī during the Safavid period itself, while the Ṣafavī order began to show Shī'ī tendencies with Junaid, who was attracted to the Musha'sha' movement, and became fully Shī'ī with 'Alī b. Junaid. In all these cases, however, a similar process was occurring. Ṣūfī orders with Shī'ī tendencies were

[1] See the series of articles by M. Molé, in *REI* during 1959–63; Shushtarī, *Majālis al-mu'minīn* II, 143–8.

[2] *Ibid.*, pp. 150–6.

inwardly transforming Persia from a predominantly Sunnī to a predominantly Shī'ī land. Therefore, sufism is the most important spiritual force to be reckoned with in studying the background of the Safavid period.

As for the intellectual background of the Safavid era, there also the theoretical and doctrinal aspect of sufism, known as gnosis (*'irfān*), plays a fundamental rôle along with schools of philosophy and theology. The very rich intellectual life of the 10th/16th and 11th/17th centuries did not come into being from a vacuum. There was a long period of preparation from the time of Suhravardī and Ibn 'Arabī to the advent of the Safavid renaissance, a period which, although spanning nearly four centuries, remains the most obscure in the intellectual history of Persia. Yet without a knowledge of this period an understanding of Safavid intellectual life is impossible.

There are four major intellectual perspectives and schools of thought, all clearly defined in traditional Islamic learning, which gradually approach each other during the period leading to the Safavid revival: Peripatetic (*mashshā'ī*) philosophy, illuminationist (*ishrāqī*) theosophy, gnosis (*'irfān*) and theology (*kalām*). It is due to the gradual intermingling and synthesis of these schools that during the Safavid period the major intellectual figures are not only philosophers but also theologians or gnostics. The very appearance of the vast syntheses such as those of Ṣadr al-Dīn Shīrāzī attest to the long period preceding the Safavid renaissance which made these all-comprehending metaphysical expositions possible.

The usual story of Islamic philosophy, according to which it was attacked by Ghazālī and after an Indian summer in Andalusia disappeared from Muslim lands, is disproven by the presence of the Safavid philosophers and metaphysicians themselves. The fact that they were able to expound philosophical and metaphysical doctrines and ideas matching in rigour and depth anything written before or after in traditional philosophy is itself proof of the continuity of Islamic philosophy after the attacks of Ghazālī and Fakhr al-Dīn Rāzī.[1] Actually, in the 7th/13th century the mathematician and theologian, Naṣīr al-Dīn Ṭūsī, who was also one of the foremost of Islamic philosophers, revived the Peripatetic philosophy of Ibn Sīnā, which had been attacked by both of the above-mentioned theologians, through his philosophical master-

[1] Nasr, "Fakhr al-Dīn al-Rāzī".

piece the *Sharḥ al-ishārāt*, which is a reply to Rāzī's criticism of Ibn Sīnā's last philosophical testament, the *Ishārāt wa'l-tanbīhāt*. Henceforth, Persia continued to produce philosophers who followed upon Ṭūsī's footsteps. His own students, Quṭb al-Dīn Shīrāzī, author of the monumental philosophical opus *Durrat al-tāj* in Persian, and Dabīrān Kātibī, author of the *Ḥikmat al-'ain*, continued the tradition immediately after him. In the 8th/14th and 9th/15th centuries Quṭb al-Dīn Rāzī and a whole group of philosophers who hailed from Shīrāz and the surrounding regions also wrote important philosophical works. Among them Ṣadr al-Dīn Dashtakī and his son Ghiyāṣ al-Dīn Manṣūr Dashtakī are particularly noteworthy. The latter, the author of *Akhlāq-i Manṣūrī* in ethics, a commentary upon the *Hayākil al-nūr* of Suhravardī and glosses upon Ṭūsī's commentary upon the *Ishārāt*, lived into the Safavid period and was very influential upon the major Safavid figures such as Ṣadr al-Dīn Shīrāzī, for whom he has been mistaken by many traditional scholars as well as by some modern historians. Many of the cardinal themes of Safavid philosophy and metaphysics may be found in the writings of Ghiyāṣ al-Dīn Manṣūr and other figures of the period, not one of whom has by any means been studied sufficiently.

Even these philosophers, who were mostly Peripatetic, were influenced by the ishrāqī theosophy of Suhravardī, especially in such questions as God's knowledge of things. After the founding of this new intellectual perspective by Suhravardī in the 6th/12th century, its teachings spread particularly in Persia and became more and more integrated with Avicennan philosophy as seen in the case of Ghiyāṣ al-Dīn Manṣūr and similar figures from the 7th/13th to the 10th/16th century. And this ishrāqī interpretation of Avicennan philosophy is one of the characteristics of the intellectual life of the Safavid period, as seen to an eminent degree in the case of the founder of the school of Iṣfahān, Mīr Dāmād.

There is also the basic question of gnosis to consider. The teachings of the founder of the doctrinal formulation of gnosis in Islam, Muḥyī al-Dīn Ibn 'Arabī, spread throughout Persia rapidly, especially through the works and direct instruction of his pupil, Ṣadr al-Dīn Qunyavī. Henceforth nearly all the masters of sufism in Persia, such as 'Abd al-Razzāq Kāshānī, Ibn 'Arabī's eminent commentator, Sa'd al-Dīn Ḥamūya, 'Azīz al-Dīn Nasafī and such famous poets as Fakhr al-Dīn 'Araqī, Auḥad al-Dīn Kirmānī and 'Abd al-Raḥmān Jāmī, were deeply influenced by the gnostic teachings of Ibn 'Arabī. Jāmī in fact wrote several commentaries upon Ibn 'Arabī's works as well as composing on the themes of gnosis independent treatises such as the *Lavā'iḥ* and *Ashiʿʿat al-lamaʿāt*.

Certain philosophers and theosophers began to incorporate this form of teaching into their schools. Ibn Turka of Iṣfahān, the 8th/14th century author of *Tamhīd al-qawā'id*, was perhaps the first person who sought to combine *falsafa* and *'irfān*, philosophy and gnosis. In the following centuries this tendency was accelerated in the hands of a few Shīʿī gnostics and sages such as Sayyid Ḥaidar Āmulī, author of *Jāmiʿ al-asrār*, which is so deeply influential in Safavid writings, Ibn Abī Jumhūr, the author of *Kitāb al-mujlī*, which is again a doctrinal work of Shīʿī gnosis, and Rajab Bursī, known especially for his *Mashāriq al-anwār*. The importance of the work of these figures for the Safavid period can hardly be over-emphasised, because it is they who integrated the sapiental doctrines of Ibn 'Arabī into Shiʿism and prepared the ground within Shīʿī intellectual life for those Safavid figures who achieved the synthesis between philosophy, theology and gnosis within the cadre of Twelver Shiʿism.

As for theology or Kalām, in its Shīʿī form it reached its peak in a certain sense with the *Tajrīd* of Naṣīr al-Dīn Ṭūsī. During the centuries preceding the Safavid period a very large number of commentaries and glosses were written upon it by Shīʿī theologians while the Sunnī theologians of Persia such as Taftazānī and Davānī – at least in his early period – continued to develop the Ashʿarī Kalām, which had reached its peak with Fakhr al-Dīn Rāzī. In fact, this outspoken theological opponent of the philosophers was also influential in many ways among Shīʿī theologians and thinkers.

In this domain also gradually philosophy and theology began to approach each other. It is difficult to assert whether a particular work of Sayyid Sharīf Jurjānī or Jalāl al-Dīn Davānī is more Kalām or Falsafa. Moreover, certain glosses and commentaries upon the *Tajrīd* such as those of Fakhrī and especially of Sammākī, who influenced Mīr Dāmād, contain many of the themes that belong properly speaking to Ḥikmat and Falsafa and were adopted by the Safavid philosophers. The long series of commentaries upon the *Tajrīd*, which has not been studied at all fully, is the source of many of the important elements of Safavid philosophy.

From this vast intellectual background there gradually emerged the tendency towards a synthesis of the different schools of Islamic thought within the background and matrix of Shiʿism, which because of its inner structure was more conducive to the growth of the traditional philosophy and theosophy which reached its full development in the 10th/16th and 11th/17th centuries. The advent of the Safavids, which resulted in Persia's becoming predominantly Shī'ī, along with temporal conditions such as peace and stability and the encouragement of the religious sciences, which in Shi'ism always include the intellectual sciences (*al-'ulūm al-'aqliyya*), aided in bringing nearly four centuries of intellectual development to fruition. And so with such figures as Mīr Dāmād and Ṣadr al-Dīn Shīrāzī, usually known as Mullā Ṣadrā, an intellectual edifice which has its basis in the teachings of Ibn Sīnā, Suhravardī and Ibn 'Arabī and also upon the specific tenets of Shi'ism as found in the Qur'ān and the traditions of the Prophet and Imāms reached its completion. A synthesis is created which reflects a millennium of Islamic intellectual life.

THE REVIVAL OF RELIGIOUS LEARNING IN THE SAFAVID PERIOD

For both religious and political reasons the Safavids sought from the very beginning of Shah Ismā'īl's reign to foster the study of Shi'ism and to encourage the migration of Shī'ī scholars from other lands to Persia. Of scholars of non-Persian origin most were Arabs either of the Jabal 'Āmila region in today's Lebanon and Syria or of the Baḥrain, which included in the terminology of that day not only the island of Baḥrain but the whole coastal region around it. There were so many Shī'ī scholars from these two regions, which had been strongholds of Shī'ī learning, that the two biographical works, *Lu'lu' al-Baḥrain* by Yūsuf b. Aḥmad al-Baḥrānī and *Amal al-'āmil fī 'ulamā Jabal 'Āmil* by Muḥammad b. Ḥasan al-Ḥurr al-'Āmilī, are devoted to the account of the scholars of Baḥrain and Jabal 'Āmila. Such men as Shaikh 'Alī b. 'Abd al-'Ālī Karkī, Shaikh Bahā' al-Dīn 'Āmilī, his father Shaikh Ḥusain, a disciple of Shahīd-i s̱ānī, and Ni'mat-Allāh Jazā'irī, all of Arab extraction, were some of the most famous of a large number of Shī'ī scholars and theologians who were responsible for the major renaissance of Shī'ī religious learning during the Safavid period.

It has often been said, even by such authorities as Browne and Qazvīnī, that the very emphasis upon religious and theological learning during the Safavid period stifled science and literature and even sufism. This is only a half-truth which overlooks previous conditions and what was actually happening in these fields. The emphasis upon the study of the *Sharī'a* and theology, while helping to unify Shī'ī Persia, did not stifle activity in other domains until the second half of the 11th/17th century, when a reaction against sufism set in. As far as literature is concerned, it is true that this period did not produce another Ḥāfiẓ or Sa'dī, but such poets as Ṣā'ib Tabrīzī, Kalīm Kāshānī and Shaikh-i Bahā'ī (Bahā' al-Dīn 'Āmilī) cannot be brushed aside as insignificant. Moreover, there are two types of poetry which reach a new mode of perfection at this time: the poetry dealing with the life, sufferings and virtues of the Shī'ī Imāms, which is particularly associated with the name of Muḥtasham Kāshānī, and poems in which the doctrinal teachings of sufism or gnosis, as well as theosophy, are set to Persian verse. In this latter case the Safavid period witnesses the interesting fact that most of its great philosophers and gnostics were also poets, some of commendable quality.

As for science, a decline had already set in in Islamic science with the Saljūqs, after which the mathematical sciences were revived by Naṣīr al-Dīn Ṭūsī and his school at Marāgha. The early Safavid period continued this tradition of mathematics and astronomy, whose centre of study in the 10th/16th century was Herat. Only in the following century did the study of mathematics begin to decline in the *madrasas*. As for medicine and pharmacology, this period, far from being one of decline, produced outstanding figures like Bahā' al-Daula to the extent that some have called it the golden age of pharmacology.[1]

The case of sufism is somewhat different and more complex. During the early Safavid period sufism flourished spiritually and even politically, until, due to the danger of a Qizilbāsh uprising and a certain mundaneness which had penetrated into some ṣūfī orders possessing worldly powers, a religious and theological reaction set in against sufism as seen in the figure of the second Majlisī. But many of the earlier religious scholars and theologians like the first Majlisī and Shaikh-i Bahā'ī were either ṣūfīs or sympathetic toward sufism. Moreover, it was because and not in spite of the spread of Shī'ī religious learning that the type of metaphysical and theosophical doctrine associated with Mīr Dāmād and Mullā Ṣadrā became current. Such forms of thought would have been inconceivable without the Shī'ī climate established by the Safavids. Even if the Shī'ī 'ulamā opposed the

[1] Elgood, Chapter 13.

mutaṣawwifa in late Safavid times, 'irfān or gnosis continued to be taught and studied within the traditional Shī'ī madrasa system itself, in which milieu it survives to this day in Persia. Those who know most in Persia even today about Islamic philosophy and even the "theology of Aristotle", or in other words Plotinus, wear the turban and belong to the class of religious scholars; they are not "free thinkers" who are *ḥakīms* in spite of being Shī'ī divines. The establishment of centres of religious learning by the Safavids and the emphasis placed upon Sharī'ī and theological learning undoubtedly diverted much of the energy of the intelligentsia to these fields and indirectly diminished activity in other fields. Not only did it not destroy the intellectual sciences, however, but it was an essential factor in making possible the appearance of the vast metaphysical syntheses for which the Safavid period is known.

SUFISM IN THE SAFAVID PERIOD

The major ṣūfī orders of the 9th/15th century such as the Nūrbakhshī, Ni'matallāhī and Qādirī, not to speak of the Ṣafaviyya themselves, continued into the Safavid period and flourished into the 11th/17th century. Naturally most of these orders acquired a purely Shī'ī colour and centred most of all around the Eighth Shī'ī Imām, 'Alī al-Riḍā, who is the "Imām of initiation" in Shi'ism and to whom most ṣūfī orders in the Shī'ī and Sunnī world are attached through Ma'rūf al-Karkhī. Many eminent ṣūfī masters of the 10th/16th century in fact lived at or near Mashhad, as we see in the case of Muḥammad al-Junūshānī, 'Imād al-Dīn Fażl-Allāh Mashhadī and Kamāl al-Dīn Khwārazmī, all spiritual descendants of 'Alī Hamadānī. All these masters expressed a special devotion to Imām Riḍā.[1] Likewise the masters of the Ni'matallāhī order, such as some of the actual descendants of Shāh Ni'mat-Allāh from whom most of the present-day orders in Persia derive, were thoroughly Shī'ī, although here the order was attached most of all to 'Alī himself.

A ṣūfī order which to this day considers itself as the purest Shī'ī ṣūfī order, the Ẓahabī, was also active during the early Safavid period. The Ẓahabīs, like most other Shī'ī ṣūfī orders, believe that even before the advent of the Safavids the basic chains (*silsila*) of ṣūfīs were Shī'ī but hid their Shi'ism through the process of concealment (*taqiyya*). The Ẓahabīs

[1] Shushtarī, *Majālis al-mu'minīn* II, 156ff.

claim that only with the advent of the Safavids did the necessity for taqiyya subside so that the orders were able to declare themselves openly Shīʿī in Persia. Among all the orders the Ẕahabīs consider themselves as being the most intensely Shīʿī; and being especially devoted to Imām Riḍā they add the title *raẕaviyya* to the name of their silsila.

An outstanding example of a ṣūfī work belonging to the Safavid period and typical of a Shīʿī ṣūfī order in its new setting is the *Tuḥfat al-ʿabbāsiyya* of the Ẕahabī master, Muḥammad ʿAlī Sabzavārī, a contemporary of Shah ʿAbbās II and, interestingly enough, the *mu'adhdhin* (he who calls the prayers) of the mausoleum of Imām Riḍā at Mashhad. The work consists of an introduction, five chapters, twelve sections and a conclusion. The titles of the chapters and sections are as follows:

Chapter I – On the meaning of *taṣavvuf* and *ṣūfī*, why there are few ṣūfīs, why they are called so and the signs and characteristics pertaining to them.

Chapter II – On the beliefs of ṣūfīs in unity (*tauḥīd*).

Chapter III – On the beliefs of ṣūfīs in prophecy (*nubuvvat*) and imamate (*imāmat*).

Chapter IV – On the beliefs of ṣūfīs concerning eschatology (*maʿād*).

Chapter V – On the dependence of the ṣūfīs upon the Shīʿī Imāms.

Section I – On the virtue of knowledge.

Section II – On continence and asceticism.

Section III – On silence.

Section IV – On hunger and wakefulness.

Section V – On self-seclusion.

Section VI – On invocation.

Section VII – On reliance upon God.

Section VIII – On contentment and surrender.

Section IX – On worshipping for forty days.

Section X – On hearing pleasing music and on that all pleasant music is not the singing that is scorned in the Sharīʿa.

Section XI – On ecstasy and swoon.

Section XII – On the necessity of having a spiritual master, and the regulations pertaining to the master and the disciple.

Conclusion – On the sayings of the ṣūfīs concerning different subjects.

An examination of the contents of this work reveals that it deals very much with the same subjects as one finds in the classical treatises of sufism such as the *Kitāb al-lumaʿ*, *Risāla qushairiyya* and *Iḥyāʾ ʿulūm al-dīn*. The only difference that can be discerned is in its relating the chain of sufism to the Shī'ī Imāms and in its relying not only upon the Qur'ān but also upon Prophetic *Ḥadīth* and traditions of the Imāms drawn from Shī'ī sources, whereas ṣūfī works within the Sunnī world are based upon the Qur'ān and Prophetic Ḥadīth mostly of the *ṣiḥāḥ* literature. As for the rôle of the Imāms, this is a major point that distinguishes sufism in its Shī'ī and Sunnī settings. In the chain of nearly all the orders that are widely spread in the Sunnī world such as the Shāẕiliyya and Qādiriyya the Shī'ī Imāms up to Imām Riḍā appear as saints and spiritual poles (*quṭb*), but not as Imāms as this term is understood specifically in Shi'ism. In Shī'ī ṣūfī orders the presence of the same figures is seen as proof of the reliance of sufism upon the Imāms, as the fifth chapter of the *Tuḥfat al-'abbāsiyya* demonstrates in a typical manner.

Besides the type of Sufism represented by the Ẕahabī and other regular orders during the Safavid period, there are two other kinds of Islamic esotericism to consider: the first is the case of those like Mīr Abu'l-Qāsim Findiriskī and Bahā' al-Dīn 'Āmilī who were definitely ṣūfīs and are recognised as such by the ṣūfī orders, but whose initiatic chain and spiritual master are not known; the second is the case of gnostics like Ṣadr al-Dīn Shīrāzī who definitely possessed esoteric knowledge usually in the form of Ḥikmat – which also implies means of attaining this knowledge – but who did not belong, at least outwardly, to any ṣūfī orders, so that the means whereby they acquired this gnostic knowledge remains problematic. Mullā Ṣadrā, while being a thorough gnostic like Ibn 'Arabī, wrote his *Kasr al-aṣnām al-jāhiliyya* against those in his times who pretended to belong to sufism and whom he calls *mutaṣavvif*, using this term in the particular context of his time and not as it has been employed throughout the history of sufism.

In fact, what we observe during the Safavid period is that as the ṣūfī orders become more popular and acquire in certain cases a worldly character, a reaction sets in against them from the quarter of the religious scholars. Henceforth within the class of the 'ulamā it is no longer socially acceptable to belong openly to one of the well known ṣūfī orders so that esoteric instruction is imparted without any outwardly declared ṣūfī organisation. Moreover, the term 'irfān, or gnosis,[1] is employed with respect in place of taṣavvuf, which from the

[1] By gnosis we mean, of course, that knowledge which is related to being and results from the union between the subject and the object, and not the Christian heresy of the 3rd century.

11th/17th to the 12th/18th centuries falls into disrepute in the circles of exoteric authorities of the religion. That is why, while Bahā' al-Dīn 'Āmilī practised sufism openly, Qāżī Sa'īd Qumī, whom a contemporary authority has called the Ibn 'Arabī of Shi'ism, refers constantly to 'irfān, but never claims to be a ṣūfī in the usual sense that is found within the *ṭuruq*, although without doubt he was a ṣūfī. To this whole situation must be added the initiatic rôle of the Twelfth Imām for the *élite* of Shi'ism in general, and the fact that the whole structure of Shi'ism possesses a more esoteric character than we find in the exoteric side of Sunnism. This fact made it possible for esoteric ideas to appear even in certain exoteric aspects of Shi'ism.

As a result, the Safavid period presents us with not only the regular ṣūfī masters of the well known orders, but also with gnostics and ṣūfīs of the highest spiritual rank whose initiatic affiliation is difficult to discern. Moreover, the gnostic dimension of Islam penetrates at this time into philosophy and theosophy or Ḥikmat, and most of the important figures of this era are thinkers with the highest powers of ratiocination and with respect for logic while at the same time seers with spiritual visions and illuminations. It is hardly possible to separate philosophy, theosophy and gnosis completely in this period.

OUTSTANDING INTELLECTUAL AND SPIRITUAL FIGURES OF THE SAFAVID PERIOD

Shaikh Bahā' al-Dīn 'Āmilī

From the point of view of versatility, Bahā' al-Dīn 'Āmilī, known to the Persians as Shaikh-i Bahā'ī (the name is quite unconnected with the heterodox Bahā'ī sect which finally broke away from Islam), is the most remarkable figure of the Safavid renaissance. Born in Ba'labakk in present-day Lebanon in 953/1546, the son of the leader of the Shī'ī community of that region, Shaikh Bahā' al-Dīn was brought to Persia by his father at the age of thirteen and soon mastered the Persian language to such an extent that he is usually considered the best Persian poet of the 10th/16th century. He studied in Qazvīn, then a centre of Shī'ī learning, and in Herat, where he mastered mathematics. His most famous teachers were his own father, 'Izz al-Dīn Ḥusain b. 'Abd al-Ṣamad, and Maulānā 'Abd-Allāh Yazdī, the author of the celebrated glosses upon the *Tahdhīb* in logic, which is studied to this day in

Persian madrasas under the title of *Ḥāshiyya-yi Mullā 'Abd-Allāh*. He also studied medicine with Ḥakīm 'Imād al-Dīn Maḥmūd. After a period of travelling in Persia and pilgrimages to Mecca, Shaikh-i Bahā'ī settled in Iṣfahān, where he gained the title of Shaikh al-Islām and where, during the reign of Shah 'Abbās, he became the most powerful Shī'ī figure in Persia. He died in 1030/1621 and is buried in Mashhad near the tomb of Imām Riḍā. His beautiful mausoleum is visited by thousands of pilgrims to this day.

The many-sided genius of Shaikh-i Bahā'ī is best illustrated by the diversity of his works, nearly all of which have become authoritative in their own domain. These works include: in the field of Qur'ān and Ḥadīth, *Arba'ūn ḥadīthan*, a collection of forty prophetic traditions with commentary, glosses upon the *Tafsīr* of Baiḍāwī, *Ḥall al-ḥurūf al-Qur'ān* on the opening letters of some of the chapters of the Qur'ān, *'Urwat al-wuthqā*, a commentary upon the Qur'ān, and *Wajīza*, also known as *Dirāyat al-ḥadīth*, on the science of Ḥadīth; in the field of jurisprudence (*fiqh*), theology, and specifically Shī'ī studies, *Ithnā'ashariyyāt* in five parts on the Muslim religious rites, *Jāmi'-i 'abbāsī*, the most famous Persian work on Shī'ī fiqh, *Ḥabl al-matīn* on the injunctions (*aḥkām*) of religion, *Ḥadā'iq al-ṣāliḥīn*, a commentary on the *Ṣaḥīfa sajjādiyya* of the Fourth Shī'ī Imām, *Miftāḥ al-falāḥ* on daily litanies and prayers, and a treatise on the necessity to perform the daily prayers (*ṣalāt*); in the sciences of language, *Asrār al-balāgha* on rhetoric, *Tahdhīb al-bayān* on Arabic grammar and *Fawā'id al-ṣamadiyya*, an advanced work on Arabic grammar still very much in use in Persia today; dozens of works on various branches of mathematics such as *Tashrīḥ al-aflāk* on astronomy, *Khulāṣat al-ḥisāb*, the most famous Muslim mathematical treatise of the last few centuries, and glosses on Chaghmīnī's astronomical treatise;[1] several treatises on the occult sciences now lost; and many works on sufism of which the most famous is the *Kashkūl* ("The begging bowl"), which as the title indicates contains, like the begging bowl of the dervishes into which bits of food were thrown, selections from masterpieces of ṣūfī literature. His poems also, such as the *masnavīs Ṭūṭī-nāma, Nān va ḥalvā* and *Shīr va shikar*, which are written in the style of Jalāl al-Dīn Rūmī's *Masnavī*, all deal with sufism. Altogether nearly ninety works are known to have been written by him concern-

[1] See H. Suter, *Die Mathematiker und Astronomen der Araber und ihre Werke* (Leipzig, 1900), p. 194.

ing nearly every domain of the Islamic sciences from mathematics to gnosis, from astronomy to theology.[1]

But the works of Shaikh-i Bahā'ī include, besides these writings, buildings and gardens which have helped leave such a vivid memory of this figure in the minds of the people of Iṣfahān and surrounding regions to this day. Shaikh-i Bahā'ī was an accomplished architect and helped in drawing the plans for the Shāh mosque in Iṣfahān, which is among the masterpieces of Islamic art. He built a bath house based on the oral and secret knowledge of masonry and architecture which he undoubtedly possessed, a bath which according to many witnesses had hot water with only a candle burning underneath its water tank. The bath was destroyed about forty years ago. He designed the plans for the beautiful Fīn Garden of Kāshān, which served as a model for the more famous Shalimar Garden of Lahore. In yet another field, he calculated the proportion of water of the Zāyandarūd to be distributed to each piece of land on the river's course to Iṣfahān, a work which is called the *Ṭūmār-i Shaikh-i Bahā'ī*. This involves a very complicated mathematical problem, which he solved so well that over three and a half centuries later his method is still used and only after the projected dam on the river is finished will his division of its waters be no longer applicable.

Shaikh-i Bahā'ī is the last eminent representative of the Muslim ḥakīm in the sense of being the master of all the traditional sciences. He was also one of the last eminent representatives of the class of 'ulamā who were outstanding mathematicians and who did not feel it below their dignity to take an astrolabe and make actual observations or measurements. After him, with only a few exceptions, the 'ulamā ceased to be interested in the mathematical sciences, with the result that the teaching of these sciences deteriorated rapidly in the madrasas.

Shaikh-i Bahā'ī was an authority in both the exoteric and esoteric aspects of Islam. He hardly hid his sufism and frequented ṣūfī gatherings openly. His *Ṭūṭī-nāma* contains some of the most eloquent and frank expositions of sufism in Persian verse. His sufism also possessed a popular aspect without itself being in any way devoid of intellectual content or the awareness that belongs only to the élite (*khavāṣṣ*) among the ṣūfīs. But in the sense that the highest is reflected in the lowest, his

[1] For his works, see Nafīsī, *Aḥvāl va ash'ār*, pp.92–110. The traditional biographies of the Safavid and later periods, such as *Amal al-āmul, Salāfat al-'aṣr, Lu'lu'at al-Baḥrain, Tārīkh-i 'ālam-ārā-yi 'Abbāsī, Rauẓāt al-jannāt, Mustadrak al-vasā'il* and *Raiḥānat al-adab*, all contain accounts of, or references to, his life and works.

sublime ṣūfī message was propagated within the popular strata of sufism and even in fact among the populace in general. To this day many storytellers (*naqqāls*) in the traditional tea houses chant his poetry, while his theological and juridical works are read by advanced religious students in the madrasas. Also his prowess and competence as a mathematician of the Pythagorean kind and fame as an alchemist have left their mark on the popular conception held of him. He is an eminent representative of the ṣūfī scientists of which Islamic history has produced many examples.

In traditional theosophy or Ḥikmat Shaikh-i Bahā'ī does not reach the level of Mīr Dāmād, his contemporary and close friend, or Mullā Ṣadrā, his student. But his contributions to Shī'ī law and theology, mathematics and sufism are sufficient to make him one of the leading lights of the Safavid period. He is one of the figures most responsible for the rapid spread of Shī'ī learning in 10th/16th century Persia and a person who, more than any other figure of his day, sought to display the harmony between the law and the way, the *Sharī'a* and the *Ṭarīqa*, which comprise the exoteric and esoteric dimensions of Islam.

Most of the well known scholars who came to Iṣfahān were students of Shaikh-i Bahā'ī: men such as Mullā Muḥammad Taqī Majlisī, Sayyid Aḥmad 'Alavī, Ṣadr al-Dīn Shīrāzī and Mullā Muḥsin Faiż Kāshānī. Over thirty of his students, many of whom also studied with Mīr Dāmād, became well known figures themselves, spreading in yet another way the influence of their teacher. Through all these channels, that is, his writings, monuments and students, Shaikh-i Bahā'ī was able to exercise widespread influence throughout nearly all classes of Persian society. There is no other figure of the Safavid period who became so well known to the élite and the common people alike, and who left such a deep mark as a national and almost mythological hero upon the people of Persia.

Mīr Dāmād

Mīr Muḥammad Bāqir Dāmād Ḥusainī, entitled Sayyid al-ḥukamā' and Sayyid al-falāsifa,[1] is the real founder and central figure of the theosophical and philosophical school which has now come to be known as

[1] These titles are mentioned in Maulavī Muḥammad Muẓaffar Ḥusain Ṣabā, *Tażkira-yi rūz-i raushan* (Tehran, 1343), p. 51, and Ḥājjī Āqā Mujtabā 'Irāqī, *Fihrist-i kitābkhāna-yi madrasa-yi faiżiyya-yi Qum* I (Qum, 1338), p. 391. Most historians, such as Tunakābunī, *Qiṣaṣ*, p. 333, agree that Mīr Dāmād was a descendant of the Prophet through Imām Ḥusain, whereas 'Alī Khān, *Salāfat al-'aṣr*, p. 485, considers him as Hasanid.

the School of Iṣfahān. As the person who established and classified the traditional sciences in the new Shīʿī setting of Safavid Persia, as Aristotle had done in Athens and Fārābī in the newly born Islamic civilisation as a whole, Mīr Dāmād has been honoured with the further title of the "Third Teacher" (*muʿallim-i s̱ālis̱*), following Aristotle and Fārābī, the First and the Second Teachers.[1] As for his title *Dāmād* ("son-in-law"), it refers to the fact that his father was the son-in-law of Shaikh ʿAlī ʿAbd al-ʿĀlī Karkī, the celebrated Shīʿī scholar of the early Safavid period.[2] Mīr Dāmād also composed fine poetry under the pen name Ishrāq, by which he is known in the annals of literary history. But this appellation also has a philosophical significance in that it demonstrates openly his attachment to ishrāqī theosophy.

The date of Mīr Dāmād's birth has not been determined with certainty: that given in the glosses upon the *Nukhbat al-ʿiqāl* of Sayyid Jamāl al-Dīn Ḥusain Burūjirdī is 969/1561–2, and appears as fairly likely considering the date of his death and the approximate span of his life, which are known. His education was carried out mostly in Mashhad, and possibly Arāk, and his best known teachers were Shaikh ʿIzz al-Dīn Ḥusain b. ʿAbd al-Ṣamad, the father of Shaikh-i Bahāʾī, and Mīr Fakhr al-Dīn Sammākī, who taught him the intellectual sciences (*al-ʿulūm al-ʿaqliyya*).[3] Mīr Dāmād travelled several times within Persia to Qazvīn, Kāshān and Mashhad and accompanied Shah Ṣafī to Iraq, where he died in 1040/1630–1; he was buried in Najaf near the mausoleum of ʿAlī, and his tomb is venerated to this day.

It was possible for Mīr Dāmād to revive the intellectual sciences and especially Ḥikmat because of his special gift in these sciences, added to the remarkable respect and authority in which he was held among the jurisprudents and theologians as well as with the king. He lived an extremely pious life and is said to have read half of the Qur'ān every night. Many of his poems are dedications to the Prophet and ʿAlī, such as the following quatrain in praise of the Prophet of Islam:

> O Seal of Prophecy! The two worlds belong to thee.
> The heavens, one is thy pulpit and nine thy pedestal.
> There would be no wonder if thou didst not cast a shadow,
> For thou art light and the sun is itself thy shadow.

[1] The title appears specifically in many works, e.g. ʿAlī Qulī Khān Dāghistānī, *Riyāẓ al-shuʿarā*, MS in the Majlis Library, Tehran.

[2] Iskandar Munshī, trans. Savory, p. 234.

[3] An account of his life and teachings is found in nearly all the standard biographies and histories such as *Luʾluʾat al-Baḥrain, Mustadrak al-vasāʾil* and *Rauẓāt al-jannāt*, as well as in more contemporary sources such as *Aʿyān al-shīʿa* and *Raiḥānat al-adab*.

In his Persian work, the *Jazavāt*, he begins with a poem dedicated to 'Alī in which he sings:

> O herald of the nation and soul of the Prophet,
> The ring of thy knowledge surrounds the ears of the intelligences.
> O thou in whom the book of existence terminates,
> To whom the account of creation refers,
> The glorified treasure of the revelation,
> Thou art the holy interpreter of its secrets.

The intensity of religious fervour in Mīr Dāmād was too great to permit his being criticised in any quarter for having revived Ḥikmat and the wisdom of Ibn Sīnā and Suhravardī. To this element must be added the abstruseness of his writings, which veiled their meaning from the eyes of the uninitiated and helped establish the banner of Ḥikmat firmly, without any opposition from the 'ulamā. No Muslim philosopher or sage has ever written works in such a difficult style and complicated phraseology, which makes access to his works well nigh impossible for all, save for those with a sound training in the tradition of Islamic philosophy and the aid of the oral instructions which accompany the texts. The difficulty of Mīr Dāmād's works is such that many stories have been told about him and it is even said that, during the first night in the grave, when the angels asked him concerning his beliefs he gave an answer that was so difficult that even they did not understand it and so went to God in search of help. The anecdote continues by mentioning the fact that even God did not comprehend Mīr Dāmād's sayings but allowed him nevertheless to enter Paradise because he was a virtuous man.

About fifty works of Mīr Dāmād are known, of which most are in Arabic and a few, including his collection of poems, are in Persian.[1] These include works on theology and jurisprudence, Qur'anic commentary and other religious sciences, and especially Ḥikmat, which is the subject of most of his writings. The most celebrated of these are *al-Ufuq al-mubīn*, *al-Ṣirāṭ al-mustaqīm*, *Qabasāt*, which is possibly his most important opus, *Taqwīm al-īmān* and *Taqdīsāt*, all in Arabic, and *Jazavāt* and *Sidrat al-muntahā* in Persian. The lattermost work may have been completed or even written by his student Sayyid Aḥmad 'Alavī, although in the *Jazavāt* Mīr Dāmād mentions it as one of his own

[1] I. al-Ṣīṣī, in a recent Ph.D. thesis at the Faculty of Letters of Tehran University (1967), which involved the preparation of a critical edition of the *Jazavāt*, mentions 52 works by Mīr Dāmād.

writings. He also wrote commentaries upon the works of Ibn Sīnā and Naṣīr al-Dīn Ṭūsī, and the collection of Persian and Arabic poems, *Mashāriq al-anvār*.

Mīr Dāmād revived Avicennan philosophy in ishrāqī dress. He may be considered as an ishrāqī interpreter of Avicennan metaphysics in the spiritual universe of Shi'ism. But his interpretation is very far from the rationalistic Avicennanism with which the occident is acquainted through the interpretation of medieval latin scholastics.[1] In fact, in a conscious manner Mīr Dāmād distinguishes between Yamanī and Yūnānī (Greek) philosophy, the first of which he associates with wisdom derived from revelation and illumination and the second with rationalistic knowledge. The "Yamanī" here refers to the symbolism of the right side (*yamīn*) of the valley when Moses heard the revelation of God. The right side or the east is therefore symbolically the source of illumination and revelation, of light and spirituality, and the left side or the occident, in accordance with the well known symbolism of ishrāqī theosophy, the source of darkness or of purely discursive and rationalistic knowledge.[2] The school of Ḥikmat thus established by Mīr Dāmād, very far from being a continuation of Muslim Peripatetic philosophy as it came to be known in the West, was a school in which illumination was combined with ratiocination and where the Avicennan metaphysics was transformed from an abstract system of thought to a concrete spiritual reality which became the object of spiritual vision and realisation.

Nowhere is this better seen than in two works of Mīr Dāmād which record two different spiritual visions he had, the first in Ramaḍān 1011/1603 and the second twelve years later in the middle of Sha'bān 1023/1614. The first, which occurred in a mosque in the city of Qum after the afternoon prayers, involved a theophanic vision of the Prophet and his five Companions, Abū Dharr, Salmān, Miqdād, Ḥuḍaifa and 'Ammār – who are so important for Shi'ism – the Twelve Imāms and the host of angels. These figures of light appeared to Mīr Dāmād with such intensity that he wrote that he would have a nostalgia for the vision of this spiritual universe until the Day of Judgment.

[1] On the difference, see Corbin, *Avicenna and the Visionary Recital*, tr. W. Trask (New York, 1960), pp. 101ff.; Nasr, *Three Muslim Sages*, pp. 46ff., and *An Introduction*, pp. 185ff.

[2] See Nasr, *Three Muslim Sages*, chapter 2, and "Suhrawardī", pp. 381ff., as well as Corbin's many studies on this theme. On the symbolism of the Yemen, see Corbin, "Le récit d'initiation et l'hermétisme en Iran", *Eranos Jahrbuch* XVII (1949), 136–7.

The second vision, which took place twelve years later at Iṣfahān, came directly from the practice of invocation (*dhikr*) in a spiritual retreat (*khalwa*). As Mīr Dāmād himself accounts in his *Risālat al-khalʿiyya al-qudsiyya al-malakūtiyya*, the vision came when he was invoking the two Divine Names, *al-Ghanī* and *al-Mughnī*. Suddenly he was taken on the wings of the spirit to the spiritual world where he was given a vision of the celestial hierarchies and the various superior states of being. In a most dramatic fashion the vision involved an actualisation of the Avicennan metaphysics and cosmology from what appears as an abstract scheme in Peripatetic philosophy to a concrete reality – in accordance with all true metaphysics, which deals not with theory in the modern sense but with *theoria*, or intellectual and spiritual vision in its original Greek sense. Moreover, the vision took place on the eve of the birthday of the Twelfth Imām, on a night which according to Shīʿī sources is the second most sacred night in the Islamic calendar after *lailat al-qadr* or the night of power. It is a night when spiritual influences descend upon man and when this very descent or deployment of grace (*faiḍ*) makes possible the spiritual ascent described by Mīr Dāmād.[1]

The two experiences described by Mīr Dāmād himself are the only witnesses we possess to the spiritual side of his life, a life which was otherwise immersed in religious and philosophical activity. But the very fact that he was able to experience such visions proves the constant presence of a spiritual life and a practice which is the same as sufism in its most universal manifestation. There is nothing closer to ṣūfī spiritual practices than the dhikr and the khalwa. This may appear strange in a sage who was especially known for his powers of ratiocination and logic and who was such an authority in the exoteric sciences. But one of the characteristics of later Persian theosophy is precisely the fact that philosophy and rational thought are tied to spiritual practices and illumination, and metaphysics becomes not the result of rational thought alone but the fruit of vision of the superior world.

An element that characterises the works of Mīr Dāmād is his concern with time and the relation between change and permanence, or the eternal and the created (*qidam* and *ḥudūth*). This problem has occupied Muslim theologians and philosophers from the beginning and many

[1] For the Arabic text and French translation, see Corbin, "Confessions extatiques", pp. 367ff.

solutions have been presented for it, although it cannot be solved through rational thought but only through the *coincidentia oppositorum* made possible through metaphysics and gnosis. Mīr Dāmād is known as the author of a novel view on this subject called *ḥudūs̱-i dahrī*. He distinguishes three realms of being which are as follows: *Sarmad*, or eternity, refers to that reality which does not change, or more exactly to the relation between the changing and the changeless. This concerns the Divine Essence and the Divine Names and Qualities, which are the self-determination of the Essence and themselves immutable. Below this world, which alone is absolutely eternal, stands *dahr* or the world which relates the immutable to the changing. The world is created not directly by the Essence but through the immutable archetypes or "lords of the species" (*arbāb al-anvāʿ*) and dahr represents precisely this relationship between these immutable archetypes and the changing world. Below dahr stands time (*zamān*), which represents the relation between changing things. The world was not created in time in the sense that there was first a time and then an event called creation which took place in it. This would be *ḥudūs̱-i zamānī* which Mīr Dāmād rejects. Rather, according to him this world was brought into being through the archetypes and with respect to dahr which stands above zamān. Creation is therefore *ḥudūs̱-i dahrī*; it is *ibdāʿ* and *ikhtirāʿ*, not *takwīn*.

This theme is amply treated by Mīr Dāmād in all its ramifications and he comes back to it again and again in his books. His works in fact are not divided into the classical four sections of metaphysics (*ilāhiyyāt*), natural philosophy (*ṭabīʿiyyāt*), mathematics (*riyāẕiyyāt*), and logic (*manṭiq*) that we find in the well known works of Islamic philosophy such as the *Shifāʾ* and *Najāt* of Ibn Sīnā or the Persian *Durrat al-tāj* of Qutb al-Dīn Shīrāzī. Rather, they treat different themes of metaphysics and philosophy whose axis remains the problem of the relation between time and eternity. Altogether these works show a Suhravardian interpretation of Avicennan philosophy in the matrix of Shiʿism, in which the most rigorous Peripatetic logic is combined with a Pythagorean interest in number and harmony and an ishrāqī attraction to the illuminative aspect of the angelic world. These are elements that were instrumental in establishing the School of Iṣfahan, which Mīr Dāmād more than any other figure helped to bring into being and which found its culmination in his disciples and students.

Of the intellectual progeny of Mīr Dāmād the most important is

Mullā Ṣadrā, whom Mīr Dāmād held in the greatest esteem and to whom we shall turn shortly. But there are a host of others such as Sayyid Aḥmad 'Alavī who became Mīr Dāmād's son-in-law and is known for his commentary upon the *Shifā'* of Ibn Sīnā and works which elucidate the thought of his master. One must also mention Mullā Khalīl Qazvīnī, a most respected scholar of his day, who has left one of the best known commentaries upon the *Uṣūl al-kāfī* of Kulainī, Zalālī Khunsārī, one of the well known poets of the Safavid period, Quṭb al-Dīn Ashkivarī, the author of the monumental history of philosophy in Persian called the *Maḥbūb al-qulūb*, which remains unedited to this day, and lesser known figures such as Aḥmad b. Zain al-'Ābidīn 'Alavī 'Āmilī Jīlī and Mīrzā Muḥammad Qāsim b. Muḥammad 'Abbās Jīlānī. One must mention also particularly Mullā Shamsā Gīlānī (d. 1098/1686–7), who continued the school of Mīr Dāmād, writing a treatise on the problem of the creation of the world, about which he also corresponded with Mullā Ṣadrā, and commenting upon the *Qabasāt* of Mīr Dāmād. The combination of Avicennan and ishrāqī elements seen in Mīr Dāmād is very much present in his works and he is among the most faithful propagators of his master's teachings.[1]

Mīr Abu'l-Qāsim Findiriskī

A contemporary and close friend of both Mīr Dāmād and Shaikh-i Bahā'ī, Mīr Findiriskī is much less known and less studied and remains to this day the most mysterious intellectual figure of the Safavid period. In his lifetime he was considered, along with Mīr Dāmād and Shaikh-i Bahā'ī, as one of the great masters of Iṣfahān and was highly revered in religious circles as well as at court. He lived a life of simplicity and asceticism and was a practising ṣūfī whose personal life can be compared in every way with those of the well known classical masters of sufism.[2] He travelled to India frequently and was highly revered by Hindu Yogis and Muslim sages alike. He is said to have journeyed often, but he also lived in Iṣfahān for a considerable portion of his life and taught philosophy, mathematics and medicine in that city. Because of his ṣūfī practices and esoteric knowledge Mīr Findiriskī came to be credited with miracles such as being in two places

[1] See Shīrāzī, *al-Shawāhid*, p. 93 of the editor's introduction.
[2] Tabrīzī, *Raiḥānat al-adab* III, 231–2; Hidāyat, *Riyāẓ al-'ārifīn*, p. 276.

at once and travelling great distances instantaneously. The very attribution of these accounts to him is of the greatest interest in understanding his personality. Even after his death his reputation would not leave him alone, for when he died in 1050/1640–1 in Iṣfahān he was buried in the famous Takht-i Fūlād cemetery, not in a regular grave, but in one which is surrounded within the earth by a metal case. Since he was celebrated as an alchemist, people were afraid that his grave would be dug up by those who sought the philosopher's stone and who would violate the sanctity of his grave in quest of physical gold.

Mīr Findiriskī wrote little. His extant works include the monumental commentary in Persian upon the *Yoga Vasiṣṭha* which had been rendered into Persian by Niẓām al-Dīn Pānīpatī and which is one of the major works in Persian on Hinduism, a treatise on motion (*Risālat al-ḥaraka*), another on sociology from the traditional metaphysical point of view (*Risāla ṣanā'iyya*) and the *Uṣūl al-fuṣūl* on Hindu wisdom. Recently his treatise on alchemy, in Persian, has also been discovered in a manuscript acquired by the Library of the Faculty of Letters of Tehran University.[1] But his most famous work is a *qaṣīda* which summarises the principles of Ḥikmat in verses of great beauty, showing Mīr Findiriskī to be an accomplished poet like Mīr Dāmād and Shaikh-i Bahā'ī. The poem begins with the verses:

> Heaven with these stars is clear, pleasing and beautiful;
> Whatever is there above has below it a form.
> The form below, if by the ladder of gnosis
> Is trodden upward, becomes the same as its principle,[2]

and continues to discuss the most essential aspects of Ḥikmat. It has been for this reason commented upon by several later ḥakīms such as Muḥammad Ṣāliḥ Khalkhālī and Ḥakīm 'Abbās Dārābī. It is also highly regarded by most of the contemporary masters of Ḥikmat in Persia.

Many later authorities believe that Mullā Ṣadrā studied with Mīr Findiriskī and learned the particular features of his doctrine such as trans-substantial motion and belief in the "imaginal world" from him. This is impossible to deny categorically, for there may have been an oral instruction imparted, but what remains of the written works of

[1] M.T. Dānishpazhūh, *Catalogue méthodique...des manuscrits de la bibliothèque privée de l'Imam Jum'ah de Kerman donné en legs à la Faculté des Lettres de Tehran* (Tehran, 1965), p. 11.
[2] Full translation in Nasr, "The School", pp. 923–4.

Mīr Findiriskī reveals that in philosophy he was a faithful follower of Ibn Sīnā and specifically denied trans-substantial motion (*al-ḥarakat al-jauhariyya*) and the archetypal world in his particularly philosophical works. Moreover, all of his students except Mullā Ṣadrā – if we do accept that Mullā Ṣadrā studied with Mīr Findiriskī – were more or less Avicennan.[1] Yet his qaṣīda affirms the reality of the archetypal world and reveals Mīr Findiriskī as a ṣūfī pure and simple. One must therefore say that Mīr Findiriskī, while a master of Peripatetic philosophy and the sciences such as medicine and mathematics, in all of which he taught the classical works such as the *Shifā'* and *Qānūn*, was a practising ṣūfī and gnostic who was also well versed in the occult sciences such as alchemy and, in addition, Hindu metaphysics. He is yet another of the remarkable intellectual figures of the Safavid period who were masters of several disciplines and expositors of different planes of knowledge.

Mīr Findiriskī trained many students, some of whom became well known figures. These include Mullā Rafī'a Gīlānī (d. 1082/1671–2), the commentator upon the *Uṣūl al-kāfī*, Mullā Muḥammad Bāqir Sabzavārī (d. 1098 or 1099/1686–7), author of several important works on jurisprudence such as the *Kifāya* and glosses upon the *Ishārāt wa' l-tanbīhāt* and *Shifā'* of Ibn Sīnā, and Āqā Ḥusain Khunsārī (d. 1080/1669–70), who was one of the greatest Shī'ī scholars of his day and wrote *Mashāriq al-nufūs* on jurisprudence and also glosses upon the *Shifā'* and *Ishārāt*. But besides Mullā Ṣadrā, Mīr Findiriskī's most famous student was Mullā Rajab 'Alī Tabrīzī (d. 1080/1669–70), who was the outstanding teacher of philosophy in the second half of the 11th/17th century. Mullā Rajab 'Alī, the author of many works including the *Kilīd-i bihisht* ("Key to Paradise") on eschatology, was opposed to Mullā Ṣadrā and did not accept his views concerning trans-substantial motion and the union of the knower and the known. Also, opposed to the great majority of Muslim philosophers, he had nominalistic tendencies and considered being (*wujūd*) to be shared only nominally by existing things without its corresponding to an objective reality. He taught the books of Ibn Sīnā and trained many well known students, including Qāżī Sa'īd Qumī and Muḥammad Rafī' Pīrzāda, who under the direction of his master composed *al-Ma'ārif al-ilāhiyya*, assembling therein the lessons given by Mullā Rajab 'Alī.[2]

[1] See Shīrāzī, *al-Shawāhid*, introduction, pp. 86–9.

[2] For all three men, see Lāhījānī, *Sharḥ risālat*, introductions by Jalāl Humā'ī and S.J. Āshtiyānī.

Ṣadr al-Dīn Shīrāzī (Mullā Ṣadrā)

The philosophical and theosophical movement of the Safavid period reaches its climax with Ṣadr al-Dīn Shīrāzī, known as Mullā Ṣadrā or Ṣadr al-muta'allihīn ("the foremost among the theosophers"), whom many Persians consider as the greatest Muslim thinker in the domain of metaphysics. His influence has been immense ever since his death and he has in fact dominated the intellectual scene in Persia during the past centuries. The present day interest in traditional Islamic philosophy in Persia also revolves around his name and many works have been devoted to him in the past few years.

Ṣadr al-Dīn Shīrāzī was born into an aristocratic family of Shīrāz in 979 or 980/1571 or 1572 and received the best education possible in his native city. Gifted from early childhood with a love for learning and being the only son of a wealthy and influential father, he was placed under the care of the best masters from an early age and was able to learn Arabic, the Qur'ān, Ḥadīth and other religious sciences early in life. This was made easier for him because of his intense devotion and religious fervour which he combined with keen intelligence from the age of childhood. At that time, although Shīrāz was a major city, the great centre of learning was Iṣfahān, to which the young Ṣadr al-Dīn decided to travel in order to benefit fully from the presence of the masters at the capital. In Iṣfahān he pursued his studies eagerly first with Shaikh Bahā' al-Dīn 'Āmilī in the religious or transmitted sciences (*al-'ulūm al-naqliyya*) and then with Mīr Dāmād in the intellectual sciences (*al-'ulūm al-'aqliyya*). It is said that he wrote a work on the order of Mīr Dāmād and when Mīr Dāmād saw it he exclaimed that henceforth no one would read his own works. Some sources have also mentioned that Ṣadr al-Dīn studied with Mīr Findiriskī but, as already pointed out, this has not been established with certainty.

After completion of his formal studies, Mullā Ṣadrā began a new phase of his life in quest of the other kind of knowledge, which comes through intuition and illumination resulting from inner purification. He left the busy life of the capital and retired to a small village named Kahak, near Qum, where he spent according to some seven and to others eleven years in ascetic and spiritual practices. He attained in this way immediate knowledge (*'ilm-i ḥuẓūrī*) as he had perfected earlier his grasp of acquired knowledge (*'ilm-i ḥuṣūlī*). At this moment he was asked by Shah 'Abbās II to come to Shīrāz to teach and train qualified students. He accepted the call and returned to public life, spending the last thirty years of his life teaching in the Khān school of Shīrāz built for him by Allāhvardī Khān, the governor of Fārs. Due to the presence of Mullā Ṣadrā, the Khān school became a great centre of learning attracting students from near and far. In fact, it became so famous that it attracted the attention of some of the European travellers of the period such as Thomas Herbert, who writes: "And, indeed, Shīrāz has a college wherein is read philosophy, astrology, physic, chemistry, and the mathematics; so as 'tis the more famoused through Persia".[1] It was also during this period that Mullā Ṣadrā wrote most of his works. On returning from his seventh pilgrimage on foot to Mecca he died in Baṣra in 1050/1640 and was buried in that city.[2]

Nearly fifty works of Mullā Ṣadrā are known, most of which were lithographed during the Qājār period and are now being republished in modern editions. Some of these concern specifically religious themes such as his Qur'anic commentaries and the monumental commentary upon the *Uṣūl al-kāfī* of Kulainī, which was left uncompleted. Others deal with Ḥikmat properly speaking, such as *al-Shawāhid al-rubūbiyya*, in many ways his personal testament and the summary of his teachings, *al-Mashā'ir* on being and *Ḥikmat al-'arshiyya* on the posthumous becoming of man. Yet another group of his writings are commentaries upon earlier philosophical works such as the glosses upon Ibn Sīnā's *Shifā'* and the commentary upon *Kitāb al-hidāya* of Athīr al-Dīn Abharī known as *Sharḥ al-Hidāya*, which became the most famous work on Islamic philosophy in the Indian subcontinent and is referred to as *Ṣadrā* in India and Pakistan to this day.[3] Mullā Ṣadrā also wrote two works in his own defence, one the *Sih aṣl*, his only Persian work in prose, in which he defended gnosis ('irfān) against the attacks of superficial doctors of law and jurisprudents, and the *Kasr al-aṣnām al-jāhiliyya*, in which he defended the Sharī'a and the exoteric dimension of religion against some of the extremists who existed within certain ṣūfī orders and to whom he refers as the *mutaṣawwifīn* of his time.[4] Mullā Ṣadrā also wrote a *Dīvān*

[1] Herbert, *Travels in Persia*, p. 72.

[2] The traditional sources for his life are the same as those mentioned above for Mīr Dāmād and Shaikh Bahā' al-Dīn: for a full discussion of them, see Shīrāzī, *Sih aṣl*, introduction, pp. 2–8.

[3] Nasr, "Mullā Ṣadrā dar Hindūstān", pp. 909ff.

[4] The term *mutaṣavvif* is perfectly legitimate in most schools of Sufism, where it refers to the person who follows the path of Sufism, but in Safavid and post-Safavid Iran it gained a pejorative connotation as referring to those who "play" with Sufism without being serious, in contrast to the real ṣūfīs who were called *Ṣūfiyya*. It thus acquired the meaning of *mustaṣvif*, a term used by some of the earlier ṣūfīs to designate those who know nothing about Sufism but pretend to follow it.

of poetry, selections of which have been published. But these poems do not compare in quality with those of his teachers Mīr Dāmād and Shaikh-i Bahā'ī or those of his students Faiż-i Kāshānī and Lāhījī.

The outstanding masterpiece of Mullā Ṣadrā is the *al-Ḥikmat al-muta'āliyya fi'l-asfār al-arba'at al-'aqliyya* ("The Supernal Wisdom concerning the Four Journeys of the Intellect"), known in Persia as the *Asfār*. This most advanced text of Ḥikmat is a final summation of traditional wisdom, including, in addition to the most thorough exposition of Mullā Ṣadrā's own vision, a vast amount of material related to the views of earlier gnostics, philosophers and theologians. It is therefore a major source for our knowledge of Islamic intellectual history and at the same time a testament to the author's remarkable knowledge of earlier philosophical, religious and historical texts. The *Asfār*, which is taught only to students who have already mastered Peripatetic philosophy, ishrāqī theosophy and Kalām, is taught in traditional schools over a six year period and is the crowning achievement in the traditional curriculum of the "intellectual sciences" in the madrasas. Numerous commentaries have been written on this work, of which some of the best known include the commentaries of Mullā 'Alī Zunūzī and Ḥājjī Mullā Hādī Sabzavārī. The *Asfār* and its commentaries are like a central river compared to which all other streams are peripheral. In such fashion has this work dominated the intellectual life of Persia; and the later philosophical and theosophical schools have been like so many tributaries that have only contributed to its expansion in its onward march.

The work of Mullā Ṣadrā, all of which except for the Persian *Sih aṣl*, a few letters and the poems are in Arabic, are written in a remarkably lucid style which in fact makes them appear as deceptively easy. There is, moreover, a mixture of logical analysis, mystical gleaming and references to religious sources, especially the Qur'ān and Ḥadīth, which characterises all of Ṣadr al-Dīn's writings. He achieved in his own life, as well as in his works which are the fruit of that life, a synthesis of the three means open to man in his quest after truth: revelation (*waḥy* or *shar'*), illumination and intellectual intuition (*dhauq*) and ratiocination (*istidlāl* or *'aql* in its limited meaning). His works reflect this synthesis. A most rigorous dialectical and logical discourse, in which type of expression Mullā Ṣadrā was an unmatched master and for which he is especially known in the Indian subcontinent, is often followed by a gnostic utterance received through illumination to which he usually refers as "truth received from the Divine Throne" (*taḥqīq ʿarshī*). In the same manner rational arguments are supported by citations from the Qur'ān, and the commentaries upon the Qur'ān and Ḥadīth are carried out through the process of hermeneutic interpretation (*ta'wīl*) in such a way as to reveal their gnostic meaning. There is but one inner, spiritual reality which manifests itself outwardly in the revealed scriptures, in the soul and mind of man and in the cosmos, or "upon the horizons" to use the Qur'anic terminology. The synthesis achieved by Mullā Ṣadrā aims at bringing man back to this one spiritual reality from all the different modes of perception and knowledge that are open to him, whether it be the given text of revelation, or ratiocination and its analysis of the externally perceived world, or the inward illumination which opens up the inner horizons of the two above modes of knowledge and is at the same time objectivised and regulated by them.

The synthesis of Mullā Ṣadrā and his intellectual progeny is based upon the integration of the four major schools of Islamic thought alluded to earlier: namely Kalām, Peripatetic philosophy, ishrāqī theosophy and ʿirfān. In Mullā Ṣadrā we find elements of Ghazālī, Ibn Sīnā, Suhravardī and particularly Ibn ʿArabī. Moreover, there is Shiʿism, especially in its gnostic aspect, which serves as the background for this whole synthesis. The *Nahj al-balāgha* of ʿAlī and the traditions of the other Shīʿī Imāms are a constant source of inspiration for Mullā Ṣadrā and a major source of his doctrines. Of course, this synthesis could not have been achieved without the work of the sages and philosophers of the two preceding centuries. But their work in turn finds its final meaning and elaboration in the doctrines of Ṣadr al-Dīn.

There are many principles which distinguish the metaphysical doctrines of Mullā Ṣadrā, not all of which can be enumerated here. Some of the most important of these principles include the unity, principiality and gradation of being; trans-substantial motion; the unity of the knower and the known and the reality of "mental existence" (*wujūd al-dhihnī*) as a distinct state of existence which makes knowledge possible; and the catharsis (*tajrīd*) and independence of the power of imagination (*khayāl*) in the soul from the body, and also the existence of a cosmic "world of imagination" which makes possible the theosophical explanation of religious descriptions of eschatology.[1]

[1] For a discussion of these points, see Nasr, "Ṣadr al-Dīn Shīrāzī". Also Corbin: introduction to *Le Livre des pénétrations métaphysiques*; "*Mundus imaginalis*"; *Terre céleste*, pp. 257–65.

The doctrine of unity of being (*waḥdat al-wujūd*) is usually associated with sufism and in fact finds its highest expression in the gnostic teachings of Muḥyī al-Dīn Ibn 'Arabī and his school. This doctrine is usually mistaken for pantheism or panentheism by those who cannot distinguish between profane philosophy and a sacred metaphysical doctrine.[1] But in reality it is nothing but the inner meaning of the *shahāda* of Islam, *Lā ilāha ill'Allāh*, made manifest by those who are given the vision of the inner meaning of things. There is nothing more Islamic than unity (*al-tauḥīd*) and waḥdat al-wujūd is the essence of al-tauḥīd and therefore of Islam. But even this doctrine has levels of interpretation; that is why in Persia a distinction is usually made between the waḥdat al-wujūd of the *'urafā* or gnostics, referring to Ibn 'Arabī and his school, and the waḥdat al-wujūd of the *ḥukamā* or theosophers, referring to Mullā Ṣadrā and his school. In order to understand this distinction it is necessary to analyse the gradual process by which man comes to understand unity. The first perception of the external world for the untrained mind or for a child is to see multiplicity and only multiplicity. The multiplicity is due to the quiddity (*māhiyya*) of each thing which distinguishes it from others, and to consider this multiplicity as ultimately real is to accept the view of *iṣālat al-māhiyya* or "principiality of quiddity" for which Mīr Dāmād and Suhravardī are known, if we do not consider that Suhravardī held to be true for light what Mullā Ṣadrā held with regard to being. Of course these sages did not negate unity, which for them stands above the world of multiplicity, but in their analysis of the world of multiplicity they stopped short at the quiddity of things without considering their existence (*wujūd*).

The next stage is to hold that within each thing, which according to Avicennan philosophy is composed of existence and quiddity or essence, it is the existence which is ultimately real and not the quiddity, but nevertheless to believe that the existence of each object is totally different from that of another. This view is *iṣālat al-wujūd* ("principiality of being"), but still falls short of fully grasping the sense of Unity. It is the view of Ibn Sīnā and his followers.

Above this view stands that of Mullā Ṣadrā and his followers, who claim that not only is the existence of each object principial *vis-à-vis* its

[1] Schuon, pp. 56ff. Burckhardt, *Introduction*, chapter 3. M. Lings, *A Moslem Saint of the Twentieth Century* (London, 1961), chapter 5. Nasr, *Three Muslim Sages*, pp. 104–8.

quiddity (iṣālat al-wujūd), but also that the existence of each object is a state and grade of Being itself, not a totally independent being. They thus believe that there is only one Being (waḥdat al-wujūd), which possesses grades and stages (*tashkīk*) while it remains transcendent with respect to these states and stages (*marātib*), and it is this being and not the quiddity of objects which gives reality to things. Mullā Ṣadrā and his followers are therefore said to believe in the unity (waḥdat), gradation (tashkīk) and principiality (iṣālat) of Being (wujūd). Above this concept of the "Unity of Being" stands the unity of gnostics, usually called *waḥdat-i khāṣṣa* (special unity), according to which Being corresponds to only one objective Reality, God. Nothing else can even be said to exist. Everything else is the theophany (*tajallī*) of this One Being, not having any being of its own, not even that of being a stage and state of the One Being.

On the basis of the doctrine of the Unity of Being Mullā Ṣadrā created the vast doctrine of the metaphysics of being, which is another version of the metaphysics of essence of Suhravardī. The interrelation between all stages of existence and the incessant deployment from the Source and return to the Source characterise the whole doctrine of Mullā Ṣadrā. There is a dynamism in his view; but it must not be in any way confused with the type of dynamism found in modern thought, which usually results from a forgetting of the immutable essences of things and terminates in a horizontal and purely temporal and secular evolution that sometimes even appears in a theological garb, as in the case of Teilhardism. The dynamism of Mullā Ṣadrā is "spatial" rather than "temporal'. It is directed not towards the achievement of a future state but towards the realisation of a higher state of being that exists here and now. The world of becoming is related to the world of being not by a temporal sequence but in a relation that can be best symbolised by the spatial circumscription of one sphere by another, as we see in the medieval cosmologies based upon the metaphysical symbolism of the Ptolemaic spheres. Interestingly enough, Mullā Ṣadrā in fact described this metaphysical relationship without having recourse to Ptolemaic astronomy: his exposition, therefore, cannot be brushed aside so easily by those who, being unable to distinguish the symbol from the brute fact, discard the medieval metaphysical doctrine of the states of being because it is tied in its exposition to the homocentric Ptolemaic astronomy.

The relationship between being and becoming, which Aristotle himself had also sought to explain, lies for Mullā Ṣadrā in the idea of trans-substantial motion (al-ḥarakat al-jauhariyya). Ibn Sīnā and the Peripatetics in general limited motion in the Aristotelian sense of the word to the four categories of position, space, quality and quantity; that is, all gradual change from potentiality to actuality or motion for them occurred not in the substance of things, but in one of the above four accidents. Ibn Sīnā in fact gave reasons in the *Shifā'* as to why the substance of an object cannot change in the process of motion. Mullā Ṣadrā, after answering the difficulties stated by Ibn Sīnā, proceeds to prove the necessity of trans-substantial motion while arguing at the same time for the "Platonic ideas" or archetypes of things which the Peripatetics had negated. It is hardly possible to analyse this difficult doctrine here.[1] Suffice it to say that for Mullā Ṣadrā motion is the means whereby gradually the substance of a thing changes until it is able to achieve a higher state of being and through man gain access to the world of immutable forms (*tajarrud*) above and beyond all change. In the same way that the cosmos receives its reality through the effusion of being from the Origin and Source of all being, the becoming and change in the cosmos are with the aim of achieving higher states of being and finally states that lie above the world of change and becoming and that lead ultimately to the Source once again. The Universe is a vast system aimed at making possible this catharsis and disentanglement from matter and becoming which the very rich term tajrīd implies (an angel being called *mujarrad* in the language of theosophy, that is one who possesses the state of tajrīd). This possibility exists here and now, at least for man who stands in an axial and central position in this world. The rôle of Ḥikmat is to make him realise where he stands and to enable him to achieve the state of tajrīd. The doctrine of trans-substantial motion, therefore, in addition to enabling Mullā Ṣadrā to construct a new form of natural philosophy, is a cornerstone of both his metaphysics and his spiritual psychology.

The problem of how we know, or epistemology, which since Descartes's dissection of reality has become both central and insoluble in Western philosophy, also occupies a central position in Mullā Ṣadrā's writings. A good part of the first journey of the *Asfār* is devoted to it. With a rigour which would satisfy a modern analyst Mullā Ṣadrā seeks to analyse the problem of knowledge from a back-

[1] See Qazvīnī.

ground which is again essentially gnostic and is based on the union between the knower (*al-'āqil*) and the known (*al-ma'qūl*). In the act of perception (*idrāk*) man becomes identified with the object of his knowledge; that is, the knower or 'āqil is at the moment of perceiving the known identified with the form of the known or ma'qūl, which is in fact its reality. Knowledge is only possible through this union.

In order to demonstrate the possibility of this union taking place, Mullā Ṣadrā must prove the existence of an independent plane of reality which he calls the mental plane (*wujūd al-dhihnī*). He is the first of the Muslim philosophers to have devoted attention to this question and to have analysed all that the reality of this plane implies. It is true that the union of knower and known had been alluded to by Abu'l-Ḥasan al-'Āmirī and some of the ṣūfīs, but here as elsewhere it was Mullā Ṣadrā who for the first time provided demonstrations for it and incorporated it into a vast metaphysical synthesis. To have found traces of this and other ideas in earlier books does not at all detract from the genius of Mullā Ṣadrā, for the important question is how these ideas are incorporated into a new intellectual perspective. Otherwise in the domain of metaphysics there is nothing new under the Sun, as Aristotle had already asserted. It is enough to compare Mullā Ṣadrā's treatment of this question with what is found in earlier Muslim sources to realise exactly what he achieved.

For Mullā Ṣadrā the mind is not a *tabula rasa* nor only a tablet on which certain "ideas" are engrained. It has several faculties and powers, one of which is to create forms, and this power is that of "imagination" as the term is understood by the ḥukamā. Mullā Ṣadrā, like Ibn 'Arabī, believes in the creative power of imagination (*mutakhayyila khallāqa*), through which the mind is able to bring forms into being in the same way that the Divine Intellect has given objective existence to things through Its own creative power. Knowledge results, not from the external form "entering" the mind, but in this external form acting as an occasion for the mind to create, in accordance with the immutable essence of the object concerned, its form. This act in turn changes the state of being of the knower itself. Therefore knowledge is inseparable from being and leaves its effect upon the being of the knower.

The catharsis or tajrīd of the imaginative faculty plays a major rôle in the eschatological doctrines expounded by Ṣadr al-Dīn. In the last part (*safar*) of the *Asfār* as well as in individual treatises on resurrection and the afterlife, especially the monumental commentary in the form of glosses upon the *Ḥikmat al-ishrāq*, Mullā Ṣadrā has expounded in the most complete fashion the esoteric meaning of the Muslim doctrine of resurrection and eschatology (maʿād).[1] His writings in this domain are probably the most thorough and systematic of any Muslim work in this area, where Muslims, in contrast to Hindus and Buddhists, have been generally laconic. It is only in the works of Ibn ʿArabī and Mullā Ṣadrā and their schools that these questions are amply treated.

The intermediate world of imagination or the "imaginal world", which he also calls "purgatory" (*barzakh*) and the world of "hanging forms" (*ṣuwar al-muʿallaqa*), is the locus of the eschatological events described in sacred scripture. It is where the events of the Last Judgment occur in a real way because this world is real and has an ontological status. This is a world possessing not only form but also matter which is, however, subtle and celestial (*laṭīf* and *malakūtī*). Man, likewise, possesses a subtle body, or what in the parlance of Western Hermeticism would be called the astral body. In his glosses upon the *Ḥikmat al-ishrāq*, Mullā Ṣadrā asserts that neither the Peripatetics like Ibn Sīnā nor the theologians like Ghazālī could really solve this problem. The one could only prove spiritual resurrection (*al-maʿād al-rūḥānī*), and the other believed in corporeal resurrection (*al-maʿād al-jismānī*) without being able to provide any demonstration for it. Mullā Ṣadrā broke this deadlock and was able to prove corporeal resurrection in accordance with Qur'anic teachings by appealing to this intermediate world where man is resurrected after death not as a dismembered soul but as a complete being possessing also a subtle body.

Mullā Ṣadrā develops fully the theme of the posthumous becoming of the soul and its resurrection beyond the imaginal world to higher states of being and finally to a station before the Divine Presence itself. He makes the science of the soul (*ʿilm al-nafs*) a branch of metaphysics (*ilāhiyyāt*) rather than natural philosophy (*ṭabīʿiyyāt*) as was the case with the Peripatetics, and he develops an elaborate science of the soul starting with the embryonic state of man and terminating in his ultimate beatitude far beyond the earthly life. In this domain no less than in metaphysics he gives an imprint of a powerful genius to a teaching that is by nature timeless and perennial.

Mullā Ṣadrā trained many students, of whom two, Mullā Muḥsin

[1] Corbin, "Le Thème".

Faiż Kāshānī and Maulānā 'Abd al-Razzāq Lāhījī, are among the first-rate luminaries of the Safavid period and will be treated below. Others less known but nevertheless significant include Shaikh Ḥusain Tunakābunī, who continued Mullā Ṣadrā's school after him, Āqājānī Māzandarānī, the author of a vast commentary upon the *Qabasāt* of Mīr Dāmād, and Mīrzā Muḥammad Ṣādiq Kāshānī, who went to India to propagate Mullā Ṣadrā's teachings. In Persia the teachings of Mullā Ṣadrā were not continued immediately after him due to difficult circumstances. But a century later men like Mīrzā Muḥammad Ṣādiq Ardistānī revived his teachings, and early in the Qājār period Mullā 'Alī Nūrī, followed by his student Ḥājjī Mullā Hādī Sabzavārī, established Mullā Ṣadrā's school as the central school of Ḥikmat in Persia.

The akhbārī – uṣūlī debate

Almost contemporary with Mullā Ṣadrā there began a debate which had some influence upon the later course of philosophy and a great deal of effect upon the further chapters of religious and theological history. This debate concerned the rôle of reason in the interpretation of religious matters. An *'ālim* by the name of Mullā Muḥammad Amīn Astarābādī (d. 1033/1623–4) established the *akhbārī* school, which opposed the use of 'aql in religious matters and relied completely on the Qur'ān and the traditions of the Prophet and the Imāms. In his *al-Fawā'id al-madaniyya* he attacked the idea of *ijtihād* or the giving of opinion based upon the four principles (*uṣūl*) of the Qur'ān, Ḥadīth or *sunna*, the consensus of the community (*ijmā'*) and reasoning or 'aql, which in Sunnism is called *qiyās*, and branded *mujtahids*, or those who practised ijtihād, as enemies of religion. The opposing school, which came to be known as *uṣūlī* and which finally won the day, continued to emphasise the importance of 'aql within the tenets of the Qur'ān and Ḥadīth.

Usually the followers of the akhbārī school were literalists and purely exoteric and outward interpreters of religion, and came to be identified as *qishrīs* (those who remain content with only the husk rather than seeking the kernel as well). They were usually opposed to sufism and Ḥikmat and even Kalām. But this was by no means always the case. There were some akhbārīs who became outstanding ṣūfīs and ḥakīms, such as Mullā Muḥsin Faiż Kāshānī, the disciple of Mullā Ṣadrā. Such men, while opposing the use of 'aql on a certain plane, were able to reach the supra-rational domain of gnosis and illumination.

The akhbārī – uṣūlī debate continued into the Qājār period in the form of the *Shaikhī – bālāsarī* disputes. Strangely enough, Shaikh Aḥmad Aḥsā'ī, the founder of the Shaikhī movement, was close to the akhbārī position and at the same time an enemy of the ḥakīms and ṣūfīs. He was particularly opposed to Mullā Muḥsin Faiż despite the fact that both may be classified as *akhbārīs*. The situation, then, is more complex than classifying uṣūlīs as pro-Ḥikmat and akhbārīs as opposed to Ḥikmat; although the refusal to consider the rôle of 'aql in the interpretation of religious matters naturally led the akhbārīs away from Ḥikmat and gnosis, in which reason serves as the first stage for a knowledge which is supra-sensible and where in any case reason is never opposed on its own plane, but is ultimately transcended.

Mullā Muḥsin Faiż Kāshānī

Of Mullā Ṣadrā's students the best known is Muḥammad b. Shāh Murtażā, known as Mullā Muḥsin Kāshānī or Kāshī, and given the title of Faiż by Mullā Ṣadrā himself, who besides being his teacher also became his father-in-law. Mullā Muḥsin was born in Kāshān in 1007/1598–9, studied for a few years in Qum and Iṣfahān, where he belonged to the circle of Mīr Dāmād and Shaikh-i Bahā'ī, and then came to Shīrāz to receive the last phase of his education from Mullā Ṣadrā and to study the religious sciences with Sayyid Mājid Baḥrānī. The last part of his life he spent in Kāshān, where he died in 1091/1680–1 and where he is buried. His tomb is to this day a centre of pilgrimage and is credited with miracle-working powers.[1]

Nearly 120 works of Mullā Muḥsin are known, of which most have survived.[2] They are in both Arabic and Persian and have become since his day a mainstay of the curriculum of Shī'ī religious schools. Like Fārābī and Naṣīr al-Dīn Ṭūsī, Mullā Muḥsin was able to place himself in the different intellectual perspectives and schools of Islam and write outstanding works in each without mixing it with the teachings of another point of view. This, of course, does not mean that he was hypocritical or without a particular point of view himself; rather it means that he observed strictly the hierarchic structure of knowledge that is such an essential element of Islam and Islamic civilisation, and

[1] On his life, see Tabrīzī, *Raiḥānat al-adab* III, 342–4; Hidāyat, *Riyāż al-'ārifīn*, pp. 388–9; Khunsarī, *Raużāt al-jannāt*, pp. 542ff.; Shīrāzī, *Ṭarā'iq al-ḥaqā'iq* I, 181ff. *passim*.

[2] Listed by Mishkāt in his introduction to Kāshānī's *Maḥajjat*.

avoided the "mixing of the arguments of different sciences" (*khalṭ-i mabḥath*), which is so disdained in traditional Islamic learning.[1]

The works of Mullā Muḥsin, of which he himself has left us with three lists, include many commentaries upon the Qur'ān such as the *al-Ṣāfī* and *al-Asfā'*; works on Ḥadīth including *al-Wāfī*, which is the most outstanding of its kind in recent centuries; treatises devoted to the principles of religion (*uṣūl al-dīn*) such as *'Ilm al-yaqīn* and *'Ain al-yaqīn*; treatises on the Muslim rites such as the daily prayers and *ḥajj* and their esoteric significance, in which this period is particularly rich;[2] collections of litanies and invocations such as *Jalā' al-'uyūn*; treatises on jurisprudence such as *al-Taṭhīr*; and works devoted to the lives and sayings of the Imāms such as his commentary upon the *Ṣaḥīfa sajjādiyya* of the Fourth Shī'ī Imām. Besides these works in the religious sciences, he wrote many works on sufism and gnosis, of which the *al-Kalimāt al-maknūna* with its summary, *al-Kalimāt al-makhẓūna*, is perhaps the outstanding example. This work, which is in Persian, is one of the outstanding expositions of gnosis in its Shī'ī setting and treats a complete cycle of metaphysics.[3] Mullā Muḥsin also summarised and commented upon earlier ṣūfī works such as the *al-Futūḥāt al-makkiyya* of Ibn 'Arabī and the *Masnavī* of Jalāl al-Dīn Rūmī. He also wrote many poems himself mostly on mystical themes and in the masnavī form. His dīvān is very well known and contains some fine verses, although all of his poems are not of first rate quality. As to Ḥikmat, he did write a few treatises on the subject, but they are not as well known as his works on religion and 'irfān.

Perhaps the most important work of Mullā Muḥsin outside the domain of Ḥadīth, where he is the undisputed Shī'ī authority of the last centuries, is his *al-Maḥajjat al-baiḍā' fī iḥyā' al-iḥyā'* ("The White Path in the Revival of the 'Revival'"), the second "Revival" (*iḥyā'*) referring to the *Iḥyā' 'ulūm al-dīn* of Ghazālī. In the same way that the *Iḥyā'* is the outstanding work of ṣūfī ethics in the Sunnī setting, the *al-Maḥajjat al-baiḍā'* must be considered as the most important Shī'ī work of ethics with a ṣūfī orientation. In fact, what Mullā Muḥsin did was to revive the work of Ghazālī in Shī'ī circles by "Shi'ifying" it. He achieved this task by substituting traditions drawn from Shī'ī sources for the

[1] Nasr, *Science and Civilization*, pp. 29ff.

[2] His treatise on the esoteric meaning of the daily prayers has been published in a beautiful edition as *Namāz, tarjumat al-ṣalāt* (Tehran, 1340/1962).

[3] For a summary, see Nasr, "The School", pp. 926–30.

Sunnī ones which serve as a prop for Ghazālī's book. Otherwise the two works are nearly the same, and of the same monumental proportions. A close comparison of the two would be a most fruitful undertaking to elucidate exactly how the Sunnī and Shī'ī religious and mystical climates are related.

Mullā Muḥsin was one of the foremost esoteric interpreters of Shi'ism. While an outstanding exoteric interpreter of the religion and an undisputed 'ālim of theology and jurisprudence, he was also a gnostic and ṣūfī of high standing and sought throughout his works to harmonise the Sharī'a and the Ṭarīqa. Of the three elements which Mullā Ṣadrā unified in his vast synthesis, namely *shar'*, *kashf* and *'aql*, or revealed religion, inner illumination and rational and intellectual demonstration, Mullā Muḥsin followed mostly the first two. Yet he was of course a ḥakīm well versed in Mullā Ṣadrā's teachings, as works such as the *al-Kalimāt al-maknūna* reveal. In fact, it is with him that the process of the integration of the school of Ḥikmat into Shi'ism is completed. It is he who identified the "celestial guide" or illuminating intellect of Avicennan and Suhravardian metaphysics specifically with the Twelve Imāms, who as heavenly archetypes reflect the "light of Muḥammad" (*al-nūr al-muḥammadī*) which is a sun that illuminates these "spiritual constellations".

Mullā 'Abd al-Razzāq Lāhījī

The other well known student of Mullā Ṣadrā, 'Abd al-Razzāq b. 'Alī Lāhījī, entitled Fayyāż, was also a son-in-law of the master and intimately associated with him. His date of birth is not known and several dates are mentioned for his death, of which the most likely is 1072/1661–2.[1] Lāhījī is known particularly as a theologian with several glosses upon different commentaries of Naṣīr al-Dīn Ṭūsī's *Tajrīd*, the *Shawāriq al-ilhām*, itself an independent commentary upon the *Tajrīd*, as well as the two Persian works, *Sarmāya-yi īmān* and *Gauhar murād*, the latter work being perhaps the best known book on Shī'ī theology of the Safavid period. But these works are theology (Kalām) that is deeply impregnated with Ḥikmat, of which Lāhījī was also a master. In fact, during the Safavid period there is not so much an independent growth of Kalām as the development of Kalām within the framework

[1] See Tabrīzī, *Raiḥānat al-adab* III, 233–4, and Shīrāzī, *al-Shawāhid*, introduction, pp. 99–102.

of Ḥikmat. Most of the glosses and commentaries upon the *Tajrīd*, such as those of Khafrī, belong more to the tradition of Ḥikmat than Kalām proper, and most of the debates that are truly theological are found within the pages of works on Ḥikmat, especially those of the school of Mullā Ṣadrā.

Lāhījī in fact developed a form of Kalām which is hardly distinguishable from Ḥikmat, although at least in his better known works such as the *Gauhar murād* he does not follow the main doctrinal teachings of Mullā Ṣadrā, as on the unity of Being and the catharsis of the faculty of imagination. Yet in other works he confirms these points in such a manner as to indicate that the condition of his times did not allow an open espousal of the teachings of Mullā Ṣadrā and that he had to adopt a more "theological" or Kalāmī dress to suit the taste of some of the 'ulamā who were by now severely criticising the ṣūfīs and the gnostics.

Lāhījī, however, has also left us with works that belong more purely to the tradition of Ḥikmat such as *Ḥudūth al-'ālam*, the commentary upon the *Hayākil al-nūr* of Suhravardī and *al-Kalimāt al-ṭayyiba*, which deals with the contending views of Mullā Ṣadrā and Mīr Dāmād on the principiality of existence or essence (*iṣālat-i wujūd* and *iṣālat-i māhiyyat*). All these works show Lāhījī to be a master in Ḥikmat and a true disciple of Mullā Ṣadrā.

Like Mīr Dāmād and Mullā Muḥsin Faiż, Lāhījī also wrote poetry which is of a high order containing many beautiful verses. His dīvān of about six thousand verses, of which the most complete manuscript is to be found in the Kitābkhāna-yi āstāna-yi quds-i rażavī in Mashhad, reveals a very different aspect of his personality from that revealed by his other works. Here one finds the gentle breeze of realised gnosis and mysticism in which pearls of wisdom are couched in verses of beauty and harmony rather than in rigorous rationalistic arguments. The poems contain many verses in the praise of the Prophet and the Imāms and also long qaṣīdas dedicated to both Mullā Ṣadrā and Mīr Dāmād, with whom Lāhījī also most likely had contacts. These are perhaps the most eloquent and telling poems ever written on these two giants of the Safavid period, and they could have been written only by a person of the stature of Lāhījī, who stood close to them both in time and from the vantage-point of ideas.

Lāhījī had many students, of whom his own son, Mīrzā Ḥasan Lāhījī, and Qāżī Sa'īd Qumī are perhaps the most important. Mīrzā

Ḥasan was a very respected religious scholar of his times, revered as an outstanding authority on the religious sciences. But he was also a ḥakīm of much merit and, at a time when Ḥikmat was being attacked by some of the 'ulamā, wrote a work in Persian entitled *Ā'ina-yi ḥikmat* to defend Ḥikmat by appealing to the traditions of the Prophet and the Imāms.

Qāżī Sa'īd Qumī

The other student of Lāhījī, Muḥammad b. Sa'īd Qumī, usually known as Qāżī Sa'īd or as the "Junior ḥakīm" (*ḥakīm-i kūchak*), is as well known as his master and belongs to the rank of the most outstanding figures of the Safavid period.[1] A student of Lāhījī, Mullā Muḥsin and also of Mullā Rajab 'Alī Tabrīzī – who represents the more Peripatetic trend of philosophy in the Safavid period – Qāżī Sa'īd was particularly attracted to sufism and gnosis, while at the same time he was the judge or *qāḍī* of Qum from which position he has gained his title. In fact, most of Qāżī Sa'īd's life was spent in Qum. It was in this holy city of Shi'ism and centre of religious studies that he was born in 1049/1639; here he passed most of his active years and also died and was buried in 1103/1691. Besides serving as the judge of Qum, he was also a well known physician in the city and was considered as a real ḥakīm in both senses of the word, as physician and philosopher.

The total attachment of Qāżī Sa'īd to 'irfān has made him the "Ibn 'Arabī of Shi'ism". This is a very apt title for him because he belongs more to the school of pure 'irfān of Ibn 'Arabī than to the school of Ḥikmat of Mullā Ṣadrā, where gnostic themes are provided with rational demonstration. The works of Qāżī Sa'īd bear this out, for they usually deal with esoteric meaning of revealed and sacred texts and rites. They include *al-Arba'ūn ḥadīthan*, which is a commentary upon forty prophetic ḥadīths dealing with divine science; *al-Arba'ūnāt li-kashf anwār al-qudsiyyāt*, which is a collection of forty treatises, again mostly concerned with the esoteric meaning of religion; *Asrār al-'ibādāt*, which deals with the esoteric significance of the Muslim rites; and commentary upon different traditions such as the famous *Ḥadīth-i ghamām*. His largest work in this domain is the monumental three

[1] See *Raiḥānat al-adab* III, 268–9; Corbin, "La Configuration", pp. 79–166; and Qumī, *Kitāb asrār*, introduction by Sabzavārī.

volume commentary upon the *Tauḥīd* of Shaikh-i Ṣaddūq, which remains unedited and is not well known except for the section dealing with rites which has become known independently as the above-mentioned *Asrār al-'ibādāt*. But he also wrote several works on logic and philosophy such as the *Asrār al-ṣanāyi'* on logic; glosses upon the "Theology of Aristotle", which is among his most important works; and also glosses upon the *Sharḥ al-ishārāt* of Naṣīr al-Dīn Ṭūsī.

The most marked feature of Qāżī Sa'īd's thought is his mastery in revealing the esoteric sense of different aspects of the Islamic tradition in both its doctrinal and practical dimensions. The process of ta'wīl, of spiritual and hermeneutic interpretation of things, which is so central to both sufism and Shi'ism, found in Qāżī Sa'īd one of its greatest masters. In his writings the inner meaning of verses of the Qur'ān, traditions of the Prophet and the Imāms, as well as Islamic ritual practices, gains the transparence and lucidity which result from the purely gnostic and metaphysical point of view held by him. In his exposition of the symbolism of the Ka'ba, he even develops a true philosophy of art, and explains the symbolic significance of forms and spatial configurations with such completeness and thoroughness that it is difficult to find its like in the annals of Islamic thought.[1] In this field also he reflects in many ways the doctrines and teachings of Ibn 'Arabī.

The two Majlisīs

It would hardly be possible to treat philosophy and theology in the Safavid period without dealing with Mullā Muḥammad Taqī Majlisī and his more famous son, Mullā Muḥammad Bāqir Majlisī, although they, and especially the son, have been dealt with elsewhere in this volume. The first Majlisī, who died in 1070/1659–60, was one of the religious scholars of his time who was attracted to sufism and was probably a practising ṣūfī.[2] The reaction against organised sufism in religious circles had not as yet set in so that Mullā Muḥammad Taqī could enjoy respect among Shī'ī scholars and yet openly espouse the cause of sufism. He rendered a great service to both in many ways. He was the first Shī'ī scholar to spread and propagate widely the text of the

[1] Corbin, "La Configuration", pp. 82ff.; Nasr, "The Concept of Space".

[2] Tabrīzī, *Raiḥānat al-adab* III, 460–2; also Bihbihānī, *Mir'āt al-aḥvāl*, which is devoted to him in particular.

traditions of the Imāms and to encourage their study, so that he must be considered in a way as the father of the science of Ḥadīth in its new development during the Safavid period. He also made the life of sufism in religious circles easier by lending to it the weight of his authority and support.

His son, Mullā Muḥammad Bāqir (b. 1037/1627–8, d. 1111/1699–1700), was in many ways a different type of personality. He was politically more influential than his father and must be considered as the most powerful Shī'ī scholar of the Safavid period. He was also much more austere and exoteric, and openly condemned and opposed organised sufism, to the extent of denying his own father's allegiance to sufism. In fact, he was the most formidable spokesman for the reaction which set in within Shī'ī religious circles during the later Safavid period due in part to excesses within some of the ṣūfī orders. With the same breath he also condemned the ḥukamā, whose teachings he saw as closely wedded to those of the ṣūfīs.

The second Majlisī is the most prolific of Shī'ī writers, and probably wrote his works with the aid of some of his own students. Otherwise these works, numbering over one hundred and including the monumental *Bihār al-anwār*, could hardly have been written by one man. The *Bihār al-anwār* itself, which is over twenty-six lengthy volumes in its modern edition, is a vast encyclopaedia of Shi'ism dealing with different aspects of Islam as a religion as well as the Islamic religious sciences and the history of the Prophets and the Imāms. It remains a treasury of information for all the phases of Shī'ī learning to this day. His other works deal with different religious sciences. Some of the most famous, such as *Ḥaqq al-yaqīn* and *Ḥilyat al-muttaqīn*, both in Persian, and *Ṣirāt al-najāt* in Arabic, are concerned with principles of religion, traditions and theology in the general sense, not in its technical sense of Kalām. In his commentary upon the *Uṣūl al-kāfī* of Kulainī, however, Majlisī turns to the intellectual sciences and seems to have been influenced by the commentary of Mullā Ṣadrā. Likewise, in his *Zād al-ma'ād* there are allusions to Islamic esoteric teachings, which implies that Majlisī was not completely alien to these subjects and perhaps spoke so vehemently against the ḥakīms and ṣūfīs because of the particular conditions of his time, which necessitated such a position for the defence of the Sharī'a and the official religious institutions. In any case Majlisī left an indelible mark upon all later Shī'ī thought while his opposition to Ḥikmat only delayed its new flowering in the Qājār period.

The later ḥakīms of the Safavid period

Although the atmosphere was not favourable to the propagation of philosophy and theosophy from the second half of the 11th/17th century to the Afghan invasion, which put an end to Safavid rule, several notable figures continued to propagate the tradition and make possible its renewal in the 13th/19th century. Among these figures one may mention Mullā Ḥasan Lunbānī (d. 1094/1682–3), a student of Mullā Rajab 'Alī Tabrīzī, who combined philosophy and sufism and even wrote a commentary upon the *Masnavī*. Due to his particular attraction to ishrāq and 'irfān he was accused by some of the exoteric 'ulamā of being a ṣūfī and wrote a treatise in his own defence.[1]

Another figure of the same period, Mīrzā Muḥammad Ṣādiq Ardistānī (d. 1134/1721–2), was more or less a follower of the teachings of Mullā Ṣadrā. Like Mullā Ṣadrā, he believed in the catharsis (tajarrud) of the inner faculties of the soul, particularly the faculty of imagination, and offers the same arguments in proof of this view. But on the question of the origin of the human soul, which he considers as a ray of the universal soul (*nafs-i kullī*), he presents a view which is different from that of both Mullā Ṣadrā and Ibn Sīnā. On the question of the unity and principiality of being also he follows Ṣadr al-Dīn.[2]

Ardistānī was the foremost teacher of Ḥikmat of his time in Iṣfahān. His *Ḥikmat-i ṣādiqiyya*, which consists of his lectures assembled by his students, is a major work on the school of Ḥikmat during the Safavid period. He was personally revered because of his extremely simple and ascetic life, but owing to the opposition of some of the religious authorities he finally fell out of favour with Shah Sulṭān Ḥusain. Yet he was able to be of much influence and to train a number of students, of whom the best known is Mīrzā Muḥammad Taqī Almāsī, a descendant of the first Majlisī. Almāsī was the first person to begin to teach the texts of Mullā Ṣadrā in official lessons of the madrasas and was instrumental in propagating his work. It was his student, Āqā Muḥammad Bīdābādī, who taught Mullā 'Alī Nūrī, the great reviver of Ḥikmat during the Qājār period, and so through him the chain of transmission of Ḥikmat is preserved between the Safavid and Qājār eras. Another of Ardistānī's students, Mullā Ḥamza Gīlānī, was also a well known

[1] See Lāhijānī, *Sharḥ risāla*, introduction by Humā'ī, p. 16; introduction by Āshtiyānī, pp. 40–1.

[2] *Sharḥ risāla*, introduction by Āshtiyānī, p 42; *al-Shawāhid*, introduction, p. 118.

master of Ḥikmat and was among the many people who lost their lives in the Afghan invasion of Iṣfahān.

During the last phase of the Safavid period, the school of Mullā Ṣadrā was as yet far from being completely dominant. A contemporary of Ardistānī, Shaikh 'Ināyat-Allāh Gīlānī, who belonged to the school of Mullā Rajab 'Alī Tabrīzī, continued the Peripatetic school of Ibn Sīnā and taught the *Ishārāt, Shifā'* and *Najāt*. Likewise, there were masters who taught pure gnosis and ishrāq. One of them, Mīr Sayyid Ḥasan Ṭāliqānī, was the outstanding gnostic of Iṣfahān at the beginning of the 12th/18th century and taught the *Fuṣūṣ al-ḥikam* of Ibn 'Arabī, as well as works of Suhravardī such as the *Ḥikmat al-ishrāq* and *Hayākil al-nūr* along with their traditional commentaries. Yet he too was to some extent under the sway of the teachings of Mullā Ṣadrā. Altogether, the general impression one has of the little known history of these last decades of Safavid rule is the gradual spread of the teachings of Mullā Ṣadrā, especially in Iṣfahān, while at the same time other schools such as the Peripatetic and the gnostic continue in a climate which became ever more hostile to both Ḥikmat and 'irfān.

The influence of the school of Iṣfahān in India

Although interest in Islamic philosophy on the Indo-Pakistani subcontinent goes back to the 7th/13th and 8th/14th centuries, the real establishment of a school of Islamic philosophy on the sub-continent dates from the Safavid period. During this epoch many Persian philosophers, scholars and scientists migrated or travelled to India, such as Qāżī Nūr-Allāh Shushtarī, author of the well known *Majālis al-mu'minīn* and *Iḥqāq al-ḥaqq*, Muḥammad Dihdār Shīrāzī, author of several gnostic treatises such as *Ishrāq al-nayyirain*, Bahā' al-Dīn Iṣfahānī, known as Fāżil-i Hindī, who summarised the metaphysics of the *Shifā'*, and the already mentioned Mīr Findiriskī. Moreover, the teachings of Mīr Dāmād and especially Mullā Ṣadrā spread far and wide in India. The *Sharḥ al-Hidāya* of Mullā Ṣadrā, to which we have already referred, became the most popular work in the sub-continent. The very large number of glosses and commentaries upon the works of Safavid masters as well as manuscripts of their writings that are found today in the libraries of the sub-continent are a witness to the remarkable spread of the teachings of the school of Iṣfahān in that region. In fact, except for Iraq, which was then as now religiously associated with

Persia, the Muslim part of the sub-continent represents the only other region of the Islamic world where this particular school of Islamic philosophy spread to an appreciable extent. The mystical and theological movements associated with such names as Shaikh Aḥmad Sirhindī and Shāh Valī-Allāh, as well as the Khairābādī school which is, properly speaking, philosophical and logical, cannot be fully understood without a study of the Safavid schools of thought.

In Persia itself after the interim period of confusion following the downfall of the Safavids, the school of Ḥikmat was revived again in Iṣfahān. The central figures of this revival were Mullā ʿAlī Nūrī, who taught the works of Mullā Ṣadrā for seventy years, and his student Ḥājjī Mullā Hādī Sabzavārī, who made the teachings of Mullā Ṣadrā so dominant and central as practically to exclude other schools of philosophy. Through him and other Qājār masters the teachings of the Safavid sages have been transmitted to the present day and continue to exercise an appreciable influence, particularly the doctrines of Mullā Ṣadrā, which have received so much attention in recent years and which act as the axis around which the revival of traditional philosophy in Persia is taking place. Furthermore, they have even attracted the attention of certain thinkers outside the orbit of Persian culture,[1] as the labour of a small group of scholars, foremost among them Corbin, has enabled the Western world to know Safavid philosophy for the first time and to study it not only for its historical interest but also as a living school of wisdom and thought, in which are combined the rigour of logic and the ecstasies of inner illumination.

[1] Corbin, "The Force of Traditional Philosophy in Iran Today", *Studies in Comparative Religion* (Winter, 1968), pp. 12–25.

CHAPTER 14

CARPETS AND TEXTILES*

I. CARPETS

The finest Persian carpets are considered to be those of the Safavid period. There are two possible reasons for this. Either this particular branch of the arts in Iran reached its zenith later than any other, or else the judgment may be explained by the fact that none of the Timurid textiles have been preserved and that their evaluation is therefore based entirely on miniatures, whereas we still possess a wealth of Safavid carpets and fabrics which attest their advanced stage of technical and aesthetic development. The miniatures leave us in no doubt as to the existence of carpets in the Timurid era. Moreover, the finest surviving knotted carpets date back to the early years of the Safavid dynasty and could not have originated spontaneously. References to precious carpets are found as early as the Sasanian period. These, however, will not be dealt with in the present survey, since the evidence does not provide any clear impression of their design or technique.[1]

Timurid carpets

Two types of carpet can be seen in Timurid miniatures, those with geometrical and those with arabesque designs. For an excellent study of these rugs we are indebted to Amy Briggs. The geometrical type is the earlier and forms by far the larger group. The geometrical carpets were replaced towards the end of the 9th/15th century by those with arabesque and floral patterns, the best examples of which are found in miniatures by Bihzād and his school. Bihzād, who lived approximately from 1455 to 1535–6, belonged to the Herat school and in 1522 he was appointed librarian to Shah Ismā'īl I in Tabrīz. On the miniature (pl. 3) attributed to him and dating from the last decade of the 15th century, both types are illustrated. The small carpet in the foreground represents the geometrical group. The designs of these carpets consist of

* The author wishes it to be known that this chapter was submitted in 1973; as a consequence more recent developments in the field have not been taken into account.

[1] For sources, see Pope, "The Art of Carpet Making", in *SPA*, pp. 2270–82.

small repeating patterns of squares, stars and crosses, hexagons, octagons or circles, thereby showing similarities to the patterns of contemporary paving tiles. The framing of these shapes by narrow light-coloured bands interwoven into stars or crosses and in between into knots is characteristic. Interlacing also occurs as a filling motif and is typical of the borders where the light drawing on a dark background is based on Kufic script. The corners are accurately worked out, using a reciprocating design divided at an angle of 45°. The ground of the inner panels is monochrome or shaded in contrasting colours like a chessboard. Arabesque motifs are rare in these geometrical carpets. Their similarity to the 16th-century "Holbein" carpets of Asia Minor is remarkable, and it is conceivable that these are a continuation of early Timurid rugs.

The later style of arabesque pattern is displayed by the other two carpets on Bihzād's miniature and by the awning in the background. (As a rule awning patterns are closely related to those of the carpets, even in the Safavid era. Unfortunately, as in the case of the carpets depicted on the miniatures, it is not clear how they were made or of what materials. Their function suggests that they were woven from silk or made of embroidered linen.) The differences between these and the geometrical carpet in the foreground are plain. The small repeating pattern has given way to a complicated and extensive quaternate symmetrical arrangement. Constructed lines cover the inner field, describing semicircles, circles, polyfoils, cartouches and ellipses. These shapes overlap to some extent and thus segments are formed which through their colouring and the arabesques specially designed to fill them stand out independently. The formalised Kufic border was replaced by a repeating pattern of elegant undulating tendrils. In the case of the awning in the background one is struck by the medallion centre piece. Further innovations include rugs and awnings with an almost isolated medallion in the centre and corner pieces resembling the quarters of a central medallion, on a ground covered with arabesques and even incorporating animal figures; and carpets with a pattern entirely of scrolling tendrils on a monochrome ground. Both these kinds too are to be seen on miniatures by Bihzād.[1] The detailed reproduction of these textiles seems to have been of particular interest to him and it may be assumed that the development of the new style,

[1] Grube, *The Classical Style*, pl. 31.2. *Iran, Persian Miniatures*, pl. XVII.

which has affinities with that of book illumination, was at least influenced by him. The three principles of composition – the division of the surface by intersecting lines into various symmetrically arranged panels, the medallion and panel design – together with individual motifs used in this context, such as tendrils, flowers and terminal arabesque leaves, form the basis of the carpet patterns of the Safavid period, at the beginning of which indeed Bihzād was still active. Carpets in the geometrical style are no longer found in this period.

Safavid carpets

As was mentioned at the outset, not even a fragment of a Timurid carpet appears to have survived. This is curious not only because there are a great number of carpets and fabrics dating from the Safavid period but also because two large carpets dating back to the years 1522–3 and 1539–40 are still extant in very good condition (pls. 6, 7). The question therefore arises whether some fragments held to be Safavid might not in fact date back to the Timurid era (e.g. pl. 5). This can scarcely be proved, for despite the abundance of examples the criteria for dating individual Safavid pieces within the two centuries in question are not very substantial and the reader who expects the assigning of precise dates and places of origin in respect of this period will be disappointed.

Dating

Four carpets with the date woven into them, two of which, alas, were produced almost contemporaneously, plus a few documents, do not provide very reliable evidence. A degree of uncertainty as to the dating existed in the case of the medallion animal carpet in the Museo Poldi Pezzoli in Milan (pl. 7), since here the date one thought could be construed as either 929/1522 or 949/1542. After intensive examination of the original I prefer nowadays the earlier reading. Thus this carpet dating from 929/1522–3 is our earliest dated example. The famous carpet produced for the tomb of Shaikh Ṣafī in Ardabīl and now in the Victoria and Albert Museum in London (pl. 6) bears the date 946/1539–40. Together with a companion piece now in the County Museum of Los Angeles, it was sold in 1886 through thc agency of Ziegler and Company to the London firm of Vincent Robinson, because money was needed for the restoration of the mosque. The carpet was restored with the help of its counterpart. Its purchase by the Victoria and Albert Museum for £2,500 – an astonishingly high price in those days – was a sensation, as is even today the carpet itself, which measures 11.52 × 5.43 metres and displays a refined drawing, a close weave of some 5,200 knots per square decimetre and subtle nuances of colour. It is one of the most important carpets of the 16th century and there can be little doubt that it was Shah Ṭahmāsp himself who commissioned such a costly pair of carpets, particularly since they were destined for the mausoleum of the founder of the Safavid dynasty.

An interval of more than a hundred years separates these two pieces from a "vase" carpet in the Sarajevo Museum dated 1067/1656.[1] The latest dating – 1082/1671 – occurs on a silk carpet from the mausoleum of Shah 'Abbās II in Qum.[2] Other inscriptions are of a purely literary nature.

The style predominant round about 1600 and in the first quarter of the 17th century is represented by the so-called "Polonaise" carpets, silk knotted carpets brocaded with gold and silver. Their production in Kāshān and particularly in Iṣfahān at this time is attested by a commission tendered in Kāshān in 1601 by King Sigismund III Vasa of Poland, by five not very typical examples in the Treasury of San Marco which were brought to Venice as ambassadorial gifts from Shah 'Abbās I, and by the contemporary reports of European travellers.

European paintings, which are useful in the dating of Anatolian rugs, cannot on the basis of research to date help us to classify Persian carpets. The pictures in which Persian carpets are depicted, for example 17th century Dutch paintings, are relatively late and merely provide examples of the "Herat" group of carpets. The Safavid miniatures show that the whole wealth of forms that recurs in textile design was already fully developed by the beginning of the 16th century. The carpets depicted represent both types, the medallion and the scrolling tendril carpets, but are not painted with sufficient discrimination to allow us to allocate them to individual sub-groups and thus employ them for the purpose of determining dates and origins.

We must therefore fall back on the two masterpieces dating from 1522–3 and 1542, the style developed under Shah 'Abbās in the first

[1] *SPA*, pl. 1238. [2] *SPA*, pl. 1259.

quarter of the 17th century which is represented by the early "Polonaise" carpets and is clearly distinct from that of the rugs of the time of Shah Ṭahmāsp, and two comparatively late examples from about 1660–70. Within this framework one must date pieces according to stylistic criteria, examining in each case the precision of the design and the craftsmanship, and the configuration and stage of evolution of individual forms. The subjectivity of such judgments explains why individual pieces have been differently evaluated by different experts.

Origin

No less difficult is the problem of origin, that is, the task of attributing to individual weaving centres the various groups which can be distinguished among Safavid carpets on the basis of their design and technical characteristics. The few inscriptions we have are of little help. Admittedly the Ardabīl carpet bears the words "produced by... Maqṣūd of Kāshān" and the silk carpet from the Qum mausoleum the words "the work of Master Niʿmat-Allāh of Jaushaqān", but this does not mean that the origin of the craftsmen is the same as that of the rugs, any more than that the destination was necessarily identical with the place of origin. Since the Safavid carpets must be the products of large establishments patronised by the Court, it may be supposed that carpets were manufactured in the workshops of successive capitals. In 1501 Shah Ismāʿīl (1501–24) conquered Tabrīz and was crowned there. In 1548 under Shah Ṭahmāsp (1524–76) the court was transferred to Qazvīn, and in 1598 under Shah ʿAbbās (1587–1629) it moved to Iṣfahān. It is likely that carpets were produced in Tabrīz under Bihzād's influence. As late as 1700 Frantz Caspar Schillinger refers to the close-woven carpets sold in that town.[1] It is surprising that hitherto scarcely any attempt has been made to trace carpets to Qazvīn, although the Court was established there for fifty years. Early in the 17th century Florencio del Niño Jesús emphasised that Qazvīn was an important trading centre where there was an abundance of silk and brocade carpets.[2] In the case of Iṣfahān there is reliable evidence from various sources of the manufacture of carpets brocaded with gold and silver threads. Indeed Jean-Baptiste Tavernier describes the exact location of the workshops in the Maidān quarter.[3] But woollen carpets

[1] Schillinger, p. 149. [2] Niño Jesús, p. 100. [3] Tavernier 1, 444.

were also woven in Iṣfahān, for Tavernier writes on another occasion: "The *Karkrone* is the house of the royal manufactories where fine carpets of gold, silver, silk and wool, together with gold and silver brocade, velvet, taffeta and other such fabrics are made."[1]

The pro-European policy of Shah 'Abbās drew many Europeans to Persia as envoys, traders and missionaries, and their reports are of great help in determining the origin of silk textiles brocaded with gold and silver. By comparison with these representative showpieces the woollen carpets seem to have been far less impressive and unworthy of detailed description. Thus we learn nothing about the designs peculiar perhaps to certain localities. A highly interesting exception is the description by Engelbert Kaempfer of the banqueting hall, probably in Iṣfahān, during an audience on 30 July 1684. He writes: "The most striking adornment of the banqueting hall was to my mind the carpets laid out over all three rostra in a most extravagant fashion, mostly woollen rugs from Kirmān with animal patterns and woven of the finest wool".[2] Other sources with which I am familiar are content with brief allusions which at best merely indicate the quality.

Kāshān is mentioned most frequently, always as outstanding for the manufacture of silk, and it was still named as the centre of this industry by Chardin as late as 1670.[3] A report for the years 1607–8 notes that here carpets of gold and silk, fine brocades and velvets, satin and fabrics of many kinds were worked.[4] D. Garcia de Silva y Figueroa, who visited the town in 1618, considers the carpets made there to be the most beautiful in all Persia and on a par with those of Iṣfahān.[5] Unfortunately, it is not clear from the account whether silk or woollen rugs are meant. Subsequently Kāshān appears to have been superseded by Iṣfahān in the manufacture of carpets. Pedro Teixeira, who left Goa in 1604 and journeyed to Europe via Persia, judges the carpets of Yazd to be the best, followed by those from the province of Kirmān and then those of Khurāsān.[6] Chardin also speaks of carpet factories in Kirmān and particularly in Sīstān.[7] On the other hand, in 1636–7 Adam Olearius avers that the best carpets come from Herat.[8] Tadeusz Krusiński, looking back in about 1720 over the reign of Shah 'Abbās, enumerates as the places where the latter established royal workshops the provinces of Shīrvān, Qarābāgh, Gīlān, Kāshān, Kirmān, Mashhad,

[1] *Ibid.*, 654.
[2] Kaempfer, p. 202.
[3] Chardin III, 3–4.
[4] Niño Jesús, p. 102.
[5] Silva y Figueroa, p. 210.
[6] Teixeira, p. 243.
[7] Chardin IV, 154.
[8] Olearius, p. 548.

Astarābād and the capital Iṣfahān.[1] Thus the following weaving centres emerge: Kāshān for brocaded silk carpets, Iṣfahān for brocaded silk carpets and woollen carpets, for the latter in addition Yazd, the provinces of Kirmān and Khurāsān with Herat. That Tabrīz is mentioned only once, about 1700, may perhaps be explained by the fact that the evidence is no earlier than the 17th century, while Tabrīz ranked as a place of importance during the first half of the 16th century.

Over against these centres we have clearly defined groups of Safavid carpets that have subsequently been distinguished. The categories are based on various criteria, so that some are named after peculiarities of design, such as the vase and garden carpets, while others are named after the provenance once attributed to them, for instance the "Polonaise" carpets, the Herats, Iṣfahāns and Kāshāns. Only in the case of these so-called "Polonaise" carpets is it possible to correlate them on the basis of the materials used, silk, gold and silver. In the case of every category it seems to me supremely difficult to assign them to one or other of the weaving centres mentioned. The assumptions as to their origin which have gained credence over the years are purely hypothetical and such designations as north-west Persia or Tabrīz, southern Persia or Kirmān, eastern Persia or Herat should be regarded as paraphrases serving to identify the various types rather than as accurate descriptions of their provenance. Hitherto the only expert to decline to make definite assertions about their origin because of the lack of evidence has been A. C. Edwards. Perhaps one day town chronicles, workshop reports or copies of designs will come to light and clarify the situation, but this is probably wishful thinking.

Principles of composition

Quite apart from the special characteristics which distinguish different types and provenances, Safavid carpets and with them all Oriental carpets, are designed according to definite principles. The most obvious of these is the division into an almost invariably rectangular inner field, and an enclosing border which consists of a main central stripe and two or more guard-stripes. In the design of the field one finds in general a continuous, usually multi-layered arrangement of small or large repeating patterns, from which a section is chosen and sur-

[1] Krusiński, chap. 232, A. 219.

rounded by the border. The attention paid to symmetry is characteristic. Most common of all is the quaternate symmetrical layout, in which the pattern is arranged like mirror images on the longitudinal and the transverse axes of the carpet and which determines the composition of the late Timurid rug and of the awning on the Bihzād miniature illustrated. This design is also apparent, though less clearly, in the small-sectioned panel design (see pl. 4) and in patterns composed of scrolling tendrils (see pl. 9). It is most easily recognised on medallion carpets. Here, in the centre of the carpet, and on a second level, as it were, a medallion is superimposed on the quaternate symmetrical section from the panel design. The composition of the ground may be formed by a small repeating pattern constantly reciprocated (see pl. 8), or alternatively the unit of design may be so large that it constitutes a whole quarter of the carpet (see pl. 6). The design consists as a rule of two layers, for instance a more broadly drawn primary tendril system with a secondary filling tendril motif (see pl. 6), or a system of tendrils on which is superimposed a design of figures and animals (see pl. 7). Sometimes the ground is filled like that of a miniature with trees, flowering shrubs, animals and hunting scenes (see pl. 13). If only one medallion is superimposed, it serves merely to emphasise the central point of the carpet. Usually, however, the central medallion is complemented by the repetition of a quarter of this medallion in each of the four corners of the field, thereby showing that it is part of a second repeating pattern and of a more extensive arrangement of offset medallions. The medallions of the early Safavid carpets have an unbroken linear contour and vary from starshaped and round to ogival. They are found on other textiles as early as the 15th century. The internal design of the early Safavid medallions is isolated from the pattern of the ground and does not extend beyond the edges of the medallion. Ancillary forms are frequently added to these medallions, generally an obliquely-set cartouche and a shield-like appendage on the longitudinal axis on either side; these are treated just as independently. In the case of 17th-century carpets, on the other hand, particularly the so-called "Polonaise" carpets, the independence of medallion and ground gives way to an interrelationship in that the tendrils of the background invade the medallion and *vice versa*. The medallions with a linear outline are replaced by formations of symmetrically arranged forked leaves which are integrated with the tendrils of the ground (see pl. 15*b*) and which go back partly to the filling motifs of the earlier medallions. Thus the medallion of this "Polonaise" carpet corresponds to the internal design of the medallion of the silk carpet illustrated on plate 15*a*.

In addition to the carpets with a quaternate symmetrical design, there are others of which the patterns form mirror images only along the longitudinal axis (see pl. 10). Examples without any axial symmetry are more rare. They are always adorned with figures and have a picture-like character. Interesting intermediate stages are seen in the carpets on plates 12 and 13.

Another type of design is the division of the surface into compartments that can be arranged both in the quaternate symmetrical fashion and in an ascending manner. These "compartment rugs" are directly connected with late Timurid book illumination and with Bihzād and the Herat school. The earliest example is probably a carpet in the Metropolitan Museum, New York (pl. 4). Here light-coloured, concavely and convexly undulating bands intersect and circumscribe shield-like panels arranged concentrically around octafoils. Rows of star motifs are produced between which other rather smaller octafoil rosettes are inserted as connecting links, so that the pattern covers the whole surface like a web. The incomplete stars on the longer sides indicate that here once again we have a section of an endless pattern. A tent in a miniature of the Herat school dating from 1486 is decorated on the same principle.[1] The larger medallions of the carpet illustrated on plate 4 depict the battle of the dragon and the phoenix; the smaller ones each contain four beasts drawn from Chinese mythology, the lions or dogs of Fo, and the shields alternately contain symmetrical spiral tendrils with terminal arabesque leaves and birds. The remaining portions of the ground are filled with scrolling tendrils and cloud-bands. The whole is framed by a border of cartouches linked by rosettes or small circular intermediate shapes. There are several examples of this among Safavid carpets. Because of the subtle design one can without hesitation ascribe this compartment rug and its counterpart in the Musée des Tissus, Lyons, to the first half of the 16th century. What is clearly a later pair of carpets has the same panel design as that upon which the medallion of the carpet on plate 8 is superimposed in the centre.[2] Another pair of carpets shows a variation in

[1] Sakisian, *La miniature persane*, pl. LXIV, fig. 109.

[2] Österreichisches Museum für angewandte Kunst, Vienna; its counterpart in *SPA*, pl. 1125.

which shields and quatrefoils are arranged in alternating rows.[1] Sections from similar patterns were also used as borders (see pl. 9). The penetration of the compartments which is familiar from the carpets in Bihzād's miniatures was repeated in the case of another carpet in the Metropolitan Museum, which has intersecting cartouches, and in the case of a pair of "Polonaise" carpets in the same collection. [2] The former carpet is so close to the vase carpets in its colouring that it could not have originated at the same period as our initial example but rather belongs – like the pair of "Polonaise" carpets – to the beginning of the 17th century. An essential difference is the fact that in these later examples the filling motif of spiral tendrils is not tailored to fit the individual fields but they overlap each other. The division of the surface into rhomb-shaped compartments formed by tendrils or lanceolate leaves is a common feature of the vase carpets.

Apart from carpets with closely corresponding patterns which may well, however, have been produced at different periods, there are many matching pairs where sometimes the one carpet is a reciprocating image of the other. At least some of these must have been intended for use in pairs. Such a pair of carpets is depicted on a miniature painted about 1540 by Mīr 'Alī Tabrīzī.[3] The so-called "Polonaise" carpets in particular often exist in pairs. The carpets featured on plates 4 and 6 also have exactly matching companion pieces and one could list a whole series of other examples.

The representation of figures shows the influence of miniature painting. The symbolic motifs of dragon and phoenix, crane, Ch'i-lin, cloud-bands and -whisps are of Chinese origin. They were already common elements in Timurid book illumination and found their way into carpet and textile patterns through Timurid and Safavid miniatures. Figured carpets reached the zenith of their development during the reign of Shah Ṭahmāsp in the 16th century. The finest example is a silk hunting carpet with an amazingly close weave of some 12,000 knots per square decimetre; formerly in the possession of the Habsburg dynasty, it is now in the Österreichisches Museum für angewandte Kunst in Vienna (pl. 13). Just as the formal medallion design characteristic of the 16th century disappears almost completely in the 17th century, so too in this same period carpets modelled on miniatures decline in importance, and the few pieces which, owing to

[1] Österreichisches Museum für angewandte Kunst; its counterpart in Sarre and Trenkwald II, pl. 17.
[2] *SPA*, pl. 1223. Dimand, *Handbook*, p. 379, fig. 249.
[3] Grube, *World of Islam*, p. 127.

the decadence of the design, cannot be assigned to the 16th century are simply offshoots of the carpets of the early Safavid era.

Prayer rugs occupy a special position, since their design is governed by their function. A characteristic feature of the field design is the niche form, the point of which is directed towards Mecca during prayer. This form is in imitation of the *miḥrāb*, which in a mosque points in the direction of Mecca, the *qibla*. There are some prayer rugs with a single niche and others with several. Scarcely any Persian examples survive from the 16th and 17th centuries. The earliest is the fragment of a prayer rug with a pattern arranged in rows in the Museum für Islamische Kunst in Berlin (pl. 5). It does not allow us to draw any conclusion as to the number of niches arranged side by side and one above the other. Stripes with light-coloured tendrils on a red ground delineate the individual fields. Narrower bands separate the niches and the surviving spandrels. The niches and spandrels are executed alternately in light and dark colours. The design of the spandrels consists in each case of scrolling tendrils with terminal arabesque leaves which in their elegance and refinement are remarkably reminiscent of a fabric serving as a coverlet on a miniature dated 1514.[1] The formation of the niches differs from one row to another. The accuracy and richness of the design indicate that it originated in the early Safavid period, but it is also possible that it dates from the Timurid era, as F. Sarre suggested.[2] There is nothing to indicate its place of origin. In the case of another type of prayer rug with only one niche, the spandrels and the borders of the upper half are adorned with verses.[3] There are thirty-seven rugs of this kind in the Topkapı Sarayı in Istanbul, clearly Turkish in origin and dating from the 19th century. It is not known whether these are copies of 16th century Persian originals or whether the examples hitherto thought to be Persian themselves belong to this Turkish group.[4] The same problem occurs with the stylistically closely related medallion carpets of the so-called "Salting" group named after a carpet from the Salting Collection in the Victoria and Albert Museum.[5]

"North-west Persian" medallion carpets

These fall into different categories which may be broadly divided into two groups of contrasting styles. In the one group, represented by the

[1] Stchoukine, *Manuscrits Ṣafavīs*, pl. V.
[2] Sarre and Trenkwald II, caption to pl. 50.
[3] *Ibid.*, pl. 51.
[4] Erdmann, review, pp. 164–5, and *Siebenhundert Jahre*, p. 162.
[5] *SPA*, pl. 1162.

Ardabīl carpet (pl. 6) which is dated 1539–40, the drawing is sinuous; in the other, best exemplified by the Milan hunting carpet of 1522–3 (pl. 7), the drawing is rigid and angular. Over against scrolling tendrils with flowing convolutions we have a lattice of straight lengths of tendril and almost rectangular offshoots. Since the inscriptions vouch for a not too long difference of time in production of both carpets, the differences cannot be ascribed to a progression or degeneration from one type to another. The reason for assigning a common origin to them was presumably the fact that both must have been produced in a court manufactory and that at the time they were woven the seat of government was still in Tabrīz.

The same disparity between figured and angular forms occurs in the case of medallion carpets with a purely representational pattern, said to have originated in north-west Persia. Examples of the former kind are an animal carpet in Milan and the so-called "Chelsea" carpet in the Victoria and Albert Museum, which is also interesting for the unusually large pattern section of offset medallions connected diagonally by pointed ovals and which, judging by its design, falls between the Ardabīl carpet and the compartment rug (pl. 4) described above.[1] The second kind is represented by a medallion carpet with a white ground, formerly in the Clarence H. Mackay Collection, and its companion piece in the Islamisches Museum, East Berlin – a rug which was largely destroyed during the last war.[2]

In a less complex type the medallions are superimposed upon a continuous, somewhat clumsily drawn design with a small repeating pattern. Figured motifs do not occur in these cases. One of the best pieces of this kind which, unfortunately, has not survived in its original size of some 10 × 3.95 metres will serve as an example (pl. 8). The plate is a photographic montage. The central portion of the carpet as far as a point just beyond the partial shield of the medallion has long since belonged to the Victoria and Albert Museum. A quarter of the missing piece with the corner was acquired a few years ago by the New York collector Joseph V. McMullan and it enabled experts to reconstruct the carpet. The pattern of the background, as is predominant in carpets of this kind, consists of a repeating pattern of very slender symmetrical scrolling tendrils terminating in arabesque leaves. At the

[1] Sarre and Trenkwald II, pls. 29–30 and 15–16.
[2] *Ibid.*, pl. 27. Erdmann, trans. Ellis, pl. 50.

point where the spirals touch, palmettes are superimposed. The medallion formed by interlocking multi-coloured fields is reminiscent of the cartouche carpets. The border characteristic of this type is composed of a repeating pattern of short reciprocating interlacing arabesques.

"Herat" or "Iṣfahān" carpets

The most outstanding features of this group are large palmettes superimposed in many variations upon a quaternate symmetrical arrangement of very slender scrolling tendrils. Medallions are rare. The ground is generally crimson, the borders dark blue or dark green. Within this group again two types can be distinguished. In the earlier kind belonging to the 16th century (pl. 9) the design is very compact and interwoven with many cloud-bands. The ends of the tendrils are not emphasised. A few pieces have details picked out with metal thread. Animals – partly creatures from Far Eastern mythology such as the stag Ch'i-lin and dragons – and beasts preying on one another are often incorporated in the pattern. The best animal carpet of this kind, together with a similar fragment, is in the Österreichisches Museum für angewandte Kunst in Vienna.[1] The Far Eastern motifs were doubtless responsible for these carpets being attributed to eastern Persia. This provenance has yet to be proved to be correct, although it is known that carpets of high quality were indeed produced in Khurāsān and its capital Herat. The carpets decorated with scrolling tendrils which are depicted on the miniatures of the Herat school lack the large palmettes and cannot be classified as "Herat" carpets.

In the later type the floral designs are simplified, cloud-bands are less frequent, and there are no animals. Along with the palmettes large lanceolate leaves attached to the ends of the tendrils and often divided into different coloured halves dominate the pattern. The borders consist mostly of repeating patterns of sinuous S-shaped tendrils terminating in lanceolate leaves, and of large palmettes superimposed at the tangential points of the single units of design. The same borders are found on the "Polonaise" carpets, and it is surely right to assume that they were produced in the same period, namely the 17th century. Whether this type of "Herat" carpet is synonymous with the woollen carpets of Iṣfahān

[1] Sarre and Trenkwald I, pl. 7.

and thus represents a style characteristic of Iṣfahān, or whether the "Polonaise" carpets are merely influenced by this group, remains an open question. It was recently suggested that some of them might stem from India, and so we find the term "Indo-Iṣfahān". We know that such carpets were exported to India and were also imitated there. In the palace of Jaipur even today there is a whole series of examples. Precise distinctions between Indian and Persian pieces of this kind have never to my knowledge been traced: at least no findings have been published.

These later "Herat" carpets must have been a commodity highly prized by Europeans, for apart from the fact that a large number are still extant they were reproduced relatively often in paintings, particularly in the pictures of 17th-century Dutch genre painters; they occurred above all in Holland and Portugal. Through the East India companies both these countries cultivated close trading links with Persia and India. Thus Joan Cunaeus, an envoy of the Dutch East India Company, reports that in 1651–2 he purchased forty-nine carpets in Iṣfahān and had them brought overland to Hurmuz, where they were shipped to the company base at Batavia and thence to Holland.[1] At the beginning of the 17th century Pedro Teixeira writes of the trade with the Portuguese in Hurmuz: "There usually come from all the provinces of Persia to Harmuz large caravans or cafilas, to trade with the Portuguese and other Christians, and the heathen and Moors that reside there, and to barter what they bring, namely gold, silver, raw and manufactured silk, brocades, carpets, horses, madder, alum, tuthiáth, rhubarb, rose-water, and divers other commodities".[2]

The "Sanguszko" group

In the case of woollen carpets the influence of miniature painting is most clearly seen in the twelve or so carpets of the so-called "Sanguszko" group. The designation derives from the carpet which at the London Exhibition of Persian Art in 1931 provided the stimulus for the classifying of this group and which belonged to Prince Roman Sanguszko.[3]

Although almost all of the carpets belonging to the group have a medallion design, I have chosen as my example the fragment from the

[1] Cunaeus, pp. 340, 346, 348. [2] Teixeira, p. 252.

[3] *SPA*, pl. 1206: at present in the Metropolitan Museum of Art, New York, on loan from Mr and Mrs E. Seley.

Maciet Collection now exhibited in the Musée des Arts Décoratifs in Paris (pl. 12), because here, independently of each other, quite definite themes from miniature painting were taken up, and the connections and influences therefore emerge particularly clearly. Thus we see – in each case twice repeated like mirror images along the longitudinal axis – in the upper zone Shīrīn discovered in the pool by Khusrau, and underneath a hunting scene, then Lailā with the dying Majnūn in the desert. On the longitudinal axis the symmetry is broken by the introduction of supplementary figures. There results a cross between a textile pattern, which through reflection and sequence is potentially capable of infinite extension, and a picture. A fine example of this is the silk hunting carpet in Vienna (pl. 13) to which the whole group is closely related formally. Since the rugs of the Sanguszko type reveal the same degree of stylistic development as the figured silk tapestry-woven carpets which we know from documentary evidence to have been manufactured in Kāshān – a stage illustrated among other things by the preference for ogival medallions and an increasing amount of stippling on animals and garments – K. Erdmann believes that they too originated in Kāshān. A.U. Pope, on the other hand, proposes Yazd or Kirmān.[1] In texture and in its individual scatter motifs the carpet illustrated corresponds to the "vase" carpets. The rugs of the Sanguszko group date back to the second half of the 16th century.

"Vase" carpets

The name derives from flower-filled vessels in the form of Chinese porcelain vases which occur on many of these carpets. On the rug illustrated (pl. 10) the vase is in the centre. Vase carpets are distinguished by a wealth of colour and vegetable forms. In addition to the most fantastically executed rosettes and facetted palmettes the characteristics include stylised lilies, naturalistic flowering shrubs and snailshell-like motifs that represent perhaps the remnants of shrunken cloud knots.

With few exceptions the patterns unfold in an ascending direction, and form mirror images along the longitudinal axis. Usually they go back to a rhomboid design. For the most part the lozenge shapes are formed as in our example by several tangential and intersecting tendrils

[1] *SPA*, pp. 2270–82, and Erdmann, review, pp. 164–5.

which, on a monochrome ground, are far less marked than the flowers. However, they may also be clearly framed by tendrils or wide lanceolate leaves and filled in different colours.[1] The symmetry of the design is quite often relieved by an asymmetrical colour pattern. There are also vase carpets without any marked rhomboid design but with interlaced rows of offset flower vases or shrubs.[2] In the case of two examples with an unusual composition in the McMullan Collection a medallion and corner pieces are superimposed on an ascending pattern of this kind, against the rules of the medallion design.[3] Pieces with an arabesque pattern and medallions are also found.[4] In the main, two borders were used. One of them, which has a repeating pattern of two interlaced arabesque tendrils, can be seen in the illustration. The other is very narrow and enclosed not by secondary stripes but merely by bands. The pattern consists of rosettes or palmettes alternating with squares of tiny flowers and a diagonal stem. The narrow borders and the elongated format have led some scholars to suppose that these vase carpets were intended for the floors of mosques. One or two examples whose irregular outlines are adapted to the ground-plan of a building,[5] the strong construction produced by a layered, so to speak double, arrangement of the warp, and the relatively large number of fragments appear to confirm this.

Regarding the chronological sequence of individual patterns and the question of which "vase" carpets to assign to the 16th century and which to the 17th, opinions vary. I cannot believe that the variations in design succeeded one another in time, but consider rather that they existed side by side and that their dating must be based on the quality of the detail. A few fragments with a luxuriant and animated design and particularly well executed detail correspond stylistically to the best "Polonaise" carpets and are doubtless contemporary with them – that is, they were woven at the beginning of the 17th century.[6] The problem is whether the more distinctly drawn, formalised pieces in the main group represent the antecedents or a subsequent development of these fragments. In some an unambiguous degeneration is seen in the impoverishment of the design; in the case of others which are still very rich

[1] *SPA*, pl. 1221; Erdmann, review, pls. 20, 21, 22.
[2] Sarre and Trenkwald I, pl. 24. *SPA*, pl. 1231.
[3] McMullan, pls. 17, 18.
[4] *Ibid.*, pls. 20, 21. Sarre and Trenkwald I, pl. 31.
[5] Erdmann, *Siebenhundert Jahre*, pl. 274. *SPA*, pls. 1238, 1218.
[6] Erdmann, review, pls. 19, 22.

despite an apparently more simple pattern, it is exceptionally difficult to reach a conclusion. Judgments will remain subjective. The vase carpet dated 1656 in the Sarajevo Museum is not a typical example and does not help us very much. Its design is to my mind remarkably good and suggests that the majority of vase carpets were produced in the 17th century.

Garden carpets

Garden carpets (pl. 33) are representations of Persian gardens with their strict geometrical and rectangular composition, with canals and ponds where ducks and fish swim and which are bordered by multifarious trees and shrubs. Between them play birds and mammals. The Persian rulers were passionately fond of splendid gardens, and so the Safavid period saw the establishment of the gardens of Hazār Jarīb near Iṣfahān, extolled by 17th-century European travellers, and the garden laid out in 1612 by Shah 'Abbās in Ashraf, in the province of Māzandarān. The carpet illustrated corresponds to the vase carpets in technique, colouring and the detail of the pattern, such as the two vases on a level with the middle watercourse and the interspersed snailshell-like forms. The quality of design is akin to that of a garden carpet measuring 28′8″ by 12′3½″ in the Jaipur Museum which is probably the earliest piece in this group.[1] On the reverse there is an inscription which records that this "foreign carpet" arrived at the Palace of Jaipur on 29 August 1632. The carpet had probably been woven shortly before and brought from Persia to India as a gift or as a commission.

The rigid formalisation and geometrical nature of every shape distinguishes what is definitely a later type from its Safavid predecessors.[2] It certainly did not develop until the 18th century and is held to be north-west Persian or Caucasian in origin.

"Portuguese" carpets

Since the same kind of design is common to them all, these constitute the most uniform group (pl. 11). Erdmann lists nine examples surviving in their entirety and three fragments.[3] They were given their name

[1] Dimand, "A Persian Garden Carpet", p. 93.
[2] *SPA*, pl. 1270. McMullan, pl. 29. Erdmann, *Siebenhundert Jahre*, p. 149.
[3] *Jahrbuch der Hamburger Kunstsammlungen* VI (1961), 156.

because of the scenes depicted in the spandrels which have been construed as the arrival of a Portuguese embassy in the Persian Gulf, and also because it was assumed that these carpets were intended for the Portuguese in Goa. They show a mixture of European and Oriental motifs in a highly unusual arrangement. A rhomboid central panel with four small ogival medallions and a serrated and pinnate outline is surrounded by concentric interlocking stripes of different colours. In the early examples they are animated and have irregular protrusions. In the later ones they are straight, run exactly parallel and are evenly stepped. The stripes fill the surface except for the spandrels in each of which there can be seen two sailing ships with people on board dressed in European fashion, and next to these a man emerging from the water and waving to the ships, the head of a sea monster and a few fish. This scene must be derived from a European model, possibly from a map. The border is related to the panel design of some arabesque carpets.[1]

As in the case of the "Herat" carpets, the origin of the Portuguese rugs has been traced both to Persia and to India. E. Kühnel believes them to be indubitably Persian. K. Erdmann and he propound southern Persia as their provenance. C. E. C. Tattersall suggests Kāshān. A.U. Pope, on the other hand, opts for Goa (Portuguese India). The latter opinion rests more on the unusual character of the "Portuguese" carpets compared with other Persian rugs than on any inherent resemblance to Indian carpets, which is itself no more convincing. The whole group would seem to belong to the 17th century.

How the same theme could subsequently be repeated in the Caucasian region is likewise a mystery.[2] Furthermore, two small silk carpets which fall between the "Polonaise" rugs and the "Portuguese" carpets are designed on the same principle, though without the scenes in the spandrels.[3]

Silk carpets of the 16th century and tapestry-woven carpets

The changes which took place between the 16th and the 17th centuries can be traced particularly clearly in the case of the silk carpets.

The earliest and most impressive example is the Vienna hunting carpet (pl. 13). It represents the climax of the rugs modelled on minia-

[1] *Ibid.*, pls. 3, 1.
[2] Bode and Kühnel, pl. 79.
[3] *Orientalische Teppiche*, Tf. LV, Abb. 73; the other is in the Walters Art Gallery, Baltimore, Inv. no. 81.5 (unpublished).

tures that were produced in the reign of Shah Ṭahmāsp. A large part of the detail is picked out in gold and silver thread. Its size – 6.93 × 3.23 metres – corresponds to that of the great woollen knotted carpets. There was a somewhat smaller silk carpet of almost identical quality in the collection of Baron Maurice de Rothschild and now belonging to the Museum of Fine Arts, Boston. The provenance is believed to be Tabrīz or Kāshān, which was famous for its silk industry. With these two carpets is associated a group of some thirteen small silk carpets (see pl. 15*a*) which K. Erdmann calls "the small silk carpets of Kāshān".[1] The majority likewise have a medallion design into which, in the case of an example in the Gulbenkian Collection, animal figures and beasts preying on one another are introduced. Apart from this example such figures rarely occur in this group, in fact on only four rugs with an ascending, asymmetrical pattern which are picture carpets pure and simple. The representation of human beings and peris is not found on these rugs.

On the other hand, these motifs do occur together with scenes of animals fighting on some woven silk carpets which with two exceptions are similarly of small format. The representational tapestry-woven carpets are closely related to the carpets of the "Sanguszko" group and reveal the same stage of stylistic development. A decisive innovation *vis-à-vis* the knotted silk carpets is the use of brocade not only to pick out detail but over whole panels. The Munich hunting carpet,[2] which unfortunately does not survive in its entirety, is outstanding among tapestry-woven carpets by virtue of its size, the excellence of the design and the hunting scenes which link it directly with the Vienna hunting carpet. In addition to the example illustrated (pl. 14) two small tapestry-woven rugs similar to our example are also associated with it, as are the remnants of a once large piece and three carpets in Berlin, Washington and Copenhagen with a dragon and a phoenix in the central medallion and slender flowering tendrils on the ground; these last three are known as "Pādishāh" carpets because of the inscription on the Berlin example.[3] The designs of all these tapestry-woven rugs contain ogival medallions with transverse cartouches and partial shields, typical secondary motifs of the early Safavid period. They are framed by borders of alternating cartouches and polyfoils.

Besides the figured tapestry-woven carpets, there is a second con-

[1] Erdmann, *Siebenhundert Jahre*, p. 143.
[2] Sarre and Trenkwald II, pl. 47.
[3] Erdmann, "Persische Wirkteppiche", p. 227, and "Ein persischer Wirkteppich", p. 62. Spuhler, "Der figurale Kaschan-Wirkteppich", p. 55.

trasting group with a purely floral design. These include a complete carpet in Munich[1] and half a carpet in Washington incorporating the arms of King Sigismund III Vasa of Poland. It is certain that these are two of the carpets which Sigismund commissioned through Sefer Muratowicz in Kāshān in 1601. An invoice dated 12 September 1602 lists pairs of carpets and a sum of five crowns for the execution of the royal coat of arms.[2] On the occasion of the marriage of the Polish princess Anna Catherina Constanza, the daughter of Sigismund III, to the Elector Palatine Philipp Wilhelm, an unknown quantity of carpets came into the possession of the Wittelsbachs in 1642 as a dowry. Among them was doubtless the tapestry-woven carpet adorned with the coat of arms, and probably the other tapestry rugs and "Polonaise" carpets now in Munich. The heraldic carpets provide evidence of the stage of stylistic development attained by tapestry-woven carpets round about 1600. In their case we perceive a simplification and a coarsening of the drawing, compared with the figured tapestry carpets and particularly with the Pādishāh carpets, in respect of the tendrils of the background, the large flowers and the lanceolate leaves. This would suggest that the figured pieces – with the exception of a tapestry-woven rug in the Louvre showing Bahrām Gūr vanquishing the dragon, and the one in the Thyssen Collection in Rohoncz castle, near Lugano, with a repeating pattern of cartouches, polyfoils and shields – date from the latter half of the 16th century. When comparing them with the knotted silk hunting carpets it must be remembered that for technical reasons a tapestry-woven rug cannot match a knotted carpet of the greatest density for delicacy of design. Correspondingly a chronological sequence can be established in the case of the floral examples by drawing stylistic comparisons with the heraldic carpets and a pair of embroidered silk carpets in the Rosenborg Castle in Copenhagen, which together with other textiles were brought to Europe in 1639 by a Persian embassy to Duke Friedrich of Holstein-Gottorp and which reveal in the centre a star-shaped medallion with two opposite phoenixes. This sequence begins with a few tapestry-woven carpets in the latter half of the 16th century[3] and continues to the end of the 17th century. It is characteristic of these pieces that the close link with the early Safavid carpets remains unimpaired by the stylistic development that occurred in silk carpets about 1600.

[1] *SPA*, pl. 1268B. [2] Mańkowski, p. 152. [3] E.g. *SPA*, pl. 1266.

"Polonaise" carpets

The production of silk knotted carpets was markedly increased under Shah 'Abbās I and these carpets form the only group in which a completely new style developed at the beginning of the 17th century, quite distinct from 16th-century rules of composition (see pl. 15*b*). The misnomer has been the subject of criticism ever since the appearance of the catalogue of the Exhibition of Oriental Carpets in Vienna in 1891, in which A. Riegl disputed the alleged Polish provenance of these carpets. There has been no lack of alternative suggestions, but none have been sufficiently apposite to replace the original name which by now has become a *terminus technicus.* The total of some two hundred and thirty extant examples shows in what numbers these rugs were produced, for they were not – as was once assumed – destined exclusively for export or as gifts for European rulers, but equally, as showpieces, formed part of the furnishing of Safavid palaces. On this point 17th-century travellers' reports leave us in no doubt.

As with the tapestry-woven carpets, large panels and often the whole ground of the "Polonaise" carpets are brocaded. Nowadays the distribution of gold and silver can be discerned only from the yellow or white silk cores of the interwoven threads, since the metal covering has largely dropped off or been oxidised. The colours of the silk pile, particularly the salmon pink, the bright tomato red, and the shades of green and yellow are as a rule badly faded. In the case of the example illustrated the original colours are still visible on the reverse. The costliness of the materials led to economies which are evident in the predominantly small size of the silk carpets and also, in the case of the "Polonaise" rugs, in the use of cotton for the foundation. A warp and weft wholly of silk is found only in those few antecedents and early examples where the style of the main group is not yet fully defined and which are very delicately and linearly drawn.[1] It is characteristic of the typical "Polonaise" carpets, on the other hand, that they transfer the emphasis from the linear to the planar, a change which finds expression above all in the abandonment of the monochrome ground. The scrolling tendrils are reduced to the function of demarcating the irregular panels which they describe and which are filled in different colours, thereby standing out independently. With this tendency to juxtapose

[1] *Ibid.*, pls. 1242, 1243.

grounds of different shades instead of contrasting them with one another as on the early medallion carpets, it is not surprising that compartment patterns are revived. Through the abandonment of the unified background and the clear delineation of the medallions, the latter are incorporated into the panel design and lose their overriding function. Where they appear to be preserved the medallions are almost always dependent upon a cartouche pattern ranged beneath them and merely serve as overlapping rosettes at the tangential points of the units of design or as filling motifs. In the detail, the abjuring of clear contours and lines is seen in a baroque luxuriance of forms and an accumulation of short encircling tendrils and fan-shaped miniature leaves. The most important individual device is the arabesque leaf which to a large extent determines the composition and acts as a terminal motif in the primary tendril system. The broad lanceolate leaves in the secondary tendril motif and the palmettes are reminiscent of the late type of "Herat" carpet.

The large number of surviving "Polonaise" carpets provides us with an insight into the technique of sketching the designs. The patterns are derived – with only one or two exceptions – from thirteen designs constantly varied by the choice of different sections, medallions or colours, so that, for instance, there is almost always a series of smaller carpets dependent upon the few large pieces. Over and above these connections we can discern fifty-two matching pairs where the companion pieces correspond even in their borders and colour schemes.

The Europeans who visited Persia in the 17th century were so impressed by the splendour of the silk carpets brocaded with gold and silver that in their reports, as I related in my introduction, they supply us with a considerable amount of evidence which enables us to assign these rugs to Kāshān and Iṣfahān and to fix their dates. The brocaded silk carpets of Kāshān were already known abroad in 1601. The transfer of the Court doubtless brought about the establishment in Iṣfahān around 1600 of the manufactories described by Tavernier in the Maidān quarter. It is probable that the uniform style revealed by the majority of "Polonaise" carpets developed as a result of the connection with the Court in Iṣfahān at the beginning of the 17th century and that the finest examples, of which the carpet illustrated is one, go back to the first quarter of the century. As far as the early examples are concerned, it may be assumed that they originated towards the end of the 16th century. In 1599 Sir Anthony Sherley was presented by Shah

'Abbās I with eighteen carpets brocaded with gold.[1] Those "Polonaise" carpets, where the quality of the design markedly deteriorates and the degeneration becomes obvious in the decline and rigid formalisation of individual motifs, were probably woven in the second half of the 17th century, and some unimportant examples as late as 1700. Krusiński reports that in 1722 the destruction of the Safavid empire by the Afghans put an end to the manufacture of brocaded textiles.[2]

On a par with the best "Polonaise" carpets is the cope knotted entirely on silk (pl. 16), which by virtue of its form, composition and themes is marked out as a commission and is the only example of figured motifs being introduced into a "Polonaise" design. The extraordinarily refined drawing, the linear tendrils on a monochrome ground and the brocaded detail stamp it as one of the earliest examples, whereas the individual devices with the numerous fan-shaped miniature leaves, the palmettes, the arabesque and lanceolate leaves and the brocaded border already reflect the style typical of "Polonaise" carpets. The tendrils incorporate on the longitudinal axis the figure of Christ on the Cross flanked by Mary and John. On the upper edge Mary on the left hand and the Angel on the right together form a tableau of the Annunciation. The reproduction of Biblical events is not an innovation in Persian art since some of them are also attested by the Qur'ān. The Annunciation is described in terms similar to the Christian tradition, but the Crucifixion of Christ's person does not occur in the Qur'ān. Moreover, the manner in which the figures on the cope are depicted is by no means Persian, unlike for instance the velvet shown on plate 34; on the contrary, the scenes correspond to a late Gothic type. It is certain therefore that this ceremonial garment was commissioned by a Christian patron who himself supplied the models for the Crucifixion and Annunciation scenes.

II. TEXTILES

Miniatures convey an impression of the wide use of the most varied fabrics. Apart from being made up into garments and turbans, fabrics were used for cushions, rugs, curtains and for tents and awnings that are apparently embroidered and often sumptuous. The garments vary

[1] Ross, *Sir Anthony Sherley*, p. 94.

[2] Krusiński, p. 219.

from the most simple to luxurious ceremonial robes which were frequently donated by guests wishing to curry favour at court or which alternatively were bestowed as a form of decoration. Velvets and brocades were also used as light rugs and as coverlets for sarcophagi. In one source, unfortunately no earlier than the end of the 17th century, the royal workshop in Iṣfahān heads the list of the most important textile factories and is described as follows: "The royal weaving mill consists of various weaving shops in which silks as well as gold and silver brocades are manufactured. The director of the establishment is the Superintendent of the traders who controls and supervises the selection of patterns, the preparation of the raw materials and the storage of the completed articles. In addition he is head of all the workshops that supply the clothing needs of the royal household". The superintendent of the traders who supervised the royal weavers, dyers, tailors and silk embroiderers was at the same time merchant and trading adviser to the King.[1]

Timurid fabrics

Again we are dependent upon miniatures for our knowledge of the appearance of Timurid fabrics since, as in the case of the carpets, no examples have survived which can with certainty be ascribed to this period. The garments have a very small pattern and are dotted with golden decorative motifs arranged in even rows. These devices include groups of dots, small rosettes, stars, peony blossoms, cloud-bands and ducks. Sometimes the shoulder area is adorned as though with a medallion. There is an ornamentation of this kind executed in gold embroidery on silk and set into the original garment in the Museum of Oriental Cultures in Moscow.[2] Ackerman attributes it to the 16th century, but equally it resembles the Timurid illustrations. Sometimes the embellishment of the robes consists of a border introduced at knee level and figured ornamentation on the chest and back. In addition there are robes and cushions covered in narrow stripes and pillows with a tendril pattern. Since pre-Timurid examples of silk-twill, satin, silkcloth and double cloth enriched with gilt thread have been preserved, and furthermore an amazing number of velvets and embroidered and printed fabrics dating back to the Safavid era, it can be

[1] Kaempfer, pp. 86, 120. [2] *SPA*, pl. 1017.

assumed that in the Timurid period the same techniques were in use. We do not possess any clues as to the location of the centres where Timurid fabrics were produced. There is not the slightest difference, for instance, between the fabrics depicted on the miniatures of the two most famous schools of painters, Herat and Shīrāz.

By comparison with the Safavid miniatures tents are less frequently reproduced. Here, as with the saddle blankets – we do not know whether these were knotted or tapestry-woven – the patterns of the Safavid medallion carpets are already emerging. Similarly the tent patterns on Safavid miniatures correspond to a considerable degree to the patterns of contemporary carpets, and the same report that supplied the evidence cited above indicates that the tents were in the charge not of the director of the royal weaving mill but of the curator of the royal carpets.[1]

Safavid fabrics

In artistic terms Persian fabrics reach their peak in the figured satins and silk velvets brocaded with precious metal of the Safavid period; in addition, however, a considerable number of outstanding silks with repeating floral patterns were manufactured at that same period. A few complete garments with patterns of this kind have survived.[2] From the travel journals it emerges that the towns of Kāshān, Yazd, Iṣfahān and Tabrīz were centres of the silk industry. The sources are in part the same as those upon which I drew in discussing the origin of the "Polonaise" carpets. In 1599 Don Juan of Persia lists in addition to Iṣfahān, Kāshān and Yazd the towns of Qum and Sāva as centres for the manufacture of silks.[3] Kāshān is the place most frequently mentioned and Niño Jesús speaks of silk carpets brocaded with gilt and of "beautiful brocades and velvets, satin and fabrics of many kinds" which were made here.[4] Olearius reports that in Kāshān and Yazd fabrics adorned with figures and inscriptions were produced, while Tavernier records that the silk workers of Kāshān weave the most beautiful "gold and silver pieces" in the whole of Persia.[5] Pietro della Valle distinguishes three sorts of silk products in Kāshān: long wide sashes for men which are wound several times around the body and

[1] Krusiński, A. 120.
[2] *SPA*, pls. 1060, 1034. Glück and Diez, p. 372.
[3] Don Juan, tr. Le Strange, p. 40.
[4] Niño Jesús, p. 100.
[5] Olearius, p. 601. Tavernier I, 80.

into which, sometimes with and sometimes without gold, stripes and delicate leaf and flower patterns are woven; silks without brocade but embellished with inscriptions and figures such as men, women and beasts; and silks which differ from the latter solely by virtue of gold and silver brocade and which were destined entirely for women's garments, cushions, bed curtains and similar domestic uses.[1] Similarly the production of figured silks in Iṣfahān is attested by Raphaël du Mans,[2] and I have already cited the fact that the royal weaving mill at Iṣfahān was responsible among other things for the clothing requirements of the royal household. Tabrīz is seldom mentioned, although Chardin claims that it ranked second in importance, size, wealth, volume of trade and population and writes that it was full of artisans specialising in the manufacture of cotton, silk and gold. Here the finest turbans and six thousand bales of silk a year were produced. These statements are largely confirmed by Schillinger round about 1700; in connection with Tabrīz he also singles out figured linen fine beyond all measure.[3] The difficulty of correlating the extant fabrics with these centres is, however, just as great as in the case of the carpets, and the lack of reliable criteria prevents me from drawing detailed conclusions about their provenance.

Fabrics bearing dates of manufacture are rare. Because of their predominantly epigraphic decoration two "silk compound clothes" dated 1545 and 1669 do not permit us to draw any inferences regarding floral and figured fabrics. Eight fabrics signed "Ghiyāṯ"(e.g. pl. 18) offer a certain amount of help. Ph. Ackerman has supplied interesting biographical details about Ghiyāṯ.[4] Regrettably, however, we do not know his dates. He is described as a *naqshband*, painter and embroiderer, he was born in Yazd, where he owned a luxurious house, and he belonged to the circle which frequented the court of Shah 'Abbās I. His name was known beyond the Persian frontiers and his fabrics were highly prized. No biographical details relevant to the problem of dating are available for other extant signatures. In the case of the figured fabrics, a stylistic comparison with miniature painting reveals a few clues which justify our assigning, for instance, various pieces influenced by the style of Riżā-yi 'Abbāsī (see pl. 35) to the early 17th century. We know the dates of presentation of the Madonna fabric illustrated on plate 34 which was brought to the Signoria of Venice by a Persian

[1] Della Valle II/1, 151 ff.

[2] Du Mans, pp. 186, 195.

[3] Chardin II, 320, 327-8. Schillinger, p. 149.

[4] Ackerman, "Ghiyath the Weaver", p. 9.

embassy in 1603, and of some fabrics which Shah Ṣafī I sent with an embassy to Duke Friedrich of Holstein-Gottorp in 1637 and which are now in the Rosenborg Castle in Copenhagen.[1] They merely confirm the dating suggested by a comparison with contemporary miniatures.

The variety of Safavid fabrics makes it impossible to examine or illustrate each kind in the present review. I shall confine my choice accordingly to a few examples which can justly be described as a supreme achievement. One of the finest fabrics of the 16th century is the brocaded velvet with a red ground (pl. 17). Two staggered rows of various peris alternate on a pattern of paired scrolling tendrils with birds and whisps of cloud. The peris with two wings in the first row sit on a carpet-like platform in front of which stands a flagon. The four-winged peris in the next row sit on thrones. The peculiar headdress of pennate leaves is already worn by peris on miniatures ascribed to the latter half of the 15th century and the Herat school,[2] and it is also worn by the Madonna on the fabric illustrated on plate 34. Peris are celestial beings from Paradise who are depicted, for instance, accompanying Muḥammad's ascension or as the retinue of Solomon and the Queen of Sheba.[3] In a sitting position and, as on the velvet shown here, in conjunction with scrolling tendrils, birds and whisps of cloud, they occur in the border of the Vienna hunting carpet (pl. 13); an enthroned peri forms the centre of the medallion of the woven Munich hunting carpet,[4] and furthermore they are familiar from the tapestry-woven rug on plate 14 and the border of the woollen knotted carpet on plate 12. To a considerable degree the border of the fabric corresponds in design to the outer guard-strip of the Vienna hunting carpet; and the pairs of fish forming a palmette occur in precisely this manner on 16th century knotted carpets. On a miniature in a manuscript dated 1556 a fabric adorned with peris serves as an awning behind Majnūn's kneeling father, and they are also seen on a camel saddle painted in 1557.[5] These parallels justify the attribution of our example to the middle of the 16th century.

The eight fabrics signed "Ghiyās̱" are among the most important silks of the middle Safavid period. With the exception of a sarcophagus

[1] Martin, *Die persischen Prachtstoffe.*
[2] Sakisian, *La miniature persane*, pl. LIX, fig. 101, and pl. LXI, fig. 105.
[3] Grube, *World of Islam*, pl. 144. Stchoukine, *Manuscrits de Shāh 'Abbās*, pls. XVI, XVII.
[4] Sarre and Trenkwald II, pl. 48.
[5] Stchoukine, *Manuscrits Ṣafavīs*, pl. XLIII. Sakisian, *La miniature persane*, pl. XLIX, fig. 85.

cover with a prayer niche and an inscription border[1] they are all figured fabrics. The themes are Khusrau glimpsing Shīrīn in the pool and Majnūn being visited by Lailā in the desert. This scene appears on the brocade with a black ground illustrated on plate 18, of which several portions have been preserved. Among other things the naturalistic portrayal of the camel on which Lailā is riding in a howdah attests the great skill of Ghiyās̱. The depictions of the camel with howdah and driver and of the poet speaking to the animals have prototypes in miniature painting.[2] The question has been raised whether Ghiyās̱ was the designer, the weaver or the director of the workshop. In fact, there is no reason to distinguish so sharply between these functions, and it is quite possible that to a certain extent he combined all three rôles. At all events he was certainly responsible for the designs of the fabric signed in his name in different styles of script. It may be assumed, however, that he did not weave them all himself but supervised their execution. With the great demand for his work it is probable that he employed assistants. We know that he lived in Yazd and it is likely that he worked there too. Nevertheless, one should not exclude the possibility of his designs having been executed in Iṣfahān, since after all he attended court there and could have occupied a leading position in the royal workshops. The introduction of his signature in a prominent place and its recurrence in the repeating pattern makes a rather obtrusive impression. This habit, rare in the east, of emphasising his personal identity is shared by his contemporaries at the court of Shah ʿAbbās I in Iṣfahān, the calligrapher ʿAlī Riżā-yi ʿAbbāsī and the painter Riżā.

The latter's style influenced a series of figured fabrics such as the velvet with a metal ground in the Badisches Landesmuseum in Karlsruhe (pl. 35), fabrics which usually depict a genre scene in the repeating pattern.[3] The scene on the Karlsruhe fabric shows a youth standing in a garden with his legs lazily crossed, leaning on a stick, and, as he smells a flower, listening engrossed to an older man on his knees before him. The latter has placed his shoes on one side and in front of him there is a shallow bowl and another, unidentifiable object. This figure has been unconvincingly interpreted as a beggar. E. Kühnel describes him as a dervish. The influence of Riżā-yi ʿAbbāsī is seen in the attitude of the figures, the delicate pleating of their garments and the large, loosely sketched turban.

[1] *SPA*, pl. 1037. [2] Stchoukine, *Manuscrits Ṣafavīs*, pls. XLII, LXVI.
[3] Sarre and Mittwoch, pls. 10, 20. Stchoukine, *Manuscrits de Shāh ʿAbbās*, pls. XXXV, XXXVI.

The brocaded silk velvet on plate 34 is closely related to the Karlsruhe fabric. In addition to its history, it is interesting for the unusual theme of the scenes it incorporates, for here, in contrast to the cope on plate 16 where the groups of figures are copied from a foreign model, the Biblical event of Christ's Nativity is depicted according to the Oriental tradition and in a purely Safavid style. E. Kühnel has produced a study of Christian motifs in Persian miniatures, in which he discusses these problems of iconography. The Nativity is also described in the Qur'ān, but it differs from the Biblical account inasmuch as Mary gives birth to Jesus in solitude under a date palm and the Lord causes a rivulet to flow at her feet in order that she might be refreshed (ṣūra xix. 24–7). In connection with this theme, which he notes is very rarely treated, Kühnel reproduces two 16th-century miniatures, and Stchoukine another dating from the beginning of the 17th century.[1] On the fabric the palm tree is replaced by a flowering shrub which with the bird perched upon it is very similar to the bushes on the Karlsruhe velvet, where indeed the spring with the fish also recurs. Mary is nursing the baby Jesus and both are adorned with the flaming halo of holiness. The figure facing this group and holding a cloth in readiness does not belong to the Nativity scene as described in the Qur'ān and cannot therefore be explained by reference to the account we find there.

The fabrics influenced by Riżā-yi 'Abbāsī, paintings and the "Polonaise" carpets represent in equal measure the courtly style encouraged by Shah 'Abbās I at the beginning of the 17th century.

Public collections of oriental carpets and fabrics

In Europe the most important collection is that of the Österreichisches Museum für angewandte Kunst in Vienna. Then comes the Victoria and Albert Museum, London. The once exemplary collection in Berlin was badly hit by extensive wartime losses. The remaining pieces are now housed in the Islamisches Museum (East Berlin) and the Museum für Islamische Kunst, Stiftung Preuss. Kulturbesitz (West Berlin). Without arranging them in order of size or completeness, I must also mention the collections of the following: the Rijksmuseum, Amsterdam; the David Collection and the Rosenborg Castle, Copenhagen; the

[1] *Ibid.*, pl. XXIII.

Museo Bardini, Florence; the Burrell Collection (recently opened to the public) belonging to the Art Gallery and Museum, Glasgow; the Museum für Kunst und Gewerbe, Hamburg; the Türk ve İslam Eserleri Müzesi, Istanbul; the Hermitage in Leningrad; the Gulbenkian Museum, Lisbon; the Musée des Tissus, Lyon; the Museo Poldi Pezzoli in Milan; the Residenzmuseum and Nationalmuseum in Munich; and the Musée des Arts Décoratifs, Paris.

In America the Metropolitan Museum of Art, New York, houses particularly splendid pieces. The Textile Museum, Washington, possesses a very large collection. To these may be added the Museum of Fine Arts, Boston; the Cleveland Museum of Art; the Detroit Institute of Arts; the County Museum of Art, Los Angeles; the Philadelphia Museum of Art; and the City Art Museum of St Louis.

CHAPTER 15(*a*)

TIMURID ARCHITECTURE

INTRODUCTION

The architectural achievements surveyed in this chapter range over four hundred years of Persian history. The first half of our period was one of constant shifts in political power accompanied by changing frontiers. Only in the second half did Persia obtain some measure of security under a single political authority. The story opens with the architectural style associated with the Īl-Khāns and its development in western and southern Persia under the successor dynasties. It was this style which was transferred to Transoxiana in the last quarter of the 8th/14th century. The part played by Tīmūr and his house is crucial to the story inasmuch as theirs was the principal building effort, first in Transoxiana and then in eastern Persia – centres of Timurid power. With the political decline of the Timurids in the middle of the 9th/15th century, the initiative in architecture returned to western Persia under the patronage of the Türkmen dynasties. Thanks to Shah Ismā'īl and his successors, the strands were drawn together and a homogeneous style was created and disseminated throughout the Safavid kingdom.

Initiative in public works was with members of the royal house and the high officers of state: many civic undertakings were due to the enterprise of local dignitaries. The religious was the most powerful of motives: for at least in the first half of our period it is only the religious foundations which survive. Apart from the public and private mosque, the *madrasa* and *khāngāh*, the principal effort was concentrated on the embellishment of the great shrines – above all, those of the Imām Riḍā at Mashhad and of Shaikh Ṣafī at Ardabīl. There is, too, as in the previous period, a preoccupation with funerary architecture. Of the builders themselves, we have an imperfect knowledge. It would seem that western and southern Persia were the source of the greatest architectural talent; and the only architect whose surviving work is sufficient to establish him as a potent creative artist with a distinctive style is Qivām al-Dīn, a native of Shīrāz.

The surviving monuments are but a partial index of the taste and aspirations of the period. With the exception of the most famous, many important monuments still await detailed and scientific study. The only secular buildings of any significance earlier than the Safavid period to have survived are a few caravansarais. There is scarcely a trace of palace architecture. There were monuments standing until a century ago which have since disappeared through wanton destruction or neglect. Natural causes, too, have taken their toll; and it is ironical that earlier buildings have survived earthquakes which reduced those of the Timurid period and later to ruins. These later buildings, conceived on a larger and more ambitious scale, lacked the structural solidity of an earlier age. Thus any survey at the present time is provisional and subject to alteration as further study leads to deeper understanding. This would apply particularly to the social and functional aspects of Persian architecture.

The most striking feature is the continuity of development. There was no sudden change of direction such as occurred in the West, where a revived interpretation of the classical tradition produced a wholly new approach to architectural forms. Building materials continued to be bricks, whether baked or unbaked, and timber. Stone was used sparingly.

The characteristic arch is pointed, struck generally from four or three centres; from two centres only rarely. The round or segmental arch is scarcely used at all. Dome profiles are elliptical or struck from three or four centres: the bulbous dome is developed in our period. The articulation of the façade is achieved by introducing blind arcades, recessed panels and pilasters. Experiment and innovation were directed to the handling of formal relationships within the accepted canons.

The principal preoccupations were, on the one hand, space and formal relationships and, on the other hand, decoration. Increased internal space was made possible by developing new vaulting systems. Much thought was concentrated on relating the dome to the other components, more particularly, the *aivān* with or without its attendant screen and minarets. It is in the nature of the great religious buildings that the architectural aspect is developed within the confining walls: thus the monumental portal (*pīshṭāq*) became the preponderant feature of the exterior façade. On the whole it was the smaller and more compact buildings, such as the mausoleum and palace kiosk, which were conceived as free standing monuments demanding a logical relationship between exterior and interior. But the most significant developments were in decoration. In our period there is an increasing tendency to conceal structural features beneath an overlay which superficially appears to have structural function but, in fact, more often than not is purely ornamental. Such are the *muqarnas* (superposed rows of prism-shaped elements in brick, plaster or wood, either covering the curved surface of a vault or acting as a cornice, and sometimes called stalactite decoration) and the complex network of ribs used to convert the square to the circle. But it is polychrome surface decoration which gives to Persian architecture of the period its unique character. Glazed ceramic tiles, applied to the wall surface in a variety of techniques, were the principal medium of decoration; gilding and painting were also used, but, vulnerable as they were to time and weather, surviving examples are rare. The three-dimensional effects of the earlier period were less and less sought after. Deeply carved and painted stucco was gradually abandoned. The interior of the mausoleum of the Imāmzāda Khwāja ʻImād al-Dīn at Qum, built in 1390, is entirely covered in polychrome plaster. It is a *tour de force* on the part of the carver but its style is already archaic.[1] A quite different technique of plaster decoration was introduced in the 15th century. The current style of decoration was rendered in very low relief in plaster which was then painted and gilded.

I. THE MUZAFFARID STYLE

The death of Sultan Abū Saʻīd in 736/1335 spelt the virtual dissolution of Il-Khanid power. From then until the coming of Tīmūr, Persia was dominated by the Jalayirids in Iraq and Āzarbāījān, the Muzaffarids in Fārs, Kirmān and Iṣfahān and the Kart dynasty in Khurāsān. The Il-Khanid style had been created in the first three decades of the century; and is represented by two remarkable monuments, the mausoleum of Öljeitü Khudābanda at Sulṭāniyya and the Great Mosque of Varāmīn. The major monuments in the period of the Mongol succession states are remarkably few. The outstanding ones are to be found in western and southern Persia and are associated with the Muzaffarid rulers. That there are no examples of the buildings raised by members of the Jalayirid house is surprising and can in part be explained by the devastations wrought by Tīmūr. The contribution of this dynasty to the development of painting was crucial, but no trace remains of the splendid palace built outside Tabrīz by Shaikh Uvais and described in detail by Clavijo.[2]

[1] Wilber, *The Architecture*, no. 144, p. 188.

[2] Clavijo, trans. Le Strange, p. 153.

The development of the Muzaffarid style can be traced in the history of two notable religious buildings, the Great Mosque of Yazd and that of Kirmān. The Great Mosque at Varāmīn, built between 1322 and 1326, had established the general plan from which subsequent public mosques in Persia rarely deviated.[1] Its exterior façade is dominated by a great arched entrance portal (pīshṭāq). In the middle of each of the four arched faces of the interior court, an aivān (an arched and vaulted niche) is introduced. Behind the aivān on the *qibla* side (i.e. that facing Mecca) is the square sanctuary chamber surmounted by a dome. Because in the ground plan these aivāns can be seen as the arms of a cross, this type of mosque has been termed cruciform. The mosque at Varāmīn was the first in which these features were adopted at its inception. At Yazd they had to be introduced into an already existing mosque structure.[2] In 1324 Rukn al-Dīn Muḥammad, a local dignitary and familiar of Sultan Abū Sa'īd, built a great square dome chamber to the north-east of this ancient mosque (pl. 19*b*). The double dome was supported on squinches concealed by stalactite pendentives converting the octagon to the circle. The outer dome springs from a relatively low drum; the inner is shallow and elliptical. In 1331 an aivān was built in front of the dome chamber. The façade of the aivān consists of a lofty arched opening set in the square-headed screen. The aivān itself extends a considerable length in depth to meet the sanctuary chamber; and the profile of its vault reproduced that of the arch. The aivāns on the other three sides of the court were never built, though it is clear enough that a cruciform plan was originally intended. Some ten years after the completion of the sanctuary aivān, the great portal was built to the east of the latter (pl. 19*a*). This is an arched opening set in a square-headed screen crowned by paired minarets. The rear wall of the shallow opening is divided into two registers. In the lower, a square-headed door is surmounted by an arched tympanum: in the upper is a hemispherical vault decorated with muqarnas above the two corner squinch arches. The same composition of portal and crowning minarets had already been used in the portal of the mosque at Ashtarjan near Iṣfahān, which bears a dating inscription of 715/1315–16.[3] The Yazd portal makes an uneasy impression by its excessive verticality.

In 1362 Shāh Yaḥyā was governing Yazd in the name of his uncle,

[1] Wilber, *The Architecture*, p. 158, no. 64.

[2] For the mosque's history, see Siroux, "Le Masjid-e-djum'a de Yezd", and Wilber, *The Architecture*, no. 66, pp. 159f.

[3] *Ibid.*, no. 49, pp. 141–5.

Shāh-i Shujā', second sovereign of the Muzaffarid house. It may have been at his instigation that his minister, the amīr Rukn al-Din Shāh Ḥasan, built in 1367 the oratory flanking the eastern side of the sanctuary dome chamber and aivān. This hall was probably intended to provide additional space within the sanctuary area. In order to roof its great width – 8.1 metres – a novel system of vaulting was used. Broad transverse arches were thrown at intervals from one longitudinal wall to the other and the space between each pair filled in to form a barrel vault. There is a similar oratory on the western side of the sanctuary chamber and aivān but, while the length is the same as that of the eastern oratory, the width is greater (9.37 m.). Transverse arches are again employed but are far narrower. At the apex of the barrel-shaped infillings are small domical heads. This western oratory may have been built at the order of the amīr Rukn al-Dīn Shāh Ḥasan or, as seems more likely, in 819/1414 during the reign of Shāh Rukh.

This system of vaulting made it possible to roof far wider areas than hitherto. Clerestory lighting could be obtained by piercing window openings in the infilled spaces between the transverse arches. The system had already made its appearance in eastern Persia, where it was adopted in the Masjid-i Kirmānī flanking the entrance portal of the shrine complex at Turbat-i Shaikh Jām (pl. 20). This masjid has been dated by Golombek to 763/1362. Unlike the oratories in the Great Mosque at Yazd where the *miḥrāb* (prayer niche) was placed on the short side, the miḥrāb was located in the middle of the longitudinal side which formed the qibla wall. The architect was a native of Kirmān and it is likely that the transverse vault was developed in western and southern Persia, for its next occurrence was in Iṣfahān when the Muzaffarid Quṭb al-Dīn Shāh Maḥmūd ordered the building of the madrasa in the Masjid-i Jāmi' in 1366.[1] This was built behind the eastern aivān of the mosque and consisted of a court, long and narrow, with two storeyed arcades on its east and west sides and an aivān on the north and on the south side. Behind the south aivān is the masjid of the madrasa, its longitudinal axis running east-west (pl. 21*a*). It is roofed by four transverse arches running north-south, the inner pair being spaced wider apart in order to accommodate the great miḥrāb which is crowned by an arch at right angles to the two transverse arches. The bays on the south side flanking the miḥrāb show how it was possible to

[1] *Ibid.*, no. 109, p. 187.

introduce clerestory lighting. Above the miḥrāb are two small cartouches containing the names of the architects; Shams b. Tāj and Fakhr b. al-Vahhāb of Shīrāz the mason (*al-bannā*).[1]

Kirmān fell to the Muzaffarids in 1340. Nine years later Mubāriz al-Dīn Muḥammad built there the Masjid-i Jāmi'.[2] The plan is cruciform; the aivāns are linked by single-storeyed arcades except on the south where they are two-storeyed. The entrance portal, square-headed with crowning minarets, leads into a dome vestibule which gives onto the shallow north aivān. The sanctuary aivān on the south side is wider and deeper than the others.

Coloured faience was now the accepted mode of surface decoration. Two techniques were employed often side by side; tile inlay and tile mosaic. In tile inlay, glazed polygonal elements were inlaid in the brick or terracotta surface to form patterns, the unglazed contrasting with the glazed areas. In tile mosaic, the entire surface is of glazed faience, each separate area of colour being carved and fitted to its neighbour. Tile inlay was already being practised in Saljūq times. Tile mosaic appears first in Öljeitü Khudābanda's mausoleum at Sulṭāniyya; and was perfected in the portal façade of the mausoleum of Bābā Qāsim completed in 1340.[3] The tilework on the portal façade of the Great Mosque at Kirmān is dated 750/1349 and has suffered much damage, although what remains is sufficient to give an impression of the original intention. The composition of the façade, logical and harmonious, was to become a standard one for succeeding generations. The arch screen is framed on all three sides by a broad band enclosing a *naskhī* inscription in white on a ground of tightly involuted scrolling in light blue, all on a dark blue background. Each of the imposts raised on a low socle is divided into three tiers of blind arcades. The voussoir of the portal arch is composed of a spirally twisted moulding which is untwisted at the two bases. The entrance door is set back within the arch, and the rectangular compartment thus formed is given a hemispherical vaulting of stalactite penditives. The tile mosaic decoration is partially preserved in the blind arcades of the imposts and their framing bands. These are decorated in white, yellow and two shades of blue with elaborate interlacings developed from a central rosette or star.

The decoration of the miḥrāb in the Masjid-i Jāmi' at Yazd was

[1] Godard, "Historique du Masdjid-é Djum'a d'Iṣfahān", p. 241. Hunarfar, *Ganjīna*, pp. 136–45.
[2] Wilber, *The Architecture*, no. 97, pp. 182f.
[3] Godard, "Iṣfahān", pp. 38–43 ("Le Tombeau de Bābā Kāsem").

executed by Ḥājj Bahā' al-Dīn Muḥammad al-Ḥusain in 1375. The tilework is far better preserved than that of the mosque portal in Kirmān. The composition of the screen is among the finest in Persia: an outer framing band with inscription, a narrow inner band of floral scrolling, bevelled voussoir band with a series of half-palmettes forming pendants, paired colonnettes supporting the arch. The treatment of the spandrel is of particular interest: a geometric roundel in each of the corner angles and a circular raised boss at the apex of the arch. The naturalistically rendered floral sprays which decorate the ground of the spandrels anticipate the style of manuscript illumination executed in Shīrāz in the first decade of the 9th/15th century.

The interior of the miḥrāb consists of five vertical faces surmounted by hemispherical stalactite vaulting. The tile mosaic panels are decorated with half palmettes arranged in the "tree of life" design or with star patterns radiating from a central rosette. In two of the faces these panels are set in a ground executed in inlaid tilework: polygonal terracotta tiles with delicate relief designs are inlaid in interlaced bands of turquoise tiles, a technique used in the mausoleum at Sulṭāniyya.

It is our misfortune that so little architecture of the second half of the 14th century has survived in Persia. The outstanding monuments are associated with the Muzaffarid dynasty and do seem to constitute a style both in structural form as well as decoration. It was the architects of Shīrāz and Iṣfahān who were to play the leading rôle in the development of Timurid architecture in Transoxiana and Khurāsān; and it is the migration of talent to Tīmūr's court which may in part explain this paucity of buildings in Persia in the closing decades of the century.

II. ARCHITECTURAL FORMS UNDER TĪMŪR

Tīmūr's conquest of Transoxiana was sealed in 1369 by the capture of Samarqand, which was declared the capital of the empire. It was Tīmūr and his family who gave the impulse to the new architectural movement. The enormous scale in public works was alone made possible by the resources of the empire in artistic talent, engineering skill and material.

The major monuments belong to the last ten years of Tīmūr's reign. His earliest efforts were directed to commemorating the deceased members of his family by the building of mausolea in the complex known as the Shāh-i Zinda. Today, this consists of some sixteen buildings grouped on either side of a narrow path which clears the crest of a hill in the north-eastern quarter of Samarqand.[1] It owes its name "the Living King" to the Prophet's cousin Qutham b. 'Abbās whose shrine had long been the principal sanctuary of the city. Here as elsewhere in Islam it was the custom to bury the dead in the vicinity of the shrine of a saint or martyr. The existing mausoleum of the Shāh-i Zinda at the northern end of the complex was built in 735/1334–5.

The Timurid mausolea are of two kinds; the domed cubical structure with a single dominating façade and a polygonal structure with dome set on a high drum and having an entrance on two or more of its faces. The earliest mausoleum to be built in the Shāh-i Zinda complex during Tīmūr's reign belongs to the first type. This is the mausoleum of Shād-i Mulk, completed in 773/1371–2 by Tīmūr's sister, Terken Āqā, for her daughter Shād-i Mulk.[2] The principal emphasis is on the portal which, with its screen, forms the façade of the mausoleum which springs from a low octagon. The dome is barely visible behind this façade. It is decorated with vertical ribs joined tangentially – a novel feature which was to be widely used in Transoxiana and Persia. Its origins have not been satisfactorily explained; and a possible connection with the stone ribbed dome current in Egypt in the 8th/14th century has yet to be investigated.

The basic scheme of the Timurid portal façade is that already developed in Persia: the screen set on a plinth, the lofty pointed arch and the vaulted entrance embrasure. The ingenuity of architect and tile worker was applied to the organisation of architectonic detail and decoration. In the façade of the mausoleum of Shād-i Mulk the decoration of the surfaces of the screen and of the flanking walls of the entrance embrasure is arranged in rectangular or square panels. Much of the decoration consists of faience carved in relief, a technique apparently unknown in Persia (pl. 21*b*). The designs were carved in the "biscuit" which was then glazed in turquoise or turquoise and white and fired. The technique was possibly developed from carved and painted stucco and had already been developed in Samarqand and Bukhārā in the earlier 14th century. In the Shād-i Mulk façade, this technique is used not only in the impost panels but also in the engaged columns

[1] For a map of the Shāh-i Zinda complex, see Cohn-Wiener, p. 24; Hrbas and Knobloch, p. 22, fig. XI. Pugachenkova and Rempel', *Vydayushchiĭsya Pamyatniki*, pp. 108–15.

[2] Cohn-Wiener, pls. XXVI–XXXIV. Hrbas and Knobloch, pls. 57, 66–7, 70. Pugachenkova and Rempel', *Istoriya Iskusstv Uzbekistana*, pp. 253ff.

which define the outer ends of the façade, the columns supporting the arch and the stalactite vaulting elements. Some of the framing bands are composed of turquoise glazed bricks laid edge above edge and the spandrel of the arch screen is decorated with sinuous leaf scrolls rendered in light relief under a turquoise glaze on a dark blue ground. There is also a framing band consisting of tiny square elements of white, turquoise and light blue faience arranged to form a series of star figures. This is the "inset" technique rather than mosaic inlay which requires that the elements should interlock.

True mosaic tilework first appears in Samarqand in the mausoleum of Shīrīn Bīka Āqā, another sister of Tīmūr. This was built in 787/1385–6.[1] It, too, is a façade mausoleum but its exterior treatment differs from that of the mausoleum of Shād-i Mulk in that the dome is slightly bulbous and rests on a sixteen-sided drum. The polygonal drum occurs in two other mausolea in the Shāh-i Zinda complex built in the 1380s. The most significant feature of the mausoleum is its portal decoration which is executed entirely in tile mosaic. The decoration is developed above the plinth and consists of vertical panels. The arch of the entrance embrasure is supported on engaged columns, and within the embrasure there are framing bands around the arched entrance door and stalactite vaulting within the portal arch (pl. 22*a*). The motifs are floral: symmetrically disposed arabesques in the vertical panels and framing bands. Within the tympanum above the arched entrance door are floral arabesques developed about a large rosette in each of the spandrels. The external niches on the sixteen faces of the drum still have traces of tile mosaic decoration. The drum itself was decorated with a network of lozenge-shaped compartments in inlays of coloured bricks. The interior of the mausoleum is painted in red, blue and black except for panels of square green tiles and light blue hexagonal tiles, the latter painted in gold with phoenixes – a rare example of "Chinoiserie" at this date.

The tile mosaic decoration on the façade of this mausoleum is related to that on the miḥrāb of the Masjid-i Jāmi‘ at Yazd and it seems probable that the technique was introduced to Samarqand by migrant tileworkers from Persia. The façade of the mausoleum of Tūmān Āqā, wife of Tīmūr, who completed it in her lifetime in 1405, is decorated with tile mosaic designs closely resembling that of the mausoleum of

[1] Cohn-Wiener, pls. XXXVI–XXXIX. Hrbas and Knobloch, pls. 61, 63, 68, 74.

Shīrīn Bīka: and it is noteworthy that they are the work of Shaikh Muḥammad b. Khwāja Beg of Tabrīz.[1]

The mausolea so far described belong to the first type of mausoleum in which the dominant external feature is the portal façade. Its form was no doubt determined by its siting in relation to other adjacent buildings. The laying out of buildings along a thoroughfare demanded a series of imposing façades since these would be the only visible features from the road. The second type of mausoleum – a polygonal structure, either square or octagonal with an entrance on two or more of its faces and a dome springing from a high cylindrical drum – was evidently intended as a free standing monument visible on two or more sides. There are examples of this type in the Shāh-i Zinda but the most famous in Samarqand is the Gūr-i Mīr which contains the tombs of Tīmūr and other members of his dynasty. It was built by Tīmūr between 1403 and 1404 to commemorate his grandson, Mīrzā Muḥammad Sulṭān b. Muḥammad Jahāngīr who died in 805/1403.[2] It was an addition to an already existing complex of buildings erected by Muḥammad Sulṭān at the close of the 14th century. These were a madrasa and khāngāh which stood to the north-east and north-west of the Gūr-i Mīr, separated by a square court. The mausoleum is octagonal in plan. The dominating feature is the bulbous dome set on the tall cylindrical drum (pl. 22*b*). With its great ribs each joined to its neighbour tangentially and appearing to rise from the stalactite corbelling of the cornice, it is a striking and bold conception. Ribs, stalactite cornice and the upper band around the drum are decorated with tile inlays of black and yellow lozenge figures on a turquoise ground. The drum is decorated with glazed and unglazed bricks arranged in zones of geometric patterns above a broad band of Kufic.

The interior is square with a projecting bay on each side. The transition from the square to the circle is achieved by the imposition of eight ribbed arches between the squinch arches and those of the four projecting bays. The resulting sixteen-sided cornice forms the base for the inner dome. The decoration of the interior is unexpectedly austere. There is a dado of hexagonal alabaster plaques framed by a guilloche moulding and above this an inscribed band of greenish grey jasper. The upper register of the walls and the surface of the dome were

[1] *Ibid.*, Abb. 73. Pugachenkova and Rempel', *Istoriya Iskusstv Uzbekistana*, pp. 268f., pl. 168.

[2] *Les Mosquées de Samarcande.* Sarre, *Denkmäler*, pp. 148–51, Taf. CXIV. Cohn-Wiener, pp. 30f., pls. LXVIII–LXXII. Hrbas and Knobloch, pp. 23f., pls. 78–80.

originally decorated with patterns in gilded paper raised in relief. The cenotaphs, including the great jade slab commemorating Tīmūr, are surrounded by a low marble balustrade consisting of exquisitely carved flower sprays and formal arabesques with low spirally twisted columns securing the balustrade to the floor. The actual interments are in the crypt.

The double dome was an established system in Persia in the 14th century. If a single dome is raised to an inordinate height, the proportions of the interior space are impaired. The shallow inner dome was the solution of this problem. In the Gūr-i Mīr the height of the ceiling dome is 22.5 m. and of the exterior dome 34.09 m. The system also made possible the development of the bulbous dome since the inner gave some measure of support to the outer. The transition from the square to the circle by the means of a sixteen-sided figure had the great advantage of reducing the transitional zone to a single register.

The mausolea of the Shāh-i Zinda are relatively modest structures. The Gūr-i Mīr must have been the crowning feature of the madrasa and khāngāh of which it was an adjunct. An example of a far more ambitious treatment of the funerary monument is the *mazār* (pilgrim shrine) of Aḥmad Yasavī in Turkistān city built in 799/1396–7.[1] This is a highly complex building designed to provide for the manifold needs of those responsible for the saint's shrine, and incorporating a masjid, library and cells of a khāngāh and a kitchen. Its plan is cruciform and centres on a great dome chamber (fig. 1). On the longitudinal axis are the deep portal aivān to the north and domed tomb chamber to the south. The remaining rooms are disposed on the east-west axis and within the four arms of the cross. The north elevation is dominated by the great portal aivān and the two flanking towers with polygonal bases. On either side of this portal are upper storeys. The principal feature of the south elevation is the portal of the mausoleum surmounted by a ribbed dome raised on a high cylindrical drum (pl. 23). Its form together with its stalactite cornice and glazed brick decoration resembles that of the Gūr-i Mīr. The roofing of certain of the rooms is by means of transverse arches – the same system employed in the oratories of the Great Mosque at Yazd and in the masjid of the madrasa in the Masjid-i Jāmi', Iṣfahān. This is the first occurrence of the system in Transoxiana and was almost certainly introduced from Persia, since

[1] See Man'kovskaya.

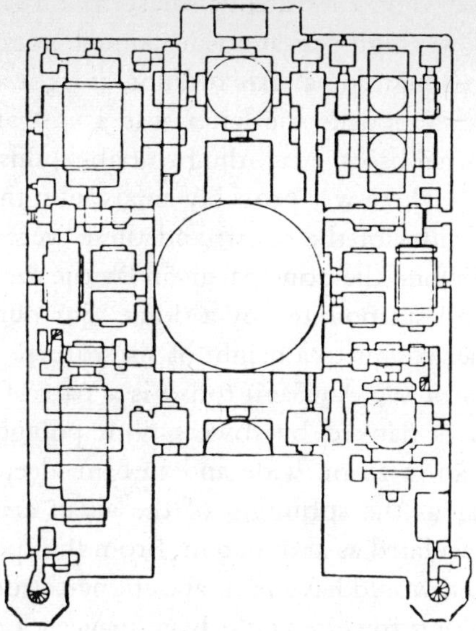

Fig. 1. Turkistān. Plan of Aḥmad Yasavī complex.

we know that the architect of the mausoleum of Aḥmad Yasavī was Khwāja Ḥasan of Shīrāz, who may have been brought to Samarqand soon after Tīmūr's conquest of that city in 795/1393.

One aspect of the mazār of Aḥmad Yasavī is indicative of the aspirations of the new style. In the exterior, the principal emphasis is on the main portal façade which dominates the great mass by its sheer weight and size. The arch screen seems to overlap the apex of the great dome itself; and the flanking minarets bonded with the outer edges of the screen suggest fortification. The manner in which the arched vault rises above the screen is a disturbing feature and it has to be assumed that this façade was never completed. It is unfortunate that there is no trace of polychrome revetment – if it ever existed.

The formula of the deep aivān with flanking towers could be applied equally well to secular architecture. It was evidently a feature of the great palace known as the Āq Sarāī which Tīmūr began to build in about 1384 at Kish, the city of his birth.[1] Renamed Shahr-i Sabz in the 14th century, Kish is situated about fifty miles south of Samarqand on the road leading to Tirmiẕ on the Oxus. The palace was still being built

[1] Cohn-Wiener, pls. LII–LVI. Hrbas and Knobloch, pls. 88, 84. Pugachenkova and Rempel', *Istoriya Iskusstv Uzbekistana*, pp. 261ff.

when Clavijo visited the city in 1404. His description gives a fairly clear idea of the layout.[1] A high portal aivān flanked by rooms led into a great court with its longitudinal axis running at right angles to that of the entrance portal. Opposite the latter was a vast aivān flanked by towers with polygonal bases. According to Bābur, this was flanked by two smaller aivāns.[2] There was probably an aivān in the centre of each of the other three sides of the court; and these were joined by two-storeyed arcades. Behind the principal aivān lay the great audience hall, probably square and surmounted by a dome. Surrounding this audience hall were lesser rooms to a height of six storeys.

All that remains of the Āq Sarāī today is a part of the great aivān portal. The aivān is flanked by towers with polygonal bases. The interior of the aivān is 22 m. wide and 12.6 m. deep; the side walls survive only as far as the springing of the aivān arch of which the height has been calculated as about 40 m. From the apex of the arch to the top of the screen would have been about one-third of the height of the arch. The flanking towers would have projected one-third of the height of the arch above the top of the screen. These dimensions give some idea of the scale of the palace.

The decoration of the flanking towers is executed in glazed bricks of two shades of blue and white: geometric patterns on the polygonal facets and Kufic seal characters arranged in diagonal patterns on the cylindrical surface. Panels of geometric ornament between inscribed bands frame the arch imposts. The interior walls of the aivān are decorated with hexagonal painted tiles; while the vaulting is ornamented with glazed brick inlays similar to the towers. One of the inscription bands bears the date 798/1395–6. In the middle of the back wall of the aivān interior is an opening into a smaller room flanked by engaged columns which certainly supported an arch. The columns consist of four spirally twisted mouldings which rise from a decorated base. These columns are also revetted with glazed tiles. The walls of the inner room are decorated with mosaic tilework which in conception and perfection of technique exceeds any of the tile mosaic in the mausolea of the Shāh-i Zinda.

The ruined portal of the Āq Sarāī at Shahr-i Sabz gives a tantalising glimpse of the new style which must have received the initial impulse from Tīmūr himself. Unquestionably his greatest monument is the

[1] Clavijo, trans. Le Strange, pp. 207–10.

[2] Beveridge, *The Bābur-nāma in English*, p. 83.

Great Mosque which he began to build in Samarqand in 801/1399.[1] It was intended as the Masjid-i Jāmī' of Samarqand and the current name "Mosque of Bībī Khānum" seems to have been applied to it from a confusion with the madrasa erected in the name of Tīmūr's wife. Of this madrasa no trace remains but we know that both the mosque and the madrasa stood within the walls of the city near the Iron Gate and that Tīmūr built a great bazaar street leading from the open space in front of the two buildings to what was later to become the Rīgistān.

At each outside corner of the mosque was a minaret (fig. 2). The entrance portal on the north façade was a vaulted aivān with cylindrical flanking minarets. This led into the rectangular court. In the centre of each side was an aivān. Parallel to the north, west and east sides were four galleries behind the arcades of the court. These galleries consisted of rows of columns of which every four supported a shallow dome. On the south side, there were nine galleries. Behind the aivāns on the west and east sides were dome chambers. The sanctuary aivān was nearly twice as wide as the others and was flanked by minarets hexagonal in section. The height of the aivān arch was 30.66 m. and of the aivān screen, 40.88 m.; the crowns of the minarets probably projected more than 10 m. above the aivān screen.

There are two dating inscriptions: 801/1398 in the sanctuary dome chamber and 808/1405 on the entrance portal. Thus we may suppose that the work was completed with the building of the main façade. The scale of the mosque is without parallel in either Iran or Transoxiana. Certain salient features require mention. The vertical effect was achieved by the eight minarets and by the great height of the sanctuary aivān screen behind which the sanctuary dome was invisible from the court. The height of the screen was further accentuated by the single-storey arcades around the court. The domes in the centre of the east and west sides are set on high cylindrical drums and projected far above their respective aivān screens which were considerably lower than that of the sanctuary. The polygonal flanking minarets of the sanctuary portal, which resemble those of the portal of the Āq Sarāī at Shahr-i Sabz, were to find their way into the mosque architecture of Iran as, too, were the dome chambers of the lesser aivāns and the corner minarets. While the aivān screens and domed structures were of brick, the vaulting as well as the columns were constructed of stone.

[1] E.E. Ratiya, *Mechet' Bibi-Khanym* (Moscow, 1950).

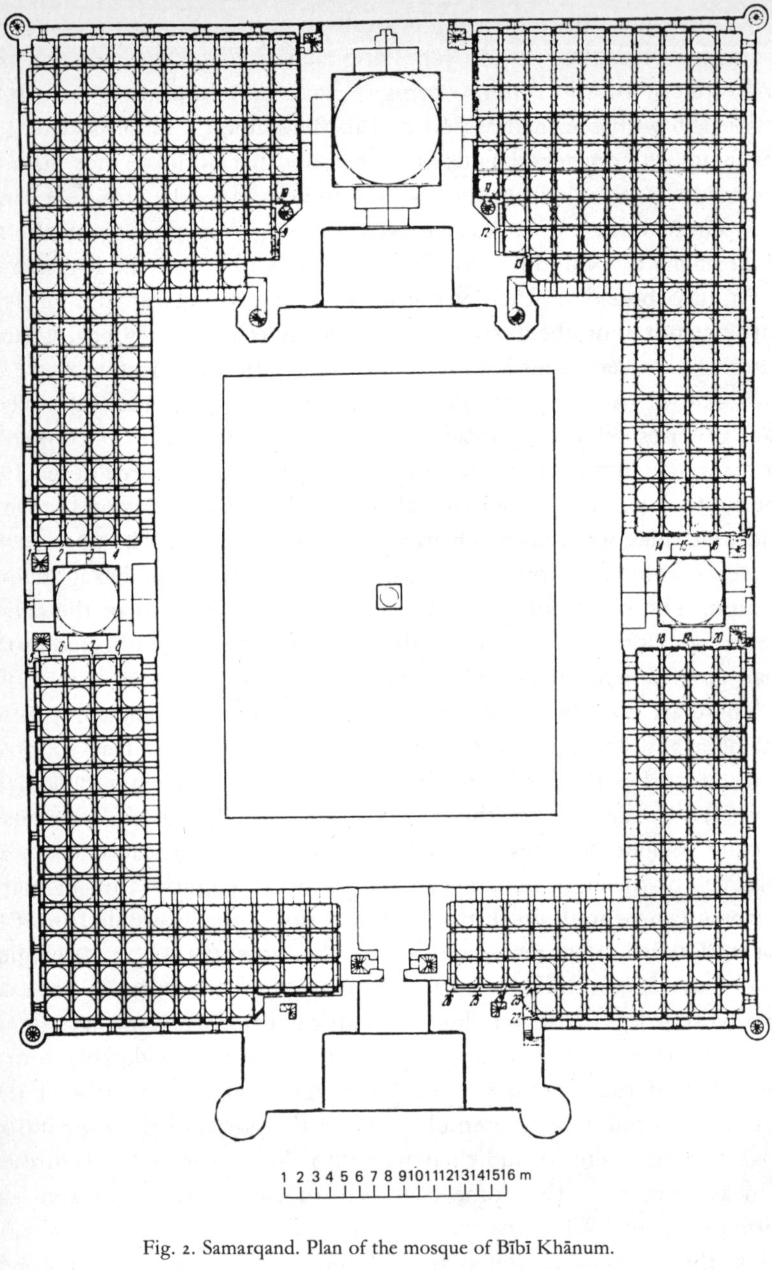

Fig. 2. Samarqand. Plan of the mosque of Bībī Khānum.

The employment of stone in Timurid Samarqand is noteworthy, for even in Iran during the Safavid period stone and marble were used sparingly, principally for flooring and lower revetments, apart of course from foundation courses which were invariably of stone. The feature was sufficiently unusual to elicit the notice of Bābur, who recalls a passage from the *Ẓafar-nāma* of Sharaf al-Dīn ʻAlī Yazdī according to which, when Tīmūr was building the Sangīn ("stone") mosque, there were stone-cutters of Āzarbāījān, Fārs, Hindūstān and other countries to the number of two hundred.[1]

No madrasa has survived that can be associated with Tīmūr; but the madrasa of Ulugh Beg in Samarqand, built between 1417 and 1420, can indicate how the new style was adapted to this type of building.[2] Since the principal function of the madrasa was teaching, the fixed requirements were living quarters, lecture rooms and prayer hall. In the madrasa of Ulugh Beg the court is laid out on a four-aivān plan. The living quarters were arranged in two storeys between the aivāns, although the upper storey has since been destroyed. There is a domed lecture hall in each of the four corners of the madrasa and on the side opposite the entrance portal and behind the aivān a long prayer gallery with its main axis parallel to the wall. There is a minaret at each of the four outside corners of the madrasa, but the wide portal screen has no flanking minarets. This portal dominates the north-eastern face of the madrasa: the width of the opening is one-third of the whole length of the latter. The entire archivolt of the aivān arch is provided with a cable moulding as in the inner entrance door of the portal of the Āq Sarāī; and each cable is faced with "cuerda seca" tiles. The minarets are decorated in glazed brick inlays with diaper patterns of Kufic seal inscriptions, and geometric glazed brick inlays form the principal decoration of the aivān screen except for the spandrels of the arch where there are still traces of mosaic inlay. The rear wall of the portal aivān consists of an arched entrance leading through a vestibule into the court and is flanked by two tiers of arched niches. It is in the entrance vestibule that the decorator concentrated his main effort. Here are panels of mosaic inlay as well as terracotta relief tiles inset with tile mosaic, a style of revetment already noted in the miḥrāb of the Masjid-i Jāmiʻ at Yazd.

[1] Beveridge, *The Bābur-nāma in English*, p. 520.

[2] Sarre, *Denkmäler*. Cohn-Wiener, pl. LXXV. Pugachenkova and Rempel', *Istoriya Iskusstv Uzbekistana*, pp. 269ff., fig. 265.

What conclusions may we draw from these examples of architectural practice by the first generation of Timurid architects? Most striking, of course, is the scale of the great monuments, which is unknown in Persia at this period. The principal forms and structural detail, however, are those of Persia. In the exterior façade, the portal entrance was the principal concern. For those of lesser buildings a tall and narrow arched embrasure was used and was often given a hemispherical vault of stalactite corbels. In the great buildings, the portal was a salient formed by a great rectangular screen in which the arched embrasure was wider and the arch sharper in relation to the height than in the portals of lesser buildings. Wall surfaces continued to be articulated by arched niches, open or blind. Arch profiles are pointed although there is some variation in form. In decoration, tile mosaic and inset tilework seem closely related to the style which was already developed in Persia.

There are certain innovations. The ribbed dome with a cornice of stalactite corbelling just below its springing seems to have been invented by the architects of Transoxiana. The high drum, too, was developed probably as a feature of the "free standing" monument. We have noticed, too, the combination of aivān screen and flanking minarets, the latter in certain cases being given polygonal bases. The squinch arch continued to be the system of effecting the transition of the square to the circle, but greater refinement was achieved by introducing ribbed arches between the shoulders of the eight arches of the octagon.

Carved faience was apparently a technique developed in Transoxiana but had gone out of fashion by the end of the 14th century. It looks on present evidence as if the technique of painted tiles was an invention of Transoxiana; and it anticipates by two centuries its use on a large scale in Persia.

Scholars of the USSR have analysed in great detail many of the monuments of Uzbekistan and Turkmenistan and, as a result, have been able to establish that the buildings discussed above were planned in accordance with a system of proportions. Designs were laid out on a grid based on a predetermined module. This practical application of mathematical knowledge is not surprising in an age in which the exact sciences were so highly esteemed; and it is revealing that the mathematical treatise *Miftāḥ al-ḥisāb*, which Ghiyāṣ al-Dīn Jamshīd of Kāshān dedicated to Ulugh Beg in 830/1427, included a chapter on the theoretical construction of arches.

1 An astrolabe made in 1127/1715 by ʿAbd al-Aʾimma, the younger, rete side.

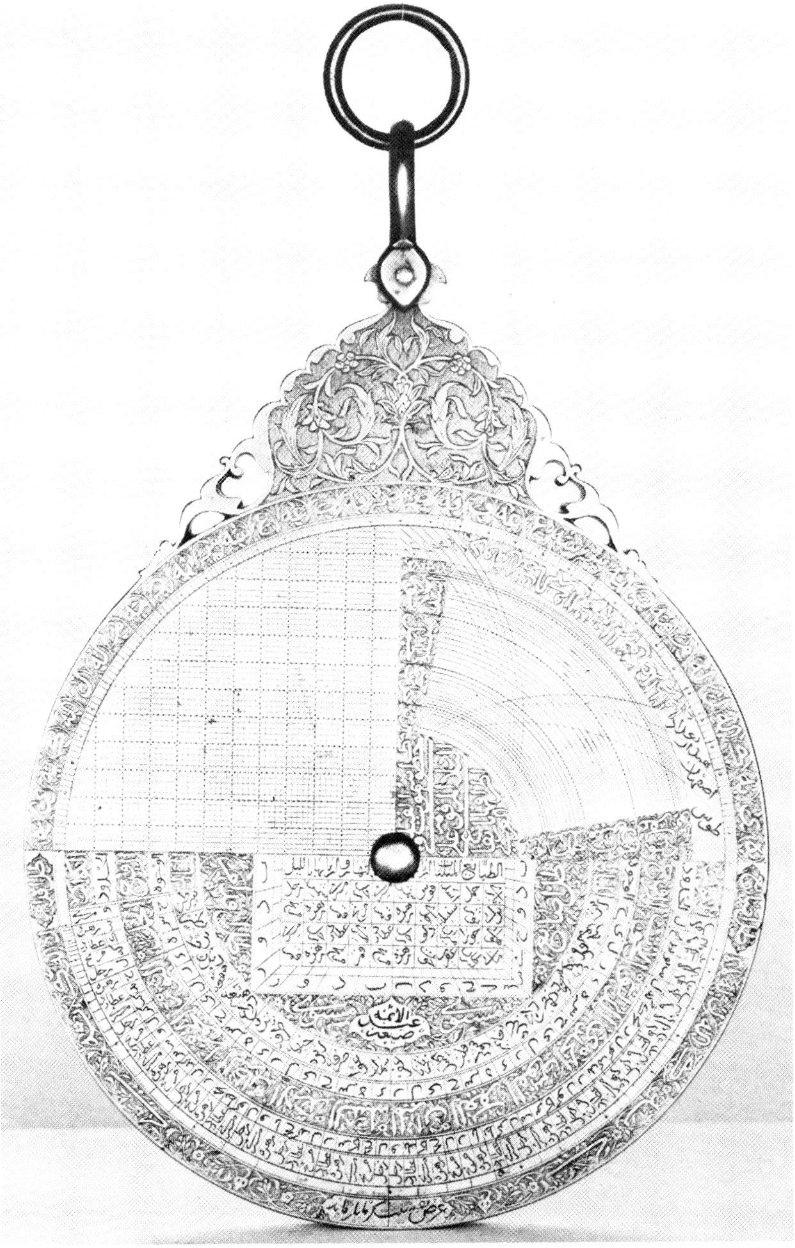

2 ‘Abd al-A’imma’s astrolabe, back, showing the alidade.

3 Khusrau and Shīrīn, ascribed to Bihzād, late 15th century.

4 Woollen knotted carpet, Persia, first half of the 16th century, 4.98 × 3.40 m.

5 Multiple woollen prayer rug, with pattern arranged in rows, Persia, first half of the 16th century, 2.74 × 1.22 m., fragment.

6 Woollen knotted carpet, the so-called Ardabīl carpet, Persia, dated 1539–40, 11.52 × 5.34 m.

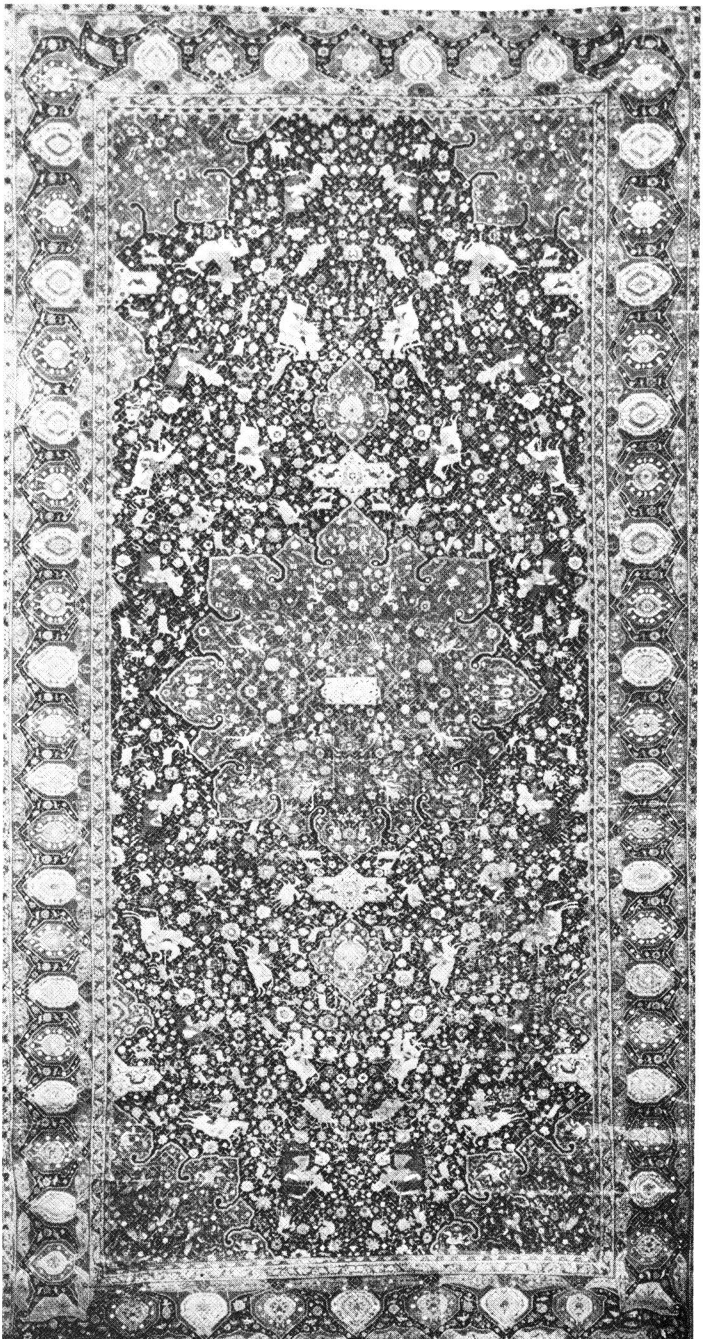

7 Woollen knotted carpet, Persia, dated 1522–3, 6.80 × 3.33 m.

8 Woollen knotted carpet, "north-west Persian medallion carpet", first half of the 16th century, two fragments, 6.04 × 3.96 m. and 2.31 × 1.55 m.

9 Woollen knotted carpet, "Herat carpet", 16th century, fragment 3.67 × 2.78 m.

10 Woollen knotted carpet, "vase carpet", Persia, first half of the 17th century, 9 ft 3 in × 6 ft 6 in.

11 Woollen knotted carpet, "Portuguese carpet", Persia, first half of the 17th century.

12 Woollen knotted carpet, "Sanguszko group", Persia, second half of the 16th century, fragment 3.75 × 2.70 m.

13 Silk knotted carpet, "Hunting carpet", Persia, 16th century, 6.93 × 3.23 m.

14 Silk tapestry-woven carpet, Kāshān, latter half of the 16th century, 2.14 × 1.46 m.

15a Silk knotted carpet, Persia, 16th century, 2.49 × 1.70 m.

15b Silk knotted carpet with gold and silver brocade, the so-called "Polonaise carpet", Iṣfahān, first quarter of the 17th century, 2.01 × 1.41 m.

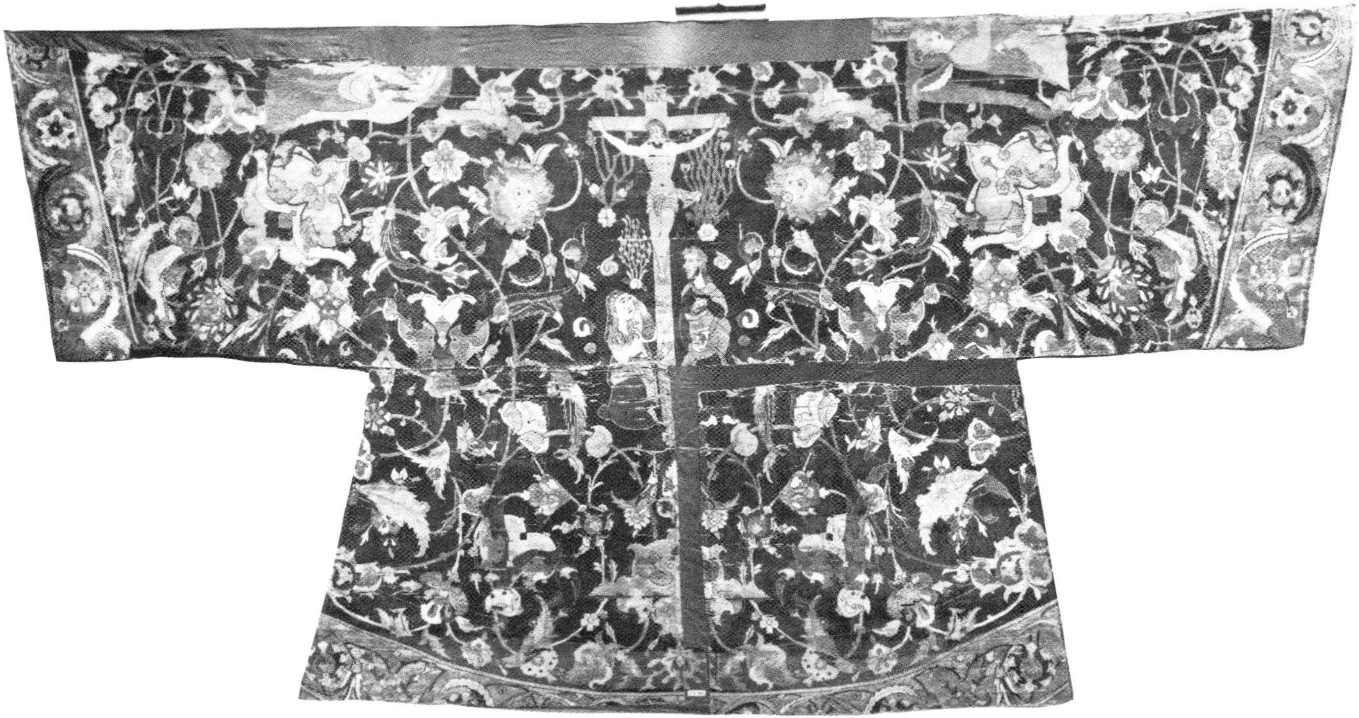

16 Cope, knotted in silk with brocade, Iṣfahān, beginning of the 17th century.

17 Velvet, enriched with metal thread, Persia, 16th century. Height of repeating pattern 34 cm.

18 Satin, Persia, beginning of the 17th century. Height of repeating pattern 24 cm.

19*a* Yazd. Masjid-i Jāmi‘, portal.

19*b* Yazd. Masjid-i Jāmi‘, view of court and sanctuary *aivān*.

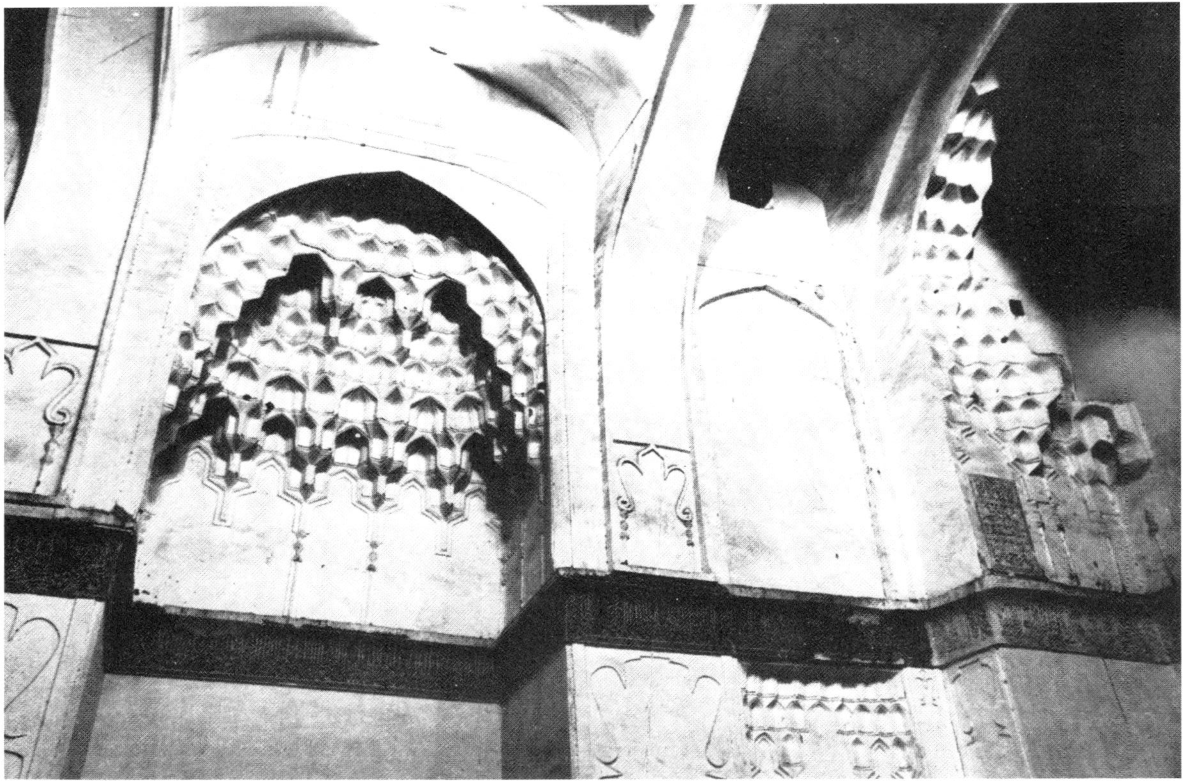

20 Turbat-i Shaikh Jām. Masjid-i Kirmānī, east wall, transverse vaults.

21 *a* Iṣfahān. Masjid-i Jāmiʿ, *miḥrāb* of the adjoining *madrasa*.

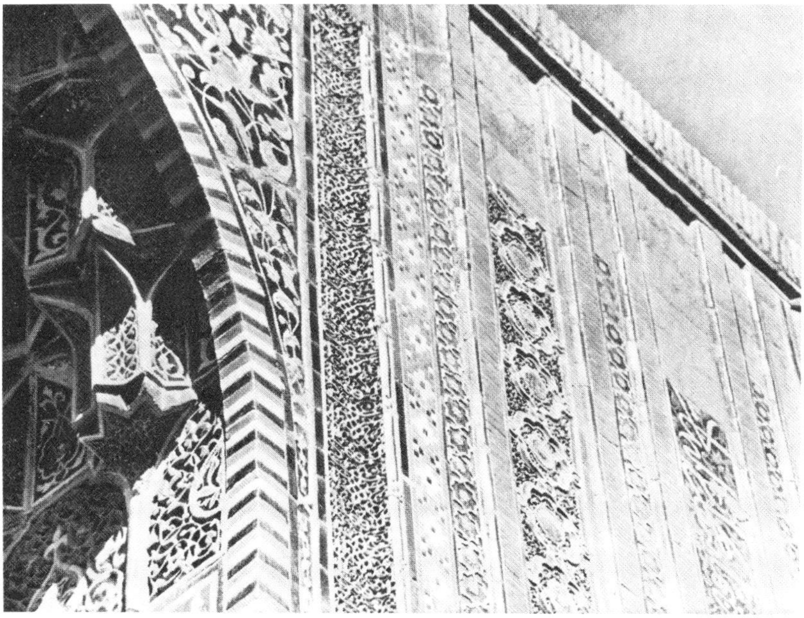

21 *b* Samarqand, Shāh-i Zinda. Detail of portal of the tomb of Terken Āqā.

22*a* Samarqand, Shāh-i Zinda. Detail of façade of the mausoleum of Tūmān Āqā.

22*b* Samarqand. Gūr-i Mīr, general view.

23 Turkistān, mausoleum of Aḥmad Yasavī, south elevation of the "complex" containing mosque, mausoleum, *khānqāh* and library.

24*a* Mashhad. Gauhar Shād mosque, sanctuary *aivān*.

24*b* Mashhad. Gauhar Shād mosque, detail of foundation inscription.

25 *a* Mashhad. Gauhar Shād mosque, southeast *aivān*.

25 *b* Herat, Gauhar Shād Muṣallā. Dome of the mausoleum of Gauhar Shād.

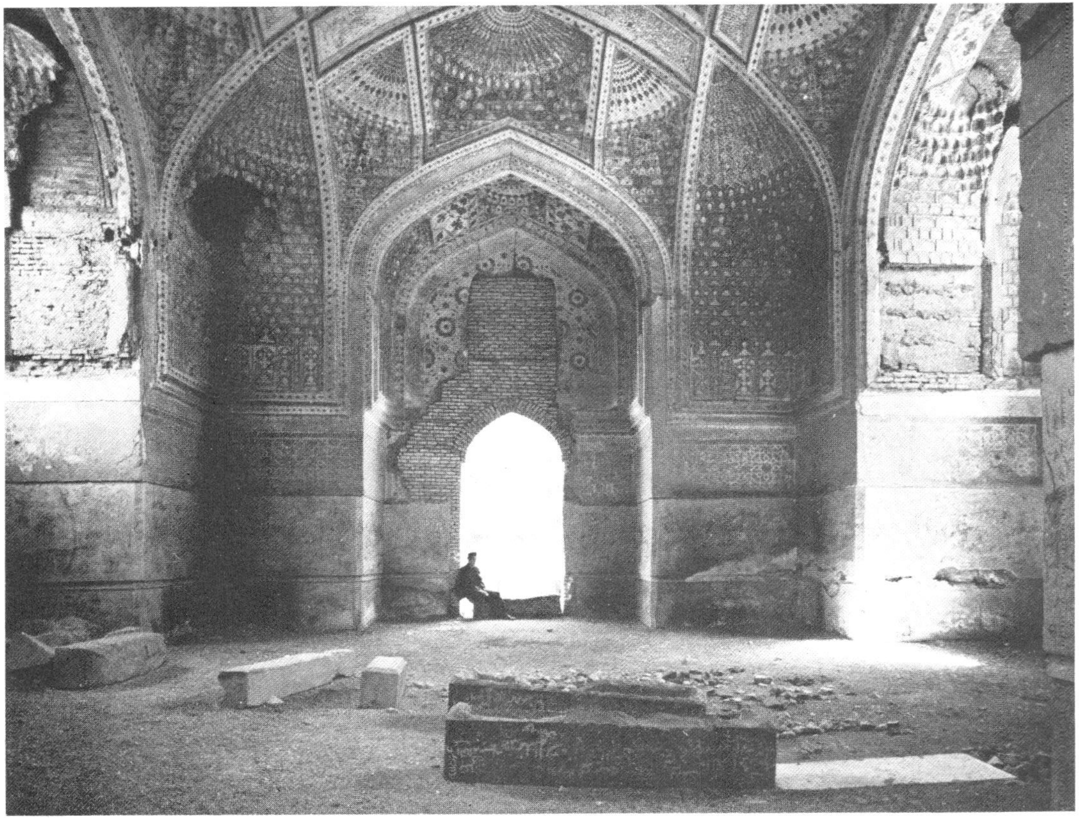

26 Herat, Gauhar Shād Musallā. Interior of the mausoleum of Gauhar Shād.

27 Herat, Gauhar Shād Muṣallā. Inside of the dome of the mausoleum of Gauhar Shād.

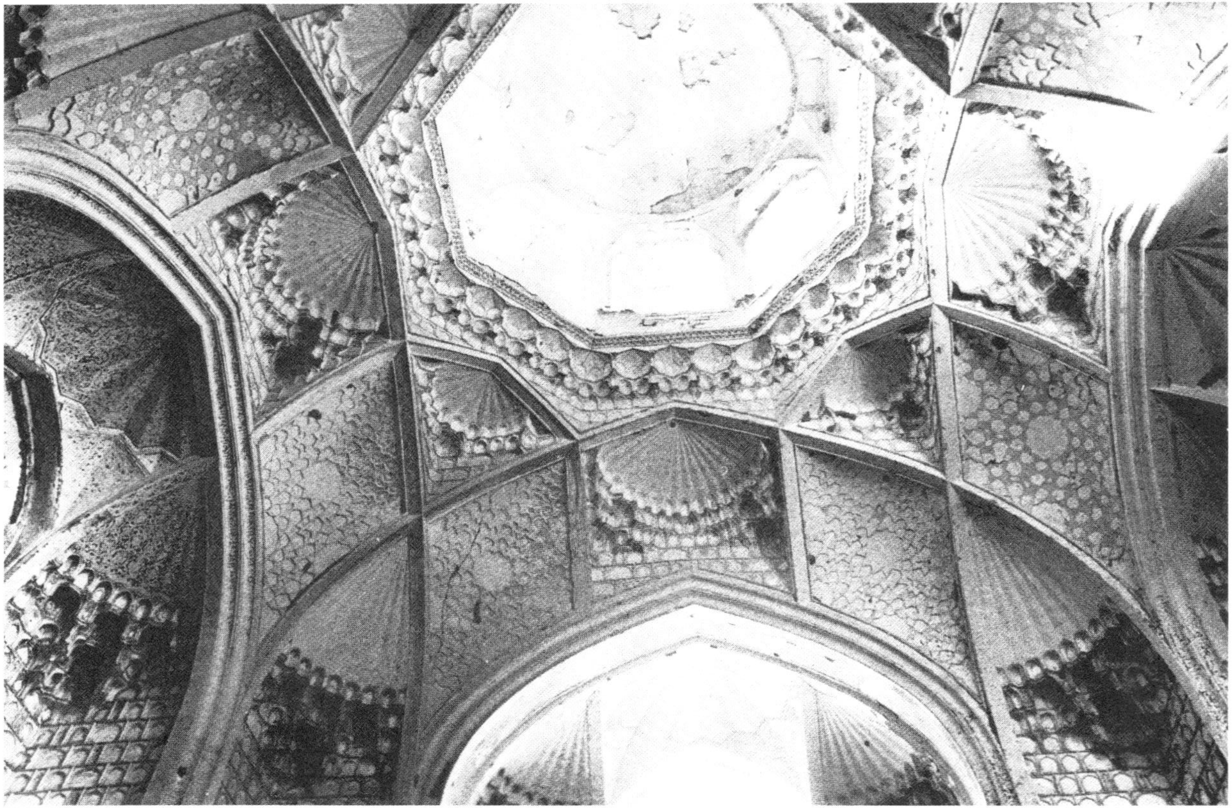

28 Khargird. *Madrasa* of Ghiyāṯ al-Dīn, interior of eastern domed room.

29 Herat, Gāzur Gāh. Detail of faience in sanctuary *aivān*.

30*a* Iṣfahān, Darb-i Imām, façade.

30*b* Iṣfahān, Darb-i Imām, detail of faience.

31 *a* Tabrīz. Blue mosque, main sanctuary, northwest side.

31 *b* Tabrīz. Blue mosque, main sanctuary, northeast side.

32*a* Tabrīz. Blue mosque, detail of main portal.

32*b* Tabrīz. Blue mosque, interior.

III. THE ERA OF SHĀH RUKH

Shāh Rukh, who succeeded to the empire on his father's death in 1405, had been governor of Khurāsān since 799/1396–7. Herat remained the seat of government until his death in 850/1447. Khurāsān was thus drawn into the cultural renaissance that was taking place in Transoxiana. Thanks to the patronage of Shāh Rukh and his consort Gauhar Shād the new architectural style was introduced into eastern Persia, where it was reinterpreted and developed by a younger generation of architects. The impact on Khurāsān is particularly striking. It is a curious fact that although the cruciform plan, that is, a court with a central aivān in each of its four sides, was adopted in domestic architecture and as a form of caravansarai and possibly of madrasa, it was only in western Iran that the cruciform plan was incorporated in the mosque and combined with the sanctuary dome chamber. The earliest example is the Masjid-i Jāmi' at Zavāra dated 530/1135–6. The known mosques of Khurāsān, however, are generally based on the two-aivān plan, the sanctuary aivān being opposed by an aivān on the north side. Such was the plan of the mosque at Furūmad (probably 13th century) and of the mosque at Zauzan (616/1219).[1]

It was due to the initiative of Gauhar Shād that the first cruciform mosque was introduced into Khurāsān. The mosque of Gauhar Shād in the shrine of the Imām Riḍā at Mashhad bears the impress of the style of Transoxiana.[2] According to the framing inscription of the sanctuary aivān which Bāīsunqur himself designed, the building was completed in 821/1418–19 by the munificence of his mother Gauhar Shād. Another inscription at the end of Bāīsunqur's inscription records that the architect was Qivām al-Dīn Zain al-Dīn of Shīrāz (pl. 24*b*). The word used here for architect is *ṭayyān* ("mason").[3] Qivām al-Dīn of Shīrāz is known to have been the leading architect at the court of Shāh Rukh.[4] Daulatshāh describes him as one of the four luminaries of the court and as one learned in mathematics, drawing and building. From another source, we know that he was versed in astrology. He must have joined the court before 1410, for in that year he built for Shāh Rukh a madrasa and khāngāh in Herat, of which neither has survived.

Gauhar Shād's mosque is built on the south side of the central core

[1] Godard, "Khorasan".

[2] *SPA*, pp. 1124–6, pls. 428–37.

[3] Sykes, "Historical Notes", pp. 1146–8.

[4] Golombek, *The Timurid Shrine at Gazur Gāh*, p. 76, n.33, for references to his life and works.

of the shrine and has, therefore, no entrance portal. The court, 55 m. long and 45 m. wide, is pierced on each side by an aivān. The sanctuary aivān on the south side is perceptibly wider than the others (pl. 24*a*). Between the aivāns are two-storeyed arcades with galleries in the rear – three on the east and west sides and seven on the sanctuary side. The dominant feature is the great south aivān arch flanked by cylindrical minarets with polygonal facets of marble around the bases. There is no screen between the domed sanctuary chamber and the aivān as in the Bībī Khānum mosque; the transition is effected by an inner nested arch. Within the chamber, the inner dome is set on four massive piers by means of stalactite net pendentives which provide a sixteen-sided seating for the circle of the dome. The miḥrāb is in a rectangular area set back from the dome chamber; and this additional chamber has a hemispherical vaulting of stalactites. The outer dome, revetted in turquoise tiles with a band of Kufic in black at its bulge, has a steep curvature and stands on a low drum. The transitional zone is concealed by a rather obtrusive four-sided structure, its three visible faces being divided into two-storeyed blind arcades. From the court the dome is barely visible behind the aivān screen.

European travellers have been unanimous in praising the sumptuous polychrome tile decoration of the court. Much of the tilework has undergone extensive restoration and a thoroughgoing analysis is required in order to realise Qivām al-Dīn's intention.[1] Mosaic tilework was used for spandrel decoration and framing inscriptions: larger surfaces were ornamented with geometric designs executed in glazed and unglazed bricks. A new technique, however, was employed in the intrados of the arches of the sanctuary and north-east aivāns: polygonal tiles were arranged to form star patterns with raised and interlaced framing bands of marble (pl. 25*a*). This use of tile decoration will occur again in Herat.

From 1417 to 1438, Qivām al-Dīn was collaborating in the building of the Muṣallā of Gauhar Shād to the north of the city of Herat.[2] Both this and the madrasa of Sulṭān Ḥusain Bāīqarā Mīrzā were almost entirely destroyed in 1885 by order of the amīr 'Abd al-Raḥmān, who

[1] Godard, in *AI* VIII, 11, mentions extensive repairs carried out in the mosque in 1087/1676–7. These included the filling in of many of the arcades flanking the sanctuary aivān as well as the addition of the parapet in order to counteract the outward thrust of the aivān arch. Perhaps, too, some of the tilework dates from this period.

[2] *SPA*, p. 1125. Yate, *Northern Afghanistan*, pp. 30–3.

thought that the buildings might provide cover for an invading Russian army. Fortunately we have detailed descriptions of the Muṣallā. It comprised a mosque and madrasa. The term muṣallā was applied to a mosque located outside the walls of a city where the citizens and inhabitants of the outlying districts congregated for the great religious festivals. Gauhar Shād's mosque in the Muṣallā was unusually large inasmuch as it was designed to accommodate such a congregation on the Feast of Sacrifices (*Qurbān bairām*) and the Feast at the breaking of the fast in Ramaḍān (*'Id al-fiṭr*). It was a large rectangular enclosure 106 m. by 64 m., with a minaret on an octagonal base at each corner. The inner court, 52 m. by 49 m., consisted of two-storeyed arcades and an aivān in the centre of each side. The sanctuary aivān, however, was flanked by two smaller aivāns, a composition recalling that of the great aivān of the Āq Sarāī at Shahr-i Sabz. An unusual feature was the addition of a smaller dome chamber behind the sanctuary dome chamber. The entrance portal on the north-eastern side was as high as the sanctuary aivān.

All that remains of the mosque today is a single minaret. These minarets must have been of great beauty. The angle of taper results from the diameter of the crown being half that of the base: the height is eight times the diameter of the base. The polygonal faces of the base were articulated by square and rectangular panels. Incorporated in these were stone panels carved in relief with intricately interlaced Kufic lettering on a ground of sinuous scrolling. The cylindrical surface above the polygonal base was entirely covered with bands of tilework and varying widths divided into three-fold divisions by three stalactite cornices. The principal bands are decorated with a network of mosaic tiles in the form of eight-pointed stars framed by a narrow marble moulding as in the court of Gauhar Shād's mosque at Mashhad. This elaborate surface embellishment of the minaret is an innovation, for the characteristic treatment in southern Persia as well as in Transoxiana was the insetting of glazed brick in the unglazed brick surface in the form of geometric designs often arranged in a spiral movement.

We do not know what part, if any, Qivām al-Dīn took in the building of this mosque; but that he was responsible for the construction of the madrasa which lies to the north of the mosque, and which was completed in 1432, we know from 'Abd al-Razzāq Samarqandī.[1] This

[1] 'Abd al-Razzāq, *Maṭla' al-sa'dain*, ed. M. Shafī' (Lahore, 1949), p. 720.

was constructed on the cruciform aivān plan, the principal façade with its vaulted entrance hall being flanked by corner minarets. The sanctuary aivān was extended in depth to the qibla wall and the miḥrāb itself was contained in a further rectangular chamber which projected from the wall. In each of the corners flanking the sanctuary aivān was a dome chamber, an arrangement already encountered in the madrasas of Transoxiana where similarly placed dome chambers performed the function of *darskhāna* (lecture room). All that remains of this madrasa is the east minaret and the right hand, that is, the western, dome chamber (pl. 25*b*). The latter is known as the mausoleum of Bāīsunqur, who was the first of his house to be buried there, in 836/1433.[1] Its external aspect resembles in certain respects that of the Gūr-i Mīr: the ribbed bulbous dome is supported on a high drum which rises from the cubical structure with no visible transitional zone. The ribs, however, are not joined tangentially as in the Gūr-i Mīr but are separated by bands of turquoise tiling. The ribs are revetted with square or rectangular tiles of black, white, red and two shades of blue arranged in diaper. Of particular interest is the extensive use of painted tiles: in the fine band of Kufic which appears to bind the base of the ribs to the dome, as well as in the stalactite corbelling and the vertical panels immediately below. The drum is lower than that of the Gūr-i Mīr, which probably required this additional emphasis.

The most striking feature, however, is the vaulting system of the interior, which must rank as a masterpiece of Muslim engineering skill (pl. 26). In the centre of each side of the square interior is an arched recess with a width of 4.5 m. The diameter of the dome is the same as the width of the recess. This is because the dome is supported on four great arches which spring from the forward edge of the recess arches, each adjacent pair intersecting to form the square. Secondary ribs spring from the haunches of the arches and effect the transition to the octagon by a series of "kite"-shaped pendentives which are so characteristic of Timurid and subsequent architecture. Above the octagon, sixteen fan-shaped pendentives complete the transition to the ceiling dome (pl. 27). The apex of each pendentive is decorated with stalactites either in relief or painted in blue, red and brown. This technique of intersecting vaulting arches was first employed in Samarqand. It had

[1] Yate, *Northern Afghanistan*, p. 31, enumerates six tombstones in the dome chamber, including that of Gauhar Shād, which is dated 861/1456–7: the latest is dated 898/1492–3.

the practical advantage of providing the structure with added strength to withstand earthquake; and quite as importantly, it had a powerful effect in the organising of the interior space. Instead of the clearly defined transitional zones of the squinch system, it produced a sense of upward motion by means of the tense rhythm of arch, rib and kite pendentive.

The attribution of the mausoleum to Qivām al-Dīn is founded not only on the statement of ʿAbd al-Razzāq but also on its stylistic similarities with the only other remaining work that can be assigned with certainty to the master. This is the Madrasa Ghiyāṣiyya at Khargird near Khwāf in Khurāsān.[1] The building was still unfinished when Qivām al-Dīn died in 1438 and according to the inscription it was completed by his associate Ghiyāṣ al-Dīn of Shīrāz in 1444. According to the portal inscription it was erected under the patronage of Shāh Rukh's minister Aḥmad b. Isḥāq and of Fakhr al-Dīn of Khwāf in 848/1444–5.

The Madrasa Ghiyāṣiyya is among the earliest madrasas in Persia. The Muzaffarid madrasa in the Masjid-i Jamiʿ, Iṣfahān, was incorporated in a larger building. The Madrasa-yi Imāmī in Iṣfahān was built probably in 1325 and is designed on a cruciform plan; but is a relatively modest structure. The madrasa at Khargird, on the contrary, although small by the standards of the madrasas of Transoxiana, was designed to fulfil all the requirements of the madrasa as it had developed in Samarqand and Bukhārā: living rooms, lecture room (darskhāna) and masjid.

The madrasa forms a rectangle 92 × 56 m. with an inner court 28 m. square (fig. 3). An aivān on each side results in a cruciform plan. Each aivān is flanked by two arcades in two storeys: and each corner is "champfered" and provided with a two-storeyed arcade. At each corner of the rectangle is a dome chamber and on the north side behind the main façade is a narthex consisting of a domed vestibule flanked by two large dome chambers. The principal façade is dominated by the slightly projecting aivān portal (pīshṭāq) which is flanked by triple arcades of which the central ones give access to the respective dome chambers. The façade is completed at each end by a tower, octagonal at the base.

The spatial organisation of the narthex is a wonderful unity of

[1] Diez, *Churasanische Baudenkmäler* I, 72–6. O'Kane, "The Madrasa al-Ghiyāsiyya at Khargird".

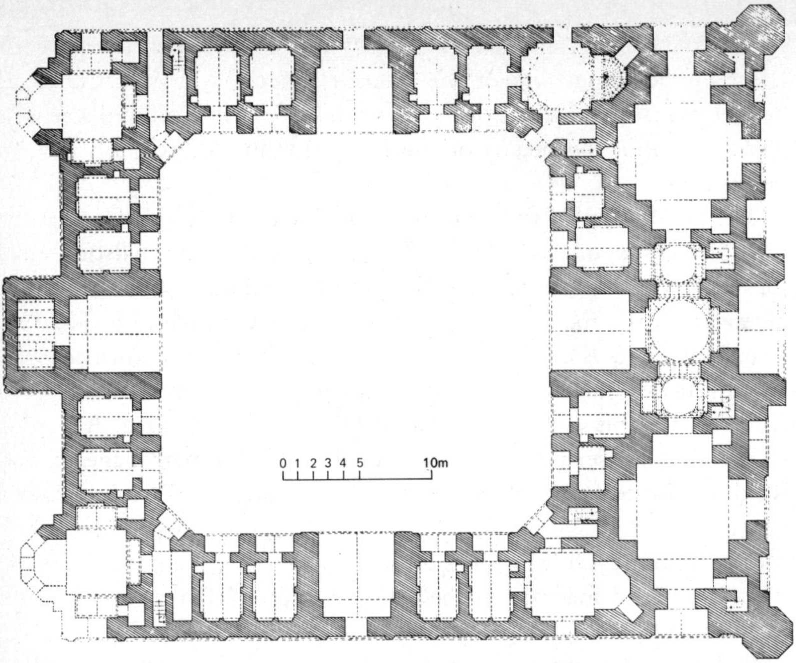

Fig. 3. Khargird. Plan of the *madrasa* of Ghiyāṣ al-Dīn.

design. The three dome chambers are joined by barrel-vaulted corridors of varying width. Of special interest are the two larger dome chambers each with a distinctive form of vaulting. That on the right, i.e., the northern dome chamber, is square with projecting niches on each side. The transition to the octagon is by means of squinches, the crowns being level with those of the niche arches. Above the octagon, stalactites effect the transition to a sixteen-side polygon. On this are set an inner and an outer row of eight piers which provide the seating for the inner and outer domes respectively.

The system of vaulting adopted in the left hand dome chamber is that of the mausoleum of Bāīsunqur in Herat (pl. 28, fig. 4). By means of intersecting arches which spring from the sides of the terminal niches, the diameter of the dome is reduced to the width of the latter. Subsidiary ribs form the characteristic "kite" pendentives just as in the mausoleum of Bāīsunqur. The work thus bears the unmistakable stamp of Qivām al-Dīn.

The Madrasa Ghiyāṣiyya served the Shāfi'ī rite and with its twenty

Fig. 4. Khargird, *madrasa*. Plan and section of the eastern dome chamber.

cells is modest by the standards of Transoxiana. Diez, who published a detailed description of the madrasa, has drawn attention to the determining effect of seasonal climate on function. As in domestic buildings, so in this madrasa distinct parts of the complex were appropriated for winter and for summer use. Those on the northern side were for summer, those on the southern for winter. This factor would account, too, for the difference in the vaulting systems of the two dome chambers in the vestibule, the smaller dimensions of the dome of the left hand one providing some measure of protection from the rigours of the cold.

Much of the building effort in the reign of Shāh Rukh was directed to the architectural development of the shrine complex. Gauhar Shād's mosque at Mashhad was introduced into a pre-existing group of buildings centred on the domed mausoleum where were interred the remains of the Eighth Imām. Other shrine complexes in Khurāsān developed around the grave of the saint which remained, however, in the open and without architectural covering. Perhaps this practice was determined by a literal adherence to the Islamic proscription of elaborate funerary monuments. Nevertheless, no scruples seem to have prevented the embellishment of such shrines by the construction of pious foundations and adjuncts in proximity to the saint's grave.

The most important of such shrine complexes is that of the eleventh century saint, Khwāja 'Abd-Allāh Anṣārī in the village of Gāzur Gāh on the northern outskirts of Herat. This shrine has been the subject of a penetrating study by L. Golombek, who has contributed not only a masterly analysis of the structure but also an illuminating commentary on the religious function. She suggests that the shrine at Gāzur Gāh is a *ḥaẓīra*. This term ("fenced enclosure") would properly refer to the tomb enclosure of the saint set on a raised platform and surrounded by a balustrade of wood or stone, but in the Timurid period was extended to cover all the subsidiary buildings necessary for the functioning of a great shrine complex of which the central feature was the ḥaẓīra proper.

The great rectangular building which forms the shrine of the saint was built by Shāh Rukh in 1425. The western and principal fâçade, with its vaulted entrance aivān flanked by blind arcades and terminal towers octagonal in section, anticipates that of the madrasa at Khargird. The pīshṭāq leads into a vaulted vestibule flanked by two rooms roofed by transverse vaults, the one a masjid, the other an assembly hall. The inner court is organised on the cruciform aivān plan with lofty arcades flanking the aivāns on the north, south and west sides. The saint's grave stands in front of the great western aivān which is both taller and wider than the other aivāns. Above the apex of the arch, the screen is pierced with a gallery of five arcades and surmounted at each end by a lantern turret. One curious feature is that while to the west of the aivāns on the north and south sides there are vaulted rooms behind the arcaded façade, to the east of the aivāns the latter is merely a curtain wall. Golombek has suggested that this, together with the great aivān, was designed to give definition to the whole east end of the court as the ḥaẓīra.

Some of these features are to be found at Turbat-i Shaikh Jām half way between Mashhad and Herat, another great shrine complex.[1] But while Gāzur Gāh was a single creation, Turbat-i Shaikh Jām developed from the 13th to 15th centuries. Successive buildings were constructed about a rectangular enclosure in the southern quarter of which lay the saint's tomb open to the sky. A square dome chamber to the south of the tomb is the earliest of these buildings. In the course of the 14th century, a mosque was built on the east side of this dome chamber, a khāngāh and madrasa on the west, and a great aivān portal on the north. In 1362, the two halls flanking the portal were built. These afford a striking parallel to the two halls flanking the entrance portal at Gāzur Gāh: these, too, are roofed by transverse vaulting. The one is an assembly hall and the other a masjid in which the miḥrāb is placed in the centre of the southern and long side. The latter, known as the Masjid-ī Kirmānī after its architect Khwāja Zakī b. Muḥammad b. Mas'ūd, has already been mentioned (pl. 20).

Tīmūr himself erected a khāngāh on the north side of the enclosure but no trace of this remains. The most important additions in the Timurid period were those of Shāh Rukh's chief amīr Jalāl al-Dīn Fīrūz Shāh. These were a madrasa on the west side of the court and a "new" mosque immediately to the south of the square dome chamber. Apparently only a part of the eastern side of the madrasa was completed: a small domed vestibule and a dome chamber to the south known as the Gunbad-i Sabz, which according to an inscription was the work of Ustād Ḥājjī Maḥmūd, here described as attached to the Jāmi' of Shīrāz, in 844/1440–1. The dome of the Gunbad-i Sabz is supported on the system of intersecting arches which we have already met in the Madrasa-yi Ghiyāṣiyya at Khargird and the Gauhar Shād mausoleum at Herat. All that remains of Fīrūz Shāh's new mosque, completed in 846/1442–3, is the domed sanctuary chamber, the remainder having been rebuilt in recent times. Its vaulting system is that of the Gunbad-i Sabz.

Shāh Rukh's minister, Aḥmad b. Isḥāq b. Majd al-Dīn Muḥammad of Khwāf, who was co-founder of the Madrasa-yi Ghiyāṣiyya at Khargird, was responsible for the so-called Masjid-i Maulānā at Tayyābād, south of the village of Yūsufābād near the present Afghan frontier.[2]

[1] Golombek, "The chronology of Turbat-i Shaikh Jām". O'Kane, "Taybād", pp. 96–103.
[2] *Ibid.*, pp. 87–96.

Completed in 848/1444–5, the same year as the madrasa at Khargird, it is described in its dedicatory inscription as a *buq'a*, a term apparently indicating a funerary function and assembly hall for a ṣūfī community. The tomb of the local saint, Zain al-Dīn, stands in the middle of a rectangular enclosure. The Masjid-i Maulānā occupies the south side of the latter and consists of a great aivān with two small flanking aivāns leading into vaulted rooms. A doorway in the near wall of the principal aivān gives access to the square dome chamber, the dome being supported on intersecting ribs. The name of the architect is unrecorded but Godard, drawing attention to the similarity in the treatment of the faience decoration to that of Gauhar Shād's mosque at Mashhad and of the Khargird madrasa, has suggested that the Tayyābād masjid was the work of Ghiyās̱ al-Dīn of Shīrāz, who collaborated with Qivām al-Dīn at Khargird.

These Khurasanian monuments retain much of their original surface decoration. Painted designs were reserved for interiors, such as in Gauhar Shād's mausoleum at Herat and Qivām al-Dīn's dome chamber at Khargird. Large external surfaces were decorated with glazed brick inlaid in the unglazed brick surface in the form of bold chevron and lozenge patterns. Mosaic faience was reserved for smaller areas such as arch spandrels and inscription bands. The patterns were generally floral. Perhaps the most felicitous use of tilework is to be seen in the interior of the great eastern aivān at Gāzur Gāh, where a lower dado is decorated with square panels of inlaid bricks arranged in Kufic "seal" forms and a upper register is composed of polygonal panels – rhomboids, hexagons and triangles – with floral, geometric and "seal" patterns rendered in mosaic faience (pl. 29).

Shīrāzī architects seem to have predominated in Khurāsān during the reign of Shāh Rukh and were probably the principal inspiration in the development of the new style. No doubt it was they who adopted the transverse vaulting system with such effect at Gāzur Gāh and Turbat-i Shaikh Jām. This, together with the use of intersecting arches as a dome support, created a new concept of interior space. The architectural forms of Transoxiana were refined: thus the ribbed dome of Gauhar Shād's mausoleum is more acceptable than that of the Gūr-i Mīr as, too, is the relation between dome and drum. The façade of the court of Gauhar Shād's mosque at Mashhad with its harmonious and rhythmic alternation of voids and solids set a standard for later generations of Persian architects. The faience decoration of the buildings we have been considering was of a quality and variety rarely equalled and never surpassed in subsequent periods.

IV. ARCHITECTURAL ACTIVITY UNDER THE TÜRKMEN DYNASTIES

In western and southern Persia during the reign of Shāh Rukh there was no building activity comparable to that in Khurāsān. Timurid power was contested first by the Jalayirids and then by the Türkmen Qarā Quyūnlū; but the political disruptions of the period are only a partial explanation of the paucity of surviving monuments. We have seen the contribution of the architects of Shīrāz in Khurāsān; yet their native city has little or nothing to offer. This is all the stranger inasmuch as Shīrāz under the patronage of its Timurid governors, Iskandar b. ʿUmar Shaikh and Shāh Rukh's son Ibrāhīm, was an active centre of manuscript illumination and painting.

In 840/1436–7 the amīr Chaqmaq built a four-aivān mosque in Yazd. The sanctuary aivān leads to a vaulted chamber containing the miḥrāb. Its most interesting feature is the oratory adjacent to the sanctuary which, with its transverse vaulting and clerestory lighting, resembles the Muzaffarid oratories in the Masjid-i Jāmiʿ at Yazd.[1] The only surviving evidence of Timurid building in Iṣfahān is the winter oratory behind the north-west aivān in the Masjid-i Jāmiʿ.[2] This was erected in 851/1444 at the order of Bāīsunqur's son, Sulṭān Muḥammad, who governed Iṣfahān from 850/1446 to 855/1451. With its groined vaulting, supported by eighteen squat piers square in section, it is an impressive building. Daylight filters through panels inserted in the middle of each vault; and the low height of the hall is designed to provide a refuge from the winter's cold. The architect of this building was a certain Shaikh Ḥasan b. Sharaf al-Dīn, a native of Ravīdasht near Kūhpāya, to the east of Iṣfahān.

The renewal of building activity was due to Türkmen initiative. In 1435 Tabrīz became the capital of the Qarā Quyūnlū and in 856/1452 Jahān Shāh occupied Iṣfahān. In the same year the Darb-i Imām was built to contain the tombs of the Imāmzādas Ibrāhīm Baṭḥā and Zain al-ʿĀbidīn. Much restored and altered in the Safavid period, it was

[1] Golombek, *The Timurid Shrine at Gazur Gah*, fig. 148. Hill and Grabar, fig. 201. *SPA*, pl. 449.
[2] Godard, "Historique du Masdjid-é Djumʿa d'Iṣfahān", pp. 245f. Hunarfar, *Ganjīna*, pp. 121–3.

originally a dome chamber preceded by a vestibule and portal.[1] The last has long been recognised as a masterpiece of tile decoration (pl. 30*a*). It is also of considerable significance inasmuch as its composition adumbrates that of the Safavid portal. The voussoir of the arch is defined by a facetted moulding which rests on low engaged columns of stone. The portal niche is treated as the halved section of a square dome chamber in which the transition to the hemispherical vault is obtained by two squinch arches each with a flanking arch. Subsidiary ribs spring from the haunches and apex of each arch and meet to form a starlike support for the hemispherical vault. The function of the ribs, however, is probably a simulated one, for the actual springing of the vault occurs at the springing of the arches which themselves incline forwards. The tile revetment is of the highest quality. The arch is framed by a band of mosaic tilework with alternate cross and cartouche figures containing single floral sprays and split-leaf arabesques. A dado of monochrome pentagonal tiles runs around the screen and the niche interior. Flanking the door, now replaced by a wood screen carved in openwork, are panels of symmetrically disposed flowers issuing from a vase (pl. 30*b*). The two side walls of the interior are decorated with polygonal mosaic tiles applied to a star-tessellated ground of polygonal tiles. A broad inscription band intervenes between these panels and the squinch zone.

The most ambitious monument of the period of Jahān Shāh Qarā Quyūnlū is the so-called Blue Mosque in Tabrīz, built by Jahān Shāh's daughter Ṣāliḥa Khānum in 1465.[2] The Blue Mosque has been regarded as a rare example of a covered mosque in Persia. One interpretation of the ground plan suggests a cruciform aivān court covered by a great dome, surrounded on three sides by vaulted and domed galleries (fig. 5). A sanctuary dome chamber projects from the south side, connected with the great inner dome court by the south aivān. The

[1] Godard, "Isfahan". See also Hunarfar, *Ganjīna*, pp. 243–353, for a revised reading of the portal inscription containing the names of both Jahān Shāh and the Timurid Sulṭān Muḥammad. The latter died in 855/1451–2, and no satisfactory explanation of the introduction of his name has been offered.

[2] To bibliography in *SPA*, p. 1130, n.4, add Dibāj, *Āṣār*, p. 76–80; also *Masterpieces of Iranian Architecture*, pp. 82–3, containing measured plans, elevations and sections. The attribution to Ṣāliḥa is given by Qāżī Ḥusain Maibudī (*SPA*, pp. 1130f., n.5); but her name does not appear in either of the two incomplete historical inscriptions, the first in the name of Jahān Shāh, the second naming Ni'mat-Allāh b. Muḥammad al-Bavvāb with the date 4 Rabī' I 870. It is not clear whether the latter was the architect or the official who supervised the building of the mosque. See Hinz, "Beiträge", pp. 58–60, 421–2; Sauvaget, "Notes épigraphiques", pp. 105f.

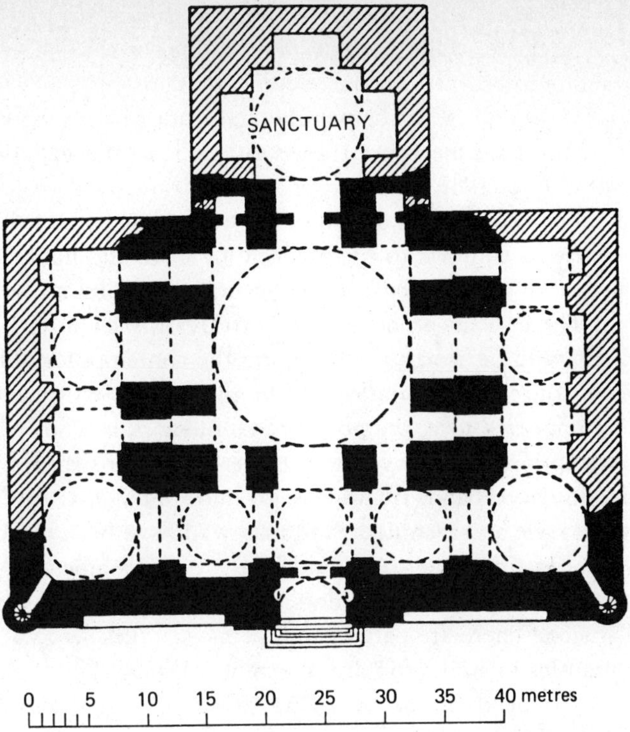

Fig. 5. Tabrīz. Ground plan of the Blue Mosque.

galleries were roofed by transverse vaults which on the east and west sides supported a dome behind the respective aivāns. The north gallery, which served as the vestibule, contained three domed vaults equal in diameter to those of the side galleries. In the north-west and north-east corners of the galleries were two larger domed vaults. The main façade of this mosque contained a lofty arched portal approached by a flight of three steps and at either end a tall tapering minaret round in section. The most interesting structural feature of the mosque is the vaulting system of the domed court. The great dome, 16.75 m. in diameter, is supported on eight arches of equal span which spring from eight massive pillars (pl. 31*a*). In actual fact, four of these are squinch arches which spring at an oblique angle from the piers. The spaces between the arches were filled in with bricks, each successive row slightly corbelled in order to secure the circular seating for the dome. In the rear wall of each aivān was an arched opening leading to the galleries and sanctuary chamber; and there were similar arched openings in the adjacent walls beneath the squinch arches. Since these arched openings occupied about one-half of the height of the great dome-supporting arches, it was possible to create window openings in the upper half, since the central mass rises above the galleries. The great dome and much of the vaulting has been destroyed as a result of earthquake, but enough remains to judge with what success the architect had realised a solution to the problem of space and light.

There has been some speculation regarding the source and origin of this design. There seems no need to look to Byzantine church architecture; and it would be worth investigating the contemporary Ottoman mosque as a source of inspiration. If the plan of the mosque was the result of an imported idea, the polychrome tilework is wholly Persian, with the exception, perhaps, of the gallery dado consisting of white geometric interlaced bands on a black ground (pls. 31*b*, 32*a*).[1] Much is distinctive in style and technique and may well have been the work of local masters. In this category would be the embellishment of mosaic tile patterns with an overlay of knots, arabesques and naskhī lettering in raised stucco. There are panels, too, of mosaic tiles set in a ground of terracotta tiles in a chevron arrangement (pl. 32*b*). Tilework of this style was introduced in the sanctuary aivān of the Masjid-i Jāmiʿ, Iṣfahān, when the Āq Quyūnlū ruler Uzun Ḥasan carried out restorations there in 1475–6.

Two years after the completion of the Blue Mosque, Jahān Shāh died in battle against Uzun Ḥasan, leader of the rival Türkmen dynasty, the Āq Quyūnlū. Apart from Uzun Ḥasan's restorations in the Masjid-i Jāmiʿ at Iṣfahān, there is no surviving evidence of the buildings with which he embellished Tabrīz. A Venetian merchant who visited the city about 1510 has described the park and palace of the Hasht Bihisht as well as the other monuments of the city,[2] but these are the work, as Woods has demonstrated, of Uzun Ḥasan's son Yaʿqūb.[3] Hinz, however, has located Uzun Ḥasan's mosque and madrasa near the Ṣāḥib al-ʿAmr mosque.[4]

[1] Seherr-Thoss, p. 170 and pl. 78, observes that this style of geometric dado is frequently found in 15th–16th century Ottoman buildings.

[2] *A Narrative of Italian Travels*, p. 177.

[3] John E.Woods, *The Aqquyunlu. Clan, Confederation, Empire* (Bibliotheca Islamica, Chicago, 1976), p. 150.

[4] Hinz, "Beiträge", pp. 60–4.

CHAPTER 15 (*b*)

SAFAVID ARCHITECTURE*

Safavid buildings are preserved in greater abundance than those of any other period in Iran. Yet Safavid architecture is far more imperfectly known than that of the Saljūqs, Il-Khanids or Timurids. Several factors help to explain this paradox. One is quite simply prejudice. The finest Safavid buildings lend themselves to uncritical panegyric and readily enter the unlovely category of tourist attractions, and perhaps for that very reason many of them have not been subjected to detailed scholarly analysis. Alternatively, one might cite the inadequate documentation of Safavid architecture: the relative dearth of monographs, technical drawings and theses in this field makes any general survey premature. A third contributory factor is the over-exposure of a few significant buildings in Iṣfahān, whose very accessibility is a snare and throws into unjust obscurity comparatively inaccessible work at Ardabīl, Māhān, Kirmān and Mashhad.

This paradoxical neglect of a richly productive period has meant that the term "Safavid" is not yet precise enough to be used safely in the context of architecture. It does not yet connote special kinds of ground plan, spatial organisation, façade composition, *muqarnas*, arch profiles or vaulting, though it is a widely used concept in the field of tilework. One of the objects of this chapter is to demonstrate that at least three Safavid styles coexisted and that only the function of the building – religious, palatial or otherwise secular – determined which of them should be used.

It is in the domain of religious architecture that the definition of a Safavid style poses the most problems, particularly in view of the eagerness of Safavid patrons to repair and extend earlier monuments. These changes are rarely recorded in detail in the inscriptions which mention them, and tile mosaic – at first sight the obvious dating control – is a potentially treacherous guide because of the innate conservatism of the medium in such matters as technique and palette. A close examination of the designs employed might lead, in Safavid as in early Islamic ornament, to the recognition of small but significant

* I am most grateful to David Gye, Dr Karīm Yūsuf-Jamālī, Bernard O'Kane and Douglas Pickett for their comments on an earlier draft of this chapter, and to Dr Ronald Ferrier for his assistance with the illustrations.

changes in apparently standard design elements and these might then be fitted into a chronological framework.[1] In the absence of inscriptions, certain types of brick and stucco ornament, fresco painting and, above all, square underglaze-painted tiles and their varied subject matter all furnish useful clues for dating. But the close resemblance between the decorated domes of the Masjid-i Shāh and the Mādar-i Shāh madrasa is sufficient reminder of the pitfalls of using ornament as a dating control. It is not surprising that, in cultic architecture, "Safavid" has become something of a collective adjective to describe work which could date from almost any time between the 15th and the 20th century.

The definition of "Safavid" in the case of palatial architecture presents rather fewer problems; fewer than ten palaces survive, most of them in Iṣfahān, and they are usually datable either by inscriptions or by literary evidence. Their ostentatiously frail architecture, their garden setting and their decoration, with its echoes of the minor arts, together lend these palaces a recognisable individuality.

Finally, the term "Safavid" is widely and often inaccurately used to describe a great range of non-palatial secular structures. In some of these buildings – dams, pigeon towers, cisterns, ice houses – the scope for innovation was slight. It is in the study of bridges and caravansarais that the search for a distinctive Safavid secular style may most profitably be pursued. But such buildings are especially hard to date. Devoid alike of ornament and epigraphy, they have an almost puritanical austerity. They obey the maxim that form follows function. They inhabit a different world from that of the imperial monuments in Iṣfahān, and their influence extended right into the present century. Numerous differences in plan, size, layout or facilities may be noted between the various caravansarais in particular, but these may reflect specific local needs or the amount of money available and are not necessarily helpful in dating these buildings or in identifying a developing style.

So much for the obstacles which currently impede a proper understanding of Safavid architecture. In such a situation the most profitable approach may well be to base a general survey on detailed discussion of a few key monuments, and thus prevent the discussion

[1] M.S. Dimand, "Studies in Islamic Ornament. I. Some Aspects of Omaiyad and Early ʿAbbasid Ornament", *AI* IV (1937), 293–337.

degenerating into a jejune list of buildings, dates and craftsmen. Only by drastic selection will the wood emerge from the trees. But – to adapt the familiar metaphor – the nature of the wood depends on the type and quantity of trees. Brief lists of buildings will therefore be included as background material at certain stages of the discussion. Buildings usually omitted from general surveys will be analysed in an attempt to bring into clearer focus the architectural activity of the 16th and the later 17th centuries, two substantial epochs in the history of Safavid architecture which have hitherto been very imperfectly known.

The accession of Shah Ismā'īl (907/1501) has commonly been regarded as a turning point in the history of Iran. It would be idle, however, to regard his reign as a comparable landmark in architectural history. Indeed, it would be hard to find any quarter-century in Iranian architecture since the rise of the Saljūqs (the aftermath of the Mongol conquests excepted) of which less material evidence survives. Architecture was of far less account to the shah than were poetry, painting, calligraphy and music.[1] Perhaps the political turmoil of Ismā'īl's reign ensured that unusually little was produced. At all events, no breath of innovation disturbed the architecture of the time, which placidly continued in the late Timurid idiom. Small-scale decorative set-pieces closely rivalled the best work of the previous age, but there seems to have been no attempt to imitate the ambitious ensembles (e.g. at Mashhad and Samarqand) popular in the previous century. Enthusiastic accounts of the palaces of Ismā'īl have been left by Western travellers, but apparently none of these structures was built to last. The random scatter of surviving early 16th-century buildings offers no clue to the magnificence of later Safavid architecture.

Undoubtedly the masterpiece of the period is the portal of the tomb of Hārūn-i Vilāyat at Iṣfahān, dated Rabī' I 918/May – June 1513. The patron, the Grand Vizier Durmīsh Khān, is mentioned in a Persian distich over the door; such poetical quotations, hitherto infrequent, quickly became a characteristic of Safavid buildings. Architecturally the complex is curious rather than distinguished, with an exterior which *in toto* falls far short of the portal, though the original layout has been overlaid by numerous later restorations. The exterior elevation of the dome chamber illustrates in miniature the piecemeal nature of the

[1] See M.K. Yūsuf-Jamālī, *The Life and Personality of Shāh Ismā'īl I (1487–1524)*, unpublished Ph.D. thesis, Edinburgh, 1981, pp. 154–70, 232–45.

whole complex. Its octagonal base gives way to a square middle storey, a reversal of the usual practice. The dome above, whose tilework is entirely of recent date, rests on a high cylindrical drum set over a modest octagon and has a slight bulge at the collar, a profile very close to that of the Masjid-i Shāh, Mashhad (855/1451). In its choicc of basic elements such as dome, courtyard and façade the building is in no sense novel.

But a distinct change of emphasis can be detected here. Attention focuses on the exterior façade rather than on the internal layout, an emphasis frequently repeated in later Safavid buildings. It is of a piece with this approach that areas which are generally seen (such as the lower part of the drum and the octagon beneath it) should be left in plain brick. The building is conceived more as a frame for lavish decoration than as an entity in which each element has its part to play; hence its defective design. Its façade, to be sure, subtly exploits the plastic potential of the arched niche, which, repeated at various scales and depths, is the leitmotif of the whole composition. But stepping through the grandiose gateway the visitor can scarcely escape a feeling of anticlimax at the restricted inner courtyard and at the imbalance of the dominant dome chamber in this cramped composition. Internally this dome chamber is unremarkable as architecture; it is notable principally for its dadoes of tile mosaic and its numerous inscription bands.

The identity of the saintly Hārūn in whose honour the tomb (*mashhad*) was built remains a mystery which the romantic confections of Chardin do little to dispel. He is referred to only indirectly by means of a *ḥadīth* quoted in a foundation inscription whose allusiveness can be paralleled in other contemporary epigraphy. Far from being a simple factual record of the date of the building and the titles of the ruler, it is an elaborate act of homage to Shah Ismā'īl. His descent from 'Alī (*jaddhu*) is brought in under cover of the ḥadīth mentioning Hārūn. His war against the Ottomans is exalted into a *jihād* by the use of the time-honoured titles *al-ghāzī, al-mujāhid fī sabīl Allāh*. His rule is twice termed a caliphate, surely intended as a counter to the Ottoman usurpation of the title. A punning reference to the name of the tomb may be detected in the use of the title *wālī al-wilāyat* for the shah, and it is surely no coincidence that this inscription, placed in a portal, mentions the ever-open doors of the shah's bounty. It is even possible that this apparently conventional eulogy is intended to bear a theological interpretation. In some of his more ecstatic verse Ismā'īl compared himself to ʻAlī, and the concept of ʻAlī as the gate to paradise was standard among Shīʻīs. Indeed, the inscription over the eastern door of the mausoleum – again the location is important – quotes Muḥammad's saying, "I am the city of knowledge and ʻAlī is its gate". Appropriately enough the name of ʻAlī joins those of Muḥammad and Allāh in a cartouche of square Kufic placed at the apex of the entrance arch. Below this, and in the tympanum of the door itself, is a panel depicting "birds of paradise" set within a radiant nimbus of Chinese clouds. The central axis of this figural panel coincides exactly with the name Ismāʻīl in the main portal inscription immediately beneath it. The name and titles of the shah are executed in dusky golden letters which stand out from the white used for the rest of the inscription. It is hard to avoid the conclusion that inscription and decoration alike have theological as well as political undertones and that they exalt the more than human status of Ismāʻīl.[1]

Yet it is not on these grounds that the building has attracted attention, for its crucial position in the history of glazed tilework has pre-empted detailed discussion of its other features. Apart from the high quality of the tilework, its dependence on earlier techniques demands emphasis. Its hints on the future development of Safavid tilework are noted below, but at the same time it exemplifies the major techniques developed previously. Thus, with the nearby Masjid-i ʻAlī, it serves as a coda to a great tradition. In addition to tile mosaic, the best established of these tilework techniques, it illustrates chequerboard work derived ultimately from Saljūq brick decoration, glazed geometric window grilles, strips of monochrome tilework outlining architectural features and the use of glazed insets against a predominantly brick background. A wide range of scripts is employed. The tall compressed cursive usually termed *thulth* predominates, but the verses over the door are a very early monumental example of *nastaʻlīq*, while *naskh* and square Kufic are also found.[2] The use of a different colour for the name and titles of the sovereign had long been standard practice, nor was it a novelty to employ living creatures in the decorative scheme. Floral compositions closely linked to carpet designs were equally familiar. Only the emphasis on thin billowing sprays, effortlessly confined to their panels and pruned of most of their leaves, is perhaps hard to

[1] Hunarfar, *Ganjīna*, p. 368: it is undated.
[2] For the inscriptions, see Godard, "Iṣfahān", pp. 64–5, 68; Hunarfar, *Ganjīna*, pp. 360–9.

parallel in earlier work, though of course the arabesque is as old as Islamic art itself. But what the façade lacks in novelty it redeems by the diverse range of styles which it fits into a limited space, and by its daring chromatic harmonies. The thin glazed strips, like much of the tile mosaic, are in line with Timurid work in Khurāsān, while the motif of glazed insets against plain brick – the single recurrent theme of the façade – finds, like the tawny marble dado, a ready parallel in the Blue Mosque at Tabrīz. Thus this early Safavid building in central Iran draws together (as does contemporary painting) the divergent threads of eastern and western Persian traditions in a harmonious synthesis – an apt symbol of this nascent pan-Iranian kingdom.

The sister building to the mashhad of Hārūn-i Vilāyat, the neighbouring and almost exactly contemporary Masjid-i ʻAlī, shares many of its characteristics. It too is renowned for the tilework of its façade, though here plain brick and geometric patterns play a much larger rôle than at Hārūn-i Vilāyat. Some of the untiled designs would not look out of place on a Saljūq building, apart from the yellow brick in which they are executed. Square Kufic is used on both a small and a large scale to spell out sacred names. Architecturally this mosque, apparently a new foundation, is of a much higher order than the nearby mausoleum, though their street façades have much in common. Internally the Masjid-i ʻAlī – the name is apparently a popular one, like its former title of the Sanjarī mosque, and is not attested by inscription – is of four-*aivān* plan, with a substantial domed sanctuary. This chamber, dated 929/1522, provides an instructive link between the Blue Mosque of Tabrīz and the Masjid-i Shaikh Luṭf-Allāh. With its numerous arched bays opening at ground and gallery level it at once recalls the earlier building. But the square ground plan, and the use of four massive pendentives to carry the dome, looks ahead to the later mosque. These pendentives are identical in size and contour to the arches along the main axes; net vaulting fills the intervening spaces, and a thick circular inscription band (Qur'ān xvii. 1–14) completes the transition to the dome. This interior is of almost unrelieved plainness; its white plaster surfaces are heightened only by the red outlining of the arch profiles. Within the bays the upper area is filled by modest decorative minor vaults. Nothing could refute more decisively the popular image of Safavid architecture dominated by applied ornament. The handsome, spacious proportions of this mosque, and its bold reworking of the traditional domed square formula, make it formally the outstanding building of this period, even though it would be rash to conclude that it exerted direct influence on later architects.

The portal inscription contains theological allusions of the same esoteric nature as those discussed earlier. Shah Ismā'īl is described as the one "on whom descends the grace of having his name repeated in the Qur'ān as many times as there are Imāms". On the face of it, this simply celebrates the pious antecedents of his name. But since the name of Ismā'īl occurs in the Qur'ān twelve times, and since it was the Twelver Shī'ī faith that Ismā'īl had instituted as the national creed, this phrasing may be seen not only as intensely topical but also as an attempt to elevate Ismā'īl to the rank of Imām at least by implication. There may be a hint too that this accords with the Divine will : hence the numerical concordance between the number of references to Ismā'īl in the Qur'ān and the number of Imāms. In this context of esoteric allusions the choice of words for the chronogram at the end of the (portal) inscription is surely also significant: "He has come, the opener of gates". For while this term usually refers to Allāh Himself, the equation of 'Alī with a *bāb* ("gate") is found in other buildings of Iṣfahān, always with a double meaning: 'Alī as a gate to spiritual enlightenment, and a punning reference to the location of these inscriptions over the entrances to religious buildings. In this mosque a third level of meaning may be intended, for the inscription has an extra appropriateness on a mosque which is itself named after 'Alī and may therefore indicate that the popular name is the correct one.[1]

Two buildings at Sāva offer further insights into the architecture of this period. The transfer of the capital from Tabrīz to Qazvīn gave the city a new importance, for important roads from the south-east and south-west met there. It would thus be natural for Shah Ismā'īl to embellish it. But the extent of early Safavid work in the Masjid-i Jāmi' has been somewhat exaggerated. The interior revetment of the dome chamber includes the name of Sa'd b. Muḥammad Kadūk (also found in the Yazd Jāmi', *c.* 1375), and this makes it premature to date even the upper structure of the dome chamber to the early 16th century. Indeed, the major new construction in the mosque at this period was apparently limited to a kind of inflated *chahār-sū* in the south-western corner, while the vaults of the two aivāns received a garnishing of

[1] Godard, "Iṣfahān", pp. 69–72. Hunarfar, *Ganjīna*, pp. 369–79. Bakhtiyar, "The Masjid Ali", pp. 1–2, argues in favour of a Saljūq date for this mosque.

clumps of stalactites. The decoration of the sanctuary area includes a probably pre-Safavid dado of hexagonal turquoise tiles and a tile mosaic inscription in the *qibla* aivān with the date 927/1520. Its *pièce de résistance*, however, is the carved stucco *miḥrāb*. The early Safavid parts of the Sāva Jāmi' use plaster decoration, whose vogue had passed one and a half centuries earlier, to a remarkable extent. This miḥrāb, for all the virtuosity of its *riqa'* inscriptions, illustrates that the attempt to revive this obsolete technique was ill-advised. Saljūq and Il-Khanid plaster miḥrābs, of which examples have been found in this mosque, are conceived sculpturally and exploit several levels of carving. This miḥrāb, by contrast, reproduces in stucco the kind of two-dimensional design originally created for tile mosaic or book-covers. In the Masjid-i Maidān nearby, whose inscriptions dated 916/1510 and 924/1518 refer to Safavid restoration work, a very similar miḥrāb, perhaps the work of the same artist, may be found.[1]

Amidst the sparse output of Shah Ismā'īl's reign one other building deserves analysis: the tomb of Shaikh Jibrā'īl (father of Shaikh Ṣafī) at Kalkhurān near Ardabīl (fig. 1). Although it bears no date, it is generally agreed to be of the early 16th century, for its style and decoration are post-Timurid while a *terminus post quem* is provided by the restoration work of Shah 'Abbās I there, dated 1030–1/1620–2. The building could most naturally be interpreted as one of the first-fruits of the virtually uninterrupted interest in Ardabīl shown by the Safavid shahs, who clearly saw the mausoleum of Ṣafī and its dependencies as a kind of dynastic shrine. Both the form and the function of the mausoleum are significant. Its form owes a general debt to the great domed squares of Timurid Transoxiana, notably the mosque-mausoleum of Khwāja Aḥmad Yasavī at Turkistān and the Gūr-i Mīr. It is much smaller than these, however, and its form is still transitional, not least in the lack of integration between its internal and external layout. A much restored dome on a high drum is set abruptly, without intermediary, on a square, flat-roofed lower storey whose box-like appearance is redeemed only by deep axial arched portals.[2] Such mausolea replaced the tomb tower, offering a far more spacious layout which encouraged large-scale pilgrimages. This decisive shift away from ostentatiously secular memorials is already evident in the burial arrangements for

[1] Godard, "Les anciennes mosquées", pp. 85–8. Pope, in *SPA*, pp. 1166–70, figs. 414–15 and 591, and pl. 460.
[2] Sarre, *Denkmäler* I, 50–2, Abb. 49–52. Dibāj, *Rāhnamā*, pp. 89–91.

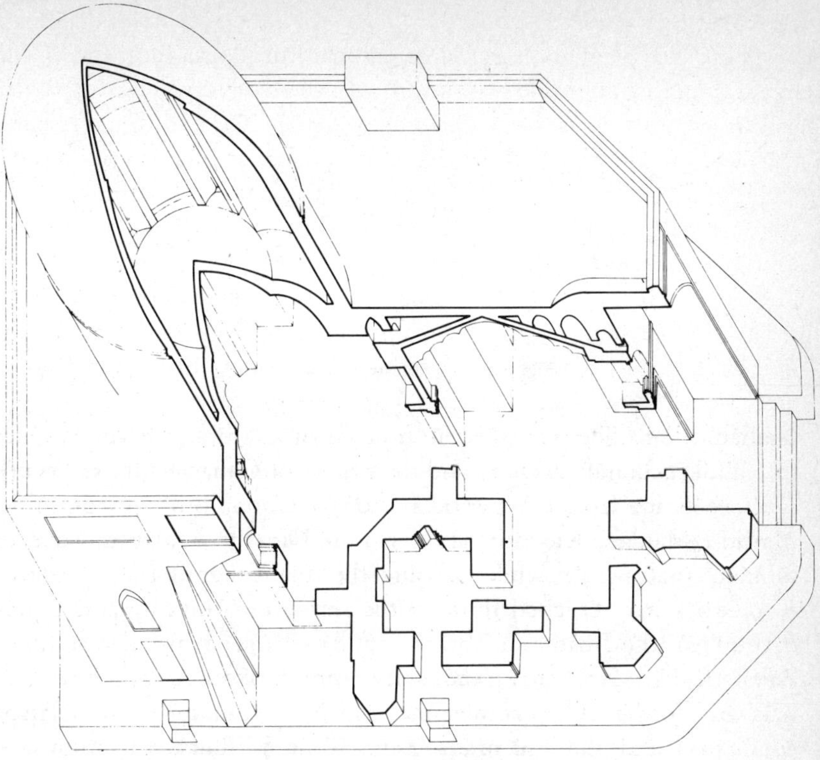

Fig. 1. Kalkhurān. Tomb of Shaikh Jibrā'īl, isometric section.

Shah Ismā'īl in the Ardabīl shrine (fig. 2). While the shah apparently continued the medieval tradition sufficiently to erect a cylindrical domed tomb tower for himself, the building was not only small but surrendered all claim to outward display by its avoidance of a free-standing site. Hemmed in amidst larger buildings, it is clearly an anachronism – a traditional architectural type transformed by a novel setting. Most subsequent Safavid shahs were buried in sacred shrines of long standing, their graves marked by sarcophagi rather than buildings.

Numerous inscriptions in buildings throughout the country testify to building activity in the reign of Shah Ismā'īl. New construction or repairs were carried out on structures as diverse as the shrines of Ardabīl, Mashhad (920/1514) and Qum (façade of the Ṣaḥn-i Kuhna, 925/1519); the Friday mosques of Damāvand (927/1520), Gaz and

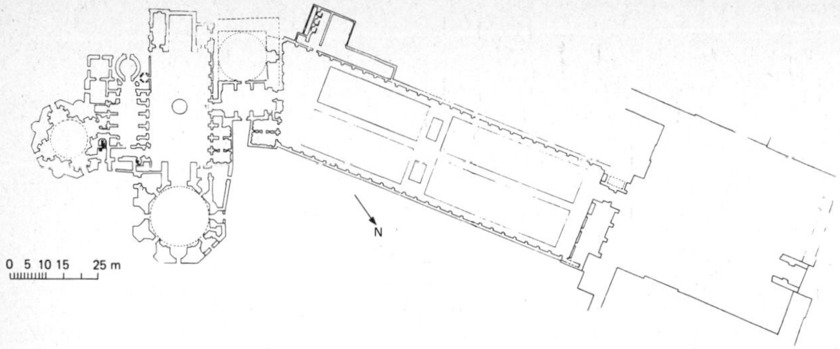

Fig. 2. Ardabīl. Shrine complex, plan.

Iṣfahān; tombs like that of Khātūn Qiyāmat at Shīrāz, Ḥusain at Qum or Chihil Akhtarān at Qum; and the bridge of Qaflan Kūh (923/1517). Decrees dating from this period are found, among other places, in the Masjid-i Maidān, Kāshān (922/1516), and in the Friday mosque of Simnān (926/1519), while among the many examples of carved woodwork may be cited those at the shrine of ʿAbd al-ʿAẓīm at Ray (918/1512), the Imāmzāda Ibrāhīm at Āmul (924/1519), the tomb of Bābā Afżāl at Maraq (912/1506) and the tomb of Sulṭān Mīr Aḥmad at Kāshān (915/1509). Tombstones include examples at Naṭanz (921/1515) and the Imāmzāda Zaid, Tehran (Rajab 920/August – September 1514). Finally, it seems appropriate in view of Shah Ismāʿīl's love of hunting to note, as a curiosity, that against all expectations a minaret decorated with the horns and skulls of game survives on the outskirts of Khūy. Contemporary accounts record the erection of such a tower here.

If, then, the reign of Shah Ismāʿīl is not so void of architectural activity as is often thought, nevertheless it represents a startling decline in productivity compared with the high level of preceding centuries. This decline characterises the lengthy reign of Shah Ṭahmāsp too. Yet this reign was incomparably more peaceful than that of Shah Ismāʿīl, and the country prospered accordingly. The continued lull in building activity must be laid at the door of the shah himself, whose apathy as a patron came to affect all the arts. Only a very few ambitious buildings or parts of buildings may be distinguished amidst the well over forty published so far and datable to his reign on grounds of epigraphy alone. Like his father, Shah Ṭahmāsp cannot be credited with a single surviving mosque for which he was wholly responsible. Not surprisingly, Iranian architecture of this period had no markedly individual style; hence the difficulty of fashioning dating controls to apply to undated buildings.

In defence of Shah Ṭahmāsp it must be said that his best work was probably concentrated in his capital city of Qazvīn, which has suffered cruelly from earthquakes. Thus virtually nothing remains of his Masjid-i Shāh and his royal palace (though a kiosk which was part of the royal palace and has recently been refurbished gives some clues);[1] while his baths (and probably his bazaar) have entirely gone. Among surviving buildings of his reign the Jannat-sarā at Ardabīl deserves special mention, though his work on the shrine as a whole is far less than was formerly thought.[2] Important mausolea survive at Nīshāpūr and Sulṭāniyya, while the best tilework of the time can be seen in the Friday mosques of Iṣfahān, Kirmān and Shīrāz as well as in the fragments of smaller Iṣfahān mosques now re-erected in the garden of the Chihil Sutūn palace. With these various exceptions, then, the majority of the work carried out under Shah Ṭahmāsp, and identifiable as such on epigraphic grounds, comprises repairs or additions to existing shrines (e.g., Mashhad and Ardabīl); mausolea (including five in Kāshān, six in the Yazd area and eight in Qum and its surroundings); mosques (Barsiyān, Qum, Yazd, Shushtar, Saravār and the Masjid-i Jāmi', Iṣfahān, along with six others in the city); tombstones, or stone slabs inscribed with decrees (e.g., at Kāshān, Masjid-i Maidān); woodwork (e.g., Tajrīsh, Imāmzāda Qāsim; Ṭabas, Imāmzāda Ḥusain; Naṭanz shrine; Kāshān, Sulṭān Mīr Aḥmad; Ray, Bībī Shahrbanū; Qazvīn, Shāhzāda Ḥusain; and Pīshva, Imāmzāda Ja'far); and a few modest tombs (Imāmzādas Abāzar, near Qazvīn, Ḥamza at Bavanāt, and Abu'l-Futūḥ at Vanshān, the last two with quantities of carved woodwork).

Although, strictly speaking, slabs with decrees, tombstones, carved doors and sarcophagi are extrinsic to the basic structure of the building in which they occur and are thus of no value in dating the structure itself, their presence is at least an indication that at the date in question the building did attract the interest of a patron. While otherwise undatable repairs cannot be dated on such evidence alone in any given case, there must be a strong presumption that in many cases these

[1] Kleiss, "Der safavidische Pavillon".

[2] Morton, "The Ardabil Shrine (concluded)", pp. 41–3, 48.

inscribed dates are contemporary with unrecorded restorations and repairs in such buildings. It will be apparent that this output has much in common with the haphazard collection of small-scale and limited work, innocent of any overall direction or momentum, which constitutes the architectural achievement of Shah Ismāʿīl.

The architectural achievements of the reign may conveniently be discussed under two headings: mosques and shrines. A Persian inscription framing the qibla aivān of the Iṣfahān Jāmiʿ and dated to the "caliphate" of Shah Ṭahmāsp mentions the beautifying and repair (*taʿzīn va taʿmīr*) of the mosque. Contemporary with this is the inscription framing the arch of the same aivān, and further nastaʿlīq inscriptions are found within the aivān. Presumably the refurbishing did not extend beyond the aivān. In the framing arch an unusual layout is adopted. Cartouches of basically *tabula ansata* form, but with rounded ends, alternate with smaller quatrefoils. The latter carry brief prayers and pious sayings, such as invocations to ʿAlī, while each of the former contains an extended litany on one of the Fourteen Pure Ones. A third inscription on the soffit of this entrance arch gives the date 938/1531–2. Significantly enough this work, executed in a mosque which for centuries had attracted the highest patronage in the land, was paid for by a certain Muḥammad al-Iṣfahānī working under the aegis of the lady Āqā Sulṭān; no credit is accorded to the shah himself. As in the previous Iṣfahānī monuments, nastaʿlīq is given some prominence.[1] At Barsiyān the Saljūq mosque, consisting presumably of an isolated dome chamber and minaret, was enlarged by the addition of a courtyard with aivāns. In the Kirmān Jāmiʿ the tile mosaic miḥrāb probably dates from the rebuilding of 967/1559–60 mentioned on the southern portal of the mosque; its arabesques recall coiled springs rather than plant life and represent a hardening of the motif in comparison with early Safavid work at Iṣfahān. For all its high technical quality, this is a very mechanical production. Finally, the Jāmiʿ of Shīrāz deserves notice for the tile mosaic dated 973/1565–6 in the qibla aivān. Its generous use of plain brick to act as a foil for tiled insets of almost *fleur-de-lys* pattern, like its emphasis on bold strapwork and lozenges spelling out sacred names in square Kufic, finds equally convincing parallels in Timurid Khurāsān and in 15th-century Āzarbāījān.

[1] Godard, "Historique du Masdjid-é Djumʿa d'Iṣfahān", pp. 256–9. Hunarfar, *Ganjīna*, pp. 88–103.

More can be learned of the architecture of this period from a study of its mausolea. An unusually grand example, though its funerary purpose is not absolutely certain and though it has lost its dome, is provided by the octagonal Jannat-sarā at Ardabīl, datable *c.*1540 (fig. 2). This was the largest single building on the site and, perhaps on account of the sanctity of the Ardabīl shrine in Safavid times and its place of honour among the monuments of the land, the building represents an unusually munificent effort on the part of the shah. With its great dome, which originally had a span of over 16 m., and its commanding position at one end of the great inner courtyard of the shrine, this spacious octagon may well have been intended by Ṭahmāsp to serve as his own tomb. Internally the plan retains its octagonal shape on both of its storeys; each side is occupied by a great blind arch enclosing narrow superposed arched niches. Subsequent alterations have disfigured the original plan, in which great arched recesses, each corresponding to one side of the octagon and reaching almost to the springing of the dome, were scooped out of the exterior façade. Only on the south-west side, which was preceded by an entrance aivān, and directly opposite on the north-east side, where the recess was internal, is the arrangement different. Whether these huge external bays held doors or windows originally can only be determined by excavation, but either way it is the open plan of the structure that deserves attention. Rather than discouraging access by a forbidding high blank wall, the architect has chosen, by this device of deep bays, to invite entry into the building. Psychologically the effect is quite different from that of previous tombs. Hints of this change are found in earlier buildings, though the new approach had not hitherto been expressed so boldly and on such a large scale.[1]

Subsequent Safavid mausolea continued to favour this open plan, though perhaps none pares down the octagon so inexorably to its eight constituent piers. In the tomb of Mullā Ḥasan Shīrāzī at Sulṭāniyya, for example, now shorn of its garden setting, the lightness and airiness of the octagon, in which broad, deep aivāns alternate with narrower and shallower arched bays (an interesting variation on the theme of the Jannat-sarā), gives way to a heavy complex interior with many walls containing staircases. The incompatible emphases of an open octagon and a closed square chamber remain unresolved. Even the multi-tiered

[1] Morton, "The Ardabil Shrine (concluded)", pp. 41–3. Weaver, *Preliminary Study*, pp. 15–18.

stalactite ceiling contrives to suggest weight rather than lightness, possibly because its many miniature spandrels have recently been picked out in red, but more likely because the inner dome is too shallow for such treatment. Quite apart from its plan, this mausoleum deserves attention for its tilework, in which may be detected a conscious antiquarianism. Thus the small glazed joint plugs with simple geometric or floral designs in two or three colours used on the exterior wall occur as early as the tomb of Öljeitü nearby and are also found in the Blue Mosque at Tabrīz. The finest work, however, is reserved for the drum of the dome, which is encircled by a band of twelve panels containing an ingenious interlocking series of inscriptions executed in square Kufic and invoking divine blessings on the Fourteen Pure Ones. The band is bordered above and below by geometrical patterns in glazed brick. The dome itself is blue while tile mosaic adorns the spandrels of the aivāns. All in all this varied decoration is an entirely appropriate reminder that Mullā Ḥasan bore the title "Kāshī".[1]

Larger tombs of the period include the Imāmzāda Sulṭān Muḥammad ʿAbīd (said to be the brother of the Imām Riḍā) at Kākh, near Gunābād, dated 960/1552, whose dominant feature is a massive dome on a high drum. A broad and low projecting façade with a central portal aivān provides a modest approach to the tomb chamber. Basically similar in layout is the shrine of Muḥammad Maḥrūq near Nīshāpūr. According to legend the saint was burned (hence his name) for converting an ʿAbbasid princess to the Shīʿī creed. Two doors within the shrine, of which one is dated 978/1570 and both are signed by Imām Qulī Najjār, give a terminus for the building itself. As with the tomb of Mullā Ḥasan, the main chamber is square, but the flanking structures are more complex and are dominated by a huge stepped portal aivān flanked by superposed arcuated niches. Moreover, despite lavish later tilework, dated 1041/1631, in the domed rooms flanking the main tomb chamber, parts of the shrine exhibit a notable simplicity. Plain brick suffices for the lower parts of the shrine's exterior, while the interior of the dome chamber, following Timurid precedent, is plain white apart from the tiled dado.[2]

An entirely unexpected find in recent years has been the richly decorated remains of a once extensive palace in Nāʾīn (pl. 41). Archi-

[1] Godard, " Le tombeau de Mawlânâ Ḥasan Kâshî".
[2] Maulavī, *Āṣār*. Pope, in *SPA*, pp. 1178–9.

tecturally its layout is unusual, with a sunken courtyard whose façades are broken by four uneven aivāns, two per long side. Living quarters are disposed in two storeys of which the upper one had a room with niches specially carved in pottery shapes, as at the ʿĀlī Qāpū. The largest aivān has an ambitious net vault executed in several planes with greatly thickened ribs to indicate the contours of the vault. Blank niches, alternately broad and narrow, form the basis from which the vault's ribs spring to form varied stellar patterns. Above a plain dado with recessed panels the entire field is decorated. Niches and stellar patterns alike contain figural ornament. The technique in these plaster panels is so fine and detailed that they seem to be paintings, but in fact the white stucco skin is cut away to reveal the dark background and thus form the design; the technique is of extreme rarity in Safavid, though not in later, times. Traces of colour survive but it is not certain whether these are original, especially as other similar decoration in Nā'īn has suffered subsequent repainting. The themes of the decoration are the common coin of miniature painting, with scenes from Niẓāmī (Farhād and Shīrīn) and Jāmī (Yūsuf and Zulaikhā), as well as games of polo, enthroned royal couples, banquets and hunts. Inscriptions of Persian poetry (Ḥāfiẓ) in densely decorated cartouches like *ʿunvāns*, and above all the style of these figures, drive home the parallel. The stellar forms created by the vault have predominantly chinoiserie themes: dragons, phoenixes, flying ducks, ch'i-lins and so on. The form and content irresistibly evoke Il-Khanid glazed star tiles. At the apex of the ceiling and of the iconographic programme is the largest such star which depicts a group of eight angels. Some reference to Paradise seems to be intended here, and the widespread ancient equation of an actual vault with the dome of heaven is emphasised by the many stars of the rib vault. A pair of much smaller rooms (some 5 m. and 3½ m. high respectively) bear broadly similar decoration to that of the aivān. The ensemble has convincingly been dated to *c.*1560 but its presence in a provincial town like Nā'īn has yet to be explained.[1]

In the dozen years between the death of Ṭahmāsp and the accession of ʿAbbās I architecture continued in the doldrums. Literary sources preserve the memory of vanished buildings erected in this period but little more survives than an occasional mosque (Iṣfahān, Masjid-i Fatḥ),

[1] Luschey-Schmeisser, "Der Wand- und Deckenschmuck", and pls. 68–81, and "Ein neuer Raum", and pls. 78–82; and Gropp and Najmabadi, pl. 82.

tombstone (Iṣfahān, Bābā Qāsim; Vanshān, Imāmzāda Abu'l-Futūḥ; Iṣfahān, Imāmzāda Ismā'īl), decree (Kāshān, Masjid-i Maidān) or sarcophagus (Pīshva, Imāmzāda Ja'far; Turbat-i Ḥaidariyya, Mazār Quṭb al-Dīn). Repairs were carried out on the Masjid-i Nau at Shīrāz in 995/1586.

The accession of Shah 'Abbās completely transformed the sorry state of affairs which had prevailed in Iranian architecture for nearly a century. His achievements in this field placed Persian work belatedly but firmly on an equal footing with the output of the Ottomans and Mughals. Around 1600 these super-powers between them controlled the Muslim world from Bengal to the Atlantic; the scale of their architectural achievements reflected this political dominance and was unsurpassed in the contemporary world. The lesson of scale was not lost on Louis XIV when his ambassadors regaled him with marvellous tales of Asian palaces.

In Iran the new spirit was symbolised by Iṣfahān. The dynamism of the new shah as a patron of building stimulated architects to recover the inspiration that had trickled away in the long stagnation of previous reigns. Appropriately enough, Timurid – and not earlier Safavid – architecture provided the springboard for fresh developments, though 'Abbās had a sense of vision beside which Tīmūr's enthusiasm for building stands exposed as merely frenetic and aimless. Such was the impetus generated by this monarch that architecture continued to thrive in spite of the progressive political and economic decline over which his successors presided. The buildings selected for extended discussion here can only hint at the wealth, variety and sheer quantity of contemporary architecture. Inevitably the monuments of Iṣfahān claim pride of place, but important works at Ardabīl, Kirmān, Māhān, Mashhad, and Shīrāz can be used to create a more balanced picture, while palaces and gardens at Ashraf, Bairamābād, Kāshān and Ṣafīābād help to reconstitute the lost splendours of the Chahār Bāgh. A local school of Perso-Armenian architecture at Julfā illustrates the pervasive influence of the Safavid aesthetic on an otherwise sturdily independent and alien tradition. Lastly, the output of public works is on such a massive scale that it reveals an entirely new dimension to Safavid architecture.

Impressive as the various provincial foundations are individually, however, they are isolated. Some of them are necessarily restricted in concept since they were conceived as additions to pre-existing ensembles; others were the work of royal governors. To assess Shah 'Abbās himself as a patron one must turn to Iṣfahān; indeed, it is in the masterpieces erected there between 1598 and 1628 that Safavid architecture found its authentic expression.

Several introductory remarks may be in order. 'Abbās had been on the throne for almost a decade when he moved the capital from Qazvīn to Iṣfahān in spring 1598. In that time he had achieved very little as a patron of architecture. It was apparently the move to Iṣfahān that roused his dormant ambitions in this field and triggered a vast programme of construction. It seems justified to conclude that Iṣfahān had his heart. At the same time the previous urban development and the natural setting of the city favoured these plans for expansion. Most of the population was concentrated in the older quarters to the north, where the natural focus was the Saljūq Maidān-i Kuhna. To the south, all the way to the river and beyond, the shah had more of a free hand. The very presence of a large river and of great tracts of unoccupied land so close to the city favoured a scheme of urban planning on the grand scale (fig. 3). Indeed, one of the most notable features of Safavid architecture in Iṣfahān after 1598 is the change of pace. Instead of the spasmodic and uncoordinated activity of earlier years a new sense of purpose makes itself felt. Much more is undertaken and some of the projects are completed with remarkable speed. As more new buildings rise, and as the outline of the royal scheme becomes increasingly clear, architecture becomes a fashionable concern. But there is little evidence that the buildings themselves were distinguished by any great originality. The concept of a city plan dominated by a great square was not new in Iran. At Shīrāz the square had, like Iṣfahān, a bazaar fronted by a *naqqāra-khāna* at one end, with the royal palace opposite. In Iṣfahān itself the Maidān-i Kuhna was a familiar sight. Fifteenth-century Tabrīz had several great squares linked by arterial thoroughfares. The maidān of Shah 'Abbās itself extended an earlier maidān on the same site. Perhaps a maidān built afresh on an unencumbered site and designedly bordered by mosques would have been oriented towards the qibla, thereby rendering otiose the ingenious shifts employed by the royal architects to accommodate divergent axes in the Masjid-i Shāh and the Luṭf-Allāh mosque.

Yet if the novelty of the Iṣfahān of 1630 has been overestimated, one must concede that it offered a unique combination of qualities. Quantities of brand new buildings, some of spectacular scale and beauty, met

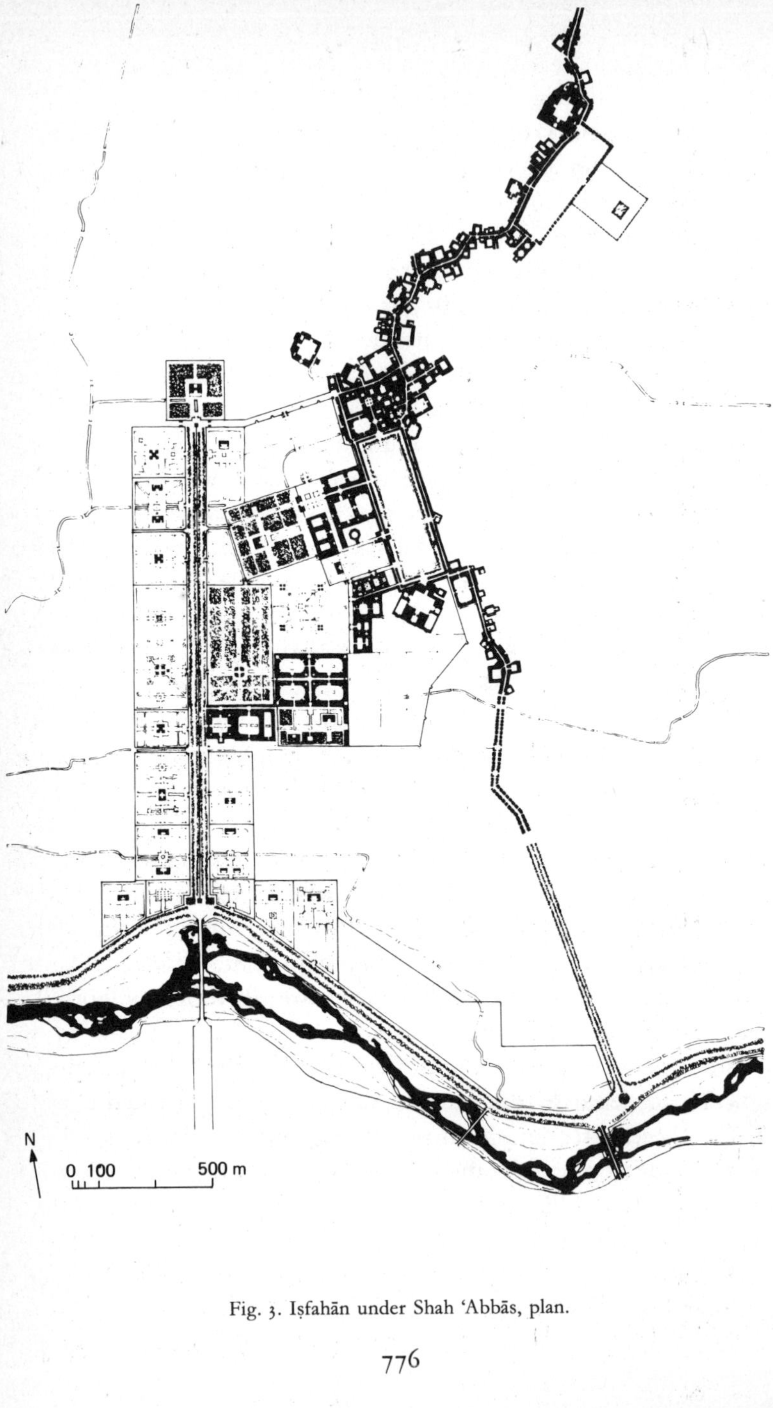

Fig. 3. Iṣfahān under Shah ʿAbbās, plan.

the eye at every turn and were often a key element in extensive and entirely man-made prospects. The reconstructed city itself was remarkably large and the maidān aptly symbolised this. Seldom was a new city so embowered in gardens; indeed, the Chahār Bāgh in its heyday was a Persian garden carpet conjured into three dimensions. It was this opulent ambience of flowers, streams, trees and fountains that surprised and delighted European visitors, and contrived to disarm even the curmudgeonly chauvinist Tavernier. Their verdict is unanimous: no contemporary city in the world could rival Iṣfahān; and these were men familiar with the greatest cities of Europe.[1]

The series of masterpieces begins with the Chahār Bāgh, where work was under way directly after Shah ʻAbbās had made Iṣfahān his capital (fig. 4). The name derives from four vineyards which he had to rent in order to carry out his plan. In form the Chahār Bāgh is a huge avenue some 4 km. long which ran on a direct north-south axis from the royal gardens bordering the centre of the maidān to the Hazār Jarīb, a royal estate some two km. south of the Zāyandarūd. Stately plane trees planted in rows divided it into three alleys, of which the central one contained a canal. Fountains and cascades punctuated its flow. Gardens spread far and wide on either side of the Chahār Bāgh and trellised rather than solid walls allowed passers-by to enjoy glimpses of them from the public thoroughfare. At intervals palaces with names like Satāra, ʻAbbāsābād, Jahān-nāma and Nastarān emerged from gardens named after thrones, nightingales, dervishes, mulberries and paradise itself. Never intended for commercial traffic, the Safavid Chahār Bāgh, as its name indicates, was essentially a garden, whose shaded walks made it a pergola on the grand scale. But it is as much an expression of architectural values as it is landscape gardening. Its use of a long vista flanked by palaces and closed at either end by a monumental building, and the use of apparently endless arcades to define the enclosed space, both find analogies in the maidān. There too nature is made part of the overall scheme, and there too the designer has blocked out his plan on the basis of adjoining rectangles. Yet there is no hint of coercion, no unnatural rigidity, in this layout; contemporary accounts stress how ideally the Chahār Bāgh was suited for the tranquil civilised pleasures of conversing, strolling – or, more often, riding – and watching the world go by.[2]

[1] Stevens, pp. 421–57.

[2] Wilber, *Persian Gardens*, pp. 102, 106. Godard, "Iṣfahān", pp. 88–94. Hunarfar, *Ganjīna*, pp. 479–93.

Fig. 4. Iṣfahān. View of the Chahār Bāgh in the 17th century.

Forming a natural pendant to the shah's work on the Chahār Bāgh and to his development of Julfā, the purpose-built Armenian suburb, is the bridge that links these two projects and continues the axis of the promenade. Erected in 1011/1602 by the shah's favourite and generalissimo, Allāhvardī Khān, and named after him, it is a remarkable 300 m. in length. As if aware of the danger of monotony, the architect garnished the bridge with pavilions at intervals, but these were not large enough to break its overall lines. Open or covered footpaths at three levels are ingeniously incorporated into the stately double arcade which is the essence of the design. As in the Chahār Bāgh itself, practical and aesthetic aims harmonise.[1]

If the Chahār Bāgh, for all its deliberate informality and its function as a promenade, imposed order on one part of the new Iṣfahān, the maidān did the same for the area to the east (fig. 5). Curiously enough, the two projects are not directly linked, although it would have been an obvious move to make the Chahār Bāgh the main pedestrian approach to the maidān. Perhaps the shah was circumscribed in both projects by land rights and the current function of the area. At all events, the avenue and the maidān were the key features of the new Iṣfahān, providing a framework within which subsequent buildings could be fitted. Much of their importance depended on their sheer size. The maidān measures 512 m. × 159 m. and thus covers over eight hectares, far outstripping comparable European urban plazas. Its apparent size is much increased by the buildings fronted with a low two-storeyed arcade which define its limits and make it a piazza rather than a sprawling field (fig. 6). These date from 1020–1/1611–12, and are primarily functional; shops took up the ground floor openings, with dwellings above. But their lowness has a further aesthetic impact in that it exalts the stature of the four buildings that break through the arcade. Though the maidān was lined with *chanār* trees and a water-channel, no buildings intruded on the cleared space and it was precisely this emptiness that allowed the maidān to play so varied a rôle in the life of the city. In turn market place, training and parade ground, execution dock, polo pitch, open-air stage, running track and arena for animal combats, it was a magnificently illuminated funfair by night and the inevitable setting for all kinds of royal entertainments. At the same time as he fixed the limits of the maidān Shah 'Abbās completed his

[1] M. Ferrante, in Zander, *Travaux*, pp. 443–50. Pope in *SPA*, pp. 1235–7.

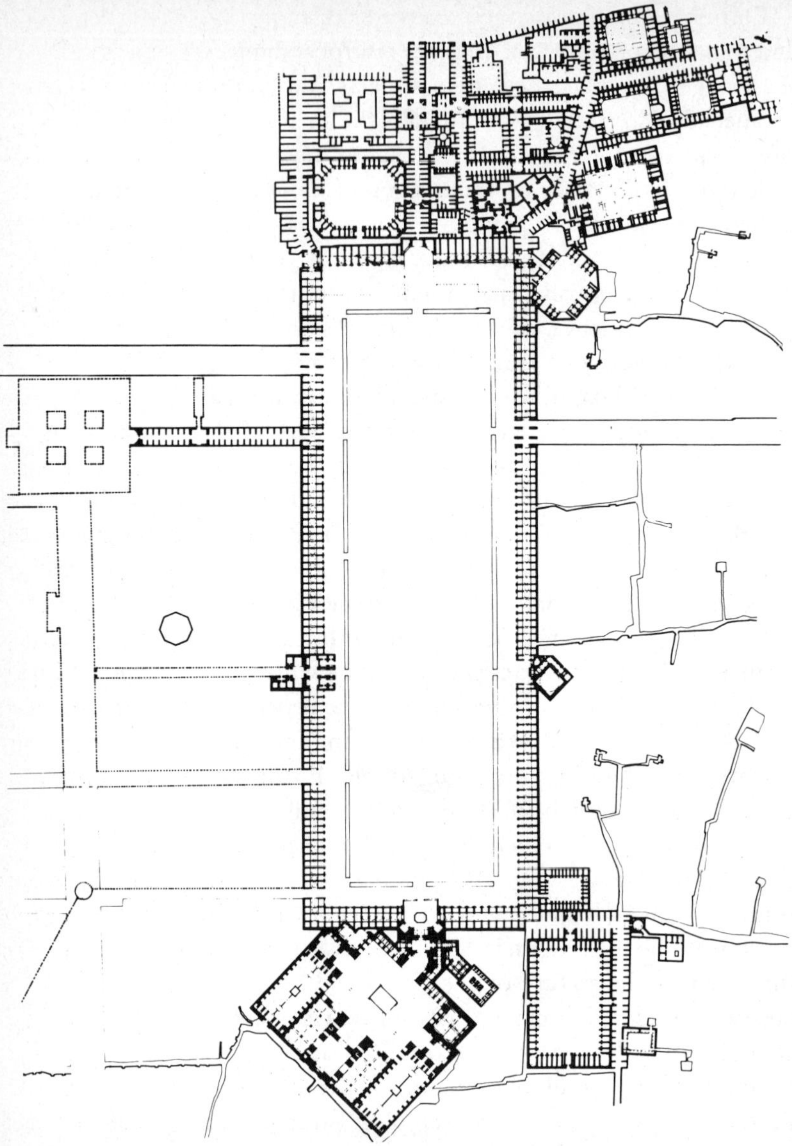

Fig. 5. Iṣfahān. Maidān area, plan.

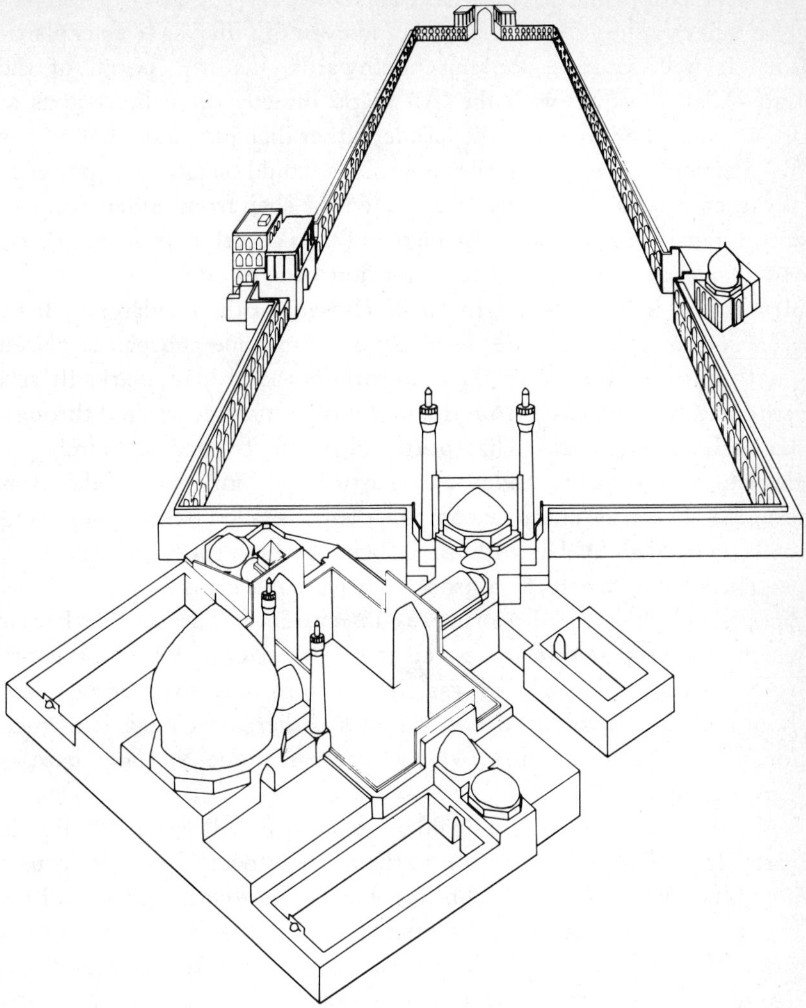

Fig. 6. Iṣfahān. Maidān area, isometric view.

plans for the façade by adding a monumental portal in the centre of each short side. These portals gave access to the Masjid-i Shāh and the Qaiṣariyya bazaar respectively. With a concentrated *corps de bâtiment* on each of its four sides, the maidān could be interpreted as a gigantic version of the courtyard with four aivāns which, found in mosques, madrasas, houses and caravansarais, maintained so tenacious a hold on the imagination of Iranian architects. Only the 3 : 1 ratio of long to short sides vitiates the comparison, and even this may have an explanation. It will be seen, looking northwards, that the portal of the Luṭf-Allāh mosque, with the ʿĀlī Qāpū directly opposite, begins at one-third of the way along the façade, rather than just under halfway as the symmetry observed on the short sides would dictate. The presence of earlier structures may have prevented the shah from undertaking an entire transformation of the maidān and thus securing axial symmetry, and it perhaps encouraged the adoption of a more subtle system of proportion. Indeed the length finally chosen for the maidān may have been determined by the desire to have the mosque and palace placed one-third of the way down the long sides of the maidān, markedly and aristocratically removed from the world of commerce entered through the Qaiṣariyya portal.[1] That portal bears in its tiled spandrels the emblem of Sagittarius, under whose astrological influence Iṣfahān was founded. The same entrance complex contains faded frescoes depicting the wars of Shah ʿAbbās with the Uzbeks. Its high galleries housed the naqqāra-khāna, where a consort of royal musicians played a daily cacophony whenever the shah was in residence. The vaulted bazaar which opens up within the portal is the finest example of the genre from the Safavid period and was erected from 1029/1619–20 onwards though no doubt planned two decades earlier; its climax is a great domed chahār-sū, a feature which recurs in numerous later bazaars (e.g. Kāshān and Qum).

On the west side of the maidān stands the ʿĀlī Qāpū ("Sublime Porte") which formerly gave on to the royal gardens (fig. 7). In form it is a rectangle some 33 m. high, too low to be a cube, preceded by a broad portico crowned by a columned verandah or *tālār*. Critics have found the junction of porch and palace proper maladroit and even absurd. Yet this is to ignore a prime component of the design; for the building faced the maidān. It was necessarily façade architecture. It backed on walled private gardens and was not intended to be viewed from behind. Moreover, its function largely determined its form. Like any modern office block it held scores of small rooms. The need to have them well lit and ventilated accounts for the lavish fenestration of the side façades, though the windows which overlooked the royal

[1] Godard, "Iṣfahān", pp. 103–6. Hunarfar, *Ganjīna*, pp. 395–401; *idem*, "Maidān-i Naqsh-i Jahān-i Iṣfahān", *Hunar va Mardum* CV (July 1971), 2–28. Galdieri and Orazi, *Progetto di sistemazione del Maydan-i Šah* (Rome, 1969); and Galdieri, "Two Building Phases".

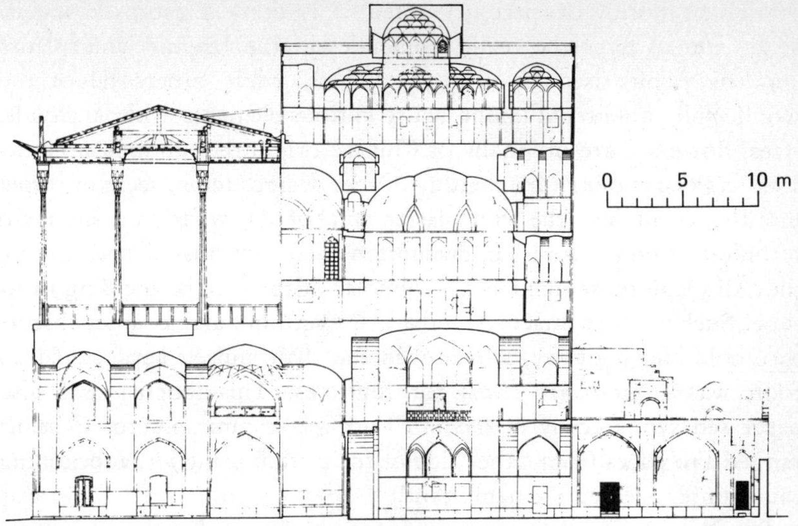

Fig. 7. Iṣfahān. ʿĀlī Qāpū, section.

harem were blocked from the outset. Each of the four upper floors is pierced by at least one deep bay. Faience spandrels and geometric window grilles variegate the busy articulation of multiple arched windows and niches. But while the main building with its six storeys looks weighty and monumental when seen from the back, the principal façade is made airy and insubstantial by the columned tālār, which takes up two entire storeys. There is even something lighthearted in combining forms as alien as the pīshṭāq and the tālār in a single building, and in transporting the tālār – traditionally a low, earth-bound architectural form – to a point forty feet above ground. Despite these incongruities the ʿĀlī Qāpū fulfils its rôle of royal grandstand to perfection. The shah could see and be seen and thus partake publicly of the life of his capital. The ancient traditions of the royal tribune and window of appearances are thus given a new dress. Royal power and royal accessibility are alike stressed.

Internally the ground plan varies markedly from floor to floor. Certain areas are easily identified: the area for judicial and administrative functions below the tālār; the reception hall, complete with water tank and fountain, at tālār level; and the music room in the top storey with its fragile stucco surround for precious porcelain. Other rooms, however, are of uncertain function. Most of them are very small, though an illusion of space is granted by vaulting. Frescoes in several styles spread over the walls: some depict the languid youths and maidens popularised by Riżā-yi ʿAbbāsī, while others develop a wonderfully unfettered idiom whose various elements – birds, clouds, trees, flowers – are originally of Chinese origin though long acclimatised in Persian miniature painting. Other designs reminiscent of carpet motifs are cut into the thin plaster skin of the walls in a sgraffiato technique found at Nāʾīn. In decoration even more than in architecture the ʿĀlī Qāpū must stand as an exemplar of the palatial building of its time. Such sanctity attached to the ʿĀlī Qāpū in Safavid times that its threshold and doorway, which even the shah himself approached on foot, was a sanctuary (*bast*) for fugitives. This sanctity was also expressed symbolically in the 110 Portuguese cannon from Hurmuz ranged 110 paces from either side of the portal: using *abjad* reckoning this number yielded the name ʿAlī.[1]

But it is above all the two mosques on the maidān that can justly claim to rank as the finest work of the time. Typically Safavid though their decoration is, in plan and elevation they are surprisingly original. Begun in 1011/1602–3 and finished in 1028/1618–19, the Masjid-i Shaikh Luṭf-Allāh, or Masjid-i Ṣadr/Masjid-i Fatḥ-Allāh as it was earlier called, is the earlier of the two and also the more unorthodox. The domed one-room sanctuary shorn of a courtyard was by now a highly unusual form as a mosque, but it fits quite naturally into the long-established Timurid and Safavid tradition of large domed mausolea. Only the central sarcophagus of such buildings is missing. This affiliation with mausolea is not the only curiosity. Much has been made of the bent entrance, and the oblique orientation of the dome chamber in relation to the maidān. One may also note the skewed relationship between aivān and dome. It is widely assumed that the two former irregularities were dictated by the need to orientate the mosque to the qibla. This is not entirely true. The aivān, for example, could lead without the least deviation to the west wall of the chamber, thereby rendering a bent entrance superfluous. Such lateral entrances to a sanctuary chamber would have been nothing new in Persian architecture, though admittedly it is standard practice to site the main entrance opposite the miḥrāb. Since a dome chamber is virtually

[1] Hunarfar, *Ganjīna*, pp. 416–26. Zander, *Travaux*, pp. 133–289; "La restauration de quelques monuments"; and "Observations". Galdieri, *Esfahān: Alī Qāpū*.

devoid of a directional emphasis internally, and entirely so externally, this oblique orientation is a problem more apparent than real. Once inside the dome chamber one would no longer be conscious of the maidān and therefore of any orientation problem, while the exterior cannot be said to be orientated or misorientated *vis-à-vis* the square. It is only when one analyses the relationship between the aivān and the dome that a discord is apparent, and it is highly significant that this discord is unnecessary. Had the dome chamber been shifted twenty metres to the north, aivān and dome would have been on a single axis and no significant alteration of the plan would have followed. Instead of this the architect did all he could to draw attention to the conflicting axes of the ensemble. Internally, the long passageway skirting the chamber, and its right-angled turn, underline the point. Externally it is the lack of correspondence between the aivān and the dome that reminds the viewer of the convergent axes at work. In the Masjid-i Shāh the presence of a courtyard with the dome chamber necessarily on its qibla side automatically emphasised the shift of direction from the portal. Thus the architect there was absolved from straining to publicise the fact that maidān and mosque faced in different directions. Clearly the architects of both buildings were at pains to reveal, not to conceal, that the dues of Caesar conflicted with those of God. The layout itself may in fact be intended as a serious call to devotion.

Shah ʿAbbās built the Masjid-i Shaikh Luṭf-Allāh in honour of the shaikh, who was his father-in-law, as a place for private prayer, though it is extremely large and ostentatious for such a purpose (pl. 43*a*). A low portal with a central arch leads to the arched entrance. The tilework here is modern. Above it broods a low single-shell dome. Its external decoration incorporates a striking feature found elsewhere in the mosque : the use of plain brick as a ground for tilework. The effect is to create the optical illusion of buff-coloured tiles. In a design of arabesques superimposed on each other as in Safavid carpets the ubiquitous blue of other Safavid domes is subordinate to buff, black and white. Once inside the building, the aesthetic purpose of the long, low, gloomy passage leading to the dome chamber becomes evident, for it is with a sense of heightened anticipation that one enters the sanctuary. Lowness gives way to soaring height and gloom is dispelled by the steady illumination of nearly a score of windows.

In all Persian architecture no more perfectly balanced interior comes to mind (pl. 43*b*). Much of this harmony is due to the dovetailing of architectural and decorative accents. This concern is already apparent in the horizontal carpet designs of the tiled dado. Above this eight huge arches carry the circular drum on which the dome rests. Each arch is outlined in a turquoise cable moulding of electric brightness, and further outlined by a broad double-decker inscription band executed in dazzling white on an indigo ground. Two more such bands mark the upper and lower limits of the collar, which is filled by thirty-two arched panels. These are alternately blind and fitted with arabesque grilles to filter the sunlight. The entire surface of the dome is covered with a network of curvilinear lozenges executed in plain brick and diminishing in size as they approach the apex of the dome, a deliberate distortion of perspective which makes it seem higher still. Each lozenge contains a tiled floral design. This novel pattern may be seen as a deliberate reduction into two dimensions of the sculptural complexity of a muqarnas vault. Yet the light and dark accents of its tilework are so situated that they create a series of concentric circles which act as a counterpoint to the main theme, the net of lozenges – a subtlety impossible in a muqarnas vault. A predominantly white sunburst design with a filigree of blue arabesques reigns supreme at the apex of the dome, like the sun in the firmament. A sovereign harmony controls the individual patterns of this interior, many of which are designed to be read in different ways depending on the viewer's distance from them. Details sharpen into precise focus or blur into some larger pattern. A similar harmony rules the elevation. Gone is the hectic piling-up of tiny vaults which characterised Timurid zones of transition and many Timurid domes. A principle of successive subdivision gives place to one of assimilation and simplification, so that the elevation resolves itself into large serene surfaces – arches, drum, dome – whose function the mind can readily grasp. The time scale of this decoration is suggested by two inscriptions: one, at the base of the dome, is dated 1025/1616 and the other, in the miḥrāb, is the signature of the builder (*bannā'*) Muḥammad Riżā b. Ḥusain, dated 1028/1619. The portal originally bore two inscriptions, one of 1011/1602–3 and the other of 1012/1603–4; the latter is signed by 'Alī Riżā al-'Abbāsī.[1]

The quality of serenity, the confident marshalling of large spaces, manifested in the Luṭf-Allāh mosque, dominates the Masjid-i Shāh

[1] Godard, "Iṣfahān", pp. 96–9. Pope, in *SPA*, pp. 1189–91, 1209–10 and pls. 481A – 485. Hunarfar, *Ganjīna*, pp. 401–15. R. Byron, *The Road to Oxiana* (London, 1950), pp. 176–8.

too. Its construction, the work of Ustād 'Alī Akbar al-Iṣfahānī, under the direction of the master of works, Muḥibb 'Alī Kika Lāla, spans about twenty years. Work began with the portal, which was started in 1021/1612–13 and completed in 1025/1616, according to an inscription signed by 'Alī Rizā al-'Abbāsī. Only in 1026/1617–18 did building on the mosque proper begin, and the date of 1040/1630 on the west aivān probably marks the end of major construction work on the mosque, though the marble dadoes (mentioned in an inscription written by Muḥammad Riżā al-Imāmī) were not installed before *c.* 1048/1638. This is a remarkably long period for an age in which the monarch was accustomed to seeing buildings completed within a year or two of being started. Popular tradition explains the delay by telling of the architect who, realising that the shah's impatience to be finished was imperilling the safety of the mosque, since the foundations needed time to settle, disappeared for five years after taking measurements and reappeared to demonstrate that the foundations had indeed sunk. It is of course entirely naïve to suppose that building would have ceased in the interim, and, besides, even twenty years is remarkably long for a project so central to the royal plans for Iṣfahān. Moreover, the mosque was indeed shoddily built in places, especially in its foundations, and has required extensive repair over the years (though it should be mentioned that subsidence has never been noted as a problem in the rocky and sandy terrain of the Iṣfahān area, and that foundations that have not been loaded have by that token not been tested). The reason for this long building campaign seems to lie rather in the unprecedented size of the mosque and in the unusually imposing form of its subordinate parts, though not all of these date from the reign of Shah 'Abbās. Essentially it is a four-aivān mosque and thus accords with the classical tradition of Persian Islamic architecture. But at every turn variations in the familiar schema meet the eye. East and west aivāns lead into domed chambers, a layout customarily reserved for the qibla side alone. The sanctuary complex includes long eight-domed winter prayer halls on either side of the main dome. Minarets crown not only the portal but also the qibla aivān. A further arcaded courtyard used for latrines opens off to the south-east of the vestibule via a domed quincunx. Perhaps the most unexpected addition, however, is the pair of custom-built madrasas flanking the sanctuary complex. Identical in form, each comprises a long narrow courtyard enlivened by pools and trees and bordered by arcades which are deeper on the sides adjoining the sanctuary complex. Diminutive aivāns at the centre of each short side reinforce the axial emphasis of the courtyard itself. They exhibit the same urge for symmetry that marks the rest of the mosque, giving it an exterior almost as streamlined as the interior layout. All these extra refinements were prodigal of space, which accounts for the huge plan area of the mosque and its dependencies – the whole measures some 140 m. × 130 m. at its greatest extent, while shorn of its entrance complex it still attains some 100 m. × 130 m. This royal mosque, with its multiple functions, in many ways harks back to the huge mosques of early Islam which served as an emblem of the Islamic community and its life.

Primarily, of course, this impression of size depends on the actual dimensions. No other Persian mosque has a double dome *c.* 52 m. high (some 14 m. above the inner dome), and the broad court, nearly 70 m. across, was a device enthusiastically copied by Qājār architects, especially those of Fatḥ ʿAlī Shāh. The sanctuary aivān is made to seem larger still because its flanking arcades are of one storey instead of two like the arcades on the other sides of the court. Similarly, the dimensions of the portal aivān (27.5 m. high) are magnified by the wings which project from each side. This device ensures that whoever enters the mosque does so not precipitately but with a proper sense of anticipation. The mosque projects its sanctity well beyond the portal, welcoming the worshipper inside, and thus there is ample time for the aivān to assert its presence gradually. The same concern with selected viewpoints ensures that subsidiary areas of the elevation are neglected, such as the rear of the entrance portal and the lateral façades of the west aivān. Many such surfaces are left in plain brick and their haphazard elevation is clear proof that in constructing vistas some Iranian architects, at least, did not have multiple viewpoints in mind. Nevertheless, it is hard to think of another building in the Islamic world with a polychrome splendour so rich and uniform as this, the reflections of the façades gleaming with redoubled effect in the extensive ablutions pool.

Apart from the entrance portal, constructed when time and money were plentiful, the ceramic decoration which predominates (marble is used for dadoes and stone for pillars in the winter prayer halls) is of overglaze painted tiles (*haft-rangī*), an understandable and practical economy given the huge surfaces to be covered. Dazzling though it is in strong sunlight, this tilework shows to poorer effect in the sanctuary chamber and worst of all when seen at close quarters in the vaulting of the winter prayer halls. Subsequent architects took to heart the evident lesson that large painted tiles are an unsuitable medium for decorating these domical and pseudo-ribbed vaults.[1]

These two great mosques mark the apogee of Safavid architecture. Although neither introduces any striking new feature into the repertory of forms and techniques, both reshuffle familiar elements into unexpected patterns. They show a concern for outward splendour that was still unusual in Persian mosque architecture, and which no doubt springs from their presence on the maidān. It says much for the architecture of this period that two such ambitious mosques so fundamentally different from each other could have been raised side by side and almost simultaneously. Their location in full view of all at the heart of one of the most prestigious capitals of the contemporary world made it inevitable that they should exert a dominant influence on subsequent Safavid architecture. Even when this influence cannot be traced *in extenso*, the basic emphasis on a lofty dome and on the sheathing of surfaces in haft-rangī tiles remained. The best of later Safavid buildings are, nevertheless, far more orthodox than these mosques, while in the many lesser mosques and madrasas erected in 17th-century Iṣfahān no very marked individual style can be detected. It could well be said that Safavid architecture had shot its bolt with the mosques on the maidān, for almost without exception the best later work is in the secular field.

The devotion of Shah ʿAbbās to Iṣfahān has tended to obscure his major contributions to the major shrines of the country, notably Mashhad, Turbat-i Jām, Ardabīl, Māhān and Qum. His work at Mashhad was on a more lavish scale than elsewhere, and extended to buildings other than the shrine, notably the mausoleum of Khwāja Rabīʿ (1030/1620). It is recorded that he made the pilgrimage from Iṣfahān to Mashhad on foot, and that after he had delivered the city (permanently) from the Uzbek threat in 1006/1597 he entered the shrine unshod to give thanks. Subsequently he encouraged his people to visit this shrine rather than Mecca, possibly for commercial reasons. A complex tangle of personal, devotional, political and economic motives may therefore have actuated his work on the shrine. Unlike

[1] Golombek, "Anatomy", *passim*. Godard, "Iṣfahān", pp. 107–16. Pope, in *SPA*, pp. 1185–9 and pls. 463–470A. Hunarfar, *Ganjīna*, pp. 427–64.

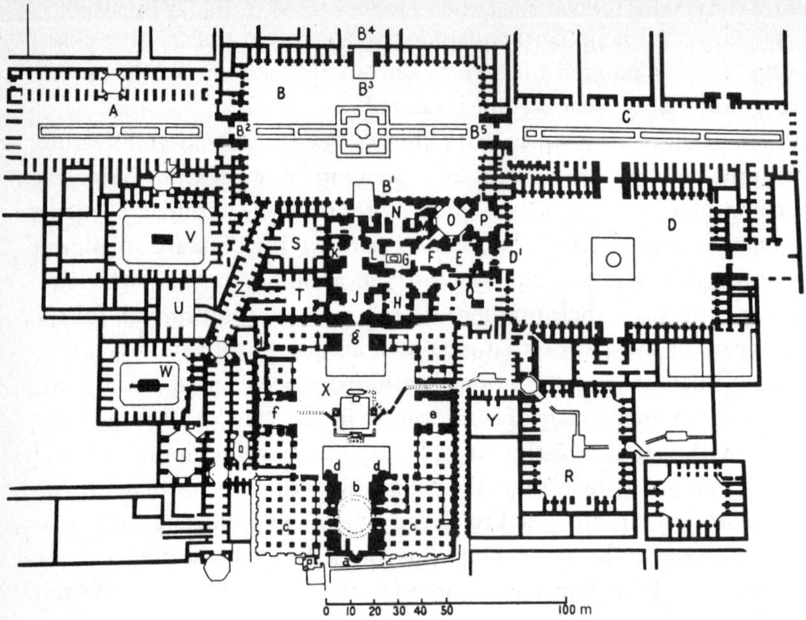

A. Bālā khiyābān (Upper esplanade)
B. Ṣaḥn-i kuhna (the Old Court)
B^1. The gold aivān (Aivān-i ṭalā) of 'Ali Shīr Navā'ī (now called the Aivān-i ṭalā-yi Nādirī)
B^2. Entrance from Upper esplanade of Shāh 'Abbās I
B^3. Aivan of Shāh 'Abbās II
B^4. Minaret of Shāh Ṭahmāsp
B^5. Entrance from Lower Esplanade
C. Pā'īn khiyābān (Lower esplanade)
D. Ṣaḥn-i nau (the New Court)
D^1. The gold aivān of Fath 'Alī Shāh
E. Dār al-sa'āda (Chamber of felicity)
F. Dome chamber of Ḥātim Khān
G. Ẓarīḥ-i Ḥaẓrat (the tomb chamber)
H. Dār al-ḥuffāẓ (Chamber of the Guardians)
J. Dār al-siyāda (Chamber of the nobility)
K. Bālā-sar (above the head (a))
L. Bālā-sar (above the head (b))
M. Mosque of the ladies
N. Tauḥīd-khāna (Chamber of monotheism)
O. Dome chamber of Allāhverdī Khān
P. Dār al-ẓiyāfa (Chamber of hospitality)
Q. Madrasa of 'Alī Naqī Mīrzā
R. Madrasa-yi pā'īn-i pā (Madrasa below the feet)
S. Madrasa-yi bālā-sar
T. Madrasa-yi Parī-zād
U. Madrasa-yi du-dar (Madrasa of two doors)
V. Caravansarai Vazīr-i Niẓām
W. Caravansarai Nādirī
X. Masjid-i Gauhar Shād
  a. Miḥrāb
  b. sanctuary aivān (aivān-i maqṣūra)
  c. oratory (shabistān)
  d. minaret
  e. aivān of Ḥajjī Ḥasan
  f. the water aivān (aivān-i āb)
  g. aivān of the nobility (aivān al-siyāda)

Fig. 8. Mashhad. Shrine complex, plan.

Iṣfahān, Mashhad did not allow him a free hand and thus his contributions to the shrine must be assessed piecemeal rather than as a unity (fig. 8). His order of 1010/1601 that the shrine be restored would lead one to expect traces of his handiwork sporadically throughout the complex, and indeed his name is associated with or found on the north aivān of the Masjid-i Gauhar Shād, the Bālāsar madrasa (repaired by his general Allāh Qulī Khān), the east and west aivāns in the Ṣaḥn-i Kuhna, the chambers of Allāhvardī Khān (1021/1612) and Ḥātim Khān

(1010/1601), the Khiyābān and the redecorated dome chamber of the Imām himself. Of these the crucial elements are the Khiyābān and the chamber of Allāhvardī Khān.

The Khiyābān, divided by the Old Court (which nevertheless continues the same axis) into an "upper" and "lower" section, traverses the entire length of the shrine at its northern extremity, and totals about 200 m. in length. A watercourse, a section of the great *qanāt* provided for the city by Mīr 'Alī Shīr, runs through its centre. The scale of the undertaking (made even more remarkable by the fact that the area was densely built-up), its bold simplicity, and the use of water as an integral part of the design, all have affinities with the much larger project of the Chahār Bāgh. Flanked on either side by shops, the two halves of the Khiyābān mediate between the shrine and the outer world. They also impose order on and knit together the otherwise ill-assorted northern façade of the shrine and thus provide a fitting and dignified approach to the Ṣaḥn-i Kuhna, the finest courtyard of the shrine proper. The east and west aivāns of this courtyard, along the axis of the watercourse, are also due to Shah 'Abbās, and here again the themes later taken up at Iṣfahān make their first appearance. In sheer scale both aivāns challenge the portal aivāns of the Masjid-i Shāh at Iṣfahān and, unlike that aivān, fulfil a double function : not only do they serve as the formal entrances to the shrine, but they also act as key components of the Ṣaḥn-i Kuhna, marking the centre of each short side. The sequence of large and small bays, of solids and voids, adopted in this inner façade is unique. The approach to the dome chamber of Allāhvardī Khān is rather unpromising, for Qājār additions have cast into permanent gloom an entrance aivān designed for sunlight. Yet the modest size of this portal, and the exterior of the dome itself, with its shallow profile and plain surface formerly crowned by a diminutive domed belvedere, show clearly enough that the building was intended primarily as an interior. Like the mausoleum of Öljeitü at Sulṭāniyya, from which it may derive, it is an octagon throughout until the springing of the dome, an unusual feature for large domed buildings in Iran. Both structures also share a marked emphasis on lighting and a preference for articulating the interior walls by deep arched recesses. The Safavid chamber, however, owes its intensity not to architecture so much as to decoration, for almost every available surface is covered in tilework. The head of each recess is crowned with cascading stalactites and they also encrust part of the dome. These broken surfaces and deep bays reflect light at every turn, while the tilework itself is spangled with tiny bright flowers, each one a pinpoint of light against the dark ground. Within each bay subdivisions are multiplied into a complex array of rectangular and arched panels, each different from its neighbour in outline and in the design or colour of its field. Net vaults of Timurid type constitute the transition zone, and the choice of this device accords with the fragmented nature of the individual parts within the grand design. Amidst a singularly rich repertoire of living creatures "birds of paradise" dominate.[1] Rectangular inscription bands frame the lower arches and provide much-needed continuity. It would be hard to discover in Safavid architecture a more concentrated display of tilework so enhanced by an original elevation.

In 1021/1612 Shah 'Abbās visited the Ardabīl shrine, to which he donated the royal porcelain collection, and various alterations to the shrine itself were made in his name from this time on, though a door dated 1011/1602–3 shows that work was already being carried out earlier in his reign. His principal contribution was the redecoration in 1037/1627–8 of the Dār al-Ḥuffāẓ, a 14th-century foundation.[2] The treatment is unusual for a shrine, for it uses exclusively the techniques of gilding, plaster ornament and painting commonly associated with Safavid palaces. The Chīnīkhāna, long regarded as entirely constructed under Shah 'Abbās, has a structure as early as the 14th century though the interior decoration, including the dado of haft-rangī tiles and of course the entire architectural surround for the porcelain (again derived from palatial models such as the 'Ālī Qāpū?), is of the early 17th century. The inner dome is unusual in that it continues the net vaulting of the "pendentives" as a decorative motif, so that the entire surface is criss-crossed with lozenge and stellar forms. Fresco paintings and carved and relief stucco in an idiom reminiscent of rocaille fill most of these panels. Again this ornament is painted and gilded.

At Māhān too the work of Shah 'Abbās is intermingled with that of earlier and later generations. To the west of the 15th-century dome chamber of Shāh Ni'mat-Allāh, which was the nucleus of the shrine and which he restored in 1010/1601, he added a covered gallery (dār al-ḥuffāẓ) and an adjoining courtyard. The long corridors thus created carry transverse vaults of the type encountered in the oratories of the

[1] Pope, "Representations".
[2] Morton, "The Ardabil Shrine", pp. 52–4. Weaver, *Preliminary Study*, pp. 18–22, 36–8.

Yazd Jāmi', which provide a structural skeleton embellished by a matchless assembly of cupolas and oculi of stellar design (pl. 42). When viewed as a continuous series, their different patterns mingle like those of a kaleidoscope in the fluid transition from one bay to the next. The dazzling white plaster finish perfectly complements these precise abstract designs; colour would be superfluous. The lower part of the gallery is, despite subsequent repairs, readily datable by inscriptions to 998/1589–90, and the vaults are probably contemporary with this, even though they are closely paralleled in the Qājār sections of the shrine, such as the Vakīl mosque, which were built at a time when spectacular vaulting, as demonstrated in the bazaars of Qum, Kāshān and Kirmān itself, was especially fashionable. Simpler forms of these probably Safavid vaults had long been established in southern Iran, while the use of pure white vaulting in cultic buildings had an equally long history. Moreover, the vaulted bays in the lower parts of the western gallery exploit the contrast between plain white stalactite vaults, lightly sprinkled with tiled insets, and the intense polychromy of tiled dadoes. Such tiled insets are a distinctively Timurid feature which might well have continued into Safavid times but would be surprising at a much later date. The evidence therefore favours a Safavid date, though more detailed discussion of the Māhān vaults must await a full monographic account of the shrine. Other decorative features include floral frescoes in the lower vaults and – in glaze – window grilles and inscribed cartouches.[1]

Apart from the great shrine complexes the outstanding Safavid ensemble in the provinces is the mosque, madrasa and caravansarai of Ganj 'Alī Khān, the governor of Kirmān under Shah 'Abbās (fig. 9).[2] The inscriptions date the work to 1007/1598, though it was probably begun as early as 996/1587, and are the work of the celebrated calligrapher 'Alī Riżā-yi 'Abbāsī. The ensemble comprises a rectangular plaza (100 m. × 50 m.) with a two-storey building, probably a caravansarai (dimensions 55 m. × 53 m.), on its east side, a small mosque adjoining it and two bazaars facing each other across the square: a Maidān-i Shāh in miniature? The bazaars comprise a series of adjacent shops each consisting of a deep domed bay, and are linked by a similar line of shops on the west side of the maidān. An impressive 12-sided chahār-sū with deep radiating niches takes up the south-west corner of the com-

[1] Bastānī-Parīzī, *Rāhnumā*, pp. 74–95.

[2] *Idem*, "L'Ensemble".

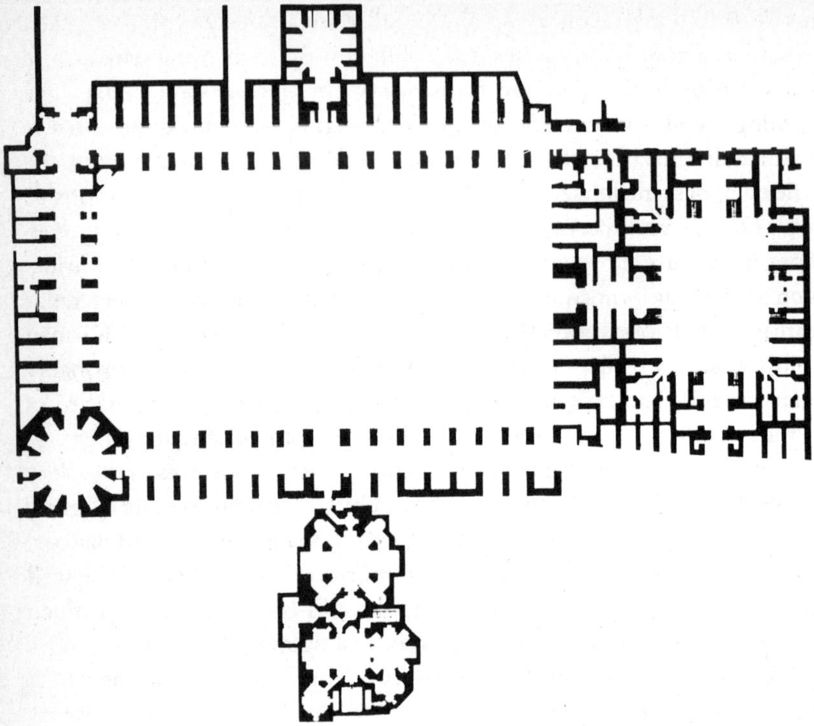

Fig. 9. Kirmān. Complex of Ganj 'Alī Khān, plan.

plex. An octagonal cistern or reservoir (*ḥauẓ*) with radiating dome chambers on each of its eight sides was also added to an earlier *ḥammām* already comprising numerous octagonal structures and adjoining the southern bazaar. Opposite the bath on the other side of the maidān is a square *darābkhāna* to which a large vestibule gives access. Numerous portals led to these various structures. The whole was made *vaqf* in 1008/1599 and again in Rajab 1024/July 1615. Apart from the bath, a very complex affair of half a dozen major elements whose chronology has yet to be established, the most remarkable element in this complex is the caravansarai, which conforms so little to the norm for this genre that it has tentatively been identified as a madrasa. It would, however, be an equally exceptional specimen of that genre too. No two sides are symmetrical or even of equal depth, and the presence of numerous rooms of uneven size and layout is hard to parallel in any public building of the period. Especially puzzling is the densely planned multi-chambered area between the courtyard and the maidān. More functions could be suggested for these various chambers, however, in the context of an urban caravansarai (with its requirement for warehouses and secure chambers for valuable goods) than of a madrasa. In the portal spandrels of this building is a series of chinoiserie themes in niched oval medallions (themselves a Chinese feature) or amidst arabesque scrolls. Dragons and phoenixes fight while cranes and Chinese clouds act as spacefillers. Other motifs include jackals, mountain sheep and felines bringing down gazelles, a repertory borrowed directly from contemporary carpets. Strangest of all, however, is the winged angel carrying a baby with a lion looking upwards from below, presumably a reference to 'Alī (who was commonly termed *ḥaidar*, "lion").

Among Safavid madrasas the Madrasa-yi Khān in Shīrāz, built between 1024/1615 and 1036/1627 by a certain Ḥusain Sammā'ī, is on several counts perhaps the most interesting. It is the only Safavid madrasa which has been subjected to a detailed historical and functional scrutiny (through its published *vaqf-nāma*) as well as to a thorough architectural analysis. It demonstrates that the best work in the provinces yielded nothing to that of the capital. Indeed, some of its details, like the fine stereotomy of its dadoes, its dragon carving in stone, above all the tilework of its vestibule, show a vital and original local style. Lastly, it provides ample evidence that the emphasis on sheer size (the madrasa measures *c.* 82 m. × *c.* 69 m.) which so often recurs in the buildings of Iṣfahān was by no means confined to that city or to royal foundations, though it is no doubt significant that the patrons here were Allāhvardī Khān and his son Imām Qulī, successively governors of Fārs and both high in the royal favour. The layout displays numerous as yet unexplained variations on earlier madrasas. While the standard four-aivān plan is employed, the general lack of symmetry within this framework is marked. Only the north and south sides agree, with their two storeys of student cells. The communal areas of the plan, including the vaulted apsidal aivān which is the cynosure of the whole building, are to the east rather than on the qibla side or within the entrance complex as at Khargird. Moreover, there is no separate mosque; the south-western aivān, located at right angles to the entrance, fulfils this function. Within the entrance complex are groups of rooms opening off central corridors, many of them difficult of access. In all its essential features the upper storey echoes the arrangement of the lower.[1]

The works of Shah 'Abbās constitute a kind of terminus. No later shah erected a tithe of the buildings which may justifiably be laid to his credit. Instead, the pattern of later building which emerges consistently is of repairs and embellishments to existing monuments. Chardin was right: when Shah 'Abbās the Great ceased to breathe, Persia ceased to prosper.[2] The dramatic fall in the quantity, scale and – to some extent – quality of architecture after his reign justifies a somewhat summary treatment of later work.

This approach is most thoroughly vindicated in dealing with the output of the immediate successor of 'Abbās, Shah Ṣafī. In his thirteen-year reign his principal achievement in the field of architecture seems to have been the modest mosques built at Shahristān and Turbat-i Ḥaidariyya; he seems also to have contributed to the gardens of Ṣafīābād and Fīn. In Iṣfahān he repaired the Imāmzāda Ismā'īl and the tomb of Bābā Qāsim, and completed the mausoleum of Bābā Rukn al-Dīn. He also put some of the finishing touches to the Masjid-i Shāh. New buildings in the city included the Masjid-i Āqā Nūr (1039/1629) and the Madrasa-yi Mullā 'Abd-Allāh.

Shah 'Abbās II was a much more zealous builder and at least two undisputed masterpieces in Iṣfahān – the Chihil Sutūn palace and the Khājū bridge – can be attributed to him. Among other buildings of high quality for which he was responsible one may cite the Talār Ashrāf and Masjid-i Ḥakīm in Iṣfahān and, in part, the Qadamgāh near Nīshāpūr. Restoration work or new building was carried out on the shrines of Ardabīl, Qum and Mashhad and on the Friday mosques of Kirmān, Gurgān and Qazvīn as well as on numerous smaller mosques and shrines. He also added the marble dadoes and great door of the Masjid-i Shāh. Finally, in Iṣfahān itself some fine smaller cultic buildings were put up during his reign: the Armenian church of the Holy Sisters (actually in Julfā), the Masjid-i Miṣrī, the Masjid-i Ṣārū Taqī, the Madrasa-yi Jadda Buzurg and the Madrasa-yi Jadda Kūchak.

The Chihil Sutūn is deservedly the most famous of Persian palaces, perhaps because it is one of the few to have kept its original garden *ambiente* (figs 10*a*,*b*). Thus some flavour of the festive, hedonistic life-style celebrated there still lingers. The prospect over the ornamental

[1] Khoubnazar and Kleiss, pls. 57–61.

[2] Chardin III, 291.

lake, closed by an axial pavilion, is integral to the architecture. Formerly the royal gardens were strewn with palaces of this kind, each drawing much of its individual quality from its surroundings. Such a tradition is at least as old as Hadrian's Tivoli palace and is found throughout the Muslim world, in Samarqand, Edirne and Granada. Kaempfer's map of the royal garden precinct at Iṣfahān gives a vivid impression of such landscape architecture (figs 11*a*, *b*).[1] But if the general tradition from which these garden palaces sprang is clear, the specific antecedents of the Chihil Sutūn type are difficult to determine. Parallels are commonly drawn with the hypostyle palaces of Persepolis and with the tālār of the typical Caspian house, but neither is very convincing. Paradoxically, despite its trabeate form it owes more to Sasanian palaces than to any other traceable source, for the deep recessed central bay leading to the throne room operates just like a Sasanian aivān.

Like many other Safavid palaces, the Chihil Sutūn has a deliberately unstable and impermanent air. Its eighteen pillars, seemingly as thin as matchsticks, seem preposterously inadequate to bear the burden of the apparently massive flat roof. There is an element of hyperbole here which finds expression in different terms in other Islamic palaces such as Saljūq Qubāẕābād or Il-Khanid Soghurluq/Saturiq, and is evoked by the very title of Chihil Sutūn – "many" rather than "forty" columns; the theory that the name refers to the reflections of these columns in the water is surely a picturesque fantasy.

Like the 'Ālī Qāpū, however, this palace offers an aspect of four-square solidity from its sides and rear which is very different from its frail and insubstantial façade. Long bays some 5 m. deep open along the lateral façades and each is punctuated by four columns. Niches with frescoes of courtly scenes break the recessed wall behind. In contrast to the main façade the rear wall presents a solid mass of masonry in which the principal break is the rear entrance. This, like all the other entrances, is stepped, for the palace is placed on a platform. The internal layout is readily grasped and has none of the bewildering complexities of the 'Ālī Qāpū. Three major spatial units are set side by side: the tālār leads into a throne room which in turn gives onto the main hall. Subsidiary chambers on the pattern of the 'Ālī Qāpū flank the throne room on its short and the main hall on its long side. Thus spacious and

[1] Galdieri, "Relecture". Luschey, "Der königliche Marstall".

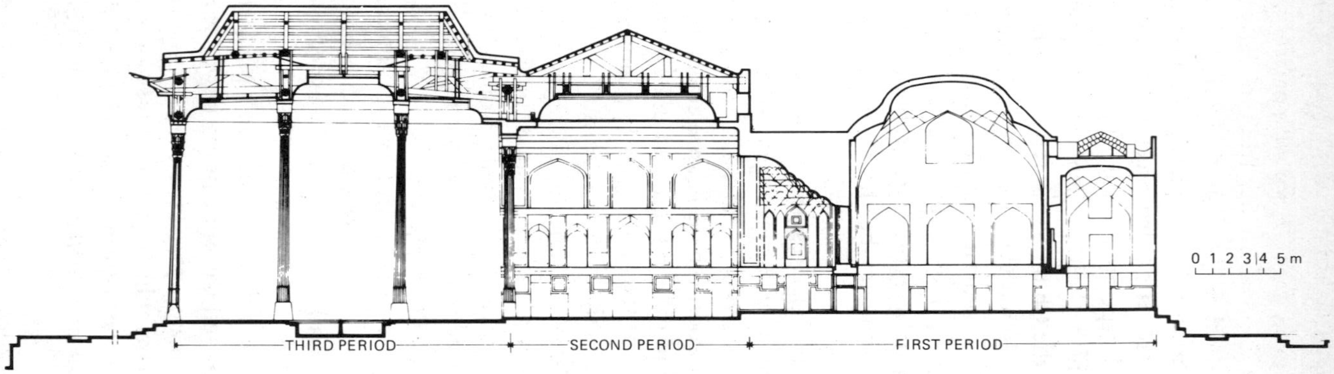

Fig. 10a. Iṣfahān. Chihil Sutūn, section.

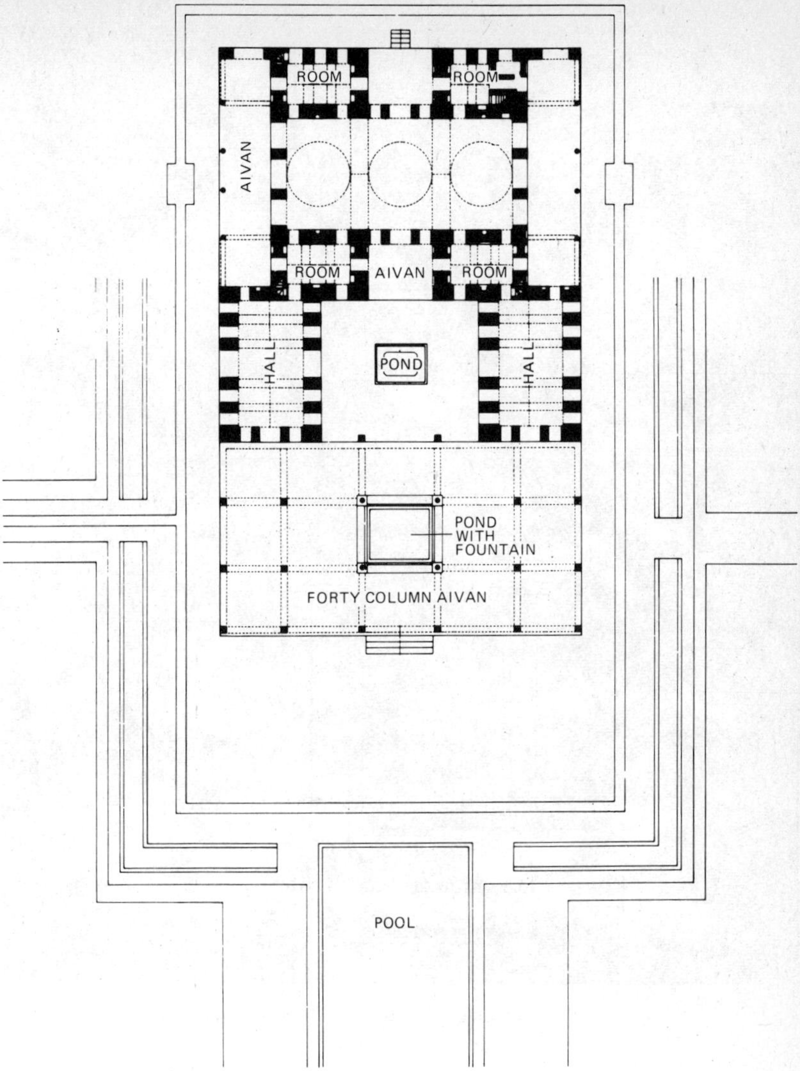

Fig. 10b. Iṣfahān. Chihil Sutūn, plan.

intimate units alternate and interact in a design of admirable compactness. They have a rich fresco decoration which recycles the threadbare repertoire of courtly scenes in the painting of Riżā-yi 'Abbāsī – vapid youths and maidens halfheartedly dallying and drinking in a landscape of eternal spring. In the large halls these themes are relegated to the

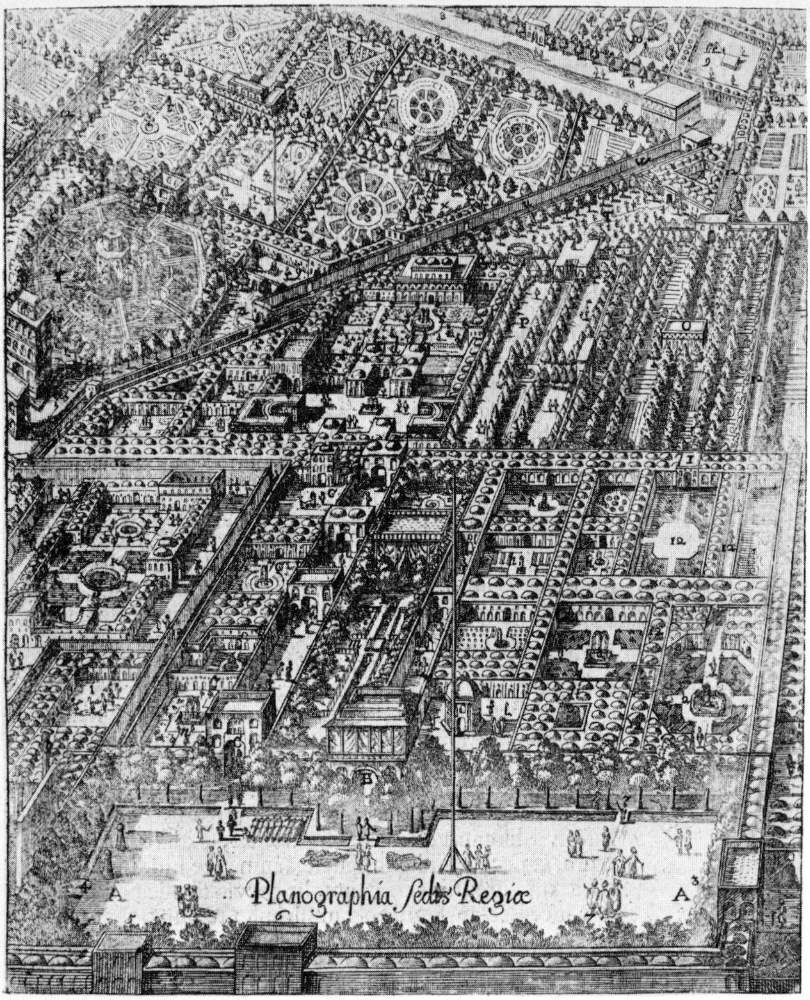

Fig. 11a. Iṣfahān. Drawing ("Planographia") of the royal precinct.

lower part of the walls, while more ambitious scenes of royal banqueting and battle claim pride of place. The tālār ceiling and eaves are prinked out in paint and marquetry work. Most of this decoration is given an architectural quality by the division of the ceiling into a grid of recessed panels, a technique earlier used in medieval vaults. Multi-tiered stalactite capitals, again a familiar medieval form, mediate between the columns and the roof. If the tālār seems somewhat bare and echoing now, in its heyday bright curtains were hung between the

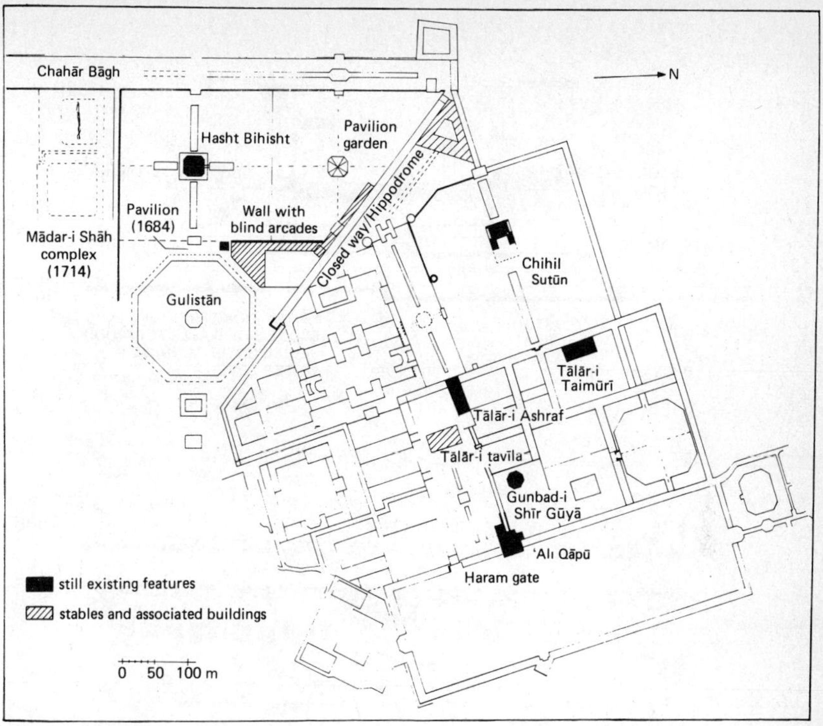

Fig. 11b. E. Galdieri's interpretation of Kaempfer's "Planographia", in a simplified drawing by H. Gaube.

columns and the floor was strewn with carpets on which courtiers reclined to watch the dancing girls frolic.

The other great masterpiece of this reign is the Khājū bridge, erected on the foundations of a Timurid bridge at the royal command, probably by the shah's general Ḥasan Beg, in 1060/1650 and named after a nearby quarter of the city (pl. 44*a*). Though less than half the length of the bridge of Allāhvardī Khān (132 m. as against *c.* 300 m.) it is lent a more imposing air by the massive octagonal pavilion which straddles it in mid-stream, and juts out on both sides like a prow. Moreover, unlike its predecessor the Khājū bridge rests on a high stone platform which to the east shelves down to the river in a series of shallow steps broken by sluices, while to the west spear-shaped *contreforts* break the river's flow. This podium on which the superposed arcades of the bridge rest transforms the structure into a massive three-

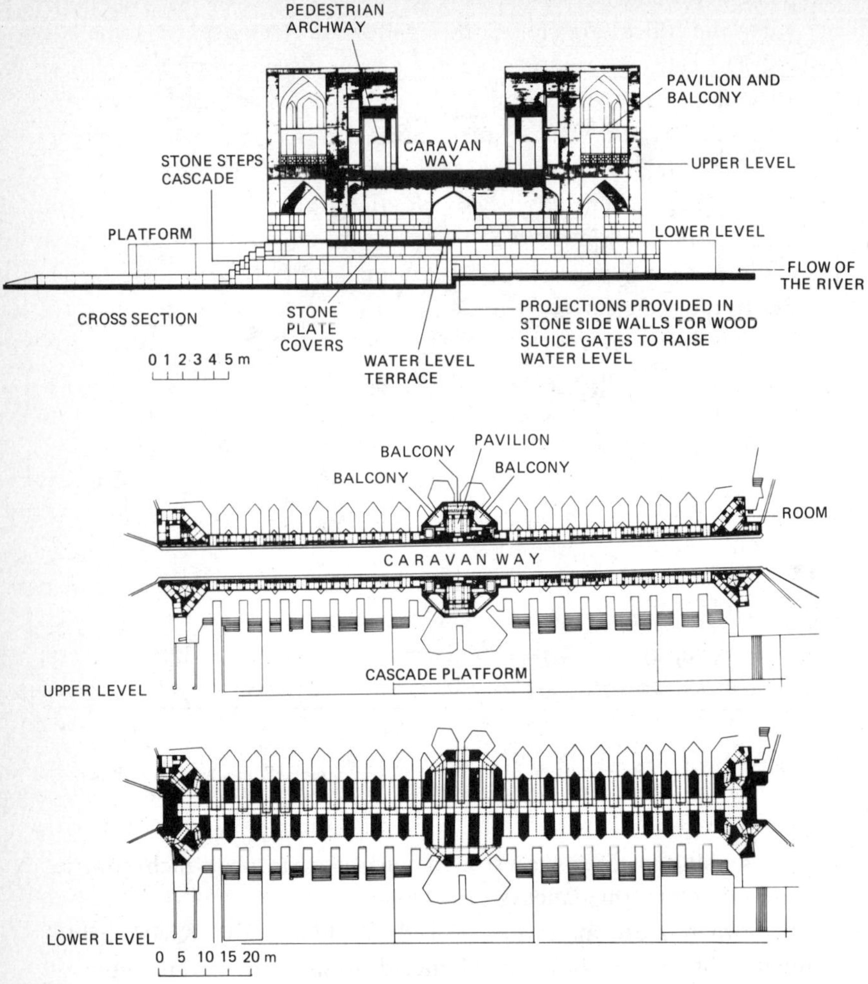

Fig. 12. Iṣfahān, Khājū bridge, section and plans.

tiered elevation conceived in highly plastic terms (fig. 12). Diminutive half-octagonal kiosks, reduced versions of the great centrepiece, terminate the bridge at each end. In purely visual terms it has a variety and compactness which is far removed from the monotonous length of the Allāhvardī Khān bridge. Functionally, too, it is a far more complex structure. The upper section is subdivided into a central track for horses and wheeled traffic with a vaulted pedestrian footway on either side. The lowest section serves as a weir which at its widest reaches 26 m.; when the sluices are closed the level of the river rises by some two metres. The central pavilion is simply a typical Safavid pleasure palace incorporated into a utilitarian structure. From this peerless vantage point the shah could watch aquatic sports, mock naval battles, water polo and regattas, while the inner rooms gave him the opportunity to retire in private when he wished. Nondescript modern tilework and stencilled carpet designs have replaced the gilded paintwork and moral saws which formerly graced these rooms. In its location the bridge testifies to the same careful planning as does its design. It is athwart the old road to Shīrāz, it provided conveniently quick access to the Zoroastrian quarter and thus effectively kept the Zoroastrians off the Chahār Bāgh, and finally it continues the axis of the east side of the maidān. A now vanished covered bazaar linked maidān and bridge.[1]

Among the many mosques erected by high officials of the Safavid court in the 17th century the Masjid-i Ḥakīm is outstanding alike for its size and for the splendour and extent of its ornament. It was erected in 1067/1656 with funds sent from India by the court physician of Shah 'Abbās II, Muḥammad Dā'ūd Ḥakīm, who had fled to the Mughal court after incurring his master's wrath by certain intrigues. Several later dates occurring in the unusually rich epigraphy – 1069/1658–9, 1071/1660–1 and 1073/1662–3 – suggest that the 1067/1656–7 date refers only to the completion of construction work on the mosque. These inscriptions were written by the finest calligrapher of the day, Muḥammad Riżā al-Imāmī. The classical formula of courtyard with axial aivāns linked by two-tier arcades and with a domed sanctuary is realised on a generous scale. While lengthy Qur'anic inscriptions from ṣūras ii, xvii, xlv and lxii are used within the aivāns and dome chamber, the courtyard façade consists largely of sacred names in square Kufic forming ingenious patterns. The virtual absence of floral motifs is marked.

This decorative scheme is notable for its avoidance of overall revetment, for it is conceived as an assembly of separate panels framed against a plain brick ground. The general effect is not of a continuously tiled surface, as in the Masjid-i Shāh, but of a predominantly brick building enlivened by touches of colour. Architectural values are begin-

[1] Pope, in *SPA*, pp. 1237–40. Hunarfar, *Ganjīna*, pp. 582–5. Ferrante, in Zander, *Travaux*, pp. 451–62.

ning to reassert themselves. Structurally the most interesting feature of the mosque is its qibla side. In the aivān preceding the dome chamber, for example, a shallow stalactite vault is suddenly resolved into an ornamental and two-dimensional squinch net etched onto the plain smooth surface of the vault. The plastic configurations of a full-scale stalactite vault are decisively rejected in favour of a smooth and indeed comparatively plain surface. Similar concerns govern the layout of the dome chamber. This owes much to the Luṭf-Allāh mosque in its virtual removal of the transition zone in favour of a ring of eight arches occupying the lower elevation, but the arches on the diagonals are much smaller than those on the principal axes and kite-shaped forms (not pendentives as they are sometimes called) are needed to fill the huge spandrels thus created. Three miḥrābs and a *minbar* sufficiently emphasise the importance of this mosque.[1]

In the field of religious architecture about half of the work associated with Shah ʿAbbās II is found in Iṣfahān, and while a few new foundations are recorded elsewhere (Vazīr mosque, Kāshān, 1055/1645; Friday Mosque, Sarm, 1062/1651) most of the dated work in the provinces consists of repairs and additions to existing structures – e.g. the Mashhad shrine (1057/1647) or the Qadamgāh near Nīshāpūr (founded 1020/1611 and refurbished 1053/1643), a domed octagon of the same general type as some of the 16th-century mausolea discussed above; whereas the activity in Iṣfahān includes many new buildings, of which three madrasas and at least eight mosques survive. This situation persisted throughout the reign of his successors, the last two Safavid monarchs.

Neither secular nor cultic architecture saw any significant advances in the last half-century of Safavid rule. Instead the trend was towards the retrospective. The major monuments erected by Shah Sulaimān are again secular, not religious – perhaps because the commanding location and scale of the mosques on the maidān, and the presence of a hoary jāmiʿ, discouraged major cultic buildings. Among the palaces the Hasht Bihisht ("Eight Paradises") of 1080/1669 is paramount (fig. 13*a*).[2] The very name, a common one for gardens in Iran, is evocative, though perhaps a more worldly paradise is intended, for the palace houses eight intimate pavilions. Its layout is a triumph of compactness,

[1] Godard, "Iṣfahān", pp. 152–4. Hunarfar, *Ganjīna*, pp. 612–20.

[2] Seherr-Thoss, pp. 204–9, figs. H–I and pls. 93–5. Hunarfar, *Ganjīna*, pp. 622–6. Ferrante, in Zander, *Travaux*, pp. 399–420.

although paradoxically the first impression is one of untrammelled space. On the principal axes huge tālārs open, extending up to roof level, so that from every part of the building views of the surrounding gardens impinge (fig. 13*b*). These tālārs are set off by sturdy polygonal corner turrents, each of which holds a complex of rooms and stairways on two storeys. Thus the private chambers of the palace and the access to them are managed within the corner blocks which carry the whole edifice. Intensively exploited areas thereby alternate with markedly open ones, while an octagonal pool with a fountain symbolically brings nature right into the building, a conceit repeated at the 'Ālī Qāpū and the Chihil Sutūn. The rather unsightly pitched roof gives no hint that it covers a huge and spectacular muqarnas vault pierced at its apex in Timurid fashion by a high drum with an inner dome. This oculus is brilliantly lit by eight windows. Like the Chihil Sutūn, the Hasht Bihisht rests on a stone-faced platform as high as a man and ascended by axial stairways, each different from the next. It is hard not to see here, as at the Chihil Sutūn, a faint echo of an ancient Iranian tradition whereby palaces were raised on platforms and thus symbolically removed beyond the ken of the common man.

The impact of the original decoration is now lost beyond recall, for over the years the building fell victim to neglect and to the misguided attentions of Qājār craftsmen whose mirrorwork and frescoes completely transformed it. But surviving parts of the original scheme (e.g. in some of the reception rooms on the second floor) go far to justify Chardin's panegyrics. Following an Iranian tradition for which early Islamic as well as Safavid parallels may be cited, the various little rooms are vaulted and ornamented in subtly different ways but bear a strong family likeness. Quite small rooms are given an illusion of size by the use of several adjoining vaulted areas. These are broken up into multiple facets which effortlessly blend into each other, and are, as Herbert would say, "pargetted with azure and gold". The decorative repertoire has a chinoiserie flavour already encountered in the 'Ālī Qāpū. Externally the accent was on tilework, some of which survives in the spandrels of the blind arches. Hunting scenes prevail. These are treated in a style akin to contemporary book painting, with the anti-naturalistic colour schemes of that medium. Thus green stags flee across a yellow ground punctuated by blue trees.

Much simpler in plan is the other important late Safavid palace to survive in Iṣfahān, the Tālār Ashrāf, which may date from *c.* 1690. It

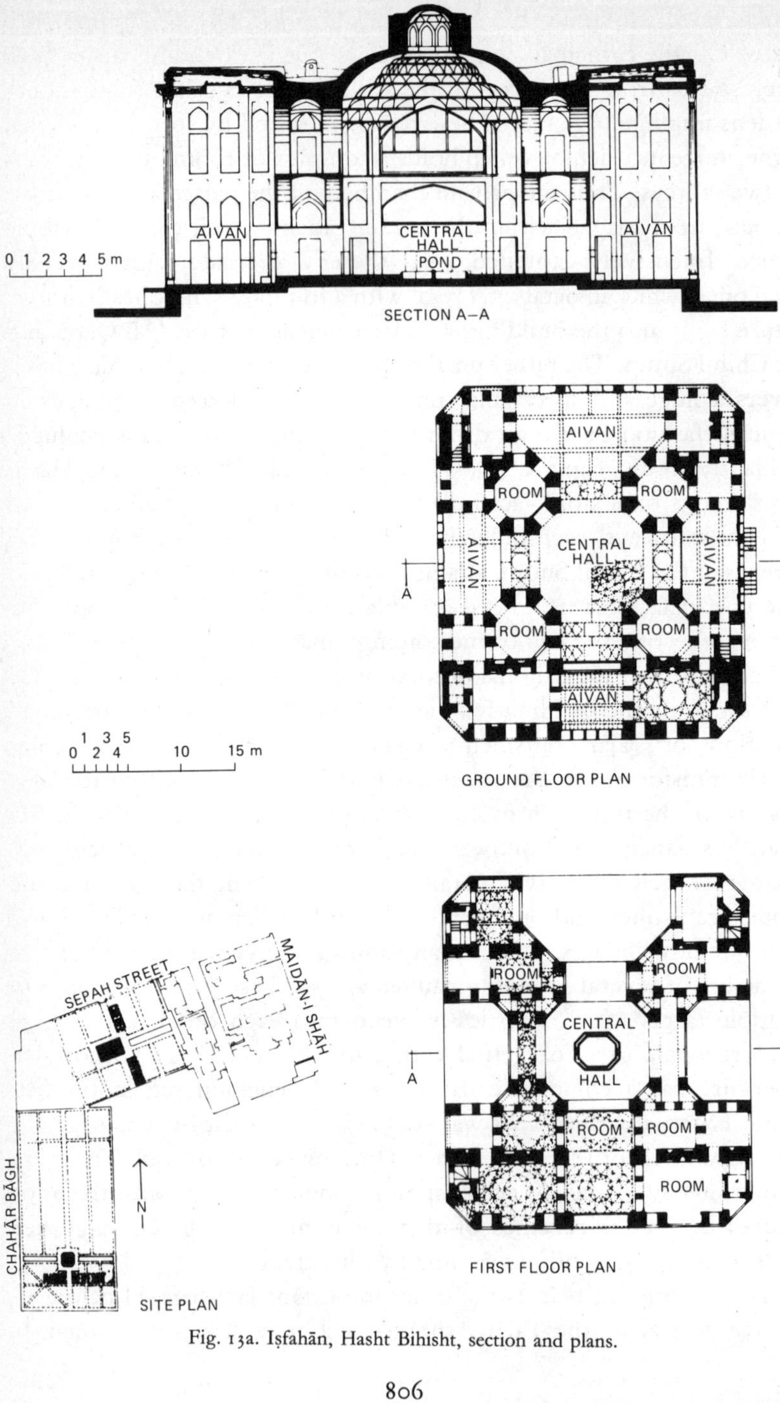

Fig. 13a. Iṣfahān, Hasht Bihisht, section and plans.

Fig. 13b. Iṣfahān, Hasht Bihisht, interior.

comprises a central pavilion, roofed with a groined vault, and a smaller room on each side, a disposition already found in the rear part of the Chihil Sutūn. Three aivāns knit together the façade. Inside, the stalactite vaulting is of the same type as that of the Hasht Bihisht, but the minutely worked stucco is something of a novelty.

Several important madrasas were built or repaired in the reign of Shah Sulaimān. In the Mashhad shrine, for example, which also received other embellishments at this time, inscriptions record repairs in the Dū Dar (1088/1677), Parīzād (1091/1680) and Bālāsar (1091/1680) madrasas (fig. 8). In Iṣfahān the Madrasa-yi Mullā 'Abd-Allāh, which was probably built in the early 17th century, was in its time, according to Chardin, "le plus grand et le plus riche collège [*sic*] d'Ispahan" – which says little for the standard of the forty-eight others, since it is somewhat humdrum. It bears a *vaqf* text of 1088/1677–8 recording the endowment of shops for the building.

It is customary to confine any discussion of the last quarter-century of Safavid architecture to a single group of monuments – the bazaar, caravansarai and madrasa on the Chahār Bāgh. Summary though this approach is, it is broadly speaking justifiable. The reign of Shah Sulṭān Ḥusain saw dated work, whether of construction or repair, carried out on something over thirty buildings, slightly less than in the previous reign and roughly comparable to the amount of work carried out under Shah 'Abbās II. But very little of this total represents new work. A miḥrāb in the Gurgān Jāmi' (1108/1696), an aivān in that of Dizfūl (1110/1698), multiple repairs – e.g. to the Imāmzāda Ismā'īl at Iṣfahān between 1100/1688–9 and 1115/1703, to the Chihil Sutūn, and to the tomb of Khwāja Rabī' (1119/1707) – these do not add up to a volume of work large enough to permit a final judgment. With the odd exception (e.g. the Friday Mosque of Chashum, 1105/1694, the nearby Faṣīḥiyya madrasa in Sabzavār, 1124/1712, or the tomb of Sahl b. 'Alī at Arak, 1110/1698) such new buildings as were erected were restricted to Iṣfahān. They include the mosque and bath of 'Alī Qulī Āghā, both of 1122/1710, the Madrasa-yi Ṣadr, the Madrasa-yi Shamsābād, founded by the merchant Muḥammad Mahdī in 1125/1713, the Madrasa-yi Kāsahgarān (1105/1694) and the Madrasa-yi Nīmāvard. The latter, built by one Zainab Begum in 1117/1705–6, is an ambitious building with a monumental tiled portal and a courtyard with bevelled corners like the Khargird madrasa. But the scale of these foundations is too modest, and their decoration too banal, to offer any insight into the quality of the best work produced under royal patronage at this time. For such an insight one can study only the complex of buildings on the Chahār Bāgh: the Mādar-i Shāh madrasa, caravansarai and bazaar (pl. 44*b*, fig. 14).[1]

[1] Coste, pp. 26–7 and pls. XVIII–XX, XXX–XXXII. Godard, "Iṣfahān", pp. 155–9. Pope, in *SPA*, pp. 1213–15. Hunarfar, *Ganjīna*, pp. 685–723.

33 Woollen knotted carpet, "garden carpet", first half of the 17th century. Size, 17ft $3\frac{1}{4}$in × 14ft $\frac{3}{4}$in.

34 Velvet, metal thread ground, Persia, beginning of the 17th century.
Total height, 1.35 m.

35 Velvet, metal thread ground, Persia, first half of the 17th century.
Height of repeating pattern 35 cm.

36 Khusrau at the palace of Shīrīn. Miniature added to a manuscript of the *Khamsa* of Niẓāmī in 1505 at Tabrīz. Size, 29 × 19 cm.

37 The court of Gayūmarṣ, by Sulṭān Muḥammad. From the *Shāh-nāma* of Shah Ṭahmāsp. Tabrīz, *c.* 1520–30. Size, 34.2 × 23.1 cm.

38 Sām and Zāl are welcomed into Kabul; Rūdāba on the balcony. From the *Shāh-nāma* of Shah Ṭahmāsp. Tabrīz, *c.* 1520–30. Size, 24.4 × 17.2 cm.

39 Iṣfahān, Chihil Sutūn. Wall-painting in a niche in the room P4. Girl seated by a stream. Attributed to Muḥammad Qāsim. Size, about 1.8 × 1.5 m. Date, *c.* 1647.

40 Iṣfahān, Chihil Sutūn. Wall-painting in a niche in the room P4. Court picnic in the country. Attributed to Muḥammad Qāsim. Date, *c.* 1647.

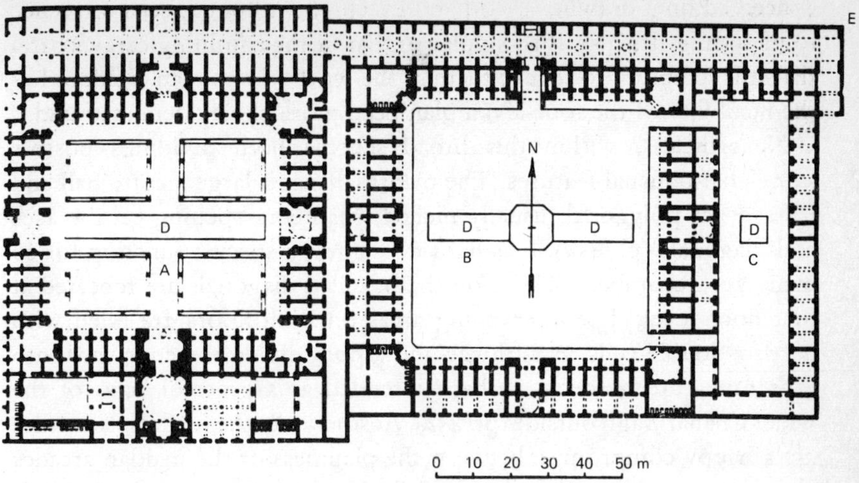

(A) Madrassa (B) Caravanserai (C) Stables (D) Canal (E) Bazaar

Fig. 14. Iṣfahān. Madrasa, caravansarai and bazaar of Shah Sulṭān Ḥusain, plan.

They are an entirely unexpected return to the grandiose planning of Shah ʿAbbās I, and together these three buildings may claim to represent the principal achievement of Safavid architecture after the 1630s. A less likely patron than the feeble and dilatory Shah Sulṭān Ḥusain can scarcely be imagined. But if the scale and ambition of the project are noteworthy, no less significant is its dependence on earlier Safavid models. Shortly before the dynasty was extinguished the familiar elements of its architecture are reshuffled on a large scale for the last time. But the result, though fine, cannot claim to be an unusually original creation. Its merits lie in the serene and rational disposition of the three constituent units. The madrasa and caravansarai are orientated along the same due eastward axis, marked by the entrance portal of the madrasa and continued in the pools of both buildings, pools which extend even to the stables closing off the complex at the east end. It will be seen that the elaborate shifts to ensure an accurate qibla in the maidān are not pursued here and the miḥrāb wall of the dome chamber points, inaccurately, due south. Presumably Shah Sulṭān Ḥusain, for all his piety, lacked the resolution to break with the long-established axes of the Chahār Bāgh and the maidān, while tradition made it virtually impossible to place the sanctuary chamber in the south-west diagonal of the building. In fact, the madrasa bears all the marks of a blueprint conceived on a drawing board and executed without special reference to its setting. Its plan is so similar to that of the adjoining caravansarai that it is tempting to regard them as the work of one man. Seldom has the flexibility of the four-aivān plan been more clearly demonstrated.

Nevertheless, within this broad schema both buildings possess somewhat unusual features. The madrasa lacks a large lecture hall and instead has polygonal, usually niched, chambers opening on the axes and diagonals (pl. 45*a*). It is hard to suggest a specific function for so many such chambers. Those on the bevelled diagonals are repeated at first floor level. The intervening areas on both floors are filled with narrow double cells. A pathway and a pool divide the courtyard into four miniature gardens, perhaps intended as a graceful echo of the wider Chahār Bāgh outside (pl. 45*b*). Aesthetically the madrasa's arcades are a happy compromise between the plainness of the maidān arcades and the somewhat oppressive overall tilework of those in the Masjid-i Shāh. Their interiors are whitewashed, with vaulting lines picked out in blue, while their court façades are tiled. The dome chamber, on the other hand, is in elevation so close a copy of the great dome of the Masjid-i Shāh that they are readily confused. But while the later architect might strive to emulate the earlier achievement, he could add nothing to it – an apt commentary on the relationship between the earlier and the later period. Only the tilework shows a marked decline from the standards of the 1620s, which themselves were not unduly high. Floral tile mosaic is almost entirely absent and muqarnas compositions, where large tiles are impracticable, are replaced by chequerwork. Coarse, indeed rather primitive, geometrical designs are frequent and are not improved by an unpleasant custard yellow which invades the colour scheme. Nevertheless, the madrasa may fairly claim to be the finest building of its kind in the country apart from the Madrasa-yi Ghiyāṣiyya at Khargird (pl. 28).

To the north the bazaar knits together the two larger buildings. It comprises a single broad corridor some 220 m. in length bordered symmetrically on both sides by multiple arcades. For the first eighty metres these open into deep recesses for shops and thereafter into shallow booths. The division between the two types of recess coincides with the eastern perimeter of the madrasa. The deeper recesses on the madrasa side serve to conceal the fact that the madrasa and the caravansarai are not harmoniously aligned to their northern end; and they ensure that the arterial passage in the bazaar runs as straight as a die.

The back walls of the southern recesses are contiguous with those of the madrasa and the caravansarai, thus permitting the back wall in each case to serve two buildings. Oddly enough no such continuity exists between the two larger buildings on the east-west axis, so that they are separated for their length by a narrow passage. Its function may have been to insulate the madrasa from noise within the caravansarai. The income from the bazaar and caravansarai was intended for the upkeep of the madrasa, and the size of the latter goes far to explain the spacious scale of the other two projects. Particularly noteworthy are the huge rectangular stables, now vanished, which ran almost the entire length of the caravansarai on the east side. Equally unusual is the placing of aivāns on the entrance axis alone, while the east and west sides are marked only by an enlarged bay which does not even embrace both floors. But, as with the madrasa and bazaar, the scale is impressive and the planning is meticulous and rational to the last detail. The confident marshalling of such large forms was a heritage bequeathed to Zand and Qājār architects and is arguably the great strength of Persian architecture in post-Safavid times.

The Safavid period has left a legacy of wall painting incomparably richer than the sum total which survives from previous periods. Most of it decorates palaces, though an important undated cycle of battle and hunting scenes adorns the upper part of the Bazaar Gate in Iṣfahān. Its relatively public subject matter is entirely appropriate to its location. The two major bridges in Iṣfahān also carry painted decorative schemes, but these are of minor interest only, while the paintings in the Hasht Bihisht, in contradistinction to its tilework, avoid figural subjects. However, in the Chihil Sutūn and ʿĀlī Qāpū palaces recent cleaning and conservation by Italian teams has revealed ambitious figural schemes in as much of their original splendour as their only partial preservation permits. They show an almost total dependence on the repertoire of contemporary book painting, with its emphasis on intimate courtly scenes and its occasional frankly erotic flavour. The artists decline to exploit the varied wall surfaces available to them and prefer to reproduce on a larger scale the rectangular and oblong frames of book illustration. In consequence the palace becomes in effect a picture gallery, an impression strengthened by the eye-level height of these artificial panels and by the deliberately muted floral or other non-figural motifs which fill the intervening spaces. This interstitial decoration operates as a kind of wallpaper. The tendency to reduce a dauntingly large wall space to a series of manageable units is found in Safavid tilework too, but there it cannot be regarded as the standard solution to the problem of dovetailing decoration with architecture.

Three major themes can be isolated in these figural schemes. The first category comprises one or more persons reclining alfresco, drinking or picnicking. The second group consists of single standing figures of courtiers or foreigners, the latter sufficiently identified by costume or attribute (thus an Englishman holds a turnip, presumably an exotic vegetable at the Safavid court). In these panels, which are usually vertical and over life-size, an attempt at realistic rather than idealised representation is made. Finally, a third group depicts busy crowded scenes of court receptions or battles. Here again an attempt at portraiture – Shah 'Abbās is instantly recognisable – and perhaps even satire (as in the cameo of a drunken youth, turban awry, reeling away from a feast supported by pages) breaks through the hackneyed conventions which govern these themes. Influences from European painting, which are themselves apparently filtered through Mughal traditions, have been detected in these large-scale paintings. So far it has not been possible to assign a date to these various figural wall-paintings, but the evidence suggests that they were produced in the reign of 'Abbās II (1052/1642–1077/1666).

It remains to consider one typically Safavid genre of building: the caravansarai (pl. 46; fig. 15*a*,*b*). The dearth of datable examples makes it desirable to treat these structures as a group rather than singly. Discussion of their variety, their utilitarian quality, the patrons who financed them, the planning devices and ideals used in their construction, and the dating problems which they present should place in better perspective the Safavid contribution to this field. By creating the abstraction of a "typical" Safavid caravansarai and describing its features, useful conclusions may be drawn from the scores of Safavid caravansarais to survive.[1]

The typical caravansarai, then, is set in open countryside and has a rectangular exterior marked by rounded towers at the corners and sometimes at intervals along the perimeter walls. The three side walls bear no decoration. At the centre of the main façade opens the single portal, sometimes flush but more often projecting boldly with its wings sometimes bevelled at the inner corners. When deep niches

[1] For useful introductory remarks on the genre, see Müller, pp. 9–30, 53–63, and *SPA*, pp. 1245–51.

articulate this façade, booths or shops may occupy them. Rings may be let into this wall for tethering animals. The provision of only one entrance has obvious advantages: traffic can be the more easily controlled and the security of the building is improved. A broad vaulted vestibule, sometimes of two storeys, mediates between the portal and the inner courtyard. If provision is made for an upper storey here, the space is often occupied by a *bālākhāna*, a well-ventilated private chamber which in some caravansarais is reserved for important guests. The inner courtyard, a spacious rectangle, is articulated by four aivāns in a cruciform disposition. Individual chambers, consisting of a broad public porch leading into a narrow private cell for sleeping, and arranged in rows at right angles to the courtyard, link these aivāns. These rooms facing the court rest on a raised platform so that the animals in the courtyard cannot intrude on the quarters reserved for travellers. Sometimes tethering rings are attached to this platform. Between the chambers for travellers and the perimeter wall run long uninterrupted galleries used for stabling. Access to these is by passages in the diagonals of the courtyard. Staircases in the thickness of the walls lead to the roof, which is also used for sleeping. Ample storage space is provided, often in the diagonals of the plan. Many caravansarais had a resident custodian, who had his private quarters adjoining or above the portal.

Certain deficiencies are apparent in this imagined blueprint. Privacy, for example, was a privilege enjoyed by the few. Generally, no facilities for cooking were available, though the individual chambers had fireplaces. Ventilation was poor. Apparently there were sometimes no latrines. Safavid caravansarais, unlike those of earlier periods, generally had no mosque. Water was frequently unavailable within the building, though if there were no cistern inside water could be obtained from a nearby well, stream, cistern or qanāt. No special provision was made for female travellers.

A few well-appointed caravansarais do, however, show that designers were aware of these imperfections and could overcome them at need. They have such extra features as shops, bakeries, baths, specially segregated quarters for women or for honoured guests, kitchens and even signal towers in which lights burned to guide desert traffic. Some of the larger examples even have two tiers of rooms; their interior façades approximate to those of mosques and madrasas.[1] Frequently

[1] E.g., Siroux, "Les caravanserais routiers", pp. 356 (Mahyār), 360 (Gabrābād), 362 (Sardahān), 364–5 (Chāh-i Siyāh Nau).

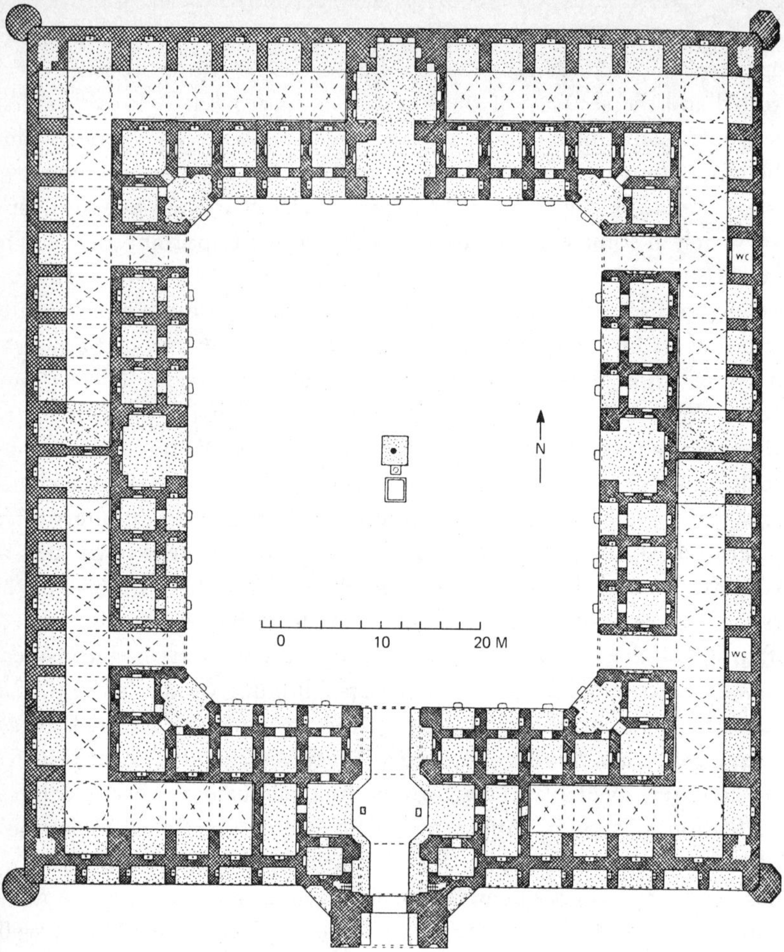

Fig. 15a. Bīsitūn. Safavid caravansarai, plan.

these improvements are grafted on to earlier Safavid or pre-Safavid caravansarais; examples are even known of Safavid caravansarais refurbished in this period.

Variety is a major characteristic of this genre of building. No two caravansarais are identical, despite their close family resemblance. A host of small, significant refinements from one caravansarai to the next can be detected even in groups of such buildings which were clearly

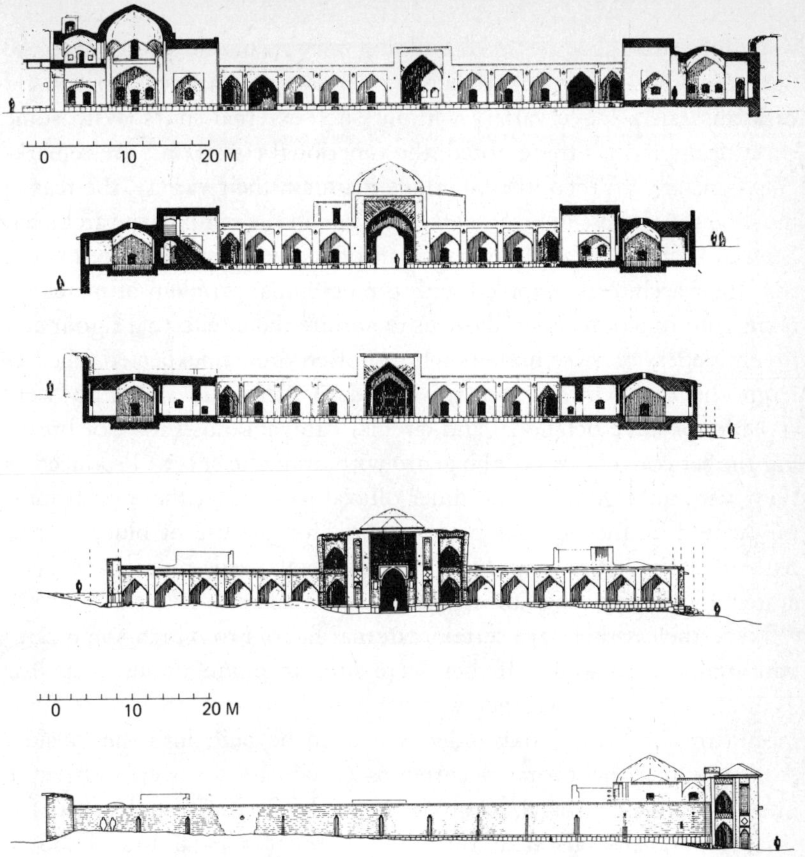

Fig. 15b. Bīsitūn. Safavid caravansarai, section and elevation.

commissioned and built together, and were usually, one presumes, the work of a single architect. This variety is particularly striking if it is recalled that these buildings, especially when they line the long, monotonous, semi-desert routes skirting the Dasht-i Kavīr, cater for a given size of caravan and so are identical in function to the others in the chain. Thus little purpose would be served by major changes in layout. Cultic structures, by contrast, were inherently open to a much wider range of functions which could be served by various elements grafted on to a nuclear plan. In addition, many external reasons account for the variety of Iranian architecture as a whole at any given period. Styles, for example, are often essentially local. Sites may be irregular. A patron may lavish interest and money on a single building. Functions in a given genre of building vary from one structure to the next. Fashions in ornament change over the generations. Yet Safavid caravansarais achieve variety without such external spurs. With some exceptions, shortly to be noted, the functional constraints are remarkably constant. If, then, the buildings maintain their variety, the reason must be sought less in external factors than in the mind of the architect. Seen as a whole, Safavid caravansarais offer silent testimony to the way that their architects grappled with the perennial problem of matching form with function. They allow us to admire the intellectual rigour and inventiveness of these masters who so often drew unexpected felicities from the deployment of a few standard elements, and who were capable, as some octagonal and circular caravansarais show, of breaking the set conventions of the genre with dramatic effect.[1] Produced as they were in large numbers under official patronage, these caravansarais would be the obvious place to look for the use of blueprints in Safavid architecture; but such blueprints, if used, must have been systematically reworked on almost every occasion.

Nevertheless there are certain external factors to which some caravansarais had to adjust. If they were sited in mountainous areas, for example, where the weather was liable to be severe, they were commonly roofed throughout and might even be built into the hillside. Routes which incorporated extremes of climate, or were otherwise uncomfortable to travel, naturally carried less traffic and called for smaller caravansarais than the more popular arterial routes. Some routes were positively dangerous, for they travelled through areas infested by brigands. Hence, probably, the trio of octagonal fortified caravansarais on the Shīrāz road. Proximity to a village might explain the reduced size of a caravansarai *vis-à-vis* others in the same chain. Conversely, if it was located close to a major town the caravansarai would probably have to deal with more than mercantile traffic, for it was an ancient custom to accompany a departing caravan to the end of the first day's stage. In the case of the Mādar-i Shāh caravansarai, some 45 km. from Iṣfahān, the needs of ambassadors on their way to the court were borne in mind; hence the unusually lavish provision of elaborate guest rooms and a ḥammām. Yet other caravansarais per-

[1] Siroux, *Caravansérails*, pp. 73–5 (Dihbīd, Amīnābād, Khān-i Khurra). Kiani, "Robat Zayn-al-Din", pp. 27–31.

formed subsidiary functions as links in the postal service, as refuges for nearby villages in time of danger or as military outposts. Exceptions apart, however, the multiple solutions that were devised within the basically simple framework of the celebrated four-aivān plan command admiration.

A second hallmark of the genre is its plainness. For elaborate decoration no Safavid caravansarai approaches such medieval examples as Ribāṭ-i Malik, Żiyā' Khātūn, Ribāṭ-i Sharaf or a whole series of Mongol caravansarais. It seems to have been a policy decision to stress the utilitarian function of these buildings. Timurid examples had probably initiated this trend, if the extensive but plain Qūsh Ribāṭ, a foundation of Amīr Shujā' al-Dīn in north-western Afghanistan dated 912/1506–7, is any guide. Internal and external façades in most Safavid caravansarais are plain, and the same austerity governs the vaulting in the covered areas. Only in the portal and in the vestibule behind it is this rule frequently broken, and then somewhat grudgingly. Portals, whether flush or salient, are decked out in ornamental brickwork or glazed tiles and often bore inscriptions, while the vestibule often boasts a stellar vault. These exceptions serve only to highlight the dominant severity of the building. So alien is this characteristic to the great public buildings of Iran that it demands an explanation. Perhaps the setting of the typical caravansarai in remote countryside, never to be seen by a large admiring public, is partly responsible, though it must be conceded that earlier patrons were not inhibited by this factor. Cultic buildings could be decorated to the greater glory of God, and palace decoration naturally reflected the luxurious life-style of the court; but the caravansarai called for display neither on cultic nor on secular grounds. Yet these reasons are insufficient to explain the plainness of these buildings. A comparison with earlier caravansarais is instructive, for the richness of many of the surviving examples and the fact that evidence for a chain of such buildings is mostly lacking suggest that they were the product of *ad hoc* patronage: hence, no doubt, the very marked differences between them. Moreover, they enabled a wealthy patron to advertise this munificence without incurring the much greater cost involved in a chain of caravansarais. The Safavid period, if not already late Timurid times, saw a total reversal of this practice. Chains of caravansarais were now built, often as part of a single building campaign. Thus the buildings were numerous and time was short. Moreover, the extensive scale of many of these structures would have made their decoration too costly. Limited funds would also have discouraged innovation. A complex of factors therefore determined the marked lack of applied ornament in this genre and its rather conservative bias. At the same time these very factors helped to perfect the "house style" marked by economy, a sense of proportion and an infallibly good taste, and founded on wide experience. In much the same way even jobbing builders in Georgian Britain achieved consistently pleasing results. In both cases the very limitations of the architectural vocabulary were turned to advantage. It is easy to understand how the caravansarai became *sui generis* in this period and why there was little interaction with contemporary religious and palatial architecture.

The Safavid caravansarai also sheds much light on the principles of design employed by architects of this period.[1] These principles are simple and practical, as befits a building intended for the daily unloading, provisioning, stabling and loading of hundreds of beasts, for the accommodation of their masters and (in the case of urban caravansarais) for the sale of goods. The building is conceived less as a whole than as a quarter, and the four quarters are planned in identical fashion. This makes it easier for the architect to block out his design. Sometimes a smaller unit is employed: thus the size of an individual bay in the stabling area, or of an individual chamber in the accommodation for travellers, is repeated in modular form for all similar elements throughout the building. In this way caravansarais of very large surface area could be laid out with rigorous exactitude. Regular subdivisions are built into the plan to keep men and animals apart, and to separate adjoining stables; this is a prime function of the aivāns. The variety of solutions devised for the treatment of the diagonal areas in the courtyards highlights the comparative sameness of the rest of the courtyard façades and suggests that architects devoted special attention to these intersections. Perhaps, indeed, the solution adopted for these passageways dictated the rest of the plan.

The construction of scores of such large and expensive buildings along the arterial roads of Iran clearly implies royal patronage. To this day most caravansarais throughout the country are confidently attributed by the local people to Shah ʿAbbās I.[2] While these identifications

[1] Kleiss, "Bericht", p. 235 and Abb. 114. Siroux, *Caravansérails*, p. 52, fig. 15. In both cases a modular layout is assumed.

[2] Siroux, *Caravansérails*, pp. 8, 24–7. For literary evidence in the case of urban caravansarais in Iṣfahān, see Kiani, "The British Museum manuscript", pp. 22–5.

are individually open to doubt, *in toto* they do deserve a certain measure of credence, the more so as no other type of building is so unhesitatingly identified. In some cases, even though no inscriptions survive, the existence of several very similar caravansarais at intervals along a given route is ample testimony – on the ground of expense alone – of exalted patronage, while the provision of caravansarais along comparatively unfrequented routes only makes sense as part of an overall policy of encouraging trade, communications and pilgrimage. Shah 'Abbās I is known to have pursued such a policy with vigour. Some groups of caravansarais are associated with particular officials, such as those on the Iṣfahān – Kāshān road built by the Grand Eunuch Āghā Kārmāl. Other single caravansarais were also built by courtiers, such as that of Gabrābād, which is associated with the royal general Mīr Sabīr. It seems likely that wealthy merchants too might have been active in this field, though there is apparently no epigraphical evidence for this.

The dating of these buildings is problematic. Until this century ample evidence was available in the form of dating inscriptions, usually in glazed tilework, set in the entrance portals of many caravansarais. Subsequently, these panels, the only decorative element of obvious value, have all too frequently been removed. Most Iranian caravansarais that bear a date are of the Safavid period, and most of those were built in the 17th century. In a chain of similar caravansarais, one dated building may allow the others to be dated by association. But these dated points of reference are rare. In a building genre where the functional element is uppermost, the detailed decoration and elaborate vaulting which serve to date anepigraphic cultic buildings are absent. Yet the presence of certain types of vault (e.g. the kite or the sunburst variety, and muqarnas semi-domes with two or three broad tiers of cells), of geometric glazed tilework in colour schemes known from other Safavid buildings, and of flush patterned monochrome brickwork, all point to a Safavid date for anepigraphic caravansarais with these features. The absence of the distinctive arch profiles of earlier centuries offers further corroborative evidence. Above all, however, the huge quantity of caravansarais for which no pre-Safavid date can be canvassed must be the crucial factor in any dating controversy. For it is plain that between 1500 and 1900 the wealth, the organisation, the internal security and the expansion of trade which this mass of buildings implies only characterised Iranian society in the Safavid centuries.

The detailed analysis of individual buildings in the previous pages must now be supplemented by a more general discussion of the wider themes expressed by this architecture. Three broad headings suggest themselves: the political context of Safavid architecture, including questions of patronage; its quantity, distribution, type and time-scale; and its characteristic styles. A discussion of the rôle of the craftsman and of foreign influence on Safavid architecture will round off this section.

THE POLITICAL CONTEXT OF SAFAVID ARCHITECTURE

At first sight the political context of these times could be regarded as well suited for great architectural projects. A good many shahs reigned for a quarter of a century or more – Ismā'īl I, 'Abbās II, Sulaimān, Sulṭān Ḥusain – while 'Abbās I and Ṭahmāsp I reigned for 41 and 52 years respectively. These long reigns provided the continuity necessary for sustained architectural campaigns. But such campaigns in fact occurred only sporadically, for several of these monarchs – e.g., Ismā'īl I and Ṭahmāsp I – failed to provide the necessary impetus from the top. As a result the period of 1500–90 is remarkably void of great architecture – more so than any century in Iran since the arrival of the Buyids. With the accession of Shah 'Abbās this situation changed dramatically; and the reason was precisely that not only the monarch but his courtiers too began to build. Apparently the menaces of the shah encouraged the laggards among them, and indeed the array of functionaries is suspiciously representative: physicians, generals, amīrs, chamberlains, major-domos and governors were all involved. But their joint activity sufficed to transform Iṣfahān beyond recognition. The European travellers comment on how these courtiers vied with each other in lavish building projects, but there is no proof that this emulation had any political edge. Thus it seems unlikely that the tribal and factional rivalries which simmered in the Safavid court found expression in competing architectural programmes. The women of the court seem to have had little hand in building, and such architectural patronage as was exercised by women in this period seems to have been directed particularly towards madrasas: there was no Safavid successor to Gauhar Shād. Beyond the orbit of the court there probably existed a class of merchant patrons whose financial support may help to explain the quantity of lavish bazaars (in Qazvīn, Kirmān, Kāshān and Qum apart from Iṣfahān itself) which were erected in this period.[1]

[1] Stevens, pp. 430–40.

In the later Safavid period, therefore, patronage was exercised on a broader basis than hitherto. But the shah himself still played the pre-eminent rôle, and his foundations often had a political motive. The establishment of Shiʿism as the national creed goes far to explain the emphasis on shrines. Ardabīl enjoyed particular prominence because of its unique status as a dynastic shrine (fig. 2), while the Mashhad shrine was lavishly embellished, evidently as part of an attempt to encourage pilgrimages there rather than to Mecca (fig. 8). Both political and economic considerations seem to underlie this scheme: Mecca was after all in Ottoman hands at this time. More surprising, perhaps, is the same shah's patronage of work on Sunnī monuments, such as Bisṭām, Turbat-i Jām and Turbat-i Ḥaidariyya. Given the solidly Sunnī population of much of Khurāsān, this support might be seen as an attempt by Shah ʿAbbās to win over these potential opponents. Economic rather than political or sectarian motives account for the extensive network of trade communications which he built up throughout Iran. In providing major roads criss-crossing the country and serviced by regularly spaced caravansarais he was realising the dream of many of his predecessors. Urban caravansarais provided a support system for the rural ones and a major port was developed at Bandar ʿAbbās. This scale of investment in trading facilities is an expression of that same capacity to think big, that same awareness of a wider world, which produced the Maidān-i Shāh.

Indeed, the imperial aspirations of ʿAbbās and his eagerness to establish contacts with Europe are the key to his architecture. He sought to make Iṣfahān rival Istanbul and Delhi, which at that very time were undergoing what might be termed an ostentatious face-lift that clearly proclaimed imperial aspirations. For once in Iranian history the greatest buildings which survive of a dynasty are those erected by its greatest ruler at the height of his power. It is of a piece with the grandiose vision of Shah ʿAbbās that the new Iṣfahān, essentially his personal creation, should attract the lion's share of resources. By the later Safavid period the capital was becoming a central feature of government and society. The ruler was apt to spend most of his time there instead of on campaign, and it was natural that the capital should be increasingly embellished. Even under Ismāʿīl I and Ṭahmāsp I most important new buildings were concentrated in Tabrīz and Qazvīn respectively. In earlier periods, distinctions between metropolitan and provincial styles in architecture may be somewhat unreal, with monuments of the first quality being built outside the orbit of the court in villages and towns all over the country. In Safavid times, however, these distinctions do begin to apply, for little fine architecture was produced in the provinces unless the monarch himself or the court was responsible for it; a similar process may be traced in book painting. Only secular architecture may provide substantial exceptions to this rule.

QUANTITY AND DISTRIBUTION OF SAFAVID BUILDINGS

So much, then, for the political context of Safavid architecture. One may now attempt to formulate generalisations about its quantity, distribution, type and time-scale. The quantity of buildings is perhaps the crucial factor, for all the other generalisations depend on it. The nearest approach to a checklist of Iranian architecture, the very incomplete gazetteer of Mishkātī, records many more monuments of the Safavid than of any other period. Its incompleteness, too, is correspondingly more marked in its coverage of Safavid buildings, as the published accounts of monuments in Iṣfahān and Yazd show. It seems likely that the 111 Safavid or partially Safavid buildings he records are less than half of those actually extant.[1]

This massive production may justify some tentative observations. Quantity alone, for example, may be deceptive. Many entries in a list of Safavid "monuments" turn out to refer to sarcophagi, tombstones, woodwork or even graffiti in buildings of uncertain date and indifferent aesthetic value. Or they may be nothing more than minor repairs. Even so, it is clear that for this – as for no other – period in Islamic Iran there exists a truly representative selection of buildings, warts and all. The contrast with earlier architecture is instructive. Almost by definition, buildings which have survived from medieval times in Iran have been of high quality. Indifferent work has gone. But in Safavid architecture a good deal of it still remains. Generalisations can thus be tested against a wide range of buildings, and panegyrics of Safavid architecture must be specifically tied to the buildings produced under royal or court patronage. Stylistic developments can be pinpointed, and it is even possible to assemble a respectable *œuvre* for individual artists, notably calligraphers. Where major blanks in the chronology

[1] An unpublished working list kindly made available to me by Dr G. D. Pickett lists 158 items.

occur (e.g. between 1520 and 1590) they can be identified as gaps in production and not confused with the vagaries of survival. Areas of active and of sluggish production emerge, as does the order of popularity of the various building types. Sufficient material is available for the large-scale collation of documentary records with the evidence of standing structures. This is a task for Iranian scholars *par excellence*, just as native Turkish scholars have brought to light and interpreted the Ottoman archival material which bears on architecture and tilework. The quantity of surviving buildings is also a reminder that – no matter what prominence is given to the finest creations of court patronage – this architecture has its roots in everyday life. A great many Safavid buildings are situated unpretentiously in villages or small towns, and even when they are found in the major cities of the land they are most often located in quarters which are essentially village or small town units transported in their entirety into an urban setting.

One conclusion, however, that cannot lightly be drawn from the large quantity of surviving Safavid buildings is that the output of this period was substantially greater than that of the preceding centuries in Islamic Iran. Contemporary records are unreliable yardsticks of building activity, but the fact that the city chronicles of Yazd and Shīrāz alone list scores of medieval monuments which have now disappeared without trace should sound a warning note. Moreover, among the great epochs of Iranian architecture the Safavid period is the most recent and one would therefore expect more to have survived than from earlier periods. Finally, the stability which Shah ʿAbbās brought to Iran may well have released into building activities – among other areas of the economy and national life – energies previously wasted in war. In such an interpretation, these hundreds of buildings spread throughout the country would reflect a land at peace. But the argument cannot be pushed very far, since the examples of Yazd and Shīrāz cited above suggest that the spate of new buildings could continue in politically self-contained towns despite political instability in the country at large.

The areas where Safavid buildings cluster most densely differ significantly from the centres favoured earlier. Āzarbāījān, so crucial for an understanding of Il-Khanid architecture, is neglected, and so too is Khurāsān, the region which produced so many fine Saljūq structures. Herat has little to show for nearly two centuries of Safavid rule. As noted above, the earlier Safavid capitals of Tabrīz and Qazvīn saw little major construction. Amidst the sea of frankly provincial work which floods the country there rise islands of more ambitious architecture, such as the great religious shrines, the buildings of Kirmān, and of course Iṣfahān itself, which offer the chance to study fine Safavid work in depth. For the rest of the country "Safavid" is more a convenient dynastic label than a precise descriptive term connoting a distinctive style.

In this chapter the rôle of the areas bordering modern Iran has deliberately been minimised because of the wealth of monuments in Iran itself. No serious distortion of emphasis seems likely to result from this neglect. But these outlying areas do show that Safavid architecture had a certain cachet and that it imposed itself even in lands with a rather different building tradition. While the Safavids held Iraq, much work was done on the four great Shī'ī shrines there (Baghdad, Sāmarrā, Karbalā and Najaf), and indeed Iraqi architecture after *c.* 1500 is in the shadow of Persian modes. This is especially clear in the minarets of the country, with their tiled geometrical and epigraphical ornament.[1] In the Caucasian provinces the Safavid style using brick and tilework and Persian forms (e.g. at Erivan) existed side by side with a local Caucasian tradition which had done much to inspire the stone architecture of medieval Anatolia. The Safavids sporadically held substantial sections of eastern Anatolia, but the architectural style there remained obstinately Ottoman. To the east Safavid influence penetrated at least to Qandahār, though it seems likely that the tiled buildings of Lahore and Multān reflect contemporary Iranian inspiration indirectly. But the major school of architecture in the Safavid style outside Iran is undoubtedly that of Shaibanid Bukhārā. It may seem ironic that the capital of the Uzbeks, the inveterate enemies of the Safavids, should be a treasury of apparently Safavid architecture. On reflection, however, it is clear that this Uzbek style was a natural outgrowth from Timurid architecture, which of course also generated – or rather, imperceptibly became – Safavid work. The Uzbek buildings conveniently fill the years 1500–1590 which are so barren in Iran, and share with their Safavid counterparts, through their joint ancestry in the Timurid style, a common vocabulary of form and decoration, though they place more emphasis on decorative brick vaulting, with flush painted joints, than was fashionable in Iran.[2]

[1] al-Gailānī, pp. 73–87.

[2] Pugachenkova and Rempel', *Vydayushchiĭsya Pamyatniki*, pp. 79–93, pls. 20–57. Hrbas and Knobloch, pls. 91–103. *Historical Monuments of Islam in the U.S.S.R.*, pls. 72–98.

TYPES

Although the Safavid period did not generate brand new types of building, its priorities did not coincide with those of previous centuries. New emphases of architectural patronage may be detected as much in what is not found in Safavid architecture as in the great achievements of the period. Perhaps the most striking feature is the virtual absence of large new mosques. A functional explanation for this – that there was by now little need for such structures – is inadequate, for the later Timurids erected numerous large and bare mosques throughout Khurāsān, many of them simply too big for the communities they were apparently intended to serve. The Timurid princes who built these mosques understood, as did Shah 'Abbās at Iṣfahān, the psychological dimension of lavish public architecture. It is only in the last century and a half, when old buildings have suffered destruction at an accelerating pace, that the need for new and large mosques has made itself felt once more. The characteristic Safavid activity in mosque architecture, as will be shown in detail below, is repair work: even in the erstwhile capital cities of Tabrīz and Qazvīn it was apparently considered sufficient to refurbish the existing jāmi', and this was at first done in Iṣfahān too. While Safavid architects did not especially avoid the challenge of sheer size, in religious architecture they were not often given the chance to meet that challenge. Large mosques were simply not fashionable. The great exception is of course Iṣfahān; once again it is clear that for all its importance that city is no satisfactory gauge for Safavid architecture as a whole. The choice of a new site on the outskirts of the city made large new mosques a necessity. In the contemporary Ottoman and Mughal empires such large mosques were, by contrast, frequently built. If such large mosques were the exception in Safavid architecture small mosques at least were a standard feature, and in Iṣfahān, where the majority of them are to be found, were built mostly at the behest of courtiers. No particular type of mosque was preferred above others; hypostyle, domed square and aivān mosques are all common.

Although madrasas were an established genre of buildings from the 11th century onwards in Iran, remarkably few medieval examples survive there, and of these few the majority are Timurid. It seems likely that purpose-built madrasas – as distinct from composite foundations, now not always recognisable as such, or mosques which served at least in part as madrasas – achieved a new popularity in the 15th century which continued throughout the Safavid period. These

Timurid madrasas are conceived on a large scale, and Uzbek madrasas perpetuated this tradition. Safavid architects, however, supplemented this type of madrasa (which remained popular) with a smaller and more intimate type of building, something perhaps more akin to the original concept of the madrasa. The courtyard remained, but was so reduced in size that the building reverted to an essentially domestic scale.[1]

But it is the shrine above all that dominates Safavid religious architecture. This is true of large complexes and even more of isolated imāmzādas; both types of building were frequently centres of pilgrimage. Many of the most celebrated shrines of Iran (such as Ardabīl and Mashhad, figs 2, 8) and of Iraq acquired their present aspect during this period. Secular mausolea gave way almost entirely to those of saints, a process traceable at least as early as the Mongol period but one which had been gathering momentum ever since then. The tomb tower form which had been such a landmark in medieval architecture had by now been decisively rejected in favour of buildings which emphasised breadth as much as height and had domes rather than conical roofs. In harmony with this revised emphasis, the square or octagonal plan had become general, replacing the variety of earlier plans. The interiors of these mausolea were comparatively spacious rather than cramped. They usually had miḥrābs and sometimes even adjoining courtyards and a garden setting. This radical change of layout was a response to the growing habit of conducting devotions in shrines and this practice helps to explain why shrines rather than mosques were the characteristic expressions of Safavid patronage in cultic architecture. The adoption of Shi'ism, with its ancient tradition of the veneration of saints, as the national creed could only accentuate this change of emphasis.

Side by side with this accent on shrines is the unexpected burst of activity in secular architecture in the 17th century. It is this which singles out the Safavid period from the rest of Islamic architecture in Iran. Bridges which have wider functions than carrying traffic are built, reviving Sasanian custom. Caravansarais in both town and country proliferate, and there are large urban bazaars. Pigeon towers were built in their thousands, mainly in the Iṣfahān oasis but also around Gulpāīgān and Kirmān. Town planning develops on a scale hitherto unequalled in Iran. Earlier, when new cities were built (like Sulṭāniyya) or old ones extended (like Tabrīz), it seems that no overall

[1] Brandenburg, pp. 64–77.

plan was imposed and thus these foundations expanded in a somewhat random way. Lastly, several princely residences have fortunately survived and make it possible, for the first time in Iranian Islamic architecture, to weigh the hyperbolic literary accounts against actual palaces. In sum, then, it seems generally true that in Safavid times secular and shrine architecture absorbed the energies of architects to a degree not found in earlier periods, and that this was to the detriment of other religious architecture which hitherto had attracted most patronage.

CHRONOLOGY

It will be seen that neither the major building types nor the areas of architectural activity were evenly spread in Safavid times, and the same patchiness marks the chronology of production under this dynasty. Periods of intense activity alternate with protracted lulls. Indeed, although Safavid rule lasted for two and a quarter centuries very few decades in this period were truly productive so far as architecture was concerned. The lack of vigorous local schools has already been noted, and it means that the Safavid, unlike the Saljūq, Il-Khanid, and Timurid periods, lacks the continuous rhythm of local traditions on which imperial foundations are occasionally superimposed. In the 14th and 15th centuries especially, the enthusiastic patronage of the later Īl-Khāns and of the Timurid princes was supplemented by that of the numerous smaller dynasties of the period: Chobanids, Muzaffarids, Āq Quyūnlū, and so on. Continuity was assured. Safavid rule brought increasing centralisation and tended to confine architecture within the orbit of the court. Such architecture thus came to depend to a dangerous degree on royal patronage. When that failed, architecture itself languished, for the continuity of provincial architecture had already been broken. This lack of continuity may help to explain why for most of the Safavid period Iran, though so rich in ordinary buildings, is comparatively barren of great ones. Interestingly enough, the obvious exception – the years from 1590 to 1630 – is also the period when there was a permanent concentration – indeed, a constellation – of talent in one place. It could very well be argued that for the rest of the century Iṣfahān lived off the resources accumulated in that creative period. Earlier, the architecture of Shah Ismā‘īl could be seen as a hangover from the Āq Quyūnlū period; but in eastern Iran the Timurid style died of inanition. In view of the doldrums of the 16th century any discussion of a developing style in this period is misplaced.

The lesson of most medieval Iranian architecture is that the necessary craftsmanship and expertise were latent and needed only the right stimulus in order to be exploited. In Safavid times it was only in the reign of Shah 'Abbās that this stimulus was forthcoming on a requisitely lavish scale. Ambitious patronage generated ambitious architecture. The grand style was lost in subsequent reigns, and while the reasons for this leave room for discussion, it seems preferable to attribute the apparent failure of nerve to the patron rather than to the architect. No matter how blame is apportioned, however, the consequences are self-evident: despite the fact that the Safavids ruled for well over two centuries, they achieved qualitatively less in that period – so far as architecture is concerned – than did the Saljūqs between 1080 and 1160 or the Īl-Khāns between 1300 and 1350.

It may be, of course, that the very scale of the larger Safavid building projects caused later architects a certain disquiet and made them chary of framing similar plans. Projects like the Ganj 'Alī Khān complex at Kirmān (fig. 9) and the redevelopment of the shrines at Ardabīl, Māhān and Mashhad – to say nothing of the great ensembles at Iṣfahān – must have brought in their train multiple problems of logistics and administration, many of them unfamiliar. Buildings on this scale were a serious drain on resources and could not lightly be undertaken. Nor was money the only problem. The time-scale adopted for some of these buildings was probably inadequate for them to be completed successfully; hence the possibly apocryphal tale about the architect of the Masjid-i Shāh noted above.[1] The change from tile mosaic to haft-rangī tilework in the same building offers independent corroboration of this story. Things were very different in the more highly organised building industry of the Ottoman empire. But Safavid architecture had no one with the genius, status or staying power of Sinān. The great achievements of Ottoman and Mughal architecture were made possible as much by efficient organisation as by great architects. In Safavid Iran, which attained imperial status appreciably later than its rivals, this fortunate conjunction was regrettably intermittent.

Clearly, therefore, the sheer size of the Safavid *œuvre* can be deceptive; and not only for the reasons just cited. An unprecedentedly high proportion of Safavid architecture all over Iran comprises repair work, not new foundations. The buildings chosen for repair and extra embel-

[1] See p. 787.

lishment were, following traditional practice, almost exclusively religious, and the great shrines especially benefited from such work. Not so secular buildings: rather than repair old caravansarais, architects preferred to build new caravansarais beside them.

Various explanations could be adduced for this emphasis on repair work. Rather than build yet more mosques and shrines Safavid patrons may have preferred the compromise solution of repairing existing structures. For a small outlay – for example, on a new portal, a façade screening earlier work, or just new decoration – they would receive disproportionate credit, especially if, as often happened, the repair was not acknowledged as such and the patron greedily claimed, implicitly or explicitly, to have erected the entire building. This seems a more likely motive than does exceptional religious piety. Alternatively, these repairs could be seen as the result of purely local initiatives prompted by the decay of some valued local building. It is of course precisely at the level of restoration and embellishment that local patronage can most fruitfully be exercised.[1]

In such repair work Safavid craftsmen acquired a close familiarity with earlier styles and this in turn may have affected their response to the task in hand. Thus at Māhān, for example, the galleries added by Shah ʿAbbās to the Timurid nucleus of the shrine ape the Timurid device of a single-colour tiled dado with plain white vaulting above (pl. 42). This could be either extreme conservatism or conscious antiquarianism, as pastiches of earlier Islamic styles can be found in Safavid lustre tilework, in the Safavid inscriptions on pre-Islamic monuments (e.g. Persepolis and Bīsitūn) which perhaps presage that wholesale adoption of and identification with the Iran of legend that was to characterise the Qājārs, or in some of the manuscripts painted for Shah ʿAbbās in the early 17th century.[2] Much of this repair work, however, was carried out on earlier Safavid buildings, which says little for their quality. The tomb of Khwāja Rabīʿ, for example, was repaired twice within a century of its original foundation. But whatever the date of the building to be repaired, redecorated, extended or subjected to some change of function, the new work was rarely identified in detail and is thus difficult to date precisely.

[1] An unpublished list of Iranian architects and craftsmen in the field of architectural decoration, drawn up by Dr G.D. Pickett and kindly made available to me, shows that most craftsmen operated in the immediate orbit of their native village or city.

[2] Watson, "Persian Lustre Ware", pp. 63–80. A.S. Melikian-Chirwani, "Le royaume de Salomon. Les inscriptions persanes de sites achéménides", *MII* I (1971), 1–41. Grube, "The Language of the Birds", pp. 344–6.

The lack of a comprehensive checklist of Safavid buildings makes it hard to pinpoint the trends underlying these repairs. It does seem, however, that repairs were proportionately more frequent in the reigns of certain rulers than of others. The evidence suggests that it was precisely the shahs who avoided large building projects – Ismāʿīl I, Ṭahmāsp I and Ṣafī I – whose reigns also witnessed a disproportionate amount of repair work. It seems, too, that the proportion of repairs *vis-à-vis* new foundations rose steeply in the reigns of Shah Sulaimān and Shah Sulṭān Ḥusain, thus suggesting that the gradual enfeeblement of the dynasty increasingly forced architectural patronage to confine itself to relatively trivial projects. But these generalisations doubtless require further refinement in the light of more evidence. Similarly, it is too early to say whether (with the obvious exception of Iṣfahān) the ratio between repair work and new foundations was constant throughout Iran, or whether some areas benefited more than others from new building within given periods.

STYLE

The foregoing remarks must suffice to establish the wider context of this architecture. Given the quantity and variety of Safavid buildings, it has seemed best to examine their style by focussing on three main areas: the buildings of 17th-century Iṣfahān; the great shrines; and secular architecture of the 17th century. The generalisations which follow have been formulated with all three groups in mind, though of course they do not apply equally to each group.

A sure sense of spatial values informs the best architecture of the period. This sense is seen at its most spectacular in the great ensembles where each building is enhanced by its neighbours. It expresses itself on the grand scale of landscape architecture in the Chahār Bāgh, where nature – even if it is nature methodised – envelopes the buildings, which function as beauty spots only and are deliberately subordinated to the landscaping of the avenue (fig. 4). The various royal gardens in Iṣfahān and elsewhere – especially the great gardens at Faraḥābād and Ashraf in Māzandarān – are also laid out with an eye for scale and for the interaction of the constituent parts. Massed plots of flowers and shrubs combine with pools, fountains and canals; trees demarcate the major divisions; uncluttered expanses rest the eye (fig. 11*a*). A ground plan tends to overemphasise the regularity of the overall design of such gardens. Within the geometrical layout so reminiscent of garden carpets there is room for surprises. Suddenly a wide prospect opens, or conversely the scale shrinks to an enclosed arbour with a central pool. Sometimes terraces bring an abrupt change of plane. A secluded pavilion, subtly at one with its surroundings, readily evokes an atmosphere of intimacy, but its plan may be open and airy with windows giving on to a series of different views, some circumscribed, others distant. Such a garden employs concepts of open and closed space, and of their interaction, which are essentially architectural; the same is true of the emphasis on vistas, directed viewpoints, and changes of plane as well as devices of anticipation and surprise.[1]

Even when the architects did not have a free hand, notably in the case of additions to extant structures, the same spatial awareness makes itself felt. Work on the great shrines illustrates this. At Mashhad the great esplanade of Shah 'Abbās imposed ideals of order and scale on the heterogeneous jumble of earlier buildings (fig. 8). The same ruler provided airy galleries to flank the domed square mausoleum of Shāh Ni'mat-Allāh at Māhān, and thus to open up the whole shrine. A huge courtyard and perimeter walls were added at Ardabīl (fig. 2). The dominant impulse in such work seems to have been to introduce a new and grander sense of scale into these foundations. This trend is of course most obvious when the architect disposed of a virgin site (Iṣfahān maidān; Masjid-i Nau, Shīrāz). Wherever possible, the essentially additive nature of the extant buildings was masked by large elements (avenues, galleries, courtyards, perimeter walls) whose scale was sufficiently bold to absorb the earlier piecemeal work. Thus an overall plan is created which takes account of standing structures but by suitable additions gives the entire shrine a more coherent and organised appearance.

Individual buildings illustrate much the same concerns. The typical free-standing mausoleum of Safavid times has a new complexity of plan and elevation. The factor of increased size alone allows far more scope to an architect interested in spatial problems. Large octagonal mausolea are in fact the ideal genre of buildings to study some typical Safavid approaches to these problems (fig. 1). A standard feature is the drastic reduction of wall surfaces, both internally and externally; deep niches are scooped out of the wall and indeed arches sometimes break through the wall altogether. Frequently the mausoleum comprises two storeys; the common arrangement in such cases is to have the ring of

[1] Wilber, *Persian Gardens*, pp. 79–140.

niches or arches on the ground floor repeated at first floor level, rather than to extend their height. Inner and outer galleries add depth to the elevation, while net or stalactite vaults and blind arches or panels articulate the individual bays. The plethora of windows ensures that the architect can exploit many contrasts of light and shade. In all these various features different levels – of light, surface, texture – are juxtaposed and the same motif is repeated along the horizontal or vertical axis. A delight in spatial diversity underlies the whole approach. A comparison with earlier mausolea reveals that the third dimension was never before so systematically exploited in this type of Iranian building. The emphasis is in some respects sculptural.[1]

Yet while Safavid architects well understood the spatial grouping of entire units and of elements within a single unit, their buildings could not fairly be described as complex. Safavid architecture is safe. It deals in large masses and prefers smooth surfaces to intricately articulated ones. With a few honourable exceptions like Māhān (pl. 42), vaulting – the essence of any curvilinear architecture – is dull and repetitive, in contrast to the pyrotechnic display of the previous period. When in doubt, the Safavid architect manufactures another few tiers of "stalactite" cells. Domes follow models known from Timurid and Il-Khanid times, if not earlier, but have a more restricted range: the melon dome, for example, disappears. Structure is reliable but not original. Estimable though this competence may be for public secular buildings such as caravansarais, especially when they are built in large quantities, it is not enough in the case of the major religious structures. Structural complexities in particular are toned down. This simplifying trend is most apparent when one compares Safavid with earlier Islamic architecture in Iran. Gone is the massive strength and vigorous ornament of Saljūq brick buildings, or the nervous tension of Il-Khanid architecture, often so close to overreaching itself. Arch forms lose the fantasy and playfulness of those produced in the previous two centuries – even Saljūq arches were much more varied. Surprises are too few in matters of structure. The vocabulary is limited; it is as if the architect voluntarily restricted himself to a few standard shapes which could be reproduced on various scales and reshuffled as required. It is not entirely unfair, then, to describe Safavid architecture as modular. The various factors which produced this situation will be analysed in more detail below.

[1] Pope, in *SPA*, pp. 1171–4, 1178–9, 1211–12.

Neither the spatial organisation nor the simplifying trend in Safavid architecture is, however, its most striking feature. Any casual visitor to Iṣfahān will confirm that the glory of this style is its decoration. No doubt this was the deliberate intention of those responsible for the buildings. This splendour aims to disarm criticism by its very profusion. But it will not bear minute examination. The common and just complaint against much Safavid tilework is that its quality is poor. In place of the many-faceted reflections of tile mosaic is the virtually unbroken sheen of large overglaze painted tiles. The deep, vibrant tones achieved in tile mosaic give way to paler, even muddy, colours. The reason for this is technical; whereas in tile mosaic each element is cut from a tile fired at the optimum temperature for that colour, overglaze painted tiles bear many colours (hence the term haft-rangī – "seven colours" – applied to these tiles, though the colours may number more or less than seven) all fired together at a "compromise" temperature. Inevitably, therefore, the quality of such a tile cannot approach that of tile mosaic.

Nevertheless it is not simply because of its technical quality that Safavid tilework is open to criticism. It is habitually used on a larger scale than ever before, several times completely enveloping an interior (Luṭf-Allāh mosque, pl. 43*b*; dome chamber of Allāhvardī Khān in the Mashhad shrine). Entire façades, too, were sheathed in tilework. Many Il-Khanid and Timurid buildings use lavish tilework, but the total exclusion of brickwork, the actual material of construction, from such large areas of the elevation is virtually without precedent. As late as the reign of Shah Ismā'īl, in the Masjid-i 'Alī, brick still plays a major part in the decorative scheme. Although tile dominates brick in many Timurid façades, brick is allowed to play several important rôles in them: it acts as a reminder of the underlying structure, provides a contrasting texture and acts as a chromatic foil to the tilework. Safavid architects surrendered these advantages and frequently relegated brick to the sides of the building. Here tilework is conspicuously absent. This is an obvious slight, and an implicit invitation to look at the building only from those viewpoints where its tilework dominates. As a result the building loses something of its three-dimensional quality and is in danger of becoming façade architecture. Courtyard façades and other subsidiary areas are either coated with plaster or left as bare brick; in either case their function is to serve as a foil (pl. 45*a*).[1]

[1] Hillenbrand, "The Use of Glazed Tilework". The Masjid-i Ḥakīm is an honourable exception to some of these strictures.

New figural themes, taken from the repertory of painting, are largely confined to palaces. Nevertheless, living creatures figure with some frequency in the tilework of religious buildings, and include, besides images that are sacred (angels) or ambivalent (peacocks), others that are quite secular (dragons). With this exception the range of tilework designs themselves is no broader than in the previous period. The themes are simply worked harder. Thulth inscriptions, for example, assume a greater prominence than hitherto.

As a whole, architectural decoration is impoverished by the comparative dearth of worked stucco, carved terracotta and ornamental brickwork. All these techniques had an important rôle in Timurid architecture. Only plain white stucco, used to cover vaults, retained a certain hold. It follows that tilework now had to serve many of the functions formerly discharged by these techniques. New colours and new combinations appear, and there are even attempts to put tilework to new uses (e.g. the tiled floor of the Luṭf-Allāh mosque). Perhaps the most distinctive new departure is the use of tiled designs, not plain tilework as hitherto, on domes. Floral arabesques were preferred here, though geometrical patterns also occur. In other, less obvious ways, too, tilework came to dominate a building, usurping functions previously reserved for brick or other media. For example, colour was now necessarily the means for distinguishing between different parts of the design or between several superimposed inscriptions. It accentuates structural features, like the turquoise cable mouldings in the Luṭf-Allāh mosque interior. Sometimes entirely glazed compositions reproduce in many colours the monochrome patterned brickwork of Saljūq times. But for all this readiness to devise different uses for tilework, the plain fact is that the medium was already past its maturity by the end of the 15th century.[1]

In its genesis and formative period glazed tilework coexisted with a booming pottery industry and it reached its zenith when that industry had already begun to decline. Late Saljūq and Il-Khanid wall tiles, especially in lustre and *lajvardīna*, benefited from developments in ceramic but there was to be no further fruitful relationship between the two sister arts. The tilework specialists of pre-Safavid times had in all probability restricted the range and combinations of glazed tones on

[1] For a survey of architectural *kāshī* in Muslim Iran until 1400, see Pickett. I am most grateful to Dr. Pickett for much information on tilework in Safavid and pre-Safavid times.

purpose. Certainly the technology for a much wider gamut of colours than they actually used was available to them.[1] Safavid inventions in this field, such as apple green and a hectic custard yellow, were rarely happy ones. Safavid decoration, then, for all its surface splendour, is in some respects the fatal flaw of this architecture.

An entirely unprecedented boom in secular buildings marks Safavid architecture in its prime as in its decline, and this fact had a direct impact on Safavid architectural styles. The buildings concerned are broadly speaking of two kinds: utility structures and palaces. The former genre has already been discussed. The palaces, however, illustrate a distinctive style which may conveniently be analysed here. The paucity of earlier examples makes it difficult to assess their originality. They are sufficiently distinct from each other, however, to allow the assumption either that they represent an original style which achieved an early flowering or that – more likely – the tradition from which they sprang was itself varied. Nearly all of them date from the period 1600–70. Numerous typological subdivisions suggest themselves, from the conception of a palace as a full-scale garden garnished with buildings, as at Faraḥābād, to the transposition of a palace on to a bridge, as in the Khājū bridge at Iṣfahān (pl. 44*a*). But in all of them a deliberate insubstantiality is the aim, a lack of emphasis on obviously solid bearing walls, a love for piercing the surface by large windows, niches or loggias and for encrusting interior walls with yet more niches as well as false low-hung ceilings and "stalactite" vaults (fig. 16). In virtually all of them the natural surroundings are brought into play. Royal Safavid miniatures conjure up in exquisite detail the courtly lifestyle to which such palaces ministered, and as a bonus they document numerous lost types of fastidiously elegant pavilions whose rickety structure sufficiently explains their disappearance. Wood here plays an important structural rôle which it is accorded nowhere else in Iranian Islamic architecture: not only are these buildings frequently of trabeate type, but wooden gratings and balconies figure largely in them. Ground plans and elevations hark back with surprising fidelity to pre-Islamic models. Seldom has the innate conservatism of Persian builders been so clearly demonstrated.

[1] Cf. the material in Lane, *A Guide*, pp. 6–26, with that in his *Later Islamic Pottery*.

Fig. 16. Royal reception at the garden pavilion at Asadābād, adjoining the Chahār Bāgh.

CRAFTSMEN

So much, then, for Safavid architectural style. What of the craftsmen who created it? While public works like caravansarais may imply the existence of teams of craftsmen travelling from one site to the next and in the process developing a "house style" which allowed little scope for individual initiative, the evidence of Safavid religious structures on the contrary suggests the primacy of local initiatives executed by local craftsmen. The evidence also suggests that the individual craftsman improved his status during this period. Two factors especially support this hypothesis. First, far more craftsmen's names survive from this period than from earlier centuries. Of course this is partly due to the large quantity of Safavid buildings extant. But buildings which would earlier have been anonymous or would have borne only a single inscription now have several. This suggests that craftsmen felt a greater self-confidence than hitherto, which itself implies an improved status. Second, the inscriptions bear witness to a new tendency to compartmentalise the labour of erecting a building. One craftsman designs, another builds, a third cuts the tiles (and draws their patterns? – hence the use of the term *al-naqqāsh*) and a fourth writes the inscriptions. Each signs himself separately and identifies the nature of his work. He may also give his *nisba* and his father's name, but very rarely anything else. Such multiple signatures appearing on a single building suggest that the master mason has been to some extent demoted and that his fellow craftsmen have benefited correspondingly. Among the specialists whose prestige increased at this time may be noted particularly the tile-cutter (now called increasingly often *kāshī-tarāsh*) and the calligrapher. Many more practitioners of the latter art are recorded than ever before; they apparently specialised in architectural inscriptions. Several of them have left their signatures on a whole series of buildings throughout Iran. Thus a chronology of their work is available and an attempt can be made to define the development of their style. Moreover, these cases provide precious evidence that the best craftsmen were in demand throughout the country. The obvious example is Muḥammad Riżā Imāmī, whose work on key monuments at Iṣfahān, Qum and Mashhad argues a very exalted status;[1] and, before him, 'Alī Riżā al-'Abbāsī was active on royal

[1] The corpus of inscriptions in this calligrapher's name has been substantially increased as a result of Pickett, "Inscriptions", pp. 91–6. See too Godard, "Muḥammad Riḍā al-Imāmī", who lists also the works of his son Muḥammad Muḥsin al-Imāmī and his grandson 'Alī Naqī al-Imāmī.

foundations at Iṣfahān, Mashhad and Qazvīn as well as the madrasa of Ganj 'Alī Khān at Kirmān.

Unfortunately, the surviving inscriptions indicate that the calligraphers were exceptional. Few other craftsmen are attested by more than one inscription. Even the builders of masterpieces acknowledged as such in their own time, such as the mosques on the Iṣfahān maidān, are known by no other buildings. This suggests that – unlike the case of most Iranian book painting – there was no royal atelier of choice craftsmen in continuous employment. But when seen in the context of the large number of names to survive, these single inscriptions bear witness to the great reservoir of talent on which Safavid patrons could draw. The signatures also pose many unresolved problems. Thus detailed study of contemporary sources might reveal whether the craftsmen were subject to any overall organisation. A checklist of the nisbas of these craftsmen would of course emphasise the unchallenged pre-eminence of Iṣfahān; but, much more interestingly, it would also permit a classification of the more important provincial centres during this period. It might even reveal that certain specialities were particularly associated with certain towns. Nisbas are of course notoriously misleading at times but the sheer quantity of examples would offset this disadvantage. Such a checklist would also indicate whether any new titles or honorifics were applied to craftsmen at this time. Until the proportion of craftsmen's names to extant buildings is established, it would be hazardous to draw further conclusions about the rôle of the craftsman at this time, and similar information is needed for preceding periods and for other contemporary Islamic lands before the full context of the craftsman's activity can be established. But, as shown above, the quantity of names available seems sufficient to isolate certain trends.

RESISTANCE TO EXTERNAL INFLUENCES

It is now time to grapple with an issue often hinted at in the foregoing pages: the reasons for the lack of development which may be detected in Safavid architecture. This has other causes than those that have been canvassed above, namely the royal neglect of the 16th century, the decay of provincial schools or the emphasis on decoration at the expense of structure. It results also from an inward-looking quality which prevented Safavid architects from looking to and learning from foreign architectural styles. The foundations of Islamic architecture in

Iran seem to have been laid in the Saljūq period at the latest. Il-Khanid architects refined, rather than expanded, the vocabulary of forms which they inherited, as did Timurid architects in their turn. Some of the excesses of 15th-century work showed that the process could not be continued indefinitely. Yet this was precisely what Safavid (and Uzbek) architects tried to do, even though their current idiom was bankrupt after centuries of intensive exploitation. It is not surprising that they were unable to introduce significant innovations and that the structural aspects of architecture stagnated. Builders had to content themselves with allotting a new and dominant rôle to decoration. A more fruitful approach might have been to look beyond the borders of Iran to some of the other flourishing traditions of the contemporary world. It may be instructive to consider why this was not done.

The lack of influences from Western Europe is entirely understandable, despite the fascination with all things Western evinced by Shah 'Abbās. Although embassies trekked back and forth between Europe and Persia, the dominant classical flavour of most contemporary European architecture would have struck no chord in Persian builders. They would not of course have seen such buildings themselves and the reports of ambassadors or the odd engraving would probably not have been a sufficient stimulus. Even in painting, where the exposure to European modes was much more sustained, it is the manner rather than the essence of the European model that is copied, as the *œuvre* of Muḥammad Zamān or the Chihil Sutūn panels depicting Europeans indicate.

Other factors, however, must explain the reluctance of Safavid architects to learn from their Ottoman and Mughal counterparts. It has been a recurrent theme of this chapter that Safavid architecture took a long time to find itself because for many decades the conditions were wrong for an original, fully integrated style to develop. Ottoman Turkey and Mughal India were favoured with one ruler after another who patronised architecture on a grand scale. Both Mughal and Ottoman architecture had a fundamentally different bias from that of the Safavids, and one that would have made imitation difficult. The use of stone rather than brick demanded different techniques, such as centering, and favoured precise calculation, whereas much of Iranian architecture depended on the eye. Ottoman architects preferred plain exteriors, which looked impressive in stone, while Iran was traditionally wedded to surface ornament. This latter bias was, however, shared by Mughal architecture, which makes the neglect of that school as a source of inspiration even harder to explain, especially as Mughal culture owed so much to Persia. Certainly Persian architects and artists went to the Mughal empire. But if they returned they apparently brought little inspiration with them, though conceivably Mughal gardens or the parkland setting of so much Mughal architecture might have exercised some influence on Safavid Persia. Both Mughal India and Ottoman Turkey were, of course, political rivals of the Safavid state, and this must have inhibited the easy dissemination of artistic styles associated with them, in architecture as in painting. Presumably this is why even those influences which would have been easy to absorb, and which had roots or parallels in the Persian tradition, such as Iznik tilework, Ottoman minarets, Mughal *chhatris* and onion domes, are absent. Chinese art, on the other hand, carried no such political liability and it is therefore not surprising that in much Safavid art, notably in pottery and in certain types of painting, a pervasive *chinoiserie* should be evident. The Chinese repertory of dragons, phoenixes, cloud scrolls, peonies and lotuses also makes frequent appearances in Safavid tilework, but these various elements had of course long been domiciled in Iran. It is not necessary, therefore, to postulate a fresh wave of influence from China.

The negative complexion of all this evidence makes it all the more surprising to find a major enclave of alien architecture in Iṣfahān itself. Nevertheless the Armenian buildings in Julfā document only the impact of Iranian modes on a sturdily independent native tradition; no influence in the reverse direction can be detected. Architecturally Julfā was as much a foreign body as it was from the standpoint of politics, religion, language and society. Armenian forms such as belfries, developed in the context of a stone architecture, look incongruous and even slightly absurd in the alien garb of Safavid brick and tile. But apart from the purely cosmetic change brought about by these local materials, the form of the churches remains entirely Armenian. They represent a curiosity rather than a true merging of the Persian and Armenian traditions.

CONCLUSION

It is now time to draw together the various threads of this chapter. The marked fluctuation in the quantity of surviving buildings from one reign to the next in the Safavid period well illustrates yet again that the finest architecture in Iran is the direct result of royal patronage. When that flagged, so did the production of major buildings. This helps in turn to explain the uneven time-scale of so much Safavid architecture, in which periods of intense activity alternate with long lulls. In fact, most of the Safavid shahs showed little interest in erecting splendid buildings, and even when some of them did engage in serious patronage their increasingly centralised state ensured that most important new construction was in the capital. It is therefore not surprising that central Iran should see the most concentrated spate of building activity, while other provinces which had earlier been of prime importance, such as Āzarbāījān, Khurāsān and Fārs, now became something of a backwater. That the quantity of structures surviving throughout much of Iran during this period is nevertheless so great reflects among other factors the replacement of royal by local patronage.

Shrines of various types, rather than mosques, were a particularly popular Safavid form and reflected a widespread veneration of saints, while in secular architecture quantities of palaces and above all of caravansarais survive. In such buildings the manipulation of scale and certain spatial devices brought new emphases to Iranian architecture. In spite of such new constructions, however, repairs and embellishments were a keynote of the period. Foreign influences are of negligible significance, for this is essentially an inward-looking style. It was too firmly rooted in the past to encourage innovation and no clear line of development can be traced throughout the buildings of the period. This conservatism in matters of structure coexisted with, and was probably linked to, a predilection for overall decoration in glazed tilework. This emphasis on applied decoration brought a new status to the craftsman which is reflected in the proliferation of signed work and of named specialists in calligraphy and in the various techniques of tilework. But the primacy accorded to ornament implied a waning interest in architecture *per se*. It can therefore be argued that, of all the styles of Islamic architecture practised in Iran before the 18th century, the Safavid seems to be the least original, notably lacking in that steady progression which characterised contemporary Ottoman and Mughal architecture.

Finally, the fact that this relative decline coexisted with a higher level of material prosperity than Iran had enjoyed for centuries demands some discussion. Perhaps it is an expression of that general artistic and cultural decline, that lack of new inspiration, which was widespread in much of Islamic culture, not least in architecture, by the early 16th century. Ottoman Turkey and Mughal India of course stand out as the exceptions.

Even so, it must be conceded that in certain areas, such as book painting, textiles and carpet manufacture, the Safavid achievement rivals that of any previous Muslim dynasty in Iran. The argument that architecture expresses a more general decline is therefore of only limited value.

Another approach would be to emphasise the destructive impact on architecture of the widespread fashion for tilework. Timurid polychrome ornament had popularised the idea that architecture was a framework, a skeleton to be fleshed out with decoration. The accumulated expertise of centuries in seeing a building as a whole was gradually lost and it could not quickly be regained. Buildings were now articulated by colour rather than structural devices. Gradually the focus of attention moved to the façade, and then to the entrance itself, a trend already well developed in Timurid architecture. The side and rear walls became of diminishing consequence and even the interior was apt to be neglected. The building as a whole was thus bound to suffer.

But perhaps the crucial factor was the conservatism which afflicted, indeed paralysed, so many Safavid architects. Earlier medieval architecture owed some of its vitality to the need to devise new architectural forms for new purposes: khāngāh, madrasa, tomb shrine and others. No such new functions make their appearance in the Safavid period. Long experience had established the optimum form of the basic secular and cultic structures. In matters of structure and decoration a similar fatigue, if not stagnation, had set in. No new structural devices appear and there is no technical breakthrough. The various emphases of earlier styles – tilework, brick patterning, stucco carving, transition zones, vaulting, large domes – had all been exhausted. The vigorous local schools of previous centuries had died, so that there was little prospect of fresh ideas from such a source. Much of provincial architecture in this period was produced at artisan level in a style which grew naturally out of provincial Timurid work. Flagging inspiration is particularly plain in cultic buildings and much of the best Safavid work is secular architecture, a hitherto less intensively exploited field. This may help to explain why in religious architecture Safavid builders so often relied on sheer scale for their most dramatic effects. The lesson was not lost on the architects of the next two centuries, who also habitually used this dimension of size and thereby partially disguised the humdrum and derivative nature of their buildings. In the context of what was to come it is thus entirely fitting that Safavid architecture should find its epilogue in the gigantic complex of Shah Sulṭān Ḥusain on the Chahār Bāgh.

CHAPTER 16(*a*)

THE PICTORIAL ARTS IN THE TIMURID PERIOD*

In his chapter in volume V of this series, Professor Grabar wrote of the present difficulty of coordinating the monuments of the visual arts with the events of the time. To some extent this is less true of the Timurid and Safavid periods, for two reasons; the existence of near contemporary literary sources for the art of the period, especially the arts of the book; and secondly the clearer relation of political events, changes of capital, the patronage of princes, the greater extent of surviving material.

Still, even for this period, there are striking gaps in our knowledge: the small amount of architecture of the 9th/15th century in western Iran; the complete disappearance of 15th century carpets; the lack of any wall-paintings or of portrait drawings which can be attributed with any security to the 15th century; and of any paintings from Samarqand or Bukhārā of the same period. Again, there has been far too little systematic publication, in spite of the marked progress during the past forty years; we still await definitive publication of the Bāīsunqur and the Ṭahmāsp *Shāh-nāma* manuscripts, for instance; even the work of Bihzād, the most famous painter of Persia, is not yet satisfactorily defined nor his life-history properly established. However, the history of miniature painting is well enough known during these two and a half centuries for an account to be given of the stylistic course and for its assessment in the scale of world art. For, with architecture, this is now the major artistic expression of Iran during this period which witnessed the rise and decline of its classic style.

When the period opens,[1] the leading centre for the arts of the book was in the west, in Tabrīz and Baghdad, alternate capitals of the

* These chapters were written in 1972. They have been twice revised to take account of subsequent research and publications, the last time in early 1981. Since then the most important event has been the publication of the monograph on the so-called Houghton *Shāh-nāma* by Martin B.Dickson and Stuart Cary Welch, Harvard University Press, in two folio volumes in which all the 258 miniatures are reproduced in facsimile size, together with 23 colour plates and extensive text. It has not been possible to take account of this book in this place. B.G.

[1] Professor Grabar has pointed out in *CHI* v, 649, that 1370 "seems to be as good a date as any other for the change to the assured style of the later fourteenth century".

Jalayirid dynasty; it then shifted briefly to Shīrāz for the opening years of the 9th/15th century, and was then fixed in Herat for the period until 853/1449, and again from about 1480 to 912/1506. In the interval the capital of the Qarā Quyūnlū under Jahān Shāh and of the Āq Quyūnlū under Uzun Ḥasan and his son Ya'qūb, Tabrīz again became a leading centre for the arts of the book and for architecture. With the rise to power of the Safavid house, Tabrīz became the leading centre for the third time, until the capital was transferred to Qazvīn and later to Iṣfahān, when this city became the capital of Shah 'Abbās the Great. After its brief glory under the governorship of Iskandar (812–817/1409–14), son of 'Umar Shaikh, Shīrāz never again assumed the leadership in Persian painting; but it remained for a hundred and fifty years a fruitful workshop, from which indeed the largest number of illuminated manuscripts emanated. This phenomenon has not so far been explained: why should the merchant class of this city have supported the art more than that of any other city of Iran? It may, however, be historically significant, because it was from this Shīrāz school that the painting styles of the Indian sultanates were mainly derived.

Both the earliest written sources which have come down to us and modern scholarship have treated of the history of miniature painting throughout the period of this volume as fundamentally a single development in time, shifting as we have indicated from one centre to another to follow the course of patronage. Anything outside this single line has been regarded as "provincial", which in effect has been taken to mean retarded, unoriginal or crude. It is a question, however, whether this scheme does not tend to overemphasise the importance of royal patronage, although no doubt economic necessity would have made some support necessary during the long period of production required for an illuminated manuscript, with the use of costly materials and the need for the collaboration of several different specialist craftsmen and artists – calligrapher, illuminator, miniaturist and binder at least. Moreover, only in princely libraries would the artists have had access to models and former masterpieces. We shall be able to show that it was not always the political leaders who provided this patronage but, on the contrary, often the less effective members of the ruling families who gave their time and money to artistic commissions. In particular, the situation in the lifetime of Tīmūr is at first sight unexpected. Although we know that he carried off from the captured cities of Iran to his new capital of Samarqand leading artists and craftsmen, including the famous calligrapher of Tabrīz, Mu'īn al-Dīn and the painter 'Abd al-Ḥaiy,[1] we do not know of a single fine manuscript produced in Samarqand during the lifetime of Tīmūr. The calligraphers and illuminators must have been fully occupied with the designing of the decoration for the many splendid buildings, permanent and temporary, which Tīmūr was putting up with feverish haste; nearly every famous scribe of these times also designed the inscriptions for public buildings, and we hear of wall-paintings in the garden pavilions and figured embroideries in the tents which still were the favourite dwellings of the conqueror. Thus it is that the Timurid style of miniature painting was not developed in Samarqand nor even in one of the seats of Timurid rule but in the precarious capitals of the last of the Jalayirids, Sulṭān Aḥmad. It was only after the death of Tīmūr that this style was adopted by his descendants, but with some modification, especially towards greater energy.

While technically the change from Mongol to Timurid painting is smoothly achieved and without radical change in visual structure, the psychological adjustment is notable. It is symbolised by the fact that romantic and lyrical poetry was not within the range of the Il-Khanid school, which, as Professor Grabar has pointed out,[2] was concerned with the *Shāh-nāma* as a mirror of the destiny of dynasties and the tragic involvement with fate. Otherwise the school was occupied by the illustration of history and of books of instruction.

The change is symbolised by the fact that the *Khamsa* of Niẓāmī was not included in the Mongol repertory; but at the end of the 8th/14th century this situation changed decisively. We now have a copy of the *Khamsa* dated 788–90/1386–8,[3] in *nasta'līq* by Maḥmūd b. Muḥammad at Baghdad when it was a capital of Sulṭān Aḥmad Jalāyir. It contains twenty-three miniatures. Then follows a very fine *Khusrau u Shīrīn* in the Freer Gallery,[4] copied by 'Alī b. Ḥasan al-Sulṭānī "in the capital of the kingdom Tabrīz" and undated, but attributable to the end of the Jalayirid period between 1405 and 1410. The new tradition is immediately taken up again in the library of Iskandar at Shīrāz, where in 813–14/1410–11 illustrations to the *Khamsa* are among the miniatures

[1] Qāżī Aḥmad, p. 63 and n.170. [2] *CHI* v, 653, 657.

[3] Christies's, *Catalogue*, 29 April 1970, lot no. 45, pp. 26–31, with four plates. Titley, "A Fourteenth Century Khamseh", pp. 8–11, 2 pls.

[4] Aga-Oglu, in *AI* IV (1937), 478–81, illustrating the five miniatures contemporary with the text. See also Stchoukine, *Manuscrits Tîmûrides*, p. 58; Gray, *Persian Painting* (1961), pp. 53–5.

of the two famous anthologies prepared for this Timurid princely patron. It may therefore be inferred that the change of subject at this time signified a change of direction in the cultural spirit of the Jalayirid court. They were of Mongol stock and claimed the main direct succession from the Il-Khanid tradition, but they lived in a completely Iranicised milieu, to which they personally contributed as writers and artists. Sultan Shaikh Uvais (757–76/1356–74) was a notable builder: his patronage of the painter Shams al-Dīn was recorded by Dūst Muḥammad.[1] With Sulṭān Aḥmad Jalāyir we enter on a period where the literary sources can be directly connected with surviving illustrated manuscripts.

Aḥmad secured the control of the kingdoms of Iraq and Āzarbāījān by 784/1382, and Baghdad and Tabrīz remained his alternate capitals so long as he was master of those cities. Coins were minted in Tabrīz in his name in 1383, but the city was seized by Tokhtamïsh of the Golden Horde in 787/1385, and it was occupied by Tīmūr in 788/1386, when Mīrān Shāh was installed as governor. It remained in Timurid hands until the death of Tīmūr in 807/1405, when it fell to the Shīrvān-Shāh for a year. Sulṭān Aḥmad was welcomed back by the inhabitants in 1406 but he survived only till 813/1410, when he was defeated and killed by Qarā Yūsuf of the Qarā Quyūnlū. Baghdad was held by Aḥmad until 795/1393, when it was taken and sacked by Tīmūr, and he fled to Syria and Egypt. However, he was soon able to return and remained in control until 803/1401, when it again fell to Tīmūr, while Sulṭān Aḥmad took refuge with the Ottoman Sultan Bāyezīd. The surviving manuscripts produced for Sulṭān Aḥmad fall in the years 1386 to 1388, 1392, 1396 and 1399, in all of which he was in control of Baghdad.

The leading master at the court of Sulṭān Aḥmad was ʻAbd al-Ḥaiy, pupil of Shams al-Dīn, until he was removed by Tīmūr in 795/1393 to his new capital in Samarqand. Junaid, pupil of ʻAbd al-Ḥaiy, remained in Baghdad, and the most famous surviving manuscript from Sulṭān Aḥmad's library, the celebrated *Khamsa* dated 1396 of Khwājū of Kirmān in the British Library, bears his signature on one of the miniatures.[2] The nine illustrations of this manuscript[3] are worthy of a

[1] Binyon *et al.*, *Persian Miniature Painting*, p. 184.

[2] Gray, *Persian painting from miniatures of the XIII–XVI centuries*, pl. 4.

[3] Stchoukine, *Manuscrits Tîmûrides*, pp. 33–5, pls. IV–VIII. Martin, *Miniature Painting* II, pls. 45–50. Barrett, pls. 8, 9. Gray, *Persian Painting* (1961), pp. 46–7.

master on account of the originality of the compositions and the brilliance of the colouring in which they are executed (pl. 47). Stchoukine considers that they are all by a single hand, but it may be that two (nos. 1 and 7) are by another painter. Two other manuscripts assigned by their colophons to the court of Sulṭān Aḥmad are an *'Ajā'ib al-makhlūqāt*, copied in 1388 and now in the Bibliothèque Nationale (Supp. pers. 332)[1], and the *Khamsa* of Niẓāmī, already referred to and dated 1386-8 from Baghdad. The twenty-three miniatures of this latter manuscript are much simpler than those of the Khwājū manuscript, but show similar, rather stiff figures of men and horses; similar conventions for the rendering of foliage and rocky ground; and in some cases similar extension of the miniature into the margins of the page. Rich colour is common to both manuscripts, with the use of gold for the sky as an alternative to a cobalt blue, but of lapis in some of the costumes and other textiles. At least one of the carpet designs is common to both, and these are among the earliest designs known to us; and the best miniatures show something of the same movement, especially apparent in the "prostration of Shīrīn (fol. 88a) before Khusrau" (pl. 48). But although all the elements of the new style are there, they are not yet developed into the spacious and romantic miniature style of the Khwājū. The *'Ajā'ib al-makhlūqāt* with its numerous miniatures shows less of this new spirit, but this is to be expected of a work of this character, with its traditional subject matter, largely astronomical. The few figure subjects are, however, quite comparable with the Niẓāmī miniatures, and there seems no need to assign, with Stchoukine, these illustrations to a later period. Another manuscript in the same library, clearly dated 1392 and apparently produced for Shāh Valad, son of Sulṭān Aḥmad, is a *Kalīla va Dimna*[2] (Pers. 913) of small format but illustrated by seventy-four miniatures contemporary with the text and therefore of the Jalayirid school of Baghdad. Some of them are more forward-looking than anything in Supp. pers. 332, especially in the importance given to landscape. There is one other manuscript dated 1399, which has been plausibly attributed to the same

[1] H. Massé, *Le Livre des Merveilles du Monde* (Paris, 1944). Stchoukine, *Manuscrits Tîmûrides*, pp. 32–3. *Arts of Islam*, no. 542.

[2] Stchoukine, *Manuscrits Tîmûrides*, p. 33, pls. II, III. S. Walzer, "The Topkapu-Saray manuscript of the Persian *Kalila wa Dimna* (dated A.D. 1413)", in *Paintings from Islamic Lands*, ed. R. Pinder-Wilson (Oxford, 1969), pp. 73–6. *Arts of Islam*, no. 543.

school. Entitled the *Kitāb al-bulhān* (Bodleian, Or. 133),[1] this is an account of the Seven Climes of the Ptolemaic cosmology and is enriched by seventy-eight miniatures, including eleven of the Seasons. These have been attributed by D.S. Rice to an Italian prototype which might have been available in the cosmopolitan capital of the Jalāyir at Baghdad, where it was produced. The flat schematic architecture might be thought primitive, but it is enlivened by shading of the tiled surfaces and rather prefigures the scenic convention that was to prevail into the early Timurid period. The tree and plant conventions are those common in the Jalayirid school, and Chinese influence is clear in the water and cloud patterns, and is shown in the dragon-headed snake (fol. 33v). These two pseudo-scientific manuscripts of 1388 and 1399 accentuate the exceptional quality of the Khwājū: they serve also to bridge the gap between the Jalayirid school of Tabrīz and Baghdad and the school of Shīrāz under the Muzaffarids.

A precursor of the *Kitāb al-bulhān* is a dispersed scientific dictionary entitled *Mu'nis al-aḥrār*, dated 1341 from Shīrāz,[2] when it was still ruled by the Īnjū dynasty. For landscape elements in the Jalayirid manuscripts we might compare the Muzaffarid *Shāh-nāma* of 1370 in Istanbul.[3] Here we see elegant little plant clumps, and above all a better relation of figures to the scale of the page than is found in either the Tabrīz or the Shīrāz manuscripts of the first half of the century. There are some fine detached *Shāh-nāma* illustrations mounted in an album in the Topkapı library (Hazine 2153),[4] which clearly develop out of the Tabrīz style of the Il-Khanid period and retain the great size of the page used in the Rashīdiyya scriptorium of Rashīd al-Dīn, but are so advanced that they can hardly be put before 1370; yet they retain the epic character of the time of Abū Sa'īd, only modified by the reduction in scale of the figures in relation to the landscape. If this date is correct, then this solution of the proper relation of figures and page was reached independently at about the same date in Shīrāz and Tabrīz.

[1] D.S. Rice, "Seasons and Labors of the Months in Islamic Art", *AO* I (1954), 1–39. Z. Janc, "Minijature iu Islamskom Astrošlokom spisu Orijentalnog Istituta u Sarajevu", 1958, *Perlozza Orijentalnu Titologiju i Istoriju Jugoslovanskiu Naroda pol. Turkskom Vladavinom*. E. Baer, in *BSOAS* XXXI (1961), 526–7.

[2] Qazvīnī, "An Account of the *Mu'nisu'l-Aḥrār*". Gray, *Persian Painting* (1961), pp. 60–2. Grube, *Miniature islamiche*, pls. 30, 31.

[3] Gray, *Persian Painting* (1961), pp. 63–4. Robinson, *Drawings of the Masters*, pl. 1. Aga-Oglu, "Preliminary Notes", pp. 191–2, pls. 5–7.

[4] Gray, *Persian Painting* (1961), pp. 41–3. See now also N. Atasoy, "Four Istanbul Albums".

Thanks to closer familiarity with Chinese painting and to more discriminating patronage, the Tabrīz landscapes are more developed. Yet the later Jalayirid miniatures seem to owe as much to the Shīrāz tradition as to that of Tabrīz. At the same time in Shīrāz, the economy of visual terms both in figures and in landscape was inherited in the early Timurid period, but refined by greater skill in draughtsmanship and enriched by freer use of gold, silver and lapis lazuli, now within the command of the rulers of an empire.

Shīrāz in the 1390s thus saw the birth of a new style, which developed naturally out of the Muzaffarid, when it was brought into touch with the achievements of the Jalayirid masters in Tabrīz and Baghdad. Twin volumes of epic poetry dated 1397 and now in the British Library[1] and the Chester Beatty Library, Dublin,[2] show the vigour and sense of striking design of Shīrāz under the Muzaffarids refined by the sensitive draughtsmanship and fine colour sense of the Jalayirid school. At Shīrāz the prince who represented the ruling house was Iskandar, son of 'Umar Shaikh. He was twice governor of Fārs, from 1394 to 1399, when in his early teens, and again from 812/1409 to 817/1414. These two volumes of epics might well have appealed to a precocious boy of thirteen, with their strongly romantic feeling and direct drama. They still keep the simplicity of composition which has all along been a characteristic of the Shīrāz school. This indeed continues in the much more sophisticated work in the miniatures illustrating the well known anthologies, or rather compendia, prepared for Iskandar by his scriptorium in 813–14/1410–11. In them the range of decoration was increased by two means: the employment, for the first time, of double-page compositions extending the full width of the open book, and the introduction of marginal decoration.[3] This practice, as distinct from the extension of the miniature into the margin, was apparently first employed in the *Dīvān* of Sulṭān Aḥmad Jalāyir, produced in the first years of the 9th/15th century. The last six pages of this manuscript, which is now in the Freer Gallery, Washington,[4] are decorated with figures in landscape, in ink with touches of blue and gold, in a closely Chinese style and medium. A similar range of colouring is to be

[1] Stchoukine, *Manuscrits Tîmûrides*, pls. XI–XV. Barrett, pl. 10. Gray, *Persian Painting* (1961), p. 66. G. Meredith-Owens, *Persian Illustrated Manuscripts in the British Museum* (London, 1965), pl. II.
[2] Binyon *et al.*, *Persian Miniature Painting*, pl. XXXI. Robinson, *Persian Miniature Painting*, pl. 7.
[3] Gray, *Persian Painting* (1961), pp. 71, 73.
[4] Martin, *Miniatures from the period of Timur*. Gray, *Persian Painting* (1961), p. 49.

seen in the margin decorations of some pages in the smaller Iskandar anthology of 1410. In the larger, there are whole pages of decorative work of this same character, veritable climaxes of illumination.[1] There are also some marginal miniatures, a feature shared with the Niẓāmī *Iskandar-nāma* of small format, now in the British Library,[2] which is later than 1410, but also of Shīrāz (pl. 49*a*). These are a witty novelty, for the artist has used the area of the text of the poem within the margins as if it were a curtain from behind which part of the action is allowed to appear in the margin: a fallen battle standard, signifying a defeated enemy; two camel-heads and a groom, a caravan; the head of a sleeping man between two candles; a harp and tambourine, to signify an orchestra. They are really thumb-nail sketches, two inches by one.

It was a time of experiment and it is therefore not so surprising to find another manuscript, dated 1398 from Bihbihān in Fārs, in which an anthology of seven poets is illustrated by eleven pure landscapes and only one figure subject (Türk ve İslam Müzesi, Istanbul, T. 1950).[3] Here the forms of trees and plants, as they are found represented in landscapes in other manuscripts of the early Timurid period, have been extracted and arranged as if they were specimens, each depicted in perfection and in fullest visibility, formed into patterns against a background of stylised hills in exotic colours. The date of these miniatures has been questioned by Stchoukine, who compares them with those of a *Khamsa* of Niẓāmī in the Topkapı Library (Hazine 1510), dated 906/1501 but with miniatures which he believes to have been added about 1570.[4] It appears, however, that not only has the date in the colophon of this manuscript been altered but the miniatures have been subsequently greatly overpainted and that their original date may have been about 1400.[5]

The full beauty of the early Timurid style of miniature is first seen in the two anthologies made for Iskandar Sulṭān in 813/1410–1. It comprehends greater freedom of handling, the figures moving in space,

[1] Gray, "Some Chinoiserie drawings", fig. 6.

[2] Robinson, "The earliest illustrated manuscript of Nizami?", *Oriental Art*, autumn 1957, pp. 96–103.

[3] Aga-Oglu, "The Landscape Miniatures of an Anthology manuscript of the year 1398 A.D.", *AI* III/1 (1937), 77-98. Çiğ, *Kataloğu*, p. 72, no. 12, pls. V, VI. Gray, *Persian Painting* (1961), p. 68.

[4] *Syria* XLII (1965), 137–40; see also his *La peinture Turque d'après les manuscrits illustrés* (Paris, 1966), p. 64, no. 27.

[5] See Pugachenkova and Rempel', *Istoriya iskusstv Uzbekistana*, p. 290 and pls. 280, 285. The patterning of the tree foliage in T. 1950 is already found in the Shīrāz *Shāh-nāma* of 1370 (Hazine 1511, fol. 105v).

experiment in rendering architectural form; the circular "Hall of Seven Images", each in a different pose;[1] the aerial view of the Kaʿba with the gay tents of the pilgrims pitched in the desert outside the walls of Mecca; Iskandar guided by a candle as he walks under the night sky over the rocky path to the hermit's cave (pl. 49*b*); or Farhād carrying Shīrīn on her horse at Bīsitūn by the rock-carvings.[2] In the other moonlit scene from the Alexander legend, in which he watches, concealed, the Sirens in their lake home, in the two versions,[3] one in each of these books, this style has reached its height. Imaginative conception and lyrical expression have found a perfect medium, perfect in scale, in feeling and in colour. This is a unique moment in the history of the Persian school: it passed all too quickly from the youth to the prime of the Timurid school. Iskandar came to an untimely end in 817/1414, and after a brief period when his cousin Ibrāhīm b. Shāh Rukh carried on the Shīrāz tradition at his capital Iṣfahān, the leadership of the school passed to his brother Bāīsunqur in his father's seat of government, Herat, in the year 823/1420.

Of Iskandar the fullest account has been given in his article "Le mécénat timouride" by Jean Aubin, who points to his great building activity both at Iṣfahān and at Shīrāz; in both cities he built fortified palaces, perhaps because of the hatred he inspired in the people by his oppressive rule. As with most of the Timurid princes his background was essentially Turki, his mother being a Chaghatai princess; and he composed poetry in Turki. Nevertheless his taste was formed by Persian culture, which is fully reflected in the two anthologies; but these also contain astronomical calculations, and in one is included a Shīʿī treatise on law. Aubin considers that his interest in mysticism was only superficial, but that would not prevent genuine feeling having been entertained by some of the artists who worked for him. The Gulbenkian manuscript includes a double-page composition showing Christians of Najrān recognise the Prophet (fols. 265–6). Both pages are resplendent in gold, light and dark clouds of glory on the right; and eleven figures writhing in flames on the left leaf.[4] This is probably a unique document for its subject: in style too it is unusual; it may be one of several miniatures in this manuscript which show Western influence,

[1] Gray, *Persian Painting* (1961), p. 75.

[2] Stchoukine, *Manuscrits Tîmûrides*, pl. XVII.

[3] Gray, *Persian Painting* (1961), p. 76. Pinder-Wilson, *Persian Painting in the fifteenth century*, pl. 2.

[4] *Persian Art: Calouste Gulbenkian Collection*, pl. 15. Professor P. Soucek has correctly identified this subject.

perhaps Byzantine, transmitted therefore through Tabrīz. For the head of Iskandar's library in Shīrāz was Maʿrūf Baghdādī, certainly not the only leading artist attracted to him from the falling power of the Jalayirid Sulṭān Aḥmad. Later Maʿrūf removed to Herat to serve Shāh Rukh, but was involved in 830/1427 in an attempted assassination of his patron by a Ḥurūfī fanatic, of which heretical movement he was an adherent.[1] It has been suggested that Iskandar may also have been affected by this heresy, which seems to have gone under the cloak of Shiʿism. One of its tenets was the mystical or divine value of certain or all of the letters of the Arabic alphabet, a doctrine likely to appeal to an aesthete and to a calligrapher. It should be stressed, however, that there is no historical evidence to support this suggestion, which remains a pure surmise.

The two anthologies produced for Iskandar Sulṭān are also of crucial importance for their illumination. The Gulbenkian book has perhaps the finest *sar-lauḥ* (frontispieces) (pl. 50) of the early Timurid school. The second double opening is laid out very like the tile mosaic decoration on the buildings of the period, and it is in fact possible to find a close parallel for these pages in the entrance gateway to the *madrasa* of Ulugh Beg, cousin of Iskandar, in the Rīgistān at Samarqand, which was built between 1417 and 1420. The central rosace, so like a Gothic rose window both in its layout and in the splendour of its floral arabesque decoration, resembles a similar feature in the architectural decoration of this gate;[2] while the stylised Kufic circles and diamonds in the framework on the page are echoed elsewhere in the décor of the madrasa. We know that other artists of the book, the calligraphers, were quite often employed to design the monumental inscriptions on buildings; and it is likely that the miniaturists also contributed to the decoration of Tīmūr's palaces and tented camps at Samarqand as they are described by the Castilian envoy Ruy Gonzalez de Clavijo.[3]

The special position of these two anthologies has already been stressed; it remains to point to two other features which distinguish them, the first of which had no continuing future, the second only to be taken up and developed in a much later period. Each manuscript contains double-page compositions which are thus not so much larger than the normal size, as different in shape and organisation. As has

[1] Aubin, "Le mécénat timouride", p. 85.
[2] Hill and Grabar, pl. 64.
[3] Clavijo, trans. Le Strange, pp. 220, 227–8, 230, 237–55, 268–76.

already been noted in one instance, the two halves can be used for contrast but in the smaller book it is also used for a panoramic view of the city of Mecca and the Ka'ba. The practice does, however, destroy the unity of the book, of text and illustration, which had just been perfectly achieved: consequently it is not surprising that the double-page composition is in future generally reserved for the frontispiece, the most striking exceptions being the illustrations to a manuscript of Sharaf al-Dīn 'Alī Yazdī's *Ẓafar-nāma*, copied in 1467 and now in the Walters Art Gallery, Baltimore.[1] The second innovation in the two anthologies is the introduction of marginal decoration, in the form of ornamental or figural thumb-pieces.

In some of the miniatures of the two Iskandar anthologies the older Shīrāz tradition still predominates, though their forthrightness is modified by the polish and sophistication of the Jalayirid school.[2] The strength of this old tradition was, however, sufficient for it to become once more dominant after the death of Iskandar and the succession to the governorship of Fārs of his cousin Ibrāhīm b. Shāh Rukh, who ruled for twenty years. This is immediately apparent in the principal surviving manuscripts from Shīrāz and Iṣfahān of this period, the anthology of the Berlin Museum of 1420,[3] which was a present sent by Ibrāhīm to his brother Bāīsunqur; and a manuscript of the *Shāh-nāma* with forty-seven miniatures in the Bodleian Library (Ouseley Add. 176) dedicated to the prince himself and probably datable to 1432–4, the last years of his life.[4] The tradition is continued in two Shīrāzī manuscripts of 839/1435-6, a *Khamsa* of Niẓāmī in the British Museum,[5] which still retains some of the romantic quality of the Jalayirid tradition; and a *Ẓafar-nāma* of Sharaf al-Dīn, whose miniatures are now widely scattered.[6] In both these manuscripts invention is still shown in the compositions, at least equal to that in the Ibrāhīm manu-

[1] For these miniatures, attributed to Bihzād, see below, p. 868 and n. 2.

[2] Stchoukine, *Manuscrits Tîmûrides*, pl. XVI. Gray, *Persian Painting* (1961), p. 74. Robinson, *Persian Miniature Painting*, pl. 8.

[3] Kühnel, "Die Baysonghur Handschrift", *Jahrbuch des preussischen Kunstsammlungen* LII (Berlin, 1931), 132–52. V. Enderlein, *Die Miniaturen der Berliner Bâisonqur-Handschrift* (Leipzig, 1969).

[4] Binyon *et al.*, *Persian Miniature Painting*, frontispiece and pls. XXXVIII–XL. Stchoukine, *Manuscrits Tîmûrides*, pls. XXI–XXVI. Gray, *Persian Painting* (1961), pp. 98–100.

[5] Gray, "A newly discovered Nizami of the Timurid school", *East and West* n.s. XIV/3–4 (1963), 220–3.

[6] Gray, *Persian Painting* (1961), p. 97. Grube, *Miniature islamiche*, pls. 32–3. Stchoukine, however, has argued for a Yazdī origin for these pages. The carcase of the MS was sold at Sotheby's in 1976.

scripts, the calligraphy and illumination also still as fine as could be found in Herat. Ibrāhīm himself designed inscriptions for the monuments of Shīrāz and Iṣfahān (but no longer extant) and he gathered about him a "numerous concourse of scholars and men of talent". It seems to have been the political decline of the Timurids which rather soon after this date made Shīrāz a provincial centre, though even as late as 1444 a *Shāh-nāma* manuscript shows a largeness of design as well as a vigour of drawing, especially in the double-page frontispiece feasting scene,[1] which is refreshing.

The finer, more sophisticated tradition had long since passed to Herat, where Bāīsunqur, Ibrāhīm's younger brother, had established himself as the leading patron of his generation, not later than 1425. Indeed in calligraphy it was clearly pre-eminent by 1420, when he returned from a punitive expedition to Tabrīz, bringing with him Maulānā Ja'far Tabrīzī, master of the nasta'līq script, Sayyid Aḥmad the painter (*naqqāsh*), Khwāja 'Alī the designer (*muṣavvir*), and Qivām al-Dīn the binder.[2] By 1421 Ja'far was using the style al-Bāīsunqurī, but the earliest of the manuscripts with minatures attested as made for him are two elegant little volumes dated 830/1426–7, a *Gulistān* of Sa'dī copied by Ja'far himself and an anthology copied by Muḥammad b. Ḥusām called Shams al-Dīn al-Sulṭānī, and a third manuscript of the following year of the *Humāī u Humāyūn* of Khwājū Kirmānī also copied by the latter scribe. The *Gulistān*, now in the Chester Beatty library in Dublin,[3] is one of the most exquisite of Persian manuscripts; its eight deceptively simple miniatures conceal a fresh and daring treatment of the picture space. Three of them show different experiments in the use of the bent wall and the open door in it, to make a closed stage for the action, while suggesting an inner world communicating with the outside through the half-open doorway. Each figure is related to the others by gestures which are quietly expressive. The stiff figures of the Jalayirid school have come alive. A similar advance has been made in the treatment of the landscape; by cutting off the line of the sky not far above the ridge of the hill. This practice had been tried out somewhat timidly in the Jalayirid *Khamsa* of Niẓāmī of 1386–8, but the effect was much reduced by bringing the figures too near the front of the compo-

[1] Gray, *Persian Painting* (1961), pp. 102–3.
[2] Dūst Muḥammad, quoted in Binyon *et al.*, *Persian Miniature Painting*, p. 185.
[3] *Chester Beatty Library, Catalogue* I, 119, pls. 27–8. Gray, *Persian Painting* (1961), p. 87. Robinson, *Persian Miniature Painting*, pl. 10.

sition; whereas now Bāīsunqur's painters had learnt how to push back the horizon. The text of the poem floats in front of the composition and serves as a curtain concealing the far distance. The colouring is cool, and has been compared by Robinson to diamonds and pearls. Actually turquoise, blue and green are predominant. Like the Junaid miniatures, these are also full-page and again, like them, introduce beautiful decorative inscriptions on the buildings depicted. The Herat court style has been born.

How much credit for this should be given to Bāīsunqùr personally is difficult to determine. Herat was now the principal seat of Timurid power under Shāh Rukh, and so would naturally have attracted the more ambitious artists. At the same time it was twenty years after the death of Tīmūr and the emergence of Shāh Rukh as his successor that this school showed its first fruits, and they were seen then only in Bāīsunqur's manuscripts.

Though overshadowed by his son Bāīsunqur, Shāh Rukh was still an important patron of the arts of the book. While Bāīsunqur was editing a new recension of the *Shāh-nāma*, his father was assuming the mantle of the great Il-Khanid minister, vizier and historian Rashīd al-Dīn. He tried to re-establish the original text by collating the manuscripts which he could find, and he entrusted Ḥāfiẓ-i Abrū with the task of bringing the history up to date in his *Majma' al-tavārīkh*. He was equally careful in having the original illustrations of the *Jāmi' al-tavārīkh* copied and in continuing this tradition of illustrated history. Ettinghausen[1] has aptly given the name of the "historical style" to this Timurid extension of the Il-Khanid style. Examples of it are to be seen in Hazine 1653 and 1654 in the Topkapı Sarayı library; in the famous *Jāmi' al-tavārīkh* of the Bibliothèque Nationale, originally published by Blochet as contemporary with the author; and in a widely dispersed manuscript of the *Majma' al-tavārīkh* of about 1423. However, the greatest surviving monument to the taste of Shāh Rukh as a patron of the arts of the book lies in the *Mir'āj-nāma* or visionary journey of the Prophet Muḥammad, copied at Herat in 1436 by Malik Bakhshī in Uighur script.[2] This mystical work is lavishly illustrated in gold and

[1] Ettinghausen, "An illuminated manuscript of Hafiz-i Abru in Istanbul, part I", *KO* II (1956), 30–44.

[2] Blochet, *Musulman Painting*, pls. LXXX–LXXXVII. Stchoukine, *Manuscrits Tîmûrides*, pls. LVIII–LXIV. Gray, *Persian painting from miniatures of the XIII–XVI centuries*, pl. 6. M.R. Séguy, *The Miraculous Journey of Mahomet, Miraj Nameh* (London, 1977).

blue. Apart from their iconographical interest, these miniatures show the continuation in Herat of the style of the Gulbenkian anthology of Iskandar of 1410, with rather large stiff figures and simple architecture and landscape. So far as the subjects allow, the colour scheme is attractive and expertly handled. So universal is its conception in illustrating the circles of heaven and hell that its miniatures have been found useful to illustrate Dante.[1] The epithet "Bakhshī" used with the name of the scribe here designates only a man who can use the Uighur script and does not imply that he was a religious devotee. This manuscript does, however, suggest that Shāh Rukh was himself inclined towards this kind of mystical gnosis. It is therefore a contrast with the epic and romantic poetry copied and illustrated for Bāīsunqur.

After the three exquisite small manuscripts of 830/1426–7, the next secure date that we have for the products of Bāīsunqur's library is 833/1429–30, in which year two famous manuscripts were completed: a *Kalīla va Dimna* copied by Muḥammad b. Ḥusām, and the *Shāh-nāma* copied by Ja'far al-Bāīsunqurī,[2] recognised since 1931, when it was first shown to the world in the great Persian exhibition at the Royal Academy in London, as the masterpiece of its age. If reflection and study now suggest some criticism of it, this does not deprive it of this title. The two outstanding features of the thirty-five miniatures which illustrate it are the skilful and varied compositions and the brilliant colouring. The drawing is not sensitive or fluent but superbly controlled. There is an expert formal relationship between the figures, but they are somewhat stiff and lack sensibility. There is a conceptual rather than a visual perspective, but it is consistently applied. The two *dīvān* scenes and the "Bedroom of Rūdāba" are rigidly frontal, with the carpets and tiled floors seen directly from above and thus in continuous line with the back wall. No attempt is made to accommodate the thrones in the layout: one is frontally seen; the other in bias, but with no adjustment of the front elevation. In the "Gulnār at the Window seeing Ardashīr" some relief is given by the irregular shape of the courtyard and the bias wall of the tower, but there is an unresolved difficulty where this should meet the top of the page. The artist has shirked this and simply continued the tiling to the margin. In the "funeral of Farāmurz" the two coffins of Rustam and Zavāra in the

[1] E. Cerulli, *Libro della Scala* (Rome, 1949).

[2] Binyon *et al.*, *Persian Miniature Painting*, no. 49, pls. XLIII–L. *Iran, Persian Miniatures*, pls. I–IX. Gray, *Persian Miniatures from ancient Manuscripts*, pls. I–IX.

domed tomb chamber are shown in a kind of aerial perspective, whereas the tiled floor on which they should stand is rigidly frontal, but apparently intended to be stepped up at each of the arcade pillars of the frontal screen. The walls of the courtyard in the foreground are impossible to reconcile with any system. On the other hand, the elaborate architecture of the Brazen Hold in which Isfandiyār is slaying the tyrant Arjāsp (pl. 51) is a very interesting attempt at aerial perspective. The throne room, which is the centre of the drama, is again seen in front view, with no allowance for the different planes of floor and wall; but all the rest of the composition is arranged so as to radiate outwards from this point. Circular composing had already been seen in the Iskandar anthology, but there the interior view permitted of a simple solution by cutting off the circle at the bottom of the page, which thus forms a hemicircle. The two encircling walls of the castle are depicted as diverging from the gateways; the re-entrant of the inner wall is depicted to show the inside, leaving an extremely awkward truncation at the corner, where the artist has covered his confusion by filling in the whole background with tilework on a straight plane. For all this difficulty, this is an able and cunning picture of a castle seen from above. It also conveys a good conceptual view of tile-mosaic clad buildings of the period, with monumental inscriptions running round the cornices.

The other Bāīsunqur manuscripts deal with these architectural problems in the same way; yet with greater trouble. For instance, in the Berenson anthology,[1] the tower in a similar love story is revealed as a cardboard piece of scenery where it meets the tiled floor of the courtyard in such a way as to make egress impossible. In the landscape scenes, the transition from low ground towards a high horizon is already an established convention, here used in an interesting way when the action requires the actors in a scene to enter into the rocky background, as in the "Combat of Gūdarz and Pīrān", "Żahhāk pinned to mount Damāvand" or "Rustam killing the White Dīv"; in all of which the mountain build-up is effectively suggested. In the Jalayirid landscapes ("Humāī and Humāyūn fighting", for instance),[2] the mountains enclose the action; in the Iskandar anthology, figures and mountains have not come to terms: the figures have to move along

[1] Ettinghausen, *Persian Miniatures in the Bernard Berenson collection* (Milan, 1961), pl. IV. Gray, *Persian Painting* (1961), p. 86.
[2] *Ibid.*, p. 47.

smooth paths leading past the rocky peaks. In each case this entry into the mountain zone is emphasised by the presence of horses or horsemen outside it, in the plain below. This more realistic approach is emphasised by the greater naturalism of the trees, though they are still partly conceptual.

The free extension of many of these miniatures into the margins has allowed the miniaturists to achieve more spacious settings without losing coherence or pictorial unity. Indeed the close-knit compositions of this great manuscript are its most striking virtue.

The second manuscript of the year 833/1429–30, the *Kalīla va Dimna* (Topkapı Sarayı library, Revan 1022),[1] has many features in common with the *Shāh-nāma*: for instance, the smooth but knotted trunks of the trees, the stiff figures and the rich colouring. The usual manner of depicting the rocky scenery, which again forms the landscape setting, is a spongy scalloped edge shading off into a neutral ground covered with small conventional plants. There is often a repoussoir of darker shaded ground in the foreground. Once more the miniatures frequently overlap the marginated area into the margin; crisply drawn and brightly coloured separate large plants are a special feature. The skies are a deep blue. Animals and birds are very precisely, even harshly, drawn.

Recently, another manuscript of the same work, copied a year later in 834/1431 by Ja'far al-Bāīsunqurī, has been discovered in the Topkapı Sarayı library (Hazine 362) by Robinson, who has put forward an interesting theory to account for the production of two copies of the same book for Prince Bāīsunqur within two years.[2] According to this theory, the Herat library, of which Ja'far was head, would have produced two classes of manuscript, one for "public" use, excelling in the academic qualities of formal accomplishment and finish, the other for the prince's private enjoyment, in which sensibility was allowed more play. In the second group, in addition to the Hazine 362 manuscript, he places the Chester Beatty *Gulistān* of 1427. It will be noticed that both these manuscripts were copies by Ja'far himself; but he also copied the *Shāh-nāma*, which is the very archetype of the accomplished academic. For this reason, as well as on the more general ground that it

[1] Aga-Oğlu, "Preliminary Notes", p. 199, figs. 10–14. Gray, *Persian Painting* (1961), p. 84. Robinson, *Drawings of the Masters*, pls. 11, 15.

[2] Robinson, "Prince Baysunghur and the Fables of Bidpai", *Oriental Art*, n.s. XVI (June 1970), 145–54.

is hard to see in what sense the academic books were "public" in a society where there was no public access to fine manuscripts of any kind, outside works of religious instruction kept in mosques or madrasas, the distinction is hard to accept in these terms. Moreover, the essential difference between these two manuscripts lies not in the quality of the calligraphy or illumination, but in the miniatures. Either, therefore, Bāīsunqur with his connoisseur's discrimination was dissatisfied with the 1430 manuscript of *Kalīla va Dimna* and commissioned another immediately, or he may have given the first away to some other bibliophile and wished to replace it. In either case the art historian's task is to seek to identify the hands of the miniaturists responsible for each of these series. Unfortunately, there is a complete absence of signed work from the Bāīsunqur *kitābkhāna*; and we can only fall back upon the names recorded in literary sources, which are not contemporary. Apart from Sayyid Aḥmad and Khwāja 'Alī mentioned already as foundation members of this library in 1420, we hear of Ghiyāṣ al-Dīn as attached by Bāīsunqur to Shāh Rukh's embassy to China in 1419–22 and of the leading master of Herat in this period, Khalīl, who may have been in charge of the production of the great *Shāh-nāma* of 1430, if this can be the manuscript referred to by Dūst Muḥammad as ordered by Bāīsunqur in rivalry with an epic volume produced for Aḥmad Jalāyir. If this is right, then Amīr Khalīl is the pre-eminent master of the "academic" style, still drawing the stiff figures of the Jalayirid tradition; mentioned by Daulatshāh as one of the "four talented artists at the court of Shāh Rukh, who in their time had no peer".[1] Robinson, on the other hand, thinks that Amīr Khalīl was the master responsible for the miniatures of the "second" *Kalīla va Dimna* of 834/1431 (Hazine 362) and also of the *Gulistān* of 1426, because of his known intimacy with Bāīsunqur. The alternative for the rôle of the "sensitive" artist is Ghiyāṣ al-Dīn or possibly Sayyid Aḥmad: we do not know. Certainly the miniatures in Hazine 362 are more forward-looking, naturalistic and sensitive, but their designer is less good at depicting animals, less dramatic, perhaps also not so good a colourist. The death of Bāīsunqur of drink and dissipation in 837/1433 brought to an end this unique combination of artists; but the Herat school held its pre-eminence for another fifteen years.

Its mastery is illustrated not only by the *Mir'āj-nāma* of 1436 but

[1] Quoted in *LHP* III, 498.

also, more typically, by the Royal Asiatic Society *Shāh-nāma* with "dedication" to Muḥammad Jūkī, younger son of Shāh Rukh. This identification was made in 1931 by J.V.S. Wilkinson[1] on the basis of an inscribed battle standard in one of its miniatures, which illustrates the shooting of Isfandiyār by Rustam: *al-Sulṭān al-aʿẓam Muḥammad Jūkī.* His cautious attribution has been amply sustained by subsequent scholarship, and it may be accepted as a work of the Herat school of about 1440. Muḥammad Jūkī is reported to have suffered from a lingering disease before his death in Sarakhs in 848/1445, perhaps hastened by the hostility of Gauhar Shād, the masterful wife of Shāh Rukh. A comparison of the miniatures in this manuscript[2] with those of the Bāīsunqur *Shāh-nāma* of only about ten years earlier indicates the change of direction which was taking place in Timurid painting at this time. The marked reduction in scale of the Muḥammad Jūkī book is an aspect of the increased importance given to landscape. This in turn indicates a new emphasis which is summed up by Laurence Binyon in the judgment that "the whole work is saturated in romantic atmosphere". This effect is achieved by the use of the same elements as before, deployed with greater freedom: the coral-like rocks have proliferated; foliage of the trees is more variegated; cloud forms are endlessly complicated with curdled and highly coloured shapes; above all architecture is now romantically related to mountains whose peaks it crowns or rivals (pl. 52). There is considerable range of quality as between the miniatures, and it is worth looking at some of the more significant pages. Robinson pointed to some clear Shīrāzī elements which appear especially in the battle scenes and has suggested that some artists from the library of Ibrāhīm Sulṭān after his death in 838/1435 may have migrated to Herat. This might explain the return of certain earlier features of the Shīrāz school, such as the use of coulisses in landscapes and the foreshortening of horses. It could also have contributed to the greater drama, even though the figures are still rather stiff. The relationship to Shīrāz has been illustrated by Robinson from the only double-page composition in the manuscript, a battle scene of which the left half is a confused *mêlée*, while the right shows an ordered array. This is essentially backward-looking; whereas another battle on a single page (fol. 430v) shows an open composition in which

[1] J.V.S. Wilkinson, *The Shah-namah of Firdausi* (Oxford, 1931), pp. 1–3.

[2] See Robinson, "Unpublished paintings from a 15th century Book of Kings", *Apollo Miscellany*, 1951. Gray, *Persian Painting* (1961), pp. 89–91.

there is balance and harmony, prefiguring in its complexity the mature art of the period of Bihzād towards the close of the century. The "Tahmīna coming to Rustam's chamber" has been exhaustively discussed by Eric Schroeder in connection with another version of this scene in the Fogg Museum, Harvard,[1] which he attributes to the period of Sultan Iskandar and to the hand of Pīr Aḥmad Bāgh-Shimālī, an artist mentioned by Dūst Muḥammad as the zenith of his time, which appears to be the early 9th/15th century. Leaving aside the justness of this attribution, we may admit the priority of the Fogg miniature and the debt of Muḥammad Jūkī's artists to the painters trained in the Jalayirid tradition. Schroeder also associated the Fogg miniature with the miniatures in a *Kalīla va Dimna* manuscript in the Gulistān library, Tehran, then generally attributed to the period 1410 to 1420. The situation of this important and beautiful manuscript[2] must now be considered in conjunction with some others.

The political confusion which followed upon the deaths of Shāh Rukh in 850/1447 and of Ulugh Beg in 853/1449 and the diminished resources of the Timurid house would already account for a break in artistic production at this point: moreover Herat which had been the centre of the school for thirty years had a particularly unstable history during the next twenty. Sultan Abū Sa'īd b. Mīrān Shāh made it his capital for the decade 863/1458 to 872/1468 (after the city had submitted to Jahān Shāh of the Qarā Quyūnlū Türkmen for six months). No manuscript with miniatures from this time is known: for the dedication of an anthology in the Chester Beatty Library to him is to be rejected on account of the date of 1475 in its colophon, eight years after his death. While this date is probably approximately correct, the evidence of the colophons is suspect and to be rejected.

In this third quarter of the 9th/15th century the leading political power in Iran and far to the west of it was that of the Türkmen, first under the Qarā Quyūnlū (Black Sheep) ruler Jahān Shāh (838–72/1435–67) and then under the Āq Quyūnlū (White Sheep) ruler Uzun Ḥasan (872–82/1467–78). Their capital was generally established at Tabrīz in Turki-speaking Āzarbāījān; but they had very wide dominions both in Anatolia and in Iran. It is only recently that important illuminated manuscripts have been identified as products at the courts

[1] Schroeder, pp. 51–74.

[2] Binyon *et al.*, *Persian Miniature Painting*, no. 44, pls. XXVII, XXXIV–XXXVI. *Iran: Persian Miniatures*, pls. X–XV. *SPA*, pls. 865–8. Gray, *Persian Painting* (1961), pp. 82–3.

of these two rulers. The earliest is a manuscript of the *Khamsa* of Jamālī[1] (India Office Library, Ethé 1284), copied in Baghdad in 869/1465, at a time when this city was in the hands of Jahān Shāh. The miniatures are in the Timurid Herat tradition with stiff but elegant figures in simple landscapes. Although they lack the compositional felicities of the Herat school of the second quarter of the century, they excel in the beauty of the colouring, mainly in a range of blues and greens, and still show a capacity for skilful arrangement of many figures. The four illuminated headings are of great beauty, fully equal to the famous tilework in the celebrated "Blue mosque" at Tabrīz of the same year. Even richer is the illumination lavished on a copy of the history of Ḥāfiẓ-i Abrū now in the Topkapı Sarayı Library (Bagdat 282), which must date from this period. It must therefore be assumed that one or two of the artists trained in the Herat library must by this date have migrated to the court of Jahān Shāh; but some of them also seem to have moved to the court of the Shīrvān-Shāh Farrukh-Yasār at Shamākhī in northern Āzarbāījān. An anthology in the British Library (Add. 16, 561) copied in 1468 in Shamākhī contains eight miniatures in a simplified style of figure drawing, but the landscapes are still completely in the Herat tradition with emphasis on beautiful flowering trees. The most remarkable of them depicts the city of Baghdad under flood,[2] a complex bird's-eye view with shifting viewpoint so that each building is seen directly in perspective. For comparison, one can turn to the "Siege of Gang-Bihist" or the "Isfandiyār slaying Arjāsp in the Iron Fortress" of the Jūkī *Shāh-nāma* of 1440, as striking examples of the same application of the principle of frontality.

Next in date comes a *Khamsa* of Niẓāmī in the Topkapı Library (Hazine 761),[3] dated 866/1461 and 881/1476 and copied by Fakhr al-Dīn Aḥmad, with sixteen miniatures and again exquisite illumination. This was produced for Pīr Būdāq at Baghdad and completed for Uzun Ḥasan in 1476; while a manuscript of the *Dīvān* of Hidāyat in the Chester Beatty Library (Turk. 401)[4] was copied in 1476–8 for the library of his son Sulṭān Khalīl (d. 1478). These also show a close connection with the Herat school; but with a certain naïvety. Uzun Ḥasan had died 882/1478 and was succeeded by his son Ya'qūb (883–96/

[1] Arnold, *Painting in Islam*, pls. XII, XIII. Stchoukine, *Manuscrits Tîmûrides*, pl. XLIV. Robinson, *Drawings of the Masters*, pl. 14.

[2] Arnold, *Painting in Islam*, pl. II.

[3] Stchoukine, "La peinture à Baghdâd sous Sultan Pir Budaq Qara-Qoyunlu", *AA* xxv (1972), 3–18.

[4] Robinson, *Drawings of the Masters*, pls. 76–7, and *Persian Miniature Painting*, pl. 41.

1479–90). Fortunately again we have a manuscript whose colophon records that the text of the *Khamsa* of Niẓāmī was copied by ʿAbd al-Raḥīm b. ʿAbd al-Raḥmān al-Sulṭānī al-Yaʿqūbī at Tabrīz the capital of the kingdom in 886/1481 (Hazine 762 in the Topkapı Library).[1] Of the nineteen miniatures in this manuscript, ten appear to be contemporary with the copying and in an enriched version of the Herat Timurid style, while the remainder have been added later, as is clear from the Safavid *kulāh* which is introduced into the costumes. The style of these is even richer and the artist has taken advantage of the margins to make delightful landscape settings. Three miniatures have been separated at some time from this manuscript and are now in a private collection.[2] One of these miniatures bears the date 910/ 1504–5 (pl. 36). By that date Tabrīz had fallen to the victorious Ismāʿīl, who was still only seventeen years old. The date seems acceptable also for the early Safavid miniatures which remain in the manuscript. They can therefore be taken to show the continuance of this Tabrīz Türkmen style into the early 10th/16th century and the Safavid period. They make a great contrast with the Bihzād style which was by then dominant in Khurāsān.

Now that a clear view of a court style under the Türkmen dynasties is possible and indeed necessary,[3] on the basis of the manuscripts mentioned it is possible also to attribute some others to this same school. The most important of these are three manuscripts of different dates. The Ṭabarī *Ta'rīkh al-rusul wa'l-mulūk*, ("Annals of the Prophets and Kings"), copied in 874/1470 (Chester Beatty P. 144),[4] the four miniatures of which are in a very conventional extension of the Herat style, can now be seen to be characteristic work of Uzun Ḥasan's library. The "Bahrām Gūr attacking a lion" (pl. 53) shows a composition[5] parallel with those of the Bāīsunqur 1430 *Shāh-nāma* (fol. 154b), while they also resemble the miniatures in a *Kulliyyat-i tārīkhiyya* copied

[1] Stchoukine, "Les peintures turcomanes et safavies d'une *Khamseh* de Nizami achevée à Tabriz en 886/1481", *AA* XIV (1966), 1–16.

[2] Robinson *et al.*, *The Keir Collection*, pp. 207–9, pls. 19–21.

[3] Robinson, "The Turkman School to 1503", in Gray, *Arts of the Book*, pp. 215–47.

[4] *Chester Beatty Library, Catalogue* I, 144, pl. 36. Robinson, *Drawings of the Masters*, pl. 20, and *Persian Miniature Painting*, pl. 12. *SPA*, pl. 880.

[5] This miniature was re-used in a MS of the *Khamsa* of Niẓāmī, copied at Herat in 849/1445–6, in the Topkapı Library (Hazine 781): Stchoukine, "Une Khamseh de Nizami". The composition was used once more in the Niẓāmī MS in the Metropolitan Museum, 1913-228-13, a *Haft paikar* long controversial for its date. Recently it has been proposed by Robinson, "Prince Bāysonghor's Niẓāmī", pp. 388–91, and by Grube, *The Classical Style*, pp. 26–7, as an original work from the scriptorium of Bāīsunqur. In spite of this weighty support, the present writer believes that these miniatures are 16th century copies after originals in early Timurid style.

for Shāh Rukh and now in the Topkapı Library. At the same time the lion and reedy stream in the foreground of this miniature recall several of the subjects of the *Kalīla va Dimna* in the Gulistān Library. As mentioned above this manuscript has been for the past forty years attributed to the early Timurid period, until recently when Robinson suggested that it might be as late as 1460–5.[1] This would bring it near the period of Bihzād, while the figure drawing is still stiff and old-fashioned. The solution may well be to attribute this, one of the most beautiful of Persian manuscripts, to the years 1450–60 under Jahān Shāh, when some masters trained in the Timurid school in Herat in the time of Bāīsunqur might still have been alive and working, and have had access to the original designs for the Bāīsunqur copies, now in Istanbul, containing miniatures with nearly identical compositions, in two cases in reverse. This strongly suggests the use of pounces, which may by this time have been part of the miniaturist's workshop equipment. It appears that they were in common use in the 9th/15th century. They were certainly then used for the gold decoration of margins, as in some poetical manuscripts, for instance an anthology in the Chester Beatty Library copied by Ja'far al-Tabrīzī in 1432.[2] At the same time there are many new compositions and the landscapes and animal drawing are more sympathetic (pl. 54) than those in either of the Bāīsunqur manuscripts. Of the thirty miniatures, seven are repeated from the 1432 book, all but two of them scenes with human figures. At latest they must have been executed before 1468, when the frontispiece composition was borrowed[3] for use in the Shamākhī anthology of that year mentioned above, in a clumsy copy, for the production of which the Gulistān *Kalīla va Dimna* manuscript must have been accessible.

Thus we must accept the idea that the court of the Türkmen rulers in Āzarbāījān provided the enlightened patronage for the arts of the book during the period when this failed in Herat owing to the disturbed political conditions in the Timurid dominions further east. Ya'qūb Beg remained a friend of Persian culture to the end of his life in 896/1490, and was exchanging manuscripts with Mīr 'Alī Shīr Navā'ī during the heyday of the Herat atelier, from which he received the gift of a complete set of the works of the poet and mystic Jāmī. Sulṭān Ḥusain Bāīqarā was able to establish his capital in Herat in 873/1469

[1] Gray, *Arts of the Book*, p. 217.
[2] Binyon *et al.*, *Persian Miniature Painting*, no. 51, pl. XLIIa.
[3] Stchoukine, *Manuscrits Tîmûrides*, pl. XLV.

and he was in undisputed possession from 875/1470, until the rebellion of his sons towards the end of the century. Mīr 'Alī Shīr Navā'ī joined him there in his first year and became his closest associate in administration, though he endeavoured as far as possible to rely upon personal collaboration rather than upon formal office. The great calligrapher Sulṭān 'Alī Mashhadī had been summoned to Herat by Sulṭān Ḥusain not later than 1477, and he probably remained there in the sultan's library until 1502. He copied many of the most famous manuscripts of this period, including both a *Gulistān* of 1486 and a *Būstān* of 1488, as well as several manuscripts which remained without miniatures until they were supplied many years later at the Shaibanid court in Bukhārā. By 1480 Herat had become that centre of culture and art which is singled out by Bābur in his memoirs for such signal praise: "Herat had no equal in the world under Sulṭān Ḥusain." Some indication of the esteem of letters there may be formed from the reputation of 'Alī Shīr Navā'ī, who was through and through a literary figure, whose own brother Darvīsh 'Alī was known as the *Kitābdār* and whose favourite Ḥājjī Muḥammad, whom he himself described as "an angel in human shape", was a painter and experimenter in the imitation of Chinese porcelain. He remained in the amīr's library until shortly before his death in 906/1501, when he followed the rising star of Badī' al-Zamān,[1] the son and for a short time successor of Sulṭān Ḥusain.

Herat then, though ruled and administered by men of Turkish blood, was a great centre of Persian culture. It was the centre of an extensive empire still including almost the whole of modern Afghanistan, eastern Iran and part of Soviet Central Asia. Mīr 'Alī Shīr Navā'ī was a great builder as well as a patron of letters, and he and his master shared the patronage of Bihzād and of his pupil Qāsim 'Alī. The sultan himself is said to have discovered the talent of the Sayyid Mīrak, who had practised calligraphy and illumination before joining the library of the court, where he became head of the painting staff.[2] Both Bihzād and Qāsim 'Alī were trained in this library and both continued to work there until the end of the reign. Both Mīrak and Ḥājjī Muḥammad died at the time of the Uzbek conquest of the city in 913/1507. This event then marks the effective end to the brilliant circle which had gathered at Herat round the sultan and his minister, Mīr 'Alī Shīr Navā'ī.

[1] Khwānd Amīr, quoted in Arnold, *Painting in Islam*, p. 139.

[2] Dūst Muḥammad, quoted in Binyon *et al.*, *Persian Miniature Painting*, p. 186.

The contemporary sources and those of the next two generations do not help us to distinguish between the contributions of these several artists to the art of the period, although they record the high esteem in which the masters were held, and the growth of the reputation of Bihzād in the next century, until he came to overshadow all other Persian painters in retrospect. Nor has it so far proved possible to arrive at a clear and accepted view of his style as distinct from that of his contemporaries in Herat from a study of the surviving material which has up to the present been available for appraisal.[1] This still continues to grow, and it would be rash at the present time to establish stylistic criteria for attribution. For these reasons it seems best to attempt here rather to give an account of the school as a whole and its main achievements during the last twenty or twenty-five years of the 15th century. By 1470 the older Herat tradition had become stereotyped, with the re-use of old motives, a stiffening of figure drawing and a lack of invention and vitality; even though in the best work there was still a good sense of colour and skilled draughtsmanship. With the return of patronage to Herat, a fresh breath was infused into the school. At the same time, it is right to emphasise the continuity with the old tradition, the terms of which were still accepted as viable for landscape and architecture, for perspective and the framework of vision. This acceptance made possible the quick advance which is to be seen in the work of the new masters. Indeed, the first of these seems to have been Shāh Muẓaffar, the son of the master Manṣūr, who had been court artist to the Timurid prince Abū Sa'īd. Since Shāh Muẓaffar is reported to have died at the age of twenty-four, he must have been active by the 1480s: his name is twice coupled by Bābur with that of Bihzād as outstandingly skilful, and he is said to have been a client of 'Alī Shīr Navā'ī. He has been thought to represent the more conservative influence at this time, but we lack proof. The earliest work of the school now identifiable can be grouped around the year 1485. This is the date of the copying of the five parts of the *Khamsa* of 'Alī Shīr Navā'ī for prince Badī' al-Zamān; of the copying of the *Khamsa* of Amīr Khusrau Dihlavī in the Chester Beatty Library; probably of the double-page composition of Sulṭān Ḥusain in his garden enclosure, in the Gulistān Library, Tehran:[2] while to the following year can be assigned

[1] Summarised by Pinder-Wilson, "Bihzad".

[2] A rather later date has been suggested by M. Lukens-Swietochowski because of the ageing face and stance of the sultan: see Gray, *Arts of the Book*, pp. 184, 207.

the *Gulistān* from the Maurice de Rothschild collection; and probably the thirteen miniatures added to a *Khamsa* of Niẓāmī copied in 1442 and now in the British Library (Add 25,900).[1] This gives a total of forty-six miniatures which provide a sufficient base for a consideration of the new style. Most are comparatively traditional, but in each group there are some new experiments, especially a more rhythmical and significant placing of the human figures. The "Khwāja 'Abd-Allāh Anṣārī with four disciples" and the "Mystics discoursing in a garden" in the Navā'ī; the "Khusrau arriving at the palace of Shīrīn" in the Amīr Khusrau; the right half of the garden scene; the "Sa'dī and the youth of Kāshghar" in the *Gulistān*; and the "Camel Fight of the Tribes of Lailā and Majnūn" in the Niẓāmī (pl. 55),[2] may be singled out for this quality in each of these compositions. Although the next group follows on only two or three years later and can be thought of as centred on the year 1490, there is a notable advance in most of the miniatures to a freer, less enclosed movement, usually with more than one centre or axis. This group consists of the four near-contemporary miniatures of the *Manṭiq al-ṭair* of 'Aṭṭār, copied in 1483, but with a date of 1487–8 on the fifth miniature;[3] of the *Būstān* dated 1488, but with a miniature dated 1489; and the *Khamsa* of Niẓāmī copied for Amīr 'Alī Fārsī Barlās, itself undated, but one of the twenty-one miniatures bears a date of 1494–5. The two earlier manuscripts in this group were prepared in the library of Sulṭān Ḥusain himself, the third for one of the Turki begs of the very powerful Barlās clan in Herat. Yet the three are knit together by frequent repetition of single figures or small groups, sometimes in reverse. They may therefore be considered the work of a single atelier or group of artists. There is a less close relation with the earlier group, although there is one clear case of the derivation of a figure in one of the Navā'ī miniatures[4] from one in the *Manṭiq al-ṭair*. It follows that the production of the *Khamsa* of Navā'ī must have continued over several years, just as no doubt did the work on the miniatures of the other manuscripts. It is characteristic of the work of

[1] The only evidence for the close dating of these miniatures is supplied by a date included in an inscription painted on the frieze on a building on fol. 77: the first two figures are clear 89; but the third digit, which has been read as both 8 and 1, appears to the present writer to be more probably 5. If so, the date would be 895/1490 rather than 1493 or 1486.

[2] Gray, *Persian Painting* (1930), pl. 6. Arnold, *Painting in Islam*, pl. XLIII. Martin, *Miniature Painting* II, pl. 77. Binyon *et al.*, *Persian Miniature Painting*, pl. LXVII. Stchoukine, *Manuscrits Tîmûrides*, pl. CXXVI. Pinder-Wilson, *Persian Painting in the fifteenth century*, pl. 7.

[3] Lukens, "The Language of the Birds".

[4] *Ibid.*, p. 324, fig. 13. Gray, *Persian Painting* (1961), p. 119.

this whole period that the execution maintains a very high standard of technical skill in every detail. This is not the place for a detailed discussion of these miniatures and of their possible attribution: this has been done frequently, most thoroughly by Stchoukine and most recently by Robinson.[1] One further manuscript must be mentioned, standing rather apart from any of those in either group and with no internal evidence for the date, except that it was copied as early as 1467 by Shīr 'Alī, though probably not in Herat since it bears the *ex libris* of Sulṭān Ḥusain, who was not yet established in the Timurid capital at that date. This is the *Ẓafar-nāma* in Baltimore University collection, but for many years in the Mughal imperial library, during which time the miniatures suffered some lamentable retouching. These are six double-page openings, which come as near to being history paintings as any of the post-Mongol period. For they are not conventional battle scenes nor romantic illustrations of heroic events, like those in the Shīrāz manuscript of 1436 of the same text; but serious attempts to reconstruct some of the outstanding events in the career of the founder of the empire of which Sulṭān Ḥusain was the last effective head. It was no doubt because of the wish to depict adequately complex military operations that the double-page format was employed. Scholars of the subject have been unanimous in praising the original conception and brilliant execution of these miniatures, so far as this is still discernible; and have with more or less conviction followed Sir Thomas Arnold[2] in accepting the attribution of them to Bihzād. He observed that the manuscript had been remarginated before the addition of the miniatures and suggested that a reasonable date for them might be about 1490, twenty-three years after the completion of the text. At least, they must be earlier than the death of Sulṭān Ḥusain in 911/1506, since his likeness is used in the representation of Tīmūr in the first and last paintings.

These are the most complete of all the miniature paintings of the school of Herat under Sulṭān Ḥusain, while they follow the second group of manuscripts in being built on more than one axis. In the battle scenes effective use is made of straight lines or rectangles to give some stability in what might otherwise have been too diffuse a composition. In the "Building of the Great Mosque at Samarqand" the

[1] Robinson, *Persian Miniature Painting*, no. 29. Stchoukine, "Les peintures de la Khamseh".
[2] Arnold, *Bihzād and his paintings*.

massive elephant moving in on the lower left gives the required sense of movement and direction in what might otherwise have been too rigid and confused a geometric scene. This painting too demonstrates the links between this manuscript and the other products of the school; for several groups of the workers depicted in it appear also in the "Building of the Castle of Khavarnaq"[1] in the Niẓāmī of 1495. Others in the first painting are found in the *Manṭiq al-ṭair* of 1483. The four contemporary miniatures of this manuscript are worthy to be ranged with the Cairo *Būstān* miniatures, especially the double frontispiece of the "Court of Sulṭān Ḥusain" and the "King Dārā and the Keeper of the royal horses",[2] in their felicities of composition and the loving treatment of animals and of the minor human figures. The ṣūfī mystical and didactic poem by Farīd al-Dīn 'Aṭṭār, the *Manṭiq al-ṭair*, was indeed well suited to express the spirit of the ruling circle in Herat at this period. Whoever illustrated the manuscript showed that he was familiar with the substance and the intention of this mystical poem, so that the allegation of Michael Rogers that the miniatures have nothing to do with the text is to be rejected.[3] The third of these miniatures (now the seventh) illustrates two stories:[4] in the foreground Sulṭān Maḥmūd aiding the woodcutter whose donkey had fallen and injured him; and in the background a passer-by saying to a drowning man, "You must get rid of your beard or you will surely drown." These stories are widely separated in the poem; one in Discourse XVII and the other in Discourse XXXIV;[5] the first pointing to the value of contact with the wise and noble ruler; the second the need for detachment from earthly ties, such as pride in a fine beard. The second miniature is equally remarkable, though it seems to have only a single reference: a funeral procession is approaching a *ḥaẓīra* (fenced enclosure for burial) near the tomb of a holy man,[6] where a grave is being dug (pl. 56); presumably illustrating the question asked of the grave-digger in Discourse XXI:[7] "Have you seen a marvel?" To which the answer was: "The dog of my [carnal] soul has seen me digging graves here for seventy years, but has neither died

[1] Gray, *Persian Painting* (1961), p. 116.
[2] Binyon, *et al.*, *Persian Miniature Painting*, pls. LXVIII, LXIX.
[3] In *Iran* VIII (1970), 137.
[4] Lukens, "The Language of the Birds", colour plate on p. 326.
[5] Nott, *The Conference of the Birds*, pp. 48, 88. See now also Swietochowski, "The Historical Background".
[6] Golombek, *The Timurid Shrine at Gazur Gah*, p. 107.
[7] Nott, *The Conference of the Birds*, p. 57, mistranslates these lines. See Hellmut Ritter, *Das Meer der Seele* (Leiden, 1955), p. 208.

nor learnt to obey me." That this miniature was believed to be by the hand of Bihzād in the 10th/16th century is shown by a Bukhārā simplified version of it in the Walters Art Gallery, which bears that attribution. Both these miniatures show the easy mastery of complex compositions with expressive stance and gesture, and loving treatment of animal life: a cat by the saint's tomb and appropriately many birds in a bare tree above it; and the patient donkey in the first scene. Matching the brilliant and sensitive handling of the horses and foals in the "Dārā with the Groom";[1] is the treatment of a yoke of ploughing oxen in the last miniature of the *Manṭiq al-ṭair*,[2] which is once more a double composition set in a country landscape, the most forward-looking of the four. The crouched figure of a Chinese mendicant monk holding a greyhound in leash, may illustrate the story in Discourse XLI,[3] of the dervish whose love for the daughter of a dog-keeper forced him to take a dog every day to the bazaar, thus showing that he preferred ridicule to insincerity. The foreground scene directly illustrates the story of Shaikh of Malinah questioning the pious old villager as he follows his ox-drawn plough.

If we seek to sum up the characteristics of the miniature art of the school of Herat at the end of the Timurid period, certain qualities stand out: the small scale and low tone of the colouring; the invention, intimacy and harmony of the compositions; the preference for lyrical, romantic and mystical poetry, rather than epic or history; and consequently the care devoted to the detail of carpet design and architectural decoration. Harmony of man and nature is the outstanding mode of the Persian miniaturist, but at no other time did the art reach the sureness of touch or the sensitive vision seen in almost every work of this school. This is the moment of fruition following the building of a tradition during the early Timurid period, and preceding the richer, more decorative, externalised art of the Safavid achievement.

Many of the Herat painters seem to have left the city after its sack by Muḥammad Shaibānī Khān in 913/1507, but at this time it does not appear that there was an exodus to Uzbekistan. It is only after 1520 and long after the death of Shaibānī in 916/1510, that miniatures in the

[1] Sa'dī, *Būstān*, National Library, Cairo: Binyon *et al.*, *Persian Miniature Painting*, pl. LXIX.

[2] Lukens, "The Language of the Birds", p. 335, fig. 30.

[3] Nott, *The Conference of the Birds*, p. 114. The detail showing the Buddhist monk is reproduced in Lukens, "The Language of the Birds", p. 334, fig. 29. Cf. this figure with that in Gray, "The Timurid Copy", pp. 35–8, which represents a further stage in reinterpretation of a Chinese theme.

Herat style appear in Bukhārā. One of the first manuscripts produced there is the *Khamsa* of Navā'ī in the Leningrad Public Library (Dorn no. 559), in which most of the miniatures have an old-fashioned mid-15th century look;[1] but in one, of "Majnūn with the wild animals in the desert", there can be seen the influence of the late Herat school. The four miniatures in a manuscript of the *Mihr u Mushtarī* of 'Assār dated 1523, and now in the Freer Gallery of Art, Washington,[2] are far more accomplished. They already show the tendency to a simplified, unstructural style which was to remain a characteristic of this school. The light-toned colour scheme of Herat is retained, but brightly coloured blossoming trees are often conspicuous. Not much later come four miniatures in a *Bahāristān* of Jāmī in the Gulbenkian Foundation, Lisbon,[3] bearing attributions to Bihzād and very close in style to the 1494–5 *Khamsa* of Niẓāmī.

A further exodus of artists from Herat followed the second Uzbek sack of 1528, but the school of Bukhārā does not seem to have reached its height until the reign of 'Abd al-'Azīz Bahādur (946–57/1539–50), who was evidently a great patron of the arts of the book, with a special admiration for the manuscripts of Sulṭān Ḥusain Bāīqarā. He commissioned miniatures to be added to manuscripts written by leading calligraphers of Herat between 1492 and 1514,[4] as well as entirely new books of fine quality and lavishly decorated with gold stencilled margins, such as the *Būstān* of Sa'dī copied for him by Mīr 'Alī Haravī in 1542 and now in the Gulbenkian Foundation.[5] Several of the miniatures in this manuscript are signed by 'Abd-Allāh and Maḥmūd *muẓahhib*, who were the leading painters at the court of 'Abd al-'Azīz. One of them derives directly from the Cairo *Būstān* of 1488, while a double-page frontispiece, signed Maḥmūd, in a *Bahāristān* of Jāmī dated 1547, derives directly from the Gulbenkian manuscript of the same work, and ultimately from the Baltimore *Ẓafar-nāma*. The Bukhārā court painters thus kept alive for two generations the tradition of the Herat school under Sulṭān Ḥusain. They did also originate; and one of the finest works of Maḥmūd is the double-page miniature in a *Mukhzan al-asrār* of Niẓāmī in the Bibliothèque Nationale (Supp. pers. 985), signed by Maḥmūd and dated 1545–6.[6] It shows Sultan Sanjar with his

[1] D'yakonova and Gyuzal'yan, *Sredneaziatskie miniatyury*, pls. 7, 8.
[2] All reproduced in Binyon *et al.*, *Persian Miniature Painting*, pls. LXXIX–LXXX.
[3] *SPA*, pl. 388. *Gulbenkian Foundation: Exhibition of Islamic Art*, no. 122.
[4] Robinson, "An unpublished manuscript", p. 231.
[5] *Gulbenkian Foundation: Exhibition of Islamic Art*, no. 123.
[6] Blochet, *Musulman Painting*, pls. CXIV, CXV.

courtiers hunting in mountain country and accosted by the old woman who complained to him of injustice, in a composition of remarkable clarity and fine handling. Similar easy skill of composition is shown in the two miniatures illustrating a manuscript of the *Shāh u darvīsh* of Hātifī dated 1540 now in the Pierpont Morgan Library, New York (MS no. 531). The first is a school scene (pl. 57) reminiscent again of the Herat school, but a good deal more lively. It bears a date corresponding to 1542 in an inscription over a doorway. How quickly the school declined after 1550 can be seen by comparing this miniature with one of a similar subject in a manuscript of the *Gulistān* of Sa'dī, dated 1566–7 in Leningrad, where the figures of the pupils are arranged anyhow.[1] It would be easy to find many parallels for this decline into jejune repetition of compositions which have lost all vitality.

METALWORK AND CERAMICS IN THE TIMURID PERIOD

Though there had been some falling away during the Il-Khanid period from the splendid traditions of metalwork and ceramic achievement of the Saljūq age, in both fields the standards were still high and production on a large scale. By the end of the 8th/14th century, however, there was evidently a reduction both in production and in variety of technique. But it is not true that silver and gold inlay on metal was then unknown. Superb monumental bronzes made by craftsmen from Iṣfahān and Tabrīz for Tīmūr himself are now in the Hermitage Museum. They were brought there, from the mosque of the city of Turkistān to which they were dedicated, in 1935 at the time of the Third International Congress of Iranian Art and published in the Memoirs of the Congress by A.G. Yakubovsky.[2] The most imposing, a huge water tank for ablutions (2.45 m. in diameter)[3] dated 801/1399, is signed by 'Abd al-'Azīz b. Sharaf al-Dīn Tabrīzī, while the equally fine candlesticks are signed by 'Izz al-Dīn b. Tāj al-Dīn Iṣfahānī with the date 1397. The ablution vessel is decorated only with engraved inscriptions in *thulth* and *kūfī* and with arabesque ornament; while three of the five candlesticks retain a good deal of the original gold and silver inlay. A similar but smaller uninscribed candlestick is in the museum of the Georgian State in Tiflis, and another example is divided between the

[1] D'yakonova and Gyuzal'yan, *Sredneaziatskie miniatyury*, pl. 17.
[2] Yakubovsky, "Les artisans Iraniens", pp. 277–85, pls. CXIX–CXXIII.
[3] First published by Veselovskiĭ and Gorokhov in *Bulletin de l'Association International pour l'exploration de l'Asie Centrale*, nos. 6 and 7 (St Petersburg, 1906–7).

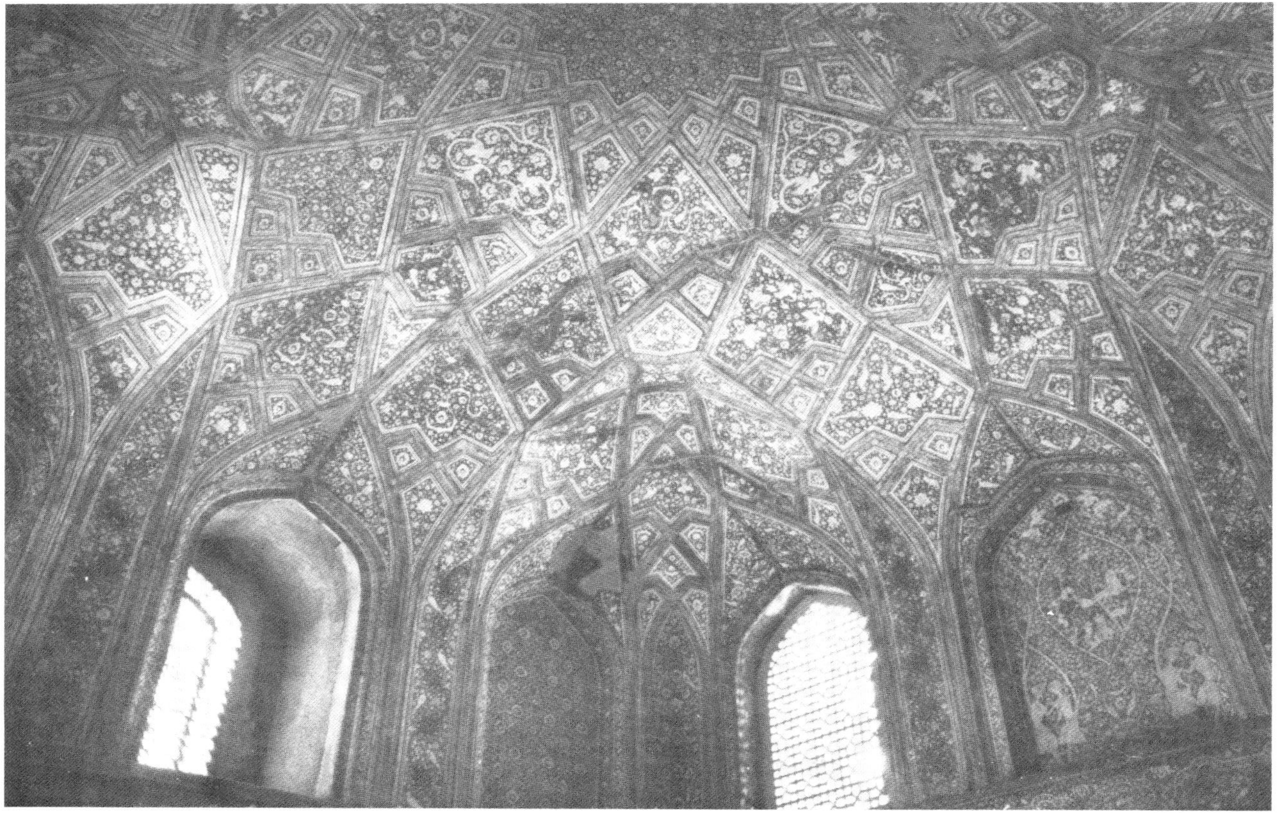

41 Nā'īn. Vault in palatial building.

42 Māhān. Vaults in shrine of Shāh Ni'mat-Allāh Valī.

43*a* Iṣfahān. Masjid-i Shaikh Luṭf-Allāh, exterior.

43*b* Iṣfahān. Masjid-i Shaikh Luṭf-Allāh, interior.

44*a* Iṣfahān. Khājū bridge, lower side.

44*b* Iṣfahān. Caravansarai and *madrasa* of Shah Sulṭān Ḥusain.

45 *a* Iṣfahān. *Madrasa* of Shah Sulṭān Ḥusain, courtyard wing.

45 *b* Iṣfahān. *Madrasa* of Shah Sulṭan Ḥusain, courtyard and dome.

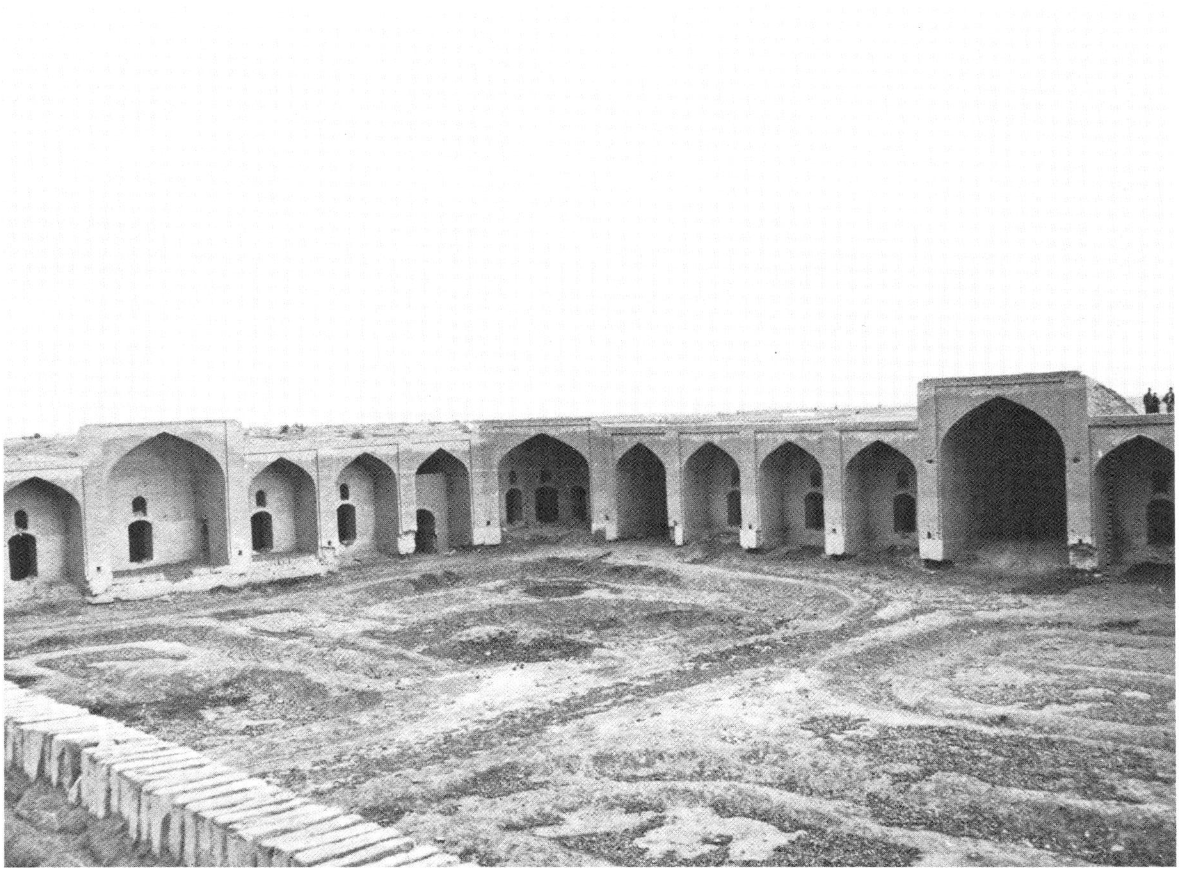

46 Gaz. Safavid caravansarai.

47 *Dīvān* of Khwājū-yi Kirmānī, wedding celebrations of Prince Humāī and Princess Humāyūn. Signed Junaid, Baghdad, 1396. Size, $11\frac{3}{4} \times 7\frac{1}{2}$ in.

48 *Khamsa* of Niẓāmī, arrival of Khusrau at the palace of Shīrīn. Baghdad, 1386–8. Size, 18.5 × 12.5 cm.

49*a* *Iskandar-nāma* of Niẓāmī, Iskandar sleeping. Shīrāz, 1440. Size, $2\frac{1}{2} \times 1$ in.

49*b* *Anthology* of Iskandar Sulṭān, Iskandar visits a hermit. Shīrāz, 1410–11. Size, $6 \times 3\frac{7}{8}$ in.

50 *Anthology* of Iskandar Sulṭān, illuminated frontispiece. Shīrāz, 1410. Size, 27.3 × 18 cm.

51 *Shāh-nāma* of Firdausī, Isfandiyār slaying Arjāsp in the Brazen Hold. Herat, 1430. Size, 38 × 26 cm.

52 *Shāh-nāma* of Firdausī, Isfandiyār slaying Arjāsp in the Brazen Hold. Herat, *c.* 1440. Size, 19.5 × 14 cm.

53 *Ta'rīkh al-rusul wa'l-mulūk* of Ṭabarī, Bahrām Gūr attacking a lion. Tabrīz, 1470. Size, 24.6 × 15 cm.

54 *Kalīla va Dimna*, The Fable of the Four Friends. Tabrīz, 1450–60. Size, 29 × 20 cm.

55 *Khamsa* of Niẓāmī, the battle of the tribes of Lailā and Majnūn. Herat, 1490. Size, $5\frac{1}{4} \times 3\frac{1}{2}$ in.

56 *Manṭiq al-ṭair* of ʿAṭṭār, funeral procession at the gate of a *ḥaẓīra*. Herat, *c.* 1487. Size, $9\frac{3}{4} \times 5\frac{1}{2}$ in.

57 *Shāhu Darvīsh* of Hātifī, Darvīsh conducting a school. Bukhārā, dated 1542. Size, 19.8 × 11.3 cm

58*a* Brass wine jar decorated with gold and silver, showing the dedication to Ḥusain Bāīqarā under the foot, with the date A.H. 903 (A.D. 1497) and signature of Muḥammad b. Ismā'īl Ghūrī. Herat, 1497. Height, 13 cm.

58*b* Silver gilt tankard, chased and engraved with the name of Qāsim b. 'Alī. Date, *c.* 1400. Height, 21.5 cm.

59 *Jamālu Jalāl* of Āṣafī, Jalāl before the turquoise dome. Tabrīz, 1504–5. Size, 30.5 × 19.5 cm.

60 *Dīvān* of Ḥāfiẓ, new moon on the feast of ʿId. By Sulṭān Muḥammad, dedicated to Sām Mīrzā, Tabrīz, 1530–5. Size, 29 × 18.5 cm.

61 *Khamsa* of Niẓāmī, King Nūshīrvān and his vizier at a ruined village. By Mīr Muṣavvir, Tabrīz, 1539–43. Size, 36.8 × 25.4 cm.

62 *Tuḥfat al-aḥrār* of Jāmī, East African with a mirror. Mashhad, 1556. Size, 34.2 × 23.2 cm.

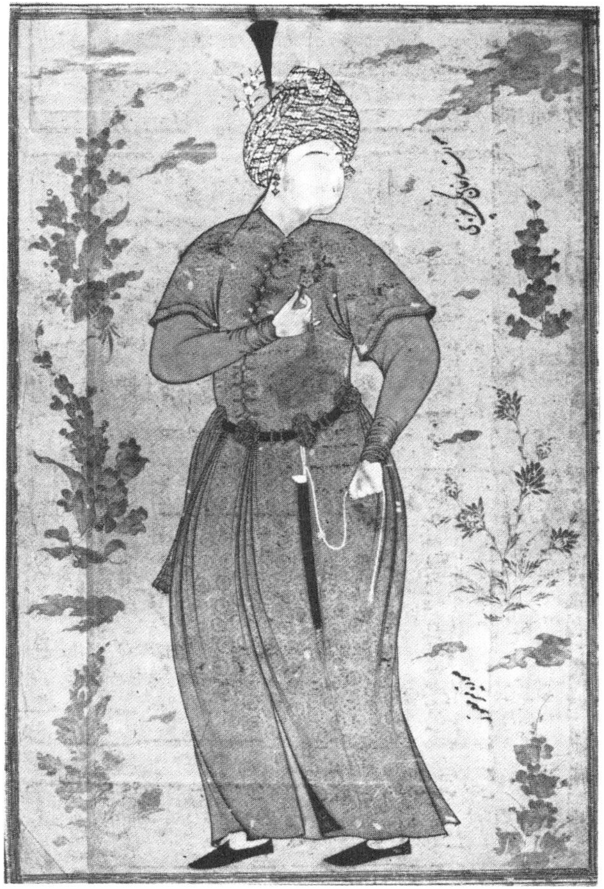

63*a* Portrait of a chamberlain, by Mīr Muṣavvir, Tabrīz, *c.* 1535–40. Size, 33 × 22 cm.

63*b* Album of the Amīr of Bukhārā, a young falconer at the court. Attributed to Ṣādiqī Beg, Qazvīn, *c.* 1590. Size, 16.2 × 7.8 cm.

64 *Shāh-nāma* of Firdausī, Bīzhan drawn up from the well by Rustam, Iṣfahān, 1614. Size, 36.4 × 20.5 cm.

65*a* A girl holding a fan, by Āqā Rīżā, Qazvīn, *c.* 1595. Size, 16.1 × 9.8 cm.

65*b* A girl holding a wine cup and flask, by Muḥammad Yūsuf, Iṣfahān, *c.* 1645. Size, 18 × 10.5 cm.

66 *Khamsa* of Niẓāmī, Shīrīn discovers the murder of her husband Khusrau, by Muḥammad Zamān, Iṣfahān, dated 1675.

67 Lacquer-painted book-cover, front side. Tabrīz, *c.* 1540. Size, 25 × 40 cm.

68 Tooled and gilt leather binding, one cover. Tabrīz, *c.* 1550–60. Size, 40 × 30 cm.

69 Panel of polychrome tiles in cuerda seca technique, from a pavilion in the Chahār Bāgh, Iṣfahān, *c.* 1640. Length, 1.98 m.

70 Steel helmet, with carved and gilt decoration: dedication to Shah 'Abbās I with the date 1625–6. Height, 27.3 cm.

71 *Shāh-nāma* of Firdausī, Rustam recovers Rakhsh. Herat style. Size, 35.3 × 28 cm. From the *Shāh-nāma* of Shah Ṭahmāsp, *c.* 1520–30.

72 *Shāh-nāma* of Firdausī, Bahrām Gūr pins the coupling onagers. Size, 20.7 × 17.2 cm. From the *Shāh-nāma* of Shah Ṭahmāsp.

Hermitage and the Louvre.[1] The restrained character of the decoration of this group which leaves considerable areas of metal plain has been attributed to the Ḥanafī milieu for which they were made;[2] but in fact it seems characteristic of the taste of the period. Already in 1374–5 a bronze ablution basin decorated only with inscriptions and arabesques was dedicated at the Friday mosque at Herat (1.74 cm. in diameter). It was signed by the maker Ḥasan b. ʿAlī b. Ḥasan b. ʿAlī Iṣfahānī made to the order of a *qalandar* in honour of his Kartid ruler, and is said to have been a model for the Turkistān basin of 1399.[3] Gold and silver inlay is also found freely applied to a numerous group of wine tankards originally supplied with covers, which were a speciality of Khurāsān in the Timurid period. The signed examples of 1457, 1461 and 1466 appear all to have been made by Khurāsānī craftsmen from Baharjan or Birjand, both within greater Khurāsān. One in the Hermitage is signed by Javān Bakht b. Ḥusain, while another in the British Museum bears under the base a dedication to Sulṭān Husain Bāīqarā, with the date 1497 (pl. 58*a*).[4] Many of these vessels include in their decoration verses by Ḥāfiẓ, and in one case by Qāsim al-Anvār (d. 837/1433–4), a mystical poet, who also freely used the symbol of the wine-cup. How early this tankard shape goes back in the 9th/15th century is not at present clear, but it is probably significant that it is found reproduced in a jade cup inscribed with the name and titles of Ulugh Beg Kūrgān,[5] and therefore datable between 1417 and 1440. The *tour de force* by which this cup is supplied with a jade handle only underlines that it must have originated in a metal shape.

Engraving alone was still used in elaborate all-over decoration in the later 9th/15th century, as on a dish with repoussé and engraved geometric interlace ornament surrounded by Persian verses in panels and stylised butterflies. This is dated 1496–7.[6] The precious metals were also frequently employed for the smaller vessels in domestic use, as we know from their representation in manuscripts, where they generally appear to be of gold. It is more likely that silver gilt was used, as in a

1 Kühnel, *Islamische Kleinkunst*, Abb. 147.

2 Yakubovsky, "Les artisans Iraniens", p. 285.

3 A.S. Melikian-Chirwani, in *Gazette des Beaux Arts* LXXIII (1969), 5–18.

4 *SPA*, pl. 1376b, dated 1461. Kühnel, *Islamische Kleinkunst*, Abb. 146, dated 1457, mistakenly attributed to Venice. Grube, *World of Islam*, p. 135, fig. 74.

5 *Gulbenkian Foundation: Exhibition of Islamic Art*, no. 28. The identification was made by R. Pinder-Wilson. *Persian Art: Calouste Gulbenkian Collection*, pl. 13. *Arts of Islam*, no. 114.

6 *Catalogue of the All-Union Exhibition on the Arts of the Timurid Period* (Samarqand, 1969), no. 106, dated 902/1496; d. 18; 5 cm. Cf. A.S. Melikian-Chirwani, *Le bronze iranien* (Paris, 1973), pp. 92–3.

pair of vessels now in the Hermitage Museum, a tall flask with a garlic mouth and a tankard (pl. 58*b*), more depressed in form than the inlaid brass ones. Both are lobed with chevron bands and both have arabesque lappets below the neck, like those on the great ablution bowl of 1399; and they probably date from the same period or rather earlier.[1] The same date is assigned to a heavy signet ring in the Metropolitan Museum with dragon-head terminals to the hoop.[2]

This illustrates the taste in Chinese design which is so conspicuous at this period in many of the arts, and above all in ceramics. Chinese porcelain had for centuries enjoyed an unrivalled reputation in Iran, and had provided a challenge to the potters which they found hard to meet. In the late fifteenth century at Herat the painter Ḥājjī Muḥammad, whom we have noted as a favourite of ʿAlī Shīr Navāʾī, succeeded after long experiments in producing vessels very similar to the Chinese in body, but less pure in colour.[3] Herat pottery of this period has not been identified, but there is little doubt that the reference here must be to blue and white,[4] since this appears as rival in esteem with the silver plate in the miniatures of the Timurid period. Naturally it is not possible to distinguish in them the Chinese imports from the local imitations. Much of the collection dedicated by Shah ʿAbbās I to the Ardabīl shrine in 1607 is of late 8th/14th and 9th/15th centuries, so that we have a good sample of the Chinese porcelain to be seen then in court circles. The copies or derivatives from them have nearly all come down to us in damaged state as fruits of excavation, and there are no more than stylistic criteria available for dating them. It can be said, however, that the majority are of later 9th/15th or 10th/16th century date and that they are less close to the Chinese prototypes than the copies made in Syria or Turkey.[5] It is probably due to the chance of more excavation of Timurid sites in

[1] *Arts of Islam*, no. 162. The tall flask (Hermitage Museum, K 586) resembles one depicted in the fragmentary *Kalīla va Dimna*, Istanbul University Library, Fy 1422, fol. 23v: Sakisian, *La miniature persane*, pl. VII. These miniatures, which depict other interesting vessels, are to be dated *c.* 1360–74.

[2] Dimand, *Handbook*, p. 154, fig. 93.

[3] Khwānd Amīr, in Barthold, *Four Studies* III, 66. Arnold, *Painting in Islam*, p. 139.

[4] A "signature" of Ḥājjī Muḥammad is found in combination with a tassel mark on a dish in the Victoria and Albert Museum decorated in Chinese taste: Lane, *Later Islamic Pottery*, pl. 81b, p. 100. Although this can date only from the third quarter of the 17th century, it may perhaps preserve an echo of a 15th century product by this master, for it is executed in green and black, an unusual colour scheme for this period; and the design of floral scrolls in the cavetto could reproduce in underglaze painting an original design incised on a black ground. If it could be shown that Ḥājjī Muḥammad worked in this style, he could be associated with the dated "Kubachi" dishes of 1465 and 1495, which could then be assigned to Khurāsān.

[5] See now Grube, "Notes".

Māvarā al-nahr than south of the Oxus that most of the blue and white so far published comes from sites now in Soviet Central Asia. In the Panjkent Museum is about half of a large dish which copies fairly closely a Chinese porcelain of the early 9th/15th century.[1] Otherwise the relationship is less direct and the dating consequently less exact. There is a good collection in the Hermitage Museum, mainly there attributed to the 9th/15th century. In one dish the Chinese motif of two fish head to tail has been added to a Chinese cloud pattern;[2] a pair of birds on another dish stand on little mounds instead of a branch, and are surrounded by a floral scroll. The most characteristic, however, show a symmetrical flower design as the centre of a formal pattern: in one case this is in the shape of a star filled with the Chinese wave pattern:[3] in others with a conventional floral design which resembles those found on the only other type of ceramics which can be attributed to the 9th/15th century. This has the design incised through a black slip ground under a turquoise on green glaze. This type also has been found in the Samarqand area, but the best known examples, bearing dates equivalent to 1468 and 1480, have been associated with the hill-town of Kubachi in Dāghistān in the Caucasus area.[4] It is improbable that this can be maintained as their place of origin; and the alternative of Tabrīz was proposed by Arthur Lane, largely on the basis of the signature of a potter called Ghaibī al-Taurīzī, who was working in Egypt in the 9th/15th century.[5] His name appears on blue and white pieces in Chinese taste, and his son signed a lamp decorated in exactly the same technique as was employed on the "Kubachi" dishes.[6] These symmetrical designs (in which calligraphy plays a significant part) are far removed from any Chinese prototype: so that it can be argued that the blue and white "Kubachi" type is earlier than the incised type with their secure dating in the second half of the 9th/15th century. It must be assumed that blue and white pottery was made in a number of different centres in the 15th century as it was also in the 16th. There is no evidence that polychrome wares in this style were made before the Safavid period.[7] Indeed, the only other type of ceramics

[1] Pope, *Chinese Porcelains*, pl. 35.

[2] *Arts of Islam*, no. 395.

[3] Pugachenkova and Rempel', *Istoriya Iskusstv Uzbekistana*, pl. 294.

[4] Reitlinger, "The Interim Period", p. 185, figs. 9, 12. Lane, *Later Islamic Pottery*, pp. 34–6, pl. 20. Zick-Nissen, "Die Tebriser Meister".

[5] Lane, *Later Islamic Pottery*, pp. 19, 31, 35, and pl. 17a.

[6] See above, p. 874 n. 4.

[7] Y. Brunhammer, in *Cahiers de la Céramique*, no. 5 (Sèvres, winter 1956–7), pp. 24–34, argues that the polychrome pieces could have influenced the early Iznik coloured wares. This seems impossible, however, in the light of recent research on the Iznik kilns by Aslanapa and others. Influence from Iznik is unmistakable in the Safavid polychrome ware.

to be attributed to the Timurid period are some residuary lustre wares of poor quality and, of course, the extremely important, varied and beautiful tiles, which must however be regarded as architectural decoration. The surviving examples of carved woodwork are also in a monumental, architectural style even when they are small objects like a Qur'ān stand in the Metropolitan Museum, dated 1360 and signed by an Iṣfahānī artist.[1] From the same mosque of Khwāja Aḥmad Yasavī in Turkistān city as the monumental bronzes already described, and contemporary with them, are two sets of doors dated 1394 and 1397,[2] in a monumental style but with freer and richer floral decoration that wood permits. A more elaborate technique with inlay in ebony, ivory and silver wire (now largely missing) was employed in the carved wood doors of the Gūr-i Mīr in Samarqand.[3] The special character of this school of architectural wood carving is achieved by counterpoint between two layers of relief arabesque.

[1] Dimand, *Handbook*, pp. 116–17, fig. 66.

[2] Denike, "Quelques monuments".

[3] Pugachenkova and Rempel', *Istoriya Iskusstv Uzbekistana*, pl. 293, for a pair of doors inlaid in ivory in the Shāh-i Zinda, Samarqand. For carved wood doors from Iran dated 1442, see *Arts of Islam*, no. 458.

CHAPTER 16 (*b*)

THE ARTS IN THE SAFAVID PERIOD

Shah Ismā'īl was of Türkmen blood on his mother's side and he deliberately made the Āq Quyūnlū capital of Tabrīz his first capital: he took over the machinery of government centred in that city, and it seems that he also took over the artists of the book from the school established there by Uzun Ḥasan and his son Ya'qūb (883–96/1479–90), which we have seen to have continued the Timurid tradition of Herat painting through the second half of the 9th/15th century. A key manuscript to illustrate the transition to the early Safavid style is the *Khamsa* of Niẓāmī copied for Ya'qūb at Tabrīz in 1481 (Topkapı Sarayı, Hazine 762),[1] to which a dozen miniatures were added later, apparently in 910/1504–5, according to a date on one of them; and evidently still at Tabrīz (pl. 36), for they show the Qizilbāsh projecting *kulāh*, the Ḥaidarī *tāj* adopted by Ḥaidar, father of Ismā'īl, as the sign of his adherents in the Ṣafaviyya. These miniatures preserve the elegance and decorative quality of the royal Türkmen school with no interest in spatial organisation. There is another well-known manuscript whose miniatures also show an early type of Safavid kulāh, one of them bearing the same date 910/1504-5 (pl. 59). This is a copy of the *Dastān i Jamāl u Jalāl* of the poet Āṣafī in the Uppsala University Library. These miniatures show the same disregard for spatial organisation, but a much greater interest in landscape, rendered in a particularly rich palette for the luxurious vegetation[2]. For all that, these miniatures are very old-fashioned compared with the contemporary school of Bihzād in Herat. These characteristics they share with a richly coloured miniature depicting the "Sleeping Rustam saved by his horse Rakhsh from a marauding Lion"[3] which has long been detached from an apparently unfinished manuscript of the *Shāh-nāma*. Here the landscape setting has become the main interest, though the animal drawing is sensitive and sympathetic. If we are correct in attributing this miniature to the opening years of Ismā'īl's reign in Tabrīz, which had become his

[1] See above, p. 863 and n. 1.

[2] K.V. Zettersteen and C.J. Lamm, *Mohammed Āṣafī, the story of Jamāl and Jalāl* (Uppsala, 1948). *Arts of Islam*, no. 591 and pl. 9.

[3] Gray, *Persian Painting from miniatures of the XIII–XVI centuries*, pl. 7.

capital in 907/1501, it can be seen what a splendid painting tradition he inherited. In 916/1510 he captured Herat from Muḥammad Shaibānī Khān, whom he killed, and so became heir also to the great Timurid school patronised by Sulṭān Ḥusain Bāīqarā and adorned by the master Bihzād. It was the union of these two traditions which made possible the achievements of the Safavid school at Tabrīz during the next thirty-five years. After 1510 we have no dated manuscript of importance from this scriptorium until the accession of Shah Ṭahmāsp in 930/1524. Although he was then only twelve years old, he showed an immediate interest in painting, for he had already received lessons in miniature painting from the leading master Sulṭān Muḥammad[1] and was ready to give his patronage to painters and illuminators. The latter part of the reign of Ismā'īl, after his defeat by the Ottoman Turks in 920/1514 at the battle of Chāldirān, was not a period when we would expect initiative or innovation, yet it is to this period that is attributed the diploma appointing Bihzād as head of the court library staff in the year 928/1522.[2] It seems that this date is not to be relied upon, for the document has been preserved only as a specimen of official style from the pen of the famous historian Khwānd Amīr (b. *c.* 880/1475, d. 942/1535). He was a protégé of 'Alī Shīr Navā'ī, the famous minister of Sulṭān Ḥusain at Herat until his death in 906/1501; and his first work was completed in 905/1499–1500,[3] from which period the farmān appointing Bihzād might well be expected to date, and not from the Safavid period.[4] Bihzād is remembered as of Herat, where he died in 942/1535-6 in the early part of the reign of Shah Ṭahmāsp, for whom he is said to have adorned a *Khamsa* of Niẓāmī with miniatures.[5] Moreover, there is sufficient evidence to show that a school of painting continued in Herat in a more conservative style than in Tabrīz. It was probably not before 1528 that the remaining artists were carried off from there to the Shaibanid court at Bukhārā, where they maintained the Bihzadian tradition well into the second half of the 10th/16th century. From the period before that date there have survived manuscripts written by Herat scribes and with miniatures in the Herat style,

[1] Qāżī Aḥmad, p. 181.

[2] Qazvīnī and Bouvat, "Deux documents inédits". Arnold, *Painting in Islam*, pp. 150–1.

[3] *LHP* III, 435.

[4] Information through Dr Paul Luft from an unpublished doctoral thesis by G. Herrmann, who discusses the contents of the *Nāma-yi Nāmī* and points out that all, including some which are certainly of the period of Ḥusain Bāīqarā, bear the same date, 928/1522.

[5] Qāżī Aḥmad, p. 135

such as a *Būstān* of Sa'dī copied by 'Alī al-Ḥusainī in 1519 at Herat and now in the Museum of Turkish and Islamic Art in Istanbul (no.1019),[1] while from a manuscript of the *Khamsa* of Amīr Khusrau Dihlavī copied by the Herat scribe 'Alā' al-Dīn Muḥammad in Balkh in 1504, some detached miniatures now in the Metropolitan Museum[2] and the Louvre[3] must be assigned to Herat about the year 1520. Soon after that date, in 1523, comes the first known illuminated manuscript of the Bukhārā school, the *Mihr u Mushtarī* of 'Assār in the Freer Gallery at Washington.[4] The transition from the first group of miniatures to the four in the 'Assār is direct; but the latter are superior in quality of design and in draughtsmanship. In both groups the simple landscape is no more than a setting for the figures, of whom even the minor ones reveal a humanity or a pathos unknown in the Safavid court style, with its interest in the rhythmical, the decorative and the gorgeous. The Herat tradition of the school of Bihzād is the purer, and, so long as it preserved the interior feeling, the most perfect expression of the miniature art in Iran, or indeed anywhere else. When it lost that integrity of vision, as it did later in Bukhārā, it became only a mirror of the old style, lacking in warmth, invention and personality.

As has been said, Shah Ismā'īl himself spent the earlier part of his reign in campaigns, but, after his disastrous defeat by the Ottomans in 920/1514, he withdrew increasingly from the personal direction of all affairs of state both civil and military. As has been pointed out in Chapter 5, the tradition of civil administration by the Persian bureaucracy was continued as a measure of policy and, although the language of the court continued to be Turki, the tradition of Persian culture was fully maintained by the Safavids. It seems that some part of the royal library was carried away as loot by the Ottomans in 1514, for there are several outstanding examples of the Türkmen royal style in the libraries of Istanbul, for instance in the Topkapı Sarayı Library a *Khamsa* of Niẓāmī dated 886/1481 (Hazine 762) and another dated 881/1476 (Hazine 761), and an Amīr Khusrau Dihlavī dated 883/1478 (Hazine 795); but it was probably only in the latter part of the reign of Ṭahmāsp that there was an exodus of artists of the book to the

[1] Çiğ, *Kataloğu*, p. 70, no. 10, pls. XV, XVI.

[2] Stchoukine, *Manuscrits Ṣafavīs*, p. 56, no. 7, where these miniatures are attributed to Tabrīz, 1525–7. Marteau and Vever 1, pls. LVII, LXIX. Sakisian, *La miniature persane*, fig. 110.

[3] Stchoukine, *Les miniatures persanes: Musée National du Louvre*, pls. VI, VII.

[4] Gray, *Persian Painting* (1961), p. 149, and *The Arts of the Book*, pls. LXXI–LXXII.

Ottoman court.[1] On the contrary, under Shah Ismāʿīl it seems that the royal library staff was strengthened by the adhesion of masters from Khurāsān. Although there is no work which can be attributed securely to the greatest of these, Bihzād, during the quarter of a century of his life as a subject of the Safavids before his death in 1535 at the age of about eighty, his influence is clearly to be seen directly in Herat and indirectly at the Safavid court.

The director of the early Safavid *kitābkhāna* seems on the other hand to have been Sulṭān Muḥammad, a native of Tabrīz and not a pupil of Bihzād or of Mīrak. The best attested fact about him is that he instructed the future Shah Ṭahmāsp in the art of painting, and was so engaged when Bihzād first arrived in Tabrīz from Herat,[2] which was not likely to have been before 1523, since Ṭahmāsp was born only in 1515. Sulṭān Muḥammad must therefore have been in charge of the court library under Shah Ismāʿīl and during the first half of the reign of Ṭahmāsp. There is good reason to think that the extraordinary achievement of the preparation of the Houghton (formerly Rothschild) *Shāh-nāma* with its two hundred and fifty six miniatures was carried out under his direction.[3] These miniatures richly illustrate the transition from the Türkmen to the Safavid court style, as well as the impact on the Tabrīz atelier of the arrival of Timurid-trained artists bringing the style of Herat to enrich it.

That Sulṭān Muḥammad himself was at work on this from an early period is strongly suggested by the miniature representing the "Court of Gayūmarṡ" (fol. 20v), in correspondence with the account preserved by Dūst Muḥammad of this artist having painted in a royal *Shāh-nāma* "people clothed in leopard skins such that the hearts of the boldest of painters were grieved" by the marvellous skill shown by the miniaturist (pl. 37).[4] This miniature is indeed a work of extraordinary finesse, and it is to be attributed to the very early 1520s. Such an immense undertaking can hardly have taken less than ten years to accomplish: the only date in the manuscript is introduced into the architecture of the miniature on fol. 516r, and is in figures "934 H.", equivalent to 1527–8. It seems fair to assume with Welch,[5] that this folio is so far on

[1] But see K. Otto-Dorn, *Das islamische Iznik* (Berlin, 1941), pp. 180–4, 194; Sakisian, in *Burlington Magazine* LXXXVII (1945), 224–32.

[2] Qāżī Aḥmad, pp. 180–1.

[3] Sakisian, *La miniature persane*, p. 108, quoting ʿAlī.

[4] Welch and Dickson, *The Houghton Shahnameh* I, colour pl. 8; *Wonders of the Age*, p. 17.

[5] Welch, *A King's Book of Kings*, p.16. There is now no colophon. Formerly it was assumed to have been copied in 944/1537 by Qāsim Ashrī : Martin, *Miniature Painting* II, 63.

in the manuscript that the work on it must have been in progress for a number of years already. He proposed a date in the early 1520s for its start and in the mid 1530s for its conclusion. I would prefer to assume dates from about 1520 to about 1530 for its production: for it seems to me that, quite apart from the numerous miniatures which echo the Türkmen court style, the majority are more closely related to two well-known manuscripts of the 1520s, the Paris Mīr 'Alī Shīr of 1526 and the Tehran *Ẓafar-nāma* of 1529, rather than to the royal *Khamsa* of Niẓāmī of 1539–43 in the British Library. A few do indeed recall the Ḥāfiẓ of Sām Mīrzā of about 1530–3,[1] but that would not invalidate the dates suggested for the temporal limits of its production. Few of the miniatures appear nearly as advanced as those in the Niẓāmī of 1539–43, which nonetheless contains two miniatures attributed by "signatures" to Sulṭān Muḥammad. One of these depicting Bahrām Gūr hunting is quite comparable with fol. 568 of the *Shāh-nāma*, which happens to treat also an exploit of Bahrām (pl. 72). The rock masses are more clearly defined, but otherwise there is no great difference between these two hunting scenes in conception of figures in landscape. Sulṭān Muḥammad was joined by his son Mīrzā 'Alī in illustrating the royal Niẓāmī, and he is likely to have given up the directorship of the library staff to Mīr Muṣavvir about 1540. He too is recorded to have worked on a royal *Shāh-nāma* manuscript which may be that in the Houghton collection. This would have allowed this latter artist a term of about ten years before his migration to the Mughal court soon after the arrival in Kābul of the emperor Humāyūn in 956/1549.

Typical of a number of the earlier miniatures in this manuscript are folios 21v, 22v and 23v,[2] which could only be the work of artists trained at the court of the Āq Quyūnlū, with their fecundity of vegetation, rather large figures in relation to the horses and with heads large in relation to the bodies. Trees, clouds and rocks are highly stylised, but both in colour and movement a certain gaiety pervades these scenes. Gold is freely used for the skies. This style is found only in the first half of the manuscript. Herat influence appears unmistakably in a few pages, which show smaller figures, more important architecture and tinted rocks in the earlier Timurid tradition (pl. 38; fol. 89v). These two kinds of miniature, both rich and exuberant, dominate the

[1] Binyon *et al.*, *Persian Miniature Painting*, pl. LXXXIVA. Welch, *A King's Book of Kings*, p. 57. *Arts of Islam*, no. 598b.

[2] Welch, *Wonders of the Age*, pp. 52–3, no. 9, and *A King's Book of Kings*, pp. 92–7.

manuscript; but there are some more forward-looking, with more open composition and fewer figures. There is an immense variety of invention and wealth of detail, so that the cumulative effect is quite overwhelming. The frame round the text area is strongly accented, even in most cases where it is exceeded by extending the miniature, generally into one of the side margins. These extensions are usually themselves rectangular and thus serve to throw the weight of the composition onto that side of the page. A few are extended rectangularly at the top as well; and the importance to the artist of the strong framing lines is demonstrated by their occasional use as architectural verticals in the compositions. Only seldom is the Timurid habit of showing the turret on a pavilion or a tree-top free against the blank paper of the upper margin still used, while a very few instances occur of a free extension on more than one side (pl. 71), a practice that was to grow towards the middle of the century. Indeed, the weakness of this new style was its diffusion, loss of concentration on the subject and consequent failure of dramatic or emotional interest. Technically they were unequalled, and in colour harmony unmatched in the art of the world.

The great achievement of this masterpiece of Persian manuscript production has been so enormously damaged by its wanton and disgraceful dismemberment that the overriding unity of the book, a sign of a mature and well-organised workshop, is greatly reduced by the extraction of the miniatures and their separation from the text. The weight and density of these near whole-page miniatures were calculated as balanced by the facing page of text. Only three out of all the miniatures occur as facing pages in a single opening. By far the greater number of pages with miniatures allow of the inclusion of some text as well: and the layout provides many alternative methods of their combination, varying from complete separation through partial continuation of miniature between the text columns to the insertion of formal arabesque illumination in these areas; in each case with the aim of preserving the integrity of both picture and text to a maximum degree. In two instances (fols. 385b and 638b)[1] the ground of four text areas has been gilded to avoid compromising the stability of the architecture depicted.

Similarly the unity of text and paintings is matched by an overall

[1] *Persian Miniatures: an exhibition of seventeen paintings from the Houghton Shahnameh* (T. Agnew & Sons Ltd., London, 1979), no. 13, pp. 36–7. Christie's, London, *Catalogue*, 17 Nov. 1976, D, pp. 28–33 (seven fols. from the Houghton *Shāh-nāma*).

unity of style and palette no doubt imposed by the director of the court atelier, Sulṭān Muḥammad. The house style may be defined as diffused and decorative; spacious and outward looking; in contrast to the Timurid style of Herat under Sulṭān Ḥusain, dominated by the introvert ṣūfī interest centred round the poet Jāmī and evident in the work of Bihzād and his school, with their tightly knit and cool harmonies and enclosed compositions.

The miniature on fol. 516b[1] is signed by Mīr Muṣavvir and illustrates the romance of Ardashīr and Gulnār, who are here seen together in bed in a brilliantly tiled pavilion at Ray. It is a scene of complete rest, with sickle moon and knotted clouds in the night sky. Passion is conveyed only by the warm colouring of the bedchamber, while the rope by which Gulnār had scaled the wall hangs slackly and the handmaids sleep. The artist's signature is in the tiled inscriptional frieze.

The other signed painting, by Dūst Muḥammad (fol. 512b),[2] whose importance as a literary source is discussed below, illustrates the story of Haftād and the Worm. This is a diffused landscape, the central feature being a town set in a valley with much coming and going at the gate. In the lower left corner the story is enacted of the finding of the magic worm by a party of girls spinning outside the gate. This is one of the most advanced compositions in the book and probably one of the latest, prefiguring the extended landscapes of the mid-century. It is also notable because it was later copied by a Mughal artist working for the young prince Salīm, afterwards the Emperor Jahāngīr, about 1600.[3]

More central in style to the Houghton manuscript and no doubt rather earlier, is the scene on fol. 42b, where Farīdūn tests the courage of his sons by confronting them with a dragon.[4] It is interesting to compare this miniature with a hunting scene in the 'Alī Shīr Navā'ī manuscript of 1526. Here Bahrām Gūr is shown performing his feats of skill before the two Greek slave-girl musicians.[5] Cary Welch has attributed these miniatures to Sulṭān Muḥammad himself, and no doubt both are of royal quality; the Bahrām Gūr composition is the more complex with its use of échelon for the file of bowmen on one side of

[1] Welch, *Wonders of the Age*, pp. 96–7, no. 30, and *A King's Book of Kings*, pp. 169–71.

[2] Welch, *Wonders of the Age*, pp. 98–101, and *A King's Book of Kings*, pp. 173–4.

[3] E. Kühnel and H. Goetz, *Indian Book Paintings from Jahangir's Album in the State Library, Berlin* (London, 1926).

[4] Welch, *Wonders of the Age*, pp. 62–3, and *A King's Book of Kings*, pp. 121–2.

[5] Blochet, *Musulman Painting*, pl. CXXIV.

the foreground and of serving men on the other side, and of heads of beaters appearing over the horizon behind; features also seen in the richly illustrated *Ẓafar-nāma* of 1529. But the Farīdūn excels in its splendid involvement of the huge dragon's body in the rocky landscape contrasted with the open plain, where the horsemen move with greater sense of space than in the tapestry-like Paris miniature.

A second miniature in this Navā'ī manuscript, the spirited battle scene, "Iskandar routing the army of Dārā",[1] illustrates the re-use of successful compositions and groupings.[2] In this case a central group of a horseman fighting off the attack of two foot soldiers was derived ultimately from a *Khamsa* of Niẓāmī datable 1490 in the British Library (Add. 25,900) and signed by Bihzād, and generally believed to be his work. This small but vigorous composition was re-used first in the Niẓāmī of 1525 in the Metropolitan Museum, for which three other groups of combatants were also taken, in addition to that in the Paris Navā'ī. That this work of 1525 was in fact the transmitter of the Bihzadian composition is proved by the presence in the Navā'ī miniature of a statuesque figure of a horseman holding an arrow on the right side, found in identical pose and position, though here bearded, in the Metropolitan page. This is a somewhat stiff work, unlike the Navā'ī Battle scene which is as vigorous as the Bihzād miniature, but fully in the open manner of the early Ṭahmāsp period.

A new more structural treatment of architecture was advanced in a painting signed by Sulṭān Muḥammad in the Ḥāfiẓ of Sām Mīrzā of about 1534.[3] In this miniature, as in the advanced paintings of the Houghton *Shāh-nāma*, large numbers of figures are introduced, each with a characteristic gesture or stance, but all related to one another, as in this depiction of the "Feast of 'Īd" (pl. 60). No doubt it was on the basis of this signed work that Welch attributed to Sulṭān Muḥammad the "Żahhāk told his fate" in the Houghton manuscript (fol. 29b).[4] The "Feast" is a far simpler composition, but the figures of courtiers and attendants show the same kind of chain relationship and the framing of the main action by a brilliantly decorated *aivān* with roof pavilion, is equally effective in both. No doubt, in spite of its early position in the manuscript, this miniature must be one of the latest in date, about 1530. Even more forward-looking is the "Bārbad hiding in a tree" on fol. 731b

1 *Ibid.*, pl. CXXV.
2 Grube, *The Classical Style*, p. 33. *Arts of Islam*, no. 595b.
3 Welch, *Wonders of the Age*, pp. 126–7, no. 43.
4 *MMAB*, April 1971, pl. 2, p. 347.

with its extraordinary night sky with wind-blown cloud streaming into the left margin. This miniature has been attributed by Welch to Mīrzā 'Alī, the son of Sulṭān Muḥammad,[1] a claim which can be supported by the two signed by this artist in the British Library Niẓāmī of 1539–43, one of which even happens to depict Bārbad, but here as court musician.

This second royal manuscript, a *Khamsa* of Niẓamī copied between 1539 and 1543 by Shāh Maḥmūd Nīshāpūrī, has survived with thirteen contemporary miniatures (British Library, Or.2,265).[2] Two royal manuscripts are mentioned by the near contemporary Dūst Muḥammad as "so beautiful that the pen is inadequate to describe their merits": he adds that the two Sayyids, Āqā Mīrak and Mīr Muṣavvir, painted the illustrations to them.[3] Evidently not all the miniatures can be by these two hands alone, but the Niẓāmī opens with an illustration to the fables of King Nūshīrvān and his vizier and the owls on the ruined village, which bears a convincing signature of Mīr Muṣavvir (pl. 61), introduced into the field of the painting, as they seldom are at this period. As in most of the illustrations to the *Khamsa*, the landscape is the most striking part, notable here for the touches of realism in the fallen tilework and the introduction of a stork's nest and snakes as well as the owls perched on the ruins. The gorgeous sunset sets a fashion which continues through the rest of the century. The other miniatures of this book bear only librarians' attributions, but several of these are acceptable, including one to Āqā Mīrak of "Khusrau enthroned": and one to Sulṭān Muḥammad of "Khusrau's first sight of Shīrīn bathing". The latter is the most beautiful illustration of this famous and favourite subject with the miniaturist that has come down to us; for in it landscape and figures alike sustain the lyrical feeling of the romantic scene. In the former the courtiers of Khusrau are depicted in the sumptuous dress of the court of Ṭahmāsp, while the great throne arch has become a mere screen through which the garden background can be better shown. Mīr Sayyid 'Alī, son of Mīr Muṣavvir, is represented by a pastoral scene of a nomad encampment in which are set the three superior tents of Lailā and her attendants, where she receives the feigned mad Majnūn led in chains by a beggar woman. This green scene is the most advanced composition of the series, built on a double axis from the corners and combining realistic detail of herdsmen and embroiderers with the romantic theme of the

[1] Welch, *Wonders of the Age*, pp. 114–5, no. 38.

[2] Binyon, *Poems of Niẓami*. Gray, *Persian painting from miniatures of the XIII–XVI centuries*, pls. 11,12.

[3] Dūst Muḥammad, in Binyon *et al.*, *Persian Miniature Painting*, p. 186.

story illustrated, in a balanced tension. In India, where he went to found a school, the realism increased, but the romance quickly faded.

There are two primary sources for the history of the arts of the book dating from the 10th/16th century, both of them reliable when writing of events and persons within their own experience but less so when dealing with earlier periods. Nonetheless, they are the best sources which have come down to us for the traditional history of miniature painting as preserved in the Safavid studios of the art. Even where they cannot be accepted literally they throw light on the manner in which the profession and its patrons looked upon that tradition.

Maulānā Dūst Muḥammad was a native of Herat, a highly esteemed calligrapher and also skilled in music and painting according to the authority of Sām Mīrzā.[1] He was employed by Bahrām Mīrzā (b. 923/1517, d. 956/1549), brother of Shah Ṭahmāsp and a notable patron of the arts of the book. His account of "Past and Present Painters" is preserved as a preface to the *muraqqa‘* bearing the name of Bahrām Mīrzā in the Topkapı library in Istanbul and is dated 1544.[2] It is naturally biased towards Khurāsān and Herat in particular, but for that reason is authoritative on the history of Herat painting under Sulṭān Ḥusain. On the early Safavid period he is also naturally well-informed. For he worked in the *kitābkhāna* of Shah Ṭahmāsp and instructed his sister Mihin-bānū, called "Princess Sulṭānim", in calligraphy. However, in general Dūst Muḥammad writes as an heir to the main stream of Timurid tradition fixed in Herat from the time of Bāīsunqur onwards.

The second source, Qāżī Aḥmad, who praises Dūst Muḥammad as a calligrapher but does not mention his preface as a source for his own account, produced the first version of his treatise on calligraphers and painters fifty years later, in 1596. He was born about 1550 into a family of Sayyids of Qum; spent his early life in Mashhad, where his father Sharaf al-Dīn Ḥusain was Mīr Munshī in the service of Ibrāhīm Mīrzā, son of the above Bahrām Mīrzā and thus nephew and son-in-law of Shah Ṭahmāsp and a man of learning and culture. The son therefore had

[1] Sām Mīrzā's *Tuḥfa*, a treatise on painters, illuminators and calligraphists dating from 957/1550–1, has been analysed by Mahfuz ul-Haq. The most valuable biographical information it supplies (pp. 242–3) relates to Āqā Mīrak, "at present... the leader and the guide of the artists of the Court" of Shah Ṭahmāsp; Mānī of Shīrāz, at first a goldsmith, later a poet, and "unrivalled in painting *(muṣavvirī)* and peerless in drawing *(naqqāshī)*"; Qadīmī of Gīlān, "good in painting, but in poetry also he does not consider himself inferior to others"; Mīr Shukrī, a Sayyid of Shīrāz, "knows book-binding and *lapis lazuli* colour work"; Qardādmish "sells china at Tabrīz."

[2] Abridged translation in Binyon *et al.*, *Persian Miniature Painting*, pp. 183–8.

personal knowledge of the patronage of Ibrāhīm until his political murder in 1577. The Mīrzā had been the principal patron of the arts of the book during the previous sixteen years following the fall of his cousin Sām Mīrzā in 1561. Apart from his personal experience in Mashhad during these years of his youth, Qāżī Aḥmad stayed in the capital Qazvīn as a minor official through the reigns of Ismā'īl II (984–5/1576–7) and Muḥammad Khudābanda (985–95/1578–87). In addition to personal knowledge Qāżī Aḥmad drew upon two written sources, a verse epistle by the famous calligrapher Sulṭān 'Alī Mashhadī, concerning the craft of writing and the rules of teaching it and possessed of little historical value,[1] and the compilation by Sām Mīrzā, son of Ismā'īl I. The treatise was first completed in 1015/1596 and was extensively revised and enlarged by 1606, when a second version was completed. It is pertinent to note how frequently leading calligraphers (including royal ones like Ibrāhīm and Bāīsunqur, the sons of Shāh Rukh, and Shah Ṭahmāsp) are recorded as having designed monumental inscriptions on buildings, for execution in tilework or glazed brick. To exemplify how closely connected the decoration of manuscripts and buildings was felt to be, it is said that Ibrāhīm Astarābādī wrote a distich in nasta'līq "as an *unvān* on the tiled gateway of the mausoleum of Fāṭima at Qum".[2] Qāżī Aḥmad also constantly illustrates the mobility of the artists of the book, in response to offers of patronage, and their intimacy with ruling princes. Professor Minorsky, who produced a valuable edition of Qāżī Aḥmad's treatise, remarks in his introduction that the plan of this book was far from original, and that it closely resembled that of a Turkish account by the poet and historian Muṣṭafā 'Alī, the *Manāqib-i hünerverān*, composed about ten years earlier. Since this was clearly no more than a compilation, it presupposes the existence of earlier sources, of which the only one mentioned by Qāẓī Aḥmad was written by Sīmī Nīshāpūrī,[3] a calligrapher of Mashhad of about the middle of the 9th/15th century, who wrote on the epistolary art and on the arts in general.

In addition to monographs, information about the history of the arts of the book is to be found in the pages of general historians; and Sir Thomas Arnold published extracts from two authors, Khwānd Amīr and Iskandar Munshī.[4] The latter carried his account down to the death of Shah 'Abbās I, whereas the former ends his account with the fatal year

[1] Incorporated in Qāżī Aḥmad, pp. 106–25.
[2] *Ibid.*, p. 89.
[3] *Ibid.*, p. 19.
[4] Arnold, *Painting in Islam*, pp. 139–44.

913/1507 when Muḥammad Shaibānī Khān captured Herat. Arnold also translated the relevant passage form Mīrzā Muḥammad Ḥaidar Dughlāt (b. 905/1499, d. 958/1551).[1] Apart from what can be deduced from these biographical accounts we know almost nothing about the organisation of the kitābkhāna until the last part of the period treated here, for which the *Tazkirat al-mulūk* of about 1725 supplies some comparative statistics for the staff of all the royal workshops, including the library. At that time we learn that the salaried staff could undertake private commissions whenever there was not enough official work to occupy all their time.[2] This may well be a practice which grew up only in this period of decadence; but, on the other hand, it might have been true of earlier periods, and thus account for duplicates of compositions by the same hand. For the later Safavid period there is also some evidence from Western travellers about the conditions of painters and other artists of the book and the way that their work was organised. Chardin gives some idea of the scale of employment in the thirty-two royal workshops, mentioning for instance that in his time there were seventy-two painters on the strength of the establishment, all enjoying an annual salary, partly paid in free messing; as compared with one hundred and eighty tailors. He also describes the manner of recruitment to these establishments by scrutiny of specimens of the work submitted by candidates first to the head of each specialist workshop, and then for confirmation by the *nāzir* in charge.[3] Appointments were normally made for life, and the children of those on the royal employ had the chance of being accepted into the establishment at twelve to fifteen years of age. This general set-up probably dates from the administrative reforms of Shah 'Abbās I and is probably more systematic than previously, but essentially throughout the Safavid period most artists of the book must have been supported out of the personal revenues of the shah or of one of the princes.

However, in Chardin's time there evidently was some private enterprise in manuscript production; for he mentions the rates charged by copyists of manuscripts, of which the highest was of four *'abbāsīs* for a thousand couplets.[4] There was also a good market for second-hand books in which high prices were paid for fine calligraphy, illumination and miniatures. Elsewhere, he writes of the supreme quality of the

[1] *BSOS* v (1930), and reprinted in Binyon *et al.*, *Persian Miniature Painting*, pp. 189–91.
[2] Minorsky, *Tadhkirat al-Mulūk*, p. 21.
[3] Chardin v, 499–500, and VII, 329ff.
[4] *Ibid.* IV, 281.

paper used for painting and of the brilliance of the pigments, which are unfading; also of the superiority of the medium, admired by Western masters, made of gum sandarac, a tree resin, and linseed oil.[1] He does not omit to mention the use of lapis lazuli, and pays tribute to the virtuosity of the line and the excellence of the arabesque work.

A third source for the history of miniature painting in the Safavid period is now available in the writings of one of the leading masters of the later 10th/16th century who was also a poet and composed in Persian verse a treatise on painting techniques, Ṣādiqī Beg (b.940/1533–4, d.1018/1609–10).[2] He belonged to one of the Turkish tribal groups which had made possible the Safavid rise to power and his native language was Chaghatai; in that language he wrote a biographical account of leading poets, painters and connoisseurs of the Safavid period. Although by family tradition a soldier, he was fired with the ambition to practise the art of Bihzād and persuaded Muẓaffar ʿAlī (d.1576), his nephew and pupil, to teach him at Qazvīn in 1568, where he was moving in court circles. He was afterwards in the employ of Ismāʿīl II during his brief reign (984-5/1576–7), but at his death withdrew to Hamadān and later to Lāhījān in Gīlān and to Yazd. He had, however, so much impressed the young Shah ʿAbbās when in Herat that on his accession in 995/1587 Ṣādiqī was made head of the library (*kitābdār*) to the shah, a post he held for the next ten years. His position and his travels gave Ṣādiqī a close knowledge of the leading personalities in the cultural world of Iran in the last third of the sixteenth century. His writings do not of course give us biographies of the leading artists of the book, but they do give vivid sketches of their personalities, reputations and accomplishments; and they are outspoken and anecodotic. His work therefore does not have the historical importance of Dūst Muḥammad or Qāżī Aḥmad.

One of the crucial artistic documents for the understanding of Safavid book-painting in the mid-sixteenth century is the manuscript of the *Haft aurang* of Jāmī in the Freer Gallery, Washington.[3] The 303 folios took nine years to complete between 963/1556 and 972/1565, and according to the colophons were divided between three centres, Mashhad, Qazvīn and Herat. It is a princely manuscript prepared for

[1] *Ibid.* IV, 271ff, and V, 204.
[2] See Gandjeï, "Notes" ; also Welch, *Artists for the Shah*, pp. 41–74.
[3] Stchoukine, *Manuscrits Ṣafavīs*, p. 127 and pls. XL, XLII, XLIII. Gray, *Persian Painting* (1961), pp.187–90.

Ibrāhīm Mīrzā, son of Bahrām Mīrzā, a favourite nephew of Shah Ṭahmāsp, who appointed him governor of Mashhad in 963/1556, when he was thirteen years old, and gave him his daughter Gauhar Sulṭān in marriage. Ibrāhīm took with him to Mashhad Maulānā Malik, a renowned master of calligraphy, to be the first head of his kitābkhāna;[1] but he was recalled by the shah to Qazvīn in 966/1559. He had meanwhile copied the first two parts of the Freer *Haft aurang*, while the rest was shared among four other leading calligraphers. That the miniatures are contemporary with the text is shown by the dedications to Ibrāhīm to be seen on three of these (fols. 38b, 132a and 162a), all of which occur in sections copied at Mashhad. We know from the account of Qāżī Aḥmad that the leading painters working in the princely governor's service at this time were Shaikh Muḥammad, 'Alī Asghar and 'Abd-Allāh.[2] The lastnamed is recorded as a master of ornamental gilding and illumination. For this reason his title was *muẕahhib* (ornamentalist or gilder), with which speciality he is also mentioned by Iskandar Munshī. The Freer manuscript is one of the first of which we can confidently say that the gold-decorated margins must be contemporary with the book.[3] Indeed, this practice of floral embellishment may probably have started only about this date, just at the time of the foundation of the Mughal school, in which also it became a special fashion. It is to be noticed that the marginal decoration of the royal Niẓāmī of 1539–43 was supplied at a date subsequent to the completion of the miniatures, which have been cut out and remounted. 'Alī Asghar, a native of Kāshān, was Qāżī Aḥmad's own instructor in miniature painting and, according to Iskandar Munshī, specialised or excelled in landscape (streets and trees). Shaikh Muḥammad was a calligrapher as well as a painter. He is said to have followed (or, perhaps, imitated) the Chinese; but that may probably be intended merely as a compliment to his skill rather than as an indication of any actual interest in Chinese painting. Indeed, on the contrary, Iskandar Munshī mentions that he introduced the fashion of imitating European painting. In any case he seems to have been especially a figure painter. There is in fact no identifiable European influence in Persian painting before the 11th/17th century. Since we may take the

[1] Qāżī Aḥmad, p. 142. [2] *Ibid.*, pp. 187–90. Arnold, *Painting in Islam*, p. 143.

[3] M.S.Simpson, "The production and patronage of the *Haft Aurang* of Jāmī in the Freer Gallery of Art", *AO* XIII (1983), 98, reports her discovery of the signature of 'Abd-Allāh al-Shīrāzī on fol. 84b, a two-page *'unvān*.

miniatures in the Freer *Haft aurang* as certain evidence for the work of this group of artists in Mīrzā Ibrāhīm's library, it is right to scrutinise it for evidence of style.

Stchoukine divided the twenty-eight miniatures into two groups, a first of sixteen which he regards as old-fashioned, not much different from the illustrations of the royal Niẓāmī of 1539–43; the other of twelve representing a further development, more dynamic and with some bold experiments in composition and striking realism in some of the figures (nos. 8, 11, 12, 14, 19, 22, 23, 24, 25, 26, 27). Nos. 23 and 24 belong to the *Lailā u Majnūn,* copied at Herat in 972/1565; no. 19 to the *Salmān u Absāl*, copied in 968/1561; while the *Yūsuf u Zulaikhā* (nos. 7–12) was copied at Mashhad in 964/1557. For comparison with the later group we have the eight miniatures of the *Garshāsp-nāma* (British Library, Or. 12,985) dated 981/1573 from Qazvīn,[1] three of them signed by the painters Muẓaffar 'Alī, Ṣādiqī Beg and Zain al-'Ābidīn, masters of the royal library of Shah Ṭahmāsp and later of Shah 'Abbās. These are, however, much more crisp in drawing and more coherent in organisation. If we can follow the distinction into two groups proposed by Stchoukine, the latter are more simplified with greater attention to figure painting (pl. 62), a characteristic which is to be taken up by Muḥammadī in his incomparably delicate drawing of 1578. Compare the "Majnūn's first glimpse of Lailā" (*Haft aurang,* fol. 231),[2] with its cow-milking in the background, with the Louvre "Pastoral Scene" of Muḥammadī and the ploughing oxen.[3] The earlier group continue the rich counterplay of numerous figures in a spacious setting which had been characteristic of the Niẓāmī of 1539–43, with some clear indebtedness to it in detail. The later group is also not far removed in style from the miniatures of a dispersed manuscript of the *Shāh-nāma,*[4] which bears contemporary attributions to Naqdī, Siyāvush, Ṣādiqī and Zain al-'Ābidīn, who are all known as court painters. All except Naqdī are mentioned by Qāżī Aḥmad[5] as men of an earlier generation than his; while Iskandar Munshī records Zain al-'Ābidīn, Naqdī and Ṣādiqī

[1] *BMQ* xxxi (1966–7), 27–31. Robinson, *Persian Miniature Painting*, no. 48, pp. 22–4.

[2] Welch, *Persian Painting*, pl. 45, an illustration to the *Lailā u Majnūn* copied in Herat in 972/1565.

[3] Robinson, *Drawings of the Masters*, pl. 40. Kühnel, *Persische Miniaturmalerei*, Taf. 34.

[4] *Chester Beatty Library, Catalogue* iii, no 256. Marteau and Vever ii, pls. CIII–CIV. Robinson, *Persian Miniature Painting*, no. 56, pl. 28. Welch, *Artists for the Shah*, pls. 14–16, 58–66, and colour-plates 1, 2, 5, 14–16: this work contains the fullest account, with bibliography on pp. 20–1. There is a succinct account in Robinson, "Isma'il II's copy of the *Shahnama*", *Iran* xiv (1976), 1–8.

[5] Qāżī Aḥmad, pp. 187, 191.

Beg as working in the library of Ismāʿīl II. Siyāvush indeed was a household servant of Shah Ṭahmāsp, a Georgian royal *ghulām* and, like Ṣādiqī, a pupil of Muẓaffar ʿAlī, whom we have seen to have been still in Qazvīn in 1573, and therefore senior to the group. Since this group of artists was probably only first brought together by Ismāʿīl II, the illustration of this *Shāh-nāma* is plausibly attributed to his reign (984–5/1576–7). The range of colouring in these miniatures is stronger and brighter than those in the *Haft aurang*, suggesting that at Qazvīn a more academic, less sensitive style was appreciated. The position of Muḥammadī in this situation remains somewhat enigmatic: he was a man of Herat and probably trained in the court style of Shah Ṭahmāsp, but, to judge from his generally accepted *œuvre,* nearer in sensibility and in preference for simple country scenes to the work of the Mashhad group of painters working for Sulṭān Ibrāhīm.[1] No doubt these too were recruited into the royal library after the death of their patron in 1577. It is therefore to be supposed that there were two or three different schools working together in Qazvīn in the last quarter of the 16th century. The *Garshāsp-nāma* and the dispersed *Shāh-nāma* represent the more brilliant and assured style of the group of painters round Siyāvush, Ṣādiqī and Zain al-ʿĀbidīn; while Muḥammadī may have been the leader of the quieter, more sensitive artists, whose work is to be seen in a number of country scenes and drawings of dervishes, and also in three detached miniatures from a manuscript of the *Gulistān* of Saʿdī in the Mahboubian collection and in a manuscript of the *Sifat al-ʿāshiqīn* of Hilālī dated 1582 in the Edwin Binney collection.[2] These sensitive miniatures represent the end of the early Safavid court style; in which landscape and figures are united in harmonious compositions, which admirably express the Persian love of natural and human beauty, and the ṣūfī tendency to see the two as equally reflecting the divine immanence.

Apart from manuscripts, there is fortunately one surviving monument to illustrate the art of wall-painting in the mid-10th/16th century, a Safavid palace pavilion at Nāʾīn, which has recently been discovered and published by Dr Ingeborg Luschey-Schmeisser. A considerable part of the decoration of the upper part of the walls and the vaulting of this building has survived, and the quality is such that one can only feel

[1] Stchoukine, *Manuscrits Ṣafavīs*, pp. 40–2, 94–7.

[2] *Exhibition of Islamic miniatures from the collection of Edwin Binney III* (1962), no. 47 and frontispiece. Grube, *The Classical Style*, no. 79. *Persian and Mughal Art* (London, 1976), no. 24.

a strong regret that so much good work of the early Safavid period must have been done on walls of which no trace remains. Shah Ṭahmāsp himself is recorded to have painted one or two scenes on the walls of the Chihil Sutūn pavilion at Qazvīn;[1] while the leading court painters Mīr Muṣavvir and Āqā Mīrak decorated for Bahrām Mīrzā an arched mirror-house *(jāmkhāna)* "making it as beautiful as paradise peopled with fair youths and hūrīs".[2] This description fits remarkably the decoration of the domed chamber in the Nā'īn palace; but this must be a building of a generation later. It is dated about 1550–60 by Luschey, who distinguishes two different hands in the work in the two rooms. On the evidence of the costume of the figures represented, and also on stylistic grounds, these paintings must be put well before 1580, and it is at present not possible to give a more definite date than that suggested by Luschey. The technique is to be noted by which these designs were carried out in relief stucco work known as *kundal*,[3] modelled and then cut to shape. Technically, therefore, these Safavid wall-paintings resemble the contemporary manner of decorating the inner surfaces of bindings with designs in appliqué, while the outer covers often show similar subjects in relief formed by pressing the leather into moulds. For the aivān arch of the pavilion is decorated with arcaded niches whose apexes form part of the interlace vaulting. Within this in star-shaped panels are depicted phoenix, *ch'i-lin*, wild geese in flight and *parīs* whose wings fit into the star shapes. On the walls are designs of animals, birds and vegetation in panels. No human figures are included in the decoration of this part of the building; but the inner domed chamber is decorated with symmetrical designs of pairs of young men drinking from a single cup, and of winged parīs, separated by floral designs – sprays growing from vases. This complex, as Luschey has pointed out, resembles some of the fine Safavid painted lacquer book-bindings in showing the sky filled with birds in flight and small stylised clouds above scenes of feasting and hunting. Thus it can be seen how closely connected this decorative wall-painting is to the contemporary arts of the book, which are primary in this period. The small scale of the designs bears this out and as final proof it can be mentioned that the Nā'īn pavilion includes in its decoration verses by

[1] Qāżī Aḥmad, p. 182.

[2] Dūst Muḥammad, in Binyon *et al.*, *Persian Miniature Painting*, p. 186.

[3] Pugachenkova, "Ishrat-Khâneh and Ak-Saray, two Timurid mausoleums in Samarkand", *AO* v (1963), 177–90. *SPA*, p. 1351, pls. 478–9.

Ḥāfiẓ in nasta'līq script in panels against a floral ground. There are two well-known drawings now in the Freer Gallery, Washington, representing a battue in mountain country and Solomon carried through the air by *jinn* and attended by parī,[1] which include all the principal elements in these wall-paintings, and of mid-16th century date, which might even be designs for similar architectural decoration. In quality there is no great difference, but the wall-paintings show faces more sharply characterised, no doubt in order to compensate for the distance from the eye of the spectator.

Although the last two decades of the 16th century saw a decline in the production of fine illustrated manuscripts, there were still some of excellent quality whose miniatures mark the transition from the late Qazvīn style to that of the new capital, Iṣfahān, which thereafter became the principal seat of the book arts. Among these, two lavishly illustrated manuscripts of the *Shāh-nāma* can be taken to exemplify the character of the period. One of these is at present known only by a fragment in the Chester Beatty Library,[2] with twelve large-scale miniatures and an illuminated frontispiece, which bears the signature of Zain al-'Ābidīn, thus marking it as a court product. It has been attributed to the last decade of the century, but should perhaps be assigned to the 1580s. The figures remain sharply focused and the detail of the architecture and landscape is fine and precise, but touches of realism fail to compensate for the loss of structural sense or of feeling. The second manuscript in the Mahboubian collection (University of Texas no. 922), also unfortunately undated, is probably slightly later. Among the twenty-three miniatures, the double frontispiece and three of the miniatures show the beginning of a new style, while the remainder are in a simplified Qazvīn style in which figures decisively dominate the landscape. This is true also of the new style, but here the figures are on a larger scale and can thus carry a more personal expression. This is emphasised by the introduction of several bare-headed men, hitherto practically unknown in this art. Gestures are expressive rather than realistic, while the setting is now entirely conventional.

Recently another illustrated manuscript, this time fortunately dated

[1] Binyon *et al.*, *Persian Miniature Painting*, no. 157, pl. XCIII. Martin, *Miniature Painting* II, pls. 57–8.

[2] *Chester Beatty Library, Catalogue* III, no. 277, pp. 49–50, pls. 478–9. On these miniatures, see now Welch, *Artists for the Shah*, pp. 106–22, pls. 8–11 and figs. 31–3, 35–41: Welch argues for a date of 1587–97, the first decade of the reign of 'Abbās I.

to 1593, has come to light, the *Anvār-i Suhailī* in the collection of the Marquess of Bute.[1] This bears a note beside the colophon that it was prepared for "Ṣādiqī Beg, the rarity of the age, the second Mānī, the Bihzād of the time". Robinson, who has published this manuscript, believes that this means that all 107 miniatures which illustrate it were painted by Ṣādiqī for his own satisfaction. I find this hard to accept, partly because they do not all appear to be by a single hand, but also because such a dedication would be more likely to represent a tribute from the artist's pupils to their master. In his recent study of the life and work of the artist Ṣādiqī, Welch has proposed that he was given by Shah 'Abbās the appointment as head of the library (kitābdār) immediately on his accession in 1587 and not as hitherto assumed in 1596, so that such a tribute might have been timely. In any case the illumination of this manuscript underlines the academic brilliance of the work in the last decade of the 16th century at the capital, Qazvīn. At the same time the miniatures, though unequal in quality, illustrate all the tendencies to be seen in the school at this time; the archaism of direct copies of the late Timurid style of Herat, the realism which is somehow connected with the contemporary Mughal style at the court of Akbar and the new style coming about at the court of Shah 'Abbās, highly mannered and with strong colouring. Other features of these miniatures include streaming, coloured clouds, strongly shaded trees and wind-blown foliage. Most of the miniatures project into the side margin of the page, as do also the miniatures in the Chester Beatty *Shāh-nāma*.

Occasionally also, even in the last years of the century, there are some manuscript illustrations of sensibility and invention, such as the four miniatures added at this time to the 1483 *Manṭiq al-ṭair* now in the Metropolitan Museum,[2] before it was dedicated by Shah 'Abbās I in 1607 to the shrine of Shaikh Ṣafī at Ardabīl. At the time of this addition the manuscript was also provided with an illuminated 'unvān signed by Zain al-'Ābidīn, as was the *Shāh-nāma* fragment mentioned above. There is, moreover, another connection between these two groups of miniatures. The most remarkable of the later series of illustrations to the *Manṭiq al-ṭair* depicts the "Conference of the birds",

[1] Robinson, "Two Persian manuscripts", pp. 50–6. Welch, *Artists for the Shah*, pp. 125–45, pls. 12, 13, figs. 42–55, and p. 66 for the appointment of Ṣādiqī Beg to the court.

[2] Grube, "The Language of the Birds: the seventeenth century miniatures", *MMAB* xxv (1967), pp. 339–47. Swietochowski, "The Historical Background", pp. 39–72, where the subjects of these miniatures are identified.

watched by a hunter carrying a matchlock in a rocky hillside. This bears the signature of Ḥabīb-Allāh, a painter recorded to have been recruited from Qum to the court workshop in Iṣfahān between 1596 and 1606; and it includes as its most conspicuous element a peacock displaying, seen frontally. This bird is exactly repeated as a decorative feature in the centre of the aivān in the best of the *Shāh-nāma* miniatures.[1] The other miniatures added to the *Manṭiq al-ṭair* are less original in composition, but in certain, as in the "Execution of a sick man by a Ghāzī", there are vivid touches of movement within traditional settings. Yet even the architecture is abreast of the times with the coffered false vaulting *(muqarnas)* of an aivān like that of the 'Ālī Qāpū reception hall. Ḥabīb-Allāh was an accomplished figure draughtsman[2] and quite capable of the swooning Christian girl in the story of the Shaikh of San'an. He shows a *fin de siècle* elegance, unlike the more relaxed stance of the 17th century. Behind the garden pavilion is the last of the 16th century garden vistas, with a pensive gardener leaning on his long-handled spade. There seems no reason why all four miniatures might not be by Ḥabīb-Allāh.

The most significant development during the last quarter of the 16th century is the rise to favour of the independent figure subject. Although a number of separate figure subjects have been attributed to the time of Sulṭān Ḥusain in Herat, and some even to the hand of Bihzād himself, there is little that can be accepted as before 1500. The well-known portrait of Mīr 'Alī Shīr Navā'ī,[3] must be posthumous, for it bears the probably genuine signature of Maḥmūd *muẕahhib,* a Bukhārā painter of the 1530s and 40s, whereas the Mīr died in 906/1501. In the time of Shah Ṭahmāsp Mīr Muṣavvir, Muḥammad Qadīmī, Kamāl al-Tabrīzī and 'Abd al-'Azīz of Kāshān are all recorded as "portraitists", though little survives of their work. The best are the figure subjects by Mīr Muṣavvir of young princes and pages in the British Museum (pl. 63*a*)[4] and the Museum of Fine Arts, Boston.[5] His son Mīr Sayyid 'Alī also made some drawings of similar fashionable youths before leaving for India with Humāyūn. The dates of these drawings must be between 1535 and 1540. Muẓaffar 'Alī also is said to have been an incomparable figure painter and to have decorated the walls of the Chihil Sutūn at

1 Robinson, *Persian Miniature Painting*, no. 60c, pl. 29.
2 Sakisian, *La miniature persane*, fig. 185. Kühnel, *Miniaturmalerei*, pl. 87.
3 Binyon *et al.*, *Persian Miniature Painting*, no. 74(d), pl. LXXVI.
4 *SPA*, pl. 901.
4 Sakisian, *La miniature persane*, fig. 137.

Qazvīn.[1] He is now known only by his manuscript illustrations already mentioned. His pupil, Ṣādiqī Beg, the first specialist in figure drawing, who "painted thousands of marvellous portraits," became in 1569 kitābdār to the shah. He was of the Afshār tribe, one of the leading Türkmen tribes, and a good warrior, but overbearing and rude, so that he finally lost his position, though not his title and salary.[2] Attributed to him are several attractive but rather mannered coloured figure drawings in the Bibliothèque Nationale (Supp. pers. 1171)[3] and elsewhere, of young beauties of both sexes. Several are included in the so-called "album of the amīr of Bukhārā" in the Pierpont Morgan Library (M. 386):[4] amongst them sketches of young men wearing loosely wound coloured turbans of the period about 1590 (pl. 63*b*), and in more sophisticated poses than became fashionable in the 17th century.

The beginning of the reign of Shah 'Abbās I thus heralds the period of the primacy of the independent miniature or drawing over the manuscript illustration. In the first part of the reign it is true that some notable manuscripts were still being produced, such as the *Duwal Rānī-yi Khiẓr Khān* of Amīr Khusrau Dihlavī of 1596 (British Library Add 7,776),[5] where the flat silhouetted figures continue the tradition of elegance introduced by Muḥammadī. This may well be a provincial manuscript, since one of the two scribes was a man from Lāhījān, chief town of Gīlān; and it has a slightly Turkish look, probably appropriate to the disputed areas of north-western Iran at this time.

Later on, after the move of the capital to Iṣfahān and the establishment of the shah as a great national leader, his personal taste becomes apparent in the miniature style of the second half of the reign; as for instance in a poetical manuscript dated 1613 in the Walters Gallery, Baltimore[6] and a *Khamsa* of Niẓāmī of 1605–26 in the Bibliothèque Nationale (Supp. pers. 1980).[7] The figures are still of considerable elegance, but their attitudes are more natural, less stylised, and could well have been taken from life; landscape and architectural setting, on the contrary, are simplified and conventional; even the famous Bīsitūn

[1] Iskandar Munshī, quoted in Arnold, *Painting in Islam*, p. 141.
[2] *Ibid.*, p. 142. For a new estimate of him, see Welch, *Artists for the Shah*.
[3] Stchoukine, *Manuscrits de Shāh 'Abbās*, pls. XXVI, XXVIII, XXIX, XXXb, XXXIb.
[4] Martin, *Miniature Painting* II, pls. 150–1. Grube, *The Classical Style*, pls. 87–9.
[5] Stchoukine, *Manuscrits de Shāh 'Abbās*, pl. IX.
[6] Gray, *Persian Painting* (1961), p. 165.
[7] Stchoukine, *Manuscrits de Shāh 'Abbās*, p. 195, pls. XLVI–XLVIII.

rock-carving, for instance, in the *Khusrau u Shīrīn,*[1] shown as a wall-painting of the lovers in a landscape found in a niche; and the clouds in the Baltimore manuscript drawn in the margins in pale blue and gold, as in the backgrounds of some of the figure drawings. The same indifference to landscape and architectural form is shown in a remarkable manuscript of the *Shāh-nāma* dated 1023/1614, which illustrates another aspect of the shah's taste, a pastiche of the great Bāīsunqur manuscript of 1430, which must have remained in the royal library. This copy contains thirty-nine miniatures, the composition of more than half of which are borrowed from the 1430 book, with simplifications.[2] The colouring and superficial resemblance are skilfully achieved, and the elements of the landscape are the same; but some figures in contemporary dress are introduced, as in the "Bīzhan drawn from the well by Rustam" (pl. 64). Here the prisoner wears the Mongol yoke (*palahang*), but his costume is of the early 17th century, and so is the water jug beside him. The background is a phantasmagoria of rocks, formed from the Timurid coral convention, but filling nearly all the sky. Rustam is a conventional Herat figure and the foreground is studded with early Timurid plants. In some of the miniatures there is no intrusive element and the landscape is a passable imitation, as in the "Rustam lassoing the Khāqān of Chīn". In others again, part of the composition is borrowed and part supplied by fresh invention, remarkably in keeping. The figure of Prince Bāīsunqur himself, on horseback, with his attendants, is adapted to a polo scene, from the double-page hunting scene which formed the frontispiece of the 1430 book. The ground is covered with an all-over floral arabesque pattern instead of vegetation, a convention which had developed in Shīrāz in the later 10th/16th century. Shah 'Abbās was determined to rival the Timurid princely patrons; and he had equal resources in materials and library staff. But the spirit of the age was no longer in tune with the romance-epic. Iran did not produce a school of history painting like India, nor of portraiture like that of the Mughals. Instead, the painters rivalled one another in virtuosity of penmanship and richness of design. For the first time in the history of the art, a majority of the drawings are signed, though not of course always in the autograph of the artist. Repetitions abound, often probably contemporary work by pupils or

1 Kühnel, *Miniaturmalerei*, pl. 90.
2 Gray, *Persian Painting* (1961), p. 164. Grube, *The Classical Style*, pls. 82 (1–4).

assistants. The question now is not so much when or where a drawing was made, as whether it is an orginal, and, if so, by whose hand. This debate continues and has proceeded farthest towards the identification of the work of Āqā Riżā.

We know from the literary sources[1] that Āqā Riżā was a son of ʿAlī Asghar and therefore, like Ṣādiqī Beg, of Türkmen stock, but unlike him born into the profession and almost certainly apprenticed in the royal library at an early age. He had an established reputation by the time that Qāżī Aḥmad completed his first version in 1596, and his birth is reasonably placed by Stchoukine about 1565, when his father was among the leading artists in the atelier of Ibrāhīm Mīrzā at Mashhad. Āqā is part of his name by which he is referred to in the sources. Qāżī Aḥmad writes: "in the flower of the youth he brought the elegance of his brushwork, figure painting and likeness to such a degree that if Mānī and Bihzād were living today they would praise his hand and brush a hundred times a day". The work of this early period which is generally accepted is not extensive. At its head are two fine coloured drawings of standing figures, one of a girl holding a fan (pl. 65*a*), the other of an elegant page in a cloak holding a fruit.[2] Both bear "signatures" of Āqā Riżā and both also the royal seal of Shah ʿAbbās with the date of his accession incorporated in the legend. The style is more elegant than that of Ṣādiqī Beg, with less sense of volume (there are no highlights on the features, as in his) but greater vitality: and we may remark a certain humour in the expressions. Then there are some pen-drawings, also of young people, a girl standing and holding a rosary[3] and a seated youth with a flowering spray in his hand,[4] which excel in the bravura of the line which moves from thick to thin, following the curves of the body and ends in a splutter of controlled ink. The first of these also bears the shah's seal, while the second comes from an album put together before the end of the 16th century, but shows a cloud formation in the background like that of the early 17th-century manuscript illustrations. Also belonging to the period about the turn of the century is another drawing in the Louvre of a young cup-bearer wearing the voluminous turban of the early ʿAbbās I period but more voluptuous in his stance than anything hitherto.[5] All these bear "signa-

1 Qāżī Aḥmad, p. 192.
2 Gray, *Persian Painting* (1961), p. 161.
3 Sakisian, *La miniature persane*, fig. 167.
4 Stchoukine, *Manuscrits de Shāh ʿAbbās*, pl. XXXIIIb.
5 *Ibid.*, pl. XXXV.

tures" of Āqā Riżā, though not all in the same hands; and evidently attributions, in spite of the humble formulae conventionally employed.

We now approach the problem of Riżā-yi 'Abbāsī, whose name is not mentioned in any of the sources, but is found, generally with a date added, on a great many 17th-century figure drawings. Some of the earliest of these according to the inscriptions, are stylistically close to the Āqā Riżā drawings last mentioned, especially the two earliest dated 1603 and 1610. There is, moreover, supporting evidence to be found in inscriptions on three other drawings, not by Riżā himself. Two are different versions of a portrait of a painter by the most productive artist of the second half of the century, Mu'īn. Both are inscribed by the artist and both give the name of the subject as Riżā-yi 'Abbāsī, the earlier dated 1673, giving the further name of Ash'ar (probably intended for Asghar), the family name of Āqā Riżā. In both, Riżā is described as Mu'īn's master, and both portraits are said to be copied after an original of 1044/1635, which, the 1673 inscription adds, was the year of his death, only one month later. The second copy, made in 1676, lacks this important additional information. The third drawing purports to be a copy made by Riżā-yi 'Abbāsī in 1618 after an illustration to the *Gulistān* of Sa'dī, which he believed to be by Bihzād. A second inscription by Riżā's son, Shafī' 'Abbāsī and dated 1064/1653, refers to him as Āqā Riżā. If we accept the genuineness of these inscriptions, we have double proof that Āqā Riżā and Riżā-yi 'Abbāsī were the same man. How then do we account for the change of name? If we turn to the second edition of Qāżī Aḥmad's treatise of 1606–8, we find an additional paragraph[1] in which his character is said to have completely changed by his consorting with libertines and taking up the vulgar sport of wrestling. He was, however, still in the shah's employ. Ten years later in 1616 Iskandar Munshī writes[2] that he was then always poor and in need and gave little time to his art, which surely implies that he was no longer in court service. His fall from grace is here attributed to the influence of Ṣādiqī Beg, whom we have seen to have had an unusually disagreeable character. Might it not be that Riżā took to using the epithet "'Abbāsī" only when he ceased to be the shah's servant, but when he wished to enhance his market value by reference to the royal patronage he had enjoyed? If his dismissal occurred about 1610, there is only one earlier dated example of the

[1] Qāżī Aḥmad, pp. 192–3.

[2] Arnold, *Painting in Islam*, pp. 143–4.

signature to account for that of 1603.[1] I would suggest that this inscription may have been added subsequently, although the date may well be correct for the making of the drawing. If this interpretation is correct, the Riżā-yi ʿAbbāsī drawings are those made for sale in the market.

This is not, however, to imply that there need have been any marked change of style at this moment, for it must be remembered that the taste of the shah was likely to be "popular": he was a good mixer and enjoyed the company of shopkeepers and such people, as we learn from the graphic pages of Pietro della Valle,[2] who visited Iṣfahān in 1617. Some index of his taste is provided by the decoration of the ʿĀlī Qāpū pavilion. Alongside of the niches intended for Chinese porcelain, for which he had a real passion,[3] are to be seen the remains of a system of arabesque decoration with birds in flight in the public rooms and of figures in the smaller rooms on a much smaller scale. That these are of the time of Shah ʿAbbās I we know once more from the pages of Pietro della Valle,[4] who considered them lascivious. They are in fact similar in style, though coarser in execution, than those of Riżā-yi ʿAbbāsī but are, from the point of view of the 20th century, gently sentimental rather than provocative. Embracing lovers are one of the themes of Riżā's work after 1610, but he was equally fond of depicting old men, especially dervishes, and of what we might call "costume pieces", young women and men wearing the elaborate modish dress of the period, including some young pages in European hats and breeches. The Persian male dress had always included trousers and by the time of Shah ʿAbbās I, as Anthony Sherley noted, breeches were a normal male dress and even worn by the shah himself. As plumes were frequently worn in turbans without any indication of rank, and as the shah favoured rich costume, such dressing up was normal and not to be attributed, as it sometimes has been, to any special Portuguese influence.

A mannerism, apparently introduced by Riżā, was to incline the

[1] Stchoukine, *Manuscrits de Shāh ʿAbbās*, pl. XXXIIa. Akimushkin and Ivanov, pl. 61.

[2] Della Valle II/2, 30–1. Cf. Blunt, pp. 185–6.

[3] Mario Ferrante argues, however, that these niches are decorative only, being formed as a plaster screen to mask the windows: "Desseins et observations préliminaires pour la restauration du palais de Ali Qapu", in Zander, *Travaux*, p. 168, fig. 73. In fact these niches closely resemble those in the Chīnīkhāna at the shrine of Shaikh Ṣafī at Ardabīl, which we know to have been prepared to receive the gift from ʿAbbās I of his large collection of Chinese porcelain in 1611: see Pope, *Chinese Porcelains*, pp. 8–11, pl. 4.

[4] Della Valle II/1, 40; Blunt, p. 126. The two upper floors were added under ʿAbbās II. Gray, "The Tradition of Wall Painting", p. 322.

standing figures forwards as if they were suddenly arrested in a forward movement. This trait is most obvious in the more complex manuscript illustrations by him such as a double-page country picnic of a young lord, dated 1612, in the Hermitage,[1] particularly rich with gold sky and gold margin decoration into which the miniatures extend. It is also to be seen in some of the miniatures in an undated manuscript of the *Qiṣaṣ al-anbiyā* ("History of the Prophets") in the Bibliothèque Nationale (Supp. pers. 1313) of about 1600, which are also by Riżā.[2] This mannerism continued through the middle of the century and is but one sign of the strength of Riżā's influence on his followers, led by his pupil Mu'īn and his son Shafī'. His personality dominates the first half of the century, no doubt partly because it corresponds so clearly to the spirit of the age, democratic, confident, delighting in display and bright colours but conservative in its respect for age and its salute to beauty.

Shah 'Abbās I died before Āqā Riżā, whose death cannot be placed prior to 1635, in the reign of Ṣafī I (1038-52/1629-42), a troubled time, from which little book art survives, though both his son Shafī' and Mu'īn must have been active. By the former is a coloured bird and flower drawing in the Hermitage dated 1634–5[3] and two pen-drawings in an album of designs dated 1640 and 1641 and signed Muḥammad Shafī' Iṣfahānī and Shafī' 'Abbāsī, the name which he received as a court artist.[4] Both are flower drawings and both seem to derive from European originals. The Hermitage drawing of a parakeet on the blossoming cherry bough, also shows Western influence in the shading. Western influence is entirely absent from his father's work, but from now on it is frequently seen for the rest of the Safavid period. Shafī' probably designed for the textile business; the silk brocades having as favourite repeat motives flowering plants and birds, such as Shafī' designed. There was an active foreign trade interest in these things: as is demonstrated by copies made by Shafī' from two English pattern books etched about 1661 in London, by John Dunstall (d. 1693), as well as by the instructions from Charles I to Nicholas Wilford in his mission to Persia in 1637.[5] This was evidently a period

[1] Stchoukine, *Manuscrits de Shāh 'Abbās*, pls. XXXVIII–XXXIX. Akimushkin and Ivanov, pls. 59, 60.

[2] Gray, *Persian Painting* (1961), pp. 162–3. Stchoukine, *Manuscrits de Shāh 'Abbās*, pls. XXI–XXIII and pp. 138–9, does not accept the attribution to Āqā Riżā.

[3] Akimushkin and Ivanov, pl. 71.

[4] Gray, "An album of designs".

[5] R.W. Ferrier, "Charles I and the Antiquities of Persia : the mission of Nicholas Wilford", *Iran* VIII (1970), 51–6.

of mutual influence between East and West, when oriental products – textiles, lacquer, ceramics – appealed to European taste, without much regard for country of origin, so long as it was east of Suez; while in India and Persia, and a few decades later in China, there was a reciprocal interest in Western painting with its perspective and chiaroscuro. The work of Shafī' 'Abbāsī of this kind extends down to 1674, which is said to have been the year of his death. At the same time he was making copies after his father's works, to some of which he probably added his father's signature. He was evidently highly skilled but without great originality.

A striking contrast to him was Mu'īn Muṣavvir, immensely prolific, dynamic and extremely personal in the virtuosity of his line. In manuscripts he excels in the vigour and originality of composition, rather than in colouring, where he showed a liking for garish contrasts, of strong primary colours. It is in his more personal, rapid sketches that he shows his genius for characterisation. The manuscripts mainly belong to the earlier part of his career under Shah 'Abbās II;[1] the style of the sketches owes nothing to the West, but is the interpretation in calligraphic line of a particularly keen observation from life. Sometimes this is combined with a traditional phantasy, as in the "Man attacked by Dragons", dated 1676, in the British Museum:[2] or under Indian influence as in the "Milking of a Cow" in the Berlin Museum,[3] of 1681. Only in the coloured drawings does the influence of his master Āqā Rižā continue until the end of his career (1689 and 1694), when he had been active for over fifty years. He kept alive the tradition of vital brushwork with a tendency to abstract calligraphic line long after it had been abandoned by most of the leading artists of the last third of the century.

The reign of Shah 'Abbās II (1052–77/1642–66)was favourable to the arts and new hands brought a revival, led by Muḥammad Yūsuf, Muḥammad Qāsim and Afżal al-Ḥusainī. The lastnamed signed sixty-two of the miniatures in a *Shāh-nāma* manuscript in the Leningrad State Library (no. 333).[4] Many of these bear dates between 1642 and 1645, while others, unsigned, excel in their dramatic effects, the figures being

[1] *Chester Beatty Library, Catalogue* III, no. 270, frontispiece and pls. 31–3. *SPA*, pls. 922–3. British Library Or. 3,248 in Stchoukine, *Manuscrits de Shāh 'Abbās*, pls. LXVI–LXVIII (mid-17th century).

[2] Robinson, *Persian Miniature Painting*, no. 84.

[3] Kühnel, "Der Maler Mu'în", *Pantheon* V (1942), 112, Abb. 6.

[4] Gyuzal'yan and D'yakonov, *Iranskie Miniatyury*, pp. 72–83, pls. 35–45.

arranged as if on a stage-set with elaborate backcloth.[1] The same dramatic effect is sought by similar means in some miniatures in a second *Shāh-nāma* dated 1648 in the Royal Library, Windsor Castle,[2] and almost certainly by the same hand. Afżal al-Ḥusainī is a very competent follower of Āqā Riżā, whereas Muḥammad Yūsuf[3] emerges more clearly as a distinct personality, of a more baroque tendency. The landscape backgrounds seem to be tormented, as if a great storm has lately passed over them, tearing the leaves from the trees and leaving the clouds in tatters (pl. 65*b*). His figures seem to carry further the inclination forwards found in Āqā Riżā's later work and to be poised for fresh movement. Muḥammad Qāsim, on the other hand, was more interested in decorative effects; his figures are static and his landscapes mere staffage, but over all attractive.[4] It seems likely that he may have been responsible for some of the best decorative and colourful wall-paintings which formed part of the improvements carried out at the Chihil Sutūn palace at Iṣfahān by Shah 'Abbās II, according to an inscription of 1647 discovered by Professor Hunarfar.[5] The most attractive of these are in one of the smaller rooms adjoining the central hall, named by the Italian restoration team who have recently cleaned and consolidated them with great skill, "P4". They fill ogival and lunette niches and show groups of picnickers in the country or single figures. The style and subject are very like those of the contemporary miniatures, and were no doubt painted by the same hands. It may be thought that such compositions gain from being carried out on a larger scale than the miniature. It perhaps becomes more obvious that the landscape elements are no more than artificial background, but the figures gain in grace and in the detailed depiction of elegant costume with patterns as lovingly reproduced as in Elizabethan portraits (pls. 39, 40). This room preserves the only complete interior of a palace decoration of Safavid times.

As the restoration of the Chihil Sutūn wall-paintings proceeds some large historical scenes in the central hall of the palace have been

1 *Ibid.*, pls. 37, 43, 45.

2 Stchoukine, *Manuscrits de Shāh 'Abbās*, pls. LVIII, LXII.

3 Binyon *et al.*, *Persian Miniature Painting*, pl. CIXc, dated 1645. Robinson, *Drawings of the Masters*, pl. 58, dated 1637. Akimushkin and Ivanov, pls. 69, 70, dated 1656 and 1658. Mahboubian collection, ten miniatures, one dated 1652.

4 Stchoukine, *Manuscrits de Shāh 'Abbās*, pls. LXXI, LXXVIII, LXXXb. Blochet, *Musulman Painting*, pl. CLXVII. Martin, *Miniature Painting* II, pl. 165c. Kühnel, *Miniaturmalerei*, pl. 91.

5 Hunarfar, *Ganjīna*, p. 566. P. Mora, "La restauration des peintures murales de Čihil Sutūn", in Zander, *Travaux*, pp. 323–8, figs. 56–81.

uncovered. These are in a style different from that of the smaller paintings in room P4 and in both composition and chiaroscuro betray Western influence. They show successive shahs receiving foreign guests identified as Humāyūn at the court of Ṭahmāsp I; the khan of Turkestan, Nadr Muḥammad, received by ʿAbbās I; and Shah ʿAbbās II with the Uzbek ambassador.[1] No attempt has been made to depict these scenes in the dress of the time, but all wear contemporary costume of the period around 1670, at the beginning of the reign of Sulaimān. It was only at this time that we begin to find evidence of Western influence in Safavid painting. The wall-paintings in the large hall are thus some twenty-five years later than those in the smaller rooms P4 and P5.

Nearer in style to the wall-paintings in the side rooms are some large panels of wall-tiles which once adorned some of the pavilions which were erected in the gardens behind the Chahār Bāgh. Several of these figural compositions are now preserved in Western museums (pl. 69), all showing similar scenes of young men and women enjoying themselves in flowery gardens. They are in the cuerda seca technique in which the colours are separated by greasy lines.

Of the work of one or two stray European painters known to have been patronised by Shah ʿAbbās I no trace now remains; but after the middle of the century there is the definite evidence in the Armenian churches and houses in Julfā, the foreign suburb of Iṣfahān, which followed not, as might have been expected, a Near Eastern tradition but a Northern European, Dutch one. It is in fact the Italianising Flemings and Dutch whose style is reflected in the semi-Western style paintings which have survived from the last quarter of the century. The two leading exponents of this style seem to have been ʿAlī Qulī Jabbadār and Muḥammad Zamān. The best collection of the work of both artists is in the Oriental Institute, Leningrad.[2] This Muḥammad Zamān is not to be confused with the calligrapher Muḥammad Zamān Kirmānī, mentioned by Qāżī Aḥmad,[3] a Tabrīzī active there at the end of the 16th century. Furthermore, it cannot unfortunately be assumed that he was the same as the "Muhamedzama" whom the Italian traveller N. Manucci met in Delhi about 1660,[4] who had been sent by Shah ʿAbbās II early in his reign as a student of theology to Rome

[1] Grube and Sims, "Wall paintings".
[2] Ivanov *et al.*, *Al'bom*, pp. 44–59.
[3] Qāżī Aḥmad, p. 166.
[4] N. Manucci, *Storia do Mogor*, ed. W. Irvine (London, 1907–8), II, 17–18. *A Chronicle of the Carmelites* I, 315ff. N.N. Martinovitch, in *JAOS* XLV (1925), 108–9.

where he had been converted to Christianity and had taken Paolo as his baptismal name. He had therefore not cared to return to Iran but had sought the Mughal court, where Shāh Jahān had given him a pension and installed him with other Persian expatriates in Kashmīr. There are chronological difficulties about this identification, for the visit to Rome seems actually to have been in the early 1630s under Shah Ṣafī, whereas the dated work of our painter in Iran falls between the years 1672 and 1697. These works are signed Muḥammad Zamān b. Ḥājjī Yūsuf, with no indication of a Christian connection. Of his forty-seven known works, four are of Christian subjects,[1] but all these appear to be copies directly from engravings (the same kind of material copied by the Mughal artists at the court of Jahāngīr and Shāh Jahān from the work of Northern artists who were trained in Rome).[2] The colouring certainly implies that Muḥammad Zamān was familiar with paintings of this school, but he used a mixed style which retains the original composition, but with the spirit and conception of a Persian miniature transposed into a Western idiom with cast shadows and plastic modelling. The trees are directly borrowed with their gnarled trunks and bunched foliage from the school of Martin van Heemskerck; while clouds are barred with shafts of sunlight. Muḥammad Zamān is best known for his three illustrations added to the royal Niẓāmī of 1539–43 in the British Library,[3] and two to the now fragmentary *Shāh-nāma* in the Chester Beatty Library.[4] All five are dated 1086/1675; and this and the two following years are the period of sixteen miniatures supplied to a manuscript of the *Khamsa* of Niẓāmī in the Pierpont Morgan Library, New York. These are smaller and in a lower tone, but they illustrate the same thoroughly mixed Westernised Persian style, as in the "Shīrīn discovers the murder of her Husband Khusrau" (pl. 66). Each element may be borrowed, but the whole remains eastern. It is hard to believe that this artist could have pursued a systematic course in the studio of a European painter in Rome. An extreme example of the mixed style is one of the miniatures added to the British Library Niẓāmī, showing Bahrām entertaining a princess,[5] a night scene with mixed candle and moonlight which the painter has used as an excuse for exaggerated chiaroscuro. The princess and one of the serving maids wear European

[1] Martin, *Miniature Painting* II, pl. 173. Ivanov *et al.*, *Al'bom*, pls. 84–5.
[2] Barrett and Gray, pp. 86–7.
[3] Arnold, *Painting in Islam*, pl. V.
[4] *Chester Beatty Library, Catalogue* III, no. 277, pl. 38. *SPA*, pl. 925.
[5] V. Smith, *A History of the Fine Arts in India and Ceylon* (Oxford, 1913), pl. CXVI.

dress, while Bahrām is dressed in the contemporary shah's costume. Since this must have been a royal commission, we are entitled to assume that this hybrid style appealed to the personal taste of Shah Sulaimān (1077–1105/1666–94).

A court scene in which a shah enthroned gives audience to a Mughal ambassador, now in the collection of Prince Ṣadr al-Dīn Agha Khan,[1] is attributed to Muḥammad Zamān and dated about 1663 by comparison with a drawing signed by Shaikh 'Abbāsī, showing a shah in similar dress and also receiving a Mughal embassy and apparently dated 1074/1663–4.[2] The Shah in this drawing is older and with a fuller beard and moustache than that in the first drawing, so that the latter would need to be earlier; yet 1663 is already very early for a work by Muḥammad Zamān. Moreover, the costume of the shah in both is that of the reign of Shah Sulaimān, who succeeded in 1077/1667 at the age of twenty; and both show notable European influence. The solution proposed is that both these court scenes date from the early 1670s, the date on the drawing by Shaikh 'Abbāsī being 1084/1673. Both Shaikh 'Abbāsī and his son 'Alī Naqī show in their work Mughal as well as European influence and this became from then onwards an element in the late Safavid painting style. [3]

The second leading figure in miniature painting in this period was 'Alī Qulī Jabbadār, who was also evidently fascinated by such Western portraits as he could see.[4] He too painted the shah surrounded by his courtiers, including a page boy in Dutch costume and, since he wears his hair over his shoulders, perhaps actually a European.[5] This artist has a less sure grasp of perspective than Muḥammad Zamān, as is betrayed by the insecurity of this group which seems to float rather than to be based on the ground; but he achieves an equally realistic finish. 'Alī Qulī may have been of Georgian origin since two of his drawings carry notes in Georgian and one, in the British Museum, signed Ghulāmzāda Qadīmī 'Alī, has been reasonably attributed to his hand.[6] It represents a couple in Georgian dress but in the Persian court style. The secular art of Georgia at this time was thoroughly Persian-

[1] A. Welch, *Collection of Islamic Art: Prince Sadruddin Aga Khan* III (Geneva, 1978), 154–7, IRM 93.
[2] Welch, *Shah 'Abbās and the Arts*, p. 98, no. 62.
[3] R. Skelton, "Shaikh 'Abbāsī and his son", in *VIth International Congress*, p. 81. Robinson *et al.*, *The Keir Collection* III, 395, pl. 90 (dated 1080/1670).
[4] Martin, *Miniature Painting* II, pl. 172.
[5] Ivanov *et al.*, *Al'bom*, pl. 99.
[6] Robinson, *Persian Miniature Painting*, no. 87, pl. 34.

ised;[1] but if 'Alī Qulī was actually Ghulāmzāda he was presumably born in Iṣfahān or Julfā.

This synthetic style was still in vogue up to the end of the century and indeed beyond through the reign of Shah Sulṭān Ḥusain (1105–35/1694–1722). There is a large manuscript of the *Shāh-nāma* in the Metropolitan Museum dated 1663–9 but with miniatures added between 1693 and 1698 and signed by the painters Āqā Nūyān, Ghulām Parmāk and 'Alī Naqī, whom we have already noted as son of Shaikh 'Abbāsī, and by Muḥammad Zamān.[2] It also contains some of the last work of Mu'īn, who naturally maintained to the end the style of his youth under 'Abbās II and was little affected by the new vogue. This style was continued after the turn of the century by the son of Muḥammad Zamān, Muḥammad 'Alī, who was working as late as 1721, when he signed a careful and no doubt official drawing of the last Naurūz present-giving of Sulṭān Ḥusain, now in the British Museum.[3] The rigidity of the architectural perspective and chiaroscuro and the conventional modelling of the faces of the depressed courtiers show the signs of artistic decadence parallel with the political decline. A drawing in the Leningrad album signed by Muḥammad Sulṭānī and dated 1694–5[4] is in the same style and may well be by the same hand. It shows the shah at the time of his accession. That this shah too favoured Western painting is proved by his commission to the Dutch painter Cornelis de Bruyn, who visited Iṣfahān in 1701 to paint his portrait.[5] Muḥammad 'Alī is known also as a painter in lacquer, a medium which was to be increasingly important during the 18th and 19th centuries. His signed work in this medium includes two *qalamdāns* signed 1701 and 1708,[6] both painted with figures in landscape in the same style as his miniatures on paper. A famous album of Mughal and Persian painting and calligraphy in the Academy of Sciences at Leningrad is enclosed in a painted lacquer binding which bears the two dates 1147/1734 and 1151/1738, during the very last years of the Safavid dynasty. The front cover has a fine over-all design of flowers symmetrically arranged around a central cartouche rather like a carpet design;

[1] Gray, "The Man in the Panther Skin", *Bodleian Library Record* III (1951), no. 32, 194–8.

[2] Robinson, "The Shāhnāmeh Manuscript Cochran 4". Stchoukine, *Manuscrits de Shāh 'Abbās*, pls. LXXXIV, LXXXV.

[3] Lockhart, *The Fall*, p. 489, pl. X.

[4] Ivanov *et al.*, *Al'bom*, pl. 92. Cf. Akimushkin and Ivanov, pl. 78 (dated 1697–8). Martin, *Miniature Painting* II, pl. 167 (dated 1700).

[5] Lockhart, *The Fall*, frontispiece and appendix.

[6] Ivanov, in *Soobshcheniya Gosudarstvennogo Ermitazha* XVIII (1960), 52–3.

the back cover shows birds and flowers confined to a central cartouche and the border. It was dedicated to a certain Muḥammad Mahdī Khān but is unsigned.[1] This is the kind of decorative lacquer painting which was to be favoured during the next hundred and fifty years.

In the sixteenth century the art of binding had kept abreast of the other arts of the book in quality of design and execution, and in rich variety of technique. Leather is always the basis, even of the lacquer painted covers, which were introduced at Herat under Ḥusain Bāīqarā. No doubt the painting was carried out by miniaturists of top rank. These bindings can never have been common and they are unfortunately easily damaged; and consequently few survive in good condition. The bigger libraries generally have examples, and in the British Library is a binding signed by Sayyidī ʿAlī on a manuscript of the Dīvān of Navā'ī (Or. 1,374) of about 1550;[2] and two detached covers of very fine quality and large size from about 1540, formerly in the Düsseldorf Museum and bequeathed to the British Museum by Sir Bernard Eckstein in 1948 (pl. 67), but these have some damage in areas of the outer faces.[3] This damage reveals that a deep blue ground was used as an undercoat, as it was also in lacquer-painting on wood. Another landscape lacquer binding on a manuscript of the Dīvān of Shāhī in the library of Trinity College, Dublin, shows the poet, who had lived at the court of Shāh Rukh, reciting to a prince in a garden. Another large pictorial lacquer binding in Hamburg (Kunstgewerbemuseum 1894.27) is enhanced with gold and silver paint. Instead of human figures it includes combats of mythical Chinese beasts and is comparable with a binding dated 1569 in the Bodleian Library (Greaves I).[4] In the Chester Beatty Library is a lacquer-painted binding with symmetrically designed decoration and not a pictorial scene; and a similar style of design is to be seen on a large tooled binding of about 1550 in the Deutsches Ledermuseum, Offenbach-am-Main (1.20.24) (pl. 68).[5]

This sumptuous type of book-cover is the gilt embossed pictorial binding made with intaglio stone moulds into which the leather is pressed. The technique seems to have been used originally by saddlers, but was extended about the middle of the 9th/15th century to book

[1] Ivanov *et al.*, *Al'bom*, pl. 98.
[2] *Arts of Islam*, no. 605 and colour plate at p. 58. It is close in style to the binding of Topkapı Sarayı Revan 999, copied in 949/1543: see Çiğ, "The Iranian lacquer technique work", fig. 5.
[3] Sarre and Martin, Taf. 30 (2 and 4). Schulz, Taf. 196–7. *Arts of Islam*, no. 606.
[4] Erdmann, Taf. 66. *Arts of Islam*, no. 602; *ibid.*, no. 611, for Bodleian binding.
[5] Size 40 x 30 cm: mid-16th century, rather than 17th as in the 1974 catalogue.

binding.[1] The use of metal stamps is older, and the austere bindings of the first half of the 15th century are generally regarded as superb examples of reticent design. In them Chinese motifs, especially the dragon and phoenix, are employed in a quite un-Chinese way in arabesque panels and combined with arabesque floral scrollwork; thus conforming to the concept of Chinoiserie, the use of Chinese elements, valued for their exotic character, in accordance with a different mode of vision and design.[2] This stylistic feature persisted in the later 15th century, when the whole face of the cover was embossed with richly gilt pattern. When this technique was first used the moulds were supplemented and finished with a good deal of hand tooling, but in the 10th/16th century this was reduced to no more than retouching and finishing off. In this field Chinoiserie design persisted much longer than in the arts of illumination, metalwork or textiles. It is only in ceramics that there is a continuous tradition of Chinese design in Persian blue and white. They are datable only by reference to the periods of the Chinese prototypes, among which the Chia-ching (1522–66) dishes and bowls decorated with cranes in flight among clouds are conspicuous. The quality of body and glaze was superior in this type to anything achieved earlier and is confidently attributed to Mashhad,[3] which remained through the 11th/17th century a leading centre for the blue and white pottery industry. In the earlier Safavid period Kirmān has been suggested as the place of origin of some blue and white vessels on which the Chinese designs have been rethought and redesigned, as on some bearing dates of 1523 and 1525.[4] Soon after this date the influence of Iznik design and colouring becomes apparent in some handsome dishes and jars and vases also attributed to the Kirmān kilns. Examples are in the Tehran archaeological museum and the Victoria and Albert. The "Kubachi" ware also shows Iznik influence at this time, though more in the colouring than the design.[5] Tabrīz has already been suggested as the centre for this ware, and it might be urged that it was more open to Anatolian influence than Kirmān. On the other hand, Tabrīz and the whole province of Iranian

[1] Ettinghausen, "Near Eastern Book Covers", pp. 123–5, pls. 6–9.

[2] Aslanapa, "The Art of Bookbinding": the earliest moulded examples on pls. 33 (dated 1407) and 42 (1442), fully pictorial.

[3] *7000 Years*, p. 176, no. 705. Lane, *Later Islamic Pottery*, pl. 74.

[4] *Ibid.*, pl. 64. There is also the purely Islamic design in blue and white on a Zodiacal plaque dated 1563–4 in the Staatliche Museen at Berlin: Erdmann, Taf. 58.

[5] *7000 Ans d'Art*, pl. CXIV.

Āzarbāījān had a troubled history throughout the Safavid period, at least until the reign of Shah 'Abbās I.

The exact date of the introduction of this polychrome ware is uncertain: the typical products of tiles or dishes with bust portraits of smart youths and girls show the fashions current at Qazvīn in the 1590s, while some dishes also copy Chinese border patterns from Wan-li porcelain (1573–1619). The attractive colouring, which includes a substitute for the brilliant Iznik red, supersedes the earlier 16th-century black painting under a green or turquoise glaze. The quality and durability of the ware at the same time decline and the products are correspondingly scarce.

The 17th century ware, which is more reliably connected with Kirmān, has a more provincial appearance[1] and may not be earlier than the middle of the century. By this time blue and white wares were being made in Iran in large quantity and especially for export through the Dutch East India Company,[2] who found that they could sell them in Europe as Chinese, especially during the years between about 1653 and 1695 when export from China was interrupted. It may be that production for the export trade encouraged the inclusion in the designs of figures in Western dress as well as Chinese and Persian; but Western figures and dress were also to the taste of Iṣfahān in the 17th century. The more freely these designs are derived from the Chinese, the more vital and amusing they are. Celadon ware was also imitated at this time in Kirmān, but the decoration, painted in white slip, sometimes with the addition of touches of blue and red, is in a purely Islamic style, with arabesque patterns or sprays of flowers.[3] No earlier a date can be given to the revival of lustre-painted decoration after a clear break during the early Safavid period; and again the designs are entirely native to Iran. The rather crowded floral patterns, often with some landscape elements, are related to the margin painting in manuscripts both in style and in the use of different tones of gold. In the earlier period a pure white ground was preferred,[4] while later blue or occasionally yellow ground was adopted. The body is finer than that of the Kirmān wares and the polychrome wares identified with that centre combine formal

[1] Lane, *Later Islamic Pottery*, pl. 69.

[2] Chardin VII, 403.

[3] Lane, *Later Islamic Pottery*, pl. 87. A variant technique is cutting through the slip to the white body, as on a blue dish in the British Museum: *Arts of Islam*, no. 399.

[4] Kühnel, *Islamische Kleinkunst*, p. 145. The name Khātim, of whom nothing is known, is often found on these pieces. For evidence of the continuation of the lustre technique in Iran, see Watson.

and geometric motifs borrowed from architectural decoration,[1] with similar floral designs as an alternative to Chinoiserie. This ware also is from the later 17th century.

In contrast to the abundance of pottery production in many different centres in the 17th century, the only significant development in metalwork is in the use and decoration of steel, whether for armour and sword-blades, or cut through as decoration, in which calligraphy usually supplies the main element.[2] Thus calligraphy, which had become more and more dominant in the decoration of brass or copper vessels, finally achieved virtual independence in the cut steel appliqué to wood or leather. On helmets (pl. 70) and body-armour chasing and intarsia were the usual methods, and some royal pieces are carved all over in low relief. Even more care was taken with the sword, the blade being of an elegant curve and the handle of jade, agate or shagreen. So the period ends with the applied arts at a high level of technical skill; closer awareness of foreign styles and markets, but with diminished originality and a loss both in ceramics and miniature painting of the inspired wealth of invention of earlier centuries.

[1] Lane, *Later Islamic Pottery*, pls. 57–61.

[2] *Arts of Islam*, nos. 234–7.

CHAPTER 17 (*a*)

PERSIAN LITERATURE IN THE TIMURID AND TÜRKMEN PERIODS (782–907/1380–1501)

This long period of 120 years was a troubled one. Tīmūr's attack on Iran, which began in 782/1380–1 with the invasion of Khurāsān and Sīstān, terminated the pre-Timurid interregnum in a period characterised by sudden alarms. Even after the conqueror Tīmūr's death, except for the comparatively peaceful reign of Shāh Rukh (807–850/1405–1447), conditions throughout the land remained unsettled; his successors could not be at peace one with another; government was the plaything of turbulent rivals. Besides numerous princes of the Timurid dynasty, there were other leaders on the scene, such as those of two Türkmen dynasties, the Qarā Quyūnlū and Āq Quyūnlū, who had established themselves in the regions of Āzarbāījān and western Persia, with occasional inroads into the eastern regions of the country. Eventually this state of affairs was ended in the east by the Shaibanids and in the west by the Safavids.

Disturbances that can be dated back to the Mongol invasions, and which finally developed into the disruption and disorder of the period after Shāh Rukh's death, occasioned a serious decline in civilisation and deterioration in thought. At the beginning of this period a few of the scholars, poets and writers of the interval between the Mongol Īl-Khāns and the Timurids were still alive and affording contributions to science and literature. But apart from these few, and with the possible exception of those who had gathered at the court of Sulṭān Ḥusain Bāīqarā at Herat and who were didactic rather than original, we hardly hear of any important or justly celebrated men of learning or science until the latter part of the 9th/15th century.

During this period the Persian language was continuing the complex evolution which had begun in the 7th/12th century. In addition to those changes in vocabulary, syntax and inflection which necessarily accompany the historical development of a language, other factors accelerated changes of a more radical nature. On the one hand, the influence of eastern Persian dialects was day by day lessened, eastern

Persian elements being supplanted by those of western Persian. On the other hand, some Arabic words and compounds which had gradually come into use in the common tongue as well as in the works of former writers became so firmly ensconced in the language that they replaced their Persian counterparts and attained permanence. At the same time the admixture of Mongol and Turkish in Persian increased; some of the many single words and compounds in use since the time of the Mongols became established features of the language. The use of the Turkish language was so prevalent during this period that, as it had been introduced into poetical works and was patronised by literature-loving but Turki-speaking rulers and notables, a Turkish prose and poetic literature eventually emerged, and this in Khurāsān, the very cradle of Persian's development as a literary language. Some exponents of literature having elected to write in this new literary medium, an argument about preferences resulted, to be expressed in a work like the *Muḥākamat al-lughatain* ("The Arbitration between the Two Tongues") of Mīr 'Alī Shīr Navā'ī, the famous minister and patron of letters under Ḥusain Bāīqarā.

The character of Persian literature at this time was decided not only by changes of this nature in the language, but also by certain factors which were leading it into new phases and simultaneously towards decline. Among these influences was the fact that before the Mongol invasion poetry and prose writing had been subject to strict rules and conventions and had been closely connected with courts, in a thoroughly "classical" situation; whereas in this later period creative writing was in the hands of the common people as well as under court influence, and ceased to be subject to former exacting literary standards. The explanation of this is that, before the Mongol invasion, a poet or writer had to learn a number of rules and examples in both Arabic and Persian. This schooling naturally resulted in a broadening of his literary horizon and an increase in his knowledge of the best models of literary techniques.[1] In the period under review, and also in later times, this concern for the great classical models either completely disappeared or at best could only rarely be discerned among the more refined and better educated. The shedding of traditional literary conventions resulted in a decline in the generally shared knowledge of the

[1] See Niẓāmī-yi 'Arūżī, *Chahār maqāla*, ed. Muḥammad Mu'īn (Tehran, 1341/1962–3), pp. 20–2, 47–8; also Safa II, 347–50.

styles, devices and disciplines of exemplary writers and poets; a consequent weakening of style was inevitable. This lapse of style and ignorance of forms are, with the outstanding exception of a writer like Jāmī, observable in most of the works of this period.

The closing down of important Persian literary centres in Khurāsān and Iraq, the break-up of courts which had supported and encouraged poets and writers, and the disappearance of great men or families who before, and even for a while after, the Mongol invasion of Persia patronised such activities, combined to cause the gradual disappearance of great masters like those of classical times without producing any worthy successors. Poetry and prose fell into the hands of men for the most part of mediocre talent.

POETRY

Persian poetry, therefore, like the language itself and, indeed, other branches of learning, was not as resplendent in this period as it might have been. In addition to the reasons already propounded, there was constant political instability and also, though admittedly to this there were exceptions, an absence of leaders and sovereigns of literary taste who enjoyed a plenitude of power and breadth or continuity of dominion that would have made for a wide and consistent cultivation of a ripely developed literature. In other words, it was a time of transition, which left the marks of unsettlement and flux on its literary products.

Among the exceptions to rulers not capable of literary patronage were such Timurid princes as Shāh Rukh, Bāīsunqur Mīrzā (d. 837/1433), Ulugh Beg (850–853/1447–1449), Abū Sa'īd (855–873/1452–1469) and especially Ḥusain Bāīqarā (873–911/1469–1506) and his minister Mīr 'Alī Shīr Navā'ī. These men, with a few others, were essayists themselves in the literary arts (or at least had works attributed to them) and admirers of men of literary talent, their courts providing centres of artistic and scientific achievement. But their fitful and regional patronage of letters in the disturbed conditions of the times seems often to have been susceptible to errors of judgment, to have lacked information on what was best; while the general dearth of notables willing to invest the weight of their influence on the side of literature made it difficult for a few, even had their taste and awareness of what was sound and what was not been of a higher order than they were, to stem the tide of decadence.

Undoubtedly the most important Timurid centre of culture was Ḥusain Bāīqarā's court at Herat, which in retrospect seems to have shone out like a beacon in lands only recently devastated by Tīmūr's own career of conquest, and which in eastern Iran afforded a refuge for the arts after Ḥusain had succeeded in carving out a realm for himself in Khurāsān, following the strife that had ensued on Tīmūr's death and his failure to consolidate an empire in Iran. Numbers of poets, writers, historians, musicians and painters were attracted to Herat, there to introduce styles and techniques that were to continue in fashion, and in their development, until Safavid times. Hence it is correct to say that Ḥusain Bāīqarā's literary, scientific and artistic circle left a great impress on Iran's intellectual and artistic life. But the high place occupied by painters at Herat evinced a new departure, and that towards the visual arts, and a new manifestation of artistic vitality, of significance in discussing the decline of literature and the absence of originality, not only in literary invention but in thought. It was as if a new channel of expression for the genius of Iran had been opened.

At the outset of the Timurid period a number of talented poets followed the methods of their predecessors of the 8th/14th century. Those who wrote poetry in the next generation adopted a style which was quite new. They even criticised the imitators of the old masters. As Kātibī has said:

He is no poet who, when he writes verses, brings together thoughts from the poems of the old masters.
No house which is built with old bricks stands on so firm a foundation as a new house.

The poetic language of the Timurid era came closer than had poetic diction hitherto to the colloquial tongue. The reason for this development was that in this epoch poetry was less, as we have seen, the speciality of the court, and, at the same time, had become more current among the common people. Since the poet had to write to suit popular taste, adherence to former poetical traditions seemed of less importance. It is possible that to this attitude may be attributed the relatively large number of poets and of poetasters of this period; reference to the biographies of this and of the early Safavid period shows the increase in their numbers after the post-Mongol, Il-Khanid times. If one examines the biographies of the poets of the Timurid era, such as Daulatshāh's *Taẕkirat al-shuʿarā*, Mīr ʿAlī Shīr Navāʾī's *Majālis al-nafāʾis* (in Turkish) and its Persian translation, entitled the *Laṭā'if-nāma*, and the *Tuḥfa-yi Sāmī* by the Safavid Sām Mīrzā, one encounters a concourse of poets who in fact represent only a part of the total. As will be also seen in connection with the Safavid period, this development cannot be divorced from the popular nature of poetry, now current among a variety of classes of people.

The prevalence of Turkish ultimately ensured its total use as a medium for poetry, or its adoption, for variety's sake, even by those who usually stuck to Persian. One of the greatest of those who usually wrote in Turkish but sometimes in Persian was Mīr 'Alī Shīr Navā'ī (d. 906/1501), Ḥusain Bāīqarā's minister. His works in Turkish include four collections (*dīvāns*) of *ghazals* (odes) and five *maṣnavīs* (rhyming distichs) in the manner of Niẓāmī's *Khamsa*, while another work, the *Lisān al-ṭair*, ("The language of the Birds"), was in imitation of Farīd al-Dīn 'Aṭṭār's *Manṭiq al-ṭair*. In his Persian poetry, which has not been praised by critics, he wrote under the pen-name (*takhalluṣ*) of Fānī.

In the poetry of the Timurid period, as for example in that of Kātibī of Turshīz, one comes across specimens of rhetorical flourishes and poetical artifices. Although some men of letters tended to adopt such conceits, it must be admitted that this was not very common, the more celebrated writers and poets of the age preferring simplicity.

Mysticism was still a favourite topic for poetry. In particular, ṣūfī expressions were in common use in ghazals. Now and again such poets as Shāh Ni'mat-Allāh Valī, Qāsim al-Anvār and Jāmī wrote long poems of a ṣūfī character. Love romances and poems consisting of anecdotes and tales on ethical and philosophical subjects were relatively numerous. They were mostly written in imitation of Niẓāmī, whose themes were sometimes versified anew with slight changes.

Furthermore, among the various poetical forms practised in the Timurid period, the ghazal received special attention. Towards the end of the Timurid era increasingly ingenious thoughts and artifices are noticeable in the ghazal. A possible reason for this development may be that the Persians, in consequence of the Mongol invasions and the massacres and plundering of the 7th–9th/13th–15th centuries, were forced to turn to spiritual matters and neglect the material world. They therefore tended to adopt far-fetched and non-corporeal, artificial themes, which they endeavoured to express as succinctly and strikingly as possible.

When this style, whose origins – chiefly in the circle of Ḥusain

Bāīqarā and Mīr 'Alī Shīr Navā'ī at Herat – are being considered here, is more fully discussed under the Safavid period, it will be seen that a balance between words and purport was not always maintained. The latter tended increasingly towards the fanciful. It was far-fetched in proportion as it departed from any basis in reality: it went beyond that realm of poetry in which the imagination's function is to transmute the world of actuality into the expression of universal ideas. Hence it became a weak and overplayed genre.

Following these general observations brief references will now be made to some of the principal Timurid exponents of the poetic art and their works, roughly in chronological order; though in the instance of the first to be singled out, he has priority of place for the merits of his achievement as well.

This was Kamāl al-Dīn b. Mas'ūd (d. 808/1405–6), who had lived in the interval between the Mongol Īl-Khāns and the Timurids and was known by his pen-name of Kamāl, Kamāl-i Khujandī, a master in the ghazal form. While to students of Persian literature he is always remembered as one of the outstanding contemporaries of Ḥāfiẓ, his own sense of his superiority to Ḥāfiẓ can hardly win support. Nevertheless, he did play an important part in perfecting the ghazal form.

Contemporary with Kamāl was Mullā Muḥammad Shīrīn Maghribī of Tabrīz (d. 809/1406–7). Mullā Muḥammad's ghazals and *tarji'-bands*[1] contain numerous references to the ideas and aspirations of the Muslim mystic: Mullā Muḥammad was himself celebrated as a ṣūfī, and his notions tend markedly towards pantheism. As a poet, however, he must be regarded as mediocre, in a class similar to that of 'Iṣmat-Allāh Bukhārā'ī or 'Iṣmat-i Bukhārī (d. 829/1425–6). 'Iṣmat left some celebrated amatory ghazals and *qaṣīdas* in addition to tarji'-band poems.

In the words of Professor Browne,[2] a poet "who offers the greatest possible contrast to Maghribī, the mystic and pantheist", was Abū Isḥāq of Shīrāz (d. 827 or 830/1424 or 1427), known as Būsḥāq Aṭ'ima because he was "the poet of foods".[3] Appropriately enough his dīvān, the collection of his ghazals, qaṣīdas, quatrains and maṡnavīs, is entitled the *Kanz-i ishtihā* ("Treasure of the Appetite"). This collection is

[1] A *tarji'-band* ("return-tie") is a poem comprising strophes of five to eleven verses in length, each verse within each strophe rhyming with the rest; the final verse of each strophe remaining the same throughout the poem as a refrain; the verse in the last strophe preceding this refrain contains an allusion to the poet in indicating his pen-name (*takhalluṣ*). Cf. *LHP* II, 23, 25, and M. Garcin de Tassy, *Rhétorique et Prosodie des Langues de l'Orient Musulman* (Paris, 1873), p. 375.

[2] *LHP* III, 344.

[3] *a'ṭima*, pl. of *ṭa'ām*, "dish" (of food).

of importance because of the details and names it gives of various foods, and of the festive occasions and eating habits associated with them. His poems and several small treatises, "The Tale of the Saffroned Rice", "The Book of Būsḥāq's Dream" and "The Glossary", are full of the old culinary terms of Iran up to his time. He was not without his imitators, for example Niẓām al-Dīn Maḥmūd Qārī of Yazd, who in the 9th/15th century also wrote verses on such subjects as dishes and dress. His poems have come down to us in his *Dīvān-i albisa* ("The Dīvān of Clothes"), which is now printed and is important because of the details to be derived from it of the dress of that century.

Also belonging to the 9th/15th century was Sayyid Ni'mat-Allāh Valī of Kirmān (d. 22 Rajab 834/4 April 1431). He was a great mystic and the founder of the Ni'matallāhī order of dervishes. His mystical poetry, which is of mediocre quality, consists of ghazals, qaṣīdas and masnavīs. Another mystic was Sayyid 'Alī b. Nāṣir b. Hārūn, better known as Qāsim al-Anvār (d. 837/1433–4), whose dīvān contains a number of poems in the dialect of the province of Gīlān as well as some verses in Turkish.

The qaṣīdas and masnavīs of Maulānā Muḥammad b. 'Abd-Allāh Kātibī of Turshīz or Nīshāpūr (d. 839/1435–6) are well known for their poetical artifices. He was the author of punning masnavīs in which he used double metres and double rhyme; these poems were entitled *Ḥusn u 'ishq* ("Beauty and Love"), *Nāẓir u manẓūr* ("The Viewer and the Viewed") and *Bahrām u Gul-Andām*. It is said that towards the end of his life he began a poetical rejoinder to the *Khamsa* of Niẓāmī.

A poet who has been praised for the beauty, effectiveness and clarity of his verse is Mīr Shāhī Sabzavārī (d. 857/1453). In particular, his ghazals are worthy of attention as they are full of meaning and beauty. Similarly, the love poems of Shaikh Āẕarī of Isfarā'in (d. 866/1461–2) are lively, graceful and full of fine ideas. A well-known poetical work which is attributed to him is the *Bahman-nāma*, about the Bahmanid rulers of the Deccan.

Maulānā Muḥammad b. Ḥusām al-Dīn, better known as Ibn Ḥusām (d. 875/1470–1), wrote poems of various kinds as well as a religious epic entitled the *Khāvarān-nāma* describing the travels and wars of 'Alī b. Abī Ṭālib. The dīvān of his qaṣīdas has been published in modern times in a printed edition.

Among the poets of the second rank of this epoch are Shihāb of Turshīz, Sīmī of Nīshāpūr, Ghiyāṣ of Shīrāz, Khiyālī of Bukhārā, Bābā Saudā'ī, Ṭālib of Jājarm and several others. At the close of the period there were other poets of this class, such as Hilālī Chaghatā'ī, Hātifī of Kharjird, Qāsimī and a few more. As, however, most of those in the latter group gained fame in the early part of the Safavid era, they will be mentioned in the later section.

By far the most outstanding literary figure of the last years of the Timurid epoch, a man who as a poet ranks as the greatest after Ḥāfiẓ, was Nūr al-Dīn 'Abd al-Raḥmān Jāmī (b. 817/1414, d. 898/1492). This poet and mystic, besides being one of the greatest writers of his age and a prolific one, a scholar in both Arabic and Persian, a critic as well as poet and one of Islam's most celebrated biographers of great figures in the path of Sufism, was also one of the leaders of the Naqshbandī order of dervishes, a fact which must attest the saintliness and studiousness of his life.

In his maṣnavīs Jāmī followed Sa'dī and Ḥāfiẓ, and in his ghazals the qaṣīda-writers of Iraq. However, one must not consider Jāmī's poetry as being empty of original ideas, power of expression and beauty of meaning. Although he cannot be said to equal his eminent predecessors, he, as the last great Persian poet, may be said to have a place and importance of his own. His poetical works include, first, the *Haft aurang* or *Sab'a* ("Septet"), which consists of seven maṣnavīs, the *Silsilat al-ẕahab* ("The Chain of Gold"), *Salmān u Absāl*, *Tuḥfat al-aḥrār*, *Subḥat al-abrār*, *Yūsuf u Zulaikhā*, *Lailā u Majnūn* and the *Khirad-nāma-yi Iskandarī*. The collection of Jāmī's ghazals, qaṣīdas and tarji'-bands is filled with mystical ideas, stories and lyrical themes; but more will be said of Jāmī in discussing Timurid prose-writers.

PROSE

Persian prose in the Timurid era had a relatively promising beginning. Since the prose works of this period were written for the most part in a simple and familiar style, they are comparatively free of the technical and rhetorical exaggerations of the 6th/12th and 7th/13th centuries: one meets with only occasional examples of ornate writing in which a highly artificial style is employed. The Timurid prose writers paid less attention to archaic Persian wording; they often used the words and compounds in common use in their own time, hence the simplicity and fluency of their style. However, the influence of the Turkish language cannot be overlooked. Also writers in this period paid little attention to the fundamental rules and conventions of the Persian language; a fact to be associated with their lack of any desire to be precise, to keep facts in view and ensure the soundness of their subject matter.

Although, generally speaking, traces of an artificial style are rare, for prefaces, the beginning of chapters and dedications to leaders and other dignitaries an ornate style was adopted. Frequently the abundance of ingenious but superficial titles and compliments obscures the real meaning of a passage. In some works one meets with dry rhyming prose and inadmissible formalities; but in others there is a refreshing directness. By and large the prose of this era lacks the firmness and succinctness of ancient writers, and appreciation of their style and adherence to their canons of taste are not, as a rule, in the least conspicuous.

There was no lack of variety in the subjects treated: they include scientific problems, history, tales, biography, commentaries on the Qur'ān, theological questions, mysticism, ethics and so on. The tendency to write on scientific subjects in Persian had been strengthened in the Mongol period and was still present. The reason was that, as the fall of Baghdad receded further into the past and the influence of the Arabic language and literature diminished, the need to employ the Persian language in the composition of scientific works became increasingly pressing.

A matter in the closing years of the Timurid period which has already been alluded to and is worthy of consideration is the use of Turkish as a literary language. The writing and compilation of books in that tongue was encouraged in the literary circles at Herat. This was in effect the strengthening of a movement which had been introduced earlier by Ḥusain Bāīqarā and Mīr 'Alī Shīr Navā'ī. Among other works, the *Majālis al-nafā'is*, the *Muḥākamat al-lughatain*, the *Maḥbūb al-qulūb*, the *Munsha'āt* and others by Mīr 'Alī Shīr Navā'ī and the *Bābur-nāma* by Ẓahīr al-Dīn Bābur were written in Turkish. Parallel to this development was the appearance of those bilingual poets to whom reference has already been made.

One of the highly regarded writers of the period was Niẓām al-Dīn Shanb-i Ghāzānī, known as Niẓām-i Shāmī, a contemporary of Tīmūr. In obedience to Tīmūr's orders he wrote the *Ẓafar-nāma*. Its style is simple, in contrast with that of Sharaf al-Dīn 'Alī Yazdī, another learned historian and writer, who made use of this biography in his own *Ẓafar-nāma-yi Tīmūrī*. His is a longer work, written in a florid and verbose manner, and was completed in 828/1424–5. Tīmūr's very last years, together with the early years of the reign of Shāh Rukh, had meanwhile been covered in the *Shams al-ḥusn*, composed by Tāj al-Dīn Salmānī in 813/1411.

A slightly later historian was Shihāb al-Dīn 'Abd-Allāh b. Luṭf-Allāh al-Khwāfī, known as Ḥāfiẓ-i Abrū (d. 833/1430), whose *Majma' al-tavārīkh* is a vast general history from the Creation down to 830/1426–7 in four volumes. Of these the last, known independently as the *Zubdat al-tavārīkh-i Bāīsunqurī*, is concerned with the period following the death of the Īl-Khān Abū Sa'īd in 736/1335. In addition, Ḥāfiẓ-i Abrū produced other historical works which are much briefer but of scarcely less importance: a history of the Kartid rulers of Herat from *c.* 732/1331–2; a history of the Sarbadārs; and surveys of the reigns of minor potentates in Khurāsān such as the Īl-Khān Togha Temür, Amīr Valī and Arghūn Shāh.[1] These pieces are included, along with a new edition of the great *Jāmi' al-tavārīkh* of Rashīd al-Dīn Fażl-Allāh (d. 718/1318) and Ḥāfiẓ-i Abrū's continuation (*ẕail*) of it, in his *Majmū'a*, or "compendium", which has fortunately survived in two Istanbul manuscripts (Bagdad Köşkü 282 and Damad Ibrahim Paşa 919). Ḥāfiẓ-i Abrū's anonymous geographical treatise, finally, is a major historical source in its own right, containing original data especially on his native Khurāsān and on Transoxiana.

Aḥmad b. Jalāl al-Dīn Muḥammad, known as Faṣīḥ-i Khwāfī, was the author of the *Mujmal-i Faṣīḥī*, which he completed in the year 845/1441–2 and submitted to Shāh Rukh. This book is of importance because it contains biographical notices of many Persian poets and scholars. Its style is of the simplest.

A writer of a different kind was Kamāl al-Dīn Ḥusain b. Ḥasan Khwārazmī, who was killed in 839/1435–6 and was the author of the book entitled the *Javāhir al-asrār u javāhir al-anvār*; it is a commentary on Rūmī's *Masnavī* and has a long preface on the history and beliefs of the ṣūfīs.

Ṣā'in 'Alī b. Muḥammad Tarka'ī Iṣfahānī (d. 836/1432–3) was a theological scholar of the age. He was well trained in speculative and

[1] These minor chronicles and the history of the Kartids were edited by Tauer as *Cinq opuscules de Ḥāfiẓ-i Abrū*. On the rulers named, see above, chapter 1.

traditional learning and achieved considerable fame during the reign of Shāh Rukh. Among his better known works are his translation of the *Milal wa'l-niḥal* by Muḥammad b. 'Abd al-Karīm Shahristānī, and the *Asrār al-ṣalavāt* and the *Tuḥfat-i 'alā'iyya* on the principles of the Islamic religion according to the four Sunnī schools. He also wrote a number of books in Arabic, in which he adopted a florid style.

Among the distinguished prose writers of this period was the poet Nūr al-Dīn 'Abd al-Raḥmān Jāmī, one of whose greatest works is the *Nafaḥāt al-uns* ("Breaths of Fellowship"), a biography of 614 ṣūfī saints. This book, written in 883/1478–9, is for the most part a translation of a collection of ṣūfī biographies by Khwāja 'Abd-Allāh Anṣārī of Herat, a work written in the Herat dialect and itself for the most part a translation of the Arabic work, the *Ṭabaqāt al-Ṣūfiyya*, of Muḥammad b. Ḥusain Sulamī of Nīshāpūr, though each of the two translators added something of his own. The *Nafaḥāt al-uns*, which is written in a simple and clear style, is one of the most authoritative works on the subject of the ṣūfīs and has a long introduction respecting their doctrine. Another of Jāmī's prose works, the *Kitāb al-bahāristān*, was written in imitation of Sa'dī's *Gulistān* and intended to teach his young son, for whose benefit he included at the end a memoir of some of the most famous Persian poets. Also deserving mention in a catalogue of Jāmī's prose works is the *Lavā'iḥ* ("Flashes"), consisting of 30 articles (*lā'iḥa*), each of which briefly describes a principle of mysticism. As a commentary on difficult points in the *Lama'āt* of Fakhr al-Din Ibrāhīm 'Irāqī,[1] a famous poet and mystic of the Mongol era, Jāmī wrote, in simple and direct language, his *Ashi''at al-lama'āt* ("Rays of the Flashes"), a highly important Persian work on mysticism. In addition to this commentary, Jāmī also wrote Persian treatises on other theological and literary works, including the *Nāi-nāma (Maṡnavī)* of Jalāl al-Dīn Rūmī, and commentaries on the poems of Amīr Khusrau of Delhi.

Another writer of this period was Ghiyāṡ al-Dīn 'Alī b. 'Alī Ḥusainī Iṣfahānī, a contemporary of Sultan Abū Sa'īd the Timurid, whose book, the *Dānish-nāma-yi jahān*, is an important work on divine and natural philosophy, written in simple Persian prose.

It will not be out of place here to mention one of the most remarkable translations into Persian prose, the translation of the *Rasā'il* of the Ikhvān al-ṣafā, from a summarised Arabic version entitled *Majma'*

[1] 'Irāqī was his *takhalluṣ* or pen-name: see *LHP* III, 124.

al-ḥikmat. This book, in clear and spirited Persian, dates from the reign of Tīmūr; several manuscripts of it are extant.

One of the greatest chronicles of this period, a work which has been used as a source by most subsequent historians, is the *Maṭla' al-sa'dain* ("The Dawn of the Two Auspicious Planets"), written by Maulānā Kamāl al-Dīn 'Abd al-Razzāq al-Samarqandī (d. 887/1482). This history covers a period of some 170 years, from the reign of the last Il-Khanid ruler of Iran, Abū Sa'īd (716–736/1316–1335), to the end of that of Tīmūr's great-grandson, his namesake, who reigned from 855/1451–2 to 873/1469. Though the author had the *nisba* "Samarqandī", he was himself born at Herat; Samarqand was the birthplace of his father, Maulānā Jalāl al-Dīn Isḥāq, who had been a jurist and divine under Shāh Rukh. The love of historical narratives and desire for annals of their own times evinced by the Mongol Il-Khanid rulers continued down to the days of Tīmūr and his successors.

The great work of Daulatshāh b. 'Alā' al-Daula Bakhtīshāh of Samarqand, the *Taẕkirat al-shu'arā* ("Memoirs of the Poets"), takes us out of the realm of history into that of a species of literary history, anthologising and even, it may be said, literary criticism. For in addition to brief biographies of the poets, written in a straightforward, bombast-free style, and to numerous extracts from their works, whence the anthologising aspect of the book is derived, Daulatshāh permits himself to make judgments on the powers of his chosen poets. Admittedly, these judgments range in degrees of praise rather than of derogation. This feature gives the work the impress of being deliberately revivalist or recollective in purpose, as if a later age was considered in need of prompting to recall the literary splendours of times past. Daulatshāh, whatever his private motives, received publicly acknowledged encouragement in the preparation of this volume from Mīr 'Alī Shīr Navā'ī, that Maecenas to whom allusion has already been made. Next to the *Lubāb al-albāb* of Muḥammad 'Aufī, Daulatshāh's work is the most important collection of biographies of poets in Persian; though there is a considerable time gap between the two compositions, for 'Aufī's work goes down only as far as 625/1228.

The date of Daulatshāh's death is uncertain: it was at some time between 896/1490–1 and 900/1494–5. While we are on the subject of this particular uncertainty in dating it is appropriate to issue the now standard warning about Daulatshāh's unreliability as a historian. His observations on the dating and his accounts of the lives of poets are so frequently inaccurate that his statements cannot, generally speaking, be accepted without caution. Legend and fact are inextricably intermingled. Nonetheless, his treatment of the lives of 105 poets comprises a volume of surpassing interest and great readability.

Returning to purely historical narrative, the *Rauẓāt al-jannāt fī auṣāf madīnat Harāt* was completed in 875/1470 by Mu'īn al-Dīn Muḥammad Isfizārī, who thus provided posterity with a book of considerable value as containing the chronicle of the Kartid rulers of Herat, and events of the Timurid period up to the reign of Ḥusain Bāīqarā, with many useful details about the notables of that time. As a stylist, Isfizārī deserves special mention for the clarity and sureness of his use of language. He was similarly a master in the epistolatory style, and was for a time in charge of the court correspondence. There are, however, decorative attempts in his "History of the City of Herat", comprised of quotations from some of the older poets, and also in the occasional adoption of a florid and prolix method of exposition, in particular in some decriptive flights and in introductory passages.

A local history such as Isfizārī's is of great importance to later historians, but much better known is the general history of Muḥammad b. Khāvand Shāh b. Maḥmūd, known as Mīr Khwānd (b. 838/1434–5, d. 903/1498). This work is called the *Rauẓat al-ṣafā fī sīrat al-anbiyā va'l-mulūk va'l-khulafā*, and is in seven volumes. The last part was added by his daughter's son, Ghiyāṣ al-Dīn b. Humām al-Dīn Muḥammad, surnamed Khwānd Amīr. Like his grandfather, Khwānd Amīr enjoyed the patronage of the Timurid rulers, to whose courts, especially that of Ḥusain Bāīqarā, Mīr Khwānd had been closely attached and by whom he had been highly respected. This last volume deals with events in the reigns of Ḥusain Bāīqarā and of his son, Badī' al-Zamān Mīrzā. But the total work had for its objective a detailed record of pre-Islamic history and of the Muslim era; while, thanks to another and later hand being engaged in completing the *Rauẓat al-ṣafā*, the last section deals with episodes that followed Mīr Khwānd's death. It is written in simple, informal language and may be said to bring to culmination the stylistic tendencies in the prose of the Timurid age.[1]

Besides completing his grandfather's *Rauẓat al-ṣafā*, Ghiyāṣ al-Dīn Khwānd Amīr (d. 941/1534–5)[2] wrote a collection of biographies of

[1] Though cf. the less favourable views expressed by Browne, *LHP* III, 433, and by Arberry, *Classical Persian Literature*, p. 390.

[2] For the date, see *PL* I/1, 101.

Muslim viziers, including those of Iran, called *Dastūr al-vuzarā*, and a general history, the *Ḥabīb al-siyar*, which comes down to the reign of the Safavid Shah Ismāʿīl I (907–930/1502–1524) and beyond. The latter work will be discussed below.

Abu'l-Ghāzī Sulṭān Ḥusain b. Manṣūr b. Bāīqarā b. ʿUmar Shaikh b. Tīmūr, the last notable Timurid prince to rule in Iran, has been mentioned so far for his patronage of literature in the capital, Herat, where he had been born and which he captured on Abū Saʿīd's death in 873/1469, to rule Khurāsān thence for thirty-eight years until his own demise in 911/1506. A dīvān of his poetry in Turki is, according to Storey, to be found in the Bibliothèque Nationale in Paris.[1] But in prose at least he must be mentioned here as possibly a Persian author in his own right. For he is the ostensible compiler of the *Majālis al-ʿushshāq* ("Conferences of the Lovers"). This work comprises an introduction treating of earthly and divine love, and seventy-six "conferences" in which, in ornate prose interspersed with verse, an equal number (or thereabouts) of mystics, famous lovers and kings are the subject-matter. The work was begun in 908/1502–3 and completed in the next year, the last person to be dealt with in it being Sulṭān Ḥusain himself. As reference to Storey's bibliography and to Browne's *A Literary History of Persia* will show,[2] the book was severely criticised by the Mughal emperor Bābur (932–937/1526–1530) in his *Bābur-nāma*. Here it is attributed not to Sulṭān Ḥusain but to Kamāl al-Dīn Ḥusain Gāzurgāhī, and described as a wretched book, full of "insipid" lies, in which carnal and spiritual loves are confused the one with the other, and from which the odour of heresy is not entirely absent. Bābur was equally incensed over the attribution made by Kamāl al-Dīn to Sulṭān Ḥusain of a work in which the verses are undoubtedly by himself and not by the sultan. The book, for all its weaknesses and despite the difficulty over its correct attribution, nonetheless deserves to be mentioned here because it serves to illustrate the taste and interests of some of the literati of the time, however lapsed the former may appear to have been, and however exotic the latter.

Although for ornateness of style, and as affording yet a further example of a decline in rhetoric,[3] he cannot be put in a superior class, Kamāl al-Dīn Ḥusain Vāʿiẓ-i Kāshifī of Sabzavār (d. 910/1504–5) was a

[1] *Ibid.*, I/2, 959.
[2] *Ibid.*, pp. 960–1. *LHP* III, 457–8.
[3] *LHP* III, 463.

much more genuine and serious writer than the compiler of the *Majālis* discussed above. As his title of Vā'iẓ implies, he was a preacher and resided in Herat, where he was a member of the ṣūfī order of the Naqshbandīs. His late work, the *Akhlāq-i Muḥsinī*, dedicated to Ḥusain Bāīqarā and composed in 900/1494–5, entitles him to rank among the writers on ethics in Persian, followers of the example set by Naṣīr al-Dīn Ṭūsī (d. 672/1274) in his *Akhlāq-i Nāṣirī* (633/1235–6). But this was by no means the sole, nor the most important, production of this typical Muslim savant, a jurisprudent, a litterateur, a Qur'anic exegetist, a man versed in astrology and the scholasticism of his time and religious environment. One of his more famous works, though more famous in India than Iran and written in a florid and turgid style, is his *Anvār-i Suhailī* ("The Lights of Canopus"), which is, in fact, a translation in a revised form of the *Kalīla va Dimna*.[1] He also wrote a *Makhzan al-inshā* ("Treasury of the Art of Composition").

Another of Vā'iẓ-i Kāshifī's works achieved considerable celebrity in the fervently Shī'ī Safavid epoch, when it was recited at the assemblies which collected to mourn the deaths of the Shī'ī martyrs. From this use of it the work became known as the *Majālis-i rauẓa-khwānī*, ("The Assemblies of the Recitations of the Martyrs' Deaths"), but its correct title is the *Rauẓat al-shuhadā* ("The Garden of Martyrs"). It deals particularly with the martyrdom of the Prophet's grandson Ḥusain, the Third Imām, and with persecutions undergone by other prophets and imāms, and is once again a work composed in a highly rhetorical style. While its historicity is not of much validity, its nature is indicative of 9th/15th century religious and stylistic impulses, of a kind which increased in prominence during the succeeding era.

In the field of Qur'anic exegesis, Vā'iẓ-i Kāshifī produced, for Mīr 'Alī Shīr Navā'ī, a Persian commentary on the Qur'ān entitled the *Mavāhib-i 'Aliyya*, completed in 899/1493–4, and representing a concise work in contrast to his other essay in the compilation of a commentary on the Qur'ān, the *Javāhir al-asrār*, also called the *Javāhir al-tafsīr* ("Gems of Exegesis"). This undertaking was planned on a more ambitious scale than the *Mavāhib*.

In yet another sphere, though one which might also be adduced as a

[1] Browne's comment is interesting, *loc. cit.*, where he states that Ḥusain Vā'iẓ "set himself to 'write up' and improve upon the work of his predecessors", this being a reference to the Persian version of Niẓām al-Dīn Abu'l-Ma'ālī Naṣr-Allāh in the 12th century, based on 'Abd-Allāh b. al-Muqaffa''s Arabic version made in the 8th century.

reason for including this author under the heading, if not of authors of ethical works, at least of those on social categories and institutions, is Vā'iẓ-i Kāshifī's *Futuvvat-nāma-yi Sulṭānī*, a work of great interest for the study of Iranian social history, since it deals with the manner of training, the beliefs and the conventions of various groups of *Fityān* (*Jāvānmardān*), "youths".

Concerning astrology he wrote the *Ikhtiyārāt* and the *Sab'a Kāshifa* ("The Seven Kashifian Discourses"). His *Lubb-i lubāb-i maṣnavī* is an abridgement of Jalāl al-Dīn Rūmī's *Maṣnavī*, itself abridged in his further work, the *Lubb-i lubb*. Besides the works mentioned, this versatile preacher's name has been appended to numerous other prose dissertations and *opera*.

His son, Fakhr al-Dīn Vā'iẓ (d. 939/1532–3), was also a writer of the late Timurid and early Safavid periods. His most famous composition is the *Rashaḥāt-i 'ain al-ḥayāt* ("Sprinklings from the Spring of Life"), a work devoted to the grace, teachings and examples of Khwāja 'Abd-Allāh, a great leader of the Naqshbandī order of ṣūfīs of the Timurid era, and of his associates. In addition, Fakhr al-Dīn wrote an interesting and informative collection of anecdotes about various classes of society: rulers, ministers, divines, ṣūfīs and others.

There remains Jalāl al-Dīn Muḥammad As'ad Ṣiddīqī Davānī (b. 830/1426–7, d. 908/1502–3), the author of the *Akhlāq-i Jalālī*, a work on ethics whose more correct title is the *Lavāmi' al-ishrāq fī makārim al-akhlāq* ("The Beams of the Suns in the Graces of Ethics"). This work, like Vā'iẓ-i Kāshifī's *Akhlāq-i Muḥsinī*, stemmed from the tradition of works on ethics established by the *Akhlāq-i Nāṣirī* of Khwāja Naṣīr al-Din Ṭūsī.

The prose works which were a feature of the Timurid period cannot be left without some reference to those connected with the sect of the Ḥurūfīs, which was founded in the reign of Tīmūr by a certain Fażl-Allāh of Astarābād. The most important work of this sect, whose scribes adopted a special literary style with symbols and idioms peculiar to their persuasion, is the founder's own *Jāvīdān-nāma*. Other Ḥurūfī texts are the *Ādam-nāma*, the *'Arsh-nāma*, the *Hidāyat-nāma*, the *Ustuvār-nāma*, the *Kursī-nāma* and the *Muḥabbat-nāma*, while there is a key to the secrets of the *Jāvīdān-nāma* entitled the *Miftāḥ al-ḥayāt* ("Key of Life").

CHAPTER 17 (*b*)

ḤĀFIẒ AND HIS CONTEMPORARIES

One of the great experiences in Iran is a visit to Shīrāz and the delightful garden that is laid out around the tomb of Ḥāfiẓ; to enter under the white marble baldachin that covers the tombstone on which some of the poet's verses are engraved in elegant *nasta'līq*, and to open the *Dīvān-i Ḥāfiẓ* to look for a *fa'l*, an augury, according to well established rules that have been followed for centuries. During such a moment the visitor may perhaps recall the beautiful lines written by the "last classical poet" of Turkey, Yahya Kemal Beyatli (1881–1958), who uses one of Ḥāfiẓ's central concepts, that of *rind* ("vagrant"), in his poem *Rindlerin ölümü*:

> In the garden at Ḥāfiẓ's tomb there is a rose
> Which opens every day with blood-like colour;
> At night, the nightingale weeps until dawn turns grey,
> With a tune that reminds us of ancient Shīrāz.
>
> Death is a calm country of spring for a vagrant;
> His heart fumes everywhere like a censer – for years ...
> And over his tomb that lies under cool cypresses
> A rose opens every morn, every night a nightingale sings.

During the long history of Islam Shīrāz was always an important centre of learning, mysticism, and poetry. In spite of frequent changes in government, numerous wars and internecine feuds of its rulers the city can boast of a long-standing cultural tradition. To be sure, the 8th/14th century, when Ḥāfiẓ lived, was no longer the time of the asceticism of Ibn-i Khafīf (d. 371/982) nor of the high-soaring mystical experiences of Rūzbihān Baqlī (d. 606/1209), and the days of Sa'dī, whose works made the name of Shīrāz known in the West before those of most other places in Iran, had long passed. But the religious tradition was embodied in one of the leading Ash'arī theologians of the later Middle Ages, 'Aẓud al-Dīn Ījī (d. 756/1355), who held the office of chief *qāḍī* under Abū Isḥāq Īnjū, although he later withdrew from Shīrāz. His *Mawāqif*, a kind of *Summa Theologica*, was to become a standard work in scholastic theology, and it is said that Ḥāfiẓ, too, studied it. The *Mawāqif* was often commented upon by later theologians; among them was – still during Ḥāfiẓ's lifetime – al-Sayyid al-Sharīf al-Jurjānī (d. 1413) who, after long wanderings in Egypt and Turkey, was called to the Muzaffarid capital in 1377 as a professor in the Dār al-shifā madrasa, and returned once more to Shīrāz after a prolonged stay in Samarqand whither Tīmūr had carried him. Jurjānī's *Ta'rīfāt* are still a helpful instrument for the understanding of theological definitions.

Poets were not lacking either in Shīrāz or in other Persian cities around 1350. E.G. Browne goes so far as to call the 8th/14th century the richest period of Persian literature, a fact which he ascribes to the existence of numerous small courts that competed with each other in attracting literati. Salmān Sāvajī (d. 778/1376), the panegyrist of the Jalayirids in Baghdad and Tabrīz, is noted for his "fluency of language" and his skilful use of *īhām* ("amphibology") which he displayed in "artistic qaṣīdas" (*qaṣīda-yi maṣnū'*). His contemporary Kamāl al-Dīn Khwājū Kirmānī settled finally in Shīrāz, where he died in 1352 or 1361; he left a dīvān with enjoyable ghazals. Certain similarities between his verses and those of Ḥāfiẓ have been pointed out by the critics. Besides lyrical poetry he composed a *Khamsa*, out of whose five – mostly mystically tinged – epics the story of Humāī and Humāyūn has attracted the interest of scholars because of the exquisite miniatures that adorn one of the early 9th/15th century manuscripts.[1] Somewhat later we find Kamāl Khujandī (d. probably in 803/1400) in Tabrīz; he and Ḥāfiẓ seem to have been acquainted, although Kamāl, an interpreter of the theory of *vaḥdat al-vujūd*, is censured as "abstruse" by the sober commentator Sūdī in the 10th/16th century. In Shīrāz itself the poetry of 'Imād al-Dīn Faqīh Kirmānī (d. 773/1371–2) was widely acclaimed. He was the chief panegyrist of the Muzaffarids, a fertile lyrical author, and also produced five mystical masnavīs. 'Imād al-Dīn and Ḥāfiẓ were allegedly not on very friendly terms, as some biographers assume, who spin out a story from Ḥāfiẓ's verse:

> Don't be duped when the devotee cat performs the ritual prayer,[2]

which is interpreted as referring to 'Imād's well-trained cat. However, as Browne pointed out, Ḥāfiẓ's expression can be more safely traced back to a verse in *Mūsh u gurba* ("Cat and mouse"), a little epic still widely read in Iran which has often been lithographed or printed with

[1] Reproduced most recently in A. Papadopoulo, *Islamische Kunst* (Freiburg i. Br., 1977), pl. 41.
[2] Brockhaus, no. 122. Aḥmad and Nā'īnī, no. 102.

simple illustrations. Its author, 'Ubaid-i Zākānī (d. 772/1371), a citizen of Shīrāz, which he dearly loved, is mainly noted for his satires; his prose satire *Akhlāq al-ashrāf* offers an interesting picture of the vices of Persian society in the 8th/14th century.

However, to speak of Shīrāz in the 8th/14th century – in fact, even to mention the city's name at all among educated Westerners – means to recall immediately the one name that has become the epitome of the Persian lyric for both Oriental and Western readers, that of Muḥammad Shams al-Dīn Ḥāfiẓ. Surpassed in popularity, particularly in the English-speaking world, only by 'Umar Khayyām, the name of Ḥāfiẓ stands in the West for everything Persian: for the apogee of uninhibited sensual delight; enjoyment of the prohibited wine; and the predominance of love in all its shades, while most of the Oriental interpreters see in him "the tongue of the Unseen World", singing of Divine Love and spiritual intoxication. In the German-speaking world, Ḥāfiẓ's name has become almost a household word since the days of Goethe. But famous as he is in both East and West, and much as he has been interpreted as the embodiment of sensuality and free thinking on the one hand, and of the highest mystical enthusiasm on the other, yet it is difficult to give a satisfactory account of his life; and the orientalist views with envy his colleagues in the field of German or English philology who can follow the development of their great writers step by step, almost day by day. In the case of Oriental poets it is next to impossible to transgress the narrow framework offered by the biographers and to infuse real life into the numerous anecdotes which are repeated time and again by the writers. A few remarks in contemporary historical sources, perhaps a tombstone, or some scattered hints in the poetry itself, may prove helpful for the chronology of a Persian lyrical poet's life. On the whole, our knowledge of Ḥāfiẓ's life is woefully inadequate.

The preface of one of the oldest manuscripts – used intensively for the first time by Qāsim Ghanī and Muḥammad Qazvīnī – contains at least some biographical material. But even the date of Ḥāfiẓ's birth is not yet established. Some authors, like Ghanī, put it in 717/1317–8, while others such as M. Mu'īn plead for 725/1325–6, a date which would agree fairly well with the statement in 'Abd al-Nabī's *Maikhāna* (written in 1626) that Ḥāfiẓ died at the age of sixty-five lunar years. Most European scholars seem to have accepted a date of *c.* 719/1319–20.

Ḥāfiẓ's father, a merchant who had migrated from Iṣfahān to Shīrāz, died early, leaving the family in straitened circumstances. Yet young

Ḥāfiẓ apparently enjoyed the traditional education in a *madrasa*. Some sources speak of his poverty, and say that he apprenticed himself to a doughmaker to earn his livelihood. It seems that he worked as a copyist for quite some time; for the library in Tashkent owns a copy of Amīr Khusrau's *Khamsa* in his hand, dated 9 February 1355.[1] That means that even in his thirties he had still to do some menial work. However, he must have been very well versed in the Qur'anic sciences; hence his nom-de-plume Ḥāfiẓ. His Arabic was excellent and in later years he taught exegesis and other theological courses in Shīrāz. According to the preface he studied Zamakhsharī's *Kashshāf* (to which he incidentally alludes in one of his ghazals), Sakkākī's *Miftāḥ* and several other Arabic works; according to A. Krymsky, some of his Arabic works are extant in autographs.[2]

A charming story tells how he received his initiation in the art of poetry at Bābā Kūhī's tomb on the hillside near Shīrāz, where 'Alī b. Abī Ṭālib appeared to him and offered him some heavenly food. The beautiful ghazal,

Dūsh vaqt-i saḥar az ghuṣṣa najātam dādand

(Yesterday at dawn I was given relief from my grief),[3]

is taken as an allusion to this event, although the story was almost certainly invented to fit the poet into the Shī'ī tradition. But in spite of Krymsky's opinion, he was not an avowed Shī'ī, for no authentic Shī'ī verse appears in the Dīvān. Several invitations from rulers outside Fārs show that his poetry attracted some interest quite early. Aḥmad Jalāyir, himself a skilful poet and talented calligrapher *inter alia*, invited him probably after Shāh-i Shujā''s death (786/1384). But before that the ruler of the Bahmanid kingdom in South India sent for him, as one century earlier the ruler of Multān, Prince Muḥammad b. Balabān, the Maecenas of Amīr Khusrau, had invited Sa'dī to leave Shīrāz for India. Ḥāfiẓ did not accept any of the invitations; but in one of his ghazals he speaks of far-away Bengal where his poetry was appreciated – poetry, which, like a perfected ṣūfī, can perform the miracle of *ṭaiy al-makān* ("ubiquity") and, though only a child one night old, can immediately make one year's journey. In this poem he says in a line that connects in a clever *murā'āt al-naẓīr* three items from the geographical sphere and

[1] Rypka, *HIL*, p. 264, following Y.E. Bertel's, "Literatura na persidskom yazyke v Sredneĭ Azii", *SV* 1948, 201.
[2] Rypka, *HIL*, p. 277, n.95.
[3] Brockhaus, no. 218. Aḥmad and Nā'īnī, no. 112.

the traditional combination of the sweet-speaking parrot with sugar:

> All the parrots of India become "sweet-spoken"
> From that Persian candy that goes towards Bengal,[1]

a line in which we find a subtle allusion to his superiority even over Amīr Khusrau, who was commonly called the *ṭūṭī-yi Hind* and whose work Ḥāfiẓ himself had copied.

Very little is known about Ḥāfiẓ's personal life. He must have been married, and one of his ghazals is interpreted as an elegy for his son, who died, probably, in 764/1362–3. According to Firishta, who is followed by an 18th-century Indian writer, the polyhistor Āzād Bilgrāmī, one of Ḥāfiẓ's sons by the name of Shāh Nu'mān came to India and is buried in Burhānpūr.

We do not know whether Ḥāfiẓ belonged to one of the numerous ṣūfī orders which were then quite active in the Middle East. The area of Shīrāz was the first part of Iran where a more closely knit community of dervishes had been formed by Abū Isḥāq-i Kāzarūnī (d. 426/1035) and his followers, who were not only active in helping the needy in Fārs but soon extended their activities as far as India and China. Ḥāfiẓ's colleague Khwājū was a member of the Kāzarūniyya. No name of any of the leading ṣūfī masters – be it 'Abd al-Qādir al-Gīlānī, the Suhravardīs, or Maulānā Rūmī – occurs in his verse, at least not overtly. Maybe the frequent use of musical terms and allusions to the *samā'* point to Ḥāfiẓ's knowledge of Rūmī's poetry, in which such imagery abounds. But this is only a vague supposition. If it is correct that one Pīr Muḥammad 'Aṭṭār was his shaikh, he would be connected with the *silsila* of Rūzbihān Baqlī, as Ritter points out.[2] The poet apparently used to attend the sessions of Maulānā Qivām al-Dīn 'Abd-Allāh. That is stated not only in the old preface but also in an account according to which the Kubravī mystic Sayyid Ashraf al-Dīn Jahāngīr Simnānī (d. 808/1405), the patron saint of Kichhaucha in eastern Avadh, met Ḥāfiẓ around 782/1380.[3] The only way to find out more details about Ḥāfiẓ's life is to look, as Ritter has done recently, for the explicit and covert allusions to political figures whom he praised or blamed with subtle allusions.

1 Brockhaus, no. 158. Aḥmad and Nā'īnī, no. 149.

2 Ritter, "Hafiz", p. 67.

3 Rypka, *HIL*, pp. 276–7, following A.A. Hikmat, "Manābi'i jadīd dar pīrāmūn-i ḥayāt-i Ḥāfiẓ", *Majalla-yi Dānishkada-yi Adabiyyāt Shīrāz* vii (1341/1962), 3–38: the source is Niẓām al-Dīn Gharīb-i Yamanī, *Laṭā'if-i ashraf*.

When the poet was still very young, the Īl-Khān Abū Sa'īd died, in 736/1335. Abū Sa'īd's successor executed Sharaf al-Dīn Maḥmūd Shāh, who had been semi-independent in Shīrāz since 725/1325; after a struggle of seven years, Maḥmūd Shāh's son Abū Isḥāq Īnjū took over. Some of Ḥāfiẓ's poems praise the tolerant and artistically-minded prince and his vizier Qivām al-Dīn Ḥasan. But soon, in 754/1353, Shīrāz fell to the Muzaffarids, whose first ruler, Mubāriz al-Dīn, was orthodox, harsh, and not inclined to spare human life. He in turn was deposed and blinded by his own son Shāh-i Shujā' after five years of reign. One usually understands those poems in which Ḥāfiẓ derides or attacks the detested *muḥtasib*, the superintendent of market police, as applying to Mubāriz al-Dīn's reign. The most famous of these poems,

> *agar chi bāda faraḥbakhsh u bād gulbīz ast ...*
>
> (Even though the wine is pleasure-granting and the wind
> scattering rose-petals,
> Don't drink wine at the sound of the harp, for the muḥtasib is
> impetuous)[1],

alludes in its last line ("for now it is time for Baghdad and Tabrīz") to the two Jalayirid capitals (both of which were later conquered by Shāh-i Shujā') as more congenial places for the poet to sing. It seems, however, difficult to place all muḥtasib poems in Mubāriz al-Dīn's time, for example, the following verse:

> Don't tell the muḥtasib my faults,
> For he, too, is continually, like me, in search of wine
> [or: of good life].[2]

The solution of these problems is left to the interpreters' understanding.

When Shāh-i Shujā' ascended the throne times changed for the better, and Ḥāfiẓ sings cheerfully:

> At dawn, glad tidings reached my ear from the voice of the
> Unseen World:
> It's the time of Shāh-i Shujā' – drink boldly wine![3]

Shāh-i Shujā' himself, though an educated man, was a mediocre poet; his

[1] Brockhaus, no. 57. Aḥmad and Nā'īnī, no. 68.

[2] Brockhaus, no. 34. Aḥmad and Nā'īnī, no. 57, reading *'aish* instead of *bāda*. The whole poem speaks of enjoyment and drinking.

[3] Brockhaus, no. 327. Aḥmad and Nā'īnī, no. 251.

court poet proper was 'Imād al-Dīn Faqīh, but Ḥāfiẓ too was one of his eulogists and it seems that *Shāh-suvār*, who repeatedly represents "the beloved", is a subtle allusion to this ruler's surname Abū'l-Favāris. When the prince left Shīrāz between 765/1363 and 767/1366 Ḥāfiẓ wrote some poems that complain of separation from the "Friend". During those years Shāh-i Shujā' had to fight his own brother Maḥmūd, who in 1365 even laid siege to Shīrāz, along with the Jalayirid Shaikh Uvais. For some time the relations between the ruler and the poet apparently cooled down; at least the view of the biographers regarding Ḥāfiẓ's verse,

Gar musulmānī az ān ast ki Ḥāfiẓ dārad
Vāi agar az pai-yi imrūz buvad fardā'ī

(If the state of a Muslim is such as Ḥāfiẓ possesses –
Woe, if there were a tomorrow after today![1]),

is that it estranged him from the ruler because of its apparently non-Islamic character. *Fardā* has of course to be interpreted as Day of Judgment, which in the Qur'ān is often called "tomorrow", just as *dūsh* ("yesterday") in Persian poetry usually points to the time before creation, the Day of the Covenant (*rūz-i alast*), when "the angels kneaded Adam's clay".[2] Ḥāfiẓ may have travelled to Iṣfahān and Yazd during the "estrangement" around 1373; but the relevant traditions are weak.

Shāh-i Shujā' was succeeded in 786/1384 by Zain al-'Ābidīn; he after a brief reign by Shāh Yaḥyā. During that time the internecine feuds in the Muzaffarid family continued. More importantly, Tīmūr, in the course of his incessant conquests, reached Shīrāz in 1387, the same year when he massacred 70,000 people in Iṣfahān. He stayed in Shīrāz for two months and may well have met Ḥāfiẓ, interested as he was in gathering learned men and artists from all over the Muslim world. The anecdote about the dialogue between the world-conqueror and the poet has been told and retold – probably spun out of the famous *maṭla'* about the *Turk-i Shīrāzī*. The story is found in a rather early source, Shujā'-i Shīrāzī's *Anīs al-nās* of 830/1426–7, so it may contain some truth; it was then popularised by Daulatshāh, from whom Eastern and Western writers alike took it.[3]

Ḥāfiẓ died in 791/1389, to which the chronogram *khāk-i muṣallā*

[1] Brockhaus, no. 525. Aḥmad and Nā'īnī, no. 374.
[2] Brockhaus, no. 222. Aḥmad and Nā'īnī, no. 115.
[3] Sayyid Muḥammad 'Alī Jamālzāda, "Ravāj-i bāzār-i shi'r u shā'irī", *Armaghān* 46, 129–42, offers a text that authenticates the meetings.

would fit, or in 792/1390 (thus the chronogram *b ṣ ẓ* in the old preface). It is said that the orthodox refused to have him buried in a Muslim cemetery because of his anti-orthodox, sensual poetry; but by means of an oracle taken from his poetry they finally agreed to a correct burial. The story may or may not be true; the custom of asking the Dīvān for good advice in every situation has been maintained.

Since Ḥāfiẓ had been too busy with teaching and scholarly work he had no time, according to the early sources, to collect his Dīvān himself; this work was left to later scholars. And here the major problem for every interpreter of Ḥāfiẓ's poetry begins: the lack of an authentic text. We do not even know the identity of the "Friend" (usually called Muḥammad Gulandām) who speaks in the preface about his acquaintance with the poet. After Boelke had made some researches into the oldest available manuscripts, Robert M. Rehder discussed once more in 1974 the textual tradition of Ḥāfiẓ's poems, in a brief, well-documented article, giving an account of fourteen dated manuscripts prior to the year 827/1423–4, which is the date of the Ghanī – Qazvīnī text. Was the "Friend" the only collector of Ḥāfiẓ's verse? Or did independent collections exist soon after the poet's death? The latter possibility seems more likely. Single ghazals of Ḥāfiẓ can be found in manuscripts written during his lifetime, for example in a collection made in 781/1379–80 in Baghdad. A *safīna*, collected a year later in Shīrāz, contains four of Ḥāfiẓ's ghazals. In 1937 Rempis drew the attention of the scholars to a manuscript dated 820/1417 that belonged to one Muẓaffar Ḥusain in Hyderabad, Deccan;[1] but, as Rehder states with regret, the whereabouts of the manuscript, which was taken to Pakistan by its owner in 1948, are at present unknown, since it is not to be found in the Library of Khairpur Mīrs, which acquired the bulk of Muẓaffar Ḥusain's library. The National Museum in Delhi has a manuscript dated 818/1415, with 358 ghazals, on loan from Hyderabad. Another manuscript, mentioned by Rehder as no. 13, consists of an anthology and was formerly in Gavanpur; since it contains the preface it seems to be the same manuscript which was carefully edited by Aḥmad and Na'īnī in 1971. It contains 435 ghazals. Ritter had studied two very valuable manuscripts in the Ayasofya Library in Istanbul (AS 3945 and 3857), dated 1410 and 1413 respectively; one of them was written for the library of the Timurid prince Iskandar b. 'Umar Shaikh,

[1] Rempis, *Beiträge*, p. 126, n.2.

from whose library another copy is preserved in the British Library with 152 ghazals which was edited by Khānlarī. The Revan Köşkü in the Topkapı Sarayı, too, owns a pre-827 manuscript of Ḥāfiẓ's poems, and an important manuscript is preserved in the library of the Tajik Academy of Sciences (no. 555) and described by Galimova.

That the text of Ḥafiẓ's Dīvān was rather garbled as early as about a century after his death is understood from the statement of the versatile Timurid author Sharaf al-Dīn Marvārīd, who writes that "through the transcribing of the text by various scribes of defective understanding many of the pearls and precious stones of that 'pattern of the praiseworthy and eminent' [Ḥāfiẓ] became the prey of the plundering fingers of a handful of fools",[1] and by the fact that one of Ḥusain Bāīqarā's sons, Prince Farīdūn Khān, decided in 907/1501–2 to produce a better edition, which found its way later into the British Library (Or. 3,247).[2]

Almost every Persian Dīvān has a tendency to become inflated; but in the case of Ḥāfiẓ's poems this process is even more natural. After all, it was the only book besides the Qur'ān out of which prognostication was taken. Therefore many poets, scholars, and eager copyists have inserted their own verses or appropriate poems in Hafizian style for the sake of gaining fame under his name or of participating in the *baraka* of the book; others may have tried to improve verses according to their own taste. Nor can we exclude the possibility, suggested by Rehder, that a certain number of variant readings exist because Ḥāfiẓ wrote more than one version of a poem or revised his words. Sūdī's commentary comprises, in one edition, 575 poems, in Brockhaus, 692 poems; the editio princeps (Calcutta, 1791) has no less than 725 poems. The inflation of the text is most conspicuous in areas where Persian was a living language, as in Iran and India.

People's admiration for Ḥāfiẓ is reflected in the care the calligraphers took to transcribe his verse on beautiful coloured paper, surrounded with margins full of delicate golden drawings. His poems were copied not only by the masters of nasta'līq but also by the specialists in *shikasta*. Did the artists perhaps think of the poet's clever use of letter-images and of his complaint that the Friend did "not send him a letter to catch the bird of his heart with chainlike script"?[3]

[1] Rehder's translation: "The text of Hafiz", p. 147. Text printed in facsimile by Roemer, *Staatsschreiben*.

[2] Ch. Rieu, *Supplement to the Catalogue of the Persian Manuscripts in the British Museum* (London, 1895), no. 268.

[3] Brockhaus, no. 247. Aḥmad and Nā'īnī, no. 203.

Several copies of the Dīvān have been decorated with miniatures, one of the finest being that in the Fogg Art Museum (Cambridge, Mass.), datable to *c.* 1527: it originally contained two miniatures by Shaikhzāda and five by Sulṭān Muḥammad. The most attractive and at the same time intriguing picture is the one by Sulṭān Muḥammad which shows the various stages of heavenly and mundane intoxication, where "Ḥāfiẓ himself, popeyed with drink or religious inspiration, sits in a window with the huge wine jar",[1] under a roof on which angels are dancing and drinking, while in the lower level wild-looking dervishes produce strange music. It is indeed a picture "which demolishes the conventional split between the effects of wine and divine ecstasy. In this extraordinary transcendental painting, low comedy and high religion meet ...".[2] And thus the problem that has puzzled generations of scholars and admirers of Ḥāfiẓ, whether to interpret his poetry as sensual or mystical, seems to be solved by the brush of one of the greatest Persian painters.

About the time when Ḥāfiẓ passed away, the Ottoman Sultan Murād I in 791/1389 vanquished the Serbs at Kossovo and thus subjugated the Balkans. Subsequently, the representatives of the growing Turkish literature began to take a more intense interest in the works of Persian poets, who became their literary masters and whose style deeply influenced the so-called *Divan edebiyatï*. Shaikhī (d. *c.* 1451) and even more Aḥmed Pasha (d. 1496) are obviously influenced by Ḥāfiẓ's lyrical style. Ottoman interpreters and commentators carefully preserved the Hafizian heritage without interfering too much with the actual text. Yet Ḥāfiẓ's poetry was apparently viewed with some suspicion in orthodox Turkish circles; otherwise it would not have been necessary to ask the famous *muftī* Abū Su'ūd (d. 1578) for a *fatvā* concerning the poet's religious attitude. The wise muftī gave an elegant ambiguous answer, explaining that Ḥāfiẓ's poetry on the whole was not really objectionable but that some expressions were prone to wrong interpretation, and it was left to the reader's discrimination to select the correct interpretation. Abū Su'ūd's judgment is important, because during and shortly after his time three most widely used commentaries were written to elucidate Ḥāfiẓ's verse. Sham'ī and Surūrī took to the mystical interpretation, while the Bosnian Sūdī gives sober,

[1] S.C. Welch, *Persian Painting* (New York, 1976), text to pl. 18; the three other extant miniatures are pl. 15, "Lovers picnicking", pl. 16, "Scandal in a mosque", and pl. 17, "The Feast of 'Īd begins".

[2] *Ibid.*, introduction, p. 20.

grammatical explanations. His dry but useful commentary was to form later the basis for most European interpreters of the Shīrāzī poet. The mystical understanding of his Dīvān was prevalent in Safavid Iran and the countries to the east. There his admirers allegorised his verse by applying the standard equations as laid down by authors like Muḥsin Faiż-i Kāshānī:[1] every curl of the beloved means the dark manifestations of contingent beings which veil and yet enhance the radiant Absolute Beauty of the Divine Face, or may pertain to the *jalāl*-side of God, His Majesty and Wrath; while every wine was only the wine of love, every tavern the non-qualified unity. This kind of mystical interpretation is the reason for some Indian ṣūfī leaders' keeping with them only three books, i.e. the Qur'ān, Maulānā Jalāl al-Dīn Rūmī's *Masnavī*, and the Dīvān of Ḥāfiẓ.

Tradition has it that the poet's own contemporaries, headed by Shāh-i Shujā', criticised a certain incoherence in his verse, and European critics of the 18th and 19th centuries followed them in complaining of the lack of a higher logical order. As Hindley wrote in 1800: "Ḥāfiẓ ... takes the liberty of glancing with the frenzied eye of inspiration from earth to heaven, from heaven to earth, in search of objects adapted to the subject of his composition ..." Gertrude Bell, who tried in the foreword to her translation to evaluate Ḥāfiẓ's greatness from a Western viewpoint, wondered why there is "almost no echo" of the political and martial events that occurred during his lifetime. She touches here a point which was to arouse major discussions fifty years later. But she concluded, "It is as if his mental eye, endowed with wonderful acuteness of vision, had penetrated into those provinces of thought which we of a later age were destined to inhabit". Friedrich Veit, who wrote his thesis *Des Grafen von Platen Nachbildungen aus dem Diwan des Hafis* in 1908, found a "unity of thought" in the poems; but his interpretation is mainly concerned with the homosexual aspects of Ḥāfiẓ's and Platen's verse. Schaeder, in his masterly book *Goethes Erlebnis des Ostens* (1938), expressed the opinion that in a Hafizian poem several themes are connected as a kind of leitmotifs. He is thus not too far from Arberry, who saw in Ḥāfiẓ's poetry a progress toward a kind of polyphony: beginning as a poet who is almost "a perfect Sa'dī" in his ghazals, he then develops the art of inserting two or more themes and elaborates them in an intricate pattern whose

[1] Examples in A.J. Arberry, *Sufism* (London, 1950), pp. 113ff.

various "melodies", so to speak, stand in a contrapuntal relationship; this art would have become more and more refined in the poet's later years.

Schaeder remained faithful to the "classical" interpretation of Ḥāfiẓ's lyrics and harshly contradicted Karl Stolz, who had claimed in an article in 1941 that one could understand Ḥāfiẓ's spiritual development to a certain extent by observing the changes in emphasis, allusions to persons, etc., referring to Maḥmūd Hūman's study *Ḥāfiẓ chi mīgūyad?* which points to the same direction of research. Stolz found strong support – though unwittingly – in the work of the French scholar Lescot, who, basing his research mainly on Ghanī and Qazvīnī, found that *un fil conducteur*, a chain of associations, connects each verse with the previous and the following one, and ascribed much of the apparent incoherence to negligent copyists. Like Stolz, Lescot discovered in Ḥāfiẓ's poetry certain cycles that can be ascribed to different phases of his life, and detected a relative chronology by disclosing the identity of people alluded to in the ghazals. Now for the first time the idea was put forth that Ḥāfiẓ was in reality a panegyrist who had cleverly used the more or less lyrical introductory part of the usual qaṣīda for his panegyrics, so that the invoked *ma'shūq*, "beloved", stands for the *mamdūḥ*, the object of the poet's praise, e.g. the prince or vizier.

Roemer in 1951 came close to Lescot's theories, defending the possibility that at least parts of the poems are datable. The problem is, however, that the application of Lescot's and Arberry's methods sometimes puts the same ghazal in two completely different categories of time, so that neither of the approaches can offer a perfect elucidation of the chronology.

One year after Roemer's useful survey of "Hafizology" there appeared two articles by Wickens, who first stressed convincingly the lack of significant or "dramatic" development in Persian poetry, a fact which he explains in the context of the Islamic way of thinking in general; his example of interpretation reads as if he were over-extending one principle of Persian rhetoric, i.e. that of *murā'āt-i naẓīr*, from one verse to a whole ghazal. Wickens went on, however, to try to find in each and every word of the oft mistreated *Turk-i Shīrāzī* every conceivable and inconceivable connotation of the written word in order to establish the underlying "Turkish" feeling of the ghazal. In a very outspoken rebuttal of this interpretation, Mary Boyce rightly stresses the fact that in the East poetry is usually recited or sung, rather than read, so that the sound is more important than the script; and indeed, how many semi-illiterate people in Indo-Pakistan or among the older generation in Turkey used to know their Ḥāfiẓ by heart and could insert quotations from his Dīvān in every conversation! She states correctly that many words, which at first reading may convey only one meaning, prove to carry secondary and associated ideas; but these ideas are either implicit in the meaning of the word itself or conveyed by delicate punning – an observation that brings her close to Schaeder's position. As a working hypothesis, Wickens' "focal theory" can prove helpful; but it should not be taken as absolute norm.

Schaeder's viewpoint was taken over, though with slight modifications, by Bausani, who stresses the *elemento non emozionale, finamente razionale* which distinguishes Ḥāfiẓ's verses from lyrics in the Western, romanticising tradition. Bausani, however, lays special stress on the two small maṣnavīs which are ascribed to Ḥāfiẓ, i.e. the *Sāqī-nāma* and the *Āhū-yi vaḥshī*, which he translates and counts among the most personal and inimitable compositions of Ḥāfiẓ; although both maṣnavīs are missing in some of the oldest manuscripts. Schaeder had branded the sweet and delicate "Wild Gazelle", which is indeed much more "personal" than the ghazals, as greatly inferior to Ḥāfiẓ's lyrical poems. The *Sāqī-nāma*, again, contains the praise of the wine of ecstasy, and stands in a tradition going back to the famous *Khamriyya*, "Wine Ode", of Ibn al-Fāriḍ (d. 632/1235).

What is it that makes Ḥāfiẓ so incomparable? He has relied upon the poetical tradition as it had been perfected by his compatriot Sa'dī, and a comparison between the motifs and metaphors used by him and his contemporaries – poets like Salmān, Khwājū, and others – proves a great similarity in their use of words and images. However, it was Ḥāfiẓ who was able to weave the best threads of the tradition into a perfect, colourful fabric.

But we have to beware of interpreting Ḥāfiẓ too much according to our own, Western understanding of poetry. Schaeder, followed by Bausani, has put his finger upon the main problem when he says, "For the German the understanding of Persian poetry begins by attempting to forget all his ideas about poetry as an expression of personality or of experience [*Erlebnis*]",[1] and he advises the reader to go back to Baroque poetry (incidentally Mas'ūd Farzād, too, drew a comparison

[1] Schaeder, "Lässt sich", p. 202.

between Ḥāfiẓ and John Donne,[1] or even to the mediaeval minnesingers who followed prescribed patterns and images to express their feelings in a stylised form. Ḥāfiẓ is after all a master of rhetoric, a *poeta doctus*, and one of the great difficulties for the Western reader is to disentangle the complicated web of allusions and rhetorical figures that make a line of Persian poetry "true poetry". Rypka has given us numerous examples of this important art of interpretation, and in his review of Nicholson's edition and translation of Rūmī's *Mas̱navī* Ritter too warned against excessive allegorising in our dealings with Persian poets.[2] For only when the rhetorical figures have been understood can a verse be interpreted correctly according to its various levels. Verses of a supreme master of this art, like Ḥāfiẓ, are like diamonds, hard and well polished so that they send out rays of different colour at every moment. We should not expect our poet to pour out his feelings in sheer lyricism, as is usually done in post-Enlightenment poetry in Europe; rather, the highest art is to condense a personal experience so perfectly that it always remains valid, just as one drop of rose-oil represents the "spirit" of hundreds of roses. The reader can use it at every moment, whether he needs a line for a drinking party or a verse that consoles him by speaking of the beloved's wisdom, of God's inscrutable will. To quote Christensen, "As the love-verses of a poet can be applied by every lover to a new individual (who differs from the person of whom the poet was thinking), so these verses can express moods which offer analogies to a love relationship, and, vice versa, mystical verses can be filled with individual contents."[3] Christensen compares the poetry of Ḥāfiẓ with the dreamlike play with rapidly changing images and thoughts; they are, thus, similar in character to the faience ornaments on Persian mosques where letters, arabesques, geometrical and floral decorations grow out of each other, and, as we may add, change colour at every moment according to the light of the sun. This comparison, incidentally, brings the Danish scholar close to Wickens' views on the "non-dramatic" character of Persian poetry, a distinctive feature which one also may call "carpet-like" – as Goethe addresses Ḥāfiẓ in the *West-Östlicher Divan*:

> Dass du nicht enden kannst, das macht dich gross,
> Und dass du nie beginnst, das ist dein Los ...,

[1] Quoted by Arberry, *Classical Persian Literature*, p. 359.
[2] *OLZ*, 1941, 247-53.
[3] Christensen, *Kulturskitser fra Iran*, pp. 88–90, quoted in Schaeder, *Goethes Erlebnis*, p. 177.

thus pointing to the "circular" movement of the Persian poem. Goethe was aware that the very character of Persian poetry is determined by the form of the ghazal; for the given rhyme scheme makes the poem assume "a tinge of quodlibet" because the poet's mind is not focussed on one point but rather turns in a number of directions in order to comply with the exigencies of the rhyme; and, continues Goethe, "We forgive him the most daring metaphor for the sake of an unexpected rhyme and enjoy the presence of mind which the poet can maintain in such a complicated position." Goethe recognised the "guiding spirit" (*das Vorwalten des oberen Leitenden*) as characteristic of this poetry, and he admired the readiness to establish human contacts (*Bereitschaft zum Geselligen*) in Ḥāfiẓ's poetry. Such poetry can lift up problems which fill the soul with extreme tension, transporting them into a realm where tension and calmness are no longer valid, namely that of pure spirit. Sensing this deeply spiritual character that underlies great Persian poetry, he knew that Ḥāfiẓ's verse should not be interpreted exclusively at face value; for the word – as he expresses it – is a fan that hides a beautiful eye and yet makes the observer feel that it exists and may suddenly smile at him.

One may claim that Ḥāfiẓ is perhaps the first poet in the Persian-speaking world who perfectly realised the unity of the mundane and the spiritual sphere. To be sure, Jalāl al-Dīn Rūmī had taken his images and symbols from every walk of life, changing even pebbles into poetical rubies, but his poetry was so deeply tinged by his experience of mystical love that it became regarded as the veritable "Qur'ān in the Persian tongue". Mystical poetry had developed particularly in Iran. Literature had been deeply affected by the introduction into ṣūfī thought of the *shāhid*, the human "witness" of Divine beauty (i.e. the charming human object of love); and we must not forget the maxim that *al-majāz qanṭarat al-ḥaqīqa*, that metaphors, and thus metaphorical, i.e. human, love, form the bridge to the Divine Reality. Already the early ṣūfīs in the time of Kharrāz (d. 286/899) and his disciple Junaid of Baghdad (d. 298/910) had developed the art of speaking in subtle hints, *ishārāt*. Ḥāfiẓ lived in the city where Rūzbihān Baqlī had composed one of the most important works on chaste love, the *'Abhar al-'āshiqīn*, and had contributed to our understanding of the theopathic utterances of early ṣūfīs, particularly Ḥallāj, in his *Sharḥ-i shaṭḥiyāt*. It would be surprising, therefore, if Ḥāfiẓ, living in Shīrāz and perhaps even related to Baqlī's *silsila*, had not been familiar with the finest art of mystical ishārāt. He would certainly agree with Rūmī, who states in the beginning of the *Maṣnavī* that "the secrets of the loved ones [*sirr-i dilbarān*] can better be expressed in the stories of others", e.g., by veiling the truth under poetical symbols. It was this art which Ḥāfiẓ has brought to perfection. In almost each of his verses, a constant oscillation between the worldly and the spiritual level can be discovered. That is why his poetry can be interpreted – and, what is more, enjoyed – on two, if not three levels (and there may be even more hidden meanings). The object can be the beautiful beloved, preferably a fourteen-year-old boy who is as cruel as he is charming and hence called by the traditional term, a *Turk*; or the object can be the Divine Beloved Who acts as He wills, and Who is loved by the poet because He combines *jamāl* and *jalāl*, Beauty and Majesty, and in spite of the fact that He is "the best of rusers" (sūra iii. 47); or the object can be the prince, whose whims are endured by the subject and who has to be flattered in terms of utter subjection (as has the beloved) and high praise. In every case the poet remains the *'abd*, the loving, admiring, and obedient servant. This intended double-entendre does not preclude, however, the possibility of discovering historical data in the lyrics.

If we approach a poem like the ever-present *Turk-i Shīrāzī* by a simple analysis of the rhetorical devices in the first verse, we certainly do not find the "charming maid of Shīrāz", although the basic idea is as simple as can be: the lover would give away even the most precious thing imaginable for a moment of kindness from his beloved, or for a moment of Divine grace, or for a sign of royal favour. The charm of this line resides not in the rather commonplace idea but in the expression: Ḥāfiẓ produces a complete *murā'āt-i naẓīr* of five geographical concepts: Turk, Hindu, Shīrāz, Samarqand, and Bukhārā, and another one from three parts of the body, i.e. heart, hand, and mole. Furthermore, the juxtaposition of Turk and Hindu is used, which is quite common in Persian poetry, particularly since Niẓāmī. The Turk supplied, from Ghaznavid times onward, the model for the beloved with his round, light-coloured moon face, a mouth like a *mīm* or a dot, and slightly slanting eyes – an ideal that appears more and more on Persian miniatures. The Hindu again was the black, lowly and often cunning slave; so much so that mystics like Majd al-Dīn Baghdādī (d. 1209) could compare angels and devils to Turks and Hindus respectively. Given this extremely lowly position of the Hindu in Persian imagery, Ḥāfiẓ's claim to give away two major cities for the "Hindu" mole of his friend gains even more momentum. Besides, the reader may think of the *Turk-i falak* (the planet Mars) and the *Hindū-yi falak* (Saturn), stars connected in astrology with minor and major misfortune, and with bloodshed and melancholia respectively. The clever combination of this verse has often been imitated, but never surpassed. But a translation that leaves out the meaningful puns can never capture its real charm. Another line that has been quoted by Oriental poets time and again, and in which mystical and profane meaning are most skilfully intertwined, comes from the ghazal that starts with the daring outcry:

> *fāsh mī-gūyam u az gufta-yi khud dilshādam ...*
> (I declare it openly and am happy about my saying:
> I am the slave of love, and free from both worlds),[1]

a *maṭla'* that makes the reader immediately think of the imminent danger of *ifshā' al-sirr*, the divulgence of the secret of loving union which, according to the ṣūfī tradition, was Ḥallāj's sin and caused his death on the gallows. The line in question reads:

> On the tablet of my heart there is nothing but the *alif*
> of the friend's stature –
> What can I do? My master did not teach me any other letter.

To play with letters is common in Persian and related poetry, and Ḥāfiẓ is no exception to this custom. The importance of the letter alif has always been stressed: as the first letter of the alphabet with the numerical value 1, and consisting of a slim vertical line, it was interpreted as the symbol of Allāh's unity and uniqueness, but is at the same time the cypher for the elegant slender stature of the beloved. Why should one go farther than this letter? The alif represents everything that is needed – as the Turkish mystic Yūnus Emre (d. *c.* 1321) says:

> The meaning of the four holy books
> is contained in one alif.[2]

Verses like this form the basis for the claim of quite a few mystics in Iran, Turkey, and Muslim India to be illiterate and to know only the alif which the great master of *'ilm ladunī*, immediate wisdom from God (Qur'ān xviii. 65), has taught them. For the mystic it is enough to

[1] Brockhaus, no. 416. Aḥmad and Nā'īnī, no. 315.
[2] *Yunus Emre Divani*, ed. A. Gölpınarlı (Istanbul, 1943), p. 200, no. XXIV.

remember God's unity as expressed in the alif; as for the lover, the slender body of his beloved completely fills his heart and mind.

One more example is taken from a poem in which Ḥāfiẓ complains of the separation from the Friend.[1] The last line mentions his pen, this instrument which he so often praises with grand hyperboles because of its miraculous powers: the pen, with severed tongue, reveals the Friend's secret only after its head is cut. Just as the reed-pen has to be cut for proper writing – which means: telling the mind's secret – so the lover will rather give his head than reveal the secret entrusted to him. "I give the head, *sar*, but not the secret, *sirr*", is a common saying. It does not matter whether the poet thinks of the secret of loving union with a human being whom he does not want to expose to blame, or of revealing, as Ḥallāj did, the secret of divine love and the experience of ecstatic extinction of the self; or whether he is one of the confidants of his prince who has entrusted him with information that should be kept secret – be it a political consideration, be it, as in the story of King Midas with the donkey's ears, a personal problem of the ruler (the pen, made of reed, is cut off from the reed-bed like the reed-flute which revealed, according to the legend, Midas' pitiable state to the world).[2] On whichever level we interpret the seemingly pleasant and easy verse, it makes perfect sense.

There is no doubt that Ḥāfiẓ, to quote Wickens, "composed some of the world's most sublime and technically exquisite poetry".[3] It is a sign of truly great poetry that every reader tries to explain it according to his own understanding, and therefore the manifold interpretations have a certain legitimacy. But it would be an injustice to Ḥāfiẓ to interpret his verse *exclusively* as an expression of a hedonistic and happy-go-lucky attitude – as wrong as it would be to see him *exclusively* as *lisān al-ghaib*, the "Tongue of the Unseen World," by applying to his verse an overall allegorical interpretation. The greatness of his poetry lies in the unsurpassable balance between the world of senses with its wine and beauty, but also its politics, and the world of unchanging Perfect Beauty, which is reflected in the changeful manifold. His "deep optimism" (Ritter) has probably to do with his talent to offer the perfect *Glasperlenspiel*, and we can see him, as did Ritter and others who followed him, as the true *rind*, a man who represents a lifestyle in

[1] Brockhaus, no. 130. Aḥmad and Nā'īnī, no. 105.
[2] Cf. for this story Ritter, "Das Proömium des Maṯnawī-i Maulawī", *ZDMG* XCIII (1939), 169-96.
[3] Wickens, "Ḥāfiẓ", p. 55.

which *ṭīb al-qalbī*, cheerfulness and goodness of the heart, is preferred to everything else; an attitude that is certainly contrary to every kind of fanaticism.

Perhaps only a poet can fully understand the secret of Ḥāfiẓ's verse – as Goethe certainly did. Therefore we owe the best explanation of Ḥāfiẓ's poetry to Rückert, the Orientalist-poet, who sings in truly Hafizian style of the double-sided fabric of Ḥāfiẓ's colourful lyrics in which sensual and supra-sensual experience are inextricably woven together:

Hafis, wo er scheinet Übersinnliches
nur zu reden, redet über Sinnliches;
oder redet er, wo über Sinnliches
er zu reden scheint, nur Übersinnliches?
Sein Geheimnis ist unübersinnlich,
denn sein Sinnliches ist übersinnlich.[1]

[1] "Where Hafiz's mere words seem supra-sensory, he speaks of the sensual; or does he speak, where he seems to speak of the sensual, only of the supra-sensory? His secret is *un*-supersensory [i.e. not beyond sense-perception], because his sensual[ity] is supra-sensory." Naturally no plain prose paraphrase can convey anything more than the vaguest hint of the word-play and verbal music of the German poet's lines.

CHAPTER 17 (c)

PERSIAN LITERATURE IN THE SAFAVID PERIOD

For the purposes of this chapter the period to be covered runs from 907/1501 to 1148/1736, one of the most remarkable ages in Iran's history. The Safavid era witnessed a political, religious and military reorganisation and unification of which Iran as it stands today is in no small degree the legacy. Socially the Safavids gave the Iranian people a sense of integration, and of recognition as an entity of consequence in the affairs of the world, which served signally to distinguish this period from the distractions and discord that had preceded it. For this period terminated the disunity and sufferings which the Mongol invasions had brought about, and which neither the Il-Khanid attempt at resettlement nor Tīmūr's subsequent reign of conquest had done anything to ameliorate; while the events of the interregnum after Tīmūr's death had only exacerbated them.

A factor which perhaps more clearly than any other marks out the Safavid period as a watershed was the establishment, during this dynasty's sway of nearly two and a half centuries, of Shi'ism as the official religion of the state. Thus a sect hitherto of secondary importance was raised to supremacy, affording a vigorous expression of Iran's identity – it might even be said, of Iranian nationalism – in face of the challenge presented by the Sunnī Ottoman empire, the Sunnī Central Asian Turkish states and the Mughal empire of India. A result of this development which must concern the literary historian was that official recognition of Shi'ism, with its active propagation by the Safavid shahs, prompted the popularisation of Shī'ī theology and hence the composition of voluminous works in the Persian, as well as to some extent in the Arabic, language. At the same time centralisation of government gave rise to a political and economic cohesion that not only served to strengthen Iran, but made possible a large-scale patronage of craftsmanship and the arts, by which the fame of Persia was spread throughout the civilised world.

In spite, however, of the form, in place of formlessness, and sense of high purpose with which it would appear that the Safavids endowed their realm, the history of Persian literature in their time, while not confined to the land of Iran itself, is by no means golden. Two reasons may be adduced to account for the way in which this period's literary products present only a qualified lustre, and both must be seen in relation to a decline in thought and learning that spells a falling-off of the essential grounds of a great literature.

The first reason is historical; the second is bound up with the religious policy of the age. The events of the preceding centuries, notably the Mongol invasions and their calamitous aftermath, had caused many scholars to leave Iran for other regions. Libraries, the repositories of the scholarship of several centuries, had been destroyed at the advent of the Mongols, and many learned men must have perished, only a relatively small proportion of the scribal and scholarly class surviving and an even lesser proportion remaining in Iran. The patrons and the security to be found in the Indian subcontinent in particular exercised an obvious attraction, to the detriment of those traditions of scholarly activity in Iran which, in any case, had been associated with urban centres – Bukhārā, Samarqand, Herat, Nīshāpūr, for instance – destroyed by the troops of Chingīz Khan. Thus despite the encouragement of learning displayed by the Īl-Khān Ghazan (694–703/1295–1304) and later by some of the Timurid princes, the ranks of the learned remained depleted and scholars of the ensuing eras were chiefly commentators and annotators, rather than originators of new ideas.

Under the Safavids the attention paid to religious questions, the patronage accorded to theologians, and the fanaticism of the *'ulamā* and exponents of a deliberately exploited new doctrinal position, all operated against freedom of thought. Reference to the life and works of Mullā Ṣadrā of Shīrāz (said to have died at Baṣra in 1050/1640–1), of whom, in the words of E.G.Browne,[1] "it is clear ... that he suffered a good deal at the hands of the orthodox divines", provides an example of the difficulties encountered in one recorded instance of an influential mind which deviated from the contemporary doctrinaire lines of thought. In Safavid times intellectual activity was cramped, to say the least, and there was a corresponding decline in language and literature.

A major factor so far as literature was concerned was the court's failure adequately to flatter the hopes of poets and authors in Persian; a

[1] *LHP* IV, 429.

failure to be contrasted with the encouragement offered Persian literature at the court of the Mughal emperors and at the hands of other notables in India. In day-to-day affairs, the language chiefly used at the Safavid court and by the great military and political officers, as well as the religious dignitaries, was Turkish, not Persian; and the last class of persons wrote their religious works mainly in Arabic. Those who wrote in Persian were either lacking in proper tuition in this tongue, or wrote outside Iran and hence at a distance from centres where Persian was the accepted vernacular, endued with that vitality and susceptibility to skill in its use which a language can have only in places where it truly belongs. In short, these authors' works can be given only qualified acceptance as examples of a living and genuinely representative Persian. The poetry and prose of the Safavid era are without the vitality characteristic of earlier ages. But, having reached this general conclusion, the opportunity will be taken here to discuss in greater detail the linguistic situation under the Safavids, with reference to what was then occurring to affect the composition of works in Persian, and also to what had happened in the preceding period.

THE PERSIAN LANGUAGE IN THE SAFAVID ERA

Of the difficulties experienced by Arabic-speaking Shīʿīs who were imported into Iran because of Safavid religious policy, and who arrived not knowing Persian, the well-known anecdote told by Professor Browne about Sayyid Niʿmat-Allāh al-Jazāʾirī and his brother on their arrival at Shīrāz is sufficiently illustrative.[1] But apart from the aspect of the situation to be inferred from the arrival of Arab divines who were expected to write and speak in Persian in order to spread Shīʿī doctrine, there was also the question of Turkish.

This aspect may be illustrated, to take one notable instance of development, by the fate of the Āẕarī dialect, an old dialect of Persian, in Āzarbāījān, where at the beginning of the Safavid period, with the exception of a few areas, it died out. This can be related to what had happened in preceding eras: it is attributable to the sojourn of Turks in the region and the domination of Turkish and Mongol tribes, dating from the 6th/13th century. By the end of the 9th/16th century Turkish was commonly spoken in Āzarbāījān's chief centres; though there is

[1] *Ibid.*, pp. 360–1.

evidence, albeit scanty, to show that at the beginning of the Safavid era Turkish had not yet gained complete sway; and even the Turkish now spoken in Āzarbāījān is a dialect composed of Āẕarī, Arabic and some Turkish words, but following the rules of the Turkish language.

So much for one notable regional development. On a larger scale what demands attention is the marked interest the Safavid monarchs themselves took in the Turkish language, in addition to the factor already touched upon, that most of the expressions used in the government, court and army were in that language. Shah Ismā'īl (907–930/1502–1524), the dynasty's founder, essayed the art of poetry under the pseudonym of Khaṭā'ī; but he composed his Dīvān in Turkish.

The situation is rendered the more strange when it is recalled that in the same period Ottoman rulers wrote ghazals and short poems in Persian. Persian at this time was widely taught in Asia Minor, where its literature was eagerly studied, Turkish literature and polite forms of address being powerfully influenced by, and deeply impregnated with, Persian images and idioms.[1] Not that this influence and currency of Persian in Asia Minor were a new departure restricted to the Ottoman era. Here once more a legacy from the past was involved. Attention to and production of Persian literature had begun in Asia Minor in the time of the Saljūq rulers of that region, i.e. from the middle of the 5th/11th century.

Persian was even more prevalent, during the Safavid period and later, in the Indian subcontinent, where again the beginnings of this, as it were, diaspora-like development must be traced much further back, to the days when Persian had accompanied the spread of Islam in India under the dynasts and military conquerors who had reached the subcontinent from eastern Iran: the Ghaznavids, Ghurids and Ghurid mamlūks, all of whom established centres in India where poets and writers in Persian received ample encouragement.

After the Mongol invasion of north-eastern and northern Iran, the use of Persian in India received a new and greater impetus. As has already been indicated, a large number of Persian poets, writers and scholars (*udabā*) fled to India from Transoxiana and Khurāsān, swelling the crowd of exponents of Persian already at Indian centres. The knowledge of Persian culture and civilisation and the numbers of poets and authors using Persian, producing ghazals, qaṣīdas and maṡnavīs in

[1] On this process of assimilation, see Gibb I, 8ff.

India were such that to the superficially informed onlooker India might well have appeared the original source and real home of Persian. Certainly one is tempted to linger over discussion of this development beyond the borders of Iran, and it is a feature of the literary history of Persian to which further reference cannot be avoided in treating literature in the Safavid period. Here, however, comment on it must be concluded with noting that, although the uses to which Persian was put in India after the end of Bābur's Mughal dynasty continued to be both elegant and widespread, its scope and popularity inevitably diminished in face of the rivalry of English and Urdu; and not least because of the lack of interest shown by Persians themselves in rescuing from oblivion this remarkable "Indian" branch of their language's power, creative susceptibility and cultural influence.

Our chief concern in this section has been to show the nature of the competition, particularly from Turkish dialects, to which Persian under the Safavids was exposed. Therefore, to digress as we have done into the realms of Persian's influence in Asia Minor and India may seem to be to neglect one objective, while irrelevantly concentrating on an altogether different topic. Indeed it says much for the strength of the Persian language that a discussion of it in decline should, in the event, conclude with references to its effects in regions well to the west and well to the south and east of its original home. But that this interim conclusion in the study of the vicissitudes of the Persian language and literature, and its achievements, during the Safavid epoch is not in fact irrelevant will emerge more clearly later. A passing reference has already been made to the effect of the transplanting of the language to other regions, and more will have to be said on, for example, how far even a high degree of eminence elsewhere had its converse in deleterious consequences upon Persian literary developments in Iran itself.

PERSIAN POETRY IN THE SAFAVID PERIOD

It must be confessed at once that, both in wording and in style, the poetry of this period lacks interest: except for a few of the more celebrated poets little of intrinsic value is to be found. There is what might be termed a "classical" reason for this in that, as with their predecessors in the Timurid era, the Safavid poets did not have the training, the thorough schooling in their art, which had been provided under the auspices of the Samanid, Ghaznavid, Saljuq and other, earlier, courts. Most of the Safavid writers were not sufficiently well-versed in either the Persian or Arabic languages and, since we are dealing with a classical literature which imposed high and rigorous standards upon its exponents, it will be appreciated that a profound knowledge of these two languages and their literary models and techniques was a prerequisite for any genuinely formative exposition of the tradition of classical Persian literature.

It will be noticed that specific reference was made above to the patronage extended by earlier courts, and in this we touch upon a matter of the utmost significance in both the development of a great classical literary tradition and its subsequent decline. For yet another cause of the decline characteristic of Safavid times was the court's failure to patronise the poet, and the latter's consequent recourse to the common people. A situation that had arisen under the Timurids became more commonplace. One aspect of this development was that it introduced variety and innovation in poetry. This might be considered as having been to the good; but, in the case of a classical tradition, its corollary of decline in standards of taste and precision cannot be ignored, and to this evil must be added the admission of abuse of grammatical rules of the language. There was novelty in subject-matter; new ideas were introduced during the Safavid period; but ill-chosen expressions and verbal infelicities have also to be encountered in this poetry.

This is a point at which we can return to the issue of the extent to which Persian was current outside Iran. Although fresh subjects and ideas were introduced because of the external areas of Persian literary endeavour, an alien environment was not without its effects on the language's customary firmness and strength. Use of Persian as a purely artistic, literary medium, and that in no small measure for the sake of novelty, away from those cities and villages where it was the medium of living speech and practical intercourse, inevitably led to artificiality and fustian.

For the purposes of this chapter sufficient information will emerge about subject-matter when authors and their works are summarised at the end. Here, in a general purview of the state of Safavid poetry, it can be noted that one effect of Safavid religious policy on poetry was to make elegies a common mode, and praise of the Imāms – that is, of the chief figures of Shī'ī hagiology – a common theme. While so much royal encouragement went into the most intense possible propagation of Shī'ī doctrine, theology and, in particular, Shī'ī jurisprudence and the traditions accompanying it did not fail to have their numerous exponents. Clearly, poetry could not remain uninfluenced: encouragement likewise went to composers of elegies and panegyrics on the descendants of ʿAlī, resulting in an upsurge of poetry of this order.

The situation is vividly brought to light by Iskandar Beg Munshī, the author of the *ʿĀlam-ārā-yi ʿAbbāsī*, where, on the subject of the position of poets during the reign of Shah Ṭahmāsp I (930–984/1524–1576), he speaks to this effect:[1]

Although His Heaven-dwelling Majesty patronised poets during his earlier life, he was, in his later years, too much occupied to give honour or withhold it; he regarded this respected class of men as latitudinarians, not as righteous and pious, and he forbade them to recite their poetry before him. Therefore, when Princess Parī Khān Khānum[2] presented him with two qaṣīdas by Maulānā Muḥtasham of Kāshān, one of which was in his praise and the other in praise of the princess, he said: "I am not pleased that poets should praise me. If they write poems in praise of the Protector of the State [the Caliph ʿAlī] and the immaculate Imāms, on Whom be Peace, then they may expect to be rewarded by those saintly souls and, in the second place, by us. When a poet writes in praise of a king, he eloquently strings together subtle thoughts, exalted notions and hyperbolical similes which, after the saying *what are his best are his lies*, seldom genuinely pertain to the matter in hand. If, however, they are applied to the Sainted Ones, then they are just, because their holy virtues are even more exalted". In short, the Maulānā received no reward.

Here is conclusive evidence of the attitude of Safavid monarchs towards poets and their offerings in the form of ghazals or panegyrics, an attitude not confined to Shah Ṭahmāsp alone. Hence the development of elegies and panegyrics on the Imāms, notably at the hands of Muḥtasham of Kāshān (d. 996/1587–8), the recipient of Ṭahmāsp's disapprobation for temporal poems. He became an adept in this type of poetry, employing an ingenuity which made his elegies (*marāṣī*) some of the foremost poetical compositions devoted to the service of religion. The specimens of his verse given in the 19th-century work, *Majmaʿ al-fuṣaḥā* ("Compendium of the Eloquent") of Riżā Qulī Khān Hidāyat, bear witness to the fact that in this genre Muḥtasham's verses continued, long after his death, to be regarded as models; in times not far removed from our own, poets have followed them.

One consequence of Shah Ṭahmāsp's and his successors' treatment

[1] Iskandar Beg Munshī, *Tārīkh-i ʿālam-ārā* I, 178; cf. Savory's trans., I, 274–5; also *LHP* IV, 172–3, where this remark is paraphrased.

[2] Shah Ṭahmāsp's second daughter: see Falsafī, *Zindagānī* I, 13; also pp. 253–5 above.

of poets was the migration of many talented composers of ghazals, maṣnavīs and romances, who withdrew from court circles and in many instances sought refuge at the Ottoman or Mughal courts. Hence the establishment of centres of Persian poetry outside Iran, particularly in India. At the court of the Mughal emperor Akbar (963–1014/1556–1605) alone there were fifty-one poets in exile from Iran. The style known as the Indian style, which had been first noticeable in late Timurid times, attained its full development in the Safavid age, when its highest exponents appeared and it enjoyed a great deal of popularity. It remained a model until the end of the Safavid period and was influential in both the Zand and the early part of the Qājār periods. Then it lost its hold and attempts were made to return to older models; though the "Indian" style still survives in India and Afghanistan.

For the poet using this style the primary objective is the expression, in language as simple as possible, of fine-spun thoughts, unusual, wonder-evoking themes, and a general conjunction of ideas the most conducive to delighted surprise in auditors or readers. The style's history dates to a gradual development in the interval between the time of the Mongol Īl-Khāns and the Timurids during the latter part of the 8th/14th century. It became the fashion during the Timurid period, notably in the literary circle centred on Herat. Its development can be attributed to the social conditions of the times, which were such that people sought to turn away from the corporeal world, desiring in preference to it a poetical diet of subtle and fanciful ideas. A second consideration is one to which allusion has already been made, namely the gradual departure of the literary language from old conventions and standards in favour of elements based on the popular idiom. Thus a fusion, at first sight of a somewhat unexpected nature, was brought about. Poetry became invested to an increasing extent with far-fetched ideas in which great striving was made after the most subtle refinements, and objects, of expression; and yet, at the same time, poetry became almost colloquial in tone. That it was also not infrequently projected into the borderlands of the absurd and worthless must in some measure be attributed to the fact that so extraordinary a fusion of stylistic aim and content could not invariably be successfully accomplished; especially in circumstances that were in numerous external ways generally adverse to the production of sound literature. Certainly poets in the "Indian" style strove hard to display bright and novel conjunctions, often enough with very considerable ingenuity. But imaginations almost as often proved to have been over-teased, and fancifulness for its own sake allowed to take precedence over strength of style, the soundness of sense and a vital grounding to exercises of the imagination, that lie at the roots of great poetry. Thus it was that, in sheer exuberance of artifice, beauty of meaning, where it existed, was sometimes in the Indian style lost to sight.

The name "Indian" was appropriated for this style because those of its partisans who lived in the time of the Safavid shahs and were adversely affected by their treatment of poets tended principally to settle in India. India and Afghanistan became its home, and the ghazal, the short lyrical piece, its most popular form, because this type of poem lent itself best to the expression of delicate and novel ideas.

More must be said about the attempt made by poets of this era to eschew ornamented language and keep close to the language of ordinary people. One result of this was that, certainly if judged by strictly classical criteria, though their verses were often fluent, they often contained colloquialisms even, as has been hinted, to the point of being grammatically incorrect. Perhaps this is not surprising when it is recalled that the aim was ever to introduce novelty; juxtapositions and forms of expression which every effort of ingenuity was stretched to make as wonder-exciting as could be. This was the process that was carried to the uttermost lengths at the Ottoman and Mughal courts, to which the dīvāns of poets such as Ṣā'ib of Tabrīz were sent as eagerly sought-after gifts.[1] And yet, if only because of this almost filigree content, and overlooking the occasional fallings-off or ineptitudes of diction, contrary to the beliefs of some of our contemporaries it may be averred that Safavid poetry does not deserve entirely to be dismissed as of no value. Its value lies chiefly in the very feature that lays it most open to the imputation of decadence: in its bold use of novel forms and original subject-matter.

Leaving aside the area of poetry that may be placed under the heading of the Indian style, the question of subject-matter brings us back to those elegies and panegyrics of the Imāms and the Immaculate Ones (i.e. their descendants), which have already been mentioned, and to consideration of such other subjects as the poetry of our period is found to have treated. For example, there were lyrical themes which

[1] See, however, *LHP* IV, 265, where it is stated that Ṣā'ib was, "like 'Urfī, one of those poets who, while greatly esteemed in Turkey and India, are without honour in their own country".

were sometimes tinged with mysticism, expressing the aspirations of hermits and dervishes, and this not without an element of the didactic. Also not absent from the period's corpus of poetry were tales and romances, especially in imitation of Niẓāmī. Throughout the period historical and religious poetry was produced in the epic form, sufficient to make a sizeable contribution to this genre. At the same time, however, for reasons which the anecdote given above about Shah Ṭahmāsp might make clear, poems in praise of earthly potentates were few, were inferior in quality to the ghazals or longer pieces dealing with holy personages or spiritual topics, and were generally dedicated to the Timurid sovereigns of India.

Before going on to discuss prose works during the Safavid era, it will be useful here to list the names of some of the principal poets and briefly to mention their more outstanding contributions.

Many of the poets of the earlier part of the Safavid era had been educated in the late Timurid period, particularly in the literary circle of Ḥusain Bāīqarā. One of them was Jāmī's nephew, 'Abd-Allāh Hātifī of Kharjird (d. 927/1520–1). One of his most important works is the *Shāh-nāma-yi Ḥaẓrat-i Shāh Ismā'īl*, an historical epic. Others of his poetical tales in imitation of Niẓāmī are *Shīrīn u Khusrau*, *Lailā u Majnūn*, *Haft manẓar* and the *Tīmūr-nāma*. The last-mentioned work describes Tīmūr's victories and wars as an answer to, or parallel with, Niẓāmī's *Iskandar-nāma*; thus it too may be classified as an historical epic.

Another poet of the beginning of the Safavid era who had been educated during that of the Timurids and in the first years of Safavid rule was Mīrzā Qāsim of Gunābād, one of the *sayyids* of that town. He also was an imitator of Niẓāmī, and his most important works comprise *Lailā u Majnūn*, the *Kār-nāma* or *Chaugān-nāma*, *Khusrau u Shīrīn*, *Shāhrukh-nāma*, *Shāh-nāma-yi māẓī* (on the subject of Shah Ismā'īl), and the *Shāh-nāma-yi navvāb 'Alī* (a description of the reign of Shah Ṭahmāsp).

Another of the well-known poets of the close of the Timurid and the beginning of the Safavid age was Bābā Fighānī, who died in 925/1519–20 and was celebrated for his graceful ghazals. He was one of the greatest poetic innovators of the ensuing age. A contemporary of his was Umīdī Ṭihrānī (d. 925/1519–20), who wrote excellent ghazals and qaṣīdas. This group of poets also included Ahlī of Turshīz (d. 934/1527–8) and his namesake of Shīrāz (d. 942/1535–6). The latter wrote fine qaṣīdas and an artificial maṣnavī entitled the *Siḥr-i Ḥalāl*. Hilālī Chaghatā'ī, who was put to death in 935/1528–9, wrote melodious and tasteful ghazals at the beginning of the 10th/16th century. Besides his passionate ghazals he was the author of three maṣnavīs entitled *Lailā u Majnūn*, *Shāh u darvīsh*[1] and *Ṣifāt al-ʿāshiqīn* ("The Attributes of Lovers").

Another of the great poets of the early part of the Safavid era was Vaḥshī (d. 991/1583–4) of Bāfq, a dependency of Kirmān: he was a contemporary of Shah Ṭahmāsp, in whose honour he composed qaṣīdas. His ghazals were celebrated for the beauty of their style and their fine sentiments. Furthermore, his short *tarkīb-bands*,[2] besides being new in Persian literature, are noteworthy for beauty and freshness and strong feeling. His unfinished maṣnavī entitled *Farhād u Shīrīn*, particularly its introduction, was much admired by later poets. It was completed in the Qājār period by Viṣāl of Shīrāz in 1265/1848–9.

A contemporary of Vaḥshī was the poet Muḥtasham of Kāshān (d. 996/1587–8), whose importance as a writer of elegies has already been mentioned. He also composed qaṣīdas and ghazals, but one of the greatest of all the writers of ghazals of this age was Jamāl al-Dīn Muḥammad b. Badr al-Dīn Shīrāzī (b. 964/1556–7, d. 999/1590–1), whose pen-name was ʿUrfī. His fame spread in Safavid times through India and Turkey. In addition to beautiful ghazals in the Indian style, he composed some qaṣīdas and maṣnavīs in imitation of Niẓāmī.

Another outstanding writer of Persian poetry in the Safavid era, though not a Persian, was Faiżī-yi Fayyiżī (b. 954/1547–8, d. 1004/1595–6), the brother of Akbar's minister Abu'l-Fażl. Like ʿUrfī, he achieved considerable fame during his lifetime and was a master of the qaṣīda, ghazal and maṣnavī. Among his well-known maṣnavīs, which were written in imitation of those of Niẓāmī, must be mentioned the *Markaz-i advār*, *Sulaimān u Bilqīs*, *Nāl u Dāman*, *Haft kishvar* and the *Akbar-nāma*.

Other poets of this time were: Saḥābī of Astarābād (d. 1010/1601–2), Naẓīrī of Nīshāpūr (d. 1021/1612–3), the author of qaṣīdas, ghazals and *tarjīʿāt*, Ẓuhūrī of Turshīz (d. 1024/1615–6), Zalālī of Khwānsār (d. in the same year as Ẓuhūrī) and Ṭālib Āmulī (d. 1036/1626–7). The lastnamed was poet laureate to the Mughal emperor Jahāngīr and author of several celebrated ghazals and qaṣīdas. Also to be included among the poets was Shaikh Bahā' al-Dīn Muḥammad ʿĀmilī, otherwise celebrated as a man of learning; he died in 1031/1622. His cele-

[1] Also known as *Shāh u gadā* ("King and beggar"): see *LHP* IV, 234.

[2] A *tarkīb-band* is a poem composed of several stanzas of equal length.

brated masnavīs, the *Savāniḥ-i Ḥijāz*, better known as *Nān u ḥalvā* ("Bread and Sweetmeats"), and the *Shīr u shakar* ("Milk and Sugar"), are both mystical and didactic in character.

Mention must also be made of Ḥakīm Sharaf al-Dīn Ḥasan (d. 1038/1628–9). A court physician and boon companion to Shah 'Abbās I, he was the author of ghazals and also of a masnavī entitled *Namakdān-i ḥaqīqat* ("The Salt-cellar of Truth"), written in imitation of Sanā'ī's *Ḥadīqat al-ḥaqīqat*. Abu'l-Qāsim Findiriskī, one of the philosophers of the Safavid period, was the author of some philosophical poems; he died about 1050/1640–1. Later there appeared Abū Ṭālib of Kāshān, poet laureate to Shāh Jahān, and an imitator of 'Urfī, greatly skilled in the Indian style. In addition to his well-known collection of ghazals, he was the author of the *Ẓafar-nāma-yi Shāh Jahānī*. He died in Kashmīr in 1061/1650–1.

A poet who brought the Indian style to perfection was Muḥammad 'Alī Ṣā'ib-i Tabrīzī (b. 1010/1601–2, d. 1088/1677-8). Even during his lifetime his fame spread through India, Persia and Turkey. He was a prolific poet: the number of verses in his Dīvān amounts to 120,000. His ghazals are noteworthy for the sureness of touch that they evince, the subtlety of ideas and, interestingly, the popular proverbs which are worked into them. As Ṣā'ib had made a thorough study of the works of his predecessors, his wording resembles theirs more than do the poems of any of his contemporaries.

Another poet to be mentioned here is Shaikh 'Alī Ḥazīn (d. 1180/1766–7). In addition to his verses he was the author of two prose works, the *Tazkirat al-aḥvāl* and the *Tazkirat al-mu'āṣirīn*.

Among the writers of epics in the 11th/17th century was Qadrī with his two historical epics, the *Jarūn-nāma* and the *Jang-nāma-yi Kishm*; these were completed in, respectively, 1031/1621–2 and the following year, the *Jang-nāma-yi Kishm* being the history of the year 1032/1622, when the Persian forces, with the assistance of the shipping of the East India Company, drove the Portuguese out of the islands of Kishm and Hurmuz.

In 985/1577–8 Bihishtī Maskūkī, another poet of this period, completed his *Shāh-nāma-yi Bihishtī* on the subject of the wars between the Turkish Sultan Murād III and Muḥammad Khudābanda, the Safavid sovereign. With verse annals of this type may be compared the *Futūḥ al-'Ajam* of Jamālī b. Ḥasan Shushtarī, an account of the capture of Tabrīz by 'Osmān Pasha in 996/1587–8. Mullā Kāmī of Shīrāz completed his *Vaqā'i'-yi zamān* or *Fatḥ-nāma-yi Nūr Jahān Bēgum*, a history of the closing years of Nūr al-Dīn Muḥammad Jahāngīr and his wars with his enemies, in 1030/1620–1.

Similarly, in this species of poetry celebrating contemporary military events, another poet named Bihishtī composed the *Āshūb-nāma-yi Hindūstān* on the wars between the sons of Jahāngīr, that is, the events of the years 1067 to 1069/1656–7 to 1658–9.

Of a different kind was the poetry of Mīrzā Muḥammad Rafī' Khān Bāẕil of Mashhad, a contemporary of the Mughal emperor Shāh Jahān. He died in 1123 or 1124/1710–1 or 1712–3, and composed a religious poem called the *Ḥamla-yi Ḥaidarī*, completed by Mīrzā Abū Ṭālib Findiriskī after his death.

These are the outstanding poets of the Safavid epoch. In addition there were many others, in Persia, India and at the Ottoman court. Each of them endeavoured to complete a dīvān or collection of poems, but by and large their works lack merit.

PERSIAN PROSE IN THE SAFAVID PERIOD

In the Safavid period Persian prose did not attain a high position as literature, despite its widespread use and popularity in Persia, India and Turkey. Although a large number of works were written during this period on many topics, it was not an outstanding one, because most of the writers cared little for style or for linguistic and rhetorical points. On the whole, the prose works of this period, in particular those of a literary character, have little to commend them. If the authors endeavoured to be simple, they tended to employ vulgar expressions; and if, on the other hand, they tried to be artificial and ornate, they employed tasteless artifices. The works which represent a compromise between these two extremes, such as the *'Ālam-ārā-yi 'Abbāsī*, are few and of little value. On the whole, Safavid prose is even more loose and superficial than that of the Timurid era; Safavid works are so full of empty titles, compliments and rhyming words that the original subject becomes lost or unintelligible. This state of affairs was even worse in the case of writers in the Indian style. Because of their tendency to pedantry more attention was paid to elaborations and superfluities than to subject-matter. In some historical books and tales an intermediate style was adopted, but even in such cases of plain writing the corrupt language of the period sometimes left its mark.

A feature of the age deserving attention was the writing of romances in prose. We have knowledge of prose romances in Persian dating from an earlier age than that of the Safavids, such as the *Dāstān-i Iskandar* (this work is to be distinguished from the *Iskandar-nāma*, written in a beautiful style in the 5th/11th century), the *Bakhtiyār-nāma*, the *Nuh manẓar*, the *Abū Muslim-nāma*, the *Dārāb-nāma*, the *Dāstān-i Samak-i ʿAyyār*, the *Ḥusn u dil*, and a number of others.

In the Safavid period the writing of romance became more common, and some important works were written such as the above-mentioned *Dāstān-i Iskandar*, the *Ṭūṭī-nāma*, the *Razm-nāma*, the translations of the famous Indian epics the *Rāmayāna* and the *Mahābharāta*, the tales of the *Hazār Gīsū*, the *Ṭālib-i pādishāh-zāda u Maṭlūb*, the *Qiṣṣa-yi Arshad u Rashīd, Ashraf u Fīrūz vazīr-zāda*, the *Shīrīn-nāma*, the *Qiṣṣa-yi chahār darvīsh*, the *Nūsh Āfarīn-nāma*, the *Qiṣṣa-yi Maryam dukhtar-i Shāh-i Purtugāl*, the *Qiṣṣa-yi haft sair-i Ḥātim-i Ṭā'ī*, and others. Some of these romances are written in a simple and agreeable style, particularly the translation of the *Rāmayāna* by Naqīb Khān and ʿAbd al-Qādir Badā'unī, carried out with skill and care in a fluent and attractive form.

From the letter-writers of this period, whether working at the Safavid court or for the Mughal emperors of India and Indian nobles, highly ornate examples of epistolatory style have come down to us. One of the greatest of these practitioners of the secretary's art was Mīrzā Ṭāhir Vaḥīd of Qazvīn (d. 1120/1708–9). He was secretary and historiographer to Shah ʿAbbās II and the vizier of Shah Sulaimān. He wrote a number of letters, in some of which he painstakingly endeavoured to exclude Arabic words and to use Persian ones instead. Mīrzā Vaḥīd was also a poet in the Indian style.

Other prose works of the period were the *Ḥabīb al-siyar* by Ghiyāṣ al-Dīn Khwānd Amīr, who died in 941/1534–5 and was one of the historians of the close of the Timurid period and the beginning of the succeeding one; his book comes down to the closing years of the reign of Shah Ismāʿīl. The *Tazkirat-i Shāh Ṭahmāsp-i Ṣafavī* is the autobiography of Shah Ṭahmāsp, the son of Shah Ismāʿīl and ruler of Iran from 930/1524 to 984/1576. His reign is also covered by Ḥasan Beg Rūmlū's *Aḥsan al-tavārīkh*. The *ʿĀlam-ārā-yi ʿAbbāsī*, by Iskandar Beg Munshī, the secretary of Shah ʿAbbās the Great, relates events up to the close of that shah's life, that is, from 958/1577 to 1038/1629, and, among the prose works of the Safavid era, is noted for the beauty of its style. The *Bahār-i dānish*, which is a revised version of the *Kalīla va Dimna*, was written by Akbar's minister, Abu'l-Fażl, who was murdered in 1011/1602. He was also the author of other books such as the *Akbar-nāma* covering the reign of that sovereign, and the *Ā'īn-i Akbarī*.

The *Hasht bihisht* and the *Tārīkh-i Āl-i 'Usmān* were written by Maulānā Idrīs of Bitlīs, a contemporary of Sultan Bāyezīd II (886/1481–918/1512), and his son Abu'l-Fażl Muḥammad al-Daftarī. The *Tārīkh-i Āl-i 'Usmān* includes some of the events of the reign of Sultan Selīm II. The *Majālis al-mu'minīn* by Qāżī Nūr-Allāh of Shushtar (d. 1019/1610–1) contains the biographies of many Shī'ī poets and scholars.

Among the products worthy of interest in the literary history of this period are the biographies of poets. One of these is the *Tuḥfa-yi Sāmī* of Sām Mīrzā, the son of Shah Ismā'īl, a work containing the lives of a number of poets from the close of the 9th/15th to the end of the 10th/16th centuries. Another is the *Laṭā'if-nāma*, a translation by Fakhrī b. Amīrī of Mīr 'Alī Shīr Navā'ī's *Majālis al-nafā'is* which he completed in 927/1520–1; another famous work by him is the *Tazkirat al-nisā* which is also known as the *Javāhir al-'ajā'ib*. There is also the *Muzakkir al-aḥbāb* by Nisārī of Bukhārā, which contains the biographies of the poets of the era of Mīr 'Alī Shīr Navā'ī up to the year 974/1566–7. Similarly, the *Nafā'is al-ma'āsir* is a biographical survey of the Persian poets who lived in India during the time of Akbar. Furthermore, there is the *Khulāṣat al-ash'ār va zubdat al-afkār*, which Taqī al-Dīn Kāshānī completed in 986/1577–8. Among the important collections of biographies of poets is the *Tazkirat-i Haft iqlīm* of Amīn Aḥmad Rāzī, which was completed towards the beginning of the 11th/17th century. We may conclude this list with the *Riyāż al-shu'arā* by 'Alī Qulī Khān Vālih-i Dāghistānī, written in the 12th/18th century.

Another feature of the literature of the Safavid period was lexicography. Besides the general need in India for such works, there was the specialised interest taken by Abu'l-Fażl, Akbar's minister, in the eloquent writing of Persian and in fostering a return to the use of the Indian style of the old writers. Such an interest necessitated a good knowledge of the use and shades of meaning of Persian words. The compilation of dictionaries was encouraged. It is clear that before Abu'l-Fażl's time compilation of dictionaries had received occasional attention, though few were produced. Among the important dictionaries which appeared in India after the time of Abu'l-Fażl, and which certainly deserve notice are, in the first place, the *Farhang-i Jahāngīrī* by Jamāl al-Dīn Ḥusain Īnjū, who lived at the court of Akbar and his son Jahāngīr, and finished this dictionary in 1014/1605–6, dedicating it to Jahāngīr, whence its title.

Prior to the compilation of the *Farhang-i Jāhāngīrī*, Muḥammad Qāsim Surūrī had completed his Persian dictionary in Iran in 1008/1599–1600 and had dedicated it to Shah ʿAbbās. Among other dictionaries compiled in India there is the *Farhang-i Rashīdī* by ʿAbd al-Rashīd al-Ḥusainī, who was a contemporary of Aurangzīb. This work is one of the most valuable Persian dictionaries and was completed in 1064/1653–4. Yet another of these works is the *Ghiyās̱ al-lughat* by Muḥammad Ghiyās̱ al-Dīn, completed in the year 1242/1826–7. Besides these, other dictionaries were compiled in India, such as the *Muʾayyid al-fuz̤alā* by Muḥammad Lād of Delhi, the *Bahār-i ʿAjam*, and the *Chirāgh-i hidāyat*. Although it is not necessary to describe them all here, one, the *Burhān-i qāṭiʿ*, must briefly be mentioned. Muḥammad Ḥusain b. Khalaf of Tabrīz, who took the pen-name "Burhān", compiled this work in India in 1062/1651–2. Since it contains many words and is fuller than other Persian dictionaries, it has been reprinted a number of times.

A serious fault in these dictionaries is that the words have not as a rule been arranged in a careful manner, so that they often lack value as works of scholarship; and in many cases it has happened that through the misreading of Arabic, Turkish or Persian words, new words have been evolved.

Another development which was a grave misfortune for the language and history of Persia was the appearance of some spurious books in Akbar's time such as the *Dasātīr*, the *Shāristān* and the *Āʾīn-i Hūshang*, all of which claimed to have a number of pure Persian words as well as material on the ancient history of the country. Such forgeries brought into existence a number of words of bogus origin and root such as *parkhīda, aparkhīda, farnūdsār, samrād*, etc. Nevertheless, these coined words were inserted in Persian dictionaries as genuine Persian words and naïvely employed by the writers of "pure Persian" in the Qājār and modern periods. It was unfortunate that the information contained in these books was used in works of the Qājār period on the ancient history of Persia and regarded as credible.

During the Safavid era many scientific and religious books were written of which some must be mentioned, beginning with commentaries on the Qurʾān. ʿAlī b. Ḥusain of Zavāra, a well-known Shīʿī theologian and a contemporary of Shah Ṭahmāsp, completed in 946/1539–40 his *Tarjumat al-Khavāṣ*, which was also known as the *Tafsīr-i Zavārī*. He further produced many translations into Persian, notably that of the *Sharḥ Nahj al-balāgha* under the title of the *Rauẓat al-anvār*; Ṭabarsī's *Makārim al-akhlāq*, entitled *Makārim al-karā'im*; the *I'tiqādāt* of Shaikh Ṣadūq, entitled the *Vasīlat al-najāt*; Ibn Ṭāūs's *Ṭarā'if*, entitled the *Ṭarāvat al-laṭā'if*; and the *Majma' al-hudā*, which was known as the *Qiṣaṣ al-anbiyā*, as well as a number of others.

There is also the *Khulāṣat al-minhaj* which is a Persian commentary on the Qur'ān by Mullā Fatḥ-Allāh of Kāshān, a pupil of 'Alī b. Ḥusain of Zavāra. He also wrote in Persian a number of other books on religion, such as the *Minhaj al-ṣādiqīn fī ilzām al-mukhālifīn*, which is a commentary on the Qur'ān in five volumes and of which the above-mentioned *Khulāṣat al-minhaj* is an abridgement. He was likewise the author of the *Tanbīh al-ghāfilīn* and the *Tazkirat al-'ārifīn*, the latter work being a commentary in Persian on the *Nahj al-balāgha*.

Shaikh Bahā' al-Dīn Muḥammad b. Ḥusain 'Āmilī, who was a contemporary of Shah 'Abbās and who is better known as Shaikh Bahā'ī, was the author of the *Jāmi'-yi 'Abbāsī*. This is one of the most important of the Shī'ī theological works of modern times in Persia; it has been annotated and explained a number of times. Since this book was left unfinished because of the author's death, Shah 'Abbās ordered Maulānā Niẓām al-Dīn Muḥammad Ḥusain Quraishī of Sāva (died some time after 1038/1628–9) to complete it.

Mullā Muḥammad Bāqir Majlisī (d. 1111/1699–1700) was one of the most influential of the theologians of the latter part of the Safavid era. He was Shaikh al-Islām of Persia during the reigns of Shah Sulaimān (1077–1105/1666–1694) and Shah Sulṭān Ḥusain (1105–1135/1694–1722). He wrote many works in Persian and Arabic on Shī'ī theology and ethics such as the *Biḥār al-anvār*, the *Mishkāt al-anvār*, the *Mi'rāj al-mu'minīn*, the *Jalā' al-'uyūn*, the *Zād al-ma'ād*, the *'Ain al-ḥayāt*, and so on.

One of the most important works on dialectics in Persian of this period is the *Kalimāt-i maknūna* by Mullā Muḥsin-i Faiż of Kāshān (d. 1000/1591–2), the pupil and son-in-law of Mullā Ṣadrā. He wrote a number of other books in Persian and Arabic on religious matters. He was also a poet, and Hidāyat has estimated the number of the couplets in his Dīvān at between 6,000 and 7,000.

Another pupil of Mullā Ṣadrā was 'Abd al-Razzāq b. 'Alī b. Ḥusain Lāhījī, who took the pen-name of Fayyāż and who also wrote on philosophy and dialectics. His most important work is the *Gauhar-i murād*, which is a compendium in Persian of religious theories.

CHAPTER 18

PERSIAN POETRY IN THE TIMURID AND SAFAVID PERIODS

Politically, this period extended from the death of the last great Īl-Khān (736/1335) to the accession of Nādir Shāh (1148–60/1736–47). It encompassed the rise and fall of two powerful dynasties, the Timurids (771–911/1370–1506) and the Safavids (907–1135/1501–1722), as well as of a number of lesser houses.

From a purely literary standpoint the era falls into two phases. The first, comprising roughly a century, was a turbulent period of wars, struggle for power, and widespread destruction, culminating in the sweeping conquests of Tīmūr and ending with his death in 807/1405. Its literature is best considered a continuation of that of the previous period, which witnessed the ascendancy of lyrico-mystical poetry (the 'Irāqī school). Beginning in the 12th century, this style reached its zenith with Ḥāfiẓ in the 14th.

The second phase, stretching from the 15th to about the middle of the 18th century, may be said to have begun with the succession of Tīmūr's son Shāh Rukh in 807/1405 and his long and relatively peaceful reign, and continued to the fall of the Safavids and the rise of Nādir Shāh. What marks the division between the two phases is the emergence of a new school, whose style is called the Indian style. This school, which had its origins in the Timurid period, produced a great deal of Persian poetry, not only in Persia, but also in adjacent countries – Ottoman Turkey, Iraq, Central Asia, Afghanistan, and especially India. The appeal of this style continued for Persian poets in these lands long after it had lost impetus in Persia.

It might appear at first sight that this second phase, which occupies a span of two and a half centuries, lacks unity, and therefore cannot be considered as a distinct literary era. This would be an erroneous assumption, based perhaps on dissociating Timurid poetry from that of the Safavids and Mughals. In fact the phase represents one of the more coherent and well-defined periods of Persian literature. Within its span the Indian style developed organically, followed a normal curve within certain limits and constraints, and finally exhausted itself into a lifeless and forced poetry.

The period ended in Persia with the appearance of a group of poets and critics in Iṣfahān about the middle of the 18th century, whose efforts led to the *Bāzgasht-i adabī* ("Literary Revival movement"). The movement sought a return to the simpler and more robust poetry of the old masters as against the effete and artificial verse into which Safavid poetry had degenerated. It should be emphasised, however, that whereas the Indian style had a clear end in Persia, it had no distinct beginning. The transition was gradual and imperceptible, and vestiges of the former style persisted for more than a century.

In the following discussion we shall focus our attention chiefly on poetry, since in Persia and the countries which came under its literary influence it was poetry that until recently was the vehicle *par excellence* of literary expression. In medieval Persia, literary effort in prose was directed chiefly at the embellishment of informative writing – histories and prefatory materials in particular – by the use of rhetorical devices. Inevitably, this led to florid or bombastic styles of writing, admired by the literati of the time but disdained today. As Persian prose grew more strident and bargained its directness and simplicity for artifice, a writer's literary fame came often to depend on his ability to engage in an excessive use of metaphors and tropes and to adorn his style with a variety of devices. Of these, the use of rhythm and rhyme (*saj'*), homonymy or alliterative play on words (*jinās*), congruence or harmony of images (*tanāsub* or *murā'āt-i naẓīr*), amphibology or double entendre (*īhām*), allusion (*talmīḥ*), allusive statement (*kināya*), antithesis (*taẓādd*), poetic exaggeration (*mubālagha*) and hyperbole (*ighrāq*), as well as an inordinate use of unfamiliar Arabic words and pedantic citations, were most frequently in evidence. As a result, an idea which could be expressed simply and clearly in two lines would be belaboured, in the worst cases, in long and tortuous pages, replete with a plethora of linguistic jugglings, semantic acrobatics, allusions, tenuous turns of phrase, forced metaphors, and complex tropes.

The taste for stylistic exertion of this kind in prose presents a literary outlook quite different from the one prevalent in the West or contemporary Persia, and although we may not enjoy the labyrynthine intricacies it often produces, it would be neither objective nor helpful to dismiss the style on the ground that it does not coincide with our own literary taste. We must allow that it is a game which is now seldom played; but as long as it was in vogue it excited wonder and literary admiration. As we shall see, the kind of taste that produced this turgid prose was not inactive in poetry either.

Imaginative prose literature, in the sense commonly understood in the West, was scarce in medieval Persia, novels, short stories, and plays being alien to Persian literary tradition. Where imaginative prose did exist, however, such as in satire and folk epics, sensible, unburdened prose was often used.

Imaginative verse, on the other hand, had a wide scope, and comprised not only amorous and mystical poetry, but also panegyric, epic, and didactic genres. Fiction normally employed verse, but the *maṣnavī* (couplet) form which was used for narrative poetry was the vehicle of other genres as well. During the period under discussion a large number of maṣnavīs were written, principally in imitation of the 12th-century master Niẓāmī, or the 13th-century Persian poet of India, Khusrau Dihlavī, or occasionally after Sa'dī's *Būstān*. They comprise narrative, mystical and ethical works.

The *qaṣīda*, a monorhyme normally between some twenty-five and seventy lines, but occasionally extended to more than twice that length, continued to be written during the whole period, although with diminishing importance. It is used chiefly for panegyrics. A good deal of qaṣīdas were written by court poets in praise of the Timurid, Türkmen, and Shaibanid princes, and of the Mughal emperors and their grandees. From the 14th century we find also a considerable amount of poetry written in praise of the Shī'ī Imāms. Among the chief Shī'ī poets of the Timurid period were Khwājū Kirmānī (d. 753/1352), Salmān Sāvajī (d. 778/1376), Luṭf-Allāh Nīshāpūrī (d. 812/1409), 'Iṣmat Bukhārā'ī (d. 829/1425–6), Ni'mat-Allāh Valī (d. 834/1431), Amīr Shāhī (d. 857/1453), Ibn Ḥusām (d. 875/1470), Fighānī (d. 925/1519), and Ahlī Shīrāzī (d. 942/1535).

The pride of place, however, belongs to the *ghazal*, which was written in abundance, overshadowing all other forms of poetry. A short monorhyme of some six to fourteen lines, the ghazal was the basic form and major vehicle of lyric poetry. It was ghazals which served as the main field where poets exhibited their true talent; it is by their ghazals that they are chiefly known. It is in the context of this form that the Indian style is discussed, and on it that this chapter is focused.[1]

[1] Prose literature of the period has been dealt with in the previous chapters, where a chronological survey of its writers and poets is given. Ḥāfiẓ is likewise treated separately in an earlier chapter.

POETRY OF THE FOURTEENTH CENTURY

This period must be considered a brilliant one in Persian letters, if for no other reason than having Ḥāfiẓ (d. 791/1389), the most celebrated lyric poet of Persia, as its pre-eminent figure. The interest of the period is not, however, confined to the figure of Ḥāfiẓ. To this century belongs also the most delightful satirist of Persia, ʻUbaid-Allāh Zākānī (d. *c.* 772/1371), whose witty satires and facetiae in prose and verse have delighted generations of readers. The period also boasts a poet, Ibn Yamīn Faryūmadī (d. 769/1368), who is generally considered the most skilful writer of occasional poems (*qiṭaʻa*s, "fragments"). The other luminaries of the period are the versatile Khwājū of Kirmān; the lyricist ʻImād al-Dīn of Kirmān (d. 773/1372); the sturdy panegyrist and able lyric-writer Salmān Sāvajī; the writer of tender ghazals, Kamāl of Khujand (d. 793 or 803/1391 or 1400); the mystical poet Maghribī (d. 809/1407); and Luṭf-Allāh Nīshāpūrī, a panegyrist of fluent verse who survived Tīmūr by some three years.

The diversity and rivalry of local dynasties which sprang up following the weakening and eventual demise of the Īl-Khāns, namely the Jalayirids in the north and west, the Muzaffarids in the centre and the south, and the Karts and Sarbadārs in Khurāsān, provided for court poets a patronage which explains the relative abundance of court poetry during this time. But this is also the period which witnessed the further spread and increasing popularity of the ghazal. Some of the poets, despite their attachment to one court or another, have written mainly ghazals (Ḥāfiẓ and ʻImād), and the *dīvān* of Maghribī consists only of ghazals. Khwājū is, however, a more representative poet of his period. He wrote engaging lyrico-mystical ghazals, panegyrics in praise of his patrons, and a *khamsa* (quintet) in maṡnavī form, as well as qaṣīdas in a mystical vein and panegyrics of Shīʻī Imāms.

In the ghazal these poets follow the norms set by Saʻdī, Rūmī, and ʻIrāqī in the previous century. In narrative poetry, however, Niẓāmī remains the main model. In qaṣīda, again, they follow the 13th-century trend, with Ẓahīr Fāryābī, Anvarī, and Khāqānī serving as frequent models. Apart from the towering figure of Ḥāfiẓ, the poets of the 14th century never reached the heights attained by the two 13th-century masters, Saʻdī and Rūmī. The poetry of the period is generally competent, smooth, melodious, and well-phrased.

The Golden age of satire

Several aspects of this literature call for comment. The first is that this is the golden period of Persian satire. Neither before nor since has Persia produced any satirist comparable to ʻUbaid or Ḥāfiẓ. ʻUbaid is a forthright satirist using not only mockery, irony, and sarcasm, but also ribaldry – without shunning obscenity – in order to expose and ridicule the corruption, injustice, bigotry, and hypocrisy of his times. Human foibles, vanity and stupidity are other targets of his satires and parodies. He often uses the device of writing scandalous parallels to the serious works of old masters. His best known work, the *Akhlāq al-ashrāf* ("The Virtues of the Nobles"), consists of short essays on various virtues, such as justice, chastity, and generosity. In the preamble of each essay he explains the meanings accorded these virtues in former times and then the interpretation offered by contemporary men of standing – all travesties of the original meanings. He illustrates these travesties with satirical and humorous anecdotes written in a most engaging mock-serious style. His prose is exemplary in its succinctness and elegance.

Ḥāfiẓ is in a sense the most accomplished satirist that Persia has produced. His is not the bitter satire of an aggressive or vengeful critic, but rather the subtle yet penetrating satire of a broadminded poet. If this aspect of his work is less frequently discussed, it is only because it is often overshadowed by his lyrical and philosophical thought. Nonetheless, satire is a major element of Ḥāfiẓ's poetry and has promoted his popularity more than is generally acknowledged. His satires come in small vignettes, in a hemistich or a line or two, in the body of his ghazals. He does not belabour his point, but delivers it succinctly with apt words and fitting images. His humour is dry compared to that of ʻUbaid. Whereas ʻUbaid aims at laughter, Ḥāfiẓ provokes a smile. Both mean to alert, subvert, and educate. The scope of Ḥāfiẓ's satire is, however, limited; it is generally directed only against the falsehood and hypocrisy of the establishment, both clerical and sufistic. Characters like the *qāḍī* (judge), *muftī*, shaikh, *faqīh* (doctor of religious law), *muḥtasib* (inspector of public morality) and ṣūfī are frequent targets of his mockery and sarcasm.

Mystical poetry

Another aspect of the poetry of the period is its increasing involvement with mystical ideas and images. ʻAṭṭār, Rūmī, ʻIrāqī, Shabistarī, and

Auḥadī, all of the 13th century, popularised mystical ideas in poetry, while Niẓāmī's *Makhzan al-asrār* and Sa'dī's *Būstān* set an example of ethical poems coloured by ṣūfī attitudes and precepts. In Timurid times the spread of sufism continued and ṣūfī *pīrs* (spiritual leaders) and their *khānaqāhs* (ṣūfī hospices), often supported by the wealthy or the powerful, could be seen everywhere. Among the poets of this period many were avowed ṣūfīs.

The mystical poetry of the 14th and 15th centuries ranges from poems devoted entirely to expounding ṣūfī ideas, through those in which a mystical thought appears here and there, to those which may only by an effort be made to bear a mystical interpretation. Expressly ṣūfī poetry is found mostly in the dīvāns of Maghribī, Kamāl Khujandī and, in the 15th century, Ni'mat-Allāh Valī and Qāsim al-Anvār (d. 837/1433), all of whom had attained a leading position in mystical orders. Their ghazals of this kind are generally abstract, dry, and sprinkled with technical ṣūfī terms. The chief – almost the sole – theme of these poems is the mystical pantheism and related ideas which were in vogue. They speak of the emanation of the One in the plurality of our world, the priority of existence (*wujūd*) over the quiddities (*māhiyyāt*), and the basic unity of all creation despite appearances, particularly in transcendence of opposites such as lover and beloved, worshipper and worshipped, the hidden and the apparent, the praising and the praised, the drunk and the sober, Moses and Pharaoh, the mote and the sun, etc. Some ghazals of this kind assume an ecstatic tone and bring to mind the rapturous utterances (*shaṭḥiyyāt*)[1] of the mystics. They are attractive and enjoyable, if not through a clear appreciation of their meanings, at least through their lively rhythms. The commoner "mystical" ghazals wrap ṣūfī thought in erotic language, or else are love poems in which the poet includes lines of either direct or oblique mystical sentiments.[2]

It is from this period that mystical interpretation of lyric poems began to become an obsession and made people look for a hidden meaning behind every image.[3] Even up to our own day dictionaries are compiled which provide esoteric sufistic meanings for the most innocent words and images.

[1] Utterances made in a state of ecstasy, sometimes seemingly blasphemous, such as identifying oneself with the divinity.

[2] See Yarshater, *Shi'r-i Fārsī*, pp. 162 ff., for examples of the varieties of mystical poems.

[3] Mullā Muḥsin Faiż, a firm *akhbārī* scholar, has written a treatise, *Gulzār-i Quds*, in which he explains the mystical meaning of the images in his ghazals; see his *Dīvān* (Tehran, n.d. [1960]), pp. 11, 18ff.

Norms and conventions of lyric poetry

Here we may pause a moment to examine the norms and conventions of the large body of lyric poetry written in the 14th century. They are also applicable to the second phase of the period under discussion.

Whereas in narrative poetry the poet writes about others, in amorous ghazals he invariably writes about himself and sings of his own love (generally in the first person singular or plural). The main motifs of love lyrics are two: the paramount beauty of the beloved and the cherished sufferings of the lover. The pleasure of union is hardly ever the lover's share. Friend and foe blame him, mock him, or pity him for having embarked on a hopeless course that brings him nothing but pain and sorrow; the guard(s) of the beloved turned rival(s) (*raqīb*) chase him as a presumptuous nuisance, and "wise" philistines waste their advice on him. He is disconsolate. He sees visions of his own consuming passion in the moth which throws itself into the candle flame, and in the enraptured nightingale that pours out its heart to the inconstant rose. The black spot in the heart of the tulip reminds him of the brand of love on his own bleeding heart, the stars share his sleepless nights of separation. The sun seems never to rise and end his interminable vigils. His sorrows are legion and his tears fall in torrents. Proud, arrogant, and fully aware of her (or, rather, his – see below) beauty, the beloved is impervious to the lover's supplications and his protestations of love and devotion. If she notices him at all, it is to humble him and inflict new wounds on him. The lover accepts all this humiliation, and more, as a token of his true, unfailing love. In his distracted passion, he is almost unaware of his wounds, hovering around her house or street, suffering the insults of his rivals, and continuing to sing her praise. To him her beauty is the marvel of the whole universe. No noble cypress tree (*sarv-i āẓād*) was ever more graceful than her figure, no gazelle walked more gracefully than she. Her lips put the reddest of rubies to shame, and her languishing (*mast*, literally "intoxicated"), melting (*bīmār*, literally "ailing") eyes, framed by the darts of her eyelashes, wreak havoc with the hearts of her lovers. With cheeks like rose-petals, night-like hair surrounding the sun of her face, and a waist as narrow as a hair's breadth, she goes about piercing lovers' hearts with the arrow of her glance. In the chains of her curls are fettered a thousand captive hearts. If only she would deign to cast a favourable glance at her lover, he would not only give up all possessions, but also his faith (*dīn*) and his life (*jān*). Perhaps in no other literature is so masochistic a picture of the lover and so haughty and cruel a portrait of the beloved presented.

Love enthroned

Resigned to the exigencies of love and to his destiny, the poet has ended up by worshipping not only the beloved, but also the sorrow and suffering of love. He boasts of them and is jealous of them. His complete and selfless devotion has led, one might say, to love's apotheosis. Love reigns supreme in Persian lyrics. It is celebrated in a half-lyrical, half-mystical manner, not only as the almighty sovereign of all existence but also as its cause and purpose.[1] The great emphasis that the mystics placed on love as the sole means of attaining the Truth and the only path to the knowledge of the divine no doubt played a part in raising the station of love to such heights. Reason (*'aql*), on the other hand, is constantly denigrated and declared impotent. The opposition between the two supplies the lyrics with one of their fertile themes.

Abstractness of the beloved

Descriptions of the beloved are neither detailed nor generally aimed at portraiture. She is described in general terms and idealised as a matchless paragon of beauty. Furthermore, her description is selective. Whereas the nose, the hands, and the feet are hardly ever mentioned, the dimple on the chin and the beauty spot (*khāl*) are frequently described. In addition to these, description of the beloved is usually confined to the hair, also the lock and curls, the face, the cheeks, the eyebrows, the eyes, the eyelashes, the *bunāgūsh* (part of the neck and face just below the ear), the lips, the mouth, the budding moustache and beard (see below), the waist, the figure, the gait, the look, the glance, the smile, and less frequently, the forehead, the teeth, the arms and the legs (*sāq*). These are described as a rule individually, without any attempt at giving an impression of the actual person of the beloved. Almost all such descriptions are variations on basic conventional metaphors. As a result, the reader, rather than getting a concrete

[1] The ṣūfīs regarded the following tradition of the Prophet as the fountainhead of their beliefs: "I was a hidden treasure; then I wished to be known; I created the creation so as to become known." Recognition of the divine, they maintained, was possible only through love.

picture of the beloved, receives an abstract image of her – an image that can fit any fancy. In Persian lyrics the beloved is a personalised concept, not a person. As an individual she remains unknown. This is true also of the other characters who populate the lyrics – the Rival, the Blamer, the Muḥtasib, the *Zāhid* (sanctimonious ascetic), the *Nāṣiḥ* (complacent counsellor), the *Rind* (ruffian), etc.

Here it may be mentioned also that in Persian lyrics many concepts such as sorrow (*gham*), patience (*ṣabr*), separation (*firāq*), and of course, love (*'ishq*) and reason, as well as the heart (*dil*) and the eye (*dīda*), are personified and treated as such, to the point that with a twist a poet, Jalāl Asīr, can curse his heart for having gone after the beloved without his knowledge and having become his rival![1]

The beloved is not a woman

Thus far I have referred to the beloved as a woman in order to avoid confusion. It should be explained, however, that, as a rule, the beloved is not a woman, but a young man.[2] In the early centuries of Islam, the raids into Central Asia produced many young slaves. Slaves were also bought or received as gifts. They were often made to serve as pages at court or in the households of the affluent, or as soldiers and bodyguards. Young men, slaves or not, also served wine at banquets and receptions, and the more gifted among them could play music and maintain a cultivated conversation. It was love towards young pages, soldiers, or novices in trades and professions which was the subject of lyrical introductions to panegyrics from the beginning of Persian poetry, and of the ghazal. A common theme in all traditional lyrical poetry is the description of the *khaṭṭ-i nau*, hair growing on the lip or face of the adolescent beloved, likened commonly to new shoots of grass. Many of the metaphors used in the description of the beloved reflected the attitude of a reluctant young man importuned by the amorous advances of his own sex.[3] His carrying of arms – particularly sword (*tīgh*, *shamshīr*), dagger (*khanjar*), bow (*kamān*) and arrow (*tīr*, *khadang*) – and his engaging in bouts of drinking are also indicative of

[1] "O heart, what were you doing in the street of my beloved?/May you bleed, have you too become my rival?": Jahānbānī, p. 155.

[2] Expressions of heterosexual love are not entirely absent from classical Persian poetry, as shown by occasional descriptions of the breast. The most common conventional metaphorical images for it are the pomegranate, the lemon, and the polo ball (*gūy*).

[3] On this question, see Yarshater, "The theme", and *Shi'r-i Fārsī*, pp. 153–60.

his sex. The following famous lines of Ḥāfiẓ give an idea of the kind of epithets that can be used for him:

Hair dishevelled, sweating, laughter on his lips, and drunk,
His shirt open in front, singing ghazals, and a jug of wine in hand,
His narcissus-like eyes eager for a brawl, and mockery on his lips,
He came to me in the middle of the night and sat by my side.[1]

Shāh Muḥammad Qazvīnī, in his translation (completed in 929/1523) of Mīr 'Alī Shīr's *Majālis al-nafā'is*, adds to the notice on Kātibī of Turshīz (d. 839/1435–6) that "Kātibī was enamoured of a youth [*pisar*], as is the wont of those cities."[2] This Kātibī, a prolific and accomplished poet, when speaking of an example of perfect love in his maṣnavī *Tajnīsāt*, does not delay in describing the "charming khaṭṭ on the lip of the beloved". *Majālis al-'ushshāq* (written in 908/1502 and attributed to Ḥusain Bāīqarā, the famous Timurid patron of the arts and literature, but in fact composed by a ṣūfī in his entourage, Ḥusain Gāzurgāhī)[3] consists of the stories of the love affairs of poets, mystics, and saints, beginning with the Sixth Shī'ī Imām, Ja'far al-Ṣādiq. Even though not much credence can be attached to them, these stories' only subject is a homosexual love which somehow led in the end to the love of the divine. In one of the better known verse romances of the century, the *Gūy u chaugān* of 'Ārifī of Herat (d. 853/1449), the subject of the narrative is again the love of a poor man (*darvīsh*) towards a young, handsome prince. Luṭf-Allāh Nīshāpūrī has a ghazal, the *radīf*[4] of which is the word *pisar*, and Kātibī in a ghazal has the following line:

My sweetheart, you ought not to be less than a woman in faithfulness
Potiphar's wife gave up her life but not Joseph's care.

It is only by bearing this circumstance in mind that some of the conventions and images of Persian lyrics can be understood. How else can one appreciate the following lines of Amīr Humāyūn of Isfarā'in (15th century)?

He was approaching, drunk, with his hat awry and his skirt
rolled-up...
Showing modesty to everyone else, but as soon as seeing me
Furrowing his brow and reaching for his dagger.[5]

[1] *Dīvān*, p. 20, no. 26.
[2] Navā'ī, *Majālis*, p. 187.
[3] See Qāsim al-Anvār, *Kulliyyāt*, Nafīsī's introduction, pp. xxii–xxiii; also Gulchīn-i Ma'ānī II, 757ff.
[4] A word or phrase which repeats itself after the rhyme at the end of each line.
[5] Yarshater, *Shi'r-i Fārsī*, p. 160.

What has been said about the ghazal is equally true of the romance, the quatrain, and lyric introductions to qaṣīdas.

The impression should be avoided, however, that Persian lyrics are mere maudlin poems populated by dipsomaniac lovers bent on self-mortification and by irritable, obstreperous youths threatening their wretched lovers with daggers and swords. Our intention is to explain, for the sake of a better appreciation, some less usual aspects of this otherwise sensitive, humane, melodious, and aesthetically superb poetry.

Wine and intoxication

In his sad plight, the lover finds solace in the liberating intoxication of wine (*mai*, *bāda*, *sharāb*). For his loneliness, the excruciating pain of love, and the afflictions of a fickle world, wine is a panacaea. It frees him from the cares of life, from himself, from the cant of hypocrites and the "wisdom" of philistines. Wine and intoxication (*mastī*) are only second to love as major themes of the ghazal. The two themes are brought together in the person of the saki (*sāqī*, "wine server") who is often the subject of the poet's longings and is generally identified with the beloved.

Poets of the Timurid and Safavid periods wrote, in addition to ghazals, poems in couplet form called *sāqī-nāma*, in which the charms of the saki, the miraculous qualities of wine, and intoxication as the antidote to the transience of life and the perfidy of destiny, are extolled. 'Abd al-Nabī of Qazvīn, a poet and anthologist of the 12th/18th century, has compiled a whole *tazkira*, or collection of notices on poets, devoted to the writers of sāqī-nāmas. The great majority of the seventy-one poets and their sāqī-nāmas mentioned belong to the Timurid and the first half of the Safavid periods. The best known is that of Ḥāfiẓ.

Cult of the tavern as a symbol of social protest

Taverns (*maikada*, *maikhāna*) were run by Magians, since Muslims were not permitted such an occupation. In their esteem for this honoured calling, the ghazal writers dubbed the tavern-keeper *pīr-i mughān* ("Magian mentor"), with broad allusions to ṣūfī *pīrs*. In a spirit of defiance and challenge, the poets treat the Pīr-i Mughān with the veneration accorded to sages and saints, and pay the tavern all the homage reseved for holy places. It is often called the Ka'ba or the khānaqāh of the lovers. Not to the mosque but to the tavern would a lover go for worship; not the hands of a shaikh, but the rim of the cup would he kiss; and not to a wooden ascetic but to the saintly tavern-keeper would he listen.

This cult of the tavern which pervades the lyric poetry of the period is in essence a symbol of protest of liberal minds against the heartless restrictions and crippling constraints of the socio-religious order. It hurls defiance at bigotry and cant. The poets go still a step further in their nonconformist attitude and associate themselves also with *kharābāt* ("ruins"), that is to say ramshackle and disreputable places where wine and drugs could be had by the dregs of society. Kharābāt are now exalted as the Mecca of the lovers, and the company of bohemians, blackguards, and ruffians (the *qalandars* and *rinds*)[1] is cherished. In a nihilistic mood, the poet professes to care not a whit about his good name, regrets the times he has ever been sober, and admires the sincerity of the open-hearted drunkards and the free spirit of the kharābāt population. He delights in the flouting of socio-religious conventions. His deeply felt antagonism towards the representatives of the establishment is seen not only in his forcefully advocating an anticulture, but also in statements which smack of sacrilege or blasphemy. He pawns his turban and his ṣūfī cloak (*khirqa*) to buy wine; he taints his prayer-rug with wine as an act of piety, and advises the people of the *madrasa* to wash off their books in wine; he chooses the arch of the beloved's eyebrows as his *miḥrāb* (the holy niche in a mosque that the believers face at prayer); he would take wine any time rather than the water of Kauthar in paradise, promised to believers; he would circumambulate the kharābāt rather than the Ka'ba in Mecca; he asks to be washed in wine, which is ritually impure, when he dies. The pleasures of paradise carry little weight with him. To him the threat of doom belies God's avowed mercy. Thus the ghazal became the repository of all sceptical, nonconformist thought. A more liberal atmosphere in Persian writing is hard to find.

[1] On the meaning of *qalandar* and *rind*, see F. Meier, "Abū Sa'īd-i Abul-Ḥayr. Wirklichkeit und Legende", *Acta Iranica* II (1976), 500–1; H. Ritter, *Das Meer der Seele*, 2nd ed. (Leiden, 1978), pp. 487–91; and C. Bürgel, "Le poète et la poèsie dans l'oeuvre de Ḥāfeẓ", *Convegno Internazionale sulla poesia di Ḥāfeẓ* (Accademia Nazionale dei Lincei, 1978), pp. 75–6. For other sources, see *HIL*, p. 277 n. 111.

THE SECOND PHASE, 1400–1750: THE INDIAN SCHOOL

The period is one of the longest in Persian letters. No conspicuous literary event marks its beginning, but the forty-two years of the relatively peaceful reign of Shāh Rukh is long enough to allow us to notice the budding of the characteristics of the Indian style.

Numerous Timurid princes, like their Türkmen rivals, combined their preocupation with sex and violence with the cultivation of arts and letters. Prominent among them were Shāh Rukh's son Ulugh Beg (d. 853/1449), a remarkable savant himself, who held court in Samarqand during his father's lifetime; Bāīsunqur, another son of Shāh Rukh and an outstanding calligrapher, who ran his father's realm until his death from excessive drinking in 837/1433; and above all, Ḥusain b. Manṣūr b. Bāīqarā (d. 911/1506), whose court, thanks to the influence of his learned vizier, Mīr 'Alī Shīr (d. 906/1501), is well-known for its generous patronage of art and literature. Its fame is associated with Jāmī (d. 898/1492), the leading poet, writer, and mystic of the period. The courts of the Qarā Quyūnlū and Āq Quyūnlū Türkmens in the west, too, furnished literary patronage in the course of the 15th century, as did those of the Ottoman sultans of Turkey.

Extensive terrain of Persian letters

When the Safavids established their sweeping power in 907/1501, their militant and fanatical Shi'ism caused a schism in the body of the Islamic world. Among other outcomes, political and cultural relations with the Uzbek Shaibanids in Central Asia (905–1007/1500–98) and the Ottomans suffered. Contrary to expectations, however, this did not affect the continued support for and production of Persian literature in their realms. It is a remarkable fact that, in spite of the religious schism and the Safavids, Persian culture and Persian literature had their widest territorial expansion during the 16th–18th centuries.

Central Asia had been a homeland of Persian literature from Samanid times, and although its importance declined somewhat during the reign of the Chaghatayids in the 13th century, it rose to prominence again under Tīmūr, who made Samarqand his capital. The city experienced considerable literary and scientific prosperity under his grandson, Ulugh Beg. Under the Sunnī Shaibanids, Persian letters continued to thrive, even though now Chaghatai (Uzbek) works were also written, following the example set by Mīr 'Alī Shīr, the father of Chaghatai poetry. The *Taẕkira-yi Muẕakkir-i aḥbāb* of Bahā' al-Dīn Ḥasan Niṣārī, written in 974/1566-7, contains the notices of 275 Persian poets who were active during the first three decades of the 10th/16th century outside Iran and more particularly in Central Asia. Among these are a large number of Shaibanid princes. These, though sworn enemies of the Safavids, still wrote Persian poetry and patronised Persian poets, as did some Ottoman sultans, notably Selīm I (d. 926/1520).[1]

Persian as the literary and administrative language was introduced in Anatolia chiefly by a branch of the Saljūqs (the Saljūqs of Rūm, 470-707/1077-1307), many of whose princes actively patronised Persian culture. Their literary legacy was taken up by the Ottomans (680-1342/1281-1924), who for the greater part of their reign followed Persian literary models (see below).

Iraq, which had been the seat of the 'Abbasid caliphs, was drawn into the orbit of Persian cultural influence after the Mongols captured Baghdad in 1258 and Iraq became a part of the Il-Khanid dominions. After the collapse of the Īl-Khāns in 736/1335 Persian literary culture continued to be supported in Iraq by the Jalayirids, a successor state of the Mongols in Iraq and Āzarbāījān (736-835/1335-1432), and after them by the Türkmen dynasties and finally by the Ottomans.

The Indian subcontinent was opened to Persian influence with Islamic missionary activities in the early centuries of Islam, and later by the conquests of the Ghaznavid Maḥmūd in the 5th/11th century. The Ghaznavids of India were among the first patrons of Persian poetry in the subcontinent. Already in the 7th/13th century, Khusrau of Delhi set the tone for a large number of poets who followed in his wake. The founding of the Mughal empire by Bābur in 932/1526 raised to unprecedented heights the level of patronage of Persian letters in the subcontinent. A host of poets flocked to the courts of Bābur's successors. The generosity of the Mughal emperors to Persian poets, and the vying of their literary-minded and art-loving dignitaries with one another in attracting and recruiting poets and artists, have become legendary. Many biographers and taẕkira writers[2] have lingered on the subject (see further below).

---

[1] See J.H. Kramers, "Selim I", *EI*[1].

[2] See, for instance, Nahāvandī III, 1ff.; Badā'unī III, 170ff.; Ṣanā'ī, pp. 89-126; Āzād Bilgrāmī, *Khiẕāna* (written in 1176/1762), on poets who have received gifts and remunerations from their patrons, under individual names; Shiblī Nu'mānī III, 4-17; 'Abd al-Ghanī I-II, 138ff., and III, 11, 38ff.

The unity of the poetry in different languages

Poetry was written also in Turkish in Turkey, in Chaghatai among the Uzbeks, and in several Indian languages in Muslim India, notably Sindhi and Urdu. An important point to bear in mind is that irrespective of the language that the poets used, the poetry was the same. In the vast territory stretching from Asia Minor to Turkestan and to Bengal, poetry employed the same outlook, literary conventions, forms, metres, rhyming patterns, and above all the same imagery. The choice of language was an accident of birth, habitat, patronage, or predilection, but the models for it were and continued to be Persian. "The first Ottoman poets – and their successors through many generations –", wrote E. J. W. Gibb in his classic *History of Ottoman Poetry*, "strove with all their strength to write what is little else than Persian poetry in Turkish words ... Of national feeling in poetry they dreamed not. Poetry to them was one and indivisible."[1]. This applies, except in folk poetry, equally well to the literature of the Turkic peoples of Central Asia and the Muslims of India; in sum, to the non-Arab Muslims that Gibb calls West Asian. "The question as to what language a writer in this West Asian literature should use," he points out, "whether this should be Persian, Ottoman, Turki, Urdu, or Pushtu, was generally, but not always, determined by the locality in which he happened to find himself ... To the Ottoman people poetry was a single entity, no more affected by question of race or language than was theology or science".[2] The languages mentioned above were all, more by cultural penetration than political dominance, pervaded by Persian, and borrowed much of their poetic vocabulary from it.

Abundance of poetry

Persian poetry was produced during this period in abundance. In his *Majālis al-nafā'is*, Mīr 'Alī Shīr names some 132 poets who experienced the reign of Shāh Rukh.[3] A 10th/16th-century Persian translator of the *Majālis*, Fakhrī Harātī, brings the number of the poets who lived in the 15th century up to 570.[4] Daulatshāh, writing *c.* 892/1487, refers in his taẕkira to the overabundance of poets and to the decline of poetry's

[1] Gibb I, 29. In writing this section, I have drawn occasionally on my "Safavid Literature".
[2] Gibb I, xxxv–xxxvi.
[3] Navā'ī, *Majālis*, pp. 1–56, 183–229.
[4] *Ibid.*, pp. 56ff.

value as a result. "Wherever you listen", he writes, "there is the murmur of a poet and wherever you look there is a tender-heart or a wit ... and it is [well] said that the abundance reduces the worth."[1] Among the vast number of practitioners of the art were not only professional poets for whom the Timurid and Türkmen courts vied, but also poets of humble birth and lowly profession. Mīr ‘Alī Shīr mentions poets who were potters, drum-players, spinners, tent-makers, bag-sweepers, binders, and simple soldiers. He even characterises two poets as ‘āmī or illiterate.[2]

As for the Safavid period, Sām Mirzā records in his *Tuḥfa-yi Sāmī* (written in 958/1551) more than 700 contemporary poets who lived under his father Shah Ismā‘īl I and his brother Shah Ṭahmāsp; and Muḥammad Ṭāhir Naṣrābādī, the 11th/17th-century anthologist and biographer of poets, writing under the Safavid Shah Sulaimān (1077–1105/1666–94), records nearly 1,000 contemporary poets. This is a considerable number, even when we allow that in taẕkiras of this kind, many poets who are recorded are no more than occasional or obscure poets who wrote only mediocre verse.

The number of poets who wrote in Persia and Central Asia was far exceeded by those who wrote in the subcontinent. Although no clear statistics are available, there is no doubt that more Persian poetry and prose was written in India under the Mughal emperors than in Persia during the same period. It will be recalled that Persian was the literary and administrative language of Mughal India. It is an indication of the extent of the popularity and productivity of Persian poetry in the subcontinent that Muḥammad Aṣlaḥ's taẕkira of the Persian poets of Kashmīr, written during the reign of the Mughal emperor Muḥammad Shāh (1131–61/1719–48), alone lists 303 poets. ‘Alī Shīr Tatavī's *Maqālāt al-shu‘arā’* (completed in 1173/1760) contains notices of 719 Persian poets of Sind alone. Of the 3,148 poets who are the subject of Aḥmad ‘Alī Hāshimī Sandīlavī's *Taẕkira-yi Makhzan al-gharā’ib* (written in 1218/1804), although this is a general taẕkira, the majority are poets who either were born in India, lived in India, or were supported by an Indian patron.

---

[1] Daulatshāh, p. 10.
[2] Navā’ī, *Majālis*, pp. 21, 23, 37, 40–4, 47; see also pp. 6, 19, 32, for instances of popular attention to poetry.

Contemporary estimation of the poetry

If in quantity the poetry of the period surpasses that of comparable periods in the past, in quality it falls behind and is associated with the decline of Persian letters. This characterisation, which reflects the standards of modern Persia and of the West, is not shared by the critics of the period. The majority of the period's taẕkiras have introductory sections on the high status of poetry and poets.[1] Sām Mīrzā, whose taẕkira has been mentioned, typically declares his contemporaries to be equal to Khusrau Dihlavī, Sa'dī, and Anvarī, and even superior to Firdausī and Sanā'ī. As to his view of the status of poets in general, he considers them "chosen by God and recipients of endless [divine] light". The very fact that men of exalted rank like Mīr 'Alī Shīr and Sām Mīrzā cared to anthologise the poems of their contemporaries and write taẕkiras on them, and the eagerness with which the Mughal princes and their courtiers sought poets, read their poems, and commented on them, attest to the high station that they accorded to the poetry of their time.

The poets themselves wrote with great confidence and thought highly of the poetry of their period. They considered it a poetry of superior ingenuity and imagination. Although not much weight may be attached to the poets' conceit, the very exaggerated views of these poets about their work[2] demonstrate at least that they saw no decline in the poetic art of their time. On the contrary, they boasted of the "new way", the "new style" peculiar to them. Several expressions are used by the poets and literary historians to refer to this new way. Among these are *ṭarz-i tāza* (or *ṭarz* for short)[3] and *tāza-gū'ī*. The latter is used by Mullā 'Abd al-Bāqī Nahāvandī in his notices on 'Urfī (d. 999/1590) and Faiżī (d. 1004/1595), suggesting that their new style was encouraged by their poetry-loving patron, Abu'l-Fatḥ Gīlānī, a high-ranking courtier of Akbar.[4]

[1] See, for instance, Daulatshāh, pp. 5 ff.; Navā'ī, *Majālis*, p. xxiv; Naṣrābādī, pp. 3f.; Tatavī, pp. 5–7.

[2] For some examples of Timurid poets' conceit, see Yarshater, *Shi'r-i Fārsī*, pp. 89–91, and Sādāt-i Nāṣirī in Āẕar, *Ātashkada* I, 125. For the conceits of Safavid and Mughal poets, see, e.g., Ṣā'ib, *Dīvān*, pp. 218, 871; Kalīm, *Dīvān*, p. 281 (ghazal no. 484); for 'Urfī, see Shiblī Nu'mānī III 78–81.

[3] Used particularly by Ṣā'ib: see his *Dīvān*, Amīrī's introduction, p. 6; Mu'tamin, *Taḥavvul*, p. 358.

[4] Shiblī Nu'mānī III, 11.

By the mid 16th century, the new style was in full swing and the fame of its major representative, Ṣā'ib (d. 1081/1675), had spread far and wide, with a large following in Persia, India, Turkey, and the other regions where Persian poetry was written.[1]

The emergence of the Indian style

In essence the Indian style is an elaboration of the 'Irāqī style into a poetry of subtle thoughts and ingenious poetic ideas, frequently at the expense of felicity of phrase and warmth of feeling.

Faint signs of the Indian style begin to appear from the beginning of the Timurid period and even in Ḥāfiẓ. In his case, however, the subtlety of imagination is matched by a perfect mastery of language and a rare power of expression. It is clear that with him the ghazal in the 'Irāqī style had actualised its whole potential. A fallow literary period ensued before a new approach made itself felt.

From about the middle of the 14th century attempts at expressing poetic ideas which would impress the reader by their subtlety, daintiness, or ingenuity become noticeable. The tendency continues during the 15th century, but it is overshadowed by efforts at formal dexterity. During the 16th century, while some poets like Vaḥshī (d. 991/1583) wrote warm, passionate poems, and others like 'Urfī composed robust qaṣīdas, the majority of the poets tended towards semantic mannerism and intricate formulation of thought. By the 17th century this had given rise in Persia and India to a style which was now distinguished from the 'Irāqī style and had adopted different aesthetic criteria. Ṣanā'ī, (d. 956/1549), 'Urfī, Faiżī, Ẓuhūrī (d. 1025/1616), Naẓīrī (d. 1021/1612), Ṣā'ib, Kalīm (d. 1061/1650), Ṭālib Āmulī (d. 1035/1626) and Bīdil (Bedil, d. 1133/1721), are among its masters.

Before discussing the Indian style in more detail, we must consider a phase in which the elaboration of the rhetorical aspects of poetry reached an unprecedented high point.

Poetry of the 15th century

The generation of poets who lived during the first half of the 15th century show no advance on their immediate predecessors. The better-

[1] See Sādāt-i Nāṣirī, in Āẕar, *Ātashkada* I, 121, for his fame.

known poets of this period, 'Iṣmat Bukhārā'ī, who wrote tender lyrico-mystical ghazals; Ni'mat-Allāh Valī, the ṣūfī leader who like Qāsim al-Anvār wrote mystical lyrics; the humourist Bushāq (Abū Isḥāq, d. 827 or 830/1424 or 1427), who has left behind a "gastronomical" dīvān; Kātibī Turshīzī (d. 839/1435–6), the prolific writer in all major forms of Persian poetry who excelled in the use of rhetorical devices; Amīr Shāhī, the writer of felicitous ghazals; and Ibn Ḥusām, who is distinguished by his well-composed qaṣīdas, are all good poets of limited interest who wrote in the style of the 14th century or earlier, but without any conspicuous originality. As in the sciences, where the scholarly endeavour tended more and more toward exegesis and annotation of earlier works rather than original writing, so also in poetry, albeit to a lesser extent, it became a current practice to write parallels to the works of older masters, emulating the metre, rhyme-pattern, and sometimes the type of content of an earlier ghazal, qasīḍa, or masnavī. This trend continued through the Safavid and Mughal period, when poets often found themselves challenged to "respond" to a poem of a past or present master.

The aspect of the poetry of the 15th century that attracts our notice is the tendency of some poets to engage in impressive rhetorical elaboration and formal artifice. The currency of this tendency in prose has already been pointed out. One of its instances in poetry is the choice of difficult radīfs. Luṭf-Allāh Nīshāpūrī, who saw the early years of this period, wrote, among others, a qaṣīda with the words *āftāb u māh* ("sun and moon") as its radīf; another one with the four elements as its radīf; and a ghazal with double rhyme plus partial homonymy (*jinās-i zā'id*) worked out in every rhyme. These efforts, however, pale before some of the tours de force performed by Kātibī. In a qaṣīda of fifty-eight lines he has managed to implant in each line the improbable pair "camel" and "chamber" (*shutur* and *ḥujra*). He also wrote three poems in couplet form of which one has a double rhyme throughout, the other employs two simultaneous metres in each line (*dhū baḥrain*),[1] and the third combines a rhyme and a jinās twice in each line, at the end of each hemistich. Amīr Islām Ghazālī wrote a parallel to one of Anvarī's qaṣīdas, from each hemistich of which a chronogram for the date of the composition of the poem can be extracted.[2] Another poet,

[1] This is achieved by playing with syllables like the *-i* of the *iẓāfa* and the conjunction *u*, which metrically can be short or long.

[2] Navā'ī, *Majālis*, p. 14 (Fakhrī Harātī's translation).

Ṣāḥib, wrote an elegy of Mīr ʿAlī Shīr, all the first hemistichs of which were a chronogram for his birthdate and all the second for his death.[1] Ibn Ḥusām, an eager practitioner of rhetorical figures, has written a long qaṣīda in every line of which some six or seven artifices are employed. Some of the rhetorical feats appear indeed beyond human capability. Ahlī Shīrāzī, who felt challenged by the maṡnavīs of Kātibī, produced an amazing maṡnavī, *Siḥr-i Ḥalāl* ("White Magic"), which combined all the three feats of Kātibī in each line, namely double metre, double rhyme, plus a jinās! As if this were not dazzling enough, he also wrote three very long qaṣīdas, in each of which a large number of subsidiary lines can be extracted and which include illustrations of practically all rhetorical figures and rhyme patterns. In India at a later date even a poet like Faiżī, who deplored exaggerated artifices in the poetry of some of his contemporaries, wrote an exegesis of the Qur'ān using only the fourteen undotted letters (out of a total of 32) of the Persian alphabet.

These few examples, chosen from many, are sufficient to show that the difficult artifices and intricate figures which were common to "literate" prose find ample expression in poetry, too. Such exertions, which indeed require great skill and practice, were admired, and many poets felt called upon to prove their dexterity in this field. Luṭf-Allāh Nīshāpūrī composed a quatrain in which he took it upon himself to mention four flowers, four gems, four weapons, four colours, four days, and the four elements, without appearing to force the meaning. Daulatshāh writes that Sīmī Nīshāpūrī, a contemporary of his, was challenged to do likewise; he spent a year trying, but failed.[2]

While a good number of poets continued to write in the fairly unencumbered style of the early Timurid period, the tendency of those who aspired to "originality" and eminence was to engage in an escalating use of rhetorical devices. An aspect of this tendency can be seen in the increasing popularity of writing chronograms and poetic riddles. Both require great straining of imagination. In chronograms the poet normally has to find a word or phrase within a poetic context that would produce the desired date when the numerical value of each of the letters is added together. In riddles, a name or concept is hinted at in a variety of ways, and the reader must solve them by following the often intricate clues. Naṣrābādī (d. *c.* 1100/1688) has a section at the end

[1] *Ibid.*, p. 244 (Shāh Muḥammad Qazvīnī's translation).
[2] Daulatshāh, p. 319.

of his taẕkira devoted solely to an anthology of chronograms and riddles, and many dīvāns of the period end with compositions in these genres.

The court of Ḥusain Bāīqarā

The poets of the next hundred years or so, from the middle of the 15th century to about the middle of the 16th century, followed the same trend. The court of the Timurid Ḥusain b. Manṣūr b. Bāīqarā is the focal point of this period, not only on account of its generous patronage of literature and the arts, but also because it boasted among its cluster of poets 'Abd al-Raḥmān Jāmī (d. 898/1492), an encyclopaedist, poet, and mystic of considerable verve and accomplishment. A most respected figure of his time, he was appreciated also at the courts of the Qarā Quyūnlū, the Āq Quyūnlū and the Ottomans. Among his better-known contemporaries were Maktabī Shīrāzī, (d. 900 or 916/1495 or 1510), writer of several maṡnavīs; Ṣanā'ī, who wrote both lyrics and panegyrics; Fighānī, composer of passionate love-ghazals; Hilālī Chaghatā'ī (d. 935/1529), who has a number of well-composed lyrics to his name; and Ahlī Shīrāzī, a master of all genres and, as we have seen, an unsurpassed practitioner of contrived rhetorical figures. Responding to the ghazals and the qaṣīdas of former masters and imitating them continued to be vigorously pursued by the poets of this period. A large number of lyrical, mystical and ethical maṡnavīs, including Jāmī's *Haft aurang* ("Seven thrones"), were written in imitation of Niẓāmī and Khusrau Dihlavī. The writing of riddles and chronograms also continued to be widely practised. The contemporary historian Khwānd Amīr mentions among Jāmī's diverse works a treatise on writing riddles.[1]

With Ahlī's wizardry at formal elaborations such feats reached a point beyond which it was hardly possible to pass. The way to the elaboration of meaning, however, which had started earlier, was open and was now taken up with relish.

Elaboration of meaning: development of the Indian style

Elaboration of the meaning, like that of the formal elements, becomes a concern of the poet when direct expression of simple poetic thoughts

[1] Khwānd Amīr IV, 338.

no longer satisfies him. Ingenuity and novelty of poetic thought in the poetry of the period manifest themselves in several ways. One common instance is to give an existing simile or metaphor a new twist or to build on its implications. Ḥazīn, for example, takes the hackneyed metaphor of calling the beloved's face a candle (light) and after reversing it (i.e. candlelight resembles her face in radiance – still a common variation of the basic metaphor) presents us with the following line:

Sweat of shame ran down from the candle's brow
When it was outshone by your radiant face.[1]

Another is to hit upon a new simile or metaphor as in the following line, attributed to Ṣā'ib:

Like a reed-riding child, in the field of choice
We see ourselves mounted on a steed; in fact we are on foot;[2]

or the following on the fertile theme of the candle:

Anyone who like the candle exalts his head with a crown of gold,
Will ofttime sit [immersed] to his neck in tears;[3]

and,

The weeping of the candle is not in mourning for the moth,
Dawn is at hand: it is thinking of its own dark night.[4]

In another line[5] Ṣā'ib compares the joy of the weary fasters when they see the new moon which ends the month of Ramaḍān and announces the feast of Fiṭr, to that of those poets who seize upon a new poetic idea after having constantly searched for it:

For us joy means to seize upon a subtle thought;
For us image makers,[6] this is the new moon of the Feast.

A third instance is to read a clever, never previously thought-of interpretation into a natural phenomenon, a fact of life, a common experience, or an observation, as in the following lines by Kalīm:

[1] Ḥazīn, *Kulliyyāt*, p. 531: the three ghazals with *sham'* ("candle") as radīf offer many elaborations and variations on the old candle metaphors.

[2] Not found in Amīrī's edition of the *Dīvān* or in Mu'tamin's selections, but quoted in Jahānbānī, p. 510.

[3] Ṣā'ib, *Dīvān*, p. 749; translation taken from *LHP* IV, 276.

[4] Ṣā'ib, *Dīvān*, p. 349.

[5] Ṣā'ib, selections ed. Mu'tamin, p. 222 (not found in Amīrī's edition).

[6] *Nāzuk-khiyālān*, literally "men of subtle imagination".

If abandoning comfort does not bring pleasure,
Why is it that the tender-bodied rose makes its bed in thorns?[1]

and,

The spark knows not of the outcome of things in this world
Look at its ashen body after being draped in satin,[2]

and again:

Those with an enlightened heart are not attached to their offspring:
Separation from spark is easy for the flame.[3]

In such verses often the observation or common experience is expressed in one hemistich, the interpretation or illustration (*irsāl al-maṣal*) in the next, so that the line is complete and self-contained, as in the following by Ṣā'ib:

When a man grows old, his greed grows young;
Slumber becomes heavy at the time of dawn.[4]

The technique often consists of illustrating a dictum or a point claimed by the poet by an undeniable parallel, as in the line by Kalīm:

The mean do not acquire nobility by proximity to the great
The thread does not become precious by its connection with the pearls;[5]

and,

If you are satisfied with your portion, the more or less of the world is the same;
When the thirsty man requires but one draught, the pitcher and the river are the same.[6]

A variation of this device is to offer a poetic justification (*ḥusn-i ta'līl*) for a statement made by the poet, a device frequently and most inventively used in the poetry of the period – for instance:

His apparent cruelty covers a hidden kindness:
He kills the prey so it will not become lean.[7]

In another variation, the poet implies validity for a poetic statement as if it were an acknowledged truth, as in the following line by Ṣā'ib:

[1] Kalīm, *Dīvān*, p. 231.
[2] *Ibid.*, p. 320: satin refers to the spark's fiery colour.
[3] *Ibid.*, p. 307.
[4] Ṣā'ib, selections ed. Mu'tamin, p. 77.
[5] Kalīm, *Dīvān*, p. 117 (no. 77).
[6] *Ibid.*, p. 192 (no. 259): the word translated "river" is *daryā* (also "sea", "ocean").
[7] *Ibid.*

To write letters to the beloved is an alien custom
The moth's letter to the candle is its wings.[1]

Yet another instance is to reach a new level of poetic exaggeration as in the line from Fighānī:

You appeared in his dream and your feet took on the hue of henna,
So much did he rub them against his eyes![2]

A further technique is that of invoking a paradox as in Ṣā'ib's line:

By bitter words he makes himself [seem] sweet;
It is a disaster to life when a coquette happens to be
sweetly foul-mouthed.[3]

Still another method is to play on the associative meanings or implications of words and images so that, apart from the more obvious purport of the line, accessory relationships and correspondences are invoked in the mind of the reader, for instance:

Oh my Joseph, how long will you place a blue beauty spot
under your lip,
This dove is not worthy of the hollow of your chin.[4]

The only raison d'être of this non-poetic and altogether vapid line is the correspondences and congruities between its elements: congruence between Joseph and pit; "blue" (*nīl*) and "the Nile" (an unexpressed homonymy), the second meaning related to Joseph; *chāh* ("pit") has invoked the image of dove on account of the expression *kabūtar-i chāhi*, "wild pigeon".

When such correspondences are not forced they add new dimensions to the line. In fact the intellectual and poetic impact of the ghazals in the Indian style is very often deepened by such implied correspondences; they invite the reader to discover and appreciate them. As long as they are not too tenuous, they afford the reader the pleasure of both wonder and discovery; but only too often the power of expression is inadequate, and the poet fails to do justice to all the relationships which crowd his mind.

An element which contributes to the intricacy of many a line is the

[1] Ṣā'ib, *Dīvān*, p. 242.

[2] Fighānī, *Dīvān*, p. 126. There is deliberate ambiguity here: henna hue either on account of tenderness of the feet's skin, or from the lover's eyes, which conventionally shed tears of blood.

[3] Ṣā'ib, selections ed. Mu'tamin, p. 192; see also the line from Kalīm, above.

[4] Ṣā'ib, selections ed. Mu'tamin, p. 119: the word translated "hollow" is *chāh*, literally "pit".

excessive use of constructs based on a metaphor. Conventional metaphors in Persian poetry are generally based on correspondence between two simple ideas, such as "glance" and "dart", "wrath" and "fire". Persian poets often combine the two elements of a metaphor in a single phrase where the second word determines the metaphorical nature of the first, such as *tīr-i nigāh* ("dart of a glance"). Such sets are often based on a simile (that is, *iẓāfa-yi tashbīhī*), but the correspondence may be otherwise and sometimes be grounded on the implications of two ideas, such as *chashm-i tama'* ("the eye of greed") or *dast-i ghaib* ("the hand of the Hidden"). The poets of the Indian School sometimes have too many of these sets in a line, as in the following from Naẓīrī's elegy on his child:

> Without the breath of morn the orchard of the flower-bud grew dry.
> Without the lip of the moist rose-petal, the milk of the clouds
> dried up,[1]

or the following line quoted by the author of *Ma'āṣir-i Raḥīmī* from Shaidā (16th century):

> When the eye of the sun finds its eyebrow in the horn of Aries,
> Night becomes the pupil and day the white, so to speak.[2]

The reader will have a hard time keeping up with such accumulated metaphors, particularly if they are unfamiliar and the links on which they are built are thin or whimsical, as in many poems of the later poets of this school, like Shaukat Bukhārā'ī (d. 1107/1696), Nāṣir 'Alī Sahrandī (d. 1108/1697) and above all, the highly imaginative, passionate, but often convoluted and occasionally undecipherable Bīdil, whose flights of fancy and his extraordinary ability to capture far-fetched correspondences often leave the reader aghast.

Despite their variety, these devices[3] can be reduced, however, to one of two basic techniques: finding new, unexpected links between unrelated notions, and orchestrating the associative meanings of words, ideas, and images. In the final analysis both come down to a single faculty: perceiving uncommon relationships. The more subtle or tenuous these are, the more ingenious and inventive they will sound, but also less easy to grasp. It is this cerebral aspect of this "imagist school" of Persian poetry which is both its great merit and its bane.

1 Naẓīrī, *Dīvān*, p. 561.
2 Nahāvandī III, 1489.
3 For more extensive examples, see Yarshater, "Safavid Literature", pp. 229–36.

Modern evaluation

The poetry of this period is generally considered one of decline, and the term "the Indian style" has assumed a mildly derogatory flavour.[1] The first to hold this view were the members of the Iṣfahānī group who began the Literary Revival movement. Luṭf 'Alī Āẕar's comments in his taẕkira on Ṣā'ib, the best-known Safavid poet, are indicative of the opinions of the group. He states that "from the beginning the way to the firm imagery of the eloquent poets of the past was blocked" to Ṣā'ib, the "founder of the distasteful new style". He considers his renown unfounded, and intimates that only with great effort had he managed to choose some poems of Ṣā'ib.[2] The harshest indictment of the Safavid style is penned perhaps by Riżā Qulī Khān Hidāyat (d. 1288/1871), the well-known Qājār scholar, historian, and anthologist. In his *Majma' al-fuṣaḥā'*, the best-known Persian taẕkira, which reflects the orientation of the qaṣīda-writers of the Qājār period, he writes:

> After the Saljūq poets no progress was obtained in poetry; on the contrary, it declined daily from the highest level until it reached a middle state with the poetry of Salmān Sāvajī and his like. A number of poets belonging to this stage attempted lyric poetry, but except for Khwāja Shams al-Dīn Muḥammad Ḥāfiẓ, whose ghazals have been well appreciated by the admirers of form and substance, there is hardly a dīvān inherited from them which could be worthy of hearing. Gradually the poetry declined further from the middle stage and reached a low level. Under the Türkmens and the Safavids, reprehensible styles appeared ...and since there were no binding rules for lyrics, the poets, following their sick natures and distorted tastes, began to write confused, vain and nonsensical poems. They placed in their poetry insipid meanings instead of inspired truths, ugly contents ... instead of fine rhetorical devices and attractive innovations ...but, since every defect is followed by a perfection, and each separation by a reunion, ...towards the end of the rule of the Lurs [the Zand dynasty] several individuals directed their tastes toward reviving the style of the old masters and demonstrated awareness of the tastelessness of the style of the later poets and their banal ways ...and endeavoured ...to divert people from their blame-worthy style.[3]

This view of Safavid poetry, which was echoed by Muḥammad Taqī Bahār (d. 1330/1951), a respected contemporary poet and literary

[1] For the views of some Western literary historians, see *ibid.*, pp. 217, 227.

[2] There are two versions of this comment in Āẕar, *Ātashkada* I, 124–5, 127, following different manuscripts: both are derogatory.

[3] Hidāyat I, 9–10.

historian,[1] has generally been followed by modern critics.[2] The distaste for this style has received further support from some contemporary literary scholars who regard the Safavid period as a barren one and hold the dynasty responsible for the decline of culture and learning in Persia.[3]

This view of the Indian school of poetry, however, has by no means been shared by all. The Literary Revival movement did not have much impact outside Persia, and the Indian, Ottoman, Afghan, and Central Asian critics continued to admire the works of ʿUrfī, Ṣā'ib, Naẓīrī, Kalīm and their like. The lively criticism we often find in works written in India of some poets of the Indian school is directed not against the school itself but against individual failings.[4] Shiblī Nuʿmānī, in the third volume of his major history of Persian literature in Urdu, *Shiʿr al-ʿAjam*, although not unaware of some of the excesses and weaknesses of the poets of this school, still shows great appreciation of them and treats them almost in the same vein as he has earlier treated Saʿdī and Ḥāfiẓ. It may be that in countries outside Persia some of the formal aspects of poetry are appreciated somewhat differently than in Persia itself.

Of late some Persian critics, too, have attempted a vindication of the Indian style.[5] The dīvāns of many of the poets of this school have recently been published, and excerpted lines from them have found their way into many anthologies, a well known example being that of Jahānbānī. These poets are now receiving kinder treatment than before, but the scepticism of the established literary critics, although moderated, has not been radically altered.

General impression of the poems

The poetry of the Indian school is too often judged – particularly by its admirers – on the basis of single lines, excerpted from the dīvāns.

[1] See his collected literary papers, *Bahār u adab-i Fārsī*, ed. M. Gulbun (Tehran, 1972), pp. 43ff.

[2] For a recent expression of this view, see Āryānpūr I, 7–13.

[3] See Muḥammad Qazvīnī's letter quoted in *LHP* IV, 26; and cf. the comments of Q. Ghanī on an anthology consisting chiefly of lines written by Indian school poets, in his *Yāddāshthā* x, ed. C. Ghanī (London, 1984), 621.

[4] A lively example is the detailed critique of Ḥazīn's poetry by Sirāj al-Dīn Ārzū (quoted by Sirishk, pp. 40–53) and a rejoinder by Āzād Bilgrāmī, *Khizāna*, pp. 194–6.

[5] Among others, Amīrī in Ṣā'ib, *Dīvān*, p. 2; Mu'tamin, *Taḥavvul*, pp. 351, 357 ff., 396; Baiżā'ī in Kalīm, *Dīvān*, introduction, p. 12; Sādāt-i Nāṣirī in Āẕar, *Ātashkada* I, 124ff.; Dashtī, pp. 133ff.

These lines, frequently met in anthologies, are generally clever, dainty, and imaginative; they are also sometimes polished and eloquent. A more comprehensive impression is gained, however, when we look at the dīvāns as a whole. Here we see the infirmity of the language, forced attempts at cleverness and novelty, crowding of lines with images, disparateness of ideas expressed in a single ghazal without any clear philosophical or even ethical focus, and a certain absence of warmth and emotional authenticity. By its preoccupation with novelty the spontaneity of this poetry suffers. Some poets like Fighānī and Vaḥshī, who were more interested in conveying their heart's feelings, still followed the models of the 'Irāqī school and their ghazals are unmistakably love poems. But more often the poets appear to be so concerned with discovering novel ideas and unexpected turns and making clever allusions that the ghazal loses some of its emotive effect and forfeits its naturalness. In the works of the later poets of the period the ghazal is often no longer an expression of the poet's feelings, but an arena for the play of poetic wit and invention. Images and ideas become almost free and assume a life of their own.

The music of the ghazals also call for some comment. Whereas the qaṣīdas generally retain their vivid musical quality, in the ghazal the lively rhythms and well-phrased modulations of the former poets are often replaced by languid, monotonous ones. This is partly because frequently longer metres, such as *hazaj* octameters (four times *mafā'īlun* to each hemistich), were chosen by the poets, possibly to enable them to express complex thought in a single line, but this cannot explain the dragging and monotonous arrangements of short and long syllables within a chosen metre. Only infrequently do we find in the ghazals of the 17th century those exciting, dance-inspiring or virile rhythms[1] we encounter in the poetry of the old masters. The music of the ghazals and the masnavīs seems to be well in tune with a spirit of meekness advocated by the mystics and the devout humility that the poet assumed *vis-à-vis* the beloved. The musical aspect of Persian poetry, however, is an area which has not been studied adequately and requires further research.

Not only in music, but also in language the ghazal lost ground. The 'Irāqī ghazal is characterised by elegance and adequacy of expression. It uses a polished, well-crafted language, the elements of which fit

[1] For an excellent example of such rhythms, see Naẓīrī, *Dīvān*, p. 195 (no. 279).

together in a grammatically sound and musically pleasing manner. With the poets of the Indian school the language becomes somewhat loose; the syntax, which is the linguistic expression of logical thought, weakens and the exclusive diction of the ghazal breaks down; common words of everyday life enter the lyrics.[1] The admission of common words is not detrimental by itself; it could even be beneficial, as in the case of Īraj (d. 1343/1924) and Parvīn (d. 1320/1941) in a later period. It is their uneasy grafting onto a select language combined with syntactic and expressive weakness that marks the poor quality of diction and is considered a negative aspect of this poetry.

On the other hand, these poems allow a variety of content which we do not find in the ʿIrāqī ghazals. They contain many universal statements, points of practical wisdom, mystical sentiments and moral advice, generally enlivened by a poetic, unexpected illustration. It must be pointed out, however, that such statements do not emanate from any system of thought. They are scattered remarks occasioned by the poet's having seized upon some congruity or elusive relationship.

Thus these poems on the one hand become less intimate, but on the other more observant. The latter quality was not lost on the critics of the period. They refer to it as *vuqūʿ-gū'ī*, which means observing and expressing real or natural situations occurring in the course of the lover's experience. The following line from Naẓīrī is a case in point:

> His kindness cannot be trusted.
> I am a new lover and his mind does not suspect me;[2]

or the following lines from Sharaf-i Jahān:

> He will answer me aloud so as to make my rival aware
> If I should ask him a question in confidence;[3]

and

> Stealthily my eyes wandered over his face
> He turned his glance toward me, and I was ashamed.[4]

But while we find many fine lines and, here and there, splendid ghazals, these hardly diminish the general impression. In view of its

[1] Mu'tamin, *Taḥavvul*, pp. 365, 380, brings together a number of these words and phrases.

[2] Naẓīrī, *Dīvān*, p. 50 (no. 79).

[3] Quoted by Shiblī Nuʿmānī III, 18, from Āzād Bilgrāmī, who expressed the view that Sharaf-i Jahān (d. 962/1555), a vizier of Ṭahmāsp I, gave an impetus to *vuqūʿ-gū'ī* and was a frequent user of it.

[4] *Ibid.*

emphasis on witty content, the Indian style poetry reads better than ʿIrāqī or Khurāsānī poetry in translation,[1] once its conventions are understood. Its language and formal qualities, lost to translation, do not match, however, the inventiveness of its thought and remain somewhat jarring.

The cause of decline

The development of Persian lyric poetry from its inception is entirely coherent and understandable. From a sturdy and joyous beginning – with a rather gratified lover as its protagonist – it develops into a passionate poetry of superb diction, and eventually leads to the intricate ghazals of the later phase of the Indian style, gradually losing its emotional force and linguistic splendour. In the end it reads more like a riddle, lost in the web of recondite thought and crowded imagery. Such a course is not uncommon in the development of many an art and literature. All manner of theories, mostly of a political nature, have been offered to account for the decline of classical Persian literature. Actually, the development of Persian poetry in the 14th to 18th centuries does not seem to have been much affected by political, social, or religious events. Neither the destructive invasion of Tīmūr, nor the religious militarism of the Safavids, nor the enlightened encouragement of the Great Mughals seems to have substantially altered its course. This course does not require much explanation, any more than do the rise, decline, and fall of political systems or social institutions. The decline simply comes with old age and the exhaustion of creative energy. Rather than having been caused by external events, it is, like some of the events themselves, a manifestation of diminishing spiritual strength.

In the period we have surveyed we are dealing with the last organic phase of "classical" Persian poetry. This phase did not come to an end without a final show of vigour. It gave us a vast body of poetry that, its flaws notwithstanding, has enriched Persian literature with gems of ingenious poetry in tens of thousands of sparkling lines.

[1] Cf. *LHP* IV, 164.

BIBLIOGRAPHIES

The abbreviations used in the bibliographies and the footnotes are given below.

AA	*Arts Asiatiques* (Paris)
AAWL	*Abhandlungen der Akademie der Wissenschaften und der Literatur* (Mainz)
Acta Iranica	Acta Iranica (Encyclopédie permanente des études iraniennes) (Tehran-Liège-Leiden)
Acta Orientalia	*Acta Orientalia* (ediderunt Societates Orientales Batava Danica Norvegica Svedica) (Copenhagen)
Acta Orientalia Hung.	*Acta Orientalia Academiae Scientiarum Hungaricae* (Budapest)
AI	*Ars Islamica* = *Ars Orientalis* (Ann Arbor, Mich.)
AI(U)ON	*Annali. Istituto (Universitare) Orientale di Napoli*
AKM	Abhandlungen für die Kunde des Morgenlandes (Leipzig)
AMI	*Archäologische Mitteilungen aus Iran* (old series 9 vols 1929–38; new series 1968–) (Berlin)
AN	*Akademiya Nauk*
Anatolia	*Anatolia* (Revue annuelle d'archéologie) (Ankara)
Anatolica	*Anatolica* (Annuaire international pour les civilisations de l'Asie antérieure) (Leiden)
AO	*Ars Orientalis* (continuation of *Ars Islamica*)
AOAW	*Anzeiger der Österreichischen Akademie der Wissenschaften* (Phil. Hist. Klasse) (Vienna)
Arabica	*Arabica* (Revue d'études arabes) (Leiden)
Armaghān	*Armaghān* (a monthly literary and historical magazine), 47 vols (Tehran 1298/1919–1357/1978)
ArOr	*Archiv Orientální* (quarterly journal of African, Asian and Latin American Studies) (Prague)
Āt̲h̲ār-é Īrān	A. Godard (ed.), *Āt̲h̲ār-é Īrān* (Annales du service archéologique de l'Iran), 4 vols (Haarlem, 1936–49)
Āyanda	*Āyanda* (A Persian journal of Iranian studies), vols 1–4 (Tehran, 1304/1925–1322/1943), vol.5 (1358/1979–)
BAIPAA	*Bulletin of the American Institute for Persian (Iranian) Art and Archaeology*, 5 vols (New York, 1930–42)
Belleten	*Belleten* (*Türk Tarih Kurumu*) (Ankara)
BEO	*Bulletin d'Études Orientales de l'Institut Français de Damas* (Damascus)
BIFAO	*Bulletin de l'Institut Français d'Archéologie Orientale* (Cairo)
BMQ	*British Museum Quarterly* (London)
BSO(A)S	*Bulletin of the School of Oriental (and African) Studies* (University of London)

BT	*Barrasīhā-yi Tārīkhī* (a journal of history and Iranian studies published by Supreme Commander Staff), 79 nos (Tehran, 1345/1966–1357/1978)
Byzantinische Zeitschrift	(Leipzig)
Byzantion	*Byzantion* (Revue Internationale des Études Byzantines) (Brussels)
Cahiers du Monde Russe et Soviétique	(Paris, 1959–)
CAJ	*Central Asiatic Journal* (The Hague – Wiesbaden)
CHI	*The Cambridge History of Iran*
DAN	*Doklady Akademii Nauk*
Der Islam	(Strassburg)
East and West	*East and West* (Quarterly published by the Istituto Italiano per il Medio ed Estremo Oriente) (Rome)
Economic History Review	(Cambridge–London)
EI[1]	*Encyclopaedia of Islam*, 1st ed.
EI[2]	*Encyclopaedia of Islam*, 2nd ed.
Endeavour	(a quarterly review of the progress of science and technology) (Oxford)
English Historical Review	(Oxford)
Eranos Jahrbuch	(Leiden)
EV	*Epigrafika Vostoka* (Moscow)
FIS	Freiburger Islamstudien (Wiesbaden)
FIZ	*Farhang-i Īrān-Zamīn*, 24 vols (Tehran, 1332/1953–1358/1979)
GETOV	*Gosudarstvennyĭ Ermitazh. Trudy Otdela Vostoka*
GMS	E. J. W. Gibb Memorial Series
Hamdard Islamicus	(quarterly journal of the Hamdard Foundation, Karachi)
HIL	J. Rypka, *History of Iranian Literature* (Dordrecht, 1968)
Historische Zeitschrift	(Munich)
HO	*Handbuch der Orientalistik*, ed. B. Spuler (Leiden–Cologne)
Hunar va Mardum	(publication of the Ministry of Culture and Arts) (Tehran)
IAN	*Izvestiya Akademii Nauk*
IC	*Islamic Culture* (Hyderabad)
ICO	*International Congress of Orientalists*
IDT	Intishārāt-i Dānishgāh-i Ṭihrān
IJMES	*International Journal of Middle East Studies* (Los Angeles – Cambridge)
IM	*Istorik-Marksist* (Moscow)

Imago Mundi	(the journal of the International society for the history of cartography) (Berlin–London)
Indo-Iranica	(the quarterly organ of the Iran Society) (Calcutta)
IQ	*The Islamic Quarterly* (London)
Iran	*Iran* (Journal of the British Institute of Persian Studies) (London)
Iranica = Īrān-Shināsī	(Journal of Iranian studies) (Faculty of Letters and Humanities, Tehran University)
IrSt	*Iranian Studies*
IS	*Islamic Studies* (Denver, Colorado)
Isis	(International review devoted to the history of science) (Cambridge, Mass., etc.)
Islamica	Islamica (dirāsāt islāmiyya) (Cairo)
İsl.Ans.	*İslam Ansiklopedisi*
IU	Islamkundliche Untersuchungen (Freiburg)
JA	*Journal Asiatique* (Paris)
JAH	*Journal of Asian History* (Wiesbaden)
JAOS	*Journal of the American Oriental Society* (New York)
JASB	*Journal of the Asiatic Society of Bengal* (Calcutta)
JASP	*Journal of the Asiatic Society of Pakistan* (Dacca)
JBORS	*Journal of the Bihar (and Orissa) Research Society* (Patna)
JESHO	*Journal of the Economic and Social History of the Orient* (Leiden)
JNES	*Journal of Near Eastern Studies* (Chicago)
JPHS	*Journal of the Pakistan Historical Society* (Karachi)
JRAS	*Journal of the Royal Asiatic Society* (London)
JRCAS	*Asian Affairs = Journal of the Royal Central Asian Society* (London)
JRCI	*Journal of the Regional Cultural Institute*
KO	*Kunst des Orients* (Wiesbaden)
KSIIMK	*Kratkie soobshcheniya o dokladakh i polevykh issledovaniyakh Instituta istorii material'noĭ kultury AN SSSR*
KSINA	*Kratkie soobshcheniya Instituta Narodov Azii*
KSIV	*Kratkie soobshcheniya Instituta Vostokovedeniya AN SSSR*
LHP	E. G. Browne, *A Literary History of Persia*, 4 vols (Cambridge, 1928)
MAIS	Mémoires de l'Académie Impériale des Sciences de St. Petersburg
MII	*Le Monde Iranien et l'Islam*
MMAB	*The Metropolitan Museum of Art Bulletin* (New York)
MOG	*Mitteilungen zur osmanischen Geschichte*, 2 vols (Vienna, 1921–6)
MSOS	*Mitteilungen des Seminars für Orientalische Sprachen*, 3 vols (Berlin, 1898–1935)
MW	*The Muslim World* (Hartford, Connecticut)
NAA	*Narody Azii i Afriki* (Moscow)
NC	*Numismatic Chronicle* (London)

Notices et Extraits	*Notices et Extraits des Manuscrits de la Bibliothèque du Roi* (Paris)
OLZ	*Orientalistische Literaturzeitung* (Berlin – Leipzig)
OM	*Oriente Moderno* (Rome)
Oriens	*Oriens* (journal of the International Society for Oriental Research) (Leiden)
Oriental Art	*Oriental Art* (quarterly publication devoted to all forms of oriental art) (London)
Pantheon	*Pantheon* (international art journal) (Munich)
Persica	*Persica* (annuaire de la société néerlando-iranienne) (Leiden)
Pismennye Pamyatniki Vostoka	(Moscow)
PL	C.A. Storey, *Persian Literature: a bio-bibliographical survey*, 2 vols in 5 parts so far. London, 1927–. Trans. Yu. E. Bregel′, *Persidskaya Literatura*, 3 vols. Moscow, 1972
PLNV	Pamyatniki Literatury Narodov Vostoka (Moscow)
Problemy Vostoka	
RAA	*Revue des Arts Asiatiques* (Paris)
REA	*Revue des Études Arméniennes* (Paris)
REI	*Revue des Études Islamiques* (Paris)
RHR	*Revue de l'Histoire des Religions* (Paris)
RK	*Rāhnumā-yi Kitāb* (Tehran)
RMM	*Revue du Monde Musulman* (Paris)
RO	*Rocznik Orientalistyczny* (Cracow)
RSO	*Rivista degli Studi Orientali* (Rome)
Saeculum	*Saeculum* (Jahrbuch für Universalgeschichte) (Freiburg-Munich)
Şarkiyat Mecmuası	
SI	*Studia Islamica* (Paris)
SPA	*A Survey of Persian Art*, ed. A.U. Pope and P. Ackerman, etc. (as vol. III)
StIr	*Studia Iranica* (Leiden)
Südostforschungen	(Leipzig)
Sumer	*Sumer* (journal of archaeology and history in Iraq) (Baghdad)
SV	*Sovetskoe Vostokovedenie* (Moscow)
Syria	*Syria* (Revue d'art oriental et d'archéologie) (Paris)
TAVO	Tübinger Atlas des Vorderen Orients
TD	*İstanbul Üniversitesi Edebiyat Fakültesi Tarih Dergisi*
TDMKV	*Trudy XXV. mezhdunarodnogo Kongressa Vostokovedov* (=Proc. 25th ICO), 5 vols. Moscow, 1963.
TMEN	G. Doerfer, *Türkische und mongolische Elemente im Neupersischen*, 4 vols. Wiesbaden, 1963–75 (VOK XVI, XIX–XXI)
TTKY	Türk Tarih Kurumu Yayınlarından
TüMe	*Türkiyat Mecmuası* (Istanbul)

Turcica	*Turcica* (revue d'études turques) (Louvain–Paris–Strassburg)
UZIV	*Uchennye Zapiski Instituta Vostokovedeniya AN SSSR*
UZLGU	*Uchennye Zapiski Leningradskogo Gosudarstvennogo Universiteta*
Vaḥīd	
Veltro	
Vierteljahrschrift für Sozial- und Wirtschaftsgeschichte	(Leipzig)
VizVr	*Vizantiiskiĭ Vremennik* (Moscow)
VOK	Akademie der Wissenschaften und der Literatur. Veröffentlichungen der orientalischen Kommission (Wiesbaden)
Voprosy Istorii	(Moscow)
WZKM	*Wiener Zeitschrift für die Kunde des Morgenlandes* (Vienna)
Yādgār	*Yādgār* (majalla-yi māhiyāna-yi adabī va tārīkhī va 'ilmī), 5 vols (Tehran, 1944–9)
ZDMG	*Zeitschrift der deutschen morgenländischen Gesellschaft* (Wiesbaden)
ZVO	*Zapiski Vostochnogo Otdeleniya Imperatorskogo Russkogo Arkheologicheskogo Obshchestva* (St Petersburg)

The following frequently quoted works are given in an abbreviated form and marked with an asterisk.

Aubin, Jean. "L'ethnogénèse des Qaraunas", *Turcica* I (1969), 65–94.

Babinger, Franz. "Der Islam in Kleinasien. Neue Wege der Islamforschung", *ZDMG* LXXVI (1922), 126–52; reprinted in his *Aufsätze und Abhandlungen* I (Munich, 1962), 52–75.

Barkan, Ömer Lütfü. "Osmanlı devrinde Akkoyunlu hükümdarı Uzun Hasan Beye ait kanunlar", *Tarih Vesikaları* I (Ankara, 1941), 91–106, 184–97.

Barthold, V. V. *Four Studies on the History of Central Asia*, trans. V. and T. Minorsky, 3 vols. Leiden, 1956–62.

Beveridge, Annette S. (ed.) *The Bābur-nāma in English*. London, 1922, repr. 1969.

Busse, Heribert. *Untersuchungen zum islamischen Kanzleiwesen an Hand turkmenischer und safawidischer Urkunden*. Cairo, 1959.

Chardin, Jean. *Voyages...en Perse, et autres lieux de l'Orient*, new ed. L. Langlès, 10 vols. Paris, 1811.

A Chronicle of the Carmelites in Persia and the Papal Mission of the 17th and 18th centuries, ed. and trans. Sir H. Chick, 2 vols. London, 1939.

Clavijo, Ruy González de. *Embajada al Gran Tamorlan*, trans. Guy Le Strange, *Embassy to Tamerlane 1403–1406*. London, 1928 (Broadway Travellers).

Della Valle, Pietro. *Viaggi*. Rome, 1658–63, 3 vols. in 4 parts.

Don Juan of Persia. *Relaciones*, trans. G. Le Strange, *Don Juan of Persia. A. Shi'ah Catholic 1560–1604*. London, 1926 (Broadway Travellers).

Du Mans, Raphael. *Estat de la Perse en 1660*, ed. Ch. Schefer. Paris, 1890.

Falsafī, Naṣr-Allāh. *Zindagānī-yi Shāh 'Abbās-i avval*, 5 vols. Tehran, 1334–52/1955–73.

Fekete, Lajos. *Einführung in die persische Paläographie. 101 persische Dokumente*, ed. G. Hazai. Budapest, 1977.

Fryer, John. *A New Account of East India and Persia, being 9 years' travels, 1672–1681*, ed. W. Crooke, 3 vols. London, 1909–15 (Hakluyt Society).

Guseĭnov, I. A., and Sumbatzade, A. S. *Istoriya Azerbaĭdzhana* I. Baku, 1958.

Hakluyt, Richard. *The Principal Navigations, Voyages, Traffiques and Discoveries of the English Nation*, with introd. by J. Masefield, 8 vols. London, 1907–9.

Herbert, Thomas. *Travels in Persia 1627–1629*, abridged ed. Sir W. Foster. London, 1928 (Broadway Travellers).

Hinz, Walther. *Irans Aufstieg zum Nationalstaat im fünfzehnten Jahrhundert*. Berlin and Leipzig, 1936.

"Ein orientalisches Handelsunternehmen im 15. Jahrhundert", *Die Welt des Orients* I (Wuppertal, 1947–9), 313–40.

"Das Rechnungswesen orientalischer Reichsfinanzämter im Mittelalter", *Der Islam* XXIX (1949), 1–29, 113–41.

"Das Steuerwesen Ostanatoliens im 15. und 16. Jahrhundert", *ZDMG* C (1950), 177–201.

Hunarfar, Luṭf-Allāh. *Ganjīna-yi āṡār-i tārīkhī-yi Iṣfahān. Āṡār-i bāstānī va alvāḥ va katībahā-yi tārīkhī dar ustān-i Iṣfahān*. Iṣfahān, 1344/1964.

Ibn Baṭṭūṭa, *Tuḥfat al-nuzzār*, trans. H.A.R. Gibb, *The Travels of Ibn Baṭṭūṭa A.D. 1325–1354*, 3 vols. so far. Cambridge, 1958–71 (Hakluyt Society, 2nd series, 110, 117, 141).

Iskandar Munshī, *Tārīkh-i 'ālam-ārā-yi 'Abbāsī*, trans. R.M. Savory, *The History of Shah 'Abbas the Great*, 2 vols. Boulder, Colorado, 1978.

Jenkinson, Sir Anthony. *Early Voyages and Travels to Russia and Persia by Anthony Jenkinson*, ed. E. Delmar Morgan and C.H. Coote, 2 vols. London, 1886 (Hakluyt Society, 1st series, 72).

Kaempfer, Engelbert. *Amoenitatum*, book I trans. W. Hinz, *Am Hofe des persischen Grosskönigs (1684–85)*. Leipzig, 1940; 2nd ed. (incomplete), Tübingen and Basel, 1977.

Lambton, A. K. S. *Landlord and Peasant in Persia. A study of land tenure and land revenue administration*. London, 1953; 2nd ed. 1969.

"Quis custodiet custodes? Some reflections on the Persian theory of government", *SI* V (1955), 125–48; VI (1956), 125–46; repr. in her *Theory and Practice in Medieval Persian Government* (London, 1980), nos. iii, iv.

Lockhart, L. *The Fall of the Ṣafavī Dynasty and the Afghan Occupation of Persia*. Cambridge, 1958.

Major, R. H. (ed.) *India in the fifteenth century*. London, 1857 (Hakluyt Society, 1st series, 22).

Malcolm, Sir John. *The history of Persia from the most early period to the present time*, 2 vols. London, 1815.

Miklukho-Maklaĭ, N. D. "Shiizm i ego sotsial'noe litso v Irane na rubezhe XV–XVI vv", in *Pamyati I. Yu. Krachkovskogo* (Leningrad, 1958), pp. 221–34.

Minadoi, Giovanni Tommaso. *Historia della Guerra fra Turchi et Persiani.* Venice, 1588.

Minorsky, Vladimir. "The Aq-qoyunlu and Land Reforms", *BSOAS* XVII (1955), 449–62.

"A Soyūrghāl of Qāsim b. Jahāngīr Aq-qoyunlu (903/1498)", *BSOAS* IX (1937), 927–60; repr. in his *The Turks, Iran and the Caucasus* (London, 1978), no. XVI.

(ed.) *The Tadhkirat al-Mulūk. A Manual of Ṣafavid Administration.* London, 1943 (GMS n.s. XVI).

A Narrative of Italian Travels in Persia, in the fifteenth and sixteenth centuries, trans. Charles Grey. London, 1873 (Hakluyt Society).

Palombini, B. von. *Bündniswerben abendländischer Mächte um Persien 1453–1600.* Wiesbaden, 1968 (FIS 1).

Petrushevsky, I. P. "K istorii instituta 'soyurgala'", *SV* 1949, no. 6, 227–46.

Pugachenkova, G. A., and Rempel', L. I. *Istoriya Iskusstv Uzbekistana s drevneĭshikh vremen do serediny devyatnadtsatogo veka.* Moscow, 1965.

Purchas, Samuel. *Purchas his Pilgrimes*, 20 vols. Glasgow, 1905–7.

Rabino di Borgomale, H. L. "Coins of the Jalā'ir, Ḳara Ḳoyūnlū, Musha'sha' and Aḳ Ḳoyūnlū dynasties", *NC*, 6th series, X (1950), 94–139.

Ritter, H. "Die Anfänge der Ḥurūfīsekte (Studien zur Geschichte der islamischen Frömmigkeit II)", *Oriens* VII (1954), 1–54.

Roemer, Hans R. *Staatsschreiben der Timuridenzeit – das Šaraf-nāmä des 'Abdallāh Marwārīd.* Wiesbaden, 1952 (VOK III).

Röhrborn, K. M. *Provinzen und Zentralgewalt Persiens im 16. und 17. Jahrhundert.* Berlin, 1966.

Schmidt-Dumont, Marianne (ed.) *Turkmenische Herrscher des 15. Jahrhunderts in Persien und Mesopotamien nach dem Tārīḫ al-Ġiyāṯī.* Freiburg i. Br., 1970 (IU VI).

Schuster-Walser, Sibylla. *Das ṣafawidische Persien im Spiegel europäischer Reiseberichte (1502–1722).* Baden-Baden and Hamburg, 1970.

Siroux, Maxime. *Caravansérails d'Iran et petites constructions routières.* Cairo, 1949.

Stchoukine, I. *Les peintures des manuscrits Ṣafavīs de 1502 à 1587.* Paris, 1959.

Les peintures des manuscrits de Shāh 'Abbās Ier à la fin des Ṣafavīs. Paris, 1964.

Les peintures des manuscrits Tîmûrides. Paris, 1954.

Tavernier, J. B. *Les Six Voyages de Jean-Baptiste Tavernier*, 3 vols. Paris, 1679.

Teixeira, Pedro. *The Travels of Pedro Teixeira*, trans. W.F. Sinclair. London, 1902 (Hakluyt Society).

Togan, A. Z. V. "Büyük türk hükümdarı Şahruh", *İstanbul Üniversitesi, Edebiyat Fakültesi, Türk Dili ve Edebiyat Dergisi* III (1949), 520–38.

Travels to Tana and Persia by Josafa Barbaro and Ambrogio Contarini, trans. William Thomas and ed. Lord Stanley of Alderley. London, 1873 (Hakluyt Society).

Yakubovsky, A. "Timur (opyt kratkoĭ kharakteristiki)", *Voprosy Istorii* 1946, nos. 8–9, 42–74.

CHAPTERS 1–4: PRIMARY SOURCES

(*a*) *Arabic, Persian and Turkish*

'Abd al-Razzāq Samarqandī, Kamāl al-Dīn. *Maṭla' al-sa'dain va majma' al-baḥrain*, ed. Muḥammad Shafī', II (3 parts with continuous pagination). Lahore, 1360-8/1941-9.

Aḥmad b. Ḥusain Kātib. *Tārīkh-i jadīd-i Yazd*, ed. Īraj Afshār. Tehran, 1345/1966.

Ahrī, Abū Bakr Quṭbī. *Tārīkh-i Shaikh Uvais*, ed. and trans. J. B. van Loon. 's-Gravenhage, 1954.

Aubin, J. (ed.) *Matériaux pour la biographie de Shāh Ni'matullāh Walī Kirmānī*. Tehran, 1956 (Bibliothèque Iranienne 7).

Bābur, Ẓahīr al-Dīn Muḥammad. *Bābur-nāma*, facsimile ed. A. S. Beveridge. Leiden and London, 1905, repr. 1971 (GMS I). Trans. eadem, **The Bābur-nāma in English*.

al-Baghdādī, Ghiyāth al-Dīn 'Abd-Allāh b. Faṭh-Allāh. *al-Ta'rīkh al-Ghiyāthī. al-faṣl al-khāmis (min sanat 656–891 H./1258–1486 M.)*, ed. Ṭāriq Nāfi' al-Hamadānī. Baghdad, 1395/1975. Trans.*M. Schmidt-Dumont, *Turkmenische Herrscher*.

Daulatshāh b. 'Alā' al-Daula Samarqandī. *Tazkirat al-shu'arā*, ed. E. G. Browne. Leiden and London, 1901.

Dughlāt, Mīrzā Muḥammad Ḥaidar. *Tārīkh-i Rashīdī*, trans. N. Elias and E. Denison Ross, *A History of the Moghuls of Central Asia*. London, 1898, repr. New York, 1970.

Giese, F. (ed.) *Die altosmanischen Chroniken (Tawārīkh-i Āl-i 'Uthmān)* I (Turkish text). Breslau, 1922. II (trans.). Leipzig, 1925 (AKM XVII/1); 2nd ed. Nendeln, 1966.

Ḥāfiẓ-i Abrū, Shihāb al-Dīn 'Abd-Allāh b. Luṭf-Allāh. *Majmū'a*, partial ed. Felix Tauer, *Cinq Opuscules de Ḥāfiẓ-i Abrū*. Prague, 1959.

Ẓail-i Jāmi' al-tavārīkh, ed. Khān-bābā Bayānī. 2nd ed. Tehran, 1350/1971.

Ẓail-i Ẓafar-nāma, ed. F. Tauer, "Continuation du Ẓafarnāma de Niẓāmuddīn Šāmī par Ḥāfiẓ-i Abrū", *ArOr* VI (1934), 429–69.

Zubdat al-tavārīkh, partial ed. D. Krawulsky, *Ḫorāsān zur Timuridenzeit nach dem Tārīḫ-e Ḥāfeẓ-e Abrū (verf. 817–823 h.)* I (text and introd.). Wiesbaden, 1982 (TAVO Beihefte, Reihe B, 46/1).

Ḥamd-Allāh Mustaufī Qazvīnī. *Nuzhat al-qulūb*, ed. and trans. G. Le Strange, 2 vols. I (text). Leiden and London, 1915. II (trans.). Leiden and London, 1919 (GMS XXIII/1,2).

Ḥusainī, Ja'farī b. Muḥammad. *Tārīkh-i kabīr*, ed. A. Zaryab, *Der Bericht über die Nachfolger Timurs aus dem Tārīḫ-i kabīr des Ča'farī ibn Muḥammad al-Ḥusainī*. Unpublished Diss. phil., Mainz, 1960.

Ibn 'Arabshāh, Abū Muḥammad Aḥmad. *Kitāb 'Ajā'ib al-maqdūr fī akhbār Tīmūr*, ed. Cairo, 1285/1868; ed. 'Alī Muḥammad 'Umar, Cairo, 1399/1979. Trans. J. H. Sanders, *Tamerlane or Timur, the Great Amir*. London, 1936.

Ibn Baṭṭūṭa, Muḥammad b. ʿAbd-Allāh. *Tuḥfat al-nuẓẓār fī gharāʾib al-amṣār*, ed. and trans. Ch. Defrémery and B. R. Sanguinetti, *Voyages d'Ibn Batoutah*, 4 vols. Paris, 1853–8, repr. 1979. *Trans. Gibb.

Ibn Bazzāz, Tavakkulī b. Ismāʿīl. *Ṣafvat al-ṣafā*, ed. Aḥmad b. Karīm Tabrīzī. Bombay, 1329/1911.

Ibn Khaldūn, ʿAbd al-Raḥmān. *al-Taʿrīf*, partial ed. and trans. W. J. Fischel, *Ibn Khaldūn and Tamerlane. Their historic meeting in Damascus. 1401 A.D. (803 A.H.)*. Berkeley and Los Angeles, 1952.

Isfizārī, Muʿīn al-Dīn Muḥammad Zamjī. *Rauẓāt al-jannāt fī auṣāf madīnat Harāt*, ed. Sayyid Muḥammad Kāẓim Imām, 2 vols. Tehran, 1338/1959.

Khunjī, Faẓl-Allāh b. Rūzbihān. *Mihmān-nāma-yi Bukhārā*, ed. Minūchihr Sutūda. Tehran, 1341/1962. Trans. Ursula Ott, *Transoxanien und Turkistan. Das Mihmān-nāma-yi Buḫārā des Faḍlallāh b. Ruzbihān Ḫunǧī*. Freiburg i.Br., 1974 (IU xxv).

Sulūk al-mulūk, ed. M. Nizamuddin and M. Ghouse. Hyderabad, Deccan, 1966.

Tārīkh-i ʿālam-ārā-yi Amīnī, partial trans. V. Minorsky, *Persia in A.D. 1478–1490*. London, 1957 (Royal Asiatic Society Monographs 26).

Khūrshāh b. Qubād Ḥusainī. *Tārīkh-i Quṭbī* (or *Tārīkh-i Ilchī-yi Niẓām Shāh*), ed. (chap. 5, from Tīmūr to Akbar) Mujāhid Ḥusain Zaidī. New Delhi, 1965.

Khwāfī, Faṣīḥ Aḥmad b. Jalāl al-Dīn. *Mujmal-i Faṣīḥī*, ed. Maḥmūd Farrukh, II (2 parts). Mashhad, 1339–41/1960–2. Trans. D. Yu. Yusupova. Tashkent, 1980.

Khwānd Amīr, Ghiyāṣ al-Dīn b. Humām al-Dīn Muḥammad. *Ḥabīb al-siyar*, ed. J. Humāʾī, 4 vols. Tehran, 1333/1954.

Kutubī, Maḥmūd. *Tārīkh-i Āl-i Muẓaffar*, ed. ʿAbd al-Ḥusain Navāʾī. Tehran, 1335/1956.

Lāhījī, ʿAlī b. Shams al-Dīn. *Tārīkh-i Khānī*, ed. B. Dorn, *ʿAly Ben Schems-Eddin's Chanisches Geschichtswerk oder Geschichte von Gîlân in den Jahren 880 (=1475) bis 920 (=1514)*. St Petersburg, 1857 (Muhammedanische Quellen zur Geschichte der südlichen Küstenländer des Kaspischen Meeres 2).

Marvārīd, Khwāja ʿAbd-Allāh. *Sharaf-nāma*, facsimile ed. *Roemer, *Staatsschreiben*.

Mīr Khwānd, Muḥammad b. Khwāndshāh b. Maḥmūd. *Rauẓat al-ṣafā fī sīrat al-auliyā vaʾl-mulūk vaʾl-khulafā*, 10 vols. Tehran, 1338–9/1960.

Mufīd Mustaufī, Muḥammad. *Jāmiʿ-i Mufīdī yā Tārīkh-i Yazd tā ibtidā-yi Shāh Ismāʿīl-i avval*, ed. Īraj Afshār. Tehran, 1342/1963.

Nakhchivānī, Muḥammad b. Hindūshāh. *Dastūr al-kātib fī taʿyīn al-marātib*, ed. A. A. Ali-zade, 2 vols in 3 parts. Moscow, 1964–76.

Naṭanzī, Muʿīn al-Dīn. *Muntakhab al-tavārīkh-i Muʿīnī*, partial ed. Jean Aubin, *Extraits du Muntakhab al-Tavārīkh-i Muʿīnī*. Tehran, 1957.

Navāʾī, Mīr ʿAlī Shīr. *Majālis al-nafāʾis*, ed. ʿAlī Asghar Ḥikmat. Tehran, 1323/1944–5.

Muḥākamat al-lughatain, trans. with introd. and notes by R. Devereux. Leiden, 1966.

Munshaʾāt. Baku, 1926.

Qumī, 'Alī b. Muḥammad (or 'Alī Shīrāzī). *Shams al-siyāq*, trans. *W. Hinz, "Ein orientalisches Handelsunternehmen".

Qumī, Qāżī Aḥmad. *Khulāṣat al-tavārīkh*, partial ed. Erika Glassen, *Die frühen Safawiden nach Qāżī Aḥmad Qumī*. Freiburg i. Br., 1970 (IU v).

Salmānī, Tāj al-Dīn. *Shams al-ḥusn*, trans. H. R. Roemer, *Šams al-Ḥusn. Ein Chronik vom Tode Timurs bis zum Jahre 1409*. Wiesbaden, 1956 (VOK VIII).

Shāmī, Niẓām al-Dīn. *Ẓafar-nāma*, ed. Felix Tauer, *Histoire des conquêtes de Tamerlan intitulée Ẓafar-nāma, avec des additions empruntées au Zubdatu-t-tawārīḫ-i Bāysunġurī de Ḥāfiẓ-i Abrū*, 2 vols. I (text). Prague, 1937. II (commentary). Prague, 1956 (Monografie Archivu Orientálního 5/1, 2).

Shushtarī, Nūr-Allāh. *Majālis al-mu'minīn*, ed. Ḥājj Sayyid Aḥmad, 1 vol. in 2 parts. Tehran, 1375.

Ṭihrānī, Abū Bakr. *Kitāb-i Diyārbakriyya*, ed. Necati Lugal and Faruk Sümer, *Ak-Koyunlular Tarihi*, 2 vols. Ankara, 1962–4.

Vāṣifī, Zain al-Dīn. *Badā'i' al-vaqā'i'*, ed. A. N. Boldyrev. Moscow, 1961 (PLNV, bolsh. ser. 5).

Yazdī, Ghiyāṣ al-Dīn 'Alī. *Rūz-nāma-yi ghazāvāt-i Hindūstān*, ed. L. A. Zimin and V. V. Barthold, *Dnevnik pokhoda Timura v Indiyu*. Petrograd, 1915. Trans. A. A. Semenov, *Dnevnik pokhoda Timura v Indiyu*. Moscow, 1958.

Yazdī, Sharaf al-Dīn 'Alī. *Ẓafar-nāma*, ed. Muḥammad 'Abbāsī, 2 vols. Tehran, 1336. Facsimile ed. A. Urunbayev. Tashkent, 1972.

(*b*) *Armenian*

Medzoph, Thomas of. *Exposé des guerres de Tamerlan et de Schach Rokh*, trans. F. Nève. Brussels, 1860. See also secondary sources (Minorsky).

(*c*) *European travellers' accounts*

Barbaro, Josafa. See **Travels to Tana and Persia*.

Clavijo, Ruy González de. *Embajada al Gran Tamorlan*, ed. F. L. Estrada. Madrid, 1943. *Trans. Le Strange.

Contarini, Ambrogio. As Barbaro.

Mignanelli, Bertrando de. *Vita Tamerlani*, trans. W. J. Fischel, "A New Latin Source on Tamerlane's Conquest of Damascus (1400/1401)", *Oriens* IX (1956), 201–32.

Moranvillé, H. (ed.) "Mémoire sur Tamerlan et sa cour par un Dominicain 1403", *Bibliothèque de l'École des Chartes* LV (Paris, 1894), 433–64.

Schiltberger, Hans. *Hans Schiltbergers Reisebuch*, ed. V. Langmantel. Tübingen, 1885. Trans. J. B. Telfer, *The Bondage and Travels of Johann Schiltberger, a Native of Bavaria in Europe, Asia and Africa, 1396–1427*. London, 1879 (Hakluyt Society).

SECONDARY SOURCES

Aka, İsmail. *Mirza Şahruh zamanında Timurlu İmparatorluğu (1411–1447)*. Unpublished Habil. thesis, Ankara, 1978.

Timur'un ölümünden sonra hâkimiyet mücadeleri ve Şahruh'un saltanatı ele geçirmesi (1405–1411). Unpublished diss. DTCF, Ankara, 1971.

Album, S. "A hoard of silver coins from the time of Iskandar Qara-Qoyunlu", *NC* 7th series XVI (1976), 109–57.
"Power and legitimacy. The coinage of Mubāriz al-Dīn Muḥammad ibn al-Muẓaffar at Yazd and Kirmān", *MII* II (1974), 157–71.
Alexandrescu-Dersca, M. M. *La campagne de Timur en Anatolie*. Bucharest, 1942. 2nd ed. London, 1977 (Variorum reprints).
Algar, Hamid. "Aḥrār", *EI*² *Supplement*.
Aliev, F. M. "O termine 'ta'yīn'", *DAN Azerb. SSR* XX/3 (1964), 93–6.
Alizade, A. A. "The agrarian system in Azerbaijan in XIII and XIV centuries", *Proc. 24th ICO* (Munich, 1957), pp. 339–49.
Andrews, P. A. "The tents of Timur: an examination of reports on the Quriltay at Samarqand, 1404", in *Art of the European steppelands*, ed. P. Denwood (London, 1978), pp. 143–81.
Arberry, A. J. "A Royal Poem", in *A Locust's Leg. Studies in honour of S. H. Taqizadeh* (London, 1962), pp. 28ff.
Arends, A. K. (ed.). *Iz istorii epokhi Ulugbeka*. Tashkent, 1965.
Arroyo, H. "Complement to the numismatic history of the Sarbadār dynasty", *Seaby's Coin and Medal Bulletin*, Sept. 1975, pp. 302-4.
Artuk, İbrahim. "Mardin'de Akkoyunlu Hamza'nın Mezarı", *Selçuklu Arastırmaları Dergisi* I (1969), 157–9.
Arunova, M. R. "K istorii narodnykh vystupleniĭ v gosudarstve Timuridov v XV v.", *KSIV* XXXVII (1960), 34–6.
Aslam, Muḥammad. "Faḍl-Ullah bin Ruzbihān al-Iṣfahānī", *JPHS* X–XI (1965), 121–34.
Atiya, Aziz Suryal. *The Crusade in the Later Middle Ages*. London, 1938.
The Crusade of Nicopolis. London, 1934.
Atti del III Convegno Internazionale sull'Arte e sulla Civiltà Islamica "Problemi dell'età timuride" (Venezia 22–25 Ottobre 1979). Venice, 1980 (Quaderni del Seminario di Iranistica 8).
Aubin, Jean. "Abū Sa'īd", *EI*².
"Comment Tamerlan prenait les villes", *SI* XIX (1963), 83–122.
"Deux sayyids de Bam au XVe siècle. Contribution à l'histoire de l'Iran timouride", *AAWL, geistes- u. sozialwiss. Kl.*, 1956, no. 7, 375–501; valuable comments by B. Nikitine, in *Der Islam* XXXIV (1959), 152–62.
"Éléments pour l'étude des agglomérations urbaines dans l'Iran médiéval", in *The Islamic City*, ed. A. H. Hourani and S. M. Stern (Oxford, 1970), pp. 65–76.
*"L'ethnogénèse".
"Études Safavides I. Šāh Ismā'īl et les Notables de l'Iraq Persan", *JESHO* II (1959), 37–81.
"La fin de l'état Sarbadâr du Khorassan", *JA* CCLXII (1974), 95–118.
"Fragments historiques concernant Bam sous les Timourides et les Qara Qoyunlu", *FIZ* II (1333), 94–232.
"Le khanat de Čaġatai et le Khorassan (1334–1380)", *Turcica* VIII (1976), 16–60.
"Le mécénat timouride à Chiraz", *SI* VIII (1957), 71–88.

"Notes sur quelques documents Aq Qoyunlu", in *Mélanges L. Massignon* I (Damascus, 1956), 123–51.
"Aux origines d'un mouvement populaire médiéval: le Cheykhisme du Bayhaq et du Nichâpour", *StIr* V (1975), 213–24.
"Les princes d'Ormuz du XIIIe au XVe siècle", *JA* CCXLI (1953), 77–138.
"La propriété foncière en Azerbaydjan sous les Mongols", *MII* IV (1976–7), 79-132.
"Quelques Notices du Mukhtaṣar-i Mufîd", *FIZ* VI (1337), 164–77.
"Références pour Lar médiéval", *JA* CCXLIII (1955), 491–505.
"Les relations Diplomatiques entre les Aq-qoyunlu et les Bahmanides", in *Iran and Islam, in memory of the late Vladimir Minorsky*, ed. C. E. Bosworth (Edinburgh, 1971), pp. 11–5.
"Réseau pastoral et réseau caravanier: les grand' routes du Khurassan à l'époque mongole", *MII* I (1971), 105–30.
"Un Santon quhistānī de l'époque timouride", *REI* XXXV (1967), 185–216.
"Un soyurghal Qara-Qoyunlu concernant le bulūk de Bawānāt-Harāt-Marwast (Archives persanes commentées, 3)", in *Documents from Islamic Chanceries*, 1st series, ed. S. M. Stern (Oxford, 1965), pp. 159–70.
"Tamerlan à Bagdad", *Arabica* IX (1962), 303–9.
Azimdzhanova, S. "Nekotorye ekonomicheskie vzglyady Zakhir ad-Dina Mukhammada Babura, izlozhennye v 'Mubaine'", in *TDMKV* III, 203–8.
al-'Azzāwī, 'Abbās. *Ta'rīkh al-'Irāq bain al-iḥtilālain* II. *al-Ḥukūmat al-Jalayiriyya 739/1338–814/1410*. Baghdad, 1354/1936; III. *al-Ḥukūmat al-Turkmāniyya*. Baghdad, 1357/1939.
al-Ta'rīf bi'l-mu'arrikhīn I, *fī 'ahd al-Mughul wa'l-Turkmān*. Baghdad, 1357.
Babinger, Franz. *Aufsätze und Abhandlungen zur Geschichte Südosteuropas und der Levante*, 2 vols. Munich, 1962–6.
"La date de la prise de Trébizonde par les Turcs (1461)", *REI* VII (1950), 205–7; repr. in *Aufsätze* I, 211–13.
*"Der Islam in Kleinasien".
"Mehmed's II. Heirat mit Sitt-Chatun (1449)", *Der Islam* XXIX (1949), 215–35.
Mehmed the Conqueror and his time. Princeton, 1978.
Bacqué-Grammont, J. L. "Une lettre du prince ottoman Bāyazīd b. Mehmed sur les affaires d'Iran en 1480", *StIr* II (1973), 213–34.
Bāqirī Sarkarātī, Mahrī. "Rūḥ al-'āshiqīn: Dahnāma-yi Shāh-i Shujā'", *Nashriyya-yi Dānishkada-yi Adabiyyāt-i 'ulūm-i Insānī-yi Āzarbāijān* XXIX (1978), 487–536.
*Barkan, Ömer Lütfü. "Osmanlı devrinde".
Barthold, V. V. "Ahmed Djalāir", *EI*[1].
**Four Studies*
Herāt unter Ḥusain Baiqara dem Timuriden, tr. W. Hinz. Leipzig, 1938 (AKM XXII/8).
"A History of the Turkman People", in *Four Studies* III, 73–170.
K istorii orosheniya Turkestana. St Petersburg, 1914; repr. in *Sochineniya* III, 97–233.

"Mīr 'Alī Shīr", in *Four Studies* III, 1–72.
Mir-Ali-Shīr i politicheskaya zhizn' – Sbornik pyatisetletiya so dnya rozhdeniya. Leningrad, 1928; repr. in *Sochineniya* II/2, 199–260.
"Narodnoe dvizhenie v Samarkande v 1365 g.", *ZVO* XVII (1906); repr. in *Sochineniya* II/2, 362-79. Tr. J. M. Rogers, "A Popular Uprising in Samarqand in 1365", *Iran* XIX (1981), 21–31.
"O pogrebenii Timura", *ZVO* XXXIII (1915), 1-32; repr. in *Sochineniya* II/2, 423–54. Tr. J. M. Rogers, "The burial of Timur", *Iran* XII (1974), 65–87.
Sochineniya. Moscow, 1963–77, 9 vols.
"Tatar", *EI*[1].
"Toḳtamish", *EI*[1].
Ulugbek i ego vremya. Petrograd, 1918; repr. in *Sochineniya* II/2, 25–196. Tr. W. Hinz, *Uluġ Beg und seine Zeit.* Leipzig, 1935 (AKM XXI/1). Tr. Minorsky, *Ulugh Beg* = *Four Studies* II.
Zwölf Vorlesungen über die Geschichte der Türken Mittelasiens, tr. Th. Menzel. 2nd ed. Darmstadt, 1962.
Barthold, V. V., and Boyle, J. A. "Čaghatai", *EI*[2].
Barthold, V. V., and Shafī', Muḥammad. "'Abd al-Razzāḳ al-Samarḳandī", *EI*[2].
Bausani, A. "Ḥurūfiyya", *EI*[2].
Bayānī, Shīrīn (Chirine). *Les Djelâirides.* Unpublished thesis, Paris, 1962.
Tārīkh-i Āl-i Jalāyir. Tehran, 1345/1966 (IDT 1093).
al-Bayati, Mehdi. *Anfänge der Prosa-Literatur bei den Irak-Türkmenen.* Unpubl. Diss. phil., Mainz, 1970.
Baykal, B. S. "Die Rivalität zwischen Uzun Hasan und Mehmed II. um das Kaiserreich von Trapezunt", *TDMKV* II, 442–8.
"Uzun Hasan'ın Osmanlılara karşı katî mücadeleye hazırlıkları ve Osmanlı-Akkoyunlu harbinin başlaması", *Belleten* XXI (1957), 261–84, with German translation pp. 285–96.
Beldiceanu, N. "Biens des Grands Comnènes en 1461 d'après un registre Ottoman", *Byzantion* XXIV (1979), 21–41.
Belenitsky, A. M. "K istorii feodal'nogo zemlevladeniya v Sredneĭ Azii i Irane v timuridskuyu epokhu (XIV–XV vv.). Obrazovanie instituta suyurgal", *IM* 1941, no. 4.
"Istoricheskaya Topografiya Gerata XV v.", in Borovkov, *Alisher Navoi*, pp. 175–202.
Bıyıklıoğlu, Ömer Halıs. *Yedi yıl harbi içinde Timur'un Anadolu seferi ve Ankara savaşı.* Istanbul, 1934.
Boldyrev, A. N. "Alisher Navoi v rasskazakh sovremennikov", in Borovkov, *Alisher Navoi*, p. 133.
"Memuary Zaĭn-ad-Dina Vosifi kak istochnik dlya izucheniya kul'turnoĭ zhizni Sredneĭ Azii i Khorasana na rubezhe XV–XVI. vekov", *GETOV* II (1940), 203–74.
"Ocherki iz zhizni geratskogo obshchestva na rubezhi XV–XVI vv.", *GETOV* IV (1947), 313–412, with abstract in English.
Bonneville, G. de. "La terrible vengeance de Tamerlan", *Mélanges de l'Université Saint-Joseph* XLIX (Beirut, 1975–6), 803–17.

Borovkov, A. K. (ed.). *Alisher Navoi*. Moscow and Leningrad, 1946.
Brandenburg, D. *Herat, eine timuridische Hauptstadt*. Graz, 1977.
Samarkand. Studien zur islamischen Baukunst in Uzbekistan (Zentralasien). Berlin, 1972.
Braun, H. *Aḥvāl-e Šāh Ismāʿīl*. See bibl. to chap. 5, primary sources.
Brosset, M. F. *Histoire de la Géorgie*. 4 vols. St. Petersburg, 1849–58.
Büchner, V. F. "Serbedār", *EI*[1].
Burn, Sir Richard. "Coins of Jahān-Shāh Kara Koyunlu", *NC* x (1950), 173–207.
Busse, Heribert. "Die Entwicklung der Staatsurkunde in Zentralasien und Persien von den Mongolen bis zu den Safawiden", *Proc. 24th ICO* (Munich, 1957), pp. 372-4.
"Persische Diplomatik im Überblick. Ergebnisse und Probleme", *Der Islam* XXXVII (1961), 202–45.
**Untersuchungen*.
Cahen, Claude. "Ardjīsh", *EI*[2].
"Artuḳids", *EI*[2].
"Contribution à l'histoire du Diyār Bakr au quatorzième siècle", *JA* CCXLIII (1955), 65–100.
Der Islam, I. *Vom Ursprung bis zu den Anfängen des Osmanenreiches*. Frankfurt, 1968 (Fischer Weltgeschichte 14).
Pre-Ottoman Turkey. New York, 1968.
Cahen, Cl., and Taeschner, F. "Futuwwa", *EI*[2].
Caskel, Werner. "Ein Mahdī des 15. Jahrhunderts. Saijid Muḥammad ibn Falāḥ und seine Nachkommen", *Islamica* IV (1929–31), 48–93.
"Die Wālī's von Ḥuvēzeh", *Islamica* VI (1934), 415–34.
Charmoy, F. B. *Expédition de Timoûr-i Lenk (Tamerlan) contre Toqtamiche, en 1391 de J.C.* St Petersburg, 1835–6 (MAIS, 6e série, Sciences Politiques, Histoire et Philologie III, v); repr. Amsterdam, 1975.
Darkot, Besim. "Hısn Keyfâ", *İsl.Ans.*
Davidovich, E. A. "Svidetel'stvo Daulatshakha o razmerakh zemel'noĭ renty pri Ulugbeke", *Pis'mennye pamyatniki Vostoka* 1971, 19–37.
"O vremeni maksimal'nogo razvitiya tovarno-denezhnykh otnosheniĭ srednevekovoĭ Sredneĭ Azii", *NAA* 1965, no. 6, 83–91.
Delaville Le Roulx, J. "Rapports de Tamerlan avec les Chrétiens", in *La France en Orient au XVe siècle* (Paris, 1886) I, 384–96.
Dennis, G. T. "The Byzantine-Turkish Treaty of 1403", *Orientalia Christiana Periodica* XXXIII (Rome, 1967), 72–88.
Deny, Jean. "Un soyurgal du timouride Šāhruḫ en écriture ouigoure", *JA* CCXLV (1957), 253–66.
Duda, Dorothea. "Die Buchmalerei der Ǧalā'iriden", *Der Islam* XLVIII (1972), 28–76, and XLIX (1972), 153–220.
Duri, A. A. "Baghdād", *EI*[2].
Erzi, Adnan Sadık. "Akkoyunlu ve Karakoyunlu tarihi hakkında araştırmalar", *Belleten* XVIII (1954), 179–221.
Ettinghausen, Richard. "Bihzād", *EI*[2].

Fallmerayer, J. P. *Geschichte des Kaiserthums von Trapezunt*. Munich, 1827.
Fedorov-Davidov, G. A. "K voprosu o denezhnom kurse zolota v Irane i Sredneĭ Azii v XIV v.", *KSIIMK* 1956, no. 66, 51–8.
*Fekete. *Einführung*.
Finster, B. "Sīstān zur Zeit tīmūridischer Herrschaft", *AMI* IX (1976), 207–15.
Fischel, Walter J. *Ibn Khaldūn in Egypt*. Berkeley and Los Angeles, 1967.
Flemming, Barbara. *Landesgeschichte von Pamphilien, Pisidien und Lykien im Spätmittelalter*. Wiesbaden, 1964 (AKM XXXV/1).
Floor, W. M. "The Guilds in Iran", *ZDMG* CXXV (1975), 99–116.
Forbes Manz, Beatrice. "Administration and the Delegation of Authority in Temür's Dominions", *CAJ* XX (1976), 191–207.
"The Ulus Chaghatay before and after Temür's rise to power", *CAJ* XXVII (1983), 79–100.
Frye, R. N. "Harāt", *EI*².
Gafurov, B. G. *Istoriya tadzhikskogo naroda*, 2 vols. Moscow, 1963–5.
Gandjeï, Tourkhan. "Il canzoniere persiano de 'Alī Šīr Navā'ī", *AIUON* IV (1952), 145–55.
"Ḥusayn Mīrzā b. Manṣūr b. Bayḳara", *EI*².
"Uno scritto apologetico de Ḥusain Mīrzā sultano del Khorāsān", *AIUON* V (1953), 157–83.
Gerasimov, M. M. "Portret Tamerlana (opyt skul'pturnogo vosproizvedeniya na kraniologicheskoĭ osnove)", *KSIIMK* 1947, no. 17, 14–21.
Ghanī, Qāsim. *Baḥs̱ dar ās̱ār va afkār va aḥvāl-i Ḥāfiẓ*. I. *Tārīkh-i 'aṣr-i Ḥāfiẓ*. Tehran, 1321/1942.
Glassen. *Die frühen Safawiden*. See primary sources, *s.v.* Qumī.
Golombek, Lisa. "The Cult of Saints and Shrine Architecture in the Fourteenth Century", in *Near Eastern Numismatics, Iconography, Epigraphy and History. Studies in Honor of George C. Miles*, ed. Dickran K. Kouymjian (Beirut, 1974), pp. 419–30.
"Urban patterns in pre-Safavid Isfahan", *IrSt* VII (1974), 18–44, with "Comments" by R. Holod, pp. 45–8.
Gölpınarlı, Abdülbâki. "Fadlallâh-i Hurûfî'nin oğluna ait bir mektûp", *Şarkiyat Mecmuası* I (1956), 37–57.
Gordlevsky, V. A. "Kara Koyunlu", *Bulletin de la Société scientifique d'Azerbaidjan* IV (Baku, 1927), 1–33.
Grousset, René. *The Empire of the Steppes. Attila, Gengis Khan, Tamerlane*, tr. N. Walford. New Brunswick, 1970.
Gülensoy, Tuncer. "24 Oğuz boyunun Anadolu'daki izleri", in *Türk Halk Bilim Araştırmaları Yıllığı* 1977 (Ankara University Press, 1979), pp. 73–98.
*Guseĭnov and Sumbatzade.
Haase, Claus P. "Probleme der Künstlerkonzentration unter Timur in Zentralasien", in *Künstler und Werkstatt in den orientalischen Gesellschaften* (Graz, 1981).
Haider, Mansura. "The sovereign in the Timurid state (XIV–XVth centuries)", *Turcica* VIII (1976), 61–82.

Ḥaqīqat-Rafī', 'Abd al-Rafī'. "Nahżat-i Sarbadārān", *Vaḥīd* III (1344–5), 744–51.

Harrison, I. B., and Hardy, P. "Bābur", *EI*².

Hashim, S. O. "Les titres exacts d'un khan de la Transoxiane", *Turcia* VIII (1976), 9-15.

Herrmann, Gottfried. "Ein Erlass von Qara Yūsof zugunsten des Ordens von Ardebīl", *AMI* IX (1976), 225–42.

"Ein Erlass des Ǧalāyeriden Solṭān Ḥoseyn aus dem Jahre 780/1378", in *Erkenntnisse und Meinungen* I (Wiesbaden, 1973), 135–63 (Göttinger Orientforschungen, I. Reihe: Syria III).

"Zur Intitulatio timuridischer Urkunden", *ZDMG Suppl.* II (1974), 498–521.

"Urkunden-Funde in Āẕarbāyǧān", *AMI* IV (1971), 249–62.

Herrmann, G., and Doerfer, G. "Ein persisch-mongolischer Erlass des Ǧalāyeriden Šeyḫ Oveys", *CAJ* XIX (1975), 1–84.

"Ein persisch-mongolischer Erlass aus dem Jahre 725/1325", *ZDMG* CXXV (1975), 317–46.

Hinz, Walther. "Beiträge zur iranischen Kulturgeschichte", ZDMG XCI (1937), 58–79, with addendum pp. 421f.

**Irans Aufstieg.*

"Die persische Geheimkanzlei im Mittelalter", in *Westöstl. Abh. R. Tschudi überreicht* (Wiesbaden, 1954), pp. 342–55.

*"Ein orientalisches Handelsunternehmen".

"Quellenstudien zur Geschichte der Timuriden", *ZDMG* XC (1936), 357–98.

*"Das Rechnungswesen".

*"Das Steuerwesen Ostanatoliens".

Hoffmann, B. *Eine Stiftsurkunde des Turkmenen Yūsuf Mīrẓā b. Ǧahānšāh Qara Qoyunlu aus dem Jahre 1464.* Unpublished M. A. thesis, Freiburg, 1979.

Hookham, Hilda. *Tamburlaine the Conqueror.* London, 1962.

Horst, Heribert. "Tīmūr und Ḫōǧā 'Alī. Ein Beitrag zur Geschichte der Safawiden", *AAWL, geistes- u. sozialwiss. Kl.*, 1958, no. 2.

Humāyūn-Farrukh, Rukn al-Dīn. "Farmānī az daurān-i Abū Muẓaffar Jahān Shāh Qarā Quyūnlū", *BT* V/3 (1348), 39–52.

Hunarfar, Luṭf-Allāh. "Iṣfahān dar daura-yi jānishīnān-i Tīmūr", *Hunar va Mardum* CLXIII (2535), 6–18.

İnalcık, Halil. "Mehmed II", *İsl.Ans.*

Jahn, Karl. "Täbris, ein mittelalterliches Kulturzentrum zwischen Ost und West", *AOAW* CV (1968), 201–12.

"Timur und die Frauen", *AOAW* CXI (1974), 515–29.

Kafalı, Mustafa. "Timur", *İsl.Ans.*

Keçik, M. S. *Briefe und Urkunden aus der Kanzlei Uzun Hasans. Ein Beitrag zur Geschichte Ost-Anatoliens im 15. Jahrhundert.* Freiburg i.Br., 1975 (IU XXIX).

Köprülü, Fuad. "Alıncak", *İsl.Ans.*

"Babur", *İsl.Ans.*

Türk edebiyatında ilk mutasavvıflar. 2nd ed. Ankara, 1966.

Köprülüzade, M. F. *Azerbaĭdzhan edebiyyatyna aid tetgigler*. Baku, 1926.
Lambton, A. K. S. "Justice in the medieval Persian theory of kingship", *SI* XVII (1962), 91–119; repr. in *Theory and Practice*, no. iv.
"Early Timurid theories of state: Ḥāfiẓ Abrū and Niẓām al-Dīn Šāmī", *BEO* XXX (1978), 1–9.
"The Evolution of the Office of Darugheh", *Majalla-yi Mardum-Shināsī* III (1338), 1–10.
**Landlord and Peasant*.
"Reflections on the Iqtā", in *Arabic and Islamic Studies in honor of Hamilton A. R. Gibb*, ed. G. Makdisi (Leiden, 1965), pp. 358–76; repr. in *Theory and Practice*, no. x.
Theory and Practice in Medieval Persian Government. London, 1980 (Variorum reprints).
Lescot, R. "Chronologie de l'œuvre de Hafiz", *BEO* x (1944), 57–100.
Malek, Khan. "Un firman d'Abū Naṣr Ḥasan Bahādur", *Athār-é Īrān* III (1938), 201–6.
Mashkūr, Muḥammad Javād. "Fitna-yi Ḥurūfiyya dar Tabrīz", *BT* IV/4 (1348/1969), 133–46.
Massé, Henri. "Ordonnance rendue par le prince ilkanien Ahmad Jalaïr en faveur du Cheikh Sadr-od-Dîn (1305–1392)", *JA* CCXXX (1938), 465–8.
Masson, M. E., and Pugachenkova, G. A. "Shakhri Syabz pri Timure i Ulug Beke", tr. J. M. Rogers, "Shahr-i sabz from Timur to Ulugh Beg", (1) in *Anatolica* VI (1977–8), 1–116; (2) in *Iran* XVI (1978), 103–26; (3) in *Iran* XVIII (1980), 121–43.
Matschke, K. P. *Die Schlacht bei Ankara und das Schicksal von Byzanz. Studien zur spätbyzantinischen Geschichte zwischen 1402 und 1422*. Unpubl. Diss. phil., Berlin, 1977.
Mazzaoui, M. *The Origins of the Ṣafawids. Šīʿism, Ṣūfism, and the Ġulāt*. Wiesbaden, 1972 (FIS III).
Shiʿism and the rise of the Safavids. Unpublished Diss., Princeton, 1966.
*Miklukho-Maklaĭ. "Shiizm".
Miller, W. *Trebizond, the last Greek Empire*. London, 1926.
Minorsky, Vladimir. "Ahl-i Ḥaḳḳ", *EI*².
"Aḳ Ḳoyunlu", *EI*².
*"The Aq-qoyunlu and Land Reforms".
"Bahārlū", *EI*².
"A Civil and Military Review in Fārs in 881/1476", *BSOAS* x (1939–42), 141–78; repr. in *The Turks, Iran and the Caucasus*, no. xv.
"The Clan of the Qara-qoyunlu rulers", in *Fuad Köprülü Armağanı* (Istanbul, 1953), pp. 391–5; repr. in *The Turks, Iran and the Caucasus*, no. xiii.
A History of Sharvān and Darband. Cambridge, 1958.
Iranica, twenty articles – Bīst Maqāla-yi Minorsky. Tehran and London, 1964 (IDT, 775).
"Jihān-shāh Qara-qoyunlu and his Poetry (= Turkmenica, 9)", *BSOAS* XVI (1954), 271–97; repr. in *Medieval Iran and its Neighbours* (London, 1982. Variorum Reprints), no. xii.

"Mārdīn", *EI*[1].
"The Middle East in Western politics in the 13th, 15th and 17th centuries", *JRCAS* xxvii (1940), 427–61.
"A Mongol Decree of 720/1320 to the Family of Shaykh Zāhid", *BSOAS* xvi (1954), 515–27; repr. in *The Turks, Iran and the Caucasus*, no. x.
"Musha'sha'", *EI*[1], *Suppl.* (Leiden, 1938).
"La Perse au XVe siècle", in *Orientalia Romana* (Rome, 1958), pp. 99–117 (Serie Orientale, Roma, xvii); repr. in *Iranica*, pp. 317–26.
"*La Perse au XVe siècle entre la Turquie et Venise*. Paris, 1933 (Publs. de la Soc. des Études Iraniennes et de l'Art Persan 7); repr. in *The Turks, Iran and the Caucasus*, no. xii.
Persia in A.D 1478–1490. See primary sources, *s.v.* Khunjī.
"The Qara-Qoyunlu and the Quṭb-shāhs (Turkmenica, 10)", *BSOAS* xvii (1955), 50–73; repr. in *The Turks, Iran and the Caucasus*, no. xiv.
*"A Soyūrghāl of Qāsim b. Jahāngīr".
"Tabrīz", *EI*[1].
"Tiflis", *EI*[1].
"Thomas of Metsop' on the Timurid-Turkman Wars", in *Professor M. Shafī' presentation volume*, ed. S. M. Abdullah (Lahore, 1955), pp. 1–26; repr. in *The Turks, Iran and the Caucasus*, no. xi.
"Transcaucasica", *JA* ccxvii (1930), 41–112.
The Turks, Iran and the Caucasus in the Middle Ages. London, 1978 (Variorum reprints).
Molé, M. "Les Kubrawiya entre sunnisme et shiisme au huitième et neuvième siècles de l'hégire", *REI* xxix (1961), 61–142.
Mordtmann, J. H., and Ménage, V. L. "Dhū'l-Ḳadr", *EI*[2].
Morton, A. H. "The History of the Sarbadārs in the Light of New Numismatic Evidence", *NC* 7th series xvii (1976), 255–8.
"Three medieval inscriptions from Ardabil", *AMI Suppl.* vi (1979), 560.
Mudarrisī-Ṭabāṭabā'ī, Ḥusain. *Farmānhā-yi turkmānān-i Qarā Quyūnlū va Āq Quyūnlū.* Qum, 1352.
"Haft farmān-i dīgar az pādshāhān-i turkmān", *BT* xi/2 (2535/1976), 85–126.
Mukminova, R. G. *Bor'ba za Maverannakhr mezhdu Timuridami i Sheĭbanidami (k istorii obrazovaniya uzbekskogo gosudarstva Sheĭbanidov)*. Leningrad, 1949.
K istorii agrarnykh otnosheniĭ v Uzbekistane XVI v., po materialam "Vakf-nāme". Tashkent, 1966.
Muminov, I. M. *Istoriya Samarkanda*, 2 vols. Tashkent, 1969.
Nasr, S. H. "Ithnā 'Ashariyya", *EI*[2].
Navā'ī, 'Abd al-Ḥusain. *Asnād va mukātabāt-i tārīkhī-yi Īrān az Tīmūr tā Shāh Ismā'īl.* Tehran, 1341/1962.
Nikitine, B. "Essai d'analyse du Ṣafvat-uṣ-ṣafā", *JA* ccxlv (1957), 285–94.
Ory, S. "Ḥiṣn Kayfā", *EI*[2].
Öztuna, Yılmaz. *1402 Ankara muharebesi*. Istanbul, 1946.
*Palombini. *Bündniswerben.*
Parry, V. J. "Bāyazīd II", *EI*[2].

Petrushevsky, I. P. "Dvizhenie serbedarov v Khurasane", *UZIV* xiv (1956), 91–162. Trans. Karīm Kishāvarz, "Nahżat-i Sarbadārān dar Khurāsān", *FIZ* x (1341), 124–224.

"Feodal'nye instituty idrar i mukasse v Irane XIII–XIV vv.", in *Pamyati I. Yu. Krachkovskogo* (Leningrad, 1958), pp. 202–5.

"O formakh feodal'noĭ zavisimosti krest'yan v Irane v XIII–XIV vv.", *SV* 1955, no. 5, 96–110.

"Gosudarstva Azerbaĭdzhana v XV v.", in *Sbornik stateĭ po istorii Azerbaĭdzhana* i (2nd ed. Baku, 1949), 153–213.

*"K istorii instituta 'soyurgala'".

K istorii podushnoĭ podati v Irane pri mongol'skom vladichestve (Terminy kupchur, sar-shumar, sarāne, dzhizye)", *Issledovaniya... I. A. Orbeli* (Moscow, 1960), pp. 413–22.

K istorii sel'skogo poseleniya i sel'skoĭ obshchiny v Irane XIII–XV vv", *UZIV* xvi (1958), 31–51.

"Izuchenie feodal'nogo obshchestva Irana v Rossii i v SSSR", in *Istoriya Iranskogo gosudarstva i kultury k 2500-letiyu Iranskogo gosudarstva* (Moscow, 1971), pp. 71–82.

"Polevye i ogorodnye kul'tury v Iran v XIII–XV vekakh (iz istorii zemledeliya v Irane)", *VizVr* ix (1956), 128–53.

"Vinogradarstvo i vinodelie v Irane XIII–XV vv. (iz istorii zemledeliya v Irane)", *VizVr* xi (1956), 163–73.

"Vnutrennyaya politika Akhmeda Ak Koyunlu", in *Sbornik stateĭ po istorii Azerbaĭdzhana* i (2nd ed. Baku, 1949), 144–52.

Zemledelie i agrarnye otnosheniya v Irane XIII–XIV vekov. Moscow and Leningrad, 1960. Trans. Karīm Kishāvarz, *Kishāvarzī va munāsabāt-i arżī dar Īrān-i 'ahd-i Mughul*, 2 vols. Tehran, 1344/1966.

Poppe, N. "Karasakpaiskaya nadpis' Timura", *GETOV* ii (1940), 185–7.

*Pugachenkova and Rempel'. *Istoriya Iskusstv Uzbekistana.*

Qā'im-maqāmī, Jahāngīr. "Farmān-i mansūb ba Sulṭān Aḥmad Jalāyir", *BT* iii/5 (1347), 273–80; repr. in *Yakṣad va panjāh sanad-i tārīkhī*, ed. J. Qā'im-maqāmī (Tehran, 1348/1969), pp. 9–15.

Qāżī, Nabībakhsh. *Die Mozaffariden in Iran. Ein Beitrag zur Hafis-Forschung.* Göttingen, 1960.

Qazvīnī, Muḥammad. "Nāma-yi Amīr Tīmūr Gūrgān ba-Shārl-i shashum pādshāh-i Firansa", in *Bīst maqāla-yi Qazvīnī* i (Bombay, 1928), 39–48.

Quatremère, Etienne. "Mémoire historique sur le règne du sultan Schahrokh", *JA* 3e série ii (1836), 193–233, 338–64.

"Notice de l'ouvrage persan Maṭla' as-sa'dain", *Notices et Extraits* xiv/i (1843), 308–41, 387–426.

Rabino, H. L. *"Coins of the Jalā'ir".

"Les dynasties alaouides de Mazandéran", *JA* ccx (1927), 253–77.

*Ritter, H. "Die Anfänge der Ḥurūfīsekte".

Roemer, Hans R. "Le dernier firman de Rustam Bahādur Aq Qoyunlu?", *BIFAO* lix (1960), 273–87.

"Die Nachfolger Timurs – Abriss der Geschichte Zentral- und Vorderasiens im 15. Jahrhundert", in *Islamwissenschaftliche Abhandlungen*, ed. R. Gramlich (Wiesbaden, 1974), pp. 226–62.
"Neuere Veröffentlichungen zur Geschichte Timurs und seiner Nachfolger", *CAJ* II (1956), 219–32.
"Probleme der Hafisforschung und der Stand ihrer Lösung", *AAWL kl. d. Lit.*, 1951, no. 3, 98–115.
Šams al-Ḥuṣn. See primary sources, *s.v.* Salmānī.
**Staatsschreiben*. See *ibid.*, *s.v.* Marvārīd.
"Timurlular", *İsl.Ans.*
"Das turkmenische Intermezzo. Persische Geschichte zwischen Mongolen und Safawiden", *AMI* IX (1976), 263–97.
Roloff, G. "Die Schlacht bei Angora (1402)", *Historische Zeitschrift* CLXI (1940), 244–66.
Ross, E. W. "Tamerlan et Bayezid en 1402", in *Proc. 20th ICO* (London, 1940), pp. 323f.
Rypka, J. "Burhān al-Dīn", *EI²*.
Salim, Necati. *Otlukbeli (1473). Türk ordusunun eski seferlerinden bir meydan muharebesi.* Istanbul, 1933.
Savory, R. M. "A 15th Century Ṣafavid Propagandist at Harāt", in *American Oriental Society, Middle West Branch, Semi-centennial volume*, ed. D. Sinor (London, 1969), pp. 189–97.
"Ḥamza Mīrzā", *EI²*.
"The Struggle for Supremacy in Persia after the Death of Tīmūr", *Der Islam* XL (1964), 35–65.
Scarcia, G. "A proposito del problema della soveranità presso gli Imamiti", *AIUON* VII (1958), 95–125.
"Venezia e la Persia tra Uzun Ḥasan e Ṭahmāsp (1454–1572)", *Acta Iranica* 1st series III (1974), 419–38; also in *Veltro* XIV/1–2 (1970), 61–76.
*Schmidt-Dumont. *Turkmenische Herrscher.*
Semenov, A. A. "Kul'turnyĭ uroven pervykh Shaĭbanidov", *SV* 1956, no. 3, 51–9.
"Nadpis' na nadgrobii psevdo-seyid Omara v Guri Emire v Samarkande", *EV* I (1947), 23–6.
"Nadpisi na nadgrobiyakh Tīmūra i ego potomkov v Gur-i Emire", *EV* II (1948), 49–62; III (1949), 45–54. Trans. Abdülkadir İnan, "'Gûr-i Emîr' türbesinde Timur'un ve ahfadının mezar kitableri", *Belleten* XXIV (1960), 139–69.
Smith, Jr, John Masson. *The History of the Sarbadar Dynasty, 1336–1381 A.D., and its sources.* The Hague and Paris, 1970. Cf. review articles by Aubin, in *JESHO* XIV (1971), 332 f., and Fragner, *ZDMG* CXXIV (1974), 177ff.
"Djalāyir, Djalāyirids", *EI²*.
Smolik, J. *Die timuridischen Baudenkmäler in Samarkand aus der Zeit Tamerlans.* Vienna, 1929.
Spuler, B. "Čingizids", *EI²*.

Geschichte Mittelasiens seit dem Auftreten der Türken. Leiden-Köln, 1966 (HO v/5).
Die Goldene Horde, 2nd ed. Wiesbaden, 1965.
Die Mongolen in Iran, 3rd ed. Berlin, 1968.
The Muslim World. A historical survey. Part II: The Mongol Period, trans. F. R. C. Bagley. Leiden, 1960.
*Stchoukine. *Manuscrits Tîmûrides*.
Stromer von Reichenbach, W. "Eine Botschaft des Turkmenenfürsten Qara Yuluq an König Sigismund auf dem Nürnberger Reichstag im März 1431", *Jahrbuch für fränkische Landesforschung* XXII (Erlangen, 1962), 433–41.
"Diplomatische Kontakte des Herrschers vom Weissen Hammel, Uthman genannt Qara Yuluq, mit dem Deutschen König Sigismund im September 1430–März 1431 zu gemeinsamem Vorgehen mit dem Timuriden Schah-Ruch gegen die Türken", *Südostforschungen* XX (1961), 267–72.
"König Siegmunds Gesandte in den Orient", in *Festschrift Hermann Heimpel* II (Göttingen, 1972), 593–609.
Stroyeva, L. V. "Serbedary Samarkanda", *UZLGU* XCVIII (1949), 270–81.
Sümer, Faruk. "Âzerbaycan'ın Türkleşmesi tarihine umûmi bir bakış", *Belleten* XXI (1957), 429–47.
"Anadolu'ya yalnız göçebe Türkler mi geldi?", *Belleten* XXIV (1960), 567–94.
"Bayîndîr", *EI*[2].
"Döğerlere dâir", *TüMe* X (1953), 139–58.
"Kara-Koyunlular", *İsl.Ans.*
Kara Koyunlular (Başlangiçtan Cihan-Şah'a kadar), vol. I only published. Ankara, 1967, (TTKY, VII. seri, 49).
"Ḳarāmān-oghullarī", *EI*[2].
"*Oğuzlar (Türkmenler). Tarihleri – Boy teşkilatı – Destanları*. Ankara, 1967.
"Yıva Oğuz boyuna dâir", *TüMe* IX (1946-51), 151–66.
Sutūda, Ḥusain-Qulī. *Tārīkh-i Āl-i Muẓaffar*, 2 vols. Tehran, 1346–7/1967–8 (IDT 1145).
Taeschner, F. "Der Achîdschuk von Tebriz und seine Erwähnung im Iskendernāme des Aḥmedī", in *Charisteria Orientalia (= Festschrift für Jan Rypka)* (Prague, 1956), pp. 338–44.
Tansel, Selâhattin. *Osmanlı kaynaklarına göre Fatih Sultan Mehmed'in siyasî ve askerî faaliyeti*. Ankara, 1953.
Tauer, F. "Timur – vojak a státnik", *Nový Orient* 1961 (Prague), 84–5.
"Timurlular devrinde tarihçilik", *Belleten* XXIX (1965), 49–69.
"Zur Korrespondenz der Muẓaffariden", *Der Islam* XXXIX (1964), 242–6.
Tekindağ, M. C. Şihabeddin. "Karamanlılar", *İsl.Ans.*
Thābitī, Sayyid 'Alī Mu'ayyad. *Asnād va nāmahā-yi tārīkhī az avā'il-i daurahā-yi islāmī tā avākhir-i 'ahd-i Shāh Ismā'īl Ṣafavī*. Tehran, 1346/1967.
Togan, Ahmed Zeki Velidi. "'Ali Şîr", *İsl.Ans.*
*"Büyük türk hükümdarı Şahruh".
"Herat", *İsl.Ans.*

"Taḥqīq-i nasab-i Amīr Tīmūr", in *Professor M. Shafīʿ presentation volume*, ed. S. M. Abdullah (Lahore, 1955), pp. 105–13; trans. as "Emîr Timur'un soyuna dâir bir araştırma", *TD* XXVI (1972), 75–84.
"Timurs Osteuropapolitik", *ZDMG* CVIII (1958), 279–98.
Tournebize, F. "Ravages de Timour-Leng en Arménie", *Revue de l'Orient Chrétien* XXIII (Paris, 1922–3), 31–46.
Treu, M. "Eine Ansprache Tamerlans", *Byzantinische Zeitschrift* XIX (1910), 15–28.
Uzunçarşılı, İsmail Hakkı. *Anadolu Beylikleri ve Akkoyunlu, Karakoyunlu devletleri.* Ankara, 1937, 2nd ed. 1969 (TTKY, VIII. seri, 2).
"Bayezid II", *İsl.Ans.*
"Eretna", *İsl.Ans.*
Osmanlı devleti teşkilâtına medhal. Ankara, 1941.
Vercellin, G. "Un 'sarbedār' del 981/1573 a Tabriz", *AIUON* n.s. XX (1970), 413–5.
Veselovsky, N. Y. "Pamyatnik Khodzhi Akhrara v Samarkande", in *Vostochniya Zametki* (St Petersburg, 1895).
Wilber, D. N. "The Timurid court: life in gardens and tents", *Iran* XVII (1979), 127–33.
Wittek, P. *The Rise of the Ottoman Empire.* London, 1958.
"Le rôle des tribus turques dans l'empire ottoman", in *Mélanges Georges Smets* (Brussels, 1952), pp. 665–76.
Woods, J. E. *The Aqqoyunlu. Clan, Confederation, Empire. A Study in 15th/9th Century Turko-Iranian Politics.* Minneapolis and Chicago, 1976.
"Turco-Iranica I: an Ottoman intelligence report on late fifteenth/ ninth century Iranian foreign relations", *JNES* XXXVIII (1979), 1–9.
Yakubovsky, A. *Samarkand pri Timure i Timuridakh.* Leningrad, 1933.
*"Timur".
Yar-Shater, Ehsan. *Shiʿr-i fārsī dar ʿahd-i Shāh Rukh yā Āghāz-i inḥiṭāṭ dar shiʿr-i fārsī.* Tehran, 1334/1955 (IDT 268).
Yınanç, Mükrimin Halil. "Ak-Koyunlular", *İsl.Ans.*
"Celāyir", *İsl.Ans.*
"Cihan-Şah", *İsl.Ans.*
"Diyarbekir şehir ve bölgesindeki vuku'âtın tarihi", *İsl.Ans.*
"Elbistan", *İsl.Ans.*
Yücel, Y. "Mutahharten ve Erzincan Emîrliği", *Belleten* XXXV (1971), 665–719.
"Timur tehlikesi", *Belleten* XXXVII (1973), 159–90; XL (1976), 249–85.
Zettersteén, K. V. "Muẓaffarids", *EI*[1].
"Shāh Shudjāʿ, *EI*[1].
Zimin, L. "Les exploits d'Emîrzâdé 'Omar Cheikh, fils de Timour, à Kachghar, en Ferghana et en Mongolie", *RMM* XXVII (1914), 244–58.
"Podrobnosti o smerti Timura", *Protokoly zasedanii i soobshcheniya chlenov Turkestanskogo kruzhka lyubitelei arkheologii* XIX (1914), 37–52, with additional data pp. 53–5.

CHAPTER 5: PRIMARY SOURCES

(*a*) *Arabic, Persian and Turkish*

Āfushta-yi Naṭanzī, Maḥmūd b. Hidāyat-Allāh. *Naqavat al-āṣār fī ẕikr al-akhbār*, ed. Iḥsān Ishrāqī. Tehran, 1350.

Arutin, Tanburī. *Tahmas Kulu Han'ın Tevarihi*. Ankara, 1942. Trans. Y. Artin Pacha, "Journal de Tanbouri Aroutine, sur la conquête de l'Inde", *Bulletin de l'Institut Égyptien*, 5e série, VIII (1914), 168–232.

Astarābādī, Mīrzā Mahdī Khān Kaukab. *Geschichte des Nadir Schah, Kaysers von Persien*, trans. T. H. Gadebusch. Greifswald, 1773.

Bidlisī, Sharaf al-Dīn. *Sharaf-nāma*, ed. V. V. Velyaminov-Zernov, 2 vols. St Petersburg, 1861. Trans F. B. Charmoy, *Chéref-nâmeh ou Fastes de la nation kourde*, 2 vols. St Petersburg, 1868–75.

Braun, H. (ed.) *Aḥvāl-e Šāh Ismā'īl. Eine unerschlossene Darstellung des Lebens des ersten Safawidenschahs*, trans. and commentary. Unpublished Diss. phil., Göttingen, 1947.

Dorn, B. (ed.) *Muhammedanische Quellen zur Geschichte der südlichen Küstenländer des Kaspischen Meeres* IV. St Petersburg, 1858.

Durrī Efendī. *Relation de Dourry Efendy*, trans. M. de Fienne. Paris, 1810. Latin trans. by T. Krusiński. Lemberg, 1733.

Fūmānī, 'Abd al-Fattāḥ. *Tārīkh-i Gīlān*, ed. Dorn, *Muhammedanische Quellen* III.

Ḥasan Rūmlū. *Aḥsan al-tavārīkh*, ed. and trans. C. N. Seddon, *A Chronicle of the early Ṣafawīs*, 2 vols. I (text). Baroda, 1931. II (trans.). Baroda, 1934 (Gaekwad's Oriental Series 57, 60).

Ibn Bazzāz, Tavakkulī b. Ismā'īl. *Ṣafvat al-ṣafā*, ed. Aḥmad b. Karīm Tabrīzī. Bombay, 1329/1911.

Iṣfahānī, Muḥammad Ma'ṣūm Khwājagī. *Khulāṣat al-siyar*, ed. W. Rettelbach, *Der* [sic] *Iran unter Schah Ṣafī (1629–1642)*. Munich, 1978.

Iskandar Munshī. *Tārīkh-i 'ālam-ārā-yi 'Abbāsī*, ed. Īraj Afshār, 2 vols. Tehran, 1334/1955. *Trans. Savory.

Iskandar Munshī and Muḥammad Yūsuf. *Ẕail-i tārīkh-i 'ālam-ārā-yi 'Abbāsī*, ed. Suhailī Khwānsarī. Tehran, 1317/1938.

Jauhar Āftāchī. *The Tezkereh al vakiat or Private Memoirs of the Moghul Emperor Humayun*, trans. C. Stewart. Lucknow, 1971.

Khafī Khān. *Muntakhab al-lubāb*, ed. Kabīr al-Dīn Aḥmad, II. Calcutta, 1874 (Bibliotheca Indica).

Khaṭā'ī (Shah Ismā'īl I). *Il Canzioniere di Šāh Ismā'īl*, ed. Tourkhan Gandjeï. Naples, 1959. *Shakh Ismayil Khetai – Sochineniya*, ed. Azizaga Mamedov, I. Baku, 1966.

Khunjī. See bibliography to chapters 1–4.

Khwānd Amīr, Ghiyāṣ al-Dīn b. Humām al-Dīn Muḥammad. *Dastūr al-vuzarā*, ed. Sa'īd Nafīsī. Tehran, 1317.

Ḥabīb al-siyar, ed. J. Humā'ī, 4 vols. Tehran, 1333/1954.

Mar'ashī, Ẓahīr al-Dīn. *Tārīkh-i Gīlān va Dailamistān*. Rasht, 1330/1912 (includes contribution by Rabino di Borgomale, "Makātib-i Khān Aḥmad Gīlānī").

Marvārīd, Khwāja 'Abd-Allāh. *Sharaf-nāma*, facsimile ed. *Roemer, *Staatsschreiben.*

Ma'ṣūm, Mīrzā Muḥammad. *Tārīkh-i salāṭīn-i Ṣafaviyya*, ed. Sayyid Amīr Ḥasan 'Ābidī. Tehran, 1351 (Intishārāt-i Bunyād-i Farhang-i Īrān 135).

Matrakī, Nasūh. *Beyan-ı menazil-i sefer-i Irakeyn-i Sultan Süleyman Hân*, ed. H. G. Yurdaydın. Ankara, 1977.

*Minorsky, V. (ed.) *Tadhkirat al-Mulūk.*

Muḥammad Hāshim Aṣaf. *Rustam al-tavārīkh*, ed. M. Mushīrī. 2nd ed. Tehran, 1352/1973.

Qazvīnī, Muḥammad Ṭāhir Vaḥīd. *'Abbās-nāma yā Sharḥ-i zindagānī-yi 22-sāla-yi Shāh 'Abbās-i sānī (1052–1073)*, ed. Ibrāhīm Dihgān. Arāk, 1329/1951.

Inshā'. Lithograph ed. Lucknow, 1265/1886.

Qazvīnī, Yaḥyā b. 'Abd al-Laṭīf Ḥusainī. *Lubb al-tavārīkh*. Tehran, 1314.

Rafī'ā, Mīrzā, and Samī'ā, Mīrzā. "Dastūr al-mulūk-i Mīrzā Rafī'ā va Tazkirat al-mulūk-i Mīrzā Samī'ā", ed. M. T. Dānishpazhūh, *Majalla-yi Dānishkada-yi Adabiyyāt-i Ṭihrān* xv (1347/1968), 504–75; xvi (1347–8/1968–9), 62–93, 198–322, 416–40, 540–64.

Sām Mīrzā. *Tazkira-yi Tuḥfa-yi Sāmī*, ed. Rukn al-Dīn Humāyūn-Farrukh. Tehran 1347/1969.

Sāqī Musta'idd Khān, Muḥammad. *Ma'āsir-i 'Ālamgīrī*, ed. Maulavī Āghā Aḥmad 'Alī. Calcutta, 1871 (Bibliotheca Indica).

Shāhnavāz Khān, Navāb Samsām al-Daula. *Ma'āsir al-umarā*, ed. A. Raḥīm and Mīrzā Ashraf 'Alī, ii–iii. Calcutta, 1890–1. Trans H. Beveridge, i. Calcutta, 1911–14 (Bibliotheca Indica).

Shushtarī, Nūr-Allāh. *Iḥqāq al-ḥaqq*, 3 vols. Tehran, 1956–8.

Majālis al-mu'minīn, ed. Ḥājj Sayyid Aḥmad, 1 vol. in 2 parts. Tehran, 1375.

Tābātāzāda, Karlū. *Mukālama-yi navvāb-i jannatmakānī-yi Shāh Ṭahmāsp bā īlchiyān-i Rūm*, text and Georgian trans. Tbilisi, 1976.

Ṭahmāsp I. *Tazkira*, ed. P. Horn, "Die Denkwürdigkeiten des Šâh Ṭahmâsp I. von Persien", *ZDMG* xliv (1890), 563–649; xlv (1891), 245–91.

Yūsuf Munshī, Muḥammad. *Tārīkh-i Muqīm Khānī*, trans. A. A. Semenov. Tashkent, 1956.

Zāhidī, Shaikh Ḥusain Pīrzāda. *Silsilat al-nasab-i Ṣafavī*, ed. Kāẓim-zāda Īrānshahr. Berlin, 1924–5.

Zain al-'Ābidīn 'Alī. *Takmilat al-akhbār*, ed. Evelin Gruner, *Die Geschichte Schah Ismā'īls I. aus der Chronik 'Takmilat al-aḫbār'*. Unpublished MA thesis, Freiburg i. Br., 1971.

(*b*) *Armenian*

Arakel de Tauriz. *Des Historiens Arméniens des 17e et 18e siècles. Registre Chronologique. Annoté par M. Brosset.* St Petersburg, 1873 (MAIS, 7e série, xix/5).

(*c*) *European accounts*

Albuquerque, Afonso d'. *Commentaries*, trans. W. de Gray Birch. 4 vols. London, 1875–84. (Hakluyt Society).

Andersen, Jürgen. *Orientalische Reise-Beschreibung 1644 ausgezogen und 1650 wiederkommen*, ed. A. Olearius, *Colligirte und viel vermehrte Reise-Beschreibungen*. Hamburg, 1696.

Barbaro, Giosafat. "Viaggi del Magnifico messer Josaphat Barbaro", in *Viaggi fatti da Venezia, alla Tana, in Persia, in India, et in Constantinopoli*. Venice, 1545.

Bizarus, Petrus. *Rerum Persicarum Historia*. Frankfurt, 1601.

Bruyn, Cornelis de. *Reizen over Moskovie, door Persie en Indie*. Amsterdam, 1711.

Busbeck, Ogier Ghiselim de. *Vier Briefe aus der Türkei*, trans. W. von den Steinen. Erlangen, 1926.

*Chardin

**A Chronicle of the Carmelites*

Dam, Pieter van. *Beschryvinge van de Oostindische Compagnie*, ed. F. W. Stapel, 2 vols. 's-Gravenhage, 1928–39.

Della Valle, Pietro. **Viaggi*. Trans. J. Beadouin, *Histoire apologétique d'Abbas, roi de Perse*. Paris, 1631, repr. 1976.

*Don Juan, trans. Le Strange.

*Du Mans

*Fryer

Hanway, Jonas. *An Historical Account of the British Trade over the Caspian Sea*, 4 vols. London, 1753.

Revolutions of Persia : Containing the Reign of Shah Sultan Hussein etc. (= *An historical account* II). 2nd ed. London, 1854.

Herbert, Sir Thomas. *A relation of some yeares travaile...especially the territories of the Persian monarchie*. London, 1634.

*Ed. Foster, *Travels in Persia*.

*Kaempfer

Kakasch de Zalonkemeny, S. *Iter Persicum. Kurtze doch ausführliche und wahrhafftige Beschreibung der Persianischen Reiss... von Georgio Tectandro von der Jabel continuiret etc.* Altenburg, 1610.

Kotov, K. F. *Khozhenie kuptsa Fedota Kotova v Persiyu*, ed. A. A. Kuznetsov. Moscow 1958.

Krusiński, Judasz Tadeusz. *The History of the Late Revolution of Persia, taken from the memoirs of Father Krusinski, Procurator of the Jesuits at Ispahan*. 2nd ed. London, 1740, repr. New York, 1973.

Manucci, Niccolo. *Storia do Mogor or Mogul India 1653–1708*, trans. W. Irvine, 4 vols. London, 1907–8.

*Minadoi

**A Narrative of Italian Travels*

Olearius, Adam. *Offt begehrte Beschreibung der neuen orientalischen Reise*. Schleswig, 1647.

Ramusio, Giovanni Battista. *Navigationi e Viaggi* II. Venice, 1583.

Sanson, N. *Voyage ou Relation de l'État présent du Royaume de Perse*. Paris, 1695.

Schillinger, Franz Caspar. *Persianische und Ost-Indianische Reis*. Nürnberg, 1709.

Silva y Figueroa, García de. *L'Ambassade de D. Garcias de Silva y Figueroa en Perse*, trans. de Wicqfort. Paris, 1667.

*Tavernier
*Teixeira, Pedro. *Relationes del origen, descendencia y succession de los reyes de Persia.* Amberes, 1610. *Trans. Sinclair.
Thévenot, Jean de. *Voyages en Europe, Asie et Afrique.* 3rd ed. Amsterdam, 1727.

CHAPTER 5: SECONDARY SOURCES

Adle, Chahryar. "La bataille de Mehmândust (1142/1729)", *StIr* II (1973), 235–41.
Aḥmad, Nāẓir. "'Ādilshāhī diplomatic missions to the court of Shāh 'Abbās", *IC* XLIII (1969), 143–61.
"Asnād-i tārīkhī dar bāra-yi ravābiṭ-i siyāsī-yi Shāh 'Abbās bā shāhān-i Quṭbshāhiyya", *FIZ* XV (1347), 277–326.
Aitchison, C. U. *A Collection of Treaties, Engagements and Sanads...*, 13 vols. Calcutta, 1933.
Aktepe, M. Münir. *1720–1724 Osmanlı-Iran münâsebetleri ve Şilâhşör Ağanın Revân fetih-nâmesi.* Istanbul, 1970 (İstanbul Üniversitesi Edebiyat Fakültesi Yayınları, 1585).
Alexandrowicz-Alexander, C. H. "A Persian-Dutch treaty in the seventeenth century", *Indian Yearbook of international affairs* 1958, 201–6.
Algar, Hamid. "Some observations on religion in Safavid Persia", *IrSt* VII (1974), 287–93.
Aliev, F. M. *Antiiranskie vystupleniya i bor'ba protiv turetskoĭ okkupatsii v Azerbaĭdzhane v pervoĭ polovine XVIII veka.* Baku, 1975.
Allen, W. E. D. *A History of the Georgian people.* London, 1932.
Amoretti, B. Scarcia. *Šāh Ismā'īl I nei "Diarii" di Marino Sanudo* I. *(Testi).* Rome, 1979.
Arjomand, Said Amir. "Religious Extremism (ghuluww), Ṣufism and Sunnism in Safavid Iran: 1501–1722", *JAH* XV (1981), 1–35.
Arunova, M. R. "Geratskoe vosstanie 1716–1732 gg.", in *Nezavisimyĭ Afganistan* (Moscow, 1958), pp. 153–63.
Ashrafyan, K. Z. "Padenie derzhavy Sefevidov (1502–1722)", in *Sbornik ocherki po novoĭ istorii Srednego Vostoka* (Moscow, 1951), pp. 188–210.
Ashurbeyli, S. B. "Seyakhat-name Evliya Chelebi kak istochnik po izucheniya sotsial'no-ekonomicheskoĭ i politicheskoĭ istorii gorodov Azerbaĭdzhana v pervoĭ polovine XVII veka", in *TDMKV* II, 474–8.
Askari, S. H. "Indo-Persian relations in the age of the Great Mughals". *JBORS* XL (1954), 323–40.
Aslam, Muḥammad. "'Ubaidallāh Khān", *JASP* IX/1 (1964), 65–70.
Aubin, J. *L'ambassade de Gregório Pereira Fidalgo à la cour de Châh Soltân-Hosseyn 1696–1697.* Lisbon, 1971.
"Études Safavides I – Šāh Ismā'īl et les Notables de l'Iraq Persan", *JESHO* II (1959), 37–81.
(ed.) *Mare Luso-Indicum*, 2 vols. Geneva and Paris, 1971, 1973.
"La politique religieuse des Safavides", in *Le Shî'isme imâmite* (Paris, 1970), pp. 235–44.

"Les sunnites du Lārestān et la chute des Safavides", *REI* XXXIII (1965), 151–71.

Babaev, K. "Voennaya reforma Shakha Abbasa I (1587–1629)", *Vestnik Mosk. Univ., Vostokovedenie*, 1973, no. 1, 21–9.

Babinger, F. "Zur Geschichte der Ṣefewijje", *Der Islam* XII (1922), 231–3.

*"Der Islam in Kleinasien"

"Marino Sanuto's Tagebücher als Quelle zur Geschichte der Safawijja", in *Oriental Studies presented to E. G. Browne* (Cambridge, 1922), pp. 28–50; repr. in his *Aufsätze und Abhandlungen* I (Munich, 1962), 378–95.

"Schejch Bedr ed-dīn, der Sohn des Richters von Simāw", *Der Islam* XI (1921), 1–106.

"Sir Anthony Sherley's persische Botschaftsreise (1599/1601)", *MSOS* XXXV (1932), 100–27.

Bacher, W. "Les juifs en Perse au 17e et au 18e siècle, d'après les chroniques poétiques de Babaï b. Loutf et de Babaï b. Farhad", *Revue des Études Juives* (Paris) LI (1906), 121–36, 265–79; LII (1906), 77–97, 234–71; LIII (1907), 85–110.

Bacqué-Grammont, J. L. "Deux rapports sur Şâh Isma'îl et les Özbeks (= Études turco-safavides X)", in *Quand le crible était dans la paille... Hommage à P. N. Boratav* (Paris, 1978), pp. 65–83.

"Un document ottoman sur la révolte des Ostâğelû", *StIr* VI (1977), 169–84.

"Études turco-safavides I: Notes sur le blocus du commerce iranien par Selîm Ier", *Turcica* VI (1975), 68–88.

"Les événements d'Asie Centrale en 1510 d'après un document ottoman", *Cahiers du Monde Russe et Soviétique* XII (1971), 189–207.

"Un 'fetiḥnâme' zû-l-Ḳâdiride dans les archives ottomanes", *Turcica* II (1970), 138–50.

"Le Kartli et ses voisins musulmans (1518–1521): deux documents inédits", *Bedi Karthlisa* XXXVIII (Paris, 1980), 186–97.

"Une liste d'émirs Ostâğlû révoltés en 1526", *StIr* V (1976), 25–35.

Ottomans et Safavides au temps des Šāh Ismā'īl et Ṭahmāsp. Unpublished D.-ès-lettres thesis, Sorbonne, 1980.

Bacqué-Grammont, J. L., and Adle, Chahryar. "Notes et documents sur Mzé-Čâbûk, Atabeg de Géorgie méridionale (1500–1515), et les Safavides (= Études turco-safavides V)", *StIr* VII (1978), 213–49.

"Notes sur les Safavides et la Géorgie (= Études turco-safavides VIII)", *StIr* IX (1980), 211–31.

Baiburtian, V. A. "Posrednicheskaya rol′ novodzhul′finskikh kuptsov v diplomaticheskikh otnosheniyakh Irana s Zapadno-evropeĭskimi stranami v nachale XVII v.", *KSINA* LXXVII (1964), 20–9.

Banani, Amin. "Reflections on the social and economic structure of Safavid Persia at its zenith", *IrSt* XI (1978), 83–116.

Bartl, P. "Marciare verso Constantinopeli – Zur Türkenpolitik Klemens' VIII", *Saeculum* XX (1969), 44–56.

Bāstānī-Pārīzī, Muḥammad Ibrāhīm. *Siyāsat va iqtiṣād-i 'aṣr-i Ṣafavī*. Tehran, 1348.

Bastiaensen, M. "La Persia safavide vista da un lessicografo europeo. Presentazione del 'Gazophylacium'", *RSO* XLVIII (1973–4), 175–203.

Bayānī, Khānbābā. *Les relations de l'Iran avec l'Europe occidentale à l'époque Safavide (Portugal, Espagne, Angleterre, Hollande et France)*. Paris, 1937.

Baykal, B. S. "Die Rivalität zwischen Uzun Hasan und Mehmet II. um das Kaiserreich von Trapezunt", in *TDMKV* II, 442–8.

Beldiceanu-Steinherr, I. "A propos d'un ouvrage sur la polémique ottomane contre les safawides", *REI* XXXIX (1971), 395–400.

"Le règne de Selīm Ier. Tournant dans la vie politique et religieuse de l'Empire ottoman", *Turcica* VI (1975), 34–48.

Bellan, L. L. *Chah 'Abbas I. Sa vie, son histoire*. Paris, 1932.

Beveridge, H. "The Author of the Life of Shāh Isma'īl", *JRAS* 1902, 170–1.

Bina-Motlagh, Maḥmūd. *Scheich Safi von Ardabil*. Unpubl. Diss. phil., Göttingen, 1969.

Boldyrev, A. N. "Tezkire Khasana Nisori kak novyĭ istochnik dlya izucheniya kul'turnoĭ zhizni Sredneĭ Azii XVI v.", *GETOV* III (1940), 291–300.

Bosworth, C. E. "Ḳandahār", *EI*².

Boxer, C. R. *The Dutch Seaborne Empire: 1600–1800*. New York, 1965.

The Portuguese Seaborne Empire, 1414–1825. London, 1969.

Boyle, J. A. "The evolution of Iran as a national state", *Hommage Universel* (1974. Acta Iranica III), 327–38, and repeated in *Belleten* XXXIX (1975), 633–44.

Braun, Hellmut. *Aḥvāl-e Šāh Ismā'īl*. See primary sources. *Das Erbe Schah 'Abbās' I. Iran und seine Könige 1629–1694*. Habil.-Schrift, Hamburg, 1967, unpublished.

"Ein iranischer Grosswesir des 17. Jahrhunderts: Mīrzā Muḥammad-Taqi", in Eilers, pp. 1–7.

"Geschichte Irans seit 1500", in *HO*, 1e Abt., VI/3 (Leiden–Köln, 1959), 98–184.

"Īrān under the Ṣafavids and in the 18th century", in *The Muslim World. A historical survey. Part* III (Leiden, 1960–9), 181–218.

"Das safawidische Königtum und der Niedergang des Reiches im 17. Jahrhundert", *ZDMG Suppl.* I/3 (1969), 941–7.

Bregel', Yu. E. "Dokument po istorii turkmen iz arkhiva Khivinskikh Khanov", *Problemy Vostoka* 1960, no. 1, 168–72.

Browne, E. G. *Account of a Rare Manuscript. History of Iṣfahān*. Hertford, 1901 (repr. from *JRAS* 1901).

"Note on an apparently unique manuscript history of the Safawi Dynasty of Persia", *JRAS* 1921, 395–418.

Brulez, W. "Venetiaanse handelsbetrekkingen met Perzië omstreeks 1600", *Orientalia Gandensia* I (Ghent, 1964), 1–27.

Burn, R. *Cambridge History of India* IV. *The Mughul Period*. Cambridge, 1937.

Bushev, P. P. "Iranskiĭ kupchina Kazim-Bek v Rossii, 1706– 1709 gg.", *Iran, Sbornik stateĭ* (Moscow, 1973), pp. 166–80.

"Iranskoe posol'stvo Fazl Ali-beka v Rossiyu (1711–1713 gg.)", *KSINA* XXXIX (1963), 33–51.

Istoriya posol'stv o diplomaticheskikh otnosheniĭ russkogo i iranskogo gosudarstv v 1586–1612 gg. (po russkim arkhivam). Moscow, 1976.

"Russko-iranskie kontakty (do kontsa XVI v.)", *Voprosy Istorii* 1973, no. 4, 130–40.

"O russkom posol'stve v Iran v kontse XVI stoletiya", *NAA* 1968, no. 2, 55–63.

Corbin, H. *En Islam Iranien. Aspects spirituels et philosophiques*, 4 vols. Paris, 1971-2.

"Sih guftār dar bāb-i tārīkh-i ma'naviyāt-i Īrān", *Revue de la Faculté de Lettres de Téhéran* v (1337/1959), 46–63.

Cottam, R. *Nationalism in Iran.* Pittsburg, 1964; 2nd ed. 1979.

Courant, M. *L'Asie centrale aux 17e et 18e siècles.* Lyon and Paris, 1912 (Annales de l'Univ. de Lyon, n.s.II. Droit, lettres, fasc. 26).

Danegyan, L. G. "Politika sefevidov po otnosheniyu k armyanskim koloniyam v Irane v pervoĭ polovine XVII v.", in *Arabskie strany, Turtsiya, Iran, Afganistan* (1973), pp. 43–9.

Danon, M. A. "Un interrogatoire d'hérétiques musulmans (1619)", *JA* XVII (1921), 281–93.

Destrée, A. "L'ouverture de la Perse à l'influence européenne sous les Rois Safavides et les incidences de cette influence sur l'évolution de l'art de la miniature", *Corresp. d'Orient. Études* XIII–XIV (1968), 91–104.

Dickson, M. B. "The Fall of the Ṣafavi Dynasty", *JAOS* LXXXII (1962), 503–17.

Sháh Tahmásb and the Uzbeks (The Duel for Khurásán with 'Ubayd Khán: 930–946/1524–1540). Unpubl. Diss. phil., Princeton, 1958.

"Uzbek dynastic theory in the sixteenth century", in *TDMKV* III, 208–17.

Digby, S. "Humāyūn", *EI*².

Dorn, B. *Geschichte Schirwans unter den Statthaltern und Chanen von 1538–1820* (=Beiträge zur Geschichte der kaukasischen Völker und Länder II). St Petersburg, 1845 (MAIS, 6e série, v).

Dzhavadova, Minaya. *Shah Ismayïl Khatainin leksikasï ("Dehname" poemasï uzre).* Baku, 1977.

Eberhard, E. *Osmanische Polemik gegen die Safawiden im 16. Jahrhundert nach arabischen Handschriften.* Freiburg i. Br., 1970 (IU III).

Edmonds, C. J. "The Belief and Practices of the Ahl-i Haqq of Iraq", *Iran* VII (1969), 89–103.

Edwards, C. C. "Relations of Shah Abbas the Great of Persia with the Mogul Emperors Akbar and Jahangir", *JAOS* XXXV (1915–17), 247–68.

Efendiev, O. A. *Azerbaĭdzhanskoe gosudarstvo Sefevidov v XVI veke.* Baku, 1981.

"O maloizvestnom istochnike XVI v. po istorii Sefevidov", *IAN Azerb. SSR ser. obshch. nauk* 1964, no. 2, 61–8.

"K nekotorym voprosam vnutrenneĭ i vneshneĭ politiki Shakha Ismaila I (1502–1524 gg.)", *AN Azerb. SSR. Trudy Instituta Istorii* VII (Baku, 1957), 151–80.

Obrazovanie azerbaĭdzhanskogo gosudarstva Sefevidov v nachale XVI veka. Baku, 1961.

"Le rôle des tribus de langue turque dans la création de l'État safavide", *Turcica* VI (1975), 24–33.

Eilers, W. (ed.) *Festgabe deutscher Iranisten zur 2500 Jahrfeier Irans*. Stuttgart, 1971.

Ergun, Sadeddin Nüzhet. *Hatayî Divanı. Şah İsmail Safevî edebî hayatı ve nefesleri*. 2nd ed. Istanbul, 1956.

Falsafī, Naṣr-Allāh. *Chand maqāla-yi tārīkhī va adabī*. Tehran, 1342/1963 (IDT 903).

"Jang-i Chāldirān", *ibid.*, pp. 1–88.

"Sarguẕasht-i Sārū Taqī", *ibid.*, pp. 285–310.

**Zindagānī*.

Fekete, L. "Zur Geschichte der Grusiner des 16. Jahrhunderts", *Acta Orientalia Hung.* I (1950), 93-133.

"İran şahlarının iki türkçe mektubu", *TüMe* V (1936), 269–74.

Ferrier, R. W. "The Armenians and the East India Company in the seventeenth and early eighteenth centuries", *Economic History Review* 2nd ser. XXVI (1973), 38–62.

"The economic dimension of the policy of Shāh 'Abbās I", *29th ICO, Paris, 1973* (Paris, 1976), pp. 63-72.

"An English view of Persian trade in 1618. Reports from the merchants Edward Pettus and Thomas Barker", *JESHO* XIX (1976), 182–214.

"The European Diplomacy of Shāh 'Abbās I and the First Persian Embassy to England", *Iran* XI (1973), 75–92.

"The trade between India and the Persian Gulf and the East India Company in the 17th century", *Bengal Past and Present* LXXXIX (Calcutta, 1970), 189–98.

Fil'roze, N. "K voprosu o formakh zemel'noĭ sobstvennosti v gosudarstve Sefevidov", in *Ocherki po novoĭ istorii stran Srednego Vostoka* (Moscow, 1951), pp. 175–87.

Fischer, K. "Zur Lage von Kandahar an Landverbindungen zwischen Iran und Indien", *Bonner Jahrbücher* CLXVII (1967), 129–232.

Floor, W. M. "Dutch painters in Iran during the first half of the 17th century", *Persica* VIII (1979), 145–61.

Forand, P. G. "Accounts of Western travellers concerning the role of the Armenians and Georgians in 16th-century Iran", *MW* LXV (1975), 264–78.

Foster, W. *England's Quest of Eastern Trade*. London, 1933.

The English Factories in India, 1630–1667. A Calendar of Documents in the India Office, Bombay Record Office, British Museum, Public Record Office, and Westminster, 9 vols. Oxford, 1910–25.

A Guide to the India Office records, 1600–1858. London, 1919.

A Supplementary Calendar of Documents in the India Office relating to India or to the Home Affairs of the East India Company, 1600–1640. London, 1928.

Fragner, B. "Ardabil zwischen Sultan und Schah. Zehn Urkunden Schah Tahmāsps II.", *Turcica* VI (1975), 177–225.

"Das Ardabīler Heiligtum in den Urkunden", *WZKM* LXVII (1975), 169–215.

"Der Schah im Schriftverkehr mit dem Abendland", *ZDMG Suppl.* II (Wiesbaden, 1974), 132–41.

Frank, C. "Über den schiitischen Mudschtahid", *Islamica* II (1926-7), 171–92.

Galdieri, E. "Les palais d'Ispahan", *IrSt* VII (1974), 511–42.

Gaube, H. "Ein Abschnitt der safawidischen Bandar-e 'Abbās-Šīrāz-Strasse: die Strecke von Seyyed Ǧemāl ad-Dīn nach Lār", *Iran* XVII (1979), 33–47.

Iranian Cities. New York, 1979.

Die südpersische Provinz Arraǧān/Kūh-Gīlūyeh von der arabischen Eroberung bis zur Safawidenzeit. Hamburg, 1973.

Geĭdarov, M. Kh. "O termine 'boniche' (k istorii polozheniya gorodskikh zemeslennikov Azerbaĭdzhana XVII v.)", *DAN Azerb. SSR* XVIII/3 (1962), 83–7.

Ghanī, Qāsim. *Tārīkh-i taṣavvuf dar Īrān.* Tehran, 1330/1951.

Glaman, K. *Dutch-Asiatic Trade, 1620–1740.* Copenhagen, 1948.

Glassen, E. *Die frühen Safawiden.* See primary sources.

"Krisenbewusstsein und Heilserwartung in der islamischen Welt zu Beginn der Neuzeit", in Haarmann and Bachmann, pp. 167–79.

"Schah Ismā'īl, ein Mahdī der anatolischen Turkmenen?", *ZDMG* CXXI (1971), 61–9.

"Schah Ismā'īl und die Theologen seiner Zeit", *Der Islam* XLVIII (1972), 254–68.

Godard, A. "Iṣfahān", *Aṯhār-é Īrān* II (1937), 7–176.

Gökbilgin, Tayyib. "Arz ve rapolarına göre İbrahim Paşa'nın Irakeyn seferindeki ilk tedbirleri ve fütuhatı", *Belleten* XXI (1957), 449–82.

"Süleyman I.", *İsl.Ans.*

Gölpınarlı, Abdülbâki. "Kızıl-baş", *İsl.Ans.*

Türkiye'de mezhepler ve tarikatlar. Istanbul, 1969.

Golschani, A. *Bildungs- und Erziehungswesen Persiens im 16. und 17. Jahrhundert.* Hamburg, 1969.

Goyau, G. "L'évêque François Picquet dans Ispahan (juillet 1682–mai 1684): son action diplomatique et religieuse", *Revue des Études Historiques* CII (Paris, 1935), 137–58.

Gramlich, R. *Die schiitischen Derwischorden Persiens*, 3 vols. Wiesbaden, 1965–81 (AKM XXXVI).

Gregorian, V. "Minorities of Isfahan: the Armenian community of Isfahan 1587–1722", *IrSt* VII (1974), 652–80.

Grohmann, A. "Masḳat", *EI*[1].

Gruner. See primary sources, *s.v.* Zain al-'Ābidīn.

Guillou, A. "Les dynasties musulmanes de Perse. Soixante-quinze ans de troubles en Iran 1722–1795", *Revista del Instituto Egipcio de Estudios Islámicos* VII–VIII (Madrid, 1959–60), 119–21.

*Guseĭnov and Sumbatzade

Haarmann, U. "Staat und Gesellschaft in Transoxanien im frühen 16. Jahrhundert", *ZDMG* CXXIV (1974), 332–69.

Haarmann, U., and Bachmann, P. (eds.) *Die islamische Welt zwischen Mittelalter und Neuzeit (Festschrift für Hans Robert Roemer zum 65. Geburtstag)*. Beirut, 1979 (Beiruter Texte und Studien XXII).

Helfgott, L. M. "Tribalism as a Socioeconomic Formation in Iranian History", *IrSt* X (1977), 36–61.

Herrmann, G. *Der historische Gehalt des "Nāmä-ye nāmī" von Ḫāndamīr*. Unpubl. Diss. phil., Göttingen, 1968.

Herbette, M. *Une Ambassade Persane sous Louis XIV, d'après des documents inédits*. Paris, 1907.

Hesenov, G. *"Dehname" nin sintaksisi (te'jini söz birleshmeleri)*. Baku, 1967.

Hinz, W. "Zur Frage der Denkwürdigkeiten des Schah Ṭahmāsp I. von Persien", *ZDMG* LXXXVIII (1934), 46–54.

**Irans Aufstieg*

"Eine neuentdeckte Quelle zur Geschichte Irans im 16. Jahrhundert", *ZDMG* LXXXIX (1935), 315–28.

"Schah Esma'īl II. Ein Beitrag zur Geschichte der Safavīden", *MSOS* XXXVI (1933), 19–100.

Hodgson, M. G. S. "Ghulāt", *EI²*.

Holod, R. (ed.) *Studies on Isfahan – Proceedings of the Isfahan Colloquium* (= *IrSt* VII [1974]).

Holt, P. M. "Irāḳ – History: The Ottoman Period", *EI²*.

Homayoun, Gholamali. *Iran in europäischen Bildzeugnissen vom Ausgang des Mittelalters bis ins achtzehnte Jahrhundert*. 2 vols. Tehran, 1969–70 (IDT, 1222/1,2).

"Iran in historisch-geographischen Werken europäischer Gelehrter im 16. Jahrhundert". *AMI* III (1970), 309–16.

Horst, H. "Zwei Erlasse Šāh Ṭahmāsps I.", *ZDMG* CX (1960), 301–9.

"Ein Immunitätsdiplom Schah Muḥammad Ḫudābandäs vom Jahr 989/1581", *ZDMG* CV (1955), 289–97.

"Der Safawide Ḥamza Mīrzā", *Der Islam* XXXIX (1964), 90–4.

Hunarfar, Luṭf-Allāh. **Ganjīna Iṣfahān*. Tehran, 1346.

"Mashāghil va manāṣib-i Arāmina-yi Julfā dar daurān-i Ṣafavī va Qājār", *Majalla-yi Vaḥīd* VIII (1343).

Hurewitz, J. C. *Diplomacy in the Near and Middle East. A documentary Record: 1535–1914* I. Princeton, 1956.

Husain, A. M. "Cultural influence of Safavid Iran over the Indo-Pakistan subcontinent under the Great Mughals", *JRCI* 1/2 (1967), 58-65; 1/4 (1968), 24–34.

Husain, Jasim M. "The role of the imamite 'wikāla' with special reference to the role of the first 'safīr'", *Hamdard Islamicus* V/4 (1982), 25–52.

Imber, C. H. "The persecution of the Ottoman Shī'ites according to the mühimme defterleri, 1565–1585", *Der Islam* LVI (1979), 245–73.

Ishaque, M. "Letter from Queen Elizabeth of England to Tahmasp I, Shah of Persia", *Indo-Iranica* XXI (1947–8), 29–30.

Ishrāqī, Iḥsān. "Ishāra'ī ba-tafrīḥāt va niẓām-i tafriḥī-yi daurān-i Ṣafaviyya", *Hunar va Mardum* XII (1353), 28–35.

Ivanov, P. P. *Khozyaĭstvo Dzhuibarskikh Sheĭkhov. K istorii feodal'nogo zemlevladeniya v Sredneĭ Azii v XVI–XVII vv.* Moscow–Leningrad, 1954.

Ja'farī, Ḥusain Mīr. "Sīstān dar 'aṣr-i Ṣafaviyya", *BT* xii/4 (2536/1977), 49–76.

"Tājlī Khānum, zan-i sitīhanda-yi Chāldirān", *Nashriyya-yi Dānishkada-yi Adabiyyāt va 'Ulūm-i Insānī, Tabrīz* xxvi (1353), 468–81.

"Zindagānī Alqāṣ Mīrzā Ṣafavī", *BT* xi/5 (2535/1976), 145–82.

Jafri, S. H. M. "al-Hillī", *EI*².

Jahānpūr, Farhang. "Farāmīn-i pādshāhān-i Ṣafavī dar Mūza-yi Britāniyya", *BT* iv/4 (1348), 221–64.

Javānshīr, Aḥmad Bey. *Qarabağ Khanlığının siyası vaziyyatina dair*, ed. A. B. *Shükürzada*. Baku, 1961.

Kasravī, Sayyid Aḥmad. "Afshārhā-yi Khūzistān", *Āyanda* i (1925), 39–44, 119–26, 199–209, 241–7; repeated in *Chihil maqāla-yi Kasravī*, ed. Yaḥyā Ẕukā' (Tehran, 1335/1956-7).

Āzarī yā zabān-i bāstān-i Āzarbāījān. Tehran, 1304/1925–6. See important review by Denison Ross in *JRAS* 1927, 148–57.

"Īl-i Afshār", *Āyanda* ii (1926), 596–603; repeated in *Chihil maqāla*, pp. 122–8.

"Nizhād va tabār-i Ṣafaviyya", *Āyanda* ii (1926), 357–65, 489–97, 801–12.

Shaikh Ṣafī va tabārash. Tehran, 1323/1944.

Shī'īgarī. Tehran, 1322/1943-4. Enlarged ed. as *Bikhānand va dāvarī kunand.* Tehran, 1323/1944–5; 3rd ed. 1336/1957–8.

Tārīkh-i pānṣad sāla-yi Khūzistān. Tehran, 1312/1933.

al-Tashayyu' va'l-Shī'a. Tehran, 1313/1934-5.

Kazi, M. I. "Sám Mirzá and his 'Tuḥfa i Sámí'", *Indo-Iranica* xiii/1 (1960), 18–39.

Kazimi, M. R. "Humayun in Iran", *IC* xliii (1969), 5–11.

Keddie, N. *Scholars, Saints and Sufis – Muslim Religious Institutions in the Middle East since 1500.* Berkeley, Los Angeles and London, 1972.

Kellenbenz, H. "Der russische Transithandel mit dem Orient im 17. und zu Beginn des 18. Jahrhunderts", *Jahrbuch für die Geschichte Osteuropas*, n.s. xii (1964–5), 481–98.

Keyvani, M. *Artisans and Guild Life in the later Safavid period. Contributions to the social-economic history of Persia.* Berlin, 1982 (IU lxv).

Khanikoff, N. "Erlass Šāh Ḥusains vom Jahre 1701", *Mélanges Asiatiques* iii (Paris, 1859).

Khubua, Makar. *Persidskie firmany i ukazy Muzeya Gruzii* i. Tbilisi, 1955.

King, J. S. "The Tāj or Red Cap of the Shī'ahs", *JRAS* 1896, 571–2.

Kırzıoğlu, Fahrettin. *Osmanlılar'ın Kafkas-Elleri'ni Fethi (1451–1590).* Ankara, 1976 (Atatürk Üniversitesi Yayınları 358).

Kissling, H. J. "Badr al-dīn ibn Ḳāḍī Samāwnā", *EI*².

"Aus der Geschichte des Chalvetijje-Ordens", *ZDMG* ciii (1953), 233–89.

"Šâh Ismâ'îl, la nouvelle route des Indes et les Ottomans", *Turcica* vi (1975), 89–102.

"Zur Geschichte des Derwischordens der Bajrâmijje", *Südostforschungen* xv (1956), 237–68.

Kiyā, Ṣādiq. "Nuqṭaviyān yā Pasīkhāniyān," *Īrān-Kūda* XIII (Tehran, 1332/1953), 1–132.

Kochwasser, F. H. "Persien im Spiegel der Reisebeschreibungen von Heinrich von Poser (1620–1625)", in Eilers, pp. 80–93.

Kohlberg, E. "The Development of Imāmī Shī'ī Doctrine of jihād", *ZDMG* CXXVI (1976), 64–86.

Köprülü, Fuad. "Avşar", *İsl.Ans.*

Kramers, J. H. "Selīm II", *EI*[1].

Kroell, A. "Billon de Canceville et les relations franco-persanes au début du XVIIIe siècle", *MII* II (1974), 127–56.

"Louis XIV, la Perse et Mascate", *MII* IV (1976–7), 1–78.

Kukanova, N. G. "Iz istorii Russko-Iranskikh torgovlykh svyazeĭ v XVII veke (po dannym ZGADA i drugikh arkhivov)", *KSIV* XXIV (1958), 41–53.

"Rol' armyanskogo kupechestva v razvitii russko-iranskoĭ torgovli v posledneĭ treti XVII v.", *KSINA* XXX (1961), 20–34.

Kusheva, E. N. *Narody Severnogo Kavkaza i ikh svyazi s Rossie vtoraya polovina XVI–30 gody XVII veka*. Moscow, 1963.

Kutsiya, K. K. "Iz istorii sotsial'nykh dvizheniĭ v gorodakh Sefevidskogo gosudarstva (dvizhenie nuktaviev)", *NAA* 1966, no. 2, 69–75.

"Gruzinskie praviteli Isfagana (1618–1722)", in *Voprosy Istorii Blizhnego Vostoka* II (Tbilisi, 1972).

Kütükoğlu, Bekir Sıdkı. "Les relations entre l'Empire Ottoman et l'Iran dans la seconde moitié du XVIe siècle", *Turcica* VI (1975), 128–45.

Osmanlı-İran siyasî münasebetleri I. *1578–1590*. Istanbul, 1961.

"Tahmasp I", *İsl.Ans.*

"Tahmasp II", *ibid.*

"Şah Tahmasb'in III. Murad'a Cülus tebriki", *TD* XI (1960), 1–24.

Lambton, A. K. S. "The Office of Kalântar under the Safawids and Afshars", in *Mélanges Henri Massé* (Tehran, 1963), pp. 206–18.

*"Quis custodiet custodes?".

"The Regulation of the Waters of the Zāyande Rūd", *BSOAS* IX (1937), 663–73.

"Two Ṣafawid Soyūrghāls", *BSOAS* XIV (1952), 44–54.

Lang, D. M. *The last years of the Georgian Monarchy, 1658–1832*. New York, 1957.

"Georgia and the Fall of the Ṣafavī Dynasty", *BSOAS* XIV (1952), 523–9.

Lockhart, L. "Abdālī", *EI* [2].

**The Fall*

Nadir Shah. London, 1938.

"The Persian Army in the Ṣafavī Period", *Der Islam* XXXIV (1959), 89–98.

"Shah Abbas's Isfahan", in *Cities of destiny*, ed. A. Toynbee (London, 1967), pp. 210–25.

Luft, P. *Iran unter Schah 'Abbās II. (1642–66)*. Unpublished Diss. phil., Göttingen, 1968.

Macdonald, D. M. "al-Mahdī", *EI*[1].

Magalhães-Godinho, V. *L'Économie de l'Empire Portugais aux XVe et XVIe siècles*. Paris, 1969.

Mamedov, Azizaga. "Les plus anciens manuscrits du dīvān de Shah Ismail Khatayi", *Turcica* VI (1975), 11–23.

"Pis'mo shakha Ismaila na azerbaĭdzhanskom yakyke", *DAN Azerb. SSR* XVI (1960), 1007–15.

Manṣūr, Fīrūz. "Pazhūhishī dar bāra-yi Qizilbāsh", *BT* x/4 (1354/1975), 145–62.

Mantran, R. "Règlements fiscaux ottomans: La province de Bassora (2e moitié du XVIe siècle)", *JESHO* x (1967), 224–77.

Martin, B. G. "Seven Safawid documents from Azarbayjan", in *Documents from Islamic Chanceries*, 1st. series, ed. S. M. Stern (Oxford, 1965), pp. 171–206.

Matuz, J. "L'accession au pouvoir des Safavides vue par un historien Ottoman contemporain", *Iranica* IV (1966), 24–44.

"Vom Übertritt osmanischer Soldaten zu den Safawiden", in Haarmann and Bachmann, pp. 402–15.

Mayer, A. E. See Mazzaoui, *Origins*

Mazzaoui, M. "The Ghāzī background of the Ṣafavid State", *Iqbāl Review* XII/3 (Karachi, 1971), 79–90.

The Origins of the Ṣafawids. Šīʿism, Ṣūfism, and the Ġulāt. Wiesbaden, 1972 (FIS III); review by A. E. Mayer in *IrSt* VIII (1976), 268–77.

"Šāh Ṭahmāsb and the Diaries of Marino Sanuto (1524–1533)", in Haarmann and Bachmann, pp. 416–44.

Shīʿism and the rise of the Ṣafavids. Unpublished Diss. hist., Princeton, 1966.

"The siege of Herat during the first year of Shāh 'Abbās' reign according to Iskandar Munshī", *ZDMG Suppl.* IV (1980), 233–4.

"From Tabriz to Qazvin to Isfahan: Three Phases of Safavid History", *ZDMG Suppl.* III (1977), 514–22.

McChesney, R. D. "Comments on 'The Qajar Uymaq in the Safavid Period. 1500–1722'", *IrSt* XIV (1981), 87–105.

"A note on Iskandar Beg's chronology", *JNES* XXXIX (1980), 53–63.

Mélikoff, Irène. "Le problème ḳızılbaş", *Turcica* VI (1975), 49–67.

Mihrābādī, Abu'l-Qāsim Rafīʿī. *Ā̱sār-i millī-yi Iṣfahān*. Tehran, 1352 (Silsila-yi Intishārāt-i Anjuman-i Ā̱sār-i Millī 101).

Miklukho-Maklaĭ, N. D. "K istorii politicheskikh vzaimootnosheniĭ Irana so Sredneĭ Azieĭ v XVI v.", *KSIV* IV (1952), 11–18.

*"Shiizm."

"K voprosu o nalogovoĭ politike v Irane pri shakhe Abbase I (1589–1629)", *SV* 1949, no. 6, 348–55.

Minorsky, V. *"The Aq-qoyunlu and Land Reforms".

"Aynallu/Inallu", *RO* XVII (1951–2), 1–11.

"Lāhidjān", *EI*[1].

"A Mongol Decree of 720/1320 to the Family of Shaykh Zāhid", *BSOAS* XVI (1954), 515–27; repr. in *The Turks, Iran and the Caucasus*, no. x.

"Mus̲h̲a'shaʿ", *EI*[1] *Suppl.* (Leiden, 1938).

Persia in A.D. 1478–1490. See primary sources, *s.v.* Khunjī.
"La Perse au XVe siècle", in *Orientalia Romana* (Rome, 1958), pp. 99–117; repr. in *Iranica* (Tehran and London, 1964), pp. 317–26.
"The Poetry of Shāh Ismā'īl I", *BSOAS* x (1939–42), 1006–53; repr. in *Medieval Iran and its Neighbours* (London, 1982), no. xiii.
"Shāh-sewan", *EI*¹.
"Shaykh Bālī Efendi on the Ṣafawids", *BSOAS* xx (1957), 437–50.
* *Tadhkirat al-Mulūk*.
"Thomas of Metsop' on the Timurid-Turkman Wars", in *Professor M. Shafī' presentation volume*, ed. S. M. Abdullah (Lahore, 1955), pp. 1–26; repr. in *The Turks, Iran and the Caucasus*, no. xi.
The Turks, Iran and the Caucasus in the Middle Ages. London, 1978.
"Tiflis", *EI*¹.
Mirzoev, A. M. "About the author of the Shāhanshāh Nāma", in *Proc. 24th ICO Munich, 1957* (Wiesbaden, 1959), pp. 449–56.
"Eshche raz ob avtore Shakhanshakh-name", *Problemy Vostoka* 1960, no. 4, 111–22.
Mordtmann, J. H., and Ménage, V. L. "Dhu'l-Ḳadr", *EI*².
"Dulkadırlılar", *İsl.Ans.*
Morton, A. H. "The Ardabil shrine in the reign of Ṭahmāsp I", *Iran* xii (1974), 31–64; xiii (1975), 39–58.
Mujīr Shaibānī, Niẓām al-Dīn. *Tashkīl-i shāhinshāhī-yi Ṣafaviyya, iḥyā-yi vaḥdat-i millī*. Tehran, 1346 (IDT, 1138).
Mukminova, R. G. *K istorii agrarnykh otnosheniĭ v Uzbekistane XVI v., po materialam "Vakf-name"*. Tashkent, 1966.
Ocherki po istorii remesla v Samarkande i Bukhare v XVI veke. Tashkent, 1976.
Munzel, K. "Ein Fund frühsafawidischer Münzen", *Jahrbuch Numismatik und Geldgeschichte* xxvii (Munich, 1977), 95–120.
Musawi, M. M. "Persian trade under the Safavids (1514–1722)", *Sumer* xxv (1969), 99–102.
Mustaufī, Mīrzā Muḥammad Ḥusain. "Āmār-i mālī va niẓāmī-yi Īrān dar 1128 yā Tafṣīl-i 'asākir-i fīrūzī-ma'āṣir-i Shāh Sulṭān Ḥusain Ṣafavī", *FIZ* xx (1353), 396–421.
Naqvi, S. M. R. "Shah Abbas and the Conflict between Jahangir and the Deccan States", *Medieval India* i ('Alīgarh, 1969), 272–9.
Nasr, S. H. "Religion in Safavid Persia", *IrSt* vii (1974), 271–86.
"Le Shī'isme et le soufisme, leurs relations principielles et historiques", in *Le Shī'isme imamite, Travaux du Centre d'Études supérieures specialisé d'histoire des religions de Strasbourg* (Paris, 1970), pp. 215–33.
Navā'ī, 'Abd al-Ḥusain. *Rijāl-i Kitāb i Ḥabīb al-siyar*. Tehran, 1343.
Shāh 'Abbās-i avval. Majmū'a-yi asnād va mukātabāt-i tārīkhī, 2 vols. Tehran, 1352/1973.
Shāh Ismā'īl-i Ṣafavī. Asnād va mukātabāt-i tārīkhī. Tehran, 1347.
Shāh Ṭahmāsb-i Ṣafavī. Majmū'a-yi asnād va mukātabāt-i tārīkhī. Tehran, 1350/1971.
Nematova, M. S. "Dva ukaza Shakha 'Abbasa I", *EV* xviii (1967), 105–12.

Nemtseva, N. B. "Istoki kompozitsii i etapy formirovaniya ansamblya Shakhi-zinda", *Iran* xv (1977), 51–73.

Niewöhner-Eberhard, Elke. "Machtpolitische Aspekte des osmanisch-safawidischen Kampfes um Bagdad im 16/17. Jahrhundert", *Turcica* vi (1975), 103–27.

Nikitine, B. "Les Afšārs d'Urumiyeh", *JA* ccxiv (1929), 67–123.

"Les valis d'Ardelan", *RMM* xlix (1922), 70–104.

Olson, R. W. "The sixteenth century 'Price Revolution' and its Effect on the Ottoman Empire and on Ottoman-Safavid Relations", *Acta Orientalia* xxxvii (1976), 45–55.

Orhonlu, C. "1559 Bahreyn seferine âid bir rapor", *TD* xvii (1967), 1–16.

Özbaran, Salih. "The Ottoman Turks and the Portuguese in the Persian Gulf 1534–1581", *JAH* vi (1972), 45–87: summary of a Ph.D. thesis, London, 1969.

"XVI. Yüzyılda Basra Körfezi Sâhillerinde Osmanılar Basra Beylerbeyliğinin Kuruluşu", *TD* xxv (1971), 51–72.

Öztelli, Cahit. "Les œuvres de Hatayî", *Turcica* vi (1975), 7–10.

*Palombini. *Bündniswerben.*

Papazian, A. D. *Agrarnye otnosheniya v vostochnoĭ Armenii v XVI–XVII vekakh.* Erivan, 1972.

Parsamian, V. A., Voskanian, V. K., and Ter-Avakomova, S. A. *Armyano-Russkie otnosheniya v 17 v. Sbornik dokumentov* i. Erivan, 1953.

Perry, J. R. "The Banū Ka'b: An ambitious Brigand State in Khūzistān", *MII* i (1971), 132–52.

"Forced migration in Iran during the seventeenth and nineteenth centuries", *IrSt* viii (1975), 199–215.

"The last Ṣafawids (1722–73)", *Iran* ix (1971), 59–71.

Petrov, P. I. "Dannye istochnikov o sostave voĭnskikh kontingentov Ismaila I", *NAA* 1964, no. 3, 76–81.

"Ferman Shakha Sultan-Khuseĭna Vakhtangu VI", *SV* 1957, no. 4, 127–8.

"Ob odnom redkom istochnike po istorii Sefevidov", *SV* 1957, no. 1, 111–20.

Petrushevsky, I. P. "Azerbaĭdzhan v XVI–XVII vekakh", in *Sbornik stateĭ po istorii Azerbaĭdzhana* i (Baku, 1949), 225–98.

"Iranskie istochniki po istorii Azerbaĭdzhana XVI–XVIII vv.", *ibid.*, 299–310.

"Narodnoe vosstanie v Gilyane v 1629 godu", *UZIV* iii (1951), 225–56.

Ocherki po istorii feodal'nykh otnosheniĭ v Azerbaĭdzhane i Armenii v XVI-nachale XIX v. Leningrad, 1949.

Persidskie ofitsial'nye dokumenty XVI-nachala XIX vv, kak istochnik po istorii feodal'nykh otnosheniĭ v Azerbaĭdzhane i Armenii. Moscow and Leningrad, 1940 (Problemy istochnikovedeniya iii).

Vakfnye imushchestva Ardebil'skogo mazara. Baku, 1947 (AN Azerb. SSR. Trudy Instituta Istorii i).

"K voprosu ob immunitete v Azerbaĭdzhane v XVII–XVIII vv.", *Istoricheskiĭ Sbornik* iv (Moscow – Leningrad, 1935), 60–6.

"Vosstanie remeslennikov v gorodskoĭ bednoty v Tebrize v 1571–1573 gg.", in *Sbornik stateĭ po istorii Azerbaĭdzhana* I (Baku, 1949), 214–24.
Pirouzdjou, Hasan. *L'Iran au début du XVIe siècle. Étude d'Histoire Économique et Sociale.* Thèse du Doctorat de 3me cycle, Univ. de Paris I, 1974.
Pistoso, M. "Qadrī di Širāz e l'epica safavide", *OM* LVIII (1978), 321–5.
Pontecorvo, V. "Relazioni tra lo Scià 'Abbās e i Granduchi di Toscana Ferdinando I e Cosimo II", *Rendiconti Accad. Lincei*, ser. 8, IV (1949–50), 157–82.
Poole, R. L. *The Coins of the Shahs of Persia. Safavis, Afghans*... London, 1887.
Puturidze, V. S. *Gruzino-persidskie istoricheskie dokumenty.* Tbilisi, 1955.
Qā'im-maqāmī, Jahāngīr. *Muqaddima'ī bar shinākht-i asnād-i tārīkhī.* Tehran. 1350 (Intishārāt-i Anjuman-i Āsār-i Millī 84).
Quiring-Zoche, R. *Die Stadt Isfahan im 15. und 16. Jahrhundert. Beitrag zur persischen Stadtgeschichte.* Freiburg i. Br., 1980 (IU LIV).
Rabie, H. "Political relations between the Safavids of Persia and the Mamluks of Egypt and Syria in the early sixteenth century", *Journal of the American Research Center in Egypt* XV (1978), 75–81.
Rabino di Borgomale, H. L. *Coins, Medals, and Seals of the Shâhs of Îrân, 1500–1941.* Hertford, 1945.
"Les dynasties de Māzandarān de l'an 50 avant l'hégire à l'an 1006 de l'hégire (572 à 1597–1598), d'après les chroniques locales", *JA* CCXXVIII (1936), 397–474.
Les provinces caspiennes de la Perse, le Guîlân. Paris, 1917.
"Rulers of Gilan", *JRAS* 1920, 277–96.
"Rulers of Lahijan and Fuman, in Gilan, Persia", *JRAS* 1918, 85–100.
Rahim, Abdur. "Mughal Relations with Persia", *IC* VIII (1934), 457–73, 649–64; IX (1935), 113–30.
Rakhmani, A. A. "Iz istorii monetnogo obrashcheniya v sefevidskom gosudarstve (XVII v.)", *Gruzinskoe istochnikovedenie* III (1971), 256–62.
Rauch, G. von. "Zur Geschichte des russischen Handels und der kolonialen Expansion im 17. Jahrhundert", *Vierteljahrschrift für Sozial-und Wirtschaftsgeschichte* XLIII (1953), 119–45.
Ray, S. *Humāyūn in Persia.* Calcutta, 1948 (Royal Asiatic Society of Bengal Monographs 6).
Reid, J. J. "The Qajar Uymaq in the Safavid period, 1500–1722", *IrSt* XI (1978), 117–43.
"The Qarāmānlū: The Growth and Development of a lesser Tribal Elite in sixteenth- and seventeenth-Century Persia", *StIr* IX (1980), 195–209.
"Rebellion and Social Change in Astarâbâd, 1537–1744", *IJMES* XIII (1981), 35–53.
Reisner, I. M. "Padenie derzhavy Sefevidov i nashestvie afgantsev na Iran (1722–1729 gg.)", *Doklady i soobshcheniya istoricheskogo fakulteta MGU* X (1950), 191–224.
"Voznikovenie i raspad Durraniskoĭ derzhavy", in *Ocherki po novoĭ istorii stran Srednego Vostoka* (Moscow, 1951), pp. 53–81.
Reychman, J. "Stosunki polsko-irańskie do końca XVIII wieku", *Przegląd Orientalistyczny* IV/80 (Wrocław, 1971), 153–62.

Riazul Islam. *A Calendar of Documents on Indo-Persian Relations (1500–1750)* I. Tehran and Karachi, 1979.
Indo-Persian Relations. A Study of the Political and Diplomatic Relations between the Mughul Empire and Iran. Tehran, 1970 (Intishārāt-i Bunyād-i Farhang-i Īrān 93).
"Iran and the Mughul frontier provinces (a study of diplomatic contacts)", in *Miscellanea in honorem Ibrahim Purdavud*, ed. Īraj Afshār (= *FIZ* XXI [1976]), pp. 109–31.
The Shāmlū Letters. A New Source of Iranian Diplomatic Correspondence. Karachi, 1971.
Richard, Fr. "Catholicisme et Islam chiite au 'grand siècle'. Autour de quelques documents concernant les missions catholiques en Perse au XVIIeme siècle", *Euntes docete* XXXIII (1980), 339–403.
Roemer, H. R. "Das frühsafawidische Isfahan als historische Forschungsaufgabe", *ZDMG* CXXIV (1974), 306–31.
"Historische Grundlagen der persischen Neuzeit", *AMI* X (1977), 305–21.
Der Niedergang Irans nach dem Tode Isma'īls des Grausamen 1577–1581. Würzburg, 1939.
"Problèmes de l'histoire safavide avant la stabilisation de la dynastie sous Šāh 'Abbās, in *Actes du Ve Congrès International d'Arabisants et d'Islamisants* (Brussels, 1971), pp. 399–409.
"Die Safawiden. Ein orientalischer Bundesgenosse des Abendlandes im Türkenkampf", *Saeculum* IV (1953), 27–44.
"Scheich Ṣafī von Ardabīl. Die Abstammung eines Ṣūfī-Meisters der Zeit zwischen Sa'dī und Ḥāfiẓ", in Eilers, pp. 106–16.
"Über Urkunden zur Geschichte Ägyptens und Persiens in islamischer Zeit", *ZDMG* CVII (1957), 519–38.
Rogers, J. M. "The Genesis of Ṣafawid Religious Painting", *Iran* VIII (1970), 125–39.
Röhrborn, K. M. **Provinzen und Zentralgewalt*
"Staatskanzlei und Absolutismus im safawidischen Persien", *ZDMG* CXXVII (1977), 313–43.
Ross, (Sir) E. Denison. "The early years of Shāh Isma'īl", *JRAS* 1896, 249–340.
Roux, J. P. "Une survivance de traditions turco-mongoles chez les Séfévides", *RHR* CLXXXIII (1973), 11–18.
Sainsbury, E. B. *A Calendar of the Court Minutes etc. of the East India Company, 1635–67*, 7 vols. Oxford, 1907–25.
Saletore, B. A. "A new Persian embassy to the Vijayanagara Court", *New Indian Antiquary* I (Bombay, 1938–9), 229–39.
Sarkar, J. N. "Correspondence between the Deccani Sultans and Mir Jumla with the Court of Iran", *JBORS* XXVIII (1942), 65–74.
"Mir Jumla – Iran Correspondence", *JBORS* XXVIII (1942), 190–7; XXIX (1943), 87–93.
Sarvar, Ghulām. *History of Shāh Ismā'īl Ṣafawī*. 'Alīgarh, 1939.
Savory, R. M. "'Abbās I", *EI*².

"Alqāṣ Mīrzā", *ibid.*
"The Consolidation of Ṣafawid Power in Persia", *Der Islam* XLI (1965), 71–94.
"A curious episode of Ṣafavid history", in *Iran and Islam*, ed. C. E. Bosworth (Edinburgh, 1971), pp. 461–73.
The Development of the Early Ṣafavid State under Isma'īl and Ṭahmāsp, as Studied in the 16th Century Persian Sources. Unpublished D.Phil. thesis, London, 1958.
"Djunayd", *EI*².
"The Emergence of the modern Persian State under the Ṣafavids", *Īrān-Shināsī* II/2 (1971), 1–44.
"The Evolution of the Safavid State": paper contributed to A Colloquium on Tradition and Change in the Middle East, Harvard University, 13 March 1968; cf. *Der Islam* LIII (1976), 230.
"Ḥaydar", *EI*².
Iran under the Safavids. Cambridge, 1980.
"Some Notes on the Provincial Administration of the Early Safavid Empire", *BSOAS* XXVII (1964), 114–28.
"Notes on the Safavid State", *IrSt* I (1968), 96–103.
"The Office of Khalīfat al-Khulafā under the Safavids", *JAOS* LXXXV (1965), 497.
"The principal offices of the Ṣafawid state during the reign of Isma'īl I (907–30/1501–24)", *BSOAS* XXIII (1960), 91–105.
"The principal offices of the Ṣafawid state during the reign of Ṭahmāsp I (930–84/1524–76)", *BSOAS* XXIV (1961), 65–85.
"The qizilbāsh, education and the arts", *Turcica* VI (1975), 188–96.
"Some Reflections on Totalitarian Tendencies in the Ṣafavid State", *Der Islam* LIII (1976), 226–41.
"Safavid Persia", in *The Cambridge History of Islam*, ed. P. M. Holt *et al.* (Cambridge, 1970), I, 394–429.
"The Ṣafavid State and Polity", *IrSt* VII (1974), 179–212; with "Comments" by H. R. Roemer at pp. 213–16.
"A secretarial career under Shāh Ṭahmāsp I (1524–1576)", *IS* II/3 (1963), 343–52; cf. comments by Aubin, in *MII* I (1971), 112–33.
"The Sherley Myth", *Iran* V (1967), 73–81.
"The Significance of the Political Murder of Mīrzā Salmān", *IS* III/2 (1964); 181–91; repeated in *26th ICO New Delhi* IV (Poona, 1970), 341–6.
"'Very dull and arduous reading': a reappraisal of The history of Shāh 'Abbās the Great by Iskandar Beg Munshi", *Hamdard Islamicus* III (1980), 19–37.
Scarcia, G. "Un documento persiano del 946/1539 nell'Archivio di Stato di Venezia", *AIUON* XVIII (1968), 338–42.
"Annotazioni Muša'ša'", in *La Persia nel medievo* (Rome, 1971), pp. 633–7.
Schimkoreit, R. *Regesten publizierter safawidischer Herrscherurkunden. Erlasse und Staatsschreiben der frühen Neuzeit Irans.* Berlin, 1982 (IU LXVIII).
Schurhammer, G. *Die zeitgenössischen Quellen zur Geschichte portugiesisch-Asiens und seiner Nachbarländer, 1538–1552.* Rome, 1962.

Schuster-Walser, S. "Ein Ehrengewand vom Safawiden-Schah", *Der Islam* LIV (1977), 126–32.
**Das ṣafawidische Persien*
Schweizer, G. "Nordwest-Azerbaidschan und Shah-Sevan-Nomaden. Strukturwandel einer nordwestiranischen Landschaft und ihrer Bevölkerung", in *Erdkundliches Wissen*, ed. E. Meynen and E. Plewe, XXVI (Wiesbaden, 1970), 81–148.
Shaibī, Kāmil M. *al-Ṭarīqa al-Ṣafawiyya wa rawāsibuhā fi'l-'Irāq al-mu'āṣir*. Baghdad, 1967.
Shubbār, Jāsim H. *Ta'rīkh al-Musha'sha'iyyīn wa tarājim a'lāmihim*. al-Najaf, 1385/1965.
Simsār, Muḥammad H. "Farmān-nivīsī dar daura-yi Ṣafaviyya", *BT* II/6 (1346), 127–52; III/1 (1347), 61–83.
Siroux, M. "Les caravanserais routiers safavids [*sic*]", *IrSt* VII (1974), 348–79.
Smirnov, J. J., *et al. Krest'yanskie voĭny v Rossii 17–18 vv*. Moscow, 1966.
Sohrweide, H. "Der Sieg der Ṣafaviden und seine Rückwirkungen auf die Schiiten Anatoliens im 16. Jahrhundert", *Der Islam* XLI (1965), 95–223.
Sourdel, D. "La classification des sectes islamiques dans le Kitāb al-Milal d'al-Šahrastānī", *SI* XXXI (1970), 239–47.
Spicehandler, E. "The persecution of the Jews of Isfahan under Shāh 'Abbās II (1642–1666)", *Hebrew Union College Annual* XLVI (Cincinnati, Ohio, 1975), 331–56.
Spuler, B. "Čingizids", *EI²*.
"D̲jānids", *ibid.*
Stchoukine. **Manuscrits Ṣafavīs*.
**Manuscrits de Shāh 'Abbās*.
Stevens, R. "European visitors to the Safavid court", *IrSt* VII (1974), 421–57.
The land of the Great Sophy. 3rd ed. London, 1979.
"Robert Sherley: the Unanswered Question", *Iran* XVII (1979), 115–25.
Stloukal, K. "Das Projekt einer internationalen paneuropäischen Liga mit Persien aus dem Ende des 16. Jahrhunderts", *Persica* I (1963–4), 53–63.
Stöber, G. *Die Afshār: Nomadismus im Raum Kermān (Zentraliran)*. Marburg, 1978 (Marburger geographische Schriften 76).
Suhailī Khwānsārī, Aḥmad. "Jalāl al-Dīn Muḥammad Yazdī, munajjim-i Shāh 'Abbās", *Hunar va Mardum* XIV/176 (2535), 28–31.
"Shāh Ismā'īl-i sivvum", *Māhnāma-yi Vaḥīd* I/3 (1342).
Sukhareva, N. M. "Sovetskie istoriki o sotsial'no-ekonomicheskikh prichinakh krizisa sefevidskogo Irana", in *Iran (Pamyati B. N. Zakhodera)* (Moscow, 1971), pp. 41–56.
Sümer, F. "Avşarlar'a dâir", in *Fuad Köprülü Armağanı* (Istanbul, 1953), pp. 453–78.
Safevî devletinin kuruluşu ve gelişmesinde Anadolu Türklerinin rölü (Şah Ismail ile Halefleri ve Anadolu Türkleri). Ankara, 1976 (Selçuklu Tarih ve Medeniyeti Enstitüsü Yayınları Tarih dizisi 2).
Taeschner, F. "Das Itinerar des ersten Persienfeldzuges des Sultans Süleyman Kanuni nach Matrakçi Naṣūḥ", *ZDMG* CXII (1962), 50–93.

Tājbakhsh, Aḥmad. *Īrān dar zamān-i Ṣafaviyya.* Tabrīz, 1340.
Tansel, S. *Sultan II. Bayezit'in siyasî hayatı.* Istanbul, 1966.
Yavuz Sultan Selim. Istanbul and Ankara, 1969.
Tapper, R. "Black Sheep, White Sheep and Red Heads. A historical sketch of the Shāhsavan of Āzarbāijān", *Iran* IV (1966), 61–84.
"Shahsevan in Ṣafavid Persia", *BSOAS* XXXVII (1974), 321–54.
Thābitī, Sayyid 'Alī Mu'ayyad. *Asnād va nāmahā-yi tārīkhī az avā'il-i daurahā-yi Islām tā avākhir-i 'ahd-i Shāh Ismā'īl-i Ṣafavī.* Tehran, 1346.
Thābitiyān, D. *Asnād va nāmahā-yi tārīkhī-yi daura-yi Ṣafaviyya.* Tehran, 1343.
Togan, Z. V. "Sur l'origine des Safavides", in *Mélanges L. Massignon* III (Damascus, 1957), 345–57.
Torabi-Nejad, M. *Die Problematik der autochthonen Genesis der modernen Wirtschaftsweise in Iran – Vergleich zwischen der sozioökonomischen Struktur des safawidischen Persien und des vormodernen Westeuropa.* Unpublished Diss. phil., Hamburg, 1979.
Tournebize, F. "Schah Abbas I, roi de Perse et l'émigration forcée des Arméniens de l'Ararat", in *Huschardzan, Festschrift aus Anlass des 100jährigen Bestandes der Mechitharisten-Kongregation in Wien* (Vienna, 1911), pp. 247–52.
Tritton, A. S. "Popular Shi'ism", *BSOAS* XIII (1951), 829–39.
Tucci, U. "Una relazione di Giovan Battista Vecchietti sulla Persia e sul regno di Hormuz (1587)", *OM* XXXV (1955), 149–60.
Turan, Şerefettin. *Kanunî'nin oğlu şehzade Bayezid.* Ankara, 1961.
Uluçay, C. "Yavuz Sultan Selim nasıl padişah oldu?", *TD* VI/9 (1954), 53–90; VII/10 (1954), 11–42; VIII/11–12 (1955), 185–200.
Uzunçarsılı, İ. H. "Şah İsmail'in zevcesi Taclı Hanım'ın mücevheratı", *Belleten* XXIII (1959), 611–16.
Vercellin, G. "Un 'Sarbedār' del 981/1573 a Tabrīz", *AIUON* n.s. XX (1970), 413–15.
Verma, B. D. "An Indian ambassador to Iran", *Indo-Iranica* XV/3 (1962), 33–8.
Vermeulen, U. "L'ambassade néerlandaise de Jan Smit en Perse (1628–1630)", *Persica* VII (1975–8), 155–63.
"La mission de Jan L. van Hasselt comme agent du Shah de Perse aux Provinces-Unies (1629–1631)", *ibid.*, 133–43.
Wädekin, K. E. *Der Aufstand des Bürklüdsche Mustafa. Ein Beitrag zur Geschichte der Klassenkämpfe in Kleinasien im 15. Jahrhundert.* Unpublished Diss. phil., Leipzig, 1950.
Walsh, J. R. "Čāldirān", *EI*².
"The Historiography of Ottoman-Safavid Relations in the sixteenth and seventeenth centuries", in *Historians of the Middle East*, ed. B. Lewis and P. M. Holt (London, 1962), pp. 197–211.
"The Revolt of Alqās Mīrzā", *WZKM* LXVIII (1976), 61–78.
Weir, T. H. "The revolution in Persia at the beginning of the 18th century (from a Turkish MS. in the University of Glasgow)", in *Oriental Studies presented to E. G. Browne* (Cambridge, 1922), pp. 480–90.

Welch, A. *Artists for the Shah: late sixteenth-century painting at the Imperial court of Iran*. Yale, 1976.
"Painting and patronage under Shah 'Abbas I", *IrSt* VII (1974), 458–507; with "Comments" by B. Robinson at pp. 508–10.
Shah 'Abbās and the Arts of Isfahan. New York, 1973.
Welch, S. C. *Persian painting: five royal Safavid manuscripts of the sixteenth century*. New York, 1976.
Werner, E. *Die Geburt einer Grossmacht – Die Osmanen (1300–1481). Ein Beitrag zur Genesis des türkischen Feudalismus*. Berlin, 1966.
"Häresie, Klassenkampf und religiöse Toleranz in einer islamisch-christlichen Kontaktzone, Bedr ed-dīn und Bürklüce Mustafā", *Zeitschrift für Geschichtswissenschaft* XII (Berlin, 1964), 255–76.
Wittek, P. *The Rise of the Ottoman Empire*. London, 1958.
Yapp, M. E. "Durrānī", *EI*[2].
Yar-Shater, E. "Safavid literature: progress or decline?", *IrSt* VII (1974), 217–70.
Yazıcı, Tahsin. "Safevîler", *İsl.Ans.*
"Şah İsmail", *ibid.*
Zekiyan, L. B. "Xoğa Safar, ambasciatore di Shāh 'Abbās a Venezia", *OM* LVIII (1978), 357–67.
Zevakin, E. D. "Persidskiĭ vopros v russko-evropeĭskikh otnosheniyakh 17 v.", *Istoricheskie Zapiski* VIII (Moscow, 1940), 129–62.

CHAPTER 6

For an annotated general bibliography of the Safavid period, see Savory, "Bibliography on the History of Iran under the Ṣafavids," in *Bibliographical Guide to Iran*, ed. L. P. Elwell-Sutton (London, 1983).

Valuable information on the Safavid administrative system may be gleaned from the immensely rich and important European travel literature relating to Iran during the Safavid period. A useful summary of the available editions of the European travellers to Safavid Iran is contained in:

John Emerson, *Ex Occidente Lux. Some European sources on the economic structure of Persia between about 1630 and 1690*. Unpublished Ph.D. thesis, Cambridge, 1969.
*Minorsky, *Taḏḏkirat al-Mulūk*, pp. 6–9, has brief assessments of the value of the main travel accounts.

Few Iranian scholars have devoted much attention to Safavid administrative institutions. An exception is:
*Falsafī, *Zindagānī*.

Works which contain a substantial amount of material on Safavid administrative institutions:

Bellan L.-L. *Chah 'Abbas I*. Paris, 1932.
*Busse. *Untersuchungen*.

*Chardin.
EI[2]:
"Dārūgha" (A. K. S. Lambton);
"Ghulām, ii. Persia" (C. E. Bosworth);
"Ḳizilbāsh" (R. M. Savory).
*Hinz, *Irans Aufstieg.*
*Lambton, *Landlord and Peasant*, chapter 5.
*Lockhart, *The Fall.*
*Malcolm, *History of Persia.*
Pearson, J. D., *Index Islamicus*, Cambridge 1958–. See articles by Jean Aubin, Hafez F. Farmayan, A. K. S. Lambton, Laurence Lockhart, V. Minorsky, J. R. Perry, H. R. Roemer, and R. M. Savory.
Savory, R. M. *Iran under the Safavids.* Cambridge, 1980.

Other works:

Keyvani, Mehdi. *Artisans and Guild Life in the later Safavid period.* Berlin, 1982 (IU LXV).
*Lambton. "Quis custodiet custodes?".
Savory, R. M. "The principal offices of the Safavid state during the reign of Ismā'īl I", *BSOAS* XXIII (1960), 91–105.
"The principal offices of the Safavid state during the reign of Ṭahmāsp I", *BSOAS* XXIV (1961), 65-85.
"Ṣafavid Persia", in *Cambridge History of Islam* I, ed. P. M. Holt *et al.* (Cambridge, 1970), 394-429.
"The Ṣafavid State and Polity", *IrSt* VII (1974), 179–212, with "Comments" by H. R. Roemer pp. 213–6.
"Some notes on the provincial administration of the early Ṣafavid empire", *BSOAS* XXVII (1964), 114–28; to be supplemented by Minorsky, *Tadhkirat al-Mulūk.*
"The struggle for supremacy in Persia after the death of Tīmūr", *Der Islam* XL (1964), 35–65.

CHAPTERS 7 AND 8

Albuquerque, Afonso d'. *Commentaries*, trans. W. de Gray Birch, I. London, 1875 (Hakluyt Society).
Allen, W. E. D. *Problems of Turkish Power in the Sixteenth Century.* London, 1963.
Aubin, Jean. "Les princes d'Ormuz du XIIIe au XVe siècle", *JA* CCXLI (1953), 77–138.
Baiao, A. *Itinerários da Índia a Portugal por terra.* Coimbra, 1923 (Scriptorum rerum lusitanarum, series B, 2).
Baiburtian, V. A. *Armyanskaya Kolonya Novoe Dzhulfa v XVII veke.* Erivan, 1969.
Balbi, Gasparo. *Viaggi di C. Federici e G. Balbi alle Indie Orientali*, ed. O. Pinto. Rome, 1962.
Barbaro. See **Travels to Tana and Persia.*

Barbosa, Duarte. *The Book of Duarte Barbosa*, trans. M. Longworth Dames, I. London, 1918 (Hakluyt Society).

Bates, E. S. *Touring in 1600*. Boston, 1911.

Beazley, C. R. *The Dawn of Modern Geography*, 3 vols. London, 1897–1906.

Bellemo, V. *La Cosmografia e le Scoperte geografiche nel Sec. XV e i Viaggi di Nicolò de' Conti*. Padua, 1908.

Berchet, G. *La Repubblica di Venezia e la Persia*. Turin, 1865.

Biblioteca Nazionale Marciana, Venice. *Mostra dei Navigatori Veneti del Quattrocento e del Cinquecento*. Venice, 1957.

Carré de Chambon, Abbé Barthélemy. *The Travels of the Abbé Carré in India and the Near East, 1672 to 1674*, ed. Sir Charles Fawcett, III. London, 1948 (Hakluyt Society).

*Chardin.

Charrière, E. *Négociations de la France dans le Levant* II. Paris, 1850.

Chesneau, Jean. *Le Voyage de Monsieur d'Armon, en Levant escript par Nobel Homme Jean Chesneau, l'un des secretaires dudit Seigneur Ambassadeur*, ed. Ch. Schefer. Paris, 1887 (Recueil de voyages et documents pour servir à l'histoire de la géographie depuis le XIIIe, jusqu'à la fin du XVIe siècle 8).

Chew, S. C. *The Crescent and the Rose*. New York, 1937.

**A Chronicle of the Carmelites*.

*Clavijo, trans. Le Strange.

Conti, Nicolò de'. *The Most Noble and Famous Travels of Marco Polo together with the Travels of Nicolo de Conti, edited from the Elizabethan translation of John Frampton*, ed. N. M. Penzer (London, 1937), pp. 125–49.
See also Bellemo.

Cunaeus, Joan. *Journaal der Reis van den gezant der O.I. Compagnie Joan Cunaeus naar Perzië in 1651–52 door Cornelis Speelman*, ed. A. Hotz. Amsterdam, 1908.

Curzon, Hon. G. N. (later Marquess Curzon of Kedleston). *Persia and the Persian Question*, 2 vols. London, 1892.

Daulier-Deslandes, André. *Les Beautez de la Perse ou Description de ce qu'il y a de plus curieux dans ce Royaume*. Paris, 1672.

*Della Valle.

Dellavida, G. L. *George Strachan: Memorials of a Wandering Scottish Scholar of the Seventeenth Century*. Aberdeen, 1956.

Dinter, Joan van. *Dagreister* of the mission of Joan Josua Ketelaar's mission to Persia, in Overgecomen Brieven 1719, Boek 3, Koloniaal Archief, bundel 1793, fols. 975–1209, Rijks Archief, The Hague.

Don Juan of Persia (Uruch Beg). *Relaciones de Don Juan de Persia, dirigidas a la Magestad Catholica de Don Philippe III Rey de las Espanas etc*. Valladolid, 1604. *Trans. Le Strange.

*Du Mans.

Dunlop, H. *Perzië: Voorheen en Thans*. Haarlem, 1912.

Bronnen tot de Geschiedenis der Ostindische Compagnie in Perzië. s'Gravenhage, 1930.

Eubel, C. *Hierarchia Catholica Medii Aevi* I. Monasterii, 1913.
Fabritius. See Konovalov.
Falsafī, Naṣr-Allāh. *Tārīkh-i ravābiṭ-i Īrān u Ūrūpa dar daura-yi Ṣafaviyya*, vol I only. Tehran, 1316/1937.
**Zindagānī.*
Ferrier, R. W. "The Agreement of the East India Company with the Armenian Nation, 22nd June, 1688", *REA* VII (1970), 427–43.
"The Armenians and the East India Company in Persia in the Seventeenth and Early Eighteenth Century", *Economic History Review* 2nd series XXVI (1973), 38–62.
"An English View of Persian Trade in 1618", *JESHO* XIX (1976), 182–214.
*Fryer.
Gabashvili, V. N. "Ioseb K'art'veli, XVIII s-is diplomati da istorikosi", in *Masalebi Sak'art'velosa da Kavkasisiis istoriisat'vis* XXXII (Tbilisi, 1955), 111–21.
Gams, P. Boniface. *Series Episcoporum Ecclesiae Catholicae.* Ratisbon, 1873.
Gärber, J. G., Major. "Nachrichten von denen an der westlichen Seite der Caspischen See zwischen Astrachan und dem Flusse Kur befindlichen Völkern und Landschaften, und von derselben Zustande in dem Jahre 1728", in G. F. Müller, *Sammlung Russischer Geschichte* (Offenbach-am-Main, 1777-9) IV, 1–147.
Journal von der Commission wegen der Grenzscheidung in Persien.
Gaudereau, Abbé Martin. *Relation de la Mort de Schah Soliman Roy de Perse et du Couronnement de Sultan Ussain son Fils, avec plusieurs particularitez touchant l'état présent des affaires de la Perse et le détail des Cérémonies observées à la Consecration de l'Evesque de Babylone à Zulpha les Hispahan.* Paris, 1696.
Relation d'une Mission faite nouvellement par Monseigneur l'Archevesque d'Ancyre à Ispaham en Perse pour la Reunion des Arméniens a l'Eglise Catholique. Paris, 1702.
Relation des Differentes Espèces de Peste que reconnoissent les Orientaux. Paris, 1721.
Gemelli-Careri, J. F. "A Voyage round the World; Containing the most remarkable Things in Turkey, Persia, in India, China, the Philippine Islands and New-Spain", in J. Churchill, *A Collection of Voyages and Travels* IV (London, 1704), 111–95.
Gibbon, Edward. *The History of the Decline and Fall of the Roman Empire*, 12 vols. London, 1838–9.
*Hakluyt. *Principal Navigations.*
Hamilton, Alexander. *A New Account of the East Indies* I. Edinburgh, 1727.
Hanway, Jonas. *(An) Historical Account of the British Trade over the Caspian Sea: with a Journal of Travels through Russia into Persia...to which are added, The Revolutions of Persia during the present century, with the particular history of the great usurper Nadir Kouli*, 4 vols. London, 1753.
*Herbert, Thomas. *Travels in Persia.*
Herbette, M. *Une Ambassade Persane sous Louis XIV, d'après des documents inédits.* Paris, 1907.

Heyd, W. *Histoire du commerce du Levant au moyen-âge*, trans. F. Raynaud, 2 vols. Leipzig, 1886.

*Ibn Baṭṭūṭa, trans. Gibb.

*Iskandar Munshī, trans. Savory.

*Jenkinson, *Early Voyages.*

Joanisian, A. *Israel Ory und die armenische Befreiungsidee.* Munich, 1913.

Klaproth, J. "Russisch-Persisch-Türkische Graenzbestimmung im Jahr 1727", in *Fundgruben des Orients* (Vienna, 1818) VI, 349–58.

*Kaempfer.

Kakasch de Zalonkemeny, S. *Iter Persicum, ou Description du voyage en Perse entrepris en 1602 par Étienne Kakasch de Zalonkemeny, Envoyé comme Ambassadeur par l'Empereur Rodolphe à la Cour du Grand-Duc de Moscovie et à celle de Chah Abbas en Perse*, trans. Ch. Schefer. Paris, 1877.

Konovalov, S. "Ludvig Fabritius's Account of the Razin Rebellion", *Oxford Slavonic Papers* VI (1955), 72–101.

Krusiński, P. Tadeusz Juda, S. J. *Histoire de la Dernière Revolution de Perse*, 2 vols. The Hague, 1728 (recension by Père J. A. Du Cerceau of Bechon's French translation of Krusiński's memoirs). Trans. anonymously as *The History of the Revolutions of Persia.* London, 1728, and Dublin, 1729.

Kukanova, N. G. "Iz istorii Russko-Iranskikh torgovlykh svyazeĭ v XVII veke", *KSINA* XXVI (1958), 41–53.

"Rol' armyanskogo kupechestva v razvitii russko-iranskoĭ torgovli v posledneĭ treti XVII v.", *KSINA* XXX (1961), 20–34.

Lebedev, V. I. "Posol'stvo Artemiya Volinskogo v Persiyu", *IAN SSSR* V/6 (1948), 528–39.

Le Fèvre de Fontenay. *Journal Historique du Voyage et des Aventures singulières de l'Ambassadeur de Perse en France.* Paris, 1715; also published in *Mercure Galant*, February 1715.

Linschoten, Jan Huyghen van. *The Voyage of Jan Huyghen van Linschoten to the East Indies*, ed. and trans. A. C. Burnell and P. A. Tiele, 2 vols. London, 1885 (Hakluyt Society).

Listov, V. P. *Persidskiĭ Pokhod Petra I. 1722–1723.* Moscow, 1951.

Lockyer, Charles. *An Account of Trade in India.* London, 1711.

Loenertz, Fr. R., O. P. *La Société des Frères Pérégrinants: Étude sur l'Orient Dominicain.* Rome, 1937.

Lucas, Paul. *Voyage du Sieur P. Lucas au Levant*, ed. C. C. Baudelot de Dairval. The Hague, 1705.

Luṭf 'Alī Beg "Āẕar". *Ātashkada.* Bombay, 1860–1.

*Major. *India in the Fifteenth Century.*

Manucci, Nicolò. *Storia do Mogor, or Mogul India 1653–1708*, trans. W. Irvine, 4 vols. London, 1907–8 (Indian Texts Series).

Maze, Père Jean Baptiste de la, S. J. "Journal du Voyage du Père de la Maze de Chamaké à Hispaham (1698–9)", in *Nouveaux Mémoires* III, 393–482; abridged in *Lettres Édifiantes et Curieuses, écrites des missions étrangères* IV (Paris, 1780), 53–112.

Meilink-Roelofsz, M. P. "The Earliest Relations between Persia and the Netherlands", *Persica* VI (1974), 1–50.

Michel, Pierre Victor. *Mémoire du Sr. Michel sur le voyage qu'il a fait en Perse en qualité d'Envoyé extraordinaire de Sa Majesté dans les Années 1706, 1707, 1708 et 1709.* MS Bibliothèque Nationale, Paris, Fonds français 7200.

Mosnier, Père Léonard, S. J. "Journal du Voyage du Père Monier d'Erzeron à Trébizonde", in *Nouveaux Mémoires* III, 314–32.

"Lettre au Père Fleuriau", *ibid.*, 1–226.

**A Narrative of Italian Travels.*

Nikitin, Afanasii. *Khozhenie za Tri Morya.* Moscow, 1958.
See also Major.

Nouveaux Mémoires des Missions de la Compagnie de Jésus dans le Levant III. Paris, 1723.

Oelschläger (Olearius), Adam. *The Voyages and Travells of the Ambassadors ... sent by Frederick Duke of Holstein to the great Duke of Muscovy and the King of Persia, Begun in 1633 and finished in 1639.* London, 1669.

Oudenrijn, Fr. M. A. van. "Bishops and Archbishops of Naxivan", *Archivum Fratrum Praedicatorum* VI (Rome, 1936), 161–84.

Page, W. S. *The Russia Company from 1553 to 1660.* London, 1911.

*Palombini. *Bündniswerben.*

Penrose, B. *The Sherleian Odyssey.* Taunton, 1938.

Travel and Discovery in the Renaissance, 1420–1620. Cambridge, Mass., 1952.

Urbane Travellers 1591-1635. Philadelphia, 1942.

Petter, Erasmus. "Een korte Beschryving van de Stad Spahan", in F. Valentijn, *Oud en Nieuw Oost-Indien* V/1 (Dordrecht – Amsterdam, 1726).

Provins, Pacifique de. *Relation d'un Voyage en Perse.* Paris, 1631.

*Purchas.

Resandt, W. Wijnaendts van. *De Gezaghebbers der Oost-Indische Compagnie op hare Buiten-Comptoiren in Azië.* Amsterdam, 1940.

Ricard, Père. "Lettre", 7 Aug. 1697, in *Nouveaux Mémoires* III, 253–71.

Roe, Sir Thomas. *The Embassy to the Moghul*, ed. Sir William Foster. London, 1926.

Ross, Sir E. Denison. *Sir Anthony Sherley and his Persian Adventure.* London, 1933.

Sanson, Père N. *Voyage ou Relation de l'État présent du Royaume de Perse.* Paris, 1695.

Santo Stefano, H. di. "The Journey of Hieronimo di Stafano Santo, a Genoese", in *Major, *India in the Fifteenth Century.*

Savory, R. M. "The Sherley Myth", *Iran* V (1967), 76–81.

Schorer, Nicolaus. "Extract uijt het Spahans' Dagregister beginnende met den eersten Mart en eijndigt den laatsten Augusto des jaars 1722", extracts in *Asiatic Quarterly Review* II (1886), 156–210.

Silva y Figueroa, G. *Comentarios de Don Garcia de Silva y Figueroa de la Embajada que de parte del Rey de España don Felipe III hizo al rey Xa Abas de Persia*, 2 vols. Madrid, 1623–5.

Stodart, Robert. *The Journal of Robert Stodart, being an account of his experiences as a Member of Sir Dodmore Cotton's Mission in Persia in 1628–29*, ed. Sir E. Denison Ross. London, 1935.

Struys, J. *Les Voyages de Jean Struys en Moscovie, en Tartarie, en Perse*. Amsterdam, 1681.

*Tavernier.

Teixeira, Pedro. *Relaciones de P. Teixeira del origen, descendencia y sucesión de los Reyes de Persia y de Hormuz*. Antwerp, 1610. *Trans. Sinclair.

Thévenot, J. *Travels into the Levant*. London, 1686.

**Travels to Tana and Persia.*

Tucci, U. "Mercanti Veneziani in India alla fine del secolo XVI", in *Studi in Onore di Armando Sapori* (Milan, 1957), pp. 1091–1111.

Uruch Beg. See *Don Juan of Persia.

Varthema, Ludovico di. *The Travels of Lodovico di Varthema*, ed. G. P. Badger. London, 1863 (Hakluyt Society).

Vaughan, D. M. *Europe and the Turk*. Liverpool, 1954.

Vechietti, Giovanni Battista. *Lettera*, ed. H. F. Brown, "A Report on the Condition of Persia in the year 1586", *English Historical Review* VII (1892), 314–21.

Vickers, E. "A Stuart Envoy in Persia", *The Blue Peter* (London, December 1924), pp. 433–7.
See also Manucci.

Worms, Johann Gottlieb. *Ost-Indien- und Persianische Reisen, oder zehenjährige auf Gross-Java, Bengala, und im Gefolge Herrn Joann Josua Kotelaar, Hollandischen Abgesandtens an den Sophi in Persien, geleistete Kriegs-Dienste*. Dresden and Leipzig, 1737.

CHAPTER 9

Arunova, M. R. "K istorii narodnykh vystupleniĭ v gosudarstve Timuridov v XV v.", *KSIV* XXXVII (1960), 34–6.

Ashraf, Aḥmad. "Historical Obstacles to the Development of a Bourgeoisie in Iran", in *Studies in the Economic History of the Middle East*, ed. M. A. Cook (London, 1970), pp. 308–32.

Aubin, Jean. *"L'ethnogénèse".

Note préliminaire sur les archives du takya du Tchima-Rud (Archives persanes commentées, 2). Tehran, 1955.

"Un soyurghal Qara-Qoyunlu conernant le bulūk de Bawānāt-Harāt-Marwast (Archives persanes commentées, 3)", in *Documents from Islamic Chanceries*, 1st series, ed. S. M. Stern (Oxford, 1965), pp. 159–70.

*Barkan. "Osmanlı devrinde".

Barthold, W. "Die persische Inschrift an der Mauer der Manūčehr-Moschee zu Ani", trans. W. Hinz, *ZDMG* CI (1951), 241–69.

Ulugh Beg = **Four Studies* II.

Becker, C. H. "Steuerpacht und Lehenswesen. Eine historische Studie über die Entstehung des islamischen Lehenswesens", *Der Islam* V (1914), 81–120.

Busse, H. "Persische Diplomatik im Überblick. Ergebnisse und Probleme", *Der Islam* xxxvii (1961), 202–45.
**Untersuchungen.*
Cahen, Claude. "L'évolution de l'iqta' du IXe au XIIIe siècle. Contribution à une histoire comparée des sociétés médiévales", *Annales: Économies, Sociétés, Civilisations* viii (Paris, 1953), 25–52.
*Chardin.
Daulatshāh al-Samarqandī. *Taẕkirat al-shu'arā'*, ed. E. G. Browne. London, 1901.
*Du Mans.
*Falsafī. *Zindagānī.*
Ḥamd-Allāh Mustaufī al-Qazvīnī. *Nuzhat al-qulūb*, ed. and trans. G. Le Strange. Leiden–London, 1915 (GMS xxiii/1,2).
Herrmann, G., and Doerfer, G. "Ein persisch-mongolischer Erlass des Ǧalāyeriden Šeyḫ Oveys", *CAJ* xix (1975), 1–85.
Hinz, W. *"Ein orientalisches Handelsunternehmen".
*"Das Rechnungswesen".
Die Resālä-ye Falakiyyä. Wiesbaden, 1952 (VOK iv).
"Die spätmittelalterlichen Währungen im Bereich des Persischen Golfes", in *Iran and Islam, in memory of the late Vladimir Minorsky*, ed. C. E. Bosworth (Edinburgh, 1971), pp. 303–14.
"Steuerinschriften aus dem mittelalterlichen Vorderen Orient", *Belleten* xiii (1949), 745–69.
*"Das Steuerwesen Ostanatoliens".
"The Value of the Toman in the Middle Ages", in *Yadnāma-yi Īrānī-yi Minorsky*, ed. M. Minovi and I. Afshār (Tehran, 1969), pp. 90–5.
"Zwei Steuerbefreiungsurkunden", in *Documenta islamica inedita, Festschrift für Richard Hartmann* (Berlin, 1952), pp. 211–20.
Horst, H. "Zwei Erlasse Šāh Ṭahmāsps I.", *ZDMG* cx (1961), 301–9.
*Iskandar Munshī, trans. Savory.
Jahn, K. "Täbris, ein mittelalterliches Kulturzentrum zwischen Ost und West", *AOAW* cv (1968), 201–12.
*Kaempfer.
Khwānd Amīr, Ghiyāṯ al-Dīn b. Humām al-Dīn. *Ḥabīb al-siyar*, 4 vols. Tehran, n.d.
Lambton, A. K. S. **Landlord and Peasant.*
"The office of kalântar under the Safawids and Afshars", in *Mélanges Henri Massé* (Tehran, 1963), pp. 206–18.
"Reflections on the iqtā'", in *Arabic and Islamic Studies in honor of Hamilton A. R. Gibb*, ed. G. Makdisi (Leiden, 1965), pp. 358–76; repr. in her *Theory and Practice in Medieval Persian Government* (London, 1980), no. x.
"Two Ṣafawid Soyūrghāls", *BSOAS* xiv (1952), 44–54.
Løkkegaard, F. *Islamic Taxation in the Classical Period.* Copenhagen, 1950.
Luft, P. *Iran unter Schah 'Abbās II (1642–1666).* Unpublished Diss. phil., Göttingen, 1969.

Martin, B. G. "Seven Ṣafavid Documents from Azarbayjan", in *Documents from Islamic Chanceries*, 1st series, ed. S. M. Stern (Oxford, 1965), pp. 171–206.
Miles, G. C. "Dīnār", *EI*².
"Dirham", *EI*².
Minorsky, V. *"The Aq-qoyunlu and Land Reforms".
*"A Soyūrghāl of Qāsim b. Jahāngīr."
**Tadhkirat al-Mulūk*.
Minorsky, V., and Minovi, M. "Naṣīr al-Dīn Ṭūsī on finance", *BSOAS* x (1940–2), 755–89; new ed. (without Persian text) in Minorsky, *Iranica* (Tehran, 1964), pp. 64–85.
Papazian, A. D. *Persidskie Dokumenty Matenadarana* I. *Ukazy*, 2 vols. Erivan, 1956–9.
Petrushevsky, I. P. *Zemledelie*, trans. Karīm Kishāvarz, as *Kishāvarzī va munāsabāt-i arzī dar Īrān-i 'ahd-i Mughūl*, 2 vols. Tehran, 1344/1966 (Intishārāt-i mu'assasa-yi muṭāla'āt va taḥqīqāt-i ijtimā'ī 34, 35).
*"K istorii instituta 'soyurgala'".
"Vnutrennyaya politika Akhmeda Ak-koyunlu", in *Sbornik stateĭ po istorii Azerbaĭdzhana* I (2nd ed. Baku, 1949), 144–52.
Rabino di Borgomale, H. L. *Coins, Medals, and Seals of the Shâhs of Îrân, 1500–1941*. Hertford, 1945.
*"Coins of the Jalā'ir".
"Coins of the Shahs of Persia", *NC* 4th series VIII (1908), 357–73; XI (1911), 176–96; XV (1915), 243–8, 351–6.
Rabino, Joseph. "Banking in Persia", *Journal of the Institute of Bankers*, January 1892, 1–56.
Roemer, H. R. "Le dernier firman de Rustam Bahādur Aq Qoyunlu?", *BIFAO* LIX (1960), 273–87.
**Staatsschreiben*.
*Röhrborn. *Provinzen und Zentralgewalt*.
Schaendlinger, A. C. *Osmanische Numismatik*. Braunschweig, 1973 (Handbücher der mittelasiatischen Numismatik 3).
*Schmidt-Dumont. *Turkmenische Herrscher*.
Schroetter, Friedrich Frhr. von. *Wörterbuch der Münzkunde*. Leipzig, 1939.
*Schuster-Walser. *Das ṣafawidische Persien*.
*Siroux. *Caravansérails*.
Smith, Jr, John Masson. "The Silver Currency of Mongol Iran", *JESHO* XII (1969), 16–41.
Smith, Jr, John Masson, and Plunkett, F. "Gold Money in Mongol Iran", *JESHO* XI (1968), 275–97.
Tehrani, Eskandar. *Die Entwicklung der iranischen Volkswirtschaft von der Zeit der Safawiden bis zu den Pahlawiden (1501–1948)*. Unpublished Diss., Munich, 1949.
*Togan. "Büyük türk hükümdarı Şahruh".
Vasmer, R. "Zur Münzkunde der persischen Schahe", *Islamica* VI (1933–4), 137–81.

Werner, E. *Die Geburt einer Grossmacht – Die Osmanen (1300–1481)*. Berlin, 1966.
*Yakubovsky. "Timur".

CHAPTER 10

Hunger, H., and Vogel, K. *Ein byzantinisches Rechenbuch des 15. Jahrhunderts*. Vienna, 1963.
Juschkewitsch, A. P. *Geschichte der Mathematik im Mittelalter*. Leipzig, 1964.
al-Kāshī, Ghiyāṣ al-Dīn Jamshīd. *Miftāḥ al-ḥisāb*, ed. and trans. B. A. Rozenfel'd, Segal, and A. P. Yushkevich, *Klyuch Arifmetiki. Traktat ob Okruzhnosti*. Moscow, 1956.
al-Risāla al-muḥīṭiyya, ed. and trans. P. Luckey, *Der Lehrbrief über den Kreisumfang*. Berlin, 1953 (Abh. d. deut. Akad. d. Wiss., Kl. für Math. u. allg. Naturwiss., 1950, no. 6).
Zīj-i Khāqānī, India Office Library MS 430 (Ethé, no. 2232).
Kennedy, E. S. "The Chinese-Uighur Calendar as Described in the Islamic Sources", *Isis* LV (1964), 435–43.
The Planetary Equatorium of Jamshīd. Princeton, 1960.
Kennedy, E. S., and Muruwwa, Aḥmad. "Biruni on the Solar Equation", *JNES* XVII (1958), 112–21.
Luckey, P. *Die Rechenkunst bei Ǧamšīd b. Masʿūd al-Kāšī*. Wiesbaden, 1951 (AKM 21/1).
Pannekoek, A. *A History of Astronomy*. New York, 1961.
Poulle, E. *Un constructeur d'instruments astronomiques au XVe siècle, Jean Fusoris*. Paris, 1963.
Price, D. J. *The Equatorie of the Planetis*. Cambridge, 1955.
Sayılı, Aydin. *Ghiyāth al-Dīn al-Kāshī's Letter*. Ankara, 1960 (TTKY, VII seri, 39).
The Observatory in Islam and its place in the general history of the observatory. Ankara, 1960 (TTKY, VII seri, 38).

CHAPTER 11

General

*Chardin. (references also to incomplete trans. by E. Lloyd, *Sir John Chardin's Travels in Persia*, 2 vols. London, 1720.)
**A Chronicle of the Carmelites.*
*Don Juan, trans. Le Strange.
*Du Mans.
*Fryer.
*Hakluyt, *Principal Navigations*.
*Herbert, *Travels in Persia*.
*Jenkinson, *Early Voyages*.
*Lockhart, *The Fall*.
*Minorsky, *Taḏẖkirat al-Mulūk*.
*Purchas.

Ross, Sir E. Denison. *Sir Anthony Sherley and his Persian adventure*. London, 1933 (Broadway Travellers).

Storey, *PL* II.

Astronomy and related sciences

Aga-Oğlu, M. "Two Astrolabes of the late Ṣafavid period", *Bulletin of the Museum of Fine Arts, Boston* XLV (1947), 79–84.

al-ʿĀmilī, Bahāʾ al-Dīn Muḥammad b. Ḥusain. *Khulāṣat al-ḥisāb*. Tehran, 1316/1898–9.

Greaves, John. *Insigniorum aliquot stellarum longitudinis et latitudinis, ex astronomicis observationibus Ulug Beigi, Tamerlanis magni nepotis*, Oxford, 1648.

Binae tabulae geographicae; una Nassir Eddini Persae, altera ulug Beigi Tatari; commentariis ex Abulfeda aliisque Arabum geographis illustratae. London, 1648, 1652; Oxford, 1712, in Hudson, *Geographiae veteris scriptores Graeci minores* III. The *commentarii* were never printed.

Astronomica quaedam, ex traditione Shah Cholgii Persae, una cum hypothesibus planetarum: item excerpta quaedam ex Alfergani elementis astronomicis, et Ali Kustigii de terra magnitudine et sphaerarum coelestium a terra distentiis: cum interpretatione Latina. London, 1652 (appeared added to *Binae tabulae* above).

The above three works are listed as published in Ward, p. 149, who gives as unpublished:

Tabulae integrae longitudinis et latitudinis stellarum fixarum, juxta Ulug Beigi observationes. See also Hyde.

Gunther, R. T. *The Astrolabes of the World*. Oxford, 1932.

Hartner, W. "The Principle and Use of the Astrolabe", in *SPA*, pp. 2530–54.

Hyde, Thomas. *Tabulae longitudinis et latitudinis stellarum fixarum*. Oxford, 1665.

Kennedy, E. S. "The Chinese-Uighur Calendar as Described in the Islamic Sources", *Isis* LV (1964), 435–43.

"A Fifteenth Century Planetary Computer", *Isis* XLI/2 (1950), 180–3; XLIII (1952), 42–50.

"A mediaeval interpolation scheme using second order differences", in *A Locust's Leg. Studies in honour of S. H. Taqizadeh*, ed. W. B. Henning and E. Yarshater (London, 1962), pp. 117–20.

Khaljī. See Greaves.

Kharegat, M. P. *Astrolabes*, ed. D. D. Kapadia. Bombay, 1950.

Luṭf-Allāh "Muhandis". See al-Ṣūfī.

Līlāwatī. Calcutta, 1827.

Mayer, L. A. *Islamic Astrolabists and their works*. Geneva, 1956.

Michel, H. *Traité de l'astrolabe*. Paris, 1947.

Needham, J. *Chinese Astronomy and the Jesuit Mission: an encounter of cultures*. London, 1958.

Price, D. J. "An International Checklist of Astrolabes", *Archives Internationales d'histoire des Sciences*, nos. 32–3 (Paris, 1955), 243–63, 363–81.

Sayılı, Aydin, "'Alâ al-Dîn al-Manṣûr's poems on the Istanbul observatory", *Belleten* XX (1956), 429–84.

"Tycho Brahe sistemi hakkında XVII. asır baslarına ait Farsça bir yazma", *Anatolia* III (1958), 79–83; English version, "An early seventeenth-century Persian Manuscript on the Tychonic system", pp. 84–7.

"Islam and the Rise of the Seventeenth Century Science", *Belleten* XXII (1958), 353–68.

The Observatory in Islam. Ankara, 1960.

Sédillot, L. A. "Description d'un astrolabe construit par Abd-ul-Aïma, ingénieur et astronome persan", *Annales de l'Observatoire Impérial de Paris, Mémoires* IX (1868), 164–71.

Seemann, H. J. "Die Instrumente der Sternwarte zu Marāgha", *Sitzungsberichte der phys.-med. Sozietät* LX (Erlangen, 1928), 17, 121–6.

Strachey, E. *Bija Ganita: or the Algebra of the Hindus*. London, 1813.

al-Ṣūfī, Abu'l-Ḥusain 'Abd al-Raḥmān. *Suwar al-kawākib*, ed. with introductions by M. Nizamuddin and H. J. J. Winter. Hyderabad, Deccan, 1954.

Stoefflerin, Johannes. *Elucidatio fabricae ususque astrolabii a Johanne Stoefflerino Justingensi, viro Germano et totius sphaeriae doctissimo nuper ingeniose concinnata atque in lucem edita*. Oppehemii, 1513.

Tekeli, S. "Nasirüddin, Takiyüddin ve Tycho Brahe'nin Rasat Aletlerinnin Mukayesesi", *Ankara Üniversitesi Dil ve Tarih-Coğrafya Fakültesi Dergisi* XVI/3–4 (1958), 301–76, 386–93, with English summary pp. 377–86.

Ward, John. *The Lives of the Professors of Gresham College*. London, 1740.

Winter, H. J. J. "The Arabic Optical MSS in the British Isles", *Centaurus* V/1 (Copenhagen, 1956), 87.

"The Muslim tradition in astronomy", *Endeavour* X (1951), 126–30.

Winter, H. J. J., and Mirza, Arshad. "Concerning the Persian version of Līlāvatī", *JASB Science* 3rd series XVIII (1952), 1–10.

Cartography

Bagrow, L. *History of Cartography*. London, 1964.

Banākatī, Fakhr al-Dīn Abū Sulaimān Dā'ūd. *Rauẓat ūlī'l-albāb*, eighth *qism* ed. Andreas Müller, *Abdallae Beidavaei Historia Sinensis*. Berlin, 1677.

Kahle, P. "China as described by Turkish Geographers from Iranian Sources", *Proc. Iran Society* II (London, 1940), 48–59.

Kātib Chelebī (Ḥājjī Khalīfa). *Jihān-numā*, ed. with additions by Abū Bekr b. Bahrām al-Dimashqī. Istanbul, 1144/1731–2.

Piri Reis. *Piri Re'is Bahrije*, ed. P. Kahle, 2 vols. Berlin and Leipzig, 1926.

Taeschner, F. "Das Hauptwerk der geographischen Literatur der Osmanen, Kātib Čelebi's Ğihānnumā", *Imago Mundi* I (1935), 44–8.

Technology and Architecture

Chaghtai, A. "A Family of great Mughal architects", *IC* XI/2 (1937), 208–9.

"Indian Links with Central Asia in Architecture", in *Indian Art and Letters* XI/2 (London, 1937), 85–104.

"Gaur-i Amir" (pseud.). "The Mosques of Samarkand", *ibid.*

Hunter, W. "Account of the astronomical labours of Jaya Sinha, Rajah of Ambhera, or Jayanagar", in *Asiatic Researches* V (London, 1799), 177–211.

Imperial Archaeological Commission. *Les Mosquées de Samarcande–Le Gur Amir*. St Petersburg, 1905.
Josten, C. H. *Catalogue of Scientific Instruments from the 13th to the 19th centuries. From the collection of J. A. Billmeir, C.B.E., exhibited by the Museum of the History of Science, Oxford*. London, 1954.
Kaye, G. R. "The Astronomical Observatories of Jai Singh", *Archaeological Survey of India, New Imperial Series*, XL (Calcutta, 1918).
Maddison, F. R. *Supplement* to Josten (above). Oxford-London, 1957.
Savory, R. M. "The Sherley Myth", *Iran* V (1967), 73–81.

Medicine

Browne, E. G. *Arabian Medicine*. Cambridge, 1921.
Elgood, C. *A Medical History of Persia and the Eastern Caliphate*. Cambridge, 1951.
Ṣafavid Medical Practice, 1500–1700 A.D. London, 1970.
Hirschberg, J. *Geschichte der Augenheilkunde*. Berlin, 1899–1918.
Nūr al-Dīn Muḥammad 'Abd-Allāh b. Ḥakīm 'Ain al-Mulk. *Alfāẓ al-adviya*, ed. and trans. Gladwin. Calcutta, 1793.
Ṭibb-i Dārā Shukūhī, Bibliothèque Nationale, Paris, MS Suppl. persan 342.
Willis, Thomas. *Pharmaceuticae Rationalis: sive Diatriba de Medicamentorum Operationibus in Humano Corpore*. London, 1674; *Pars secunda*. Oxford, 1675.

CHAPTER 12

Aubin, J. "Deux sayyids de Bam au XVe siècle. Contribution à l'histoire de l'Iran timouride", *AAWL, geistes- u. sozialwiss. Kl.*, 1956, no. 7, 375–501.
"Études Safavides I. Šāh Ismā'īl et les Notables de l'Iraq Persan", *JESHO* II (1959), 37–81.
Matériaux pour la biographie de Shāh Ni'matullāh Walī Kermānī. Tehran, 1956.
"Notes sur quelques documents Aq Qoyunlu", in *Mélanges L. Massignon* I (Damascus, 1956), 123–51.
"Les Sunnites du Lāristān et la chute des Safavides", *REI* XXXIII (1965), 151–71.
Babinger, F. "Schejch Bedr ed-dīn, der Sohn des Richters von Simāw; ein Beitrag zur Geschichte des Sektenwesens im altosmanischen Reich", *Der Islam* XI (1921), 78–92.
"Marino Sanuto's Tagebücher als Quelle zur Geschichte der Safavijja", in *Oriental Studies presented to E. G. Browne* (Cambridge, 1922), pp. 28–50.
"Firište-Oghlu", *AIUON* n.s. V (1954), 153–5.
Barthold, W. "Khalif i sultan," in *Sochineniya* VI (Moscow, 1966), 17–78.
Bausani, A. "Ḥurūfiyya", *EI*².
Birge, J. K. *The Bektashi Order of Dervishes*. London and Hertford, 1937.
Caskel, W. "Ein Mahdī des 15. Jahrhunderts. Saijid Muḥammad ibn Falāḥ und seine Nachkommen", *Islamica* IV (1931), 48-93.
Daulatshāh al-Samarqandī. *Taẕkirat al-shu'arā'*, ed. E. G. Browne. London, 1901.

Della Valle, Pietro. **Viaggi*. Also ed. L. Lockhart and F. Gaeta, *I Viaggi... Lettere dalla Persia* I. Rome, 1972.

*Don Juan, trans. Le Strange.

Efendiev, O. A. "K nekotorym voprosam vnutrenneĭ i vneshneĭ politiki Shakha Ismaila I", *AN Azerb. SSR. Trudy Instituta Istorii* XII (1957), 151–80.

*Falsafī, *Zindagānī*.

Gardet, L., and Anawati, M.-M. *Introduction à la théologie musulmane*. Paris, 1948.

Gölpınarlı. A. "Fadlallâh-i Hurûfî'nin oğluna ait bir mektûp", *Şarkiyat Mecmuası* I (1956), 37–57.

Gordlevsky, V. "Iz religioznoĭ zhizni Kyzylbasheĭ Maloĭ Azii", *Novyĭ Vostok* I (Moscow, 1922), 259–78.

*Hakluyt. *Principal Navigations*.

Ḥamd-Allāh Mustaufī al-Qazvīnī. *Nuzhat al-qulūb*, ed. and trans. G. Le Strange. Leiden–London, 1915 (GMS XXIII/1, 2).

Ḥasan-i Rūmlū. *Aḥsan al-tavārīkh* I, ed. C. N. Seddon. Baroda, 1931.

*Hinz. *Irans Aufstieg*.

Horst, H. "Tīmūr und Ḫōğä 'Alī. Ein Beitrag zur Geschichte der Ṣafawiden", *AAWL, geistes- u. sozialwiss. Kl.*, 1958, no. 2.

Huart, Cl. *Textes persans relatifs à la secte des Houroufis...suivis d'une étude sur la religion des Houroufis par le Dr Riza Tevfiq*. Leiden, 1909 (GMS IX).

*Ibn Baṭṭuṭa, trans. Gibb.

*Iskandar Munshī, trans. Savory.

Kasravī, Sayyid Aḥmad. *Shaikh Ṣafī va tabārash*. 2nd ed. Tehran, 1342/1963.

Tārīkh-i pānṣad-sāla-yi Khūzistān. 3rd ed. Tehran 1330/1951–2.

Kiyā, S. "Nuqṭaviyān yā Pāsīkhāniyān", *Īrān-Kūda* XIII (Tehran, 1332/1953), 1–132.

"Āgāhīhā-yi tāza az Ḥurūfiyān", *Majalla-yi Dānishkada-yi Adabiyyāt, Tehran* II/2 (1334/1955), 39–65.

Kutsiya, K. K. "Iz istorii sotsial'nykh dvizheniĭ v gorodakh Sefevidskogo gosudarstva (dvizhenie Nuktaviev)", *NAA* 1966, no. 2, 69–75.

Le Coq, A. von. "Kyzylbasch und Yäschilbasch", *Orientalisches Archiv* III (Leipzig, 1913), 61–5.

al-Majlisī, Muḥammad Bāqir b. Muḥammad Taqī. *Biḥār al-anwār* XII. Tehran, 1305/1887–8.

Membrè, Michele. *Relazione di Persia*, ed. G. Scarcia. Naples, 1968.

*Miklukho-Maklaĭ. "Shiizm".

*Minadoi.

Minorsky, V. "Jihān-shāh Qara-qoyunlu and his Poetry", *BSOAS* XVI (1954), 271–97.

Persia in A.D. 1478–1490. London, 1957.

"The Poetry of Shāh Ismā'īl I", *BSOAS* X (1939–42), 1006–53.

Molé, M. "Les Kubrawiya entre sunnisme et shiisme aux huitième et neuvième siècles de l'hégire", *REI* XXIX (1961), 61–142.

Mordtmann, J. H. "Sunnitisch-schiitische Polemik im 17. Jahrhundert", *MSOS* XXIX/2 (1926), 112–29.
Muḥammad Ḥasan Khān Sanī' al-Daula. *Maṭla' al-shams* II. Tehran, 1302/1884–5.
Petrov, I. P. "Dannye istochnikov o sostave voĭnskikh kontingentov Ismaila I", *NAA* 1964, no. 3, 76–81.
"Ukaz Nadir-Shakha o pochitanii chetyrekh pravednykh khalifov", *KSINA* XXXIX (1963), 52–5.
Petrushevsky, I. P. "Dvizhenie serbedarov v Khorasane", *UZIV* XIV (1956), 91–162.
Qumī, Ḥājj Shaikh 'Abbās. *Kulliyāt-i mafātīḥ al-ẓinān*. Tehran, 1316/1937–8.
*Ritter. "Die Anfänge der Ḥurūfīsekte".
Ross, Sir E. Denison. "The Early Years of Shāh Ismā'īl, Founder of the Ṣafavī Dynasty", *JRAS* 1896, 249–340.
Sanuto, Marino. *Diarii* IV. Venice, 1880.
Scarcia, G. "Intorno alle controversie tra Ahbārī c Usūlī presso gli Imamiti di Persia", *RSO* XXXIII (1958), 211–50.
"Annotazioni mušă'ša'", in *La Persia nel Medioevo* (Rome, 1971), pp. 633–7.
Scarcia Amoretti, B. "Una polemica religiosa tra' ulama' di Mashad e' ulama' 'uzbechi nell'anno 977/1588–9", *AIUON* n.s. XIV (1964), 647–71.
"Ibn 'Inaba", *EI*².
Sohrweide, H. "Der Sieg der Ṣafaviden in Persien und seine Rückwirkungen auf die Schiiten Anatoliens im 16. Jahrhundert", *Der Islam* XLI (1965), 95–223.
Togan, Z. V. "Sur l'origine des Safavides", in *Mélanges L. Massignon* III (Damascus, 1957), 345–57.
Tunakābunī, Mīrzā Muḥammad. *Qiṣaṣ al-'ulamā*. Tehran, n.d. (Kitābfurūshī-yi Islāmiyya).
Walsh, J. R. "The Historiography of Ottoman–Safavid Relations in the sixteenth and seventeenth centuries", in *Historians of the Middle East*, ed. B. Lewis and P. M. Holt (London, 1962), pp. 197–211.

CHAPTER 13

'Alī Khān, Sayyid Ṣadr al-Dīn. *Salāfat al-'aṣr*. Cairo, 1324.
Amīn, Sayyid Muḥsin. *A'yān al-shī'a*. Damascus, 1927– .
Āshtiyānī, S. J. *Hastī az naẓar-i falsafa va 'irfān*. Mashhad, 1379.
Sharḥ-i ḥāl va ārā-yi falsafī-yi Mullā Ṣadrā. Mashhad, 1381.
Aubin, J. *Matériaux pour la biographie de Shāh Ni'matullāh Walī Kirmānī*. Tehran, 1956 (Bibliothèque Iranienne 7).
al-Baḥrānī, Yūsuf b. Aḥmad. *Lu'lu'at al-baḥrain fi'l-ijāẓa li qurrat al-'ain*. Tehran, 1269.
Bihbihānī, Aḥmad. *Mir'āt al-aḥvāl-i jahān-nāma*.
Burckhardt, T. *Introduction to Sufi Doctrine*, trans. D. M. Matheson. Lahore, 1959.
Sagesse des prophètes. Paris, 1955.
Corbin, H. "Confessions extatiques de Mīr Dāmād", in *Mélanges L. Massignon I* (Damascus, 1956), 331–78.

"La configuration du temple de la Ka'ba comme secret de la vie spirituelle", *Eranos Jahrbuch* xxxiv (Zurich, 1967), 79–166.
L'imagination créatrice dans le soufisme d'Ibn 'Arabi. Paris, 1958.
Le Livre des pénétrations. See Shīrāzī.
"*Mundus imaginalis* ou l'imaginaire et l'imaginal", *Cahiers internationaux de symbolisme* vi (1964), 3–26.
"La place de Mollâ Ṣadrâ Shîrâzî (ob. 1050/1640) dans la philosophie iranienne", *SI* xviii (1963), 81–113.
"Sayyid Ḥaydar Āmolī, théologien shi'ite du soufisme", in *Mélanges H. Massé* (Tehran, 1963), pp. 72–101.
"Le thème de la résurrection chez Mollā Ṣadrā Shīrāzī (1050/1640) commentateur de Sohrawardī (587/1191)", in *Studies in Mysticism and Religion presented to Gershom G. Scholem* (Jerusalem, 1967), pp. 71–115.
Terre céleste et corps de résurrection : De l'Iran mazdéen à l'Iran shī'ite. Paris, 1961.
Dānishpazhūh, M. T. *Fihrist-i kitābkhāna-yi ihdā'ī-yi Āqā-yi Sayyid Muḥammad Mishkāt*, 7 vols. Tehran, 1330/1951–1338/1959 (IDT 123, 168, 169, 181, 299, 303, 533).
Elgood, C. *A Medical History of Persia*. Cambridge, 1951.
Gobineau, Comte de. *Les religions et les philosophies dans l'Asie centrale*. Paris, 1923.
Gramlich, R. *Die schiitischen Derwischorden Persiens, Erster Teil: Affiliationen*. Wiesbaden, 1965.
*Herbert. *Travels in Persia*.
Hidāyat, Riżā Qulī Khān. *Riyāż al-'ārifīn*. Tehran, 1316.
Horten, M. *Das philosophische System des Shīrāzī*. Strasbourg, 1913.
*Iskandar Munshī, trans. Savory.
Izutsu, T. *The Key Philosophical Concepts in Sufism and Taoism* i. Tokyo, 1966.
Kāshānī, Faiż. *Maḥajjat al-baiżā' fī iḥyā' al-aḥyā*, ed. S. M. Mishkāt, 4 vols. Tehran, 1380–1.
Khunsārī, Muḥammad Bāqir. *Raużāt al-jannāt*. Tehran, 1306.
Lāhijānī, Mullā Muḥammad Ja'far. *Sharḥ risālat al-mashā'ir*, with introduction by S. J. Āshtiyānī. Mashhad, 1342.
Langarūdī, M. J. *Sharḥ al-mashā'ir*, ed. S. J. Āshtiyānī. Mashhad, 1384.
Nafīsī, Sa'īd. *Aḥvāl va ash'ār-i fārsī-yi Shaikh-i Bahā'ī*. Tehran, 1316.
Nasr, S. H. "Fakhr al-Dīn al-Rāzī", in Sharīf, *A History of Muslim Philosophy* i, 642–56.
Ideas and Realities of Islam. London, 1966.
An Introduction to Islamic Cosmological Doctrines. Cambridge, Mass., 1964.
Islamic Studies. Beirut, 1967.
"Mullā Ṣadrā", in *The Encyclopaedia of Philosophy* (New York, 1967).
(ed.) *Mullā Ṣadrā Commemoration Volume*. Tehran, 1340.
"Mullā Ṣadrā dar Hindūstān", *RK* iv (1340), 909–13.
"Sabziwārī", in Sharīf, *A History of Muslim Philosophy* ii, 1543–56.
"Ṣadr al-Dīn Shīrāzī", *ibid.*, pp. 932–61.
"The School of Ispahan", *ibid.*, pp. 904–32.

Science and Civilization in Islam. Cambridge, Mass., 1968.
"Seventh Century Ṣūfism and the School of Ibn 'Arabī", *JRCI* I/1 (1967), 45–50.
"Shi'ism and Ṣūfism : their relationship in essence and in history", *Religious Studies* VI (London 1970), 229–42.
"Suhrawardī", in Sharīf, *A History of Muslim Philosophy* I, 372–98.
Three Muslim Sages. Cambridge, Mass., 1964.
"'The World of Imagination' and the concept of space in the Persian Miniature", *IQ* XIII (1969), 129–34.
Nūrī, Ḥājj Mīrzā Ḥusain. *Mustadrak al-vasā'il*. Tehran, 1321.
Qazvīnī, Ḥājj Sayyid Abu'l-Ḥasan. "The Life of Ṣadr al-Muta'allihīn Shīrāzī", in Nasr, *Mullā Ṣadrā Commemoration Volume*, pp. 7–21.
Qumī, Qāżī Sa'īd. *Kitāb asrār al-'ibādat va ḥaqīqat al-ṣalāt*, ed. Sayyid Muḥammad Bāqir Sabzavārī. Tehran, 1339.
Sabzavārī, Muḥammad 'Alī. *Tuḥfat al-'abbāsiyya*. Shīrāz, 1326.
Sajjādī, S. J. *Muṣṭalaḥāt-i falsafī-yi Ṣadr al-Dīn Shīrāzī*. Tehran, 1340.
Sharīf, M. M. (ed.). *A History of Muslim Philosophy*, 2 vols. Wiesbaden, 1966.
al-Shībī, M. K. *al-Fikr al-shī'ī wa'l-naza'āt al-ṣūfiyya*. Baghdad, 1966.
al-Ṣilah bain al-taṣawwuf wa'l-tashayyu', 2 vols. Baghdad, 1963–4.
Shīrāzī, Maṣ'ūm 'Alī Shāh. *Ṭarā'iq al-ḥaqā'iq*, 2 vols. Tehran, 1339.
Shīrāzī, Ṣadr al-Dīn. *Dīvān*. Printed at the end of *Sih aṣl*, ed. Nasr (below).
al-Ḥikmat al-muta'āliyya fi'l-asfār al-arba'at al-'aqliyya, ed. A. S. M. H. Ṭabāṭabā'ī, 5 vols. so far published. Tehran, 1358/1978–.
Kasr al-aṣnām al-jāhiliyya fī radd 'alā mutaṣawwifī zamānihi, ed. M. T. Dānishpazhūh. Tehran, 1340.
Kitāb al-mashā'ir, ed. and trans. H. Corbin, *Le livre des pénétrations metaphysiques*. Tehran and Paris, 1964.
al-Shawāhid al-rubūbiyya, ed. S. J. Āshtiyānī, with English preface by S. H. Nasr. Mashhad, 1967.
Sih aṣl, ed. S. H. Nasr. Tehran, 1340.
Shushtarī, Nūr-Allāh. *Majālis al-mu'minīn*. Tehran, 1375.
Suhravardī, Shihāb al-Dīn 'Umar b. Muḥammad. *Opera metaphysica et mystica*, ed. H. Corbin, 3 vols. Istanbul, 1945; Teḥran and Paris, 1952–70.
Tabrīzī, Muḥammad 'Alī. *Raiḥānat al-adab*, 6 vols. Tehran, 1331–3.
Ṭihrānī, Āqā Buzurg. *al-Ẕarī'a*. al-Najaf, 1936–.
Tunakābunī, Muḥammad Ḥusain. *Qiṣaṣ al-'ulamā*. Tehran, 1313.
al-Zanjānī, A. *al-Failasūf al-fārsī al-kabīr Ṣadr al-Dīn al-Shīrāzī*. Damascus, 1936.

CHAPTER 14

For a general survey one should refer to the following large volumes of illustrations. In connection with the first Exhibition of Oriental Carpets in Vienna in 1891 the three-volume *Orientalische Teppiche* (Vienna, London, Paris) appeared in 1892. The first proposed classification was published by F. R. Martin in *A History of Oriental Carpets before 1800* (Vienna, 1908, 2 vols.). Two years after the Exhibition of Mohammedan Art in Munich in 1910 there appeared F. Sarre and F. R. Martin, *Die Ausstellung von Meisterwerken Muhammedanischer Kunst in München 1910* (Munich, 1912, 3 vols. and a supplement), a work equally important for both carpets and fabrics. The best colour plates are to be found in F. Sarre and H. Trenkwald, *Alt-orientalische Teppiche* (2 vols. Vienna, 1926–8): Volume I by Trenkwald is devoted entirely to the exhibits of the Österreichisches Museum für angewandte Kunst in Vienna, while in Volume II Sarre deals with important carpets in various public and private collections. The comprehensive Exhibition of Persian Art in London in 1931 led to the publication of **SPA*, which contains the largest compendium of Safavid carpets and fabrics.

Fundamental information is also supplied by W.v. Bode and E. Kühnel, *Vorderasiatische Knüpfteppiche*, (4th edition Braunschweig, 1955); trans. C. G. Ellis, *Antique Rugs from the Near East* (Braunschweig, 1958); by A. U. Dilley, *Oriental Rugs and Carpets* (New York, Philadelphia, 1954, revised by M. S. Dimand); and by K. Erdmann in *Der orientalische Knüpfteppich* (Tübingen, 1955), trans. C. G. Ellis, *Oriental Carpets*, New York, 1962. K. Erdmann here compiles an extensive bibliography of Oriental carpets which is a splendid source of information, not least because it is a classified list. On the subject of carpet techniques a useful handbook is C. E. C. Tattersall, *Notes on Carpet-Knotting and Weaving* (London, 1961, Victoria and Albert Museum).

Specifically on the fabrics see also O. v. Falke, *Kunstgeschichte der Seidenweberei* (Berlin, 1913, 2 vols.), F. R. Martin, *Die persischen Prachtstoffe im Schlosse Rosenborg in Kopenhagen* (Stockholm, 1901) and – particularly for their bibliography – H. J. Schmidt, *Alte Seidenstoffe* (Braunschweig, 1958) and A. C. Weibel, *Two Thousand Years of Textiles* (New York, 1952). Information about the technique of Persian fabrics is supplied by N. A. Reath and E. B. Sachs, *Persian Textiles and their Technique from the Sixth to the Eighteenth Centuries* (New Haven, Conn., 1937).

The most comprehensive bibliography of Islamic art is K. A. C. Cresswell, *A Bibliography of the Architecture, Arts and Crafts of Islam to 1st January 1960*, The American University at Cairo Press (London, 1961).

Ackermann, P. "A Biography of Ghiyath the Weaver", *BAIPAA* VII (1934), 9–13.

Briggs, A. "Timurid Carpets", *AI* VII (1940), 20–54; XI–XII (1946), 146–58.

*Chardin

Cunaeus, J. *Journaal der Reis van den Gezant der O.I. Compagnie Joan Cunaeus naar Perzië in 1651–52 door Cornelis Speelman*, ed. A. Hotz. Amsterdam, 1908.

*Della Valle

Dimand, M. S. *A Handbook of Muhammadan Art*. 3rd ed. New York, 1958.

"A Persian Garden Carpet in the Jaipur Museum", *AI* VII (1940), 93–6.

*Don Juan, trans. Le Strange

*Du Mans

Edwards, A. C. "Persian Carpets", in *The Legacy of Persia*, ed. A. J. Arberry (Oxford, 1953), pp. 230–58.

Erdmann, K. "Ein persischer Wirkteppich der Safawidenzeit", *Pantheon* XXI (1938), 62–6.

"Persische Wirkteppiche der Safidenzeit [*sic*]", *Pantheon* x (1932), 227–31.
Siebenhundert Jahre Orientteppich. Herford, 1966.
review of Pope, "Art of Carpet Making", in *AI* VII (1940), 121–91.
Glück, H., and Diez, E. *Die Kunst des Islam*. Berlin, 1925 (Propyläen-Kunstgeschichte 5).
Grube, E. J. *The Classical Style in Islamic Painting*. New York, 1968.
The World of Islam. London, 1967.
Iran, Persian Miniatures – Imperial Library. Paris, 1956.
*Kaempfer
Krusiński, Tadeusz. *Tragica vertentis belli Persici Historia per repetitas clades, ab anno 1711 ad annum 1728*. Leopoli, 1740.
Kühnel, E. "Christliche Motive in der persischen Malerei", in *Kunstgeschichtliche Studien für Hans Kauffmann* (Berlin, 1956), pp. 120–6.
McMullan, J. V. *Islamic Carpets*. New York, 1965.
Mańkowski, T. "Note on the Cost of the Kashan Carpets at the Beginning of the Seventeenth Century", *BAIPAA* IV (1936), 152–3.
Niño Jésus, Florencio del. "A Persia (1604–9)", in *Biblioteca Carmelitana-Tere-siana de Misiones* II (Pampluna, 1929).
Olearius, Adam. *Vermehrte Beschreibung der Muscowitischen und Persischen Reyse*. Schleswig, 1656.
Pope, A. U. "The Art of Carpet Making. History", in *SPA*, pp. 2257–430; see also Erdmann (above).
Ross, Sir E. Denison. *Sir Anthony Sherley and his Persian Adventure*. London, 1933.
Sackville-West, V. "Persian Gardens", in *The Legacy of Persia*, ed. A. J. Arberry (Oxford, 1953), pp. 259–91.
Sakisian, A. B. *La Miniature Persane du XIIe au XVIIe siècle*. Paris and Brussels, 1929.
Sarre, F., and Mittwoch, E. *Zeichnungen von Riza Abbasi*. Munich, 1914.
Schillinger, Franz Caspar. *Persianische und Ost-Indianische Reis*. Nürnberg, 1709.
Silva y Figueroa, Don Garcia de. *L'ambassade de D. Garcias de Silva Figueroa en Perse*, trans. de Wicqfort. Paris, 1667.
Spuhler, F. "Der figurale Kaschan-Wirkteppich. Aus den Sammlungen des regierenden Fürsten von Liechtenstein", *KO* v (1968), 55–61.
*Stchoukine. *Manuscrits de Shāh ʿAbbās*.
**Manuscrits Ṣafavīs*.
*Tavernier
*Teixeira

CHAPTERS 15(a) AND (b)

Afshār, Īraj. *Yādgārhā-yi Yazd*, 2 vols in 3. Tehran, 1348–54/1969–75.
Akten des VII. Internationalen Kongresses für Iranische Kunst und Archäologie. Berlin, 1979.
Ardalan, N., and Bakhtiar, L. *The Sense of Unity. The Sufi Tradition in Persian Architecture*. Chicago and London, 1973.

Bakhtiyar, A. A. "The Masjid Ali of Isfahan", *Bulletin of the Asia Institute of Pahlavi University* I (1969).

Bāstānī-Parīzī, M. E. "L'Ensemble de Ganj Ali Xân à Kerman", in *VIth International Congress of Iranian Art and Archaeology. Memorial Volume* (Tehran, 1976), pp. 13–20.

Rahnumā-yi āṣār-i tārīkhī-yi Kirmān. Tehran, 1335/1956.

Baudouin, E. E. "Isphahan sous les grands Chahs", *Urbanisme* x (Paris, 1932), 1–47.

*Beveridge. *The Bābur-nāma in English*.

Brandenburg, D. *Die Madrasa, Ursprung, Entwicklung, Ausbreitung und künstlerische Gestaltung der islamischen Moschee-Hochschule*. Graz, 1978.

Bruin, C. de. *Voyages*, 2 vols. Amsterdam, 1718.

Carswell, J. *New Julfa: The Armenian churches and other buildings*. Oxford, 1968.

*Clavijo, trans. Le Strange.

Cohn-Wiener, E. *Turan. Islamische Baukunst in Mittelasien*. Berlin, 1930.

Coste, P. *Monuments modernes de la Perse*. Paris, 1865.

Daridan, J., and Stelling-Michaud, S. *La peinture séfévide d'Ispahan. Le palais d'Ala Qapy*. Paris, 1930.

Dībāj, Ismā'īl. *Āṣār-i bāstānī va abniyā-yi tārīkhī-yi Āzarbāījān*. 1346.

Rāhnumā-yi tārīkhī-yi Āzarbāījān-i Sharqī. Tabrīz, 1343/1955.

Diez, E. *Churasanische Baudenkmäler* I. Berlin, 1918.

Foroughi, M., *et al. Masterpieces of Iranian architecture*. Tehran, n.d. (*c.* 1975).

al-Gailānī, 'Abd al-Raḥmān. *Islamic Art and the Role of China*. Unpublished Ph.D. thesis, Edinburgh, 1973.

Galdieri, E. *Esfahān: Alī Qāpū; an architectural survey*. Rome, 1979.

"Relecture d'une gravure allemande du XVIIe siècle comme introduction à une recherche archéologique", in *Akten des VII. Internationalen Kongresses*, pp. 560–70.

"Two Building Phases of the Time of Šāh 'Abbās I in the Maydan-i Šāh of Isfahan. Preliminary Note", *East and West* n.s. xx (1970), 60–9.

Galdieri, E., and Orazi, R. *Progetto di sistemazione del Maydan-i Šāh*. Rome, 1969.

Godard, A. "Historique du Masdjid-é Djum'a d'Iṣfahān", *Athār-é Īrān* I (1936), 213–82.

"Les anciennes mosquées de l'Īrān", *Athār-è Īrān* I (1936), 187–210, and *AA* III (1956), 48–63, 83–8.

"Iṣfahān", *Athār-é Īrān* II (1937), 1–176.

"Khorasan", *Athār-é Īrān* IV (1949), 7–150.

"Muḥammad Riḍā al-Imāmī", *Athār-é Īrān* III (1937), 267–74.

"Le tombeau de Mawlânâ Ḥasan Kâshî à Sulṭânîyè", *AA* I (1954), 23–39.

Golombek, L. "Anatomy of a mosque – the Masjid-i Shah of Isfahan", in *Iranian Civilization and Culture*, ed. C. J. Adams (Montreal, 1972), 5–11.

"The chronology of Turbat-i Shaikh Jām", *Iran* IX (1971), 27–44.

"The Cult of Saints and Shrine Architecture in the Fourteenth Century", in *Near Eastern Numismatics, Iconography, Epigraphy and History. Studies in Honor of George C. Miles*, ed. D. Kouymjian (Beirut, 1974), 419–30.

The Timurid Shrine at Gazur Gah. Toronto, 1969 (Royal Ontario Museum Occasional Papers 15).
"Urban patterns in pre-Safavid Isfahan", *IrSt* VII (1974), 18–44.
Grabar, O. "Isfahan as a Mirror of Persian Architecture", in *Highlights of Persian Art*, ed. R. Ettinghausen and E. Yarshater (Boulder, Co., 1979), pp. 213–41.
Gray, B. "The Tradition of Wall Painting in Iran", *ibid.*, pp. 321–7.
Gropp, G., and Najmabadi, S. "Ein Gedicht von Hafez in einem Safavidenpalast", *AMI* II (1969), 193–6.
Grube, E. J. "The Language of the Birds; the seventeenth-century miniatures", *MMAB* XXV (1967), 339–52.
Grube, E. J., and Sims, E. G. "Wall paintings in the seventeenth century monuments of Isfahan", *IrSt* VII (1974), 511–42.
Hill, D., and Grabar, O. *Islamic Architecture and its Decoration, A.D. 800–1500*. London, 1964.
Hillenbrand, R. "The Use of Glazed Tilework in Iranian Islamic Architecture", in *Akten des VII. Internationalen Kongresses*, pp. 545–54.
The Tomb Towers of Iran to 1550. Unpublished D.Phil. thesis, Oxford, 1974.
Hinz, W. "Beiträge zur iranischen Kulturgeschichte", *ZDMG* XCI (1937), 58–79.
Historical Monuments of Islam in the U.S.S.R. (Muslim Religious Board of Central Asia and Kazakhstan) Tashkent, 1962.
Hrbas, M., and Knobloch, E. *The Art of Central Asia*. London, 1965.
Hunarfar. **Ganjīna*.
"Maidān-i Naqsh-i Jahān-i Iṣfahān", *Hunar va Mardum* CV (July 1971), 2–28.
Kaempfer, E. *Amoenitatum exoticarum*. Lemgo, 1712.
Khoubnazar, H., and Kleiss, W. "Die Madrasa-yi Ḫān in Schiras", *AMI* VIII (1975), 255–78.
Kiani, M. Y. "Robat Zayn al-Din: a masterpiece of Safavid architecture", *Bāstān-shināsī va Hunar-i Īrān* IX–X (1972), 27–31.
"The British Museum manuscript on Safavid caravansarais in Isfahan", *Bāstān-Shināsī va Hunar-i Irān* V (Tehran, 1970).
Kleiss, W. "Bericht über Erkundungsfahrten in Iran im Jahre 1971", *AMI* V (1972), 135–242.
"Der safavidische Pavillon in Qazvin", *AMI* IX (1976), 290–8.
Lane, A. *Later Islamic Pottery*. 2nd ed. London, 1971.
A Guide to the collection of tiles. London, 1960.
Luschey, H. "Der königliche Marstall in Iṣfahān in Engelbert Kaempfers Planographia des Palastbezirkes 1712", *Iran* XVII (1979), 71–9.
Luschey-Schmeisser, I. "Ein neuer Raum in Nayin", *AMI* V (1972), 309–14.
The Pictorial Tile Cycle of Hašt Behešt in Isfahan and its Iconographic Tradition. Rome, 1978.
"Der Wand- und Deckenschmuck eines safavidischen Palastes in Nāyīn", *AMI* II (1969), 183–92.

Man'kovskaya, L. Yu. "K izucheniyu priemov sredneaziatskogo zodchestva, kontsa XIV v. (Mavzoleĭ Khodzha Akhmeda Yasevi)", in *Iskusstvo zodchikh Uzbekistana* (Tashkent, 1962).

Masterpieces of Iranian Architecture, published by the Ministry of Development and Housing with cooperation of Society of Iranian Architects. Sept. 1970.

Maulavī, A. *Āṣār-i bāstānī-yi Khurāsān*. Mashhad, 1354/1975.

Mechkati, N. *Monuments et sites historiques de l'Iran*, trans. I. Sepahbodi and I. Behnam. Tehran, n.d.

Mora, P. "La restauration des peintures murales de Čihil Sutūn", in Zander, *Travaux*, pp. 323–82.

Morton, A. H., "The Ardabil Shrine in the Reign of Tahmasp I", *Iran* XII (1974), 31–64; (concluded) XIII (1975), 39–58.

Les Mosquées de Samarcande, fasc. 1. *Le Gour-Emir*. (Commission Impériale Archéologique) St Petersburg, 1905.

Müller, K. *Die Karawanserai im Vorderen Orient*. Berlin, 1920.

Narāqī, H. *Āṣār-i tārīkhī-yi shahristānhā-yi Kāshān va Naṭanz*. Tehran, n.d.

**A Narrative of Italian Travels*.

O'Kane, B. "The Madrasa al-Ghiyāsiyya at Khargird", *Iran* XIV (1976), 79–92.

"Taybād,Turbat-i Jam and Timurid Vaulting", *Iran* XVII (1979), 87–103.

Orazi, R. *Grate lignee nell'architettura safavide. Studi e restauri a Esfahān*. Rome, 1976.

Pickett, G. D. *The efflorescence of Persian kāshī: the glazed architectural decoration of Islamic Iran in the Mongol and Muzaffarid periods*. Unpublished Ph.D. thesis, London, 1981.

"Inscriptions by Muḥammad Riḍā al-Imāmī", *Iran* XXII (1984), 91–102.

Pope, A. U. *Persian architecture*. London, 1965.

"Representations of living forms in Persian mosques", *Bulletin of the Iranian Institute* VI–VII (1946), 125–9.

Pope, A. U., and Katchadourian, S. *Persian Fresco Paintings*. New York, 1932 (Publications of the American Institute for Persian Art and Archaeology 4).

Pugachenkova, G. A., and Rempel', L. N. **Istoriya Iskusstv Uzbekistana*.

Vydayushchiĭsya Pamyatniki Arkhitektury Uzbekistana. Tashkent, 1958.

Ratiya, E. E. *Mechet' Bibi-Khanym*. Moscow, 1950.

Rempel', L. I. *Arkhitekturnyĭ Ornament Uzbekistana*. Tashkent, 1961.

Sa'ādat, Bīzhan. *Bārgāh-i Rizā (The Holy Shrine of Iman Reza, Mashhad)*, 4 vols. (Persian and English). The Asia Institute, Pahlavi University, Shiraz, 1976.

Sarre, F. *Denkmäler persischer Baukunst*. Berlin, 1901–10.

Sauvaget, J. "Notes épigraphiques sur quelques monuments persans", *AI* V (1938), 103–6.

Seherr-Thoss, S. P. and H. *Design and Color in Islamic Architecture*. Washington, 1968.

Serajuddin, A. *Architectural Representations in Persian Miniature Painting during the Timurid and Safavid Periods*. Unpublished Ph.D. thesis, London, 1968.

Shokoohy, M. *Studies in the Early Mediaeval Architecture of Iran and Afghanistan.* Unpublished Ph.D. thesis, Heriot-Watt University, 1978.

Siroux, M. **Caravansérails.*

"Les caravanserais routiers safavids [*sic*]", *IrSt* VII (1974), 348–75.

Anciennes Voies et Monuments Routiers de la Région d'Ispahan. Cairo, 1971.

"La Masjid-e djum'a de Yezd", *BIFAO* XLIV (1947), 119–76.

Stevens, Sir Roger. "European visitors to the Safavid court", *IrSt* VII (1974), 421–57.

Sutūda, M. *Az Āstārā tā Astarābād*, 2 vols. Tehran, 1349–51/1970–2.

Sykes, P. M. "Historical Notes on Khurasan", *JRAS* 1910, 1146–8.

Ṭabāṭabā'ī, M. *Turbat-i Pākān*, 2 vols. Qum, 1354/1975.

Watson, O. "Persian lustre ware from the 14th to the 19th centuries", *MII* III (1975), 63–80.

Weaver, M. E. *Preliminary Study on the Conservation Problems of Five Iranian Monuments.* Paris, 1970.

The Conservation of the Shrine of Sheikh Safi at Ardabil: Second Preliminary Study. Paris, 1971.

Welch, A. *Shāh 'Abbās and the Arts of Isfahan.* New York, 1973.

Wilber, D. *The Architecture of Islamic Iran, the Il-Khanid Period.* Princeton, 1955.

"Aspects of the Safavid ensemble at Isfahan", *IrSt* VII (1974), 406–15.

"The Development of Mosaic Faience in Islamic Architecture in Iran", *AI* VI (1939), 16–47.

Persian Gardens and Garden Pavilions. Rutland, Vermont, and Tokyo, 1962.

Yate, C. E. *Northern Afghanistan, or Letters from the Afghan Boundary Commission.* London, 1888.

Zander, G. "Observations sur l'architecture civile d'Ispahan", *IrSt* VII (1974), 294–319.

"La restauration de quelques monuments historiques d'Ispahan: une nouvelle lumière sur les problèmes d'histoire de l'architecture s'y rattachant", in *Vth International Congress* II, 246–59.

(ed.) *Travaux de restauration de monuments historiques en Iran.* Rome, 1968.

Vth International Congress of Iranian Art and Archaeology. Memorial Volume II. Tehran, 1972.

CHAPTERS 16(a) AND (b)

Aga-Oğlu, M. "Preliminary Notes on some Persian Illustrated MSS. in the Topkapu Sarayi Müzesi, part I", *AI* I (1934), 183–99.

Akimushkin, O. F., and Ivanov, A. A. *Persidskie miniatyury XIV–XVII vv.* Moscow, 1968.

Arnold, T. W. *Painting in Islam.* Oxford, 1928.

Bihzād and his paintings in the Zafar-nāmah MS. London, 1930.

The Arts of Islam. Exhibition Catalogue, The Hayward Gallery. (Arts Council of Great Britain) London, 1976.

Aslanapa, Oktay. "The Art of Bookbinding", in Gray, *Arts of the Book*, pp. 59–91.

Atasoy, Nurhan. "Four Istanbul Albums and some fragments from fourteenth century Shah-namehs", *AO* VIII (1970), 19–48.
Aubin, J. "Le mécénat timouride à Chiraz", *SI* VIII (1957), 71–88.
Barrett, D. *Persian Painting in the fourteenth century*. London, 1952.
Barrett, D., and Gray, B. *Painting of India*. Geneva, 1963 (Treasures of Asia v).
Barthold, W. "Mir Ali Shir", in **Four Studies* III.
Binyon, L. *The Poems of Nizami*. London, 1928.
Binyon, L., Wilkinson, J. V. S. and Gray, B. *Persian Miniature Painting, including a critical and descriptive catalogue of the miniatures exhibited at Burlington House, Jan.–March 1931*. Oxford, 1933, repr. 1972.
Blochet, E. *Musulman Painting, XII–XVII century*. London, 1929.
Blunt, W. *Pietro's Pilgrimage*. London, 1953.
Boase, T. S. R. "A Typological Cycle of Paintings in the Armenian Cathedral in Julfa", *Journal of the Warburg and Courtauld Institutes* XIII (London, 1950), 323–7.
Carswell, J. *New Julfa : the Armenian churches and other buildings*. Oxford, 1968.
*Chardin.
Chester Beatty Library. Catalogue of the Persian manuscripts and miniatures, 3 vols. Dublin, 1959–62.
Çiğ, Kemal. *Türk ve Islam Eserleri Müzesi'ndeki Minyatürlü Kitapların Kataloğu*. Istanbul, 1959.
"The Iranian lacquer technique work in the Topkapi Saray Museum", in *Vth International Congress* II, 24–33.
*Clavijo, trans. Le Strange.
*Della Valle.
Denike, B. "Quelques monuments de bois scupltés au Turkestan occidental", *AI* II (1935), 69–83.
Dimand, M. S. *A Handbook of Muhammadan Art*. New York, 1958.
D'yakonova, N. V. and Gyuzal'yan, L. T. *Sredneaziatskie miniatyury XVI–XVIII vv*. Moscow, 1964.
Erdmann, K. *Iranische Kunst in Deutschen Museen*. Wiesbaden, 1967.
Ettinghausen, R. "Near Eastern Book Covers and their Influence on European Bindings", *AO* III (1959), 113-31.
(ed.) *Islamic Art in the Metropolitan Museum of Art*. New York, 1972.
Gandjeï, T. "Notes on the Life and Work of Ṣādiqī : A Poet and Painter of Ṣafavid Times", *Der Islam* LII (1975), 112–18.
Golombek, L. *The Timurid Shrine at Gazur Gah*. Toronto, 1969 (Royal Ontario Museum Occasional Papers 15).
Gray, B. "An Album of Designs for Persian Textiles", in *Aus der Welt der islamischen Kunst : Festschrift für Ernst Kühnel*, ed. R. Ettinghausen (Berlin, 1959), pp. 219–25.
(ed.) *The Arts of the Book in Central Asia, 14th–16th centuries*. London, 1979.
Persian Miniatures from ancient Manuscripts. New York, 1962.
Persian Painting. London, 1930.
Persian Painting. Geneva, 1961 (Treasures of Asia II).
Persian Painting from miniatures of the XIII–XVI centuries. London, 1947.

The Shahnameh of Ferdowsi, the Baysonghori manuscript : an album of miniatures and illuminations. Tehran, 1971.
"Some Chinoiserie drawings and their origin", in *Forschungen zur Kunst Asiens; in Memoriam K. Erdmann*, ed. O. Aslanapa and R. Naumann (Istanbul, 1969), pp. 159–71.
"The Tradition of Wall Painting in Iran", in *Highlights of Persian Art*, ed. R. Ettinghausen and E. Yarshater (Boulder, Co., 1979), pp. 321–7.
Grube, E. J. *The Classical Style in Islamic Painting*. New York, 1968.
Miniature islamiche dal XIII al XIX secolo. Venice, 1962.
"Notes on the Decorative Arts of the Timurid period", in *Gurarājamañjarikā: studi in onore di Giuseppe Tucci* (Naples, 1974), pp. 233–79.
The World of Islam. New York, 1966.
Grube, E. J., and Sims, E. G. "Wall paintings in the seventeenth century monuments of Isfahan", *IrSt* VII (1974), 511–42.
Gulbenkian Foundation: Exhibition of Islamic Art. Lisbon, 1963.
Gyuzal'yan, L. T., and D'yakonov, M. M. *Iranskie miniatyury v rukopisyakh Shakh-Name leningradskikh sobraniĭ*. Leningrad, 1935.
Hill, D., and Grabar, O. *Islamic Architecture and its Decoration, A.D. 800–1500*. London, 1964.
*Hunarfar. *Ganjīna*.
Inal, Güner. "Artistic relationship between the Far and Near East as reflected in the miniatures of the Gami' at-Tawarikh", *KO* x (1976), 108–43.
Iran, Persian Miniatures – Imperial Library. (UNESCO) Paris, 1956.
Ivanov, A. A., Grek, T. V., and Akimushkin, O. F. *Al'bom Indiĭskikh i Persidskikh Miniatyur XVI–XVIII vv*. Moscow, 1962.
Kühnel, E. *Islamische Kleinkunst*. Braunschweig, 1963.
Miniaturmalerei im islamischen Orient. Berlin, 1923 (Kunst des Ostens 7).
Lane, A. *Later Islamic Pottery*. 2nd ed. London, 1957.
*Lockhart. *The Fall*.
Luckey-Schmeisser, I. "Der Wand- und Deckenschmuck eines safavidischen Palastes in Nāyīn", *AMI* II (1969), 183–92.
Lukens, M. G. "The Language of the Birds; the fifteenth-century miniatures", *MMAB* xxv (1967), 317–38.
Mahfuz ul-Haq, M. "Persian painters, illuminators, and calligraphists, etc., in the 16th century A.D.", *JASB* n.s. XXVIII (1932), 239–49.
Marteau, G., and Vever, H. *Miniatures persanes exposées au Musée des Arts Décoratifs*, 2 vols. Paris, 1913.
Martin, F. R. *The Miniature Painting and Painters of Persia, India and Turkey from the 8th to the 18th century*, 2 vols. London, 1912.
Miniatures from the period of Timur in a MS of the Poems of Sultan Ahmad Jalair. Vienna, 1926.
*Minorsky. *Tadhkirat al-Mulūk*.
Nott, C. S. *The Conference of the Birds, by Farid ud-Din Attar: a translation of the Persian poem Mantiq ut-Tair*. London, 1954.
Özergin, M. Kemal. "Temürlü sanatına âit eski bir belge: Tebrizli Ca'fer'in bir arzi", *Sanat Tarihi Yıllıgı* VI (1974-5), 471–518.

Persian Art: Calouste Gulbenkian Collection. Lisbon, 1972.
Pinder-Wilson, R. "Bihzad", in *Enciclopedia Universale dell'Arte* (Venice and Rome, 1960), pp. 600–4.
Persian Painting in the fifteenth century. London, 1958.
Pope, J. A. *Chinese Porcelains from the Ardebil Shrine.* Washington, 1956.
*Pugachenkova and Rempel'. *Istoriya Iskusstv Uzbekistana.*
Qāżī Aḥmad. *Calligraphers and painters; a treatise by Qāḍī Aḥmad, son of Mīr-Munshī,* trans. V. Minorsky. Washington, 1959.
Qazvīnī, Mīrzā Muḥammad. "An Account of the *Mu'nisu'l-Aḥrār*", *BSOS* v (1928–30), 97–108.
Qazvīnī, Mīrzā Muḥammad, and Bouvat, L. "Deux documents inédits relatifs à Behzâd", *RMM* xxvi (1914), 146–61.
Reitlinger, G. "The Interim Period in Persian Pottery: an essay in chronological revision", *AI* v (1938), 155–78.
Robinson, B. W. *Drawings of the Masters; Persian Drawings.* New York, 1965.
Persian Miniature Painting from collections in the British Isles. London, 1967.
"Prince Bāysonghor's Niẓāmī: a speculation", *AO* ii (1957), 383–91.
"The Shahnameh Manuscript Cochran 4 in the Metropolitan Museum of Art", in Ettinghausen, *Islamic Art in the Metropolitan Museum*, pp. 73–9.
"The Tehran manuscript of *Kalīla wa Dimna.* A reconstruction", *Oriental Art* n.s. iv (1958), 108–15.
"Two Persian manuscripts in the library of the Marquess of Bute: part II. *Anwar-i Suhayli* of 1593", *Oriental Art* n.s. xviii (1972), 50–6.
"An Unpublished Manuscript of the Gulistan of Sa'di", in *Beiträge zur Kunstgeschichte Asiens. In Memoriam Ernst Diez*, ed. O. Aslanapa (Istanbul, 1963), pp. 223–36.
Robinson, B. W., Grube, E. J., Meredith-Owens, G., and Skelton, R. W. *The Keir Collection: Islamic painting and the arts of the book*, 3 vols. London, 1976.
Sakisian, A. B. *La Miniature Persane du XIIe au XVIIe siècle.* Paris and Brussels, 1929.
"Maḥmūd Mudhahib – miniaturiste, enlumineur et calligraphe persan", *AI* iv (1937), 338–48.
Sarre, F., and Martin, F. R. *Die Ausstellung von Meisterwerken muhammedanischer Kunst in München 1910*, 3 vols. Munich, 1912.
Schroeder, E. *Persian Miniatures in the Fogg Museum of Art.* Cambridge, Mass., 1942.
Schulz, P. W. *Die persisch-islamische Miniaturmalerei.* Leipzig, 1914.
Stchoukine, I. "Une Khamseh de Niẓāmī de la fin du règne de Shah Rokh", *AA* xvii (1968), 45–58.
Les miniatures persanes: Musée National du Louvre. Paris, 1932.
"Les peintures de la Khamseh de Nizami", *Syria* xxvii (1950), 301–13.
Les peintures des manuscrits de la 'Khamseh' de Nizami au Topkapi Sarayi Müzesi d'Istanbul. Paris, 1977.
**Manuscrits Ṣafavīs.*
**Manuscrits de Shāh 'Abbās.*
**Manuscrits Tîmûrides.*

Swietochowski, M. L. "The Historical Background and illustrative character of the Metropolitan Museum's *Mantiq al-Tair*", in Ettinghausen, *Islamic Art in the Metropolitan Museum*, pp. 39–72.

Titley, N. "A Fourteenth Century Khamseh of Nizami", *BMQ* xxxvi (1972), 8–11.

Varkhotov, D. "Newly found ceramics of the xv-end of xvi centuries in Tashkent" [in Russian], *Obshchestvennye Nauki v Uzbekistane* viii–ix (Tashkent, 1969), 86–9.

Watson, O. "Persian lustre ware from the 14th to the 19th centuries", *MII* iii (1975), 63–80.

Welch, A. *Artists for the Shah: late sixteenth century painting at the Imperial court of Iran.* Yale, 1976.

Shah 'Abbās and the Arts of Isfahan. New York, 1973.

Welch, S. C. *A King's Book of Kings, the Shah-nameh of Shah Tahmasp.* New York, 1972.

Persian Painting: five royal Safavid manuscripts of the sixteenth century. New York, 1976.

Wonders of the Age: masterpieces of early Safavid painting, 1501–76. New York, 1979.

Yakubovsky, A. G. "Mastera Irana v Sredneĭ Azii pri Timure", in *IIIe Congrès d'Art et d'Archéologie Iraniens: Mémoires* (Leningrad, 1939), pp. 277–85.

Zander, G. (ed.) *Travaux de restauration de monuments historiques en Iran.* Rome, 1968.

Zick-Nissen, J. "Die Tebriser Meister und Kunsthandwerkliche Produkte in Berliner Sammlungen", in *Festschrift für Peter Wilhelm Meister*, ed. A. Ohm and H. Reber (Hamburg, 1975), pp. 62–70.

Vth International Congress of Iranian Art and Archaeology. Memorial Volume, 2 vols. Tehran, 1972.

VIth International Congress of Iranian Art and Archaeology. Memorial Volume, Tehran, 1976.

7000 Ans d'art en Iran. Paris, 1961.

7000 Years of Iranian Art. Washington, 1964.

CHAPTERS 17(a), 17(c) AND 18

As the poets mentioned in these chapters are numerous and their works are very often available in more than one edition, only those who have been examined in some detail are represented in this bibliography. For the chroniclers, see the bibliographies to chapters 1–5 (primary sources); and for writers on religious or philosophical matters, see those to chapters 11 and 12.

'Abd al-Ghanī, Muḥammad. *A History of Persian Language and Literature at the Mughal Court (Bābur to Akbar)* i–ii. Allāhābād, 1929; iii, Allāhābād, 1930.

'Abd al-Nabī Qazvīnī. *Tazkira-yi maikhāna*, ed. A. Gulchīn-i Ma'ānī. Tehran, 1961 (includes Muḥammad Shafī''s introduction from his Lahore edition of 1926).

Arberry, A. J. *Classical Persian Literature.* London, 1958.

Āryānpūr, Yaḥyā. *Az Ṣabā tā Nīmā*, 2 vols. Tehran, 1972.

Aṣlaḥ, Muḥammad. *Tazkira-yi shu'arā-yi Kashmīr*, ed. Ḥusām al-Dīn Rashīdī. Karachi, 1967.

Badā'unī, 'Abd al-Qādir. *Muntakhab al-tavārīkh*, ed. M. A. 'Alī, 3 vols. Calcutta, 1868–9.
Dashtī, 'Alī. *Nigāhība Ṣā'ib*. Tehran, 1977.
Daulatshāh b. 'Alā' al-Daula Samarqandī. *Taẕkirat al-shu'arā*, ed. E. G. Browne, Leiden and London, 1901.
*Falsafī. *Zindagānī*.
Faṣīḥ-i Khwāfī. *Mujmal-i Faṣīḥī*, ed. Maḥmūd Farrukh, 3 vols. Mashhad, 1339–41/1960–2.
Fighānī. *Dīvān*, ed. S. Khwānsarī. Tehran, 1937.
Gibb, E. J. W. *A History of Ottoman Poetry* I. London, 1900, repr. 1965.
Gulchīn-i Ma'ānī, A. *Tārīkh-i taẕkirahā-yi Fārsī*, 2 vols. Tehran, 1969–71.
Ḥāfiẓ. *Dīvān*, ed. Qāsim Ghanī and Muḥammad Qazvīnī. Tehran, 1320/1941–2.
Ḥāfiẓ-i Abrū. *Cinq opuscules de Ḥāfiẓ-i Abrū*, ed. Felix Tauer. Prague, 1959.
Ẕail-i Jāmi' al-tavārīkh, ed. Khān-bābā Bayānī. 2nd ed. Tehran, 1350/1971.
Ḥazīn, Shaikh 'Alī. *Kulliyyāt*. Cawnpore, 1893.
Taẕkirat al-aḥvāl, ed. F. C. Balfour. London, 1831. Trans. *idem*, *The Life of Sheikh Mohammed Ali Hazin*. London, 1830.
Hidāyat, Riżā Qulī Khān. *Majma' al-fuṣaḥā*, ed. M. Muṣaffā, 6 vols. Tehran, 1957–61.
**HIL*
Isfizārī, Mu'īn al-Dīn. *Rauẓāt al-jannāt fī auṣāf madīnat Harāt*, ed. Muḥammad Kāẓim Imām, 2 vols. Tehran, 1338/1959.
Iskandar Beg Munshī. *Tārīkh-i 'ālam-ārā-yi 'Abbāsī*. Tehran, 1314/1935–6; *trans. Savory.
Jahānbānī, Muḥammad Ḥusain. *Gulchīn-i Jahānbānī*. Tehran, 1937.
Kalīm. *Dīvān*, ed. P. Baiżā'ī. Tehran, 1957.
Khwānd Amīr. *Ḥabīb al-siyar*, ed. M. Dabīr-Siyāqī, 4 vols. Tehran, 1333/1954.
**LHP*
Mīr Khwānd. *Rauẓat al-ṣafā*, 10 vols. Tehran, 1338–9/1960.
Mu'tamin, Zain al-'Ābidīn. *Taḥavvul-i shi'r-i Fārsī*. Tehran, 1960.
Nahāvandī, 'Abd al-Bāqī. *Ma'āṡir-i Raḥīmī*, ed. M. Hidāyat Ḥusain, 3 vols. Calcutta, 1910–31.
Naṣrābādī, Muḥammad Ṭāhir. *Taẕkira*, ed. Vaḥīd Dastgirdī. Tehran, 1938.
Navā'ī, Mīr 'Alī Shīr. *Majālis al-nafā'is*, Persian translations ed. 'Alī Aṣghar Ḥikmat. Tehran, 1323/1945 (pp. 1–178, Fakhrī Harātī's trans., *Laṭā'if-nāma*; pp. 179–409, Shāh Muḥammad Qazvīnī's trans.).
Muḥākamat al-lughatain, trans. R. Devereux. Leiden, 1966.
Naẓīrī. *Dīvān*, ed. M. Muṣaffā. Tehran, 1961.
Niṡārī, Bahā' al-Dīn Ḥasan. *Taẕkira-yi Muẕakkir-i aḥbāb*, ed. M. S. Fażl-Allāh. New Delhi, 1969.
Qāsim al-Anvār. *Kulliyyāt*, ed. Sa'īd Nafīsī. Tehran, 1957.
Ṣafā, Ẕabīḥ-Allāh. *Tārīkh-i adabiyyāt dar Īrān*, 4 vols. Tehran, 1959–77.
Ṣā'ib Tabrīzī, Muḥammad 'Alī. *Dīvān*, ed. Amīrī Fīrūzkūhī, 2nd impression Tehran, 1957. Selections ed. Z. Mu'tamin, *Ash'ār-i barguẓīda-yi Ṣā'ib*. Tehran, n.d. [1941].

Ṣanā'ī, Ḥasan.
ed. S. M. Fażl-Allāh. Hyderabad, 1969.
Sandilavī, Aḥmad 'Alī Hāshimī. *Tazkira-yi Makhzan al-gharā'ib*, ed. Muḥammad Bāqir, 3 vols. Lahore, 1968–72.
Shiblī Nu'mānī. *Shi'r al-'Ajam*, ed. Mas'ūd 'Alī Ṣāḥib Nadvī, 5th impression A'ẓamgarh, 1956, III.
Sirishk, M. *Ḥazīn Lāhījī*. Mashhad, 1963.
Tatavī, 'Alī Shīr. *Maqālāt al-shu'arā*, ed. Ḥusām al-Dīn Rashīdī. Karachi, 1957.
Yarshater, Ehsan. "Safavid Literature: Progress or Decline?", *IrSt* VII (1974), 217–70.
Shi'r-i Fārsī dar 'ahd-i Shāh Rukh. Tehran, 1955.
"The theme of wine drinking and the concept of the beloved in early Persian poetry", *SI* XIII (1960), 43–53.

CHAPTER 17 (b)

Editions

Aḥmad, Nāẓir, and Nā'īnī, S. M. Riżā Jalālī. *Dīvān-i Ḥāfiz*. Tehran, 1971.
Brockhaus, H. *Die Lieder des Hafiz*. Leipzig, 1854–60; repr. 1969.
Ghanī, Qāsim, and Qazvīnī, Mīrzā Muḥammad. *Dīvān-i Ḥāfiz*. Tehran, 1320/1941–2.

Secondary Material

The main sources are: *LHP* III, 271–319; H. Ritter, "Hafiz", *İsl. Ans.*; A. J. Arberry, *Classical Persian Literature* (London, 1958), chapter XIII; A. Bausani, "Letteratura Neopersiana", in A. Pagliaro and A. Bausani, *Storia della letteratura Persiana* (Milan, 1960), pp. 437–50; and *HIL*.

Boyce, M. "A Novel Interpretation of Ḥāfiẓ", *BSOAS* XV (1953), 279–88.
Christensen, A. *Kulturskitser fra Iran*. Copenhagen, 1937.
Galimova, G. "The oldest manuscript of the poems of Hafiz", *SV* 1959, pp. 105–12.
Lescot, R. "Chronologie de l'œuvre de Hafiz", *BEO* X (1944), 57–100.
Rehder, R. M. "The text of Ḥāfiẓ", *JAOS* XCIV (1974), 145–56.
"New Material for the text of Ḥāfiẓ", *Iran* III (1965), 109–19.
Rempis, C. *Beiträge zur Chajjam-Forschung*. Leipzig, 1937 (AKM XXII/1).
Roemer, H. R. "Probleme der Hafizforschung und der Stand ihrer Lösung", *AAWL, Kl. d. Lit.*, 1951, no. 3, 98–115.
**Staatsschreiben*.
Schaeder, H. H. *Goethes Erlebnis des Ostens*. Leipzig, 1938.
"Lässt sich die 'seelische Entwicklung' des Dichters Ḥāfiẓ ermitteln?", *OLZ* XLV (1942), 201–10.
Wickens, G. M. "An analysis of primary and secondary significations in the third ghazal of Ḥāfiẓ", *BSOAS* XIV (1952), 627–38.
"Ḥāfiẓ", *EI*².
"The Persian Conception of Artistic Unity", *BSOAS* XIV (1952), 239–53.

INDEX

The system used in this index is word-by-word. Italic figures denote illustrations and bold figures denote main entries. A figure followed by letter 'n' indicates a footnote.

East India Company (English):
contacts with Armenians, 469; financial affairs, 399, 458–9, 463, 468, 488; trading arrangements, 297, 393, 444–5, 449–50, 459–62, 480, 486–7
Edwards, Arthur, English merchant, 431, 432
Egypt, relations with Türkmens, 158, 160–1
Elizabeth I, queen of England, 383
England, English, 268, 296, 297, 375, 392
trade with Persia, 383–5, 430–1, 432–5, 446, 449–51, 452, 457–8; travellers in Persia, 383–5, 393, 395–6, 403
see also East India Company
Erivan, fortress of, 284–5
Erzerum, 154, 159, 243, 416
Esen Buqa, Chaghatayid khan in Mughalistān, 115
eunuchs, 355, 404
Euphrates, river, as a frontier, 180
Europe:
books on Persia, 388; diplomatic contacts with Persia, 314, 443; influence on Persian art, 314, 812, 839; relations with Safavids, 271, 636–7; relations with Türkmens, 175–6, 177, 179; religious missions from, 375, 389, 396–8, 403–4, 587, 608; trade contacts with Persia, 296–8, 309, 383, 393, 394, 400, 458
see also individual countries

Fabre, Jean-Baptiste, French envoy, 405, 466
Fabritius, Ludwich (or Ludvig), Swedish envoy, 402–3
faience, 143, 733, 744, 754
Faiżī-yi Fayyiżī, poet and scholar, 593, 958, 981, 984
Fakhrī b. Amīrī, writer, 962
Faraḥābād, castle of, 320, 322, 324
Faraj, amīr, 66
Faraj, Mamlūk sultan (1399–1412), 67, 74, 76, 79
Farghāna, 120
Farrukh-Yasār, Shīrvān-Shāh, 116, 183, 209, 211–12, 862
Fārs province, 61, 94, 181, 282
Fatḥ ʿAlī Khān Dāghistānī, Grand Vizier to Safavids, 318, 319–20
Fatḥ ʿAlī Khān Qājār, 327
Fatḥ-Allāh of Kāshān, Mullā, theologian, 964
Fażl-Allāh, founder of the Ḥurūfī sect, 62, 623
Ferdinand II, Hapsburg Emperor, 284
Ferreira, Miguel, Portuguese envoy, 380
fiefs, *see suyūrghāl*; *tiyūl*
Fighānī, Bābā, poet, 957, 967, 985, 988, 992
Findiriskī, Mīr Abu'l-Qāsim, ṣūfī, 665, **675–7**, 696, 959
works of, 676
Fīrūz Shāh, Jalāl al-Dīn, amīr, 104, 753
Fīrūzābādī, Abū Ṭāhir b. Yaʿqūb al-Shīrāzī, lexicographer, 96
Fitch, Ralph, English traveller, 385, 388
Folk Islam, 135, 136, 191, 196–7
France, French:
missionaries, 396–8, 403–4; trade contacts, 298, 453, 455, 465–7; travellers in Persia, 382–3, 399–40, 404–7; treaties with Persia, 375, 406, 407, 465
Francus of Perugia, archbishop of Sulṭāniyya, 374
Friedrich, duke of Holstein, 397, 462, 479, 717, 724
Fryer, Dr John, English physician and traveller, 403, 464, 477, 607
fur trade, 429, 448

Gaikhatu, Īl-Khān, 3
Galonifontibus, Johannes de, 375
Gamrū (Gombroon), *see* Bandar ʿAbbās
Gardane brothers, Ange and François, 407
gardens, 777, 830–1, *836*
Garshāsp-nāma (manuscript), 891, 892
Gaudereau, Père Martin, French priest, 404, 406
Gauhar Shād, wife of Shāh Rukh, 104, 106, 117, 142, 616, 745–7, 860
Gāzur Gāh, shrine at, 752, 754
Gāzurgāhī, Kamāl al-Dīn Ḥusain, poet, 926, 974
Georgia:
and the Safavids, 245–6, 268, 269, 285–6, 296, 309, 327; invasions by Tīmūr, 59, 71, 75, 79–80; invasions by Türkmens, 163, 172
Georgians in Persia, 246, 271–2, 285, 286, 363–5
Ghalzai tribe, 314–15, 316, 317, 318, 320–1, 324
Gharchistān, 238
Ghazālī, Amīr Islām, poet, 983
Ghazan, Īl-Khān, 53, 155, 181, 501, 534–6, 538–9, 556–7, 949
ghāzī (soldier of the faith), 203, 208, 211, 312, 338
Ghāzī Khān Takkalū, 237, 242
"Ghiyāṣ", fabric designer, 723, 724–5
Ghiyāṣ al-Dīn, painter, *see* Naqqāsh
Ghiyāṣ al-Dīn of Shīrāz, architect, 749, 754
Ghiyāṣ al-Dīn Muḥammad, b. Rashīd al-Dīn, vizier to the Īl-Khāns, 20, 22
Ghujduvān, battle of (1512), 127, 217, 230

Muḥammad Mahdī al-Yazdī, astrolabe maker, 597–8
Muḥammad Mu'min b. Badī' al-Zamān (Timurid), 123
Muḥammad Mu'min-i Ḥusainī, physician, 606
Muḥammad Muqīm al-Yazdī, astrolabe maker, 598
Muḥammad Qāsim, artist, 903, 904
Muḥammad Qāsim b. Muḥammad Jūkī (Timurid), 107
Muḥammad Qulī Khān Shāmlū, Grand Vizier to Sulṭān Ḥusain, 321
Muḥammad Riżā Beg, Persian ambassador, 404, 406–7, 467
Muḥammad Riżā al-Imāmī, 787, 803, 837
Muḥammad Shaibānī, Uzbek khan, 119–20, 124–6, 217, 227, 870
Muḥammad Sulṭān, nephew of Tīmūr, 59
Muḥammad Sulṭān b. Jahāngīr (Timurid), 83, 737
Muḥammad Sulṭān b. 'Umar Shaikh (Timurid), 93
Muḥammad Yūsuf, scribe, 903, 904
Muḥammad Zamān (17 c.), artist, 310, 905–6, 907, 908
Muḥammad Zamān Khān Shāman, 316
Muḥammad Zamān Kirmānī (16 c.), artist, 310, 598, 839
Muḥammadī, Āq Quyūnlū ruler (d. 1500), 183
Muḥammadī b. Jahān Shāh (Qarā Quyūnlū), 164, 173
Muḥandis, Luṭf-Allāh, astronomer, 593, 603
Muḥtasham Kāshāni, poet, 954, 958
Mu'izz al-Dīn, *see* Ḥusain
mujtahid (influential theologians), 337, 346, 351, 362, 368, 655
Mukhranids, dynasty in Kartlia, 309
mulk (possession of land), 517–18
Mullā Qāsim, Nuqṭavī sectary, 273–4
Mulūk Sabzavārī (Sarbadār), 50, 62
Mu'nis al-aḥrār (manuscript), 848
muqāṣṣa (grant of property), 503
Murād, Āq Quyūnlū ruler (1498–1503), 183, 212
Murād III, Ottoman sultan (1574–95), 257, 589
Murād IV, Ottoman sultan (1623–40), 283, 284
Murshid Qulī Khān Ustājlū, governor of Mashhad, 261, 262, 264
Murtażā Qulī Khān Bījarlū, 293
Murtażā Qulī Khān Shāmlū, 259
Mūsā, Īl-Khān (1336–7), 12, 20
Mūsā al-Kāẓim, Seventh Imām, 198, 342
musallamī (tax exemption), *see mu'āfī*
Muṣavvir, Mīr (16 c.), artist, 881, 883, 885, 893, 896
Muṣavvir, Mu'īn (17 c.), painter, 310, 903
Muscat Arabs, 296, 461, 464, 468, 470
Muscovy Company, *see* Russia Company
Musha'sha' movement, 136–7, 216–17, 245, 283, 318, **625–9**
mushrif al-mamālik (financial official), 554
musta'jir (tenant farmers), 512, 520, 555
Mustaufī, Ḥamd-Allāh, historian and geographer, 19, 614, 617, 618
mustaufī al-mamālik (head of finance chamber), 290, 354, 554
mutavallī (administrator), 509, 519–21
al-Mutawakkil I, 'Abbasid caliph at Cairo, 16, 42
Muẓaffar 'Alī, painter, 891, 892, 896–7
Muẓaffar Ḥusain b. Ḥusain Bāīqarā (Timurid), 124, 125
Muẓaffar-i Kāshī, 15, 60
Muzaffarids:
  architectural style, 730–4; culture and religion, 16, 63–4, 144; history of, 4, 11, **13–16, 59–63**; genealogical table of, 10

Nādir Shāh Afshār (Nadr Qulī Beg), 127, 325, 327–8, 407, 654
  biography of, 408
Nadr Muḥammad, Uzbek khan of Bukhārā, 286–7, 299, 905
Nā'īn, palace at, 772–3, 892–4
Najaf, 282, 654, 670
Najm-i s̱ānī (Yār Aḥmad Khūzānī), Grand Vizier/army commander, 127, 217, 230, 343n
Nakhchivān, archbishopric of, 374
Naqd 'Alī Beg, Persian envoy, 396, 452
Naqqāsh, Ghiyās̱ al-Dīn al-, painter, 594, 859
Naqshbandiyya, religious order, 136, 920, 928
Naṣrābādī (d. 1688), poet, 980, 984–5
naṣṣ (legitimate nomination), 337, 338, 340, 342, 346
Navā'ī, Mīr 'Alī Shīr, statesman and poet, 123–4, 136, 139, 145, 864–5, 896; buildings of, 143, 791; general works of, 917; *Khamsa*, 866, 867, 870; *Muḥākamat al-lughatain*, 914
nāẓir al-mamālik (financial official), 554
Naẓīrī, of Nīshāpūr, poet, 958, 982, 989
Negüderis, Mongol tribal group, 11, 44
Newberie, John, English traveller, 384–5
Nicholas V, Pope, 175
Nicopolis, battle of (1396), 74, 77
Nikitin, Afanasiĭ, Russian merchant, 377, 419–20, 422